Society and Education

Society and Education

Eighth Edition

DANIEL U. LEVINE
University of Missouri at Kansas City

ROBERT J. HAVIGHURST

ALLYN AND BACON
Boston   London   Toronto   Sydney   Tokyo   Singapore

Series Editor: *Sean W. Wakely*
Series Editorial Assistant: *Carol L. Chernaik*
Production Administrator: *Annette Joseph*
Production Coordinator: *Susan Freese*
Editorial-Production Service: *Grace Sheldrick, Wordsworth Associates*
Composition Buyer: *Louise Richardson*
Manufacturing Buyer: *Megan Cochran*
Cover Administrator: *Linda K. Dickinson*

Copyright © 1992, 1989, 1984, 1979, 1975, 1967, 1962, 1957 by Allyn and Bacon
A Division of Simon & Schuster, Inc.
160 Gould Street
Needham Heights, Massachusetts 02194

Library of Congress Cataloging-in-Publication Data

Levine, Daniel U.
    Society and education / Daniel U. Levine, Robert J. Havighurst. —
8th ed.
        p. cm.
    Includes bibliographical references and index.
    ISBN 0-205-13371-1
    1. Educational sociology—United States. 2. Educational
equalization—United States. 3. Minorities—Education—United
States. 4. Pluralism (Social sciences)—United States.
    I. Havighurst, Robert James. II. Title.
LC191.4.L48 1991
370.19′0973—dc20   91-33082
                                                            CIP

Printed in the United States of America

10 9 8 7 6 5 4 3 2 1   96 95 94 93 92 91

Brief Contents

Contents

Chapter 6
The Transition from Adolescence to Adulthood   177

Chapter 10
Cultural Pluralism and Minority Education   341

The eighth edition of *Society and Education* continues the emphasis found in previous editions on delineating and assessing social changes that have major implications for education. Because education was the object of increasing concern and attention nationally during the 1980s and continues to be during the early 1990s, critical problems in society and the educational system are emphasized throughout the volume, and considerable material has been added on school reform. Every chapter has been revised to include new or updated information. Sections on the following topics are entirely or almost entirely new:

- *Chapter 1*—perceived decline of blue-collar culture; recent developments in underclass neighborhoods; and poverty, race/ethnicity, and family structure
- *Chapter 2*—achievement of suburban minority students; purposes and problems of community colleges; financing of students in higher education; and the college admissions test controversy
- *Chapter 4*—child neglect and abuse; serial-marriage children; skip-generation families; disappearing fathers; the postnuclear family and self-fulfillment; latchkey children; homeless children and youth and runaways; foster-care children; and effects of crack cocaine
- *Chapter 5*—aggressive and insensitive children and youth; cliques in classrooms; and benefits of participation in the Boys and Girls Clubs of America
- *Chapter 6*—employment training for disadvantaged youth in the 1990s; Worklink, apprenticeships, and related proposals for reform; possible negative effects of students' employment; personal capital/educational equity accounts; and community support for youth development
- *Chapter 7*—mobility of ethnic, racial, and religious groups; assimilation of European ethnic

groups; factors affecting group status and mobility: discrimination, availability of resources, effectiveness of mediating institutions, compatibility of ethnic culture with mainstream institutions, family structure and networks; recent trends in socioeconomic mobility; growing importance of college attendance and graduation; and critical pedagogy
- *Chapter 8*—cost/benefit analysis of preschool programs; deficiencies in the organization and operation of Chapter 1; and comprehensive ecological intervention
- *Chapter 9*—research on magnet schools; magnet-school selectivity; and controlled choice in small urban districts
- *Chapter 10*—recent immigration patterns and developments; importance and value of recent immigration; difficulties in maintaining subcultural identities; European ethnic identification and affiliation; historic importance of cultural pluralism; the plight of underclass black males; background differences related to minority achievement; recent research on instruction for LEP and NEP students; academic performance of Asian American subgroups; discrimination against Asian Americans in higher education; economic development among Alaskan Natives; status and problems of Native American education; and recent multicultural education developments and controversies
- *Chapter 11*—the continuing plight of displaced homemakers; recent feminist theory; and feminist theory in education and social science
- *Chapter 12*—community orientation of rural schools; diversity of rural districts; district cooperatives; effective-schools projects in rural districts; and privatization and contracting-out of educational services
- *Chapter 13*—achievement levels and trends; importance of numeracy; teacher licensing and preparation; tomorrow's teachers and schools; assessment and testing of student performance;

the rise and stagnation of merit pay and career ladders; school performance incentives and differential treatment; restructuring, deregulation, waivers, and school-based management; national goals; participation of external organizations; higher education students as tutors; assured college access for high school graduates; recent school choice proposals and developments; manifest/latent functions and unforeseen consequences; accelerated schools; Higher-Order Thinking Skills (HOTS) program; success for all; reading recovery; and instructional resource personnel

As in previous editions, much of the emphasis in *Society and Education,* eighth edition, is on the education of disadvantaged students, particularly of minority students in big cities. In accordance with the changes and challenges emerging as the United States moves further into the postindustrial age, improving the performance of the growing proportion of disadvantaged students has become a critical task facing both our schools and our society. Systematic attention throughout the text also is given to the increasing importance of enhancing higher-order skills among all groups of students.

The eighth edition of *Society and Education* continues to emphasize assessment of relevant research in drawing conclusions about the role and functioning of schools in U.S. society and on presentation of a range of perspectives and conclusions based on differing and even contradictory studies, rather than on a single ideological point of view. When we describe our own conclusions and the data or analysis on which they are based, we are conscientious in identifying other views and in providing pertinent sources for further information.

Although the presentation and summaries of research throughout *Society and Education* are nontechnical, we provide enough information to give the reader a sense of the complexities and uncertainties in conducting and interpreting research. Many readers have viewed this effort as a particular strength of previous editions.

We also stress social-systems considerations that affect the functioning of schools and the context in which they operate. Such considerations are, after all, among the major factors that help distinguish educational sociology and study of the social foundations of education from educational psychology or social psychology. Examples of this emphasis include:

- Analysis of threshold forces in the functioning of schools as institutions
- Analysis of promotion/retention policies in terms of their effects on students as a group, not just on individual students
- Description of the (limited available) research on home environment differences between students in magnet schools and so-called regular schools
- Cooperation between schools and other social institutions
- Analysis of the peer group as a reference group inside and outside the schools
- Analysis of desegregation in terms of social class mixture
- Description of effective-schools research dealing with the importance of schoolwide characteristics
- Identification of the educational implications of major social and economic trends
- Importance of unforeseen consequences in efforts to reform education

Related to our efforts to avoid dogmatic positions and in order to encourage the reader to seek further information and opposing points of view, this latest edition of *Society and Education* also continues the practice in previous editions of explicitly avoiding either-or propositions or solutions when considering problems involving the educational system and its place in the larger society. Complex problems in the real world of the schools seldom if ever are amenable to understanding or solution through relatively simple analysis that postulates a dichotomous explanation or response. For example, it is not true that the educational system either functions universally to provide socioeconomic mobility or else does nothing but reinforce inequality, that desegregation plans must be either all mandatory or all voluntary, or that the increase in the number of single-parent families either must cause insurmountable problems for the schools or can have no probable negative consequences. These and other current issues in research and analysis involving education and society are discussed at length in a balanced presentation.

That does not mean, however, that we never take a position. For example, we believe that the education system has entered a period of crisis involving national and societal requirements to improve the performance of disadvantaged students in big cities and to upgrade the system as a whole with respect to teaching of higher-order skills and understandings. We have endeavored to portray this crisis as clearly and convincingly as possible but without ignoring contrary evidence indicating that genuine progress is being registered in some locations.

As in previous editions, information on references cited in the text and on the list of suggested readings at the end of each chapter is provided in the extensive Bibliography. To assist the reader further, each reference in the Bibliography concludes with the page number(s) (in parentheses) indicating where in the text it is cited.

Acknowledgments

Special thanks in preparing this eighth edition of *Society and Education* are extended to Anita Jennings of the University of Missouri at Kansas City School of Education; to Sean Wakely, Carol Chernaik, and Sue Freese of Allyn and Bacon; and also to Grace Sheldrick, Wordsworth Associates, whose indispensable editorial assistance and encouragement resulted in a variety of improvements and refinements in preparing the text.

Robert J. Havighurst

Born in 1900, Robert J. Havighurst was a man of and for the twentieth century. His first career was in the emerging field of physical chemistry, in which he obtained a doctorate and worked with some of the world's leading physicists. During a postdoctorate assignment in Europe, he became interested in the humanities and social sciences; he subsequently made important contributions in sociology, educational psychology, and several other fields. After World War II he continued his earlier work and also played a leading role in developing the disciplines of educational sociology, human development, and gerontology and in building interdisciplinary bridges that helped keep numerous fields alive and vibrant. He also served as director of the Rockefeller Foundation's European Rehabilitation Program and worked in countless other ways to help improve social and civic institutions and organizations.

But this remarkable man's vision never became fixated in the century to which he contributed so much. In his later years Professor Havighurst urged social scientists to identify problems and trends that would be prominent in the future, and in the early 1980s, he recast Chapter 1 of *Society and Education* to emphasize developments most likely to be prominent in the twenty-first century.

My initial contact with Bob Havighurst was in the late 1950s, when I heard him tell an audience of educators that the serious teacher shortage with which they were struggling would become a surplus that would create different problems. In many subsequent contacts I learned that his capacity to think in the future was the product of sound judgment that systematically worked through the logical consequences of past and current developments. His ability to help identify and address the most important issues of tomorrow's world will be missed.

Professor Havighurst was internationally renowned for the breadth and depth of his scholarship, the acuity of his insights, and the amazing capacity he had to encapsulate and summarize complicated materials and theories within an easily understandable and communicable framework. But those of us who were fortunate to know him will most remember and honor his generosity of spirit, his dedication to civil liberties and civil rights, his respect for the dignity and humanity of all persons, and his quiet encouragement and support, which he unfailingly provided to everyone with whom he came in contact.

D. U. L.

1

Socioeconomic Trends and the Social Class Structure

THE SOCIAL CLASS HIERARCHY

A social-class group consists of people who have similar social habits and values. One test of membership in a social class is that of association, actual or potential. In a small community, the members of a particular social class tend to belong to the same social organizations and to entertain one another in their homes. If they live in a big city, their numbers are so large that only a few can actually associate with one another; yet, even in large cities, if members of the same social class meet as strangers they soon recognize a good deal of similarity in their ways of life and recognize each other as social equals.

The various social classes are organized into an overall hierarchical structure. Most persons recognize that they occupy a position on a social scale. They acknowledge that there are other people and other groups that have more or less economic or political power or social prestige than their own group. Within a particular community, people can rank themselves and their neighbors according to power or prestige; that is, they can assign different individuals to particular positions on a social ladder.

All societies, large or small, primitive or modern, show this phenomenon of rank: the leaders and people of high prestige occupy positions at the top; others occupy intermediate positions; and still others are at the bottom of the social scale. This is true regardless of the political form of government. A democracy has rank; so does an absolute monarchy; so also does a communist society such as the Soviet Union. The king and the nobility are at the top in a monarchy; the top people in the Soviet Union are the leaders of the Communist Party and the high government and military officials. In a democracy, the people at the top are those who have earned or inherited economic power or social prestige.

Studying the Social Structure

Various sociologists have chosen to highlight one or another of the dimensions listed above in undertaking studies of social stratification; this text focuses on studies of American communities according to the methods developed by W. Lloyd Warner and his associates (Warner, Meeker, and Eells 1960). These investigators stressed the dynamics of community organization; that is, they focused on prestige and the patterns of social interaction that constitute the social life of a community.

The usual procedure was for the social scientist to move into the community and live there for a time, talking with people and observing the social scene. He or she discovered the social groups that existed, talked with the members of various social groups, and asked about the social structure of the community. The social scientist learned who associated with whom, who were considered the top people, who the bottom, and why. Gradually he or she pieced together a picture of the community as it was viewed by its members. Seldom did any one citizen see the whole structure of the community clearly, but the social scientist combined the views of many people into a single composite picture representing the consensus. This picture showed groups of people arranged in a network, as well as on a social scale from top to bottom in terms of the status assigned them by their fellow citizens.

After the major lines of the social structure had been delineated and the positions of a few key people had been agreed on, it was possible to locate other people in relation to the original persons. Eventually, the majority of the population could be located on the social map in this way.*

This method, of course, worked well only in small communities, where it was possible to meet with, or at least find out about, practically every adult inhabitant. Somewhat different methods had to be devised for use in larger, more urban communities. To conduct larger studies of social status in urban communities, sociologists identified four types of socioeconomic measures that seemed particularly useful in determining the social class of individual respondents: occupational prestige (i.e., occupational status as determined originally by asking people to rank occupations according to their prestige), education (usually in number of years), income, and housing and/or neighborhood prestige (as determined by the value of one's house and/or the prestige of the neighborhood) (Warner, Meeker, and Eells 1960). Men who scored high on all these indices were considered high in status or upper class, and

those who ranked low were considered lower class, with many possible social-class or social-status levels in between. Women and children generally were assigned the social-class score of the male head-of-household.

Most research involving social status or social class uses only one or two of the possible measures of social status in categorizing individuals on some scale of status. One of the most frequently used approaches asks respondents to indicate occupation and education using categories devised by August Hollingshead (1957) as part of his Two Factor Index of Social Position; respondents are then placed in social-class categories I (High) to V (Low). Many other studies use only occupational status scores such as the North-Hatt scale (Reiss 1961), which ranks occupations on a scale of 8 (shoe shiner) to 93 (Supreme Court Justice), particularly when other measures of social position are difficult to obtain for a large sample of respondents. In recent years, some studies of children from female-headed families in poverty neighborhoods have had to use education of the mother as the sole measure of social class because other information was unavailable.

Researchers often feel justified in using only one or two measures of social status because occupation, education, income, housing/neighborhood, and other social-status variables generally are highly correlated with one another. Income, for example, is partly a function of occupation, and amount of education helps determine a person's occupation and income. Research by K. Hope (1982) indicates that occupation prestige scores are based partly on the economic rewards people believe are associated with an occupation and partly on its perceived value to society. Physicians, for example, rank very high on both measures. Thus, it is not surprising that occupational prestige is highly correlated with income. On the other hand, some occupations, such as priest or minister, generally have relatively high prestige/status but relatively low income, whereas others (e.g., categories of skilled craftspersons) may have high income but relatively low prestige.

---

*This method of mapping the social system and of discovering the social class of a particular person is called the "method of evaluated social participation," often abbreviated as E.P. First, by interviewing members of the community, the major lines of social structure were ascertained, and the names obtained of a few people who interviewers agreed occupied given positions in the structure. It was then noted with whom these people associated in social clubs, informal social cliques, service clubs, church associations, and so on. Thus, other people were placed in relation to the original group. Eventually, the majority of the population was placed in this way. Then, if the social scientist wished to know the social status of Mr. X, whose name had not previously been brought into the study, he asked who Mr. X's friends were, what clubs or associations he belonged to, and then found that Mr. X was close to one of the groups already defined on the social map. Mr. X's social participation was thus evaluated in relation to that of others in the community, and his place in the social structure was determined.

D.J. Treiman (1977) has examined and conducted cross-national and historical studies of occupational prestige and other measures of social status. Among his major findings are the following:

1. Occupations that have high prestige in one country tend to have high prestige in other countries, regardless of differences in political, social, and economic characteristics. For example, rankings of occupations are almost exactly the same in the United States and Chile, in Brazil and West Germany, in Poland and the Ivory Coast, in New Zealand and Spain, and in Yugoslavia and Argentina.

2. Within and across countries, there are high correlations between occupational status and education and between occupational status and income.

3. An International Standard Occupational Scale has high correlations with scores from local occupational scales developed in individual countries.

4. Occupational status is stable over time. Although there have been vast changes in the types of occupations in which people worked at different historical periods—there were many chimney sweeps two hundred years ago and there are many computer operators today—occupations that have continued to exist over long periods of time generally undergo little change in relative status. For example, ruling warriors were the highest caste in Nepal in 1395, just as high military officers are now near the top of the International Standard Occupation Scale (see Table 1-1). Similarly, saddlers and tanners were ranked near the bottom among guilds in fifteenth-century Florence, just as tanners and leather workers rank near the bottom today on the international scale.

5. The close relationship between occupation and income or wealth also has been very stable over time. For example, income data associated with differing occupations in the United States in 1776 correlate highly with income data associated with London occupations in 1890, with income data on English occupations in 1688, and with wealth data on Florentine guilds in 1427.

Social Class Categories

It is important to note that measures of occupational status and other status indicators are not exactly the same as measures of social class. Strictly speaking, the term *social class* refers to large groups of persons who have common political and economic goals and interests related to their position in the social structure. Probably the most influential conception of social class has been that of Karl Marx and his followers, who made the following distinctions:

> *Capitalists:* those who controlled large amounts of capital
> *Bourgeoisie:* middle-class persons with significant amounts of property and some control over investment, the means of production, and the labor powers of others
> *Petitbourgeoisie:* lower-middle-class persons with significant control of property, investments, and production but not the labor of others
> *Proletariat:* manual workers with no real control of property or production
> *Lumpenproletariat:* very poor, unskilled workers
> *Intelligentsia:* persons whose influence and wealth derive from working with knowledge rather than material goods

In the early industrial period, the large majority of individuals in most societies were proletarians with little real control over production or their own labor power. With occasional interruptions, the proportion of unskilled proletarian workers has been steadily decreasing in the United States and other developed, industrialized nations during the twentieth century (Steinmetz and Wright 1989).

The most fundamental distinction between social classes in most conceptualizations has been

TABLE 1-1 *Comparison of Occupational Caste Rankings in Nepal in 1395 with Contemporary International Occupational Scale Scores*

Rank	Nepali Caste Title	International Standard Occupational Scale Title	Score
63	Bhupa, raja (ruler or warrior)	High armed forces office	73
59	Mantrin (state official, minister)	High civil servant, head of dept.	71
57	Pujita (temple priest)	Clergyman	60
56	Deva cinta (God thinker)	Religious teacher	56
48	Sajakara (tailor)	Tailor	40
45	Marikara (confectioner)	Banker	33
44	Silpikara (craftsman)	Skilled worker	42
42	Napika (barber)	Barber	30
41	Lepika (plasterer)	Plasterer	31
40	Daukara (wood carver)	Cabinetmaker	31
39	Taksaka (carpenter)	Carpenter	37
36	Kumbhakara (potter)	Potter	25
34	Karnika (weaver)	Weaver	30
33	Kansyakaya (bell maker)	Metal caster	33
31	Tamrakara (copper smith)	Copper or tin smith	32
30	Gopaka (cowherd)	Livestock worker	26
21	Gayane (bard singer)	Musical entertainer	32
20	Citrakara (painter)	Building painter	31
15	Mali (gardener)	Gardener	21
14	Mansabikri (butcher)	Butcher	31
5	Dohbi (washerman)	Launderer	22
2	Matangi (elephant driver)	Animal driver	18
1	Charmakara (leather worker)	Leather worker	22

Source: Adapted from Treiman 1977.
Note: Nepali caste rankings varied from 1 to 63. Contemporary international occupation scores vary from 6 to 90.

that between manual workers, who are relatively unskilled and have relatively little power to influence economic decisions, and nonmanual workers with relatively greater education, occupational status, or knowledge that yields at least some degree of control over the disposition of their labor. If social classes do exist and have some importance in determining—or reflecting—what happens to people, social class should be more closely related to various measures of behavior and outcomes than should single status measures such as occupational prestige. That is, knowing a person's social class—for example, a classification according to manual or nonmanual occupations or a classification of lower class or upper class according to occupation prestige and education—should be more highly related to behaviors and outcomes than a

simple score on occupational prestige. Research continues to show that social class is a meaningful concept from this point of view (Wright 1985).

The terminology most commonly used to categorize social classes uses the distinction between upper (high status), middle, and lower or working classes. Sociologists frequently distinguish between the lower working class and the upper working class and between the lower-middle and the upper-middle class (see below). In some cases, a distinction also is made between upper-upper and lower-upper class groups.

In recent years, a number of observers have argued that a "new class" has emerged that has distinctive political and economic interests and cultural patterns within modern, postindustrial societies (Lasch 1990). Bruce-Briggs (1979) has reviewed this literature and identified three major overlapping groups that have been identified as the new class. First is the new middle class, consisting of white-collar workers who generally are not highly paid but have gained access to secure and physically nondemanding jobs through education. Second are the managers, who have considerable power and high income but do not own the property of the corporations they work for, as did the capitalists of the industrial era. Third is group *X*, which Bruce-Briggs describes as earning its living "by the use of learning, especially the ability to use words" (1979, 16).

Bruce-Briggs and other researchers believe that the latter group *(X)* of people who work with symbols is becoming larger and more important in the postindustrial period and may be a pivotal force in contemporary society because it does so much to shape the society's ideas and policies. Sociologist Peter Berger, for example, believes that this new class of intellectually oriented citizens adheres to "secular humanism" in its value structure; that is, this class advocates pluralism in values rather than acceptance of traditional values and attitudes. While this orientation helps the intellectually oriented to learn and adapt flexibly as society changes, it also challenges and antagonizes large segments of society that support traditional values and cultural patterns (Berger 1979).

Other observers, however, dispute the conclusion that there really is a new class defined in terms of a separate part of the population with distinctive political and economic interests (Lasch 1990). Andrew Hacker has summarized this argument as follows:

> *Do people afflicted with the rationalist attitude constitute a "new class?" . . . The individuals in new occupations entered them because the openings were there. They produce words and numbers and notations because that output is expected of them. If anything, they belong to a very old class: they work for a living, just as most people always have. The color of their collars may have changed. They have larger vocabularies and greater verbal facility. They receive comparatively generous salaries; many live varied and interesting lives. Yet when all is said and done, they remain workers beholden to the organizations employing them . . . and do not constitute a special class by themselves. (Hacker 1979, 167)*

In recent years, social analysts have been trying to identify long-range implications of the growth of occupations concerned primarily with manipulation of words, ideas, and symbols. For example, in discussing the prevalence and role of knowledge workers in the emerging symbol economy organized around information, Peter Drucker (1989) called attention to their high mobility in moving from job to job within and across businesses, hospitals, universities, government agencies, and other institutions. According to Drucker, this phenomenon has greatly changed the political system, which no longer centers on competition among labor, agriculture, industry, and other occupation-based interested groups. In addition, knowledge has replaced capital (i.e., financial resources for investment) as the most fundamental determinant of economic expansion and prosperity. Because acquisition of knowledge depends on advanced education and training, possession of college degrees has become a major consideration in determining whether individuals and societies succeed economically.

Economist Robert Reich (1989, 1990, 1991) also views symbols and information as playing an increasingly important part in contemporary society. According to Reich's analysis, jobs in the emerging economy can be classified into three basic categories: *symbolic-analytic services* provided by such persons as lawyers, consultants, researchers, teachers, real-estate developers, art and design specialists, media personnel, and innumerable others who manipulate data, words, and symbols; *routine production services* involving tasks that are repeated over and over as one step in completing a product; and *routine personal services* that are provided by such persons as restaurant and hotel workers, cabdrivers, barbers, retail clerks, hospital attendants, truck drivers, and others who tend to be relatively unskilled and are usually paid by the hour. Reich estimates that symbolic analysis now accounts for more than 40 percent of gross national product in the United States, and almost 20 percent of jobs.

Persons in the new class of symbolic analysts have a high standard of living in part because they "increasingly are part of a global labor market . . . [in which] the services they offer are quite scarce in the context of the whole world" (Reich 1989, 26). "In the emerging economy" of the twenty-first century, he further concluded, the most important asset a nation will possess will be the "problem-solving, problem-identifying, and strategic-brokering skills" of its citizens. (Reich 1991, 42). Routine production workers, by way of contrast, have faced a declining standard of living that will continue to fall as the global economy places them in competition with their counterparts worldwide, while providers of routine personnel services, though somewhat sheltered from international competition, also face relatively bleak prospects because they compete with displaced production workers, new immigrants, and illegal aliens. Reich believes that systematic efforts should be launched to transform (technologically empower) jobs that involve routine production and personnel services so that they reflect greater control over tasks and output, introduction of new technologies, and other aspects of symbolic analysis that can make them more attractive and rewarding. (Numerous examples of how that might be done are provided in Zuboff 1988). After acknowledging that such a transformation will require major improvements in education, Reich generally concluded that

> it is now possible for the most fortunate fifth to sell their expertise directly in the global market, and thus maintain and enhance their standard of living, even as that of other Americans declines. . . . [This population of symbolic analysts has] been able to insulate themselves from the less fortunate, by living in suburban

> enclaves far removed from the effects of poverty. (Reich 1989, 26–27)

SOCIAL STRUCTURE IN THE UNITED STATES

The results of many community studies have enabled social scientists to draw certain general conclusions about social structure in the United States. In general, there is a basic five-class structure (see Figure 1-1). The proportion of people in each class varies depending on the size, the age, and the economic character of a given community. Thus, in comparison with the country as a whole, a community in a coal-mining or steel-mill area is likely to have a higher proportion of working-class people, whereas a community with a college or university is likely to have a higher proportion of upper-middle-class people. If the economic situation of a community changes drastically, the social structure of the community also is likely to change.

Small Communities

It is very common for people, particularly if they live in small, self-contained communities (that is, communities that are not satellites of big cities), to stress equalitarianism and to play down, or deny, the existence of social classes. At the same time, they recognize that there are different types of people in their community. As a respected citizen of Jonesville, a city of 6,000, explained:

> Almost everyone in this town is rated in some way; people can rate you in just a few minutes by talking to you. It's remarkable how you can size people up in a hurry—suppose I use a rating scale of zero to 100 and rate people on it. You can be sure this is not a hypothetical thing either. Not to the people of Jonesville. People like the Caldwells and Volmers . . . rate 100. The Shaws would be up there, too. People like me, oh, a 70 maybe, and people like John (a janitor) about a 40, no better than that. Remember, this is the social rating. If we rated

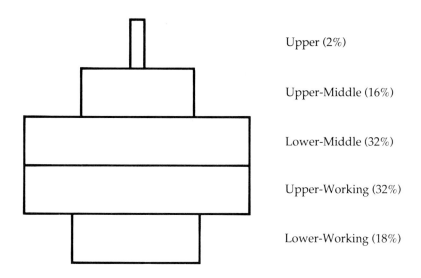

Upper (2%)

Upper-Middle (16%)

Lower-Middle (32%)

Upper-Working (32%)

Lower-Working (18%)

FIGURE 1-1   *The Social-Class Structure in the United States (*Source: *Authors' estimates based on a variety of national and community studies and data sets.)*

them financially, some of them would rank differently. (Warner and associates 1949, 22)

This man did not speak of social classes as such; however, he recognized that his community reflected a social hierarchy.

The Small Rural Community.   Studies of extremely small communities, villages ranging from a few hundred in population up to about 1,500, generally showed a three-class structure consisting of an upper-middle class, a lower-middle class, and a few families at the very bottom. Class lines in these communities were relatively indistinct as compared to larger communities, and there was more social intercourse between classes (Havighurst and Morgan 1951; West 1945).

The Small City

Cities with a population from about 5,000 to 15,000 tended to exhibit a five-class structure. A good example is a midwestern community that was described under the names of Jonesville, Elmtown, and Midwest (Warner and associates 1949; Hollingshead 1949; Warner, Meeker, and Eells

1960). This city had a population of about 6,000 and represented the most common type of small city in the north central states—a county seat, with both an industrial and an agricultural population.

In this community, the upper class constituted about 3 percent of the population. Some members of this class were the descendants of a pioneer settler who, a hundred years earlier, had acquired large tracts of farmland that had now become the best real estate in the city. Others were executives of a small factory, or they were the owners of the banks, the largest farms, and the most profitable businesses.

The upper-middle class contained about 10 percent of the population and consisted mainly of professional men, business executives, and owners of businesses and of large farms. The lower-middle class, about 30 percent of the whole, consisted mainly of white-collar workers, owners of small retail businesses, a few foremen and skilled manual workers, and the bulk of the prosperous farmers. These people were said by those in the classes above them to be "nice people" but social "nobodies."

The upper-working class, numerically the largest group (with 35 to 40 percent of the population), were described as "poor but honest" people who worked as skilled and unskilled laborers or as tenant farmers.

The lowest class, about 15 percent, consisted partly of people who were working hard to maintain a respectable kind of poverty and partly of people who seemed to the rest of the community to be generally immoral, lazy, and defiant of the law.

After the Jonesville studies were made, two other midwestern communities, one of 40,000 and one of 100,000, were studied. In these communities essentially the same picture of social structure emerged (Havighurst 1962).

A somewhat more complicated six-class social structure was found, however, in a New England community of about 17,000 called "Yankee City" (Warner and Lunt 1941). In that community, there were two upper-class groups: an upper-upper, consisting of families who traced their lineage back to colonial times and who had had wealth and high social position for several generations; and a lower-upper group, or *nouveaux riches,* families who had moved into the community more recently and whose money had been acquired for the most part in the present generation or in the one just preceding. There was a clear separation between these two groups in terms of their social participation.

The Large City

In a large city, it is impossible for the sociologist to analyze social-class differences on the basis of actual social participation (who associates with whom), for only a handful of people are known to each other and any given pattern of face-to-face interaction can involve only a small number of the total population.

In attempting to study the social structure of the metropolitan area of Kansas City in the late 1950s, however, investigators found that residents made consistent evaluations of various symbols of status (Coleman and Neugarten 1971). Kansas Citians had a highly developed awareness of the status hierarchy in their community; and, although

average citizens could name only some of the persons who were at the top and some who were at the bottom of the social ladder, they nevertheless ranked their fellow residents on the basis of such dimensions of status as area of residence, quality of housing, occupation, club membership, ethnic identification, and so on. Thus, for example, Kansas Citians were particularly aware of the prestige ranking of various neighborhoods and tended readily to place persons on the social ladder according to their home addresses.

As anticipated, the heterogeneity and complexity of the large city produced a much more highly differentiated social structure than found in a small town. Thirteen different social strata were visible, each stratum representing a gradation on the social scale. At the same time, the basic five-class system seemed applicable. There were five core groups of people, readily distinguishable on the basic social characteristics mentioned above; with each of the other eight groups forming a variant of one of the basic patterns; and with greater differences appearing between the five larger groups than between the thirteen smaller ones.

Large cities, then, can be described in terms of the basic five-class structure, granted that there will be many subgroups. The proportions of people in the five classes are probably roughly the same as those for small cities. In Kansas City in the 1950s, for instance, the percentages of the population in the five social classes were estimated to be, from upper to lower, 2.5, 11, 32, 40, and 14. In the same way, Hodges (1968), after studying the peninsula area of California (from San Francisco to and including San Jose) and after studying data obtained from almost 2,000 heads of households in the area, summarized the social structure as a five-class structure.

THE OCCUPATIONAL STRUCTURE

Another way to examine social-class structure is by studying the occupational structure—one of the main components of social class. Table 1-2 shows the development of the U.S. occupational structure between 1910 and 1988. In 1910, the large majority of the population was in working-class occupations involving either farming or blue-collar work in such fields as manufacturing. Throughout the twentieth century, however, the proportion of middle-class occupations has increased. By 1988, 29 percent of employed persons were in professional or managerial occupations, and the relative percentages of clerical and sales workers also had increased. The growth of the middle class led some observers to conclude that by 1970 or 1980 the United States had become perhaps the first very large nation in history in which the modal population was middle class. Although there are indications that the United States has become more bifurcated with a diminishing middle class in the 1980s, the long-range trends historically have been toward growth of the middle-class segments and relative decline of the working class.

PERSPECTIVES ON SOCIAL CLASS STRUCTURE

Not all sociologists agree that the social structure of the United States is fairly represented by the five-class hierarchy shown in Figure 1-1. For one thing, the economic and technological changes occurring in our society are raising standards of living and changing relations among various classes. From certain perspectives, the differences between classes are becoming obliterated. For instance, the lines between the upper class and the upper-middle class seem to be disappear-

ing, with less emphasis given to lineage in all but the oldest and most conservative communities, and with upper-status people taking active leadership roles in community affairs. Blue-collar workers have had greater relative gains in income during the past three decades than have white-collar workers, and patterns of buying and spending have become more similar between these two groups.

From other perspectives, the differences between social classes are becoming sharpened—as, for instance, between the group on public assistance in metropolitan and rural areas and all the other groups in the society.

Some observers describe the social-class structure in the United States as a three-class system in which there is a growing upper-middle class that encompasses the old upper class; then a huge, increasingly undifferentiated "common man" or blue-and-white-collar working class; and an "under class" of unskilled, public-assistance families. Karl Mayer (1963), for one, describes the changing social-class outlines of the United States not as a pyramid but as approximating a diamond in which there are small groups of nonmobile people at both the top and the bottom, with all the rest of society in between, and in which gradations in the undifferentiated middle are so numerous and so gradual that class lines are relatively obliterated. Alternately, Ralph Whitehead (1990) believes that the baby-boom generation of the 1940s and succeeding generations in the United States can be categorized most usefully in terms of *upscale*

TABLE 1-2   *United States Occupational Distribution by Sex, 1910 to 1988*

Occupational Grouping	Percentage of Men					Percentage of Women				
	1910	*1930*	*1950*	*1970*	*1988*	*1910*	*1930*	*1950*	*1970*	*1988*
Managers, professionals, proprietors	11	13	19	28	29	11	16	16	19	29
Clerical, sales, technical and administrative support	09	13	13	13	19	14	29	35	41	43
Service workers, including unskilled household	02	03	06	07	08	25	22	22	22	16
Precision workers, including crafts and foremen	15	16	18	20	21	01	01	01	01	02
Operators, including semiskilled laborers	29	30	29	27	20	29	24	19	15	09
Farming-related, forestry, and fishing	34	25	15	05	04	20	07	06	02	01

Source: U.S. Bureau of Labor Statistics; U.S. Bureau of the Census; *Statistical Abstract of the United States* 1990.
Note: Percentage totals vary from 100 due to rounding. Percentage distributions for 1988 do not include small proportions of employed persons from racial groups other than black and white.

America consisting of a wealthy overclass, a *new middle class* consisting of bright collars (knowledge workers), blue collars, and new collars (non manual workers who earn less than bright collars), and *downscale America* consisting of the poor and the underclass.

Other sociologists go further. Although they do not deny differences in rank, they feel that class lines cannot be drawn at all in an open society like our own, where there is so much movement or mobility up and down; where networks of informal social interaction overlap friendship, clique, and membership groups to form a series of gentle gradations; and where, accordingly, the concept of social class itself lacks meaning.

Social classes can be thought of, however, as conceptually discrete, even though, in an increasingly urbanized society, the social scientist finds it difficult to establish empirically the boundaries between classes. In this view, social classes can be described in terms of averages; social classes differ, on the average, by income, by occupational level, by attitudes toward education, and by other value systems that we have been describing. People who rank high on one class indicator such as education will tend to rank high on others such as occupation or income; yet there will be many exceptions. Probably everyone has met such exceptions: a successful businessperson who never completed high school; a service station operator who has a college degree; a social worker who lives in the slum neighborhood in which he or she works; a graduate student who is scraping along on a very meager income. There are many people who share socioeconomic characteristics of a given social class but who do not follow its characteristics in all respects. There are also large numbers of persons who will show status discrepancies, or inconsistencies; that is, they will rank higher on some dimensions of status than on others.

However, people whose characteristics are very different from the average on many characteristics of their class will be very possibly in the process of moving into the class immediately above or immediately below their own. As we show later, there is much movement between classes.

SUBCULTURES OF THE SOCIAL CLASS

Finding that people can be described as belonging to different classes is only a first step. How do the class groups differ in behavior, in beliefs, in attitudes, and in values? In other words, what is the subculture that characterizes each social-class group?

In describing subcultures, we use the five-class structure found to be useful in studying communities in the United States, even though this structure is an oversimplification, especially of the complex metropolitan area. The following descriptions are based on studies carried out in large cities (such as Kansas City) and in larger geographical areas (such as the San Francisco peninsula) as well as in smaller communities. Even though they are only thumbnail sketches and thus cannot do justice to the variety of patterns found at each class level, they do point out the most salient differences in life-styles as these differences bear on the educational system. A more expansive portrayal of social-class subgroups appears in the Appendix at the end of this chapter. The Appendix presents a useful portrayal by the Claritas Company of twelve major social groups subdivided into forty life-style clusters in the U.S. social structure.

It should be remembered that the classes are in many respects more alike than they are different. People of all classes, for instance, share the modern mass culture of the United States: they read the same newspapers, go to the same movies, listen to the same music, and watch the same television programs and commercials. Riesman et al. (1950), Hodges (1968), and Bronfenbrenner (1977) concluded that the mass culture is obliterating class differences, particularly between the lower-middle and the working classes.

The Upper Class

Upper-class people generally have inherited wealth and usually have a family tradition of social prominence that extends back several generations. A few may not be wealthy, but as the respected cousins, nieces, or nephews of upper-class families, they also belong in the upper class. All these people will be listed in the *Social Register* (if the community has one) and will belong to the most exclusive social clubs. They are likely to be well versed in family history.

Upper-class people belong to the boards of directors of art museums, of symphony and opera associations, and/or of Ivy League colleges. They tend to support charitable organizations and chambers of commerce. In older New England communities, their support was often silent ("the power behind the throne") and they left the offices in these organizations to be filled by upper middle-class people. In newer and in larger cities, however, they are likely to be indistinguishable from upper-middles in this respect and are visible as community leaders. Upper-class people usually belong to the Protestant Episcopal, Presbyterian, or Congregational churches in the Midwest, or to the Unitarian or Congregational churches in New England. Relatively few are Catholics or Jews.

Only rarely do upper-class people indulge in conspicuous consumption—showy parties, ostentatious mansions with numerous servants, jewels, and furs. Their houses, gardens, summer places, automobiles, and clothes are more likely to be conservative and inconspicuous (but of good quality).

In the eyes of upper-class people, education is a matter of proper rearing; formal schooling is no more important in this connection than are other aspects of training that children need if they are to fill their adult roles properly. Young men and women go into business or into one of the higher status professions such as architecture, medicine, law, and (infrequently) the ministry in an upper-status denomination. Children generally attend private schools and the prestigious Ivy League and selective coeducational and women's colleges (Kingston and Lewis 1990).

The Upper-Middle Class

Many adult members of this class have climbed to their present status from lower beginnings. Hence this class seems to include many active, ambitious people. The men are business executives and professional men; the women are active in club work, PTA, and civic organizations, and many work as professionals or technicians. The members of this class do not have aristocratic family traditions. Although some are interested in building up such traditions, the typical comment is, "We do not care about our ancestors. It isn't *who* you are, but *what* you are."

The majority of positions of leadership in civic, business, and professional organizations are held by upper middle-class people— organizations such as Rotary and Kiwanis clubs, the League of Women Voters, the Chamber of Commerce, the Medical Society, the Ministerial Association, the Bar Association, and the National Association for the Advancement of Colored People.

The upper-middle-class family may be quite wealthy, with money earned in the present generation; more commonly, the income is adequate, enough to pay for a comfortable home, a new automobile every few years, a fair-sized insurance and pension plan, and college education for the children.

Most such families patronize the theater and the symphony concerts, and they read such periodicals as *Harper's Magazine,* the *Atlantic Monthly,* and the *New Yorker.*

Many active church leaders come mainly from this class, and upper-middle-class persons frequently predominate in the membership of Episcopalian, Methodist, Presbyterian, and Unitarian churches (Mims and Lewis 1989). There are also many Catholics, Jewish, and Lutheran upper-middle-class persons.

The Lower-Middle Class

This large group is often called the common-person group by those above them in the social scale, although they themselves think of the working-class people below them as being the common person.

The lower-middle class consists of white-collar clerical and sales workers. Some are factory foreman or members of the labor aristocracy, such as railroad engineers, conductors, and photo-engravers; some are small building, electrical, and plumbing contractors. Most farm owners who operate their own farms are also in this class. These people tend to be at the national average; their income is at about the middle of the national income range, and the magazines, sports, television programs, movie stars, and comic strips they prefer tend also to be the national favorites.

Lower-middle-class people stress thrift and are proud of their economic independence. Their houses are usually comfortably furnished and well-kept but are small to medium in size and located nearer the wrong part of town or in inexpensive suburban tracts.

This group makes up the bulk of members of fraternal organizations such as the American Legion and their corresponding women's auxiliaries. They are fairly active in the PTA, and they furnish much of the membership in the Protestant and Catholic churches. They also furnish the lay leadership of some churches, especially the Baptist, the Lutheran, and in many places the Methodist churches. Many lower-middle-class people are Catholics, and some are Jews. Appreciable numbers of this class are children or grandchildren of immigrants.

Most members of the lower-middle class finished high school, and more than 75 percent of their children go on to college. Schooling is considered essential for a good job, and the children are expected to be obedient pupils. In the suburbs, lower-middle-class and working-class people often live in the same developments and have many characteristics in common. In time, the two classes may become enough alike to be considered together as the common-person group.

The Upper-Working Class

The respectable working people, the skilled and semiskilled blue-collar (as opposed to white-collar) workers, make up the upper-working class.* They are often Catholics, but there are also considerable numbers in the fundamentalist Protestant denominations such as the Assembly of God, the Pentecostal, and Holiness churches. They are also frequently Baptists and Methodists. At the same time, a considerable minority of this group are not church members, and some are hostile to churches.

Working-class people in small towns and cities live across the tracks or on the wrong side of town in small houses that are usually well kept. Particularly in the big cities, the working class has enjoyed a considerable increase in real income in recent decades, which has enabled increasing numbers to buy homes in inexpensive suburban tracts. Working-class people are fond of labor-saving gadgets as are middle-class people and frequently show concern about keeping up with the Joneses by buying more household equipment and newer and bigger cars and by frequently remodeling their homes.

Working-class men provide much of the membership in veterans' organization and fraternal orders. Their wives join the ladies' auxiliaries and are often members of PTA when the children are small. The men enjoy hunting and fishing; most working-class people, however, spend their leisure time at home, watching television or fixing up around the house. They seldom read more than the local newspaper and one or two magazines.

Typically, working-class adults put little value on learning for learning's sake; but they do

---

*In earlier studies of social structure undertaken by Warner's methods, the upper-working class was referred to as "upper-lower," and the bottom class as "lower-lower." It is not easy to find substitute terms that are free of implied derogation; we have chosen the terms *working class* and *upper-working class* and *lower-working class* as at least somewhat less biased and as reflecting more accurately the fact that most persons at the lowest social level are also workers. At the same time, to do as certain other sociologists have done and draw no distinctions within the working class is to obliterate some very significant differences between the large group of stable, blue-collar workers at the common person level and the smaller group who in many respects stand apart from all the other levels of society due to poverty and other social and economic deprivations.

recognize that education is the key to a good job, and they want their chldren to go further in school than they themselves have gone. At present, most of the children from this social class complete high school, and many go on to the local college or junior college.

The Lower-Working Class

Lower-working-class people are easy to stereotype because they live in highly visible and often shockingly poor quarters—big city slums or low-income public housing developments; shacks at the edges of cities; or tenant farmers' cabins. Miller (1964) has distinguished four groups within this class: the stable poor, unskilled workers who have steady jobs and a stable family life; the strained, who have steady jobs but who have major family or personality difficulties; the copers, people who have economic difficulties but strong family relations and who manage to get along most of the time; and the unstable, people who have both financial and familial or personal problems and who may end up on the welfare rolls as multiproblem cases.

Historically, the lower-working class included the newest immigrants who perform the most menial tasks of the society while they are learning the ways of life in the United States. In the past, such people were frequently Irish, German, Swedish, or Polish. Today, they frequently are Hispanic or Asian immigrants or black Americans with recent rural origins.

Lower-working-class people have few occupational skills and frequently have less than a high school education. Many have difficulty finding jobs because of their color. Because they are the last to be hired and the first to be fired, they have difficulty acquiring job seniority. A business recession that has only a slight effect on the other classes will put many lower-working-class people out of work, swelling the welfare rolls. Many people in this class spend a great deal of time seeking work that will provide a decent living for the family. It is not surprising that many believe that diligence and thrift have little to do with getting ahead and that only by luck or connections will they ever better themselves.

Families of this class produce a disproportionate share of problem children in the schools: the slow learners, the truants, the aggressive, and the delinquent. These children draw a good deal of attention from educational authorities. Identified as needing compensatory education, some get considerable help from remedial reading specialists, counselors, truant officers, and volunteer tutors.

Perceived Decline of Blue-Collar Culture

Some observers, such as Ralph Whitehead of the University of Massachusetts-Amherst, believe that growth in the percentage of upper-income groups together with standardization of culture in the mass media, economic problems in working-class communities, and other factors have caused a decline in the manifestation and integrity of traditional blue-collar cultural patterns. Whitehead believes that diminishment of blue-collar culture also may operate to reduce the power and opportunities available to working-class citizens:

> *Upscale yuppie haunts spring up: the health club, the gourmet takeout shop, the pricy boutique, the atrium building. Downscale blue-collar haunts wither: the union hall, the lodge, the beauty parlor, the mill. The guys with red suspenders began showing up in the beer commercials right about the time the loggers and guys with air hammers began to disappear . . . stock portfolios began to get fat just as blue-collar families were losing their pensions and health insurance. Condo prices were climbing in Atlanta just as bungalow prices fell in Buffalo. . . . This situation intensifies the shift of power in society as a whole. The dominant forces in society become . . . Upscale America versus Downscale America [italics in original]. Upscale America uses its power to secure privileges such as proposed cuts in the capital gains tax. Downscale America strikes back blindly through rising rates of crime. (Whitehead 1990, 53)*

DEVELOPMENT OF A BIG-CITY UNDERCLASS

Our description of social class has used a frequently used classification including five categories ranging from lower-working class to upper class. This classification has been widely followed in analysis and research dealing with the social class structure.

However, in recent years many social scientists have begun to identify and refer to a sixth class of individuals at the very bottom of the class structure: an underclass. As the term implies, this group can be considered as the lowest status and most depressed segment of the lower-working class. The term *underclass* also is used to connote a degree of permanency greater than is implied in referring simply to a lower class. People in the underclass are stuck at the bottom of the social structure and perceive themselves as having little chance of ever escaping from a pervasively poverty-ridden environment (Wilson 1987, 1990; Whitman 1989/1990).

Demographic analyses of census data indicate that there are two to four million persons in the United States who can be characterized as *underclass* using a definition that focuses on geographic concentration of families and individuals for whom poverty is persistent across one or more generations (Mincy, Sawhill, and Wolf 1990; DeParle 1991). As we stress throughout this book, concentrated poverty neighborhoods tend to be located in heavily minority, inner-core areas of big cities and generally rank high on indicators of social problems associated with unemployment, drug use, delinquency, dropping out of school, teen-age pregnancy, and violent crime. Although many residents of underclass communities are not poor and do not engage in dysfunctional or debilitating activities, by definition, all residents of such neighborhoods live in environments that are distressing for adults and "even worse for children and adolescents who normally cannot choose where they live and who are especially likely to be influenced by the patterns of behavior that are commonplace in their communities"

(Mincy, Sawhill, and Wolf 1990, 451). Recent deterioration in many poverty neighborhoods is summarized in this description of a public housing project in New York City:

> *For the most part, the people of King Towers are working men and women living ordinary lives despite the nightmare raging outside their doors. They are the New Yorkers who catch the early bus to work: the maintenance man, cleaning women and nurse's aides. They are the short order cooks and low-level clerks. They wash the clothes and empty the bedpans.*
>
> *After work, they rush home, a series of locks clicking behind them. Rarely are they caught on the street when darkness falls. Some even plot trips to the store as though mapping a route through a minefield . . . . [According to a researcher at City University, the increasingly-severe problems at King Towers are related to] "the decline of the social environment of the city and the society. There has been an enormous erosion of opportunities for people who are at the lower end of the scale."*
> *. . . . One result has been to turn young men into targets, mother love into despair and hope into skepticism. (Terry 1991, C10)*

The concentrated poverty neighborhoods in which the big-city underclass live are characterized not just by low income but also by a variety of other indicators of disadvantaged status, such as the following:

1. Many but not all of their inhabitants are from disadvantaged minority groups (Murray 1990). White families who live there and can be considered part of the underclass tend to be problem families, in which urban poverty has been transmitted across a number of generations, or relatively new urban in-migrants from economically depressed sections such as Appalachia.

2. There is a very high percentage of female-headed families, so high that in some concentrated poverty neighborhoods as many as 90 percent of the families are classified as female-headed. This high a degree of family disorganization exists in concentrated poverty neighborhoods, for many reasons, including (a) the existence of welfare policies that reduce assistance for families in which the husband remains in the home; (b) many unemployed or underemployed adult males who give up looking for a good job and become part of a street culture whose members drop out of normal family life; and (c) high rates of crime and personal violence that result in the incarceration of a relatively high percentage of the male population (Wilson 1987, 1990; Lemann 1991b).

3. Social institutions such as the family, the school, and the law enforcement system frequently appear to have broken down and no longer function effectively to achieve their traditional social purposes. Parents find it increasingly difficult to control their children, educators are overwhelmed with the problems of teaching a concentrated poverty population, and law enforcement agencies are unable to cope with relatively high rates of juvenile delinquency and adult crime (Terry 1991).

The problems of concentrated poverty neighborhoods are discussed in greater depth in Chapters 2, 3, 8, and 10, but at this point it is important to emphasize that such neighborhoods also are characterized by a sense of hopelessness and powerlessness. This attitude appears to be both a result and a cause of the social disorganization that exists in big-city slums. Reasons that this vicious circle of psychological despair and social disorganization has become so pronounced include the following:

1. In some ways, inhabitants of concentrated poverty neighborhoods are more segregated from the larger society than was true in the past, if only because the poverty area is now physically larger and the middle classes are more removed from it due to suburbanization than was true in previous generations (Goldsmith 1982; Hacker

1988; National Research Council 1989; Lemann 1991b). Data illustrating the increase in the number of persons in poverty areas in big cities have been compiled by Winard (1970), who found that the population of poverty areas in a sample of fifty-nine big cities increased by 18 percent between 1960 and 1970, and the percentage of city residents who lived in these areas increased from 32 percent to 39 percent. Wilson and Aponte noted that the number of poor people in central cities increased from approximately 8 million in 1969 to 12.7 million in 1982. They concluded that this increase represented a "remarkable change in the concentration of poor people in the United States in only slightly more than a decade" (1985, 239).

In addition, the proportion of low-income neighborhoods in which rates of unemployment, crime, and other social problems are very high nearly tripled after 1970 (Mincy, Sawhill, and Wolf 1990). Even though the overall population of some of these neighborhoods has declined in some cities, much of this decline has been due to further withdrawal of upwardly mobile families, leaving still fewer models of successful families for children to emulate than had been available in the 1960s. Wacquant and Wilson (1989) have referred to the outcome of this process as "hyperghettoization."

2. For young people lacking specialized skills and knowledge, it is more difficult to become mobile now than it was in earlier periods of United States history. As the number of unskilled and semiskilled jobs has decreased relative to highly skilled jobs, young people entering the economy in a low-level job have fewer prospects for advancement than did unskilled workers in the past (Howe 1988; National Research Council 1989; Wilkerson 1990a; Cotton, J. 1991). In addition, movement of industry to the suburbs has made many jobs geographically inaccessible to poverty populations in the central city (Suro 1991).

3. Forty or fifty years ago, inner-city parents striving to persuade their children to work hard to attain long-range goals in schools and society were aided by newspapers, magazines, and other mass media that told the child to save for the future and to view the satisfaction of many impulses as sinful and pagan. Today, the messages communicated to children by the mass media tell them to buy now, pay later, and to regard the satisfaction of worldly desires as the most glorious of human pursuits (Kamarck and Galston 1990). These messages also are directed, of course, at children outside of concentrated poverty neighborhoods, but it is the children of the poor who tend to be most victimized because such messages reinforce feelings of isolation in a have-not environment.

4. Many of the opportunities that enabled residents of poverty neighborhoods to become economically and socially mobile in earlier periods no longer exist. For example, street entrepreneurs who sell vegetables from pushcarts or provide unlicensed jitney taxi services are no longer allowed to function or are severely restricted in many cities, and stringent housing codes frequently result in relatively high-cost rentals that make it difficult to save money to start a small business. Although restrictions and regulations that hamper small business opportunities are well intentioned and often contribute to important public purposes, some also limit socioeconomic mobility to a much greater extent than was true in the past (Martin 1990). Decline of labor unions and of political patronage also has reduced opportunities that historically provided employment and mobility for large segments of the low-income population in big cities (Edsall and Edsall 1991).

5. The high proportion of low-income, female-headed families in many concentrated poverty neighborhoods in itself is both a cause and an indicator of intergenerational poverty in these neighborhoods (Mickelson and Smith 1989; Lemann 1991b). Because families in this situation generally are dependent on the income of one typically unskilled adult, it is perhaps inevitable that a very high percentage will be below the poverty level. Because so many husband-wife families escape the problems that exist in these neighborhoods at the first opportunity, a big-city

neighborhood with a high proportion of female-headed families tends to become progressively more characterized by the problems associated with concentrated poverty. Thus, it is not surprising to find that female-headed families not part of the labor force constitute an increasing percentage of the poverty population and a substantial proportion of the underclass in big cities:

> *The low-income population is becoming less and less similar to the population as a whole. . . . Poverty reduction has been more successful for those with a strong attachment to the labor force. In 1959, two-thirds of the heads of poor families had worked at least part time; the proportion had fallen to just over half in 1972. . . . Poverty among the aged and among male-headed families was dropping both absolutely and proportionately.*
>
> *The implications of these data for public policy are sobering. Those who remained poor in the early 1970s were increasingly those for whom it has been most difficult to design and implement effective social programs. (Lynn 1977, 98)*

In short, the slums of earlier years have become concentrated poverty neighborhoods characterized by intergenerational transmission of low status. Since World War II, suburbanization has left many of the poor to inhabit the inner core of central cities. Where big-city slums once functioned significantly as staging areas from which children of the poor perceived themselves as having a good chance to fight their way out, today they appear to many of their inhabitants as symbols of an oppression they have little chance to escape. There is still some mobility out of the underclass, but thousands of youngsters who grow up in big-city poverty areas believe there is little real possibility they will escape. The result, according to Mark Hughes, is that historically U.S. cities that functioned as "machines for mobility" of low-income persons now are less effective in serving this purpose (quoted in Wilkerson 1991, pA12).

Street Cultures and a Dual Labor Market

The preceding discussion of how the big-city underclass is locked into the lowest status position in the social structure makes it clear that the causes of the situation are both cultural and structural. The causes are cultural in the sense that they involve the attitudes of a group of people who develop distinctive modes of behaving in a shared environment. They are structural in the sense that they involve the ways in which opportunities and statuses are provided and determined within a large social and economic structure. Social scientists who have been studying big-city working-class and underclass groups have found it useful to view their situation and problems from both points of view. In particular, they have examined two related phenomena that appear to be important in understanding the plight of the underclass—the street culture, within urban society in the United States, and the operation of a dual labor market in the United States economy.

The street culture in low-status sections of United States cities has attracted the attention of many sociologists. One of the best descriptions of the street culture and its effects on underclass blacks in big cities has been provided by Elliott Liebow, who spent months as an observer documenting the day-to-day events in the lives of men whose interaction centered on a street corner in Washington, DC. In a poignant book named after one of its principal characters, *Tally's Corner* (1967), Liebow summarized the major events and beliefs that seemed to characterize the lives of these young men as follows:

> *Making a living takes on an overriding importance at marriage. . . . He wants to . . . support a family and be the head of it, because this is what it is to be a man in our society. . . . Although he wants to get married, he hedges on his commitment from the very beginning because he is afraid, not of marriage itself, but of his own ability to carry out his responsibilities as husband and father. His own father*

> *failed and had to "cut out," and the men he knows who have been or are married have also failed or are in the process of doing so. He has no evidence that he will fare better than they and much evidence that he will not. However far he has gone in school, he is illiterate or almost so; however many jobs he has had or how hard he has worked, he is essentially unskilled . . . jobs are only intermittently available . . . [and] are almost always menial. . . . He has little vested interest in such a job and learns to treat it with the same contempt held for it by the employer and society at large. From his point of view, the job is expendable; from the employer's point of view, he is. . . . Sometimes he sits down and cries at the humiliation of it all. . . . Increasingly he turns to the street corner. (pp. 210–214)*

Liebow's description of the major life events of men in a big-city street culture makes it clear that even though statistics on the problem of the underclass center on females as family heads, the underlying difficulty is as much or more a problem involving the situation of males growing up in concentrated poverty neighborhoods. (See Chapter 10.) Statistics on inner-city males are not as frequently scrutinized as those on females, but in general it is known that females are overrepresented compared to males in graduating classes in poverty-area high schools and in employment training programs for the big-city poor, both of which should be improving economic and social opportunities for the underclass. Without the participation of males, it is difficult to see how much progress can be made in alleviating the plight of the underclass (Wiley 1990).

Additional information about the street culture of male youth in underclass neighborhoods has been provided by Elijah Anderson (1978, 1989), whose ethnographic studies have examined interrelationships between male-female interactions, peer culture, limited employment opportunities, and other social aspects of life in inner-city communities. Anderson has described how the "lack of family-sustaining jobs or job prospects" helps reinforce peer-group emphasis on "sexual prowess as a mark of manhood, at times including babies as its evidence." After providing considerable detail regarding the consequent emergence and elaboration of a "sexual game" in which girls are "lured by the boys" often vague but convincing promises of love and marriage," Anderson reported that many girls "end up pregnant and abandoned, but eligible for a limited but sometimes steady income in the form of welfare, which may allow them to establish their own households and, at times, attract other men in need of money." At the same time, many of the young men "cling to the peer group" and end up in intermittent, low-paid employment or participants in an underground economy built on drugs and crime (Anderson 1989, 59, 76).

Economists use the term *dual labor market* to refer to the division of jobs between the primary market, consisting of jobs with relatively high wages and skill requirements, high tenure of employment, and opportunities for promotion to higher-status positions, and a secondary market, in which jobs barely provide a living wage and are characterized by low skill requirements, high absenteeism and turnover, and low opportunity for advancement (Kuttner 1989). Many or most jobs available to big-city poor—particularly the black poor—are in the secondary labor market (Harrison 1972b; Mickelson and Smith 1989; Wilson 1990).

Employment-training programs that the government has sponsored for low-income groups in big cities generally have not succeeded in helping a high percentage of enrollees enter the primary labor market. In general, these programs have been designed to provide unskilled persons with beginning skills required for jobs realistically available to them. In most cases, these jobs pay very little, and for various reasons the trainees who fill them do not stay employed for very long. "Government institutions designed to place low-income workers into 'good' jobs," Harrison concluded (1972b), have succeeded only in "recirculating the poor among the very low-paying, unstable jobs which they already held" (p. 123).

The street culture and the secondary labor market are closely interrelated. On the one hand, the irregular economy of the street culture (gambling, narcotics, hustling) is an attractive alternative to low-paid jobs in the secondary labor market for some residents of concentrated poverty neighborhoods (Williams and Kornblum 1985). In recent years, this irregular or "underground" economy increasingly has centered on crack cocaine and escalating rates of violence in the inner city (Bourgois 1989). Conversely, the availability of this alternative helps account for the tendency toward high turnover among some workers in poverty neighborhoods. The interaction between these phenomena was apparent in Glasgow's study of *The Black Underclass* in the Watts section of Los Angeles. Based on interviews reminiscent of those Liebow conducted in Washington, DC, Glasgow concluded that

> the trap in which these youths are caught cannot be fully understood in terms of theories, statistics, or comparison. It must be seen as a way of life. . . . It means having high aspirations but having to find the ways to achieve them outside the mainstream. It involves feeling capable of handling the task if opportunity were available but believing the chances are limited. . . . Still more unfortunate is the man who no longer even hopes for a legitimate opportunity. . . . His struggle for economic survival has shifted to another arena, the world of hustling, thugging, and burglary.
>
> Defensive behavior such as limited investment in goal striving, limited aspirations, and assumption of a psychological readiness for failure are some of the devices employed. . . . Hence institutional racism (which involves ghetto residence, inner-city educational institutions, police arrests, limited success models) . . . destroys motivation and, in fact, produces occupationally obsolete young men ready for underclass encapsulation. (Glasgow 1980, 81–84)

The Underclass in Big-City Poverty Neighborhoods

To avoid misunderstanding and neither to exaggerate nor underestimate the magnitude of the problems faced by the big-city underclass, it is important to be as clear as possible about its composition and also about its situation in the inner core of large metropolitan areas. The underclass includes members of white ethnic groups, but the majority of its members probably are from racial and ethnic minority groups that have been confined and piled up in the older, deteriorating, inner core of big cities (Magnet 1987). In Los Angeles, Houston, New York, and some other cities, a high proportion of the underclass is Hispanic; but in other cities the underclass is predominantly African American. Perhaps for this reason most research involving the emergence of an urban underclass has been focused on the black population. Mitchell Sviridoff has pointed out that although most of the poverty population in the United States is not in the underclass, the underclass is "making a disproportionate contribution to violent crime, the decay of inner-city neighborhoods, school failure, family disruption, illegitimate births, [and social welfare] dependency" (quoted in Brotman 1982, 1).

Ken Auletta (1982) has studied a group of underclass youth and adults participating in a work-training program in New York City and has also reviewed the research and analysis dealing with the development of an underclass in big cities in the United States. (Auletta additionally provides a comparison of the urban poor with the rural underclass among whites in Appalachia and blacks in Mississippi.) He cites data indicating that the underclass is about 70 percent nonwhite and that a majority of its members are children under age eighteen. His overall conclusions include the following:

> If we strip away the rhetoric of the right and left, a surprising consensus emerges. There is broad agreement that America has developed an underclass. . . . Those on the right tend to use words like 'pathology,' 'passivity,' and 'hostility'; those on the left tend to speak of 'despair,' 'hopelessness,' and 'alienation.' . . . For the first time in America's relatively young history, the ghetto has become a permanent home for too many broken families. For some, upward mobility is a lie, and organized society is the enemy; for others, the temporary crutch of welfare has turned into a straitjacket of permanent dependency. Whether you are compassionate or scared, the underclass should command your attention. . . . Pushing aside the pieties, charts, and stereotypes, one sees that a segment of the poor are sometimes victims of their own bad attitudes, and sometimes the victims of social economic forces. Neither the right's desire to blame individuals, nor the left's to blame the system, addresses the stubborn reality of the underclass. (Auletta 1982, 50, 319)

Auletta's portrayal of the underclass and its distinguishing characteristics agrees with the findings of a study Glaser and Ross (1970) conducted to identify the characteristics of successful men who had been upwardly mobile from seriously disadvantaged backgrounds. Glaser and Ross compared the histories and attitudes of successful and unsuccessful black and Mexican-American men from working-class communities. They found that compared to the unsuccessful group, the successful men had more positive attitudes toward representatives of mainstream society, exhibited relatively more loyalty to their families than to peers or street groups, experienced more stable and satisfying marital relationships, had more specific long-range goals and realistic strategies for achieving these goals, and based their self-esteem more on achievement than on "the good opinion of peers on the streets" (p. 74).

Improving Opportunity for the Underclass

The solutions one proposes for any problem depend, or should depend, on one's diagnosis of its causes. If the causes of the plight of the under-class in big-city poverty neighborhoods are both cultural and structural, it is legitimate to con-clude that solutions that do not take both types of phenomena fully into account will not have much chance to succeed. Our argument here and else-where in this book is that educators have an im-portant part to play in working to eliminate both the cultural and structural causes of intergener-ational poverty in big cities, as in other commu-nities in the United States.

The structural causes of big-city underclass status are relatively easy to enumerate, though extremely difficult to modify with social pro-grams. As we have seen above, interrelated causes include residence in a concentrated pov-erty neighborhood, isolation from the wider so-ciety and from resources such as jobs in the suburbs, lack of access or failure to enter the primary labor market, lack of material re-sources required to get a start in the economy, and discrimination or other barriers to employ-ment and education.

To a degree, naming the causes implies the direction for a solution. If a primary cause of underclass status is isolation from the larger so-ciety and residence in a concentrated poverty neighborhood, then efforts to help the big-city underclass should give some priority to reducing its isolation and deconcentrating big-city poverty. If the structural causes also include failure to enter the primary labor market, then efforts also should be made to change the economy so that better opportunities are available to the poor (Wilson 1990). Herbert Gans (1976) summa-rized this argument as follows:

Since jobs, particularly for the unskilled, are now scarcer than they were during the time the immigrants escaped poverty, it will be neces-sary to resort to deliberate job-creation. The jobs to be created should mesh with the needs of the private and especially the public econ-omy, but they must also mesh with the long-range need of the poor: to become part of the primary labor market. In other words, such

jobs must provide enough income, security, and opportunity for advancement to enable their holders to feel that they are participants in the economy and the society, so that their children will be able to advance further through education.

The historical record suggests that parental establishment in the primary labor market was a prerequisite and a takeoff point for using education to achieve further mobility, but whether history must repeat itself, or whether a different takeoff point can be found is as yet an unanswered question. No one knows where the take off point is at which people feel that they are participants in the economy and the society so that their children will feel it is useful to go to school. (Gans 1976, 66—67)

Along with programs to provide employ-ment and income, education also is a central component in carrying out a comprehensive program to improve conditions for the under-class in big cities. Desegregation of the public schools, for example, should be concerned with reducing the social isolation of the poor. Whether the poor acquire good jobs in the future will depend to an extent on what low-status youth learn in the schools. These issues are discussed at much greater length in subsequent chapters, but at this point it is important to emphasize that education should be seen as one key component in a larger effort to improve the quality of life for the residents of poverty areas in big cities.

The social and cultural causes of underclass status also must be explicitly addressed if pro-gress is to be made in alleviating the problems of big-city poverty. Because these causes involve such phenomena as are exemplified in the street culture, efforts to improve the conditions and sta-tus of the underclass must take into account the sense of hopelessness of people in the inner city and the difficulties that the family, the schools, the labor market, and other institutions encoun-ter in working with young people attracted to the street culture (Hacker 1988; Bourgois 1989; Raspberry 1991). To help citizens escape from the underclass, according to Lawrence Mead (1989, 1991), will require social policies that "aim to create competence," instead of simply "assuming it" (Mead 1989, 111). Our discussion in subsequent chapters of efforts to improve the effectiveness of education for disadvantaged students places considerable emphasis on the social and cultural causes of low performance among students in concentrated poverty neighborhoods.

Recent Developments in Underclass Neighborhoods

Recent developments have made underclass neighborhoods an increasingly difficult environment in which to lead a productive life and raise children. Among the most important of these developments are:

- The hyperghettoization that is occurring as upwardly-mobile residents flee and poverty becomes still more concentrated in low-income enclaves (Wacquant and Wilson 1989).
- The spread of crack cocaine and other drugs that increasingly have been victimizing women and children (Blakeslee 1989; London 1991).
- The growing incapacitation of health institutions, law enforcement agencies, and social-welfare organizations that are overloaded struggling to deal with drugs, family breakdown, and other problems (Berger 1990; London 1991).
- The increase in crime and delinquency to still higher and virtually epidemic levels (Di-Iulio 1989; Gross 1990).
- The growth in the negative influence of peer groups engaged in antisocial behavior.
- The spillover of the effects of drugs and crime into and around schools.
- The resulting demoralization, frustration, and feelings of powerlessness among inner-city residents (Berger 1990).

ECONOMIC, SOCIAL, AND DEMOGRAPHIC CHANGES

Many of the economic, social, and demographic changes occurring in the United States have important implications for the social structure and for education. This section describes and discusses some of the most significant changes. Much of the material in this book is concerned with the past and future effects of these changes on the educational system and with how the schools have responded or might respond most productively in the future. Trends considered involve the occupational structure, the age structure, racial/ethnic minority population, and poverty and female-headed families.

The Occupational Structure, Employment, and Education

A general name for the new society into which we are now moving is the postindustrial society. Daniel Bell (1973) and David Riesman (Riesman et al. 1950) used this term to denote the coming nature of our society, which began two hundred years ago as an agricultural society and changed in the period around 1900 to an industrial society. The personnel and wealth of an industrial society are devoted to transforming raw materials into many forms of material goods and selling or trading a part of these products for the goods and services wanted by the people of an affluent society.

As shown in Table 1-2 and in Figure 1-2, the number of jobs in manufacturing rose slightly between 1959 and 1984 and is expected to hold relatively steady at slightly more than 20 million through 1995. However, the proportion of manufacturing jobs to all jobs has declined substantially as numerous other types of jobs have expanded (Kilborn 1990; Nasar 1991). (Due to the introduction of technology and higher productivity, the *proportion* of manufactured goods in the Gross National Product has been relatively stable during this period.) The largest increase has been in service occupations, where the number of

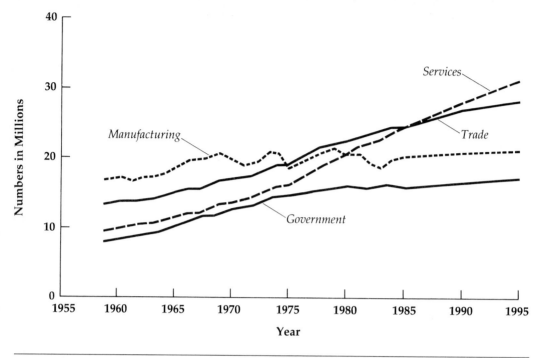

FIGURE 1-2 *Total Employment in Selected Major Economic Sectors, 1959–84, and Projected, 1985–95 (*Source: *Personik 1985).*

jobs increased from less than 10 million in 1954 to about 25 million in 1984. These occupations are expected to employ more than 30 million people by 1995, and seven of every ten new jobs in the 1990s will be white collar (Crispell 1990).* The service occupations in which job opportunities have increased most rapidly generally involve health, education, commerce, legal services, clerical work, and sales. The numbers of jobs in trade and in government also have increased significantly and are expected to increase slightly more in the future. The largest declines generally have been in extraction industries, such as agriculture, fishing, forestry, and mining (not shown in Figure 1-2). Because service and government both involve white-collar occupations, there has been an increase in the ratio of white-collar to blue-collar jobs.

Many of the services inherent in postindustrial society involve processing of information, so that some observers view current trends as evolving toward the emergence of an information society. For example, some social scientists (e.g., Beniger 1986) have shown that the percentage of workers in information-processing jobs (teachers, secretaries, accountants, insurance, etc.) grew substantially after 1950. Marc Porat (1977) prepared a U.S. Department of Commerce report that explicitly analyzed the information-processing components within the service segment of the economy. He was unable to say exactly how much the information sector has increased, but he did point out that it has grown by "leaps and bounds" (Naisbitt 1982). Analysis provided by the Education Commission of the States indicated that this trend toward emphasis

*The term *service occupations* refers to mostly middle-class jobs different from the service workers category used by the Census Bureau and others in classifying occupations. As shown in Table 1-2, jobs classified as carried out by service workers involve mostly unskilled persons who usually are working class in status.

on information-processing in the economy will require that workers possess "improved skills in the selection and communication of information .... Attention given only to the minimum competencies as currently defined shows a lack of foresight and leaves many students without adequate preparation for future learning and employability" (Gisi and Forbes 1982, 1–2). For this reason, editors of *The Economist* have called recent change in the occupational structure a cerebral revolution.

Trends regarding growth in the service economy and information processing have been accompanied by accelerating emphasis on high technology involving computers, automation and robotics, introduction of new media, and other aspects of work based on advanced scientific knowledge and methods. Electronics is now the largest industry in the United States, employing nearly three million people. All of these trends are expected to continue during the 1990s (Howe 1988; Christensen 1990). Young people entering the labor markets in the 1990s may have an easier time obtaining employment than has been true in the recent pass because the large cohort of baby boomers born after World War II are now adults, and there may be less competition for jobs among the smaller cohorts that followed (Levy and Michel 1991). However, shortage of workers may further stimulate employers to accelerate trends toward replacing low-wage labor with automated machinery and other labor-saving equipment. Jobs in this type of economy likely will pay more, but they also will require more advanced skills and higher levels of training and education (Morris 1989; Christensen 1990).

Employment Trends and Education

Technological changes in recent years thus suggest that future economic prosperity will depend on comprehensive efforts to prepare young people and to retrain many adults for employment in jobs that require new skills. In this regard, an assessment of national technology trends estimated that 42 percent of U.S. workers will re-

quire additional training to prepare them for work-place changes in the 1990s. The business sector is already spending many billions of dollars each year on training, but its expenditures in preparing workers for jobs in today's economy undoubtedly will have to be substantially greater if the United States is to compete internationally in high-technology industry (Reich 1991).

Even though there are many disagreements and uncertainties regarding the future of technology and its effects on society and the schools, all or nearly all informed observers would probably accept several conclusions. Among these conclusions are the following:

1. Computerization and other aspects of new technology are "deskilling" some jobs (e.g., bank teller) but increasing the skill requirements in many fields, such as military service (Burke and Rumberger 1987; Zuboff 1988; Kilborn 1990; Bailey 1991).

2. Jobs with relatively high pay and status will require higher levels of skill and knowledge. Success in the economy will depend even more than it does now on mastery of increasingly more complex and abstract information and skills (Howe 1988; Morris 1989; Bailey 1990; Reich 1991).

3. Accelerated introduction of new technology is bringing about major changes in the occupational structure and the social-class structure. Leontief (1985) studied recent trends and concluded that continuing emphasis on new technologies such as computer-based automation may require 20 million fewer workers in the year 2000 than would maintenance of the old technology, but at the same time the percentage of professionals in the work force will be about 38 percent higher (1985, 39). This would mean that even though millions of persons would have higher status jobs, many millions of others either would be unemployed or would have to be absorbed in new jobs—many of them low in pay and status—in other fields (Barton and Kirsch, 1990). Similarly, Castells (1985) reviewed developing trends and concluded that the impact of automation on the occupational structure may result in a "bifurcated labor market, with the upgrading of a minority of workers and rapid growth of professional sectors, while a majority of workers are deskilled and reduced to low-paying jobs, either in labor-intensive services or in down-graded manufacturing" (1985, 21).

4. Both general education and vocational education at the secondary and postsecondary levels should place greater stress on providing students with broad learning and problem-solving skills as contrasted with narrow training for specific occupations in order to prepare them for a range of occupational possibilities that will become important in the future (Panel on Secondary School Education for the Changing Workplace 1984; Commission on Workforce Quality and Labor Market Efficiency 1989; Barton and Kirsch 1990).

5. The groups most hurt by introduction of high technology will include African American and Hispanic youth. As pointed out by Xerox Corporation Chairman David Kearns, more than "a third of tomorrow's work force will be minorities . . . [half of whom now either drop out of school or] don't come close to having the skills to survive in an advanced economy" (Fiske 1989b, l).

In addition to these direct implications for the educational system, developments now impacting the occupational structure point to a multitude of important questions about the functioning of the schools in society. Do students from differing social-class and racial/ethnic backgrounds receive equal or even adequate opportunity to pursue success in our postindustrial economy through the schools? Are women disadvantaged in pursuing equal opportunity through education? How are trends in the family and the home affecting students' opportunities to succeed academically and economically? What problems do youth encounter in striving to become productive adults? What can the schools do in responding to such questions? What should they do? Changes involving the occupational

structure provide the background and context for much of the succeeding presentation and discussion of material throughout this book.

Bifurcation in the Social Structure

As indicated above, many scholars believe that new technologies are causing a bifurcation such that the high-income, high-status segment of U.S. society is becoming larger at the same time that the low-income, low-status segment also is becoming larger. In other words, the rich are getting richer and relatively more numerous, the poor are getting poorer and relatively more numerous, and the middle segments thereby are shrinking (Whitehead 1990). Analysts at the U.S. Bureau of the Census (and elsewhere) hesitated for years to view this trend as long lasting, because it might have been due to temporary considerations, such as initial absorption by the economy of large numbers of poorly paid young workers, immigrants, and women in entry-level jobs. However, persistent increase in wealth/poverty differentials throughout the 1980s eventually led Bureau analysts to refer to this trend as "the growing inequality of the income distribution" (Pear 1990c; 1991). Economists point particularly to increased Social Security taxes and declining demand for unskilled, poorly educated workers as causes of recent bifurcation (Shabecoff 1991). Support for concluding that bifurcation has occurred includes the following factors:

• The relative difference in income between the highest income groups and the lowest increased by more than 25 percent between 1978 and 1989 (Pear 1990c, 1991).

• Forty-four percent of the new jobs created between 1979 and 1985 paid poverty-level wages (Bluestone and Harrison 1987).

• An increasing economic squeeze on the middle class has, among other things, increased the percentage of income young families spend on home mortgages from about 15 percent in 1949 to about 33 percent in 1989 (Nasar 1989; Levy and Michel 1991). As pointed out by Dreier and Hulchanski (1990), this pattern has left many lower-income families "only one rent increase, one hospital stay, one lay-off, or other emergency away from becoming homeless" (p. 123).

• The relative proportion of the median income spent on taxes more than doubled between 1965 and 1990. Taxes that increased substantially in the 1980s generally were regressive, that is, sales taxes and Social Security taxes that take a higher percentage of the income of low-income than of higher-income individuals. Conversely, federal income tax reductions were much more rewarding for the rich than for the poor (McIntyre 1991).

• Between 1980 and 1990, the average pretax income of families in the top 5 percent increased by 45 percent, and their tax rate decreased 10 percent. For families in the bottom 5 percent, pretax income declined by 9 percent and tax rates increased by 28 percent (DeParle 1990a).

• The percentage of poor and near-poor families served by Medicaid decreased from 65 percent in 1969 to 46 percent in 1985 (New Republic editors, 1986).

• Young adults appear to be having increasing difficulty obtaining a college education and purchasing a home unless their parents are able (and willing) to make a large financial contribution (Kuttner 1987; Frances 1990; Levy and Michel 1991).

• The spread in wages among persons in the same type of job increased by about a third between 1970 and 1990. This dispersion in wages, in turn, means that persons at the low end have increased difficulty maintaining an adequate standard of living (Uchitelle 1990b).

Levy and Michel (1985, 1990, 1991) have pointed out that one group most affected by social and economic changes has been the baby boomers entering adulthood and middle age, and that many persons in this generation believe they will never live as well as their parents and are part of a vanishing middle class. "In summary," Levy and Michel concluded, "the baby boomers . . . see themselves portrayed in television commercials which tell them that they can 'have it all.' But the living standards they saw as children—a single-family house, two or three children, provision for retirement, and all this on one salary—seem wildly out of reach" (1985, 40–41). Subsequent data indicated that due to rising housing costs and falling relative income, the percentage of householders between twenty-five and twenty-nine years of age who own a home fell from 43 percent in 1980 to 36 percent in 1988 (Crispell 1989). Similarly, the home-ownership rate for married couples aged twenty to twenty-four fell from 32 percent in 1983 to 27 percent in 1988 (Hughes and Sternlieb 1990).

Some other observers disagree with the conclusions and implications drawn from data indicating that the social structure may be growing more bifurcated. Levels of consumption, they point out, have continued to rise for most people in the United States despite the financial difficulties and obligations thereby incurred; the U.S. economy has created new jobs at a rate faster than ever before; millions of women have entered the labor force in little more than one generation; and the generations following the baby boom should be in greater demand in the labor market because there will be fewer young adults competing with each other (Kosters and Ross 1988; Edmondson 1990). These observers also argue that discouraging data for the 1980s (such as reported above) have been largely due to a significant economic recession in the first part of the decade and, in any case, represent temporary dislocations and setbacks as the nation adjusts to a new technological age and to increased foreign competition.

Time will allow for determining whether or to what extent the social structure in the United States has become permanently more bifurcated in recent years. Meanwhile, it is difficult to determine the extent to which bifurcation in the social structure may be having, or subsequently may have, negative effects on the educational system. On the one hand, an increase in the percentage of children in low-status families may exacerbate problems educators face in working with disadvantaged students, taxes for education may decline if low- and middle-income citizens are unwilling or unable to take on additional burdens, and young adults who experience severe economic problems may become more alienated from the schools and society as a whole. On the other hand, bifurcation may be much less important in determining such outcomes than other social, political, economic, and educational developments that involve

1. The adequacy of tax policies and structures.
2. The extent to which the economic system is internationally competitive and provides improved job opportunities.

3. The effectiveness of the schools in delivering improved instruction.
4. The large increase that has occurred in immigration.
5. The functioning and correction of deficiencies in health-care arrangements.
6. Numerous other issues and problems.

The Age Structure

The population of the United States is becoming older as the baby boomers advance into and through middle age. As Figure 1-3 shows, the polygon representing age distribution will look less like a pyramid and more like a square

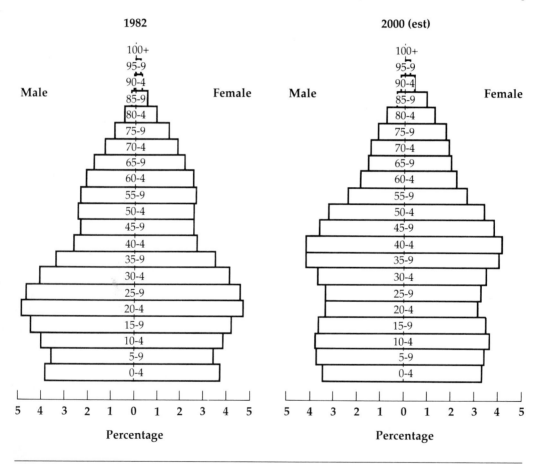

FIGURE 1-3 *Estimated and Projected Percent Distribution of the U.S. Population, by Age and Sex, 1982 and 2000 (est)* *(Source: U.S. Bureau of the Census.)*

TABLE 1-3 *Recent and Projected Changes in the Labor Force, Percentage Distributions by Age and Race/Ethnicity*

Age Group	Percentage Distribution		
	1976	*1988*	*2000*
16 to 24	24.3	18.5	15.9
25 to 54	60.8	69.1	71.1
55 and over	14.9	12.4	12.3
Race/Ethnicity*			
White	88.2	86.1	84.3
Black	9.9	10.9	11.7
Hispanic	4.4	7.4	10.1
Asian and other	1.9	3.0	4.0

Source: Adapted from Fullerton 1989.
*Race/ethnicity sums total more than 100 because black and white Hispanics are counted twice. Other includes Native Americans and Pacific Islanders.

TABLE 1-4 *Estimates and Projections of the Population of the United States, 1985–2000*

Age Group	Numbers in Millions				Percent Change 1985–2000
	1985	*1990*	*1995*	*2000*	
Under 15	52.0	54.6	56.7	55.9	08
15–24	39.5	35.6	34.1	36.1	−09
25–34	42.0	43.5	40.5	36.4	−13
35–44	31.8	37.8	42.0	43.7	37
45–54	22.6	25.4	31.4	37.1	64
55–64	22.3	21.1	20.9	23.8	07
65 and older	28.5	31.7	33.9	34.9	22

Source: U.S. Bureau of the Census.

(through the mid-fifties) as generational progression proceeds during the remainder of this century. By the year 2030, 21 percent of the population is expected to be sixty-five or older, compared with 9 percent in 1960 (Beck 1990). As this happens, young people will constitute a decreasing percentage of the labor force (Table 1-3).

Government projections also underline changes that will occur in the school-age population. As shown in Table 1-4, the size of the cohort under fifteen years of age is expected to increase by 8 percent between 1985 and 2000, as the baby boomers raise their own children. Some demographers studying population change in the early 1980s thought that this echo of the baby boom would become much more pronounced, but it now appears to be a relatively small and transient blip in long-range trends functioning to reduce the relative percentage of children and youth in the United States.

Figure 1-4 provides a graphic representation showing government projections of the size of four cohorts of youth under twenty-four years of age. Conclusions and implications that can be drawn from Figures 1-3 and 1-4 and Table 1-4 include the following:

1. Enrollment at the preschool level probably will rise slightly until about 1992 and then decline slightly before levelling off.

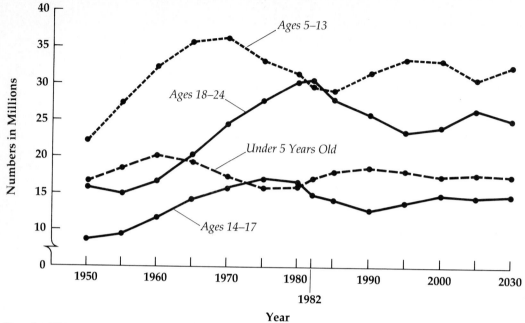

Data for 1950 to 1982 are estimates; data for 1983 to 2030 are midrange projections.

FIGURE 1-4 *Estimates and Projections of the Population under Twenty-Four Years of Age, 1950 to 2030, by Age Group* (Source: *U.S. Bureau of the Census.*)

2. Enrollment at the elementary level probably will rise until 1995 or 2000 and then decline.

3. Enrollment at the secondary level probably will continue declining until shortly after 1992 and then rise.

4. Enrollment in postsecondary institutions of youth between eighteen and twenty-four years of age probably will decline until about 1995 and then rise.

5. It may be easier to finance education in the year 2000 than it was in the year 1985 because the percentage of persons under twenty-four will be smaller and the percentage of persons in the most productive working years (ages twenty-five to sixty-four) will be larger.

6. Young adults entering the labor market may have an easier time obtaining employment than has been true in recent decades, because the size of this cohort will not be increasing rapidly as it has in the past twenty years (Howe 1988; Christensen 1990).

Racial/Ethnic Minority Population

Another major change taking place in the social structure involves the relative increase in the percentage of racial and ethnic minority groups. The largest of these groups include African Americans, Hispanics (Cuban, Mexican American, Puerto Rican, and others of Hispanic background), and Asian Americans (Chinese, Cambodians, Eastern-origin Indians, Filipinos, Hmong, Japanese, Koreans, Laotians, Vietnamese, and other subgroups).

The Hispanic minority is growing more rapidly than is the black population and may become the largest U.S. minority group in the twenty-first century (see Chapter 10). The percentage of whites in the United States population is expected to decline from 85 percent in 1982 to 82 percent in 2010 and then to 77 percent in 2050. (Hispanics constitute an ethnic group most of whose members are classified as white or black, depending on their racial background. The term *Hispanic American* usually includes both black and white Americans of Hispanic origin.) The number of U.S. residents in the "black and other races" classification is expected nearly to double between 1982 and 2030 (U.S. Bureau of the Census 1984).*

The increase in the number and proportion of minority population in the United States is due primarily to relatively high fertility in some minority groups—particularly the Hispanic and African American subgroups—and to in-migration of Asian, Hispanic, and other groups. Increase occurring due to relatively high fertility and to in-migration of families with young children means that minority citizens will constitute an increasing proportion of the labor force (see Table 1-3), and that minority students will constitute a rapidly increasing proportion of the future school-age population. For example, the percentage of births classified as black, Hispanic, or Native American increased from 14 percent in 1950 to 35 percent in 1991 and may increase to more than 40 percent by the year 2010 (Marriott 1991a). Reflecting this trend, the percentage of non-Hispanic whites in public school enrollment declined from 80 percent in 1968 to 70 percent in 1988 and will decline still more in the future. During this period, the number of Hispanic students in public schools increased by 80 percent, enrollment of Asian students increased by 412 percent, and the number of native American (Indian) students increased by 105 percent (Orfield 1987). Just as the educational system was a main agency for the socioeconomic mobility of European immigrants from 1840 to 1915, it will be challenged to perform a similar function for minority children and youth who will constitute a substantial proportion of the school-age population during the remainder of this century and thereafter.

*Terminology and definitions used to designate racial and ethnic populations are sometimes confusing. The majority of (ethnic) Hispanics in the United States are considered to be white in terms of racial background, but many have predominately black or other ancestry. Data for the Hispanic population sometimes exclude those with predominately African origins, and data for whites frequently include those who are Hispanic. Insofar as possible in this book, we use classifications that include black Hispanics under the general "Hispanic" heading, but some data sets tabulate this part of the Hispanic population only with other African Americans. In some data sets, black Hispanics are counted twice, once in each category.

Some data sets include tabulations of "Black and Other" racial groups, which means that Asian Americans, Native Americans, and /or other smaller racial groups have been tabulated with African Americans. In many instances the groups so tabulated are those officially designated as minority for various government purposes, namely *American Indians or Alaskan Natives, Asian or Pacific Islanders,* and *Black or African Americans.* When *other* is used in a set of terms also including Asians, blacks, and whites, it usually refers to persons who have mixed or uncertain ancestry or are unwilling or unable to designate their racial background. There was a 45 percent increase in the other category between the 1980 and 1990 census. The Census Bureau uses a formula to allocate others to one of the four major racial groups specified above.

Poverty, Race/Ethnicity, and Family Structure

The percentage of people living in poverty in the United States, as defined by federal income guidelines, declined substantially from 23 percent in 1959 to 12 percent in 1969, held steady at 12 to 13 percent throughout the 1970s, increased slightly to 14 percent during the recession years of the early 1980s, and then fell back to 13 percent in 1988 and 1989 (Pear 1990c). The percentage of children and youth between six and seventeen years of age who were in poverty followed the trend of large decline in the 1960s, decreasing from 26 percent in 1959 to 14 percent in 1969, but then rose substantially to 20 percent throughout most of the 1980s—an increase of 43 percent from 1969 to 1989.

The poverty rate for African American and Hispanic children and youth has been and remains much higher than the rate for non-Hispanic whites. In 1989, the rate of 36 percent for Hispanics between six and seventeen years of age was more than 2.5 times higher than the rate for non-Hispanic whites (14 percent), and the rate for blacks (42 percent) in this age group was three times the white rate. (However, because the white group is much larger, whites comprise nearly 50 percent of U.S. children and youth whose families live in poverty.) In addition to being disproportionately minority, children and youth in poverty are much more likely to live in poorly-educated female-headed families than are their more fortunate peers. Approximately nine of ten families headed by a female high-school dropout are poverty families, compared with one in twenty among couples who have attended college. Much of the increase in the percentage of children and youth in poverty after 1969 was associated with a simultaneous increase in the percentage of children in families headed by females, which approximately doubled between 1969 and 1989. Nearly three-quarters of the increase in the number of children in poverty after 1970 has oc-

curred in households headed by women. During this same time period, the percentage of African American children who live in female-headed families increased from 33 to 51 percent.

Interaction of some of the trends described above is illustrated in Figure 1-5, which shows that family structure and race/ethnicity are independently associated with children's poverty. Approximately two-thirds of children under eighteen in one-parent minority families lived in poverty in 1989, compared with 8 percent of the non-Hispanic white children in two-parent families. The most direct consequence of these trends for the public schools has been that the percentages of poverty students, minority students, and students from female-headed families in elementary and secondary enrollments generally have increased substantially. All these trends have been particularly pronounced in big-city school districts. Much of this book discusses the effects and implications of these trends.

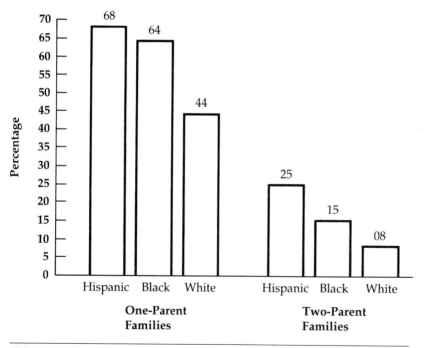

FIGURE 1-5 *Percentage of Children under Eighteen Years in Age in Poverty, by Race/Ethnicity and Family Type, 1989 (Source: U.S. Bureau of the Census.)*

Generational Conflict and Poverty

As noted above, the percentage of children and youth in poverty has increased greatly since 1969, while the percentage of poor persons in the population increased only slightly. One major reason for this discrepancy is that the percentage of the elderly (individuals more than sixty-five years old) who live in poverty decreased almost as rapidly from 1969 to 1984 as it had from 1959 to 1969. By 1984, only 11 percent of the elderly were living in poverty, compared with 36 percent in 1959. This percentage remained stable at 11 to 12 percent throughout the late 1980s (Congressional Budget Office 1988; Gleckman 1990; Pear 1990c; Kaplan 1991).

The causes of this impressive decline in poverty among the elderly include the expanded functioning of federal Social Security and health-care programs, growth of pension plans, relaxation of retirement regulations, and general economic prosperity through much of this period (Langbein 1991). At the same time, state and federal budget deficits led to reductions in various programs for children, including nutrition and day-care services and financial support for low-income parents. By the 1990s, total per capita expenditures by the federal government on the elderly were more than ten times as great as per capita expenditures on children under age seventeen (Lamm 1990). Between 1977 and 1987, the average net worth of persons over sixty-five increased more than half, while the net worth of persons seventeen to twenty-four years of age declined by about one-third (Carlson 1987). Such data led George Miller, Chair of the U.S. House of Representatives Select Committee on Children, Youth, and Families, to remark, "We've spent 25 years lifting the elderly out of poverty. . . . [In so doing] we've become a nation of rich adults and poor kids" (quoted in Borger 1989, 18).

The coincidence of a large decline in poverty among the elderly and a large increase among children and youth has raised a number of important questions involving the social structure and political arrangements in postindustrial society. Longman (1985) has described shifts that have been occurring in postindustrial patterns involving the needs of differing generations:

> *The middle generation in any given era either must strike a prudent balance between the demands of its parents and the demands of its children or prepare itself for an unhappy retirement. . . . [If] the government spends so much on the elderly that it must skimp on the education of the young or an investment in economic growth, then . . . [the young later may be unable to provide] enough support. Alternatively, if the government is stingy with the elderly, the young may come to feel . . . free to shirk their responsibilities to the old. (Longman 1985, 78)*

After pointing out that the elderly in preindustrial society frequently maintained some economic power and security by retaining title to land or other property, Longman noted that industrialization changed the balance of power between the generations: "Factory workers could . . . achieve a tolerable standard of living without first inheriting an estate. But, by the same token . . . most could not save enough out of their wages" to provide for their own old age. For this reason, economic arrangements shifted so that each generation could tax its own children through such programs as Social Security and Medicare.

As in earlier periods, however, each generation thus "appears simply to appropriate by law some share of the next generation's wealth." However, this arrangement cannot succeed unless each generation also provides the resources to ensure the future economic productivity of its children. "Each generation, in exchange for support in its old age, still must provide its children with a legacy" (Longman 1985, 81). Indeed, in contrast to earlier historical periods in which inheritance primarily took the form of property and other material resources, today the major resource parents help children acquire for the future is education—preferably a college degree.

As a result, fewer children expect to inherit wealth, and fewer parents feel obliged to save it to pass on to the next generation (Langbein 1991).

Preston (1984) also reviewed data on poverty differentials between generations and called attention to underlying economic and social forces that function to generate relatively more poverty among the young. The elderly, he pointed out, have increased their relative political influence as the percentage of older persons in the population has increased and as persons under age sixty-five realize that they will benefit later from programs designed to assist the elderly. Children and youth, on the other hand, cannot vote and must depend on the political influence of parents acting on behalf of their progeny. However, Preston also argued, the conjugal family

> has begun to divest itself of responsibility for the young, just as it earlier abandoned much of its responsibility for the elderly. Absent fathers are the main factor in this divestiture. . . . It is unrealistic simply to wish away the possibility that there is direct competition between the young and old for society's resources . . . . U.S. society has chosen to place almost exclusive responsibility for the care of children and youth on the nuclear family. Marital instability, however, has much reduced the capacity of the family to care for its own children. Hence insisting that families alone care for the young would seem to be an evasion of collective responsibility. (Preston 1984, 46, 49)

Preston and other authors (e.g., Longman 1989; Will 1989; Gleckman 1990) have also pointed out that increase in the proportion of minority groups among children and youth in general and low-income youngsters in particular may reduce the likelihood that the white adult population will be willing to assume and discharge its collective responsibility for the welfare of the young. The problem may be particularly acute because, as we point out in many parts of this book, a high proportion of low-income children and youth are now concentrated in big-city poverty neighborhoods and schools characterized by massive social disorganization and very low academic achievement; given the continuation of current patterns, many of these youngsters will not be in a position to contribute productively to the welfare of subsequent generations.

In addition, the percentage of U.S. households with no children increased steadily from 26 percent in 1870 to nearly 70 percent in 1990 (Coleman 1990b). This trend, too, may reduce taxpayers' willingness to provide education and other services for children.

The possibility that serious generational conflict will occur in the future has been made more likely in recent years by controversies and developments regarding health care for the elderly. Partly due to health-care costs, federal expenditures for each citizen over sixty-five years of age are more than ten times greater than for young people less than eighteen years old (Peterson 1990). As the costs of such care have escalated rapidly, disagreements have arisen concerning the burden of paying for it. For example, Congress passed a 1988 law that initiated a surtax on relatively high-income elderly citizens to pay for long-term catastrophic hospitalization, but it rescinded this legislation in 1989. What happened, according to Phillip Longman (1989, 27) and some other observers, was that

> Congress dared to ask today's wealthy and middle-class senior citizens to pay for this new protection . . . rather than, as usual, pushing the cost on to the young in general. These seniors refused . . . . The spectacle of healthy retirees denouncing even the concept of helping fund their own needs . . . threatens to extinguish the good will the young now feel toward the elderly as a whole . . . . As the population ages, all of us will have to bear a much greater burden to support the truly needy in old age. If affluent retirees hope to hold on to the subsidies they are already collecting from younger workers, including

the working poor, they had best show they are willing to share in the general sacrifice required.

Concerned with these developments, the executive director of the American Association of Retired Persons called attention to the importance of bringing about an equitable distribution of benefits and responsibilities across generations. In an editorial in that organization's monthly bulletin to members, Horace Deets (1990) concluded that

> *the real inequity in this country today is not between the elderly and children. It is the growing gap between the rich and poor of all ages. That gap is wider today than it has been in a half-century. It is the result of 10 years of tax cuts that benefit higher-income people, disproportionate cuts in domestic programs for the poor, significant increases in defense spending, rampaging medical costs, stagnant wages and the loss of millions of high-paying manufacturing jobs.*
>
> *One reason for America's greatness is that— throughout our history—one generation has helped another. Other times it's been indirectly through programs like Social Security and Medicare, guaranteed student loans or Head Start. With the many problems our nation faces*

today, Americans of all ages must work together as never before. (Deets 1990, 3)

CONCLUSION

After describing the social-class hierarchy and the occupational structure of postindustrial society in the United States, this chapter identified several major trends that have important implications for the educational system. Trends discussed included a growing emphasis on high technology, the increasing average age of the population, increase in the percentage of minority groups in schools and society, and growth in the proportion of children and youth in poverty.

The confluence of these trends is likely to generate enormous problems and challenges for the educational system in the future. At the same time that education is becoming a more decisive factor in determining the success of individuals and social groups (see Chapter 7), an increasing proportion of students are disadvantaged by their socioeconomic and/or racial/ethnic background. Also, commitment to providing children and youth with a good start in life may be declining as the adult population grows older and less similar demographically to subsequent generations. The full extent and nature of these problems and challenges are reviewed and analyzed in the following chapters.

EXERCISES

1. A person's social position as measured by socioeconomic indices (occupation, income, level of education, etc.) does not always coincide with social position as evaluated by the people in the community. (For example: a poor, but upper-class woman; or a wealthy, but lower-class businessman.) Have you known such a person? What does that case illustrate about the bases of rank in the community?

2. Obtain a map of your community. Interview a few people and ask them to point out the

   areas that are best, average, and worst neighborhoods. (One of the best persons to interview will be a real estate agent.) How much agreement do you find among your informants? On what kinds of factors are their judgments made?

3. Select an elementary school in your community and make an informal investigation of the community from which it draws its pupils. Walk up and down the streets of the neighborhood, observing the houses, lawns, alleys; look at the names on doorbells; go

into stores and notice what kinds of food, clothing, and other goods are sold; and so on. From what social classes would you say the school draws? How heterogeneous is the neighborhood?

4. Think about the community in which you grew up. (If it was a large city, interpret this to mean your neighborhood.) Write a description of that community in terms of its social-class structure. How many social classes were there? Were class lines clearly drawn? What kinds of people occupied positions of highest and lowest status? Does it make sense to think of your community as a system of social classes? Why or why not?

5. Read *The New Class?* edited by B. Bruce-Briggs, and outline the main points in a debate between an advocate and an opponent of the conclusion that a new class of intellectuals is distinguishable within a modern society.

6. In a school to which you have access, make a list of the children in a given classroom. Estimate their socioeconomic positions. Compare these positions with such things as their school grades, their extracurricular activities, and their vocational goals.

SUGGESTIONS FOR FURTHER READING _____

1. There are a number of studies of social structure in various United States communities. The first and most elaborate was of a New England community, reported in a serious of volumes called the Yankee City Series. Volume 1 of the series, *The Social Life of a Modern Community,** by W. Lloyd Warner and Paul S. Lunt, is the most appropriate for studentrs of education. A midwestern community is reported in *Democracy in Jonesville* by W. Lloyd Warner and associates. A small agricultural town in a border state is described in *Plainville, U.S.A.* by James West; the same community studied again is described by Gallaher in *Plainville Fifteen Years Later.* The social structure of the San Francisco peninsula is described in Hodges, *Peninsula People.* For a discussion of the social-class structure in the United States at large (rather than a study of a particular community), read *American Life: Dream and Reality* by W. Lloyd Warner. The most comprehensive study of the social structure of a large city (Kansas City) is reported in *Social Status in the City* by Coleman and Neugarten. Chapter 12 in that book summarizes studies of social-class structure in eight different communities.

2. The methods of investigating and measuring social status are described in *Social Class in America,* by W. Lloyd Warner, Marchia Meeker, and Kenneth Eells; *Social Status in the City,* by Richard Coleman and Bernice Neugarten; and Chapters 1 and 2 in Kahl's book, *The American Class Structure.* Also, *Class, Status and Power: A Reader in Social Stratification* edited by Bendix and Lipset is a good reference for the student who wishes to explore further the theoretical issues of social structure, or to study different theories of stratification.

3. A number of books analyze value patterns and life-styles of particular social classes. For example, C. Wright Mills's book, *White Collar,* is a penetrating analysis of the American middle class. Spectorsky's *The Exurbanites* describes the lives of upper-middle-class suburbanites. Chinoy's *Automobile Workers and the American Dream;* Walker and Guest's *The Man on the Assembly Line;* and Rainwater, Coleman, and Handel's *Workingman's Wife* are all interesting studies of the working class, as is *Whitetown* by

---

*For each of these references, see Bibliography for facts of publication.

Binzen. *Blue-Collar World,* edited by Shostak and Gomberg, reports research findings on working-class life prepared by various authors. Baltzell's *Philadelphia Gentlemen* deals with a national upper class. *Social Standing in America,* by Coleman and Rainwater, reports on preceptions of social class in Boston and Kansas City.

4. Religious groups function as subcultures in U.S. society. A book by Lenski comparing Protestants, Catholics, and Jews in Detroit shows that different religious subcultures exist within a given social class. Also, Rossi and Rossi have studied the effects of a parochial school system on the attitudes and beliefs of Catholics. Gordon's *Assimilation in American Life* deals with religious as well as ethnic factors. Greeley's book, *Religion and Career,* is a study of differences between Catholics, Protestants, and Jews in a large sample of college graduates.

5. The heterogeneity of suburban life is described in Dobriner's *Class in Suburbia.* Berger's book, *Working Class Suburb,* describes a relatively homogenous blue-collar suburb. *The Levittowners* by Gans reports on the public schools in a Philadelphia suburb.

6. The effect of the social-class structure on education earlier in this century is treated at length in *Elmtown's Youth* by August B. Hollingshead; in *Children of Brasstown* by Celia B. Stendler; in *Social-Class Influences upon Learning* by Allison Davis; and in *Growing Up in River City* by Robert J. Havighurst and colleagues.

7. Numerous authors have described the street culture in various racial and ethnic groups. *Street-Corner Society* by William F. Whyte describes this culture in an Italian community, and *Down These Mean Streets* by Piri Thomas describes it in a Puerto Rican community. *The Social Order of the Slum* by Suttles contrasts several Chicago communities with respect to the operation of a street culture and other, related manifestations of social behavior in low-status neighborhoods. *Strategic Styles: Coping in the Inner City* by Janet Mancini describes five differing coping styles among inner-city youth.

8. One of the best discussions of the dual labor market can be found in *Internal Labor Markets and Manpower Analysis* by Peter Doeringer and Michael J. Piore. An excellent summary on this and related topics is available in A. Dale Tussing's 1975 article in *Intellect* magazine.

9. *In the Age of the Smart Machine* by Shoshana Zuboff provides a wealth of information and examples concerning effects of computer technology on the nature of work.

10. Many of the trends considered in this chapter are discussed in an essay by Mickey Kaus (1990) entitled "For a New Equality."

11. An essay by Burt Saxon (1991) provides an analysis of *Tally's Corner* and describes how he has used the material in it to teach social studies at the high-school level.

12. Aspects of intergenerational conflict and possibilities for dealing with it productively are analyzed in a comprehensive and balanced manner in George Kaplan's 1991 article titled "Suppose They Gave an Intergenerational Conflict and Nobody Came."

APPENDIX *Twelve Social Groups Subdivided into Forty Community or Neighborhood Life-Style Subgroups*
(Claritas Company PRIZM Cluster System for Market Segmentation and Targeting)

Social Group	Subgroup Nickname	Modal Location*	Modal Education Level**	Modal Employment Classification***	Modal Adult Age Groups****
1. Educated, affluent executives & professionals in elite metro suburbs	1. Blue Blood Estates	Subs	CG	WC	4/3
	2. Money & Brains	Subs	CG	WC	4/5
	3. Furs & Station Wagons	Subs	CG	WC	3/4
2. Pre- & postchild families & singles in upscale, white-collar suburbs	1. Pools & Patios	Subs	CG	WC	5/4
	2. Two More Rungs	Subs	CG	WC	6/5
	3. Young Influentials	Subs	CG	WC	1/2
3. Upper-middle, child-raising families in outlying, owner-occupied suburbs	1. Young Suburbia	Subs	CG	WC	3/2
	2. Blue-Chip Blues	Subs	SC	BW	3/2
	1. Urban Gold Coast	City	CG	WC	2/6
	2. Bohemian Mix	City	CG	WC	2/1
4. Educated, white-collar singles & couples in upscale, urban areas	3. Black Enterprise	City	SC	WC	3/4
	4. New Beginnings	City	SC	WC	2/1
5. Educated, young, mobile families in exurban satellites & boom towns	1. God's Country	Town	CG	WC	3/2
	2. New Homesteaders	Town	SC	BW	1/2
	3. Towns & Gowns	Town	CG	WC	1/2
	1. Levittown, U.S.A.	Subs	HS	WC	5/6
6. Middle-class, postchild families in aging suburbs & retirement areas	2. Gray Power	Subs	SC	WC	6/5
	3. Rank & File	Subs	HS	BC	5/6
7. Mid-scale, child-raising, blue-collar families in remote suburbs & towns	1. Blue-Collar Nursery	Town	HS	BC	3/2
	2. Middle America	Town	HS	BC	5/4
	3. Coalburg & Corntown	Town	HS	BC	6/3
	1. New Melting Pot	City	NC	WC	6/5
8. Mid-scale families, singles & elders in dense, urban row & hi-rise areas	2. Old Yankee Rows	City	HS	BW	6/5
	3. Emergent Minorities	City	SH	BS	1/2
	4. Single City Blues	City	SC	BW	1/2
9. Rural towns & villages amidst farms & ranches across agrarian mid-America	1. Shotguns & Pickups	Town	HS	BF	3/4
	2. Agri-Business	Farm	NC	BF	6/5
	3. Grain Belt	Farm	HS	BF	6/5

36

10. Mixed gentry & blue-collar labor in low-mid rustic, mill & factory towns	1. Golden Ponds	Town	NC	BW	6/5
	2. Mines & Mills	Town	HS	BC	5/4
	3. Norma Rae-Ville	Town	SH	BC	1/4
	4. Smalltown Downtown	Town	HS	BW	6/1
11. Landowners, migrants & rustics in poor rural towns, farms & uplands	1. Back-Country Folks	Town	SH	BC	6/3
	2. Share Croppers	Town	GS	BF	6/5
	3. Tobacco Roads	Town	GS	BF	6/5
	4. Hard Scrabble	Farm	GS	BF	6/5
12. Mixed, unskilled service & labor in aging, urban row & hi-rise areas	1. Heavy Industry	City	SH	BC	6/5
	2. Downtown Dixie-Style	City	SH	BS	1/6
	3. Hispanic Mix	City	GS	BC	1/2
	4. Public Assistance	City	GS	BS	1/6

Source: Adapted from "PRIZM the 40 Cluster System." Reprinted with permission of Claritas, Alexandria, VA

*City = dense, urban row or high-rise; Subs = suburban or urban-fringe residential; Town = outlying towns or satellite suburbs; Farm = farms, ranches, or other rural.

**CG = college grad and above; SC = some college; HS = high school grad; SH = some high school; GS = grade school; NC = not classified.

***WC = white collar; BC = blue collar; BW = mixed white and blue collar; BS = blue collar and service; BF = blue collar and farm.

****1 = 18–24; 2 = 25–34; 3 = 35–44; 4 = 45–54; 5 = 55–64; 6 = 65+

Educational Selecting and Sorting in Postindustrial, Metropolitan Society

Since the landing of the Pilgrims in Massachusetts more than 350 years ago, the United States
has been perceived as a land of opportunity. During the eighteenth and nineteenth centuries,
good land could be obtained at low prices and
jobs were available in the expanding economy.
New cities were being built and new industries
were being established. Since 1900, the areas of
economic opportunity have shifted to expanding
industry and to the expanding professional, managerial, technical, and service professions. These
postindustrial occupations generally require
postsecondary education. The professions all require at least a college degree, and executive positions in business and industry are awarded
more and more to college graduates.

SORTING AND SELECTING IN THE EDUCATIONAL SYSTEM

Realizing that an avenue of opportunity is provided by the educational system, parents have
encouraged their children to continue further
and further in school. Since 1910 the proportion

of young people attending high school has more
than tripled, and the proportion attending college has multiplied by more than seven. Table
2-1 shows the increase in high school and college
attendance since 1910.

Amount of education is a good indicator of
socioeconomic status, from lower-working class
up through upper-middle class, because education leads to economic opportunity. Young people, through education, secure higher-status jobs
than their fathers. With greater incomes, young
adults from lower-status families tend to associate with persons of higher status and adopt their
ways. It may be concluded, consequently, that
education provides a channel not only to better
socioeconomic status, but also to social mobility
in the broader sense.

These statements are so widely accepted
that few people, even those most critical of the
educational establishment, disagree with them.
Research on amount of schooling in relation to
success in adult life (Levin, Guthrie, Kleindorfer,
and Stout 1971) affirms the view that amount of

TABLE 2-1 *Change in the U.S. Education System as a Selecting Agency*

Educational Level Reached	Number (per thousand)					
	1910	*1940*	*1960*	*1970*	*1980*	*1990*
First year high school	310	800	910	960	990	995
Third year high school	160	580	750	860	885	900
Graduation from high school	93	450	720	770	810	850
Entrance to college or other postsecondary institution	67	150	330	465	465	490
Graduation from college (Bachelor's degree)	22	70	170	255	270	290
Master's degree	1.5	9	35	75	75	85

Source: Author's estimates from various sources.

education (not school marks) is linked with later success. These authors concluded their report by saying, "The evidence is overwhelming in support of the proposition that the post-school opportunity and performance of a pupil are related directly to his educational attainment" (p. 14). In 1985, for example, the average college graduate earned nearly twice as much as the average high school dropout (Cohany 1986).

The American educational system is expected to provide opportunity for social and economic mobility by selecting and training the most able and industrious youth for higher-status positions in society. Insofar as the school system does this job efficiently and fairly, it equips youth for career opportunities and it contributes to the success of democracy.

The degree of selection can be observed in Table 2-1, which shows our estimates of the number of students per thousand born in a given year who reach various levels of the educational ladder. It will be seen that the high school is much less selective than it was 40 to 50 years ago; and the college, too, while still selective, is less so than before. This pattern reflects the fact that the focus of selection in the social structure has shifted somewhat from the high school to college. That is, the main prerequisite for obtaining a relatively high-status job used to be possession of a high-school diploma, but many jobs now require completion of two or more years beyond high school.

The process of selection is not carried on in a formal sense by the school alone. Several factors determine how far a student goes in school: the parents' wishes, the individual's aspirations and ability, the financial status of the family, as well as the school's effects in encouraging some students and discouraging others. The end result, however, is selection.

Intellectual Ability and Postsecondary Participation

As mentioned, one goal of the educational system is to select and carry along the most able young people. The extent to which the system suc-

ceeds in this regard can be assessed in part by examining data on relationships between students' performance and their continuing participation in the system. Data of this kind are provided in Table 2-2, which indicates that high school seniors high in test performance are much more likely to attend college than are those low in test performance. (Test performance is an indirect, though, of course, imperfect measure of intellectual ability.) Only 19 percent of students in the highest quartile on test performance did not attend college.

However, data on college completion indicate that many students high in test performance do not complete college. As shown in Table 2-2, only 35 percent of 1972 seniors in the highest quartile on test performance graduated from college four years later. Although this figure should be interpreted cautiously because many college students graduate after the fourth year and because college graduation rates have improved in the 1980s, many high-achieving students undoubtedly do not graduate due to lack of financial support, poor motivation, personal problems, or other causes. Dropout from college is particularly a problem for high-achieving students in the bottom quarter on social class, of whom only 20 percent graduated in four years. Thus, it appears that the educational system has substantial room for improvement in facilitating the progress of high-ability students.

More recent data continue to indicate that large numbers of high-performing students do not obtain postsecondary degrees or diplomas, despite the increasing importance of college completion in obtaining rewarding employment (see Chapter 7). Schmitt (1989) analyzed the subsequent careers of 1980 high-school graduates and found that only 57 percent of those in the highest test-performance quartile had attained a postsecondary degree by 1987.

Postsecondary Participation, Social Status, and Race/Ethnicity

Table 2-2 also demonstrates that both intellectual ability and participation in postsecondary

TABLE 2-2 *Percentages of 1972 High School Graduates Who Entered and Graduated from College, by Socioeconomic Status (SES) and Test Performance*

Socioeconomic Status (SES) Level	Percentage Entered in College Test Performance				Percentage Graduated from College in 1976 Test Performance			
	Lowest 25%	Middle 50%	Highest 25%	Total	Lowest 25%	Middle 50%	Highest 25%	Total
Lowest 25%	21	33	63	30	02	05	20	05
Middle 50%	23	47	73	47	02	10	27	12
Highest 25%	46	76	93	82	03	18	47	31
Total	24	50	81	51	02	10	35	15

Percentage of lowest socioeconomic group in highest test performance level	11
Percentage of middle socioeconomic group in highest test performance level	25
Percentage of highest socioeconomic group in highest test performance level	60

Source: Computed and adapted from Bruce E. Eckland, Louis B. Henderson, and Andrew J. Kolstad 1981.
Note: College attendance refers to entry in an academic program in 1972. College graduation refers to acquisition of a bachelor's degree four years later. Test performance is measured by a composite reading and mathematics score. Socioeconomic status scores are a composite of father's and mother's education, father's occupation, parental income, and types of items in the home. Data were collected as part of the National Longitudinal Study of the High School Class of 1972.

schooling are related to socioeconomic status (SES). Regarding intellectual ability, 50 percent of high-school graduates in the highest SES quartile have test scores in the highest 25 percent, compared with only 11 percent of graduates in the bottom SES quartile. As regards participation in postsecondary schooling, 82 percent of graduates in the highest SES quartile entered college and 31 percent completed college four years later, compared with 30 percent and 5 percent, respectively, for low-status graduates.

After taking account of socioeconomic status, postsecondary participation does not appear to be related systematically to race and ethnicity. As shown in Table 2-3, recent data (Peng 1990) indicate that about one-quarter of African American, Hispanic, and non-Hispanic white students from the bottom quartile of SES families are attaining postsecondary certificates or degrees within six years of high-school graduation. The major exceptions to the generalization that race/ethnicity is not much related to postsecondary participation independent of social class involve the high attainment rates of Asian American students, regardless of their SES,

and a tendency for middle- and high-status (non-Hispanic) white students to have higher rates of attainment than do black and Hispanic students with comparable SES backgrounds.

Data further indicate that low-status students are even less likely than otherwise to attend or graduate from college if they attend high schools in which other students generally have low test scores. Regarding 1980 high-school seniors, for example, Paula Knepper (1991) found that only 48 percent of low-SES graduates who attend high schools with low average test scores completed more than one year of postsecondary education by 1984, compared with 68 percent of low-SES graduates of high-quality schools.

Recent data also indicate that the relative college attainment of economically disadvantaged students has declined rather than increased over the past few decades. Although the college entrance rates of unmarried high-school graduates from the lowest and highest quartiles on family income (of their parents) were mostly unchanged between 1970 and 1989 (about 45 percent for the low quartile and nearly 80 percent for the high quartile in each of those years), the

TABLE 2-3 *Highest 1986 Level of Educational Degree or Certificate Attained by 1980 High-School Seniors, by Socioeconomic Status (SES) Quartile and Race/Ethnicity*

Socioeconomic Status Quartile and Race/Ethnicity	Percentage with High-School Diploma or Less	Percentage with Postsecondary Certificate or Degree
Lowest 25%		
Asian	53	47
non-Hispanic black	73	26
Hispanic	74	25
non-Hispanic white	75	24
Middle 50%		
Asian	51	49
non-Hispanic black	68	32
Hispanic	67	32
non-Hispanic white	62	38
Highest 25%		
Asian	43	57
non-Hispanic black	56	44
Hispanic	60	40
non-Hispanic white	45	55

Source: Adapted from Peng 1990.
Note: Socioeconomic status is a composite variable based on family income, parental education and occupation, and household characteristics. Totals vary from 100 due to rounding. Hispanics may be of any race.

baccalaureate-attainment rates for the low quartile category remained under 10 percent whereas the baccalaureate rate for the high quartile category increased from 39 to 50 percent (Mortenson and Wu 1990; Mortenson 1991). Thomas Mortenson of the American College Testing Program interpreted these trends as constituting a "staggering" decline in the relative opportunities available to low-income youth:

> *In 1989 a student from the bottom quartile of the family income distribution . . . had a 6 percent chance of graduating from high school, enrolling in college, and graduating by age 24. . . . [Since high-income students' college completion rates increased, the relative attainment of the bottom quartile has] actually declined, especially during the second half of the 1980s. . . . High school graduates from the bottom quartile . . . experienced extraordi-*

> *nary difficulties with college access . . . and college completion. (Mortenson 1991, 124)*

Ability Grouping and Tracking

Sorting and selecting for further success in the educational system take place in part through ability grouping and tracking. At both the elementary and secondary levels, many schools use ability grouping (or homogeneous grouping) in attempting to facilitate teaching and learning (Passow 1988b; Slavin 1991). Students with high academic performance are placed in a class of high achievers or in a subgroup of high achievers within the classroom; those with low performance are placed in low-achieving classes or subgroups; and those in between are placed in average groups. In many schools, the high, average, and low levels are further subdivided according to previous achievement.

Tracking refers to the practice in high schools of enrolling students in college preparatory classes (usually high-achieving students), or general, business, or vocational tracks for lower achievers or students not intending to go to college or preferring to pursue less academic subjects. (The general curriculum usually includes little mathematics and no advanced science or foreign language courses.)

Ability grouping or tracking in schools enrolling a socially diverse population tends to be correlated with social class and racial/ethnic status. Partly because economically and socially disadvantaged students have lower average achievement scores than do middle-class students and nonminority students (documented later in this chapter), they are found disproportionately in low-achieving classes and nonacademic tracks, while middle-class students are disproportionately represented in higher-achieving classes and college preparatory courses and tracks. In 1990, only 39 percent of high-school seniors from families with annual income below $12,000 completed a college-preparatory curriculum, compared with 55 percent of students from families with more than $42,000 income (Mortenson 1991).

In addition, social class has an independent effect on track placement beyond its association with achievement. In 1982, 80 percent of high-achieving seniors high in socioeconomic status were in an academic track, compared with only 52 percent of seniors who were high in achievement but low in status (Vanfossen, Jones, and Spade 1987).

The pattern of grouping varies from community to community and school to school. In some schools, ability groups are formed only in particular subject-matter areas, as when those children in a grade who are poor in reading, or those who are particularly good in science, are given special instruction as a group. In such schools, the child may spend only one period a day with a special group; the rest of the time, with his or her regular group. This modification of homogeneous grouping tends to counteract the possible social-class biases that may otherwise operate (Barr and Anderson 1991).

To take another example, schools in homogeneous parts of a large city, where the school population is drawn from one or two social classes, may use a scheme of sectioning by ability that brings together those children with the most motivation for education. The children who consistently work hard often seem to teachers to be the abler ones and will tend to be grouped together.

Ability grouping has been severely criticized since about 1965 on the basis of the double-barrelled argument that (1) the ability tests as they now exist tend to favor middle-class children and (2) the tests now in use tend to segregate students by social class and by race/ethnicity. In some school districts, ability grouping has been disallowed by federal judges who ruled that it resulted in unconstitutional segregation, and school boards in some large districts have abandoned or reduced the extent of ability grouping.

This trend became widespread after the Supreme Court's 1967 ruling in *Hobson* v. *Hansen*, which stated that separation of Washington, D.C., students into fast and slow tracks resulted in unconstitutional segregation of minority and nonminority students. After 1967, the courts and the federal government frequently required desegregating school districts to reduce or eliminate grouping of students based on ability test scores, previous achievement, or other measures that might reflect a student's disadvantaged background rather than his or her true academic potential. In 1991, the U.S. Office of Civil Rights introduced guidelines stating that districts cannot receive federal funds if their grouping practices result in segregation and cannot be shown to have clear educational benefits (Schertschuk-Armstrong 1991.)

Although ability grouping usually has been introduced in order to facilitate teaching and learning, much research indicates that it generally has not improved student achievement. Reviews of research on this topic have most often concluded that ability grouping has little or no consistent overall effect (Good and Marshall 1984; Slavin 1990a). Some studies, however, indiate that homogeneous grouping promotes better performance among high achievers (Kulik and Kulik 1987), and/or that it further depresses the performance of low-achieving students (Dar and Resh 1986; Sorensen and Hallinan 1986; Gamoran 1990). Instances in which ability grouping appears to be harmful to the performance of low achievers are thought to occur because:

- Teachers have low expectations for students and thus pace instruction at a very slow rate (Gamoran 1986a).
- The content of instruction emphasizes low-level skills (Peterman 1990).
- Students are stigmatized and thus are not motivated by being placed in slow classes or groups.
- Low achievers frequently reinforce each other's negative attitudes and behaviors (Gamoran 1990).

Detrimental phenomena associated with ability grouping and tracking have been documented by Jeannie Oakes in a study of the school experience of students in more than 1,000 classrooms (Oakes 1985; Oakes and Lipton 1990). Using data collected as part of A Study of Schooling in thirty-eight nationally representative districts, including both elementary and secondary schools, Oakes found that students in high-ability classes generally had more challenging instruction than did those in low-ability classes, which tended to emphasize "simple memory tasks" and literal comprehension. Oakes concluded that the rudimentary curriculum content in low-ability classes "was such that it would be likely to lock students into that track level . . . [by omitting topics] that constitute prerequisite knowledge and skills for access to classes in . . . higher track levels" (Oakes 1985, 77–78).

Oakes also found that students in higher-ability classes were significantly more "involved" in their learning than were those in low-ability classes. The latter students, she concluded, "reported that they were far less concerned about completing classroom tasks . . . [and] also reported far greater degrees of apathy—not caring about what goes on in class or even concerned about failing" (Oakes 1985, 130). One of her

overall conclusions was that given the correlation between economically and socially disadvantaged background on the one hand and low-track placement on the other, ability grouping and tracking frequently constitute "in-school barriers to upward mobility for capable poor and minority students. . . . [Once placed in low-level classes, their] achievement seems to be further inhibited by the type of knowledge they are exposed to and the quality of learning opportunities they are afforded" (Oakes 1985, 134).

Ability grouping and tracking thus frequently seem to reinforce the low performance of disadvantaged students as part of the educational system's general arrangements for sorting and selecting meritorious students who are likely to be successful at the next level. Tracking at the high-school level also operates to depress further low-status students' self-esteem, contact with highly motivated peers, participation in extracurricular activities, and subsequent enrollment in postsecondary education (Vanfossen, Jones, and Spade 1987). Therefore, what begins as an attempt to ensure that instruction is appropriate for students given their previous performance (Nevi 1987) may be harmful for low achievers who might achieve more in heterogeneous classes with more challenging instruction.

This problem in the sorting and selecting process raises a number of complicated and difficult questions for which there are no simple answers. (Barr and Anderson 1990; Page and Valli 1990). For example, how can the pace of instruction in heterogeneous classes be maintained at a level that challenges high achievers without frustrating low achievers? How might instruction in low-ability classes be improved to avoid the detrimental effects frequently associated with homogeneous grouping of low achievers? How can high expectations be maintained in low-level classes so that grouping and tracking function to provide remediation and special assistance for selected students rather than increasing the gap between high and low achievers? We return to these types of questions elsewhere in this book, particularly in Chapters 8 and 13.

Reading Achievement

Because reading is important to success in most academic fields, reading achievement probably is the best single measure of academic achievement in general. Data on the reading performance of students nine, thirteen, and seventeen years of age have been collected periodically since 1971 by the National Assessment of Education Progress (NAEP). The NAEP uses a sophisticated sampling design and advanced technical methods to obtain estimates of reading proficiency that allow comparison of performance over time and among subgroups in the national population. Reading proficiency is categorized according to the following scores and definitions (NAEP 1985):

150: *Rudimentary*. Readers can follow brief written directions. They can also select words, phrases, or sentences to describe a simple picture and can interpret simple written clues to identify a common object.

200: *Basic*. Readers can locate and identify facts from simple informational paragraphs, stories, and news articles and can combine ideas and make inferences based on short, uncomplicated passages.

250: *Intermediate*. Readers can search for, locate, and organize information in relatively lengthy passages and can recognize paraphrases of what they have read.

300: *Adept*. Readers can understand complicated literary and informational passages and can analyze and integrate less familiar material.

350: *Advanced*. Readers can extend and restructure the ideas presented in specialized and complex texts.

The NAEP data in Figure 2-1 portray large differences in the reading proficiency of students according to their level of socioeconomic status. (Most NAEP reports have used parental education to represent social class background.) At nine years of age, students whose parent(s) did not complete high school have an average proficiency score of 193 (basic level), compared with an average of 220 (halfway between basic and intermediate) for nine-year-olds whose parent(s) had postsecondary education. Similar differences in reading proficiency by socioeconomic status (SES) are apparent for thirteen-year-olds and seventeen-year-olds. The average reading proficiency of seventeen-year-olds whose parent(s) did not complete high school is only 267 (between intermediate and adept), which places them at about the same level as high SES thirteen-year-olds. Because 267 is far below the 300 level at which readers are described as being able to "understand complicated literary and informational passages," average seventeen-year-olds from low SES families presumably would experience many problems if they sought to obtain additional education after high school.

However, the patterns shown in Figure 2-1 underestimate differences in reading performance by SES because the parental education categories are crude indicators of social class that do not consider such factors as occupational status and income, neighborhood location, interactions between social class and race/ethnicity, and disadvantages associated with underclass status. To obtain a more refined understanding of differences related to social class and other variables, NAEP data can be analyzed taking more account of the characteristics of students and schools included in the national sample. The results of such an analysis are shown in Table 2-4, which presents data from our analysis of the 1984 reading proficiency scores of thirteen-year-old students in public schools.

As shown in Table 2-4, the average reading proficiency score of students who attend schools with more than 60 percent poverty and minority enrollment in so-called disadvantaged urban areas (defined by the NAEP as having a population greater than 200,000 and a high proportion of residents on welfare or unemployed) and whose parent(s) did not continue with education beyond high school is 229. (*Poverty* is defined in this analysis as eligibility for federal lunch subsidy.) Students who live in the same type of community and whose parents have the same education level

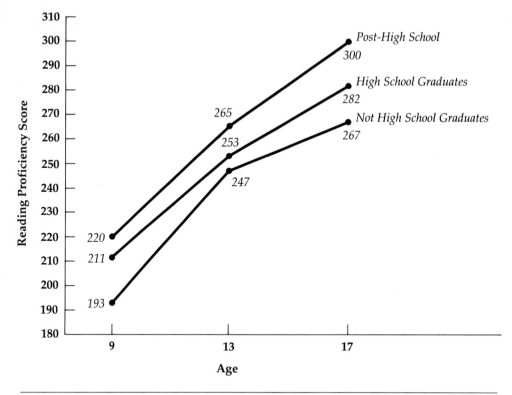

FIGURE 2-1   *NAEP Reading Proficiency Scores of Nine-, Thirteen-, and Seventeen-Year-Olds, by Parental Level of Education, 1988* (Source*: Mullis and Jenkins 1990.)*

but who attend schools with enrollment less heavily poverty and minority have an average of 260. Students whose parent(s) attended college and who live in advantaged urban communities (more than 200,000 people but low on welfare and unemployment) have an average score of 233 if they attend heavily poverty/minority schools and an average of 278 if their schools are relatively low in poverty/minority enrollment.

It should be noted that the average reading proficiency scores of thirteen-year-olds in public schools with enrollment more than 60 percent poverty and minority (scores of 229 and 233 in disadvantaged and advantaged urban areas, respectively) are only slightly higher than the 1984 average of 224, which the NAEP reported for all nine-year-olds whose parents had acquired some education beyond high school (Mullis and Jenkins 1990). Conversely, the 278 registered by thirteen-

year-olds whose parents had at least some college education and who attended schools relatively low in poverty/minority enrollment in advantaged urban communities is approximately the same as that for seventeen-year-olds whose parents graduated from high school but did not attend college.

In addition, the scores for the thirteen-year-olds in heavily poverty/minority schools are considerably below the "intermediate" level of 250, which the NAEP defines as characterizing readers who can "search for, locate, and organize the information they find in relatively lengthy passages." The standard deviation of NAEP reading scores is approximately 35. This means that only about 10 percent of urban thirteen-year-olds attending disadvantaged urban schools with heavily poverty/minority enrollment have scores as high as the average student in advantaged urban schools with lower minority/poverty enrollment, and only

TABLE 2-4 *NAEP Reading Proficiency Scores for Public School Thirteen-Year-Olds, by Type of Community, Parent Education, and School Percentage of Poverty/Minority Students, 1984*

Disadvantaged Urban Community		Advantaged Urban Community	
Parent(s) graduated from high school or less		Parent(s) some college or more	
School percentage poverty/minority		School percentage poverty/minority	
More than 60	229	More than 60	233
Less than 60	260	Less than 60	278

Source: Author's analysis using data tape available from the National Assessment of Educational Progress.
Note: Disadvantaged urban refers to communities with a population greater than 200,000 and a relatively high proportion of residents on welfare or unemployed. *Advantaged urban* refers to communities above 200,000 with lower percentages of residents on welfare or unemployed. *Poverty* is defined as eligibility for federal lunch subsidy. Minority students in this analysis are black or Hispanic.

about 10 percent of thirteen-year-olds in advantaged urban schools relatively low in poverty/minority enrollment have scores below the average student in disadvantaged urban schools with high poverty/minority enrollment. There thus is little overlap between the two groups, and a large proportion of urban students attending public schools high in poverty/minority enrollment are not acquiring reading skills adequate to learn well in high school.

Given that students in schools high in poverty/minority enrollment constitute a significant proportion of the high school population, it is not surprising to learn that average reading performance levels of high-school seniors are cause for concern regarding national needs for an increasingly better educated and more highly skilled citizenry. Archie Lapointe, director of the NAEP, called attention to this problem when he reported that only about 40 percent of high school seniors are "comfortable" with academic track textbooks and "relatively sophisticated magazines," that the "bulk of our population seems stuck at the three lowest levels of reading skill achievement," and that the majority of students do not write "adequate responses to the informative, persuasive, or imaginative tasks included in the assessment" (Lapointe 1987, 76–77). More information on NAEP patterns and trends in achievement of racial/ethnic subgroups is provided in later chapters, particularly Chapters 10 and 13.

Assessments conducted by the NAEP also indicate that the reading performance of students whose parents have not attended college have improved at relatively low proficiency levels but have not improved or have even declined at more advanced levels. For example, as shown in Table 2-5, there was an increase of six points (from 38 percent in 1971 to 44 percent in 1988) in the percentage of students at or above the intermediate reading proficiency level among thirteen-year-olds whose parents were not high school graduates, but the percentage at or above the adept level among seventeen-year-olds whose parents were not high school graduates declined from 20 to 15 percent.

Other data collected by the NAEP have examined the literacy skills of young adults between twenty-one and twenty-five years of age. Among the findings are that less than half of young adults whose parents did not graduate from high school and only 53 percent of black young adults had reading proficiency scores above the national average for eighth graders in 1985 (Kirsch and Jungeblut 1986; Barton and Kirsch 1990). Richard Venezky, Carl Kaestle, and Andres Sum (1987) reviewed these data for the Educational Testing Service and concluded not only that the "literacy skill levels found in the NAEP survey are not adequate, on average, for maintaining world leadership in a changing, technological society," but also that the poor performance of many black and Hispanic high school graduates who did not go to college should be

TABLE 2-5 *Percentages of Students at or above Designated NAEP Reading and Mathematics Proficiency Levels, Various Years, by Parent Education and Age Group**

	Reading						Mathematics					
	Percentage at or above Basic Level (200 proficiency)		Percentage at or above Intermediate Level (250 proficiency)		Percentage at or above Adept Level (300 proficiency)		Percentage at or above Beginning Skills/Under-standing Level (200 proficiency)		Percentage at or above Beginning Problem-Solving Level (250 proficiency)		Percentage at or above Moderately Complex Procedures Level (300 proficiency)	
Age Group/ Parent Education	1971	1988	1971	1988	1971	1988	1978	1986	1978	1986	1978	1986
Nine												
Less than high school	38	48	07	06	00	00	51	49	08	06	02	00
Graduated high school	60	60	13	17	01	01	72	73	19	17	01	00
At least some college	74	71	26	23	02	02	81	81	30	25	02	01
Thirteen												
Less than high school	87	92	38	44	03	06	90	97	44	56	06	06
Graduated high school	95	95	59	54	08	06	96	99	65	69	15	08
At least some college	98	97	75	66	17	15	99	99	80	81	28	21
Seventeen												
Less than high school	91	98	61	70	20	15	96	100	82	90	26	20
Graduated high school	97	99	78	82	36	32	98	100	91	94	43	39
At least some college	99	100	90	92	53	52	100	100	97	98	65	62

Source: Adapted from Dossey et al. 1988; Mullis and Jenkins 1990.

*Reading proficiency levels represent the following: 150—can carry out simple, discrete reading tasks; 200—can comprehend specific or sequentially related information; 250—can search for information, interrelate ideas, and generalize; 300—can find, understand, summarize, and explain relatively complicated information; 350—can synthesize and learn from specialized reading materials.

Mathematics proficiency levels represent the following: 150—knows some basic addition and subtraction facts; 200—can add and subtract two-digit numbers; 250—can add, subtract, multiply, and divide using whole numbers; 300—can compute with decimals, fractions, and percents, recognize geometric figures, and solve simple equations; 350—can solve multi-step problems and use basic algebra.

viewed as a "major national concern by educators and economic policymakers" (pp. 7, 35). These authors also extracted NAEP data demonstrating that among young adults who did not attend post-secondary schools, those with high literacy scores had much higher income and much lower unemployment than did those with low literacy scores.

It also should be noted that NAEP data agree with other sources of information. Data collected by the College Board using the Degrees of Reading Power (DRP) Test indicate that less than 33 percent of high school seniors can fully comprehend front-page and editorial material in newspapers (Burrill 1987), and that students disadvantaged by poverty or race/ethnicity have much lower performance levels on the DRP than do more advantaged students (Cooper 1986).

Mathematics Achievement

The situation with respect to mathematics achievement in U.S. schools is similar to that for reading achievement. As portrayed and reported in the second international study of mathematics (Crosswhite et al. 1985; McKnight et al. 1987), students in the United States perform at an acceptable level as long as the curriculum narrowly emphasizes arithmetic and relatively mechanical skills through the eighth grade, but compared to students in other industrial countries, they perform poorly with respect to higher-order mathematics skills at the senior-high level. Analyses of the data for U.S. students (McKnight et al. 1987; Stigler and Stevenson 1991) indicated that reasons for this low performance included a "fragmented" curriculum combined with slow-paced, "low intensity" instruction, and the United States had become a "nation of underachievers" as regards achievement in mathematics (Rothman 1987). A follow-up study of mathematics and science achievement among thirteen-year-olds in six countries found that U.S. students ranked lowest in math and second lowest in science. Only 9 percent of U.S. students demonstrated an understanding of advanced concepts in geometry and measurement, compared with 40 percent of Korean students, even though about 67 percent of U.S. students compared with 23 percent of their Korean counterparts said they were "good in math" (Rothman 1989).

As in the case of reading achievement, math achievement is highly correlated with socioeconomic status and racial/ethnic group membership. Thus, the National Center for Education Statistics has reported that high-status eighth graders are three times as likely to be enrolled in algebra or other relatively advanced math classes as are their peers low in socioeconomic status, and data from the most recent NAEP assessment of mathematics performance show that average proficiency levels of students whose parents have relatively more education are higher than are those of students whose parents have less education. As portrayed in Table 2-6, seventeen-year-olds whose parents have not graduated from high school score at about the same level as do thirteen-year-olds whose parents are college graduates. In addition, as shown in Table 2-5, it appears that the mathematics performance of students whose parents have not attended college did not increase consistently between 1978 and 1986. Mathematics proficiency levels by race/ethnicity are described and discussed in Chapter 10; trends in performance in mathematics and other subject areas are summarized and analyzed in Chapter 13.

In addition, fewer female students than male students score at a very advanced level in mathematics. After reviewing this discrepancy as well as the data indicating that Japanese and Chinese high-school students perform much higher in mathematics than do U.S. students, Steen (1987) concluded that, except for Asian students, advanced mathematics achievement in the United States is "primarily part of white, middle-class male culture, readily available only to those who have the nourishment, solitude, and luxury

TABLE 2-6   *Average 1986 NAEP Mathematics Proficiency Scores, by Parent Education and Age Group**

	Age Group		
Parent Education	*Nine*	*Thirteen*	*Seventeen*
Less than high school	201	252	279
Graduated high school	218	263	293
Some education after high school	229	274	305
Graduated college	231	280	314

Source: Adapted from Dossey et al. 1988
*Mathematics proficiency levels represent the following: 150—knows some basic addition and subtraction facts; 200—can add and subtract two-digit numbers; 250—can add, subtract, multiply, and divide using whole numbers; 300—can compute with decimals, fractions, and percents, recognize geometric figures, and solve simple equations; 350—can solve multistep problems and use basic algebra.

to spend time in concentrated thought." Steen also concluded that the "practice of tracking students . . . introduces substantial variation in their opportunity to learn and magnifies the range of achievement from grade to grade," and that overcoming our international competitive disadvantage in mathematics education will require an "extraordinary redirection of energy by the American political and economic systems" (pp. 251–252).

Achievement of Suburban Minority Students

As noted, reading and mathematics performance in schools with high concentrations of low-income minority students generally are distressingly low. Most of these schools are largely black and/or Hispanic and are located in inner-city neighborhoods. Because many African American and Hispanic students in suburban areas are from middle-class families and the schools they attend do not have high concentrations of poverty, their average achievement presumably is much higher than that of their central-city counterparts and should approximate that of nonminority students.

Although data are not available to provide a comprehensive assessment of achievement levels among suburban minority students, the limited data reported suggest that average performance among African American and Hispanic students in suburban districts is not as high as considerations cited above might lead one to expect. For example, Levine and Eubanks (1990a) reviewed data from the NAEP and from several suburban districts that reported achievement scores separately for minority and nonminority students. They concluded that at the elementary and middle-schools levels black and Hispanic students had language mechanics scores (i.e, grammar, punctuation, and spelling) and math computation scores close to those of their nonminority peers; however, the reading comprehension and math problem-solving scores of the minority students were noticeably lower. (This pattern probably would generate relatively low achievement levels among minority students after they enter high school, and performance depends relatively

more on comprehension and problem solving.) Among the reasons that may help account for this pattern are the following:

- Many suburban minority students may be having trouble in academic studies that require a strong background in standard English.
- Many teachers may be devoting disproportionate time and energy to improving minority students' performance with respect to narrow, relatively mechanical skills (e.g., spelling, math computation) that are most easily taught and tested.
- Some suburban minority students may have moved from central-city school districts where their previous education emphasized small, mechanical skills rather than higher-order learning focused on comprehension and problem solving.

Regardless of which explanation or set of explanations is valid, improving the higher-order skills of suburban minority students is critically important in preparing them for college and success in later life. Although this generalization can be made for all groups of students, it is particularly relevant regarding suburban minorities because they will constitute an increasing proportion of minority enrollment nationally in the future. Thus, Levine and Eubanks (1990a) recommend that steps be taken to bring about fundamental improvement in the education provided for suburban minority students. Possibilities and direction for major reform of public schools are discussed at length in the last chapter of this text.

Dropout from High School

Due in part to relatively low achievement levels, students from families low in socioeconomic status and racial/ethnic minority students (except Asians) are much more likely to drop out of high school than are high SES students and nonminority students. Approximately one-third of young people, aged eighteen to twenty-four, who were from the lowest quartile in family income (of their parents), were high school dropouts in 1988, compared with less than 10 percent of students in the highest quartile and about 15 percent from the middle quartiles (National Research Council 1989). As regards race and ethnicity, in 1988 more than 40 percent of Hispanic youth, aged eighteen to twenty-four, were high school dropouts, compared with 24 percent of black yough and 18 percent of white youth (Carter and Wilson 1989; Magner 1991).

However, it should be noted that the dropout rate among African American students has been declining steadily in recent decades. Whereas the rate for high-school noncompletion among whites between eighteen and twenty-four years of age remained stable between 1973 and 1988, the rate for blacks in this age group declined from 35 percent to 24 percent (Carter and Wilson 1989; Magner 1991). The rate for Hispanic students during this period fluctuated around 40 percent. A follow-up component in the High School and Beyond Study indicated that approximately 30 percent of the black and Hispanic students who dropped out subsequently returned to and completed high school or obtained an equivalency diploma (Kolstad and Owings 1986). Analysis conducted for the National Research Council (1989) indicated that differences in socioeconomic status entirely account for differential dropout rates of black and non-Hispanic white students.

Despite impressive gains that have been registered in high-school completion rates among African American students, dropout rates in some big cities with large proportions of low-income minority students are still close to 50 percent (Kass 1990). At poverty high schools in these cities, the dropout rate sometimes is 70 to 80 percent (Simon 1990). The challenge involved in reducing dropout rates and providing productive secondary eduation for low-income minority students in big cities is likely to prove enormous. The sons and daughters of low-income immigrant families who preceded them fifty to one hundred years ago did not have high secondary school completion rates at a time when high schools

were still relatively elite institutions and unskilled jobs were available and accessible for most working-class youth (Cotton, J. 1991). Unfortunately, today's emerging postindustrial economy provides relatively limited opportunities for unskilled high-school dropouts, and the educational system thereby has been given the responsibility vastly to upgrade the education and skills of inner-city students in an historically telescoped period of time. Fernandez and Vellez reviewed past and current trends bearing on this challenge and reached the following general conclusion:

> *The dropout problem has existed for a long time and is likely to continue to plague major urban school systems in the years to come. Second, . . . most of the studies about dropouts have a very short longitudinal range, usually four years, when it is clear that the problem needs to be studied across generations. Is it possible for a socializing agency such as the school to do for newcomers and for racial and language minorities in general what it failed to do for earlier generations of immigrants? (Fernandez and Vellez 1985, 138)*

Sorting and Selectivity by Type of College

As delineated above, students who are high in SES and test performance, are non-Hispanic white or Asian, and/or are enrolled in the academic track or, to a lesser extent, in the general track in high school are the most likely to attend college and, in so doing, enroll in four-year colleges. It thus is not surprising to find that students in four-year colleges are higher in test performance and SES than are those at two-year colleges. These patterns are shown in the information presented in Tables 2-7 and 2-8.

As shown in Table 2-7, in the early 1980s 18 percent of public four-year colleges and 27 percent of private four-year colleges had student bodies with an average combined SAT score of 1,000 or above, but only 1 percent of two-year colleges (public or private) had enrollment with

TABLE 2-7   *Average SAT Score by College Type*

College Type	Average Combined SAT Scores (percentage of colleges by type)			
	1150 or above	*1000–1149*	*850–999*	*Less than 850*
Public 4-year (N = 496)	02	16	50	33
Private 4-year (N = 1033)	07	20	53	19
Public or private 2-year (N = 1161)	00	01	16	84

Source: Adapted from Astin 1985.
Note: Percentages do not add to 100 due to rounding.

this level of SAT performance. Conversely, 84 percent of two-year colleges, as compared with 33 percent of public four-year colleges and 19 percent of private four-year colleges, had student bodies with average SAT scores below 850. Public four-year colleges are thus much more likely to enroll students with SAT scores below 1,000 than are private four-year colleges.

As indicated in Table 2-8, colleges at which the average combined SAT score was 1,150 or higher had student bodies in which 40 percent of students were from families with annual income of $50,000 or more (in the early 1980s), as compared with 23 percent at colleges in which the average SAT score was between 1,000 and 1,149, and 10 percent at colleges with average SAT scores below 1,000. Conversely, 28 percent of students at colleges with low SAT average scores were from families with annual income below $15,000, compared with 7 percent at colleges with high SAT averages. Similarly, 66 percent of students at high SAT colleges had a high-school grade-point average of A or A–, compared with 12 percent at low SAT schools. Subsequent analysis for the latter part of the 1980s indicated that 55 percent of students at four-year colleges with SAT averages below 1,175 came from families below $40,000 in annual income, compared with 30 percent at four-year colleges with average SAT scores above 1,175 (Kingston and Lewis 1990).

In addition, data reported in Table 2-8 indicate that annual per pupil expenditures related to instruction were $9,395 at the highly selective colleges (i.e., those with high average SAT scores), as compared with $5,326 at colleges with intermediate selectivity, and $3,688 at nonselective colleges. It is unlikely that these patterns have changed much since the early 1980s (Astin 1990).

Other statistics that can be calculated from the data presented in Tables 2-7 and 2-8 include the following:

1. Eighty-six percent of the colleges included in the data set had average SAT scores below 1,000. Of the 14 percent with average SAT scores above this level, 75 percent were private four-year colleges, even though this group constituted only 38 percent of the colleges in the study.
2. Seventy-three percent of the colleges with average SAT scores below 1,000 were two-year colleges, even though this group constituted only 43 percent of the colleges in the study.
3. Colleges with average SAT scores above 1,000 had an average annual per pupil expenditure of $6,137 for instruction, whereas those with average SAT scores below 1,000 had an average expenditure of $3,683.

Available research also indicates that social-class advantages and disadvantages in type of college attended are transmitted thereafter into graduate school patterns. Stated differently, and despite numerous exceptions, social class and the prestige of college attended are the best predictors of the prestige of graduate schools in which students eventually enroll after college (Lang 1987; Kingston and Smart

TABLE 2-8 *Percentage of Students at Three Annual Family-Income Levels, Percentage of Students with A or A– High-School GPA, and Average per Pupil Expenditure for Instruction at Colleges, Classified by Average SAT Score*

Colleges Classified by Average Level of SAT Scores	Percentage of Students by Annual Family Income Level			Average Annual per Pupil Expenditure on Instruction	Percent of Students with A or A – High-School GPA
	Over $50,000	$15–50,000	Under $15,000		
1150 or above (N = 81)	40	53	07	$9,395	66
1000–1149 (N = 293)	23	64	13	$5,236	35
850–999 (N = 983)	13	66	21	$3,932	16
849 or below (N = 1333)	10	62	28	$3,500	12

Source: Adapted from Astin 1985.
Note: Expenditures for instruction include those classified as *instruction, academic support,* and *student services* and exclude those classified as *administration, physical plant,* and *research.*

1990). Research further indicates that college selectivity (measured by average SAT score) is related to subsequent earnings. That is, after taking account of students' test scores, those who attended selective institutions with very high average test scores have much higher earnings than do those who attend less selective colleges. However, this relationship is present only with reference to the most elite colleges (Kingston and Smart 1990).

The overall pattern emerging from this information on sorting and selectivity in postsecondary education is that students low in social status are much less likely to enter and graduate from college than are high-status students with the same performance level. In addition, low-status students tend to be concentrated in two-year colleges with low expenditure levels, whereas high-status students are relatively concentrated in four-year colleges—frequently in elite private colleges—with much higher average expenditures and student bodies with much higher academic performance. Baccalaureate aspirants entering community colleges subsequently have lower educational and economic attainment than do comparable students who attend four-year colleges, probably in part be-

cause this aspect of tracking contributes to attrition and later difficulty in transferring to four-year colleges (Dougherty 1987). Problems involving transfer are discussed later in this chapter.

ADDITIONAL TOPICS INVOLVING SORTING AND SELECTING

The preceding sections of this chapter describe the results of sorting and selecting in the educational system with respect to reading achievement, dropout from school, and participation in higher education. This section briefly discusses additional topics that involve the process of sorting and selecting in the U.S. educational system: vocational education, community colleges, proprietary schools in postsecondary education, financing of students in higher education, and ability tests in relation to social class, race, and sex.

Secondary and Postsecondary Vocational Education

Millions of young people participate in one or another form of vocational education at the high-school and postsecondary levels of schooling in the United States. (Precise data are not available due to the diversity of programs and the lack of standard classifications and information at the national level.) Most of these students either participate in vocational education courses in comprehensive high schools and community colleges or attend vocational and/or technical education high schools and postsecondary institutions. Most students in vocational education participate either in general programs (e.g., consumer/homemaking; prevocational studies in industrial arts, agriculture, or other subjects; basic skills coordinated with vocational exploration; and employability skills, such as communications) or in specific programs emphasizing preparation for a particular occupation.

In 1984, Congress passed the Carl D. Perkins Act in order to improve the effectiveness and equity of vocational education at the secondary and postsecondary levels. To help access the Perkins Act's operation and effects before reauthorizing additional billions of dollars annually in the 1990s, Congress mandated that a National Assessment of Vocational Education be carried out in the late 1980s. The resulting report (Wirt, Muraskin, Goodwin, and Meyer 1989) included the following conclusions regarding the Perkins Act and the status and future of vocational education:

> *In its current form, the Perkins Act is a weak mechanism for achieving its goals. One reason is that little has been done in the regulatory or implementation process to convert the goals and provisions of the legislation into effective guidelines for states and localities. Little additional direction has been forthcoming from federal or state levels on the targeting of federal funds for supplementary services to disadvantaged and handicapped students, nor has technical assistance been provided on effective practices for serving these populations. . . .*
>
> *The breadth of participation in vocational education presents major challenges to educators. One challenge is adapting the vocational curriculum to provide a range of courses with the right mix of job-specific and transferable occupational skills to serve stu-*
> *dents with different educational and work goals. Much of the secondary vocational curriculum may need to be broadened for the many students who plan to obtain further education, or who have not committed themselves to an occupational field, by placing greater emphasis on transferable skills. On the other hand, too many vocational courses could jeopardize its value for work-bound (and other) students seeking immediate skills needed to get good jobs. Arriving at a sound balance of offerings to meet the needs of students with different goals appears to require significant change in the vocational curriculum.*
>
> *A second challenge invited by the amount of vocational education taken by both work-bound students and students planning further education is to expand the contribution of vocational education to academic education. . . .*

Policy Recommendations

> *We find major needs for improving second-ary vocational education and promising opportunities for proceeding. The results of our analyses lead us to propose six major objectives for federal policy on secondary vocational education. The intent of the policy would be to stimulate reform in vocational education comparable in scope to that of the academic reform movement. The six objectives are:*
>
> Revise and build the high school vocational curriculum *to upgrade skill levels and provide students with the mix of occupationally specific and transferable skills they need to get good jobs or to pursue further training and education at the postsecondary level.*
>
> Integrate high school academic and vocational curricula *so that students come to vocational programs well equipped with fundamental academic skills and that vocational courses provide an applied context, based on broad and specific job training, that reinforces and enhances academic skills and*

motivates students to excel in both academic and vocational courses.

Accelerate the education of at-risk students *by providing them with the extra assistance they need to succeed in demanding and highly rewarding vocational courses.*

Expand efforts to place students in good jobs *that make full use of their vocational and academic training.*

Improve the linkages between secondary and postsecondary training *so that training is highly complementary for the group of students who obtain instruction at both levels.*

Raise the quality of vocational programs in schools with high concentrations of poor and low achieving students. . . .

[To help accomplish these objectives, federal policy should:]

Improve rates of program completion and placement *in training-related jobs.*

Provide special assistance to at-risk populations *for whom the problem of noncompletion is most serious.*

Improve the transition from secondary to postsecondary vocational education *in a way that results in more coherent and indepth training for students. (Wirt, Muraskin, Goodwin, and Meyer 1989, ix–xix.)*

As noted in conclusions of the National Assessment of Vocational Education, problems exist with respect to organizing and delivering vocational education in an equitable manner that is efficient and effective for various groups of participants. Paul Barton (1990) of the Policy Information Center at the Educational Testing Service reviewed research on problems in vocational

education and reached the following conclusions regarding students who do not intend to enter postsecondary institutions:

> *[The] watered-down general track produces a thin education and no occupational skills. Those in the vocational track may get some occupational education, but are not likely to get the mathematics, science, and communication skills they will need to progress beyond entry-level employment . . . [and their chances for postsecondary education frequently are curtailed]. The occupational courses are not offered in a planned sequence that leads to a skill in demand in the market place; . . . [instead, students] end up with little more than a sampling of occupational content. (Barton 1990, 19)*

After describing several leading programs in which vocational educators are attempting to introduce a more coherent set of courses and requirements that coordinate and integrate academic and vocational learning objectives, Barton further concluded that these programs are "beginning to build a solid foundation . . . for a restructured program at the high school level, particularly for those who do not expect to go the academic route . . . [and who should receive preparation] for employment without limiting options for postsecondary education" (Barton 1990, 21).

In addition, other major innovations for revamping vocational education and preparation also are being explored and introduced. For example, the Pittsburgh Public Schools now require high-school sophomores to choose between the academic and vocational tracks, thus eliminating the general track in which students dropped out of school and/or too seldom received adequate preparation for either further academic studies or occupations (Niederberger 1990). If Pittsburgh high schools succed in reducing their dropout rates and helping students function well in academic and vocational studies, many school districts elsewhere may try the same approach.

Another alternative for improving vocational preparation is to place non-college-bound students in apprenticeships in which they receive pay increases and greater responsibility as they learn the skills of a trade or occupation over several years. Apprenticeship has long been the predominant approach in preparing young adults for productive jobs in West Germany and several other countries (Hamilton 1990a). In the United States, the Department of Labor has created an Office of Work-Based Learning to support the development of pilot apprenticeship programs, and Secretary of Labor Elizabeth Dole worked with business and labor leaders and other government officials to expand apprenticeship training (Uchitelle 1990a). We review other possibilities for improving occupational preparation for youth in the Chapter 6 discussion of the transition from school to work.

Other improvements in vocational preparation and in coordination between academic and vocational education also may occur as a result of the Carl D. Perkins Vocational Applied Technology Education Act of 1990. Based on experience and research involving the Perkins Act of 1984, Congress modified and expanded federal vocational education funding and programs in order to attain a range of objectives, including the following:

1. Concentrate federal assistance more systematically to help schools that specialize in vocational preparation.
2. Improve services for "the economically disadvantaged, the disabled, the limited English proficient, and . . . training [of] women and men in nontraditional occupations.
3. Bolster vocational education in correctional institutions and thereby help "end the horror of the revolving door from prison to society and back to prison."
4. Improve integration of academic and vocational education.
5. Strengthen guidance and counseling, including hiring of more high-school counselors and provision of part-time and summer job counselors and assistance programs.

6. Target postsecondary funds to institutions where the need is greatest.
7. Retain and protect sex equity programs and services for single parents, displaced homemakers, and pregnant women.
8. Provide for new state government roles in monitoring and evaluating programs.
9. Strengthen the state role in curriculum development and teacher and administrator training and retraining.
10. Provide support for apprenticeship training and for "tech-prep" degree programs that link the last two years of high school with two-year programs in community colleges (Pell 1990a, S12011–S12011).

Purposes and Problems of Community Colleges

Two-year community colleges and equivalent postsecondary institutions have played an important part in providing higher education during the past sixty years. Three important objectives that community colleges have tried to carry out in enlarging and equalizing educational opportunities have been identified as follows (Brint and Karabel 1989; Zemsky 1990):

1. Providing opportunities accessible to what some observers call "the new majority" of higher-education students (i.e., African American, Hispanic, and other minority students, students above the age of twenty-five, and students who did not graduate from high school or did not proceed to colleges directly after graduation). This function of community colleges has been viewed as a central part of our nation's partially successful efforts to achieve and maintain greater "openness and fluidity" in the system of higher education than has been attained in any other country (Brint and Karabel 1989, 220).
2. Providing training that can lead to immediate, worthwhile employment in a variety of technical fields, particularly for students uninterested in academic careers.

3. Serving the community by helping prepare employees for local businesses and industries, offering a range of noncredit courses and programs of interest or assistance to local citizens, providing and encouraging cultural resources and development, and offering technical and consultant services for organizations and community agencies.

Community colleges and equivalent two-year institutions proliferated and grew rapidly as they attempted to attain these diverse objectives. Although the number of nonpublic community, junior, and technical colleges declined from 309 to 154 between 1937 and 1987, the number of public colleges in these categories (henceforth referred to simply as community colleges) increased from 553 to 1222. Between 1940 and 1990, annual enrollment in public community colleges increased from less than 150,000 to nearly 5 million. Nearly one-half of minority students in higher education attended community colleges in 1990, compared with little more than a third of nonminority students. (This disproportion exists largely because many community-college students are minority persons above the age of twenty-three. Among those aged twenty-two and twenty-three, there is much less difference in the proportions of minority and nonminority students who attend four-year colleges.) Conversely, minority students comprise 30 percent of enrollment in community colleges (Carter 1990; Watkins 1990).

The large scope and complexity of goals inherent in the varied missions of most community colleges have made it difficult for them to attain their objectives. In many cases, the concentration on problems in fulfilling one goal, such as preparing the disadvantaged for subsequent transfer to four-year colleges and universities, has made it difficult to fulfill other goals, such as providing technical training leading to immediate employment or conducting numerous noncredit programs. Similarly, concentrating on vocational or technical training may lead to neglect of severe academic deficiencies among disadvantaged students who desire or should be counseled to prepare for further academic studies. Resources, including faculty time and energy, seldom have been available to carry out each function well.

Steven Brint and Jerome Karabel (1989) have analyzed the development of two-year community colleges since 1900 and concluded that many of them became increasingly "vocationalized" in the 1960s and thereafter, in large part because they could not compete with the "existing better-endowed, higher-status institutions." Instead, community-college officials determined to

use vocationalization to bring a stable flow of resources linked to a distinctive function, a unique institutional identity, and above all a secure—indeed, expanding—market niche. . . . [The larger result] of vocationalization was that . . . [it addressed] a far broader societal problem: that of managing ambition in a society that generates far higher levels of aspiration for upward mobility than it can possibly satisfy. Faced with unprecedented numbers of students clamoring for access to a traditional four-year college education . . . the system of higher education responded by channeling many . . . into two-year community colleges.

. . . Today, powerful forces both inside and outside the community college are pushing to move it still further away from its popular function of serving as a pathway into four-year colleges and universities; indeed, some would like the two-year institutions . . . [to focus even more thoroughly] on terminal vocational programs. Yet those who are unhappy with the transformation . . . into a predominantly vocational institution . . . should nonetheless acknowledge the powerful organizational logic behind this development [of a vocational market niche] . . . [as well as the fact most community college students] in fact never transfer to a four-year institution. . . . [If present trends continue] transfer programs may break down altogether; already astronomical attrition rates may increase; and private corporation may . . . [contract for training

*that transforms more community colleges]
into virtual trade schools. (Brint and Karabel
1989, 17, 213)*

Some observers are not as negative concerning historical developments of the community college movement as are Brint and Karabel, particularly with respect to community colleges' contributions in providing vocational skills among students who otherwise would have had few prospects either for meaningful employment or completion of higher education. For example, Richard Richardson (1990) concluded that although many community colleges have gone "overboard in their pursuit of vocational programs and their benign neglect of the transfer function," many colleges also have offered a large array of career-preparation programs that provide a "democratizing function" for numerous students who have few realistic alternatives (Richardson 1990, 52–53).

Transfer Function.   As indicated above, one issue in assessing opportunities provided by community colleges involves the extent to which they should or actually do prepare students for transfer to four-year institutions. Many observers believe that they perform this function poorly, instead diverting many motivated students into vocational programs and thereby sorting them out of higher education. As higher education becomes more important for later success (see Chapter 7), such sorting could become increasingly detrimental to community college students and to society as a whole.

Concerned with transfer issue, researchers as well as educators and public officials have sought to determine how well community colleges prepare students for transfer and how many of them proceed to obtain four-year degrees. Community-college associations report that from one-third to one-half of students who enroll say they intend to transfer, but most do not proceed to transfer to four-year institutions upon completion (Pincus and Archer 1989; Watkins 1990). Beyond these approximate data, however,

little information has been available that would help assess how well community colleges have been functioning and what should be done to improve their operation with respect to the transfer function.

To obtain data that could be useful in addressing transfer issues, Fred Pincus and Elayne Archer (1989) conducted a systematic investigation of transfer patterns and problems. After reviewing previous research and several data sources, Pincus and Archer reached the following conclusions:

1. The transfer rate declined in the 1970s and 1980s.
2. Rates are highly variable both within and among community college systems.
3. The current transfer rate is only about 15 to 20 percent of all students and 20 to 30 percent of those who express the desire to transfer.
4. About half of the students who transfer (therefore only 10 to 15 percent of all community college students) eventually obtain a B.A.

Pincus and Archer also tried to determine why transfer rates have dropped to what they characterized as a very low level. They identified the following considerations that frequently hamper transfers:

- *Institutional* explanations and characteristics, such as lack of concentration on preparing students to transfer, uninterested or inadequate faculty, complex transfer procedures and arrangements, tracking of students into low-level courses, high costs to attend, and ineffective remedial programs.
- *Student* explanations and characteristics, such as poor academic skills, low aspiration, and inability to pay financial costs.
- *Social and political* forces, such as economic recession, political neglect, and growth in demands for technical (as contrasted with professional) employees.

Acknowledging the difficulties created by these numerous, interacting consideations, the authors underlined the importance of identifying potential transfer students at entry, providing effective remediation for those with academic deficiencies, and providing additional help if needed after students transfer. They prepared a set of recommendations for future improvement that included the following (Pincus and Archer 1989, 3–8):

1. The culture of the urban community college [where much of the problem is focused] should be transformed to emphasize intellectual rigor and critical thinking.

2. Urban community colleges must aggressively promote the development of a vibrant on-campus community, especially for minority students.

3. Dual admissions programs should be established so that any student who completes an approved associate degree program will be guaranteed admission with junior status to any four-year institution in their state, and will not be required to repeat any course. . . .

4. Data bases should be established at all community colleges and a common definition of 'transfer' and 'transfer student' should be agreed upon.

5. After upgrading the transfer curriculums, community colleges should aggressively promote their prebaccalaureate programs among high school students, teachers, counselors, and administrators.

6. Each state should develop a set of financial incentives to reward community colleges which have successful transfer programs.

7. A special federally funded scholarship program for low-income students who transfer to four-year colleges should be established.

Remedial Education. As indicated above, provision of remedial services to overcome students' academic deficits is a centrally important function at many community colleges. Nearly half the English and mathematics taught at community

colleges appears to be at the remedial level (Cohen 1989, 1990). One scholar who has been analyzing the development of community colleges for several decades describes the general approaches that have emerged in response to this far-reaching remedial challenge:

> *A major issue in remedial education has been whether to offer less than collegiate level composition and arithmetic studies through the academic departments or to set up a separate division through which all noncollegiate activities are presented. . . . In some colleges where remedial studies are still the responsibility of the academic departments, supplemental instruction designed to teach students to read the textbooks and write the types of papers required in the college-credit courses has been introduced . . . [thus limiting students to only one or two regular courses per term] . Whether remedial studies are offered in separate divisions or . . . in college level classes, the decline in student abilities has affected the level of discourse. (Cohen 1989, 7–8)*

The Cooling-Out Function and Dynamics. Related to the relatively poor record community colleges have registered with respect to preparing students for successful transfer, some observers have viewed the two-year college system as serving to cool-out weak students who aspire to college degrees but are not well prepared to succeed in higher education. The classic statement of this viewpoint was provided by Burton Clark (1960). He argued that community colleges provide a soft response to low academic performance in the sense that rather than rejecting poorly qualified students, many community colleges use pre-entrance tests, counseling interviews, probation policies, and other mechanisms to reduce students' expectations and steer them to vocational fields. Many knowledgeable observers agree that too many community colleges (and four-year colleges) at which high attrition rates are taken for granted do function to lower low achievers' expectations and divert them from academic careers (Crook and Lavin 1989). This viewpoint is obviously compatible with the analysis and interpretation of Brint and Karabel.

Central City Challenges.   For several reasons, problems involving preparation of students for transfer or entry-level employment, provision of remedial education, responsiveness to community needs, and other community-college functions are most severe in the case of large-city institutions that enroll high proportions of low-income students. Many students at these colleges are poorly prepared for either academic or vocational programs. In addition, high dropout rates, relatively low loan repayment rates (discussed later in this chapter), and inadequate institutional financing combine to hamper institutional efforts to expand higher education opportunities for the big-city poor.

Maurice Weidenthal conducted a study of community-college responses to these challenges and reported to the study's sponsor (The American Association of Community and Junior Colleges) that "because of the enormous burdens and responsibilities assumed by central-city campuses, they have become different kinds of institutions with missions different from and, in a sense, greater than their sister campuses serving suburban areas and other populations" (Weidenthal 1989, 23). The author proceeded to illustrate some of the complicated problems faced by city colleges that provide many of their students with the "sole opportunity to elevate themselves from the hopelessness" of their surrounding neighborhoods:

> *In rapidly changing Los Angeles, City College now enrolls students who speak 62 different languages and whose levels of education and ability represent the entire academic spectrum. . . .*
>
> *At the downtown campus of Miami-Dade Commuity College . . . [many students from Nicaragua and elsewhere lack] basic language or economic survival skills. . . . In Cleveland, Pittsburgh, and Detroit, dramatic*

> *efforts have been under way to train and retrain a work force devastated by the industrial revolution of the 1980s. (Weidenthal 1989, 5)*

After describing numerous examples of outstanding programs, such as a job retraining effort for 20,000 students who attended the Kansas City Metropolitan Community Colleges, Weidenthal concluded that community colleges "in the central cities continue to be vibrant, exciting, committed centers of education and training." He also concluded, however, that the additional responsibilities they have had to assume have created "sizable additional financial burdens that must be recognized and dealt with. In some cases heroic efforts to train and educate our central city citizens are being hampered by lack of funds, particularly in states where funding is limited to traditional credit programming" (Weidenthal 1989, 23).

Suitable Vocational/Occupational Preparation. As already noted, providing students with skills and knowledge for meaningful employment is a primary activity at many community colleges— some think too central an activity at too many colleges. But regardless of their views concerning the proper role and balance of various activities at community colleges, all observers agree that occupations for which students receive training should be those in which good jobs are now, or will in the future, be available, and that many shortcomings have existed with respect to vocational and occupational training provided at community colleges. Among the problems cited most frequently by Arthur Cohen (1989, 1990), Sonia Nazario (1990), and other authors are the following:

- Continuing preparation for fields in which there is an oversupply of qualified applicants. Examples involve data processing and auto mechanics, for which community colleges sometimes have continued to churn out workers for whom there has been little or no demand.

- Failure to prepare students for fields in which demand is large or growing locally or nationally. Examples of this converse phenomenon have occurred with respect to various health-care specialities and fields involving new technologies.
- Lack of coordination among training programs at nearby colleges, which helps to produce both oversupply in some fields and shortages in others.
- Overconcentration on vocational skills to the extent that graduates still lack basic academic skills required to obtain or hold jobs.
- Neglect of placement and other supportive services that will help students obtain jobs after completion of training.
- Failure to monitor and/or report placement and employment rates and outcomes for persons who have completed training programs, thus making it more likely that problems related to oversupply and shortage will continue and recur in future decades.

Policies for the Future.   As suggested by the preparation and publication of numerous recent studies and reports on the problems and future of community colleges (e.g., Pincus and Archer 1989; Weidenthal 1990; Zemsky 1990), educators and government officials are well aware of the importance of clarifying and improving the role of two-year colleges within the system of higher education. Much analysis and thinking on this topic were summarized by Zemsky (1990) as follows in recommendations prepared for The Pew Charitable Trusts Higher Education Research Program:

- *"Move beyond marketing"* to introduce "new programs and programs . . . that ensure that those students so vigorously recruited actually gain the education they seek."
- *"Rethink learning paradigms"* so that collegiate learning is not viewed as "necessarily a one-time opportunity confined to the season of late adolescence."

- *"Build and enhance partnerships . . .* among and between institutions of higher education, primary and secondary schools, local community groups, and local industry."
- *"Recognize the diversity of educational missions"* so that community colleges are able to restructure based on the "recognition that not all higher education should look the same."
- *"Emphasize educational substance rather than educational process"* by giving "less attention . . . to minimum numbers of class hours or credits and more to demonstrated competencies." (Zemsky 1990, 7–8. Italics in original.)

Proprietary Schools in Postsecondary Education

Many students receive some or all of their postsecondary education at tuition-charging proprietary schools. Wilms (1987) estimated that there were more than 6,000 proprietary institutions (other than correspondence schools) in the United States in 1986. His extensive analysis of these institutions included the following four observations and conclusions:

1. Proprietary schools are the largest provider of postsecondary vocational education. Although they offer instruction in many subjects from accounting to zookeeping, the bulk of the programs fall in the four major categories of trades (e.g., aviation, allied health), business and secretarial, cosmetology, and barbering.
2. Enrollment is directly related to prevailing wage rates and unemployment rates.
3. Most proprietary schools enroll fewer than 200 students and operate on very small profit margins. Their main competition is from public two-year community colleges. This competition has become more intense as the number of eighteen- to twenty-one-year-olds has declined.
4. Enrollment at proprietary schools is disproportionately low-income and minority.

Dropout rates frequently exceed 50 percent. However, dropout rates for similar students at public two-year colleges probably are even higher.

Major controversies involving proprietary schools have centered on whether they should receive governmental support in the form of grants or loans for their students. Many observers believe they make an important contribution in providing opportunities for students who otherwise would not have the financial capacity or motivation to continue their education (Chosky 1989; Blair 1990). Others believe that many proprietary schools place too much emphasis on vocational training to the exclusion of other educational goals, fail to provide many of their students with usable skills, are providing undesirable competition for nonprofit colleges, and/or are earning high profits from students who attend for short periods and then default on government loans (Wilson 1989; Cage 1990). Katherine Boo (1991) has described some particularly egregious examples of the latter phenomenon, such as a Florida travel agent and secretarial academy that spent 52 percent of its revenues on advertising/marketing. The few students who graduated and obtained employment generally were placed in menial jobs.

Several issues were considered in an investigation and report prepared for a U.S. Senate subcommittee on governmental affairs. The root of the underlying problems, the report concluded, is that because there has been inadequate regulation of proprietary trade schools, some have been able to function mostly in order to earn profits from students (and their government loans), regardless of whether students acquire useful skills or are prepared for subsequent employment or futher education. In the absence of effective licensing and other state and federal regulatory measures, according to this report, profit-seeking trade schools were largely regulating themselves in a manner that put the "prisoners in charge of running the prison." Officials of the National Association of Trade and Technical

Schools responded that the basic problem arose not from culpable acts of proprietary institutions, but rather from the failure of state and federal regulators "to adequately fulfill their own roles" (DeParle 1990b).

Financing of Students in Higher Education

The first chapter pointed out that success in the occupational structure and the economy increasingly requires acquisition of advanced knowledge and skills through postsecondary education. In Chapter 7 we summarize research supporting this conclusion, particularly for black students. Because higher education has become so important for later success, financing higher education for students from economically or socially disadvantaged families has become an increasingly central issue in determining whether equity is present in the process of sorting and selecting within the educational system.

Problems involving participation in higher education have become prominent in part because the costs of going to college have escalated rapidly while federal budget deficits have led to changes in policies and practices for helping students participate in higher education. Between 1980 and 1990, average tuition and fees increased by about one-half (Hartle 1990). During this same period, federal grants and scholarships declined by nearly half, loans replaced grants as the most common form of federal support for college students, a significant proportion of loans was diverted from colleges and universities to proprietary institutions, and the percentage of students receiving federal loans for postsecondary education more than doubled (Jaschik 1990a). By 1986, the average indebtedness of students graduating from four-year colleges was more than $7,000 (Evangelauf 1987). In addition, frugal parents who saved money to send their children to college were penalized because the increase in their assets meant their children could not obtain federal grants (Frances 1990). Such consideration led the Congressional Joint Economic Committee to commission a 1986 report that reached the following conclusion regarding borrowing for higher education:

> *Growing student indebtedness has raised questions about the implications of the debt burdens for the national economy, for the economic well-being of borrowers, for equality of access to higher education and even for the educational process itself. . . . The federal strategy for fostering equality of opportunity in higher education, which initially focussed on a balanced array of grants, loans, and work opportunities for the disadvantaged, has been transformed, with uncertain and largely unexamined implications for the groups who were the original focus of federal concern. (Quoted in Evangelauf 1987, 1, 18.)*

Data collected several years later by Mortenson and Wu (1990) also called into question the effectiveness of federal strategies for improving postsecondary opportunities for students low in socioeconomic status. After reviewing information on postsecondary enrollment and completion rates between 1970 and 1989 among high-school graduates from low-income families, these analysts reached the following conclusions:

> *Federal programs . . . were targeted on those [students] from low family income backgrounds. . . . The results are profoundly disappointing: low family income students actually lost substantial ground compared to high family income students during the 1980s. . . . If the federal programs had been successful there would have been at least an increase in the level of participation of disadvantaged students. (Mortenson and Wu 1990, xxiii)*

Escalation of both costs and borrowing for higher education also raises even broader questions regarding general societal arrangements for preparing youth for the future in a postindustrial society. For example, D.A. Hansen (1986) studied recent trends and concluded that growing in-

debtedness may discourage college students from entering socially important but relatively low-paid fields such as teaching and social work. After examining data on recent trends, economist Michael McPherson pointed out that large debts being incurred to participate in higher education probably will make it more difficult for graduates to save for their own children's higher education in future generations, and that the issues thereby raised "go beyond the merely financial." A parental savings strategy, he further concluded, "might strengthen generational bonds, but it could also sour familial relationships by making parents feel too burdened and children too dependent. Also, parents and students may have different ideas about which educational investments to make; who's paying for the education may affect the balance of power between them" (McPherson 1986, 9).

Major equity issues involved in the escalation of college costs include the question of whether minority students and low-income students are being increasingly foreclosed of the opportunity to attend relatively prestigious and well-funded colleges, and whether low-income citizens thus are receiving a fair return for their investment in taxes for higher education. In considering these questions we have noted that working-class students are disproportionately represented at two-year colleges, which generally have smaller expenditures per pupil and enroll lower-performing students than do four-year colleges; declining availability of grants for low-income students in the 1980s may have significantly exacerbated tendencies toward development of a two-tiered system in higher education (Orfield 1990). Regarding this possibility, the president of the Consortium for the Advancement of Private Higher Education reviewed recent trends and concluded that

> *cutbacks in federal student aid combined with greater than inflationary increases in tuitions are pushing more and more colleges beyond the reach of low-income students. . . . [Private college's ability to maintain access] unaided is*

limited. For this reason, we must be unflagging in our efforts to convince state and federal governments that society, and not just students and their families, must pay the price of accomplishing that goal. (O'Keefe 1986, 8)

In addition, the switch from grants to loans has played an important part in limiting the percentage of African American students and low-income students in higher education in the 1980s. Nationwide surveys indicate that the percentage of African American college students dependent on financial aid is much higher than that for white students, and that the percentage of African American students able to obtain loans has not increased sufficiently to compensate for reduction in the percentage who receive federal grants (Jaschik 1990a). Considerations such as these were analyzed in a report prepared for the American College Testing Program by Thomas Mortenson (1990). Mortenson delineated the history of college attendance and financing of college costs for low-income students in the 1960s, 1970s, and 1980s, and reached the following conclusions:

First . . . the college enrollment rates of students from poor family income backgrounds increased when net college attendance costs were decreased through the expansion of student aid programs based on grants between the mid 1960s and the late 1970s. Then, during the 1980s, when net college attendance costs were greatly increased by the substitution of loans for grants . . . [much of the enrollment gain in the 1960s was lost].

Second . . . some low income students moved down the price ladder of higher education—from universities and four-year colleges to two-year colleges—to attend college at a more affordable cost.

. . . loans are not substitutes for grants for low income students. Only grants achieved the enrollment gains made by students from low income families between 1966 and the late 1970s. When loans were substituted for

grants . . . college access dropped, college choice deteriorated, and default rates increased. . . . To the extent that the aims of student aid are to enhance higher educational opportunity for those with financial need to pay college costs, loans have been counterproductive for some groups seeking the benefits of higher education. (Mortenson 1990, iii)

Responding to such critics as Mortenson and, perhaps more important, to Congressional dissatisfaction and uncertainty regarding the extent to which federal aid for higher education has been helpful to low-income students and others who need considerable assistance, the Congressional Budget Office (1991) conducted a comprehensive analysis of student-aid expenditures related to costs and distributions in postsecondary education in 1989. Results of the study indicated that students from low-income families were much more likely to receive financial aid (from federal, as well as other sources) than were students from middle- or high-income families, and recipients from low-income families received a much higher amount of help than did those from higher-income families. For example, about 85 percent of students whose families earned less than $17,000 annually and who attended public four-year colleges received assistance, compared to 25 percent of high-income students ($50,000 or more family income) at these schools. In addition, the low-income recipients received about twice as much per student as did the higher-income students. Similar patterns were reported at two-year schools, private four-year schools, and proprietary schools, and for loan aid and grant aid when analyzed separately.

Nevertheless, the Budget Office analysts recognized that various other considerations, such as ability of families to pay nonassisted costs, effects of high debt loads on students' motivation and enrollment, effects of loan defaults on individuals and on society, and differences in the value of education acquired at differing institutions, also have important implications in considering the adequacy of federal and other sources of financial assistance for postsecondary education. Therefore, authors of the study proceeded to discuss, as follows, some implications of their data in answering such central questions as Are actual costs reasonable for meeting financial-aid objectives involving provision of access and choice for students? and What should be the federal role in providing aid?

Some people argue that the basic school of access should be the public two-year institution, widely known as the community college, because these institutions receive substantial (primarily state) subsidies to keep tuitions low and they provide a wide range of academic and vocational programs. Others argue that it should be the public four-year institution, since they believe postsecondary education should be primarily academic in nature and a four-year degree has traditionally been the goal of postsecondary education. By implication, more expensive types of institutions become schools of choice—namely, proprietary schools and private four-year institutions, as well as public four-year institutions—if public two-year institutions are schools of access.

The standard of net cost equal to or less than EFC [Expected Family Contribution] is not, however, appropriate for evaluating the degree to which choice has been achieved. The basic problem is that this standard assumes that aid should meet all need—that is, the difference between total costs and the resources available to students in the form of their EFC. But unmet need will generally exist because, if it did not, students would have strong incentives to choose the most expensive school that would admit them. Similarly, schools would have incentives to increase their tuitions, knowing that the EFC would be the maximum cost to the student. Evaluating whether choice is being achieved, then, requires determining how much larger net cost can be than EFC at schools of choice and still be reasonable. . . .

[On the one hand, our data support the conclusion] that the current aid system is working well in achieving equal educational opportunity because, on average, students were able to enroll in public two-year institutions without paying more than their EFCs. Furthermore, students from families with the lowest incomes were able to choose private four-year schools over public two-year institutions for an additional net cost that averaged only about $800.

On the other hand, one could conclude that the current aid system is not working well because, on average, students from families with income between $11,000 and $30,000 enrolling in public four-year institutions had net costs greater than their EFCs. . . .

[In addition] one could argue that the costs of choosing a proprietary or private four-year institution are unreasonable, since on average net costs significantly exceeded EFCs for students who did so.

If one judges that the net costs for some students are either too high or too low . . . [one option is to lower the EFC] for some or all students . . . if sufficient aid were available to meet the resulting increase in financial need . . . . In contrast, the EFC could be raised . . . [which would result in higher student costs that] could prevent some students from attending postsecondary institutions and result in others choosing less expensive schools. . . . [Another alternative is that] the mix of aid and loans could be changed . . . [for example, by increasing grants and reducing loans, which would] encourage more youth to attend postsecondary institutions . . . [but] would be extremely expensive. . . .

The issue of whether student aid should be in the form of grants or loans is linked to the issue of whether postsecondary education produces social benefits or primarily results in private gains (such as higher earnings) to the student. . . . Various analysts have interpreted differently the empirical research on this issue. . . . A variation on this issue . . . concerns schools of choice. Some analysts argue . . . that convincing evidence does not exist that enrollment in schools of choice produces any greater social benefits than enrollment in schools of access. . . . [But others argue that schools of choice] provide a special atmosphere in which some students . . . [are more likely to realize their potential, and therefore] . . . relatively more aid should be available as grants for schools of choice to encourage a broad range of students—especially those from low-income families—to enroll in them. (Congressional Budget Office 1991, xx–xxiii, 80, 81)

Ability Tests in Relation to Social Class, Race, and Sex

The school system could sort and select more or less mechanically if there were a close relationship between intellectual ability and social status, or between intellectual ability, ethnicity, race, sex, or other student background characteristics. In the absence of such relationships, sorting and selecting that eliminate economically or socially disadvantaged students may reflect serious inequity in the educational system and in society as a whole.

Until the middle of the twentieth century, it was widely believed that there was an inborn intellectual inferiority in people of lower-class status and in people of nonwhite skin color. Many white people believed that whites had the highest innate intelligence and that the intelligence of other races descended in order of their departure from this color, with the darkest-skinned blacks lowest on the intelligence scale. This idea was supported by some early intelligence-test studies, in which it was found that black children scored lower than white children, with children of mixed white and black parentage scoring in between.

However, critical studies of intelligence testing (Eells et al. 1951) have shown that the ordinary intelligence tests favor children whose parents are of middle- or upper-class status. The problems in the tests are ones for which life in an upper-class or middle-class home give superior preparation.

For example, in the following test item,

A symphony is to a composer as a book is to what?

( ) paper   ( ) sculptor   ( ) author
( ) musician   ( ) man

the problem is probably easier for middle-class children. They are more likely to have heard their parents talking about symphonies than are working-class children.

On the other hand, the following item is probably as difficult for high-status as for low-status children:

A baker goes with bread the same way as a carpenter goes with what?

( ) a saw   ( ) a house   ( ) a spoon
( ) a nail   ( ) a man

The ordinary intelligence test contains many items of the first type. As a consequence, the test, by bringing in words that are less familiar to them, tends to penalize children of low socioeconomic status or distinctive cultural backgrounds (Miller-Jones 1989).

Furthermore, children of upper- and middle-class families are more often pushed by their families to do good work in school. School training itself helps one to do well in most intelligence tests. Therefore, many social scientists now believe that the differences in intelligence test performance between black and white children are mainly due to the fact that more black children are working-class. When middle-class black children are given intelligence tests, they do about as well as middle-class white children. Innate differences exist between individuals within these groups, but most social scientists believe that the average innate intelligence of differing groups is the same, if the groups have equal opportunity and similar experience and training in solving the ordinary problems of life (Zuckerman 1990).

However, the possibility of racial group differences in intelligence has not been ruled out by all scientists. A vigorous controversy developed in 1968–69 over the publication by Professor Arthur R. Jensen, a distinguished educational psychologist, of his conclusions from his own and other research on intelligence in relation to heredity, social class, and race (Jensen 1968; 1969). Jensen concluded that intelligence is inherited to a considerably larger degree than most other psychologists believe. He also concluded that certain research studies demonstrate a genetic difference between whites and blacks in the quality of abstract intelligence.

Peggy R. Sanday (1972) took issue with Jensen by supporting the following three propositions:

1. The magnitude of the genetic contribution to a given trait cannot be measured with present methods if the trait is determined by more than one gene, as is true for intelligence.
2. The methods used to measure intelligence (the ordinary tests) are not equally valid for various socioeconomic groups.
3. When the sociocultural factors for different socioeconomic and racial groups are equated, the measured intelligence does not differ reliably, or differs very little.

This last proposition is disputed because a variety of published researches give a variety of results. However, several important studies, in which black and Chicano children of middle-class status have been studied in sufficient numbers to give stable results, appear to support this proposition. For example, in a study of school-age children in Riverside, California, Mercer (1973) found that when the sociocultural factors (such as home background and education of mother) were kept equal, there was no difference between the intelligence of Hispanic, black, and white elementary school children. But Jensen's response to Mercer is that sociocultural factors are themselves determined at least partly by the innate intelligence of the parents. That is, parents who are more intelligent create a favorable sociocultural environment for their children; but it is their own innate intelligence passed on to their children that gives the children high intelligence test scores. (See also Herrnstein 1990).

Most social scientists agree that intelligence is determined substantially by heredity (McGue 1989), but they assign a greater influence to a person's experience and environment than do Jensen and his supporters. In technical terms, what proportion of the variance on an intelligence test is to be attributed to heredity, and what proportion to environmental influence? Jensen and some of his supporters have designated the percentage of variance in intelligence test scores accounted for by heredity at about 80 percent (Herrnstein 1982, 1990); their opponents frequently place this percentage at 50 to 60 percent or less (Jencks 1987; Plomin 1989). Jensen (1980) also argues that intelligence tests provide valid data on respondents' innate intellectual capabilities, but his opponents believe that the tests are susceptible to environmental bias associated with race, social class, and other considerations.

Critics of the hereditarian position generally argue that environmental influences on mental development are not fully taken into account in most research comparing the effects of heredity and environment on IQ. Flynn (1980; 1987), for example, has reviewed much of the research on each side of the issue and concluded that such factors as relatively poor nutrition and relatively less verbal parent-infant interaction among blacks as compared to whites of the same socioeconomic status may account for much of the fifteen-point differential. "Not one piece of evidence" on either the environmentalist or the hereditarian side, he further states, is "so firm that it is proof" against exacting criticism (p. 214). Similarly, Scarr (1981a; 1981b) has summarized the thrust of this viewpoint:

A growing literature on black socialization indicates that there are important differences from the socialization of white families that affect the intellectual development of children as measured by tests. . . . Black families emphasize affect, non-verbal communication, motor activity, willfulness, and tolerance for high levels of sensory stimulation for their children. By contrast, white families stress object orientation, verbal communication, low motor activity, obedience, and tolerance for low levels of sensory output, such as working quietly alone in a classroom. . . . Intelligence tests sample predominantly from the object-oriented, abstract world of the white child, rather than the interpersonal, affective world of the black child. (Scarr 1981a, 335–336)

Those who support the environmentalist position also point to changes that have occurred in IQ scores nationally and in average IQ scores for various racial and ethnic groups. For example, Kotkin and Kishimoto (1988) point out that, in the early twentieth century, more than 80 percent of Russian-Hungarian and Italian Americans scored in the "feeble-minded" range, but scores for these groups are now above average. Gould (1980; 1981) reported that United States IQ scores averaged 100 in 1937 but 106 in 1972 and concluded that

this general gain can hardly be ascribed to genetic causes; it reflects whatever improved literacy, earlier access to information through radio and television, better nutrition, and so forth have wrought in just thirty-five years. When we recognize that the average black-white difference is 15 points, and that gains of up to two-thirds of this amount have occurred in certain age groups as a result of general changes in environment not specifically directed toward this end, then why should we be ready to conclude that group differences are ineluctable? (Gould 1980, 43)

Similarly, Sowell (1978) has studied data on changes in the average IQ scores of various racial and ethnic groups. He found that between 1920 and 1970, average IQ scores for Italian Americans increased from 92 to 100, and scores for Polish Americans increased from 91 to 109, but scores for Mexican Americans and Puerto Ricans remained in the 80s. The absence of a significant increase among the latter groups might be explained, according to Sowell, by (a) genetic differences; (b) relatively static socioeconomic position; (c) enduring prevalence of Spanish as the language spoken in the home; or (d) the high incidence of return migration. He rejects the genetic explanation and cites 1958 data from the New York City Board of Education showing that average IQ was 93 among Puerto Rican students with 9 or 10 years in mainland schools, but the average was only 72 among students with only 1 or 2 years of mainland schooling.

The related argument concerning the validity of IQ tests became a raging controversy in the 1980s. Jensen's books *Bias in Mental Testing* (1980) and *Straight Talk about Mental Tests* (1981) provided many arguments indicating that the tests do measure general intellectual ability, but critics have not been convinced and have offered a variety of rebuttals and counterevidence. Hafner and White (1981), for example, criticized Jensen's data and conclusions as follows: "By ignoring the evidence that tests are biased, educators who measure student progress with test scores do their students a disservice, especially if these tests are better at discriminating subgroups than in reflecting educational attainment or predicting accomplishment" (p. 585).

Similarly, a four-year study conducted by the Committee on Ability Testing (1982) of the National Academy of Sciences concluded that standardized ability tests do not measure the "inborn, predetermined capacity" or "potential" of an individual, but rather reflect his or her previous learning and achievement. The Committee also concluded that such tests are not inherently or intentionally biased against minority groups, but instead reflect the general socioeconomic disadvantages that minorities and the poor suffer in United States society as a whole. The Committee cautioned against indiscriminate use of such tests to make educational or employment decisions about individuals based solely on test scores. After reviewing arguments and research supporting and opposing the use of intelligence tests for selection in schools and other institutions, Weinberg (1989, 102) reached the following general conclusions in a summary paper prepared for *The American Psychologist*:

> *Intelligence test development generally has lacked theoretical foundations, being driven instead by attention to measurement and statistical requirements. . . . The use of an IQ as a primary basis for decisions about a child's future must be discouraged. Objective assessment can inform, but cannot replace, judgment. Scores must be interpreted within the context of a child's total record, including classroom observations and behavior outside the school milieu, taking into account the instructional options available to the child.*

The College Admissions Tests Controversy. Criticism of aptitude tests in educational decision making has focused on general effects in terms of restricting the opportunities of disadvantaged students with relatively low scores. As discussed in this and other chapters, many observers view aptitude tests as advancing a "hidden agenda of social control" that harms disadvantaged students by placing many of them in slow classes in elementary and secondary schools—where they are not expected to achieve—and denying them admission to prestigious postsecondary institutions, especially four-year colleges (Banks 1991, 32).

In recent years, much concern about ability testing in relation to student background characteristics has centered on use of the Scholastic Aptitude Test (SAT) and the American College Test (ACT). Devised to measure respondents' acquisition of knowledge and skills required for postsecondary education, the SAT and the ACT are used widely in making decisions regarding admissions to college and reward of financial aid to successful applicants.

Because low-income students and disadvantaged minority students tend to have lower mean scores on the SAT and the ACT than do economically or socially advantaged students with the same GPA, rigid use of these test scores favors the advantaged groups in admissions and financial-rewarded decisions. In addition, young women graduating from high school have lower SAT and ACT scores, on the average, than do young men, largely because the mean math scores of males are substantially higher than are those of females. (In 1990, males registered an average of 499 on the SAT math section, compared with 455 for females.) Thus, use of college-aptitude scores in decisions about admissions and financial aid favors men over women.

Opposition to use of the SAT and other aptitude tests in making college-admissions and other educational decisions has been led by the FairTest organization and several smaller groups. Among the arguments and assertions most frequently articulated by these opponents of college aptitude tests are the following (Nairn 1980; Crouse 1985; Crouse and Trusheim 1988, 1991; Verhovek 1990):

- The tests do not contribute anything of value in college admissions because they generally do little or nothing to improve predictions of success after account is taken of students' high-school GPAs. Instead, their main effect is to screen out some capable students who score low.
- For reasons we enumerated in the preceding section, the SAT, the ACT, and other postsecondary screening tests do not provide a valid measure of candidates' intelligence.
- The tests do not, as their sponsors claim, frequently help low-status and minority students gain admissions or financial assistance by identifying disadvantaged applicants who have high ability but relatively low GPAs.
- The tests are particularly discriminatory against young women because they screen out female applicants who score low in math but otherwise have achievement and grades as high or

higher than those of men. (See Chapter 11 for information on achievement patterns and trends by sex.)

▪ The content of the tests favors mainstream students; therefore, the tests are biased against African American, Hispanic, and other minority students whose cultural and educational background has provided inadequate preparation to obtain high scores.

Sponsors of the SAT and the ACT have actively provided counterarguments against criticism of college aptitude tests. Among the justifications and responses they offer most frequently are the following (Cole 1990; Goldberg 1990; Hanford 1991):

▪ Although the tests do not add much accuracy to the overall prediction of college success among a large group of applicants, they do uniquely identify some students who most likely will not succeed, but who would be admitted on the basis of GPAs.

▪ College admissions tests do not pretend or attempt to measure innate intelligence, but only the acquisition of knowledge and skills required for success in higher education.

▪ Disadvantaged minority students who score relatively high thereby improve their chances to gain admission to a prestigious college and obtain financial support.

▪ Although low scores among minority students frequently do reflect cultural differences and limitations in educational background, such differences and limitations also signify inadequate preparation for higher education. Thus, attacking the tests for cultural bias is equivalent to blaming the messenger who delivers bad news.

▪ The lower scores of females compared with males reflect less adequate mathematics preparation, which subsequently hampers the college performance of many women. In addition, the lower average scores of women reflect the fact that a high proportion of students who obtain extremely high math scores are male students

(see Chapter 13) particularly likely to succeed at prestigious colleges.

Many arguments for and against college admissions tests involve complicated analyses of complex data bearing on a wide variety of interrelated issues. Given the importance of the tests in determining students' subsequent careers, these data and issues have been reviewed in numerous research papers and discussed by many educators and policymakers, but proponents and opponents continue to disagree on their meaning and interpretation. Meanwhile, important recent developments have occurred with respect to college aptitude testing, including the following (Glaberson 1989; Blumenstyk 1990a; Solomon 1991):

▪ More than 100 colleges and universities have either eliminated use of aptitude tests or made them optional.

▪ The College Board voted to revamp the SAT and change its name to the Scholastic Assessment Test. Between 1991 and 1994, the SAT will be modified substantially so that it will consist of two major parts. The SAT-I Reasoning Tests will revise and expand the verbal and math sections to emphasize critical reading and production of responses rather than simple selection of multiple-choice alternatives. The SAT-II Subject Tests will revise and expand the achievement sections to emphasize writing, introduce Asian languages, facilitate entry-level placement in basic English and math, and provide for other enhancements.

▪ Several legal suits have challenged policies and practices involved in use of the SAT and other college aptitude tests. Some of the most important litigation has been in New York, where a 1989 judicial ruling prohibited the state department of education from awarding scholarships solely on the basis of SAT scores, which were viewed as discriminating against women, and a 1990 ruling overturned a New York law aimed at bringing about "truth in testing" by requiring publication of the Medical College Admission Test. The College Board, the Educational Testing Service, and other agencies also have sued to overturn other New York laws that require them to disclose questions and answers from a number of other tests.

THE CRISIS IN SORTING AND SELECTING

The confluence of several trends has led to a crisis in the functioning of the educational system in the United States. Education is becoming more important for later success as the postindustrial economy introduces high technology and reduces blue-collar employment. (See Chapters 1, 7, and 13 for additional information on these topics.) At the same time, strong associations persist between social-class background and racial-ethnic status on the one hand and educational achievement and attainment on the other. The combination of these factors is making it relatively more difficult for many low-status citizens to take advantage of economic opportunity, and meanwhile the percentages of poverty students and minority students in the public schools are increasing steadily and will continue to increase in the future.

In addition, education has become increasingly central in determining whether the United States will be successful economically, particularly with respect to international competition. Growing emphasis on services in the economy and the introduction of new technology have created needs for a better educated work force in general and for additional highly educated personnel in many occupations involving delivery of services or use of science and technology. Thus, some recent research indicates that substantial proportions of workers do not now possess the problem-solving and decision-making skills required for adequate performance in many occupations (e.g., fire fighter, police officer, financial clerk, textile worker) that have become increasingly complex (Gottfredson 1984; Bailey 1990). Also, the National Assessment of Educational Progress has reported that although the "overwhelming majority of young adults (twenty-one to twenty-five years of age) adequately perform tasks at the lower level [of literacy] . . . sizable

numbers appear unable to do well on tasks of moderate complexity" (Kirsch and Jungeblut 1986, 4; see also Mullis, Owen, and Phillips 1990 and Barton and Kirsch 1990). Information on these trends and problems has led influential business groups, such as the Committee on Economic Development, to demand and support major reforms in the educational system, with particular emphasis on strengthening academic preparation to ensure acquisition of abstract thinking and independent learning skills:

> *For most students, employers would prefer a curriculum that stresses literacy, mathematical skills, and problem-solving skills: one that emphasizes learning how to learn and adapting to change. The schools should also teach and reward self-discipline, self-reliance, teamwork, acceptance of responsibility, and respect for others. (Committee for Economic Development 1985, 15)*

Political leaders also have become increasingly concerned with making the educational system more effective for a larger proportion of children and youth. For example, President Reagan made international competitiveness the major theme of his 1987 State of the Union address, emphasizing the importance of education in improving the nations' ability to compete. Presidential aspirant Gary Hart (1987) also emphasized education in his campaign platform. He released a paper entitled "Education: The Key to the Third Century" in which he stated that "fate and circumstance have now seen fit to bind that future to our willingness to inform the minds of our citizens" and to reverse "the emerging colonialism of ignorance and economic domination" (pp. S1527–S1528).

As documented earlier in this chapter, much of the problem of lower performance in the educational system centers on and reflects the disadvantaged status of students from low-income families and racial/ethnic minority groups, particularly in concentrated urban poverty areas. This outcome of the sorting and selecting process not only detracts from the nation's capacity to prepare a highly skilled work force capable of improving our competitive position internationally, but it also raises the prospect that the United States will become even more divided into a prosperous, largely nonminority segment on the one hand and an embittered segment of low-status citizens with mostly working-class and substantially minority family background on the other. Arkansas Governor Bill Clinton was concerned with this and other trends documented in Chapter 1 when he told members of the American Association of Colleges for Teacher Education in 1987 that "we don't have as much time as most people think" to improve the schools; if recent trends continue, "40 percent of the U.S. population will be worse off economically in the year 2000, while 20 percent will hold their own and 40 percent will better their lot" (quoted in Teske 1987, p. 4).

METROPOLITAN EVOLUTION

Urbanization is the most characteristic aspect of modern society. Urbanization is the process of making people into city-dwellers. Until 1800, the people of even the most powerful societies were mainly engaged in getting food and fuel from the land—some 80 percent of the working population were tillers of the soil, or sheep and cattle tenders, or fishermen, or foresters. Then the growing technification of society enabled fewer and fewer people to raise more and more food, until, today, less than 10 percent of the working force in the United States produces enough fuel and food to provide a high standard of living for all the population.

The farm, the home, the office, as well as the workshop, have all been technified, and with this process has come increasing urbanization. Larger and larger proportions of the population have come to live in cities and suburbs. Together, the city and the suburbs comprise the metropolitan area, defined as a central city of 50,000 or more people plus the surrounding county or counties in which the population has

significant economic, social, and cultural contact and interchange with the city.

As shown in Table 2-9, the population of the United States became steadily more concentrated in metropolitan areas between 1910 and 1988. By 1988, 77 percent of the U.S. population was located in 284 metropolitan areas. Thirty-nine of these metropolitan areas were Consolidated Metropolitan Statistical Areas with more than one million people each. The 1990 census showed that, for the first time, more than half the U.S. population lived in metropolitan areas with a population greater than one million. The United States had become a predominantly metropolitan society.

Another result of these long-range trends has been the creation of massive strip cities, that is, urban settlements that usually are near major highways or beltways and cross numerous municipal jurisdictions. Lacking a coherent residential, commercial, or industrial center, many of these sprawling strip settlements are generating traffic congestion and high development costs throughout metropolitan areas (Fishman 1990).

Population shifts underlying these changes constituted an important development in the United States in the 1970s and 1980s. For the first time in U.S. history, some older and larger metropolitan areas—including their suburbs—lost population, and for the first time in this century nonmetropolitan counties gained rather than lost population (Johnson 1989). These trends in turn reflected at least three major developments: (1) a lower birthrate; (2) out-migration from central cities and, in some cases, from interior suburbs in older and larger metropolitan areas, particularly in the East and Middle West; and (3) general movement of population from economically depressed regions in the snowbelt to economically vigorous or otherwise attractive regions in the sunbelt.

As a result of these changes, approximately one of every three U.S. residents lives in a metropolitan area that declined or registered virtually no population growth since 1970. This unprecedented situation in U.S. history both

TABLE 2-9 *Growth of Urban Population in the United States*

Year	Rural (under 2,500)	Total Urban (2,500 and over)	Cities over 100,000	Metropolitan Areas
		Distribution of Total Population (by percentage)		
1790	95	5	–	–
1810	93	7	–	–
1830	91	9	2	–
1850	85	15	5	–
1870	74	26	11	–
1890	65	35	15	–
1910	54	46	22	46
1930	44	56	30	54
1950	36	64*	29	59
1960	30	70*	29	63
1970	37	73*	28	69
1980	26	74*	25	75
1988	27	73*	25	77

Sources: U.S. Bureau of the Census; Statistical Abstract of the United States, 1990.
*Current U.S. Census definition of *urban* adds about 5 percent to numbers based on pre-1950 definition.

reflected and caused serious problems in metropolitan schools and society, particularly in the central cities. However, population decline in many metropolitan areas also opens up possibilities for urban renewal and revitalization of deteriorating SMSAs.

Movement to the Suburbs and Deterioration of the Central City

By 1920, a number of U.S. cities were developing into complex metropolitan areas. Choice residential suburbs were being established outside many central cities, at first strung out along the railway lines that led into the city. These suburbs were exclusive residential areas, expensive to live in, with more living space and with superior schools provided at no greater cost to the taxpayer than in the central city. These suburbs were heavily upper-middle class, with fringes of upper-class and of lower-middle-class residents. Their schools, elementary and secondary, were relatively homogeneous along socioeconomic, racial, and ethnic lines.

Because the suburb is a part of the metropolitan complex, the fact that some suburbs draw mainly middle- and upper-class people results in an increase in the proportion of both working-class population and poverty families in the central city. As more persons move into metropolitan areas, the working-class and poverty areas of the central city expand, creating obsolescence and reduced monetary values in former middle-class residential areas. The area of solid middle-class residences becomes smaller and is often cut up into small islands contiguous to lower status areas.

The poverty areas of the central city expand during this stage of metropolitan development partly because the dynamics of the housing market lead to a deterioration of entire neighborhoods where there is substantial segregation of low income groups in separate communities (i.e., socioeconomic stratification). Abandoned housing has become a key factor in the spiral of deterioration that has been occurring in many big cities in the United States (Wilkerson 1990b). Sternlieb and Burchell (1973) have studied the process of residential abandonment in big cities and concluded that the root cause is the lack of buyers for housing units that become vacant or in tax arrears, particularly in homogeneous lower-working-class neighborhoods. Sternlieb and Burchell also addressed the next logical question, "Why are there so few buyers for vacant housing in these neighborhoods?" and concluded, "The environment of abandonment is the key here. This is illustrated by both growing fiscal incapacity of the city and by a fear on the part of remaining residents that they will be victimized by either crime or fire" (p. xxix).

Socioeconomic Stratification Intensified by Racial Segregation

Because many of the families migrating to the cities were from racial or ethnic minority groups that were confined to segregated neighborhoods, racial and ethnic segregation also increased during the period of rapid suburban growth after World War II, with minority families concentrated in the central cities. At the same time, families moving from the central city were predominantly white. Thus, the metropolitan area as a whole became increasingly both stratified and segregated, with working-class families and minority families concentrated in the central city, and middle-class white families predominating in the suburbs. The intensification of racial segregation on a metropolitan basis is shown in Table 2-10 which portrays a ninety-year trend toward racial differentiation between the central city and suburbs. As of 1980, blacks constituted 70 percent of the central city population in Washington, D.C., 67 percent in Atlanta, and 63 percent in Detroit, but they constituted only 17 percent, 14 percent, and 5 percent of the respective suburban populations in these metropolitan areas.

Stratification of the metropolitan area has been compounded by racial segregation (Massey and Eggers 1990). As the population of working-class minority communities increased, pressure built up to open additional housing opportunities in surrounding neighborhoods. A few racial minority families would begin to move into these neighborhoods, realtors would steer even more minority families toward them, and before long these neighborhoods were undergoing racial transition and soon became predominantly minority. A variety of real estate and housing practices, including "blockbusting" tactics designed to scare whites into leaving changing neighborhoods, discriminatory covenants that prevented minorities from purchasing property in white neighborhoods further away, and refusal of banks and federal agencies to support loans to minority families seeking to move into predominantly white neighborhoods, combined to cause increasingly rapid turnover.

Geographic segregation of African Americans thus expanded rapidly during the 1950s and

TABLE 2-10 *Proportion of Population in Metropolitan Areas That Is Nonwhite, 1900–1980**

Year	Metropolitan Area	Central City	Outside Central City
1900	7.8	6.8	9.4
1910	7.3	6.9	8.1
1920	7.2	7.3	7.0
1930	8.1	9.0	6.4
1940	8.6	10.1	6.0
1950	10.0	13.1	5.7
1960	11.7	17.8	5.2
1970	12.8	21.4	4.9
1980	16.4	29.4	8.8

Source: U.S. Bureau of the Census.
*Hispanics may be either white or nonwhite.

thereafter, as black families from the rural South moved to cities and as nonminority families settled largely white suburban areas. As shown in an analysis of 22,000 neighborhoods in 66 cities conducted by Massey and Denton (1989), by 1980 this geographic separation according to race reached the level of hypersegregation, in the sense that a substantial proportion of blacks not only are mostly isolated from the larger metropolitan society, but also are concentrated in predominantly black sections of the largest central cities. (Massey and Denton also reported that many Hispanics are geographically segregated, but with the exception of Puerto-Rican Americans in older cities in the Northeast and Midwest, they are not segregated nearly as systematically as African Americans.) Massey and Denton (1989) summarized implications of their analysis as follows:

> *[Even if blacks] go to the adjacent neighborhood, or to the neighborhood adjacent to that, they are still unlikely to encounter a white resident. These agglomerations of monoracial [census] tracts are densely settled and geographically restricted, comprising a small portion of the urban environment closely packed around the city center, a zone known for poverty and social disorganization long before blacks arrived there. . . .*
>
> *This extreme level of residential segregation across multiple dimensions is important because of the social isolation it implies. For blacks in large ghettos of the north, this isolation must be extreme. Unless a resident of these ghettos works in the Anglo-dominated economy, he or she is unlikely to come into contact with anyone other than another black ghetto-dweller. Indicators of the accompanying social isolation . . . [include data suggesting that] black ghetto speech has grown progressively more distant from the standard English [used by most whites] . . . black marriage, fertility, and family patterns have diverged more sharply from the mainstream . . . [and] poverty, labor force withdrawal, and unemployment*

> *have come to be increasingly concentrated in inner-city black neighborhoods. (Massey and Denton 1989, 389)*

However, it is important to emphasize that the socioeconomic stratification of metropolitan areas in the United States was exacerbated but not created solely by racial segregation. According to urban analysts such as George Sternlieb, considerable stratification and its accompanying "defunctioning" of the central city "would have occurred even if there had not been a problem of race" (1974, 225). On the other hand, racial segregation not only speeded up socioeconomic stratification but also helped obscure the real nature of what is going on in the central city, that is, the effects of concentrating poverty so heavily in one part of the metropolitan area.

Stratification and segregation combined with suburbanization have continued to concentrate low-status minority groups in the central cities in the 1970s and 1980s and thus to generate an increasingly high proportion of economically disadvantaged minority students in central city school districts. In the fifty largest U.S. cities, for example, the overall population declined between 1970 and 1980, but the number of low-income black Americans living in poverty areas increased by 23 percent (Herbers 1987).

The Stratified and Segregated Metropolitan Complex

The movement of population to the suburbs has continued through the 1970s and 1980s. In the 1950s and 1960s a new and more complicated pattern appeared wherein working-class migration to the suburbs also became significant. Most of these working-class families were white, and many settled in areas that became predominantly working-class suburbs. But in many metropolitan areas one or more centers of black working-class residence also existed or began to form in the suburbs. Thus, even though most of the suburbs do not include the lowest socioeconomic group found in the central city, many suburban regions have become differentiated into communities that are either predominantly upper-middle class, lower-middle class, or working class (Hess, Lewis, Laine, and Gilbert 1991). In recent years, *technoburbs* consisting of expensive planned communities organized around commercial and financial services or emerging high-tech industries have been established at the outer edges of large metropolitan areas (Lemann 1989; Johnson 1991). The overall results of this stage of metropolitan evolution are that within the larger pattern of metropolitan stratification, working-class residents constitute a major part of the central-city population, and the suburbs also have become increasingly stratified according to social class.

Another complicating factor in metropolitan evolution emerged in the 1970s, when many middle-class black families began to move out of the central city (Fox 1990). Commenting on this trend, Detroit Urban League Director Francis Kornegay noted, "it's a human urge as a person climbs the economic ladder to spend and get the best for his family. And where is the best now? In the suburbs" (quoted in Wolman 1976, 27). By 1990, African Americans constituted about 6 percent of the suburban population in metropolitan areas with more than one million people (Frey 1990).

An analysis of African American suburbanization indicates that in some metropolitan areas, black population—particularly the middle class— is dispersing to some degree throughout the suburbs, but in other metropolitan areas black movement appears to be mostly spillover of central city population into first-ring and adjacent suburbs. This latter pattern appears to be particularly the case in the largest metropolitan areas, which have the largest black populations and have had the greatest black migration to the suburbs. It is clear that first middle-class and then working-class black families in Atlanta, Chicago, Cleveland, St. Louis, and other big cities have been moving to the inner tier of suburbs adjoining the central city ghetto, and that some of these inner suburbs now are becoming heavily black (Rose 1982; Nathan 1991). What has been happening, in other words, is that middle-class and upwardly

mobile black families have been escaping from the inner-city ghetto, but the same pattern of socioeconomic and racial segregation that had marked the decline of the central city is appearing in some suburbs (Lake 1981; Kerr 1989; Suro 1991).

Looked at in a slightly different way, the deteriorated inner core of the metropolitan area has expanded into the suburbs just as it previously had grown to consume large parts of the central city. If these trends continue, African American and white middle-class families who now live in inner suburbs will move farther out as working-class families begin to move in, and the overall stratification of the metropolitan area will be further reinforced.

The pattern of metropolitan development described here is typical of older and larger United States metropolitan areas that have evolved toward a high degree of socioeconomic stratification and racial segregation (Massey and Eggers 1990). However, it should not be assumed that all metropolitan areas in the United States have followed the same pattern of development or necessarily will evolve in the same direction as those that best illustrate the pattern. Metropolitan areas differ considerably in accordance with their age, size, region, unique history, and other characteristics. For example, small metropolitan areas tend to be less stratified than larger ones and may not necessarily become highly stratified in the future if steps are taken to prevent this from happening. Metropolitan areas in the south historically exemplified an opposite pattern than those in the north, with high status population tending to be concentrated in the central city and very low status population residing in the periphery. However, larger metropolitan areas in the south have begun to follow the northern pattern.

Stratification, Segregation, and the Underclass

One of the most important facts about racial segregation in larger and older metropolitan areas is that it appears to have become self-perpetuating despite attempts made to ensure that racial and ethnic minorities have equal access to housing throughout the city and the suburbs. Federal, state, and local open housing laws were passed in the 1960s, and government programs in housing and other activities since then have included an emphasis on reduction of racial segregation. As noted, substantial numbers of black families have begun to move to the suburbs, thereby bringing about a slight decline in residential segregation on a national basis (McKinney and Schnare 1987; Taeuber 1990).

However, the movement of middle-class minority families out of segregated city ghettoes has *increased* concentration of poverty in the inner city. As noted earlier in this chapter and elsewhere in this book, socioeconomic stratification and racial segregation thus have placed many minority citizens into underclass communities in big-city poverty neighborhoods (Wacquant and Wilson 1989). By definition, the underclass consists of individuals locked into a cycle of poverty, welfare dependency, and social despair. But the negative effects of having a large underclass in the heart of our metropolitan areas damage not just the individuals directly involved but also the larger communities in which they live (De Parle 1991). In a paper titled "The Black Community: Is There a Future?" Orlando Patterson has examined the broader consequences of this demographic pattern and reached the following conclusions:

> On the whole . . . the range and variety of black ghetto styles are rapidly declining. . . . The "achievers" have almost all left or are scrambling to leave. The activists and revolutionaries of the sixties are now almost nonexistent. . . . What remains . . . are the "defeated," the 'rebels without causes' or criminal elements, and, most pervasive of all, the 'street people.' . . . For the mass of the black poor, and for the poor generally, this . . . must seem like a social nightmare. . . . What in the world will the post-industrial world do with them? (Patterson 1979, 274, 278)

Effects on the city and metropolitan area as a whole have been similarly dysfunctional and foreboding. In 1982, the staff of the Joint Economic Committee of the U.S. Congress analyzed the fiscal condition of the big cities and concluded that patterns of stratification and segregation had combined with economic decline to produce grave problems for much of urban America:

> The outlook for the cities is bleak. In the declining cities where capital deferrals are accompanied by reductions in service levels and large tax increases, it appears that crises cannot long be avoided. . . . This will not only leave these cities in a deepening state of distress, but will render these cities home for the most dependent segments of society—the undereducated, the unemployed, the aged, and the minorities. These individuals have neither the means to leave nor the skills to improve their plight if they did. This scenario makes it difficult to imagine that the private sector in these cities—even those firms that remain— will make a dent in training or employing the unemployed or in significantly enhancing the local tax base. (Galbraith 1982, xiii–xiv)

Recommendations and opinions concerning possible responses to the problem of stratification and segregation in United States metropolitan areas differ greatly in accordance with each observer's social, politial, and economic philosophy. Patterson's (1979) analysis concluded that long-range improvements in opportunities for twenty million blacks in urban ghettoes will require a much greater emphasis on full employment policies at the federal and state levels, even if this reinforces inflationary tendencies in the economy, and a much greater government effort to combat discrimination and ensure economic growth in the cities. President Jimmy Carter's Commission for a National Agenda for the Eighties first noted that "a sizeable portion of the urban underclass" have become "relatively permanent," and then offered a number of recommendations including emphasis on "a guaranteed job program for those who can work and a guaranteed cash assistance plan for both the 'working poor' and those who cannot work" (Panel on Policies and Prospects 1980, 15, 102).

In further recommending that "federal urban policy efforts should not necessarily be used to discourage the deconcentration and dispersal of industry and households from central urban locations" and that "relocation of population and economic vitality to nonmetropolitan and previously rural areas also should not be discouraged" (p. 104), the commission set off a storm of controversy pitting those who would concentrate on developing or redeveloping deteriorated cities in the North and Middle West against those who would encourage migration of population to more prosperous metropolitan areas in the South and West. Many political leaders—particularly big-city mayors—expressed disagreement with this policy and argued that deteriorating older cities are too large and important a part of the United States thereby to "abandon" or "neglect." Probably the only policy direction on which there has been widespread agreement since the 1970s is that revitalization of the United States economy as a whole is badly needed if progress is to be made in overcoming patterns of decay and decline in many of our metropolitan areas (Fox 1990).

Derek Shearer (1989) reviewed developments with respect to urban policy in the 1980s and concluded that some improvements had been made through federal community-development grants tied in with local initiatives and priorities for renewal and growth. Although very uneven from city to city, progress was registered in many locations through emphasis on "increased public participation, job creation and retention, increased technical assistance to community economic organizations, and increased job placement of city residents" (p. 291). Shearer also perceived a "new urban populism" emerging as part of this process, based on a "vision of the city as a place where people should be given priority over buildings, cars, and businesses," and where all segments of the population share in gains that previously had gone mostly to affluent citizens who benefited from gentrification of deteriorated neighborhoods and demolition of housing to make way for highways (p. 293).

Big-City Schools Reflect Stratification and Segregation

Due to concentration of working-class/underclass and minority populations in central cities, public school districts in the central cities generally have much higher proportions of low-status students and minority students than do surrounding suburban districts. An example illustrating this pattern is shown in Figure 2-2, which provides data on the Milwaukee Metropolitan Area. (Milwaukee is a medium-sized metropolitan area that in many ways is typical of others in the United States.) Data for 1983–84 were available for 141 city and suburban elementary schools from which the Study Commission on the Quality of Education in the Metropolitan Milwaukee Public Schools was able to collect appropriate information (Witte and Walsh 1990).

Figure 2-2 arranges the percentage of low-income students against the percentage of minority students for a random sample of one-third of the schools in the data set. As shown in Figure 2-2, only two of the sixteen suburban schools have a percentage of low-income students as low as the city schools that scored lowest on this variable,* and none of the suburban schools had a percentage of minority students even half as high as the lowest city school. The average percentage of low-income students among the thirty-one city schools was 30 percent, as compared with 6 percent for the sixteen suburban schools. The average percentage of minority students for the city schools was 57 percent, while the average for suburban schools was 4 percent.

---

*Most big cities have a number of elementary schools with enrollment virtually all poverty and minority, but Milwaukee's desegregation plan has nearly eliminated this type of school.

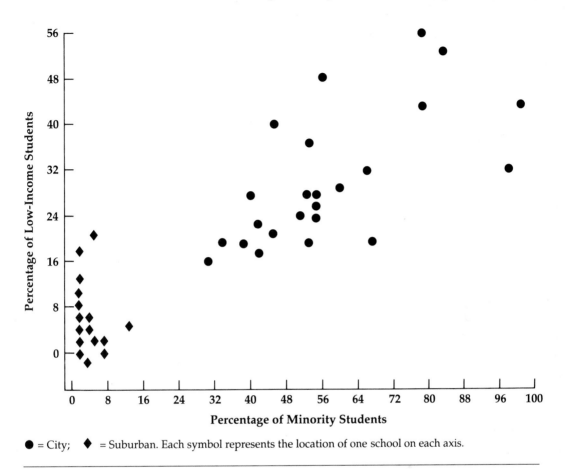

● = City;   ◆ = Suburban. Each symbol represents the location of one school on each axis.

FIGURE 2-2   *Percentage of Low-Income Students Plotted against Percentage of Minority Students, Milwaukee Metropolitan Area Elementary Schools, 1983–84 (Source: Analysis of data available from the Study Commission on the Quality of Education in the Metropolitan Milwaukee Public Schools; Witte and Walsh 1990.)*

Consequences for the educational system are illustrated in Figure 2-3, which shows the percentage of low-income students plus the percentage of minority students at high schools in the Milwaukee Metropolitan Area plotted against average tenth-grade achievement scores at high schools for which the Study Commission was able to collect appropriate information. Achievement scores are composites showing the percentage of students in the top half nationally in reading and math. The percentage of low-income/minority students in the suburban schools is slightly exaggerated and the percent-

age of high achieving students there is slightly deflated because some suburban schools receive transfer students from the city. The data for the city are averages across city high schools.

As shown in Figure 2-3, the average percentage of low-income students plus the percentage of minority students in city high schools is more than four times higher than that at the suburban high school with the highest score on this variable. Conversely, the achievement score at the lowest suburban high school is much higher than the city average of 38 percent. All of the suburban high schools have achievement far

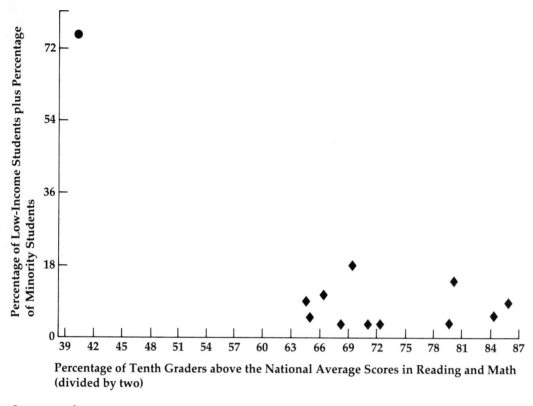

FIGURE 2-3 *Percentage of Low-Income/Minority Students Plotted against Average Reading and Math Achievement, Milwaukee Metropolitan Area High Schools, 1983–84 (*Source: *Analysis of data available from the Study Commission on the Quality of Education in the Metropolitan Milwaukee Public Schools; Witte and Walsh 1990.)*

above the national average, whereas the city is far below. The fact that more than half the city tenth-graders are in the bottom 38 percent nationally also means that a larger proportion of city students are reading below grade level, and that many students are not learning much in high-school courses that require students to learn through reading.

Another major consequence for central-city school districts involves the high concentrations of high-school dropouts. As shown in Figure 2-4, the average dropout rate at city high schools during the 1983–84 school year was approximately five times as high as those at suburban high schools in the Milwaukee Metropolitan Area.

(The low-income/minority percentage and the dropout percentage are slightly exaggerated at suburban schools due to the fact that some enroll low-income, minority students as part of a city-to-suburban transfer program.) Because some students leave school at each high-school grade each year, the percentages of students who drop out before graduation is much higher than the one-year percentage. At some individual city schools with mostly poverty/minority students, the percentage of students who leave before graduation is higher still—in the range of 40 to 60 percent.

These data for the city of Milwaukee are in line with those from other big cities. For example,

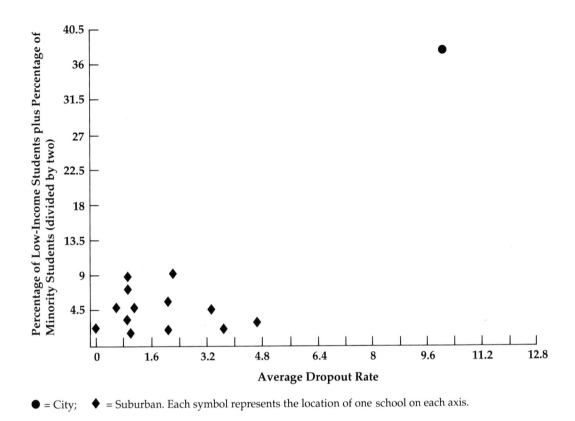

● = City; ◆ = Suburban. Each symbol represents the location of one school on each axis.

FIGURE 2-4 *Percentage of Low-Income/Minority Students Plotted against Average Dropout Rate, Milwaukee Metropolitan Area High Schools, 1983–84* (Source: *Analysis of data available from the Study Commission of the Quality of Education in the Metropolitan Milwaukee Public Schools; Witte and Walsh* 1990.)

data from Chicago indicate that nearly 45 percent of high-school students citywide do not graduate from high school, and some Chicago high schools have dropout rates above 60 percent (Hess and Lauber 1985). The dropout rate in New York has been estimated at more than 50 percent (Snider 1987), and a few high schools in that city may have a rate above 80 percent.

National data on the percentage of students who are members of minority groups indicate that most big-city school districts now enroll a preponderance of minority students. (The official federal definition of *minority* students includes those designated as American Indian, Asian, black, and Hispanic, as well as several

much smaller groups.) The Council of the Great Cities Schools, which includes 47 of the largest school districts in the United States, has reported that in 1990, 42 percent of the students in its members' schools were African American, 24 percent were Hispanic, 6 percent were Asian, and 3 percent were "other" minority. The Council further reported that 57 percent of the students enrolled in its schools were from low-income families eligible for federal lunch subsidies (Waste 1989; Casserly and Kober 1990; Rist 1990a).

Note that the metropolitan educational structure as portrayed in this section is compatible with the view (described in Chapter 1) that the United States recently has become increasingly bifurcated, with an increasing proportion of low- and high-income persons and a decreasing proportion of middle-income persons. In any case, regardless of whether bifurcation is increasing or decreasing in society as a whole, increasing stratification and segregation by socioeconomic status and race/ethnicity do appear to be defining characteristics of metropolitan evolution in the past five or six decades.

URBAN RENEWAL

During the 1950s, civic ills accompanying metropolitan growth led to social action called urban renewal. The emphasis on urban renewal in this early period was on tearing down the worst of the slums and building large blocks of public housing for low-income families. For example, much of Boston's oldest housing was torn out to make room for expressways. Hundreds of acres of tenement houses were torn down on Chicago's South Side, on New York's Lower East Side, and in the area of Washington south of the Capitol. Los Angeles cleared the area on which the new Civic Center was built. The Golden Triangle of Pittsburgh was modernized with new office buildings, hotels, and expressways.

Not only were slums cleared, but a good deal also was done to arrest and reverse the process of decay of the downtown business district. This meant building a second generation of ultramodern skyscrapers to replace those erected in the early 1900s. It also meant building expressways to provide easy automobile transportation for commuters who do not use old-fashioned public transit services. In addition, new and attractive apartment housing was built within walking or taxi distance of the downtown offices and stores for those people who have the money and the inclination to live in upper- or middle-class style without going out to the suburbs or the city fringes.

In the 1960s, 1970s, and 1980s, the federal government continued to award significant sums of money to what is now called Housing and Urban Development. An Act of 1965 provided a variety of aids for housing, including substantial numbers of new low-rent public housing units, rent supplements to aid low-income families to secure better private housing, and subsidized low interest rates for housing for people of moderate income. Community development legislation was updated in the 1970s to place a greater emphasis on *conservation* of neighborhoods that might otherwise become slums, and on *redevelopment* of deteriorated or unused land as part of a long-range plan for the improvement of the central city and the entire metropolitan area. The federal government also began to place some stress on reducing metropolitan stratification and segregation, for example, by refusing to approve some applications for housing projects that would concentrate more low-status population in the central city and by requiring suburbs to consider low-cost housing in their plans for future development. These emphases were foreshadowed in the 1960s by Robert C. Weaver, who served in President Lyndon Johnson's Cabinet:

> *I am convinced that the recent decline in the population of central cities has been due, in large part, to the concentration of new construction in the suburbs and the scarcity of competing living facilities in the central cities.*
>
> *The city today is, or should be in my opinion, the heart, and in a sense the soul, of a metropolitan area. The suburbs around it, to a large degree, draw their life and their spirit from the city's economy and culture. The city should be revitalized as the anchor holding together our metropolitan areas. It does not perform this function effectively today. (Weaver 1964, 6)*

However, urban renewal activities through the 1970s and 1980s generally have not yet succeeded in reversing the process of segregation and decay in large metropolitan areas (Applebome 1991). Part of the reason is that most housing built for or made available to low-status families has been in or next to low-status neighborhoods and has compounded as much as it has alleviated the problems generated by stratification and segregation. Slums were cleared in many cities, but in the absence of long-range plans for metropolitan development there was no place for evicted families to move except to nearby low-status neighborhoods, which then experienced accelerated deterioration. Most public housing built in the 1950s was in the form of high-rise apartments, which magnified the problem of concentrated urban poverty. Housing programs since that time have not contributed as blatantly to additional stratification and segregation, but neither have they succeeded in greatly reducing the concentration of low-status families in the central city and in some of the suburbs.

Redevelopment of Deteriorated Neighborhoods

Several forces favor the redevelopment of large sections of the central city as stable neighborhoods with a substantial middle-status population base. Redevelopment of this sort can take place either through renovation of older housing in which middle-class families are willing to invest large sums of time and money or through the construction of new housing on land previously nonresidential or cleared of slums by government action. Most big cities already have some housing that fits this description, where a neighborhood with old mansions has become a prestige address for young couples interested in renovation or middle-class apartments and townhouses have been built in or near the downtown (Fishman 1990; Frey 1990). These clusters of redevelopment generally could serve as nuclei for much larger renewal efforts, provided that potential residents have confidence in the future viability of neighborhoods in the central city.

An example of redevelopment of a well-situated but deteriorated central city area is the project for twenty-first century renewal by the Chicago 21 Corporation. Favored by city government, this organization with private financing is in the process of buying and developing vacant areas close to the downtown business district of Chicago. There are about four square miles of mainly vacant land to the south and west of the Chicago Loop.

The first phase of the plan has been carried through by the Dearborn Park Corporation. This corporation bought a 51.5 acre site, including the old Dearborn Station and unused railroad tracks. The Corporation has built several hundred town houses and two high-rise apartment buildings, with a total of 3,000 residential units, which have been rented or sold either to young married couples or to older families who are employed in the central business district.

The Problem of a Viable Economic Mixture

The confluence of trends such as those described means that it now may be possible to redevelop deteriorated central city neighborhoods into attractive communities for people of varied racial and ethnic background and socioeconomic status. Paul R. Porter, formerly administrator of the Marshall Plan for the redevelopment of Europe after World War II, has examined some of these trends and written a book on *The Recovery of American Cities*, which concluded that they represent

> *a superb opportunity for cities . . . as long as low-income housing was in acute short supply, and as long as there was a strong stream of migration from the countryside, renewal policy (with some exceptions) has been to preserve this land for low-income residents. The policy, like most buildings on the land, is obsolete. The proper goal should be to transform the decaying districts into new neighborhoods attractive enough to* compete with suburbs *as a place of residence for people who work in the central business district. (Porter 1976, 14)*

It is clear that the restoration of middle-income housing contiguous to the downtown core of the big city is a part of the larger problem of maintaining a viable mixture of social classes within the central city of the metropolitan area. The problem is partly one of racial and ethnic residential integration, and of desegregation of public schools, considered at length in Chapter 9. In general, the position of the public schools is likely to become more and more strategic. William G. Colman, an authority on the structure of the metropolitan area, has written:

> *Until central city schools become as good as, or somewhat better than, suburban schools, few middle and higher income families with school-age children will remain in the city, particularly if the public school servicing their neighborhood is attended by children who are all or mostly from low income families. . . . Undoubtedly the public school is a major, if not the dominant factor, in restoring a socioeconomic balance in central cities. (1977, 34)*

To a significant degree, the problems of city and metropolitan revitalization are centered in the older and larger metropolitan areas in the northern, eastern, and middlewestern parts of the United States. Constructive revitalization will be difficult to bring about, but scholars studying urban development in the United States are not entirely pessimistic. For example, Richard Knight has examined recent developments and has tried to identify the major actions and policies required to rebuild United States cities for the twenty-first century. His overall conclusions are as follows:

> *Industrial cities are easily misread. If one thinks of them in terms of plant and equipment, all one sees is abandoned plants and neighborhoods in the center of the city, and thus their image of inevitable decline is reinforced. . . . [But, viewed] in perspective, the worst is over. Most of the production jobs that will be lost have already . . . [been lost]. The challenge they now face is one that all cities have faced in history: to rebuild. This requires a clear vision of how their role has*

changed so that they can be redesigned in ways that are supportive of their expanding functions.

> *The real success of any city in the future, as in the past, will depend on its ability to pass on its knowledge base from one generation to another, to retain its young once they have been educated . . . to recruit talent to apply and advance the wide range of technology that is required. . . . [Thus] development strategy for cities in the future will have to be oriented toward rebuilding a city that is . . . attractive to the middle class. Although this may seem like the obvious direction, it would require a major shift in values, behavior, and policies. (Knight 1982, 64)*

CONCLUSION: THE CRISIS IN SORTING AND SELECTING

This chapter has documented that much of the crisis in educational sorting and selecting in the United States involves and reflects recent trends that have concentrated working-class and underclass students, many of whom are disadvantaged minority students, in the inner-city portion of a postindustrial, metropolitan society. Scott Miller of the Exxon Education Foundation has surveyed developments regarding the differential development of inner-city schools and communities and has summarized them in the trenchant observation that "several of our inner cities have effectively become the planet's first truly international multicultural, multilingual 'developing countries.' . . . The nation-building agenda concerning nonwhites [in the inner city] has been transformed in recent years into a much larger concern for the overall moral, political, and economic health of the nation" (Miller 1986, 52).

Miguel Castells also has examined recent patterns of metropolitan development in relation to larger economic and social trends and noted that "we are witnessing the rise of urban schizophrenia . . . [involving] the contradictory coexistence of different social, cultural, and economic logics within the same spatial structure . . . [thereby inducing] a *new territorial division of labor*, based on *polarized growth* and *selective development*, which reflects itself in the interregional cleavages, intrametropolitan dualism, and *simultaneous* life and death of our great cities" [italics in original]. He further pointed out that much of the problem involving schools and society in inner-city poverty neighborhoods has its origins in the "upgrading of professional and technical jobs in advanced service and high technology manufacturing . . . [which require] a fundamental retraining of labor, something the educational system is hardly able to assure, particularly in the secondary public school" (Castells 1985, 22, 24, 32, 33).

Concerned with both the international economic challenge faced by the society as a whole and the equity issues raised by the inadequate performance of many disadvantaged students, educators also are reviewing the trends that have produced the crisis in educational sorting and selecting. One of the most useful analyses of the general problem in education has been provided by Daniel and Lauren Resnick. They have reached the conclusion that traditional arrangements for sorting and selecting are no longer functional for the United States. The Resnicks first recognize that our historic efforts to provide equal educational opportunity and to stimulate national growth involved the movement to make high-school education not just available but compulsory for all students. With the exception of contemporary Japan, no other large nation has established a system of comprehensive high schools providing some common academic emphasis for nearly all its youth.

The Resnicks also point out, however, that traditional efforts to provide a common curriculum for all secondary students were possible only because ability grouping and tracking allowed the schools to differentiate within the comprehensive public-school system. "Where do American schools stand," they ask, "with respect to curriculum and tracking?" After reviewing the history of the comprehensive high school in the twentieth century, their answer is that

we have compromised. Our rhetoric and our provision in most school systems of an undifferentiated high school diploma all suggest a decision against tracking. However, in reality we have considerable tracking . . . even if it is not always formally so labeled. Comprehensive high schools usually house several quite different sets of courses in which expectations and standards vary considerably. (Resnick and Resnick 1985, 10)

According to the Resnicks and many other observers, the most destructive consequence of the compromise educators reached in trying to provide opportunity for all while maintaining high standards for only a few has been that the great majority of students have not been challenged and helped to attain a high level of academic performance. Some students in the top track become advanced, independent learners, while the vast bulk of students receive relatively low-level instruction emphasizing passive learning, memorization and regurgitation of factual material, and mastery of only very minimal standards (Goodlad 1984; Resnick 1990). This basic pattern has been significantly reinforced during the past fifteen years by introduction of minimum competency testing, continuing and probably growing reliance on simplified textbooks, and mandated reforms that require or at least encourage teachers to emphasize such low-level skills as computation in math and the mechanics of language (Madaus 1988). To do otherwise would have required truly fundamental system reforms involving introduction of active learning methods, reduction of class size in many schools, continuous and expensive teacher-retraining, provision of much more administrative support, and many other costly and difficult interventions.

In addition, the traditional pattern appeared to be producing relatively acceptable results for most students, until the emergence of postindustrial society and escalation of international competition substantially magnified the need to attain a higher level of performance on a more equitable basis that ensures improved achievement on the part of economically and socially disadvantaged students. After reviewing the current status of curriculum and instruction in elementary and secondary schools as well as of recent national and state efforts to improve instruction, the Resnicks conclude that an important first step in raising educational standards is to improve the level of instruction through a non-tracked curriculum that sets strong intellectual requirements for all students. "Nobody knows," they argue, "whether a strong intellectual program" for all students could work—whether most students would remain in school and perform successfully. The idea of a high-level, academically oriented common curriculum" is radical because it "takes seriously the goal of a fully educated citizenry" (Resnick and Resnick 1985, 18).

Later chapters describe efforts to provide compensatory education to improve the performance of low-status students (Chapter 8), the role of desegregation in improving educational opportunity for minority students (Chapter 9), problems and obstacles that make it difficult for educators to overcome disadvantages in students' home environment (Chapters 3 and 4), and other topics bearing on improvement of students' performance. The entire final chapter is devoted to an examination of recent educational reforms and of promising approaches for improving achievement. Indeed, much of the remainder of this book constitutes in effect an extended meditation and commentary on the causes and consequences of the crisis in sorting and selecting that is occurring in post-industrial, metropolitan society, and the actions that can or should be taken to deal with this crisis.

EXERCISES

1. Describe the steps being taken for urban renewal in a metropolitan area, and discuss the relations you think the schools should have to urban renewal in this area.

2. If you live in a city of fewer than 50,000, study it and its county as an example of tension between urban and rural styles of life. How do the schools fit in? Do they tend to work toward urbanization?

3. After reading Paul R. Porter's book on *The Recovery of American Cities*, describe ways in which education might affect the success of comprehensive plans to bring about systematic renewal in the metropolitan area.

4. Select a college you know. Analyze the student body in terms of socioeconomic backgrounds. What is the relation of socioeconomic background to fraternity membership, participation in athletics scholarship awards, participation in religious organizations, and enrollment in various curricula or courses of study?

5. Interview several high-school students of different social backgrounds to find out what their attitudes are toward the school and its various curricula.

SUGGESTIONS FOR FURTHER READING

1. A number of classic books deal with the growth of metropolitanism and the problems of the city. The book by Bollens and Schmandt, *The Metropolis*, is particularly relevant, as is also *Anatomy of a Metropolis* by Hoover and Vernon, and *The City Is the Frontier*, by C. Abrams. The book *Metropolis, 1985* by Raymond Vernon is one of a series describing the New York Metropolitan Region Study. Jean Gottmann's *Megalopolis*

gives a striking account of metropolitan development in the chain of urban areas that stretches from Boston to Washington, D.C.

2. The American metropolis is rather different in its history and structure from the great cities of other parts of the world. To see the range in types of cities, the following books are useful: *The Urban Community: A World Perspective* by Nels Anderson; *The City* by Rose Hum Lee; and *The City in History* by Lewis Mumford.

3. Patterns of resegregation in suburban areas are among the topics documented and discussed in *The New Suburbanites* by Robert Lake.

4. Many key aspects of urban evolution and policy are discussed in *Cities in the 21st Century* edited by Gary Gappert and Richard V. Knight. Chapters dealing with "The Evolving Dynamics of Urban Development," "The Hispanic-American Urban Order," "The Future of Black Ghettos," "New Technologies and Their Urban Impact," "Toward the Androgynous City," and "Changes in the Provision of Public Services" are particularly useful to educators.

5. *Making Inequality* by James E. Rosenbaum is a case study of a white, working-class school in which the academic track into which students were assigned had substantial independent effects on their subsequent careers. Rosenbaum shows how tracking is used to select and sort secondary students and discusses implications for public policy. He concludes that tracking sets up a tournament mobility system that successfully eliminates students on meritocratic grounds such as ability and effort but also on other grounds such as efficiency and convenience in organizing the public schools.

6. A critical analysis of the community colleges and their role in higher education was published in the *Harvard Educational Review* by Fred L. Pincus in 1980 under the title "The

False Promises of Community Colleges: Class Conflict and Vocational Education." A somewhat more balanced report on Community Colleges was presented by Virginia Robinson: "Community Colleges: Education's Biggest Growth Industry Has an Uncertain Mission," *Education Times*, Nov. 23, 1981.

7. A good summary of the issues and of the research program that attempted to create culture-fair tests of intelligence (tests that would not penalize children from lower socioeconomic level) is given in "Social Class and Intelligence Tests" by W. W. Charters, Jr., and N. L. Gage, in *Readings in the Social Psychology of Education*.

8. The important questions about relative influence of heredity and of environment in the production of intelligence cannot be answered in simple terms. There is always an interaction of heredity and environment. In the United States, the practical question concerns the relation of IQ to race and to social class. But no two racial groups have the same social-class or social environmental experience. Therefore, information about racial status is mixed up with information about the social environment. A student who is reasonably knowledgeable about statistics and about socioeconomic status could usefully study the recent publications of Jensen and of those who disagree with him. See Sanday, Scarr-Salapatek, Mercer, and Herrnstein.

9. *The New Heartland* by John Herbers describes recent changes in urbanization and metropolitan evolution in the United States. Topics dealt with include the growth of exurbs, deindustrialization in the East and North, long-range commuting, and movement to small towns and cities.

10. *The Diverted Dream* (subtitled "Community Colleges and the Promise of Educational Opportunity in America, 1900–1985") by

Brint and Karabel (1989) provides a detailed account and explanation of how and why community colleges increasingly concentrated on developing vocational skills among relatively low-status and low-achieving students.

11. Kenneth Fox (1990) argues that postindustrial society in the United States is evolving toward a new geographic pattern wherein continuous urban settlements reflectig a "diffuse economy" constitute a "megalopolis" or "consolidated urban region."

12. Problems that have been emerging in sprawling strip settlements in suburban areas are described and analyzed in the article "Megalopolis Unbound" by Robert Fishman (1990).

13. Katherine Boo (1991) describes ripoffs of students and the federal government that have been perpetrated at some low-quality proprietary schools. She concludes that the government's willingness to fund such schools without adequate supervision has been undermining U.S. productivity as well as the aspirations of the relatively low-status students who attend them.

14. The August 1990 issue of the *American Journal of Education* is devoted to the topic of changing patterns of opportunity in higher education.

Problems of Children and Youth in Differing Social Class Environments

This chapter describes some of the most important problems children tend to encounter in three differing types of environments categorized by social class: working class, underclass, and middle class. Describing and discussing environments in this way necessarily oversimplifies reality. For example, implying that there are no major differences between differing working-class communities and suggesting that all families in a given working-class neighborhood behave and react the same way obviously is incorrect. The reader should keep in mind the fact that we are trying to portray general tendencies rather than implying that communities and families can be universally categorized according to social class.

EVOLUTION OF THE CHILD-NURTURING, MODERN FAMILY

Before describing the problems that children and youth encounter in differing types of communities categorized by social class, it is important to review how the family has evolved toward greater emphasis on nurturing children for success in the educational system and later in life. This evolution is connected with larger patterns of change that have occurred in family structure and in the relationship between the family and other social institutions (Alwin 1989).

We begin by noting that the family was much more of an economic unit in earlier times than it is now (Zelinger 1985; Stone 1991). Before industrialization, most families lived on the land, and children grew up in close contact with their parents and other adults (Chartier 1989; Pearcey 1990). All members of the family contributed to production, and education for most children consisted largely of learning how to function as a member of the family and the community in which they lived. Thus, the family together with the larger community was the major educational influence in the life of the child and worked in conjunction with other community institutions such as the church and the apprenticeship system in preparing young people for their roles as adults.

The family as a social institution has undergone marked changes, particularly in the past 100 years. In contrast to the rural or frontier family, the modern urban family remains the unit of economic consumption but is no longer the unit of economic production (Pearcey 1990). Formal education, as well as many types of informal education, have been taken over by the school, the mass media, and other agencies. Even the function of character building has been taken on more and more by such nonfamily agencies as the church, the school, and such special youth-serving organizations as the Boy Scouts and Girl Scouts, the 4-H clubs, Future Farmers of America, and the YMCA and YWCA. In this sense, the family can be thought of as a less important educational institution today than it was in traditional society.

In other aspects, however, the educational role of the family has become even more important today than it was in the past. Change in this direction has been associated with changes in the role the family plays in society as a whole. These latter changes involve the historical evolution of the family in the direction of (1) setting itself apart from the life of the larger community and (2) specializing to a greater extent than it did in satisfying the emotional needs of its members (Pearcey 1990).

A number of historians have been struck by the degree to which the family and the community in traditional and early industrial society were more closely intertwined than they tend to be in Western society today (Ariès 1989). On the one hand, people participated in communal activities and events such as festivals and open-air marketing to a greater extent than most adults do now. People lived their lives more in the immediate local community than is true today, in the company of others from their community at work, at church, and in other settings in which children became a part of the adult world at an early age (Chartier 1989). In addition, in many parts of the Western world the home was penetrated much more frequently by outsiders—particularly boarders, guests, and apprenticed youth—than is true today. In early industrial England, for example, families frequently sent their children to work for other people at an early age and accepted the children of others as servants or apprentices in their own homes (Boswell 1989). Phillipe Ariès has summarized the preindustrial community as follows:

The historian who studies iconographic documents . . . promptly makes the acquaintance of . . . the crowd—not the massive, anonymous crowd of our overpopulated cities, but the assembly of neighbors, women and children, numerous but not unknown to one another. . . . It is as if everyone had come out instead of staying at home: there are scenes depicting streets and markets, games and crafts, soldiers and courtiers, churches and tortures. . . .

Life in the past, until the seventeenth century, was lived in public. We have a good many examples of the ascendancy of society. The traditional ceremonies which accompanied marriage and which were regarded as

more important than the religious ceremonies . . . the visit paid by the guests to the newly-married pair when they were already in bed . . . afford further proof of society's rights over the privacy of the couple. What objection could there be when in fact privacy scarcely ever existed, when people lived on top of one another, masters and servants, children and adults, in houses open at all hours to the indiscretion of callers? (Ariès 1965, 405)

Closely related to the tendency for premodern families to "live life in public" as compared with families today was the relative overcrowding in housing which was typical of traditional and early industrial families. Collomp (1989) and other historians have examined data on housing in several countries and have concluded that both in traditional rural areas and in early industrial communities, family members generally lived and slept in much more confined quarters than do families today.

In addition, families in traditional society were in much closer contact with relatives; partly as a consequence, much more emphasis was placed on family heritage and honor than is true of most families in today's geographically and socially mobile society. Shorter has summarized this aspect of traditional society and the change that has occurred during the past 400 years as follows:

People in traditional families are willing to renounce a number of personal ambitions. They're ready to postpone marriage until late in life, or indeed forego it entirely so that the farm may prosper under the eldest; they're willing to overcome whatever strivings towards privacy slumber in their breasts, and go to the communal bonfire on St. John's Day. . . . [in the] Old Days—let us say the sixteenth and seventeenth centuries—the family . . . was held firmly in the matrix of a larger social order. One set of ties bound it to the surrounding kin, the network of aunts and uncles, cousins and nieces who dotted the old regime's social landscape. Another set fastened it to the wider community, and gaping holes in the shield of privacy permitted others to enter the household freely and, if necessary, preserve order. A final set of ties held the elementary family to generations past and future. . . . In its journey into the modern world the family has broken all these ties. (From The Making of the Modern Family, *by Edward Shorter, © 1975 by Basic Books, Inc., Publishers, New York, pp. 3, 18. Reprinted by permission.)*

Along with this change from looking outward to looking inward, the modern family became more child-centered than had been true before (Boswell 1989; Gèlis 1989). In addition, middle-class families began to place some stress on raising children to think independently, as contrasted with traditional emphasis on obedience and authority. Whereas in the traditional and early industrial periods the family had been oriented to the larger community, the modern family appears to be relatively oriented more toward interactions among its members, and much of this interaction centers on the welfare of the children. (Ariès 1989; Stone 1991). Children probably receive at least as much individual attention from parents in the modern family as was true in earlier periods, even though parents in modern society are at work, away from children a high percentage of the time.

What has been responsible for the change from the community- and heritage-oriented family of the preindustrial and early industrial periods to the conjugal family more typical of modern times in which husband, wife, and children are largely set apart from the outside world? Historians disagree on which causes are the most important (Pollock 1983), but most would list a number of developments that helped either bring about or make possible this change. Among these are:

1. Industrialization and urbanization, which had the effect of detaching people from the communities in which their families previously had been rooted.
2. Economic progress, which made it possible

for many families to have larger housing units with more private accommodations.
3. Loss of economic and other family functions to other institutions, which freed the family to specialize more in meeting the psychological needs of its members (Zelinger 1985). "The modern family," according to Frank Musgrove, "specializes in affection. It can do this job precisely because it need do little else" (Musgrove 1966, 37).
4. Reduced family size, which made it possible for parents to devote more resources and individual attention to children than could be done in large households (Alwin 1984).
5. Reduced child mortality, which made it more rewarding to lavish attention and resources on children than was the tendency when a high percentage of children died at an early age (Zelinger 1985).
6. Spread of the idea of "romantic love," which Shorter describes as unseating "material considerations in bringing the couple together. Property and lineage . . . [gave] way to personal happiness and individual self-development as criteria for choosing a marriage partner. . . . Domesticity, beyond that, sealed off the family as a whole from its traditional interaction with the surrounding world" (Shorter 1975, 5, 228).

Whatever the relative importance of these and other interrelated causes, it seems safe to conclude that the emergence of the inward-looking, child-nurturing, conjugal family was a development that spanned several centuries and proceeded at a different rate among various social groups in Western societies (Chartier 1989). It also is apparent that this development was at first substantially a middle-class phenomenon and indeed was simultaneous if not actually synonymous with the rise of the middle class. In this regard, Young and Willmott (1973) have described how "domesticity" and separation from the larger community did not become characteristic of the English working class until the late nineteenth or early twentieth centuries, and

Stone (1974) has explained that it was the propertied and bourgeois families that first turned inward because these were the "families which were not so grand as to be able to maintain a small army of nursery staff to take care of the children for them, but rich enough to indulge in the luxury of sentiment" (p. 31).

The analysis to this point has described the evolution of the family in the direction of modern emphases on privacy, child nurturance, and sentiment. It also has linked this evolution to the emergence of the middle class, as part of a long-term change in society toward the creation of contemporary social classes that to a significant extent pass the advantage of wealth and the disadvantages of poverty on to following generations. When one views these developments as part of a single, larger pattern, it appears as if the middle-class family historically acted to shelter its children from the outside world and to provide relatively permissive nurturance of a kind that would give the child good preparation for succeeding in school and later in life. "Family and school together," Ariès has observed, "removed the child from adult society" (p. 413). The working-class family, by way of contrast, was not as quickly able and willing to shut out external influences that might be deleterious in terms of preparing children to function independently in the classroom and the economy; instead, it continues to this day to place more stress than middle-class families do on obedience and authority—values that parents apparently perceive as more functional in a difficult and often threatening low-income environment.

The reader should not conclude that stress on authority and obedience in child raising is necessarily or universally inimical to the development of skills that will help children succeed in society. Stone (1974, 1991) has described how the "nuclear child-centered" family was relatively authoritarian in the sixteenth and seventeenth centuries, more "permissive and affectionate" in the eighteenth century, and again relatively more authoritarian in the nineteenth century, thus indicating that emphasis on child nurturance for

success in school and society is not strictly a function of permissive versus authoritarian family relations. Stress on obedience probably does not damage a child's cognitive development unless this stress is so insistent and pervasive as to inhibit exploration of the social, intellectual, or physical environments in which the child grows up. The following chapter summarizes what is known about home environments that contribute to achievement in the educational system. Before turning to this topic, more should be said about the efforts of contemporary families to isolate their children from external influences that might have a negative effect on their performance in school.

The ability to achieve this latter goal probably is more directly linked with social class than are variations in the actual learning environment provided in the home, because social class plays such an important part in determining how a family relates to the surrounding community and whether it is able to shield children from negative external influences (Cohen 1981). Middle-class families typically are more successful in this regard than are working class families, because their economic level and their emphasis on sentiment and nurturance have enabled them to attain a relatively high level of separation (privacy) from the outside world. However, middle-class families appear to be having more difficulty protecting their children from external influences now than they did in the past few generations before television invaded their homes, and before automobiles and drugs became more important parts of the subculture of teenagers. Like the family, the school confronts similar difficulties in a modern urban environment (Gabarino and Plantz 1980).

Is it better to shelter the child from the adult environment than to have the child learn how to get along in it at an early age? Is it desirable to separate the family from the community in order to nurture the cognitive growth of children and make the family a more self-sufficient unit emotionally? The answers to these types of questions depend on many considerations, including the goals established for children and other family members and the nature of the environment in which the family functions. Examining such questions from the viewpoint of social-class differences among families and communities can help us understand the problems children encounter growing up and going to school.

WORKING-CLASS ENVIRONMENTS

The upper working-class family frequently is still a traditional family in many respects. Although in some ways it is gradually becoming more similar to "modern" middle-class families (Young and Wilmott 1973; Rubin 1976), particularly when it is located in suburban parts of the metropolitan area (Tallman and Morgner 1970), it still emphasizes close ties with kin and segmentation of family roles by age and sex. These patterns have been described by Gans (1962) in his study of a working-class Italian community in the West End of Boston:

> *The* working-class subculture *is distinguished by the dominant role of the family circle. Its way of life is based on social relationships amidst relatives. The working class views the world from the family circle, and considers everything outside it as either a means to its maintenance or to its destruction. (Gans 1962, 244)*

There are definite advantages for child rearing in the upper working-class style described above. (Gans uses the term *lower class* to describe the lower-working class.) Children receive much more support from a variety of adults, and many parents do succeed in protecting their children from negative influences in the environment. However, one might almost say they do so by shutting out the world beyond the family and neighborhood as long as possible. This type of childhood tends to result in limited preparation and aspirations for education, and it does not help children learn to function independently in institutions like the modern school.

In addition, working-class children in an urban setting tend to be drawn into the lower working-class street culture that has the effect, among other things, of reducing the likelihood that they will succeed in the school. This is particularly a problem for young males, and for children from those working-class families that exemplify considerable marital instability and detachment from the primary labor market (i.e., which may be part of a culture of poverty). Gans calls these the "action-seeking" families and youth and reports that

> *mothers do attempt to teach their departing children rules of proper behavior, namely the rules of the adult-centered and routine-seeking home. . . . During this time, however, the child is also learning what are called the rules of the street, that is those of the peer group. Thus, for some years, parents fight the ascendancy of street rules over home rules. . . .*
>
> *Interestingly enough, the home-rules that are preached to the child differ little from those held by the middle class. . . . The extent to which these rules are enforced, however, varies between action-seeking and routine-seeking or mobile families. The former, for instance, seem to surrender earlier, with less resistance to the child's inevitable adoption of the rules of the street. Moreover, the child himself reacts differently to the enforcement of these ideals. The child of a routine-seeking family, discovering that there are home rules and street rules, soon learns therefore to act accordingly in both places. In an action-seeking family, however, the child learns that the rules which the parents preach and those which they themselves practice diverge sharply. (Gans 1962, 58–59)*

UNDERCLASS ENVIRONMENTS

Problems that parents experience in trying to protect children from the environment in which the big-city underclass lives represent a different order of magnitude. Poverty is more concentrated in these inner-city neighborhoods, social disorganization is more widespread, and families find it even more difficult to protect their children from negative forces in the environment than do upper working-class families that have built a compact family circle around the child. "It is not poverty itself," according to one informed observer, but "the condition of poverty—the squalor, the crime, the brutality and helplessness and anger—that spin a web that ensnares whole families for generations (King 1990, A16). Rainwater (1970) has studied an underclass housing project in St. Louis and has shown that the environment for children in this setting is highly stimulating and anxiety producing, particularly with regard to frequency of violent behavior and exposure to adult sexual activities. Rainwater found that early sophistication thus acquired by the children bothered their mothers, who then tried to

> *keep their children within the apartment as much as possible. . . . One often gets the impression that mothers try to hold them virtual prisoners within the house, so great is their fear for their physical and moral safety outside.*
>
> *However, mothers know they cannot succeed with this strategy as the children grow up. Children get a taste of freedom as they walk to and from school and they increasingly demand the right to come and go as their peers do. . . . Only parents who remain energetically vigilant can isolate their children through adolescence. Teenage girls, for example, may not be allowed to spend time outside the home (except for school) unless they are accompanied by a responsible adult. But few mothers can maintain sufficient authority to carry out such strict discipline more than intermittently. . . . The parents try to teach the child what life is supposed to be like and how he is supposed to live it. In doing so they communicate an image of conventional American family and community life, but always in the*

> *context of the quite different life actually experienced by both parents and child. . . . Parents communicate to the child that only if he does right he may be safe, but in fact, he discovers that when he does right he is not safe, and very often he does not want to do right because the things that are wrong are more interesting and stimulating. (Rainwater 1970, 223, 225, 226)*

As Rainwater's account makes clear, the socialization of underclass children in concentrated poverty neighborhoods generally is not conducive to success in the school and the economy. It seems almost as though the inner-city environment reproduces some of the most important social characteristics of premodern communities that offered children little protection from the dangers as well as rewards of adult society, before the modern family came into prominence partly to provide refuge for its members and develop resources required for success in a modern economy. The difficulty of raising children in the inner city is underlined when it is recognized that the brightest and most talented youngsters frequently tend to be the ones who are most quickly destroyed, perhaps because they may be most likely to become leaders among their peers and are quickest to perceive the hopelessness of their situation. It is no accident that the most common refrain among parents of teenagers in the inner city is, "I can't control my children anymore," (Ianni 1989b) or that children asked to write essays in the inner-city classroom frequently respond like the teenager who titled his story "In Hell," or another who ended her story with the comment, "Earth is Hell to live on. I wonder if we could live on the moon."

Many underclass neighborhoods in big cities have deteriorated in many respects since Rainwater, Elliot Liebow (1967), and other writers described conditions there in the 1950s and 1960s. Claude Brown in *Manchild in the Promised Land* has described some of the negative developments as follows in contrasting current conditions with those he encountered growing up:

In the forties, each block in Harlem would be the population from some town in South Carolina or Georgia or Alabama. . . . Aunts, uncles, cousins—everybody knew each other. . . . [Although there were drugs, the dealer was an outcast; although there was poverty, there also were jobs available, affordable housing, and functional community institutions.] The gangs fought mainly over girls and territory. . . . [but] they didn't have easy access to guns the way gang members do today. . . . We also carried switchblades, but we were experts at cutting a guy just on his hand or arm. We weren't killers. We weren't crazy the way they are today. (Quoted in Stone 1989, 36, 38)

Some persons familiar with the big city underclass believe that many of the children and youth in the inner city will never have an adequate opportunity to succeed unless they are removed from their families and neighborhoods and placed in an entirely new environment somewhat as many middle-class children historically were placed in boarding school to give them special preparation for education and careers (Coleman and Hoffer 1987; Proctor 1989; Coleman 1990a). Even today, governments in some countries take the brightest teenagers from their homes and send them to schools in communities distant from their families and neighborhoods (Joyce and Showers 1987). However, there obviously are disadvantages in removing children from their families even if this is thought to be legally and morally acceptable, and there are other alternatives for improving the home environment of children in the inner city. Some of these alternatives are discussed elsewhere in this book, particularly in the sections in Chapters 4, 8, and 9 dealing with home environments and the schools and with deconcentrating the poverty population in big-city schools.

MIDDLE-CLASS ENVIRONMENTS

In many respects, the environment in predominantly middle-class communities is more oriented toward preparing children and youth for success in modern society than is true in working-class communities. Several such aspects of many middle-class environments have been described as follows by Francis Ianni (1989b), based on interviews that he and his colleagues conducted in ten different types of U.S. communities:

Like the other [middle-class] suburban areas we studied, Sheffield is child-centered . . . its resources are directed to advancing the lives of its children as extensions of the family. . . . [In the case of one of the teenagers interviewed] his friends' parents . . . had the same expectation for him . . . as teachers at school. Even the occasional contacts he had with the local police always reinforced these expectations . . . . Communities like Sheffield mold their teenagers into a particular kind of person and start most of them off along well-prepared routes to college and careers. (Ianni 1989b, 59–61)

The dangers to children growing up in a middle-class environment are quite different than those faced by children in working-class or underclass environments. Whereas underclass environments pose clear threats to physical, cognitive, and emotional growth, and working-class environments tend to limit the child's range of experience and opportunities to become well prepared to participate in the school, many youngsters in predominantly middle-class neighborhoods now face an excess of opportunities that sometimes make it difficult to attain a stable and authentic sense of identity.

In general, middle-class children are well prepared to enter and succeed in school, and they tend to acquire much information about the world beyond their immediate neighborhood (Lasch 1990). However, their families tend to have few real roots in the communities in which they live. Their parents attempt to develop self-direction but frequently are unable to provide very much actual direction for the future, and the knowledge that they acquire is difficult to integrate into a coherent set of values to guide growth and development. Orr and Nichelson (1970) have described some of the characteristics of this type of environment, which they call the *radical suburb*, in terms of its emphases on openness to new experience and on empirical testing of reality as contrasted with acceptance of traditional opinion:

> It is a very short step from the empirical notion that truth is what is verifiable by experience to the expansive belief that experience itself is valuable. . . . From there it is but another short step to the notion that the richest life is one that includes the most varied kinds of experiences. The style of the suburban radical is not as it appears—a backlash against the stainless-steel grayness of a scientific atmosphere—but instead is the predictable spin-off from a culture that is infatuated with scientific experimentation. (Orr and Nichelson 1970, 50)

As Orr and Nichelson suggest, emphasis on new experience may lead to a lack of regard for the quality and effects of experience, to the feeling that "a bad trip may be better than no trip at all" (p. 62). It may provide children with a large amount of information about the world, but this knowledge, as Ortega y Gasset has pointed out, may be "in a form so intricate, so overloaded with distinctions, classifications, arguments, that . . . [there is] no way in so overgrown a forest to discover the repertoire of clear and simple ideas which truly orient man in his experience" (Ortega y Gasset 1958, 100).

The very fact that abundant opportunities for personal and career growth are available to the middle-class child presents problems of its own. When "anybody can be anybody," Klapp has observed, it may be that "nobody can be somebody" (Klapp 1969, 122). Young people in this type of environment have an opportunity to develop a multitude of identities, but too much impermanence in self-definition can destroy the sense of self that is to be fulfilled. The environment in which a person with shifting or unfinished identity functions also is likely to seem abstract and unreal, thus generating a ceaseless search for a more satisfying definition of self.

Emphasis on new experience and opportunity to experiment with a variety of identities can also lead to feelings of satiation and boredom with the world. Young people who are satiated with the everyday world and perceive their environment as unreal or plastic, who lack a stable sense of identity and the simple ideas which truly orient man in his existence, are likely to have problems in working to attain long-range goals in the school and the economy. As Klapp has summarized the situation,

> identity is a delicate psychosocial equilibrium requiring various kinds of support for its maintenance. But in the very society that proclaims abundance for everybody, we see interactional and symbolic deficiencies; . . . . the wiping away of traditions and places; shallow, inconsistent relationships. . . . an inability of people to get through facades and roles to each other. . . .
>
> A person whose interactions lack psychological payoffs will find life unutterably boring. The success symbols, though he has them, will seem empty. . . . He will, therefore, have a tendency to become a dropout or a deviant, turning to escapes or kicks for compensation. (Klapp 1969, 318–319)

In a sense, the dangers to youth most characteristic of a contemporary, middle-class environment tend to be manifested in ways similar to those in an underclass environment. In both situations, though for different reasons, the problems young people experience growing up tend to result in the formation of peer subcultures emphasizing drugs and escape from institutions in the local community. This is why alienation from school has been particularly evident and problematical in inner-city, poverty schools on the one hand and in homogeneous middle-class schools on the other. Middle-class youngsters tend to do

well in the elementary school, but many are experiencing problems connected with alienation
at the secondary level. To some extent, of course,
the problems of youth subcultures are similar
across social-class groups and present challenges
to educators in any secondary school, because
they represent age-based problems in growing up
in a modern society. Brake has summarized this
relatively universal aspect of youth development:

> *Youth culture also offers a collective identity,
> a reference group, from which to develop an
> individual identity, 'magically' freed from the
> ascribed roles of home, school and
> work. . . . Once they have made this separa-
> tion, which makes a dramaturgical statement
> about their difference from those expectations
> imposed upon them by others, they feel free to
> explore and develop what they are. They will
> create an image, often of a quasidelinquent,
> or rebellious style, which marks them apart
> from the expectations in particular of their
> family and other adults. (1980, 166)*

It is interesting to consider in the context of
this discussion some possible ways in which
middle-class families with their emphasis on privacy sometimes may overprotect their children
from the world outside the home. Sennet (1973)
has identified this type of situation in his study of
late nineteenth-century families in Chicago, at a
time when industrial growth was rapid and many
opportunities were available for upward mobility. Based on his study of family records, Sennett
found that sons who grew up in large middle-
class homes including relatives of the husband
and wife generally equalled or exceeded their
fathers in social status, whereas sons who grew up
in small, nuclear families showed less upward
mobility and frequently experienced downward
mobility. Sennett's conclusion was that sons in
the latter families had been given security at the
cost of opportunity: "the intensive family . . . became a shelter from the work pressures of the
industrial city, a place where men tried to institute some control and establish some comforting

intimacies in the shape of their lives, while with-
drawing to the sidelines as the new opportunities
of the city industries opened up" (Sennett 1973,
127–128).

IMPLICATIONS FOR EDUCATION

Dangers or deficiencies in differing social-class
environments have implications for the types of
approaches to curriculum and instruction that
should be emphasized in the schools. Some of
these implications are considered with reference
to the three types of environments described in
the preceding pages.

Inner-City Schools

Implications for inner-city schools attended by
underclass students in concentrated poverty
neighborhoods follow primarily from the fact
that the inner-city environment is an unstable
and damaging one for many children. Children
who grow up in this environment frequently are
unable to function effectively either in a traditional school setting or in an educational environment in which they are expected to work auton-
omously before being given preparation to work
in this way. They need a good deal of close guidance from supportive adults, in an environment
that provides both structure and consistency. In
addition, action must be taken to help inner-city
students and parents gain greater control of the
forces that operate both inside and outside the
inner-city school.

*Structure and Consistency in the Educational
Environment.*   One reason structure and consistency are necessary in inner-city schools involves the fact that a large proportion of students
in these schools have failed to master basic academic skills; they require close guidance and support in overcoming gaps in their education. Another reason involves the fact that the inner-city
environment tends to be chaotic for children.
Chaos in daily life is a direct effect of poverty. For

example, the world, and the future, obviously will seem disorderly and unpredictable to the members of families constantly on the verge of being evicted from their living quarters for inability to pay rent.

It is difficult to see how very much learning can take place in an inner-city school that recapitulates the chaos of the world outside. Herndon has described some of the effects such an external environment has on the inner-city elementary school:

> *Why would a kid, or a whole row of kids, become frantic because they weren't getting any pencils? Why was it no one could pass out paper for a routine assignment without all the kids in the back pushing up to the front, grabbing at the paper, crumpling it, and spilling it out onto the floor out of fear they wouldn't get any? They always did, every day, every period, all year long.*
>
> *[One reason for this behavior was their] concern to get their fair share of whatever was being passed out. . . . What was being passed out today, what probably would be passed out tomorrow, but on the other hand just might not be. (Herndon 1968, 62–65)*

Few teachers in the inner city would disagree that structure is a prerequisite for productive learning there, but it is difficult to define just what structure means, or should mean, for the conduct of instruction in the classroom. Doll and Levine (1972) have tried to work out a definition of structure for application in the classroom and have identified some of the key elements of structure as involving

> *the choice and sequencing of instructional experiences and materials in accordance with the particular learning problems and characteristics of disadvantaged students. . . .*
>
> *The initiation of procedures and arrangements to obtain order, so that teaching and learning can begin to take place. . . .*

> *The use of requirements and ground rules in such a way as to (a) clearly define what students are expected to do; (b) require initial participation on the part of the students; (c) provide for increasing student participation in setting subsequent ground rules; and (d) ensure that students understand . . . the rationale underlying the instruction. (Doll and Levine 1972, 152–154)*

It also is important to emphasize what structure is not. It is not repression of pupils, exclusion of pupils from decision making in the classroom, or simple provision of busywork to keep pupils occupied. Nor should it be defined as preventing a teacher from building on or encouraging the expression of students' spontaneous interests. Structure does not in any way obviate the need for inner-city teachers to be flexible in working with their students and to treat each student as a worthwhile human being.

One danger in emphasizing the importance of structure for inner-city students is that teachers will equate structure with order and will fail to move beyond the attainment of order to provide suitable activities to achieve the goal of improved learning. Another danger is that structure and guidance will not be provided consistently from one teacher or classroom to another. Levine (1968) has pointed out that consistency is particularly needed in inner-city schools because of the unusually large gap that exists between the students' competence and motivation to fulfill the role of student and the need to hold students to high standards of performance in order to overcome their relative lack of preparation for learning in the classroom:

> *Ambivalence in the child's orientation is reflected in the way he fulfills the role of student. . . . On the one hand he tends to accept the demands and expectations of the teacher as legitimate, at least to the extent that in general he outwardly acquiesces when instructed in what he should do and even when berated for not doing. Though he often fails in*

trying to carry out his intentions, he does aspire to do well in his work and often he almost pitifully resolves to do better even after an unbroken record of years of failure to act on this resolution. Unfortunately, however, he has developed only fragments of the intellectual skills and the [academic self-discipline necessary to succeed] . . . .

Students make more or less superficial attempts to live up to expectations, but fall far short. The exasperated teacher may either lower the level of expectations set for students and/or admonish them to overcome the personal 'defects' responsible for their failure. To protect their egos from further attack, students withdraw psychologically or become ever more resistant to the demands of teachers. They learn to play off the behavior of one teacher against that of another, by protesting against the threat in one classroom of requirements which "other teachers don't make us do" or which are unfairly "forced on us only because we are poor." (Levine 1968, 208–210)

Before a person is able to perform satisfactorily in any role, he or she must know what is expected, must be able to meet the role requirements, and must practice the behavior appropriate to the role. The inner-city school in which teacher behaviors and expectations differ from one classroom to another fails on all three counts to provide a social situation in which the child can learn to perform well in the role of student. Less certain of what is expected, less proficient in carrying out the tasks that define the role, and less committed to devoting serious effort to reach distant academic goals than is the middle-class pupil, the inner-city child needs to be continually reinforced in mastering clearly defined aspects of the role of student. Thus, one major problem faced by the teacher is "not to overcome a hostile set of values, but to help pupils whose values [related to the role of student] are confused and underdeveloped to clarify their values and to work

effectively toward the realization of them" (Havighurst 1966, 56).

Control of the Inner-City Environment. In using this phrase we have in mind the need to help inner-city parents and students gain control over the forces that presently reduce the effectiveness of educational programs inside the school and are part of the out-of-school conditions—that is, the street culture—that are detrimental to the development of children and youth. As indicated above, much can be done to design a school environment suitable to the needs of inner-city students, but in the end such efforts are not likely to be successful unless inner-city parents and students acquire and act on a belief that they can control their general environment and can work with the school to make learning more productive there.

It may be thought naïve to advocate action based on the belief that inner-city residents can gain more control over their future inside and outside the school, given the fact that for various reasons individuals in the inner city presently exercise very little power over the development of their neighborhood and its institutions. Indeed, a defining characteristic of the inner city is the sense of powerlessness people develop in adapting to the reality they see around them. But even though this is a defensible sociological explanation, which accounts in part for the situation in the inner city, it is not a sound ideology to govern the behavior of individuals and groups. Unless and until individuals in any community take responsibility for what happens to them and begin to perceive a possibility that they can improve their environment, it is hard to see how they can make good use of opportunites that may be available now or can be gained in the future.

Some organizations in inner-city neighborhoods thus are arguing that reform must come partly from within, through exercising greater control over what happens in families, schools, and other institutions in the inner city. In the 1970s and 1980s, the foremost of these groups has been the People United to Save Humanity organization, founded by the Reverend Jesse L. Jackson. Jackson and PUSH have worked in a number of big cities to reform schools and other community institutions, particularly in the inner city (Eubanks and Levine 1977). The PUSH Program for Excellence in Education has been described as aiming at "total involvement" to improve the conditions of teaching and learning in the inner city program. Information about the PUSH program is provided in Chapter 5.

Working-Class Schools

At the outset, we should emphasize that in many respects the problems students and teachers face in working-class environments are similar to those in underclass neighborhoods. (By our definition, the underclass is the lowest-status segment of the working class.) Working-class neighborhoods are those in which there is a preponderance of upper and lower working-class residents, with some underclass families whose children are most in danger of being drawn into the street culture. Because children in working-class neighborhoods come to school poorly prepared as compared with middle-class youngsters, and because lack of economic resources and other environmental influences in these communities impede the scholastic performance of children growing up there, we view structure and consistency in the educational environment and control over the child's socializing environment as desirable developments not just in inner-city schools but in other working-class schools as well.

If students in working-class schools are to have a greater opportunity to succeed academically and, if so desired, go to college and become professional or white-collar workers, then schools in working-class neighborhoods must do a better job of teaching basic skills, enlarging pupils' horizons to understand the opportunities that later could be available to them, and guiding students toward careers that will provide them with security and with opportunity for mobility in the future. At the present time, academic perfor-

mance in working-class schools tends to be very low, frequently as low as in inner-city schools, and a high percentage of students in working-class high schools drop out or graduate with minimal skills needed for success in the future.

Part of the reason this happens is that parents in working-class schools tend to press local school officials to provide an environment with considerable stress on obedience to authority and continuation of tradition. There is nothing inherently wrong with these goals, but in the school they frequently are translated into rote learning of traditional curricula and minimal expectations for achievement on the part of children. Like underclass students and, indeed, any group of students, working-class students can benefit from a certain amount of drill and an emphasis on mastery of traditional material, but continuing success in a modern education system requires more than this. It also requires some mastery of the skills involved in self-directed learning and understanding of many types of subject-matter that are not included in the traditional curriculum.

To the extent that parents in working-class neighborhoods tend to resist potentially more effective approaches to curriculum and instruction, educators in these neighborhoods face the same types of obstacles as do other public-service workers who endeavor to introduce "modern" institutional patterns and technologies into traditional communities. Many working-class parents can be viewed as wishing to preserve the traditions of the past while at the same time gaining access to the benefits of modern technology. This is a praiseworthy goal, but it also is true that modernization of local institutions cannot be achieved without changing them to some extent. Failure to institute an appropriate degree of change in local institutions can make them ineffective in carrying out their goals in a modern society, thereby depriving their clients of an opportunity to make good use of institutional resources. Peter Binzen, who has sympathetically studied working-class schools and communities in a number of large cities, has summarized this situation as follows (Binzen refers to these neigh-borhoods as "Whitetown," but he does make it clear that they include many upper and lower working-class minority families):

> *In this period of sexual permissiveness, God-is-dead theology, student revolts, . . . their [Whiteowners'] old-fashioned patriotism, reli-gious fundamentalism, and family together-ness has gone out of style. . . .*
>
> *Whitetown was not ready for the techno-logical revolution, either, having traditionally valued brawn over brains. . . .*
>
> *[Whitetown] appears to be on the skids. Its housing is deteriorating. It is losing popula-tion. . . .*
>
> *Any attempt to help the "stepchildren" of Whitetown should start with their schools. For in our . . . society education is the passport to progress. . . .*
>
> *[But in] changing times, the Whitetowners oppose change. . . . They tend to reflect-. . . the "Little Red Schoolhouse Ideal" [and] look back to a "past golden age which has been lost. . . . What was good enough for me is good enough for my children." And at a school meeting one night I heard a hard-core Whitetowner utter those very words. (Binzen 1970, 27–28, 36–37)*

From this point of view, what appears to be most important in working-class schools is for administrators and teachers to take the lead in helping parents and students understand that ed-ucational approaches designed to help each stu-dent become a more independent learner and to acquire broader horizons do not completely con-flict with community emphasis on authority and traditions. Parents also must be helped to under-stand that modern instructional approaches that aim at diagnosing and solving each student's learning problems can, if properly implemented, result in more rather than less success in master-ing basic skills and attaining other traditional goals of the school. It is true that there is likely to be some degree of tension between a community

that emphasizes tradition and an educational ap-proach that may be thought of as "innovative," but appropriate explanation of the purpose and potential benefits of new approaches can help to minimize this tension.

Another major problem typically found in working-class schools is more straightforward: many working-class schools have too few re-sources to introduce and operate an outstanding instructional program effectively. This is partly because working-class schools tend to be located in big-city school districts with an inadequate fi-nancial base for public education. Financial pres-sures in big-city schools have become very severe in the 1970s and 1980s; working-class schools, which generally have students who need a large amount of extra help but do not have enough below-poverty-level pupils to qualify for special government assistance, have borne much of the brunt of these budget problems. In addition, school buildings in working-class neighborhoods are among the oldest in the cities, and their teachers tend to have been trained in out-dated methods.

Middle-Class Schools

Many students in a predominantly middle-class neighborhood tend to have difficulty in school if placed in a classroom in which social control and instruction are highly structured or are externally imposed in a teacher-centered curriculum. Be-cause middle-class home environments tend to stress egalitarianism and development of self-direction, a highly structured, teacher-centered classroom can be not only discrepant for middle-class students but also can cause them to lose interest and motivation in learning. However, classrooms in middle-class elementary schools tend not to be highly structured, because parents and school administrators there tend increas-ingly to push for the development of instructional programs stressing student-centered learning and self-direction.

At the secondary level, however, school tends to become more problematical for students from a middle-class environment. Secondary schools tend to be large and impersonal, maintaining rules and traditions designed to provide external coordination of the activities of a thousand or more people; and because the problems of middle-class youth tend to become manifested most clearly during adolescence, alienation in middle-class secondary schools has become widespread. Levine (1972) has analyzed the middle-class environment in the modern metropolis and concluded that the following guidelines should be considered in designing educational programs—particularly secondary programs—for students growing up in this environment:

> *Every young person [should be provided] with opportunities to test and define himself against difficult challenges in the physical and social environment. . . .*
>
> *Students' educational experiences should be provided in a setting which brings them into close and continuing contact with others of differing social, racial, ethnic, and religious backgrounds. It is all very well to teach students about other people who reflect or embody the diverse character of the metropolis, but learning about them is too abstract an activity to counteract perceptions of isolation from metropolitan reality. . . .*
>
> *Much of the curriculum . . . should be explicitly concerned with the study of urban and metropolitan affairs.*
>
> *[Much more should be done] to provide adolescents and young people with opportunities to perform socially important and personally meaningful work in the metropolis. . . .*
>
> *Students should have more scope in choosing what to learn and in deciding how to learn it. (Levine 1972, 41–44)*

SOCIAL CLASS ENVIRONMENTS AND CLASSROOM SOCIAL CONTROL

Chapter 7 indicates that there is a tendency for schools with many lower-status students to place more stress on rote learning and discipline than do middle-class schools, which put relatively more emphasis on creative and independent learning. The material in this chapter helps in understanding why this difference between working- and middle-class schools gets built into the educational system. Teachers frequently emphasize discipline and authority in working-class schools partly because students are accustomed to this type of emphasis, and their parents also tend to demand it (Tyler 1991). Thus, some research indicates that children from homes with coercive interactions perform better in coercive classrooms than in classrooms based on cohesive or laissez-faire interactions (Hansen 1986). Schools in middle-class communities, by way of contrast, frequently emphasize the development of self-directed learning, in response to the perceived needs of and preferences of students and parents. Bernstein (1975, 1990) describes this difference as involving a lack of distinction between work and play in middle-class schools, in line with the intermingling of work and play that characterizes the culture of the middle class.

From our point of view, the issue is not so much whether these differences tend to exist in differing types of schools but what if anything should be done to improve the effectiveness of education for students from differing backgrounds. In recent years, attempts have been made in some working-class and inner-city schools to introduce instructional programs emphasizing independent, self-directed learning. Most such attempts at innovation have not succeeded; conditions in these schools have been extremely chaotic, and both students and teachers have ended up feeling frustrated and defeated. Typically, however, neither teachers nor students in these innovative projects have been well prepared to participate in them. Without a substantial amount of special training, continuous staff development, and appropriate supporting resources, teachers cannot be expected to implement them successfully. Without careful and substantial preparation, students who are not used to working independently cannot be expected to function successfully as self-directed learners. We discuss these topics at greater length in Chapter 13.

In a few instances, such programs do appear to have worked well for working-class and underclass students when they have been carefully planned and expertly implemented based on the premise that appropriate learning arrangements can provide internal structure in an "open" environment. Some elementary-school programs for economically disadvantaged students seem to have been most successful when emphasizing direct instruction (see Chapter 8), but this type of instruction can be provided within a program that also emphasizes the development of self-directed learning skills. Thus, it would seem desirable to work toward the goal of helping students in low-status schools become more self-directed, beginning with carefully structured instructional experiences and shifting later, when students are ready, to less structured learning environments.

However, relatively few attempts seem to have been made to work in stages toward the development of self-directed learning skills in low-status schools. Instead, programs emphasizing self-direction and creativity frequently have been initiated by sponsors imbued with an ideology of freeing the low-status child from the oppression of the school. Such projects have seldom involved careful longitudinal planning goals; as a result, most have failed abjectly.

The problem behind simpleminded attempts to move instantly from structured to unstructured school environments sometimes can be traced back to confusion about concepts such as *structure, oppression*, and *freedom*. Proponents of unstructured schooling who equate structure with oppression and lack of structure with freedom fail to recognize that structure can be as liberating if properly provided as it is restricting in other circumstances. To the extent that ideologues who confuse structure with oppression have organized structureless free schools that quickly failed, ideology has discredited what might have been a productive movement to modify and reduce structure gradually as pupils are helped to become more self-directive.

Other ideological positions that may serve to block serious attempts to help low-status students develop more competence in self-directed learning are represented by people who believe either that those students are inherently incapable of developing such skills or that improved instructional programs for low-status students will not help them much in the absence of a political and social revolution to correct underlying inequalities in society. The first position may be true for some low-status students, but it clearly is not legitimate to conclude that most cannot become autonomous learners when few systematic, longitudinal attempts have been made to achieve this goal. The second position is equally narrow in not recognizing that millions of low-status people have achieved mobility through education, and many more can be helped to do so in the future if the schools can succeed in developing their skills and competence to function more successfully in the educational system. How the schools can help to do this is discussed in Chapters 8 and 13 and elsewhere in this book.

EXERCISES _____

1. Read Oscar Lewis's account of slum communities in Puerto Rico and Mexico, respectively (*La Vida* and *Children of Sanchez*), and Lee Rainwater's account of a predominantly black inner-city housing project in the United States, *Behind Ghetto Walls: Black Families in a Federal Slum.* Compare and contrast these manifestations of the cultural patterns associated with intense poverty.

2. What are some of the causes of alienation toward society among children and youth from: (1) lower working-class communities and (2) upper middle-class communities? In

what ways are the causes and consequences of alienation among these groups different? In what ways are they similar?

3. Read James Herndon's *The Way It Spozed to Be* and prepare a list of the ways in which environmental conditions in the lives of the children described in it affect their behavior in schools.

4. Why do underclass parents encounter so many problems in trying to raise their children to be good students? What do you think can or should be done to give their children a better chance to succeed in United States schools and society?

5. Frank Reissman's *The Culturally Deprived Child* argues that as compared with middle-class students, disadvantaged students frequently have learning styles that are physical or visual rather than aural, content-centerd rather than form-centered, and problem-centered rather than abstract-centered. He sees these and other aspects of their "mental style" as qualities that teachers should consider in designing effective instruction. Read Reissman's analysis and discuss the merits and demerits of his proposals.

6. Read *To Kill a Mockingbird* by Harper Lee, and describe how the classroom lesson portrayed in Chapter 26 created special problems for disadvantaged children.

SUGGESTIONS FOR FURTHER READING

1. *White Ethnics: Their Life in Working-Class America*, edited by Joseph A. Ryan, includes chapters describing the social environment of Italian-American and Polish-American working-class families, as well as analyses of religion, employment, and school conditions in white working-class neighborhoods. Descriptions of the environment for youth in underclass neighborhoods can be found in Claude Brown, *Manchild in the Promised Land*, and Roger D. Abrahams, *Deep Down in the Jungle . . . Negro Narrative Folklore from the Streets of Philadelphia*. *The Autobiography of Malcolm X* provides an excellent account of the problems such an environment creates for children and youth, and the unusually difficult time a youngster encounters in surmounting them. Lillian Rubin's *Worlds of Pain: Life in the Working-Class Family* reports the results of interviews with a sample of working-class adults, and the author's thoughtful comments and evaluations of the interview information. *The Children of the Counterculture* by John Rothchild and Susan Berns Wolf provides a fascinating account of the social environment of children growing up in a variety of countercultural settings. The problems involved in trying to create a new kind of social environment are vividly portrayed, and considerable attention is given to the issue of educating the young in circumstances that markedly differ from those characteristic of normal working-class and middle-class environments.

2. Oscar Handlin's books on *The Newcomers* and *The Uprooted* and Bernard Bailyn's *Voyagers to the West* describe how migration to the United States modified people's sense of community and identity. *The Hunger of Memory* by Richard Rodriguez provides a vivid account of this process from the viewpoint of an Hispanic American.

3. *Past, Present, and Personal* consists of essays by John Demos on the history of the family, with particular emphasis on the United States.

4. *Children of the City* by David Nasaw (1985) describes the environment experienced by working-class children in New York City between 1900 and 1920.

5. *Pricing the Priceless Child* by Viviana Zelizer argues that the historical evolution of the family from an economic to a "sentimental" institution became apparent when child-death awards, adoption practices, and child-insurance patterns began to stress emotional bonds and considerations.

6. Subtitled "The Abandonment of Children in Western Europe From Late Antiquity to the Renaissance," John Boswell's (1988) *The Kindness of Strangers* documents why and how children frequently were abandoned in many periods of history, to be raised in orphanages, by other families, or in various church-supported institutions.

7. *Within Our Reach: Breaking the Cycle of Disadvantage* by Lisbeth Schorr (1989) summarizes various strands of international research, examining how poverty environments damage many children and youth and the possibilities for concerted action to improve early-childhood environments for the disadvantaged.

8. Ralph Tyler (1991) has discussed the need for a balance between structure and independent learning: "As John Dewey once said to me, 'an environment in which everything is rigidly structured produces slaves; an environment in which there is no structure produces chaotic, whimsical behavior.'"

9. Based on hundreds of interviews and aptly titled *There Are No Children Here*, a recent book by Alex Kotlowitz describes the difficult struggles faced by children and youth living in a public housing project in Chicago.

10. *Teenage Wasteland* (Gaines 1991) describes and discusses the diminishing career opportunities available to young people and the increasing difficulties they experience growing up in blue-collar communities.

Home Environment and Cognitive Development

The relationship between social-class background and achievement has been emphasized in preceding chapters. Working-class children are less prepared for school and less successfully sheltered from influences detrimental to school achievement than are middle-class children. An average working-class child performs less well academically than does the average middle-class child, and the educational system helps to sort children of differing backgrounds into higher- or lower-status careers in accordance with their performance in school. Hess and Shipman (1965) summed up the results of many studies documenting these kinds of differences:

> *Children from deprived backgrounds score well below middle-class children on standard individual and group measures of intelligence (a gap that increases with age); they come to school without the skill necessary for coping with first grade curricula; their language development, both written and spoken, is relatively poor; auditory and visual discrimination skills are not well developed; in scholastic achievement they are retarded an average of two years by grade six and almost three years by grade eight; they are more likely to drop out of school before completing a secondary education; and even when they have adequate ability, are less likely to go to college. (Hess and Shipman 1965, 869)*

Thus, it has long been observed that children from lower socioeconomic groups provide by far the greater share of a school's academic failures and dropouts. These phenomena were explained away in earlier periods as due, first, to lower native intelligence of these children; and second, to lack of concern on the part of their parents. Today, it is known that neither explanation is adequate. The likely explanation is that although parents of all classes realize the importance of education and prize good schooling for their children, different families create environments that influence children's intellectual growth and educational motivation in different ways. When one parent ignores the child's questions but another parent makes a point of reading to the child every day, two different environments are created. The first parent has created an environment that operates against learning; the second, one that promotes learning. Because the social classes tend to provide differing home environments, their children tend to be more or less prepared for or helped to do well in school (Holmes 1988; Schaefer 1991).

Conversely, even though family socioeconomic status is statistically correlated overall with children's school achievement, there are many exceptions. The exceptions show that the causes of the relatively low achievement of lower-class children are characteristics of individual families and are not universally connected with low socioeconomic status. This was demonstrated in a study of children from a working-class population in New York City's Harlem, where high-achieving and low-achieving fifth-grade pupils were compared (Davidson and Greenberg 1969). Eighty boys and eighty girls were selected from twelve elementary schools; all children met the following criteria:

- Parents were of low socioeconomic status according to occupation, educational level, and type of dwelling unit.
- Parents were all born in this country.
- Child attended school in a northern city since first grade.
- IQ between 75 and 125.
- Age between 9 years, 11 months and 11 years, 4 months.

The forty boys and girls who were high achievers averaged at the 6.45 level in reading and the 5.4 level in arithmetic. The forty boys and forty girls who were low achievers averaged 2.85 in reading and 3.35 in arithmetic.

The two groups—the high achievers and the low achievers—were compared on a variety of psychological and social characteristics. High achievers were superior to low achievers on a number of psychological characteristics, as would be expected. But the striking thing was the relationship of certain home or family characteristics within this working-class group to school achievement. An experienced interviewer visited in the homes and talked with the mother about the child and about the mother's behavior. He was not informed as to the achievement level of the children. The families of high achievers were rated as substantially superior to those of low achievers in "Concern for the Children's Education," "Thinking and Planning for the Child as an Individual," "General Social-Civic Awareness and Concern of the Parent," and "Structure and Orderliness of the Home." Thus, within the black lower-class group some children score above the national norms on educational achievement, and they tend to come from homes that prepare them well for school achievement.

Home environment and other family characteristics constitute one of the four most important factors that influence a child's level of achievement in school. Another is the inborn ability of the child. A third is the quality of the schooling the child receives. The fourth is the child's self-concept or aspiration level, which grows out of family and school experiences. After several years of school experience, the child determines how hard he or she shall work in school and toward what goals.

Inborn or biological differences of intelligence exist, but between individuals, not between large social or racial groups. Inborn differences in intelligence exist among children in a single family; and every school class of thirty children includes thirty different levels of intellectual potential.

Once a child is born, a home environment that promotes learning can operate so that a child with only average inborn ability does well in school. A very good school can operate so that a child with only average innate ability does well; and it can operate also to compensate a child for a poor home environment.

IMPORTANCE OF EARLY ENVIRONMENT

Research on the cognitive development of children summarized by Bloom (1964), Hunt (1979), Schorr (1989), and Schaefer (1991) points to the family as the major influence and to the preschool years as crucial for mental development. A dramatic illustration of the importance of early environment on later cognitive and social development was provided by a study of a group of children first studied in the 1930s by Skeels and Dye (1939). The study compared experimental children who were raised in an institution for the retarded and children raised in an orphanage. Among the first group, there were thirteen infants ranging in age from seven to thirty months who were considered unfit for adoption because of mental retardation (mean IQ, 64.3). These children were removed from an orphanage and placed in the institution for retarded persons. Another group of twelve children, who came from comparable family backgrounds but who seemed of better intellectual endowment (mean IQ, 90.0), remained in the orphanage where they were periodically observed and tested.

The orphanage nursery, as it was being operated prior to the study, was limited to a small playroom with additional dormitory rooms. The children were cared for by two nurses assisted by two young girls. Contacts with adults were largely limited to feeding, bathing, dressing, and toilet details. The girls who assisted the nurses accepted the work as a necessary evil and took little personal interest in the children as individuals. Few play materials were available. The children were seldom out of the nursery room except for short walks for fresh air.

At age two, the children moved on to "cottages," where thirty to thirty-five children of the same sex under age six lived in the charge of one matron and several untrained girls aged thirteen to fifteen. Most of their waking hours were spent in an average-sized room, a sun porch, and a cloakroom. The duties falling to the matron involved caring for the children and also included cottage maintenance, cleaning, mending, and so forth. The result was a necessary regimentation. The children sat down, stood up, and did many things in rows and in unison. They spent considerable time just sitting on chairs.

The experimental situation in the school for the retarded provided quite a different environment. Generally one (and no more than two) of the experimental children was placed in a ward that contained only older, brighter girls. The attendants and the other girls became very fond of the child placed in their ward and took great pride in the child's achievement. There was considerable competition between wards to see which one would have their baby walking or talking first. The girls would spend a great deal of time with the children, teaching them to walk, talk, and play with toys. They also spent their small allowances to buy special foods, toys, picture books, and clothing for the infants.

Similarly, attendants frequently took the children on excursions, care rides, and trips. In addition, it was the policy of the matron in charge to single out certain children whom she felt were in need of individualization and permit them to spend a portion of time each day visiting her office. This furnished new experiences, including special attention and affection, new play materials, additional language stimulation, and contacts with other office callers.

The so-called retarded children were sent to the school kindergarten as soon as they could walk. As part of the school program, the children each morning attended chapel exercises, which included group singing and music by the orchestra. They also attended the dances and other school programs.

First Follow-Up

Results of the first follow-up study conducted several years later were unexpected (Skeels 1966). All experimental children (who had been considered mentally retarded by the trained members of the orphanage staff as well as by a psychiatrist) achieved the normal range of intelligence within six to fifty-two months. The average gain in IQ was 27.5 points, with three children gaining 45 points or more. A year after the experiment ended, two of these children were above average in intelligence and only one had an IQ below 80.

The children who remained in the orphanage, on the other hand, fell increasingly behind in intellectual development. Except for one child, all suffered losses ranging from 8 to 45 IQ points.

The radical improvement in the experimental children cannot be attributed solely to environmental enrichment. Nine children who became greatly attached to one or two adults gained an average of 34 IQ points, while the four children who did not develop close personal attachments to an adult made an average gain of only 14 points. A parent surrogate whom the child learns to love and imitate is apparently an important factor in optimum development.

When these results became known, the orphanage staff made heroic efforts to improve conditions by adding more personnel to the staff, cutting down the numbers of children in the cottages, and initiating a preschool program in the nursery. Nevertheless, the damage to the orphanage group could not be undone; and the differences persisted between the children who had received special attention in infancy and the children who had not.

Second Follow-Up

Twenty-one years later, all the children were located and restudied (Skeels 1966). Every one of the thirteen children of the experimental group had eventually been placed in a family and was now found to be living a normal life. They had completed, on average, the twelfth grade; four had entered college, and one had received a B.A. Eleven had married, and nine of these had children.

In contrast, of the orphanage group (originally the better endowed), one had died in adolescence after prolonged institutionalization for mental retardation, and three others were still inmates of such institutions. One was in a mental hospital. Of the two who had married, one was divorced. In conformity with state law, three girls, classified as retarded, has been sterilized before they had been permitted to leave the institution. On the average, this group had completed less than third grade in school. Half were unemployed; of those who were working, all but one held the lowest of menial jobs.

Even though the Skeels and Dye findings are dramatic, they should be interpreted cautiously because they do not themselves prove that the effects of early enrichment generally are pervasive or permanent. The two groups studied by these investigators were different not only in early childhood experiences, but also with regard to the experiences that intervened between early childhood and the time of follow-up some twenty years later (Spitz 1986). In addition, the research dealt with severe intellectual retardation produced by severe environmental deprivation. One should not simplistically conclude that mild intellectual retardation is due mostly to environmental degradation, or that it necessarily can be sub-stantially modified by moderate amounts of special training or improvements in environment (Weinberg 1989).

HOME ENVIRONMENT, COGNITIVE DEVELOPMENT, AND ACHIEVEMENT

During the past three decades, sociologists and psychologists have tried to identify home environment characteristics that are directly related to cognitive development and to achievement in schools. Skeels and others had shown that the amount and quality of stimulation provided for infants was associated with their intellectual development, but beyond that little was known about how home process variables are related to children's intellectual and scholastic performance. Thus, researchers began to examine a whole set of additional variables in order to identify home and parent characteristics that are consistently related to intellectual development (Schaefer 1991). For example, Dave (1963) and Wolf (1964) devised interview protocols that could be used to categorize the home environment on a number of characteristics likely to be related to performance on tests of ability and school achievement. Data they collected on fifth graders showed that information on the following six home environment characteristics accounted for nearly two-thirds of the variation in scores on the Metropolitan Achievement Battery:

1. Achievement pressure: (a) parental aspirations for the education of the child; (b) parents' own aspirations; (c) parents' interest in academic activities; (d) knowledge of the educational progress of the child; (e) preparation and planning for the attainment of educational goals.
2. Language models: (a) quality of language usage of the parents; (b) opportunities for the enlargement and use of vocabulary and sentence patterns; (c) keenness of the parents for correct and effective language usage.

3. Academic guidance: (a) availability of guidance on matters relating to schoolwork; (b) quality of guidance on matters relating to schoolwork; (c) availability and use of materials and facilities related to school learning.
4. Activeness of the family: (a) extent and content of the indoor and outdoor activities of the family; (b) use of television and other such media; (c) use of books, library, and other such facilities.
5. Intellectuality in the home: (a) nature and quality of toys, games, and hobbies made available to the child; (b) opportunities for thinking and imagination in daily activities.
6. Work habits of the family: (a) degree of structure and routine in home management; (b) preferences for educational activities over other pleasurable pastimes.

In several studies examining relationships between students' social background and academic achievement, the single best predictor of achievement has been the amount of reading materials in the home. (The reader should keep in mind that social class, level of education, occupation, income, and other indicators of social status are highly correlated with reading materials in the home and with other measures of home environment.) The extent of this relationship is shown in Figure 4-1, which uses 1988 data on nine-, thirteen-, and seventeen-year-olds sampled by the National Assessment of Educational Progress (NAEP). As indicated in Figure 4-1, students in each age group who reported that there were fewer reading materials in their home scored lower than those who reported that there were more materials (Mullis and Jenkins 1990).

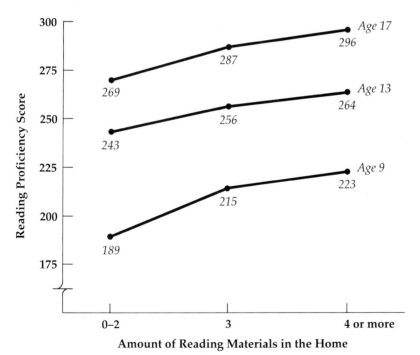

Reading materials = Newspapers, magazines, encyclopedia, more than 25 books.

FIGURE 4-1 *Reading Proficiency Scores of Nine-, Thirteen-, and Seventeen-Year-Olds, by Amount of Reading Materials in the Home, 1988 (Source: Adapted from Mullis and Jenkins 1990.)*

The NAEP data also indicate that this relationship between reading materials in the home and students' reading proficiency is strong even after taking account of parental level of education. For example, students who report having a dictionary, more than twenty-five books, and numerous magazines in their homes have an average reading proficiency score approximately fifteen points higher than those whose parents have the same educational level but report fewer reading materials at home (our analysis of NAEP data tapes).

Home environments supportive of cognitive growth provide not just reading materials, but also a variety of opportunities and encouragements to develop and use oral and written language skills (Adams 1990). Some of the language-learning opportunities available to children in families that promote cognitive and academic growth have been illustrated as follows by Heath and McLaughlin:

> *[Such children] have extensive experience in learning by listening to others tell how to do something, they themselves know how to talk about what they are doing as they do it, and they know how to lay out plans for the future in verbal form. On command, they know how to display in oral or written formats the bits and pieces of knowledge that the school assumes represent academic achievement. (Heath and McLaughlin 1987, 578).*

Research on the relationship between parental behavior and children's cognitive development and achievement has been summarized by Rollins and Thomas (1979), who carefully reviewed and assessed studies carried out during the previous three decades. Among the generalizations for which they found solid research support were the following:

- Greater parental support is associated with higher cognitive development of children.
- Greater parental coercion is associated with lower cognitive development.

- Greater parental support is associated with higher instrumental and social competence of children.
- Greater parental coercion is associated with lower instrumental and social competence.
- For girls, high parental support and frequent parental control attempts are associated with low academic achievement.
- For boys, high parental support is associated with high academic achievement when parental control also is high, and high parental control is associated with low achievement when parental support is low.
- In general, conclusions regarding the relationship between parental behavior and development of the child are stronger for boys than for girls.

Additional evidence regarding the influence of parental control techniques on children's cognitive and academic performance has been provided in a longitudinal study conducted by Hess and McDevitt (1984). After collecting and examining appropriate data on mothers' behaviors and their children's "school-related abilities" at ages four, five/six, and twelve, Hess and McDevitt reported that "in both teaching and disciplinary situations, direct control tactics were negatively correlated with children's school-relevant performance" (1984, 2017). They also found that children of mothers who used a high proportion of direct control techniques performed more poorly than did children whose mothers used a combination of direct and indirect interventions, and that boys seemed to be less affected than did girls by their mothers' control techniques.

Note that parental child-raising techniques appear to interact with social class, environmental setting, gender of the child, and, probably, with race and other variables in affecting children's cognitive development and school performance (Holmes 1988; Berry and Asamen 1989). For example, Rollins and Thomas (1979) reviewed the literature and concluded that high parental support in combination with high control internalized by the child function to encourage academic achievement for boys but not for girls. Sue and Okazaki (1990) reviewed research indicating that although authoritarian parental attitudes are negatively correlated with school performance among non-Hispanic whites, this relationship does not appear to be present for Asian American students. Clark (1983) hypothesized that girls in inner-city communities benefit as much as boys from the combination of high support and control in a threatening environment. He then collected data that provided support for the hypothesis. Wentzel (1990) studied sixth-grade boys and their families and found that "harsh and inconsistent" discipline by the mothers was directly and negatively related to their sons' grades and achievement, whereas similar discipline by the father had these effects only for sons for whom it weakened self-restraint.

In recent decades, much has been learned about how differing home environment conditions are related to intellectual development at different ages, though much more remains to be discovered about the interactions between parent behavior, cognitive growth, and school achievement as the child grows older. For example, Wachs, Uzgiris, and Hunt (1971) reported that although intensity and variety of stimulation in the home and opportunity to hear vocal labels for objects, actions, and relationships were significantly correlated with cognitive development in the first two years of life, there also was a tendency for over-stimulation to have harmful effects. Four years later, Elardo, Bradley, and Caldwell (1975) reported that stimulation in the physical environment is strongly related to mental test performance in the first year of life but after that time maternal involvement with the child becomes a stronger indicator of cognitive development. These findings suggest that differing aspects of the home environment affect mental capabilities in a complex fashion.

Other research has focused on further identifying longitudinal relationships between home environment variables, particularly maternal behavior, and specific cognitive abilities. For example, Saxe (1987) and his colleagues studied the maternal interactions and numerical performance of preschool children and found that performance improved most rapidly when mothers adjusted their assistance in accordance with the child's level of success. Similarly, Shipman and her colleagues (1976) studied the home environments and development of disadvantaged youngsters in the preschool and elementary grades and concluded that the mother's level of aspiration for the child may be

> *directly tied to the child's* early *signs of intellectual alertness. If so, the implication is that early cognitive stimulation from within or outside of the home is important for the mother* subsequently *to provide a continuously stimulating climate. . . . The present findings suggest that as the mother interacts more, she feels less powerless, more optimistic and is less likely to resort to status and authoritarian appeals for controlling her child. Thus, programs reducing alienation may in turn increase the child's educability. (Shipman et al. 1976, 173–174)*

Numerous investigators have been carefully examining the parental behaviors that appear to be related to cognitive and emotional development in young children (Karen 1990). They are finding that the ways in which children explore their environment and use objects and concepts are related to the actions of adults who arrange and structure the environment. Conducted through intensive observation of parents or other adults and young children, these types of studies generally take years to carry out and analyze. One of the most important series of investigations along these lines was carried out by Jean V. Carew of Harvard University. After studying a socioeconomically heterogeneous group of twenty-three white children between the ages of one and three in Boston, Carew concluded that there are four types of activities or experiences involving (1) language skills, (2) spatial skills, (3) practical reasoning, and (4) expressive skills that seem to be "intellectually valuable" for the child; children's activities in these areas correlated with IQ and were distinguished from other activities involving simple play-exploration, routine task, basic care, and gross motor functioning, which did not correlate with IQ.

Carew was further interested in determining whether it matters if the child constructs the intellectually valuable experiences for himself or herself, or whether they are received from the environment. Based on theories of Piaget, it was hypothesized that "the child's active construction of his own experiences is central to his intellectual development," but other learning theories indicated that "structure and appropriateness" of the environment might be more important than the child's active exploration. The results of this study were described as giving "some support to both camps, full comfort to neither":

> Briefly we found that it does matter a great deal how the child's intellectual experiences are derived but different sources of intellectually valuable experiences become important at different periods in the child's life. The earliest forms of intellectual experiences that were correlated with . . . [tested and observed intellectual competence] at age three (and earlier) were experiences in which the child interacts with another person. These intellectual experiences included reciprocal interaction in which the child and the interactor contributed jointly to the child's intellectual experience, but most important were encounters in which the interactor was the primary source of the intellectual experience and the child the attentive but basically non-contributing partner. It is not until age two and a half that the intellectual experiences that the child fashioned through his own activity began to be significantly correlated with his tested intellectual competence . . . it was the role played by the interactor in creating intellectual experiences for the child or reciprocally sharing them with him that was first and most highly related to the

> child's later intellectual competence. (Carew 1976, 9–11)

Carew emphasized that understanding the role of the interactor in providing intellectually valuable experiences for the child requires a knowledge of how this role was specifically defined in the study:

> An interactor is considered to be the primary or joint source of the child's intellectual experiences only when he uses a participatory technique of interaction. The specific techniques defined as participatory include teaching, helping, entertaining, conversing and sharing in the intellectual activity like a playmate. The common feature of these techniques is that the interactor plays a direct, active, and integral role in creating, guiding and expanding the child's intellectual experience. . . . His behavior is not merely facilitative (in the sense, say, of praise or approval), or incidental to the intellectual experience. Rather, the interactor's behavior literally creates or helps to create its intellectual content. This content is often judiciously chosen, well structured and attractively presented. But the same or better can be said of certain children's television programs, which we found related not at all to intellectual development in these young children. What seems to distinguish these two types of environmental inputs are two features that are highly salient in the interactor's behavior and seldom present in television programs. These are the individualized and responsive quality of the interactor's behavior and its affective subtext.
>
> When an interactor engages in an intellectual activity with a child he typically tailors his input to the individual child's needs. He tries to match its content and style to what he knows of the child's capabilities and interests. He is responsive to questions, problems, inadequacies in the child's understanding.
>
> This point brings us to the affective aspect of interactive experiences. By the very fact of sharing in intellectual experiences with the child

the interactor conveys that such experiences are valued and pleasing. It is not necessary that the interactor express approval or affection overtly. The essential message is already transmitted by the sheer fact that the interactor participates positively in the experiences. When the interactor is a parent, a sibling or a friend to whom the child is emotionally attached, it seems very likely that the child will come to value and engage in such activities for the simple reason that these are the ones that people he likes prefer. (Carew 1976, 11–12)

The importance of home learning environment also has been underlined in a 1979 review of research on home-based reinforcement of school behavior, a 1982 analysis of research on the effects of school programs that have attempted to improve students' home and family learning environments, and a 1989 study of adopted children. Richard Barth's (1979) review of twenty-four studies dealing with home-based reinforcement showed that many kinds of behavioral and academic problems have been successfully reduced by helping parents learn to deal with the problems at home.

In the analysis of home and family intervention programs, Graue, Weinstein, and Walberg (1982) reviewed twenty-nine studies of school projects that worked with parents to encourage and reinforce targeted child behaviors. Projects examined worked with parents at various grade levels and assessed a number of subjects and skills, particularly reading and math. The authors found that the average experimental student scored at the 76th percentile compared with an average at the 50th percentile for control-group children. They then pointed out that effects so large and consistent are very seldom encountered in connection with educational treatments.

The 1989 study of adopted children was the first to provide data on children whose biological parents were high on SES but who were raised in low-SES families. The authors (Capron and Duyme 1989) found that these children had average IQ scores 12 points lower, at age fourteen, than did children whose biological and adoptive parents were high in SES.

RECENT TRENDS IN THE FAMILY AND YOUTH DEVELOPMENT

Trends occurring in family structure, family relations, and related phenomena have implications for the development of children and their treatment in the educational system and other modern socializing institutions. Some important trends are described here.

1. *Increase in single-parent families.* The percentage of U.S. families that include a married couple declined from 74 percent of all families in 1960 to slightly less than 60 percent in 1990. A large majority of the families with only one parent are female-headed households. As shown in Table 4–1, the rise in the percentage of single-parent families was accompanied by a steady decrease in the percentage of children and youth growing up in two-parent families. By the year 2000, more than half of all children will spend part of their lives in single-parent homes (Waldrop 1990).

The increase in single-parent families reflects increases in the divorce rate and in the proportion of out-of-wedlock births (Footlik 1990). Divorce rates rose each year during the 1960s and 1970s, setting a new record in 1981 of 109 per 1000 married women—up from 47 in 1970. Divorce rates dropped slightly from 1982 thru

TABLE 4-1 *Percentages of Children under Age Eighteen Living with Two Parents, by Race and Ethnicity, 1960 to 1988*

Race/Ethnicity	1960	1970	1980	1988
Hispanic	–	–	75	66
Non-Hispanic black	67	59	42	39
Non-Hispanic white	91	90	83	70

Source: U.S. Bureau of the Census.
Note: Data for Hispanic families were not collected in 1980 and 1970.

1984 but rose again in 1985 to nearly the 1981 rate. Some demographers now predict that nearly two-thirds of newly married couples eventually will be divorced and that one-half or more of all children under age eighteen will live with a divorced or unmarried parent at some point in their lives (Carlson 1990). Between 1950 and 1990, the number of out-of-wedlock births per 1000 babies nearly tripled. Because many of the mothers of out-of-wedlock children did not subsequently marry, the percentage of female-headed families showed a concomitant increase. Some of the effects of divorce on children have been reviewed and summarized by Bianchi and Spain:

> *In sum, an increasing number of children are growing up in situations other than the "typical" two-parent nuclear family. . . . Kramer and Kramer aside, most children still end up in their mother's custody when a marital break-up occurs, and a sizable portion will have little or no contact with their father from that time on. In addition, family income in these mother-only households is low. And there is evidence of school problems and poorer health among children who are separated from their parents. (Bianchi and Spain 1986, 47)*

It also should be noted that the proportions of children living with both biological parents vary substantially by race and ethnicity. According to federal estimates, 86 percent of African American children, compared with 42 percent of white children, will spend at least some of their childhood in single-parent homes (Waldrop 1990). The percentage of black children living in female-headed families increased from 24 percent in 1960 to slightly more than 50 percent in 1990.

2. *Increase in the percentage of working mothers.* The percentage of women who have children under age eighteen and are employed has been increasing fairly steadily since at least 1950, for reasons including the breakup of husband-wife families, improved opportunities in the labor market for women, desire for increased dispos-able income, financial pressures requiring mothers to work, and changes in cultural and social patterns that formerly dictated that many women remain in the home. Fifty-two percent of mothers with children under age one were in the labor force in 1990, compared with 24 percent in 1960 (Uchitelle 1990c; Wingert and Kantrowitz 1990; Perry 1991). Along with this change there was a major shift in childcare arrangements for the children of working mothers (Kamerman 1991). In 1958, 57 percent of the young children of employed mothers were cared for in their own homes. This responsibility has shifted to outside caregivers. Today, less than 30 percent of such children are cared for in their homes.

Effects of maternal employment on parents' interaction with their children have been investigated by Nock and Kingston (1988), who analyzed data on a national sample of married couples with children. Based on a carefully controlled analysis taking account of various activities, such as "play/education," "child care," "fun," "home-making," and "talking," Nock and Kingston concluded that "Dual-earner couples have lesser parental time with children for the simple reason "that they work more than do single-earner couples." These authors also found no evidence to support the hypothesis that "working mothers with young children substitute 'quality' *types* of time for lesser quantities of overall contact with their children" (Nock and Kingston 1988, 59, 81).

3. *Smaller family size.* The birthrate in the United States and other Western societies generally has been falling for many decades, interrupted only temporarily by increases such as the one following World War II. As shown in Table 4-2, the total fertility rate fell from 704 in 1800 to 248 in 1970, and after 1972 dropped below and has remained below the population replacement rate of 211 (Koretz 1991). Due to the availability of contraceptives, changing attitudes toward marriage, delayed childbearing, and other causes, this decline in the fertility rate means that women are giving birth to fewer children spread

TABLE 4-2 *Estimated Total Fertility Rates in the United States, 1800 to 1982*

Year	Rate	Year	Rate
1800	704	1960	365
1840	614	1970	248
1880	424	1975	177
1920	317	1980	184
1940	230	1985	184
1950	304	1990	195

Sources: Rates through 1920 are estimated in Coale and Zelnik (1963). Rates from 1940 are based on estimates in U.S. Bureau of the Census, *Social Indicators 1976* and data presented in the *Statistical Abstract of the United States,* 1990, and other sources.
Note: Rates represent live births per 1,000 women of childbearing age.

over the whole of their childbearing years; as a result, the average number of children per family also has decreased markedly since 1800. Some demographers predict that birthrates will rise substantially during the 1990s as youth in the relatively small baby-bust group now proceeding through the schools perceive enlarged opportunities for themselves and their children (Easterlin 1980; Barringer 1989; Koretz 1991). Most observers, however, believe that the long-range decline in fertility rates and the increase in the age of persons marrying for the first time reflect a fundamental change in social attitude and technology and, hence, are not likely to be reversed substantially (e.g., Westoff 1981; Riche 1990).

4. *Child neglect and abuse.* According to a report prepared by the United States Advisory Board on Child Abuse and Neglect (a panel of experts appointed by the U.S. Department of Health and Human Services), nearly one million substantiated cases of child mistreatment were identified in 1989, a figure many times higher than annual figures in the 1960s and 1970s (Tolchin 1990). Much of this increase was related to the passage of laws that require physicians, social-service professionals, educators, and other persons who have contact with young people to report suspected cases of neglect or abuse to

state and local authorities. (In this context, false allegations also have become a severe problem in many communities.) The Advisory Board also reported that more than 150,000 children are seriously harmed each year. Although neglect and abuse occur at all socioeconomic levels, it is much more frequent in poverty families than in middle-class families (Levitan, Magnum, and Pines 1989).

Neglect, maltreatment, and abuse of children have important implications for the schools, if only because many victimized children will have trouble attending to their school work and attaining a satisfactory level of performance. In particular, psychological maltreatment can generate depression and other pathological symptoms as debilitating as severe physical abuse. In addition, as many as 20 percent of abused children become child abusers themselves as adults (Widom 1989). Accordingly, some schools have initiated activities and programs intended to help identify and prevent child neglect and abuse. In some instances, these activities seek to warn preschoolers and primary-grade students about sexual abuse. The limited research that has been conducted to assess such instruction suggests that it may be counterproductive for very young children, in part because the concepts taught are difficult for preschoolers to understand and may be interpreted to mean that no family members are to be trusted (National Monitor staff 1989; Reppucci and Herman 1991).

5. *Increases in the proportion of households without children.* Beginning more than 100 years ago, there has been a steady increase in the percentage of households without children and youth living at home. As the U.S. population moved from farms to towns and cities, as family size decreased, and as the adult life span increased, this proportion increased from slightly more than one-quarter to approximately two-thirds today (Coleman 1990b). As discussed elsewhere in this text, increase in the proportion of households without children appears to have combined with other considerations in producing

recent declines in willingness to pay to support education, social services, and other activities that benefit young people.

6. *Serial-marriage children.* High divorce rates in recent decades have produced a concomitant increase in the number of "serial-marriage" children—children whose parents have divorced, remarried, and then divorced and remarried again. Brody, Neubaum, and Forehand (1988) analyzed the situation of serial-marriage children, and the available research dealing directly or indirectly with their development, and concluded that more systematic attention should be given to this topic in the future. After defining serial-marriage children as those whose parents have been married three or more times as a result of multiple divorces and/or multiple widowhood, they identified studies indicating that attitudes and behaviors developed during an unsuccessful marriage tend to be "amplified" in subsequent marriages, and that children involuntarily exposed to several divorces suffer from bewildering "multiple periods of diminished parenting capacity" (Brody, Neubaum, and Forehand 1988, 216–218). Their overall conclusion was that serial-marriage children thus exposed to a "consistently-negative child-rearing environment" are likely to encounter

> unequally high levels of interpersonal conflict, which may result in heightened levels of anxiety and aggressive behavior. Repeated separations from attachment figures may also result in behavioral disturbance . . . [and] a view of close relationships as transitory and untrustworthy . . . which could lead to difficulty in establishing and maintaining intimate relationships through life. . . . Periods of disrupted parenting . . . may produce intellectual, social, and emotional difficulties and increase the likelihood of antisocial behaviors. The accumulation of negative life events and the consistent history of disrupted, unstable family life . . . [may result in] behavior problems, suicide propensity, poor parent-child relationships, learned feelings of helplessness, depression, and feelings of incompetence . . . all

> these outcomes will be mediated by the child's personality characteristics. (Brody, Neubaum, and Forehand 1981, 219)

7. *Skip-generation families.* As family structures and patterns have diversified rapidly in recent decades, many social workers and other people who provide family services have become concerned about skip-generation families. In these families, children are raised largely by a grandparent or grandparents because their parents are deceased or are unable or unwilling to provide appropriate guidance and support. Although the occurrence of skip-generation families has been particularly stimulated due to the havoc wrought by crack cocaine and other drugs among inner-city mothers (Blakeslee 1989), such families apparently are appearing more frequently in middle-class city and suburban communities as well (Seligman 1990). Psychologists dealing with skip-generation families worry about potentially negative consequences for children's general development and well-being. For example, Sylvia de Toledo of the Reiss-Davis Child Study Center in Los Angeles has found that although children in skip-generation families usually are very attached to their grandparents, they "have a profound sense of abandonment . . . [worry] that they may once again be abandoned . . . [and] often do poorly in school, defy authority, have problems making friends and exhibit physical aggressiveness or feelings of isolation" (quoted in Seligman 1990, 46).

8. *Disappearing fathers.* A large proportion of divorced fathers disappear from their children's lives in the sense that they maintain little or no contact after the divorce. In addition, many children whose parents had not married seldom, if ever, have contact with their fathers in later years. In many cases, fathers who do not live with their children fail to maintain meaningful contact; in many other cases, fathers may want or try to maintain a continuing relationship, but opposition by the mother, travel and geographic distance considerations, or other obstacles make that exceedingly difficult. Thus, recent studies indicate that more than nine out of ten divorces result in sole custody of the children being given to mothers, that only about one in six children whose fathers are not at home see them an average of once a week or more, and that about half the children in custody of their mothers have not seen their fathers in a year or longer (Popenoe 1988; Lewin 1990a; Nordheimer 1990).

9. *Increased prominence of peer cultures among youth.* Although peer cultures have constituted an important phenomenon in nearly every society, there is reason to believe that they have become more prominent and influential among youth in the United States in the past four decades (Ascher and Coie 1990). This development is discussed more fully in Chapter 5, but at this point we should emphasize that the prominence of peer cultures today probably is related to increases that have occurred in the percentages of female-headed families and of working mothers, if only because all these developments reflect an apparent decline in the ability and desire of family members to maintain a conjugal family as a refuge from the outside world.

10. *Increased influence of television and other media.* Another important historical change affecting family relations and the socialization of children involves the increased importance of the mass media—particularly television, comic books, radio, and movies. In 1960, Schramm, Lyle, and Parker studied a sample of children in the United States and Canada and reported that the average child spent as much time watching television as attending school. Siegal (1975) estimated that the average child had spent 15,000 hours watching television by age sixteen, and the American Academy of Pediatrics (1990) has reported that children and youth over six years of age watch an average of twenty-two to twenty-three hours of television each week.

An activity that consumes this amount of time clearly can play an important part in changing children's attitudes and behaviors, if only because much of this time probably would have been spent interacting with parents and other

family members in earlier generations. Comic books also have an important influence in the lives of many children, and radio as well as movies are very effective in influencing the attitudes and interests of teenagers and their peer groups. In recent years, videotapes and games have become a time- and money-consuming activity for many children and youth, and many adults are concerned that the effects may be damaging to development.

In particular, violence in commercial videotapes has been a matter of increasing concern among parents of young adolescents. Following an incident in which a grocery store allowed children younger than thirteen to rent a "slasher" tape ("I Spit on Your Grave") graphically portraying five castrations and four rapes, the Missouri legislature passed a law designed to prevent minors from renting or buying tapes that exceed community standards for "acceptable violence." After representatives of the videocassette industry challenged the law on constitutional grounds, one informed observer commented that growing "public frustration . . . may force video stores" to set and enforce more meaningful voluntary standards for restricting rentals and sales to children and youth (Therrien 1989). The Missouri law was ruled unconstitutional by a federal judge who concluded that it could be used to prevent distribution of such violence-ridden works as "Bambi" and "Roadrunner."

Another recent media trend that may have major effects on the family involves the development of teletext, videodisks, and videotext technology. As defined in a report from the Institute for the Future prepared for the National Science Foundation (1982), teletext provides one-way communications services, and videotext is the provision of two-way communications services that deliver information to the home. Presently exemplified by personal computers that instantly draw on sources of knowledge and entertainment anywhere in the world, this developing technology has been described as beginning to change many aspects of daily life as well as the relationship between the home and other institutions. The electronic home of the future, the report concluded, may give the family much greater capacity than it has now to influence the education of children and the careers of youth and adults. Schools, too, will feel the impact, because information technology at school and at home will facilitate rote learning and free teachers to concentrate on development of creative problem-solving skills (Marriott 1990), and parents will be responsible for helping their children become generalists who can work with a fantastic variety of information tools.

11. *Increase of violent crimes among youth.* Criminologists are quick to point out that rising crime rates in the United States reflected an increase in the number of teenagers and young adults during the 1960s and 1970s. Delinquency and crime rates have long been substantial in these groups, which account for a substantial proportion of all crimes. Within this pattern, probably the most important development involving crime rates among youth is the increase in the number and proportion of violent crimes (aggravated assault, armed robbery, forcible rape, and murder). Approximately 30 percent of all serious crimes committed in the United States are committed by youths under nineteen years of age (Hindelang 1981). Much of this increase has taken place in big cities, particularly among underclass youth in concentrated poverty neighborhoods (Jencks 1991).

Interrelationships among Trends

Changes in the structure of the family and other phenomena clearly are interrelated. For example, the increase in the proportion of working mothers is related to higher rates of divorce and the formation of female-headed families: mothers who must support their children alone are more likely to work, other things being equal, than those who have a husband working. The increase in youth crime appears to be related to the growing prominence of peer cultures, increase in drug use, and the influence of television

and other media, particularly in concentrated poverty neighborhoods in which these influences are related to the functioning of a destructive street culture among children and youth. Hubert Williams, director of the Newark Police Department, has summarized some of the interrelated effects on inner-city children and youth:

> *Although crime may have been lower in the 1950s, seeds were being planted in our cities that would grow and flourish. . . . Narcotics . . . is the most obvious one. . . . But the drug problem points to deeper changes . . . which together constitute an enormous shift in the values and norms that determine how people behave. During the 1950s people in the inner city still generally believed that by working hard they could improve their lives—jobs were available; unemployment was much lower . . . and television . . . was not so influential then. Today, inner-city kids are well aware of the symbols of success—the fancy cars and clothes. . . . [In addition] in the inner cities kids were growing up without the guidance they'd had in the past . . . [as] the number of single-parent households increased tremendously. (Quoted in Harper's editors 1985, 41)*

PROBLEMS RELATED TO FAMILY EVOLUTION

In some ways, trends delineated in the preceding pages probably represent a culmination of earlier developments in the evolution of the family. As we note in the previous chapter, the modern nuclear family as described by Stone (1974, 1991), Gellis (1989), Pearcey (1990), and others is based on a shift from predominantly economic to predominantly emotional bonding, but the emphasis on emotional bonding seems to be evolving toward a greater emphasis on emotional satisfaction as compared with an emphasis on privacy and child nurturance in earlier periods. As described by Shorter, who sees in this the emergence of a "post-modern" family, recent developments are particularly characterized by

a growing instability of the couple. Since the mid-1960s, divorce rates have accelerated dramatically in every country in Western society. To be sure, ever since the mid-nineteenth century when divorce first started to be eased, the rates have been inching upwards. But that long, gradual climb (interrupted in the 1950s by a plateau in most places) gave way in the 1960s to an unprecedented explosion. . . . Behind these dry statistics lies a major upheaval in the life of the couple. . . . The conventional explanations for increases in the divorce rate are all inadequate. The upthrust has simply been too powerful and universal to be dismissed as a result of more liberal divorce laws. . . . We may also reject the hysterical proposition that 'the family' is breaking up, for the fact is that all these divorcing people turn right around and marry again. . . .

Two developments in the 1960s and 1970s have weakened the force of the permanent union. . . . First, the intensification of the couple's erotic life . . . has injected a huge chunk of high explosive into their relationship. . . . To the extent that erotic gratification is becoming a major element in the couple's collective existence, the risk of marital dissolution increases. . . .

Second, women are becoming more independent economically, and can afford to extract themselves from undesired unions. (Shorter 1975, 277–278)

In other respects, however, current trends in family structure represent a reversal of earlier developments in the history of the family in Western societies (Day 1988). The modern family emerged as a result of centuries of evolution directed partly toward protecting children from external influences in the environment and nurturing them for success in the school and the economy (Chartier, 1989). But it also generated new problems in social relationships and social-

ization. In some ways it cut children off too drastically from the life of the larger community, and it has been described as constituting a kind of emotional "hot-house" in which its members became too dependent on each other for affection and support (Pearcey 1990).

It frequently did succeed, on the other hand, in ensuring that children received the type of protection, guidance, and stimulation they needed to succeed in the larger society in which it functioned. Some authorities, such as Ryder (1974), see both the earlier evolution toward the modern family and recent trends toward its restructuring or dissolution as inevitable within the overall context of the history of Western society:

The conjugal family serves as an oasis for the replenishment of the person, providing the individual with stable, diffuse and largely unquestioning support, assuaging the bruises of defeat and otherwise repairing whatever damage may have been done in the achievement-oriented struggles of the outside world. . . . The conjugal family is a relatively efficient design for supplying the kind of labor force a productive society needs and for providing comfort to the individual exposed to the consequences of participation in that system. . . . Yet any attempt at further attenuation of family ties, in the interest of optimal allocation of human resources, would probably be self-defeating because of the high psychological cost to the individual. The family is an essentially authoritarian system persisting within an egalitarian environment. The growth of industrialism has been closely linked to the development of the ideology of individual liberty. Family political structure—the authority of male over female and of parent over child— has no immunity to the implications of this ideological change. Grave internal difficulties may therefore be expected. (Ryder 1974, 128)

Regardless of whether changes now occurring in the family are seen as continuations or reversals of earlier trends, it is important not to exaggerate their impact. Bane (1976), for example, has pointed out that children in earlier periods were involved in marital disruption due to the death of a parent and other disrupting events during the course of their childhoods as frequently as are children today, and that working mothers frequently spend about as much time with their children as do nonworking mothers.

Nevertheless, general indicators of family structure and juvenile behavior have changed substantially, and one can speculate on the implications of these changes for the schools. On the one hand, decreasing family size may signify or result in improvements in the cognitive development of children and their preparation for school, since children thus may be receiving more undivided parental attention than was true in the past (Zill 1982; Stafford 1987). In addition, the average parent today has more education than in earlier decades. On the other hand, there is reason to be concerned about the effects on children and youth of increases in the percentage of female-headed families, particularly in working-class and concentrated poverty neighborhoods. It appears that recent increases in the incidence of divorce and female-headed families among middle-class populations are only now beginning to reach a level high enough to detect a consistent and noticeable impact on the development of their children.

Along these lines, Mahoney (1976) views such recent trends as part of a larger pattern and has concluded that their effects are most likely to be detrimental:

> We have seen that families are much smaller than they once were; that there are fewer adults in the household with whom children can interact; and that even those adults who remain are absent much of the time, working in full-time jobs. What do these long- and short-term changes mean for the education of the nation's children? All of these changes combine to produce one important result: the isolation of children from adults. . . . The schools cannot possibly bear the full responsibility for the education of children. Cultural values cannot be transmitted en masse to a classroom of thirty. The enterprise takes the commitment of one human to another over a lifetime. . . . But because adults have less and less time and support for their roles as parents, what children experience now is a cultural void that is filled, even created, more by television and peers, than by parents or teachers. (Mahoney 1976, 10)

Somewhat similarly, Zinsmeister (1990) has stressed the difficulties other socializing institutions experience when family conditions deteriorate and the concomitant importance of working with and bolstering parents rather than trying to replace or supersede them. "If you house the child, and feed him his hot meals, and provide all his intellectual and moral instruction at school, you run the risk of persuading marginally involved parents that they are superfluous" (Zinsmeister 1990, 55). However, Zinsmeister also argues that when parents are unable to provide adequate care and oversight, child-protection agencies "must have the resources and will to act." Too often, he concludes, they do not; instead,

> many child-protection agencies are now doing little more than preventing murder, and sometimes they fail even to do that. . . . [In Washington, DC] one social worker says, "Prevention is not a word that exists in our agency anymore. . . . When we define tragedy, it is not a child's failure to thrive. It is either they are maimed or they are dead." Asked why he hadn't acted to remove a six-year-old boy from a known crack house run by the child's mother . . . an investigator in Maryland explained that he had twenty similar cases on his desk, and that he didn't have time to go through the time-consuming process of taking a child from a parent unless there was "immediate danger." (Zinsmeister 1990, 56–67)

The central role of poverty environments in damaging the development of young people and the difficulties families in general are experiencing in raising children in our complex postindustrial society have been described by the Carnegie Council on Children in a major report published in 1977. Established by the Carnegie Corporation, the Council spent four years studying the problems of contemporary family life and preparing a set of recommendations that its members believed could be implemented by the end of the 1980s. The Council stressed that at least one-quarter of the children in the United States were growing up in poverty environments that severely limit their opportunities to succeed later in life. In a section titled "The Theft of the Future," the Council pointed out that

> *poor children live in a particularly dangerous world of broken stair railings, of busy streets serving as playgrounds, of lead paints, rats and rat poisons, or a rural world where families do not enjoy the minimal levels of public health. . . . It is frequently a world of intense social dangers, where many adults, driven by poverty and desperation, seem untrustworthy and unpredictable. Children who learn the skills for survival in that world, suppressing curiosity and cultivating a defensive guardedness toward novelty . . . may not be able to acquire the basic skills and values that are needed, for better or worse, to thrive in mainstream society. (Keniston et al. 1977, 33)*

But it is not just poverty families and children who experience severe problems in contemporary society; many others also are having trouble in an environment that has made child raising "demanding and complex." As schools, television, the peer group, and other institutions have become more important in socialization, parents have had to take on something like an "executive function . . . choosing communities, schools, doctors, and special programs that will leave their children in the best possible hands" (p. 12). It is

not so much that parents are abdicating, the Council pointed out; instead they are being "dethroned, by forces they cannot influence, much less control" (pp. 22–23).

Based on this analysis, the Council's major recommendations included proposals stressing the following four goals for family policy:

1. Elimination of discriminatory employment practices and a national full-employment strategy combined with arrangements of family income supports designed to provide nearly all families with children a minimum income of at least half the current median in any given year;
2. A major national push for flexible and "family-conscious" work arrangements including flexible scheduling of working hours, more and better part-time employment opportunities, and time off for child rearing;
3. An improved range of comprehensive and universally accessible public services— especially in health care—to support and strengthen rather than replace the child-raising efforts of parents; and
4. Introduction and implementation of a variety of legal protections to assist troubled families.

In 221 pages of closely reasoned text, the Council set forth a persuasive list of specific proposals to accomplish these goals. The focus of these recommendations was primarily on the structural rather than the cultural causes of poverty and other family problems associated with poor performance in the school and the economy. The Council explained its reason for emphasizing structural forces affecting the development of children and youth:

> *Schools, the institutions traditionally called upon to correct social inequality, are unsuited to this task; without economic opportunity to follow educational opportunity, the myth of equality can never become real. . . . It is on*

questions of income, health, and family sup-ports that much of a child's early development and later success will turn. (pp. 47, 80)

Council Chairman Kenneth Keniston has stated that this emphasis on structural solutions to problems of family and child development was deliberate. In an interview published in the *Car-negie Quarterly*, Keniston stated:

Money, we would grant, is no guarantor of a decent life—other things, having to do with the human qualities of parents or with the neighborhood in which one grows up may be more important—but if one thinks what a society can do to support children, the promise of work and a modest income would em-power families with at least the minimum authority to control their lives. (Carnegie Cor-poration 1977, 11)

More than a decade later, an independent Commission on Work, Family, and Citizenship was established by the William T. Grant Founda-tion to examine developments during the 1980s (Halperin 1988; Howe 1990). After expressing agreement with "the position taken by . . . the Carnegie Council for Children that nothing is gained by blaming families for changes caused by broad economic and social forces that lie, for the most part, beyond their control," the Commis-sion concluded that employers, governments, community agencies, and other institutions should do "much more to enable families to ac-commodate to a changing world. These efforts must begin by supporting both the families that young people are born into and the families they create as adults." The Commission further con-cluded that "poverty is the worst threat to family effectiveness," particularly in the case of single-parent families that experience multiple obsta-cles in trying to prepare children for success in school and society (Howe 1990, 298–299).

Actions of the kind recommended by the Carnegie Council on Children and the Commis-sion on Work, Family, and Citizenship are indis-pensable in overcoming the structural forces that hamper the cognitive and social development of children and youth, particularly among under-class groups in big cities. However, for reasons explained in the preceding chapters, the cultural aspects of poverty and poor performance in the school and the economy also must be taken into account in working to improve educational and economic opportunities for low-status stu-dents. Educators in particular must formulate policy and practice for improving opportunity in terms of all the major causes that limit the mobility of underclass and other working-class students. Taking account of cultural aspects of poverty will require attention to issues involv-ing desegregation as well as major efforts to change the schools and their programs so that low-status students will be more successful than they are now.

THE POSTNUCLEAR FAMILY ADRIFT ON A SEA OF SELF-FULFILLMENT

Preceding sections of this chapter describe a number of ways in which the nuclear family struc-ture has been unraveling in recent decades: high divorce rates, increase in single-parent families, growth in serial marriages, and greater incidence of skip-generation families are some of the most striking indicators of this trend. After examining the growing incidence of such phenomena in the United States and other industrialized countries, David Popenoe (1988, 1991) concluded that we are experienc-ing the emergence of a "postnuclear family" pattern in which emphasis on families has been replaced to a substantial extent by concern for individual "self-fulfillment" (i.e., "individual-ism" oriented toward "pleasure, self-expression, and spontaneity," p. 239). In contrast to the nuclear-family system's emphasis on limiting sex-ual activity to married couples who engage in long-term "pair-bonding" initiated partly for the purpose of raising children, postnuclear families are more focused on the needs not of children, but of adults. A high percentage of all pair bonds in a post nuclear system do not involve children . . . [and even those units with children] have become less child centered. . . . With the rise of outside-the-family day-care facilities, child rearing has become less of a family enterprise. . . . parents spend an increasing portion of their family lives in other than child-rearing pursuits. . . . [High family dissolution rates also indicate a reduced child-centered orientation because parents] seldom break up a relationship to benefit the children . . . [but rather to benefit themselves because] typically their needs for intimacy are not being met. (Popenoe 1988, 302)

Although Popenoe recognizes the positive aspects of postnuclear family trends, including improvement in opportunities for and treatment of women and availability of medical care and other professional services for children as well as adults, he also is concerned that decreased child-centered "familism" may be harming the development of children and youth. As we note earlier in this chapter, for example, reductions in time parents spend being with and supervising their children and increased influence of peer groups and mass media may be having frequently negative effects in terms of preparing children to function well in school and later life. Noting the contrast between today's neighborhood environment, in which most adults either are not present during the day or are unfamiliar to children, and earlier times when the immediate neighborhood included responsible adults who helped provide social control outside the home, Popenoe pointed out that social control provided by "impersonal mechanisms," such as the police and the school, are "inadequate replacements for the older mechanisms administered by parent, aunt, neighbor, and pastor" (p. 339). He further concluded that the postnuclear family pattern may be generally beneficial for adults but harmful for children:

This is the first time in world history that the masses have been able to achieve the degree of self-fulfillment previously possessed only by rich males. In the past, familism was one of the principal cultural elements posing a powerful constraint on such individualism. . . . [But since self-fulfillment has become a central value] familism and the family today face . . . an unprecedented, adverse cultural climate. . . . [The modern nuclear family] has been cast adrift from the kinship groups to allow the emotional relationship between husband and wife to flourish . . . [and replace economic-production goals that previously guided family organization. But now it] has become clear that adults no longer need children in their lives, at least not in economic terms. The problem is that children . . . still need adults . . . who are motivated to provide them with . . . an abundance of time, patience, and love. (Popenoe 1988, 329–330)

Ensuring that the family and community institutions will provide a positive environment for children and youth requires more than glibly stating that parents should "achieve a better balance between career and domestic roles" (Popenoe 1988, 330). Actually to attain a productive balance, Popenoe concluded that "some shift in values is required, namely a partial retreat from the predominance of self-fulfillment" (p. 331). After speculating that in the future parents may place greater stress on stable parenting because they may lament its absence in their own childhood, Popenoe (1988, 340) also called for greater societal stress on diverse obligations of:

Parents, who should create strong family units.

Employers, who should take account of what their activities do to families.

Government, which should provide services and facilities in a manner that supports rather than weakens the family.

Men, who should play a "much more active role in family life."

Influential decision makers, who should be sure that "in the process of protecting 'alternative life-styles,' " the ideal of "good family life" in which parents "share responsibility for their children and for each other" is not downgraded.

Given the fragmentation (i.e., denuclearization) that has occurred in the family and between the family and other community forces that socialize the young, some social scientists have asked whether the schools might help restore a more unified approach in working with the family and other local community institutions. For example, Thomas Hoffer and James Coleman (1990) have considered possibilities for having educators, families, and employers establish small schools at sites where parents are employed and can cooperate with teachers in providing a positive environment for children's growth and learning. Noting that some firms "apparently have adopted this model with some success" at the preschool level and even in the primary grades, Hoffer and Coleman concluded that it would be "worthwhile to see if success can generalize" to later grades (1990b, 130). Elsewhere, Coleman (1990c, 36) has stressed the potential of such "workplace" schools in "building strong intergenerational communities in which groups of parents with similar values can support each other's childrearing." Some workplace schools for young children up to eight or nine years of age have been established in Dade County (Florida) and several other locations, and many corporate officials are considering creating such schools to help their employees as well as financially strapped school districts (Arrarte 1990; Pipho 1991).

HOME ENVIRONMENT AND INTELLECTUAL DEVELOPMENT

Researchers are making progress in identifying the specific home environment variables that affect cognitive and scholastic performance and the ways in which home environment is related to performance at differing stages of development. Research in this area has particular relevance for the design of preschool and elementary school programs to improve educational opportunity for economically disadvantaged children. Such programs are discussed in Chapter 8, but at this point it is relevant to mention several major unresolved issues involving the relationship between home environment and intellectual development.

Father Absence and Achievement

Partly because the percentage of children raised in female-headed families has been increasing, there is considerable interest in the issue of whether, other things being equal, children from homes with a father present perform better in school and have fewer emotional problems than do children without a father in the home. Family structure and its effects are of particular concern because low socioeconomic students and students from some minority groups are disproportionately likely to grow up in homes without a father present (Tables 4-1 and 4-3). Presumptively it can be argued that a single parent tends to have less time, energy, and material resources to devote to a child than does a husband-wife family.

A large number of studies have examined this issue, with various results and conclusions. That is, some researchers have found that children without a father in the home do not show lower achievement or other indications of impaired development than do children with a father (e.g., Svanum, Ringle, and McLaughlin 1982; Desai, Chase-Lansdale, and Michael 1989), but numerous other researchers have reached opposite conclusions (e.g., Guidubaldi 1984; Milne, Myers, Rosenthal, and Ginsburg 1986; Myers, Milne, Baker, and Ginsburg 1987; Dawson 1990; Goodyer 1990; Zill and Schoenborn 1990).

Marino and McCowan (1976) have usefully defined the issue in larger terms by asking whether parent absence rather than just father absence has effects on the development of

TABLE 4-3   *Percentages of Eighth Graders from Different Types of Households, by Socioeconomic Status Quartile and Race/Ethnicity**

Socioeconomic Status Quartile**	Mother or Female Guardian Only	Other Single Parent	Mother and Father, or Mother or Father and Guardian
Lowest	26	09	66
25–49 Percent	17	06	77
50–74 Percent	15	05	80
Highest	09	04	88
Race/Ethnicity***			
African American	36	10	54
Asian American	08	06	87
Hispanic	18	06	77
Native American	21	10	70
White	13	05	83

Source: Adapted from Hafner, Ingels, Schneider, and Stevenson 1990.

*Percentages sometimes do not add to 100 due to rounding.

**Socioeconomic status is measured in terms of mother's and father's occupations, mother's and father's educational levels, and family income.

***African American refers to non-Hispanic black students. White refers to non-Hispanic white students. Native American refers to American Indians and Alaskan Eskimos and Aleuts.

children and have reviewed the large body of research bearing on this issue. They pointed out that conclusions on parent absence are very difficult to reach because one should take into account the duration and cause of separation, the age and sex of the child, the quality and quantity of interaction with remaining adults, the context in which separation occurs, and other factors that may influence the child's reactions. They concluded that "parent absence may be a major contributing factor to low achievement . . . [and] personal maladjustment, but clearly not the only factor" (Marino and Mc-Cowan 1976, 177).

Clarke-Stewart (1977) also reviewed the research on parent absence and child development. She concluded that one-parent families are not necessarily harmful to the child's development, but she also found evidence to support the conclusion that husband-wife families may be more effective because both parents have an opportunity to exert a positive influence. Shepherd-Look (1982) reviewed the research dealing specifically with the effects of father absence and concluded that "separation of the father from the home environment, either temporarily or permanently, has definite negative effects upon male children. . . . Boys who were separated from their fathers early in life show a sex-role disruption pattern characterized by high verbal aggression, low physical aggression, more dependent behaviors, and a more feminine self-concept" (p. 423). She also concluded that this pattern occurs partly because many mothers who are single parents tend to treat their preadolescent sons in an overprotective manner; when single mothers do not discourage adventurous behavior, problems in sex-role development are minimal.

Additional information concerning relationships between parents' marital status and problematic behavior and outcomes among children has been provided by several major studies conducted by research teams in the United States and Great Britain (Cherlin 1991). Based on data collected in 1976 on 1,747 U.S. families with children ages seven to eleven and follow-up information obtained five years later, the researchers concluded that boys whose parents had divorced or separated during this period exemplified somewhat more parent-rated behavior problems (e.g., telling lies, difficulty concentrating, disobedience at home and school, depression, negative peer relationships) than did boys still in intact families. However, taking account of behavior problems reported by parents and teachers in 1976 greatly reduced this relationship to a barely reliable level, largely because boys in the divorced/separated families ranked high in problematic behavior *before* the subsequent family disruption. For girls, there was little reported difference in the relatively high behavioral-problems scores of the two groups (from divorced/separated compared with intact families) at either time period.

Largely similar results were found in a study of all children who were born in 1958 in England, Scotland, and Wales during the first week of March and whose families and teachers provided behavioral and achievement data in 1965 and again in 1969. However, girls from divorced/separated families had lower math achievement and lower behavioral ratings from teachers than did girls from intact families. The researchers summarized the results and implications of these U.S. and Great Britain studies as follows:

> *Overall, the evidence suggests that much of the effect of divorce on children can be predicted by conditions that existed well before the separation occurred. . . . Just when children begin to experience the process that precedes a divorce we cannot say. . . . [but] the British and U.S. longitudinal studies suggest that those [persons] concerned with effects of divorce on children should consider reorienting their thinking. At least as much attention needs to be paid to the processes that occur in troubled, intact families as to the trauma that children suffer after their parents separate. (Cherlin 1991, 1388)*

One particularly worrisome aspect of single-parent families that has been delineated in research is a "powerful tendency" for parents without a spouse at home to "permit adolescent youth earlier control over their own behavior" in such areas as "choice of friends . . . and time they must come home" (Dornbusch and Gray 1988, 285). After presenting data indicating that this phenomenon was present at all social-class levels, the authors of this national study concluded that

> *early decision-making . . . may be a reasonable response by single parents to the difficulties encountered by one parent attempting to monitor the behavior of an adolescent- . . . . [but] it has an unfortunate consequence, an increased probability to engage in deviant acts on the part of the youth. . . . [from this point of view] single parents are injuring the child through permissive parenting and the too-early granting of sole responsibility for decision making. It will not be easy to inform single parents of these problems or of appropriate ways of dealing with them. (Dornbusch and Gray 1988, 285–86, 293)*

Complicated methodological problems have made research on father absence difficult to conduct and interpret (Webster-Stratton 1989). Because low social class is associated with both father absence and low scores on achievement or other outcomes, research should control for the effects of social class in estimating the relationship between family structure or disruption and student outcomes. However, father absence lowers the social class of many families that become female-headed; in this case, controlling for social class may incorrectly eliminate a true relationship. Similarly, divorce generally reduces the economic resources of families that become single-parent (Goodman 1990), but controlling for income in research on educational effects will tend to reduce or eliminate (true) relationships between family types and educational performance (Desai, Chase-Lansdale, and Michael 1989).

In addition, the growing incidence of father absence in United States society may mean that family disruption is having a much more widespread effect on child development, but it may also mean that effects are lessened when disruption is perceived or experienced as more nearly a normal phenomenon. Svanum, Ringle, and McLaughlin (1982) have pointed out that these and other opposing or contrasting patterns may all be having differential effects on subgroups within a sample of children, and that in any case most research uses only "crude indexing of familial processes" (e.g., measures of family structure to represent child-parent interaction) that perhaps should not be expected to disclose strong effects of father absence on child outcomes (p. 142).

Finally, important longitudinal studies by Judith Wallerstein (1989) indicate that a variety of detrimental outcomes, including impaired interpersonal functioning, depression, poor adjustment in school, and declining school performance, were not immediately or very soon apparent among children of recently divorced parents but were frequently and strongly manifested ten or more years later. For some of these young people, part of their problems apparently originated in overburden associated with feelings of responsibility to care for their unhappy custodial parents. If such patterns are common beyond the middle-class, white children included in Wallerstein's sample, then negative effects of divorce and separation probably have been greatly underestimated by previous researchers (Kamarck and Galston 1990).

Although general research on single-parent families has had to contend with complicated variables and has not always supported the generalization that children in female-headed households perform less well in school than do children in husband-wife families, the situation in poverty neighborhoods appears to be particularly complex. A high percentage of children in concentrated poverty neighborhoods grow up in female-headed families, many of which do not have a male adult permanently in the home; but several studies (e.g., Wasserman 1972) have not found a relationship between family structure

and school achievement in these types of neighborhoods. We believe this is because low school achievement in such neighborhoods represents not so much a deficiency of female-headed compared to husband-wife families as it does a concentration of underclass families whose children tend to perform poorly in school regardless of family structure.

Faced with a rapid increase in the percentage of children from single-parent families, educators have been attempting to identify and take account of implications for elementary and secondary schools (Barney 1990). As part of their Study of School Needs of Children from One-Parent Families, the National Association of Elementary School Principals and the Kettering Foundation made recommendations such as the following for change in the schools: (1) Schools should review and update student records to identify children from one-parent homes so that guidance counselors and teachers can become more sensitive to their needs; (2) Schools should revise their calendars to provide easier after-hours access for working single parents; and (3) School systems should assume a major leadership role in conducting more effective parenting programs (Brown 1980). Similarly, the National Committee for Citizens in Education (Clay 1981) surveyed 1,237 single parents in 47 states and offered recommendations including the following:

- Copies of report cards and school activities notices should be sent to the noncustody parent.
- Single-parent families should be represented in textbooks and curriculum materials.
- School libraries should include materials that show varied life-styles and should help children deal with death and divorce.
- Schools should cooperate with other agencies in providing child care arrangements before and after school.
- In-service workshops should help teachers become aware of negative expectations they

may have for children from single-parent families.

Family Size, Birth Order, and Cognitive Development

Research on home environment and cognitive development also has been concerned with such variables as size of the family, number of siblings, and order of birth of children within the family. Some studies, such as those by Walberg and Marjoribanks (1976), Steelman and Doby (1983), and Judith Blake (1989) have found that after controlling for socioeconomic status, children in small families with few brothers and sisters are superior in cognitive development and educational attainment, compared with children who have more siblings. In addition, Walberg and Marjoribanks found that measures of home support and stimulation for learning were correlated both with cognitive development and number of siblings, after controlling for social status. In other words, it appears that other things being equal, parents with few children seem able to provide a more intellectually stimulating environment than do parents with many children, perhaps because parents' time, attention, and resources are spread much thinner in large families.

Zajonc (1976; 1986) has been studying these types of variables using several large cross-national samples. He has found that the brightest children generally are those born early in the smallest families, perhaps because they have a large amount of undivided adult attention in their early years. Birth spacing also appeared to make a difference, because longer spacing between children makes it possible to give each child more attention in the early years of life. And, in some samples, children with no brothers or sisters have IQs slightly below those of children with one brother or sister, perhaps because the second child in a two-child family with adequate spacing has the advantage of having an older brother or sister as an additional teacher in the home. Support for these conclusions also has been reported by some other authors (Desai,

Chase-Lansdale, and Michael 1989; Powell and Steelman 1990).

However, the Zajonc research findings have been challenged by other researchers who have reported opposite or conflicting results (Stafford 1987; Blake 1989a; Goleman 1990). For example, Page and Grandon (1979) analyzed data from a large national sample and concluded that if one takes account of social class and ethnicity, the independent effects of birth order and family size on ability are trivial, and that children are not necessarily "dumber by the dozen" (p. 270). In addition, data collected by the National Assessment of Educational Progress do not show a decline in performance among later-born children as is predicted by Zajonc's hypothesis and other earlier studies, and a study reported by Steelman and Mercy in 1980 concluded that birth order and intelligence are not related. Steelman (1985) reviewed the research on this topic and concluded that, in general, it tends to refute the conclusion that birth order has an independent effect on cognitive or academic outcomes. Blake (1989b) also concluded that although number of siblings is spuriously associated with educational outcomes because low-status families have more children than do high-status families, there is not a consistent independent relationship between family size and academic or cognitive outcomes.

Thus, at this time, it is not entirely clear how or whether family characteristics such as family size and birth order are independently related to specific home environment variables such as degree of intellectual or verbal stimulation provided by the parents or parental aspirations for the child, other than that the two types of variables appear to be connected. Also, much remains to be learned concerning their interactions with school achievement and with other environmental characteristics such as type of neighborhood in which a child grows up and how well the child does in school. The complexity of these issues is suggested by a 1976 study (Nuttall et al.) of teenagers in four suburban communities near Boston, which found "sex-specific patterns" indicating that after controlling for IQ, small family size was related to school grades for boys but not for girls, and firstborn status was related to academic achievement among girls but not among boys.

Race and Ethnicity, Home Environment, and Intellectual Development

Chapter 2 discusses the issue of whether reported racial differences in intelligence are due to heredity or environment and concludes that innate differences if they exist are limited and should not determine educational policy. However, even granted this conclusion, it still is important to learn more about the relationships between race or ethnicity, home environment, and intellectual development, in order to identify and understand the effects of home environment on achievement.

Because families of differing racial and ethnic groups differ in both social class and home environment, it is difficult to determine whether differences found in cognitive development and school achievement among their children are independently related to race or ethnicity or are artifacts of the social-class and home environment differences (Berry and Asamen 1989; Sanders-Phillips 1989). We already have mentioned that a number of studies (e.g., Mercer 1973) have shown that most of the IQ and achievement differences among groups of students classified by race or ethnicity can be accounted for by differences in social status and home or neighborhood environment. However, other researchers have found that racial and ethnic differences in ability or achievement persisted after controlling for differences in social status or family environment. For example, Epstein (1972) found that ethnic group membership was a better overall predictor of academic performance than was social-class status among a sample of fifth-grade children in Peru, and Marjoribanks (1972) studied mental ability scores among children from five Canadian ethnic groups after controlling for home environment and found that significant ethnic group differ-

ences persisted in verbal, number, and reasoning ability scores.

The problem of interpreting these findings is compounded not only by the fact that ethnic groups differ in social class and home environment but also by the possibility that various social-class and home-environment characteristics may have differing meaning or effects in differing groups. Even if it is assumed that social class and home environment are correctly and comprehensively measured for the purpose of understanding or explaining differences in intellectual development (which obviously is very difficult to do), differences in the saliency of a characteristic for a given group and interactions between all these variables may make it almost impossible to disentangle their separate or unique effects.

For example, parental education may result in high achievement only in families in which there is high verbal interaction with children, and income and high achievement may go together only when parents spend money on intellectually stimulating materials. Peterson and DeBord (1966) found that home and family variables predictive of achievement were different for black and white eleven-year-old males, and Carter and Levine (1977) found that home environment characteristics such as reading to the child appeared to have differential effects on achievement among Anglo, black, and Chicano third- and sixth-graders in a large midwestern city.

In addition, some studies (e.g., Laosa 1977) suggest that social-class measures such as parental education or occupation have different meaning for differing ethnic groups, and that these differences may be related to children's performance on tests of ability or achievement. For example, a position as postal supervisor may be indicative of relatively high status for a black male in a big city but not for a white male in the suburbs, and children's performance may reflect more the status achieved by parents in the local community than the ranking of an occupation on a national index of occupational status. Furthermore, parental action to provide a more positive home environment probably has differential effects depending on the social class of the home as well as on the influence of neighbors and peers and other factors. Thus, Benson (1979) studied family background and other variables in a large black ghetto and found that home environment was not closely associated with student achievement among students relatively high in social class (other considerations overrode the effects of negative home environment) or relatively low in social class (positive home influence was overwhelmed by other factors), but that home environment did appear to influence achievement significantly among students in the middle social-class group.

In view of all these difficulties, it does not now appear possible to make definitive statements about relationships between race or ethnicity, social class, home environment, and intellectual development, but it is possible to conclude that both home environment and social class are closely related to the cognitive and scholastic performance of children within most if not all ethnic groups. Research to date also suggests that race and ethnicity may be more closely related to achievement among working-class than among middle-class students, perhaps because individuals from a given ethnic group who attain middle-class status resemble individuals from other groups who have been upwardly mobile. In the process of upward mobility, people who formerly were working class have acquired a middle-class style while losing some of their ethnic characteristics (Havighurst 1976).

Home Environment, Brain Damage, and Cognitive Retardation

Another aspect of home environment known to be related to cognitive development involves malnutrition, lead poisoning, and other indicators of poor health conditions, such as low birth weight, high incidence of birth complications, inadequate medical care during pregnancy, and high rates of physiological disability among infants (Sanders-Phillips 1989; Hilts 1990b; Chris-

tensen 1991a). Lead poisoning is a particular concern because it affects a large percentage of low-income black children; health officials know how to eliminate lead poisoning from urban environments, but funds have not been made available to deal effectively with the problem (Jaroff 1991). Malnutrition and related indicators of health problems also are associated with severe poverty. Malnourished children are most frequently from low-income families, particularly one-parent households. Havighurst (1971b) surveyed the research on malnutrition and child development and concluded that severe, early malnutrition does have an effect on development of the brain. Serious impairment of normal cognitive and psychological development is most likely to occur to the extent that malnutrition is severe up to about six months of age. Severe malnutrition after this time also affects the child's learning development by causing irritability and inattentiveness, but it seems to result in little or no permanent brain damage (Bejar 1981).

However, very few children in the United States and other industrialized countries suffer from severe malnutrition. A number of low-status children probably do experience less severe malnutrition—particularly anemia—which affects their performance in school (Read 1976; Sanders-Phillips 1989), but a more debilitating cause of impaired cognitive development is lack of adequate or appropriate environmental stimulation during the early years of life. Lack of appropriate intellectual and social stimulation is associated with deficiencies in cognitive growth substances in the brain. Thus, infants who do not receive adequate environmental stimulation may be impaired in mental functioning when they grow older. A 1977 report to Congress by the Comptroller General concluded that 75 percent of the 100,000 new cases of mental retardation diagnosed each year are due to this type of sociocultural impairment.

These findings suggest that there probably is considerable sociocultural retardation (as opposed to inherent biological retardation) among low-status children in homes that do not provide appropriate stimulation during the early years or in which nutritional or other related health problems result in inattentiveness or irritability. These conditions in turn cause children to fall behind in acquiring basic learning skills and to develop a poor self-concept as a learner. Such conclusions also suggest, however, that cognitive retardation among low-status students can be avoided by working with parents to (1) improve nutrition and other indicators of physical well-being, and (2) provide appropriate environmental stimulation during the early years of life.

These conclusions further suggest that much of the learning deficit among low-status students in countries like the United States can be overcome or reversed, particularly if action is taken to provide appropriate home environment conditions during the early years (Hunt 1979; Schorr 1989). Scientists who believe that much of the intellectual retardation evident among many low-status students is reversible cite studies that indicate that brain damage may not be as widely prevalent or as long-lasting in its effect as some scholars previously believed. Read (1976), for example, believes that much retardation is substantially reversible. In support of this conclusion, he cites studies of Korean children who were severely malnourished early in life and after adoption by families in the United States were "normal in intellectual performance by American standards" and of Colombian children who were chronically undernourished but "improved their performance markedly on various behavioral indices" (pp. 30–31) following nutritional supplementation and educational stimulation beginning about age three. We already have cited Skeels's (1966) findings concerning the improvements in cognitive functioning made by children removed from a nonstimulating institutional environment at an early age.

Kagan and Klein (1973) also cite studies including their own research in Guatemala indicating that children who perform poorly on various cognitive tests during early childhood show marked gains after participating in an environment that provides stimulation and experience of the kind they previously lacked and is required for high performance on the tests. They concluded that children who are not too severely retarded have the capacity to overcome most of their learning handicaps when placed in an appropriate environment.

Taken together, these studies all suggest that much can be done to overcome intellectual retardation not just among low-status students but also among any large group of students with impaired cognitive development or low scholastic achievement. It may be true that a significant number of cognitively retarded pupils have brain damage that is basically irreversible and it may even be true that a substantial proportion of youngsters who grow up in physically unhealthy and intellectually nonstimulating environments will never achieve their full cognitive or scholastic potential. On the other hand, there is little or no solid evidence to contradict the conclusion that most such children can learn enough to meet standards of academic performance that would allow them to succeed in the school and in a modern economy.

Classification of Minority Students as Mentally Retarded

Many school districts try to provide special classes for students with an IQ below 70 (the American Association of Mental Deficiency defines the 55 to 69 range as "educable mentally retarded"), and some try to provide such classes for children below 80 in IQ. In some cases, students are placed in special classes for pupils with learning disorders if they have a relatively low IQ and also are diagnosed as emotionally disturbed, since emotional disorders are known to be associated with mental retardation. The number and percentage of students classified as mentally retarded increased regularly for about three decades after World War II and then began declining slowly in the mid-1970s.

Minority students are much more likely than nonminority students to be placed in several special-education categories such as "educable mentally retarded" and "seriously emotionally disturbed" (Lytle 1988; England, Stewart, and Meier 1990). In addition, research indicates that black students and Hispanic students but not nonminority students are much more likely to be in classes for the mentally retarded if they live in states that are high on poverty and other indicators of low socioeconomic status (Gelb and Mizokawa 1986). This pattern points to the possibility that minority students are being disproportionately classified as mentally retarded due to educational disadvantages associated with their social-class background. Low-income black students in big cities may be particularly vulnerable because they are disproportionately victimized by lead-paint poisoning, which in turn is associated with high frequencies of learning disabilities, hyperactivity, and other disorders (Schmidt 1990).

However, controversy exists over whether children classified as mentally retarded have been correctly diagnosed and the types of arrangements that should be made for their education. Some observers point out that intelligence tests have been constructed for use particularly with middle-class white populations and that as a consequence minority and low-status children may be diagnosed as retarded partly or largely because they are unfamiliar with the terminology and procedures of the tests (Quantz 1981–82). Some support for this conclusion has been provided by Garrison and Hammil (1971), who found that at least 25 percent and as many as 68 percent of the children—many of them minority—who had been assigned to educable mentally retarded classes in a five-county area in Philadelphia had been misassigned. The federal government Office of Civil Rights investigated 148 school districts between 1975 and 1979 and concluded that the special education placement of minority students frequently could not be justified educationally (Education Advocates Coalition 1980). This outcome can be damaging because children misclassified as retarded may be treated as such and expected to perform at a low level by teachers, parents, and classmates, thus generating a self-fulfilling prophecy wherein children work below their capacity in accordance with their own or other people's expectations (National Academy of Sciences 1982b). If this happens, then classification as retarded is racially discriminatory to the extent that minority students may be misclassified relatively more frequently than majority-white students.

Various groups concerned with the rights and welfare of minority students have raised this issue. Following a study of special education placement in five southern states, for example, the Children's Defense Fund issued a report saying that

we do not want to state that, based on these facts above, there were over 32,000 black students in these five states who have been misclassified and misplaced in educable mentally retarded classes. In order to make such a statement we would have to know the proportion of black and white students who should be in EMR [educable mentally retarded] classes in each of these districts, a figure which has not yet been derived even on the national level. . . . Such facts clearly warrant immediate further examination and investigation by local school officials and federal OCR [Office of Civil Rights] compliance officials. (quoted in Klein 1977, 13)

Some courts have been sympathetic to this type of criticism and have acted to reduce the possibility that students will be misassigned to special education classes. In a 1970 case (*Diana* v. *Board of Education*), for example, a California court examined the claim of nine Mexican-American children who felt they had been improperly classified as mentally retarded on the basis of an IQ test on which their scores ranged from 52 to 68. When tested by a bilingual psychologist and allowed to respond in Spanish or English, their IQs increased by an average of 15 points. The court ruled that (1) all children whose primary language is other than English must be tested in both their primary language and English; (2) the tests must not depend solely on vocabulary, general information, or other experience-based content; and (3) school districts that have a disparity between the percentage of Mexican-American students in regular classes and in classes for the retarded must submit an explanation. In another case (*Larry P.* v. *Riles*) in 1972, a California court ruled that black students could not be placed in EMR classes on the basis of IQ tests "as currently administered," after hearing evidence that the family environment and dialect of many black students caused them to have misleadingly low scores on the tests.

The federal government also has acted to avoid misclassification and misplacement of mentally retarded and other handicapped students, through sections of Public Law 94–142 (the Education of Handicapped Children Act). This law not only mandates and furnishes assistance to the states to provide a free appropriate public education for handicapped children but also establishes due process procedures regarding the classification of students. Educators gradually are being placed in the position of having either to prove that approaches that classify and segregate children as mentally retarded really provide the most effective means to overcome deficits in cognitive development or to try other approaches for improving the performance of children who previously would have been placed in special classes.

Effects of Television

There has been grave and growing concern with the question of whether the media—particularly television—may be encouraging violence and other antisocial behaviors among children and youth. The average teenager in the United States has seen tens of thousands of violent acts depicted on TV (Simon 1989; Plagens 1991). The Surgeon General of the United States appointed an advisory committee that studied this issue. The committee reported that the scientific data were not conclusive about whether television vi-

olence causes aggression in most children, although the members said evidence indicated a relation between viewing violence on television and aggressive behavior among children who had a tendency toward aggressive behavior (U.S. Public Health Service 1972). The American Academy of Pediatrics also has concluded that repeated exposure to violence on TV promotes a tendency to violence (Simon 1989).

Recent reviews of research (Comstock 1977; Dorr 1986) also have indicated that effects are largely dependent on situational factors such as "frustration or anger; similarities between the available target and the target in the portrayal; expected consequences such as success, failure, pain, or punishment; and opportunity to perform" the act of violence (Comstock 1977, 195). Ten years after the Surgeon General's 1972 report, a committee of behavioral scientists reviewed subsequent research for the National Institute of Mental Health and concluded that a relationship between viewing of violence on television and aggressive behavior in children was not well established. The committee further concluded that "television violence is as strongly correlated with aggressive behavior as any other behavioral variable that has been measured," and that children "learn to behave aggressively from the violence they see on television in the same way they learn cognitive and social skills from watching their parents, siblings, peers, teachers, and others" (U.S. Department of Health and Human Services 1982, 6, 38, 39). Recent longitudinal research also has found that heavy viewing of televised violence during childhood is associated with adult participation in violent crimes (Plagens 1991).

That television can be an important force for positive socialization also is apparent and has been supported by some research indicating that "Sesame Street" has been helpful in developing vocabulary among both middle- and lower-status children (Leifer, Gordon, and Graves 1975; Almeida 1977; Walsh 1989), and that children can become more cooperative and nurturant after viewing programs emphasizing these behaviors

(Poulos, Rubenstein, and Liebert 1975; Dorr 1986). Recognizing the promising as well as the potentially damaging effects of television on children and youth, critics have been organizing and pushing for changes in commercial programming in the United States. The National Congress of Parents and Teachers has made reform in television one of its principal national demands, and such groups as the National Citizens Committee for Broadcasting have been organized to collect data and lobby for change. Critics of television have blamed it for a variety of social ills including the promotion of unintelligent consumerism (Lasch 1990), sexual perversion (Plagens 1991), declining performance on academic tests in the schools (Healy 1990), and the promulgation of stereotypes regarding low-status minorities and women (Pierce, Carew, and Willis 1977; Rockwell 1990; Pollitt 1991). Even "Sesame Street"

has been severely criticized on the grounds that it harms children's growth by emphasizing trivial cognitive skills and produces distractible learners with short attention spans (Healy 1990). Winn (1977, 1989), Willis, Thomas, and Hoppe (1985), and others present some evidence and strong arguments suggesting that television may be helping to make children physically and intellectually passive and dependent, with detrimental effects on both cognitive development and social functioning. In this context, it is depressing to note that more than 60 percent of U.S. students say their parents rarely or never limit their television viewing (Bacon 1990).

Research on television viewing and school achievement indicates that there is a relationship, but causes of the relationship are somewhat unclear. The overall relationship between television viewing and reading is shown in Figure 4-3,

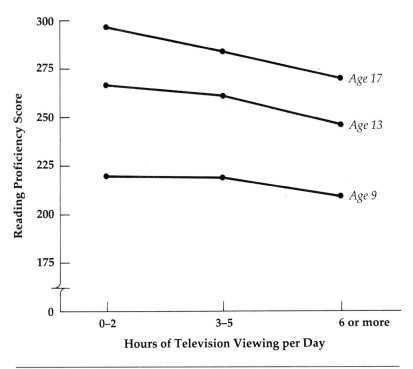

FIGURE 4-2   *Reading Proficiency Scores of Nine-, Thirteen-, and Seventeen-Year-Olds, by Hours of Television Viewing, 1984 (*Source: *Adapted from National Assessment of Educational Progress [NAEP] 1985.)*

which presents 1984 data collected by the National Assessment of Educational Progress (NAEP) for nine-, thirteen-, and seventeen-year-olds. As shown, students either nine or thirteen years of age who watch television six or more hours per day have lower reading proficiency than their peers who report less viewing. For seventeen-year-olds, this trend also is present, and those who watch three to five hours per day have clearly lower reading scores than those who view television two hours or less per day. More recent NAEP data analyzed by Langer, Applebee, Mullis, and Foertsch (1990) displayed similar patterns.

However, the NAEP study and other research (e.g., Walberg and Tsai 1985) reporting that low reading scores are associated with excessive viewing are correlational studies that have not been able to disentangle cause and effect. In general, children and youth who are doing poorly in school may retreat to television and other nonacademic activities, or television viewing may be a manifestation of family and home environment variables that also affect school achievement.

Recent research indicates that relationships between achievement, television viewing, age of the student, home environment, and other variables are complex and multidimensional (Anderson and Collins 1988). For example, a 1981 study of television viewing among more than 12,000 sixth graders in California indicated that heavy viewing was associated with lower achievement in reading, mathematics, and writing, lower social class, and preference for light entertainment. Viewing in excess of five to six hours per day was associated with low achievement for all social-class groups, but for students of lower social class, watching television up to three to four hours per day was associated with higher achievement (California Assessment Program 1982). (One can speculate that the television environment is more productive of achievement than are working-class home and neighborhood environments.) Findings from a 1981 survey of 580 students in Northern California further indicate that social class is more strongly related to read-

ing achievement among third than sixth graders, and effects of viewing on achievement depend on such considerations as reasons for viewing (e.g., to learn or to escape from other activities), reasons for reading, and degree and type of involvement in reading and television viewing. The investigators concluded that "amount of viewing and amount of reading, although important variables in their own right, are but parts of a larger complex of related television or viewing constructs" (Bachen, Hornby, Roberts, and Hernandez-Ramos 1982, 31).

High amount of television viewing also is associated with relatively poor social skills and peer relations. On the average, children and youth who are less popular and spend less time with peers devote more time to watching television. Dorr (1986) examined this relationship and reported that as in the case of television and achievement, cause and effect are difficult to delineate:

> Children with less satisfactory relationships may watch television simply because other children avoid them. . . . Or they may watch so much television that they do not leave enough time to learn to get along with peers. Or they may be less satisfactory companions because they spend more time watching television's bad examples. . . . Or all three things may account for the association. Or another as yet unidentified variable may cause both amount of viewing and quality of peer relationships. (Dorr 1986, 105)

The television industry has not been completely unresponsive to criticism (Waters 1990). Between 1975 and 1983, there was a slight reduction in violence and other adult themes during prime viewing hours, and efforts were being made to portray the antisocial nature of violence more meaningfully. However, violence in children's programs increased rapidly after 1985 (Walsh 1990b). Turow (1981) reviewed three decades of network television programming for children and reported that criticism of the television industry had been generally ineffective at changing basic programming criteria, though it has "eked out" some concessions involving "slightly fewer action-adventure series, a few more live-action shows, a few more realistic dramas about children, [and] more children of both sexes in the programs" (p. 12). But in 1989, not one of the major networks provided regular, weekday programming for children (Walsh 1990b).

Responding to such issues, Congress passed a 1990 law limiting advertising during children's programs and requiring that the quality and quantity of programming for children be considered in awarding broadcast licenses. All things considered, however, the effects of television on children and the family still pose an important national issue, though little can be said conclusively beyond the truism that television promises extraordinary benefits for education but also sometimes undermines family interaction and other forms of learning, such as play and reading (Charren 1990).

Effects of Maternal Employment

Growth in the percentage of women working outside the home has generated concern that maternal employment may be harmful to the development of their children. Partly because the proportion of employed mothers with young children was small until recent decades, relatively little research has been conducted on this topic. Rollings and Nye (1979) reviewed the research on effects of maternal employment and concluded that there is "little evidence of appreciable effects, positive or negative" (p. 217). A panel of the National Academy of Sciences (182a) reviewed available research on maternal employment and children's school achievement and reached the same conclusion; with some exceptions, most studies show little or no difference in the achievement of children of employed and nonworking mothers. However, some recent studies have reported negative effects on children's intellectual development, particularly among boys (Desai, Chase-Lansdale, and Michael 1989), and some summaries of research on the effects of daycare on the preschool children of working mothers have identified a wide range of negative outcomes (Perry 1991).

Latchkey Children

As maternal employment has increased, the percentage of latchkey children who return to empty homes or apartments also has increased (Schorr 1989). Some national data indicate that there may be more than ten million such children between the ages of five and thirteen (Rosenberger 1985; Lawson 1990). Other data indicate that the number may be much lower—perhaps not many more than two million (U.S. Bureau of the Census 1987).

Considerable attention to the potential problems of latchkey children was generated by 1985 Congressional hearings at which psychologist David Elkind testified that as adults we should "not kid ourselves that this is a beneficial experience that builds independence" (quoted in Bridgman 1984). In general, problems seem to center on children who wander freely after school and whose parents accordingly do not know where they are (Goleman 1989). Several researchers have reported that latchkey children have abnormally high levels of fear and some even lock themselves in closets (Dwyer 1990); other researchers have reported that there are no significant differences in personality or behavior between supervised children and latchkey children (Goleman 1989). Those who favor expanded government services for latchkey children argue that millions of children would benefit, but opponents maintain that too little is known about effective organization and delivery of such services. Meanwhile, however, schools in Independence (MO), Tulsa (OK), and some other locations have initiated before- and after-school programs for many elementary students whose parents work or want their children to engage in additional enrichment learning experiences (Lawson 1990).

Strother (1984) reviewed the literature related to the school's role in providing assistance to latchkey children. After delineating the pros and cons "regarding the involvement of public schools in child care" (1984, 290), Strother pointed out that schools engaging in provision of before- or after-school child care will have to deal with legal and policy issues involving such matters as licensing and liability. She then described a number of programs and practices that might be undertaken, including provision of space and other resources for other nonprofit agencies, direct sponsorship of before- and after-school supervision, busing of children to after-school programs elsewhere, conduct of seminars for parents, encouragement of home-based support services and telephone hotlines, training for children in coping skills, and cooperation with youth-serving organizations such as Camp Fire. Strother concluded her review with the following three specific recommendations for educators:

> *First, they should concentrate on structuring homework carefully . . . [and should] consider starting telephone hotlines for homework, staffed by teachers or by parent volunteers.*
>
> *Second, educators should allow time during the school day for children to discuss personal concerns.*
>
> *Third, school officials should establish better procedures for contacting working parents in an emergency. (Strother 1984, 293)*

Concern with the situation of latchkey children has grown as drug use and crime escalated in many communities in the late 1980s and early 1990s. Such concern is magnified by data indicating that teenagers who care for themselves after school are much more likely to consume marijuana and alcohol than are those who are supervised, even after account is taken of socioeconomic status, race, and other demographic factors (Kutner 1989; Weisman 1990a). Experts believe that parents of latchkey children should not panic, since the majority of latchkey children

do not use drugs; but parents whose children are unsupervised after school should do whatever they can to make productive activities available, to ensure that their children can reach relatives or neighbors in an emergency, and to stay in regular contact through the telephone or other means (Goleman 1989; Kutner 1989).

Homeless Children and Youth and Runaways

Along with economic recession and major reductions in federal housing programs in the early 1980s, a nationwide increase occurred in the number of homeless persons in the United States. Economic conditions improved in the mid-80s, but the homeless population remained relatively high and may have increased even more. Rising housing costs and deinstitutionalization of the mentally ill also contributed significantly to homelessness (Moynihan 1989; Rossi 1989; Ludtke 1990). Whatever the numbers and causes, the homeless population appears to be more diverse than in earlier decades, when it generally was portrayed as consisting primarily of unattached, older adults. As shown in Table 4-4, many of the homeless are high school graduates who have at least occasional employment but still are unable or unwilling to find affordable housing. Richard Ropers (1985) has described the general situation of the homeless population:

> *The homeless seem to be everywhere. Some are obviously homeless, like the bag-ladies, the shopping-cart people, the disheveled who huddle in doorways, and others who seem to wander aimlessly in streets and alleys. Those whose homelessness is apparent, however, and who look as though they fit the long-held stereotypes of bums, derelicts, winos, or the insane, are only the tip of the iceberg. There are also the invisible ones, many of whom are indistinguishable from the rest of us, and who "pass" during the day, roaming shopping malls or university hallways. At night they try to rest in rat- and roach-infested movie theaters,*

TABLE 4-4 *Characteristics of the Adult Homeless Population in Chicago and Minneapolis*

Sex	Percentage
Male	79
Female	21

Race	
Non-Hispanic white	35
Non-white and/or Hispanic	65

Education Level	
Did not complete high school	48
High school graduation or more	52

Marital Status	
Now married	07
Not now married	93

Employment Status	
Employment during previous month	38
Not employed during previous month	62

Source: Adapted from Westerfelt 1987–1988.

in lonely schoolyards, in their cars, on subways, or in the cold restrooms of public buildings. Most of the contemporary homeless are in fact difficult to detect because of their diversity and "invisibility." (Ropers 1985, 1)

Data collected in recent years show that many families and children are among the contemporary homeless population (Braccidiferro 1991). Children constitute a particularly high proportion of the homeless in many suburban areas (Schmitt 1988; Stronge 1991). Studies examining the problems of homeless children indicate that, as a group, they suffer from relatively high rates of child abuse and low rates of school enrollment and attendance, low achievement, and high incidence of poor health and learning disabilities (Barden 1990b; Lorch 1989; Stronge 1991). Such data are not surprising inasmuch as many homeless children share bathrooms in shelters with drug addicts, and they generally live in environments that are physically and morally destructive.

Local governments frequently have been unable or unwilling to deal effectively with the problems of homeless families and children, and the federal government in the face of a large budget deficit also has provided only limited assistance to address this important national problem (Rossi 1989; National Law Center 1990). Some school districts have tried to initiate special programs to help homeless students, but lack of funds, high rates of turnover, and the severity of students' educational and psychological problems have made it difficult to respond effectively (Friedman and Christiansen 1990). Wells (1989a) and Stronge (1991) have identified some of the programs and services that schools can initiate to help homeless children:

- *School-shelter liaisons* who meet with families moving into temporary housing and help them transfer academic records and enroll their children
- *After-school and extended-day programs* that provide a quiet place to study, cultural enrichment, and/or opportunities for recreation
- *Special tutoring programs*, particularly for those homeless students who have missed weeks or months of school
- *Workshops* to help parents find housing and jobs
- *In-school social workers* who can help obtain food, clothing, and other necessities
- *Counselors* to help overcome severe psychological problems associated with homelessness
- *In-service training* to help teachers become aware and sensitive concerning homeless children's special problems

A significant number of homeless youth are runaways who have left or been expelled from their homes, many of which exemplify serious levels of child neglect or abuse. Although some observers have estimated the runaway youth population as exceeding half a million per year, most runaways leave for only a relatively short time and then return home. Those who remain homeless for a longer period, however, frequently end up in dangerous environments in or near downtown areas in big cities. Youth in the latter situation frequently are victims of severe physical and sexual abuse (Archambault et al. 1990).

Foster-Care Children

Partly as a result of homelessness, child abuse, growth in single-parent families, drug use among pregnant women, and other current social maladies discussed elsewhere in this chapter, the number of children in foster-care homes and institutions has increased rapidly (Barden 1991). Based on a survey in eleven states, the U.S. House of Representatives Committee on Children, Youth, and Families reported that between 1985 and 1988 the number of foster-care children increased by 23 percent to nearly 350,000. Committee Chairman George Miller interpreted these numbers as indicating that "we are devastating hundreds of thousands of [foster-care] children . . . [many of whom] are becoming candidates for long-term dependency on our social welfare system . . . [or are situated in what amount to schools] for future penitentiary residents" (Associated Press 1989:15). Overburdened by the increase in many kinds of family problems, the foster-care system has been characterized as a "multibillion dollar system of confusion and misdirection, overwhelmed by the profusion of sick, battered and emotionally scarred children who are becoming the responsibility of the public" (Barden 1990b, A1).

Effects of Crack Cocaine

As indicated in Chapters 1, 2, 3, 6, 8, and 10, environments for raising children and youth recently have become still more difficult as poverty neighborhoods have become increasingly homogeneous, single-parent families have proliferated, and young people have been drawn into a peer-oriented street culture. In particular, drug use and addiction associated with the spread of crack cocaine have accelerated rapidly. Effects on children and the family frequently have been devastating (London 1991; Reed 1991). As summarized by Morgenthau crack has

> *proven to be an illicit bonanza for those who sell it and a curse on those who use it. Unlike heroin, crack is widely used by women. That fact alone has disastrous consequences for low-income families. If single-parent households have contributed to the intractability of poverty in the past, no-parent households may be poverty's appalling future. And crack is a catastrophe for the young. It has touched off an explosive increase in birth defects and an epidemic of child abuse and parental neglect. Its profits, in neighborhoods where the standard of living is very low, have led or forced thousands of inner-city youngsters into hard-core crime, and many others into addictions from which they may never recover. It has bankrupt parental authority and it is destroying the fraying social fabric of inner-city neighborhoods all over the United States. (Morgenthau 1989, 17)*

In addition to effects on families and their environments, crack has harmed a significant number of young children whose mothers consumed it during pregnancy. Many of these so-called *crack babies* appear to have suffered physiological damage that, in turn, produces disabilities that actually or potentially impede their cognitive development and learning in school. Health officials estimate that more than 300,000 infants a year were prenatally exposed to crack and other addictive drugs in recent years. Although it is difficult to determine how many of these infants and children will develop severe inattentiveness, hyperactivity, or other symptoms associated with prenatal crack consumption, teachers and administrators in numerous cities have been reporting a rapid increase in the drug-related incidence of kindergarten students who function very poorly. Educators are beginning to identify instructional approaches and related services that may help many such children, but it is not known what methods are best and how well they can be expected to work (Daley 1991).

PARENTAL INVOLVEMENT AND COOPERATION WITH THE SCHOOL

Most teachers are very aware that cooperation with and support from parents is an important determinant of students' success in school. When parents provide a positive environment for learning at home, reinforce school rules and expectations, and require or at least attempt to require their children to work hard and complete their assignments, the teacher's job is made easier and his or her effectiveness can be greatly enhanced.

As we discuss earlier in this chapter and elsewhere, it appears that socialization of children and youth is much more fragmented in postindustrial society than it was in preceding eras, when the family, neighbors, the church, teachers, and other influential adults could work together more easily in small communities to provide consistent and intensive supervision and guidance of youth. Aware of the importance of home-school cooperation and the negative outcomes that frequently occur when parents, teachers, and other socializing agents function at cross-purposes, the Council of Chief State School Officers (1990a) has urged state governments to require every school to develop and implement plans for increasing parental and community involvement in schools, improving collaboration between the schools and other public and private agencies, and sponsoring more comprehensive parental education programs.

Evidence regarding contemporary deficiencies in parental support for the work of the schools has been provided in the National Education Longitudinal Survey of nearly 25,000 eighth graders and their parents. Conducted for the U.S. Department of Education, the survey found that almost half the students reported rarely discussing school with their parents, and only about half of their parents reported having any contact with their children's teachers. Nearly two-thirds of the students also reported that their parents rarely or never limit the amount of TV they watch (Bacon 1990). Commenting on the results, one federal official said that the data indicated a "disengagement of parents from the schools and from their children's performance," and another stated that many students are "doing pretty much as they want, which is to say, not much at all" (Bacon 1990, 82).

Data collected from nationwide samples of teachers suggest similar conclusions and implications. For example, more than half of teachers responding to a Metropolitan Life Insurance survey expressed the opinion that "most" or "many" parents fail to discipline their children adequately, provide insufficient motivation so that their children "want to learn in school," and "take too little interest in their children's education." For their part, parents generally rated the "availability and responsiveness of teachers when you need to contact them" as "excellent" or "good" (Olson 1990b, 18–19). But many parents responding to a PTA survey reported that lack of time and obligations at work severely limit their involvement with their children's teachers and schools (Jennings 1990).

Just as there are many ways that parents can help their children improve their chances of succeeding in school, educators can engage in a wide variety of activities to improve home-school cooperation and to help involve parents productively in their children's education. Joyce Epstein (1990, 1991) and her colleagues at Johns Hopkins University have been studying parental involvement in education and ways to increase it. They have identified five major types of parent involvement along with numerous practices schools can employ to promote each type:

1. **Type 1**—*Parenting*. Illustrative practices include providing information and suggestions about home environments that support learning, and sponsoring workshops, videotapes, or computerized phone messages on parenting and child rearing.
2. **Type 2**—*Communicating*. Illustrative practices include holding parent-teacher

conferences, providing translators for parents who speak or read little or no English, and sending home weekly or monthly student-work folders.

3. **Type 3**—*Volunteering*. Illustrative practices include sponsoring of parental volunteer activities and committees at the classroom level, sending postcard surveys to identify talents and contributions of potential volunteers, and making available a resource room for volunteers and other community members.

4. **Type 4**—*Learning at home*. Illustrative practices include sending parents information on skills being taught in each subject at every grade level, establishing and disseminating homework schedules, and publishing calendars with daily topics parents can discuss with their children.

5. **Type 5**—*Representing other parents*. Illustrative practices include cooperating with and encouraging participation in school-related parent organizations, organizing advisory committees dealing with curriculum, safety, and other matters, and helping recruit and train parents for independent advisory or advocacy groups.

As stressed by Epstein and her colleagues, educators can choose from many possible actions and practices in working to advance each type of parent involvement. For example, Ascher (1988) illustrated a few of the possible "first steps" that can be undertaken to foster parenting and learning at home among low-income urban families:

- Conduct a "media campaign on the important role of the home in educating children."
- Build support for home learning from "ministers and other respected leaders."
- Establish "family learning centers in schools, storefronts, and churches."
- Operate "bilingual hotlines for parents who need help in helping their children with their homework."

- Design "learning activities that parents and their children can do together" (Ascher 1988, 4).

Many studies have shown that, for various reasons, middle-status parents are more frequently involved with and cooperate more closely with their children's schools than are low-status parents (e.g., Hoover-Dempsey, Bassler, and Brissie 1987). Although there are numerous individual exceptions to this generalization (Eisenhart 1989; Epstein and Dauber 1991), working-class parents on the average have less knowledge of how to work with the school and how to help their children and feel less comfortable with teachers and administrators than do middle-class parents (Menacker, Hurwitz, and Weldon 1988; Comer and Haynes 1991). In many cases, very low-income parents may be too preoccupied with survival or may be too disorganized in their own lives to maintain consistent contact with the school or to help their children learn to function well in education. On the other hand, many low-income parents express the desire to cooperate more closely and productively with their children's schools and teachers (Dauber and Epstein 1989; Epstein 1991). Thus, there appears to be great potential and scope for improving home-school cooperation in schools that enroll the children of the poor.

Elsewhere we describe major projects and programs being initiated partly to enhance involvement and home-school cooperation among parents of economically disadvantaged students (see the section on comprehensive ecological intervention in Chapter 8). Here, we want to emphasize that efforts to bolster parent involvement and cooperation with the schools are growing nationally, in accordance with evidence cited earlier indicating that inadequate involvement constitutes a pervasive problem. For example, Tennessee is implementing and assessing eleven different approaches to build parent-school partnerships at schools throughout the state, and by 1990, twenty states had enacted some kind of legislation to promote home-school collaboration (Jennings 1990).

Although most activities and programs still tend to be fragmented and perhaps of questionable effectiveness, educators are beginning to identify the kinds of "essential elements" (Jennings 1990), such as the following, that can help bring about more successful programs in the future:

1. Build parent involvement activities on written school and district policies.
2. Through funding in the regular budget, provide needed materials, equipment, and space, as well as designation of persons to implement activities.
3. Provide appropriate training for staff and parents.
4. Provide for joint planning, goal setting, and assessment by teachers, administrators, and parents.
5. Encourage frequent two-way communications, in part by welcoming parents in a setting conducive to participation.
6. Link with social-service agencies and other resource and information sources.
7. Undertake regular evaluations and revisions.

Research

Although it clearly is desirable to have high levels of parental involvement and cooperation, research has not conclusively identified what schools can do to bring this about or whether more involvement and cooperation will bring about substantial achievement gains.

Regarding issues involving the best ways to enhance involvement and cooperation, researchers seldom conducted systematic studies before the 1980s. However, a series of studies being carried out at Johns Hopkins University has provided some support for the potential efficacy of school initiatives. For example, a Johns Hopkins study of inner-city elementary and middle schools found that parents who received teachers' guidance on how to help at home spent more time assisting their children with homework than did other parents, and that school practices aimed at informing and involving parents are more important in determining whether parents stay involved with their children's education than are parental education, marital status, or family size (Dauber and Epstein 1989; Epstein and Dauber 1991). Researchers conducting these studies also have concluded that designing homework so that parents can help—particularly on weekends—can increase parental support, and that the strongest involvement programs usually have a part- or full-time coordinator to work with parents and teachers (Brandt 1989; Epstein and Dauber 1991).

Regarding the potential impact of involvement and cooperation on student performance, research demonstrates that students whose parents are involved have better grades and test scores (Peterson 1989). However, positive home environment in general is related both to involvement and performance; for this reason, the involvement-performance relationship may be a spurious consequence of home environment, and involvement may have little or no independent effect after taking account of other aspects of environment (Silvern 1988). At the school level, research indicates that schools that have higher achievement than most other schools with students similar in social class seem to rank high on parental involvement and home-school cooperation, but exactly what these usually effective schools do to encourage and work with parents and community groups is not very clear and probably depends on considerations somewhat unique to each school (Levine and Lezotte 1990).

In addition to studies that inquire whether parent involvement generally is related to high student or school achievement levels, researchers have identified and documented examples of schools at which active parent and community groups played a part in introducing improvements that resulted in enhanced student performance. For example, Sizemore (1987) and her colleagues described several inner-city elementary schools in which teachers' and administrators' systematic efforts to improve instruction were strongly supported by parents and community leaders. Similarly, James Comer (1980, 1988, 1990) and other observers (e.g., Boger 1990; Gursky 1990; Hall and Henderson 1990; Davies 1991) have described developments at improving inner-city elementary schools at which parents have been involved in all aspects of their children's education, including service on school policy-making councils and special working groups (i.e., "Mental Health Teams") in which parents, teachers, psychologists, social workers, or other child-development specialists design and supervise individualized learning arrangements for students experiencing and/or causing unusual problems. Combined with curriculum modifications and instructional changes that emphasize active learning, language development and thinking skills, and improvement in students' social skills and discipline, these comprehensive parent involvement efforts have helped to produce large gains in student learning (Comer and Haynes 1991).

Participation in School Governance

As mentioned previously, one way parents can work more closely with educators involves participation in decisions regarding provision of education at local school buildings. In recent years much attention has been given to possibilities for including parents and other community representatives in school-level councils or committees established for this purpose. In some cases such councils or committees are purely advisory, but in other cases their decisions determine how funds are expended and whether and in what ways designated educational services are provided and delivered. Approaches for involving citizens in school-level decision making also differ with respect to whether citizens constitute a minority or majoriy on a committee or council and whether decision-making powers include a role in selecting administrators, teachers, and other staff.

In the Chicago Public Schools, for example, 1988 state legislative changes resulted in the establishment at every school of a council with a majority of parents who help in developing and implementing a three-year improvement plan, selecting the school's principal, and determining how available funds will be expended. In Seattle and some other districts that have established advisory councils at each school, parents and other nonstaff must constitute half the membership. By way of contrast, requirements that councils be established at each school in the Dade County (Miami, Florida) and Los Angeles school districts provide only for significant representation of parents and do not specify council powers as extensive and detailed as those established for councils in Chicago. Many other school districts, both large and small, have either mandated or encouraged the establishment of local school councils or committees with varying degrees of parental participation in a diverse array of decision-making and advisory roles and functions.

School-based councils that include parents have been functioning at schools in Florida, South Carolina, and other locations since the 1970s, and researchers have inquired about their operation and effectiveness. We discuss the rationale and results of this approach to educational improvement in our consideration of school-based management reforms in Chapter 13, but here we should note that lack of adequate training for parents and other participants appears to have constituted a serious problem at most schools where it has been attempted (Levine and Eubanks 1992). For this reason, training has become a key component in working to establish or improve local councils or committees in many schools and school districts in the 1990s.

CONCLUSION

Home influences on intellectual development have been examined in this chapter, and we have concluded that home-environment differences that underlie social-class differences are related to cognitive and scholastic performance. In conjunction with the previous chapter, the material in this chapter suggests that families influence the intellectual development of their children particularly through the adequacy of their efforts to protect the child, if necessary, from detrimental external influences, and the kinds of verbal and intellectual stimulation and encouragement they provide inside the home.

Several important issues involving relationships between home environment and intellectual development also were examined. The conclusions reached in this section can be partly summarized by saying that large family size, malnutrition and other indicators of physical health problems, and, probably, father absence (i.e., female-headed family structure), seem to be implicated to some degree as causes of the below-average intellectual development and performance of students from working-class backgrounds. However, family structure measures such as father-absence and large size do not directly hamper cognitive development but exert their influence through effects on home environment or are themselves indicators of environmental conditions that hamper learning. In addition, malnutrition and related health indicators do not appear to result in permanent brain damage for a very high percentage of children in the United States, thus suggesting that efforts to make home environments more conducive to cognitive development would not be likely to fail for this reason alone.

Our discussion of home environment and cognitive development included an analysis of trends in family relations because these trends have great importance for the future development of children and youth. As pointed out by Kamarck and Galston (1990), U.S. society has moved in one generation from Ozzie and Harriet to the Simpsons, from

one breadwinner to two, from child-centered nuclear families that stayed together for the sake of the children to the struggling one-parent families of today.... The signs are everywhere around us that America's children are suffering—economically, educationally, and emotionally.

Today we stand at a crossroads. We are just beginning to understand the full range of costs that society bears when families raise children less effectively.... Public programs cannot fully substitute for healthy families and should not try. Instead, government should work to stabilize families and to enhance their child-rearing capacity. In so doing, government will have to provide substantial resources. But at the same time it must minimize bureaucratic cost, complexity, and intrusion. (Kamarck and Galston 1990, 1–2)

Developments regarding home environment and learning are inseparable from larger trends in society affecting the evolution of families and social classes. From this point of view, it is very important that society develop national policies and programs to ensure that families are able to provide their children with an environment conducive to success in later life. No one can draw up a master plan that ensures that this will happen for all children or that takes full account of pluralistic values concerning the development of children and youth, but policies can be worked out to provide the resources and nurturance young people need to function effectively in a modern society. It is this possibility that former U.S. Commissioner of Education Terrel H. Bell had in mind when he recommended that proposals for government or private action in United States communities should include a "family impact" statement to go along with required "environmental impact" statements that Congress wrestles with in deciding what types of day-care arrangements to finance in the United States.

From the viewpoint of the educational system, the most important national policies dealing with families and children will include those that affect working-class populations, particularly underclass residents of concentrated poverty neighborhoods in big cities. Our analysis of social mobility and education (see Chapter 7) indicates that the schools need to become more effective in providing opportunities for working-class children in general and underclass children in particular. Our analysis of social-class environments and home environments in relation to intellectual development indicates that steps should be taken to improve home, neighborhood, and school learning environments for working-class children and others who are poorly prepared to function in school, if such children are to have a reasonable chance to succeed later in school and society. Much will depend on what other institutions such as the federal, state, and local governments do to solve problems of poverty, segregation, and big-city deterioration that are connected with the educational problems of working-class children. Much also will depend on what schools do to provide more effective learning opportunities for low-status students. This latter topic is addressed in Chapters 8 and 13.

EXERCISES

1. The Dave-Wolf home environment scale described in this chapter has been widely used in research relating home environment to performance in school. It is administered by interviewing a child's mother and giving a score on each dimension from high to low. A copy of a similar instrument incorporating additional items on home environment is available in a paper by Levine, Eubanks, and Roskoski (1980). The reader may write for a copy and use it to measure home environment in nearby communities. (Write to Daniel Levine, University of Missouri—Kansas City, 5100 Rockhill Road, Kansas City, Missouri, 64110.)

2. What procedures are being used in nearby school districts to classify students as mentally retarded? What safeguards are being used to avoid misclassification? To what degree are minority and/or low-status students overrepresented in classes for the mentally retarded in comparison to their proportion in local schools?

3. If you were asked to advise friends on how they can provide an intellectually stimulating environment for their young children, how would you respond? What specific suggestions would you give to encourage optimal cognitive development?

4. What are the main arguments suggesting that children from female-headed families are not likely to do as well in school as those from husband-wife families? What are some of the major counter-arguments? Why do researchers have a difficult time determining the answer to this question?

5. After reading *The Nature of the Child* by Jerome Kagan, list things you believe that parents should and should not do to promote their children's development.

SUGGESTIONS FOR FURTHER READING

1. *The American Family in Social-Historical Perspective* edited by Michael Young includes a number of essays that describe historical trends involving the family in the United States and discusses their implications for the present and the future.

2. Many Jo Bane's *Here to Stay: American Families in the Twentieth Century* and *Haven in a Heartless World: The Family Besieged* by Christopher Lasch provide background data and thoughtful discussion dealing with the status of the family in the United States.

3. For an account of how the family acts to produce differences in personality between children of different social classes, read

Father of the Man by Allison Davis and Robert J. Havighurst.

4. *The Changing American Parent* by Daniel R. Miller and Guy E. Swanson and *Patterns of Child Rearing* by Robert E. Sears, Eleanor E. Maccoby, and Harry Levin are reports of two large-scale studies of child-rearing practices. For an account of how methods of child rearing have changed in America in the past 100 years, read Chapters 9 and 10 in *Childhood in Contemporary Cultures*, edited by Margaret Mead and Martha Wolfenstein. See also the article by Urie Bronfenbrenner, "Socialization and Social Class through Time and Space," in *Readings in Social Psychology* by Eleanor E. Maccoby.

5. There are a number of good textbooks on the family as a social institution. A useful survey of much research on the family as an agent of socialization has been prepared by Clausen (1966). A book of readings on the *Family in Transition* (Skolnick and Skolnick) deals with the changing family in the 1970s. *Family Studies Review Yearbook* edited by Olson and Miller (1983) reports many aspects of research on the family.

6. Research on the family's role in child development is reviewed and summarized in Alison Clarke-Stewart's 1977 monograph on *Child Care in the Family*.

7. For a comprehensive survey of research on the socialization process, see the review by Edward Zigler (1970) entitled "Social Class and the Socialization Process." See also the chapter "Sociological Correlates of Child Behavior" by Clausen and Williams in the NSSE Yearbook, *Child Psychology*.

8. *Education and the Brain* edited by Jeanne Chall and Allan Mirsky, the 1978 yearbook of the National Society for the Study of Education, includes a large amount of material dealing with the cognitive development of children.

9. The entire November 1977 issue of *Educa-*

tion and Urban Society is devoted to television and education. Authors explore a number of important issues on this topic.

10. *Contemporary Theories about the Family*, edited by Wesley R. Burr and others, provides a wealth of information on family dynamics and processes.

11. *The War over the Family: Capturing the Middle Ground*, by Brigitte Berger and Peter Berger, argues that the nuclear, middle-class family has been a major force in modernizing and developing a stable, productive society. The authors take a middle ground between liberals and conservatives on family policy issues involving public and private rights and responsibilities.

12. Nearly all of the July 1986 issue of *Sociology of Education* is devoted to research on effects on children and youth of single-parent families and maternal employment.

13. Aimée Dorr's *Television and Children* (1986) is a short but comprehensive and succinct review of the many ways television affects children and their implications for schools, families, and society as a whole.

14. *Family Life and School Achievement* by Reginald Clark identifies and analyzes differences between the families of high- and low-achieving urban black students.

15. A special Winter/Spring 1990 issue of *Newsweek* titled "The 21st Century Family" is devoted to a wide range of family-related developments including variation in types of families; implications of changing patterns regarding childhood, adolescence, and old age; problems with respect to day care, housing, and cultural change; and implications of genetic testing.

16. An extensive study and report on *Volunteers in Public Schools* (Michael 1990) documents the diverse ways in which parents and other community persons can help improve the quality and effectiveness of education.

17. The January 1991 issue of *The Elementary School Journal* is devoted to the topic of parent involvement in education.

18. Research on school programs to prevent sexual abuse of young children and provide sexuality-related education for older students is described and assessed in a 1991 paper by N. Dickon Reppucci and Janna Herman.

5

The Peer Group

The importance of the peer group in elementary and secondary schools was underlined in data John Goodlad and his colleagues collected in the early 1980s as part of their national research project titled "A Study of Schooling." Information was collected from 17,163 students and 1,350 teachers at 38 representative public schools (Goodlad 1984). In response to the question, "What is the *one* best thing about this school?" students in junior and senior high schools were much more likely to cite "My friends" than anything else about their schools. As shown in Table 5-1, 35 percent selected the response dealing with peers; no other aspect of their schools was selected by more than 13 percent of the students responding. It may be noteworthy that only 11 percent selected either "Classes I'm taking" or "Teachers."

THE NATURE AND IMPORTANCE
OF THE PEER GROUP

A child grows up in two social worlds. One is the world of adults: parents, relatives, teachers, club leaders, store clerks, and friends of the family. The other is the world of peers or age-mates: friends, play groups, clubs and gangs, and school groups. For any child, of course, "the" peer group means a succession of specific groups of children with whom he or she interacts, just as "the" family is, for a child, one particular family. Peer groups are of many different kinds—from the informal play group to the organized Scout troop or organized gang, from the clique of three or four members to the wide school group—and

the average child will interact with a variety of particular peer groups as he or she grows up. Each group has its own rules, implicit or explicit; its own social organization; and its own expectations for group members (Ascher and Coie 1990).

The adult is always, to greater or lesser degree, excluded from the peer group of the child and adolescent. At one extreme, a peer group may be in open conflict with adults, as in a delinquent gang in a slum neighborhood whose activities may be in express defiance of community standards of law and order; or as in groups of adolescents whose standards of dress, speech, and behavior while by no means delinquent, nevertheless conflict with expectations set by parents. The situation in which a teenager argues with his or her parents that, "The other kids stay out until midnight, why can't I?" has countless variations. Yet the variations are on the same

TABLE 5-1 *High School Students' Response to the Question, "What Is the One Best Thing about This School?"*

Response	Percentage
My friends	35
Sports	13
Good student attitudes	11
Nothing	8
Classes I'm taking	7
Teachers	4
Other	22

Source: Compiled and adapted from Goodlad 1984, 76–77.

theme, that of reconciling two sets of expectations: one set from the peer world, the other from the adult world (Ianni 1989a, 1989b).

The other extreme is the situation in which the peer-group expectations are in full accord with adult expectations and are even a direct outcome of adult planning, as in a neighborhood play group formed under the watchful eyes of mothers; or a Boys Club organized through a settlement house, or an urban renewal project; or a high school Hi-Y group meeting under the leadership of a respected teacher. Even in such situations, however, the adult is to some measure excluded, with youngsters reserving certain areas of communication and interaction to themselves. The child or the adolescent feels comfortable with age-mates in a way that he or she is not comfortable with the adult, however acceptant and understanding the adult may be. Unlike the family and the school, the peer group is not a formalized, institutionalized agent of society. It has no legal definitions, no formally ascribed functions or duties. Yet it pervades the life of the child to a greater extent as he or she grows older, and it performs increasingly important functions in teaching the ways of society.

Importance of Peer Acceptance and Rejection

Research indicates that acceptance by peers is an important consideration in predicting whether children and youth will experience problems later in life. Parker and Asher (1986, 1990) have examined the literature on this topic and concluded that acceptance/rejection by peers is strongly associated with social adjustment problems and later outcomes such as dropping out of school and criminality. One general conclusion of their review of research is that

> *children with poor peer adjustment are at risk. . . . Some idea of the incidence of later maladjustment among children with peer relations problems can be gained by considering the dropout area. The most consistent predic-*

> *tor in this area was low acceptance per se. In study after study, children identified as having low peer acceptance dropped out at rates 2, 3, and even 8 times as high as other children. (Parker and Asher 1986, 7–8)*

Recent research also supports the conclusion that peer rejection is closely linked to a relative insensitivity that many children demonstrate with respect to nonverbal communication. For example, studies of children aged nine to eleven indicate that as many as 10 percent of children may have so much trouble interpreting and communicating nonverbal signals that they experience serious social and academic problems (Ascher and Coie 1990). According to psychologist Stephen Nowiski, such children typically are unable to approach other children without antagonizing peers, and because "they are unaware of the messages they are sending or misinterpret how other children are feeling . . . unpopular children may not even realize that they are initiating many of the negative reactions they receive from their peers" (quoted in Goleman 1989, 21).

FUNCTIONS OF THE PEER GROUP

As a socializing agency, the peer group serves the child in a number of ways (Schunk 1987). Adults generally expect the peer group to teach a child how to get along with others, as witnessed by the distress of parents and teachers over a child who is not accepted by other children and who is therefore denied many opportunities for social learning (Kutner 1990).

Teaching the Culture

Even though a peer group may be said to have a subculture that is particularly its own, it nevertheless reflects the adult society and reinforces most of the values held by the adult society.* A

---

* The distinction should be made between an organized gang and other types of peer groups. The gang may be defined as an organization of preadolescents or adolescents that does not

child learns through peers the prevailing standards of adult morality—competition, cooperation, honesty, responsibility—which, while they may at first be childlike versions, become adultlike with increasing age. Research indicates that the peer group becomes increasingly important in the development of moral reasoning as children grow older (Lerner and Shea 1982; Ascher and Coie 1990). For example, Gerson and Damon (1978) studied children who took part with peers in a discussion of how to distribute candy and found that older children (eight- to ten-year-olds) were more likely to distribute it equally.

The peer group teaches children their sex roles, building on but changing and elaborating the earlier teaching of the family. A child learns from peers what behavior is acceptable and admired in a boy and what is accepted and admired in a girl. Thus, the peer group is a powerful agency in molding behavior in accordance with current versions of manhood and womanhood (Eder and Parker 1987; Smilansky 1991).

The peer group is also an important source of information in areas other than social relations. Our modern sophisticate, aged ten, has obtained much up-to-the-minute knowledge of outer space and satellites from television, it is true; but it is after discussion with age-mates that the information takes on value and becomes part of the child's intellectual equipment. It is the peer group that often decides what knowledge is important, and what is not.

Certain areas of teaching and information giving have become the special province of the peer group: for instance, to teach a child by actual experience how rules are made, how they can be changed and, along with this, an understanding of the individual's responsibility in a group situation. The peer group also is important in imparting sex education to the child.

The Peer Group as a Shifting Phenomenon

In the adult world, the child is always in a position of subordinate status. In the peer world, the child has equal status with others and learns from persons who are not removed from him or her by wide differences in age, maturity, or prestige (Hartop 1989). Deference and respect for authority are largely irrelevant issues. Among peers, the child is relatively free to express his or her own attitudes, judgments, and critical faculties, and to explore personal relationships (Ianni 1989b).

One special characteristic of the peer group is the transitory quality of relationships. These relationships may be intense, but not necessarily long lasting. An eight-year-old, for example, may suddenly switch allegiance from one child to another and report to his family that it is now Richy, rather than Don, who is the paragon of all virtues. A twelve-year-old girl said, in similar vein, "I used to think Ellen and Nancy and I would always be friends. We spent a lot of time together, and did our homework together, and all. But now Ellen seems kind of silly, and we get into a lot of arguments. So I've become friendly with Kathy and Jill, and I like them lots better. They're my best friends now."

There are, of course, long-enduring friendships formed in childhood. Still, except in a relatively isolated setting where there are few age-mates, most children form new relationships and break old ones as their level of social and emotional maturity shifts in relation to others, as interests change, and as needs for new social experiences change (Kutner 1990).

A third differentiating characteristic of the peer group as a socializing agency is that its influence tends to become more rather than less important with the advancing age of the child (Ianni 1989b). Unlike the family, whose influence becomes less influential with time, the peer

---

relate itself positively to adult leadership. A gang may or may not engage in delinquent behavior, but in the eyes of most adults, gangs are undesirable because they are at least potentially antisocial, if not actually so. The efforts of most social agencies in dealing with gangs are directed toward the transformation of gangs into groups by providing adult leadership and thus to guide their activities into socially acceptable channels.

group becomes more influential. The eight- or ten-year-old wants to do things "like the other kids do." By the age of sixteen, this desire may become an obsession. In adolescence, the peer group takes a certain precedence in many ways over any other group that influences the individual (Smilansky 1991).

Peer Group Serving as Reference Group

Every person wants to look good in the eyes of certain other people and does not care what impression he or she makes on still other groups for which there is no respect or interest. The groups to which he or she wants to be favorably known and seen are called *reference groups*. She sees herself through their eyes; he judges himself as they would judge him; she learns from them her attitudes and aspirations.

Most people have several reference groups. Their family is generally the first, and most important when they are quite young. Then come their friends, their teachers, their peers, their neighbors, and their fellow citizens. Their peer group is generally quite important to them by the age of seven or eight, and it becomes more important as they move into adolescence, reaching its greatest effectiveness as a reference group when they are fifteen to twenty years old.

Still, the parents remain an effective reference group for some purposes (Ascher and Coie 1990). Brittain (1963) studied the relative importance of friends and of parents on various issues. He found that peers are more influential in deciding some things, like what course to take in school; but parents are more influential when, for instance, a girl decides which of two boys to date.

The peer group helps the adolescent become independent of adults—especially of parents. It appears that the adolescent peer group acts as a kind of shock absorber in the relations between adolescents and adults. It defends youth from too stringent demands for scholarly behavior or for adultlike behavior, but it also presses youth to become more mature in their behavior. The research evidence is mixed on this matter.

The so-called adolescent society is not simply a group that glorifies athletic skills, social skills, and student leadership.

The peer group also reflects the social-status structure of the wider society. Social-class differences not only operate in the adult society but operate also in the society of children and adolescents.

The first study of social-class differences in the child's society was made in Jonesville. There, Neugarten (1949) found that fifth- and sixth-grade children (all of whom were together in the same school), when asked who were their best friends, most often named children above them in social class, then, second, children from their own social class. Few choices were made downward in the social scale, with the result that most working-class children were chosen only by others of their own social status. Similarly, as regarded reputation, children ascribed favorable personality traits to children from lower social classes. There was a consistent relationship between social class and reputation: as one moved up the social scale, from lower-working to upper-middle class, children received consistently higher proportions of mentions on favorable characteristics and consistently lower proportions on unfavorable ones (Neugarten 1949).

Research also suggests that middle-status youngsters generally have been more likely than working-class children to designate parents rather than peers as their primary reference group. In line with earlier studies, Curtis (1975) reported this result in a study of nearly 10,000 junior and senior high school students in North Carolina and Ohio. We already have seen (in Chapter 3) that one problem of growing up in a working-class environment is the temptation to participate in antisocial peer groups. It is probable that middle-class adolescents in some subcultures (e.g., homogeneous middle-class suburbs) have become as oriented to peers as are working-class youth, but little systematic research has been carried out to document such convergence if it is taking place.

THE ADOLESCENT PEER GROUP
AND PROBLEM BEHAVIOR

The problem behavior that becomes relatively frequent during adolescence is generally supported by some members of the peer group who thus serve to help adolescents break away from behavior standards set by their parents (Elliott, Huizinga, and Ageton, 1985). A major research paper by Jessor and Jessor studied high school students of a Colorado city, starting with grades 7, 8, and 9, in 1969 and following them to grades 10, 11, and 12 in 1972. They secured confidential reports of problem behavior from the students, including drinking, marijuana, and sexual intercourse. They found the frequency of these behaviors to be closely related to concern for approval by friends as opposed to approval by parents. They report, "adolescents who are likely to engage in problem behavior perceive less compatibility between the expectations that their parents and their friends hold for them, they acknowledge greater influence of friends relative to parents, they perceive greater support for problem behavior among their friends, and they have more friends who provide models for engaging in problem behavior" (1977, 12–13). These results later were replicated with data from a national sample of 10,405 adolescents (Jessor, Chase, and Donovan 1980).

Research indicates that influence of the peer group as compared with parental influence depends on the type of problem behavior and influence being investigated. Biddle, Bank, and Marlin (1980) studied a diverse group of twelve-, fifteen-, and eighteen-year-olds in a large metropolitan area and found that peer behavior was relatively more important than parental behavior in predicting adolescents' preference for and use of alcohol, but parental norms were more important than peer norms in predicting attitudes involving achievement in school. They also concluded that adolescents' own preferences are more important in their decision making than usually has been taken into account in previous research.

THE GROWING INFLUENCE
OF THE PEER GROUP

Even though the peer group operates informally, as we have said, in the United States its influence has grown more important over the last 100 years. Data collected by Boocock (1976) on the daily lives of children in a variety of communities showed that when not in school, most children spend most of their time with friends or alone, watching television or "fooling around." Boocock concluded that in contrast to earlier times, "relatively few children of the 1970s seem to have strong linkages with the larger society" (p. 10). There are a number of factors involved. More and more children and adolescents live in urban rather than rural settings today, the number of youth organizations of all types has grown, a large percentage of mothers are now employed, and adolescents spend increasingly more years in school rather than at work—children and adolescents thus are thrown together in groups of agemates to an ever increasing extent. (Ianni 1989a, 1989b; Ascher and Coie 1990).

In our society, adolescents as an age group play a relatively insignificant part. Their labor is not required in economic production, and they remain in positions of economic dependence on the family for longer and longer periods. As adolescence tends to be prolonged, and as youth are excluded from participation in the adult society, young people turn more and more to the peer group for recognition. In return, the peer group takes on an increasingly larger role in the socialization process.

THE PEER GROUP AND THE FAMILY

Trends toward increasing influence of the peer group are due in part to larger changes taking place in the structure and condition of the family in the United States. Chapter 4 notes that trends in the family include an increase in the proportion of female-headed families and working mothers as well as other changes that appear to be reducing interaction between parents and their children. As a result, parents exercise less influence over their children and the peer group becomes concomitantly more important (Ascher and Coie 1990).

Some support for this point of view can be found in data that Condry and Siman (1974) collected on 766 sixth graders in and around Syracuse, New York. The authors administered questionnaires designed to determine the degree to which children were oriented toward peers and adults, and the types of activities engaged in by respondents with differing orientations. They found that peer-oriented children were more likely than adult-oriented children to say they sometimes were truant from school, smoked and used foul language, and engaged in other activities disapproved by adults, whereas adult-oriented children were more likely to engage in adult-sanctioned activities such as "helping someone" and "making or building something."

Further exploration of their data suggested that peer-oriented children interacted less with their parents and received less adult supervision than did adult-oriented children. Particularly for boys, Condry and Siman also found evidence suggesting that some children were turning to their peers because they were neglected by their parents, or their parents were unwilling or unable to control them. The Family Research Council estimates that total contact time between parents and their children decreased by 25% between 1965 and 1990 (Hewlett 1990).

Data such as Condry and Siman's, which were collected with paper-and-pencil instruments administered to students at one time, must be interpreted cautiously. They cannot conclusively demonstrate that lack of effective parental contact and supervision is a main cause of peer orientation or that young people thereby are pushed rather than pulled into peer-group activities for this or other reasons. Nevertheless, they do help advance understanding of the problems and dangers inherent in a society in which parental supervision over and interaction with children may be undergoing a long-range decline. During the past century, the family has lost much of its control over socialization to other institutions (Ianni

1989b). Responsibilities for children's learning have been transferred largely to the school, and parents' rights to raise their children as they see fit are now at least partially superseded by educators, child-care specialists, truant officers, and other professionals concerned with the welfare of children (Kamarck and Galston 1990).

To some extent, these changes are desirable or even necessary responses to the problem of socializing children in a complex, modern society. However, to the extent that they indicate a long-term decline in the family's capacity to control the socialization of children, they suggest that the peer group will continue to become more important in the socialization process in the future.

THE PEER GROUP AND THE SCHOOL

The school is expected to help the child bridge the gap between the child's world and the adult world. This is, in one sense, the expressed function of the school as a socializing agency. Even though this is also a function of the family, the important difference between school and family in this respect is that the school deals with children and moves them along toward adulthood, not as individuals, but as groups. Consequently, the influence of the school on the individual child is always mediated in the setting of the peer group. It is from this point of view that the school and the peer group are inextricably bound together in their influences on the child.

Because peer groups are important in the development of children and youth, and because peer relations affect the child's educational development, educators should give explicit attention to helping youngsters establish positive peer relationships (Webb 1987; Hilke 1990). After pointing out that poor peer relations in elementary school predict psychological disturbance and delinquency in high school, and that poor peer relationships in high school predict adult pathology and dysfunctioning, Johnson and Johnson (1981) cited sixteen steps that educators and adults should take to promote effective socialization through peer relationships.

1. Ensure physical proximity between children and their peers.
2. Structure cooperative interdependence, and encourage activities that stimulate working or playing together.
3. Emphasize joint rather than individual products whenever possible.
4. Directly teach interpersonal and small-group skills.
5. Give children meaningful responsibility for the well-being of their peers.
6. Encourage feelings of support, acceptace, concern, and commitment.
7. Hold children accountable for discharging their responsibilities to their collaborators.
8. Ensure experiences of success in a cooperative setting.
9. Promote the appropriate exchange of personal information.
10. Occasionally structure appropriate interpersonal and intergroup competition.
11. Occasionally structure appropriate individualistic activities.
12. Encourage perspective-taking dialogues with peers.
13. Provide opportunities for prosocial action.
14. Provide opportunities for participation in decision making appropriate to the child's age.
15. Suppress peer pressure for antisocial behavior.
16. Provide opportunities for older children to interact with and supervise younger ones.

Educators have been developing systematic instructional appproaches for improving peer relationships and related aspects of positive social behavior in the classroom. Among the best known of these approaches are cooperative student-team-learning techniques developed by Elizabeth Cohen (1986, 1990), David and Roger Johnson (1984, 1990), and Robert Slavin (1987, 1990b, 1991) and his colleagues. Information concerning several of these approaches is provided in Chapters 9 and 13. One of the most ambitious of recent approaches is the Child Development Project (CDP), which uses a wide range of instructional techniques designed to develop childrens's prosocial behavior involving cooperative learning, discipline, social understandings, values, and helping activities. Data collected during a five-year implementation following a group of students from kindergarten through fourth grade in three suburban elementary schools supported encouraging conclusions regarding attainment of CDP goals (Solomon 1988; Battistich 1989; Watson 1989; Kohn 1990, 1991).

Aggressive and Insensitive Children and Youth

Available data indicate that the children most likely to be rejected by their peers are those who are high in aggressiveness and low in cooperative behavior (Coie and Kupersmidt 1983; Hartup 1989; Ascher and Coie 1990). Research by Coie and Whidby (1986) found that this generalization was true in a study of predominantly black and low-income third-graders, just as had been the case in a number of previous studies of white and middle-class elementary students. The authors also found that the results were more pronounced for boys than for girls, perhaps because there were relatively few highly aggressive girls. The dynamics of gender in the operation of elementary peer groups are discussed in Chapter 11 dealing with women and education.

Bullies are a subset of aggressive children and youth who regularly harass other students and seem to derive satisfaction from harming others, whether psychologically or physically (Roberts 1988). Research on bullies suggests that many are no more anxious or insecure than other children, but they frequently are larger, stronger, and more accustomed to using physical force to get what they want or to try to solve their problems. Research also indicates that bullies tend to continue aggression into adulthood, frequently becoming spouse and child abusers (Tony 1990).

The National School Safety Council views bullying as "perhaps the most underrated problem in our schools." Council surveys indicate that about one-third of eighth- and tenth-graders report having been threatened at school or on a school bus during the previous year. Pointing out that adults placed in a similar situation frequently would call in the police or take legal action, the Council has cautioned educators to communicate and enforce clear standards for acceptable behavior, closely monitor playground and hallway activitiy, and watch for symptoms of victimization by bullies, such as withdrawal from activities, decline in grades, and bruises or torn clothing (Tony 1990, 3).

Cliques in Classrooms

Peer-group phenomena in classrooms and schools frequently are manifested in the formation and operation of cliques of students who interact among themselves and exclude other students. Defining cliques as "densely connected networks of peers who are tied to each other by positive sentiment," Hallinan and Smith (1989, 898) studied friendship choices and interactions among students in grades four through seven and found that the development and functioning of cliques are dependent not just on individual preferences but also on the characteristics of classrooms. Specifically, the data indicated that class size, racial composition, grade level, classroom climate, and achievement level are among the variables that influence the formation and characteristics of cliques. The authors also concluded that two of their findings were particularly important:

Classrooms with a higher mean achievement level have fewer friendship cliques. . . . . [Second], in classes where teachers place less emphasis on objective measures of achievement, friendship cliques show greater diversity in ability. If fostering positive social ties with peers of diverse achieved characteristics is a school goal . . . [teachers may be hindering its

attainment through their efforts] to improve academic achievement. Further study . . . is called for to suggest ways for teachers to maximize student learning while at the same time fostering positive peer relationships. (Hallinan and Smith 1989, 916–917)

Schools, Social Interaction, and the Transition to Adolescence

Many young people who are entering adolescence experience particular problems related to variations in their physical development and how these variations affect their peer relationships. Adolescents generally are very concerned with their standing and interactions with their peers, and negative attitudes or self-concepts trouble many of them during the middle school years, when there is most variation in physical maturation and development. Nottelmann (1982) has reviewed the research on this topic and also reported results of a recent study of adolescents' transtion to the sixth and seventh grades. She concluded that being "off time" (early or late in physical maturation) at early adolescence damages children's social competence (relationships with peers), particularly among "less mature" boys and "more mature" girls. Given that "we cannot synchronize children's biological clocks," she further concluded, it appears that "we might be able to soften the impact of puberty and the negative social comparison effects on the self-perceptions of children who are 'off time' by helping all children to understand (a) that the process of physical maturation during adolescence is idiosyncratic in onset and rate of progression . . . and (b) that eventually in later adolescence, individual differences in physical maturity will disappear" (Nottelmann 1982, 12).

Thornburg (1979) has offered specific recommendations for educators working with preteens and teens during the middle school years. First, he identified four important developmental requirements and characteristics of early adolescence: develop friendships with others; became aware of increased physical changes; show interest in planning one's own educational experiences; and begin to develop a system of values. Based on these characteristics, he recommended that teachers in middle schools should emphasize making learning functional to the student, provide learning experiences that develop social contact and responsibility, and include material on environmentally relevant issues in the classroom.

Peer Groups in Secondary Schools

In secondary schools, one can usually find diverse peer groups such as the "leading crowd," the "brains," and the "wild ones." Among these groups an informal hierarchy will exist so that everyone will know which group has the greatest prestige and which the least. The group, with its common values, gives the individual an identity and a sense of belonging (Smilansky 1991).

Not all students, of course, are members of groups; some never become identified with any particular clique, but remain on the fringe, perhaps with one or two friends, perhaps not. These are the "Outs," and their marginal positions may have deleterious effects. Some of these individuals may have no need for group association; but for others, this lack of group identity will affect self-confidence and may retard the normal process of social and emotional development (Tucker-Ladd 1990).

Part of the importance the peer group assumes for the adolescent has been documented by James Coleman (1961) in a study of student bodies in eleven different high schools. Even though the schools were carefully picked to reflect a wide range of differences in terms of the size of the community and the social-class backgrounds of the students, there was considerable agreement on major values from one adolescent group to the next as expressed in responses to questionnaires. Thus, for boys, the importance of being a "brilliant scholar" was secondary to be-

ing a "star athlete" in all schools in the study; and, for girls, it was less important than being an "activities leader." For both sexes, it was better to be popular than to be intellectually outstanding.

Coleman summarized his data, at one point, in the following terms: "Despite wide differences in parental background, type of community, and type of school, there was little difference in the standards of prestige, the activities which confer status, and the values which focus attention and interest. In particular, good grades and academic achievement had relatively low status in all schools" (Coleman 1959, 338).

Coleman's conclusion regarding widespread peer de-emphasis on academics at secondary schools in the United States has been supported in a number of later studies, including research conducted by Cusick (1983) and by Clasen and Brown (1986). The latter researchers studied a suburban junior high school and identified the major types of peer groups or crowds as consisting of "Brains," "Dirtballs/toughs," "Jocks," "Populars," "Unpopulars," and "Unknowns." Their overall conclusion was that

crowd pressure needs to be considered in regard to school performance. Brains, who do best in school, reported receiving significantly more pressure from peers toward school involvement than did dirtballs and unpopulars. . . . Pressures regarding misconduct also seem to play an important role in school performance. Both jocks and dirtballs reported perceiving significantly more pressure to be involved in misconduct activities, such as drinking, smoking, sex, and vandalism, than did brains. Conversely, brains perceived significantly more pressure against misconduct. . . . There does not seem to be a commitment to outstanding school performance on the part of the student body as a whole. If academic performance is to improve for all, educators must attend to this inertia. (Clasen and Brown 1986, 11–12)

Coleman's general conclusions regarding the sources of popularity in secondary schools also were supported in the national data collected as part of the Study of Schooling mentioned earlier in this chapter. Kenneth Tye (1985) has analyzed the responses junior high students included in the study provided when asked to identify the most popular types of students in their schools. As shown in Table 5-2, 37 percent said "good-looking students," 23 percent pointed to "athletes," 15 percent specified "gang members," and only 14 percent selected "smart students." However, the distribution of responses varied considerably from school to school and community to community.

Penelope Eckert (1989) also has collected data on the major groupings of students that were apparent at five high schools in suburban Detroit. The two largest groups consisted, on the one hand, of active, "leading crowd" students who "enthusiastically participate" in and "receive the sponsorship" of the school and, on the other, of alienated students who "reject the hegemony of the school and in turn feel largely rejected" (Eckert 1989, 2). (Using terminology she found widespread among the students, Eckert referred to these groups as "Jocks" and "Burnouts," respectively.) As shown in Table 5-3, students who participated enthusiastically in clubs, student government, athletics, and other school activities were disproportionately enrolled in more difficult academic classes, whereas alienated students (who were disproportionately

TABLE 5-2 *Junior High Students' Responses When Asked to Identify the Most Popular Students in Their Schools*

Response	Percentage
Good-looking students	37
Athletes	23
Gang members	15
Smart students	14
Members of student government	08
Wealthy students	03

Source: Adapted from Tye 1985.

working-class in family background) tended to enroll in less difficult academic courses, vocational subjects, and elective courses. What the alienated students tended to learn in school, Eckert also reported, is "how to be marginalized. . . . [They tend] to regard the academic classroom as a center of received knowledge of no great relevance" and to reject the norms of an institution that fails to provide them with a "meaningful experience" (Eckert 1989, 181–183).

The School as a Reference Group

Among people who interact again and again, certain norms develop and tend to influence the behavior of these people. This is the *reference-group postulate*, and it can be seen to operate especially in secondary schools. This postulate leads to the hypothesis that a school from which most of the pupils will graduate and go to college would influence its pupils to adopt this pattern of behavior, whereas a school whose pupils drop out early would influence pupils to drop out.

Where an entire school is seen as a reference group, it must be assumed that students and teachers have a general consensus about the desirable forms and outcomes of the school program. There may be subgroups of students who do not share this consensus, but they have little prestige and little power. The average student feels a pressure from the school as a whole to adopt certain attitudes about education, or clothing, or career, or political activities. Examples are a school with a strong tradition of musical and dramatic performance that will lead its students to value music and dramatics and a school with a strong athletic record that will lead its students to value sports, both as participants and spectators.

However, the majority of schools probably are too heterogeneous to view as reflecting the presence of a single, predominant reference group. Instead, there are multiple reference groups within the school, and an individual student will tend to be influenced by the one with which he or she identifies and interacts most strongly. Some students may be influenced by a

TABLE 5-3 *Percentage Distribution of Suburban Male and Female Active and Alienated Students by Type of Courses*

	More Difficult Academic Courses	Less Difficult Academic Courses	Vocational Courses	Miscellaneous Elective Courses*
Male actives	76	12	5	7
Female actives	81	7	0	13
Male alienated	36	23	33	9
Female alienated	19	35	9	37

Source: Adapted from Eckert 1989.
* Miscellaneous elective courses include art, business, foreign language and music
Note: Percentages do not add to 100 due to rounding. In Eckert's terminology the active students are Jocks and the alienated students are Burnouts.

group of peers who reinforce antiacademic aspirations or values; others may be influenced primarily by friends who stress academics or extracurricular activities.

Reference-Group Influence on College Attendance.   Because high school graduation and college attendance are becoming more and more frequent, especially for middle-class students, it might be expected that high schools with a substantial middle-class population would exert a reference-group effect on their students to cause them to graduate from high school and go to college. A study of high school seniors in the Kansas City metropolitan area was designed to test this hypothesis.

The high school seniors in nearly all of the high schools of the Kansas City area were asked by Levine, Mitchell, and Havighurst (1970) to answer a questionnaire in the spring of their senior year, telling about their home backgrounds and telling whether they expected to enter college the next autumn. The fifty-five high schools in the study were categorized as described in Table 7-8.

The college expectations of those high school seniors were related to the socioeconomic composition of their school, as well as to the socioeconomic status of their families. For example, students from middle-class families who attend various types of high schools show decreasing percentages planning to enter college

as we go down from "middle-class" to "socially comprehensive" to "working-class" type schools, and the same rule applies to students from lower middle-class families. This is true for both sexes.

Very similar finding were reported by Alan Wilson (1959) from his study of college aspirations of boys in eight public schools in Oakland, California. More recently, Alexander and McDill (1976) and Hallinan and Williams (1990) confirmed the importance of peer influences in affecting the college aspirations and orientations of high school students. Analyzing 1964 and 1965 data on both male and female students at twenty high schools, Alexander and McDill found that peer relations along with a student's previous academic performance have "considerable unique importance . . . in the determination of subjective orientations to school and schooling" (p. 976). Successful academic performance and "acquiring friends who evidence college plans" appeared to "reinforce or induce commitment to scholarship, a sense of competence and high educational goals" (p. 976). In follow-up research designed to extend Alexander and McDill's study, Alexander, Cook, and McDill (1977) showed that peer relations in the junior high school played a large part in determining whether students later enrolled in college-preparatory curricula and reported friendships leading subsequently to high aspirations, high achievement, and enrollment in college. Hallinan and Williams examined the subsequent careers of high-school seniors and found that peer influence has an important effect on their college plans and enrollment. Thus, available data continue to suggest that association with middle-status peers can help improve the college aspirations and plans of low-status students.

In addition, there also is reason to believe that peer influence on the college plans and aspirations of high school students frequently operates through an intervening mechanism, namely the curriculum placement or type of curriculum in which a student is enrolled. According to this theory, students enrolled in a college-preparatory curriculum come into contact with highly motivated peers who reinforce their own motivation to succeed in high school and go to college. Students in noncollege tracks associate mostly with less motivated peers and are not reinforced in their academic aspirations. Stress on curriculum placement as a factor influencing subsequent academic plans is compatible with data showing that peers play an important part in determining college plans and expectations.

Because middle-class students are more likely than low-status students to enroll in college-preparatory programs, it frequently is argued that discriminatory placement is one means by which the middle class maintains its advantage over the working class. That is, it is argued that school counselors and other decision makers in the educational selection system place middle-status students of a given ability level in college tracks more frequently than low-status students with the same academic ability and history. Critics of the educational system argue that this gives middle-status students the benefit of more highly motivated peers and thereby functions to perpetuate the social structure (Vanfossen, Jones, and Spade 1987). Other observers disagree and argue that curriculum placement gives little or no advantage to middle-status students after taking account of background, ability, previous academic performance, and type of academic program (Gamoran 1986b; Bryk, Lee, and Smith 1990).

The evidence on this issue is somewhat mixed. Rehberg and Rosenthal (1975) reviewed the results of four major studies and concluded that most showed the high school to be basically meritocratic (i.e., curriculum placement depended on ability rather than social background). They also concluded that high schools probably were more meritocratic in this regard in the 1960s and 1970s than was true in earlier periods. On the other hand, these results were not consistent across all studies, and Alexander and McDill's (1976) study indicated that socioeconomic background was more important than academic ability in predicting curriculum placement. Alexander and McDill concluded that "curriculum differentiation may indeed serve as an important mechanism for maintaining status advantages through the educational system" (p. 973), in part by giving middle-status students more access than low-status students to highly motivated peers. The contradictory nature of research on this issue in turn suggests that counselors and other school faculty should be careful not to help steer working-class students away from college-preparatory courses without very good reasons for doing so.

Extracurricular Activities

It has been difficult to determine whether participation in extracurricular activities benefits students in other aspects of their development. The main reason for this difficulty involves uncertainty regarding cause and effect. Research has shown, for example, that students with a high participation level have higher grades than do nonparticipating students (see Table 5-4). However, students who have high grades are more likely to participate than are students with low grades (Holland and Andre 1988; Lewis 1989b). Thus, research must consider whether participation leads to or reflects high grades, or whether there may be a reciprocal relationship between the two variables.

In addition, students high in socioeconomic status are more likely to participate in extracurricular activities than are those low on this variable. As shown in Table 5-4, this pattern held among 1982 high school seniors for ten of eleven activities for which participation rates were surveyed; the only activity in which socioeconomic status and participation were inversely correlated was "Vocational Education Clubs." However, it is difficult to determine whether high status has a causal, independent effect on extracurricular participation, because status also is related to grades in school.

A considerable amount of research on the effects of participation in extracurricular activities has been conducted in the past twenty years. For example, Braddock (1981) studied data from the National Longitudinal Survey of high school students moving into adulthood and concluded that for both white and black males, participation in high-school athletics is positively associated (controlling for ability and social-class background) with grades, academic self-esteem, educational plans, college enrollment, and college attainment. Using the same data, Hanks (1979) found that participation in athletics had a much smaller effect on the college enrollment of females than males, and that the influence of athletic participation on college enrollment is mediated by the influence of college-oriented peers. Recent data also indicate that participation in athletics can reduce dropout rates among minority students and improve college attendance among disadvantaged minority students (Mallozzi 1989; Nettles 1990). Brown, Kohrs, and Lazarro (1991) collected and analyzed data on students in California and Wisconsin and reported that participation in various extracurricular activities has a small but independent effect in terms of improving academic performance. Otto (1982) has reviewed the research in this area and reached the following conclusions:

Participation in extracurricular activities contributes to a number of important social and behavioral outcomes measured as late as fifteen years after high school. Though the magnitude of the effect is modest, the breadth of effect on later life outcomes is remarkable. No consistent evidence indicates that participation . . . has negative effects on the variables measured.

. . . Several explanations have been offered. One is that useful content is learned—

TABLE 5-4 *Percentages of 1982 High-School Seniors Participating in Extracurricular Activities by Grade Point Average and Socioeconomic Status*

Activity	Socioeconomic Status			G.P.A.				
	High Quartile	Middle Quartile	Low Quartile	2.00 or Less	2.01–2.50	2.51–3.00	3.01–3.50	2.50–4.00
Any activity	85	79	75	68	76	81	88	96
Varsity athletics	44	35	29	30	34	35	40	42
Cheerleaders, pep clubs, majorettes	14	15	12	9	12	13	18	21
Debate or drama	19	12	9	9	11	13	18	19
Band or orchestra	16	15	10	9	11	14	19	23
Chorus or dance	22	19	18	18	19	19	21	24
Hobby clubs	21	21	18	21	20	20	16	16
Honorary clubs	25	14	9	3	3	7	32	75
Newspaper, magazine, or yearbook	25	17	15	9	14	20	24	33
Subject-matter clubs	22	20	20	16	17	18	26	37
Student council, government, political clubs	23	15	12	8	12	16	23	31
Vocational education clubs	14	22	39	23	27	24	22	20

Source: Sweet 1986

"attitudes," "capacities,"... or "interpersonal skills."... A second is that participation gives a young person visibility and important future "contacts."... A third explanation is that participation in extracurricular activities, especially athletics, elevates a students' peer status.... A fourth explanation is that some individuals are born achievers.... None of these explanations, however, has been supported by research.... [A fifth explanation that does have research support is that] students assess their achievement potential, set their own goals, and significant others provide encouragement to them on the basis of the youth's past performance in extracurricular activities as well as performance in the formal academic curriculum. (Otto 1982, 224–225)

Educators and researchers also have been trying to determine why many students do not participate in extracurricular activities and what can be done to encourage greater involvement. Thus, some researchers have concluded that preschool children who lack good coordination or have poor physical skills tend to avoid athletic activities and show a general disinclination to participate by age eight or nine (Nelson 1989). At age eleven or twelve nonparticipation rates increase as many students conclude that they are unable to compete with talented peers (Watkins and Montgomery 1989). Experts in physical education and school sports believe that participation can be increased if students are given appropriate instruction, encouragement, and opportunities to develop their athletic and social skills (Nelson 1989).

Such conclusions have great importance for educators because participation in extracurricular activities frequently is more manipulable than many other variables related to educational outcomes. For example, we have pointed out that home environment is related to student aspirations, but influencing or changing home environment is difficult and expensive. Facilitating participation in extracurricular activities may be one of the most feasible steps educators can take to improve students' aspirations and attainments (Holland and Andre 1988).

THE PEER GROUP AND THE COMMUNITY

The discussion in this chapter has indicated that the peer group is one of the major forces in the socialization of children and youth. In conjunction with the family, the school, and other institutions, it helps prepare the young for the society in which they will live. Relationships between the peer group and other social institutions change over time. Understanding of the nature and implications of these changes is important in developing policies to prepare children and youth for adulthood (Ianni 1989a, 1989b; Ascher and Coie 1990).

Many sociologists believe that the most important of these changes is that the community of traditional small towns and villages became the society of the industrial and postindustrial periods. Population multiplied and became urbanized, contacts between people became impersonal, young people as well as adults found it easier to travel outside one's immediate vicinity, and large organizations replaced the network of families and small units that were responsible for the conduct of economic activity within the relatively narrow boundaries of the traditional community. As noted in Chapter 3, the family and the community were much more intertwined in traditional settings than generally is true today. Most social activity involved interaction with nearby kin and neighbors, and the community was knit together through churches and interdependent economic enterprises. The family and the community in this setting were hardly separable.

Another characteristic of many traditional communities was that the school functioned directly under the influence of the community and, frequently, the church. In many such communities, only a few years of schooling were provided for most youngsters, through church schools organized to propagate local religious beliefs. Even where the schools were formally independent of the church, they frequently taught religious doctrine that was most prominent in the surrounding community (Luke 1989).

The peer group in traditional settings clearly functioned as one of the community's institutions for socializing the young. Peer associations frequently were formed through the church and the school, and many youth activities were organized through the church, but peer groups independent of the church and the school also functioned to socialize youth in the traditions of the community. Peer groups played an important part, as they do today, in governing courtship and sexual relationships among youth, but the morality they developed and transmitted was more clearly attuned to local community standards than is true today (Shorter 1975; Chartier 1989).

The network in which the peer group functions is now very different from what it was in traditional society. Where formerly the peer group, the family, the church, and the school tended to operate in a complementary and reinforcing manner to prepare youth for roles in a specific community, today the major socializing institutions transmit much more divergent influences reflecting their specialized roles within the wider society. The family still is responsible for preparing children to participate in society, but much of its former educational function has been taken over by the school. The church has become much less important in socialization than it used to be, though it still is a major influence in the lives of many youth (Cremin 1977; Kamarck and Galston 1990).

More youngsters of a given age group live near one another in an urbanized than a rural setting, leading to an expansion in the size of peer societies and with this expansion greater autonomy from local adult institutions. Most important, mass media such as television, radio, and films have become key factors in disseminating cultural understandings among young people, but attitudes and values developed through these channels do not necessarily reflect those of the family, the church, the school, or other institutions in the local community. Instead, they frequently constitute the core of a distinctive youth culture that has become a relatively autonomous segment of the larger society. Historian Lawrence A. Cremin has summarized much of this transformation in discussing changes that have occurred in the "relationships among educative institutions":

> *As the household declined in size and influence, the school increased in holding power and effect. And the school's new potency was both direct and indirect. On the one hand, children spent more time with their teachers and were doubtless more profoundly influenced by them. . . . On the other hand, children, and particularly adolescents, also spent more time with one another, creating a newly powerful element in their education, namely, the peer group. Children had always had friends, to be sure; but now there was a discernible age-structured group that gathered daily in a particular institution, the school. Moreover, that group became the target of special films, special radio programs, and special advertising campaigns for special products; put otherwise, that group became a special market clientele, which was systematically taught styles of dress, entertainment, and . . . consumption. The household mediated this educative influence to some extent, but the influence was powerful nonetheless and in many ways competed with the purposeful efforts of parents, pastors, and school teachers. (Cremin 1977, 111)*

These generalizations are, of course, greatly oversimplified. Relationships between socializing institutions varied from one community and one time period to another. At some times and locations, such as the early industrial period in England, the apprenticeship system played a major part in the socialization of youth. Libraries, museums, and other cultural institutions have been and remain an important factor in socialization. Arrangements varied among religious groups, social classes, and ethnic segments within a given community. Some families still exercise predominant influence over all aspects of socialization through adolescence, and some families in traditional communities exercised so little influence that laws had to be passed requiring them to supervise their children (Cremin 1977). The organization and the role of the peer group vary greatly according to whether it is sponsored or facilitated by another institution and the degree to which its members are free to come in contact with other young people (Ianni 1989b). Nevertheless, a fundamental change has occurred in industrial and postindustrial society, wherein the peer group has tended to become a more important influence, and the family, the church, and the community have lost some of their control over socialization. Some implications of this change are explored further in the following chapter.

Inner-City Peer Groups

In recent years, it has become apparent that the peer group among underclass youth in the inner city is a critical component in socialization processes that frequently lead to the formation of an antisocial street culture and hamper efforts to improve education for young people in concentrated poverty areas (Anderson 1989; Ianni 1989b). Chapters 1, 3, 7, and 8 describe the difficulties that parents and other socializing institutions confront in working to provide a constructive environment for growing up in these neighborhoods and present some of the data indicating that delinquent gangs constitute a major problem for parents and teachers in the inner city. The role of delinquent peer groups has been described in Williams and Kornblum's study of children and youth in four inner-city communities:

> The child who is afraid to fight faces endless threats: money is extorted; bicycles are taken away. . . . Under these conditions, parents naturally seek to protect their children, most often by keeping them home, calling them from work, and begging them to stay off the streets. But this is a losing proposition as the kids reach adolescence and turn to the peer group for protection and identity. . . . In some situations a peer group may develop into what youth call a crew, the contemporary descendant of the adolescent fighting gangs of the 1950s and 1960s. . . . The root cause of the formation of a crew is a pressing need of some sort: money, protection, recognition, success. For poor teens, all of these things are hard to come by. (Williams and Kornblum 1985, 74–75)

Recognizing the importance and the destructiveness of much peer-group behavior among underclass youth in the big cities, many community leaders and educators are trying to bring about improvements in the environment in which inner-city children and youth grow up and go to school (Ianni 1989b). The best known effort in this direction has been initiated by Reverend Jesse L. Jackson and the People United to Save Humanity (PUSH) organization he founded in December 1971. By 1978, PUSH had outlined a program for improvement in education that was being initiated in parts of Chicago, Detroit, Hartford, Kansas City, Los Angeles, New Orleans, Washington, and other big cities. Although not necessarily limited to minority or inner-city neighborhoods, the PUSH Program for Excellence is aimed particularly at improving the socializing and educative environments and institutions for minority youth in concentrated poverty neighborhoods. Evaluation of PUSH work with schools indicated that participating students had improved in motivation and self-concept (Nettles 1990).

Efforts of PUSH and some other organizations trying to improve the environment for inner-city youngsters are promising because they are based on an explicit identification of the harmful influences that destroy so many children and youth in concentrated poverty neighborhoods. Jackson has repeatedly pointed out that improvements in academic performance among youth in the inner city depend on a concerted effort of all major socializing agents.

Parents, he insists, must exercise more control over their children, for example by turning off the television at least two hours each night while children study. Recognizing the traditional importance of the church among black families in the United States, he argues that ministers must play a central part in working with parents and teachers to improve the environment for growing up in the inner city. Peer-group influence must become positive rather than negative, with "Peace Brothers and Sisters" organized as monitors and supervisors of behavior in inner-city schools, and "teams of students" functioning to instill pride and achievement in academics in the same way that peer groups now emphasize nonacademic values such as excellence in athletics or antiacademic behavior such as truancy or delinquency. Teachers and administrators must join with the community to improve the effectiveness of instruction and overcome negative influences in the environment. Nor are the mass media neglected: local disc jockeys and other persons exercising influence over inner-city youth through the media also must be involved in establishing a constructive environment for growing up (Eubanks and Levine 1977).

The most striking thing about the PUSH Program for Excellence is its recognition that inner-city youth suffer so severely from fragmentation among the major socializing institutions in modern society. Parents and teachers generally try to provide a positive environment, but the peer group, the mass media, and other influences in the inner-city setting have defeated their efforts to socialize children for mobility in a modern society. Inner-city youth have been particularly victimized by socialization forces that work at cross-purposes: the school versus the streets; parents versus peers. Jesse Jackson perceives the problem in these terms and wants to enclose the inner-city child in a "love triangle" bounded by home, the school, and the church.

It is not all clear whether the PUSH Program for Excellence or other comparable efforts will or even can succeed in greatly improving the socialization of youth in the inner city. It is possible that no solution short of large-scale deconcentration of the population in big-city poverty neighborhoods will succeed in making the inner city a constructive environment in which to grow

up for most children who now live there. Newspaper columnist William Raspberry summarized both the promise and the inherent difficulty of PUSH-type efforts when he wrote that

that sense of entrapment in love may have been a good deal easier to achieve in tiny Greenville, N.C. (pop: about 12,000 when Mr. Jackson was born there in 1941) than in the teeming cities where uprootedness and unconnectedness combine to produce the very anomie Mr. Jackson is trying to attack.

To a significant degree, what he is proposing is the establishment of small towns in the city, a series of caring communities in which every adult is parent to every child.

Jesse Jackson is, in short, proposing a miracle. And yet, with a little luck and a lot of focused commitment, it could take hold. Not that thugs would suddenly become young gentlemen and hallrovers instant scholars.

But it just may be possible to reestablish in the classrooms a situation where serious scholarship, mutual respect and discipline are the norm, and where peer pressure serves to reinforce that norm.

It certainly is worth trying.*

Youth-Serving Agencies

The peer group is so important to children and youth that adult society attempts to work through it whenever the opportunity appears. This is especially noteworthy in the case of churches and of youth-serving organizations.

Religion-Oriented Agencies. Besides the youth organizations of individual churches, several large-scale organizations have a religious orientation and have had broad support from religious groups. Chief among these are the Young Men's

---

*William Raspberry, "The discipline revival," *Washington Post,* February 2, 1976. Used with permission of the *Washington Post.*

Christian Association (YMCA), Young Women's Christian Association (YWCA), and the Jewish Community Centers. These organizations all provide settings for the social and physical development of boys and girls, settings in which the aim is to promote character development. Usually such an organization will have a building with gymnasium, swimming pool, indoor recreational facilities, and, often, dormitory quarters for older youth.

Originally these agencies were widely separated from the school. They offered programs on Saturdays and on weekdays in after-school hours. Then, about 1915, the YMCA began experimenting with clubs of in-school youth at the secondary school level. Many of the club leaders were high-school teachers. The Hi-Y Clubs thus formed were often closely associated with the school program, even though their meetings were generally held in YMCA buildings or in members' homes. A boy did not usually need to be a member of the YMCA to belong to a Hi-Y Club. In communities that did not have a YWCA, the YMCA launched into work with girls. There, Tri-Hi-Y clubs for both boys and girls were started. Later, a type of boys' club at the grade school level was formed, under the name of Gra-Y. Often these clubs met in the school building after school hours.

The YMCA has grown into a huge organization, with programs and buildings around the world to serve men and boys of various ages. The other organizations have also grown tremendously, and all have strong programs for the social and physical development of youth. The specific religious emphasis of earlier programs has tended to decrease, concomitant with the growing secularization in the middle class.

Since 1940, a new group of religion-oriented youth organizations has emerged. These are nonsectarian, with a Protestant Fundamentalist theology. They encourage their young people to carry the Bible with them to meetings and to rely on it entirely for religious guidance, without using other books that might favor one interpretation of Christian theology over another. Organizations of this type include Youth for Christ,

Young Life, and Campus Crusade for Christ. Meetings are held on Sundays and weekdays; there is a social as well as a religious fellowship; and summer camps provide an important part of the program. Possibly, these new organizations perform somewhat the same functions that were performed by the YMCA and YWCA in earlier years, before the latter organizations became more secular in orientation.

Other Agencies.   An important group of youth-serving agencies has less specifically religious motivation. These agencies are primarily interested in bringing adults into active and supportive relations with youth peer groups. There are, for example, the Boy Scouts, Girl Scouts, Camp Fire, Girl Reserves, Junior Achievement, Junior Optimist, Key Club (sponsored by Kiwanis), and DeMolay (sponsored by the Masonic Order). Somewhat similar to these are such organizations as the 4-H Clubs, Future Farmers of America, Future Homemakers of America, and Junior Grange. In general, these organizations do not have buildings of their own but form small units under local leaders and meet in churches, community centers, schools, and homes.

In the big cities, a number of youth-serving organizations have been established in underprivileged areas (Ianni 1989b). For example, settlement houses, in addition to providing recreational facilities for boys and girls whether they are club members or not, usually organize clubs for children and adolescents. Boys Clubs and Girls Clubs have been established in many urban neighborhoods. The sponsors and financial supporters of these agencies are usually people of middle-class or upper-class status who give time and money to provide better opportunities for underprivileged and other youth. These organizations seldom have any connection with the schools, and they serve children from both public and parochial schools.

Changes in Youth-Serving Organizations

The earliest youth-serving agencies were designed for boys and girls aged about twelve to sixteen. It was expected that boys and girls of these ages wanted to associate with each other outside of the family circle and under the leadership of adults who were neither parents nor teachers. In most of these agencies, boys and girls were organized into separate groups.

On this basis, there was a tremendous growth of youth-serving organizations with the bulk of the membership aged twelve to fifteen. By age fifteen there was a tendency for boys and girls to drop out of these organizations, in spite of vigorous efforts by leaders to keep them as members (Macleod 1983). Programs were developed for older youth, such as the Explorers (Boy Scouts). Some of these groups kept the sexes separated; others included both sexes. With more and more young people staying in school through the twelfth grade, and with many having no after-school employment, there is clearly a large pool of youth aged fifteen to eighteen or twenty who have a good deal of spare time, yet who do not take part in youth organizations. It has become a major source of concern to the leaders of youth-serving organizations to do a better job of holding youth in the middle and late teens.

At the same time, there has been a downward reach of youth-serving agencies into the age range from age seven or eight to twelve, and some, such as Camp Fire, include infants and young children. This is accomplished partly by lowering the entrance age in some organizations. Responding to rapid increase in the employment of mothers with young children, the Girl Scouts changed its rules to allow for entry of five-year-olds (Neugarten and Neugarten 1987; Drucker 1989).

More generally, however, this is done by organizing services for younger children in conjunction with the child's family. The Boy Scouts, for instance, organized the Cub Scouts, with a Den Mother in charge of a group of six- to ten-year-olds, a woman who generally has her own son in the group. The Girl Scouts organized the Brownies on a similar basis. In addition, the Girl Scouts started special programs for preschool girls in Head Start (Helgesen 1990). The YMCA not only has organized classes for boys and girls as young as nine to ten, but it has also started the Indian Guide and Indian Princess units for younger children, with fathers and mothers leading the groups that meet in their homes.

This downward reach of youth-serving agencies into middle childhood probably reflects two attitudes on the part of parents; first, the realization that the peer group, if left unaided and unwatched by adults, either would not develop adequately or would move in directions opposed to adult norms (Ianni 1989b). Second, it reflects the intense desire of middle-class parents that their children become socially well adjusted during the elementary school period (Macleod 1983).

Most youth-serving organizations increased in membership during the 1950s and 1960s as the number of young people in the United States rose dramatically, and then declined in the 1970s as the baby-boom generation moved into adulthood. The Boy Scouts, for example, reached a high of 4.8 million members in 1972 but then dropped to 3.1 million in 1979. However, youth-serving organizations generally stabilized their membership in the 1980s, and some have registered gains: membership in the Boy Scouts now is back above 4 million (Whitman 1991).

Key factors in reversing the membership decline apparently include:

- A greater willingness among children and youth to participate in adult-sponsored activities.
- Contributions from active volunteers.
- Reduced antagonism toward authority figures.
- Recent increase in the number of children and youth related to immigration and to child-bearing among adult baby boomers.
- An increased organizational effort to provide appropriate services for contemporary youth (Drucker 1989; Whitman 1991).

Along these lines, the 4–H Clubs have reached out to disadvantaged students in urban areas (only about 20 percent of 4–H members now live on farms), and the Girl Scouts teach urban survival skills, such as shopping at the supermarket. In 1970, the Girl Scouts were predominantly white. By 1989, the proportion of black girls who participated had increased rapidly and matched that of white girls (Drucker 1989; Byrne 1990).

Some of these trends have been apparent in the recent history of the Boy Scouts. During the early 1970s, the Boy Scouts attempted to enhance their appeal and service to urban youth by reducing emphasis on outdoor skills that had exemplified scouting since the organization was founded in 1907. However, this change in direction seemed to reduce the organization's attractiveness and membership. Participation in scouting has been increasing since the original emphasis on outdoor skills was restored in 1979. Now, many Boy Scout units emphasize urban topics, such as analysis of traffic, environmentalism, and avoidance of drug abuse, along with traditional outdoor skills (Whitman 1991).

Similar trends and difficulties have been reported for other youth-serving organizations. Konopka (1977) studied a group of adolescent girls and found that 83 percent had belonged at one time to a youth organization but had dis-affiliated. The primary reasons given for dropping out were that activities were childish or boring, adult leaders were domineering, or groups were too large for close personal contact. In a report prepared for the Ford Foundation, Lipsitz (1977) reviewed these and other data and concluded that adult-supervised youth organizations "have been unsuccessful in adjusting to the social dilemmas of our urban and ethnic post-industrial society" (p. 173).

Although this interpretation was somewhat exaggerated and premature, it underlines the need for youth-serving agencies to modify existing programs and services. One unanswered question is whether traditional youth organizations can be very helpful to young people who historically have had relatively low participation rates, such as working-class, minority youth in big cities (Whitman 1991). Related to this question is the issue of whether public funds or money collected through united-charity solicitations should be diverted to new organizations established to help young people not currently served. If the traditional organizations are not successful in revising their approach to reflect change in society, then other institutions may have to be established to help in the socialization of youth, especially beginning in the teenage years when many young people are now disaffiliating in favor of informal peer groups. Lipsitz offered the following six recommendations to improve the effectiveness of existing organizations:

1. Allowing adolescents to participate actively in planning and executing youth projects;
2. Furnishing opportunities for adolescents to discuss their problems;
3. Establishing coed activities;
4. Reducing organizational structure to leave groups small, informal, and fairly autonomous;
5. Active recruiting of "youth in trouble"; and particularly,
6. Encouraging significant participation in the public life of the community. (Lipsitz 1977, 181)

Phelps (1980) pointed out that many youth-serving agencies have begun to make changes in directions specified above. For example, the Boy Scouts began admitting girls to full membership in its Explorer division in 1971, and both Future Homemakers and Camp Fire have become coeducational. In addition, women are now allowed to serve as leaders of Boy Scout troops (Kimmel 1988). The Boys Clubs of America officially became the Boys and Girls Clubs of America in 1990. Many organizations, such as Future Homemakers, Camp Fire, and the YWCA, also have begun asking youth members to serve on their major decision-making bodies, at both the local and the national levels. Some local chapters of national organizations have initiated peer counseling programs. The Girl Scouts, Camp Fire, and other organizations are doing more than they previously did to reach youth who are delinquent or self-destructive, and the Girls Clubs of America has initiated projects to help develop interests in science and math (Nicholson and Hamm 1990). Phelps concluded that "in recent years, through profound reexamination of purpose, through restructuring organizations and programs, and sometimes through sheer will and determination, the major youth organizations have begun to reach larger numbers and more diverse groups of young people" (1980, 113).

Benefits of Participation in the Boys and Girls Clubs

Effects of participation in youth-serving organizations have seldom been studied comprehensively and scientifically, but available data suggest that such participation is beneficial for many children and youth. For example, the Boys Clubs of America (now called the Boys and Girls Clubs) commissioned a study by the Louis Harris polling organization and found that alumni reported the following perceptions (Boys Clubs of America 1985):

- Nine of every ten reported that Boys Clubs had a positive effect on their lives.
- Hispanic alumni as well as those who grew up in low-income communities were among the most likely to report a positive impact.
- Six of every ten alumni reported that they had few other options for constructive activity outside of school.
- Eight of ten believed that participation had enhanced their ability to work with other people.
- Three of every four alumni believed that participation had helped avoid difficulty with the law.
- Eighty percent reported benefits in terms of health and fitness.
- A substantial majority reported that participation had improved their leadership skills.

OUT-OF-SCHOOL SERVICES FOR CHILDREN AND ADOLESCENTS

Private and public youth-serving agencies historically have offered a variety of services and programs for children and youth. Activities conducted at community centers and neighborhood facilities typically have ranged from athletics and arts to leadership training and scholarly hobbies. After-school and weekend programs have played an important role in providing older children and adolescents with opportunities for learning to function away from the familiar settings of the home and the school, usually in conjunction with other young people in their community. Participation is voluntary, and participants typically engage in activities that teach both cooperation and self-discipline. These opportunities have become more important as the proportion of working mothers has increased, thus helping generate more of a void in supervision of adolescents in the after-school hours before parents return home (Heath and McLaughlin 1991).

Elliott Medrich and his colleagues conducted a study to determine how sixth-grade children in Oakland, California, spend their time after school. They found that the average distribution of time was as follows: television viewing—three to four hours a day; activities "on their own" (alone or unsupervised with friends)—two to three hours a day; activities with parents—less than 1½ hours per day; chores and responsibilities—less than one hour a day; and participation in organized recreational and cultural activities supervised by adults—four to five hours a week. They also found that about 20 percent of the children did not participate in organized activities, a few were very heavily involved in a number of activities, and nearly 80 percent participated in at least one organized activity during the school year. Level of participation was not much related to social class, but upper-status children tended to participate in activities that required significant fees and parent involvement (particularly regarding transportation), whereas lower-income children depended more on free activities at nearby locations. Medrich has summarized some of the fundamental conclusions and implications of the study:

> Over several generations community services for children have developed very successful ways of meeting a wide variety of needs for a large proportion of the young adolescent population. In our survey, almost 80 percent took advantage of community-sponsored organized activities on a regular basis; well over 60 percent used parks and schoolyards for unstructured activities; and 43 percent used neighborhood public libraries on their own. . . .
>
> Despite the obvious importance of community facilities for the young, there is reason to believe that children's interests and activity patterns are being compromised as communities respond to economic auster-

> ity . . . and the needs of children, the kinds of after-school programs described here are in great jeopardy. Ironically . . . [retrenchment comes] at a time when more and more families have a greater need for the services. . . .
>
> Reductions will not affect all children to the same degree. Those from lower-income homes who can least afford private or fee-paying alternatives will be left with the fewest opportunities (Medrich 1982, 33, 36, 37)

Conclusions Medrich and his colleagues reached concerning out-of-school activities have been mostly reinforced and confirmed by data from the National Education Longitudinal Study (NELS) of eighth graders (Hafner, Ingels, Schneider, and Stevenson 1990). Based on questionnaires administered to a nationally representative sample, NELS researchers

TABLE 5-5 *Percentage of Eighth Graders Participating in Out-of-School Activities, by Race/Ethnicity and Socioeconomic Status*

									Activity
Race/Ethnicity*	Any	Scouting	Boys' or Girls' Clubs or Neighborhood Clubs	Y or Other Youth Groups	4-H	Religious Youth Groups	Hobby Clubs	Summer Programs	Nonschool Team Sports
African American	66	20	47	23	14	30	22	30	34
Asian/Pacific	68	13	21	13	05	27	17	24	32
Hispanic	60	11	27	14	06	25	16	20	31
Native American	61	17	36	16	10	28	21	22	34
White	74	14	19	14	09	37	14	17	39
*Socioeconomic Status**									
Lowest quartile	60	13	29	14	11	23	16	17	30
25–49 percent	69	14	24	16	10	30	15	17	36
50–74 percent	74	14	21	15	09	36	15	19	38
Highest quartile	83	16	20	17	07	46	16	25	45
All students	71	14	23	15	09	34	16	19	37

Source: Adapted from Hafner, Ingels, Schneider, and Stevenson 1990.

* "African American" refers to non-Hispanic black students. "White" refers to non-Hispanic white students. "Native American" refers to American Indians, Alaskan Eskimos, and Aleuts.

** Socioeconomic status is measured in terms of mother's and father's occupations, mother's and father's educational levels, and family income.

found a relatively high participation rate: more than 70 percent of eighth-graders report participation in one or more organized activities outside of school. As shown in Table 5-5, the activities cited most frequently by respondents were Nonschool Team Sports and Religious Youth Groups. Scouting, Boys' or Girls' Clubs or Neighborhood Clubs, or Other Youth Groups, and Summer Programs were cited relatively more frequently by African American students than by respondents from other groups, while non-Hispanic white students were relatively most likely to report participation in Religious Youth Groups and Nonschool Team Sports. Unlike Medrick and his colleagues, however, NELS researchers found some strong relationships between social class and participation: high SES students were much more likely to report participation in at least one activity, in Religious Youth Groups, in Summer Programs, and in Nonschool Team Sports, than were low SES students. Conversely, low SES students reported participating relatively more frequently in Boys' or Girls' Clubs or Neighborhood Clubs, perhaps because many low SES students are concentrated in big cities where clubs are accessible.

CONCLUSION

Peer groups play an important part in the socialization of children and youth in school and elsewhere in society. Among the functions served by the peer group are its roles with respect to teaching the culture, helping children learn to live in society, and providing a reference group that affects attitudes and aspirations. Some research indicates that the peer group has become a more important socializing agent today than was true in earlier periods, but research also indicates that the influence of peers as compared with other reference groups depends on a variety of considerations and circumstances.

Recognizing the importance and centrality of peer groups and peer influences in the school, educators have a responsibility to help students establish positive relationships and to benefit from extracurricular activities and opportunities. Other agencies in the community that can help young people and their peer groups develop in positive directions include such traditional youth-serving organizations as the Boy Scouts and the YMCA. In inner-city communities, groups that provide constructive adult influence may help counteract negative forces in the socializing environment of children and youth.

EXERCISES _____

1. Are there any learning experiences offered by the peer group that could *not* be offered by other socializing agencies? Explain.

2. Give an example, from your own experience, in which the peer group's standards of behavior for a child (or adolescent) were at variance with adult standards. What did the child do to resolve the conflict?

3. Thinking back over your own experience as a child, were children in your elementary school more or less democratic as regards social-class differentiations than your high school group? Cite examples.

4. Describe briefly a case in which a boy or girl dropped out of school before graduating. How did the attitudes of classmates toward the child affect his or her decision to leave school? Was there anything the school might have done to change the situation for that child?

5. Have you been in a school that had conflicting peer groups? If so, what were the differences among the groups, and how did the various groups relate to the authority of the school or the teacher?

6. Locate a youth-serving agency in your community and find out how it serves children and youth of different ages, sex, and social class.

7. Select a minority peer group that you know something about and compare the formal and informal teaching within this group to the formal and informal teaching of the school.

8. Many books on classroom management provide instructions for constructing sociograms that show the friendship patterns among students in a class. How might the teacher use a sociogram to identify peer groups in his or her class, and how might this be useful? If you have access to an elementary or junior-high class, construct a sociogram showing the friendship patterns among students and discuss their possible implications for working with particular students.

SUGGESTIONS FOR FURTHER READING

1. Jean Piaget, in *The Moral Judgment of the Child*, describes how children learn through games (and thus through the agency of the group) how rules are made and changed, and how children move through various stages of maturity in the development of moral judgment. See especially Chapter 1. Also, Kohlberg (1966) summarizes his theory of moral development as it is affected by the school.

2. A very useful book of readings edited by Muuss (1971) contains articles on the influence of the peer group in adolescence, especially articles by Brittain, Gronlund, Bronfenbrenner, Costanzo and Shaw, Coleman, and Himes.

3. Edgar Friedenberg in his interestingly written little book, *The Vanishing Adolescent*, sounds a note of caution for those who would like to increase adult control over adolescents. Friedenberg views adolescent conflict with adult society as necessary if the adolescent is to mature and become independent.

4. *The Adolescent Society* by James S. Coleman describes in nontechnical language a study of the students in ten different high schools and the implications for education of the differences between adult and adolescent values.

5. For a review of research on peer socialization in elementary schools, see the article by John C. Glidewell, Mildred B. Kantor, Louis M. Smith, and Lorene H. Stringer, "Socialization and Social Structure in the Classroom."

6. Read C. Wayne Gordon's *The Social System of the High School* for more details of the social organization that exists within a socially comprehensive high school.

7. *Growing up Forgotten* by Joan Lipsitz (1977) includes several chapters dealing partly with research on peer group influences among children and youth.

8. *Rites of Passage* by Joseph F. Kett includes a systematic description of the influence of the peer group, youth-serving agencies, and other institutions affecting the development of adolescents in the United States from colonial days to the 1970s.

9. *Learning to Labour* by Paul Willis describes how peer influence among working-class youth counteracts the efforts of teachers who attempt to raise their educational achievement.

10. David Macleod's outstanding history of the Boy Scouts and other youth-serving organizations draws explicit implications for contemporary practice. Titled *Building Character in the American Boy*, Macleod's book focuses on the period from 1870 to 1920.

11. *Sunday School: The Transformation of an American Institution 1790–1880* describes

the growth of the Sunday school movement and the part it played not just in socialization of children but in helping develop literacy as well.

12. *The Nurturing Neighborhood* by Gerald Sorin recounts the history of an urban Boys Club from 1940 to 1990.

13. *Cooperation and Competition* by David and Roger Johnson (1990) provides a comprehensive analysis and summary of research and practice involving cooperative arrangements to improve classroom learning.

14. *Peer Rejection in Childhood*, edited by Steven Ascher and John Coie (1990), examines the topic from a wide variety of perspectives.

15. Considerations that are important in encouraging adolescents to participate in youth-serving organizations are described in a paper by Heath and McLaughlin (1991).

16. *Friendship in Adolescence and Young Adulthood* by Moshe Smilansky (1991) includes a detailed description of an approach schools and other institutions can use to help adolescents develop peer positive relationships. Smilansky believes that loneliness is a serious problem for many adolescents and that educators and other people who work with youth have a responsibility to help them learn to develop and maintain friendships.

The Transition from Adolescence to Adulthood

The educational system in the United States has come to dominate the lives of most young people. Of the fourteen to seventeen age group, 95 percent were enrolled in school in 1988. Approximately 76 percent of both sexes complete a high school course, and 48 percent enter college. This situation contrasts with the beginning of the century, when only 11 percent of the fourteen to seventeen age group were in school, and only about 3 percent entered college.

Thus, most young people spend much more time in school than did their grandparents, and substantially more than their parents did. This means less time in employment, less time associating with a variety of adults, and more time in what might be called preparing for adult living (Riche 1990). A federal government Panel on Youth described the situation as follows:

> As the labor of children has become unnecessary to society, school has been extended for them. With every decade, the length of schooling has increased, until a thoughtful person must ask whether society can conceive of no other way for youth to come into adulthood. If schooling were a complete environment, the answer would properly be that no amount of school is too much, and increased schooling for the young is the best way for young to spend their increased leisure, and society its increased wealth.
>
> But schooling, as we know, is not a complete environment giving all the necessary opportunities for becoming adult. School is a certain kind of environment: individualistic, oriented toward cognitive achievement, imposing dependency on and withholding authority and responsibility from those in the role of students. So long as school was short, and merely a supplement to the main activities of growing up, this mattered little. But school has expanded to fill the time that other activities once occupied, without substituting for them. These activities of young persons included the opportunities for responsible action, situations in which a youth came to have authority over matters that affected other persons, occasions in which he experienced the consequences of his own actions, and was strengthened by facing them—in short, all that is implied by "becoming adult" in matters other than gaining cognitive skills. (Coleman et al. 1974, 5)

Many of the problems youth face in becoming adults are associated with the long transition to work and the rapid changes characteristic of contemporary society. Before describing some of these key problems, background information is provided on youth as a stage of life in modern society and on the size of the youth group. Other sections of this chapter discuss changes in the attitudes and values of youth, major problems many young people encounter in the transition to adulthood, and a constructive role for the schools in helping youth make a successful transition.

YOUTH AS A SEPARATE STAGE OF LIFE

As indicated in the next few pages, it is useful to think of the age period from fifteen through twenty-four as a stage of life that is a transition between early adolescence and adulthood. This period is different from what is ordinarily called adolescence, for the latter has usually a biological meaning, referring to puberty and the immediate postpubescent years up to about eighteen. For the period of youth, we are dealing with a psychosocial period of transition.

The proposal to designate this as a separate stage of life was made in 1972 by Keniston, in his book entitled *Youth and Dissent*. In the prologue to this book, Keniston says:

> *Millions of young people today are neither psychological adolescents nor sociological adults; they fall into a psychological no man's land, a stage of life that lacks any clear definition. . . .*
>
> *The very fact that so many millions of young people are in a stage of life that lacks even a name seems to me one of the most important psychohistorical facts about modern societies. In this essay I argue that the unprecedented prolongation of education has opened up opportunities for an extension of psychological development, which in turn is creating a "new" stage of life. . . .*
>
> *The opening up of youth as a stage of life to millions of young people seems to me a human advance, whatever its perils and dangers. A prolonged development can make possible a more autonomous, more individuated position vis-à-vis the existing society and can permit the individual to achieve a degree of inner complexity, differentiation, and integration not vouchsafed those whose development is foreshortened or foreclosed. Furthermore, the extension of human development means that we are creating—on a mass scale—a "new" breed of people whose psychological development not only inclines them to be critics of our own society, but might even make them potential members or architects of a better one than ours.*

This transition period, according to Keniston, is one of tension between the selfhood of the young person and the existing social order. The resolution of this tension leads to adult status. During this transition period, which for individual persons may be as short as five years or as long as fifteen, a youth settles a set of questions for himself or herself and thereby becomes an adult: questions of his or her relation to the existing society, of vocation, of life-style and characteristic social roles.

SIZE OF THE YOUTH GROUP

Fluctuations in the absolute and relative size of the youth group are a striking feature of the population in the United States during the twentieth century. The birthrate was very high (above 30 per 1,000 population) from 1900 to 1910 and then dropped steadily (to about 18 per 1,000) in 1933, influenced partly by the economic depression of that decade. The birthrate remained at the relatively low level of fewer than 20 per 1,000 until 1945, when it shot up to 25 per 1,000 by 1955, remaining at about that level for about eight years. Then it dropped again in 1968 to a level below the 1933 depression figure, where it has remained into the 1990s. During this time, the death rate decreased steadily from 17 per 1,000 in 1900 to 9 per 1,000 in 1955, where it has remained to the present.

The result of these phenomena is indicated in Table 6-1, where the absolute numbers of the 15–24 group are shown as well as the ratio of the 15–24 group to the 25–64 group. This ratio clearly presents the problem for the 1980s and 1990s. The 15–24 group is ready to move into the productive labor force, to do the work of the society. But society has changed since World War II; it now needs relatively fewer workers to do the necessary work. Even though the society has increased its gross production, especially in the 1950–70 period, the vast increase in size of the 15–24 group from 1960 to 1970 was more than the labor force could easily absorb. As Table 6-1 shows, the ratio of 15 to 24 to 25 to 64 jumped from .29 in 1960 to .41 in 1970 and stayed at that level through the 1970s and early 1980s. This development created serious problems for youth, and for society as a whole.

THE VALUES AND ATTITUDES OF YOUTH

Given the pervasive changes that have occurred in the lives of youth as society moved into the present postindustrial phase, we might expect the values, aspirations, and expectations of young people to change. Some of the earliest information on this topic was collected by Daniel Yankelovich, a psychologist who has been conducting surveys of youth since the 1960s. In 1968, Yankelovich asked a sample of youth eighteen to twenty-four years of age to say whether they agreed or disagreed with a number of value-statements. About half of this sample were college students, and the others had not attended college. The college students were asked to select one or the other of the following statements as representing their views about college education.

1. For me, college is mainly a practical matter. With a college education I can earn more money, have a more interesting career, and enjoy a better position in society.

2. I'm not really concerned with the practical benefits of college. I suppose I take them for granted. College for me means something more intangible, perhaps the opportunity to change things rather than make out well within the present system.

Those who chose the first statement were called "practical minded." Those who chose the second were called "forerunners." After studying the survey data, Yankelovich concluded that there had been a substantial increase in the proportion of youth who were forerunners. He also concluded that the forerunners have acquired a system of beliefs and behaviors that attempts to place nature and the natural at the center of existence. To be natural means:

To place a sensory experience ahead of conceptual knowledge . . . [and to] de-emphasize aspects of nature illuminated by science; instead to celebrate all the unknown, the mystical, and the mysterious elements of nature.
To stress cooperation rather than competition.
To devalue detachment, objectivity, and noninvolvement as methods for finding truth,

TABLE 6-1 *Population Aged Fifteen to Twenty-Four, 1890 to 2000*

Year	Number (Millions)	Percent of Total	Percentage Change in Preceding Decade	Ratio, 15–24/ 25–64
1890	12.8	20.4	–	.51
1900	14.9	19.5	+ 16	.47
1910	18.2	19.5	+ 22	.45
1920	18.8	17.6	+ 3	.39
1930	22.5	17.0	+ 20	.39
1940	24.0	18.2	+ 7	.36
1950	22.2	14.6	− 8	.29
1960	24.1	13.3	+ 9	.29
1970	36.5	17.8	+ 51	.41
1980	42.5	18.7	+ 16	.40
1990 (est.)	35.6	14.3	− 16	.28
2000 (est.)	36.1	13.4	+ 01	.26

Sources: U.S. Bureau of the Census: 1960 *Final Report* PC1-1B, 1961; *Current Population Reports* Series P–25, No. 601, 1975; No. 998, 1986.

instead . . . [to seek truth] by direct experience, participation, and involvement. (Yankelovich 1972, 35)

University of Chicago Professor Jacob W. Getzels (1978) reviewed the Yankelovich and other findings and concluded that in addition to incorporating "emergent" attitudes characteristic of the forerunners, youth had become more oriented toward an emphasis on greater personal and social responsibility. Getzels also concluded that emergent values did not continue to grow more prominent in the late 1970s (i.e., the forerunner group did not continue to grow larger) and that it was difficult to characterize the mixture of traditional, transitional, and emergent values that prevailed among youth in the late 1970s.

Data collected in the late 1970s and 1980s indicate that there has been a shift back to the practical-minded emphasis in the values and attitudes of youth. For example, surveys of college freshmen conducted for the American Council on Education show that the percentage of respondents saying that "being well-off financially" was one of their most important goals increased from 39 percent in 1970 to 74 percent in 1990 (Jaschik 1991). In addition, adults under forty-five years of age report that they are more family-oriented and more concerned with their careers than they thought would be true when they were younger (Greider 1988). These changes probably were due in part to occasional recessions and growing economic problems in the United States in the 1970s and 1980s.

In some other respects, the values and attitudes of youth appear to have remained mostly constant over the past few decades. The 1960s and 1970s brought a shift away from and then back to practical mindedness, but overall, the majority of youth throughout this period were primarily oriented toward success in the economic system and toward traditional values. Throughout the 1970s and 1980s, a large majority of young people ages eighteen to twenty-four consistently reported that they either were

"pretty happy" or "very happy" with their lives in general (Palmer, Smeeding, and Torrey 1988; Rodgers and Backman 1988). In addition, data collected in various surveys indicate that marriage and parenthood continued to be designated as very important life goals by a large majority of young people. For example, in 1990 nearly two-thirds of men aged eighteen to twenty-four said that their family is the most important part of their lives (Cutler 1990).

Within this pattern of relative stability in some important attitudes, what long-range changes have occurred in the values and attitudes of young people? In addition to several described in the preceding pages, Veroff, Douvan, and Kulka (1981) have identified the following five "generational shifts" large enough to have important implications for United States society:

- Increased concern about an uncertain future.
- Movement from social to personal sources of well-being, including an increased focus on self-expression and a shift in concern from relationships in social organizations to relationships involving interpersonal matters.
- A shift away from perceiving marriage and parenthood as critical prerequisites for personal success and a lessened tendency to view fulfillment of societal expectations as necessary for personal happiness.
- For women, increased importance attached to meeting standards of excellence in performing activities in competition with others or with the self.
- For both men and women, increased fear of being controlled by others.

It is useful to compare recent data on the attitudes and values of youth in the United States with information on long-range trends that appear to be taking place in Europe and industrialized nations elsewhere. Ronald Inglehart (1990) has been analyzing and comparing attitude surveys conducted periodically since 1970 in more than two dozen countries and has reached the general conclusion that the "values of Western publics have been shifting from an overwhelming emphasis on material well-being and physical security toward greater emphasis on the quality of life." Although he acknowledges that the causes and implications of this shift undoubtedly are complex, the fundamental reason is that to an increasing extent in recent decades, an "unprecedentedly large portion of Western populations have been raised under conditions of exceptional economic security." Consequently, although economic and physical security continue to be "valued positively . . . their relative priority is lower than in the past" (Inglehart 1990, 5).

Inglehart's book, *Culture Shift in Advanced Industrial Society*, proceeds to delineate contrasting sets of attitudes that, respectively, embody materialist values emphasizing such goals as economic growth, stable prices, strong national defense, maintenance of order in society, and crime reduction, and postmaterialist values focused on such goals as freedom of speech, increased participation in decision making at work, more voice in government, and reduced impersonalization in society. Greater tolerance toward divorce and homosexuality, heightened concern for ecology and protection of the environment, working with people one likes, searching for "interesting experiences," and other noneconomic values also are part of the postmaterialist outlook. Attitude survey data from many nations including the United States indicate that each new cohort of young people entering adulthood has been relatively more inclined than their predecessors to emphasize postmaterialist as compared to materialist values. Furthermore, the overall trend is not simply one in which young people are less materialistic (by the definition given above) than are middle-aged and elderly citizens, and then become equally materialistic as they grow older. Instead, each new cohort of youth continues to place greater relative emphasis on postmaterialist values as they move into adulthood.

Inglehart's analysis indicates that sustained prosperity characteristic of the postindustrial era is a central underlying cause that stimulates (or allows) individuals to worry less about economic security, national defense, and other materialist goals, and to focus greater attention on postmaterialist concerns. However, other influences also are important. For example, as shown in Table 6-2, respondents classified as postmaterialist are more likely to have fathers who completed postsecondary education than are materialists. In addition to ranking higher on this measure of social class, Postmaterialists also have higher education levels themselves and higher income than do Materialists. Thus, postmaterialism is related to and seems to emerge in part from the increase in education and social class levels that occurs as a growing proportion of each new youth cohort has benefitted from sustained prosperity.

TABLE 6-2 *Father's Level of Education of Respondents Classified as Materialist, Postmaterialist, or Mixed Materialist/Postmaterialist*

Attitude Classification	Percentage Whose Fathers Did Not Complete Secondary Education	Percentage Whose Fathers Completed Secondary Education	Percentage Whose Fathers Completed Post-secondary Education
Materialist	70	26	4
Mixed	61	31	8
Postmaterialist	41	43	16

Source: Adapted from Inglehart 1990.
Note: Data are from surveys in the United States, West Germany, the Netherlands, and Austria. See text for definitions of materialist and postmaterialist.

However, Inglehart also reports that nations that score relatively high on postmaterialism now have relatively low economic growth rates, possibly at least partly because their citizens emphasize noneconomic rather than economic goals. One can speculate that reduced economic growth may generate greater insecurity in the emerging international economy, and that dissatisfaction with economic accomplishments may then increase and generate a resurgence of materialist attitudes in the future.

Influence of Societal Contradictions on Values and Attitudes

Conclusions cited in the preceding pages are reminiscent and supportive of Daniel Bell's analyses of emerging problems in contemporary United States society. Following his influential *The Coming of Post-Industrial Society* (1973), Bell published a book titled *The Cultural Contradictions of Capitalism* (1976), in which he called attention to fundamental problems inherent within the nature of modern urbanized societies. Among the most general of these problems is the contradiction between an economic system organized to stimulate, direct, and reward hard work, and economic-cultural forces that generate demand for material goods:

> On the one hand the business corporation wants an individual to work hard, pursue a career, accept delayed gratification—to be, in the crude sense, an organization man. And yet, in its products and its advertisements, the corporation promotes pleasure, instant joy, relaxing and letting go. One is to be 'straight' by day and a 'swinger' by night. This is self-fulfillment and self-realization! . . . One can discern the structural sources of tension . . . between a social structure . . . that is organized fundamentally in terms of roles and specialization, and a culture which is concerned with the enhancement and fulfillment of the self and the "whole" person. (pp. 71–72, 14)

Bell's analysis portrays many of the interactions and the reciprocal influences among the major systems and strands (economic, cultural, political, social, educational, etc.) in modern society. Emphasis on science and rationality has reduced the influence of the church and the family, thus stimulating a growing orientation toward personal satisfaction. Mass consumption and mass media undermined traditional cultural standards that gave common direction in raising children and youth, geographic mobility required by the economic system cut people off from traditional influence, and economic prosperity further reinforced stress on individual happiness and self-fulfillment. In Bell's words, mass consumption "meant the acceptance, in the crucial area of life-style, of the idea of social change and personal transformation, and it gave legitimacy to those who would innovate . . . in culture" (p. 66). In addition, discretionary income "allowed individuals to choose many varied items to exemplify different consumption styles" (p. 38). Mass education also was required to provide skills for the economy and to maintain a political consensus in a democratic framework, but more education also widened the scope of "discretionary social behavior [so that] more and more individuals want to be identified . . . by their cultural tastes and life-styles" (p. 38).

Like other citizens, social scientists disagree on the meaning and implications of changes in the values and attitudes of youth. For example, as mentioned earlier Inglehart (1990) reached a generally positive conclusion in documenting increase in tolerance, concern for the environment, and other postmaterialist values, but other observers, such as Christopher Lasch and John Leo (1991b), are not at all optimistic. In three books providing an extended analysis of twentieth-century changes in values and attitudes (*The Culture of Narcissism*, 1978; *Haven in a Heartless World*, 1977; *The True and Only Heaven*, 1991), Lasch argues that the emphasis on personal satisfaction in consumerism has done much to destroy traditional values. Lasch also believes that the stress on personal satisfaction and individualism is creating disastrous consequences for individuals and society. Parents are abdicating child-raising responsibility to outside specialists, and withdrawal of the father to the world of work has interfered with the development of children's superego and thereby further stimulated emphasis on fulfillment of individual desires and impulses. The likely outcome of additional movement toward emphasis on personal satisfaction, he finally concludes, is the development of totalitarian government: "The only alternative to the superego, it has been said, is the superstate" (1977, 189).

If there is little agreement on the extent and meaning of changes taking place in values and attitudes, there is even less agreement on what to do about them (Kamarck and Galston 1990).

Some citizens believe that the family should be strengthened by recreating traditional environments, but others believe that government should intervene to provide economic support or professional assistance (Popenoe 1988; Howe 1990). Some believe that the school should take the lead in helping students understand and assess moral philosophies and social change, but others believe that teachers either should indoctrinate students in traditional values or should leave these tasks entirely to the family and the church. Some believe that the curriculum should help students self-consciously learn to pursue goals involving personal happiness and satisfaction, but others believe that the school has no business emphasizing anything but traditional academic goals.

The preceding discussion has barely scratched the surface of a large volume of material that describes or interprets changes in the values and attitudes of youth. Because there has been relatively little research designed to identify the appropriate function of the school, the family, and other institutions in helping youth respond to the perplexing problems of modern society, it is not possible to provide definitive guidelines concerning the role of differing institutions. Elsewhere in this chapter and this book some implications have been drawn for the school and other agencies, but it also must be rec-ognized that insufficient knowledge is available to justify conclusive statements about many aspects of the overall problem that society faces in helping youth make a constructive transition to adulthood.

Work Satisfaction

There has been a great deal of interest in the attitudes of U.S. workers toward their work, instigated by the general perception that the postindustrial society carries with it some changes in work attitudes compared with the industrial society. It is fairly clear that the great majority of our youth want to work and report satisfaction with their work. These are conclusions from the national Monitoring the Future surveys of high-school seniors and follow-up surveys of their responses several years later, which have been conducted regularly since 1976. Young adults and employed youth who have taken part in these surveys generally and consistently have reported that they are satisfied with their jobs (Rodgers and Bachman 1988).

Regarding young adults, Veroff, Douvan, and Kulka (1981) also have examined data from two large national studies conducted in 1957 and 1976 respectively, and reported that only about 30 percent of the younger male workers (ages twenty-one to thirty-four) said they were not satisfied with their jobs. However, the percentage of female workers who were dissatisfied with their jobs increased from 18 percent in 1957 to 35 percent in 1976. The investigators attributed this change among younger women to increased entry of women into the labor force. In addition, the data suggested that highly educated workers are relatively more insistent that work will fulfill inner desires for interesting and exciting experiences. These patterns led Veroff, Douvan, and Kulka to question whether college-educated persons are coming to expect too much satisfaction (i.e., to have unrealistically high expectations) from their work roles. A recent national survey of adults between the ages of eighteen and forty-four also indicated that many college-educated persons are dissatisfied with their work (Sheff 1988).

Thus, the evidence suggests some cause for concern that youth in the United States—particularly women and the college educated—may be growing somewhat more dissatisfied with work roles and opportunities. The data do not, however, support the proposition that most young people in the United States are *alienated* from work. They are *dissatisfied* with some things about the society, especially with the high level of unemployment among youth. But most do not appear to be resentful about their jobs or seriously unhappy at work.

SUICIDE

Suicide rates among youth in the United States have risen sharply since 1955, particularly during the 1970s among white males (Wynne and Hess 1986). More than 49,000 youth and young adults between the ages of fifteen and twenty-four took their own lives during the 1970s. The suicide rate among young people ten to fourteen years of age increased by 112 percent between 1980 and 1985 (Waller, Baker, and Szouska 1989).

The suicide rate in a country or a society was thought by the French sociologist Emile Durkheim (1956) to be related to the amount of social solidarity in a society. He thought a high suicide rate was indicative of people's uncertainty about the future and a lack of external social rules and expectations on which people could depend. He viewed a high suicide rate as going together with a high degree of loneliness and a low degree of social interaction. Some social scientists thus believe that suicide among youth is partly a result of anonymity, secularism, and impersonality in modern, postindustrial societies (Trovato and Vos 1990). Data on suicide rates in various countries suggest that Durkheim's theory has some support. For example, suicide rates of males aged fifteen to twenty-four about the year 1970 were high in developed countries such as Austria, Sweden, Canada, and Japan, and much lower in Mexico and Colombia.

Hobinger and Offer (1982) have examined data on increase in the suicide rate among ado-

lescents in the United States and found that it is highly correlated with changes since 1933 in the number and percent of youth within the general population: as the number and percent of youth aged fifteen to nineteen rose or fell, the suicide rate among this group rose or fell. They speculate that this relationship may be due to at least two psychodynamic explanations:

> *The first involves issues of competition and failure. As the number of adolescents initially increases, there are more competitors for the same number of positions: jobs, positions on varsity sports teams, places in the freshman class of good colleges, access to various social services (e.g., school counselors . . . probation officers, vocational counselors). . . .With an increased adolescent population relatively more adolescents will fail to achieve their goals, will see themselves as failures, will be unable to reestablish a balance in this self-esteem equilibrium, and will begin the downhill slide. . . . Second . . . it may be more difficult for an adolescent to gain a sense of self-worth and to find friends in the large impersonal high schools of today. . . . The lonely, emotionally depleted, depressed adolescent may see most of his peers as functioning relatively well, sharpening his awareness of his personal problems and increasing his loneliness and isolation. (Hobinger and Offer 1982, 306).*

Information on trends among youth in the United States tends to support the argument that increase in the suicide rate during the past few decades may have been due to at least in part to increase in the number and percent of youth. These data indicate that the suicide rate for young people age fifteen to nineteen leveled out and then declined slightly in the 1980s as the size of the youth group declined (Wynne and Hess 1986).

Other causes cited in accounting for the increase in suicide among youth include the infectious effects of media coverage (Simon 1989), the diminishing role of religion, increased family disruption, and general rapidity of social change

(Kamarck and Galston 1990). In any case, school officials in many locations have become concerned with the problem and have begun to work with mental health agencies in trying to alleviate it. Some educators, such as Pfeifer (1986) and Barrett (1989), have described programs through which schools might help young people learn coping skills to avert suicide. However, a U.S. Department of Education assessment of school-based efforts to prevent suicide concluded that little is known concerning the effectiveness of programs introduced in the 1970s and 1980s. Also, a former president of the American Association of Suicidology criticized most such programs for using a "one-shot approach" that allows school officials to "feel like they're doing something . . . [without] asking any tough questions and thinking it through" (Jennings 1989:20).

HOMICIDE

Homicide in the United States is a serious problem among young men between fifteen and twenty-four years of age, who account for about one-fifth of all homicides. The annual homicide rate of more than 20 per 100,000 men in this age group is much higher than in other industrialized countries, in which rates range from .3 per 100,000 in Austria to 5 per 100,000 in Scotland (Rosenthal 1990). About one in every ten deaths among young people involves homicide using firearms (Center to Prevent Handgun Violence 1990). The firearms death rate for U.S. teenagers increased by 43 percent between 1984 and 1988 (Lawton 1991).

Social scientists who have been studying homicide among youth in the United States attribute the high rate to a variety of causes, including increased use of crack cocaine in the 1980s, availability of firearms, influence of the mass media, residence in underclass communities, and growing up in violent homes and environments. Several of these forces have been most evident among young black males, for whom the homicide rate increased from about 60 to slightly more

than 100 per 100,000 during the 1980s. But the problem is not confined to black youth; the rate of homicide among young white males is more than twice that in Scotland or other countries that have relatively high youth homicide rates (Rosenthal 1990; Jencks 1991).

YOUTH AND EMPLOYMENT

Major questions exist concerning how society should provide employment training for youth who do not graduate from high school or who do not obtain rewarding employment or go on to colleges and technical schools after high school. The problem of helping youth prepare for and enter productive employment is particularly difficult with respect to minority youth in concentrated poverty neighborhoods within the inner city. But it has become increasingly severe for many other youth as well, as up-grading of skill and certification requirements for employment have reduced opportunities for obtaining unskilled employment leading to subsequent acquisition of skills and promotions (Kilborn 1990). Rist (1981) has summarized the overall problem as follows:

> *For most of the youth who want to work when they leave high school—with or without a diploma—they are simply on their own. There is no social net below them as they attempt to make their way. There is no social infrastructure to which they can turn for assistance. Youth have no ombudsman in the United States, as they do in New Zealand and Sweden, to whom they can turn for advocacy on their behalf as they seek housing, employment, training opportunities, social welfare, and health benefits. In America, unless one is sponsored by one's friends, or neighbors, finding adult roles is a lonely endeavor. (Rist 1981, 5–6)*

One approach that appears to have had some success in helping youth prepare for and obtain employment is the Jobs for America's

Graduates (JAG) program, which began in Delaware in 1979 and expanded to a number of other states in the 1980s. In the JAG approach, a single professional person works with about 35 high-school seniors to improve their skills in finding and keeping jobs and to identify and develop jobs in which students are placed (Wichess 1984). Research on the employment status of seniors from four states (Delaware, Massachusetts, Missouri, Tennessee) that participated in 1981–82 indicated that only 16 percent were unemployed the following autumn, as compared with 41 percent of students in a comparison group. In addition, 81 percent of the employed JAG students had jobs rates as "positive placements," as compared with 67 percent of the comparison students (Newitt 1984). By the end of 1990, 350 schools in nineteen states were involved in the JAG approach, and assessment data collected nationally indicated that more than 80 percent of graduates were gainfully employed (Weisman 1991a).

Disadvantaged and Minority Youth

Unemployment rates among young people in the United States are substantial, particularly among minority youth in the inner city. The unemployment rate for white males between sixteen and twenty-four years of age increased from about 7 percent in the late 1960s to the range of 10 to 15 percent in the 1980s. The comparable rate for black males between the ages of sixteen and twenty-four generally has been from two to three times as high as the rate for white males during the past thirty to forty years and has been above 30 percent in some years during the 1980s.

The pattern for females sixteen to twenty-four years of age is somewhat similar: for white females, the unemployment rate increased from 7 percent in 1955 to 10 percent or more in some recent years, while the rate for black females generally was two to three times higher and at times reached 20 percent or more in the 1980s.

High rates of unemployment remain persistent among black youth: among black males six-teen to nineteen years of age, 42 percent were unemployed in 1986, and 35 percent of black females in this age group were unemployed.

Hahn and Lerman have reviewed these data for the National Planning Association's Committee on New American Realities and concluded that although the U.S. economy was able to create millions of jobs for the large cohorts of young people who were entering adulthood in the 1960s and 1970s, a "devastating job situation . . . has hit poor and black youth" (1985, 2). Other conclusions they reached included the following:

Unemployment is highly concentrated among . . . poor and minority youth who had dropped out of school . . . or graduated from high school [but] are ill-prepared for the bulk of available jobs. . . . The job problems of disadvantaged youth are of particular concern because of their close association with crime, teenage pregnancy, poverty, and long-term unemployment. . . . Failure to cope with the problems of these youth tends to perpetuate an underclass with the all too common mix of family instability, involvement in or exposure to crime, poverty, unemployment, and a difficult home environment for children. . . .

The evidence clearly points to low educational achievement as one of the primary factors contributing to the employment problems of low income and minority youth. . . . Family factors also complicate the ability of low income youth to take advantage of increased job opportunities. Many disadvantaged youth live with nonworking adults, which limits their connections to jobs and the world of work. . . . Many of these factors . . . are the result of complex social problems not easily addressed through employment policies. However, employment policy can lessen some of the problems and help overcome the effects of others. (Hahn and Lerman 1985, 2, 7, 31)

Other researchers who have studied the problem of unemployment among low-income minority youth have reached similar conclusions.

For example, Williams and Kornblum studied inner-city communities in Cleveland, Louisville, Meridian (Mississippi), and New York City, and concluded that "adolescents who fail in school, work in marginal (at best) employment, or drop out of the labor market as teenage parents, all need structures of opportunity within which they can realize their potential" (1985, 113). Freeman and Holzer (1985; 1986) examined the research on black youth unemployment and concluded that "the overall picture . . . is one in which black youth clearly want to work, but only at jobs and with wages that are comparable to those received by their white counterparts. Unfortunately . . . with increased job market competititon from women and other groups . . . the youths have had trouble obtaining such jobs . . . [and] many have been led into alternative modes of obtaining money 'on the street' and to leisure activities that will not get them back on track" (1985, 30–31).

With regard to the specific problem of improving employability and employment of economically disadvantaged youth, much has been learned through national and local programs that have attempted to identify the types of approaches that are most successful. Robert Taggart, who played a major part in designing and evaluating a number of national demonstration projects for disadvantaged youth, has assessed their results and concluded that

> *jobs can reduce the likelihood and consequence of negative events such as crime. Findings from work programs featuring intensive support services for youth in the criminal justice system suggest a noticeable in-program decline in arrests. Findings from another federally supported experiment guaranteeing jobs to low-income youths who stay in high school or return indicate that jobs can be used to lure youth back to school and to forestall early leaving. It is estimated that . . . one-third of eligible dropouts have been lured back to school. (Taggart 1982, 259)*

Taggart also concluded that programs that are well designed and well implemented to provide linkages between education and training, skilled supervision, and adequate materials and funding can substantially improve the employability and subsequent employment history of disadvantaged youth. He further concluded that employment experience can help prevent disadvantaged youth from becoming more alienated and that postsecondary training can provide them with skills and knowledge that lead to significant employment gains.

Other lessons Taggart identified as resulting from various national and local projects included the following: (1) one must provide careful structuring of career-entry experience to assure subsequent access to regular jobs; (2) youth who have left school may need some "aging" before they are ready to return to the classroom; those who have left and return voluntarily do better than those who are enrolled immediately; (3) alternative settings should be available to provide educational remediation through self-paced learning and individualization; (4) basic employability skills should be developed through job search assistance, counseling, vocational exploration, and other means; and (5) work activities should be structured and demanding, but second and third opportunities should be provided for youths who do not meet meaningful performance standards (Taggart 1982, 264–271).

Another major employment-training demonstration project was carried out for single mothers in San Jose, California, in the 1980s. Called the Minority Female Single Parent Demonstration, the San Jose project included mostly young, inner-city mothers who had relatively little education, work experience, and family resources. Applicants were randomly assigned either to a control group that received no assistance or to a treatment group that received comprehensive services including assessment and diagnosis, training in specific job skills, remediation of basic reading, math, and communications skills, job-search training and job placement, child-care help, counseling, and other needed support services, such as transportation and food for the most impoverished. Initial evaluation results indicated that after only one year of enrollment, mothers who received services were more likely to be employed and had much higher monthly earnings than did those in the control group (Burghardt and Gordon 1990). The evaluators also concluded that program design elements that appeared to be most important included the following:

- The integrated training design . . . which emphasized training for all regardless of educational skill levels . . . [and] offered remedial education within the context of job skill training
- The attention . . . [to ensuring] that training is offered in demand occupations and that trainees are well prepared to meet the employer needs
- An on-site child care center
- The dedication of the organization to its primary mission of job training for disadvantaged individuals
- The relatively large scale . . . [of the organization and main center, which thus allowed for provision of] training in a range of occupations and gave the organization the financial capacity to acquire equipment. (Burghardt and Gordon 1990, 34–35)

Generalizations that are supported most frequently by studies cited here and others that have assessed programs to prepare disadvantaged youth for employment include conclusions regarding the importance of (1) integrating or coordinating basic learning skills and job training education and (2) providing a comprehensive set of services in the overall training program. Regarding the first point, the director of the Brandeis University Center for Human Resources examined the relevant research and concluded that successful employment-related instruction for youth requires "opportunities to apply problem-solving skills on the job and utilize basic skills in carrying it out" (Curnan 1990, 26). Regarding the

second point, the Commission on Workforce Quality and Labor Market Efficiency (1989, 23) established by the U.S. Department of Labor has stated that the responsibility for education and training programs should be "shared by a variety of federal, state, and local agencies," including private industry councils, the U.S. Departments of Labor and of Health and Human Services, and state and local agencies that administer various education and welfare programs. Considerable coordination is needed, the Commission further concluded, to overcome existing "fragmentation and associated administrative complexity [that] make it difficult to integrate training services, [to] respond strategically to evolving workforce needs, and [to] use limited resources efficiently."

It should be emphasized that recommendations, such as those described here, generally are based on the results of demonstration-type programs that tell us what can be achieved through successful implementation of well-planned approaches. In practice, however, many or most programs do not appear to have been successful, even when based on the findings of previous theory and research. As in the case of federal funding for compensatory education (see Chapter 8), as a society we know a lot more about what is required to make programs for disadvantaged youth successful than we have been able to put into practice on a widespread basis. As one example, analysts of employment training programs long ago recognized that linking training to the prospect of a guaranteed job with subsequent advancement opportunity can be highly motivating for disadvantaged youth or adults, and the U.S. Department of Labor's Youth Incentive Entitlement program was designed to determine whether this type of approach would induce disadvantaged youth to remain in or return to school and to reduce their rate of unemployment. However, the U.S. General Accounting Office investigated implementation of Entitlement projects and concluded that many sponsors experienced "serious operational problems" regarding job quality, supervision, job development, counseling, worksite monitoring, and other matters, and in the end questioned "whether sponsors are capable of implementing complex programs such as Entitlement" (U.S. General Accounting Office 1980, i–ii). "Real world" improvements in implementation, the report concluded, would require much more oversight, monitoring, and technical assistance than usually are provided in most youth employment training projects.

In this context, the important underlying question regarding social policy in the United States is whether the nation can develop the will and know-how to provide effective elementary and secondary education and employment training for disadvantaged youth throughout the country. As we note in Chapter 7, neo-Marxist and other critics of United States society do not believe our existing political and economic arrangements are capable of providing effective opportunity for underclass and working-class students. Developments in education and related fields during the 1970s and 1980s demonstrated that we now can specify the types of programs and approaches that can deliver effective education and employment training (Smith, Blank, and Bond 1990). On the other hand, billions of dollars are spent each year on programs and approaches (e.g., "make-work" summer jobs) that do not result in any measurable improvement in fundamental learning skills and employability. The result of this situation, as summarized by Julia Wrigley of the University of California at Los Angeles, is reinforcement of a cycle of lack of opportunity that provides alienated, disadvantaged youth with further "daily evidence of their superfluity." Thus, our national efforts to date have not come to grips with the problems of youth whose experience has taught them a "message of marginality." As long as this remains the case, many such youth will continue to remain at the end of the labor queue, "on the edges of the productive institutions of the economy" (Wrigley 1982, 256–257).

It also should be noted that employment training programs generally have accomplished very little in combatting the isolation from mainstream culture and economic activity that severely hamper opportunity for disadvantaged inner-city youth in large metropolitan areas. Stated differently, growing up in a depressed poverty neighborhood in a big city in itself constitutes a major handicap in terms of learning about and gaining productive employment, particularly in many metropolitan areas with large central city-suburban distances and limited public transportation. Part of this pattern that restricts employment for inner-city youth has been summarized in testimony before the U.S. Civil Rights Commission:

> *What are the industries that employ large numbers of young people? [These are] the retail establishments and the restaurants and that kind of activity. . . . The growth of retail business in our society is in the suburbs. . . . The McDonalds and the Kentucky Fried Chickens, they are not in the middle of the ghetto; they are on the periphery, on the border. But when you really go out down Rockville Pike and you see a hundred fast-food places, the majority of the youngsters that work there are white, the vast majority of them, and those are the youth industries.*
>
> *Where you get the babysitting money is the suburbs. Youth are also able to get some income mowing lawns. No one is paying, I don't think, in the inner city barrio to have their lawns mowed. . . . I really cannot say what the impact of working at an early age is. But I would venture to say that at least that youth is getting some notion of the world of work, getting some income, some positive reward. (U.S. Commission on Civil Rights 1982, 32–33)*

Employment Training for Disadvantaged Youth in the 1990s

Much of the employment training provided for disadvantaged and other youth in the 1980s was made available through the federal government's Job Training and Partnership Act (JTPA). Because financing and implementation of the act clearly were not satisfactory, Congress made important revisions as part of the Job Training and Basic Skills Act (JTBSA) of 1990. Senator Paul Simon (1990) summarized some of the major deficiencies and problems that had become apparent in operation of the JTPA as follows:

- Funding after taking account of inflation declined by one-third between 1980 and 1990, and fewer than 10 percent of eligible youth were able or willing to participate.
- Program administrators frequently "creamed" the target population in the sense that they enrolled high "proportions of high school graduates and others who might find employment on their own, while underserving high-school dropouts, the disabled, long-term welfare recipients and others who comprise the hard-core unemployed" (Simon 1990, S18130).
- Short-term training was overemphasized in order to provide favorable statistics indicating that local programs were successful.

In attempting to improve the effectiveness and efficiency of federal employment training, Congress included the following eight JTBSA provisions designed to help economically disadvantaged youth:

1. Seventy percent of participants under the age of twenty-two must be persons facing "a barrier to employment" because they have inadequate basic skills or a poor school record, a disability, limited English proficiency, or a criminal record, or have children or have dropped out of school or are homeless. At least half of these participants must be out-of-school youth, but those under eighteen must return to school or an alternative educational program.

2. Authorized funding was increased substantially.

3. Participants must be "individually assessed and a service strategy must be implemented that provides . . . basic skills and occupational training whenever necessary" (Simon 1990, S18127).

4. Services must be coordinated with local educational agencies.

5. Program evaluation measures must include assessment of basic and occupational skills attainment.

6. An increased percentage of local allocations may be spent on support services.

7. Special grants (known as the "Fair Chance Program") are to be awarded to "high poverty communities" in order to make services for disadvantaged youth more comprehensive.

8. Funds were provided to begin replicating "successful and innovative models" in additional locations (Simon 1990, S18131).

Summarizing congressional concerns that led to passage of the JTBSA, Senator Simon emphasized the following considerations:

> *It is all too clear that new workers and the unemployed must be properly educated and trained to participate fully and productively in a high-tech economy. We must target our limited Federal funds on the truly disadvantaged, who have never entered the labor force and have no means to do so without the direct intervention of this program. [The new legislation encourages rather than discourages] local areas to train and educate hard-to-serve populations and provide a comprehensive array of services that have a lifelong impact in terms of improving one's income earning potential instead of a short-term impact in dead-end minimum wage jobs. (Simon 1990, S18132)*

THE TRANSITION FROM SCHOOL TO WORK

Data reviewed in preceding sections indicate that this nation faces serious problems preparing young people for a successful transition from school to employment. Many young persons who do not continue education beyond high school are unemployed or do not have sufficient income to provide adequate support for family life and children (see Chapter 1). At the same time, the vocational education system is beset with many deficiencies, and too few systematic and effective opportunities for advancement through on-the-job training are available, particularly for disadvantaged youth (Chapter 2). Paul Barton analyzed the overall situation with respect to opportunities for noncollege youth in the early 1990s and reported the following major conclusions:

> *Unlike other developed countries, the United States does very little to smooth the transition from school to work for high school graduates, while it spends large sums on those who continue their education. For the non-college-bound, the road to employment is, and long has been, a bumpy one. . . . Education and work remain two separate worlds. . . . Students graduate, leave school, and search for full-time jobs, largely with the poorly informed advice of their friends and relatives. . . . [By 1980 the United States Employment Service] had, for budgetary reasons, abandoned the start it made 30 years earlier in bringing counseling and placement services to the schools, after having implemented programs in half the nation's schools by the early 1960's. Only vestiges remain . . . [and new] arrangements are not likely to come solely from ad hoc projects between a few businesses and a few schools . . . . [Changes must be made] to create workplace skills employers demand, and students going directly into the workplace must be given the preparation they need without foreclosing opportunities for further education. (Barton 1990, 27–30)*

Given this situation, there has been growing concern regarding the adequacy of arrangements to ensure a positive transition from school to work in the United States. Examples (see Olson 1990a; Lewis 1991a) of this increasing concern include the following:

- The U.S. Secretary of Labor noted that the United States is one of the few industrial-ized countries without strong and consistent social institutions and arrangements to ensure a successful transition for young people who do not attend college.
- The president of the American Association of Community and Junior Colleges called attention to the lack of adequate remuneration and status for persons in occupations that do not require a college diploma.
- The president of the Council of Chief State School Officers described current efforts to facilitate the school-to-work transition as being about as useful as "perfuming a pig."
- The director of the National Institute for Work and Learning cited research indicating that many students perceive little connection between schoolwork and their future employment opportunities.
- A U.S. government study found that competing nations "invest extensively in out-of-school youth . . . [whereas] U.S. employment and training programs reach only a modest proportion of youth in need" (Nilsen 1990, 3).
- The Commission on the Skills of the American Work Force (1990), chaired by two former U.S. Secretaries of Labor, concluded:

> *Because employers have not set training standards, few students can be sure that there is a market for the courses they pursue. Education is rarely connected to training and both are rarely connected to an effective job service function.*
>
> *While the foreign nations we studied differ in economy and culture, they share an approach to the education and training of their workers and to high productivity work organization.*
>
> *They insist that virtually all of their students reach a high educational standard. We do not.*
>
> *They provide "professionalized" education to non-college bound students to prepare them for their trades and to ease their school-to-work transition. We do not.*

They operate comprehensive labor market systems which combine training, labor market information, job search and income maintenance for the unemployed. We do not.

They support company based training through general revenue or payroll tax based financing schemes. We do not.

They have national consensus on the importance of moving to high productivity forms of work organization and building high wages economics. We do not.

Our approaches have served us well in the past. They will not serve us well in the future. (Quoted in Pell 1990b, S16012–S16014)

Concern with the transition from school to work has been spurred by the work of researchers who have identified specific problems regarding the employment prospects of young workers. For example, John Bishop (1989, 1990) of Cornell University has analyzed or reviewed various data sets dealing with linkages between high schools and the workplace. His primary conclusion has been that many students put forth relatively little effort to learn challenging material in secondary schools (see Chapter 13 in this text), in part because the "labor market fails to reward effort and achievement ... [so that] *most students realize few benefits from working hard while in school*" (Bishop 1989, 7. Italics in original.).

In support of this argument, Bishop presented data indicating that young men and women with high scores on a number of achievement measures generally do not earn higher hourly wages than those with low scores. As shown in Table 6-3, young women with high scores in each of seven skills areas tested have about the same hourly wage as the average young women who participated in the National Longitudinal Surveys. For young men, the only instances in which scoring at the 67th percentile was associated with wages more than 3 percent above those for the average young male were for the Computational Speed and Mechanical Skills subtests, and even here the wage enhancements, respectively, amounted to only

6 percent and 4 percent. Bishop summarized his conclusions from these and other data as follows:

During the first eight years after leaving high school, young men who do not go to college receive no rewards from the labour market for developing competence in science, language arts and mathematical reasoning. ... For the non-college-bound female ... competence in science, language arts, and the technical area does not ... [increase wage rates]. The tendency of so many American high school students to avoid rigorous mathematics and science courses and their poor performance on international science and mathematics tests, may, therefore, well be a rational response to the lack of labour market rewards. (Bishop 1990, 122–123)

Bishop's analysis also suggests that one major reason high-school performance is not related to wage rates among young workers is that employers have little or no useful information on the previous careers of their new employees. Although research conducted by Bishop and others

TABLE 6-3 *Percentage of Hourly Wage Increase or Decrease Associated with Test Scores at the 67th Percentile Compared with the 50th Percentile, by Sex and Subtest*

Subtest	Males	Females
Clerical	0%	2%
Computational speed	6	3
Electronics	3	0
Math	−1	3
Mechanical skills	4	−1
Science	−1	0
Verbal	−3	2

Source: Adapted from Bishop 1990.
Note: Data are from National Longitudinal Surveys of young people who were tested in 1980, did not attend college, and were interviewed in subsequent years. Hourly wage increases and decreases are calculated controlling years of schooling, age, work experience, region, metropolitan residence, and ethnicity.

clearly indicates that young workers who performed well in high school are more productive on the job than are those who did not (even after other considerations are held constant), employers generally know only whether young applicants have graduated or not graduated from high school. Few large companies and hardly any small companies test job applicants, and high-school transcripts hardly ever are available to employers. Even in the few cases in which companies request transcripts from high schools, such requests generally are ignored, in part because "Most high schools apparently have designed their systems for responding to requests for transcripts around the needs of college-bound students rather than the students who seek jobs immediately after graduating" (Bishop 1989, 8).

After noting that Australia, Canada, Japan, and most other industrialized countries administer curriculum-related achievement tests that play an important part in employers' hiring and initial-wage decisions, Bishop recommended that "competency profiles be prepared for U.S. students and made available to potential employers as well as postsecondary education institutions." In addition, employers "should start demanding high-school transcripts and give academic achievement . . . greater weight in hiring," so that high-school graduates would less likely "be relegated to sales clerks jobs simply because of their age [and instead would be] allowed to compete for really attractive jobs on the basis of the knowledge and skills they have gained in high school" (Bishop 1989, 10).

Worklink, Apprenticeships, and Related Proposals for Reform

Responding to data and problems, such as those cited previously, government and business leaders have begun to develop and implement proposals for improving the transition from school to work. The best known and most fully developed of these proposals is the Worklink Project sponsored initially by the National Alliance of Business (NAB), the National Urban League, and the

Educational Testing Service (ETS). A computerized information system designed to link employers and schools, Worklink has been described by an NAB senior vice-president as follows:

WORKLINK aims . . . to enable young people to build a portfolio that will provide their transcripts and employability records on a national information system easily accessible by employers.

WORKLINK would include assessments in prose reading, document reading, numeracy, applied mathematics and applied science. Students would decide which assessments they would take, and would decide which results would be reported. Results would be reported in the form of descriptions of proficiency—in terms that employers can relate to job openings. . . . Students would begin developing their WORKLINK resume while in high school and continue adding to it after they graduate. Work experience and transcripts would be included along with academic assessment.

[Employers could] search this new database for candidates that match their job needs. . . . At the same time, WORKLINK would allow young people to use all of their work and training-related experience to advance themselves . . . [and would give them] a clearer idea of the importance of education in their own lives, and a greater incentive to increase their efforts in school.

However, schools and students will only have an incentive to use WORKLINK if young people who use it gain an advantage in the job market over those who don't. Schools need a clear message from business to become involved in the WORKLINK project. (Schaeffer 1989, 4)

Although planning for Worklink is still in its early stages, pilot efforts to test some aspects have been either considered or initiated in Indianapolis, Spokane, Tampa, and other locations. However, some observers estimate that even if

Worklink proves successful and expands rapidly, national implementation will not be possible for five to ten years.

Meanwhile, developers must deal with many uncertainties and must avoid potentially negative consequences. For example, it is not clear whether apathy toward academics among high-school students is due more to perceived lack of later incentives among non-college-bound students (as Bishop argues) or to irrelevance in the current curriculum, bargains between teachers who keep requirements minimal in return for students' agreement to behave in class (see Chapter 13), and other causes. If perceived lack of incentives is not the central problem, then efforts to bolster incentives through Worklink or similar approaches may not make much difference.

Among the many dangers in the Worklink approach is the possibility that it may generate additional obstacles to mobility and success among disadvantaged students in big-city schools. As noted in Chapters 2, 7, 8, and 10, there is reason to believe that academic standards are very low at many high schools in concentrated poverty neighborhoods, and that many of their graduates have not acquired adequate skills. If Worklink results in documentation of very low performance when such students seek jobs, they may have even greater problems obtaining employment than they do now. Thus, systems for collecting and disseminating information on student performance could be counterproductive in the absence of massive (and successful) efforts to reform high schools, particularly those in big cities. We review possibilities for such reform in Chapter 13.

Other approaches similar or related to Worklink also are being proposed or developed by various organizations and individuals. For example, the American Business Conference has been working on incentive systems for students in California, and the Commission on the Skills of the American Workforce has recommended that national performance-based examinations should be prepared and administered to all students at age sixteen. Students with an acceptable score would receive a Certificate of Initial Mastery that would qualify them for "going to work, entering a college preparatory program, or studying for a Technical and Professional Certificate" that would lead to full-time work in a wide "range of service and manufacturing occupations . . . after completing a two-to-four-year program of combined work and study." As part of this approach, Youth Centers would be established to "enroll school dropouts and help them reach" the standards, and a "system of Employment and Training Boards" would be established by "Federal and state governments, together with local leadership, to organize and oversee the new school-to-work transition programs and training systems" (Pell 1990b, S16012–S16014).

This proposal by the Commission on the Skills of the American Workforce and similar proposals and plans advocated by other organizations involve the incorporation of *apprenticeship* arrangements modeled to some degree on approaches that have been used in numerous societies for several centuries. One scholar who has been studying apprenticeships has defined them as involving the "ancient practice" of preparing youth for employment and adulthood through practical activity conducted under the close and personal supervision of experienced crafts workers (Hamilton 1990a, 1). In particular, Germany has long provided comprehensive apprenticeship opportunities for young people who do not participate in higher education. In the United States, some young people have been prepared for employment through apprenticeships, but arrangements have been by no means as successful or wide-ranging as those in Germany and some other countries (Hamilton 1990a). After presenting evidence indicating that noncollege youth trained through apprenticeships in Germany are much more successful than their U.S. counterparts in acquiring technical skills and obtaining well-paid jobs, Barton (1990), Hamilton (1990a), Lerman and Pouncy (1990), and other analysts have argued in favor of a comprehensive, national apprenticeship system.

Not simply a transplanted copy of arrangements in Germany or elsewhere, a comprehensive apprenticeship system in the United States would be "more flexible and reflective of American values and traditions" (Hamilton 1990a, 16). Designed particularly to use not just workplaces but also "other community settings as learning environments" that link work experience, academic-skills development, and training for an occupation, such a system would offer a "means of directing the resources of an entire community" to providing young people with a "clear vision of a desirable future and a well-marked path to an adult career" (Hamilton 1990, 133). Unlike traditional apprenticeship arrangements, this system could include community service assignments for early adolescents, a much wider range of community locations and mentoring personnel, periodic chances and support to switch to colleges and other postsecondary institutions, coordination with social services and health agencies, and other components designed to maximize opportunities available to youth. Through coordination with the educational system, it also could "contribute to school credentials rather than substituting for schooling," making sure that preparation for work is sufficiently general to avoid making training for a particular job "the sole end" of apprenticeship assignments (Hamilton 1990a, 152).

Possible Negative Effects of Students' Employment

Before the 1940 to 1950 period, few high school students had paid employment, but part-time employment of students has increased enormously in the past forty years. Today a majority of high school students over sixteen years of age have part-time jobs, and national surveys indicate that approximately half of seniors work more than eighteen hours per week (Woodward 1990).

Employment of high school students frequently has been perceived to be desirable because it provides young people with additional income, offers them an opportunity to learn about work and develop dependable habits and transferable skills for later employment, and reduces the dependency associated with prolonged adolescence in modern society. In addition, the limited research that has been conducted suggests that employment less than about twenty hours a week is not academically harmful (Barton 1990). In recent years, however, some educators, social scientists, and other observers have begun to question whether the overall consequences are generally positive for most young people and for society (Mihalik 1990).

For example, Jerald Bachman of the Survey Research Center believes that employment may be encouraging adolescents to place too much emphasis on cars and other material possessions, and some school superintendents have reported that employment of students not only results in low academic performance in many cases, but also may be stimulating teachers to require less homework and otherwise decrease academic standards. In addition, many observers wonder whether most students are acquiring transferable skills and positive work habits in jobs typical of the fast-food industry and other low-level employment (Viadero 1987b; Manges, 1990; Woodward 1990).

In general, many school officials as well as other concerned citizens are concluding that action should be taken to limit the number of hours students work and to ensure that jobs are meaningful and productive. Regarding the extent to which teenagers' jobs provide positive work experience, available data suggest that many jobs offer very little challenge. For example, two national studies (Table 6-4) have indicated that only about half of working teenagers perceive their jobs as being useful for their future work (Sterns 1990). Note, however, that employed students whose jobs are supervised as part of their school program are more likely to say their work is meaningful and career-enhancing (Stone, Stern, Hopkins, and McMillan 1990).

TABLE 6-4 *Percentage of Employed High-School Seniors Who Indicate Their Jobs Exemplify Selected Characteristics at Least "To Some Extent"*

Job Characteristics	Monitoring the Future Survey, 1984	National Center for Research on Vocational Education Survey, 1990
Teaches you new skills that will be useful in your future work	50%	47%
Makes good use of special skills you learned in school	30	31
Lets you get to know people with social backgrounds very different from yours	59	59
Uses your skills and abilities— lets you do the things you do best	50	52
Causes you stress and tension	40	39

Source: Adapted from Stern et al. 1990.

DELINQUENCY

As adolescents pass through the period of youth on the way to adulthood, many of them engage in delinquent behavior, and most outgrow it (Gottfredson and Hirschi 1989). One can view delinquency as a kind of contagious disease, like mumps, that most youth catch and get over with few permanent disabilities. But to treat delinquency so lightly is a mistake, for two reasons: first, it hinders a youth from developing into a competent adult, even though he or she does not become a criminal; and second, some youths become seriously delinquent and go on into an adult life of crime or serious maladjustment.

Boys are delinquent much more frequently than girls. In all societies for which delinquency data are available, boys outnumber girls in the delinquency statistics by a ratio ranging from between 4 to 1 and 10 to 1. Boys at the beginning of adolescence are likely to do some mischief to property in the neighborhood and may be warned by the police.

There has been a large increase of juvenile and young adult arrest rates since 1960. Total annual arrest rates for juveniles under age 18 approximately tripled between 1960 and 1985. Worse still, arrest rates for youth 18 to 24 years of age approximately quadrupled during this period (Wynne and Hess 1986).

Generalizations about Juvenile Delinquency

1. Violent delinquency is much more common among working-class youth than among middle-class youth (Glaser 1979; Guyer 1989; Sullivan 1990). In addition, low-status youth in low-status neighborhoods—particularly inner-city neighborhoods—are more likely to be delinquent than are low-status youth in other neighborhoods (Mayer and Jencks 1989; Jencks 1991).

2. A large proportion of crimes is committed by youth under the age of twenty-five. However, most youthful offenders settle down to a stable adult work life (Gottfredson and Hirschi 1989; Sullivan 1990).

3. Violent delinquency is associated with participation in a violent subculture that tends to be perceived by some participants as neither illegal nor immoral (Austin 1980; Dennis 1990).

4. There is a relationship between youth crime and unemployment. Poverty and desire for money combine to favor money-making forms of crime (Williams and Kornblum 1985; Gurr 1989; Myers 1990). Regarding this relationshiup, Daniel Glaser has summarized research on factors leading to delinquency and concluded with the following statement: "To combat youth crime is largely futile unless an effort is also made to assure legitimate employment for youth. To deal effectively with both youth crime and youth unemployment in the United States today, however, major social, cultural, and political developments must be taken into account" (1979, 79).

5. The best predictor of serious delinquency is association with delinquent peer groups (Elliott, Huizinga, and Ageton 1985). Some recent research also indicates that delinquency is particularly frequent in communities in which youth peer groups are unsupervised (Sampson and Groves 1989).

6. Young persons who exemplify a discrepancy between high economic goals and low educational attainment are most likely to be delinquent (Farnsworth and Leiber 1989).

7. Perceived certainty of punishment is significantly related to the frequency of delinquency (Paternoster 1989; Jencks 1991).

8. Rates of delinquency have been increasing much faster for girls than for boys. In particular, delinquent acts involving violence by females increased rapidly in the 1980s (Crittenden 1990).

9. Participation in delinquent gangs appears to be associated with growing up in a home environment that provides relatively few family rituals to build positive attitudes and relationships (Pearsall 1990).

10. Boys who are aggressively antisocial in the first years of elementary school are most likely to become delinquent teenagers and drug users (Flax 1990a).

11. Violence and crime portrayed in the mass media probably stimulate and increase youth delinquency (Gurr 1989; Dennis 1990; Plagens 1991).

12. Much delinquency is related to problems in the family (Wilson and Herrnstein 1985; Kamarck and Galston 1990). Reflecting this relationship, recent research indicates that violence in the family is the most useful predictor of membership in a delinquent group (Rosewater 1989).

Delinquency as a Subcultural Phenomenon

The most common type of juvenile delinquency in the United States and other industrialized countries seems to arise from certain disjunctions in the society itself. People in power in the society regard certain types of behavior as undesirable and they label it "delinquent," although the same behavior may appear natural to other people who belong to special subcultural groups. From this point of view, delinquent acts are primarily carried out by subgroups of youth who are at odds with the value system of the greater society in which they live. In a sense, these young people are alienated from society and, feeling rejected by the community at large, they do not wish to obey its rules.

According to this theory, working-class boys grow up with standards of behavior that get them in trouble with the authorities who represent middle-class standards. Kvaraceus and Miller (1959) favor this theory and list the following characteristics of working-class culture that tend to get a boy in trouble with the authorities: high value placed on toughness, outsmarting others, seeking excitement, maintaining one's autonomy, and attributing events to fate. In contrast, the middle-class culture places high value on the following traits: achievement through hard work, responsibility, desire for education, respect for property, cleanliness, ambition, belonging to formal organizations, and ability to defer present pleasure in favor of future gratification.

Since most working-class boys do *not* become delinquent, Kvaraceus and Miller (1959) concluded that not all working-class families have typical working-class values and that some boys from working-class families learn middle-class modes of behavior in school, in church, or in recreational settings. With the aid of education, these boys move out of the working class.

School Failure and Delinquency

There is certainly a positive correlation between failure in school and delinquency; but it is not certain which is the cause and which is effect (Mickelson and Smith 1989). Some students of the problem believe that youth with learning problems tend to become delinquent. For instance, the Comptroller General of the United States in 1977 reported that there is growing "evidence, being established by experts in education, medicine, law enforcement, and juvenile justice ... [indicating] a correlation between children experiencing academic failure (learning problems) and children demonstrating delinquent behavior" (p. 2). The report went on to say that the research did not definitely establish a causal link between learning problems and delinquency.

Related research also has supported the conclusion that delinquency is associated with the existence of learning disabilities (LD) among male teenagers (Fiske 1989a). Based on a three-part study initiated by the National Institute for Juvenile Justice and Delinquency, Dunivant (1982) reported a significant relationship between learning disabilities and delinquent behavior among teenage boys in Baltimore, Indianapolis, and Phoenix, after taking account of socioeconomic differences between learning disabled and nondisabled subjects. Youth with LD reported more acts of violence, theft, alcohol and marijuana use, and school misbehavior and had more contact with the criminal justice system. The study provided support for the "susceptibility" hypothesis, which argues that personality characteristics (e.g., lack of impulse control) that are associated with LD contribute directly to increases in delinquency.

An experimental study in which adjudicated delinquents were randomly placed in remediation and control conditions showed that a relatively large amount of instruction (at least 40 to 50 hours) to improve basic skills reduced the recidivism of black youth, of teenagers with a relatively mild history of official delinquency, and of participants whose performance IQ was below average. The investigators concluded that this reduction in delinquency probably was due to bonding with the LD specialists who provided remediation (Fiske 1989a).

The Peer Group Interacting with Other Causes

The various causes of delinquency have been studied and delineated systematically in research Elliott, Huizinga, and Ageton (1985) conducted using longitudinal data from the National Youth Survey. The authors found support for a causal model in which problems involving socialization and social disorganization in the home, neighborhood, and school lead to involvement with delinquent peers. In particular, they concluded that "bonding to delinquent peers is the most proximate cause of delinquency and drug use," while "strain" and low "conventional bonding" in the family and the school have indirect effects mediated by the level of bonding to delinquent peers (p. 142). "Strain" involves the "discrepancy between a set of cultural expectations endorsed by the subject as important" in the home and the school and "his or her perceived realization of these goals." Youngsters who perceive themselves as not meeting important goals of the home and school experience strain. "Conventional bonding" involves the "amount of time spent with the family and on academic concerns at school" and the belief that one must not violate the rules of the home and school in order to achieve personal goals or aspirations (Elliott, Huizinga, and Ageton 1985, 95–96). Youngsters who experience strain and low conventional bonding in the family and the school are more likely to develop strong bonding with delinquent peers and then engage in delinquency and drug use (Thornberry 1987; Gardner and Shoemaker 1989; Sherry, Gomez, Rush and Sobocinski 1991).

Genetic Factors

James Wilson and Richard Herrnstein (1985) argue that some crime and delinquency is genetically based. Others such as Jencks (1987) and Zuckerman 1990) reject this explanation but agree that genetic factors may predispose some individuals to be highly aggressive, and in some cultures aggressiveness is channeled into antisocial outlets.

Inequality

Evidence presented by Currie (1985), Massner (1989), and Blackwell (1990) indicates that inequality in wealth and power is positively correlated with crime and delinquency in working-class populations. This relationship is not present in all societies and cultures. Crime and delinquency frequently become more prevalent as gaps between the poor and the wealthy grow larger (Schwartz and Exter 1990).

General Social and Cultural Forces

As indicated above, much of the analysis that addresses the genesis and manifestations of juvenile delinquency involves general social and cultural developments in society. Arrangements for socializing youth, influence of the mass media, availability of economic and educational opportunity, the size of the delinquency-prone youth group, and other social and cultural forces help determine whether and how young people attain productive roles and positions in their communities (Malcolm 1990). Roger Lane (1989) reviewed historical trends involving violent crime and delinquency over the past century and concluded that general social and cultural forces generated a relatively steady decline in interpersonal violence as the United States became urbanized and industrialized. Beginning in the 1960s, however, there has been a "post-industrial surge in violence" associated with major economic changes in society. As a result,

> whatever created the earlier, urban-industrial decline [in violence] is no longer working. The new economy makes unprecedented educational demands on its successful participants, as large numbers trade down these good old industrial jobs for [low-wage, marginal employment] . . . . Until the post-industrial economy offers some equivalent of the kind of socialization that their parents and grandparents experienced, many descendants of the old white working class will face a [bleak

> future] . . . . Here and indeed across the post-industrial world the history of the American "underclass" may represent the future of millions more. That is a recipe for trouble of many kinds. (Lane 1989, 76–77)

DRUG ABUSE

A major aspect of the life of youth since 1955 is the so-called drug culture—the vastly increased use (or abuse) of psychedelic (consciousness-expanding) and other drugs by youth. Data on drug use among youth have been provided annually since 1975 in national surveys of high-school seniors conducted by the University of Michigan Institute for Social Research (e.g., Johnston, O'Malley, and Bachman 1990). Three major findings from the surveys include:

1. *Marijuana.* Marijuana use by high-school seniors declined in the 1980s. The percentage of seniors who report having used marijuana within the previous year fell from a peak of 54 percent in 1978 to little more than 40 percent in 1991. This decline probably was due in part to an increasing concern about the effects of marijuana on health. The percentage of seniors who attributed "great risk" to regular marijuana use increased from 35 percent in 1978 to 78 percent in 1989.

2. *Cocaine.* The percentage of seniors who reported using cocaine during the previous year increased from 7 percent in 1975 to 17 percent in 1985, but it then declined to less than 7 percent in 1991.

3. *Alcohol.* More than 80 percent of 1991 high-school seniors reported using alcohol during the previous year. Use and abuse of alcohol by young people continues to be a very serious problem, and the average beginning age for alcohol drinking has dropped to thirteen. Alcohol is involved in all three of the leading causes of death among young people: accidents, homicide, and suicide (Saunders 1989).

Even though recent declines in use of marijuana and cocaine have been encouraging, the use of cocaine has been troubling, particularly because evidence has been accumulating concerning serious negative effects of cocaine on mental and physical health. In addition, cocaine has become much more easily available in the form of crack. Lloyd D. Johnston of the Institute for Social Research has summarized some findings and implications of the Institute's surveys on cocaine use:

> *It is important for the general public to recognize the insidious way in which a severe cocaine dependency develops, or we are going to see an already serious epidemic expand even further. . . . We have suggested to those in policy positions that changing people's complacency about experimental and occasional use of cocaine may be an important step toward controlling the rising casualty rate of this drug. . . . Trying to publicize the vast network of corruption and human suffering associated with cocaine may be an effective way of getting potential users to think twice. (quoted in* Editors of ISR *1985–86, pp. 5, 7–8)*

The Institute for Social Research surveys of high-school seniors also showed that illicit drug use is highest in large metropolitan areas, in the Northeast, among males, and among students who do not plan to go to college. In addition, the surveys found that the great majority of students say their friends do not condone the use of illicit drugs other than marijuana, and most say their friends do not approve of regular marijuana use. The data further indicated that the rise that had been occurring in peer approval of marijuana use was sharply reversed in 1980–81 and thereafter. The researchers concluded that the decline they found in marijuana use among seniors was due to greater recognition of both the physical and the psychological damage that may accompany abuse of this drug.

Both alcohol and marijuana are not just widely used but also are widely abused by many adolescents and youth. Concern with marijuana, alcohol, or other relatively mild drugs arises partly from the possibility that they may stimulate or reinforce alienation from major social institutions and hinder the transition to adulthood among many adolescents and youth (Hawley 1990). Thus, a report on marijuana by the Secretary of Health, Education and Welfare pointed out that many "of the factors which have been found to be related to drug use—low academic performance, rebelliousness, depression or criminal activity—appear more often to precede rather than to follow the use of drugs." There is reason to be concerned about use among adolescents, especially "when such use become an escape from the demands of preparing for later life" (National Institute on Drug Abuse 1977, 9, 11, 27). Recent research regarding the effects of marijuana supports the conclusion that frequent use has a variety of detrimental consequences including impairment of learning ability and memory, damage to the body's immune system, and infertility. Some authorities now believe that contrary to earlier conclusions, heavy use of marijuana frequently is a stepping stone to use of other drugs such as heroin and cocaine (Mills and Noyes 1984; Saunders 1989).

Several researchers have been trying to identify the forces that lead to or are associated with the use of illicit drugs (Stein, Newcomb, and Bentler 1987; Sherry, Gomez, Rush and Sobocinski 1991). For example, Huba and Bentler (1980) surveyed 1,634 students in the seventh, eighth, and ninth grades and concluded that adolescents become more susceptible to peer encouragement to try various drugs as they proceed through these grades, and that the relative effects of peer and adult influences depend on the student's age and sex and on the type of drug considered. Jessor, Chase, and Donovan (1980) have analyzed data on seventh- through twelfth-grade students who participated in the National Study of Adolescent Drinking Behavior, Attitudes, and Correlates, and concluded that proneness to marijuana use

> *appears to consist of a rather coherent and integrated pattern of psychosocial attributes: in the* personality system, *greater value on*

independence than on academic achieve-ment, lower expectations for academic achievement, greater tolerance of deviance, and less religiosity; in the perceived environment system, *less compatibility between the adolescent's two major reference groups— parents and friends, less influence of parents relative to friends, and greater approval for and models for marijuana use and other problem behaviors; and in the* behavior system, *greater actual involvement in other problem behaviors and less participation in conventional activities. (p. 610)*

Jessor and his colleagues also found that essentially the same pattern accounted for problem use of alcohol, that marijuana involvement and abuse of alcohol were highly correlated, and that these patterns held regardless of sex, age, or ethnic group. After noting that similar conclusions have been reported with respect to adolescent vandalism, stealing, and other forms of deviance, they further concluded that prevention approaches should consider the syndrome or cluster of problem behaviors, rather than trying to deal with adolescent problem behaviors in isolation from one another.

Concern for drug abuse among adolescents and teenagers probably should be somewhat tempered by recognition that most users apparently do not suffer long-range harm from participation in youth subcultures that sanction relatively mild drugs. In this regard, Ramos (1980) has examined research on the drug subcultures of the 1960s and 1970s and concluded that one should not underestimate the "extent to which illicit drug users naturally reform once the adolescent peer group supporting the deviant behavior matures, weakens, and inevitably disbands" (p. 242). After citing research indicating that most young drug abusers eventually "mellow out" or "mature out," he concluded that "it is of some consolation, no doubt, to recognize that . . . going straight, not staying deviant, is the rule rather than the exception" (p. 244).

Nevertheless, drug and alcohol abuse among youth is a serious national concern. As mentioned, cocaine use involves a vast network of corruption and human suffering that increasingly afflicts the young. In addition, the spread of smokable cocaine in the form of crack appears to be increasing the number of youth addicted to cocaine. Use of other drugs is still substantial and frequently has harmful physical and psychological effects on young people (Hawley 1990).

As is true with delinquency, teenage pregnancy, and several other youth problems, drug use is particularly a problem with underclass youth in big cities (Treaster 1991). Inciardi (1980) has examined research on this aspect of the drug problem and concluded that at least since the 1940s, most inner-city communities "have maintained large populations of drug users that are heavily involved in crime" (p. 199). Because youth crime in the inner city has a number of causes other than drug addiction (e.g., high rates of unemployment and poverty), one cannot say that delinquency and crime are caused primarily by drugs. Rather, illicit use of hard drugs is both a manifestation of underclass environments and a cause, for some users, of additional deviance. Unless this environment is changed, youth drug abuse will continue to be characteristic of inner-city communities in the future, with occasional epidemic use occurring as social, political, and economic forces escalate the underlying conditions that lead to abuse.

Much of the responsibility for education about drug use and its prevention has been given to the schools, but educators apparently have not been very successful in providing effective programs to prevent drug use (Buscemi 1985; Miller 1988; Flax 1990b). Thus, Hanson (1980) has provided the following summary of conclusions from early research on drug education:

Research has demonstrated that while it is relatively easy to increase drug knowledge, it is more difficult to modify attitudes. A number of studies have reported greater changes in knowledge than in attitude, or have reported changes in knowledge unaccompanied by changes in attitude. . . . By far the largest number of studies have found no effects of drug education upon use. (p. 273)

However, indications are that some antidrug programs devised in the 1980s have been more effective than earlier programs (Viadero 1986; Treaster 1990). In general, such programs place greater emphasis on younger students, on longitudinal instruction for more than a year, on helping students learn to resist peer pressure and to understand how drugs have negative effects in daily life, and on coordination between efforts of the school and the community (Buscemi 1985; Rose 1986; Ellickson and Bell 1990). On the other hand, this also means that successful antidrug education tends to be relatively complex and expensive, in contrast to ineffective earlier programs that frequently consisted of little more than occasional lectures and provision of information (Viadero 1986; Rose 1986; Ellickson and Bell 1990).

National concern about the negative effects of drug use among young people and adults greatly escalated in the late 1980s, in part because many observers felt that cocaine use had reached epidemic proportions in some communities and was having increasingly detrimental effects on individuals and society. In this context, the President's Commission on Organized Crime issued a report stating that the "menace of drugs" has become "a threat to national security," and the National Association of Secondary School Principals issued a statement referring to drug abuse as the most "pernicious and persistent" problem faced by contemporary youth (Rose 1986). In 1990, the National Commission on Drug-Free Schools recommended a large expansion of antidrug programs in elementary and secondary schools, with greater parent involvement and extension of such efforts beyond regular school hours (Flax 1990b).

TEEN PREGNANCY

The teenage pregnancy rate rose significantly between 1950 and 1970 but then declined through most of the 1970s and 1980s. In 1989, however, the decline was reversed, with a particularly sharp rise for young women between the ages of fifteen and seventeen (Barringer 1990a). Even though the number and rate of births among all teenagers fell during recent decades due to decline in the youth population, availability of abortion, use of contraceptives, and other causes, the percentage of births to unwed mothers among babies born to teenagers increased explosively from 15 percent in 1960 to nearly 70 percent in 1989 (Select Committee 1986; Mydans 1989; Caldas 1991).

The Select Committee on Children, Youth, and Families (1986) of the U.S. House of Representatives examined these trends in the context of other information bearing on teenage pregnancy and identified five related problems.

1. Families headed by young mothers are much more likely to be living below the poverty level than are other families.
2. Teen mothers suffer higher rates of marital separation and divorce than do women giving birth at later ages. The risk of marital dissolution is carried on through later life, showing up in increased risks of marital dissolution in second marriages.
3. Infants born to teenage mothers, particular those under age seventeen, are much more likely to have a low Apgar score—the summary measure used to evaluate the newborn infant's overall physical condition—than are babies born to older mothers.
4. Pregnant teens who give birth are much less likely to receive prenatal care in the first trimester of pregnancy than are other mothers.
5. Children of teenage parents tend to be less healthy on the average than other children and tend to exhibit learning difficulties more frequently in school. These effects result principally from the severe social and economic consequences of early childbearing. (Select Committee n.d., 1)

Kingsley Davis (1980) has studied the data on teenage pregnancy in the United States and stressed the following four conclusions: (1) teenage births constitute a higher proportion of births in the United States than in other industrial nations; (2) this proportion is particularly high in the black population and in the younger ages; (3) the proportion of out-of-wedlock births is nearly five times greater for women under twenty than for older women; and (4) out-of-wedlock fertility has risen steadily for adolescents while falling for older women. Davis attributes the rise in illegitimacy among teenagers to such interrelated considerations as wider availability of contraceptives, earlier and more frequent sexual intercourse, decline in parental and community influence over the behavior of youth, changes in ideology that no longer require or pressure the father to marry a pregnant teenager, assumption by society and social agencies of responsibility for assisting young mothers with out-of-wedlock children, and greater community and societal acceptance of teenage sexuality and illegitimacy.

Regarding international comparisons, studies conducted for the Guttmacher Institute (Jones 1986; Hilts 1990) found that the teenage pregnancy rate for white females in the United States is much higher—in most cases two to five times higher—than the rates reported for Canada, England, France, the Netherlands, Sweden, and other industrialized nations. The authors' analysis concluded that "two factors are key to the location of the United States with regard to teenage fertility: an ambivalent, sometimes Puritanical attitude toward sex [which discourages fertility control], and the existence of a large, economically deprived underclass" (Jones 1986, 230).

As mentioned, the teenage pregnancy rate in the United States is higher among black females than among white females (Ellis 1990). In addition, the rate of out-of-wedlock births among women under age twenty is much higher for African Americans than for white (Bennett, Bloom, and Craig 1989). Because a higher percentage of the black population is relatively low in socioeconomic status, one can assume that the racial dis-

crepancy in illegitimacy is due partly to this social class difference (Caldas 1991).

Although research has not conclusively identified racial differences in teenage pregnancy after taking account of social class, Davis (1980), Farber (1990), and other analysts believe that some of the differences probably involve racial factors; that is, that oppression and discrimination associated with race have produced social conditions conducive to relatively high illegitimacy rates among African Americans. After reviewing research on the very high rates of teenage pregnancy among black youth in the United States, Moore, Simms, and Betsey (1986) reached the following conclusions:

Many of the factors found independently to predict early childbearing—less information, more poorly educated parents, school dropout, poor employment prospects, single-parent families—are found to be concentrated in those neighborhoods in which black children are particularly likely to be growing up. The aggregate influence of these separate factors may be greater than the single sum of the separate effects.... A realistic approach to the problem of early pregnancy in the black community will need to confront the attitudes of contemporary black youth which seem to be relatively accepting of early sex and out-of-wedlock parenthood. However, it is important to recognize that blacks, like other social groups, are very heterogeneous and that the adult generation does not support or encourage early sexual activity or pregnancy. (Moore, Simms, and Betsey 1986, xii, 136–137)

In any case, it appears that pregnancy and illegitimacy are particularly likely to cause other problems and to be symptomatic of destructive social environments among black youth in inner-city communities (Hulbert 1990). The association between teenage motherhood and later-life disadvantage is well established, and many observers believe this association is bidirectional: young women who are poor and have limited opportunity are more likely to have babies at an earlier age, but having a baby also reduces the future opportunities of many young women (Hulbert 1990). Furstenberg (1977; 1988; Furstenberg, Brooks-Gunn, and Morgan 1987; Furstenberg, Levine, and Brooks-Gunn 1990) has conducted longitudinal research working with low-income, teenage, black females in Baltimore and has found that in many cases motherhood had a negative impact on their subsequent careers:

> *Early pregnancy created a distinct set of problems for the adolescent parent that forced a redirection of her intended life course. In particular, we established a number of links connecting early childbearing to complications in marriage, to disruption in schooling, to economic problems and, to some extent, to problems in family size regulation and childbearing as well. . . .*
>
> *Some women had been able to repair the disorder created by an untimely pregnancy. . . . Still other participants were not so successful in coping with the problems caused by precipitate parenthood. . . . Poorly educated, unskilled, often burdened by several small children, many of these women at age 20 or 21 had become resigned to a life of economic deprivation.*
>
> *. . . Almost all the young mothers in our study wanted to complete high school, but most were not so inspired to remain in school whatever the difficulties. . . . Similarly, with few exceptions, the young mothers wished to avoid a rapid repeat pregnancy, but few were so anxious not to conceive that they continued to use birth control methods when events in their lives made contraception difficult or frightening. (Furstenberg 1977, 297–298)*

Furstenberg provided a portrayal of young inner-city women trapped in a destructive environment in which a variety of forces generate and reinforce underclass status; teenage pregnancy and childbearing constitute one force that fre-

quently is a devastating hurdle for all but the most supermotivated young women (Furstenberg, Levine, and Brooks-Gunn 1990). He also pointed out that although the federal government emphasizes that pregnant teenagers have a right to continue their education and although many programs have been initiated to reduce or eliminate teenage pregnancy and related problems, opportunities and programs vary in scope and effectiveness, and services generally are too timid and fragmented to deal with the inner-city situation. Jaffe and Dryfoos (1980) and Nettles (1990) reviewed fertility control programs in the United States and concluded that it was not yet possible to determine whether preventive educational services (family life, population, or sex education) were having any substantial effect on adolescent sex patterns, fertility control practices, pregnancy experience, abortion use, or childbearing.

However, some subsequent research has reported encouraging results concerning the efficacy of school-based clinics and other public-school programs to help prevent or alleviate the problems associated with teenage pregnancy (Zabin 1986; Buie 1987; Miller, D.F. 1990). On the other hand, these problems seem to have become increasingly severe and widespread in the 1980s, and public recognition of their importance expanded rapidly in the 1980s. For example, popular journals carried articles with such provocative titles as "Children Having Children" and "Children As Parents" (Hulbert 1984); and the National Education Association published a paperback book (Compton, Duncan, and Hruska 1986) emphasizing the widening scope of teenage pregnancy problems and recommending that, among other responses, schools expand sex education and related staff development activities, bolster antidropout programs for pregnant adolescents, help sponsor advocacy and day-care programs, and offer appropriate prenatal care and social support services. The U.S. House of Representatives Select Committee on Children, Youth, and Families surveyed the situation and reported that "there is no focused approach to solving the complex problem of teen pregnancy.... The efforts that do exist are too few, uncoordinated, and lack significant support. In short, the system is broken" (Select Committee 1986, ix).

Shortly thereafter, a National Research Council Panel appointed by the National Academy of Sciences and the National Academy of Engineering issued a 337-page report recommending widespread distribution of inexpensive contraceptives to teenagers, beginning sex education at an early age, establishment of more school-based clinics, and life-planning courses as part of the curriculum, media help to emphasize "sexual responsibility," and availability of abortion to teenagers (Panel on Adolescent Pregnancy and Childbearing 1986). The Panel's report drew attention to controversial aspects (e.g., information about contraceptives and abortion) of school-based clinics established or proposed in many school districts. Highly publicized conflicts over school-based clincs have taken place in numerous cities (Miller, D.F. 1990).

COMMUNITY AND NATIONAL SERVICE

During the 1980s, a number of influential organizations and individuals expressed support for comprehensive programs to provide national and/or local community service opportunities for children and youth. In 1985, for example, the Youth Policy Institute issued a report advocating that service opportunities be expanded sufficiently to constitute a national system with a "demonstrable impact" on society. Pointing out that the United States already operates an ad hoc program including the Peace Corps and VISTA (Volunteers in Service to America), the authors of the report described a model system based in part on programs in West Germany, Nigeria, and Israel and incorporating components such as the following (Foley, Manaker, and Schwartz 1984):

- Voluntary opportunities for all young people past the age of compulsory schooling.

- Inclusion of a wide variety of opportunities such as military service, care for the elderly, and tutorial assistance to children.
- Contributions to goals unmet by the marketplace, such as support for health care and conservation of public lands.
- Involvement of all sectors and every level of society in planning and operation of a national service.

Two years later, a study conducted for the Ford Foundation analyzed four approaches to national service, including a mandatory school-based program, a national draft, a federally supported volunteer service, and universal service with income-tax penalties for nonparticipants (Danzig and Szanton 1986). Among the most important benefits of such programs, the authors concluded, would be promotion of a sense of citizenship as well as personal development and socially useful activity on the part of youth and young adults.

While national reports and recommendations were being prepared and released, service programs for youth were being introduced or expanded in numerous communities. For example, the Campus Outreach Opportunity League and Youth Service America were active in promoting service opportunities for high-school and college students; school districts in Atlanta, Detroit, Washington, DC, and elsewhere initiated programs for high-school students; and consortia of public and private organizations in Boston, New York, and other communities also helped sponsor or established service programs (Bandow 1990; Schapiro 1990). As interest continued to build, nine differing proposals for federal sponsorship of community-service and related activities were introduced in Congress.

Following considerable debate and deliberation as well as negotiation with the Bush administration, Congress passed the National and Community Service Act of 1990. With nearly $400 million authorized for 1991 through 1993, the Service Act will provide grants that elementary and secondary schools, institutions of higher education, and community-based groups can use to develop and implement service projects. Student assignments can include a wide range of activities involving environmental conservation, hospitals, child-care facilities, public-facilities rehabilitation, law-enforcement institutions, schools, and many other social- or human-service agencies. Another major section in the Act will enable as many as eight states to offer programs that will provide students $5,000 worth of educational benefits for each full-time year of volunteer service, or $2,000 for each year of part-time service (Blumenstyk 1990b). Participating youth also can receive remedial instruction to upgrade their basic skills.

The extent to which the National and Community Service Act of 1990 will prove valuable for participating communities and youth will depend on many considerations involving the design and implementation of individual programs. In this regard, analysts at the Children's Defense Fund have examined a number of service programs and concluded that effective programs exemplify the following five "key elements":

1. Careful adult supervision within a well-defined structure to maximize learning and maintain the quality of service provided for young people.
2. Ample opportunity for participants to reflect and discuss their service experience to reinforce the benefits of such activities.
3. Basic academic training for young people who need such assistance.
4. Close consultation with local officials and public employee unions to ensure that projects do not conflict or interfere with the efforts and responsibilities of public agencies.
5. [Awareness of] the risks of substituting service programs for job creation efforts . . . [so that service opportunities are not] advanced as a less expensive way of providing jobs for young workers who have no other employment prospects. (Heffernan and Taylor 1989, 13)

PERSONAL CAPITAL / EDUCATIONAL EQUITY ACCOUNTS

As already mentioned, one component in the National and Community Service Act of 1990 will provide participating youth with a specified amount of funding to continue their education for each year of voluntary community service they are willing to perform. Recognizing the growing importance of postsecondary education (see Chapter 7) and the difficulties low-income youth encounter in obtaining a college or other postsecondary education (see Chapter 2), some social scientists have long advocated such an approach to help provide more equitable opportunities and ensure a more productive transition to adulthood for disadvantaged youth.

Expanding on this theme, several economists have called for a comprehensive national program that would provide every young person with a specified sum of money set aside in a special bank or entitlement account to allow him or her to obtain useful education and training. Typically referred to as *personal capital* or *educational equity accounts*, such an entitlement would counteract inequities arising from the fact that the families of low-income children and youth pay considerable taxes for higher education while their sons and daughters historically have been underrepresented in enrollment at colleges and universities. For example, Robert Haveman (1988) has proposed that the federal government provide citizens with a more "even start" in life by giving every eighteen year old a $20,000 personal account to spend as he or she chooses for approved purchases of health-care services and of education and training options most suitable to his or her personal goals. Among other benefits, this approach would replace and, hopefully, vastly improve currently problematic financial assistance programs for postsecondary students (see Chapter 2). More recently, Bluestone, Clayton-Mathews, Havens, and Young (1990) proposed expansion of Social Security to include an Educational Equity Program that would establish an Educational and Training

Bank functioning with the following five eligibility and repayment policies and characteristics:

1. Maximum awards would be $10,000 per year and $40,000 lifetime (in 1990 dollars).
2. Actual awards could not exceed tuition plus room and board and a stipulated amount for miscellaneous education-related expenses.
3. Awards would be transferable across accredited schools and could be used at any state-accredited or licensed postsecondary institution, including vocational schools and apprenticeship programs.
4. Repayment each year during subsequent employment would be arranged through Social Security deductions and would be based on the amount of the previous awards and the age and income of the recipient, that is, persons who earn less would repay a lower percentage.
5. The program would be implemented through an agency called the Equity Investment in American Fiduciary Trust, which would coordinate activities with the Internal Revenue Service and the Social Security Trust Fund.

COMMUNITY SUPPORT FOR YOUTH DEVELOPMENT

Based on information from hundreds of intensive interviews and other data on the situation of young people in ten U.S. communities, Francis Ianni (1989a, 1989b) concluded that a community's overall support or lack of support for the development of children and youth can make a great difference in determining how well they are prepared for later life. More specifically, Ianni concluded that the socializing institutions in the community should function together to provide a "caring structure" that produces positive behavioral standards and expectations. Such standards and expectations are not "so much a set of rules sanctioned by the community" as they are "a loose collection of shared understandings [that

limit] the variability of permissible behavior." Ianni and his colleagues decided to call this "unwritten, 'sensed' set of expectations and standards the community's 'youth charter' " (Ianni 1989a, 680). A productive youth charter provides "patient, guided tutoring," rather than "only benign neglect or outraged moralizing" (1989a, 682).

Ianni and his colleagues particularly recommended that communities do much more to provide constructive *mentoring* programs for children and youth. Such programs can and do take many forms, ranging from "continuous and very intense encounters," when young people are paired with an adult mentor, to less structured participation in various kinds of learning networks. Apprenticeship training, tutoring aspects of school-business partnership efforts, adult guidance in youth-oriented, community-service programs, and adult supervision of peer-counseling services also constitute examples of potentially productive mentoring. Comprehensive and intensive mentoring approaches are especially needed in the inner city because positive "formal role models" tend to be less available there to help young people attain a productive adult identity (Ianni 1989b, 269–271).

SCHOOLS AND OTHER INSTITUTIONS IN A CONSTRUCTIVE PROGRAM FOR YOUTH

To be constructive and realistic at the same time is the goal we must set for ourselves as we consider the situation of youth in the 1990s. The transition from adolescence to adulthood is more difficult than it has been in earlier periods. The weight of helping young people make this transition has been shifting away from the family to other institutions, including government, employers, mass media, and social-service agencies. As pointed out by James Coleman and Torsten Husen (1985), the industrial pattern wherein

> *the economy produces, the family consumes, and the State redistributes, is not adequate any longer. The traditional meanings have*

changed. The economy educates as well as produces, the family produces (with most women in the labor force), and the State is drawn into the productive system as a major provider of services. This also means that the relationships between the three have changed profoundly. . . . However, the shift . . . does not take place without problems: the process of transition from youth to adult appears to be increasingly taken over by youth-oriented commercial interests. . . . It is evident that if the difficulties are not to increase, society as a whole must, especially through its educational institutions, devise new mechanisms for aiding youth entering the labor market. (Coleman and Husen 1985, 9, 47)

Changes and problems with respect to the situation of youth recently have been analyzed by The National Commission on the Role of the School and the Community in Improving Adolescent Health (1990). Sponsored by the National Association of State Boards of Education and the American Medical Association, the Commission first examined data on increased drug use, violence, sexual activity, suicide, unemployment, and other aspects of serious social problems among adolescents and young adults. The Commission then characterized the situation as constituting an "unprecedented health crisis" that has serious consequences for society because for "the first time in the history of this country, young people are *less* healthy and *less* prepared to take their places in society than were their parents" (The National Commission on the Role of the School 1990, Executive Summary). The Commission then proceeded to issue a "CODE BLUE," which it viewed as analogous to the medical signal of a life-threatening emergency that requires "extraordinary actions to save a patients' life." It also sketched the outlines of a unified approach in which the educational system would work in cooperation with other social institutions to "substantially improve the health and achievement" of young people and the opportunities available to help them become produc-

tive adults (The National Commission on the Role of the School 1990, 18). Recommendations for carrying out intensive national efforts to achieve these goals were organized as follows (pp. 18–48):

I. Guarantee access to health services to all adolescents regardless of income or ability to pay.
   1. Restructure health insurance to give all youth access to benefits including family, medical, and psycho-social services.
   2. Establish adolescent health centers at convenient locations, including schools.
   3. Expand school health services as well as other services for adolescents.
II. Focus on communities as the front line in the battle for adolescent health.
   1. Establish coordinating community councils for children, youth, and families, with a major focus on adolescent health in devising local solutions.
   2. Make radical changes in federal and state policies and programs in order to support collaboration on behalf of individual children, youth, and families.
   3. Transform fragmented and disparate neighborhood organizations and individuals into a caring community.
III. Organize and provide services around people, not the other way around.
   1. Take bold action and modify "business as usual" to improve collaboration among agencies and professional disciplines.
   2. Take extraordinary steps, including the creation of Neighborhood Health Corps, to provide service to the most vulnerable low-income youth.
   3. Train many more professionals to work collaboratively and effectively with each other and young people.
IV. Urge educators and schools to take a more central role in improving adolescents' health.
   1. Make schools less impersonal in order to treat adolescents as individuals and

increase their affiliation. (Characteristics of a more "personal school" include identifying and providing help to students who are having difficulties, relatively small enrollment or division into smaller subunits, and "reaching out" more directly to families.)

2. Provide a more positive learning environment to motivate adolescents.
3. Develop a new approach to health education, including a planned, sequential K–12 curriculum addressing drug education, emotional health, and a wide range of other issues.
4. Increase collaboration inside and outside the school to reduce physical, social, and emotional problems that interfere with learning.
5. Appoint and assign approrpriate responsibilities to health coordinators at every school.
6. Conduct school staff development focused on health issues and collaboration.

Analysts also have been trying to identify approaches that already have had some success linking schools with other human-service agencies to help children and adolescents and to determine how such linkages can be improved systematically in the future (Lewis 1991b). After reviewing recent research and analysis on this topic, Carol Ascher (1990a) concluded that the most frequent and promising activities at the local level include:

1. Assigning a teacher or social worker to help students obtain services from community agencies.
2. Integrating programs and services through placing nurses, social workers, teachers, and other professionals at a common site, usually within or near the school and/or
3. Creating a community coordinating council representing mental health, adult education, social welfare, and other services.

Ascher also pointed out that difficulties frequently arise when personnel from several bureaucratic organizations try to work together using diverse sets of rules and regulations. Such collaborations have been most successful, she further concluded, when they exemplify the following characteristics:

- They are generally comprehensive, either directly offering a wide array of services, or providing an easy entry point to services, delivered flexibly and coherently.
- They move beyond crisis management and even early intervention to focus on prevention and development.
- They cross professional and bureaucratic boundaries to offer coherent services, often in nontraditional settings and at nontraditional hours.
- They provide staff with the time, training, and skills necessary to build relationships of trust and respect.
- They hire one staff member who is from the local community and can act as a facilitator.
- They involve both teachers and parents in the communication loop.
- They deal with the child as part of the family, and the family as part of the neighborhood or community.
- They build in accountability, with creative and meaningful measures. (Ascher 1990a, 2)

CONCLUSION

Trends reviewed in this chapter indicate that the transition to adulthood has become more difficult for many young people than was true earlier in the twentieth century. The prolonging of adolescence is a problem for many youth. In the past few decades it has been associated with substantial increases in unemployment, suicide, crime and delinquency, drug use and abuse, teenage pregnancy, and out-of-wedlock birth rates. These problems have been particularly evident and devastating among economically disadvantaged minority youth in the inner city. Thus the problems young people encounter in their transition to adulthood and the high incidence of destructive behavior such as crime, drug abuse, and teenage pregnancy are causes for serious concern. This chapter also identified the kinds of national and local programs and actions that governmental and nongovernmental agencies and the schools might take to address the problems systematically and comprehensively. Many such programs and actions are required in the future if more youth are to make a successful transition to productive adulthood.

EXERCISES

1. Write a paper arguing for or against the following proposition: Education at the secondary school and college levels should be mainly concerned with the development of knowledge and intellectual skills necessary for the professions and for business leadership.

2. Assuming that everybody at age 16 was given a voucher, equivalent in value to the average cost of education through four years of college, to be used at his or her discretion for schooling or skill acquisition at any subsequent time, describe how you think four quite different persons, two women and two men, might use these vouchers.

3. From your observation and experience in your own institution, what is the drug situation?

4. Read what you can find on delinquency among girls. What differentiates it from delinquency among boys?

5. Find an example of a work-experience program for predelinquent or delinquent boys; describe and evaluate it.

6. Is it valid to say that youth are less mature now than they were two or three decades ago? What arguments support this conclusion, and what arguments counteract it? Which arguments do you think are most defensible?

SUGGESTIONS FOR FURTHER READING

1. A set of essays on the transition from youth to adulthood has been edited by Ralph W. Tyler. Entitled *From Youth to Constructive Adulthood*, these essays describe and analyze the situation of youth from the points of view of educators and social scientists.

2. A thought-provoking four-year longitudinal study of high-school and college students has been conducted by Richard and Shirley Jessor, entitled *Problem Behavior and Psychosocial Development*. This study reveals a great deal of deviant behavior in a middle-sized college town.

3. The values of a work-experience program for boys in the prevention of delinquency are explored thoroughly in the book *400 Losers* by Ahlstrom and Havighurst, which describes a five-year experimental study in Kansas City.

4. Much of the analysis in James Q. Wilson's *Thinking about Crime* (1983) is devoted to juvenile delinquency and drug abuse.

5. *Student Pregnancy* by Compton, Duncan, and Hruska (1986) offers many suggestions regarding how the schools might help address problems related to teenage pregnancy.

6. *Finding Work* (1986) edited by Ray Rist provides information and analysis regarding youth employment and training in Australia, England, Japan, the United States, and other countries.

7. A report on *Student Service* (Harrison 1987) prepared for The Carnegie Foundation for the Advancement of Teaching describes many programs providing voluntary and assigned community service for high-school students and also offers suggestions for initiating and conducting such programs.

8. *The Case for School-Based Health Clinics* by Dean Miller (1990) focuses on services involving teen pregnancy and includes chapters dealing with the history of clinics, their structure, staffing, and funding, and the role of parents.

9. *Substance Abuse in Children and Adolescents* by Schinke, Botvin, and Orlandi (1991) describes approaches to prevention as well as evaluation of interventions.

10. The June 1991 issue of the *Phi Delta Kappan* reviews research on school-based community service and describes a variety of outstanding programs.

7

Mobility and Education

In a complex, democratic society, many people will move upward from one social class to another during the first half of their lifetime. This kind of movement is implied in the ideal of equality of opportunity. However, social movement downward from one class to another is also implied for some people.

A substantial amount of upward mobility is evidence of the existence of opportunity. Education is widely believed to help young people move up the social scale by preparing them for a higher status occupation than that of their parents, by increasing their earning power, and by giving them more of the general knowledge of the past and the present that marks middle-class people.

In a democratic society, there is bound to be much competition for the prized middle- and upper-class positions because they have so much that most people desire. Children born to upper- and middle-class families have some advantage in this competition, because they probably learn much in the family that will help them maintain the family position. Children from lower-status families may be able to compete successfully for some of the higher-status positions if they have certain favored qualities of mind and personality and if they get sufficient help from the educational system.

It is widely believed that democratic societies reward young people on the basis of merit, where *merit* is defined as ability plus effort. Such a society is called *meritocratic* and should display a good deal of upward social mobility for its young people. However, difficulties do block the path of upward mobility for children of lower-status families and for children of some minority groups.

This chapter examines the nature and amount of social mobility and the relationships of education to social mobility. First, we report on the actual amount of social mobility and on several aspects of this general phenomenon. Then, major research studies on the relations of education to social mobility are described. This chapter also describes major controversies among researchers on the relationship of education to the socioeconomic structure of the United States.

THE NATURE AND AMOUNT OF SOCIAL MOBILITY

Even though much upward social mobility today occurs through education, other channels are important. The self-made businessman whose wife guides him up the social ladder is one example of an alternative pattern of mobility. Athletic prowess in a boy often provides a good base for mobility, as when a boy becomes a professional baseball or football player. Although there are notable exceptions, in most cases athletic ability combines with a college education if the young man is to become a successful middle-aged man. The mobility patterns of girls have increased in variety as the world of business and professions opened more widely to women in the 1970s.

The people who rise on the social scale are those who have talents, abilities, and motives their society values. In the highly instrumental and materialist society of the past 100 years, these values were ambition, economic foresight, habits of industry, and verbal or mechanical intelligence. Today's period of rapid technological and social change is likely to see a change in the human qualities that gain favored status for people. It is difficult to predict the future, but we should keep this possible change in mind as we examine the mobility data for recent decades.

Mobile Youth at Midcentury

Teachers and other observers often feel confident that they can spot the talented or the ambitious students and that they can predict which ones will and will not get further in life than their parents. At the same time, there are relatively few studies in which a large group of youngsters have been followed to find which ones actually do, in adulthood, follow patterns of upward mobility and thus to identify the characteristics leading to mobility.

One such study was carried out on a group of boys and girls who in 1951–52 constituted all the sixth graders in the public schools of a community called River City. They were followed until 1964, when they were approximately twenty-three years old. Some of the original 450 left the city and were lost to the study, but fairly adequate data are available on almost 400 of the group (Havighurst 1962).

Table 7-1 shows the social and intellectual characteristics of the group when studied at age twenty-three. By this time, almost all of those who expected to go to college had at least started. Of those who had not gone to college, the men and some of the women had been working for four to seven years. Most of the women had married and were homemakers.

Each person in the group was evaluated in comparison to family of origin with regard to educational level, occupation, occupational

TABLE 7-1 *Characteristics of Mobile and Stable Twenty-Three-Year-Olds in River City (N = 399)*

| | | *Mean Percentile Scores** | | |
	N	*IQ†*	*High School Grades*	*Social Effectiveness‡*
Upwardly mobile:				
Men	52	71	59	70
Women:				
Not married	11	75	75	77
Married between ages 21 and 24	18	65	75	77
Married by age 20	36	50	51	64
Total	117			
Stable:				
Men	101	42	45	42
Women:				
Not married	10	86	66	80
Married between ages 21 and 24	17	59	71	57
Married by age 20	72	42	47	46
Total	200			
Downwardly mobile:				
Men	44	28	26	40
Women:				
Not married	4	42	41	44
Married between ages 21 and 24	4	34	52	—
Married by age 20	30	50	48	42
Total	82			

* Based on the entire group of students.
† Based on a number of tests given in sixth grade.
‡ A combination measure including popularity, friendliness, and leadership as evaluated by both teachers and peers.

performance, and reputation in the community. On this basis he or she was identified as upwardly mobile, stable, or downwardly mobile. (The women who had married were assigned the status of their husbands; those who had not married were evaluated in the same way as the men.)

The data on *intelligence* are based on a battery of tests administered when the group was in the sixth grade. The data on *social effectiveness* came from sociometric tests and teachers' descriptions obtained when the students were in the sixth grade and again when they were in the ninth grade. The combination measure shown in Table 7-1 includes popularity, friendliness, and leadership as evaluated by both teachers and peers.

Among the men, the upwardly mobile as compared to the socially stable had been markedly superior in high school on measures of intelligence, school grades, and social effectiveness. The downwardly mobile had been the poorest on these measures. Thus, a teacher who knew this group of students could have predicted with considerable accuracy which boys would be upwardly mobile and which would be downwardly mobile.

For the women, however, predictions would have been more difficult. Although the upwardly mobile women had been superior in high school to the stable and to the downwardly mobile, the patterns were complicated by differences related to age at marriage. With a few exceptions, in the stable and upwardly mobile groups the late-marrying women (those who had not yet married by age twenty-three) had been superior to those who married between twenty-one and twenty-four; the latter, in turn, had been superior to those who married early (before age twenty).

At the same time, the woman who was upwardly mobile as the result of an early marriage to a higher-status man was higher on social effectiveness than were other early-marrying women, though not higher in intelligence or school grades. The early-marrying downwardly mobile women had the same IQ as the early-marrying upwardly mobile women. In short, social effectiveness, but not IQ, differentiated between early-marrying women who married "above" and early-marrying women who married "below" their own social status levels.

All in all, the River City study clearly showed two main paths of social mobility earlier in this century. Men, and some women, ascended the social ladder by making use of superior intelligence and superior social effectiveness to succeed in school and college and on the job. The more frequent path for women (as of 1960) was by marrying a relatively successful young man. Today, the path for upwardly mobile women is much more similar to that of men than was true in 1960.

The data and case study just described appear to indicate that education is a means to upward mobility for many young people, but not for others. Some people are downwardly mobile, and others achieve upward mobility through social resources other than education and through abilities other than intelligence, or through a combination of education or intelligence with other resources and personal qualities.

Group Mobility

The preceding section considers the phenomenon of individual social mobility, one mark of democracy in our social-class system. Group mobility affects and qualifies individual mobility. Group mobility occurs when a social group moves as a whole in relation to other groups. The mobile group may be a large or a small one. For example, skilled workers in the United States have gained greatly in economic status relative to minor white-collar workers and relative to farmers. The wages of electricians, plumbers, railroad men, and others of the so-called aristocracy of labor have risen more since 1900 than have the incomes of clerical and retail sales-workers, teachers, farmers, and other groups. This economic gain has enabled many of these blue-collar workers to move up, using their money to purchase the symbols of lower middle-class living.

Upward group mobility tends to favor individual mobility of members of the group, but the two movements are not identical. Thus, as the standard of living has risen, some working-class people have come to enjoy fancy automobiles, the newest home appliances, high school educations, and paid vacations, all of which would have marked them as middle class in 1920. Indeed, this phenomenon has caused some foreign observers to refer to the United States as a nation of middle-class people. However, those working-class people who now possess certain material and nonmaterial goods that in 1920 would have symbolized middle-class status have not thereby been turned into middle-class people. This is true because many of the symbols of middle-class status have changed in the interim. Today, middle-class people quite generally have a college education rather than the high school education characteristic of the middle class in 1920. Quite a few travel to Europe. These things have now become symbols of a middle-class life-style, a life-style not shared by working-class people. Thus, the system of rank continues in a changing society even though the bases or signs of rank are shifting.

Mobility of Ethnic, Racial, and Religious Groups

There has been a great deal of group mobility among the various ethnic and religious groups that have come to this country: first, English, then Irish, German, Scandinavian, French, Dutch, Polish, Hungarian, Italian, Bohemian, Serbian, Rumanian, Armenian, Chinese, Japanese, and Spanish American. People came in groups and made settlements either in the new lands on the frontier or in the cities. Gradually, they joined the main cultural stream of life in the United States. The schools hastened this process by teaching the new language and the new ways to their children.

Generally, a new immigrant started at the bottom of the social scale and worked up. For example, the Irish, the lowest status group in the midnineteenth century, were employed in digging canals and building railroads in the expanding country. They moved up, leaving room at the bottom for Scandinavians, Italians, and Bohemians, who in turn worked their way up.

Some immigrant groups came into the social system at a level above the bottom, either because they possessed capital, or because they brought with them a culture that was enough like that of the middle class to enable them to participate at once at that level. For example, numerous Germans came after 1848 because of political unrest and persecution in Germany. Some of them were middle-class people who started businesses and built up cities such as Milwaukee, St. Louis, and Cincinnati.

The Jews came with their religion and with a compound Jewish ethnic culture from Holland, France, Germany, England, Poland, and Russia. Some, with business skills and a willingness to go alone into new communities, moved into small towns and cities, where they rapidly rose to middle-class status, though their religious culture set them apart from other middle-class people. Many others remained in big cities, where, although they now occupy a wide range of social-class positions, a significant proportion work mainly as factory workers. Today, the Jewish people themselves comprise a variegated set of cultural subgroups. Some have become liberal in their religious views; others have remained Orthodox.

The Jews have probably made more use of education as a means of moving up in the social-class structure than has any other immigrant group, although education alone does not account for their mobility. According to studies by Sowell (1981), even when education is held constant, Jews as a group still outdistance non-Jews in occupational mobility.

Upward mobility among African Americans also has been substantial in recent decades. However, although the black middle class has greatly increased, many blacks are trapped in the big-city underclass. This situation is discussed extensively in Chapters 2 and 10 and also elsewhere in this book.

The displaced persons who fled into Germany at the close of World War II from Lithuania, Estonia, and Latvia and later came to the United States, were mainly middle-class people.

So also were the Hungarian refugees of the mid-1950s. Although they took whatever working-class jobs they could get, they quickly integrated themselves into the culture of the United States. Their children adopted middle-class ways of life relatively quickly.

During the 1960s, 1970s, and 1980s, there was substantial in-migration of Hispanics and Asians. Most Hispanic immigration has been from Mexico and Cuba, but some has been from South America. Asian immigrants have come particularly from Southeast Asia—Vietnam, Laos, and Cambodia; but significant numbers of in-migrants have also come from Korea and the Philippines. Mexican immigrants have tended to be low status and unskilled, whereas many of the immigrants from Cuba and the various Asian countries have been persons with relatively high levels of education and occupational skills. Recent immigrants from Russia, India, Israel, and some other countries also had relatively high skill levels. Because the immigration laws generally require that applicants possess skills or contacts likely to result in gainful employment, immigrants who enter the United States legally tend to be in a relatively good position to pursue social mobility for themselves and their children, compared to most who came during the high tide of immigration before 1920.

Thomas Sowell (1981) has studied the research on ethnic patterns of immigration and mobility in the United States. He cites many studies and historical records to support the following conclusions:

> *Perhaps the most striking pattern among American ethnic groups is their general rise in economic conditions with the passage of time. . . . In many parts of the world, people still live at an economic level not much above that of their ancestors. But in addition to absolute rises in living standards . . . American ethnic groups have typically also risen in relative terms.*
>
> *Every ethnic group has encountered obstacles to its progress. But the obstacles and suffering they experienced before arriving here usually exceeded anything experienced on*

> *American soil. Anti-Semitism in the United States meant encountering snobbery and occupational restrictions, but not living under the threat of mass expulsions and massacres. Even . . . slavery was worse for Africans enslaved to the Arabs or in the rest of the Western Hemisphere, where slaves died off faster than they could reproduce. In short, America has never been exempt from the age-old sins that have plagued the human species. What has been distinctively American is the extent to which other factors have also been at work, usually for the better. (p. 275)*

Assimilation of European Ethnic Groups

Data on the status of U.S. citizens whose ancestors immigrated from Central, Eastern, and Southern Europe indicate that they generally are productively assimilated within social and cultural patterns characteristic of the nation as a whole. Millions of ethnics from these regions came to the United States during the latter part of the nineteenth century and the early decades of the twentieth. Facing language and other cultural barriers, they struggled to prepare their children to enter the mainstream of U.S. society. By 1960, this goal had been fundamentally accomplished.

For example, until the 1930s, men whose ancestors came from Central, Eastern, and Southern Europe had substantially lower rates of college attendance than did men with British ancestry. For men born after 1946, however, college attendance rates for these ethnic groups have been virtually indistinguishable from those for men of British ancestry (Table 7-2). Data assembled by Richard Alba (1988) also indicate that the percentage of Central-, Eastern-, and Southern-European ethnics whose spouses have the same ancestry has diminished rapidly (Table 7-2), and that the percentage of ethnics who were raised as Catholic or Jewish declined from 91 percent for men born before 1916 to 77 percent for men born between 1946 and 1960 (not shown in Table 7-2). Information of this kind led Alba to the conclusion that among Central-,

Eastern-, and Southern-European ethnics, the typical younger person

> comes from the third or a later generation, was raised in a home where only English was spoken, has an ethnically mixed ancestry, and has attended college.... The breadth and strength of these differences ... imply a transformation of the ethnicity of these groups. ... Critical ethnic markers—for example, undivided ancestry, exposure to a mother tongue, endogamous marriage—are concentrated in older cohorts. During the next few decades, these cohorts will be greatly reduced by mortality so that the frequency of such characteristics will be reduced as well. (Alba 1988, 226)

Evidence indicating that religious differences associated with larger ethnic-group differences have diminished during recent decades also has been provided by Alwin (1989). After analyzing data dealing with values that parents emphasize in raising their children, Alwin concluded that in 1964 Catholics placed significantly greater emphasis on *obedience* and *conformity* than did Protestants, but by 1984 this difference had virtually disappeared.

Differences in Group Status and Mobility

Various racial and ethnic groups have differed in the rates with which they have moved up the social scale. Among immigrant groups in the northeast-

ern section of the United States, for instance, the Greeks as well as the Jews attained middle-class status more quickly than did French Canadians or southern Italians (Strodtbeck 1958; Rosen 1959).

There are probably several reasons for such differences. One is the extent to which the immigrant group possesses certain work skills that are valuable in the economy; another is the degree to which the dominant group is willing to permit newcomers equal access to jobs, housing, and schooling; another is the differences between the immigrant groups in psychological and cultural orientations toward achievement (Caplan, Whitmore, and Choy 1990). In a study of six ethnic and racial groups (Rosen 1959), historical and ethnographic data showed that differences between the groups in achievement motivation, values, and aspirations existed before these groups arrived in the United States, and that these differences tended to persist. The differences are related to the variations among the groups in rates of upward mobility.

Demographic and cultural considerations also play a part in determining the amount and rate of a group's mobility. Some of these considerations include the following:

Age Structure. Groups that have a relatively high proportion of young people, as do Mexican Americans and Puerto Ricans today, are likely to have lower than average current mobility because many members are just getting started in occupations and careers.

TABLE 7-2   *Twentieth-Century Changes in Educational Attainment and Spousal Similarity among U.S. Men with Eastern-, Central-, and Southern-European Ancestry, by Age Cohort*

	Percentage Attended College		
Age Cohort	Eastern, Central, and Southern European	Third Generation British	Percentage with Spouse of Same Ancestry
Born before 1916	21	30	43
Born 1916–1930	28	41	29
Born 1913–1946	49	53	16
Born 1946–1960	56	55	12

Source: Adapted from Alba 1988.

Region.   Although differences in wealth, education, and other indicators of status in regions of the United States are diminishing, these differences are still important; thus, groups such as Mexican Americans that are concentrated in low-income parts of the southwest will score lower on many socioeconomic measures (Waldinger 1990).

Fertility.   Historically and still today, high fertility rates and large numbers of children per family not only reflect poverty but also help perpetuate it (Kasarda and Billy 1985). Other considerations equal, groups such as African Americans and Hispanic Americans, which have higher than average fertility rates and relatively low incomes, will have problems transmitting socioeconomic advantages to their children.

Circumstances Involving In-Migration.   Those groups that have been in the United States longest will have had more time to become mobile, and those that enter under favorable economic conditions will have relatively greater opportunities for mobility (Waldinger 1990). In this regard, Sowell (1978a, 1978b, 1981) has pointed out that African Americans from the West Indies rank above the United States average in social status, whereas "native" blacks rank far below.

Sowell believes that the reasons for this difference involve historical patterns wherein slaves in the United States were made dependent on external support and were deprived of opportunities to obtain educational and occupational skills. Even though slavery in the West Indies was harsher in some respects, its effects were not so systematically perpetuated in terms of dependency and related cultural patterns. In addition, blacks who migrated to the United States from the West Indies have been among the most ambitious and motivated persons in their original communities, a pattern that also has characterized other ethnic groups (Ogbu 1990). However, recent migration of West Indians to the United States has included a growing percentage of un-

skilled very low-income persons in recent years (De Witt 1990a).

Geographic Concentration.   Differences in the degree to which ethnic groups are concentrated in a geographic area or are in high- or low-density settlements may also have effects on mobility. These effects can vary according to group history and circumstances. For some groups, concentration in a community can contribute to mobility through reinforcement of intergroup contacts and support, provided that opportunities for mobility are present in the society and group cohesion is not stressed to the exclusion of contact with the mainstream. For other groups, effects may be largely negative, particularly if the group is low in status and geographic concentration reinforces its separation from the larger society (Hacker 1988).

Discrimination.   Nearly all groups other than those with British background initially have encountered considerable discrimination against their being so-called foreigners and/or inferiors. As noted here and elsewhere in this book, most groups appear to have been largely assimilated in terms of such mobility indicators as occupational status and educational attainment. However, African Americans and some other non-white minority groups have faced much greater and more blatant levels of discrimination that have functioned to retard their mobility (National Research Council 1989; Waldinger 1990). The dynamics of this pattern have been described by Joel Perlmann (1988), who conducted a detailed and painstaking analysis of historical developments involving the Irish, Italians, Jews, and African Americans in Providence, RI. Perlmann concluded that although blacks were relatively successful with respect to educational attainment (i.e., high-school entry in the early twentieth century), this was partly because they faced "uniquely virulent" economic and social discrimination that limited other opportunities and mobility. He further concluded that racial discrimination, more than "cultural attributes," appeared to account for relatively low mobility rates among blacks in Providence during the industrial period (Perlmann 1989, 218).

Availability of Resources Useful in an Appropriate Environment. Analysis by Roger Waldinger (1990) indicates that immigrant groups are most likely to be successful when they have access to resources that are useful in their particular environment. For example, Greek Americans have succeeded in the restaurant business because they have been able (and willing to work hard) to direct economic and cultural resources to this type of enterprise in communities where demand has been favorable and entry opportunities have been available.

Effective Mediating Institutions. As pointed out by Peter Skerry (1991), some immigrant groups succeeded in part because effective institutions—particularly churches, labor unions, and local political organizations in big cities—were available to mediate between the family or kin groups on the one hand and economic, educational, and other large, formal institutions on the other. Skerry also points out that these mediating institutions no longer function as widely or effectively to assist recent immigrant groups as in the past.

Compatibility of Immigrant Culture with Mainstream Values. Some immigrant groups achieve success more rapidly and markedly than do others in part because attitudes, expectations, and values stressed in their cultures fit in well with those in the mainstream of the society to which they emigrate. Kvisto (1989) has summarized this factor in pointing out that an ethnic culture provides a "tool kit" of "symbols, practices, and world views" that constitute cultural components used to construct "strategies of action" in the new society (Kvisto 1989, 19–20). For example, Kotkin and Kishimoto (1988) and Waldinger (1990) have described how entrepreneurial attitudes and practices characteristic of many Chinese families have helped them succeed in the United States and other countries that welcome

private economic initiative. Similarly, Caplan, Whitmore, and Choy (1990) have described how an emphasis on family cohesion and the authority of parents over children has helped Vietnamese and other boat people from Cambodia and Laos succeed in the United States after fleeing from Indochina in the 1970s and 1980s.

Family Structure and Network. Some immigrant groups have relied successfully on close-knit family structures and networks to gain access to economic opportunities. For example, some Asian groups finance new businesses through financial sharing among relatives, and Koreans in New York have been able to operate small food stores when parents and their children work around the clock to keep them open (Roberts 1990).

Consistency among Socializing Institutions. Many social scientists believe that the degree to which there is consistency among institutions that socialize children and youth plays an important part in determining whether the group will be successful in the educational system and the society. For example, De Vos (1982) has studied the family and the peer group in several cultures and concluded that consistency among the peer group, the family, and the school is a major force in determining whether youth will take advantage of educational and economic opportunities in postindustrial society. "What one sees in contemporary Japan as well as in many Japanese-American children in the United States," De Vos observed, "is a peer-group orientation that mutually reinforces" an intense educational commitment developed in the family and the school (p. 97). Caplan, Whitmore, and Choy (1989) have reached similar conclusions regarding Vietnamese and other Indochinese groups that migrated to the United States in recent decades. De Vos further points out that the development of and interactions between socializing institutions reflect an ethnic group's relationships to the larger society. If adults in the group are powerless or discriminated against in the larger society, then young people may be relatively less willing to follow their parents' entreaties to work hard in school and the economy; in this case, the peer group may be especially at odds with the family and the school (also see Ogbu 1978, 1982, 1990). If both family and peer group encourage teenage males to be aggressive but the school stresses passivity, education may not function effectively as a route to economic mobility. These types of inconsistencies—particularly among disadvantaged minority groups—are described more fully in Chapter 5 and elsewhere in this book.. The preceding examples raise the question of how group characteristics involving ethnicity and race are related to social class in affecting status and mobility. Clearly, a group's opportunity for mobility reflects its participation in and situation as an ethnic or racial group in the larger society. Just as clearly, a group's social class standing influences its participation and opportunity in society.

Stephen Steinberg (1981) has been studying the issue and has reached the conclusion that social class interacts with race and ethnicity in determining group status and mobility. Steinberg's book, *The Ethnic Myth*, points out that the historic position of ethnic and racial groups within the social class structure has played a major part in determining whether they would succeed economically. Black Americans, for example, were denied opportunities to own land in the rural South and to compete for industrial employment in the nineteenth and early twentieth centuries. Other groups, such as Jews from Eastern Europe, were not as hampered by social forces that maintained low social class status among blacks in the United States. Some of Steinberg's major conclusions in this regard are as follows:

> *Where the class theory differs from the cultural theory is in its emphasis on the* primacy *of class factors . . . cultural factors have little independent effect on educational outcomes, but are influential only as they interact with class factors. Thus, to whatever extent a reverence for learning was part of the religious and cultural heritage of Asians and Jews, it*

> *was . . . given existential significance by their social class circumstances . . . without which it is hardly conceivable that these groups could have sustained their traditional value on education. . . . Had immigrant Jews remained in poverty and deprived of educational opportunities, it is unlikely that Jewish intellectual life would have advanced beyond the archaic scholasticism . . . carried over from Europe. Conversely, other immigrant groups that started out with less favorable cultural dispositions with respect to education rapidly developed an appetite for education once they achieved a position in the class system comparable to that of Jews a generation earlier. . . . As in the case of Jews, Catholics had to secure an economic foothold before their children could make significant advances up the economic ladder. (Steinberg 1981, 132, 138, 144)*

Differences in group status are evident in Table 7-3, which shows whether groups are above or below the national average as measured by the occupational status scores on a scale of 2 (coal miner) to 96 (physician) of men ages twenty-one to sixty-four in a national study conducted in 1973 (Featherman and Hauser 1978). Hispanic groups and blacks were far below the national average of 40; men whose background was from English-speaking countries, Russia, and China or Japan were substantially above the average. However, taking account of years of schooling, father's occupation, and generational status (number of generations in the United States) greatly reduces group differences from the national mean. This finding means not only that groups low in social status generally are low in social background (as measured by father's occupation), education, and generational status; it also indicates that low status is transmitted by or through low status background, low educational level, and recency of immigration to the United States. The implications of this pattern are analyzed and discussed in the next chapter and elsewhere in this book.

Table 7-3 shows that several racial-ethnic minority groups—namely, the black and the Hispanic

TABLE 7-3   *Occupational Status of National Heritage Groups, U.S. Men Aged Twenty-One to Sixty-Four, 1973*

	Difference from the National Mean	
Group	Gross Difference	Considering Education, Father's Occupation, and Generational Status
Mexican	− 16.01	− 4.60
Puerto Rican	− 14.70	− 3.09
"Other" (includes blacks)	− 7.10	− 2.14
Italy	− .36	− 1.03
Ireland	.96	1.21
Germany	1.92	.61
Poland	3.12	.83
England, Scotland, Wales	7.03	2.74
USSR (includes Jews)	15.04	3.20

Source: Adapted from Featherman and Hauser 1978.

populations—are seriously disadvantaged in socioeconomic status. One must keep in mind that a large proportion of both groups is now urban but was living in rural poverty only one or two generations ago. As regards black Americans, Sowell (1981) has pointed out that massive movement from the rural south to cities in the 1940–1970 period constituted the kind of "traumatic social change" that required generations of adjustment among other ethnic groups: "The social pathology that other groups experienced—violence, alcoholism, crime, delinquency—all reappeared in the transplanted black populations of the cities" (p. 211). Sowell also points out that established middle-class black families in the cities tended to separate themselves from the newly urbanized migrants, but forces generating segregation have concentrated both middle- and low-status blacks in racial ghettos in the core parts of metropolitan areas. Results and implications of this pattern are analyzed in detail in succeeding chapters.

Mobility Analysis by Race/Ethnicity Complicated by Intermarriage

Although the U.S. census and other sources provide a wealth of data for assessing and understanding mobility patterns among social and ethnic groups, conclusions sometimes are difficult to reach because increase in intermarriage has complicated analysis. Increase in intermarriage across racial and ethnic lines has been associated with increasing rates of intermarriage across religious barriers. The rate of intermarriage among Catholics has increased from less than 20 percent in the early part of the twentieth century to about 40 percent today; more than 70 percent of Protestants now marry outside of their denominational backgrounds; and more than one-half of Jews now marry non-Jewish partners (Schumer 1990; Goldman 1991).

The Extent of Mobility in the United States

Returning now to individual mobility, its extent can be studied by measuring the degree and kinds of mobility that have occurred within the lifetimes of adults.

Several studies have been made of the family socioeconomic origins of certain occupational groups. For example, a major study has been carried out by Featherman and Hauser (1978), using data from two large national surveys in 1962 and 1973. Both surveys included men from twenty-one to sixty-four years of age, thus the time period included in the study spanned the entire twentieth century. The focus of the study was on occupational status, as measured by Duncan scale scores ranging from 2 to 96 and by 17 groupings of occupations arranged hierarchically. Socioeconomic status (i.e., social class) was designated by five groupings of occupational strata including these seventeen occupation categories:

I. *Upper Nonmanual:* 1) Professionals, self-employed; 2) Professionals, salaried; 3) Managers; 4) Salesmen, other.
II. *Lower Nonmanual:* 5) Proprietors; 6) Clerks; 7) Salesmen, retail.
III. *Upper manual:* 8) Craftsmen, manufacturing; 9) Craftsmen, other; 10) Craftsmen, construction.
IV. *Lower manual:* 11) Service; 12) Operatives, other; 13) Operatives, manufacturing; 14) Laborers, manufacturing; 15) Laborers, other.
V. *Farm:* 16) Farmers; 17) Farm laborers.

There are many difficulties in conducting this type of research, including problems in collecting data and measuring occupations, ambiguity in measuring "mobility," uncertainty in interpreting floor and ceiling effects, and selection of statistics to analyze and portray complicated situations. Featherman and Hauser worked out sophisticated methods that seem to be an improvement over previous research and reported the following data as regards mobility for men in 1962 and 1973 across the five social-class strata and the seventeen occupational-status categories: in both years, approximately 51 percent of the men had moved up across stratum boundaries and 60 percent had moved up in occupational categories. Fifteen percent of the men in 1962 and 17 percent in 1973 had moved down in stratum level, and 24 percent in 1962 and 26 percent in 1973 had moved down in occupational category. Among the major conclusions Featherman and Hauser drew from their data and analysis were the following:

1. There has been a trend toward greater occupational mobility in the United States. Although there was little change between 1962 and 1973 from the father's job to the son's first job, mobility from the first job to current occupation has increased.

2. Upward mobility is much more common than is downward mobility.

3. Trends in mobility are partly but not entirely explained by change in occupational distribution. That is, though some mobility has occurred largely because there are relatively more high-status jobs than there used to be, some mobility seems to be due to opportunity for sons to advance beyond their fathers' occupations.

4. There is great immobility at the top and bottom of the occupational hierarchy, among the upper nonmanual and the farm occupations, respectively. (Relative immobility at the top is not unexpected since children of upper-status families have nowhere to move but down.) According to Featherman and Hauser, this immobility is "far more extreme than had heretofore been supposed by most students of the mobility process; it may even be consistent with the beliefs of the most extreme critics of rigidity in the American class structure" (p. 179).

5. There is also considerable immobility into or out of occupations adjacent to the top and bottom. "In this sense," Featherman and Hauser conclude, the data "suggest the existence of barriers to movement across class boundaries" (p. 179).

6. On the other hand, there is very little immobility in the middle range of occupations, from upper blue-collar through middle-class, white-collar jobs. In particular, there is "no evidence" of class boundaries "limiting the chances of movement to or from the skilled manual occupations" (p. 180).

7. Historically, mobility rose for groups entering the labor market from the 1920s to 1940, declined during the war years, rose again after World War II, and then gradually dropped to the pre-Depression level in the early 1960s.

Studies reviewed here indicate that there has been considerable upward mobility in the United States during the twentieth century. Although there has been relatively less upward mobility from the lowest social class positions and although opportunities for mobility have increased or decreased in accordance with economic conditions, technological change, population growth or decline, and other factors, it may generally be concluded that the social structure in the United States is not hardening in the sense that class lines have become systematically and consistently more rigid at all levels of the social structure.

Net Mobility versus Exchange Mobility

In an open society with relatively free educational opportunity and with a tradition favoring social mobility, the amount of individual mobility is relatively high. Upward and downward mobility, considered together, can be called *exchange mobility*. The amount of one kind of mobility over the other can be called *net mobility*.

The amount of exchange mobility may be a better index of equity in a society than is the amount of upward mobility. Exchange mobility signifies openness to individual mobility and therefore signifies that people succeed in relation to their ability and effort. A society may have considerable exchange mobility and yet, if industrialization is not rapid and if upward and downward mobility are approximately equal, there may be very little net upward mobility. Glass (1954) found this condition to exist in Great Britain between 1920 and 1950. During that time, given the more rapid economic and industrial expansion in the United States, it probably required less intelligence, drive, and social effectiveness to be upwardly mobile in the United States than it required to be be upwardly mobile in Great Britain. For the same set of reasons, those who were downwardly mobile in the United States were probably less able and less ambitious than those who were downwardly mobile in Great Britain.

Reviewing Featherman and Hauser's 1973 data on social-class movement across five occupational strata, the rate of exchange mobility was 68 percent (51 percent up and 17 percent down); the net rate of upward mobility was 34 percent. Goldthorpe (1980) and his colleagues have carried out a similar analysis using 1972 data from a national survey in Great Britain. After classifying occupations into seven social class categories and then determining the amount of mobility into and out of three larger groupings (classes 1 plus 2; 3, 4, and 5; and 6 plus 7), they found that 32 percent of the men in their sample had been upward mobile and 17 percent had been downward mobile. Thus, the exchange mobility rate was 59 percent, and net upward mobility was 15 percent. Caution must be exercised in comparing these figures with data from the United States due to differences in collecting, analyzing, and interpreting the information; however, the data do suggest that while there has been substantial mobility in both the United States and Britain, there probably has been greater exchange mobility and net upward mobility in the United States.

A low degree of net or upward mobility is interpreted as a hardening of the social structure and a lessening of opportunity. On the other hand, too high a degree of mobility may indicate a revolutionary or chaotic quality in the society. The latter may be unhealthy because people cannot count on holding and passing on to their children the gains they have made. No one can say what precise degree of individual mobility would be most desirable in a modern society, but there would probably be general agreement that the present amount of mobility in the United States generally should not decrease and should be enhanced for the working class and, particularly, for the underclass.

Recent Trends in Socioeconomic Mobility

Data collected in 1983 enabled Goldthorpe (1987) to reassess and update his earlier analysis of mobility trends in Great Britain. Analysis of these data supported the following eight conclusions (Goldthorpe 1989, 327–348):

1. The "net association between the class position of individuals in the present-day population and their class origins remains essentially the same in its extent and pattern as that which existed" in the first half of the twentieth century.

2. Because technological, economic, and related changes have created increasing "room at the top," there has been substantial upward mobility among persons with working-class and lower-middle-class origins.

3. However, persons with middle-class origins are much more likely to attain high occupational status than are persons with working-class backgrounds. From this point of view, the "class structure" appears to offer strong resistance to attempts to make it substantially more egalitarian.

4. Although the upper-middle-class (which Goldthorpe calls the "service class") has diverse class origins, there has been "no sign of any falling off in the capacity of its members to transmit social advantage to their offspring. On the contrary, even while expanding [it has tended] to 'solidify' in the sense that its families have become less likely to be detached . . . from one generation to the next."

5. Mobility patterns for women in Great Britain have been fundamentally similar to those for men.

6. "Direct routes of access" to upper-middle-class positions have become *proportionately more important* [italics in original] than indirect ones from all class origins." Stated differently, an increasingly higher proportion of upper-middle-class persons have entered their occupations soon after having attained appropriate educational credentials and qualifications, regardless of their social-class origins.

7. Although the "significance of the division between the skilled and nonskilled sections of the working class has much diminished," in part because both segments have similar opportunity for upward mobility, the existence of widespread

and continuing unemployment has been generating a "major division . . . within the working class" in the sense that the "long-term unemployed are increasingly set apart from those in work in their standards and styles of living" and are beginning to constitute an underclass "concentrated . . . within the inner cities and the areas of most widespread industrial decay."

8. The British mobility patterns described here generally are similar to those in France, Germany, Hungary, Ireland, Poland, Scotland, and Sweden, countries for which Goldthorpe provides comparative data. Based on comparison with the conclusions of other researchers, these general patterns also are similar to those in the United States and other industrialized countries as well.

Recent indications that significant socioeconomic mobility is continuing to occur in the United States have been provided in an analysis by Michael Hout (1988) of national data collected between 1972 and 1985. As shown in Table 7-4, Hout found that for persons employed between 1982 and 1985, the percentage of men who were classified as professionals nearly doubled compared to the percentage of professionals they reported among their fathers and other "family head," and the comparable percentage for women more than doubled. Conversely, a smaller percentage of men and women were laborers than had been true among their fathers and other family heads. After extensive analysis of these and other data that also dealt with respondents' socioeconomic origins and destinations (i.e., their own attainment) by level of education, Hout (1988, 1388–1391) concluded that "the effect of origin status on destination status declined in the past fifteen years. . . . The association between men's and women's socioeconomic origins and destinations decreased by one-third between 1972–75 and 1982–85." Furthermore, this trend is

related to the rising proportions of workers who have college degrees—the more college graduates in the work force, the weaker the association between origin status and destination status. The relationship between origin status and destination is nil among college graduates but strong among workers without degrees. . . . This finding provides a new answer to the old question about education's overcoming disadvantaged origins. A college degree can do it. Of course, a higher probability of attaining a college degree is part of the advantage in high-status origins, but labor market inequities do not compound these advantages for college graduates in the way that they do for workers with less education.

EDUCATION, OPPORTUNITY, AND MOBILITY

Confirmation that there is still substantial upward mobility in the United States does not in itself indicate whether the United States is now a meritocratic society in which most young people have realistic opportunities to succeed socioeconomically in accordance with their abilities and efforts. The facts are clear that the social-class position held by a young person growing into adulthood is determined to a significant extent by how the parents rear the child and by what economic assistance is given. Parents who are in middle- or upper-class positions naturally do a great deal to pass their favored status on to their children. Many working-class parents also are of significant help to their children, though they cannot give much economic assistance.

The school system seeks to help young people from lower-status families rise on the social scale, and the extent to which a society is meritocratic depends partly on how effective the educational system is in this effort. Thus, the social class of young adults is determined partly by what they make out of their schooling, and partly by their social class origins. The preceding sections present evidence indicating that many young people do use education to overcome disadvantages associated with their family background, but a more systematic examination of the issue and of the role of the schools in advancing or retarding opportunity requires additional analysis.

Sociologists have been active in conducting research on these topics, especially since about 1960. Research has attempted to find out how mobility is related to the socioeconomic status of an individual's family, mental ability, level of school achievement, and the kind of schools he or she attends. Researchers also have attempted to determine whether the schools and other social institutions function to provide opportunities on a meritocratic basis.

An extensive review of the research on social mobility and education was reported in 1976 by Shea, with a set of approximately 150

TABLE 7-4 *Distribution of Occupational Origins and Destinations for Men and Women in the Labor Force between 1982 and 1985*

Occupational Grouping	Origins		Destinations	
	Men	Women	Men	Women
Professionals	09.6%	09.4%	18.9%	22.5%
Managers and Proprietors	17.9	20.2	19.9	13.5
Clerical and sales	05.3	04.7	07.5	37.0
Crafts	25.1	24.4	22.8	02.8
Operatives	20.9	21.1	22.6	22.5
Farmers	13.4	11.7	02.8	00.2
Laborers	07.8	08.5	05.5	01.5

Source: Adapted from Hout 1988.

Note: Origins refers to the respondent's report of the occupation of his or her father or other family head. *Destinations* refers to the respondent's own occupation.

references. Shea summarized the consensus of these studies as follows: "An increasing body of evidence suggests that schooling is indeed meritocratic, i.e., operates in a classless way to make destination status independent of origin status" (p. 511). Featherman and Hauser's studies (1976, 1978) of 1962 and 1973 data on the occupational status of adult men further support the conclusion that education increasingly is functioning to provide mobility for many persons. However, the authors found that education also is implicated in the transmission of low status from one generation to the next: although more Americans are acquiring more years of education and although more education yields more occupational status, the greatest payoff now comes from acquisition of a college education, and individuals from low-status families are less likely to go to college than are those from high-status families:

> *Demands for a more highly skilled labor force, rising GNP, and more favorable social origins combined . . . to enable ever larger fractions of each cohort to attend high school. But . . . the historical educational differentials by socioeconomic status have not disappeared. Rather, they have shifted from the precollege to college years. (Featherman and Hauser 1978, 302).*

On the other hand, Featherman and Hauser also stress the conclusion that the relationship between social origins and college attainment is far from perfect (p. 251). In addition, it should be kept in mind that gains in higher education for the disadvantaged that may have been associated with open admissions policies, increasing federal support for students, and other equalizing measures in the 1970s could not have had much effect on the 1973 data.

Jencks and his colleagues (1972, 1979) also have been studying the relationships between family background, education, and occupational attainment and additionally have tried to delineate relationships of these variables with data on the earnings of adult men. Using the 1962 and 1973 data sets analyzed by Featherman and Hauser as

well as nine other major United States sources of data collected in the 1960s and 1970s, Jencks's 1979 book, *Who Gets Ahead? The Determinants of Economic Success in America*, concluded that family background accounts for nearly half of the variation in occupational status and somewhere between 15 and 35 percent of the variation in earnings, depending on the nature of the data available and the statistical approach used in analysis. Family background and amount of education, which, of course, is related to family background, together explain 55 percent of the variation in occupational attainment. Other conclusions involving the relationships between family background and education on the one hand and occupational attainment and earnings on the other included the following:

1. Men from advantaged families have more cognitive skills and noncognitive traits valued by employers.
2. Comparing men with similar cognitive and noncognitive traits, those from advantaged families have more education than do men from disadvantaged families.
3. Men from advantaged families are relatively successful economically partly because they obtain more education than do men from disadvantaged families.

In addition to confirming Featherman and Hauser's conclusion that higher education has become the more important factor (as compared to acquisition of a high school diploma) in influencing later career success and in translating high status background into occupational attainment, Jencks and his colleagues analyzed data on cognitive skills (e.g., IQ scores) and noncognitive traits (such as are measured in teachers' ratings of students' personality traits) in examining the question of whether the schools and society are providing equal opportunity on a meritocratic basis for talented and motivated students. Their major conclusions included the following:

> *If we define 'equal opportunity' as a situation in which sons born into different families have*

the same chances of success, our data show that America comes nowhere near achieving it. . . . But . . . in contemporary America . . . inequality between families or individuals is acceptable so long as it derives from 'merit' of some sort. We doubt that merit runs in families to anything like the extent necessary to reconcile our results with 'meritocracy.' But our data do not speak on this issue directly.

We have shown, for example, that a nontrivial fraction of background's effect on success derives from the fact that background affects cognitive skills. But it is not clear that cognitive skills are, or should be, synonymous with 'merit.' . . . The same logic applies to educational attainment. Educational credentials are essential for obtaining some lucrative jobs. But it does not follow that educational credentials ought *to be essential for these jobs. . . . Our surveys do not measure these attitudes or values [associated with success in obtaining top jobs] . . . . Without evidence on this, our data constitute neither an indictment nor an endorsement of the status quo. (Jencks 1979, 82–83)*

It should be noted that Jencks and most others who have been studying relationships between family background, education, and occupational or economic attainment have been examining data collected before the mid-1970s. Thus, *Who Gets Ahead?* concluded with the statement that "past efforts" through education and other efforts aimed at "equalizing the personal characteristics known to affect income have been relatively ineffective." As pointed out in Chapter 8 and elsewhere in this book, compensatory education to overcome the disadvantages of low-status students has been relatively unsuccessful on a national basis, but much has been learned concerning the changes needed to make it more successful in providing more effective and equal educational opportunity. Definitive conclusions about the equity and adequacy of education in helping accomplish the fundamental

goals of United States society therefore will depend on the success of efforts to improve compensatory education in the future.

Results of mobility studies in other Western nations also indicate that the structure of society is stable enough to encourage people to expect to pass on their social-class position to their children, while there is enough individual social mobility to change the composition of the social classes as many individuals move from one class to another. Assessing studies conducted in the 1950s in Britain and in the 1960s in France, Boudon (1973) concluded that both a "meritocratic and a social heritage effect appear very clearly. . . . Let us be content to note that both effects seemed to be relatively important" in both societies.

Another major analysis of family background, education, and occupational attainment in Great Britain has been conducted by Halsey and his colleagues. Conclusions were basically similar to those reported above (Halsey, Heath, and Ridge 1980; Winfield 1989). However, the authors also concluded that whereas higher education in the United States is now the attainment point that best distinguishes the advantaged from the disadvantaged, in Great Britain the comparable dividing line is still at the secondary level:

Cultural capital influences selection for secondary school, but thereafter its importance is minimal. . . . This picture of unequal access to the superior secondary schools has remained depressingly constant over time. For the selective schools as a group, chances of access rose at all levels in the middle of our period, leading to some slight narrowing of class differentials, but then they fell back again to levels like those of a generation earlier. . . . In summary, school inequalities of opportunity have been remarkably stable over the forty years which our study covers. Throughout, the service [white-collar] class has had roughly three times the chance of the working class of getting some kind of selective secondary schooling. (Halsey, Heath, and Ridge 1980, 200, 203, 205)

Growing Critical Importance of Postsecondary Education and Graduation

As noted in preceding sections, studies of mobility in the United States indicate that college attendance and graduation have become increasingly important considerations in providing opportunities for economic and social success in later life (Hout 1988). Additional support for this conclusion recently was provided by Kevin Murphy and Finis Welch (1989). They examined data on wage differentials from 1963 to 1986 between persons who graduated from high school and had or had not graduated from college. (Graduation was defined as attainment of sixteen or more years of schooling.) As shown in Table 7-5, Murphy and Welch found that between 1981 and 1986 both men and women who graduated from college earned considerably more money relative to those who had graduated from high school but not college than was true in the preceding eighteen years. (The authors attribute the dip in differentials between 1975 and 1980 to the large number of college-educated baby boomers who entered the labor market during this period, along with related factors, such as college deferments during the Vietnam war.) These and other data led Murphy and Welch to conclude that the increasing advantage enjoyed by college graduates has been due to increase in demand for college-trained workers associated with international competition, advances in technology, decline in the number of young adults, and other economic and social factors (also see Kaus 1990). At the same time, the high-school diploma has become devalued because a higher proportion of young people attend college and employers thus can pick and choose among applicants with postsecondary education to fill jobs formerly available to high-school graduates or dropouts. New college graduates can now expect to earn more than one-half million dollars greater lifetime income than nongraduates (Passell 1990). These trends probably will become still more pronounced in the future (Ottinger 1990; Levy and Michel 1991).

TABLE 7-5 *Percentage Gain in Wage Returns Associated with College Degrees among Men and Women with One to Five Years Experience, 1963–68 to 1981–86*

Time Period	Women	Men
1963–68	48%	41%
1969–74	50	38
1975–80	41	28
1981–86	57	53

Source: Adapted from Murphy and Welch 1989.
Note: Wage returns of obtaining a college degree represent the percentage of excess of the average of employees with sixteen or more years of schooling relative to those of employees with twelve to sixteen years of schooling.

Later data analyzed by social scientists at the Economic Policy Institute also underscore the increasing importance of a college education. For both men and women who graduated from college within the previous five years, income increased by 11 percent between 1979 and 1987 after adjusting for inflation, but for high-school graduates of the same age income declined by 18 percent among males and 4 percent among females (Kilborn 1990).

Schools Both Perpetuate and Modify the Social Class Structure

The preceding sections indicate that many young people use education to become upwardly mobile, but we also have seen that many lower-status students are disadvantaged before they ever enter school and are not able to achieve much success through the schools or other social institutions. There is no logical reason to believe that the schools cannot function both as a route to mobility for some students and a barrier for others, even though some social scientists and educators habitually speak of the "educational system" as being either a force for meritocracy and egalitarianism or a means by which the existing social structure perpetuates itself.

Nor is there a logical contradiction in the conclusion that the schools are becoming more of a force for upward mobility than they have been in the past and at the same time are becoming more of a barrier to the mobility of some segments of the population. Indeed, this is exactly what one would expect if the schools are playing a larger part in the mobility process than they did before. In this case, both the mobility generating and the mobility limiting roles of the school could be simultaneously more pronounced. We shall see that there is evidence for accepting both propositions.

Preceding sections have noted that the educational system as a whole does appear to be an increasingly important part of the social mobility process. This is not surprising inasmuch as industrial society places growing emphasis on the attainment both of the skills acquired in elementary, secondary, and higher education and on the education credentials that presumably provide short-hand certification that a person has acquired the skills for a given job. Evidence for the growing importance of education has been provided by a variety of studies in several western nations, particularly the United States.

However, it is still true that the family also helps determine the amount of education its children receive, more in some countries than in others. For instance, in Great Britain, family status has been more closely linked to educational level of the children than in the United States. A 1972 British study conducted at Nuffield College (Halsey 1976) suggests that the effects of education on mobility in recent decades may have been as much or more in the direction of perpetuating as unfreezing the social class structure.

> *Clearly there are both ascriptive and achievement forces at work in the passing of occupational status between generations. We live neither in a caste society nor one in which the generations are severed from each other by random reallocation of status. . . . What has happened is the weighting of the dice of social opportunity according to class, and "the game" is increasingly played through strategies of child rearing refereed by schools through their certifying arrangements. The direct effect of the class hierarchy of families on educa-tional opportunity and certification has risen since the war. And at the same time the articulation of education to the first entry into the labor market has been tightening. Thus education is increasingly the mediator of the transmission of status between generations. It commands the passage from school to work more completely than it did a generation ago, and it is a mediator with power independent of the family. Institutionally, education is the principal agent of achievement. (p. 184)*

The school's role in bringing about mobility and/or transmitting status appears to depend on a variety of factors, such as the characteristics and development of the society in which it functions, the definition of mobility and status attainment, and the social subgroups that are studied. For example, Tinto (1981) studied the 1968 occupational status of 1961 male college graduates and found that variables such as father's status and type of college attended accounted for much of the variation in status of men in professional occupations but almost none for the men in business-managerial occupations.

The Transmission of Status

How is social status transmitted from one generation to the next? This can be seen both as a simple process involving mainly the family and a more complicated process involving schools and the economic and political systems of a society (Holmes 1988; Fuller 1991). Practically everyone realizes that growing up in a low-income environment is not conducive to attaining higher social status later and that high-status families pass on certain advantages to their children. The resources that families and society make available to promote the development of children and youth and that are related to their success in the school and other institutions are clear in their broad outlines. These resources include:

- Material resources, useful or necessary for success in later life.

- Values and attitudes, which help determine how one behaves in social institutions.
- Knowledge and understandings, required for success in socializing institutions, particularly the school.
- Cognitive and verbal skills, required for success in the school.

Material and Cultural Resources.   Much of the process of status transmission involves the transfer and use of material and cultural resources that help young people get a good start toward achieving or maintaining middle- or upper-status positions in society (Schaefer 1991). Material resources can take such forms as funds spent on helping children do well in school through tutoring or the pursuit of intellectually enriching hobbies, access to middle-class public and private schools, financial support to remain in high school or attend college, assistance in establishing a business or entering a profession, or availability of time to work with teachers in establishing positive home-school relationships (Lareau 1989; McGue 1989). Cultural resources include:

- Contact with adults who can provide a youngster with a part-time job.
- Knowledge in identifying and having children removed from the classrooms of weak teachers.
- Family acquaintances who can help gain admission to professional training or full-time employment when jobs are scarce.
- Parental experience in understanding teachers' communications.
- Guidance or role models in deciding what career to pursue and how to go about preparing for it (Lareau 1989; Epstein and Dauber 1991).

Values and Attitudes.   Children in differing social classes grow up not only with different levels of material support but also with different attitudes toward society and the schools. An important analysis of the overall process by which low status is transmitted through values and attitudes

passed on from one generation to another has been worked out by sociologist Melvin L. Kohn, who collected and analyzed data on the values, status, and child-raising orientation of men and women in Washington, DC, and in Turin, Italy. Kohn began by asking parents to pick the characteristic they valued most highly in their children and then compared the responses of parents of differing social classes. The data showed that middle-status parents placed relatively more value than did low-status parents on having their children demonstrate interest in how and why things happen, whereas low-status parents placed relatively more emphasis on children being obedient and well mannered (Kohn 1969, 1987, 1990).

Kohn also found that middle-status men attached more importance than did low-status men to how important their work is, the amount of freedom they have at work, and the chance to use their abilities fully on the job. Understandably, low-status men attached relatively more importance than did middle-status respondents to pay, fringe benefits, and job security. "Self-direction," Kohn concluded, "is a central value for men of higher class position, who see themselves as competent members of an essentially benign society. Conformity is a central value for men of lower class position, who [have] an orientational system premised on the dangers of stepping out of line" (Kohn 1969, 233).

Kohn interpreted his data along with information he and his colleagues have collected since the original studies to mean that the conditions of middle-class life, particularly on the job, tend to place a high value on self-direction and intellectual flexibility. Middle-class parents not only perceive that these qualities are important for success but also become committed to them as values in their own right. Their methods of child-rearing reflect these values, with emphasis on rearing children to function independently in an intellectually complex world.

Working-class parents, by way of contrast, have tended to place relatively greater emphasis on obedience and conformity to accepted opinion, placing relatively less stress in their child rearing on the development of intellectual flexibility and self-direction. The demands of the job thus generate values and attitudes that parents strive to pass on to their children (Kohn and Schooler 1973; Alwin 1988, 1989; Kohn 1990).

The conclusions regarding middle-class versus working-class emphasis on the value of self-direction versus conformity agree with the results of decades of research on differences in child-raising practices between classes. As long ago as 1958, Bronfenbrenner summarized twenty-five years of research on this theme:

> *The data on the training of the young child show middle-class mothers, especially in the postwar period, to be consistently more permissive toward the child's expressed needs and wishes. The generalization applies in such diverse areas as oral behavior, toilet accidents, dependency, sex, aggressiveness, and freedom of movement outside the home. . . .*
>
> *In matters of discipline, working-class parents are consistently more likely to employ physical punishment, while middle-class families rely more on reasoning, isolation, appeals to guilt, and other methods involving the threat of loss of love. At least two independent lines of evidence suggest that the techniques preferred by middle-class parents are more likely to bring about the development of internalized values and controls. . . .*
>
> *Over the entire 25-year period studied, parent-child relationships in the middle class are consistently reported as more acceptant and equalitarian, while those in the working class are oriented toward maintaining order and obedience. (See Maccoby, 1958, 424–425)*

There is reason to believe that working-class values and child-rearing practices have shifted somewhat away from a stress on order and obedience since the 1940s and 1950s. This is not very surprising inasmuch as Bronfenbrenner found that working-class values in child-rearing tended to be influenced by middle-class patterns becoming dominant in the mass media, reflecting the recommendations of prominent authors of books on child care. For example, a general shift toward greater emphasis on self-direction in parental values for children was reported in 1976 by Wright and Wright based on a national sample of data collected in 1973. Subsequent analysis by Duane Alwin (1989) of data collected between 1964 and 1984 has confirmed the conclusion that parental values have moved away from an emphasis on obedience and toward greater stress on autonomy and individual judgment. As shown in Table 7-6, relative emphasis on good manners, neatness, and obedience declined substantially, while relative parental stress on sound judgment and individual responsibility clearly increased. However, it is not clear to what degree this shift represented changes in the occupational and educational structures of the U.S. population (a relatively higher proportion of middle-class population) as compared to actual changes in values within social classes.

Knowledge and Understanding.   Socialization for success in an industrial society can be seen as learning to participate in an ever-expanding social environment. The social environment, in turn, can be viewed in terms of the life space in which a child or an adolescent lives and grows. The concept of life space, as used here, involves physical space, and the psychological sense of freedom or constraint in exploring and expanding one's social and intellectual environment.

The life space of the growing individual expands—from the crib, to the living room, to the street in front of the house, to the neighborhood, and then to the community. From here, it enlarges partly through the child's travel experience and partly through vicarious experiences by way of movies, television, magazines, books, maps, and geography lessons. At the same time, the child's psychological and intellectual life space expands to include new ideas, new attitudes, and new values.

It is obvious that neighborhoods and communities vary in the extent to which they provide a variety of opportunities for learning. Cohen

TABLE 7-6   *Mean Rankings of Thirteen Child Characteristics Specified as Important by Fathers, 1964 and 1980–1984*

Child Characteristic	Average Rank		Probability of a Difference
	1964	1980–84	
1. Has good manners	3.18	3.03	00
2. Tries hard to succeed	2.70	2.95	00
3. Is honest	3.78	3.98	00
4. Is neat and clean	2.70	2.50	00
5. Has good sense and sound judgment	3.04	3.51	00
6. Has self-control	2.83	2.94	00
7. Acts like a boy (or girl) should	2.76	1.91	00
8. Gets along well with other children	3.20	2.95	00
9. Obeys his or her parents well	3.66	3.39	00
10. Is responsible	2.79	3.29	00
11. Is considerate of others	3.14	3.23	02
12. Is a good student	2.59	2.64	03
13. Is interested in how and why things happen	2.64	2.68	47

Source: Adapted from Alwin 1989.
Note: The probability of a difference represents the number of times in 100 samples in which a difference in ranking as large and consistent as reported in the table would occur by chance, even if the responses in the populations sampled were the same. Rankings were obtained by asking respondents to place characteristics in five categories scored as follows: (1) least important; (2) one of the least but not least important; (3) neither one of the three least or most desirable; (4) one of the most but not most important; (5) most important.

(1981), for example, has shown how English parents moving from working-class neighborhoods to a new middle-class housing estate developed a "collective estate culture and life-style" conducive to the academic success of their children, and how mothers both adapted their child-raising methods and worked with the local elementary school to achieve this goal. Sociocultural patterns developed by the parents included segregating children from nearby working-class neighborhoods, grooming children for success beginning at an early age, sharing of responsibility for education-oriented child-development activities, and providing a variety of growth experiences for children.

In a study of families who live in a large public housing project in Chicago, mothers often reported to the interviewers that their ten-year-olds were not allowed out of the apartment alone, except to go back and forth from school; or they were limited to playing on the small balcony of the apartment. Often these children were not allowed even to play in the playgrounds below, because, as one mother said, "I can't keep my eyes on him all the time, up here on the tenth floor; and he might get into trouble with some of the bad kids that live in this project."

Another mother said, "I tell her she can't walk through this neighborhood. It isn't safe. Especially she is *not* to play in the elevators or on the stairs of this building. That means she can watch television, and she can do her school work, and she can wait for me or her daddy to take her out. Of course I don't get out much because of the younger kids. . . ."

One interviewer reported an extreme case in one of these families: "There are four children, all under five. Each time I arrived, all four were lined up on the bed, watching television and not moving. I couldn't get even the oldest one to respond to me, even after several visits and after I tried repeatedly to bribe him with candy. I couldn't lure him from the fixed position on the bed."

A middle-class mother, on the other hand, living within several blocks of the same housing project, described to the same interviewer the activities of her ten-year-old daughter: "She has to check in after school, of course, but then she usually goes down the block to play with her friend . . . or else the two get on their bicycles. (Interviewer: Where do they go?) Oh, around the neighborhood. Sometimes they ride over to the lake. They have to stay on the streets, of course, and they have to be home by five o'clock. They don't go into any deserted areas. But they're sensible by this age, and I don't worry. Then one day a week she takes the bus after school and goes to her piano lessons . . . and Saturdays she goes down to the Art Institute for her art class."

These considerations indicate that young middle-class children are likely to acquire more knowledge of the world outside their home and immediate neighborhood than are working-class children. This knowledge becomes important when children enter school and when they are required in later years to make choices concerning their educational and vocational careers.

Cognitive and Verbal Skills. The child-rearing practices of the middle class favor a more rapid development of cognitive skills than do those of the working class. This is a conclusion reached by Edward Zigler, who ended a systematic review of social class influences on cognitive development (1970) with the statement: "There are real class differences in intellectual functioning and these are produced by class differences in environment." According to Zigler, there is a general development sequence in cognitive function that is common to all social classes, but the middle-class children move along this sequence more rapidly than do lower-class children; and lower-class children may end up at a lower level as adults.

In addition to being at a disadvantage in mastering cognitive skills, which are needed to understand the increasingly abstract material children encounter as they proceed through school, working-class children tend to lag behind middle-class children in mastering standard English, or, in other countries, whichever formal language is the primary medium of communication for learning in the classroom (Bowman 1989; Taylor 1989). Moreover, mastery of verbal skills in the language of the school probably is related to development of cognitive skills inasmuch as the student whose linguistic preparation does not allow for clear understanding of classroom material is placed at an additional disadvantage in trying to understand and manipulate concepts inherent in the material (Heath 1983; Heath and McLaughlin 1987; Shields and Shaver 1990).

How verbal patterns handicap students from working-class families has been studied by Bernstein (1961, 1975, 1986, 1990), who has analyzed the language used by working-class and middle-class children and found considerable differences. Children of both classes learn adequately the language of ordinary conversation, which is grammatically simple, uses stereotyped expressions, does not permit precise statment of ideas or emotions, and relies on gestures, inflection, and further explanation to make meaning clear. Bernstein calls this language "public," or "restricted." Middle-class children learn, in addition to the restricted language, what Bernstein calls the "formal" or "elaborated" language—the grammatically complex language of the schoolroom, which permits precise expression and provides greater potentiality for organizing experience than does the restricted language.

The elaborated language characteristic of many middle-class children is based on general principles that are relatively context-independent, compared with the restricted language more typical of working-class children (Holland 1981; Bredo, Henry, and McDermott 1990). The child who learns only the restricted language, according to Bernstein, is limited in his or her ability to learn new things and to interact with other people because one's language restricts the ability to organize experience. The child who masters the elaborated language possesses a tool that permits expression of complex ideas and distinctions between feelings and ideas.

In an effort to understand why some children learn a more elaborate language than others, Hess and Shipman (1965) studied the ways in which mothers teach their own four-year-old children. They found that the techniques used by mothers vary by the amount of education the mothers have had—and thus also by social class. The middle-class mothers, as compared with the working-class mothers, talked almost twice as much to their children in teaching them, and used more abstract words, more adjectives, more complex grammar, and longer sentences. Furthermore, they more frequently gave explicit instructions, let the children know what was expected of them, and praised them for their accomplishments. The children from the middle-class homes learned much better than did the children from the working-class homes; and the middle-class children were more frequently able to explain correctly the principle behind the task they had learned.

Later studies further specified some ways in which working-class children are disadvantaged because of language development in the home. Snow, Dubber, and De Blauw (1982) have found that middle-class mothers are more likely than working-class mothers to establish intellectually productive conversational *routines* and to provide *responsive talk* that is semantically contingent on the child's own speech. Snow summarizes these differences in concluding that middle-class youngsters are more likely than working-class youngsters to learn "impersonal" and "decontextualized" language (Snow 1991, p. 3).

Analysis by Feagans (1982) and others indicates that school-like narratives and dialogues may be relatively infrequent in the homes of poverty children, thus placing them at a disadvantage when they enter school. In addition, Snow, Dubber, and De Blauw believe that problems associated with poverty may be even more important than are parent-child language interaction style *per se* in retarding the verbal development of children from low income homes: "Social class is a *package variable*, a shorthand term for describing many differences" in income, financial security, parental education and occupation, goals for children, access to interaction with parents, and parents' style of interaction with children. "It is not yet clear," they concluded, "to what extent and how these different components of social class differences may interact; whether, for example, a particular style of interaction with children is caused by financial insecurity or by the parents' ideology" (Snow, Dubber, and De Blauw 1982, 70).

The preceding analysis indicates that working-class children tend to be educationally and socially disadvantaged relative to middle-class children. Their families possess fewer material and nonmaterial resources that could help them succeed in school and later in life, and their attitudes, cognitive and verbal skills, and early experience in the world also tend to place them at a disadvantage in school and society (Schaefer 1991). An excellent summary of the nature and implications of social class differences in child-rearing has been provided by John and Elizabeth Newson, based on their intensive study of 700 children and their parents in Nottingham, England:

> *Parents at the upper end of the social scale are more inclined* on principle *to use democratically based, highly verbal means of control, and this kind of discipline is likely to produce personalities who can both identify successfully with the system and use it for their own ends later on. At the bottom end of the scale . . . parents choose* on principle *to use a highly authoritarian, mainly non-verbal means of control, in which words are used more to threaten and bamboozle the child into obedience than to make him understand the rationale behind social behavior. . . . Thus the child born into the lowest social bracket has everything stacked against him* including his parents' principles of child upbringing *(1976, 406).*

In addition, differences in socialization by social class almost certainly are much more pronounced among parents who live in predominantly working-class or middle-class neighborhoods, as contrasted with relatively heterogeneous neighborhoods. Since metropolitan areas have become relatively more stratified (i.e., middle-class and working-class families live in different locations), social-class differences in socialization may be a more potent determinant of future success than was true in earlier periods.

Schools in the Upward Mobility Process

The process by which social mobility is attained through schools and other institutions has been painstakingly investigated by Alex Inkeles and his colleagues, who have been studying modernization in six developing countries (Argentina, Chile, East Pakistan, India, Israel, and Nigeria) as well as in other parts of the world. Inkeles has been trying to identify characteristics of the "modern man" and to determine how and why some people acquire the skills needed for upward mobility in an industrial or industrializing society and others do not. Even though he has carried out most of his research in developing nations, Inkeles and many other social scientists believe that the same process has occurred earlier and is still occurring among some segments of the population in industrialized nations. Inkeles and Smith (1974) have summarized the characteristics of the "modern man":

The modern man's character . . . may be summed up under four major headings. He is an informed participant citizen; he has a marked sense of personal efficacy; he is highly independent and autonomous in his relation to traditional sources of influence . . . and he is ready for new experiences and ideas, that is, he is relatively open-minded and cognitively flexible. . . . Our results provide definite evidence that . . . modern man is not just a construct in the mind of sociological theorists. He exists and can be identified with fair reliability within any population where our test can be applied. (p. 290)

It is apparent that the "modern man" as defined by Inkeles and Smith tends to be well educated and resembles the middle-class or upwardly mobile type of individual whom Kohn (1969, 1987, 1990; see preceding section) portrayed as valuing and exemplifying self-direction and intellectual flexibility in his attitudes and his work. After examining the forces that seem to be most important in producing modernity and mobility, Inkeles and Smith summarized their conclusions:

Some of the institutions most commonly associated with the process of modernization failed to substantiate their claim to standing as important schools for making men modern. Most notable of these was the city, whose failure to qualify as an important independent modernizing influence was not corrected by taking into account either the size or the cosmopolitanism of different urban centers. . . .

Since a whole set of institutions, including the school, the factory, and the mass media, all operated to make our men modern, the question arises: Must a nation be able to bring all these forces to bear, and do so simultaneously, in order to stimulate the development of individual modernity?

. . . Our experience suggests that it is not necessary that all, or even most, of the more effective agencies be available and working simultaneously . . . any one modernizing institution seems to be able to operate independently of the others. (p. 311)

Inkeles and his colleagues thus stress the conclusion that although the schools are not the only modernity-generating institution in modern society, they can have an effect even when nonschool conditions work against the acquisition of attitudes and behaviors associated with middle-class status and upward mobility (Inkeles 1983). In addition, the conclusion that living in cities is not in itself a very potent generator of modernity implies that educational and economic opportunity and other social resources are needed to improve the condition of working-class people in big cities. These points are considered further in a later section of this chapter on mobility and the underclass, but first there is need to review some ways in which schools may function to help transmit low status from one generation to the next.

Schools in the Perpetuation of Low Status

We have seen that the schools appear to function effectively in helping many middle-class youth acquire skills and attitudes they will need later and that historically they have helped many working-class youth in the United States and elsewhere beome upwardly mobile. This means that many working-class youth use the schools to retain respectable upper working-class status. Working-class children tend to enter school lacking some of the knowledge, attitudes, and skills that would help them succeed there; afterward, many of them are sorted at one or another level into career lines leading to blue-collar jobs similar in status to those of their parents. Middle-class students, by way of contrast, tend to enter school with a head start that they maintain in later years and then enter college to prepare for white-collar and professional jobs for which family and school have worked to prepare them.

In addition, there are other ways in which the schools may be thought of as actively helping to lock low-status youth into the same social class as that of their parents. To the extent that what is taught in school is not adapted as fully as possible to the special learning problems that many working-class students encounter in the classroom, the schools become as much a cause as a conduit of low status transmitted from generation to generation. To the extent that educators do not do everything they can to help working-class students develop their talents to the fullest in accordance with the demands and opportunities of a modern economy, the schools can be viewed as making an unnecessary and gratuitous contribution to the transmission of low status. These considerations are discussed much more fully in Chapter 13, but at this point we want to emphasize how

the educational system helps reproduce low status if it groups working-class students into relatively homogeneous low-status schools and thereby helps isolate them from the wider society in which they will have to function later.

The issue of whether predominantly working-class schools handicap working-class students over and beyond the disadvantages associated with their family background has been extensively investigated in research examining attitudes and achievement of students in differing types of schools. Although some researchers disagree, most have reached the conclusion that working-class students who attend a middle- or mixed-class school tend to achieve more and develop more productive aspirations than do students of equivalent background who attend working-class schools. James S. Coleman and his colleagues (1966; Coleman 1990a) reached this conclusion in carrying out one of the largest studies ever conducted on the schools or other social institutions. A number of other researchers have reached the same conclusion based either on their own data (e.g., Wilson 1967; Chubb and Moe 1990; Orland 1990) or on years of additional analysis of the data collected by Coleman and his colleagues (Mosteller and Moynihan 1972; Mayeske 1971).

Why is it that students in working-class schools tend to perform less satisfactorily than do working-class students in other types of schools? In part, the answer seems to involve a tendency for working-class students in middle-class or mixed-status schools to develop more adequate motivation than do working-class students in low-status schools. Researchers have shown that the influence of other students who are significant others in the sense of influencing a young person's attitudes and behaviors is nearly as important as the influence of parents in predicting school-related attitudes and behaviors (Alexander and McDill 1976; Shea 1976; Hallinan and Williams 1990); thus, it seems probable that the influence of middle-class peers can make a valuable contribution to mobility among working-class youth.

Other ways in which predominantly working-class schools may hamper the status attainment process for their students involve the attitudes students develop in attending such schools and the classroom behaviors of students and teachers. At one time it was thought that students in working-class schools achieved poorly because they received fewer resources per pupil (books, teachers, etc.) than did mixed- or middle-class schools, but the Coleman report tended to discredit this as the only or major explanation, and federal as well as state funds for low-income schools have helped somewhat in equalizing the resources available in differing types of schools. The school's social environment is as important as or even more important than differences in physical resources in accounting for very low performance levels in working-class schools (also see Chubb and Moe 1990).

Negative social environments appear to be particularly problematical in inner-city schools attended by minority students: Coleman and his colleagues found that among black and Hispanic students, a sense of control over one's future and one's chances in life was more highly related to learning than was one's view of oneself as a competent learner; the reverse was true among white students. The latter pattern is what educators would predict, given the established fact that students who believe they can learn tend to perform better, other things being equal, than do students who say they are not capable of learning much in their classroom. It is reasonable to conclude that for minority students in working-class schools, and probably also for white students in the inner city as well, growing up in a predominantly low-status environment and/or attending a low-status school tends to generate feelings of exclusion and powerlessness that inhibit success both in school and later life.

In addition, teacher expectations for students tend to be lower in working-class than in middle-class schools. For a variety of reasons, it appears that students in working-class schools are not required to perform at a level as high as are students of comparable background in other types of schools (Payne 1984, 1989; MacIver and Epstein 1990). Related to differences in student behavior patterns and teacher expectations (i.e., requirements), educational climates in schools differ according to the socioeconomic composition of the student body. These differences are explored more fully in Chapter 8, but at this point it is important to notice that there tends to be a much greater emphasis on external discipline in low-status schools than in high-status schools, whereas teachers in the latter schools stress academic excellence, independent work, and self-discipline to a much greater extent than do teachers in low-status schools (Chubb and Moe 1990).

For example, Wilcox (1978) studied classrooms in so-called open elementary schools and found that despite the use of instruction emphasizing such approaches as multiple learning centers and individualized contracting with students, teachers used more "authoritarian control mechanisms" in working with lower-status than with higher-status classes. Similarly, Anyon (1983, 1988) studied students' work tasks in five elementary schools that differed greatly in social class: two working-class schools in which the majority of fathers were unskilled or semiskilled; a mixed-status school (which she called "middle class") in which most parents were well-paid blue-collar workers or were white-collar workers; an "affluent professional" school in which parents were predominantly upper middle-class professionals; and an "executive elite" school in which most of the fathers were high-level executives. Her descriptions of task assignments and activities in mathematics, language arts, social studies, and other subjects included the following portrayal of modal tendencies:

> [In the Working-Class Schools] work is following the steps of a procedure . . . usually mechanical, involving rote behavior . . . the children [copied mathematical terms] in their notebooks. . . . Work in language arts is mechanics of punctuation, . . . capitalization, and the four kinds of sentences. [In history,

the teacher] put information . . . on the board and the children copied it. . . .

[In the Middle-class School*] work is getting the right answer. . . . One must follow directions . . . but there is . . . some choice, some decision making. [In math] one may do two-digit division the long way, or the short way. . . . In social studies the daily work is to read the assigned pages . . . and answer the teacher's questions. . . .*

[In the Affluent Professional School*] work is creative activity carried out independently. The students are continually asked to express and apply ideas and concepts. [In history, children] wrote and exchanged a letter in hieroglyphics. [In language arts, the students] wrote editorials [and] radio plays . . . to read on the school intercom. . . .*

[In the Executive Elite School*] work is developing one's analytical intellectual powers. Children are continually asked to reason through a problem, to produce intellectual products that are both logically sound and of top academic quality. A primary goal . . . is to conceptualize rules by which elements may fit together. (Anyon 1988, 363–375)*

Using Kohn's terminology for analyzing education in the status attainment process, one might say that middle-status schools tend to receive youngsters who have been prepared at home to work independently, and then the schools help them develop their skills further so youngsters can pursue self-directed jobs in the economy. Working-class schools, by way of contrast, receive students who have not been prepared or are otherwise not ready to work independently in the classroom, and then use external discipline of the kind students are familiar with at home to provide guidance in the classroom.

Recent confirmation indicating that middle-status schools continue to place greater emphasis than do working-class schools on independent learning of meaningful subject matter has been provided in Johns Hopkins University national surveys of intermediate schools (i.e.,

schools with a combination of grades from five through nine). As summarized by principal investigator Henry Becker (1990a), these studies found that compared to their working-class counterparts, middle-class intermediate schools placed more stress on scientific methods of discovery, regular editing and rewriting of English assignments, weekly laboratory work in science, study of literature, and discussion of controversial issues in social studies.

Based on the results of these studies, the Chicago School Survey (Havighurst 1964), and other sources (e.g., Bernstein 1990), schools can be distinguished according to the types of students they enroll and the kinds of discipline they stress or exemplify. As shown in Table 7-7, discipline in middle-class schools tends to be relatively informal, whereas teachers in schools with a large proportion of working-class students attempt to impose strict discipline in the hope that this will facilitate instruction in basic skills. The descriptions in Table 7-7 are, of course, prototypical: not all schools can be placed in such clear-cut categories, and disciplinary emphasis will vary from teacher to teacher and according to the age of students, the type of leadership, and other conditions in a given school. There is enough truth in the descriptions, however, to make them useful summaries of the disciplinary emphases that exist in differing types of schools. There also is empirical support in research such as that conducted by Anyon (above) and by Howell and McBroom (1982), who found significant correlations between emphasis on "openness" versus control in the family patterns and the school experience of a national sample of high school students. These findings underline how elementary and secondary schools reinforce family background in preparing or not preparing young people for upward mobility in a modern economy.

There also is reason to believe that many community colleges and other higher-education institutions that are disproportionately working class in student composition extend the emphases on control and on low-level learning into the

TABLE 7-7 *Disciplinary Approaches Emphasized in Differing Types of Schools*

Type of School	Economic Background of Students	Disciplinary Emphasis
Middle class	Upper- and lower-middle class	Students work independently in the classroom; discipline is informal; emphasis is on developing a variety of scholarly and creative skills.
Mixed	Lower-middle class and working class	Emphasis is on developing self-discipline and greater capacity to work independently.
Working class	Upper- and lower-working class	Emphasis is on obedience to authority; students work in structured situations with stress on developing mastery of basic academic skills.

postsecondary level. Richardson, for example, cited evidence indicating that "open-access" colleges—including many community colleges and other colleges and universities in big cities—minimize "activities involving the synthesis or comprehension of large issues," thereby detracting from development of "students' abilities to read and write" (1985, 45). He also concluded, however, that "urban areas are threatened by the absence of critical literacy skills among high percentages of their population. Urban universities and colleges represent the best hope for interrupting the channeling process through which those who lack such literacy skills gain credentials as teachers and return to perpetuate their own inadequacies through the public school system" (1985, 49).

Social Mobility, Education, and the Underclass

Our analysis to this point suggests that schools along with other social institutions provide successful routes to upward mobility for a substantial percentage of the population by equipping talented and ambitious young people with skills and opportunity to enter and advance in the economic system (Holmes 1988). However, another segment of the population—particularly the big-city underclass—has relatively little realistic opportunity to succeed because the family, the schools, the economy, and other social institutions serving this population apparently are not

functioning successfully to generate mobility. Some members of the underclass are able to escape from extremely disadvantaged circumstances and enter the stable working class or the middle class. Many others, however, are not succeeding, and their numbers have become sufficiently large to make the inner core part of our cities a social tinderbox.

If this analysis is correct, our conclusions should be reflected in data showing that education for the underclass is not working as effectively to generate upward mobility as it is for the national population as a whole. To our knowledge, social scientists have not framed and pursued this question precisely in these terms, but several lines of research do suggest that this is exactly what has been happening in the United States during the past three decades.

This research generally examines differences between the white and black population. Since the black population until fairly recently included only a small middle class, research comparing whites and blacks tends to constitute a comparison between a mixed-status population (whites) and a low-status population (blacks). Some research conducted during the past few years also has singled out the black population of big-city ghettos for special study, thus focusing more directly on the urban underclass. Other studies have begun to focus on social-class differences emerging among the black population, to an extent thereby highlighting the black underclass (e.g., Landry 1987). The results of these studies provide indirect support for the conclusion that the schools and other mobility-generating institutions are not working as well for the underclass as for the population as a whole.

1. A study by Harrison (1972a) concluded that although the gap between the school completion rates of young whites and blacks had nearly disappeared by 1972, blacks in urban ghettos were not benefiting as much from schooling as were other segments of the population. Harrison speculated that this difference may reflect the strong influence of a "street culture" among the black underclass: "Clearly, education has a very high opportunity cost for non-whites living in the urban ghetto. There are any number of (largely illegal) activities out 'on the street' which are capable of returning more money than can be obtained through a high school diploma" (p. 806).

2. We already have mentioned the studies by Featherman and Hauser (1976, 1978) that found that the occupational status attainment of whites had become more meritocratic between 1962 and 1973. Featherman and Hauser also examined attainment for blacks and concluded that the pattern for blacks had begun to resemble the pattern for whites:

> In 1962, black men of all ages, except those 35–44, were not able to advance in the status hierarchy much beyond the position of their family heads. [In 1973] black men were far more likely to be upwardly mobile than their counterparts a decade earlier . . . black men recently have begun to experience status mobility in their life cycles which more closely duplicates the circumstances of whites. (1976, pp. 629–630)

However, Featherman and Hauser also stress that the increasing utility of education in the status attainment process for blacks is linked to the emergence of clearer social-class lines among the black population. Before the 1960s, the great majority of the black population was either working class or underclass; but economic classes are more visible among the black population now than in 1962. "Black families seem increasingly able," they concluded, to "transfer their socioeconomic statuses to sons" (1978, p. 381). We interpret this situation as indicating that it is the black middle class that is translating educational attainment into social mobility, while large segments of the black population still are immobilized in the working and underclass groups, particularly in big cities and metropolitan areas.

3. A study by Camburn (1990) found that graduates of predominantly black metropolitan high schools are less likely to persist in college than are graduates of other high schools, in part because they apparently are receiving "inadequate preparation for the academic rigors" of higher education (p. 566).

4. Portes and Wilson (1976) have examined black and white differences in educational attainment and have come to conclusions that shed further light on the role of education in the status attainment process for both groups. Analyzing data collected in the late 1960s and early 1970s from a national probability sample of 87 high schools, they stressed the "crucial fact" that

> for the white majority academic grades, apart from the psychological effects, appear to "carry along" individuals toward predictable levels of achievement. Black grades . . . appear to be more irrelevant as marks of achievement within the schools themselves and as criteria of selection for higher education. Institutional administrators seem to do so much "discounting" of the value of inner-city and other black school grades as to render their importance for admission almost nil. (pp. 428–429)

"Discounting" of the grades of inner-city students could operate in either or both of two directions. High grades might be discounted because it is felt that they do not represent very high achievement levels, or low grades might be disregarded because it is believed that their possessors can perform more adequately if given opportunity and support in undertaking a career after high school. It is probable that both tendencies are at work in the status attainment process for students in low-status schools, but for our purposes here the most important point is that educational attainment as measured by grade point average does not seem to be as accurate an indicator of academic achievement among inner-city students as it is among the population as a whole.

The same generalization can be made for educational status as measured by attainment of a high school diploma or number of years completed in the public schools. Much research has indicated that for the population as a whole, number of years of schooling completed is an excellent measure for characterizing educational attainment. Based on an extensive survey of the literature, Shea (1976) summarized the justification for this generalization as follows: "Those who attain more years of schooling score higher on most measures of achievement anyway, including intelligence tests, grade point averages, and achievement test scores" (p. 477). As noted earlier, however, neither grade point average (Portes and Wilson) nor attainment of a high-school diploma (Camburn 1990) seem to represent very useful measures of attainment for the ghetto segment of the black population. Instead, data on the status of black Americans indicate that college attendance rather than high-school graduation is associated with social-class mobility (Smith 1989). In our view, this means that partly due to inadequate school performance, blacks in the underclass are highly dependent at this time on nonschool routes to mobility, but they also are in a poor position to take advantage of even these channels because they tend to be cut off geographically and socially from opportunities to become mobile through the job market (Hacker 1988).

5. Analyses of the status attainment process for whites and blacks have provided additional data to support the conclusions enumerated above. For example, J. P. Smith (1982) reviewed census information on educational attainment collected in 1940, 1970, and 1979 and related this information to data on income and literacy among men and women born in five-year groups from 1865–1870 to 1946–1950. His overall conclusion was as follows:

The tale being woven in this paper is a relatively optimistic one of slow progress. It is also a story of the long lags before changes in the home and school are reflected in outcomes in the labor market. . . . The long-term historical process has been one in which black incomes have risen relative to whites in all schooling classes. . . . The largest black gains relative to whites [now] are concentrated among black college graduates. But the most intriguing trend documented . . . is the post-1973 deterioration in relative black incomes among new entrants with a high school diploma or less. This deterioration represents the first significant reversal in the gradual trend toward income convergence between the races that has occurred in the last few decades. . . . We may be picking up the first signals of problems with the relative quality of Northern inner-city black schools. A substantial part of the well-documented improvement in the quality of black schooling in the twentieth century reflected black migration from the South to the better schools of the North and also the overall rise in the quality of Southern schools. These factors having largely run their course, further improvement in black schooling depends critically on what is taking place in Northern urban black schools. (J. P. Smith 1982, 29–30)

This pattern also suggests that the public school system is not operating very effectively to help the underclass achieve mobility. Students who are sufficiently motivated tend to finish high school, but even among this group many are not acquiring adequate academic and occupational skills. Neither grades nor a diploma appear to represent much achievement in schools enrolling high proportions of poverty students, apparently because students are able to move along from one grade to another without actually learning much.

This critical situation is discussed in more detail in succeeding chapters, but at this point it is important to emphasize that schools and society in the United States appear to be generating too little mobility for underclass students in big-city school districts.

EDUCATION AND THE SOCIOECONOMIC POWER STRUCTURE: THE NEO-MARXIST AND REVISIONIST CRITIQUES AND CRITICAL PEDAGOGY

A number of economists and political scientists have challenged the conclusion that schools and society in the United States and in other western nations really function to provide meaningful opportunity for the working class. Because their major conclusions are that education in a capitalist society is bound to work against the interests of the poor and that reforms within the capitalist system fail to provide adequate opportunity for the working class, their point of view can be described as Marxist or neo-Marxist. Henry Levin, a leading advocate of this position, has described its basic thrust in the following summary of the central arguments on both sides:

> *The role of education in creating a just and productive society is very much a topic of controversy today. On the one side are those who see the educational system as that institution of modern society which develops, sorts, and selects persons according to their productive proficiencies to fill the hierarchical positions of modern, large-scale bureaucratic organizations in a rational and meritocratic manner.*
>
> *On the other side are those who see the schools as agencies for reproducing the social relations of production for monopoly capitalism and its supportive state structures. . . . In their view the schools serve the role of preparing wage-labor for capitalist enterprise with its*

> *attendant needs for docile and disciplined workers who are socialized and certified for particular places in the work hierarchy with an awareness only of their individual relations to the enterprise rather than of solidarity with other workers as a class. . . .*
>
> *While other important versions of the role of the school exist, the poles of the present debate are represented by the functionalists who see schooling as the essential institution for preparing competent members of a modern, rational, efficient, and meritocratic society and the Marxists who see schooling as one of the most important instruments of the state for supporting the capitalist hegemony over the worker. (Levin 1976, 148–149)*

As described by Levin, the neo-Marxists view the schools as part of a larger system designed primarily to produce "disciplined" workers certified for a position at the bottom of the social structure. The schools do this partly by emphasizing external discipline in teaching working-class children, in the same manner as does the family in which they grow up and the factories in which many work as adults. The neo-Marxists frequently refer to this arrangement as the *correspondence principle*: the social relations of schooling and of family life correspond to the social relations of production; the social relations of the larger society are reproduced in the school in a way that tends to reproduce the social class structure later (Carnoy 1974; Bowles and Gintis 1976).

In other words, the economic and technological characteristics of a society cause the families and the schools to take on characteristics that fit in with the socioeconomic structure. Bowles (1975) developed this idea as follows:

> *I will argue that the social division of Labor—based on the hierarchical structure of production—gives rise to distinct class subcultures. The values, personality traits, and expectations characteristic of each subculture are transmitted from generation to generation*

through class differences in family socialization and complementary differences in the type and amount of schooling ordinarily attained by children of various positions. . . . This outline, and what follows, is put forward as an interpretation, consistent where testable with the available data, though lacking as yet in firm empirical support for some important links in the argument. . . .

These personality attributes are developed primarily at a young age, both in the family and, to a lesser extent, in secondary socializing institutions such as schools. Because people tend to marry within their own class (in part because spouses often meet in our class-segregated schools), both parents are likely to have a similar set of these fundamental personality traits. . . . The children of managers and professionals are taught self-reliance with a broad set of constraints. The children of production-line workers are taught obedience.

Although this relation between parents' class position and child's personality attributes operates primarily in the home, it is reinforced by schools and other institutions. Thus, . . . the authoritarian social relations of working-class high schools complement the discipline-oriented early socialization patterns experienced by working-class children. The relatively greater freedom of wealthy suburban schools extends and formalizes the early independence training characteristic of upper-class families. (pp. 58–60)

Bowles, Gintis, and some other neo-Marxists subsequently moderated their views on the correspondence principle by recognizing that the schools can and sometimes do function to develop habits of independent thought among disadvantaged students, rather than simply reproducing labor market relations aimed strictly at obedience and acceptance of the status quo (Bowles and Gintis 1981; Carnoy 1982, 1989). Similarly, Michael Apple (1991, p. xiv) has pointed out that teachers in public schools can undercut what he views as the "state's overt in-

terests." (For discussion of this viewpoint, also see Jennifer Gore's 1990 essay on empowerment in critical and feminist pedagogy.)

Recent works of some neo-Marxist analysts also have given more adequate attention to other disjunctions between the educational system, the economic system, and the larger social system. These disjunctions indicate that schools do not simply reproduce the existing social order through the mechanical operation of a universal correspondence principle. For example, *Schooling and Work in the Democratic State* by Martin Carnoy and Henry Levin (1985) recognizes that although schooling functions partially to reproduce the unequal class relations of a capitalist economy, it also is "more democratic and equal than the workplace for which it prepares students" (p. 4). Specific contradictory tendencies in the relationships they describe between the educational system and the economy include the effects of schooling in (1) alienating students, thereby undermining the school's role "as a producer of trained labor" (p. 156); and (2) deprofessionalizing the teaching force, thereby making teachers less effective in training the labor force. In addition, Carnoy and Levin concluded that conflicts over spending on education may result in improved funding to enhance the performance of disadvantaged students. Thus, in contrast to some of their previous writing, Carnoy and Levin's later analysis allows for greater progress toward economic equality through reform of the educational system (also see Carnoy 1989).

The discussion in this chapter has shown that some criticisms of the neo-Marxists have a certain amount of validity. Many working-class children have little realistic opportunity for mobility through the schools and other social institutions; this problem has become particularly acute among the underclass population of big cities.

However, if the neo-Marxist position that schooling mainly reproduces the existing social order is correct, then there should be very little social mobility upward and downward between the working class and the middle class, and most working-class children should be attending predominantly working-class schools and be enrolled in vocationally oriented programs in which they are being indoctrinated in the discipline of the capitalist order. But we have seen that the evidence available from a large number of studies suggests not only that there is considerable mobility occurring in the United States and in other western societies, but also that these societies seem to be growing more meritocratic and education seems to be accounting for an increasing share of mobility.

In addition, there is reason to question the extent to which working-class children are generally penalized by being shunted into vocationally oriented programs or by attending predominantly working-class schools in which consistent emphasis is placed on external discipline. For one thing, the climate in working-class schools varies to an extent from one school or classroom to another, and many such schools have made serious attempts to enhance the quality and effectiveness of curriculum and instruction (Cuban 1990). Second, it is far from true that all working-class children are enrolled in different courses based on their voca-tional aptitudes or attend schools that are predominantly working-class in socioeconomic composition.

There has been some research on the social class composition of secondary schools in the United States. One such study is summarized in Table 7-8. First, small-town and rural high schools serve the entire community without regard to the socioeconomic status of the students. They do not have vocational education courses much beyond agriculture and home economics. Approximately one-fourth of our youth attended such schools in the early 1970s. Elsewhere in the United States, the "comprehensive" high schools in cities and suburban areas enroll perhaps 40 percent of youth. In these schools, working-class and middle-class youth take the same courses, except for a small minority who take vocational education courses. An ambitious and reasonably successful working-class youth will attend the same classes and go on to a university in company with the middle-class youth. It is certain that many upwardly mobile working-class youth learn the same material and associate intimately with middle-class youth in these comprehensive schools.

TABLE 7-8 *Social Class Composition of High Schools in the 1970s*

| Type of School | Socioeconomic Status of Students Percentage Distribution | | | | | Number (000) | Percentage of Total |
	I (HI)	II	III	IV	V(LO)		
Middle-class	33	33	29	5	—	2,000	13.1
Independent	45	50	5	—	—	100	0.7
Working-class or poverty	3	10	28	46	13	1,200	7.9
Vocational	—	5	50	40	5	400	2.6
Comprehensive urban	12	20	36	28	4	6,300	41.5
Small-town & rural	3	14	30	38	15	4,000	26.3
Church-related	8	17	34	35	6	1,200	7.9
Total American high-school students	11	19	33	30	7	15,200	100.0

Source: Adapted from Levine, Mitchell, and Havighurst 1970.
Note: The five Socioeconomic Categories are *not* identical with the five social classes we have defined previously. The categories are based on a specially devised scale of socioeconomic status used with high-school seniors in the Kansas City metropolitan area. Class I is actually mainly upper middle-class students and Class V students from very low-status families.

National data collected by Jeannie Oakes (1990b) and her colleagues at the Rand Corporation similarly indicate that substantial proportions of working-class students and poverty students attend schools that have socioeconomically diverse enrollment. Based on information from a nationally representative sample of 977 schools, the data indicated that at 29 percent of elementary schools and 35 percent of secondary schools, between 10 and 30 percent of students' parents were unemployed or received welfare assistance. At an additional 27 percent of elementary schools and 33 percent of secondary schools, less than 10 percent of students' parents were unemployed or received welfare, but less than 30 percent worked in professional or managerial occupations.

National data sets also indicate that a large majority of low-status students attend suburban schools and rural schools, which seldom are predominantly working-class in socioeconomic composition. Thus, data from the National Education Longitudinal Study (NELS) of eighth graders show that 72 percent of the approximately three-quarters of a million eighth graders in the bottom quartile on socioeconomic status attend suburban or rural schools (Valdivieso 1991).

Other research also has countered some arguments of the neo-Marxist position regarding the correspondence principle. For example, Olneck and Bills (1980) analyzed information from a study of Kalamazoo youth and found that among men from middle-class families, those who were rated uncooperative by their teachers had higher initial occupational status than those who were rated cooperative. In addition, there was no relationship between teachers' ratings of cooperativeness and initial job status among working-class youth. The authors concluded that these findings are inconsistent with Bowles and Gintis's contention that the same behaviors are rewarded at work as in school.

Part of the problem in the neo-Marxist critique seems to be that many of its proponents tend to take an either-or position on issues involving social mobility. As Levin himself states in describing the Marxist point of view, functional-ists such as Inkeles and critics such as the Marxists are seen as representing "the poles of the present debate." Once debate has been polarized to force a choice among contending positions, one tends to lose sight of the evidence indicating that although education is reinforcing the low status of too many working-class students, it also is serving as a route to mobility for substantial numbers of others. Thus, even though the neo-Marxists have added a useful and important perspective to the debate on education and social mobility, their overall conclusions are too limited and one-sided to yield a validated position on what should be done to provide more equal opportunity in schools and society (Liston 1990; Fuller 1991).

On the other hand, preceding sections indicate that the schools and other institutions do not seem to be functioning at all adequately for the underclass in big cities. Children from this group generally are enrolled in predominantly low-status schools, and the schools thus appear to be reinforcing their isolation from the larger society. Evidence we present in later chapters indicates that there is a real question whether schools are working effectively for underclass students in the cities.

The Revisionists: Who Controls the Public Education System?

Another important strand of criticism regarding how schools function in capitalist societies has been developed by a group of revisionist historians. They argue that the public schools have served to make the children of the poor and of ethnic minorities satisfied with failure in school and with low-status occupations. If this proposition is true, it might be supported by data indicating that the children of the poor have now, and have had in the past, very little upward social mobility, that education has not and does not lead to upward social mobility, and that the teaching of United States history and social studies in the schools has been systematically false in many respects.

There has been much controversy over the work of the revisionists; the student can find and read books and articles by Michael Apple (1982, 1990), Michael Katz (1968, 1975), Paul Violas (1978) and other authors identified with revisionist viewpoints. One problem in most revisionist writings is that a reader looks in vain for a consideration of this question: What amount of upward and downward social mobility is viable in a democratic society in which middle-status families believe they have the right and the obligation to help their children maintain the same or a higher social status? The basic problem of a balance between social fluidity and social stability seems to be ignored. Do the revisionist historians favor a complete social revolution every generation, so that every child of a new generation stands on an equal basis with every other, with respect to economic support and to home support for school achievement? If not a revolution, how do they propose to equalize the differential opportunity that comes from different home backgrounds?

A useful summary and analysis of the arguments of the neo-Marxist writers on education and society and of the revisionist historians can be found in the monograph *The Revisionists Revised: Studies in the Historiography of American Education* by Diane Ravitch. Professor R. Freeman Butts of Teachers College, Columbia University, published a thoughtful review in 1974 of the revisionist position in *The History of Education Quarterly* (1990), while Henry Aaron (1977) and Daniel Liston have prepared short reviews of the evidence for and against the neo-Marxist revisionists. In addition, Donald Warren has put together a set of articles that report the contributions of history to the broader study of education and public policy in the United States. Historian Sol Cohen has summarized some problems in the methods and conclusions of the revisionists (whom he called the "new reconstructionists"):

> *To the new reconstructionists the function of history of education is clearly to serve the cause of social reconstruction. . . . Novel can-*

ons of historical writing are introduced. Katz ingenuously states: "Our concerns shape the questions that we ask and, as a consequence, determine what we select from the virtually unlimited supply of facts," and, "in any event, the burden of proof no longer lies with those who argue that education is and has been unequal. It lies, rather with those who would defend the system. . . . The new reconstructionists ask such loaded questions of the evidence that they can be pretty sure at the beginning what answer they will emerge with at the end. There is a finality and rationality about their work that terribly oversimplifies the ambiguity, the incompleteness, the complexity of historical events. . . . Karier has said that history speaks only very cautiously and modestly to the present, that in history one seldom finds answers which are completely satisfying. But despite these caveats, the ideological commitment of the new reconstructionists has become a strait jacket." (Cohen 1976, 327–329)

Critical Pedagogy

The neo-Marxist and revisionist and other broad critiques that question the extent to which opportunities for mobility are available to low-status citizens frequently are referred to under the broader term *critical theory*. Applied to the education system, critical theories often are presented and discussed as part of an analytic framework that is concerned with "critical pedagogy" (Henricksen and Morgan 1990). Critical pedagogy particularly rejects the so-called banking approach to instruction, which it perceives as stressing deposit of knowledge into the student and thereby recapitulating the "oppressive paradigm of a dominant culture" that separates students' lives from their education (Ewell 1990, 52).

Much of the best-known analysis associated with critical pedagogy has been developed by Henry Giroux and various collaborators in the 1970s and 1980s. Although Giroux and his colleagues seldom provide a precise definition of critical pedagogy, their writings generally delineate various ways in which it challenges educators and students to make educational opportunities more effective for disadvantaged persons and groups. A number of terms, including *critical literacy*, *critical engagement*, *critical educational theory*, *critical understanding*, *critical discourse*, *critical dialogue*, and *critcial analysis*, are used almost interchangeably in considering what can and should be done to reduce inequality of opportunity in the schools and in society (Giroux 1988a, 1988b, 1991).

As in the case of economic, political, and other aspects of critical theory (that Giroux sometimes refers to as "radical theory" or "radical criticism"), critical pedagogy begins with analysis asserting that the "dominant culture" embodies a "privileged" system that makes opportunities available to historically dominant groups and excludes the disadvantaged. Reminiscent in many ways of Basil Bernstein's analysis of language codes (see preceding parts of this chapter), critical theory in education concludes that far "from being neutral, the dominant culture in the schools is characterized by a selective ordering and legitimating of privileged language forms, modes of reasoning, [and] social relations" that exemplify the imposition of a "specific set of ruling-class codes and experiences." Thus, critical pedagogy is a strand of critical theory inasmuch as it portrays the "transmission of a dominant culture in schools" through actions that "disconfirm the histories, experiences, and dreams of subordinate groups," as well as other "ways in which the State, through its selective grants, certification policies, and legal powers, influences school practice in the interest of particular dominant ideologies" (Giroux 1988b, xxx–xxxi).

But, Giroux insists, critical pedagogy must "move beyond the language of critique and domination." The "tragedy" of critical theory limited to viewing the schools "almost exclusively as agencies of social reproduction" is that it inhibits educators from "developing a programmatic language for either pedagogical or school reform . . . a progressive, political educational strategy" (Giroux 1988b, xxxxi). In a series of articles and books intended explicitly to move beyond the portrayal of socioeconomic reproduction, Giroux particularly emphasizes the goal of *empowerment* of students and educators (1991, 47). Because schools do not just reproduce the larger society but are locations in which to "resist its dominating logic," teachers and administrators should view themselves as "transformative intellectuals" who work not only to provide students with the "knowledge and social skills they will need to function in the larger society," but also to educate students for "transformative action." Such an education, according to Giroux, will emphasize both "pedagogical transformation" within the school and "struggle against forms of oppression in the wider society" (Giroux 1988b, xxxiii). Thus, the "notions of struggle, student voice, and critical dialogue are central to the goal of developing a critical pedagogy" (Giroux 1988a, 132).

Giroux also has sketched out some aspects of a critical pedagogy that is "fundamentally concerned" with student voice and "takes the problems and needs of the students themselves as its starting points." In addition to introducing students to "a language of empowerment . . . that permits them to think about how community life" can be vastly improved and to helping students "understand why things are the way they are and how they got that way," critical pedagogy must go beyond "celebration of plurality" by unifying diverse student voices through shared study of "human suffering . . . and the conditions that perpetuate such suffering" and through use of popular culture as central content in the curriculum (Giroux 1988b, 164–166; Giroux and Simon 1989, 223). The role of popular culture in critical pedagogy is discussed later in this section.

Regarding the role of teachers who strive to achieve the goals of critical pedagogy, Giroux believes it is "especially important that teachers critically engage how ideological interests structure their ability both to teach and to learn with others. . . . Educators need to take as their first concern the issue of [their own] empowerment, and the route to that goal . . . depends on the ability of teachers in the future to struggle collectively in order to create those ideological and material conditions of work that enable them to share power, to shape policy, and to play an active role in structuring school/community relations" (Giroux 1988a, 167, 214).

Critical Pedagogy and Popular Culture. As noted, one emphasis in critical pedagogy is on drawing on and incorporating "popular culture" in working to improve opportunities for disadvantaged students through education. This aspect of critical pedagogy is described and discussed comprehensively in a book titled *Popular Culture, Schooling, and Everyday Life* (Giroux and Simon 1989). Arguments and conclusions set forth by the authors focus on possibilities for drawing on popular culture to help students "critically assess the role they might take up as engaged and democratic citizens living in a world of increasing cultural diversity and conflict," and to "expand rather than limit their potentialities" to become culturally literate, not only with respect to their local communities but also to the larger world. Particularly for disadvantaged students, this emphasis on a critical pedagogy would mean "affirming those histories, traditions, stories, and everyday events that have been denied their rightful place as important legacies in the struggle for democracy and cultural justice" (Giroux and Simon, 1989, xi).

The introductory chapter (by Paolo Freire and Henry Giroux) in *Popular Culture, Schooling, and Everyday Life* emphasizes the importance and value of developing educational practices and approaches that allow and help students to grasp the "standpoint of others while simultaneously recognizing the partial nature of all discourses, including their own" (Giroux and Simon, 1989, xii). Contributors repeatedly insist that the goal of such a critical pedagogy is not to reject all aspects of "high culture," but rather to incorporate both popular culture and traditional high culture in a more meaningful approach to curriculum and instruction, thus moving critical

theory beyond its original emphasis on how schooling reproduces the social order.

In their initial chapter, "Popular Culture as a Pedagogy of Pleasure and Meaning," and again in their concluding chapter, Henry Giroux and Roger Simon wrestle with the difficulties involved in determining how critical pedagogy can build effectively on popular culture in part through attending "to ways in which students make both affective and semantic investments as part of their attempts to regulate and give meaning to their lives" (1989, 3). Because much of popular culture is concerned with experiencing pleasure, affect, and "corporeality" (i.e., the physical existence of the body) and with "active involvement in popular forms such as neighborhood sports, punk dancing, or working-class weddings," a critical pedagogy built in part on popular culture necessarily will give considerable attention to themes and materials that traditional pedagogy rejects as insignificant, vulgar, and, frequently, obscene. Although appropriate use of such themes and materials can help engage students in meaningful learning, critical pedagogy also confronts numerous pitfalls involving temptations to overly romanticize popular culture and to treat its themes and materials as ends in themselves. Instead, according to Giroux, Simon, and other contributors, critical pedagogy should view popular culture as a means to develop students' broader understandings and analytic capacities.

Among the possibilities introduced and discussed in *Popular Culture, Schooling, and Everyday Life* are use of films, television programs, rock music, concerts, and other mass-media resources that can constitute a "significant basis of knowledge" on which students and teachers can draw to create "a space for mutual agreement of lived difference that does not require the silencing of a multiplicity of voices by a single dominant discourse" (Giroux and Simon 1989, 24). But educators working to develop a critical pedagogy will have to give serious attention to a variety of difficult questions and issues, such as the following (Giroux and Simon 1989, 266–231):

1. Can educators "incorporate aspects of students' lived culture into the work of schooling without simply confirming" students' existing knowledge?

2. Can educators do this without trivializing the "cultural resources important to students?"

3. Can this be done without "singling out groups of students as marginal, exotic . . . 'others' "?

4. How can educators "sustain the notion of popular culture as a terrain of possibilities" rather than a threat posed by "profane" desires?

5. How can educators avoid having encouragement of "student voice" through emphasis on popular culture become a form of "voyeurism"?

6. Will putting "popular cultural practices . . . up for discussion" basically change their character by repressing their vitality? How can popular culture become part of a critical pedagogy that does not "ultimately function to police its content and forms"?

7. Given that much of popular culture involves materials that are sexist, racist, or otherwise "reactionary," can such material be used productively in the service of a "progressive pedagogy . . . How can one avoid the conservatism inherent in simply celebrating personal experience and confirming what people already know . . . [and instead] acknowledge previous experience as legitimate content and challenge it at the same time?"

Resistance Theory.   One major strand of critical pedagogy involves what some analysts call "resistance" theory. This theory seeks to explain and interpret the genesis and meaning of working-class students' tendencies to resist participating in learning opportunities available to them in the typical public school. Robert Connell and his colleagues (1982) interviewed working-class teenagers and some of their teachers and parents in Australia and concluded that resistance is the "*main* relation to the school" for many working-

class students who struggle against "oppressive futures" (p. 88).

Resistance to the school arises partly because many working-class students reject the authority of both their parents and their teachers (Connell, Ashenden, Kessler, and Dowsett 1982, 172; Connell 1989), partly because school rules and norms contradict working-class students' definitions of and emphasis on masculinity and femininity (p. 98), and partly because an "oppositional peer life" reinforced by the mass media stimulates them to resist being treated as children by adults in the school (p. 164). Equally important, these authors concluded, many working-class students have little or no interest in the "hegemonic" traditional curriculum of the schools, which "marginalizes" the knowledge acquired by working-class students in daily life. "The main form of dissent" in the school thus reflects the

> *working-class tradition of resistance to power and authority . . . [and is] pitted against the bearers of knowledge. It becomes anti-intellectual, and, partly for that reason, open to commercial exploitation. Everyone comes to agree that the resisters are 'stupid'—that's even a word they use themselves for what they do in classrooms and outside the school with their friends. . . . [Thus mass education] is a mechanism of hegemony in class relations: it divides the working class, [and] undermines its self-confidence. (Connell 1982, 172, 197).*

Robert Everhart (1983), in a study of a similar group of working-class students attending a junior high school in the United States, reached much the same conclusion as did Connell and his colleagues in Australia. In particular, Everhart studied the behavior and attitudes of three teenagers named Don, Steve, and Roger; he summarized some of his observations as follows:

> *Don, Steve, and Roger were finding the requirements of school to be unfulfilling and alienating. They resisted teacher attempts to*

involve them in the classroom because to become so involved would be tantamount to admitting that the reified knowledge of the school was legitimate. . . . Don and his friends were interested in the present, not the future, and no amount of cajoling or ridiculing by teachers could convince them that this alienative work was for the better. Their goals were simply to consume as much of the products that liberal capitalism had produced as possible. (Everhart 1983, 115)

Henry Giroux has been analyzing the implications of resistance theory for improving the education of working-class students and disadvantaged minority students. Giroux believes that resistance theory is useful and potentially liberating because it "redefines the causes and meaning of oppositional behavior," and in so doing "points to a number of assumptions and concerns about schooling that we generally neglect in both traditional views of schooling and radical theories of reproduction" (Giroux 1983, 289). The theory of resistance, he says, calls attention to the need to "unravel the ideological interests embedded in the various messages of the school, particularly those embedded in its curriculum, systems of instruction, and modes of evaluation" (p. 292). It further suggests taking seriously the "counterlogic that pulls students away from schools into the streets, the bars, and the shopfloor culture" (p. 293). In this and other papers (see our preceding section), Giroux argues that improving education for working-class students is dependent on developing curriculum and instructional approaches that are relevant to them in terms of their own experience, interests, and personal knowledge (Giroux and McLaren 1986; Giroux 1988, 1991).

Important research involving key aspects of resistance theory also has been carried out by Lois Weis. After a year as a particpant-observer at a big-city high school, Weis (1987, 1990) concluded that changes seem to be occurring in the attitudes and behaviors of working-class white students. She reported that working-class males

generally resist institutional authority in the school and "attempt to carve out their own space- . . . which can then be filled with *their* fundamentally anti-school meanings" (87), as had working-class secondary students in several other studies in the United States and Great Britain. However, Weis also found that male students she interviewed perceived schooling as offering utilitarian opportunities for acquiring skilled jobs and thus were willing to "put in their time" in school and even go to college (1987, 93). Noting that this finding differed from earlier research, Weis viewed this change in attitudes as reflecting students' recognition that unskilled manual labor provides decreasing opportunity for success in postindustrial society.

Regarding females, Weis reported that the working-class girls she interviewed generally did not aim for a marginal "wage labor identity" as had girls in earlier studies. Instead, they had a positive perception of the usefulness of education and wanted to prepare themselves for high-paying jobs that would provide a measure of independence and autonomy. Rather than pursuing romantic fantasies focused on the traditional family, as working-class females in previous research had done, the girls in this study challenged a "fundamental premise of patriarchy—that woman's primary place is in the home-family sphere." Because the boys she studied still held to this traditional premise, Weis concluded that changes in "female culture" may "therefore hold the greater promise of challenge to the traditional role and conception of the working class" (1987, 113–114).

CONCLUSION

The educational system in the United States helps both to change and perpetuate the existing social class structure. The social structure probably is even more fluid now than it has been at some times in the past, and education—which is increasingly a prerequisite to upward mobility in modern societies—is a major route to status advancement for many young people, including working-class youth.

However, the public schools and other social institutions are not providing sufficient mobility for the underclass population in big cities.

Research on developing countries suggests that living in cities is not enough to generate modern attitudes and behaviors associated with upward mobility among working-class populations. Educational and economic opportunity and other social resources are required to improve the conditions of life of the working class. Because education in modern societies is a more important route to mobility than it was in premodern societies, effective education is required to generate mobility for the working-class in the United States.

On their own, the public schools cannot provide equal opportunity in life for underclass students, or for working-class students in general, but together with other institutions the schools may be able to help them succeed in accordance with their talents and ambitions. The role of the schools in working with other institutions for this and other purposes is analyzed in more detail in succeeding chapters.

EXERCISES

1. In what ways is a youngster with high academic ability better off in a modern society than a premodern society? What considerations determine whether high ability will be translated into success later in life?

2. If there is a low-status school nearby, interview several students and/or teachers to determine the extent to which grades that students receive reflect high levels of performance. Do teachers in this school give good grades for low-quality performance? If they do, is it because they do not care about the quality of performance? What problems would teachers encounter if they graded more directly according to performance?

3. Interview several parents to determine the kinds of child-rearing practices they advocate and use with their children. To what degree do these practices agree with the information in this chapter on differenes between the social classes?

4. Describe the group mobility of one subgroup in your own community during the past 100 years.

5. Interview a dozen adults, selected more or less at random, asking them what they think is happening to social mobility in the United States. Is it increasing or decreasing, and why?

6. Identify three or four people who have been upwardly mobile and interview them to determine whether education has helped them achieve this mobility. What other factors or qualities played a part in their success? How do their goals for the education of their children compare with their own educational backgrounds?

7. Analyze the want ads in the employment section of a Sunday newspaper to determine what kinds of educational background are required for differing jobs. Do some of the ads list or assume the completion of high school or college? To what degree do you think some of the skills required could be learned on the job?

8. *Choosing Sides* by Cary Goodman and *Muscles and Morals* by Dominick Cavallo present contrasting interpretations of the movement to establish playgrounds and leisure activities for urban children from 1875 to 1925. Goodman emphasizes reformers' motives involving preparation of young people for "industrial discipline" (e.g., stress on punctuality, team play, following rules and regulations), while Cavallo stresses broader goals involving development of positive mental and moral habits. Which author provides better evidence for his conclusions and interpretations?

SUGGESTIONS FOR FURTHER READING

1. *Power, Ideology and Education* (1977), edited by Jerome Karabel and A. H. Halsey, includes a number of chapters bearing on the schools and the social structure. The volume contains a wide range of viewpoints on issues involving education and mobility in different societies. Various authors report the results of research on these issues, and others analyze the implications and adequacy of this research.

2. In *Class and Merit in the American High School*, Richard A. Rehberg and Evelyn R. Rosenthal report the results of a longitudinal study indicating support for the meritocratic position that scholastic ability, educational ambition, and academic performance are at "least as important as social class in the determination of ultimate educational attainment" (1978, 250). The book also contains a useful summary of both the meritocratic and revisionist viewpoints, basic research approaches that are being used to examine the issues, and previous research conducted by other investigators.

3. In *The Training of the Urban Working Class*, Paul C. Violas reviews the history of urban schools in the United States during the first part of the twentieth century. He concludes that a number of developments associated with the "progressive" movement actually were intended to enable working-class children "to adapt more easily to the assembly lines and production teams in the modern factory" (1978, 15). He argues that compulsory attendance laws, the establishment of playgrounds, "learning by doing," and the development of extracurricular activities, differentiated curricula, and vocational guidance were all designed to develop disciplined and obedient workers for business and industry. For example, he argues that the "playground movement implanted in the child behavior patterns appropriate for an industrial worker" (p. 14). Whether or not one accepts this neo-Marxian revisionist interpretation, the book contains useful historical information on the social purposes of United States schools.

4. Christopher J. Hurn's *The Limits and Possibilities of Schooling* includes concise summaries of the neo-Marxist and meritocratic positions (which he calls "radical" and "functional," respectively) and a thoughtful analysis emphasizing an alternate explanation of the role of education in modern society. Hurn believes that the importance of formal education is best explained by "shared beliefs" that it yields occupational status and "high quality people" (1978, 261) rather than by its actual accomplishments in achieving these goals (the functional explanation) or its role in reproducing inequality (the radical explanation). Hurn offers many thoughtful insights and perspectives in the course of his analysis.

5. Arthur M. Cohen's 1977 paper on "The Social Equalization Fantasy" reviews some of the research on the meritocratic versus neo-Marxist positions regarding the functioning of the educational system at the postsecondary level.

6. The November 1980 issue of the *American Journal of Education* includes several articles reviewing and critiquing *Who Gets Ahead?* by Jencks, as well as some of the research and conclusions reported by Bowles, Gintis, and other neo-Marxists.

7. Several books and papers by Michael Apple (1981, 1982, 1985, 1990; Apple and Jungck 1990) provide an analysis emphasizing neo-Marxist perspectives on curriculum. Neo-Marxist and revisionist scholars are well represented in the book he edited on *Cultural and Economic Reproduction in Education.*

8. Based on participant observation and interviewing of working-class youth in England,

Learning to Labour by Paul Willis describes how working-class culture and the larger society lead students to adopt counter-school attitudes that devalue education and how educators develop a custodial orientation in responding to the problems of teaching in working-class classrooms. David Hogan's essay on social-class formation and reproduction in the United States also provides perspectives on the development of working-class attitudes toward school and society.

9. *The Language of Children Reared in Poverty* edited by Lynne Feagans and Dale Farran analyzes and discusses recent studies and intervention projects dealing with language development of low-status children.

10. *The Hidden Curriculum and Moral Education* edited by Henry Giroux and David Purpel (1983) describes and discusses differing viewpoints on a number of issues involving neo-Marxist and revisionist analysis of education. Many of their points are updated in Giroux (1988) and Purpel (1988).

11. *Ideology and Practice in Schooling* (1983), edited by Michael W. Apple and Lois Weis, provides a variety of perspectives on reproduction of the social classes through education. The chapter by Weis on students at a black community college in the United States provides a useful analysis related to higher education and an interesting contrast with white working-class youth in England. Compared to white youth described in *Learning to Labour* by Willis, black college youth studied by Weis seemed more willing to cooperate with teachers and administrators, provided that the latter groups were perceived as being sincerely concerned with the interests and goals of their students.

12. The book by Coleman and Neugarten, *Social Status in the City*, is an empirical study of the social-class structure of a large midwestern city, with special attention to social mobility.

13. *The Social Order of the Slum* by Gerald Suttles discusses some of the reasons that various ethnic and racial groups have found it more or less easy to attain social mobility in the United States.

14. A wealth of important and fascinating information on the history and status of ethnic groups in the United States is provided in *American Ethnicity* by Bahr, Chadwick, and Strauss, and in *Ethnic America* by Sowell.

15. Two essays in the *Harvard Educational Review* (Giroux 1983, Giroux and McClaren 1986) summarize and extend much of recent critical theory and its implications for education.

16. *The Politics of School Reform 1870–1940* by Paul Peterson (1985) and *The Origins of Public High Schools* by Maris Vinovskis (1986) criticize much of the data and interpretations of the revisionist historians.

17. An essay by Mark Holmes (1988) provides useful perspectives and analyses regarding education and mobility in contemporary society.

18. Subtitled *Critical Theories and Pedagogies, Reorientations* (Henricksen and Morgan 1990) provides a series of essays dealing with critical approaches to humanities teaching. The editors view critical pedagogy as a form of "postpedagogy" compatible with postmodern and poststructural analysis.

19. Jennifer Gore's (1990) essay on "critical and feminist pedagogy" discusses various perspectives on implications of critical theory for empowering students in educational settings. Gore is skeptical concerning theoretical approaches that seem to place responsibility for empowerment on teachers but do not provide "much in the way of tangible guidance" (p. 19) for accomplishing that goal. In particular, she concludes that attempts to "share power" in the "name of empowerment might be misdirected. [Instead, energies] of those of us who advocate critical and feminist

pedagogies might be better directed at seeking ways to exercise power toward the fulfillment of our espoused aims, ways that include humility, skepticism, and self-criticism" (p. 21).

20. After reviewing the theories and arguments of "radical educators who are informed by Marxist theory," Daniel Liston (1990) concludes that this group of educational Marxists frequently has offered facile explanations that "either assume the truth of their propositions or are framed in a manner immune to empirical examination" (pp. 14, 72). While generally sympathetic to neo-Marxist goals and analytic frameworks, Liston criticizes what he views as the narrow theoretical base and lack of empirical accuracy in some major works of critical theorists.

21. Bruce Fuller (1991) portrays the contemporary state as an entity that must "look modern" (p. 95) by attempting to provide educational opportunity for all children. By thus expressing its commitment to modernity, the state hopes to acquire or retain the legitimacy it needs to survive and function. From this point of view, state motivations and actions in providing education do not primarily or comprehensively involve an attempt to serve the interests of advantaged social classes, but rather reflect *institutional* imperatives associated with modernity. However, lacking sufficient resources to provide effective schooling for disadvantaged students through decentralized approaches that recognize and respond appropriately to local problems and needs, the state resorts to standardized, bureaucratic methods that perpetuate many advantages and disadvantages of students' home and family backgrounds. Based in part on research in developing countries by the World Bank, Fuller's analysis is relevant for understanding education in the Third World; he also points out its applicability in considering social forces and prospects for school reform in postindustrial societies.

8

Low-Status Students and Compensatory Education

The material in the preceding chapters helps explain why many students from low-status homes are not well prepared for success in a modern school and why it is important to improve their performance in the educational system. One purpose of this chapter is to identify some reasons that low-status students continue to perform poorly in school despite efforts made recently and in the past to improve their academic performance.

At the outset, it is important to emphasize several points to avoid misleading conclusions or implications. First, much of the discussion is concerned in one way or another with the reasons that schools have not been sufficiently effective in helping low-status students achieve at a more satisfactory level and what can be done to make them more effective in this regard in the future. In considering these questions, we necessarily consider what makes schools or schooling relatively effective or ineffective in general.

Second, it should be clear by now that such terms as *working-class students* and *inner-city schools* are concerned with differences that exist between differing groups of students and schools but do not mean that all students with similar background or all schools with similar student composition are necessarily alike. Thus, our concern is with averages and modal patterns; but exceptions can be found to any generalization involving relationships between social class or other sociological background variables and achievement in the schools.

REASONS FOR POOR PERFORMANCE

We already have described some ways in which schools differ with regard to student control patterns and the kinds of behaviors emphasized in working with students. Schools in working-class neighborhoods tend to emphasize conformity and order in the classroom, whereas schools in middle-class neighborhoods tend to provide less external structure and to emphasize the development of self-directed learning. Students who do not eventually acquire self-directed learning skills experience increasing difficulty as they proceed to higher levels of education.

We also have noted that teachers in working-class schools sometimes confuse order with learning; that is, teachers have had a relatively difficult time maintaining order, and once this goal has been accomplished, many have been unwilling or unable to move beyond it toward the development of self-directed learning skills. This latter phenomenon helps account for the low-achievement patterns found in most working-class schools, but it provides only a partial explanation of the widespread failures teachers have experienced in working to improve the performance of low-status students. Additional reasons involving poor nutrition (Schorr 1989), peer-group influence (Hale-Benson 1989), lack of material resources (Lareau 1989), and other factors are discussed in Chapters 2, 4, and 7 and elsewhere in this book. Some of the most central considerations are discussed in detail in the following pages.

1. *Inappropriate curriculum and instruction.* Because their home environment frequently has not exposed them to the kinds of materials teachers have been trained to use in instruction (see Chapter 7), many low-status students lack basic "print awareness" and respond uncomprehendingly to the lessons teachers try to develop in the classroom (Adams 1990; Snow 1991). This is true in the early grades, when teachers are introducing terminology and concepts with which low-status students may have little familiarity; it frequently becomes even more of a problem in later years when teachers introduce more advanced vocabulary and concepts dependent on earlier understandings that students did not master in earlier grades.

Lack of congruity between disadvantaged students' cultural background and the school's expectations in curriculum and instruction involves not just vocabulary and terminology but also general linguistic patterns important for successfully functioning in the classroom (Bowman 1989; Adams 1990). In this regard, Judith Green of the University of Delaware has surveyed the research on linguistic process in the classroom and concluded that "surface-level" linguistic problems may be less important than "pervasive linguistic patterns" that inhibit many students' "acquisition of strategies for participating in school activities . . . and learning how to learn." She also concluded that successful students not only know "academic information" but also know "how and when to display this information. Being accurate or right was not enough; students needed to present information in appropriate form at the appropriate time" (Green 1983, 207, 227). Many low-status students are disadvantaged in school because they lack knowledge and experience involving such linguistic expectations (Cazden 1988; Bredo, Henry, and McDermott 1990).

2. *Lack of parental and peer reinforcement of school norms and learning experiences.* We have seen that the home environment in early childhood among working-class families frequently is less intellectually stimulating than among middle-class families, and that relatively many working-class parents encounter serious difficulty protecting children from educationally distracting external influences. These tendencies continue to hamper preparation for and interest in school as the child grows older, and their effects make it difficult for the school to function effectively with working-class children.

In many cases, working-class parents physically punish their children or ask the school to use corporal punishment when their children misbehave or do not pay attention, but this approach frequently is not as effective as the middle-class approach emphasizing understanding and internalization of school behavior and academic achievement norms. Working-class parents who are too busy earning a living or are otherwise not able or inclined to visit the school and work closely with teachers in solving their children's problems frequently find that neither physical punishment nor verbal exhortation has much permanent effect. Working-class youth who get into trouble in school or drop out before completing high school frequently mention an early involvement in antischool peer groups as the crucial turning point in their educational careers.

3. *Mismatch between classroom expectations and students' behavioral and learning styles.* Although they may have not been adequately researched, explanations involving a mismatch between students' behavioral and learning styles and school expectations may help account for the relatively low academic performance of many low-status students (Tharp 1989). For example, Boykin (1978; 1983) has examined the research on home and school behavioral characteristics of black children and concluded that the "psychological/lbehavioral verve" that he believes many black youngsters display interacts with the typical classroom environment to produce failure and misbehavior in school (see Shields and Shaver 1990). According to this interpretation, many black children show a higher-than-average "chronic activation level . . . through exposure to more constant high and variable stimulation" in

homes characterized by "televisions on continuously, stereos constantly blaring, a steady stream of people coming in and out of the home, [and] a greater number of people per living space" (1983, 346). (Recall Aries's description in Chapter 3 of preindustrial community in England.)

Boykin believes that the increased "behavioral vibrancy" and "psychological affinity for stimulus change" produced in many children in such an environment place them at a disadvantage in classrooms that are "relatively unstimulating, constraining, and monotonous" (p. 347). In support of this conclusion, he cited research such as that of Greenberg and Davidson (1972), which showed a high correlation between school achievement and orderliness of the home among inner-city black students, and research by Guttentag and Ross (1972), which concluded that low-status black students learned verbal concepts better through an instructional method that used movement than through traditional passive learning. Similarly, DePalma (1990) cites African American educators who believe that many black children have an unusually high energy level, and Morgan (1980) described classrooms in which "management for docility" appears to lead many black children, particularly males, to "disengage from the mainstream of academic tasks" (p. 51). The schools' failure to take children's activity level into account may thus be an example of "blaming" or "victimizing" the child for the institution's failure to make appropriate adaptations in classroom practice.

Although Boykin limits his consideration to black students and refers to "certain cultural and ancestral" factors that may result in high behavioral verve we believe that his description of their home environment is not accurate for many or most middle-class black children but is characteristic of the family setting of many underclass children whatever their racial or ethnic group. For example, descriptions by Oscar Lewis (1961) and Piri Thomas (1967) of the environment of underclass Hispanic children indicate that many probably will encounter classroom problems related to a relatively high activation level. In addition, the fact that regardless of racial-ethnic background, many more boys than girls experience school problems associated with hyperkinetic behavior may indicate that underclass boys generally face more severe problems in adjusting to traditional school environments than do underclass girls.

It should be noted that some researchers believe that overstimulation in the home environment frequently interferes directly with learning by making students unusually distractible and inattentive (Diamond 1988). But whether analysis places emphasis on ways in which high activity level may detract from cognitive learning or on behavioral problems that many low-status students experience in a traditional classroom, there is little doubt that mismatch between home environments and classroom environments and expectations plays an important part in accounting for the low academic performance of many low-status students. Social class differences in nutrition, such as a greater working-class dependence on junk food, may also play a part in producing unusually high activity levels that detract from learning in traditional classrooms.

Another perspective on possible learning style differences that may affect the development and achievement of disadvantaged students has been provided by Barbara Shade and others (e.g., Hilliard 1989/1990) who have been studying cognitive patterns among black children. Shade (1982; 1986) has reviewed research bearing on the cognitive style of black students and has concluded that part of their achievement deficit involves an "Afro-American cognitive or perceptual style preference" that emphasizes a *person* rather than an *object* orientation (p. 236). Such an orientation, which appears to be relatively common among economically disadvantaged students in general, may in turn create or magnify difficulties experienced by disadvantaged students in elementary and secondary schools:

For Afro-American learners . . . [there appears to be] a preference for people-oriented situations and for spontaneous and novel stimuli and situations . . . and a highly affective orientation toward ideas, things, situations, and individuals. . . . [which may be associated with a relatively great need for] constant encouragement, recognition, warmth, and reassurance in order for them to continue participating in the schooling process. . . . It is postulated that an enhanced ability in social cognition may work to the detriment of individuals within an object-oriented setting such as the school. (Shade 1982, 237–238)

Madge Willis (1989) also reviewed previous analysis dealing with learning styles among African American students and concluded that "observations, theories, and research" on this topic can be "integrated into four groupings of characteristics." In addition to the *social/affective*, people-oriented emphasis cited earlier, Willis described groupings dealing respectively with a "*harmonious*" emphasis on "communal" aspects of society and holistic seeking of knowledge "sought for practical, utilitarian, and relevant purposes"; preference for *expressive creativity* emphasizing "novel, stylistic, intuitive stimulation . . . [and] oral expression"; and stress on "*nonverbal*" communication based on "intonation, body language . . . [and] movement" (Willis 1989, 54; italics in original). Willis recommended that educators should find ways to take these aspects of learning style into account in teaching black students, and also that black students should receive assistance in learning how to respond in terms of stylistic preferences favored or required by teachers.

4. *Lack of previous success in school.* Failure to learn adequately in the early grades is damaging not just to a student's chances to understand later material but also to the student's perceptions of himself or herself as a capable learner and his or her confidence in having a chance to succeed later in school and in life (Ames and Ames 1991). Partly for this reason, many low-status students have a low self-concept as a learner and low feelings of control over what happens to them in the school (Broderick and Sewell 1983). As shown in Table 8-1, students low in SES have scores about twice as high as high SES students in expressing agreement to such statements as "Good luck is more important than effort for success" and "Every time I try to get ahead, something or somebody stops me." Other things being equal, such feelings will be associated later with even more failure, because students who feel they cannot or do not have a chance to learn are less likely to work hard

TABLE 8-1 *Percentages of Eighth Graders in High External, Neutral, and High Internal Locus of Control Groups, by Socioeconomic Status Quartile*

| Socioeconomic Status Quartile** | Locus of Control* | | |
	High External	Neutral	High Internal
Lowest quartile	45	30	25
25–49 percent	37	31	32
50–74 percent	28	36	36
Highest quartile	22	35	43

Source: Adapted from Hafner, Ingels, Schneider, and Stevenson 1990.

* Locus of control refers to the degree of control the student feels over his or her life. High External students are those who agreed with and High Internal Students are those who disagreed with three statements: "In my life, good luck is more important than hard work for success"; "Every time I try to get ahead, something or somebody stops me"; and "My plans hardly ever work out, so planning only makes me unhappy."

** Socioeconomic status is measured in terms of mother's and father's occupations, mother's and father's educational levels, and family income.

toward this end than are students who feel confident about their learning abilities (Ames 1990).

5. *Difficulty of teaching conditions and lack of adquate preparation for teachers in low-status schools*. As implied in the preceding discussion, it is difficult to teach low-status students because many need extra help and assistance to function effectively as learners. Middle-status students tend to benefit from traditional curricula more than do low-status students, and in any case they generally make some academic progress even if the quality of their instruction is poor. Low-status students, in contrast, tend to fail academically, and their teachers, like the students themselves, are frustrated and defeated by lack of success in the classroom. As students fall further behind in their classwork, they tend to lose interest in school and many cause behavior problems in the classroom. Teachers become still more frustrated dealing with both academic and behavioral problems and experience difficulty establishing a productive learning environment in the classroom (Payne 1989; Page and Valli 1990; Knapp 1991).

The problem is compounded by the fact that few teachers have had adequate preparation for solving the learning or behavior problems they encounter among low-status students, since neither preservice nor in-service training programs generally develop much practical skill in dealing with these types of problems. As a result, some teachers either give up trying to teach low-achieving students or try to obtain less frustrating positions teaching higher achieving students who may present fewer overt problems (Liston and Zeichner 1990).

The difficult problems encountered by a teacher—particularly a new teacher—in working-class schools have been illustrated by Binzen in an account of his experience as a new fourth-grade teacher in a predominantly white working-class school. Binzen describes how he received a note from a teacher next door, who said:

> "Will you please keep your kids quiet? We can't hear ourselves think!" Very funny. Well, I couldn't think either. The kids simply ran

> roughshod over me. . . . Somehow it became two o'clock. Time for physical education. The gym instructor awaited my little band of hardened criminals. The class lined up raggedly and, on my signal, raced down the stairwell as though shot from a cannon . . . the class came trooping back. The physical-education teacher had refused to accept such a disorganized, uncontrolled horde. I really couldn't blame him. (Binzen 1970, 178–179)

6. *Teacher perceptions of student inadequacy*. Related to the frustrations and failure experienced both by students and teachers, teachers of low-status students easily can conclude that their pupils are inadequate learners and have little capacity for attaining academic success (Dorr-Bremme 1991; Stallings and McCarthy 1990). This perception tends to become a self-fulfilling prophecy because teachers who believe their students cannot learn are less likely to work hard in designing appropriate learning experiences than are teachers who believe that their pupils can perform much better if properly taught (Good 1981; Brophy and Good 1986). In addition, students are influenced by the views and treatment of their teachers and other significant figures in their lives, such as parents and peers; students whose significant others treat them as inadequate learners will tend to internalize this perception and perform still more poorly in the future. It was this probability that led a U.S. Office of Education Task Force on Urban Instructional Strategies (1977) to conclude that too many "teachers and administrators in communities with high concentrations of poor children believe these children cannot learn. All too often this has become a self-fulfilling prophecy. . . . The need to create positive teachers' attitudes about and responses to the learning styles and aptitudes of the urban pupil cannot be overemphasized" (p. 8).

7. *Homogeneous grouping, tracking, and differential treatment of low-status students within schools and classrooms*. Related to the lack of success and problems in self-concept as a learner that low-status students experience in school is

the tendency to set low-achieving students apart in special classes or in separate classroom groups, generally as part of an effort to provide special instruction appropriate to their current level of performance. However, as noted in Chapter 2, many educators believe that separate grouping of low-achieving students tends to create more problems than it solves, and that it is better to deliver instruction within heterogeneous groups rather than risk reinforcing feelings of incompetence generated by singling out low achievers to be part of a group of so-called dummies. Rist illustrated some of these problems in his study of classroom dynamics in a predominantly low-status elementary school in which he found that some teachers tended to fail with the lowest-status students and wound up focusing most of their energy helping the few high-achieving students who they perceived would benefit most from instruction:

> *The class was divided into groups: those expected to succeed ("fast learners") and those expected to fail ("slow learners"). . . . this categorization had the following results:*
>
> *(1) Differential treatment was accorded the two groups in the classroom, the group designated as "fast" learners receiving the most teaching time, rewards, and attention from the teacher. Those designated as "slow learners" were taught infrequently, subjected to more control, and received little if any support from the teacher.*
>
> *(2) The interactional patterns between the teacher and the various groups in her class became increasingly rigidified, taking on caste-like characteristics, during the course of the school year. . . .*
>
> *(3) The consequence of the differential experiences of the children within the same kindergarten classroom was that they were differentially prepared for the first grade. The first grade teacher grouped the children according to the amount of "readiness" material they had completed in kindergarten. (Rist 1973, 91)*

This kind of development occurs frequently in working with low-status students, but sometimes an opposite pattern develops. In some cases, teachers confronted with a significant number of low-achieving students concentrate their efforts on this group and as a result tend to neglect the higher-achieving students, hoping that the latter group will make progress without much guidance from the teacher. In a few instances, this approach may work out satisfactorily; but much more frequently, it results in unsatisfactory performance among both groups (Barr and Anderson 1991).

Although the hazards of homogeneous grouping of low-achieving students are clear, implications for practice are not at all clear (Slavin 1990a). On the one hand, some degree of individualized instruction in heterogeneous classes may make it possible to provide effective instruction for both low- and high-achieving students. On the other hand, it is both difficult and expensive to provide individualized instruction effectively (Bennett and Desforges 1988), and efforts to do so in schools with a high percentage of poverty students generally have not been very successful. Instead, teachers confronted with heterogeneous classes in the inner city typically have not been able to work effectively with relatively large numbers of low achievers (Levine and Lezotte 1990; Knapp 1991).

One possible solution is to group low achievers for reading and language arts instruction but to make sure these groups are small and are taught by skilled and well-trained teachers (Slavin 1987; 1988, 1990a). This alternative is in line with recent analysis indicating that unusually successful inner-city elementary schools have particularly effective arrangements for teaching low achievers (Levine and Stark 1982; Levine, Levine, and Eubanks 1985; Levine and Lezotte 1990), and that "restrictive" school settings (i.e., separate or "isolated" settings for low achievers) may have either positive or negative outcomes, depending on what is done to make instruction effective (Leinhardt and Pallay 1982; Page and Valli 1990).

8. *Ineffective delivery of services in classrooms with many low-status students.* The preceding discussion suggests that instructional services generally are difficult to deliver effectively in classrooms with a significant number of low-status students. Although few studies have been conducted bearing directly on this question, those that have examined differences between low-status and middle-status schools suggest that for whatever reason, instruction in low-status classrooms generally is not being carried out as effectively as in predominantly middle-status classrooms. One study was conducted by Deutsch (1964), who found that teachers in low-status schools spent only about half as much time actually teaching as did teachers in middle-status schools, apparently because a much greater proportion of their time was spent dealing with the diversity of classroom problems that arose in the former group of schools as compared with the latter.

Recent research has continued to delineate and document the difficult problems that teachers face in providing instruction in schools with a high proportion of low-achieving students. For example, Dreeben and Barr (1988) examined arrangements for teaching reading in seven elementary schools and concluded that the usual approach of dividing a class into several subgroups does not seem to work well in difficult classes that have a high proportion of low achievers. In this situation, the lowest reading group is inordinately large; students in this subgroup therefore receive relatively little attention from teachers who have too many low achievers to help individually and who also have "to deal with . . . the remainder of the low-aptitude class whose members, without strong skills themselves, had to work independently" (Dreeben and Barr 1988, 138). Similarly, Lewis and Moore (1990) found that low-achieving students made smaller reading gains in homogeneous, low-achieving classes than in mixed-ability classes, probably in part because there are a "greater number of discipline problems in classrooms with a majority of low-achieving students . . . lack

of adequate opportunities for students [in such classrooms] to learn from each other . . . and a relatively poor school climate for learning in schools containing many classrooms with a majority of low-achieving students" (Lewis and Moore 1990, 15).

Overcoming such delivery-of-service problems, however, is not simply a matter of somehow increasing or speeding up instruction in the classroom. Given the gaps in the background knowledge and previous learning typically encountered in a class with relatively many low achievers, teachers confront difficult decisions about how to proceed. For example, according to the author of a major federally funded review of decades of research on reading instruction, teachers of "low-readiness" readers are caught in a bind:

> *They can only speed progress through the stories by accepting higher error rates or by skipping stories. Across the lessons of the basal readers, however, sight vocabulary and readability are built up, story by story. Teachers cannot, therefore, skip stories without accepting an accelerated increase in difficulty in those stories that are read.* (Adams, 1990, 113)

9. *Overly large classes.* As implied in the preceding discussion, one reason delivery of instruction frequently is ineffective for low-status students in low-achieving schools or classes is that classes are too large to allow teachers to provide appropriate assistance for students who are experiencing learning problems. Overly large classes are likely to be particularly problematical with respect to learning goals focused on reading comprehension, mathematics problem solving, critical thinking, and other higher-order skills. As we point out in Chapter 13 and elsewhere in this book, improving mastery of higher-order skills among low achievers appears to require systematic *mediated* assistance from teachers or others who help students develop their cognitive functioning and learning-to-learn strategies individually or in small groups.

Support for this conclusion regarding the importance of class size, at least in the primary grades, has been provided by a major study of achievement in differing types of Project STAR classes in Tennessee (Finn and Achilles 1990, Word 1990). Carried out with several million dollars provided as part of a state legislative mandate, Project STAR worked with eighty schools to assign students to kindergarten through third grade classes respectively organized as small (thirteen to seventeen students), regular (twenty-two to twenty-five students), or the regular plus a full-time teacher aide. Previous research regarding the possible achievement effects of class size had been controversial and difficult to interpret, but the Tennessee study allowed for relatively firm conclusions because students initially were assigned to classes on a random basis, most students in the study participated for more than one year, and each participating school included all three types of classes so that differences in achievement by type of class could not be attributed to or obscured by the probability that some schools generally were more effective than others.

Characterizing their results as definitive, researchers assessing Project STAR found that students in the small classes scored substantially higher in reading and math in kindergarten and first grade and maintained their advantage in the second and third grades. Although achievement in small classes was higher than in other classes at all four types of schools in the study (i.e., inner-city, rural, small-town, and suburban), gains associated with small class size clearly were greatest at inner-city schools, which had high proportions of low-income, minority students. "Few well-defined interventions," the researchers noted, "have shown as consistent an impact as this one on the performance of minority students in inner-city settings." They also cited data collected in other parts of the study that suggested that the gains in small classes were connected with greater teacher opportunities for providing individual attention to students and for increasing "the extent to which individual pupils attend to and become involved in learning activities" (Finn and Achilles 1990, 574–575).

10. *Low standards of performance.* By standards of performance, we mean the requirements for promotion or advancement from one level to another either within a classroom, as when students are moved to a more difficult unit of work without having mastered earlier skills, or within a school or educational system, as when students are promoted to the next highest grade or from elementary school to high school without having accomplished as much as their abilities would allow.

There are many reasons why low-achieving students are advanced from one level to another without having been required to achieve adequately at the earlier level. These reasons include "sympathy" for students who do not appear to be suceeding; low expectations among teachers who believe that low-status students cannot meet minimum standards; doubt whether retaining students at a current level would stimulate them to perform better in the future; recognition that repeating a given level might involve wasted time going over material already found to be not stimulating or useful; higher financial costs seemingly involved in retaining students at an earlier grade level; and, of course, difficulties encountered in trying to "force" students to work harder in school when they reject teacher demands or live in an environment that is not conducive to study. For reasons such as these, schools have tended to promote students from one level to another without requiring them to do their best work inside the classroom or to complete assignments for outside work, with disastrous results on academic performance.

At the high school level, evidence is available indicating that low-status students tend to be expected and required to accomplish very little, and that they frequently are led to believe that low performance is acceptable to their teachers. This tendency is most pronounced in schools with a preponderance of low-status students, because students then reinforce each other in resisting demanding requirements and teachers are most likely to lower standards when they have many pupils who are not meeting them. Whether in a working-class or mixed-status school, however, many low-status students appear to be making very little effort to meet demanding academic requirements by the time they reach the secondary level. Wrigley (1982) has summarized the way in which student-teacher interactions reinforce low standards of performance:

> *[Low-track students] dislike teachers who do not trouble to maintain educational illusions. . . . The frequency with which even students who are doing very poorly in school say that they aspire to middle-class professional occupations indicates that it is difficult to give up the idea of success through schooling; the student may well have given it up in a practical, day-to-day sense . . . but it is far more devastating to have teachers who . . . have already given up. . . .*
> *. . . As academic work requires steady application in the absence of much immediate return . . . it is hard for many ghetto youth to muster this application in the face of the unemployment and low earnings that are pervasive in their milieu. Educational ambivalence is essential to the functioning of many ghetto schools; if the students lose faith entirely, they become impossible to control, yet the teachers do not want to foster hopeless illusions about their students' possible success. Thus, students are praised for work that might actually be below par, even while a climate of failure and misdirected application hangs over the entire school. (pp. 242, 245)*

Massey, Scott, and Dornbusch (1975) studied student attitudes at eight high schools in San Francisco and provided data indicating that academic requirements for low-status students were very low and that low standards appeared to have detrimental effects, overall, on student attitudes. These authors compared the attitudes of black, Spanish surname, other white, and Asian-American students and found that black students seemed to be most frequently victimized by systematically low expectations; hence, they titled their report "Racism without Racists: Institutional Racism in Urban Schools." However, it is likely that their black sample was lower in status than were the other three groups, so that their findings can be attributed as much or more to classism as to racism, and in any case they found the low standards pattern operating among low-status students whatever their racial or ethnic group:

> *A curious irony is presented. Black students . . . were doing the least amount of work in school. Yet . . . they believed they were trying extremely hard. How is it possible . . . that black students are allowed to kid themselves on their level of effort . . . given their low academic achievement and grades?*
> *. . . About half of the students believed they would not usually get poor grades if they did poor work or did not try. . . . The students did not feel that grades operated as mechanisms of control to encourage greater effort. (Massey, Scott, and Dornbusch 1975, 8–9)*

11. *Lack of parental knowledge and power to influence their children's school careers.* Numerous observers have concluded that low-income parents frequently lack knowledge, time, energy, and/or other resources that allow middle-class families to influence what happens to their children in the school and classroom. This differential has been summarized as follows, under the heading "Absence of Educational Legacy," in a report prepared for the Quality Education for Minorities Project (1990, 44): "Low-income parents typically have less formal educational and often find it difficult or impossible to help their children navigate through school. . . . [or] to challenge the system on behalf of their children."

12. *Overcrowding in the home environment.* Several studies of conditions characteristic of the home environments of many disadvantaged urban students suggest that overcrowding constitutes an additional negative influence on their

school performance. One study of inner-city elementary students found that those living in high-density apartments had less adequate study space and were more hyperactive and antisocial than peers in lower-density apartments. A study in Chicago found that students in crowded households had less adequate study space and were supervised less often by their parents than were neighboring children in less crowded households (Nettles 1990).

Attitudes and Performance in School

Conclusions enumerated here regarding expectations for students and their response to these expectations underline the importance of examining student attitudes in conjunction with conditions in the schools they attend when trying to identify the reasons pupils fail in the classroom. In general, it is desirable that students feel they are competent learners in the classroom, but this feeling of competency should be based on actual accomplishment; otherwise high self-concept as a learner may be an inflated perception that does not signify high motivation to succeed. High self-concept as a learner is not very useful unless it signifies attainment of learning goals in the past and understanding of what is required to attain more difficult goals in the future. From this point of view, one of the most damaging effects of segregating students by social class and race may be that such segregation frequently causes low-status students to develop an unrealistically high self-concept as a learner. In the terminology of Massey, Scott, and Dornbusch, this is part of the process wherein low-status students "are allowed to misinterpret feedback on their level of effort and achievement."

These considerations help to explain why research relating self-concept to achievement frequently reports only a small association between measures of the two variables (Powell 1989). In the first place, it is difficult to measure self-concept accurately, since respondents tend to give positive responses even if they have considerable doubt about their abilities. In addition,

there are many aspects or dimensions of self-concept, including self-image in general and competence in social activities and athletics. A child's self-concept also may change substantially from day to day or year to year, in accordance with maturational factors or with things that happen to the child inside or outside the classroom. But probably as important as any of these in accounting for low relationships between measured self-concept and achievement is the tendency for academic self-concept scores to be grossly inflated among low-achieving students who are led to believe their performance is adequate even when they are allowed to perform far below their capacity.

Self-concept also is related in complex ways to other aspects of attitude and behavior in the classroom. It is likely, for example, that a student who has a low self-concept as a learner due to previous failure in the classroom also will feel that he or she has little chance to do better in the future, and these feelings may result in reduced effort and still lower self-concept and sense of control. If, on the other hand, the students' self-concept is lowered due to higher demands for performance but higher demands result in higher performance, then self-concept, a sense of control, and other attitudes toward school may all improve later (Graham 1989).

Attribution theory suggests that students who take responsibility for their failures may benefit from having a high sense of control over what happens to them in school, whereas students who blame "unfair" teachers or other outside forces may not work harder to achieve success even if their teachers look for ways to build a feeling of confidence in the future (Graham 1989). All these considerations also may be related to the inferences a student may make concerning his or her opportunity to be successful in life based on the fact that he or she lives in a segregated, low-status community or attends a segregated, low-status school.

The preceding discussion has shown that student attitudes, teacher expectations, and previous failure in school play an important part in limiting the academic performance of low-status students. These and other considerations such as inappropriateness of learning materials interact in complex ways in reducing motivation to succeed and reinforcing initial disadvantages associated with home and family background, particularly in schools in which the overall school climate exemplifies low expectations for students and a sense of futility that anything can be done to improve achievement. This type of climate is not inevitable in a low-status school or classroom, but it does tend to be prevalent in situations where students have experienced repeated failure in the past.

Implications for Instruction

The most important implication of the preceding discussion is that it is critically important to structure the learning experiences of low-status students so they succeed in school and develop a substantively based sense of competence as learners who are able to perform at an acceptable level in the classroom. This need was mentioned in Chapter 3, and its importance is underscored when we consider what happens to low-achieving students from nonstimulating home environments after they enter the schools.

Does this conclusion suggest that low-status students should be given high grades in order to bolster their sense of adequacy in the classroom, regardless of whether their actual effort or achievement is high or low? Keeping in mind the evidence indicating that automatic promotion policies have been detrimental to the performance of students in the public schools, it is better to conclude that success must follow from meaningful effort and achievement if it is to generate a cycle also characterized by improved performance and a positive but realistic self-concept as a learner. Teachers should work in any way they can to strengthen the academic and nonacademic self-concepts of low-status students, but their foremost effort should be to stimulate and help students master academic skills in the classroom.

Does it then follow that teachers should fail to promote low-status students from one academic level to another in order to encourage them to work harder, achieve success, and thereby raise their academic self-concept and later performance? This solution, too, is unsatisfactory, because failure generally helps a child very little and may destroy his or her motivation to succeed in the future (Levine and Lezotte 1990). Just as the arguments in favor of automatic promotion have been one-sided in taking into account the negative effects of retention in grade on a failing pupil but not considering the effects on others in the classroom when a student who makes little or no effort is promoted from one grade to the next (Levine 1966; Natale 1991), so, too, it is simpleminded to believe that merely failing to promote students whose effort or achievement is below their capacities will help many of them attain higher levels of performance later (Natale 1991).

What this discussion suggests, then, is that to improve the academic performance of low-status students requires the development and implementation of new systems of instruction and organization that carefully structure learning experience to ensure successful mastery of academic skills required for later academic work. One alternative for doing this is the *mastery learning* approach, which is being developed and tested in many types of schools at various educational levels. The mastery learning approach has been described at length in a 1976 book on *Human Characteristics and School Learning* by Benjamin S. Bloom. His central argument is that 95 percent of students can "master" what the schools have to teach at practically the same level of mastery, with the slower 20 percent of students needing 10 to 20 percent more time than the faster 20 percent. Though slower students require a longer period of time than others to achieve mastery, they can do so if their knowledge level is diagnosed accurately and if they are taught the material with appropriate methods.

Bloom and his colleagues believe that quality of instruction should be defined in terms of the cues or directions provided to the learner, the reinforcement that the learner secures, and the feedback or corrective system instituted for overcoming problems that arise in the learning process. He and his colleagues have found that individual assistance to the slower students in the early stages of a new learning experience helps more than does the same amount of assistance at a later stage. They cite several studies that show substantial achievement gains by classes using these procedures (Bloom 1988). Several of these studies have been carried out with low-status students in big cities, and reports of successful implementation of mastery learning programs are present in the literature on research and evaluation in big-city schools (Smith and Wick 1976; Levine 1985; Abrams 1988; Levine and Ornstein 1989).

Even before data on these projects were available, Rosenshine (1976; 1986) had surveyed the research on the effectiveness of various teaching methods and concluded that the most successful approach for students of low socioeconomic status uses "direct instruction," which he defined as including "a drill pattern consisting of questions that the students could answer, followed by feedback and subsequent questions," and a pattern consisting of "small steps at the students' level" (1976, p. 368).

However, we also should emphasize that improving the academic performance of low-status students is likely to require (1) a broader approach than simply working on basic skills, in order to develop students' capacity for learning increasingly abstract subject matter as they proceed through the grades; (2) explicit matching of learning experiences with the individual style of students who are at somewhat different stages in conceptual development; and (3) development of self-regulated learning skills among students who currently function at a low conceptual level.

1. *Abstract thinking skills*. Direct instruction seems to be effective in helping low-status students master essential skills, such as word recognition in reading, but the students also will have to acquire more abstract skills if they are to remain successful in school (Passow 1990). Lack of development of abstract thinking skills may be one reason many special preschool and primary programs for low-status students have been suc-

cessful in improving academic achievement, but gains made by students at these levels disappeared later when students entered higher grades (Bronfenbrenner 1974; Chira 1990b).

A number of educators working with low-status students are aware of this problem and are trying to find ways to develop abstract thinking skills, in addition to such basic skills as word recognition in reading and fundamental operations (multiplication, division) in mathematics. For example, Kessler and Quinn (1977) have found that instruction in hypothesis testing, which they refer to as an "inquiry approach" to "cognitive development," improved the language development of low-achieving sixth graders; and Levine and Sherk (1990, 1991) have described an inner-city junior high school at which faculty use of appropriate instructional strategies resulted in large gains in students' higher-order comprehension. A variety of such instructional strategies are described briefly in the last chapter of this book.

2. *Matching instruction with student's conceptual level*. We have mentioned that direct instruction in a structured learning environment appears to be the most effective approach for improving the academic performance of low-status students. However, this generalization should not be applied mechanically, because any group of students is likely to show considerable variation in conceptual development and in responses to differing types of instructional approaches. For this reason, efforts should be made whenever possible to provide a learning environment that is appropriate to each student's learning needs and stage of development.

Researchers who have been studying the relationships between student characteristics and learning environments believe that appropriate matching of environments and students can result in improved academic performance, whatever the ability level or social background of the student involved. David E. Hunt, for example, has investigated students' "conceptual level" in relation to the learning environments that are most effective in the classroom. By "conceptual level," Hunt refers to "both cognitive complexity (differentiation, discrimination, and integration) as well as interpersonal maturity (increasing self-responsibility)" (Hunt 1975, 218). Hunt's studies also indicated that conceptual level is significantly higher in middle-class groups of students than in working-class groups at the same grade level, though working-class groups tend to have more variability than do middle-class groups (Hunt 1965).

Hunt and his colleagues conducted a number of studies to identify the effects of differing learning environments categorized by the "*degree of structure*, or the degree of organization provided by the learning environment. In high structure, the environment is largely determined by the teacher, and the student himself has little responsibility, whereas in low structure, the student is much more responsible for organizing the environment" (Hunt 1975, 219). In one study conducted at junior high schools, Hunt and his colleagues showed that low conceptual level students placed in classes in which teachers were requested to provide a structured environment learned more than did low conceptual level students in unstructured classes, whereas high conceptual level students learned more in classes where teachers provided low structure than they did in structured classes. Hunt also found that students low in conceptual level "can develop skill in self-directed learning," but only if their learning environment provides "step-by-step instructions" (Hunt 1974, 29).

3. *Development of self-regulated learning skills and strategies.* As indicated here and in earlier chapters, students' perceptions of their learning ability and their capacity to work independently in mastering abstract skills are important in determining whether they succeed or fail in the classroom (Idol and Jones 1991). In recent years researchers have begun to develop a comprehensive analysis of these phenomena and related perceptions and behaviors that affect academic performance as part of self-regulated learning. Much of this research has been summarized by Barry Zimmerman (1990) in a paper that

distinguishes between *self-regulation processes*, such as "perceptions of self-efficacy," and *self-regulated learning strategies*, which help a student attain his or her learning goals and outcomes. According to Zimmerman and other analysts, successful learners tend to be unusually insightful in understanding relationships between their self-perceptions and their learning activities, thereby constructing "self-oriented feedback loops" that help them monitor the effectiveness of their learning methods and modify both their self-perceptions and their learning strategies in accordance with information on how well they are proceeding (Zimmerman 1990, 5).

After further noting that students' motivation to expend effort in regulating their own thinking and learning depends on a variety of considerations, Zimmerman summarized the results of several studies indicating that low-achieving students are less likely than high achievers to demonstrate high levels of internal motivation and to use self-regulated strategies, such as "self-evaluation," "goal setting and planning," internal "verbal elaboration," "information seeking," "self-monitoring of learning processes and performance," "seeking social assistance" from peers or teachers, and "reviewing" of notes, books, or themes. Taken together, these studies indicated that use of self-regulated learning strategies makes a "distinctive contribution" to academic performance apart from the effects of measured learning ability (Zimmerman 1990, 6–9).

Although researchers studying self-regulated learning have introduced diverse theoretical refinements and use varying definitions of self-regulation strategies, they generally agree that there is a reciprocal relationship between perceptions of self-efficacy, which motivate a student to use such strategies as goal setting, and successful use of strategies, which in turn enhances self-concept (Zimmerman 1990). Recognizing this interdependence between perceptions, motivation, and learning strategies, researchers have been developing approaches for improving *metacognitive* functioning (i.e., awareness, monitoring, and control of one's own thinking processes and progress toward a learning goal) and for acquiring instructional strategies to improve comprehension and thinking. David Pearson and his colleagues at the University of Illinois (Pearson 1985; Garcia and Pearson 1991) view the widespread development of such strategies in the 1980s as constituting virtually a "revolution" in our knowledge of how to improve the cognitive performance of low achievers. Many such strategies emphasize helping students succeed in taking greater responsibility for their own learning, moving incrementally from teacher-initiated activities to student participation in all aspects of learning during a lesson. Additional information involving several self-regulated learning approaches (e.g., emphasis on metacognitive processes, cooperative student teams) is provided in the last chapter of this book.

CONCENTRATED POVERTY SCHOOLS

Earlier in this chapter, we mentioned that there is reason to believe that instructional services are delivered less effectively in low-status schools than in mixed or middle-status schools, apparently because the concentration of learning and behavioral problems in low-status schools makes teaching and learning problems particularly difficult there. This generalization suggests that low-status schools tend to be dysfunctional compared to other types of schools. Social-class segregation in the schools makes it more difficult to provide an adequate education for students from low-status families.

This phenomenon can be seen most clearly by looking at inner-city schools, which we have defined as schools located in concentrated poverty neighborhoods in big cities. Poverty in these neighborhoods is more concentrated on a larger scale than is true in most other low-status neighborhoods; families and students there tend to be particularly isolated within a distinctive urban subculture, and schools tend to face particularly severe problems related to the difficult living conditions that characterize these neighborhoods. Recent data (see Table 8-2) on the composition and lo-

cation of a nationally representative sample of public and private schools suggest that about 7 percent of elementary schools are concentrated poverty schools with heavily-minority enrollment in the inner-core sections of urban areas. Because poverty schools in big cities tend to have unusually high enrollment—sometimes several thousand at the elementary level—their students probably constitute 10 or 12 percent of national enrollment. Numerous schools with high proportions of poverty students are located elsewhere in metropolitan areas and in rural communities.

Levine and his colleagues (1979) studied achievement patterns in big-city schools and found that there appears to be a "threshold point" involving the concentration of urban poverty beyond which most schools as presently organized are unable to function effectively. Evidence for this conclusion was found by examining measures of poverty status among students in elementary schools or poverty-related characteristics of neighborhoods they serve and relating these scores to average reading achievement for students in grades three through six. For each elementary school in a given district, the poverty score was plotted on a graph that also showed the average achievement for a particular grade level. For example, Figure 8-1 shows the percentage of students eligible for subsidized lunch in 1976 (an indicator of poverty) and average sixth-grade reading achievement scores for each of sixty-one schools in Kansas City, Missouri.

As shown in the figure, there appears to be a threshold point of 35 to 40 percent poverty pupils beyond which none of the schools have high achievement scores. None of the forty-two schools that had 40 percent or more of their students eligible for subsidized lunch had achievement scores above 5.7, whereas thirteen of nineteen schools with less than 40 percent poverty pupils had scores higher than 5.7. This means that at least half the pupils in the forty-two schools with 40 percent or more poverty pupils scored below 5.7, which in turn is more than a year below the national norm of 6.8 for the date the test was administered. Clearly, a significant

TABLE 8-2   *Numbers of Elementary Schools (N = 346) in Metropolitan/Rural Location by Poverty/Nonpoverty Status and Racial Composition* *

	Inner City			Other			Suburban			Rural		
Percentage White Students	*High Poverty*	*Low or Moderate Poverty*	*High Wealth*	*High Poverty*	*Low or Moderate Poverty*	*High Wealth*	*High Poverty*	*Low or Moderate Poverty*	*High Wealth*	*High Poverty*	*Low or Moderate Poverty*	*High Wealth*
0–10	13	2	0	2	2	0	0	0	0	2	1	0
10–15	12	2	0	9	12	0	4	6	0	3	3	0
50–90	10	3	0	7	23	4	1	29	12	7	12	2
90–100	1	5	2	4	11	10	1	37	26	10	49	7
Total	36	12	2	22	48	14	6	72	38	22	65	9

Source: Adapted from Oakes 1990b.

* Location was determined by asking principals to specify whether their schools could best be described as (a) inner-city, (b) urban but not inner-city, (c) suburban, or (d) rural.

Poverty status was determined by asking principals to specify the percentages of their students whose parents were unemployed or receiving welfare and/or work in various occupational categories. Based on this information, schools were classified as follows: High Poverty = 30 percent or more of students' parents are unemployed or receive welfare; Moderate Poverty = 10 to 30 percent of students' parents are unemployed or receive welfare; Low Poverty = less than 10 percent of students' parents are unemployed or receive welfare and no more than 30 percent work in professional or managerial occupations; and High Wealth = less than 10 percent of students' parents are unemployed or receive welfare and more than 30 percent work in professional or managerial occupations.

number of the students in these concentrated poverty schools are not learning to read. Similar patterns regarding reading comprehension have been found for Chicago, Cincinnati, Cleveland, Houston, Los Angeles, Milwaukee, Rochester, and other big cities for which Levine and his colleagues obtained appropriate data. A recent analysis (Levine 1992) of 1989 reading scores in Kansas City elementary schools also revealed similar patterns.

Other socioeconomic factors related to poverty also characterize the neighborhoods in which school achievement is low. For example, the schools with lowest sixth-grade reading scores were in neighborhoods with the highest percentage of households with 1.51 or more persons per room. Similarly, almost all schools in neighborhoods in which 3 to 5 percent or more of the adult women were separated from their husbands had low reading scores.

The authors of this study interpreted their indicators of neighborhood socioeconomic status as measuring not just concentrated urban pov-

erty but also high social and family disorganization in the neighborhoods that had a high proportion of poverty residents. Crime rates, for example, were highly correlated with poverty and were related to achievement in the same way as was percentage of poverty students. High density (people per room), housing deterioration (percentage of year-round vacant housing units), and family disorganization (separated females; female-headed households) were interpreted as indicating general social disorganization in a neighborhood. Measures such as percentage of separated females were interpreted not as measuring the "adequacy" of individual female-headed families but as denoting the existence of socially disorganized communities. (There was little relationship between percentage of separated females and achievement either above or below the threshold point that isolated the concentrated poverty schools from other schools in the six cities.)

Three additional aspects of this area of research should be emphasized in considering the

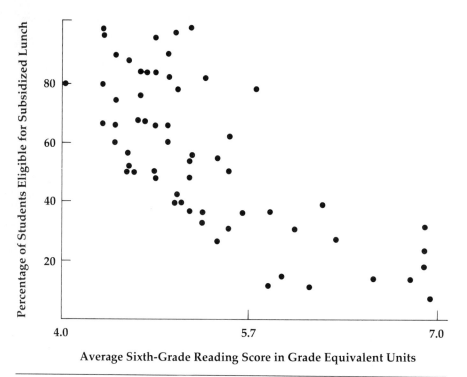

FIGURE 8-1 *Average Sixth-Grade Scores Plotted against Percentage of Students Eligible for Subsidized Lunch, Sixty-One Kansas City, Missouri, Elementary Schools, 1976 (*Source: *Kansas City, Missouri, Public Schools.)*

relationships between concentrated urban poverty and school achievement. First, although a large proportion of the concentrated poverty population in many big cities are racial minorities, there also are concentrated poverty schools that are predominantly white. These schools meet the concentrated poverty criteria specified above, such as having a threshold percentage of their students eligible for subsidized lunch, and also have reading scores in the bottom part of the achievement distributions in their respective cities.

Second, threshold points can be found among groups of schools that are predominantly minority in the same manner as they are found in the samples for the cities as a whole. Among a group of sixty-four predominantly black schools in Chicago, for example, none of the thirty-six in neighborhoods in which 3 percent or more of households had 1.51 or more people per room

had sixth-grade reading scores above 5.2 in 1969, as contrasted with nineteen of twenty-eight schools with lower density scores that had achievement scores above 5.2. This finding suggests that socioeconomic status and concentrated poverty, not race and ethnicity, are the key determinants of low achievement in big-city schools.

Third, in line with what one would expect given the relationships enumerated above, achievement scores in big-city schools are highly predictable based on information about the socioeconomic and concentrated poverty status of the neighborhoods in which they are located. Table 8-3, for example, shows the actual and predicted tenth-grade achievement scores for twenty-six city and suburban high schools in the Milwaukee metropolitan area. (Achievement scores are a combination of reading and math scores.) These predicted scores are based on information reporting the percentage of low-income students in each high school. The statistics used in the analysis took into account a threshold point denoting concentrated poverty. As shown in the table, none of the predicted scores is more than 9 percentile points different from the corresponding actual score, and 61 percent are within 3 points of the actual scores.

Relationships between concentrated poverty and school achievement also have been assessed by Martin Orland (1990) of the National Center for Education Statistics. After analyzing a national data set collected as part of the Sustain-

TABLE 8-3 *Actual and Predicted Tenth-Grade Achievement Scores (Median Percentiles) for Milwaukee Metropolitan High Schools*

School Number	Actual Achievement	Predicted Achievement	Difference
1	69	68	1
2	71	72	1
3	81	81	0
4	77	81	4
5	64	64	0
6	72	72	0
7	32	34	2
8	36	41	5
9	44	44	0
10	33	37	4
11	45	46	1
12	44	38	−6
13	15	16	1
14	41	38	−3
15	33	27	−6
16	20	22	2
17	43	43	0
18	30	32	2
19	80	77	−3
20	66	58	−8
21	66	68	2
22	71	72	1
23	58	64	6
24	84	77	−7
25	86	81	−5
26	68	77	9

Source: Levine 1992.

ing Effects Study, Orland reported that 56 percent of the poverty students attending schools at which more than 25 percent of students were poor had achievement scores in the bottom quartile, compared with only 28 percent of poverty students at schools with a lower proportion of low-income enrollment. Extensive analysis indicated that this pattern was not due primarily to other social background differences, such as a tendency for poverty students in nonpoverty schools to have better educated parents than poverty students in concentrated poverty schools. Orland also reported that the proportions of African American and Hispanic students who attend poverty schools are much higher than is true for non-Hispanic white students, and that large urban districts have a much higher percentage of concentrated poverty schools than do other types of school districts.

THRESHOLD PHENOMENA IN INNER-CITY SCHOOLS AND SOCIETY

If it is true that concentrated urban poverty is associated with the existence of threshold points beyond which inner-city schools do not function effectively, it is important to understand why this may happen and what it may mean in terms of implications for the improvement of academic performance in the inner-city school.

No research has been conducted explicitly to determine at what point learning and behavior problems in low-status schools may make it extremely difficult to deliver instruction effectively, but research by Deutsch and by Behr and Hanson, cited earlier in this chapter, does indicate that teachers in low-status as compared to middle-status schools tend to spend relatively more time on non-instructional tasks and have greater difficulty providing appropriate instruction at each student's current level of performance.

If this is so, as seems likely in view of the relatively high incidence of learning and behavior problems among low-status students, it probably also is true that teachers in low-status schools experience growing difficulty as the number of problems to be solved approaches and exceeds a point at which problems are being compounded faster than they are being solved. For example, where a teacher in a middle-status school may have two or three academically retarded students, a teacher in a low-status school may have eight or ten such students and may have to spend so much time helping this group that the majority of students in the class are neglected.

Similarly for administrators, counselors, and other school personnel, concentrated urban poverty appears to be associated with a proliferation of problems beyond the point at which educators are able to carry out their jobs successfully and the schools are able to function effectively. High school counselors, for example, will be unable to discharge responsibilities such as providing personal advice for students or guiding high school students into appropriate postsecondary careers if most of their time is spent keeping track of truancies and suspensions (as frequently happens in inner-city schools). In other words, doubling the number of problems in a school may triple or quadruple the difficulty of dealing with them and may result in dysfunction throughout the institution.

The much greater incidence of problems at schools with a substantial percentage of low-status students than at schools with few such students is shown graphically in Figure 8-2. This figure shows the percentage of low-income students in relation to teachers' perceptions of certain problems at high schools in the Milwaukee metropolitan area. The average for the central-city high schools is represented by a "C"; suburban high schools are represented by "S." The problem score is based on teachers' responses to four types of problems following the question, "To what degree do you consider each of the factors below to be a problem that detracts from your ability to do the best possible job of teaching your students?" The four problems dealt respectively with "inadequate student preparation," "students cannot read," "classroom discipline," and "English is students' second language." A higher score on the problems scale represents a perception that problems are severe rather than unimportant.

Figure 8-2 shows the clear tendency for teachers at high schools with a higher proportion of low-income students to report a greater incidence of problems present in their schools than do teachers at schools with higher-income students. (The percentages of low-income students at the suburban schools are slightly exaggerated because they enroll small percentages of transfer students from the city school district.) In addition the high schools in the city exceed the suburban high schools both in percentage of low-income students and in teachers' perceptions that problems involving student preparation and discipline interfere with the effectiveness of their teaching.

Knowledge of the high incidence and severity of teaching/learning problems at concentrated poverty schools helps us understand why many researchers have concluded that socioeconomic rather than simple racial integration can improve educational opportunities for low-income minority students. For example, Coleman and his colleagues (1966), O'Reilly (1969), Crain and Mahard (1982), and Orland (1990) reviewed research on desegregation and concluded that schools with predominantly low-status students do not provide a positive educational environment. When carried out effectively, socioeconomic desegregation can reduce the number of students who attend concentrated poverty schools.

These speculations also help explain why enormous expenditures to improve the performance of students in inner-city schools frequently appear to have had little discernible impact on the academic achievement of students in these schools. Pouring additional money into these schools for whatever purpose—more materials, more teachers, new equipment—may make little difference if the school as a whole is not changed sufficiently to deal successfully with learning and behavior problems in the classroom. Fiddmont (1976) studied a group of seventeen Kansas City elementary schools eligible for federal assistance for low-income students and found that 25 million dollars in special federal, state, and local funds were spent to improve education between

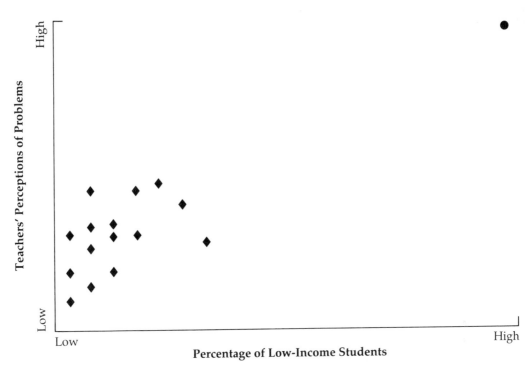

● = City;   ◆ = Suburban. Each symbol represents the location of one school on each axis. Problems that teachers assessed included "inadequate student preparation," "students cannot read," "classroom discipline," and "English is students' second language."

FIGURE 8-2   *Relationship between Teachers' Perceptions of Problems and Percentage of Low-Income Students at High Schools in the Milwaukee Metropolitan Area, by City and Suburb (Source: Authors' analysis of data available from the Study Commission on the Quality of Education in the Metropolitan Milwaukee Public Schools; Witte and Walsh 1990.)*

1965 and 1975 in addition to regular per pupil expenditures, but achievement levels in these schools changed hardly at all. Similarly, Rand Corporation researchers analyzed eleven inner-city schools in New York City that had received 40 million dollars in federal money over a period of four years and found no improvement at all in academic achievement or truancy rates.

It should be stressed that other social institutions in the inner city face comparable problems in handling the multiple problems characteristic of concentrated poverty neighborhoods (Wilson 1987; Gross 1990). In the law enforcement system, for example, police and probation officers have less time to deal effec-

tively with any given offense; as a result, their morale tends to deteriorate, offenders are apprehended and punished relatively less frequently than in low-crime areas, counseling and other support services are not provided for parolees, young people do not perceive that there is much connection between crime and punishment, and conditions favorable to the spread of delinquency then become as destructive as the most virulent physical epidemic (Labaton 1990). Social welfare agencies, hospitals in low-income areas, and other public institutions also deteriorate rapidly when confronted with an overload of problems associated with concentrated poverty (Zinsmeister 1990).

Institutions concerned with maintenance of the physical environment are similarly impacted by conditions in the inner city. Savings and loan associations, for example, may be unable to make a profit when the default rate on home loans doubles from 2 or 3 percent to 5 or 6 percent; one result is that residents of the inner city are unable to obtain loans to maintain or improve their property, except, perhaps, at exorbitant rates that lead to still more defaults. Once a few properties become deteriorated and unsalable, property values nearby go down and lending institutions become still more reluctant to approve loans. Before long, a threshold point has been reached beyond which occurs a spiralling cycle of further deterioration and deflation.

Furthermore, it also should be recognized that dysfunctioning in one inner-city institution such as the school tends to lead to dysfunctioning in others, such as the law enforcement system or the housing maintenance system. A full analysis of insitutional functioning in the inner city would consider the interrelationships between differing institutions and urban systems, as when abandoned housing provides a breeding ground for delinquency among teenagers or when students who can barely read drop out of school and begin looking for work that requires a higher level of literacy. Inner-city schools, for their part, are faced with the problem of teaching large numbers of students whose main concern frequently is that of survival in the neighborhood outside the school. Overloaded with too many students who themselves are overloaded with a multitude of individual and family problems, the public schools as traditionally organized and operated sometimes then may all but cease functioning educationally.

VIOLENCE IN THE SCHOOLS

One of the most serious problems confronting many schools in concentrated poverty neighborhoods is the tendency for violence in the community to affect teaching and learning conditions in the schools. Violent and other antisocial behavior of one sort or another is more prevalent there than in most other neighborhoods, and it is difficult if not impossible to prevent problems in the community from impinging on the schools. At the elementary level, vandalism and extortion against younger students are frequent problems, and physical assaults against students and teachers frequently constitute additional problems at the secondary level. At either level, a climate of violence outside the school is not conducive to study or learning on the part of students whose attention is bound to be distracted by this type of detrimental environment (Rubel 1980; Lee 1990).

Violence in and around big-city schools has constituted a growing problem since the early 1960s. Part of this trend is reflected in an increase in assaults on teachers, particularly in urban schools (Foley 1990). Rates of violence in the public schools were relatively stable through the early 1980s (Baker 1985) but increased again in some locations in the late 1980s (Smith 1990).

Increasing violence in the schools appears to be closely associated with parallel increases in the size and severity of problems in concentrated urban poverty neighborhoods during the past two decades (Viadero 1987a). Undoubtedly, these trends are most apparent in big cities in general and in poverty neighborhoods in particular (Menacker, Weldon, and Hurwitz 1990). Violence in and around schools in big cities also is associated with a series of related problems that are particularly characteristic of poverty neighborhoods in these cities—the operation of gangs of teenagers and young adults, the infiltration of schools by intruders and trespassers, and crime associated with drug sales and abuse. As regards the functioning of gangs in and around the schools, a 1973 study on youth groups "as a crime problem in major American cities" concluded that although this problem had waxed and waned for decades, there was reason to believe that it became very severe in the 1970s:

In many instances, several gangs, often rivals, operate within the same school—often two or three, in extreme cases eight or more. This creates a high potential for intergang conflict.

Gang members above school age or out of school for other reasons customarily frequent school environs, impeding or interdicting passage or entry by non-gang students, attacking rival gang members leaving or going to school, engaging in gang combat, and defacaing and destroying school property. (Miller 1973, 52–53)

Violence in the schools also is related to the extremely high absence and truancy rates now characteristic of low-status secondary schools in big cities. Thus, studies of Chicago high schools have concluded that absence from classes exceeds 30 percent and that a "culture of cutting" of late morning and early afternoon classes not only was prevalent at the schools studied but also had been institutionalized at one school by assigning students to nonexistent study halls (Wells and Prindle 1986; Robinson 1990). Many students who are absent or truant from their classes congregate near schools and participate in delinquent activities.

There obviously are many reasons for high absence rates, which signify a breakdown in the functioning of the inner-city high school. One cause is simple fear of going to school. Lalli, Savitz, and Rosen conducted a three-year study of 1,000 male students in the Philadelphia Public Schools and reported that nearly half the black students and one-fourth of the whites "viewed the streets to and from schools as extremely dangerous" (quoted in Delaney 1975). A later study of elementary schools in concentrated poverty neighborhoods in Chicago found that nearly half the students did not feel safe in school (Menacker, Weldon, and Hurwitz 1990). National studies indicate that tens of thousands of high-school students regularly carry guns to school (Witkin 1991).

Since the mid-1970s, school officials have moved vigorously to contain violence in big-city schools and to make them more secure places in which to teach and learn. Steps taken to accomplish this have included:

1. The provision of building security personnel, elaborate security systems, and creation of safety corridors to provide protected access to and from the street
2. Intensification of counseling services for students in trouble
3. Programs to help students acquire basic skills in the classroom
4. Organizational modifications, such as dividing a school into several independent communities (Ianni 1980; Foley 1990)
5. "Mediation" assistance and training that helps students learn to resolve disputes peacefully (Feinblatt 1991).

Research conducted for the National Institute for Juvenile Justice and Delinquency Prevention reported that the overwhelming majority of school administrators who had initiated a combination of such approaches for reducing school violence felt that these actions had been helpful in attaining their goal (Marvin 1976, 46). Nevertheless, the overall effects on education of violence and related problems in concentrated urban poverty neighborhoods are still generally detrimental to learning, as summarized in this eloquent statement by former Chicago Superintendent of Schools Manford Byrd:

The losses . . . cannot be measured in terms of dollars. No one has measured the immediate and long term effects on the education of children resulting from the climate of fear generated by these conditions. Many hours of education are lost because of false fire alarms and bomb threats. Much harm is done to educational programs when classroom windows are shattered, teaching materials destroyed or stolen, and schools damaged by fire and other acts of vandalism. When students and teachers are fearful of going to school . . . a healthy environment for learning is lost. (U.S. Senate Subcommittee 1977, 17)

The existence of threshold phenomena and the problem of violence in and around inner-city schools suggest that the goal of improving the education of students in these schools is related to the larger goal of improving general social conditions and opportunities for the underclass residents of concentrated poverty neighborhoods. Unless radical improvements are made in the education available to students in these neighborhoods, and unless systematic national efforts also are made to attack both the structural and cultural causes of underclass status, the typical difficulties of teaching and learning in low-status schools will continue to be compounded in concentrated poverty schools, and achievement in these schools may continue to be extremely low even after substantial sums of money are spent to conduct compensatory education programs there.

THE STATUS OF COMPENSATORY EDUCATION

It had become clear, by 1965, to most educators that the majority of children from low-income families, particularly from low-income black families, were achieving poorly in the schools and were probably headed for a lifetime of poverty. Hence, there arose a number of proposals and experiments for working with such children to help compensate for their unfavorable start in life and for their disadvantages in school. The federal government put relatively large sums of money into this field, first through the War on Poverty and the Office of Economic Opportunity, beginning just before 1965, and then through Title I of the Elementary and Secondary Education Act of 1965.

It was then, and still is, uncertain what balance of effort should be placed on preschool children as compared with school-age children, and how much relative emphasis should be placed on working to improve the home environment as compared with the school in providing compensatory education.

Those who emphasize the family factor wish to expand preschool classes for socially disadvantaged children, educational work with their mothers and fathers, and a variety of other forms of assistance and support. Those who emphasize the school factor demand new forms of education, not merely more of the old forms. They call for radical changes in the schools and ask that the schools find new ways of teaching working-class children. Research has identified approaches to improve the effectiveness of schools for disadvantaged students, but most inner-city schools are not yet systematically providing effective education for the urban poor.

Here, we review the status of compensatory education efforts at various levels including the preschool, elementary, secondary, and postsecondary levels. Particularly successful projects for each level are described in order to illustrate the kinds of improvements possible in outstanding programs for improving the academic performance of low-status students.

Preschool

Several variants of preschool programs have been tried, in which children in the experiments are matched with similar children in comparison groups. The age of children ranges from infancy to five. Some experiments involve training the mothers; others take the children to a preschool site where a variety of educative procedures are used. The most widespread program is Head Start, which has operated in some areas on a six- to eight-week summer basis but now generally functions on a year-round basis and provides two years of preschool instruction for most participants. Children are tested for mental ability as well as for physical health when they enter Head Start programs. They are tested again at the close of a program, and the results are reported to state and federal agencies.

Between 1965 and 1990, Head Start served more than 11 million children, approximately one-fifth of the population from families below the income level that determines eligibility for the program. In recent years Head Start has had a budget of about 1 billion dollars and has served approximately 4,500,000 disadvantaged students per year, about one-quarter of the children eligible under federal income guidelines (Beatty 1990). In 1990, Congress authorized substantial increases in future Head Start funding, aiming to include most eligible children by 1994 (Mundy 1989; Oden and Ricks 1990).

The director of the office of Child Development from June 1970 through July 1972 was Edward Zigler, professor of psychology at Yale University. In 1973, he wrote an article entitled "Project Head Start: Success or Failure?" in which he gave a limited positive evaluation. He argued that Head Start's main goal was social competence, and that this had been improved substantially:

> *Whether Head Start is seen as a success or a failure is determined by the factors one chooses to weigh in making such an assessment . . . . If one assesses Head Start in terms of the improved health of tens of thousands of poor children who have been screened, diagnosed, and treated, Head Start is clearly a resounding success. . . . I believe that a realistic and proper assessment of Head Start demonstrates that it has been a success. (Zigler 1973, 3)*

However, several major evaluations of Head Start have indicated that it is not generally successful in terms of bringing about lasting improvement in students' IQ scores (Caruso and Detterman 1981; Haskins 1989) or academic achievement (C.S.R. 1985; Chira 1990b). This conclusion generated widespread pessimism concerning the potential of preschool efforts to enhance cognitive functioning. On the other hand, educators and researchers have continued to develop and evaluate preschool programs designed to achieve this goal. In 1974, Bronfenbrenner examined the impact of those programs that appeared to have incorporated the most promising approaches for this purpose and had been most carefully implemented and evaluated; he concluded that some of these programs were resulting in significant IQ gains among the students who participated.

Bronfenbrenner's 1974 review of preschool compensatory education led to encouraging conclusions about the potential of such efforts, but it was not enough to dispel the pessimism that had become widespread as a result of the Head Start

evaluations. Although widely cited, Bronfenbrenner's conclusions were drawn mostly from study of a few outstanding programs that improved the IQ scores of participating students, but little evidence was available to indicate that these gains could be sustained after the children graduated from them and entered regular school classes (Chira 1990).

Since Bronfenbrenner's review of research on early intervention, even more encouraging results have been reported concerning the effects of outstanding preschool programs to enhance the cognitive development of low-status students (Caldwell 1991; Eckroade, Salehi, and Wode 1991). In general, these data suggest that low-status students who have participated in outstanding cognitively oriented preschool programs subsequently perform substantially better in school than do children of comparable background who did not participate (Schorr 1989; Palmer 1990; Kennedy 1991).

For example, one of the most carefully developed and evaluated programs for disadvantaged youngsters was the cognitive-development oriented Perry Preschool Project conducted by David Weikart and his colleagues in Ypsilanti, Michigan, between 1962 and 1967. Since 1967, longitudinal analysis of the subsequent performance of participants and comparable "control" group children has been carried out, with initial results leading to the discouraging conclusion that substantial IQ gains participants showed at age three and four disappeared by the third grade (National Research Council 1990b).

However, subsequent research showed that scores of participants in reading, language, and arithmetic began to exeed those of the control group beginning at grade three (Haskins 1989). By grade eight, the children who had been in the preschool, although still averaging more than two years below grade level, were more than a year ahead of the control group (Schweinhart and Weikart 1977; Eckroade, Salehi, and Wode 1991). By the time students had graduated from high school, 39 percent of the control group as compared with only 19 percent of the preschool students had required special education services for at least one year, and still later data showed that the preschool group was more likely to find and hold jobs or enroll in college and less likely to be on welfare or to be arrested (Schweinhart and Weikart 1980; Farnsworth, Schweinhart, and Berrueta-Clement 1985; Schweinhart and Weikart 1989; Frazier 1990). Similar results have been reported for the Syracuse Preschool Project operated in the early 1970s (Neinhuis 1986; Schorr 1989; Kennedy 1991).

This phenomenon, sometimes referred to as the sleeper effect, also has appeared in other longitudinal studies of the subsequent school careers of low-status students who had received preschool compensatory education (Olmsted and Syegda 1988; Caldwell 1991). For example, Francis H. Palmer studied the subsequent performance of black youngsters in Harlem who had participated at age two or three in preschool programs respectively emphasizing *concept training* and *discovery training*. ("Concept training" emphasized teacher presentation of concepts. "Discovery training" encouraged students to learn concepts through inquiry methods.) Both groups attended one-hour sessions twice a week for eight months. After an intensive search to locate the children nearly ten years later, he found that the fifth-grade reading scores of children who had received concept training were significantly higher than those of children in discovery training or a control group, and that training at age two was more potent in improving reading than training at age three (Palmer n.d., 24). Average differences between the two groups in some cases were substantial, as in the results for students in the fifth grade in 1975: 47 percent of concept training training students were reading at or above grade level, as compared with 37 percent of the discovery training students, and a little more than 30 percent of students in comparison groups.

Longitudinal gains in achievement also have been reported for children whose mothers participated in special training and assistance programs for the parents of infants in low-status

families. For example, the Florida Parent Education Project conducted by Ira J. Gordon and his colleagues began work with poverty-level mothers of children who were three months old in September 1966. Families were randomly assigned to experimental and control groups, and those in the experimental group participated for either one, two, or three years. The intervention consisted of home visits approximately once a week by paraprofessional parent educators. They demonstrated home learning activities to the parent so the parent in turn would engage in instructional interaction with her child. Children in the experimental group at age two also were enrolled in home learning centers in their neighborhoods, where five children at a time spent eight hours a week working with the parent educator. Three to five years later, children in the experimental groups were found to score seven or eight points higher in IQ than did control children (Guinagh and Gordon 1976, 20).

Thus, a number of preschool programs such as Weikart's, Palmer's, and Gordon's appear to have had encouraging longitudinal results. Summary conclusions also have been reported by Irving Lazar and other researchers who examined the results found in studies of twelve early childhood programs for youngsters who participated in the early and mid-1960s and were subsequently studied at ages nine to eighteen (Lazar 1977; Darlington 1980; Cotton and Conklin 1989; Haskins 1989). Lazar and his colleagues reported that for most of the twelve programs, students who had participated in the compensatory education preschools had IQ scores generally about four to eight points higher three to six years later than did students in the control groups. They also were less likely to be placed in special education or to experience failure in school (Eckroade, Salehi, and Wode 1991).

However, some researchers have challenged the validity of data available on the results of well-known preschool programs, particularly those data dealing with IQ gains (see Spitz 1986). Also, keep in mind that programs reporting positive results appear to have been unusually well-implemented. One cannot assume that the average program has been run well or has had permanent effects (Schweinhart 1987; Chira 1990b).

Cost/Benefit Analysis. Having concluded that well-implemented preschool programs for disadvantaged students can have positive effects, some researchers have attempted to estimate respective costs and benefits in order to determine whether such programs are worth the relatively high financial expenditures likely to be required. The most comprehensive and systematic analysis of this kind was prepared by Barnett (1985) in connection with the Perry Preschool Project (described earlier) in Ypsilanti, Michigan. After estimating a variety of short- and long-range costs and benefits, he concluded that the project more than paid for itself in terms of reduced subsequent special-education costs, reduced delinquency, fewer retentions-in-grade, increased high-school graduation rates, and other beneficial, longitudinal results among children who participated. Barnett and Escobar (1987, 1989) later reviewed these data along with less comprehensive information obtained from other preschool programs. After acknowledging the difficult problems and numerous assumptions inherent in estimating costs and benefits, they concluded that

> *we would be disappointed if our review and cautions about the limitations of early educational intervention were interpreted as dampening enthusiasm for increased public support of early childhood programs for children in low-income families. Even with its limitations, the evidene that quality early educational intervention is a sound public investment is far stronger than the evidence that the savings and loan bail out . . . or the proposed cut in the capital gains tax are economically sensible policies. Moreover, in an era when tensions between equity and efficiency are expected from educational and social programs, a program that promises to reduce inequality and repay the*

> *costs to the taxpayer should find almost universal support. (Barnett and Escobar 1989, 34–35)*

Elementary- and Secondary-Level

Research reported in the previous section regarding the sleeper effect of some preschool programs in generating academic gains found years after the programs ended should not be interpreted as indicating that later support is unnecessary to ensure sustained gain of a substantial nature. The Head Start evaluations along with data from big-city school districts showing consistent later declines among students with improved academic performance in kindergarten or even first and second grade (Fuerst 1977; Caldwell 1991) both indicate that it is desirable to continue compensatory education after early childhood.

Primary Grades and Follow Through. Data from a number of school districts show that compensatory education in some locations has been effective in raising the academic performance of low-status students to the national average in the primary grades, even in some inner-city schools in which achievement deficits generally have been most sizable. For example, primary grade achievement very close to national norms was reported for inner-city schools in Chicago's sub-district ten in 1974 (Fuerst 1976), and citywide achievement in the third and fourth grades in Philadelphia was reported as "approaching national norms" in 1977 (Philadelphia Public Schools 1977, 11).

Research on the results of Follow Through projects also shows that compensatory education can be effective in improving the performance of low-status students in the primary grades (Adams 1990). These projects were initiated in 1967 to "follow through" on Head Start after evaluation indicated that gains from early childhood programs frequently were not being maintained after kindergarten and first grade. President Lyndon Johnson requested 120 million dollars to conduct Follow Through programs for 200,000 low-income, primary grade students in 1968, but only 14 million was made available by Congress.

Appropriations increased to 70 million dollars in 1970 but declined to a much lower level in subsequent years (Schmidt 1990a).

Follow Through has been organized and implemented on a national "planned variation" basis. A number of different instructional approaches (models) have been tried in a variety of locations, with an unusually thorough evaluation to determine which approaches are most effective. Local parents and educators have selected among twenty-two approaches ranging from the Cognitive Curriculum model stressing teaching of concepts, to responsive education using the so-called talking typewriter, and a behavior analysis approach emphasizing positive reinforcement through award of tokens for success.

The Follow Through evaluation, like the program itself, has been difficult, expensive, and controversial (Caldwell 1991). By 1977, more than 30 million dollars had been spent on evaluation, and the difficulties encountered in reaching firm conclusions were exceeded only by the difficulties encountered in administering the program in many different settings spread throughout the United States. Major problems in carrying out the evaluation included questions involving the comparability of groups of students of somewhat different socioeconomic status (severely versus moderately disadvantaged), high attrition of students, teachers, and sites, complicated technical issues involving comparison of gain scores at differing levels of performance, and uncertainty whether a given model at a particular site was implemented well enough to be considered a good test of its potential effects.

Despite such problems, evaluations of Follow Through have yielded useful knowledge about instructional approaches for improving the performance of low-status students. Tucker (1977) reviewed the results of many Follow Through studies and derived a set of conclusions including the following:

Educational philosophies based on a well defined curriculum with emphasis on the development of basic skills generally produce meaningful gains over a variety of cognitive and affective outcome measures. . . .

Models based on the use and development of the . . . language [used in the child's home] and culture produced meaningful effects over the range of outcome measures. Models with a definite set of instructional objectives in the cognitive and conceptual domains produced expected outcomes. (p. 17)

Several recent examinations of the data base on Follow Through continue to indicate that many projects produce positive results but that whether a project is implemented well is more important than the particular instructional approach used at a particular site (Caldwell 1991). For example, Wang (1988) reviewed data available from a number of sites at which Follow Through programs had been implemented for "a period of time." She concluded that successful operation depended more on use of a "core" of effective instructional practices than on the particular instructional approach followed (Wang 1988, 34). After noting that these core practices were similar to those cited in effective teaching research examining the methods of unusually successful teachers in general (see Chapter 13), Wang identified some of them:

- Availability of diverse, appropriate materials.
- High allocation of class time for curriculum-related activities.
- Learning tasks that are suitable in terms of students' achievement levels and learning needs.
- Considerable student choice in selecting learning activities.
- Constructive interaction among students.
- Individual diagnosis and prescription.

It should be emphasized here that although Follow Through research has helped identify the characteristics of successful compensatory education in the primary grades, this research does not indicate that the problem of improving the academic performance of low-status students at this level has been definitively solved, particularly in concentrated poverty schools. Richard Anderson of Abt Associates has examined the effectiveness of differing models. He concluded, "The most succesful model, in this respect, achieved this heroic level with only a minority of groups. If educators know how to close the performance gap between disadvantaged children and the nation in general. . . . Follow Through has not proved that they can do it reliably" (Anderson 1977, 4). It also is known that much of the Follow Through gain, where it does occur, is lost when students enter the middle grades, just as Head Start gains frequently are lost when students enter the primary grades (Adams 1990). This failure to maintain gains is sometimes referred to as the fade out effect (Caldwell 1991).

Through the Middle Grades.   Although many school districts are reporting substantially improved academic achievement in the primary grades, few schools or programs have been able to sustain these gains through the middle grades. Examination of achievement data in these situations suggests that there frequently is a third- or fourth-grade dropoff in the achievement of students attending low-status schools. This pattern is particularly obvious in the case of concentrated poverty schools in big cities, where middle-grade achievement levels almost always are very low.

One reason that achievement levels for low-status students who gained in the primary grades tend to fall in the middle grades may be insufficient attention given in their previous compensatory education to developing abstract thinking skills that become important in the middle grades (Adams 1990; Anderson and Pellicer 1990). As pointed out in Chapter 7, direct instruction seems to be most effective in developing basic learning skills such as decoding of words and computation in arithmetic, but other instructional emphasis such as inquiry training also may be necessary to develop cognitive thinking abilities that become more important later. This explanation suggests that it is easier—as one would

expect—to improve basic learning skills than to develop abstract thinking abilities. It also suggests that preschool and primary compensatory education programs have not yet identified the optimal mix between direct instruction and emphasis on more complex cognitive skills.

However, there also are other plausible explanations for the dropoff in achievement of low-status students in the middle grades, including two such possible reasons as the following: (1) much less has been done in the middle than the primary grades to improve instructional materials and approaches, train teachers in how to use them, or otherwise provide effective compensatory education; and (2) academically negative influences from peer and neighborhood sources may become much more important in the middle grades than in the early years of school. Systematic research is needed to determine which of these or other factors are most important in producing a plateau in achievement where compensatory education seems to have been effective through the primary grades. Even without such research, it is apparent that new instructional approaches are needed if early academic gains are to be extended into the middle grades.

Until recently, about all that could be said with confidence about this goal was that substantial academic gains in the middle and upper grades would need the same educational components required to make any innovation work successfully, namely, outstanding administrative leadership, large-scale staff development, systematic organizational changes in support of the innovation, and competent planning and evaluation. Fortunately, much has been learned during the 1980s about how to make instruction more effective for economically disadvantaged students beyond the primary grades. The status of efforts to improve the achievement of disadvantaged students in the middle grades and high schools is described in the section on effective schools research in Chapter 13.

Title I/Chapter 1.   Since the Elementary and Secondary Education Act of 1965 was passed by

Congress, more than 40 billion dollars have been spent to improve the academic achievement of low-status students in elementary and secondary schools. Approximately three-fourths of all public elementary schools in the United States receive some Chapter 1 funding for this purpose. Originally called Title I, these funds were re-titled Chapter 1 in 1981. Nearly 4 billion dollars were budgeted for Chapter 1 in 1990 (Beatty 1990).

Every school district that receives Chapter 1 money must collect evaluation data, and surveys of these school district reports have formed the basis for most of the national evaluations. One frequently used criterion for attainment of the academic objectives of Chapter 1 programs has been the goal of having participants achieve one month of gain for every month in the program. Such month-to-month gains would mean that low-status students no longer were falling progressively further behind national averages each year in school.

Early evaluations of Chapter 1 during the late 1960s were similar to the Head Start evaluations in suggesting that compensatory education was not very effective in improving the performance of disadvantaged students. Students in Chapter 1 programs did not appear to be achieving normal month-to-month gains or to be catching up with higher-status students. However, it also became apparent that one reason Chapter 1 programs were having little impact was because funds were being dispersed on a variety of services and activities that often were clearly incapable of improving participants' mastery of fundamental learning skills. Federal, state, and local guidelines for the conduct of Chapter 1 programs were revised to concentrate funds on students with the greatest learning deficiencies, to introduce planning and monitoring procedures, and to incorporate instructional approaches aimed particularly at improving academic performance.

Since 1973, several studies of Chapter 1 achievement effects have been carried out by analyzing data from state department of education reports to the federal government. Findings by Thomas and Pelavin (1976) replicated the con-

clusions of other researchers who reported that students in Chapter 1 programs by that time generally were meeting or exceeding the month-to-month gain standard within a given school year. Hendrickson (1977) reviewed the history of Chapter 1 evaluations and concluded that they "justify cautious optimism" in the capacity of Chapter 1 to raise the achievement of disadvantaged children within a given school year.

On the other hand, national data clearly indicate that although Chapter 1 has had some positive impact, it has not substantially improved the achievement of disadvantaged students on a long-range basis (Passow 1988a; Walmsley and Allington 1990). For example, studies conducted by the National Assessment of Educational Progress showed that the difference between the reading performance of black nine-year-olds in schools eligible and not eligible for Chapter 1 services declined by less than 1 percentage point between 1971 and 1980. Continuing inadequacies in the achievement of students at Chapter 1 schools in part reflect that many students who improve in achievement do not receive help the following year and many others are not helped at all due to national funding limits (Kennedy, Jung, and Orland 1986; Anderson and Pellicer 1990).

In addition, the final report of the national Chapter 1 evaluation (i.e., the Sustaining Effects Study) found that even though Chapter 1 students gained in mathematics in grades one through six and in reading in grades one through three, reading scores of students beyond grade three did not improve (Stonehill and Anderson 1982; Mullin and Summers 1983; Carter 1984; Passow 1988a; Miller 1991a). A second national evaluation released in 1987 came to the same conclusion, reporting that Chapter 1 students appear to make small gains in reading and math but that these gains do relatively little to offset their large learning deficits (Kennedy 1987; Miller 1991a). The fact that millions of poverty students are still entering high school each year with very low scores in reading, mathematics, and other skills also indicates that Chapter 1 and other compensatory programs have not yet generally succeeded in overcoming the academic problems experienced by disadvantaged students (Anderson and Pellicer 1990).

Secondary Level. Evidence is available supporting the conclusion that compensatory education can be effective in improving the academic achievement of low-status students beyond the middle grades. This conclusion has been explicitly confirmed by a study the U.S. Office of Education commissioned to separate out and assess data on the effectiveness of programs for secondary students. One purpose of this study was to provide data for policy makers struggling with the question of whether to set aside more funds for secondary programs on the grounds that low-status students at this level have a very large achievement deficit, or to continue to concentrate Chapter 1 funds on early childhood and elementary programs in order to prevent learning problems that many educators believe become insoluble among older students.

The study (Larson and Dittman 1975) found that achievement gains equal to or greater than the month-to-month criterion were attained in a number of projects, but critics suggested that much of this gain represented a "rebound" effect that appears when older students enter a skills development program in which they reacquire skills and knowledge they had previously forgotten. However, the study concluded that this type of explanation did not account for most of the gain and that there was no basis

> *for the claim that compensatory projects for adolescents are less effective than those for children in primary grades. Grade equivalent gains in reading skills are consistently higher for students in grades 7–12, with both mean and median gains of over one month per month. . . .*
>
> *Other data show with equal clarity that there are large numbers of adolescents who vitally need special assistance if they are to achieve basic skill levels and to function effectively as adults. The present concentration*

> *of compensatory funds on the early grades is neither eliminating nor meeting these needs. (Larson and Dittman 1975, xii, 53)*

Larson and Dittman also examined the characteristics of the most successful secondary programs in California and found that these programs generally did more than provide individual instruction from remedial education specialists, which is the typical approach used in most Chapter 1 programs. In addition, the successful projects included an intensive effort to "involve regular teaching staff, through in-service training" and attempted, in some cases, to improve the "whole curriculum" of the school (p. 59).

This conclusion helps explain why national evaluations of Chapter 1 and other compensatory educational programs have found that low-status students seem to gain a good deal while participating but frequently are found to be falling further and further behind national averages in subsequent years. Because most Chapter 1 secondary students are dropped from the program after they are judged to have made enough progress to function adequately in regular classes, and because few secondary schools have made systematic adjustments to address their learning needs after they return to regular classes, whatever they gained during Chapter 1 is soon washed out (Miller 1991a).

Secondary compensatory education also has been provided through the federally sponsored Upward Bound Program and similar efforts to offer special help to disadvantaged students at the senior high level. The goal of Upward Bound programs is to improve participants' preparation and motivation for postsecondary education. Analysis of data on Upward Bound students indicates that the program "continues to enhance youths' preparation for post-secondary education. . . . [UB students are] more likely to be planning to attend and complete college, and more likely to have made concrete plans for attending college" (Steel and Schubert 1983, 18).

Deficiencies in Chapter 1.   As noted, Chapter 1 programs at both the elementary and secondary levels have been hampered by a variety of problems that have severely limited their effectiveness. Lorin Anderson and Leonard Pellicer (1990) reviewed more than two decades of research dealing with Chapter 1 and other compensatory and remedial approaches for helping low achievers and reached the following conclusions regarding problems in their organization and operation:

> *Chapter 1 programs are often so poorly coordinated with regular programs that student learning is actually impeded. Along with some federal programs for the handicapped and state programs for the gifted, Chapter 1 programs contribute to a fragmentation of the curriculum.*
>
> *Although they generally lack qualifications, teacher's aides often serve as instructional staff in Chapter 1 programs because they are less expensive than certified teachers—they are chosen for pragmatic, rather than educational reasons.*
>
> *Students in remedial and compensatory classes often spend inordinate amounts of time working alone at their desks.*
>
> *Chapter 1 teachers often have low expectations for their students and a tendency to teach to their present levels of functioning rather than to the levels they will need to be successful in the future. As a result, Chapter 1 students may do well on classroom tests and worksheets, but they often perform poorly on state or national tests.*
>
> *Chapter 1 programs are substantially less effective for students with severe learning problems than for "marginal" students, whose problems are associated with an inability or unwillingness to learn in regular classroom settings. (Anderson and Pellicer 1990, 11)*

However, Anderson and Pellicer also concluded that much has been learned about delivery of effective compensatory education for low achievers and that some Chapter 1 programs have been successful when they were organized and operated to avoid or overcome inherent obstacles and pitfalls. To attain more success in the future, Anderson and Pellicer further concluded that Chapter 1 and other compensatory education programs should be fully integrated into and coordinated with arrangements for curriculum and instruction throughout the school. In doing so, emphasis should be on providing challenging instruction at a more rapid pace for low achievers, on providing active rather than passive learning experiences, on incorporating higher-order thinking skills, and on not treating students who may be relatively slow learners as if they had severe mental handicaps. In the absence of such changes, according to these analysts, we will continue to be satisfied with "merely slowing the rate" at which low achievers "fall further and further behind," and we will continue devoting "huge financial commitments to programs that simply don't work very well, year after year after year" (Anderson and Pellicer 1990, 15).

Open Admissions and Compensatory Education in College

By 1970, there was a broad movement toward admissions procedures that would admit at least a substantial minority of students who could not qualify by the earlier aptitude test or high school course record requirements. For example, the City College of the City University of New York (CUNY), long known as even more highly selective than some Ivy League colleges, in 1970 adopted an open admissions policy that admitted any applicant with a high school diploma. The policy applied to the four-year senior colleges of CUNY as well as to the two-year community colleges. The CUNY consisted of nineteen colleges, all with free tuition in 1970.

It should be understood that open admissions is standard practice in many state-supported colleges and universities, which are required to admit any graduate of an accredited high school. However, it is well known that this form of open admissions frequently results in a kind of so-called revolving door phenomenon, with a considerable number of entering students failing in their first-year course work and dropping out of the college.

The New York City College faculties undertook to meet this situation with a number of remedial courses and arrangements for tutoring students who were below average in reading and mathematics. There was substantial growth in enrollment, indicating that the policy was drawing youth who could not have gained admission under the earlier requirements. For example, from 1969 to 1974 the undergraduate enrollment at four-year state universities in the State of New York increased by 33 percent, while the enrollment increase at CUNY four-year colleges was 60 percent. And enrollment at state two-year institutions increased 36 percent while the two-year colleges of CUNY increased 103 percent. Blacks comprised 14 percent of the freshman class in 1969, and 31 percent in 1977. Puerto Ricans represented 6 percent of freshmen in 1969 but 16 percent in 1972. It was also found that the numbers of applications and admissions of students from poverty families more than doubled (Crook and Lavin 1989).

Based partly on earlier programs that had been initiated to provide remedial services for disadvantaged students, City College initiated and expanded a variety of efforts to help poorly prepared applicants succeed. Special program adjustments included placement of many students in ESL (English as a Second Language) courses; assistance to minority students in science, engineering, and health sciences; and establishment of urban-oriented centers for academic skills, biomedical education, legal education, and performing arts.

Robert E. Marshak, President of CUNY from 1970 to 1979, reviewed developments in connection with open admissions. He reported data suggesting that CUNY generally had maintained high-quality education. For example, CUNY students continued to score at or above national norms on all national college exit exams, and high percentages of graduates gained acceptance into graduate schools. Marshak offered the following "general statements" about the achievements of the open admissions program:

> One must first acknowledge that the open admissions experience brought about invaluable educational changes at the college. Many of the remedial programs added measurably to the college's ability to bring poorly prepared high school students through the difficult transition to the intellectual demands of a college education that would meet traditional graduation requirements. The relaxation of 'entrance' requirements was not accompanied in any significant fashion by a relaxation of 'exit' requirements. What is true is that the attrition rate before graduation increased substantially—especially in the freshman and sophomore years—not a surprising result if graduation standards were to be maintained.
>
> . . . The experiment must be judged a success. Given the emergency conditions under which open admissions was instituted, the constant underfunding of the program, the lack of experience of faculty dealing with large numbers of underprepared students, the economic, physical, and social handicaps of the students, the problems of overcrowding on campus, the constant sniping by a vocal minority of the faculty, the disproportionate burden assigned to City College through CUNY's allocation policies, the college not only survived open admissions but showed how to turn it to academic innovation as well as social good. (Marshak 1981, 52)

Later evaluations of the CUNY open admissions program by David Lavin and his colleagues (1981, 1986; Crook and Lavin 1989; Lavin and Crook 1990) also support the conclusion that it has been successful in several respects. The authors concluded that minority students were not disproportionately channeled into dead-end community college careers as a result of open admissions, and that opportunities for students from low-income families were substantially increased and improved. Their overall assessment is that *the open-admissions policy probably has altered forever historic patterns of ethnic access to the University. . . . Open admissions substantially boosted the number of graduates from every group, but its contributions were critical to the proportion of black and Hispanic graduates. . . . The program more than doubled the number of black students who received a degree of some kind . . . nearly doubled the number of black students placed on the threshold of graduate or professional school. . . .*

But at the same time that many minority students were gaining the opportunity for a college education under open admissions, so were even more whites. (Lavin, Alba, and Silberstein 1981, 271, 276–277)

It has been understood from the outset that an open admissions policy requires a special program of instruction to help compensate for the disadvantages of the low-scoring students. This has been done in various ways at many colleges and universities and has met considerable opposition from some outstanding scholars who argue that relaxation of admissions standards will either lower the intellectual quality of higher education or will cause a great deal of frustration for students who are first admitted and then failed.

However, the director of research for the American Council on Education, Alexander W. Astin (1969, 1990) has made a thorough study of the relation between test scores, high school grades, and college dropouts, and has come to the conclusion that a considerable fraction of students do make it in college in spite of low aptitude scores or low high school grades. He concluded, furthermore, that "the model of selective admissions based on test scores and grades is inappropriate for institutions of higher education. Presumably, educational institutions exist in order to educate students. They should strive in their admissions practices to select those applicants most likely to be favorably influenced by the particular educational program offered at the institution" (Astin 1969, 69).

Early experience and research on college compensatory education also indicated that although low-status students who participated certainly were greater risks than the average student who was admissible under the usual standards, they generally had attained fairly high grades in high schools. In other words, they seldom were among the hard-core disadvantaged but came from low-status families that had been relatively successful in motivating and preparing them for higher education. As found in one study of special programs for disadvantaged students in the late 1960s, the students who were succeeding in these programs "seemed to have a pervasive middle-class orientation, and in most cases a parent, brother, sister, or other close relative who had college experience. For such students, even what seemed to be severely limiting personal circumstances—for example . . . living at home with four younger brothers under miserably crowded conditions, and without a means of convenient transportation—did not prove to be a roadblock" (Klingelhofer and Longacre 1972, 7).

Since 1975, a growing volume of research on college compensatory education also has provided a degree of positive evaluation. Edmund W. Gordon, director of the Clearinghouse on Urban Education at Teachers College, Columbia University, has been periodically reviewing research on this topic and has provided the following summary of research on compensatory education at the collegiate level:

Where programs have been implemented with full systems of student support services (financial aid, adjusted curriculum, tutorial support, remediation where necessary, and counselling and continuous social/psychological support), special opportunity students showed equal or higher grade-point averages than regular students of comparable ability and showed equal or higher retention than regular students. . . . Where programs with full systems of student support services have been implemented special opportunity students show increased self-esteem and motivation. (Gordon 1976, 12)

A systematic review of evaluation studies of college compensatory education also supports the conclusion that such programs frequently result in substantial gains for participants. Kulik, Kulik, and Shwalb (1982) examined evaluation on sixty special college programs for high-risk students and concluded that in general these programs "had basically positive effects" (p. 1). Students who participated had higher grade-point averages and completed more years of college than comparable students who did not participate. Although differences in the majority of programs were small, some programs had large positive effects. The investigators also reported that compensatory education appeared to be more successful in four-year colleges than in community colleges. Research also indicates that the retention rates have improved substantially at some institutions providing strong compensatory education programs (Foster 1982; Richardson 1991).

Additional evidence of the efficacy of postsecondary compensatory education at some locations is apparent in data on individual colleges. For example, research at Chicago State University indicates that three-quarters of the students who failed academic entry tests passed subsequent competency exams after participating in compensatory courses; a computerized Academic Alert system that identifies and monitors the impact of special support services for low-achieving students has helped improve the performance of many at Miami-Dade Community College; and entry-level placement tests and strong compensatory programs have improved the performance of many students at Santa Fe (FL) Community College and helped them graduate (Foster 1982; Zwerling 1988; Rendon and Taylor 1990; Smittle 1990). Such examples indicate that where outstanding leadership, adequate funds, and a dedicated faculty combine to focus on overcoming the learning problems of low achievers, compensatory education can be successful at the postsecondary level.

COMPREHENSIVE ECOLOGICAL INTERVENTION

For many children in particularly difficult environments, preschool classes and later compensatory education opportunities limited entirely or mostly to school-based interventions cannot be expected to overcome severe environmental disadvantages, even when such interventions are designed and implemented competently. In this case one must aim for *ecological* intervention, that is, comprehensive efforts to improve the family environment of severely disadvantaged young children (Bronfenbrenner 1974; Smith, Blank, and Bone 1990). One major goal of ecological intervention is to assist the family in order to help the parents become more effective "socializers" of the child" (Zigler 1991, 164).

Lizbeth Schorr (1989) has reviewed several decades of research dealing with early childhood environments and their effects and concluded that some environments jeopardize development to the extent that a "threshold" level is crossed beyond which there frequently are serious negative consequences. (Also see our discussion in this chapter on the operation of negative threshold phenomena at concentrated poverty schools in big cities and our description of the Skeels and Dye study in Chapter 4.) In the absence of external intervention, she further concluded, "economic stress," "lack of social support," a "fragile, impaired, or immature parent, and sometimes a difficult infant can combine . . . to create an environment so bad that it prejudices normal development of the child." Specific childhood-environment factors that place a child particularly at risk and signify a possible need for "intensive intervention" include "persistent poverty," "neighborhoods of concentrated poverty and social dislocation," "families that are homeless," and a "mentally ill, alcoholic, or drug-addicted parent" (Schorr 1989, 143, 286).

The good news from research, according to Schorr, is that ecological intervention effectively carried out to provide comprehensive family support and related services frequently can counteract and overcome the negative effects of severely damaging environments. However, she also found that programs successful in helping at-risk families and their children are "more intensive, more comprehensive, and sometimes more costly than those typically needed" by less disadvantaged families (Schorr 1989, 285). In general, available research indicates that successful comprehensive programs for severely disadvantaged children must:

- move beyond custodial care to offer intellectual stimulation.
- include nutrition, health care, and other social services.
- provide systematic support for parents.
- be provided by "competent staff, with a staff-child ratio high enough that children at each developmental stage get the attention they need in order to thrive" (Schorr 1989, 202).

Unfortunately, Schorr also found that few programs provide the quantity and quality of comprehensive services associated with successful ecological intervention for severely disadvantaged families and their children. In the words of George Miller, chairman of the U.S. House of Representatives Select Committee on Children, Youth, and Families, "what we keep finding" in congressional hearings and from other sources is that "when it comes to services for kids and families in poverty, where it is done in a first-class fashion, it succeeds beyond our wildest dreams. And everywhere we've tried to do it on the cheap, everywhere we've tried to cut a corner, we end up spending money with no appreciable results" (quoted in Schorr 1989, 293–294). Among the promising comprehensive interventions identified and described by Schorr, Cohen (1989, 1990, 1991), and others are the following:

- An expansion to New York City of the Tacoma, WA, Homebuilders projects, which provides intensive social services coordinated by staff members who have very small caseloads.
- The Beethoven project, at a large housing project in Chicago, which provides coordinated

and comprehensive services involving health, adult education, employment training and job-search assistance, parent training, support for children's intellectual and psychological development, and other forms of assistance for all members of families with very young children.

- A State of Missouri pilot project in which specially trained teachers visit the homes of the preschool children every six weeks to help parents learn how to provide a supportive environment for learning (Baker 1989; McGuire 1990). Titled Parents as Teachers, this approach also has been introduced in other states (Cohen 1990).
- A set of Tennessee programs that deal respectively with screening prekindergarten students for physical and mental problems, readiness-improvement and enrichment for three- and four-year-olds, and promotion of active parenting and new parents as teachers (Lueder 1989).
- The Parent and Child Education (PACE) programs at numerous Kentucky sites at which parents of three- and four-year-olds receive literacy instruction, parenting education, and adult basic education while their children attend preschool classes (Smith, Blank, and Bond 1990).
- Programs in Independence, MO, and Tulsa, OK, in which elementary schools not only provide before- and after-school day-care arrangements for students but also serve as neighborhood child-care centers that offer preschool classes and various support services for parents of young children (Lawson 1990).
- The New Beginnings project in San Diego, in which school and county personnel are working together closely to overcome bureaucratic obstacles and coordinate a multitude of services in order to foster the success of low-income families and students at a pilot elementary school (Cohen 1991).
- A multicity program in which the families of children low in birthweight receive various services beginning at birth and the children participate in educationally oriented day care beginning at the age of one. At age three, participating children have IQ scores thirteen points higher than control-group children (Kolata 1990).

▪ The Giant Step program sponsored by the Human Resources Corporation and the Board of Education in New York City, which enrolls four-year-olds at more than 100 sites. Using a curriculum approach similar to Head Start, Giant Step includes a more intensive parent involvement and assistance component, greater staff training, small classes, a teacher's assistant and a family aide for every class, and a program director as well as a social worker for every three classrooms. Initial results assessing students' behavior and intellectual growth have been very promising (Layzer, Goodson, and Layzer 1990; Goodson and Layzer 1991).

The importance and value of ecological intervention also have been apparent in results from The Milwaukee Project, which was carried out and described by Howard Garber (1988) and numerous colleagues. Working in a concentrated poverty neighborhood in Milwaukee in the 1960s and 1970s, sponsors of the project demonstrated that IQ of the mother was the best predictor of "sociocultural" mental retardation, which they defined as IQ in the 50–70 range with no identifiable nervous system disorder. In an attempt to determine whether sociocultural retardation could be overcome by very early intervention, The Milwaukee Project selected forty inner-city black children whose mothers had IQ scores below 70, randomly placed half in an experimental group and half in a control group, and began an intensive rehabilitation program with two primary components: educational and vocational rehabilitation for the mothers, and individualized enrichment for the children beginning in the first few months of life.

The program began shortly after birth with daily visits to the home by a paraprofessional teacher who established rapport with both the mother and the child and helped the mother develop parenting skills and establish a positive home environment. After about three months, the infant began to attend a learning center every day from nine until four, five days a week, on a year-round basis until entering first grade. Meanwhile, vocational training as well as remedial education and instruction in homemaking and child-care skills and crisis counseling and assistance were provided for the mother. The mothers were trained to work in local nursing homes and were given assistance obtaining jobs there. Health services also were provided for the mothers and their children.

The children's learning program had a cognitive-language orientation implemented though a planned environment using informal prescriptive teaching techniques in which teachers:

1. Observed each child's strengths, weaknesses, and preferences.
2. Geared tasks and experiences specifically for the child.
3. Evaluated the effects of the task or experience on the child.

Explicit attention also was given to social and emotional development of the children and to developing achievement motivation by creating an atmosphere designed to maximize their interest and ensure success experiences. The learning program continued until the experimental children were old enough to enroll in school.

The results of this experiment have been very impressive. Experimental-group children attained average IQ scores above 120 at various testings from ages four to six, compared with average scores in the low 90s for control-group children. (Both sets of scores probably are somewhat inflated due to relative unreliability of testing arrangements and tests available for preschool children.) At six years of age, 39 percent of control children but none of the experimental children had scores below 85. In addition, data from various sources indicated that the experimental children "demonstrated more sophisticated early problem-solving behaviors," greater verbal facility and verbal interaction with their mothers, and more use of abstract categories on sorting tasks, than did the control children (Garber 1988, 120, 199, 223).

Collecting additional data on performance as students moved through Milwaukee elementary schools, Garber and his colleagues also found that experimental children had average IQ scores slightly above 100 at several testings up to age ten, whereas average scores for control children were in the low 80s. However, the researchers also reported that although experimental children had relatively high achievement scores in the first grade, their achievement "slowly but consistently declined across the four elementary grades" (Garber 1988, 280). After noting that this pattern was typical for the inner-city elementary schools the children attended, Garber drew attention to the overall conclusions and implications of the study as follows:

> The experimental group in this study was provided with an intensive intervention program assumed to be similar to the microenvironment provided naturally by mothers with high IQs. . . . [The results support] our basic premise that mild retardation can be prevented by offsetting the negative influences of the microenvironment created by the low IQ, low verbal skilled mother. . . . It is these children who [otherwise] are most likely to demonstrate the dramatic declines in intellectual performance previously believed to be characteristic of the majority of children from deprived environments.
>   . . . It seems therefore that although it is possible to achieve improved intellectual performance or prevent expected declines in IQ test performance in children at risk for mental retardation, considerable questions remain as to the nature of intellectual growth . . . [and the approaches that can maintain] performance benefits over time that result from intervention treatments. (Garber 1988, 310, 403–404)

It also must be acknowledged, however, that the spread in the late 1980s and early 1990s of crack cocaine and related phenomena involving crime, delinquency, and other aspects of social disorganization in poverty neighborhoods seems to be making it substantially more difficult to deliver comprehensive ecological intervention successfully. For example, social scientists and various governmental officials have reported that infants whose mothers smoke crack are displaying signs of unusually serious developmental damage (Blakeslee 1989), and drug addiction among inner-city women has reached unprecedented levels (Greene 1989). In addition, recent increase in social disorganization has overloaded hospitals, social-welfare agencies, probation and parole services, and other social institutions serving the inner-city poor, well beyond the previous situation in which many already were understaffed and functioning poorly in the face of multiple problems (DiIulio 1989). The growing scope and severity of social disorganization in poverty neighborhoods indicate that it may be even more difficult to design and implement effective ecological intervention in the future than has been true in the past.

In addition, research on ecological intervention in the preschool years suggests that disadvantaged children who receive its benefits frequently do not maintain high or adequate achievement gains later as they proceed through elementary school, particularly when they attend concentrated poverty schools in the inner city (e.g., Garber 1988). Issues involving the provision of effective compensatory education for low-achieving disadvantaged children and youth at all grade levels are discussed elsewhere in this chapter, in Chapter 13, and in other chapters.

SOCIAL POLICY AND COMPENSATORY EDUCATION

The discerning reader may have noted that the preceding discussion introduced a variety of criteria for determining the goals and success of compensatory education. At some points, early childhood programs seem to have been considered successful if they resulted in any longitudinal gain beyond what low-status children would have attained in the absence of compensatory intervention. At other points, the implicit goal was to help inner-city youth become sufficiently literate to obtain a good job; and at still others, it was to prevent disadvantaged students from falling further and further behind middle-status peers as they proceed through school.

Lack of clarity and agreement regarding the goals of compensatory education is an important issue because definition of the goal to be sought has important implications for the design of compensatory programs. If the major goal is to be functional literacy, then programs that stress direct instruction may be successful in developing basic skills subsumed under this goal.

However, Resnick and Resnick (1985) have examined the history of efforts to develop literacy and concluded that the criterian of *comprehension*—which is a step beyond the mastery of basic skills required for functional literacy—may not be attainable through traditional methods emphasizing basic skill development. In a later paper, Lauren Resnick (1990) argues that higher-order skills can be taught best for many students through a literacy "apprenticeship" in which they produce and critique written texts on topics about which they are enthusiastic. Moreover, Singer (1977) has reviewed the research on instructional strategies and skills development and concluded that although "guided" learning is appropriate in developing a basic skill, some form of "discovery" or "problem-solving" learning may be necessary to develop the capacity to apply the skill in new situations (p. 494). These conclusions suggest that methods to develop comprehension skills and high-cost early ecological intervention focusing on conceptual development will need to receive much more stress in compensatory education programs if their goal is to develop a high level of literacy and the ability to become a self-directed learner (Passow 1990).

One reason the goals of compensatory education tend to be shifting and poorly defined is that compensatory education is a major national issue involving fundamental values in society. As education has become more important in determining a person's chances for success in life,

greater stress has been placed on ensuring that low-status students really do have a chance to succeed educationally in accordance with their inherent talent and ability. Everyone can agree on the goal of equal educational opportunity stated at this level of generality, but disagreement occurs as soon as the goal is stated in operational terms. Is society responsible for providing low-status children a chance to proceed as far in the educational system as middle-status children, even though parents of the latter expend a great deal of their own time and money to give their children educational advantages?

In addition, unanswered questions regarding the conditions necessary for successful compensatory education make it difficult to work out comprehensive social policies for more effective compensatory education in the future. We have seen that compensatory education can achieve at least some of its goals at any level from preschool through college, and this research has led to concomitant changes in social policy. For example, many Head Start programs now stress work with parents in accordance with research suggesting that home-based components are vital in the early years. Follow Through was established after research suggested that Head Start participants lost ground following entry into regular primary classes. Nevertheless, uncertainties involving the design and implementation of compensatory education still make it difficult to work out a coherent national approach.

One uncertainty involves the degree to which *massive ecological intervention* in the early years may be prerequisite to later success. It seems clear that many youngsters, particularly those in concentrated poverty neighborhoods, require this type of intervention in order to have a real chance to succeed later in life, but no one knows just what proportion of disadvantaged students fit in this category or how much continuing intervention they may require after the preschool years (Zigler 1991).

A second and related uncertainty involves the issue of *costs*. It is easy to see that massive early intervention is expensive, but the costs of successful compensatory education in elementary and secondary schools generally have been underestimated in practice. Expenditures per child from Chapter 1 and other sources typically amount to six or seven hundred dollars per student per year, but we have presented evidence suggesting that compensatory education may have to continue at the same intensity as Head Start and Follow Through (which are considerably more expensive than Chapter 1), and that secondary schools may need to provide a consistently improved learning environment for low-status students rather than merely providing short-term remedial instruction. Many authorities believe that it requires two or three times as much money per student to provide effective compensatory education at the elementary and secondary levels as it does to educate nondisadvantaged students (McLure and Pence 1971, 26), whose education already costs well over $4,000 per student per year in many big cities. How much would this figure be decreased if early childhood compensatory education were more effective? The answer is not known, and meanwhile the problems of paying for compensatory education on an adequate scale in big cities have been compounded by fiscal crises that have forced schools in Chicago, Cleveland, Detroit, Los Angeles, New York, and many other big cities to cut back their general instructional programs.

Also related to the issue of ecological intervention is that of *racial and socioeconomic integration in the public schools*. One purpose of desegregation is to provide equal opportunity for minority students and, presumably, thereby help improve the academic performance of low-status or low-achieving minority students. Since the 1960s, compensatory education has tended to be seen as an alternative to integration. From our point of view, desegregation—particularly socioeconomic desegregation—should be viewed as an ecological intervention designed to improve the environment of the school, by reducing the number of low-status students who attend classes in a dysfunctional environment.

Another issue regarding compensatory education involves the extent to which *alternatives outside the regular educational system* may be necessary to provide effective educational opportunities for low-status students at the secondary and postsecondary levels. We have discussed compensatory education in the educational system at these levels, but other alternatives also have been or can be made available to improve opportunity for disadvantaged students. One of the most important of these has been the Job Corps, originally established as part of the War on Poverty to provide low-income youth sixteen to twenty-one years of age with educational and vocational skills required to escape from poverty.

The Job Corps is an ecological intervention designed to remove young people from poverty neighborhoods in the hope that this together with suitable instruction will enable them to function effectively in a job training program and, afterward, the economy. Assessments of the first few years of the Job Corps were discouraging, indicating that graduates were not clearly more successful than were control group youth who had not participated (Levitan and Mangum 1969). Later evaluations, however, have been considerably more positive, indicating that the Job Corps has had some success recruiting and retaining hard core disadvantaged youth, and that graduates of some centers had made significant gains in acquiring basic academic and vocational skills that helped them make an improved entry into the economy (Burbridge 1983; Frazier 1990). Even though it is a relatively expensive program, the Job Corps appears to be paying for itself on a cost-benefit basis to the degree that it is helping some participants avoid life-long dependence on the public welfare system (Dervarics 1985; Commission on Workforce Quality and Labor Market Efficiency 1989; Quality Education for Minorities Project 1990).

FINANCING OF CENTRAL-CITY SCHOOLS

A particular problem in working to improve education for disadvantaged students in most metropolitan areas is the inequality of financial support for schools between the central city, on the one hand, and the wealthier suburbs, on the other hand. Where public schools are paid for mainly by local property taxes, it happens that some wealthy suburbs have twice as much or more taxable property for each pupil as does the central city (Archer 1989). Thus, one district may support its schools with $7,000 or $8,000 annually per pupil, while a neighboring district in the same metropolitan area, although it taxes its property owners at a higher rate, is able to provide only $3,000 or $4,000 per pupil (Toch 1990).

At the same time, central city school districts generally have greater financial needs than do other metropolitan school districts. Reasons for this differential include the following:

1. *Greater proportion of low-status students.* Effective compensatory education for working-class students is expensive because it requires, among other things, purchase of a range of diversified learning materials, intensive staff development and specialized personnel such as reading supervisors, counselors, and school security officers. Because most central city school districts have a much higher proportion of low-status students than do most suburban districts, their financial requirements are correspondingly greater (Casserly and Kober 1990).

2. *Teacher salaries.* Because the teaching staff in big-city districts tend to be more militant than is true in most suburban districts, salaries in the central city tend to be among the highest in the metropolitan area (Ascher 1989). Teacher salaries typically constitute from 75 to 85 percent of a school district's overall budget.

3. *Cost for buildings and maintenance.* Central city school districts have had relatively high costs because land values historically have been higher than in most of the suburbs, and because older buildings are relatively expensive to maintain (Casserly and Kober 1990). School buildings in many big cities are in a deteriorated state that will cost billions of dollars to repair or replace (Boyd 1991).

4. *Difficulty of increasing property taxes.* Central city school districts generally have had even more of a problem gaining approval for property tax increases than have suburban school districts

(Ascher 1990). Part of the reason is that a higher proportion of voters in the central city tend to live on low or fixed incomes. In addition, central city residents tend to suffer from what political scientists have called "municipal overburden." This means that central city taxpayers tend to pay proportionately more than most suburbanites for fire, police, and other municipal services, thus making it difficult to obtain approval for additional school taxes.

5. *Higher absence rates.* Central cities with large numbers of low-status students have much higher absence rates than do most suburban districts. Because state funding for public schools generally is based on the number of pupils in average daily attendance, both these tendencies result in reduced operating budgets for central city schools. Central city schools, like their suburban counterparts, are struggling to close unneeded school buildings and reduce the size of the teaching staff in line with falling enrollment, but a variety of obstacles make this difficult to accomplish very quickly (Casserly and Kober 1990).

One solution is for the state to take more of the financial responsibility for public education and to pay 50 percent or more of the school bill. Most states have reviewed or are reviewing their school finance arrangements, in many cases, such as California and New Jersey, because courts have required them to reduce inequities in per pupil expenditure levels. The general trend has been toward a school finance formula that brings about power equalization in the sense that impoverished districts with tax rates set above a designated minimum level receive additional state funds so that per pupil expenditures approach those of wealthier districts (Hollifield 1990).

However, this basic reform in state school finance arrangements generally does not address the differential caused by higher costs and special needs in central city districts (Ascher 1989). Equality in per pupil expenditures does not take into account the factors leading to significantly higher per pupil needs in the central city. Federal funds for compensatory education and instructional improvement provide central city schools with some of the additional money they need for these and other purposes; but as noted above, the financial condition of many city school districts remains precarious.

In addition, depressed economic conditions and reductions in federal funding for elementary and secondary schools further magnified the financial problems of central city school districts in the 1980s. St. Lous, for example, lost 86 percent of its federal funding between 1982 and 1983. Reduced federal appropriations for education in 1982 resulted in an average reduction of 16 percent in the total operating budget of twenty-eight of the nation's largest school districts and in elimination or curtailment of compensatory education services provided for several hundred thousand students in these districts. Problems involved in providing effective education in the big cities thus were intensified in Boston, New Orleans, Philadelphia, and other big cities (Roberts 1982; Casserly and Kober 1990).

CONCLUSION

Low-status students face many problems in the schools in addition to initial learning disadvantages associated with their home and family background. Problems of teaching and learning in working with low-status students include inappropriate curriculum and instruction, lack of parental and peer reinforcement of school norms and learning experiences, loss of motivation associated with lack of previous success in school, teachers' lack of preparation for solving the learning and behavior problems of low achieving students, teacher perceptions of student inadequacy, homogeneous grouping of low achieving students, ineffective delivery of instructional services, and low standards of performance.

These problems begin to be apparent in the earliest grades in school and generate a cycle of failure characterized by poor academic performance, low or inaccurate self-concept as a learner, and lack of a sense that one can succeed in school by trying harder in the future. Implications for instruction include the conclusion that

schools must provide structured success experience for low-status students. Because low-status students tend to lack essential academic skills, some "direct" instruction should be provided to develop these skills. Research on teaching low-status students supports this conclusion, but theory and research also suggest that additional goals such as development of self-directed learning skills, enhancement of conceptual skills through an inquiry approach to learning, and appropriate matching of teaching methods with students' conceptual level must be given much attention in working to improve the academic performance of low-status students.

Schools in concentrated poverty neighborhoods confront teaching and learning problems that are even more difficult to solve than those in other low-status schools or classrooms. Evidence from research in a number of big cities suggests that academic performance in concentrated poverty schools almost always is very low, possibly because the schools and other social institutions in these neighborhoods are unable to function effectively in the face of multiple problems that exceed their capacity to handle successfully. Violence in a variety of manifestations including assaults on students and teachers, operation of gangs in and around the schools, and invasion by intruders and trespassers makes the teaching and learning environment even more difficult than in other low-status schools. For reasons such as these, there is a real question whether compensatory education can be made to work effectively in inner-city neighborhoods in the absence of successful efforts to improve general economic and social opportunities, reduce social disorganization, and deconcentrate the poverty population that lives there.

Many efforts have been made throughout the United States to improve the academic performance of low-status students in general and inner-city students in particular. These efforts have had some success at the preschool, elementary, intermediate, secondary, and postsecondary levels. However, the general level of achievement among low-status students is still inadequate, particularly among students in concentrated poverty schools.

A number of problems, including value disagreements, high costs, and inadequate information for key policy decisions, make it difficult to work out and implement a comprehensive program for compensatory education. This goal is particularly difficult to attain in a large, relatively decentralized country like the United States, where most educational decisions are made at the local level and a tradition of individualism conflicts with some actions that might have to be taken to make compensatory education effective on a carefully planned and sequenced national basis. The United States is still far from having attained a rational system of compensatory education wherein each child who needs massive ecological intervention receives it in the early years, thereby minimizing the costs of school-age programs later, and appropriate funding and alternatives are available to ensure that effective compensatory education is provided at each educational level from preschool through postsecondary.

EXERCISES

1. If data are available on achievement in a nearby big-city school district, examine the results to determine whether a threshold effect appears to be operating. In addition to reasons listed in this chapter, what other causes could help account for the threshold effect? How would one go about determining whether these causes actually are present in low-status schools?

2. Read Jonathan Kozol's *Death at an Early Age* or James Herndon's *The Way It Spozed to Be*, both of which describe the experience of relatively successful inner-city teachers, and make a list of the understandings and abilities needed to be successful in teaching in an inner-city school.

3. In what ways and situations would high self-concept as a learner probably contribute to improved academic performance as a learner? When might high self-concept contribute to poor performance? What, if anything, do you think educators should do to improve the academic self-concept of low-status students?

4. In recent years, there has been a trend to place learning-handicapped students in regular classrooms (i.e., "least restrictive environments") as much as possible, while gifted and talented students more frequently are separated in special classes or learning activities. Are these trends in conflict? Why are these differing grouping arrangements frequently prescribed for "slow" and "fast" students? What do you think is the best policy for each group?

5. It is sometimes said that by the time a child enters school it is "too late" to make any real changes in his or her personality. A teacher may say, especially of a lower-class child, "I can't undo what the family has done." Do you agree with this point of view, generally speaking? Why or why not?

6. What are the main arguments for and against spending more money for compensatory education at the secondary level? Interview local school officials to find out how effective such programs have been in nearby schools.

7. Make a list of the most important actions or guidelines needed to make compensatory education effective. Visit a school that receives Chapter 1 funding and analyze its programs in terms of your list of guidelines.

8. If a nearby school district has a compensatory education program for economically disadvantaged students under Chapter 1 of the Elementary and Secondary Education Act, ask to see the evaluation reports that have been submitted to the federal government. Has any progress been reported in raising the achievement of eligible

students? If yes, what types of programs or program elements seem to have been effec- tive? How do these results fit with the data and conclusions in this chapter?

SUGGESTIONS FOR FURTHER READING

1. Much of Bronfenbrenner's review of re- search regarding the effectiveness of com- pensatory education is easily accessible in his article titled "Is Early Intervention Ef- fective?" which appeared in the October 1974 issue of the *Teachers College Record*.

2. *Reforming Metropolitan Schools* by Orn- stein, Levine, and Wilkerson includes a chapter on the history of compensatory ed- ucation in the United States and an analysis of the most important issues the schools have encountered in trying to implement it.

3. An excellent short summary of the research on Follow Through is available in Mary M. Kennedy's paper describing the problems encountered in carrying out and evaluating the program.

4. Wesley C. Becker's paper on "Teaching Reading and Language to the Disadvan- taged: What We Have Learned from Field Research" includes a description of the DISTAR program and discusses ways to ex- tend direct instruction methods in improv- ing the achievement of disadvantaged stu- dents. Much of what was learned in the Follow Through program has been summa- rized in W. Ray Rhine's *Making Schools More Effective: New Directions from Follow Through*.

5. The functioning—and dysfunctioning—of inner-city high schools are convincingly de- scribed and analyzed in *Getting What We Ask For* by Charles Payne. Mary Haywood Metz (1986) and James Herndon (1968) each describe comparable situations at inner-city elementary and middle schools.

6. *Implementing Mastery Learning* by Guskey (1985) is written primarily by teachers and administrators who may want to use mastery learning. *Improving Student Achievement through Mastery Learning Programs* edited by Levine (1985) provides information on the theory and practice of mastery learning and includes case studies dealing with im- plementation at inner-city schools.

7. *Educating Urban Minority Youth* by Kathleen Cotton (1991) summarizes much of the re- search on effective education for disadvan- taged minority students.

8. A recent yearbook (Kagan 1991) of the Na- tional Society for the Study of Education is devoted to early childhood education both in and outside school settings.

9. Major sections of *Better Schooling for the Children of Poverty* (Knapp and Shields 1991) deal with literacy, mathematics, class- room management, and broad educational issues.

10. The January 30 1992 issue of *Black Issues in Higher Education* focuses on programs and approaches to help disadvantaged minority students.

Desegregation

In 1954 the U.S. Supreme Court ruled in *Brown* v. *Topeka Board of Education* that "separate but equal has no place" in education, and that government-imposed or government-supported segregation unconstitutionally violates the rights of black students. Effects of the *Brown* decision soon became apparent in many areas of U.S. society, including voting, employment, and all public services. After Rosa Parks refused in 1955 to sit at the back of a bus in Montgomery, Alabama, protests against segregation were launched in many parts of the nation. Reverend Martin Luther King, Jr., along with other civil rights leaders, emerged to challenge deep-seated patterns of racial discrimination. Fierce opposition to civil rights made the headlines in the late 1950s and early 1960s as dogs and fire hoses were sometimes used to disperse peaceful demonstrators. After three civil rights workers were murdered in Mississippi, the U.S. Congress passed the 1964 Civil Rights Act and other legislation that attempted to guarantee equal protection under the laws for minority citizens.

STATUS OF SCHOOL DESEGREGATION

The history of public-school desegregation since 1954 can be divided into three major phases. Little desegregation was accomplished during the first phase through about 1965. Much desegregation was accomplished in the South and in smaller cities and towns during the second phase, between 1966 and 1973. Since 1973, some progress has continued to be made outside the largest cities, and desegregation plans in big cities with many segregated minority students have included an increasing emphasis on improvement of instruction, particularly for minority students in segregated schools.

The courts have been petitioned by parents and civil rights organizations to step in and order desegregation of the schools in ways that will be helpful to minority racial and ethnic groups. There is a language problem here, since the so-called minority groups that need assistance are mainly African American and Hispanic or Spanish-speaking children. These are minority groups in terms of national population, but generally they are segregated locally so that they are majorities in many schools. The white children are really in the majority of the national school population, but they are a minority of students in many schools that are mainly black or Hispanic.

Our practice in this book, as in the literature on school desegregation, is generally to use the term *minority* to refer to nonwhite children and to Hispanic children, and to refer to white children of the majority group as *nonminority* or sometimes as non-Hispanic white.

Phase I: 1954–1965

The Supreme Court decision in the *Topeka* case rested in part on the argument that segregation had damaging psychological effects on black children, even when the school facilities themselves were supposedly equal to those of white schools. The consensus of social scientists was that segregation of blacks has been an obstacle to their competence in an urban, industrial, democratic society. This conclusion was based on research on the social psychology of race relations (summarized by Katz 1964), which indicated that where the races are systematically segregated, black children thereby learn that they cannot expect to be treated as equals by most white people. This proposition, when read today, has a dated quality. It reflects the thinking that prevailed at the time of the Supreme Court decision of 1954. The economic and educational situation of the black population has changed so much during the 1960s, 1970s, and 1980s that a substantially different set of propositions has now come to the forefront. These propositions are developed in this chapter.

Initially, after 1954, the focus of attention by educators and by government officials was on the process of desegregation. There were two aspects of this problem—*de jure* segregation and *de facto* segregation. *De jure* segregation refers to segregation brought about in one way or another by government action. This was clearly the situation in southern states, where state laws long prevented white and black children from attending the same schools. *De facto* segregation is caused by private decisions rather than government action. This is one major cause of the problem in big cities, where, because most blacks live in segregated housing areas, many schools are attended entirely by black children.

Although the Supreme Court in 1955 ordered school districts to desegregate with "all deliberate speed," desegregation proceeded slowly (National Research Council 1989). The U.S. Office of Education reported that at the beginning of the 1965 school year, at most only 7.5 percent of black students in the South were attending schools with white children. In most parts of the North and West, some black students who lived in integrated neighborhoods continued to attend desegregated schools, but there was little additional desegregation because the official policy in most school districts was that the schools should be "color blind." This meant that the school system would take no formal notice of the color of pupils or teachers but would strive to do the best job possible of educating all children in accordance with their needs and abilities.

Phase II: 1966–1973

The second phase of desegregation was a period during which much desegregation was accomplished in the South (National Research Council 1989). At the same time, major efforts were begun elsewhere to improve public schools for economically disadvantaged students regardless of their race.

The major legislative forces were the Civil Rights Act of 1964 and the Elementary and Secondary Education Act of 1965, which together gave government officials and public school educators a great deal of power. The Civil Rights Act of 1964, among other things, required all state and local agencies as well as private persons or agencies *who receive federal government funds* to give written assurance that "no person shall be excluded from participation, denied any benefits, or subjected to discrimination on the basis of race, color, or national origin." The requirement that school systems receiving any federal payments must submit "assurance of compliance" with the law had the effect of stimulating desegregation in the schools.

The Deep South.   Given these new legislative changes, most school systems of the South had begun the process of integration by 1966. The *New York Times* of September 4, 1965, reported, "Under the threat of a loss of Federal assistance, the South is admitting probably 7 percent of its Negro children to classes with white children this fall—a percentage that compares reasonably with the national average. And for the first time school desegregation has come to the Black Belt and to hundreds of rural southern towns, with virtually no violence or resistance." Faculty desegregation also got under way in some southern cities.

Border and Northern Cities.   The drive for desegregation in the border cities and northern and western industrial cities also was accelerated in this period. Civil rights organizations joined together and were aided by federated church groups acting through such agencies as a Council on Religion and Race. Civic organizations became involved. The most prominent domestic issue in the country during this period was the issue of change in the schools. Most big cities saw school boycotts aimed at inducing the board of education to take more active measures to hasten desegregation.

The majority of school boards, while issuing statements saying that they favored integrated school experience for as many pupils as possible, added, however, that there were limits beyond which the school system would not go in fostering integration. They said the major limiting factor was the "neighborhood school policy," which places a high priority on the pupil's attending school near home. Because the big cities have a great deal of residential (i.e., *de facto*) segregation by race, the neighborhood school policy makes it difficult to get integrated schools, especially at the elementary level (National Research Council 1989).

Nevertheless, during the latter half of the 1960s, the more positive forms of integrative procedure were being pushed forward and tried in some locations. This was partly due to a mounting series of court decisions, for after 1965 the courts were increasingly throwing their weight against *de facto* segregation or were beginning to define government action such as building new schools in segregated neighborhoods as *de jure* segregation. In New York and New Jersey, the courts upheld the actions of school boards in fixing boundary lines of schools so as to produce an ethnic balance among students. In 1965, Massachusetts went further than any other state had gone up to that time by passing a law aimed at the *elimination* of racial imbalance in the public schools.

In spite of efforts made in a number of cities to reduce segregation, the proportions of African American pupils in schools that were all-black or nearly so continued to increase and the black population became more densely concentrated. Between 1950 and 1980 the black population increased between 100 and 300 percent in New York, Chicago, Los Angeles, Oakland, Detroit, Boston, and other cities. It simply was not possible to get a racial balance in more than a few of the schools in these large cities, unless mass transportation of as many as a third of the pupils was to be undertaken. The migration of white families to the edges of the cities and to the suburbs was defeating the policy of school desegregation.

Small Cities. Many small cities successfully desegregated their schools as students from formerly segregated schools were reassigned to schools with a stable racial balance. An example of this type of city is Evanston, Illinois, a predominantly middle-class suburb north of Chicago. The black minority in Evanston was less than 25 percent—large enough to fill several elementary schools before desegregation was carried out. Many black families in Evanston are working-class families whose adult members work at nearby industrial plants that employ a large part of the local population. Few, however, are lower-working class, and the median income for black families in Evanston in the 1960s was about double that of all black families in the United States. Thus, cities like Evanston did not have the high concentrations of very low-status minority students as did many of the big cities.

Phase III: 1974–1992

During the third phase of desegregation, emphasis shifted significantly to large urban school districts. Much desegregation had been accomplished successfully in the South and in small cities and towns throughout the nation, but desegregation of minority students in big cities was relatively uncommon and segregation was increasing as their minority population increased (Taeuber 1990).

Much of the impetus toward desegregation efforts in urban school districts with widespread *de facto* segregation was supplied in 1973 by the U.S. Supreme Court's decision in *Keys* v. *School District No. 1, Denver.* Plaintiffs charged that the school board had followed policies that intentionally brought about segregation (i.e., *de jure* segregation caused by foreseeable government action) in the Park Hill section of Denver. They also argued that segregation of black and Hispanic students in some schools and of non-Hispanic whites in others throughout the district was caused partly by the segregated patterns originating in Park Hill and partly by "purposeful and systematic" action of the school board. Where there has been intentional segregation of students in "substantial" portions of a district, they concluded, it is likely that segregation throughout the district is intentional, if only in the sense that the school board could have taken action to reduce or eliminate segregated attendance patterns.

Even though the Supreme Court did not directly rule that *de facto* segregation is unconstitutional, it did accept much of the plaintiffs' argument and concluded that clear evidence of intentional segregation in one part of a district suggests that other instances of segregation also are intentional. In ordering district-wide reassignment of students in Denver, the Supreme Court provided a spur for desegregation suits in other cities in which it could be shown—as it usually can—that there has been some intentional segregation that helped generate or reinforce larger patterns of residential segregation.

The situation with respect to desegregation of black students is shown in Table 9-1, which reports U.S. Department of Education surveys of racial and ethnic enrollments. Table 9-1 shows less segregation of black students in the South than in other parts of the United States. This condition is the result of school districts' actions in the southern states to combine formerly all-black and all-white schools into mixed schools that reflect the local population ratios. Because many schools were in rural counties that had long transported pupils by bus, there was no major change in the school-attendance routine for most families except that the children would now attend a biracial school. As Table 9-1 shows, 43 percent of the southern black pupils attended schools in 1984 where they were in the minority. During the 1970s and 1980s, all regions except the Northeast reduced segregation of black students to some degree. The Northeast, with many large urban concentrations of black population, increased in segregation and is the most heavily segregated region in the United States. Gary Orfield examined these data and concluded that "as the United States becomes an increasingly multiracial society, racial segregation remains the prevailing pattern in most regions with significant minority populations. Progress in desegregation for blacks in the South is offset by increasing segregation in the North" (1982, 9).

TABLE 9-1 *Percentages of Black Students in Public Elementary and Secondary Schools More Than 50 Percent and 90 Percent Minority, 1968 to 1984, by Region*

	Percentage of Black Students in Schools 50 Percent or More Minority			Percentage of Black Students in Schools 90 Percent or More Minority		
	1968	1976	1984	1968	1976	1984
National	77	62	64	64	36	33
9 Northeast states	67	73	73	43	51	47
11 Midwest states	77	70	71	58	51	44
11 West states	72	67	67	51	36	29
6 border states and DC	72	60	63	60	43	37
11 Southern states	81	55	57	78	22	24

Source: Orfield and Monfort 1987.

Note: National figures are for the continental United States (i.e., excluding Alaska and Hawaii). The definition of *minority* is the official federal classification, which includes the following groups: Black (Negro); American Indian; Spanish-surnamed; Portuguese; Asian (Oriental); Alaskan; and Hawaiian.

As the percentage of Hispanic population in U.S. schools and society has increased during the past three decades, segregation of Hispanic students has become a growing problem for the educational system and the nation (Taeuber 1990). The percentage of Hispanic students in public school enrollment increased from 5 percent in 1968 to 9 percent in 1984, while the percentage of non-Hispanic white students declined from 80 percent to 71 percent. Increase in Hispanic enrollment was particularly pronounced in the western states, where the percentage of Hispanic students increased from 12 percent in 1968 to 21 percent in 1984 (Orfield 1987).

In tandem with the increase in Hispanic enrollment, the percentages of Hispanic students in schools more than half minority and more than 90 percent minority also steadily increased (see Table 9-2). By way of contrast, segregation of black students decreased substantially in the early 1970s and then held mostly steady (see Tables 9-1 and 9-2). Both patterns reflect the fact that Hispanic and black enrollment has become increasingly concentrated in large metropolitan areas, particularly in central city school districts that are most difficult to desegregate.

The problem of desegregating schools in the practical sense—that is, of putting white and minority pupils in the same school building with both groups having at least 20 to 30 percent of the enrollment—is now particularly a problem for the large cities, where residential segregation has developed to such an extent that a minority child who attends a neighborhood school is likely to be in a school that is nearly all black or Hispanic. Given the segregated housing patterns and the high percentages of minority students in many big-city school districts, most minority students in these locations still attend segregated schools. Possibilities for desegregation of students in big-city school districts are discussed more fully later in this chapter.

Development of Desegregation Planning

Another important development during the past two decades was the accumulation of knowledge concerning approaches to successful desegregation. Educators and researchers have learned a great deal about the types of programs and policies most likely to produce stable desegregation in which both minority and nonminority students benefit from integration in the school and classroom. Much of this knowledge has been summarized in papers by Willis Hawley and his colleagues (Hawley et al. 1982; Hawley 1983; Hawley and Smylie 1988) and by Carol Ascher (1990). These analysts have concluded that the following actions are particularly important in

TABLE 9-2 *Percentage of Black and Hispanic Students in Public Elementary and Secondary Schools More Than 50 Percent and 90 Percent Minority, 1968 to 1984*

| | Percentage in Schools More Than 50 Percent Minority | | Percentage in Schools More Than 90 Percent Minority | |
	Black Students	Hispanic Students	Black Students	Hispanic Students
1968	77	55	64	23
1972	64	57	39	23
1980	63	68	33	29
1984	64	71	33	31

Source: Orfield and Monfort 1987.
Note: National figures are for the continental United States (i.e., excluding Alaska and Hawaii). The definition of *minority* is the official federal classification, which includes the following groups: Black (Negro); American Indian; Spanish-surnamed; Portuguese; Asian (Oriental); Alaskan; and Hawaiian.

designing and implementing effective pupil reassignment plans:

- Begin desegregation as early as possible.
- Provide educational options within and among schools.
- Enrich and improve instruction in all schools.
- Implement a plan for all ages of children at one time rather than phase in desegregation at different educational levels.
- Take account of special needs (e.g., bilingual education, development of pride in one's culture) of different racial and ethnic groups.
- Encourage stability in student-student and teacher-student relationships, and otherwise reduce or eliminate uncertainties parents have about where their children will attend school and who will be responsible for their education.
- Provide a safe school environment.
- Retain a "critical mass" (15 to 20 percent) of students of any racial or ethnic group at a given school.
- Allow the percentage of minority population to vary in accordance with the nature of residential patterns and other factors.

Considerations that were cited as helping to improve achievement and race relations as part of a desegregation plan included the following:

- Create schools and instructional groupings within schools of limited size that provide a supportive environment in which teachers know students personally and can provide continuity in learning.
- Develop multiethnic curricula.
- Make human relations a fundamental component involving everything that is done in a school.
- Maximize direct parental involvement in the education of their children.
- Discourage interstudent competition while holding high and attainable expectations for individual students.
- Maintain discipline through clear rules of student behavior that are consistently and fairly enforced.
- Maximize participation in extracurricular programs that provide opportunities for interracial interaction.

DESEGREGATION GOALS AND OBSTACLES

The desegregation programs and procedures ordered by courts or by state or local boards of education, and some of the problems connected with them, can be summarized as follows:

1. *Racial isolation and racial balance*. There should not be one-race schools. Local school boards should draw school boundary lines to achieve a mixture of students from various racial and ethnic groups. There is no universal definition of a *one-race school*, but in some districts the courts have ruled that schools that are 80 or 90 percent or more minority or nonminority are one-race schools that must be eliminated through all practicable means, including reassignment of students. This must be done even though the arrangements to eliminate segregation may seem administratively "bizarre," as in the 1971 court case of *Swann* v. *Charlotte-Mecklenburg Board of Education*.

In seeking to eliminate one-race schools, judges frequently have required a more balanced racial composition than is found in a school 80 percent or more minority or nonminority. Some courts have required that each school be within about 15 percent of the districtwide racial composition. Applying this guideline in a school district that has 55 percent minority students, each school must have between 40 and 70 percent minority students. The federal executive branch, particularly the Department of Education, the Department of Health and Human Services, the Justice Department, and the Office of Civil Rights, is obligated to work toward the elimination of segregation in accordance with laws passed by Congress and the rulings of the courts. No school district may receive federal funds if it is not in compliance with constitutional mandates for desegregation.

It is clear that in a big-city school system where the school population has a majority of black and Hispanic pupils, such as Chicago or Los Angeles, there are severe limits on the extent of desegregation practicable. Such a school system will continue to have many one-race schools unless desegregation is carried out on a regional or metropolitan basis including suburban schools (Taeuber 1990).

2. *Increase in segregation.* The percentage of minority students in many school districts has been steadily increasing for decades. Due to white suburbanization, minority migration to urban areas, and other factors, schools in some districts first have been desegregated and then have become resegregated as nonminority enrollment decreased and minority enrollment held steady or increased. As noted elsewhere in this chapter, there also is reason to believe that desegregation sometimes has accelerated white and middle-class withdrawal in school districts with a high percentage of low-status, minority students (Coleman 1990a). Thus, steps that have been taken to desegregate the public schools frequently have been only temporarily successful.

In 1976, the Supreme Court ruled in *Pasadena City Board of Education* v. *Spangler* that school districts do not have to take new action each year to desegregate schools that have become resegregated following implementation of a constitutionally acceptable desegregation plan. As long as the population shifts that cause resegregation are not attributable to segregative action on the part of the school system, the system need not take continuous action to maintain racial balance.

3. *White flight.* The Supreme Court has said that school district desegregation plans must "promise realistically to work." School officials frequently have tried to minimize student reassignment and transportation on the grounds that larger efforts would result in the withdrawal of whites and thereby defeat the purposes of desegregation. The courts generally have been alert to the possibility that potential white flight will be used as an excuse to avoid desegregation and have insisted that the right of minority students to attend desegregated schools should not depend on whether desegregation is convenient for nonminority students or on the cooperation of families that threaten to leave the schools if constitutional guarantees are extended to minorities. The counter-arguments on this issue have led to a delicate legal and practical balance: school district officials are allowed to take the possibility of white withdrawal into account in formulating a desegregation plan which has a reasonable chance to succeed, but this possibility cannot be the only major consideration in determining the extent to which busing or other techniques will be used to desegregate the schools.

The outcome of these difficult legal decisions has been considerable uncertainty regarding the types of court-ordered desegregation plans appropriate in big-city school districts. One type of relatively comprehensive plan has been put into effect in Boston, Denver, Memphis, and several other cities where courts have ruled that nearly every school must be within 10 to 20 percent (depending on the city) of the overall racial composition of the district, even if this requires extensive pupil reassignment and transportation. At the other end of the continuum, courts have allowed Dallas, Houston, and some other cities to implement plans involving much less student reassignment, with substantial numbers of schools remaining one-race on the grounds that additional desegregation would be impractical. Most one-race schools remaining in this latter situation are minority schools, because courts generally require action to desegregate schools that have a preponderance of nonminority students.

During the first half of the 1970s, big-city desegregation orders appeared to be going in the direction of the first type of plan. Recognizing that millions of minority youngsters still attended segregated schools, the courts along with concerned officials at various levels of government tended to push for the complete desegregation of big-city school districts. In general, it was not difficult to show that government action had played a major part in segregating the schools, and courts in a number of locations ordered the implementation of comprehensive plans to eliminate these patterns "root and branch." Boston's comprehensive plan was implemented in the fall of 1975, and similarly comprehensive plans were introduced in San Francisco, Denver, and other cities.

At the same time, however, the potential pitfalls of implementing extensive student reassignment plans in big cities with a high proportion of minority students also were becoming clear. Analysis of desegregation plans in Detroit and some other cities suggests that large-scale reassignment of students sometimes would involve the transportation of minority students from schools 90 percent or more minority to schools 60 to 90 percent minority, with unclear benefits for any of the participants. Recognizing the dilemma, many desegregation planners systematically began to reexamine the possibilities and prospects for big-city school desegregation (Armor 1988; Rossell 1990a).

In this context, viewpoints regarding alternatives for big-city desegregation were undergoing inevitable change. On the one hand, it was apparent that the courts could and sometimes did take a legalistic approach to desegregation. The constitution would be satisfied either by making the racial composition in each school similar to the district as a whole or by reassigning students such that every minority student was enrolled in a school with 10 percent or more nonminority students assigned to it. White or middle-class families might continue to withdraw from schools with a majority of minority and working-class students thus assigned to them, leaving working-class minority students still more racially and economically isolated, but the courts and other government bodies could then walk away from the problem because the constitution had been upheld.

On the other hand, it was apparent that less extensive student reassignment plans also would leave many working-class minority students racially and economically isolated, and that other alternatives would have to be pursued if segregation and stratification were to be reduced. For example, magnet schools might be helpful in retaining white or middle-class students in big-city schools, and desegregation pursued on a metropolitan basis would be more stable than plans limited to the central city (see below). Armor (1988) and Rossell (1990a) have reviewed the research on white withdrawal from school districts undergoing desegregation and concluded that mandatory desegregation can accelerate the withdrawal of nonminority students, particularly in larger school districts with accessible white suburbs. Acceleration of white withdrawal is most pronounced in large central city districts in which there is a high concentration of minority students and the desegregation plan calls for substantial two-way busing of students. Recent research (Ascher 1990; Rossell 1990) indicates that voluntary plans including magnet schools and other nonmandatory components can bring about more desegregation than do large-scale mandatory plans.

4. *Mandatory busing.* During the 1970s, many big-city desegregation programs were going in the direction of extensive pupil reassignment to schools often some distance from the local neighborhood school and requiring transportation by bus as much as half an hour or more one way. There was a growing opposition to mandatory busing on the part of parents and also of many members of the general public. An example of this was the referendum called for in California by a member of the California legislature. This referendum called for an amendment to the state constitution that would bar mandatory busing for the sake of desegregation. (However, federal courts could still require mandatory busing in California.) In 1979, voters approved the referendum by a large margin. However, civil rights organizations charged that such an amendment to the state constitution was contrary to the United States Constitution and appealed to the U.S. Supreme Court for a ruling.

The U.S. Supreme Court in 1982 ruled that the proposed amendment to the state constitution was acceptable under the U.S. Constitution. Also, at about the same time in the early 1980s, the United States Congress passed several laws that would deny federal government financial support for desegregation programs that included mandatory busing of students.

Thus, in the late 1970s and early 1980s, it became clear that additional assignment of pupils to schools outside of their own neighborhoods would not be widely supported by mandatory busing. Consequently, many districts that were highly segregated turned to a variety of procedures that were more acceptable to many pupils and their families and involved freedom of choice and voluntary transportation if distances of travel were great. In addition, while racial or ethnic desegregation was still emphasized in some programs, others placed equal or greater emphasis on improving the quality of instruction in segregated minority schools and/or desegregated schools (Hawley and Smylie 1988).

For example, court orders in Chicago, Detroit, Los Angeles, St. Louis, and several other cities placed as much or more emphasis on improving instruction in minority schools as on reassigning minority students to desegregated schools. In most cases, state government was required to pay half the cost of both the instructional improvement and the student reassignment components in this type of desegregation plan. Instructional improvement components of desegregation plans are discussed more fully later in this chapter.

Segregation and Resegregation within Schools

A different kind of obstacle to successful desegregation involves problems that result in maintenance or reappearance of segregation within schools that enroll both nonminority and minority students. In many cases schools have become desegregated in terms of building racial composition, but various indications of internal segregation and related problems still are present. Desegregation planner Perry Bates (1990) has identified some of these indicators, which require continuing work and vigilance to counteract, as follows:

- Counseling arrangements and practices that create classes that are entirely or mostly minority or nonminority.
- Grouping arrangements that create within-class subgroups that are entirely or mostly minority or nonminority.
- Extracurricular and cocurricular policies and practices that create or allow segregation in honor societies, athletics, cheerleading, school-sponsored clubs, and other activities.
- Disproportionate and sometimes discriminatory suspension or expulsion of minority students.
- Assignment of faculty to courses or other duties according to race or ethnicity.

Socioeconomic Mixture and Middle-Class Withdrawal

Figure 9-1 shows the social compositions of three general types of high schools. School A is a typical high school in a town or small city that has only one high school; it therefore receives all the children of secondary school age. Most of the students are lower-middle and upper working-class, but there also are significant numbers of upper, middle and lower working-class students.

School B is a high school in an upper middle-class suburb, where there are very few working-class people. This type of school is sometimes called a "comprehensive" high school because it offers several curricula, including commercial and vocational courses, but it is not representative in the sense that its students represent a cross section of the social structure.

School C is a big-city high school with mostly working-class students. It serves a community in which there are no upper middle- and only a few lower middle-class families. In such an area there may be a majority of lower working-class residents, but since their children tend to drop out of school early, the composition of the high school shows a preponderance of pupils from upper working-class homes.

There is probably a critical point involving the socioeconomic mixture of most big-city schools, a point at which middle-class parents are likely to become anxious and will consider removing their children from the school and moving to a higher-status area. If the proportion of working-class students increases beyond this point, middle-class parents may fear there will be a drop in the academic standards of the school, or changes in curricular offerings, or unwelcome influences on their own children's motivation for school achievement (Roth 1990).

We should note that such attitudes on the part of parents are not altogether unfounded. A study by Wilson (1959) supports the generalization that when student bodies vary in their proportions of middle and working class, students develop different educational and vocational aspirations. The study showed that in predominantly lower-status schools, *higher*-status children have lower educational and occupational aspirations than in predominantly higher-status schools, and in predominantly higher-status schools, *lower*-status children have higher aspirations than in predominantly lower-status schools. Wilson says, "The *de facto* segregation brought about by concentrations of social classes in cities results in schools with unequal moral climates which likewise affect the motivation of the

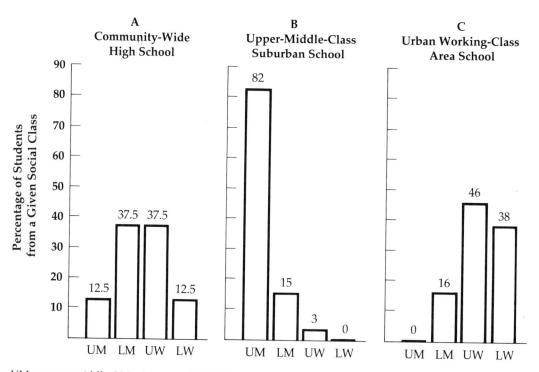

UM = upper-middle; LM = lower-middle; UW = upper-working; LW = lower-working

FIGURE 9-1   *Social Class Composition of Various Types of Secondary Schools* (Source: *Authors' estimates.*)

child . . . by providing a different ethos in which to perceive values" (Wilson 1959, 845).

The point at which a school becomes undesirable in the eyes of middle-class parents is subjective and variable, depending on the attitudes and experience of a particular parent, and depending also on such factors as the tradition of the school, the racial composition of the school, the type of curriculum, and the quality of the teachers. However, in practice there seems to be relative consensus among middle-class parents on the question of when a school becomes a "poor" school and when they begin to move out of the school district. As this happens in big-city school districts, a higher proportion of the schools become predominantly working-class.

The phenomenon of middle-class withdrawal from schools that have a substantial number of working-class students appears to be as characteristic of black neighborhoods as of white neighborhoods. One primary reason that middle-class black families have been moving to the suburbs has been to remove their children from concentrated poverty schools and neighborhoods (Wolman 1976; Boyd 1991). Middle-class black families that remain in the city frequently send their children to parochial or other nonpublic schools if there is no predominantly middle-class public school nearby (Walsh 1991).

White Withdrawal from Desegregated Schools

Just as middle-class families rapidly withdraw their children from schools they perceive are becoming predominantly working-class, nonminority families (i.e., non-Hispanic white families) tend to withdraw their children from schools that have a substantial proportion of minority students. These two tendencies frequently are difficult to disentangle, because many minority students are from working-class families and because nonminority parents often have confused socioeconomic status and race, that is, they have assumed that minority students entering their children's schools are from lower working-

class homes. However, the two phenomena can be distinguished both conceptually and in practice, as is shown by some cases in which middle-class black families withdraw from schools with an increasing proportion of working-class students and other cases in which working-class nonminority families withdraw from schools that have become racially balanced.

There is some uncertainty concerning the possible existence of a so-called tipping point at which schools that are growing in minority percentage tend to become rapidly resegregated. Some studies such as one conducted in Kansas City by Levine and Meyer (1977) have indicated that big-city schools that reach about 30 percent in minority enrollment subsequently tend to become resegregated at a rapid rate, but other studies such as one in Baltimore (Stinchcombe, Medill, and Walker 1969) suggest that schools with a small percentage of minority students subsequently experience continuing nonminority withdrawal with no discernible point at which to prevent the segregation of big-city schools.

However, most big cities also have had a few schools with a relatively stable minority percentage ranging from 30 to as much as 70 percent, indicating that it is possible to prevent the segregation of big-city schools. As in the case of socioeconomic integration, much depends on such aspects of the situation as the degree to which parents have confidence that the student composition of local schools will remain stable, the availability of alternatives such as private schools or affordable housing in the suburbs, and the leadership of educators in maintaining attractive instructional programs (Ascher 1990b).

It is certain, however, that middle-class families still were leaving schools in many big cities during the 1980s. In addition to unwillingness to send their children to working-class schools, middle-class families leave big-city schools for a variety of reasons, including dissatisfaction with instructional offerings, deterioration of local neighborhoods, and general unhappiness with conditions in the city. In general, school and other government officials not only have failed to intervene effectively to stop this process of segregation and deterioration but in some ways have also aided it through policies that helped to concentrate low-status population in the central city.

INSTRUCTIONAL IMPROVEMENT COMPONENTS IN DESEGREGATION PLANS

The situation in the 1970s forced educators to define the goals of desegregation in larger terms. Emphasis began to be placed on improving instruction in an effort to reduce the achievement gap between minority and nonminority students and courts began to include more instructional components in desegregation plans designed to overcome the effects of past and current racial isolation of minority students. (Components of this kind frequently are referred to as *ancillary relief components*.) This trend was particularly apparent in the big cities, where it had become clear that many minority students would continue to attend predominantly minority schools in the absence of metropolitan remedies involving nonminority students outside the central city.

Judicial insistence on improvement of instruction as part of desegregation plans was particularly evident when Judge Robert E. DeMascio, Jr., issued a 1975 desegregation order requiring, among other things, that "the Detroit Board of Education and the General Superintendent . . . shall design, develop and institute a comprehensive instructional program for teaching reading and communication skills. Such educational program shall be characterized by excellence and shall be instituted in every school in the system." Judge DeMascio further ordered that the state government, which with the board of education was responsible for segregation in Detroit, should pay half the costs of carrying out the remedial program. The Supreme Court opinion upholding DeMascio's order said the Detroit schools had been so "pervasively and persistently segregated" that the constitutional violation could not be remedied by student reassignment alone.

Since 1975, Detroit has implemented a desegregation plan limited almost entirely to ancillary relief components designed primarily to improve instruction in predominantly minority schools. Major components have dealt respectively with reading, in-service training, guidance, testing, student conduct, bilingual education, vocational education, and school-community relations.

A good example of a central-city district attempting to implement an ambitious program of ancillary relief is Kansas City, Missouri, which designed many of the components in its first court order (1985) to improve the effectiveness of instruction. As shown in Table 9-3, ancillary relief components were designed to make funds available for individual school needs; reduce class size; provide additional staff development; expand summer school; meet state standards for art, music, physical education, libraries, and teacher planning time; conduct all-day kindergartens; carry out early childhood education; and improve capital facilities for the district's approximately 35,000 students. In general, these components were designed to enhance desegregation by making the district more effective and attractive.

EFFECTS AND OUTCOMES

There have been considerable disagreement and confusion concerning the effects of school desegregation on students. Some observers, including researchers familiar with the fairly extensive literature on this topic, firmly believe that desegregated schools provide an indispensable means for improving the achievement of minority students or for developing positive interracial attitudes. Others, also including researchers familiar with the literature, confidently state that desegregation either has not generally had positive effects or has not been shown to have positive effects. Conclusions differ a good deal according to one's selection and reading of the research and its meaning.

Achievement of Minority Students

In addition to the larger disagreement on whether desegregation has had a positive effect on the achievement of minority students, there

TABLE 9-3 *Ancillary Relief Components in the Three-Year Court Order for Desegregation of the Kansas City, Missouri, Public Schools, 1985–1987*

Component	Three-Year Expenditures
Discretionary school funds*	$17,175,000
Reduction in class size	12,000,000
Staff development	500,000
Summer school	1,131,500
Meet state standards**	5,207,750
All-day kindergarten	1,638,000
Early childhood development***	1,850,022
Capital improvements	27,000,000

Source: Eubanks and Levine 1987b

* Discretionary school funds to improve student achievement were provided for 1985–86 on the basis of $50,000 per school less than 90 percent black and $75,000 per school 90 or more percent black, with the respective allocations increasing to $125,000 and $100,000 per school in 1987–88.

** Standards addressed include minimal provisions for the highest State of Missouri classification with respect to art, music, and physical education teachers, libraries and librarians, and teacher planning time.

*** Early childhood development refers to a variety of preschool programs including expansion of Head Start–type activities, screening of young children for learning problems, and parental education to improve home learning environment.

has been a dispute over the reasons that achievement gains occur where they do appear to have been documented. Some observers believe that such gains are primarily or entirely due to socioeconomic mixture; achievement gains are brought about when low-status minority students attend schools with middle-status nonminority students. Other observers, however, believe that racial desegregation sometimes improves the achievement of minority students apart from the effects of socioeconomic desegregation. (It should be noted that most desegregation research deals with black students; very little deals specifically with Hispanics or other minorities.) Most researchers agree that desegregation has not harmed the achievement of nonminority students (Hawley and Smylie 1988), but it also should be noted that middle-status white parents generally withdraw their children from predominantly working-class schools in which their achievement might decline.

Disagreements regarding achievement effects underline the complexity and difficulty of school desegregation research. Problems arise in measuring and controlling for the effects of socioeconomic status, in distinguishing between students who improve in achievement and those who do not, in measuring changes that may be relatively small but meaningful over a one- or two-year period, in comparing results for students who participate in different types of desegregation settings (e.g., voluntary transfer programs or mandatory assignment; urban or rural), and in assessing gains in different subject areas such as reading or mathematics. Among these and many other methodological problems, probably the most important involves the comparison of results in situations in which desegregation has been well implemented with results in situations—probably the vast majority—in which little has been done to prepare teachers to work with students of diverse performance levels and backgrounds (National Research Council 1989).

Given these problems, it is not surprising that scholars have reached such differing conclusions concerning the achievement effects of desegregation. St. John (1975) carefully reviewed the major studies on school desegregation and concluded that due to methodological weaknesses and problems in data interpretation, one could not say that desegregation had been either successful or unsuccessful in terms of raising minority students' achievement. Weinberg (1977) also has analyzed this research and concluded that overall, desegregation does have a positive effect on minority achievement. Bradley and Bradley (1977) analyzed studies that had been reported through 1976 and concluded that there are "well designed" studies both supporting and disconfirming "the use of school desegregation as an intervention strategy" (p. 444). Their general conclusion was that "the data collected since 1959 regarding school desegregation has been inconsistent and inadequate" (p. 444).

A later review by Krol (1980) of 129 studies dealing with effects on minority-student achievement also raised questions about the effectiveness of desegregation. Krol concluded that even where desegregated minority students made greater achievement gains than did comparable groups of segregated students, these gains generally were small and not statistically significant.

However, Crain and Mahard (1982) also reviewed available research on desegregation effects and came to somewhat different conclusions. (To a substantial degree, conclusions in this type of research review frequently depend on the studies one selects as worth review, the methods used to assess them, interpretation of the research design and statistics in a given study, and other considerations.) After analyzing 93 studies reporting on 323 samples of black students, Crain and Mahard selected 45 that met the standards they had established for adequate research design. Their main conclusions included the following:

> Studies that avoided . . . [major] methodological errors show consistent results. We found positive effects of desegregation in 40 of 45 such studies. . . . the effect of desegregation, when measured properly, is a gain of about .3 standard deviations (about one grade-year). . . . The 93 studies of black achievement after desegregation were used to identify the most successful types of desegregation plans. These are metropolitan plans, either voluntary or mandatory, which result in schools that have a minority, but not a small minority, of black students—in the North, schools that are 10 to 20 percent black; in the South, schools that are 10 to 30 percent black. These estimates cannot be considered precise, but they clearly imply that schools should have a majority of white students and more than a token number of black students.
> . . . These findings are quite consistent . . . with the hypothesis that the benefits of desegregation are the result of socioeconomic desegregation. . . . [In addition, studies of His-

panic achievement suggest] that any low-income group will benefit academically from attending a school whose students are predominantly higher status, regardless of the ethnicity of either the higher-status or the lower-status group. (Crain and Mahard 1982, v, vi, 35)

Taking account of the reported discrepant research interpretations, it is not possible to offer either conclusive generalizations about desegregation or facile predictions that desegregation will improve the achievement of minority students in the future. However, in view of the facts that some well-designed studies have reported positive outcomes from desegregation and that desegregation typically has not been combined with effective systematic efforts to improve instruction for students of differing performance levels, we believe the research literature supports two conclusions.

1. Desegregation accompanied by instructional improvement efforts can be an effective technique for raising the achievement of low-status minority students. The National Evaluation of the Emergency School Aid Act (ESAA), which provided hundreds of millions of dollars to facilitate desegregation, has shown that some local ESAA projects were quite effective in improving both basic skills and school racial relations, though the success of those projects was obscured by the failure of other projects (Coulson 1976). This evaluation also indicated that successful programs had the following characteristics: there was a greater focus of resources on attaining the goals of the program; administrative leadership was stronger and more assertive; classroom lessons were more highly structured; parents were more heavily involved in the classroom; and administrators and teachers made greater efforts to promote positive interracial attitudes. Several of these characteristics resemble those identified in Chapter 8 as being required for successful compensatory education.

The similarity between characteristics of successful compensatory education and successful desegregation projects makes it difficult to determine whether desegregation has a separate impact beyond effectively implemented compensatory education. In addition, the finding that desegregation projects that were successful in raising achievement also tended to improve interracial attitudes may mean either that minority students who feel accepted in the school may become more motivated and improve in achievement or outstanding leadership accounts for both achievement gains and improvements in interracial attitudes. In view of these difficulties in interpretation, it probably is best to view desegregation as a condition facilitating the implementation of compensatory education or other instructional reforms.

This conclusion is congruent with the fact that compensatory education has not been very effective in concentrated poverty schools. Although some gains have been reported, for the most part achievement in concentrated poverty schools continues to be very low above the primary grades, regardless of whether their enrollment is white or black or integrated. Thus, positive effects of desegregation on minority students' achievement probably are due much more to socioeconomic mixture than to racial desegregation per se. Several major studies, such as a five-year experiment in Israeli elementary schools (Klein and Eshel 1980), indicate that socioeconomic desegregation *plus* instructional improvement can improve the achievement of low-status students.

2. However, it is possible that racial desegregation also can help improve minority achievement beyond the effects of socioeconomic desegregation. Arguments in favor of this conclusion depend on the premise that racial isolation has a negative effect on minority students' motivation separate from the effects of socioeconomic isolation among low-status students, perhaps by reinforcing feelings of powerlessness associated with racial segregation or by shielding minority students from competitive pressures that support high achievement among nonminority students. Supporting this conclusion, Anthony Pascal

(1977) reviewed the research on desegregation and found that even after socioeconomic status and previous achievement are taken into account, the "gains for minority students are real" (p. 4). However, Pascal also concluded that gains from racial desegregation per se are modest and contribute relatively little to narrowing the achievement gap between blacks and whites.

It should be emphasized that few scholars have concluded that desegregation without effective compensatory education can substantially eliminate achievement differences that exist between low-status minority students and higher-status nonminority students (National Research Council 1989). A typical estimate of the potential effect of desegregation is that offered by Pettigrew (1973), who believes desegregation by itself can close approximately only one-fourth of the achievement gap between minority and nonminority students. A similar estimate has been provided by Jencks and Mayer (1989). On the other hand, gains of this magnitude represent one or more years of achievement on standardized performance tests. For many students, such gains constitute the difference between functional literacy and illiteracy. It also should be kept in mind that contact with middle-status students frequently appears to have an important positive influence on the academic aspirations of low-status students. (Evidence for this conclusion is presented in Chapter 5 and elsewhere in this book.) Together with effective compensatory education programs beginning in the early years, desegregation may be an indispensable precondition for bringing about widespread improvement in the academic performance of low-status minority students, particularly above the elementary level, when peer dynamics and influences become increasingly important.

We also should emphasize that the impetus for desegregation does not depend primarily on whether research has demonstrated it has been consistently effective in raising minority achievement. Courts have reviewed the complicated and sometimes contradictory research on this topic, and judges have found the results as difficult to interpret as have other observers. Faced with this complex literature, judges have had little recourse but to begin from the starting point established in *Brown et al.* v. *Board of Education of Topeka, Kansas*, in 1954 and elaborated in subsequent Supreme Court decisions: state action that places minority students in segregated schools is unconstitutional because segregated schools are inherently unequal and discriminatory.

Interracial Attitudes and Relations

Research on the race-relations effects of school desegregation has not shown a consistent tendency for results to be positive. Schofield (1991) assessed nearly thirty years of research on this issue and reported that

> in general, the reviews of desegregation and intergroup relations were unable to come to any conclusion about what the probable effects of desegregation were. . . . Numerous studies found generally positive effects [but at least] as many found generally negative effects [and a] substantial number found mixed [effects or no effects at all] Thus, virtually all of the reviewers determined that few, if any, firm conclusions about the effects of desegregation on intergroup relations could be drawn. (Schofield 1991, 356)

However, as is true with respect to research on achievement effects, there is reason to believe that this conclusion understates the potential utility and efficacy of desegregation in improving interracial attitudes and relationships. Failure to find positive relationships frequently may be due to serious methodological and analytic problems in conducting this type of research (Schofield 1991). Equally important, desegregation typically has not been implemented very well, so it is not surprising that it has frequently been ineffective. In cases in which it has been well implemented, it frequently appears to have some positive effects in terms of interracial relationships (National Research Council 1989).

Recognizing this need to distinguish between successful and unsuccessful desegregation efforts and to determine why some are more successful than others, Forehand, Ragosta, and Rock (1977) conducted a systematic study to identify successful projects and the factors responsible for their success. Data for the study were obtained from a 1974 survey of 168 schools and a 1975 follow-up in 43 schools. Data collection methods included site visits and interviews to obtain information on successful school practices and problem-solving techniques. This examination of successful desegregated projects showed that these projects tended to have outstanding administrative leadership, achievement gains among minority students, and improved interracial attitudes and relationships. The study examined teaching and administrative practices in considerable depth and reported the following three major conclusions:

1. Low-status black students often attend desegregated schools characterized by negative teacher attitudes and by absence of teaching practices to improve race relations. At both the elementary and secondary levels, teacher attitudes toward race seemed to be the crucial determinant of white students' attitudes.

2. Successful schools have adopted specific practices and policies effective in improving race relations among students. Examples include use of multiracial curriculum materials, teaching of minority group history and culture, open classroom discussions on race, and assignment of black and white students to work and to play together in organized activities.

3. High schools that have good race relations tend to have principals supportive of both black and white teachers. A principal's impact in improving race relations results from leadership to adopt effective practices and policies and the effects this leadership has on teachers. This happens because principals' racial attitudes have a direct effect on the attitudes of teachers, and because desegregation appears to be most successful when the principal demands unbiased behavior of the staff.

It should be noted that these findings concerning the kinds of instructional practices that lead to successful school desegregation are well in line with decades of research in which social psychologists have identified some conditions necessary for producing positive attitude and behavior change as a result of intergroup or interracial contact (National Research Council 1989; Schofield 1991). Psychologist Gordon Allport and others have studied this issue in some detail and concluded that personal contact is much more important than is information in generating change in attitudes and behavior, but contact can have either positive or negative results depending on its nature and quality. Positive change (i.e., favorable toward members of other groups) is most likely to occur when contact is "equal status"; an "authority" and/or the social climate are in favor and promote it; the contact is sustained and intimate rather than fragmented and casual; it is pleasant and rewarding; and the members of interacting groups cooperate in functionally important activities or develop common goals or superordinate goals that are more important than individual goals (Amir 1969; Jones 1988; Grant 1990; Goleman 1991).

Desegregated schools provide an opportunity that did not previously exist for positive intergroup contact, but they also provide an opportunity for neutral or negative contact (Hallinan and Teixeira 1987; Grant 1990). Depending partly on the leadership in a school, contact may tend to be unpleasant or unrewarding for many students and teachers, and it may result in little meaningful interaction in working on common goals. In many situations, minority students enter desegregated schools or classrooms far below nonminority students in academic achievement, and partly as a result they may be placed in separate learning groups where there is relatively little personal contact. If low-achieving minority students are placed in desegregated classrooms, stereotypes and negative perceptions and self-perceptions regarding their ability may be reinforced rather than alleviated. Unless desegregation is implemented to avoid these outcomes, its effects on race relations and interracial attitudes may be more negative than positive. Scott and McPartland (1982) have reviewed the research on this topic and concluded that "although desegregation under some conditions may foster more positive race relations, favorable conditions may not exist in all schools, in all classes of the same school, or for both races in the same class. . . . The different ways in which desegregation has been implemented and is practiced from one community to the next virtually insures that the quality and amount of face-to-face contact cannot be predicted from racial composition alone" (pp. 399–400).

Scott and McPartland also examined data from the National Assessment of Educational Progress 1976 survey of nine-, thirteen-, and seventeen-year-olds, in order to identify relationships between desegregation and interracial attitudes. Racial tolerance was assessed with items inquiring about willingness to engage in interracial contact. They found that despite vast differences in implementation of desegregation among schools in this national sample, desegregation is positively associated with racial tolerance for both blacks and whites. They also found that although both black and white nine-year-olds responded less tolerantly than did the older students, desegregation had a stronger relationship with tolerance among the younger students.

Researchers have been working to develop systematic approaches for achieving the goals of desegregated education. By organizing instruction and other school activities to bring about equal status contact and cooperative work on common educational goals, they hope to generate positive interracial interrelationships and also to improve the achievement of low-achieving students who otherwise tend to be frustrated by competitive practices of the traditional classroom (National Research Council 1989). For example, Aronson and Gonzalez (1988) report that a classroom technique called the jigsaw method, in which students work interdependently as members of teams, increases the academic achievement of black and Mexican-American students. Rosenholtz (1977) found that the self-fulfilling prophecy wherein students low in reading performance tend to withdraw from instruction and hence continue to perform poorly can be altered by a "multiple abilities curriculum" wherein every student is provided with some degree of competence in at least one skill and is expected to improve in subsequent performance. Emphasis in the multi-ability classroom involved the installation of groupwork, task activities that do not make reading a prerequisite for success, use of multi-ability definitions of the situation, individualization of academic tasks, private evaluation of students, and reduction in comparative and competitive marking and grading. Cohen (1980, 1986, 1990) reported that use of small groups and multi-ability activities has led to a dramatic increase in the classroom participation rates of low-achieving students in desegregated classrooms.

Much work along these lines also has been done by Robert E. Slavin and his colleagues at the Center for Social Organization of Schools at Johns Hopkins University, where researchers are developing the Teams–Games–Tournament (TGT) approach and the Student Teams–Achievement Divisions (STAD) approach for equalizing probability of success in learning. Using the TGT approach, students compete as individuals to contribute points to their teams in three-person competitive situations in which the highest three students in past performance compete with each other, the three next highest compete with each other, and so on. Using the STAD approach, team points are earned based on competitions in which student scores on twice-weekly quizzes are compared to the scores of other students of similar performance. Thus, both TGT and STAD contain a (cooperative) team component and a comparison-among-equals component. Slavin (1977b) described an experiment using STAD in a 70 percent black junior high school in Baltimore in which black student achievement was improved more markedly than white student achievement. He speculated that this difference may have been due to a tendency

for black participants to be lowest in social class and for low-status students to be more peer oriented than are middle-status students.

Slavin also conducted a comparative study (1977a) in three junior high schools in which it was found that STAD methods were more effective than were control methods in increasing academic achievement, peer support for academic performance, liking of others, and number of students cited as friends. The study also indicated that there were team effects at the two schools that were overwhelmingly white but team effects were most apparent at the predominantly black working-class school. Slavin concluded that the "present study joins a steadily growing body of literature supporting the use of student teams in classrooms to achieve multiple outcomes, including increased time on task, academic performance, and most dramatically increased interpersonal attraction among class members . . . including friendships across racial lines" (p. 18).

These findings are not surprising inasmuch as research consistently indicates that cooperative learning arrangements in the public schools contribute to the improvement of student achievement and to the attainment of other goals, such as social development, positive school attitudes, and good interpersonal relationships (Brandt 1989/1990; Kagan 1989/1990; Johnson and Johnson 1990; Slavin 1980, 1989/1990, 1990b, 1991; Hilke 1990). David and Roger Johnson also have been studying cooperative learning arrangements and reached the following conclusions based on an analysis of available research: "Teaching students interpersonal small-group skills" through cooperative learning produces improvements in learning and thus can contribute subsequently to "greater employability and career success" (Johnson and Johnson 1989/1990, 32).

Opportunity Networks

Another major purpose of desegregation is to help minority youth enter so-called opportunity networks that can help them gain access to social and economic resources in mainstream society (Braddock and McPartland 1987; National Research Council 1989). Thomas Pettigrew of the University of California at Santa Cruz has summarized research on opportunity networks:

Labor economists . . . have long noted that blue-collar workers, clerical workers, engineers, lawyers, and even college professors typically secure their positions through such indirect methods as personal contacts . . . rather than such direct methods as employment agencies and advertisements. The important thing is to be in the informational flow about jobs, to hear about openings and new occupational possibilities.

Earlier work on this problem assumed that it was close ties with relatives and intimate friends that were crucial for this network phenomenon. But Mark Granovetter found that job information flowed typically through 'weak ties.' . . . Two-thirds of these contacts were work-related rather than family members or social friends. . . . Granovetter reasons that the importance of weak ties in the flow of job information is related to the fact that they are maximally informative because the networks minimally overlap, while relatives and close friends are likely to share much the same knowledge of the world. (Pettigrew 1978, 44–45)

The possible role of desegregation in providing minority students with access to opportunity networks has not been widely researched. A study by Robert Crain (1970) that examined the postsecondary experience of blacks who had attended segregated compared with desegregated schools indicated that the latter group was more fully in the white-dominated job information flow than the former, but Crain's study did not address the issue systematically. Henry Becker of Johns Hopkins University reviewed the research related to desegregation and opportunity networks and concluded that "Obtaining a job re-

quires much more than having certain attributes like the ability to read and write. . . . To the extent that racial segregation in housing, schooling, and employment continues to prevent young blacks from having access to the information channels used to fill job vacancies and to the extent that employers continue to demand greater degrees of sponsorship for unknown black youth than for whites, the gap between the employment prospects of white and black youth will remain" (Becker 1979, 22–23).

Subsequent Desegregation Participation

One of the most important benefits of desegregation is that it appears to generate greater willingness and capacity to participate in additional subsequent desegregated experiences. For example, Hallinan and Williams (1990) analyzed a national data set and found that interracial friendship has a positive impact on the college aspirations and enrollment of African American students (Liebman 1990). Increasing minority students' likelihood of participating in subsequent desegregated experience may be particularly important in encouraging their attendance at schools and colleges with high academic standards and high levels of student aspirations, as well as subsequently enlarging their socioeconomic opportunity networks. Jomills Braddock (1987) has reviewed the research bearing on this potential benefit of desegregation and reached the following four conclusions:

1. Individuals who grow up in segregated environments are "more likely to lead their adult lives in segregated situations . . . be it in education, residential location, employment or informal social contacts." The research provides "impressive evidence that segregation is perpetuated from elementary-secondary schools to colleges, neighborhoods, jobs, and other adult social settings. . . . Earlier desegregated schooling breaks this self-perpetuating cycle."

2. School desegregation generates "positive

reactions among blacks and whites to future interracial situations."

3. School desegregation helps develop "interpersonal skills that are useful in interracial contexts."

4. Desegregation of schools thus may be a "uniquely necessary ingredient to open up fairer career opportunities, to penetrate barriers to adult desegregation, and for students to develop skills at working successfully in multiracial settings." (Braddock 1987, 8, 14, 15, 18, 31).

URBAN SCHOOLS

As noted at the conclusion of Chapter 2, declining cities and metropolitan areas cannot be renewed successfully without attractive, high-quality public schools. Smaller metropolitan areas are likely to proceed through the same stages of deterioration as have older and larger areas unless central city schools remain attractive and can provide effective instruction for children of all social classes, particularly for lower working-class students who otherwise may constitute a segregated underclass. This section discusses what can be done to make urban schools a positive force for desegregation in the long-range development of metropolitan society.

We also note earlier in this chapter that desegregation is closely related to the issue of social class in the schools. The academic benefits of desegregation for minority students tend to be associated with socioeconomic mixture, that is, with situations in which low-status minority students go to school with higher status nonminority students. Desegregation also is primarily a social-class issue to the degree that withdrawal of middle-class families from desegregated schools follows from fear that instructional standards will decline as schools become increasingly working class.

Despite the importance of socioeconomic mixture, courts and school officials have given little systematic attention to it in formulating and carrying out plans for desegregation of the public schools. In part, this is because the Supreme Court has ruled that economic discrimination is not prohibited by the federal constitution. There is no recognized constitutional requirement that the poor must have a chance to attend economically desegregated schools.

Big-City School Districts

After about 1950, African American neighborhoods in large cities experienced a very rapid increase in child population that soon overcrowded the schools in these areas. By the early 1950s, schools that had formerly stood partially empty in many central cities were full to overflowing with black children. The rapid in-migration of black population into central cities ended during the late 1960s in most parts of the country, but suburbanization of whites continued at a steady pace; as a result, African Americans have constituted a steadily increasing proportion of the population of central cities. The percentage of the black population residing in central cities increased from 44 percent in 1950 to 57 percent in 1988, while the comparable percentage for non-Hispanic whites declined from 35 percent to 27 percent.

During the 1960s the Hispanic population of the cities began to increase rapidly in many parts of the United States. The Hispanic population is concentrated in central cities almost as heavily as is the African American population, and the percentage of Hispanics is still increasing at a rapid rate in many cities. The result of movement of blacks and Hispanics to big cities together with non-Hispanic white movement to the suburbs is that the largest central cities and their school systems now have about 80 percent minority enrollment (Rist 1990a). With most big cities now enrolling a large majority of minority students, the general pattern is that most of their minority students attend predominantly minority schools.

Big-city school officials have been trying to find policies that might result in sustained movement to reduce segregation. We discuss key elements of plans that have emerged in several cities, with special emphasis on the situation in Dallas, Texas, where more has been done than in most other localities to develop a plan systematically addressed to the goal of improving the quality of education in the central city. We believe that plans similar in some respects to the Dallas plan, but adapted to the situation in individual cities, provide a promising approach for advancing the goals of big-city school desegregation in the remainder of this century.

Student Assignment Patterns

The court-ordered plan for desegregation in Dallas was implemented in 1976. The plan does not reassign students in grades K–3, on the grounds that it is inappropriate to transport young students beyond a nearby school and that emphasis at this level should be mostly on developing basic skills so students are prepared to participate fully in instructional programs offered in desegregated settings at the middle-grade levels. Effective compensatory education programs emphasizing parent involvement along with improvement in instruction must be introduced to make this goal attainable.

Working within this broad policy, it may be desirable to pair or cluster K–3 enrollment in nearby schools in some cities, in situations where predominantly minority schools are adjacent to predominantly majority schools. Pairing and clustering involve "pooling" of students from such schools and reassignment to campuses with desegregated enrollment. Care should be taken in these circumstances to make sure that travel times are short and that each campus has a potentially stable racial mixture (i.e., generally not more than 40 to 60 percent minority students). In addition, middle-status students should not be assigned to schools with more than 30 to 40 percent working-class students. Few middle-status parents—white or black—will send their children to this type of school.

At the middle-grades and above, students should be reassigned wherever practical to schools with a desegregated student body. Reorganization of the schools at these levels provides an opportunity to improve education greatly for older children and young adolescents, with special emphases on providing multicultural experience to prepare students for life in a pluralistic society and on introducing students to career possibilities in the wider society. The Dallas plan, which established intermediate schools for students in grades 4–6 and grades 7–8, is a good example of movement in this direction on a district-wide basis.

Within this policy, it is important to maintain a potentially stable racial balance in desegregated schools and to offer options to parents who might otherwise withdraw their children from the public schools. Schools in integrated neighborhoods that already are 40 to 60 percent minority should be basically left alone, since natural desegregation of this sort can provide a nucleus for expanding neighborhood and school desegregation on a stable foundation. Leaving them undisturbed also may begin to give parents a vested interest in living in integrated communities, because middle-grade students in predominantly minority or nonminority neighborhoods will have to be transported to schools outside their communities for purposes of desegregation.

Particularly in school districts that have more than 50 or 60 percent minority students, implementation of this type of policy means that some students will remain racially isolated in schools more than 80 or 90 percent minority. The initial Dallas plan left many students in one of the school system's six administrative subdistricts racially isolated in this way, and some judges elsewhere have accepted similar arrangements in districts where there appear to be too few nonminority students to achieve anywhere near an even racial balance in most schools.

In addition, emphasis should be placed on reducing racial isolation through the establishment of magnet schools and programs. There is an important difference between a magnet *school* and a magnet *program*. As defined here, a magnet school is a desegregated school that students voluntarily attend on a full-time or half-time basis in order to participate in instructional programs not available in their local school. A magnet program is a part-time educational experience, as in the case of a two-week assignment at a science center with special instructional resources. As defined here, a magnet program also can be a course or set of courses that students from a variety of schools voluntarily attend for one or two hours a day at a desegregated magnet location.

Voluntary magnet arrangements should be particularly stressed at the secondary level. In most big cities, many or most desegregated high schools already have 50 percent or more minority students, making it difficult to assign minority students to them much more extensively without upsetting their stability. In addition, as demonstrated in the next section, magnetization is a particularly promising approach to improving the quality of instruction for secondary students. By establishing magnet schools and programs at the high-school level, school officials hope to reduce the number of minority students at racially isolated schools. Magnet schools are discussed at more length later in this chapter.

Variations on the Larger Theme

The emerging desegregation pattern described above can be summarized as follows:

1. Little or no mandatory reassignment of students in grades K–3, with emphasis at this level on improving basic skills through instructional reform and parent involvement.

2. Substantial reassignment and transportation of students in grades 4–8 or 4–9, with emphasis at this level on multicultural experience and programming but not so much student reassignment as to disturb schools that already have 40 to 60 percent minority students. This approach leaves many minority students in racially isolated schools in school districts that have more than 50 or 60 percent minority students.

3. Establishment of voluntary magnet schools and programs to increase desegregation and reduce racial isolation at the high-school level, with mandatory reassignment of students if necessary

to ensure there are at least 35 to 40 percent minority students at each school.

Within this larger pattern, there are many variations developing in line with the situation, issues, and possibilities that characterize a given school district. Several of these variations and considerations are as follows:

1. *Desegregation goals*. The goal implicitly being used to develop the kind of desegregation plan described above is to reduce racial isolation of as many minority students as possible without precipitating further withdrawal of white or middle-class families. In a few cities, this goal has been stated explicitly and has even been enlarged to aim at attracting students from suburban and nonpublic schools. Minimum and maximum percentages of minority enrollment in desegregated schools may vary somewhat from city to city, but generally the minimum is set at about 30 percent and the maximum at about 70 percent.

2. *Nonblack minority groups*. The size and status of nonblack minority groups in a school district also affect the formulation of desegregation plans. Except in a very few cities, the largest groups of this type are Hispanic—Puerto Ricans on the East Coast and in some midwest cities, Cubans in Miami, and Mexican Americans in the West and Southwest. Hispanic students are the largest racial-ethnic group in some cities such as Los Angeles, where there were nearly 335,000 Hispanic students (57 percent of the overall enrollment) in 1988.

The presence of relatively large numbers of Hispanic or Asian students obviously is a complicating factor in striving to desegregate big-city schools. Members of these groups tend to be located in ethnically distinct neighborhoods. Desegregation thus requires bringing students together from three or four rather than from two neighborhoods if black and non-Hispanic whites also are present and are to be mixed on a multiethnic basis. Additional complications arise because Hispanic groups tend to be more divided than are blacks on the steps that should be taken to advance desegregation. Although only about 50 percent of black parents indicate much enthusiasm for transporting their children to reduce segregation, and although some community groups in most black neighborhoods oppose busing for desegregation, predominantly black organizations and the most respected leaders in black communities generally have continued to support vigorous action toward desegregation. Hispanic communities, by way of contrast, appear to be much more divided. As a result, local political circumstances appear to be more influential among Hispanics than among blacks in determining the extent to which there is pressure for desegregation.

3. *State and federal initiatives.* Actions at the state and federal executive levels also continue to play a large part in shaping big-city desegregation efforts. For example, disposition of desegregation suits in some cities depends partly on whether they are filed under the state or federal constitution. Suits such as the Los Angeles case brought under the California constitution are governed by state supreme court decisions, which place greater emphasis on long-range reduction of *de facto* segregation (not caused by governmental action) than have most federal courts. Decisions in many cities are affected by congressional limitations on magnet school expenditures. The impact of these limitations varies a great deal according to the circumstances in local communities.

This analysis of student desegregation patterns emerging in big cities describes the situation as it developed in the 1980s. We believe that in some respects these developments were positive inasmuch as they opened up possibilities for reducing metropolitan segregation and stratification. In particular, emerging desegregation trends in some cities appear to be taking account of the need to strengthen instructional programs and to retain multiracial and economically diverse populations in central city schools and neighborhoods.

Magnet Schools

We have defined magnet schools and programs as voluntary approaches in which there is an attempt to attract a desegregated student body to schools that offer instructional opportunities not available at local neighborhood schools. Magnet-type schools have been operating in some cities for many years, although they generally were not so designated until recently. New York has long had specialized district-wide high schools in science and in the arts. Boston's Latin School traditionally has attracted top students from throughout the city. Rochester, San Diego, and other school districts have provided specialized, magnet-type programs for elementary students for a number of years, sometimes for decades. Many cities have offered advanced vocational programs at schools similar to some high schools now being established as magnet schools (Blank 1990).

Because magnet-type schools are well established in many cities, it is appropriate to ask whether there is anything new about the current magnet-school movement, which has seen magnet schools established in Cincinnati, Dallas, Dayton, Houston, Milwaukee, St. Louis, Seattle, and many other cities. For four reasons, we believe this movement is distinctive.

First, it places definite emphasis on attracting desegregated student enrollment, if necessary using quotas to facilitate the attainment of this goal.

Second, the magnet-school movement aims to serve a much larger clientele than the selective magnet-type schools of the past. (This seems to be true of alternative schools in general; see Raywid 1987; 1990, 1991.) Opportunities are offered for average-achieving students and for students whose special talents were generally ignored until recent developments in diversified programming. At the high-school level, a much greater range of specialized topics is pursued in greater depth than was true in magnet-type vocational schools operated years ago. The range and depth of a good district-wide magnet program are shown in Table 9-4, which lists the magnet high schools and fields of study operating in 1978 in the Dallas Independent School District.

TABLE 9-4 *Magnet High School Enrollment and Selected Fields of Study in the Dallas Independent School District, 1978**

Jobs for Which High School Students Are Fully or Partially Prepared by the School Programs

---

Arts High School
Art Gallery Employee
Window Designer
Interior Decorator
Internship with: Musician, Sculptor, Potter,
   Jeweler, Dancer
Enrollment: 670 (44% NM; 49% B; 7% H.)

Health Professions High School
Dental Hygienist
Medical Lab Technician
Dental Technologist
X-Ray Technologist
Practical Nurse
Medical Office Assistant
Enrollment: 837 (28% NM; 64% B; 8% H.)

Human Services Center
Social Work Assistant
Media Aide
Rehabilitation Assistant
Child Care Aide
Mental Health Assistant
Child Welfare Assistant
Recreation Assistant
Geriatrics Aide
Enrollment: 108 (32% NM; 56% B; 12% H.)

Skyline Career Development Center
(A magnet-type high school opened in 1971) 27 Career
Clusters including Architecture, Aviation,
Cinematography, Computer Technology, Cosmetology,
Electronics, Horticulture, and Plastics
Enrollment: 4,329 (55% NM; 37% B; 8% H.)

Business-Management Center
Bank Teller Aide
Stenographer
Legal Assistant
Administrative Assistant
Office Assistant
Machine Transcriber
Real Estate Sales Aide
Enrollment: 1,226 (13% NM; 73% B; 14% H.)

Transportation Institute
Auto Sales Assistant
Equipment Sales Assistant
Parts Distributor
Body Repair Aide
Front-End Aide
Tune-Up Specialist Aide
Enrollment: 518 (26% NM; 55% B; 19% H.)

Law and Police Administration
Police Officer Aide
Law Clerk Aide
Security Officer Aide
Probation Officer Aide
Tax Collector Asssistant
Enrollment: 206 (34% NM; 45% B; 21% H.)

Source: Dallas Public Schools.

* Abbreviations following enrollment figures denote racial-ethnic members, NM = Nonminority; B = Black; H = Hispanic

At the elementary level, magnet schools and programs also offer a variety of distinctive educational options for students of varied ability levels. Whereas earlier magnet-type schools such as Boston Latin usually had rigorous entry requirements, most of the magnet schools established since 1970 place greater emphasis on students' interests than on test scores or previ- ous academic record. District emphases in the elementary grades can include themes as divergent as foreign language, the Montessori approach to primary instruction, and organizational patterns for individualizing instruction. Houston is operating magnet elementary schools specializing in such subjects as music, literature, math, and science; and other school districts are establishing their own or comparable variants providing specialized instruction and resources in areas of particular concern to parents and students. Opportunities of this nature have been offered here and there in the past, but they seldom were available for substantial numbers of students and they frequently lacked the specialized staff and resources to make them successful. Some big-city school districts are aiming to enroll a substantial proportion of their students—both elementary and secondary—in magnet alternative programs (Estes, Levine, and Waldrip 1990).

A third feature of the magnet school movement is its frequent emphasis on using resources in the wider community to a much larger extent than has usually been the case in public education. This is particularly true at the high-school level, where some outstanding magnet schools are organized and operated in conjunction with business or professional leaders and resources in the fields of study available in the school. In Dallas, for example, the first director of the Arts Magnet High School was one of the metropolitan area's most respected leaders in that field. The Business and Management Center has equipment—much of it donated by business—more advanced than is available in regular high school business or commercial courses. Students develop their skills using the latest equipment for word and data processing and also have a chance to attend training programs conducted by employers for their own employees. In their senior year, students are placed in appropriate, supervised internships paying anywhere from the minimum wage to $6 or $7 per hour. It is hoped that opportunities such as these will attract enrollment from regular high schools.

The fourth major distinguishing characteristic of the magnet school movement is its emphasis on retaining middle-status population in central city schools. Even though this goal is seldom stated explicitly in these terms, it is clearly an important objective in cities in which a variety of educational options or alternatives are being made available. Establishing an attractive magnet school may retain white and black middle-class students whose parents are unwilling to send them to a local neighborhood school, whether racially segregated or desegregated. Magnet schools also attract upwardly mobile working-class students who are dissatisfied with educational opportunities or security arrangements in inner-city schools. From this point of view, some magnet schools may be thought of as the big city's attempt to compete with suburban and nonpublic schools (Morgan 1991).

The magnet school movement continued to expand throughout the 1980s and early 1990s. Virtually all big-city districts and most medium-sized urban districts now operate at least a few magnet schools (Estes, Levine, and Waldrip 1990; Wells 1991b). Consequently, it is important to determine whether they are functioning to enhance desegregation, improve the quality and effectiveness of instruction, bolster community confidence and retain middle-class enrollment in public schools, and help accomplish other goals of educational systems.

Research.   The limited research conducted on effects and contributions of magnet schools has been generally encouraging. For example, the federally funded National Survey of Magnet Schools (Blank 1984, 1990; Dentler 1990) concluded that magnet schools can improve the quality of education while offering expanded choices to students and parents and enhancing desegregation. Students, teachers, and external observers tended to give magnet schools relatively high ratings on instructional effectiveness, curriculum, teacher-student interaction, and general climate. One of the authors summarized some of the survey's specific findings as follows:

> *When a magnet has solid support from its district administration and solid leadership from the principal or magnet program leader, and when it has formed a coherent and definite identity of its own, it is able to deliver educational quality. . . . Magnet plans can have great desegregative impact if they were*

intended to have it and if the school board and administration make a strong effort to carry through on this intention.... magnet plans can revitalize equity in a district, contribute to the build-up of public confidence in the system, diversify opportunities for students, and redistribute both staff and students district-wide in desegregative ways. (Dentler 1990, 71, 75–76)

Seven years after the 1983 National Survey, Rolf Blank examined the subsequent development of magnet schools and plans in fifteen urban districts included in the earlier study. After analyzing a variety of data and reports, Blank (1990) reported the following conclusions:

• Magnet school enrollment increased significantly in thirteen of the districts and more than doubled in seven. By 1990, magnet students constituted one-third or more of the enrollment in Buffalo, Cincinnati, Kankakee, St. Paul, San Diego, and Seattle.

• Districts that have increased the numbers of magnet schools and students tended to avoid using selective admissions criteria, such as high previous achievement scores. Selective criteria probably are being applied less frequently than in 1983. However, the resulting "self-selection of students through voluntary enrollment tends to produce an entering student group with better academic achievement than the district average." Thus "it appears that most magnet schools serve students that are not 'at-risk' in terms of academic problems."

• Magnet students generally have positive attitudes toward and are satisfied with the schools they attend.

• Although few studies of achievement in magnet schools have taken account of students' socioeconomic background or the probability that applicants have more parental support and more positive home environments than nonapplicants of similar social class, the limited research that addressed these considerations indicates that students tend to improve in achievement after enrolling in magnet schools.

One of the most intensive studies of a sizable group of magnet schools was conducted to identify outcomes of magnetization at more than one hundred magnets in fourteen districts in the State of New York. Among the major conclusions of the study (Musumeci and Szczypkowski 1991, 139–142) were that magnet schools in the sample "fared exceptionally well" in as much as they generally were functioning successfully to attain the following results:

• A "dramatic" reduction in racial isolation. "Schools that once were segregated, deviating substantially from their districts' minority enrollment averages, became significantly less so as a result of magnet implementation."
• A "significant impact" in helping to bring about more desegregation districtwide.
• An increase in opportunities for additional contact among students of different races.
• An improvement in the achievement of students attending magnets and a narrowing of the achievement gap between schools high and low in minority enrollment.
• A reduction in the dropout rate among students attending magnet high schools.
• An increase in the percentage of students planning to pursue some form of postsecondary education.

Selectivity.   One of the most important issues regarding the establishment of magnet schools involves their potentially negative effects on educational opportunities available to students elsewhere in a school district. If magnet schools are highly selective in the sense that they admit only or mostly high-achieving students, and/or if students who apply to attend are generally the most highly motivated students, other (nonmagnet) schools in a district may lose their best and thereby become or remain poorly functioning, low-status schools (see Chapters 2 and 8). In addition, if substantial additional funds are provided to implement magnet themes, other schools may receive less money to improve their operations, unless the magnet programs are funded through external sources (Wells 1991b).

Concerns regarding possible negative effects of selectivity have been expressed since the earliest years of the magnet-school movement (e.g., Levine and Campbell 1978; Rossell 1978). Early analysts also recognized that operation of a few selective magnet schools in a large district could not have much negative effect on the composition of schools elsewhere, but in this case such elitist magnets also could not provide much help in increasing or improving desegregation on a systemwide basis.

Analysis of magnet schools and programs in several school districts has indicated that their negative effects sometimes do seem to outweigh their benefits. For example, Moore and Davenport (1989) studied magnets in Boston, Chicago, and New York and concluded that substantial creaming of the best students is taking place, with some negative consequences for schools elsewhere. Similarly, a leading desegregation planner reviewed data on developments in urban districts and concluded that although good magnet plans have helped some dedicated educators enhance desegregation, magnets in some other locations have been part of a "shell game" that enabled school officials to desegregate a few schools while avoiding more comprehensive desegregation (Dentler 1990, 82).

If magnet schools can enhance desegregation and other aspects of high-quality education but also detract from broader efforts to improve instruction and reduce segregation throughout a school district, then it is important to design and implement magnet plans that produce overall positive results. Several guidelines can help attain the latter outcome:

1. *Establish magnet schools as part of a larger plan that also includes mandatory desegregation components, if necessary*. In districts with a preponderance of nonminority students or a relatively even balance between minority and nonmi-

nority students, it frequently is possible to desegregate and/or to maintain desegregation at many schools through mandatory actions, such as assignment of students in desegregated neighborhoods to local schools, pairing of adjacent minority and nonminority schools, and busing of students short distances to schools with a majority of middle-class enrollment. In this situation, establishing magnets can bring about substantial additional desegregation on a voluntary basis, as long as students are not allowed to transfer to magnets if this might segregate their previous schools. Thus, the underlying mandatory components can help attain and protect widespread desegregation, while the magnets further enhance desegregation (Ascher 1990).

2. *To the extent possible, avoid selectivity and elitism in magnet-school entrance criteria*. As noted, one goal of the magnet-school movement is to motivate students by providing specialized learning opportunities that historically were available mostly to a relatively small proportion of the academically elite. In addition, although rigorous achievement criteria for admission to magnets can attract middle-class students reluctant or unwilling to attend their neighborhood schools, this approach may harm regular schools by skimming their best students. Accordingly, rigorous admissions criteria should be avoided, except, perhaps, in the case of a few schools carefully designed to function as part of a much larger plan to enhance desegregation and instructional opportunity.

3. *To the extent possible, convert the entire district to magnet schools while working to improve instruction at schools that may be left unmagnetized*. In districts with minority enrollment as high as 50 or even 60 percent, it may be possible to achieve substantial desegregation through converting all or most schools to magnets and utilizing racial composition criteria as part of the enrollment process. Provided that distances across the district are not large and funds are available to support strong magnet themes, voluntary enrollment then can result in desegregation throughout all or most of a school district. A good example of this approach is in Richmond, California, where all fifty schools have been converted to System of Choice schools that emphasize Montessori education, classical studies, international studies, "whole-language" learning, gifted and talented education, or future studies (Rist 1990b).

In districts with more than 50 to 60 percent minority enrollment, it may not be possible to desegregate all or nearly all schools through magnetization because some may not attract enough nonminority students unless the district and the distances between schools are very small. (When there are more than about 80 percent minority students, a plan that tried to distribute nonminority students across all schools would not result in much meaningful desegregation and probably would stimulate withdrawal from predominantly minority schools and concentrated poverty schools.) A good example of a district that stresses magnetization of most but not all schools is in Kansas City, Missouri, where all twenty-one middle and senior high schools and thirty-five of the district's fifty-three elementary schools became magnets between 1986 and 1990 (Hale 1990).

When the Kansas City plan was initiated in 1986, the district enrolled 72 percent minority students and was becoming slowly resegregated as neighborhoods became more heavily minority and middle-status families moved to suburban areas or sent their children to nonpublic schools. Magnet enrollment guidelines generally require that racial composition will be no more than 60 percent minority or nonminority, except that magnet schools at which enrollment has been mostly minority may have more than 60 percent minority students as long as that percentage declines by at least 2 percent each year. Even if the Kansas City district is largely successful in attracting nonminority students from the suburbs and nonpublic schools, it is unlikely that sufficient numbers will be available to desegregate all the elementary schools before the mid-1990s or later (Hale 1990).

In this context, it was important to avoid allowing the magnet elementary schools to become elitist institutions that are well funded and attract most of the high-achieving and well-motivated students, while nonmagnet schools remain or became segregated poverty schools with poorly functioning instructional programs. The overall desegregation plan in Kansas City is designed to avoid this type of two-tier system by providing various fundamental improvements (e.g., reduced class size, building rehabilitation, ongoing staff development, and other components described earlier in this chapter) at *all* district schools, whether magnet or nonmagnet.

Controlled Choice in Small Urban Districts

During the 1980s several school districts in small cities introduced or began to consider initiation of *controlled-choice* plans that allow students to select the school they will attend within the district, with free transportation provided. Parents are required to designate three or four schools of choice for each child, and the district attempts to place every student in a school selected by the parents. Enrollment in each building is controlled in order to enhance or maintain desegregation. This approach is somewhat analogous to a magnet plan in that each school must function like a magnet in order to attract students to meet its enrollment goals. Alternately, a comprehensive magnet plan can include controlled-choice arrangements, as in the case of the Kansas City and Richmond plans.

The controlled-choice approach was first adopted on a districtwide basis in 1981 in Cambridge, Massachusetts. Data on implementation indicate that, in 1988, 80 percent of parents received their first choice of schools and another 10 percent received their second or third choice. Research on the Cambridge controlled-choice plan indicates that it appears to be stimulating improvements in instruction and school climate, that a significant number of students have been attracted from nonpublic schools, and that the positive impact on desegregation has been substantial (Peterkin 1990, 1991). Data collected in Montclair (NJ) also indicate that controlled-choice along with establishment of magnets in a small district can help produce both stable desegregation and improvement in instructional effectiveness (Clewell and Joy 1990).

Districtwide controlled choice appears most feasible in relatively small districts in which minority enrollment is not more than 40 to 50 percent and distances between schools in the plan are not too large to dampen parents' willingness to select a school outside their immediate neighborhood. Elements of the controlled-choice approach are now being implemented in Boston, Buffalo, Little Rock, San Jose, and several other urban school districts (Glenn 1991).

Desegregation in a Central-City District: Seattle

The Seattle Public Schools began voluntary efforts to desegregate in 1963, but the percentage of minority students in the district and in segregated schools increased steadily in the 1960s and 1970s. By 1977, civil rights groups and many civic leaders were urging district officials to take more vigorous action to desegregate the schools. The Board of Education responded by issuing a statement specifying that no school should be more than 20 percent above the districtwide average in percentage minority (then 35 percent), and initiating six months of activities involving the community in planning for desegregation.

The desegregation plan adopted in December 1977 includes both voluntary and mandatory components to desegregate the schools. When voluntary efforts such as magnet schools and permissive transfer prove ineffective, schools are desegregated through pairing and clustering and through mandatory transportation. Nonminority enrollment in Seattle decreased from 85 percent in 1963 to 65 percent in 1977, and then declined further to 45 percent in 1990.

In order to enhance desegregation in this situation, the Board of Education introduced controlled choice guidelines that disallow enrollment of more than 50 percent of a single minority group (e.g., black, Hispanic, or Asian) and limit each school's total population to 70 percent minority or 65 percent white. However, new guidelines proposed for 1992 would allow 75 percent enrollment from a single racial group. Although there apparently has been significant white withdrawal associated with the plan, desegregation has been maintained in most of the district (Egan 1988; Miller, J.A. 1990).

Several efforts were made to block implementation of the mandatory component of the Seattle plan. The most serious was a statewide referendum in which Washington voters supported prohibition of mandatory transportation to bring about desegregation in education. However, in 1982 the U.S. Supreme Court ruled that such a prohibition is not constitutional when a state intervenes in local school board decisions in a manner inconsistent with the fourteenth amendment to the Constitution. Because the explicit goal of the referendum was to prevent desegregation, the Supreme Court ruled, the State of Washington could not prevent the Seattle Board of Education from implementing mandatory action to provide more equal opportunity for minority students.

As shown in the contrast between the following description of the status of school desegregation in Chicago and the situation in Seattle, desegregation is much easier to attain in moderate-sized cities than in very large districts with a very high proportion of minority students. Short of a metropolitan or regional remedy, many minority students in the latter districts will remain in predominantly minority schools no matter how much emphasis is placed on mandatory student reassignment. In smaller urban districts with a moderate percentage of minority students, by way of contrast, it is possible to provide desegregation for most or all minority students.

Limited Desegregation in a Very Large Central City: Chicago

A good example of the development of a deseg-regation plan in a very large urban school district is provided in the case of Chicago. Like Detroit, Houston, Los Angeles, New York, Philadelphia, and other very large districts enrolling a prepon-derance of minority students, Chicago has been unable to provide desegregated education for most of its minority students. Many of the larger urban school districts in the South and the West have been able to provide desegregated educa-tion for most minority students, because school districts there tend to be county-size units that include relatively large proportions of nonminor-ity students. However, although there is a great variation nationally in the degree to which deseg-regated education has been attempted and at-tained, in general there is a tendency for deseg-regation to be most limited in very large Northern and Midwestern districts with a high proportion of minority students.

The percentage of non-Hispanic whites in the Chicago Public Schools decreased substan-tially, declining from 62 percent in 1950 to 13 percent in 1990 (see Table 9-5). The percentage of African American students grew rapidly from 1950 to 1978, as did Hispanic enrollment in both the 1970s and 1980s. Concerned observers pointed out that there was a growing number of

elementary schools with 90 percent or more black pupils.

The Chicago Urban League, an organiza-tion that worked to improve the economic and educational condition of the black population, began to exert influence against school and resi-dential segregation. From this time, the Chicago Board of Education came under increasing pres-sure to adopt procedures that would reduce the racial-ethnic segregation.

In April 1976, the Illinois Board of Educa-tion placed the Chicago Public Schools on Pro-bationary Recognition Status. The State Board of Education was in a position to cancel or reduce state financial aid and asked for action by the Chicago Board of Education sufficient to show that some progress was being made to reduce segregation. Early in 1977, Superintendent Jo-seph Hannon appointed a City-Wide Advisory Committee to produce a desegregation plan that might satisfy the State Board of Education. CWAC, as it was called, produced a 200-page report entitled *Equalizing Opportunities: Pro-posed Plan.*

This Plan contained sixteen components aimed at substantially reducing segregation. A crucial question was whether the program would produce enough desegregation if the movement of students to desegregated schools was volun-tary on the part of students and their parents.

TABLE 9-5   *Racial-Ethnic Composition of the Chicago Public Schools, 1950–1990*

Year	Percentages				Total Enrollment
	White	*Black*	*Hispanic**	*Asian/Pacific Is.*	
1950	62	36	—	0	372,000
1960	55	42	—	0	480,000
1970	35	55	1	1	578,000
1978	22	61	16	2	495,000
1981	17	61	20	2	443,000
1987	14	60	23	3	429,000
1990	13	60	24	3	421,000

Source: Chicago Board of Education.
* Nearly all Hispanics are included in the white category before 1970. Numbers may not add to 100 percent due to rounding.

The CWAC plan included the following statement: "*Voluntary/Mandatory Process*. This component provides for each component in the plan to become mandatory if the voluntary process fails to bring about the amount of integration expected."

Superintendent Hannon appointed an Administration Management Committee of members of his staff to study the CWAC Plan. This committee produced an alternative plan entitled *Access to Excellence*, which contained material from the CWAC Plan but did not have a mandatory clause. The Board of Education approved the *Access to Excellence* plan by a vote of six to five.

Access to Excellence was put into action in the autumn of 1978. There was evidence of some progress toward desegregation in the spring of 1979. During this period, Superintendent Hannon requested the federal government to provide money to support the cost of Access to Excellence under the Emergency School Aid Act. This was part of a continued attempt by the Chicago Public Schools to secure federal government assistance, which had been denied several times on the ground that the Chicago Schools had not satisfied all the criteria stated in federal legislation. An exchange of letters and consultation between Superintendent Hannon and staff of the Office of Civil Rights of the Department of Health, Education and Welfare did not produce agreement.

At this point, the Department of Justice of the federal government filed a complaint in the United States District Court of Northern Illinois alleging that the Chicago Board of Education had engaged in acts of discrimination in violation of federal laws. A series of conferences between representatives of the Department of Justice and members of the board of education and lawyers for the board resulted in a *Consent Decree* signed by the Justice Department and the Chicago Board of Education in September 1980. Essentially, the consent decree established a procedure whereby the board of education would create an aggressive desegregation program and the federal government would provide financial assistance.

In October, the board voted to employ as chief desegregation consultant Robert L. Green, dean of the College of Urban Development of Michigan State University, a black educator with broad experience in the field of school desegregation. From December 1980 until May 1981, a series of public meetings and conferences was conducted by Green and his staff. These meetings resulted in a plan for desegregation, which was submitted to Judge Milton Shadur of the Federal District Court. A desegregated school was defined as one with an enrollment between 30 to 70 percent non-Hispanic white. This would leave many schools all or nearly all black or Hispanic; they would receive additional federal funds to improve instruction.

In December 1981, the board of education issued a plan implemented in the spring of 1982. The plan's most important components were to (1) desegregate predominantly white schools (more than 70 percent non-Hispanic white) through a variety of techniques including creation of magnet schools, voluntary transfering of minority students, pairing and clustering of schools, redrawing of attendance areas, and closing of old buildings; (2) expend approximately 25 million dollars extra per year for improvement of instruction at more than 400 predominantly minority schools; (3) allocate an additional $72,000 per school to target schools high in minority percentage and very low in achievement; and (4) continue to create and expand magnet-type schools and programs.

In January 1983, Judge Shadur accepted the board's desegregation proposal, even though it would leave approximately two-thirds of the district's schools predominantly minority. Judge Shadur's ruling stated that districtwide desegregation did not seem feasible in a system with nearly 85 percent minority students. He further stated that "it would be tragic if a well-intentioned desegregation plan" that involved extensive student reassignment and busing in Chicago "were to cause accelerated resegregation—so that the common desegregation goals of the board and its critics were defeated" (Mirga 1983).

By the fall of 1983, the Chicago school district had 50 magnet schools in operation and had also initiated 50 magnet programs that provided some part-time desegregation. In addition, nearly all the district's approximately 600 schools were more than 30 percent minority, and hundreds of schools more than 70 percent minority were participating in a variety of compensatory-education programs. This overall program has remained basically stable since that time. In 1990, Chicago operated 47 magnet schools, provided magnet programming (i.e., partial magnets) within 133 schools, and provided additional funds to improve instruction at low-achieving poverty schools, but 280 of 604 schools were 90 percent or more African American (Kass 1990).

Metropolitan Arrangements

It is obvious that central-city school districts that have 70 to 80 percent or more minority students and a high proportion of concentrated poverty schools are not going to achieve full racial or socioeconomic desegregation within the confines of their own boundaries. No matter how elaborate or well worked out their overall desegregation plans or how successful their magnet-school programs, such districts will have a significant percentage of their students attending racially isolated and concentrated poverty schools. Most big-city school districts are now approaching or have passed the 70 percent minority figure. Many have half or more of their students in concentrated poverty schools. Full racial and socioeconomic desegregation in these districts will require arrangements involving white and middle-status students from a region larger than the central city (Taeuber 1990).

Metropolitan arrangements fostering desegregation can take either of two forms. They can be brought about through *court orders requiring regional solutions* to problems of unequal educational opportunity in the metropolitan area or they can be accomplished through voluntary *cooperation* between the central city school district and surrounding suburban districts. Levine and Levine (1977) have identified two reasons that metropolitan arrangements are desirable in addition to the

fundamental goal of counteracting deterioration in the central city and its public schools:

1. Some inner city suburbs in large metropolitan areas are now becoming heavily minority as black families escape the inner city. Unless a regional approach to desegregation is formulated and implemented, some of these suburbs will become an extension of the inner city and the pattern of central-city decay will be repeated in the suburbs. Regional arrangements can help achieve or maintain desegregation in these suburbs.

2. Metropolitan arrangements for desegregation frequently are more feasible than are plans limited to the central city. In situations where predominantly white suburbs adjoin minority sections of the central city, it is much more efficient to transport students a couple of miles across the city border than to bus them ten or fifteen miles between a nonminority neighborhood at one end of the city and a minority neighborhood at the other end. The greater feasibility of desegregation arrangements when suburbs are included has been demonstrated by the fact that city-only plans proposed in Cleveland, Kansas City, Los Angeles and some other cities either have to bus city students *across* suburban districts or route buses along inconvenient detours to avoid leaving the city.

Court-Ordered Regional Solutions. Prospects of mandatory action to reduce big-city and metropolitan school segregation through the courts were being explored in a number of other metropolitan areas in the late 1970s and 1980s. Earlier efforts to bring about regional solutions received setbacks in 1973, when the Supreme Court in a 4–4 decision refused to approve District Judge Robert R. Merhige's order consolidating the Richmond Public Schools with adjoining districts in Henrico and Chesterfield Counties and in 1974, when the Supreme Court voted 5 to 4 in *Bradley* v. *Milliken* to reverse U.S. District Judge Stephen J. Roth's decision requiring cross-busing of students between Detroit and fifty-two suburban districts. In the *Milliken* decision, the Supreme Court stated, "Before the boundaries of separate and autonomous school districts may be set aside by consolidating the separate units for remedial purposes or by imposing a cross-district remedy, it must first be shown that there has been a constitutional violation within one district that produces a significant segregative effect in another district."

However, the *Milliken* decision did not completely close the door on suits petitioning for regional solutions. In subsequent years, the Supreme Court approved lower-court orders requiring merger of the Louisville Public Schools with the surrounding Jefferson County Public Schools and interdistrict remedies for the segregation of minority students in the Wilmington, Delaware, Public Schools and the Indianapolis Public Schools. Evidence submitted and judicial decisions in these court cases suggested that constitutional violations justifying an interdistrict remedy for big-city segregation can include such government actions as the following:

1. Required transportation of minority students into central-city schools where southern and border states practiced *de jure* (legally mandated) segregation before 1954. Where school district boundary lines were disregarded for the purpose of segregation, they cannot be considered as impermeable boundaries to prevent desegregation.

2. State laws that had the effect of exempting segregated city schools from plans to improve the organization of school districts in the metropolitan area.

3. Housing practices supported by state and local governments that had the effect of establishing or reinforcing segregated residential patterns on a multijurisdictional basis. Included under this heading might be actions that concentrated public housing for minorities within the central-city school district, state support of restrictive housing covenants that forced minority families to settle in segregated city neighborhoods, and zon-

ing practices that intentionally prevented minority families from moving to integrated locations.

Depending on subsequent court decisions, it is possible that regional remedies eventually may be ordered in a number of metropolitan areas, particularly in southern and border states in which it can be shown that minority students were transported across school district lines before 1954 for the purpose of segregation. For most of the United States, however, regional approaches to reduce segregated schooling will come about only as a result of voluntary cooperation between cities and suburbs.

Metropolitan Cooperation. Given the strength of forces that work against cooperation between city and suburbs, there would not be any hope of achieving this goal in most large metropolitan areas except for the fact that developments during the 1970s and 1980s were such that cooperative arrangements now can contribute directly to the solution of serious problems in suburban schools. Primarily this is true because:

1. Many suburban districts are losing enrollment. Rather than close schools or maintain undersized classes, it may be more efficient for districts to work with central-city schools when allocating space for the future.

2. Magnet high schools in the central city can offer educational opportunities far superior to those now available anywhere in the metropolitan area. Few suburban high schools can draw on a sufficiently large and heterogeneous population base to offer the types of curricula that a regional magnet high school can make available for youth throughout the metropolitan area. For example, few, if any, suburbs are in a position to establish a magnet high school devoted to science or the performing arts. Conversely, inclusion of the suburban population base for the central-city, magnet high schools will improve their chances of attracting a student body large enough to be cost-effective. This suggests that

magnet high schools should be planned and operated on a regional basis, with some located inside and others outside the central city, but all easily accessible to both city and suburban students.

However, regional cooperation for desegregation and related purposes is not likely to come about—no matter how desirable it may be objectively—without strong leadership and incentives from the state and the federal government. It is true that school districts in many metropolitan areas already have cooperative arrangements for providing services such as special education, teacher training, and instructional television, and that these arrangements provide a model, and in some cases an existing mechanism, for further cooperation involving desegregation. In addition, a few metropolitan areas such as Boston, Hartford, Milwaukee, and Rochester have had city-suburban transfer programs for fifteen years or more, with significant numbers of central-city minority students transported to suburban schools on a voluntary basis (Armor 1989). On the other hand, it also is unlikely that most suburban districts will cooperate voluntarily on thorny and controversial issues like desegregation unless incentives for doing so are strong and obvious (Levine and Eubanks 1990b).

Wisconsin. Leadership on the issue of city-suburban cooperation for desegregation has begun to emerge in a few states and at the federal level. Probably the best example of what can be done at the state and local level has been provided in Wisconsin, where in April 1976 the state legislature passed a law providing incentives for intra- and interdistrict transfer of students for desegregation. Financial help is given both for transfer of minority students from districts or schools 30 percent or more minority to districts or schools less than 30 percent minority and for transfer of nonminority students following the same formula in reverse. In the case of interdistrict transfers, the sending district receives the normal amount of state aid per student and the

receiving district also receives additional state aid for each student plus a bonus of 20 percent if more than 5 percent of its enrollment are transfer-in students. The state also pays transportation costs.

Results in Milwaukee.   Court action accusing Milwaukee Public School officials of unconstitutional segregation began in 1965. As in many other cities, the case (*Armstrong* v. *Brennan*) dragged on for years, until in 1976 Judge John Reynolds issued a ruling finding the district in constitutional violation. Judge Reynolds also directed public school officials to formulate and implement a plan to desegregate the schools. The court defined a desegregated school as one that is between 25 and 45 percent black. (Hispanic students have not been defined as minority students who must be desegregated in Milwaukee.) The board of education responded by indicating an intention to use voluntary approaches and incentives to bring about as much desegregation as possible.

Between 1976 and 1979, the court set annual targets for increasing desegregation in the Milwaukee Public Schools, and the school district made modifications in school attendance areas and grade organization, established elementary and secondary magnet schools and developed a voluntary city-suburban transfer program, and encouraged both minority and nonminority students to attend desegregated schools. These steps appear to have been relatively successful inasmuch as the number of desegregated schools (redefined in 1978 to be 25 to 50 percent black) increased from 14 in 1976 to 101 in 1978 (Bennett 1979), and the percentage of black students in desegregated schools increased from 16 percent to 71 percent.

In May 1979, the court accepted a settlement in which the plaintiffs and the school district agreed to withdrawal of the litigation as long as desegregation goals are met as specified in the agreement. The board of education agreed to have at least 75 percent of the district's black students in desegregated schools as long as the percentage of black students in the district as a whole remains 50 percent or less. (If the district exceeds 50 percent black, the goals may be readjusted.) The district also agreed to continue notifying students still in segregated schools that they have the right to free transportation to attend desegregated schools, and to make instructional and organizational improvements in schools remaining predominantly black.

The magnet-school component in Milwaukee's desegregation plan has grown to include twenty elementary and middle schools, five senior high schools, and twenty-five career specialty programs at the remaining ten high schools. Ten percent of the seats in the magnet programs are set aside for suburban students. By 1990, nearly 1000 suburban students were attending schools in the city, and more than 4300 minority students were attending suburban schools (Levine and Eubanks 1990b).

The ancillary relief component to improve education for black students choosing to remain in segregated schools in the inner city also has had some success at the elementary level. Implemented primarily through the RISE project at sixteen elementary schools, efforts to improve the achievement of students at inner-city schools resulted in a gain in average fifth-grade reading scores from the 43rd percentile in 1979 to the 68th percentile in 1984. The comparable gain in fifth-grade math scores was from the 57th to the 79th percentile (McCormack-Larkin 1985).

However, decline in Milwaukee's white population makes it increasingly difficult to maintain desegregated environments for 75 percent of the district's black students. (By 1985, student enrollment was 48 percent black and 45 percent white.) "Looking ahead to 1990 and beyond and seeing a growing minority student population and isolation in the city," and also concerned with the quality of education provided for minority students who transfer to suburban schools, members of the Milwaukee Board of Education initiated litigation in 1984 requesting a mandatory interdistrict remedy for school de-

segregation in the Milwaukee metropolitan area (McMurrin 1985, 32). A voluntary settlement reached in 1987 requires the suburban districts to work with the city district in order to increase interdistrict transfers substantially.

Massachusetts.   Massachusetts also has been a leader in providing financial incentives and other forms of support (e.g., in planning and communications) for city-suburban cooperation on desegregation. In 1976, the Massachusetts legislature appropriated up to $3 million to support magnet schools and programs, many of which involve cooperative exchange and transfer of students in the Boston and Springfield metropolitan areas. These funds supported such activities as the Metropairways program, in which approximately 500 city and suburban elementary and middle-school students were in paired groups studying environmental science, ethnic history, and other subjects. Also, under the METCO program (Metropolitan Council for Educational Opportunities), approximately 3,000 minority students from racially unbalanced schools in Boston have attended suburban schools each year since 1976.

St. Louis.   St. Louis also has implemented a plan to provide desegregation for many black students, largely through cooperation with suburban districts. (The plan is only semivoluntary in that a federal court required suburban districts to accept sufficient black students from the city to reach a minimum percentage of 15 percent black.) The St. Louis desegregation plan also includes emphasis on instructional improvement and on establishment of city magnet schools to attract suburban students. Implemented in 1981, the plan has been expanded each year so that nearly 13,000 black students from the city were attending suburban schools and more than 800 suburban white students were attending city schools during the 1990–91 school year. Altogether, more than 15,000 city black students were attending either predominantly white suburban schools or desegregated city magnet schools

(Levine and Eubanks 1990b; Tompkins 1990; Gillerman 1991).

San Diego.   Probably the best example of successful voluntary desegregation on a metropolitan scale involves the multifaceted desegregation plan in the San Diego Unified School District. (Although San Diego is a city school district, it is a very large regional district that includes a number of suburban areas that would be separate school districts in many other parts of the United States.) Desegregation of the San Diego schools has been carried out almost entirely on a voluntary basis.

After initiation of a court-ordered desegregation plan, 45 magnet schools were established in San Diego between 1978 and 1987 (among 130 schools in the district), and more are being opened each year. As of 1988, approximately 14,000 minority students who otherwise would have attended segregated schools attended desegregated magnets, and another 5,000 participated in a voluntary program through which they transferred to predominantly white outlying schools in the district. Altogether, nearly 90 percent of the minority students living in racially isolated attendance areas participated in these two desegregation programs in 1988. The percentage of minority students attending racially isolated schools was reduced from 35 percent in 1977 to 24 percent in 1988, despite a large natural decline in enrollment of white students and a continuous Hispanic in-migration during this period (Levine and Eubanks 1990b).

In addition, San Diego's court-ordered plan for improving instruction at inner-city, minority schools has had outstanding success. Components and effects of the instructional-improvement plan are described in the last chapter of this book.

Magnet Schools in Urban Development: The Webster School

One example of the use of a public school as a major factor in the strategic redevelopment of a deteriorating neighborhood close to the downtown area of a large city is the Webster School in St. Paul, Minnesota. In 1975, St. Paul school officials designated the Webster Elementary School as a desegregated magnet school as part of the overall plan for desegregation of the schools in the district. At that time, enrollment at Webster was 74 percent minority. Most pupils were economically disadvantaged, and the neighborhood was considered so unsafe that students had to ride a bus only a few blocks to school. There is no doubt that Webster was a typical inner city school that would have trouble attracting students from other neighborhoods.

Planning for the desegregation program at Webster was carried on during 1975–76 with the aid of a citizens' committee and publicity for the program. New students were bused to Webster on a voluntary basis, with 25 minutes as the longest bus ride. A $600,000 addition to the school building was constructed and opened in 1978. During this time enrollment increased from 362 to 975, with minority students constituting 34 percent of the student body.

According to the principal, the main attraction for parents was an outstanding instructional program that involved a split-day schedule according to which approximately one-half of a student's day is devoted entirely to basic skills instruction and the other half is spent in application of skills. The applied skills part of the program allows for a variety of enrichment activities building on the particular learning interests and requests of students. Thus, the overall program can be equally attractive both to parents who want what they call "the basics" stressed for their children and for those whose greatest stress is something they refer to as "openness" or "humaneness." Subjects that have been taught in minicourses as part of the applied skills program include Ceramics; Photography; Creative Writing; Classical Literature; Children's Theater; Drama; Dance; Vocal Music; Instrumental Music; Spanish; French; Computer Logic; Typing; Business; and Environmental Science.

At the same time the Webster School was being improved, neighborhood redevelopment was being promoted by community groups, a number of substantial old homes were rehabilitated, and a Control Data Corporation plant was located there.

The construction of a new building at a school that previously had been underenrolled seems to have helped convince middle-class parents that the magnet school would not be a predominantly working-class school. Before 1975, a high proportion of the students were from poverty families, and there was little likelihood that middle-class parents would send their children to Webster even if it had an attractive magnet program. Addition of the new building, however, suggested that there would be a critical mass of new students when the magnet school opened. This perception helped make it possible to obtain enough nonpoverty students to reopen as a mixed-class school.

HOUSING AND SCHOOL DESEGREGATION

Both educators and lay leaders recognize that school desegregation is much easier to achieve when blacks and whites live in the same community served by a naturally integrated neighborhood school. Conversely, school desegregation can contribute to desegregation in housing, particularly if schools are desegregated on a metropolitan or regional basis so that there is no point in nonminority parents' moving to avoid sending their children to desegregated schools (Pearce 1980; Wells 1991a).

Gary Orfield has been studying the relationship between desegregation in schools and housing and has concluded that although there is much to be gained by coordinating school and housing policies in an effort to maximize stable desegregation, little has been done to develop and implement coordinated policies. After studying the situation in twelve communities that had relatively effective school desegregation plans and a reputation for relatively progressive leadership, Orfield (1981) reached these six general conclusions:

1. School and housing officials agreed on the need for coordinating policies for desegregation but had done little to formulate or carry out effective coordinated action.
2. Most school desegregation plans and orders neglect possibilities for encouraging desegregation in housing.
3. In most cases, there has been no serious attempt to stabilize existing integrated neighborhoods.
4. The common assumption that subsidized housing in the suburbs automatically will lead to desegregation is incorrect.
5. The urban revitalization process that is bringing middle-class whites back to some central city neighborhoods has not generally resulted in much desegregation of schools.
6. However, solutions for parts of the problem have been found in a few cities, and officials elsewhere express strong interest in learning about such possibilities.

Orfield's discussion of possibilities for coordinating desegregation in schools and housing emphasizes three major policy goals: (1) achieving stable integration in communities that already have both minority and nonminority residents; (2) opening nonminority neighborhoods, schools, and jobs to blacks and Hispanics; and (3) maintaining desegregation in neighborhoods where revitalization is forcing out low status, minority families. He describes many actions such as the following, which can be taken and in a few communities are being taken to achieve or maintain desegregation in schools and neighborhoods: penalize realtors who steer clients to segregated neighborhoods; establish housing counseling centers that emphasize desegregation; exempt integrated neighborhood schools from busing; give preference to integrated neighborhood schools in closing schools; provide scattered-site subsidized housing for families; provide loans to maintain and improve housing in desegregated neighborhoods; guarantee the safety of children in desegregated schools; improve the quality of instruction in desegregated schools; and carry out school desegregation on a regional or metropolitan basis.

WHEN INNER-CITY FAMILIES ARE RELOCATED IN THE SUBURBS

One of the potentially most important social developments occurring in the United States involves the movement of inner-city families from Chicago to its suburbs. This movement followed the 1977 decision in *Hills* v. *Gautreaux*, in which the U.S. Supreme Court ruled that black families had been unconstitutionally concentrated in inner-city public housing. To remedy this constitutional violation, the federal government made rent subsidies available for black families who would move to outlying Chicago neighborhoods. By the early 1990s, more than 4000 had taken advantage of this opportunity to relocate in desegregated neighborhoods and 118 suburbs, and thousands more swamped the program's telephone lines to add their names to a long waiting list (Schmidt 1989; Johnson 1990b).

James Rosenbaum and his colleagues at Northwestern University have been collecting data on black families participating in the Gautreaux remedy and have prepared several reports dealing with the experience of people relocated in the suburbs. Rosenbaum has reported that there were no differences in the number of friends made by children and youth in these families when compared with a city control group and that they were as "well-integrated in their new neighborhood as in their former neighborhood, or as the city control group was" (Rosenbaum, Rubinowitz, and Kulieke 1985, 10/12).

In addition, the mothers of the suburban black students reported that peer influences were significantly more positive than in the city, that the students had more positive attitudes about their suburban schools than about their former city schools, and that peer influence was strongly and positively associated with the grades

students received in school (Rosenbaum, Kulieke, and Rubinowitz 1987). The authors summarized much of the school experience of the relocated black students:

> *The mothers reported that their children's academic performance relative to their classmates did not change from the city to the suburbs. Despite the greater demands of the suburban schools, teachers also offered more help in the suburbs and this sometimes had great benefits, according to the reports of some mothers. (Rosenbaum, Rubinowitz, and Kulieke 1985, 10/16–10/17)*

Rosenbaum and his colleagues also have reported that single mothers are finding suburban employment and that their sense of control over their fate is strongly associated with their aspirations for their children (Rosenbaum and Popkin 1991). That is, among black families in the Gautreaux project, mothers who responded that they had some control over their future have higher educational expectations for their sons and daughters than did mothers perceiving less control over their future. In addition, mothers who perceived relatively low amounts of physical danger in their environment had higher educational aspirations for their sons than did those who perceived greater danger. These generally encouraging findings indicate that relocation to the suburbs may provide an improved setting for inner-city families and for the social and educational development of their children. Relocation to the suburbs may be one of the most potent and successful social policies for alleviating the plight of underclass children and youth growing up in concentrated poverty neighborhoods in big cities (Rosenbaum and Popkin 1991).

CONCLUSION

Considerable desegregation of elementary and secondary schools has been attained in much of the United States, particularly in rural areas and in small towns and cities. However, segregation is still prevalent for many minority students, particularly in large Northern and Midwestern cities that have many concentrated poverty schools enrolling a substantial proportion of the nation's black and Hispanic children and youth.

Research on desegregation, although somewhat ambiguous, indicates that it can help improve minority students' achievement, motivation, and aspirations and can also help improve subsequent social and economic opportunities and outcomes. One major mechanism for explaining this result appears related to the fact that socioeconomic desegregation frequently removes minority students from poorly functioning, concentrated poverty schools.

Some big-city districts with a relatively small minority enrollment or that serve a regional population are providing desegregated education for most minority students. Other urban districts with a high percentage of minority students have enhanced desegregation through magnet schools and cooperative arrangements with suburban districts. In addition, instructional improvement has become a major emphasis in many big-city desegregation plans.

However, given the existing widespread pattern of segregation of minority students, much more remains to be accomplished in order to help alleviate the plight of the underclass, to reverse metropolitan trends toward segregation and stratification, and thereby to bolster the health of the city and the metropolis as a whole. Attaining these goals will require metropolitan arrangements for dealing with the segregation of millions of minority students within the educational system in accordance with perspectives articulated by President Lyndon Johnson in a 1965 message to Congress on "The Problems and Future of the Central City and its Suburbs":

We begin with the awareness that the city,* possessed of its own inexorable vitality, has ignored the classic jurisdictions of municipalities and counties and States. That organic unit we call the city spreads across the countryside, enveloping towns, building vast new suburbs, destroying trees and streams. Access to suburbs has changed the character of the central city. The jobs and income of suburbanites may depend upon the opportunities for work and learning offered by the central city. Polluted air and water do not respect the jurisdictions of mayors and city councils, or even of Governors. Wealthy suburbs often form an enclave whereby the well-to-do and the talented can escape from the problems of their neighbors, thus impoverishing the ability of the city to deal with its problems.

The interests and needs of many of the communities which make up the modern city often seem to be in conflict. But they all have an overriding interest in improving the quality of life of their people. And they have an overriding interest in enriching the quality of American civilization. These interests will only be served by looking at the metropolitan area as a whole, and planning and working for its development. (Johnson 1965)

EXERCISES

1. What are the arguments for and against stressing desegregation of schools in the primary grades? What arguments can be made for giving it particular stress for high school students?

2. Talk to some of your relatives or neighbors about their views on school desegregation. To what degree do you think they make a distinction between racial-ethnic and socioeconomic integration? To what degree do they assume that desegregation automatically assumes mixing working-class minority students with high-status nonminority students?

---

* In this message, the word *city* is used to mean the entire urban area—the central city and its suburbs.

3. What do you think are the major obstacles in persuading students to attend magnet high schools? How do you think these obstacles might be overcome?

4. The Supreme Court has ruled that school segregation must have been caused by intentional state action to justify a court order for desegregation. Consult a law library to see if you can find any material on the legal definition of *intent*.

5. What are the reasons that school desegregation seems to have been achieved much more widely in towns and small cities than big cities?

6. What part do you think private elementary and secondary education plays in the development of social and geographic patterns in the metropolitan area? In what ways might private schools contribute to stratification and segregation? In what ways might they contribute to reducing or minimizing the effects of stratification and segregation?

7. Investigate a school that has had a successful program of racial integration. Talk with some teachers and parents as well as with the principal. Analyze the reasons for success.

8. Investigate a school in which efforts at racial integration have been unsuccessful. What are the reasons for failure?

9. Contact city or regional planning officials to obtain information on the movement of black families to the suburbs. Is such movement occurring on an integrated or segregated basis? How rapidly is it taking place? What do planning officials see as its most important implications?

SUGGESTIONS FOR FURTHER READING

1. *School Desegregation in Metropolitan Areas: Choices and Prospects*, edited by Ronald D. Henderson and Mary von Euler, includes papers and discussion originating at a 1977 conference dealing with most major aspects of desegregation in central cities and metropolitan areas. The topic is examined from a number of vantage points ranging from legal and political to instructional and financial.

2. *The Future of Big-City Schools*, edited by Daniel U. Levine and Robert J. Havighurst, includes chapters dealing with desegregation policies and developments, magnet school programs, and related topics in urban education. Major sections are devoted to describing developments in Cincinnati and Dallas.

3. *The Integration of American Schools* by Harris, Jackson, and Rydingsword reviews a wide range of data and viewpoints on desegregation in the 1970s.

4. *School Desegregation: Past, Present, and Future*, edited by Stephan and Feagin (1980), includes chapters on a variety of topics involving desegregation.

5. B. Smith's book, *They Closed Their Schools*, tells the story of the closing of public schools in Prince Edward County, Virginia, an extreme example of a community that attempted to avoid, then delay, school integration. The story is told in the personal terms of the people involved.

6. A conservative analysis of school desegregation rationales and effects is provided in *The Burden of Brown* by Raymond Wolters.

7. A positive view of the St. Louis desegregation plan is described in "County and City Transfers," a 1987 paper by Willie and Uchitelle. A negative interpretation is put forward in *A Semblance of Justice* by Daniel Monti.

8. Case studies of urban magnet schools are provided in *Different by Design* by Mary Haywood Metz.

9. Methodological issues in studying desegregation are described and discussed in *School Desegregation Research*, edited by Jeffrey Prager, Douglas Longshore, and Melvin Seeman.

10. *Cooperative Learning* (1990b) by Robert Slavin describes and analyzes several cooperative learning approaches and summarizes research dealing with achievement effects for disadvantaged minority students.

11. *Magnet Schools*, edited by Estes, Levine, and Waldrip (1990), includes chapters describing plans in Kansas City and San Diego. Other chapters discuss marketing, placement of students, and related operational topics.

Cultural Pluralism and Minority Education

Even though Anglo-Protestants have constituted the largest subgroup, the population of the United States has always included a number of different national, racial, and religious groups. The diversity of population in the United States today is underlined in Table 10-1, which provides an enumeration of the population of the major racial groups and Hispanics designated in the 1980 Census.

Relationships between groups in the United States population frequently have been antagonistic, but the expressed ideal of many Americans historically has been to anticipate and support reduction of group differences through various forms of common activity within a framework of a democratic society. Thus, it was common to speak of the United States as a "melting pot."

However, in recent years the attitude toward the continued existence of subgroups and subcultures has become more approving and more appreciative. Educational systems are now expected to help various groups maintain their cultural differences and achieve their cultural goals within a cooperative framework. Thus, James E. Allen, Jr., former United States Commissioner of Education, observed that

the day of the melting pot is over. No longer is it the ideal of each minority to become an indistinguishable part of the majority. Today, each strives to maintain its identify while seeking its rightful share of the social, economic, and political fruits of our system. Self-help and self-determination have become the rallying cries of all minorities.

Separate and different group cultures and traditions are now generally regarded as healthy

TABLE 10-1 *Estimated Population of Major Racial Groups and Hispanics in the 1990 Census*

Group	Percentage of Total Population	Percentage Increase in Population Since 1980
White	80	6
Black	12	13
Hispanic	9	53
Asian	3	108
Native American	1	38
Other	4	45

Source: U.S. Bureau of the Census.
Note: Hispanics may be of any race. For this reason, percentages given above add to 109 percent. The estimated percentage of non-Hispanic whites in the population in 1990 was 76 percent. Many persons in the Other category are reassigned to the major groups specified above after additional analysis. In previous census reassignments, more than 90 percent were classified as White.

in a complex democratic society. They enrich the society. At the same time, the mainstream offers many rewards to members of minority groups who reduce their allegiance to a minority group. Thus, there is an inherent tension between the societal forces that push for a democratic cultural pluralism and those that work toward a democratic social integration.

In the period since 1965, the slogans of pluralism have been popular, but integration continues to be an important social goal. By *social integration* we mean the mixing of various racial and cultural groups through association in business, education, government and cultural affairs, and some degree of intermarriage with the goal being one common culture. By *democratic cultural pluralism* we mean the amicable coexistence of a variety of racial, ethnic, religious, and economic groups, each group keeping its subculture partially intact.

If equal respect and equal opportunities and privileges are accorded to all groups, then a condition of democratic pluralism may be said to exist, as it does in Switzerland, with its French, German, and Italian cantons, and in Holland, where religious subcultures set themselves apart in political and civic as well as social and religious affairs. The dynamics of the burgeoning pluralism and diversity characteristic of contemporary society and education in the United States have been captured and celebrated by Otto Friedrich in a special *Time* magazine issue dealing with immigration:

The American schoolroom has traditionally provided a hopeful glimpse of the nation's future. . . . Come for a moment to the playground of the Franklin elementary school in Oakland, where black girls like to chant their jump-roping numbers in Chinese. 'See you manana,' one student shouts with a Vietnamese accent. 'Ciao!' cries another, who has never been anywhere near Italy. And let it be noted that the boy who won the National Spelling Bee . . . was born in India . . . and speaks Tamil at home. . . . Graffiti sprayed in

a nearby park send their obscure signals in Farsi. . . . Such changes require adaptation not only in the schools and the marketplace but throughout society. The Los Angeles County court system now provides interpreters for eighty different languages from Albanian and Amharic to Turkish and Tongan. (Friedrich 1985, 29).

RECENT IMMIGRATION PATTERNS AND DEVELOPMENTS

Until late in the nineteenth century, most immigrants to the United States were from England, France, Germany, Ireland, Scotland, Sweden, and other places in Northern Europe. From the 1870s until the 1920s, when Congress severely restricted immigration, large number of immigrants also came from Italy, Poland, Russia, and other parts of Eastern and Southern Europe. After provisions of 1965 legislation liberalized immigration, the number of in-migrants increased rapidly. More than 6 million legal immigrants entered the United States in the 1980s (Hall 1990). In 1990, Congress once again increased immigration quotas, from about one-half million to approximately 700,000 per year. The Census Bureau estimates that the proportion of U.S. population growth accounted for by immigration will increase from about one-fourth in the 1980s to more than one-third in the year 2005 (Pear 1990b).

Like previous newcomers to the United States, a majority of immigrants since 1965 have settled in or near old coastal cities and have been willing to accept relatively low-paid work to make their way in a new land. Unlike the bulk of previous immigrants who were mostly European whites, many recent newcomers have been from Asia and Central and South America. Alejandro Portes and Rubén Rumbaut (1990) studied the data on recent in-migration to the United States and concluded that the most striking overall characteristic of new immigrant groups is their *diversity*. Significant numbers of immigrants now arrive from more than 100 locations throughout the world, and "contemporary immigration features a bewildering variety of origins, return patterns, and modes of adaptation to American society." "Never before," they further concluded, "has the United States received immigrants from so many countries, from such different social and economic backgrounds, and for so many reasons" (Portes and Rumbaut 1990, p. 7).

Although many immigrants are still struggling as their predecessors did to gain a foothold on the ladder leading to economic and social mobility, many others are succeeding or beginning to succeed in diverse fields of economic activity. Arab Americans involved in food distribution in the Detroit area, Korean American professionals in Los Angeles and New York, Vietnamese fishermen in Texas, African Americans from Jamaica and other Caribbean islands now operating a variety of small businesses on the East Coast, Russian computer scientists flocking to California and New York, Cuban Americans in every occupational field in Florida—these are but a few of the groups and fields of endeavor associated with recent immigration. The view that there is a "uniform assimilation process" that different immigrant groups are experiencing in the "course of several generations as a precondition for their social and economic advancements. . . . [is thus] increasingly implausible" (Portes and Rumbaut 1990, 8). Instead, there "are today first-generation millionaires who speak broken English, foreign-born mayors of large cities, and top-flight engineers and scientists in the nation's research centers; there are also those, at the other extreme, who cannot even take the first step toward assimilation because of the insecurity linked to an uncertain legal status" (Portes and Rumbaut 1990, 8).

Within this diverse pattern, it is clear that a substantial proportion of immigrants in recent decades have been relatively well educated and have entered the United States with a strong determination to work hard and succeed. The latter quality has tended to characterize in-migrants willing or forced to leave their homelands

throughout our history, but the relatively high levels of education among many recent groups of immigrants is a newer development associated with 1965 legislative preferences given to skilled applicants. As a result, half or more of U.S. citizens born in Bangladesh, Egypt, India, Kenya, Pakistan, Taiwan, Zambia, and several other nations have had at least some college education (Portes and Rumbaut 1990).

Some immigration-related controversies since 1965 have involved the total number of immigrants to be admitted annually, the extent to which political refugees and relatives of previous migrants should be given preference, the maximum quotas to be allocated to various countries, and the actions that should be taken to impede and/or assist persons who enter illegally. Major legislation enacted in 1986 included steps to prevent illegal entry, along with provisions to assist and legalize undocumented entrants already well established in the United States. In 1990, Congress established additional preferences for applicants with relatively high occupational skills, educational background, and/or good job prospects in the United States. But in the end, according to one point of view, the

> *precise number and type of immigrants to be admitted aren't important. Raising the current 650,000 per year to a million and allowing more skill-based Hong Kong and Soviet sorts seems a reasonable step. Whatever: so long as they keep coming. Because immigration is the defining fact of American life, as central to our national identity as the royal family is to England's. The Korean grocers, working like slaves to build a future, and all the others in their kaleidoscope of hues and tongues, serve to remind us who our grandparents were. They are our future and our past. (Klein 1990, 19)*

Importance and Value

Expanded immigration into the United States in the 1970s and 1980s generated widespread concern about possible significant negative consequences. In particular, many citizens worried that immigrants might be reducing employment opportunities for native-born workers and might be creating tax increases and deficits to pay for education, health care, and other added social services (Skerry 1991).

Some economists who have examined effects of immigration in recent decades have concluded that the overall consequences have been positive rather than negative. For example, George Borjas (1990) concluded that there is no evidence that competition from immigrants has substantially harmed native workers in recent decades. Julian Simon (1990, 1991) concluded that immigrants are making important economic and social contributions that outweigh their consumption of government services. Most informed observers do agree, in any case, that immigration policy should place emphasis on encouraging entry of highly skilled and educated newcomers in the future (Mandell 1990). In line with this viewpoint, federal legislation passed in 1990 greatly increased quotas set aside for in-migrants with high levels of technical and professional skills (Pear 1990a, 1990b).

In addition to contributing to internal economic and social development, many immigrants have been making important contributions that help the United States become stronger and more competitive internationally. Probably the most important and visible benefits involve the relatively high rates at which the children of immigrants from China, Cuba, India, Korea, the Philippines, the Soviet Union, Thailand, and other countries are entering computer science, engineering, medical research, physics, and numerous other technical and scientific fields, at a time when enrollment in these fields at U.S. colleges and universities has been otherwise declining (Kotkin 1991b). One consequence is that there are now more than 6,000 (East) Indian-surnamed and 10,000 Chinese-surnamed engineers and scientists employed at Silicon Valley firms in California (Kotkin and Kishimoto 1988; Kotkin 1991a). In addition,

population growth associated with immigration (immigrants plus their children) now accounts for more than one-fourth of U.S. population growth. The Census Bureau predicts that this will increase steadily in the future (Pear 1990a).

Beyond direct contributions to U.S. national development and international competitiveness associated with engineering, science, and the professions, immigrants are helping maintain and build the image and influence of the United States as a leading nation in world affairs. As summarized by Joel Kotkin (1989), the importance of these developments can be viewed as follows:

> *Since the 1970's the United States has accepted more* legal *immigrants than the rest of the world combined . . . [largely for this reason, the United States] will have a younger population than any of our rivals. . . . Perhaps more important than mere numbers, however, is the racial makeup of America's new immigrants, the vast majority of whom hail from Latin America and Asia. . . . We are moving from being a "melting pot" of Europeans to a "world nation" with links to virtually every part of the inhabited globe.*
>
> *In a world where the economic center of gravity is rapidly shifting away from the Atlantic toward the Pacific Basin, the emergence of the American world nation provides a major advantage in adjusting to the new world reality. As a world nation, the United States can transcend its European identity and emerge as a multiracial role model in an increasingly nonwhite economic order. . . . [Already] Hispanic influence has transformed Miami into the banking capital of Latin America, while on a smaller scale boosting San Antonio and San Diego into business centers for rapidly industrializing Northern Mexico. Asian immigrants have turned Los Angeles and San Francisco into dynamic centers of Oriental capitalism. (Kotkin 1989, 23–24)*

PLURALISM

The United States was a pluralistic society from its very beginning, with the thirteen colonies representing a variety of European nationalities and a variety of religious groups, with Indians who were being pushed out of their lands, and with Africans who were held and sold as slaves. This pluralism could hardly be called democratic. For many of the European immigrants who came to this country in the nineteenth century, there was blatant discrimination. For example, the large Irish immigration between 1840 and 1860, resulting partly from famine in Ireland, produced a lower class of Irish in the United States, who were given only the most menial jobs. Advertisements in the newspapers for an office boy or for a parlor maid often carried the letters "NINA" (No Irish Need Apply). Subsequent to this period, immigrant Hungarians, Poles, Italians, Croatians, and Russian Jews arrived and lived in poverty under brutal conditions of employment.

What saved the situation for the newcomers and led to their upward mobility were the constant demands for unskilled and semiskilled labor in the expanded economy, the free schools that enabled many immigrant children to move into white-collar jobs, the almost free land on the frontier, and the expansion of local government and business, which created roles into which many of the immigrants could move with little formal schooling. A mixture of social integration and cultural pluralism was at work. Each wave of European immigrants who arrived without money or position improved its status rapidly, although leaving behind in its rise, after one or two generations, some members who were not so fortunate.

Several groups, however, did not share equitably in the nineteenth-century blend of democratic pluralism and social integration: the American Indians, who were pushed into inferior lands and decimated by the U.S. Army if they chose to fight; and the freed African slaves. Smaller groups in some regions were also virtually excluded from participation.

The period of United States social history up to about 1900 was dominated by a policy that sociologist Milton Gordon calls *Anglo-conformity*. This policy assumed the desirability of maintaining the social institutions of England, the English language, and English-oriented cultural patterns as dominant in American life (Gordon 1964). The society was also heavily Protestant, and there was much prejudice against Catholics and new Catholic immigrants. The German, Scandinavian, and Irish immigrants who predominated during the 1840 to 1890 period were accepted with some misgivings. Most of the Irish and some of the Germans were Catholic. The Scandinavians were regarded as clannish and they maintained their home languages. Still, the country was large, a growing industry needed labor, and the frontier was open. The society became in fact more pluralistic than before.

Around the beginning of the twentieth century, there developed the concept of a new, composite nationality being formed through the agency of frontier life as it spread across the middle of the country and onward to the west. The historian Frederick Jackson Turner in his influential book, *The Frontier in American History,* said the western frontier acted as "a solvent for national heritages and separatist tendencies" of the European immigrants (Gordon 1964, 118). Yet the vast flow of immigration from southern Europe after 1880 made it clear that neither Ango-conformity nor the frontier life could be a feasible social or political model. The eastern cities were filling up with a polyglot population. This reality had to be reckoned with in any conception of the structure of American society.

An English Jewish writer, Israel Zangwill, stated the new theory through his popular drama, *The Melting Pot,* first produced in 1909. The hero of the play is a Russian Jewish immigrant who falls in love with a Gentile girl. The hero, in the rhetoric of his day, proclaims that

> *America is God's Crucible, the great Melting Pot where all the races of Europe are melting and re-forming! Here you stand, good folk,*

think I, when I see them at Ellis Island, here you stand in your 50 groups, with your 50 languages and histories, and your 50 blood hatreds and rivalries. But you won't be long like that, brothers, for these are the fires of God you've come to—these are the fires of God. A fig for your feuds and vendettas! Germans and Frenchman, Irishmen and Englishmen, Jews and Russians—into the Crucible with you all! God is making the American. (Zangwill 1909, 37)

The melting pot theory accepted the eastern and southern European immigrants as good material for making Americans, just as good as the English and north European stock.

Integration and Pluralism after 1920

After the close of World War I, the socioeconomic condition of the country changed markedly. Restrictions were placed on immigration, thus opening the job market in heavy industry to migrants from the South and the Appalachian states and to Mexican Americans from the Southwest. Puerto Ricans came to the eastern cities. These groups did not integrate readily into the mainstream. At the same time, technological development reduced the proportion of jobs that required high-school and college education. Industrial productivity increased so much that after 1950 the economic-industrial complex could not employ all the available labor, thus producing a substantial group of unemployed who had to live on welfare payments.

In effect, socioeconomic changes since about 1920 have worked to restrict opportunities for groups with the lowest incomes to integrate themselves into the mainstream of economic, social, and civil life. This was occurring at the same time that the United States was becoming in some respects more of a melting pot than it had ever been. Overt racial and ethnic discrimination was reduced on an historically dramatic scale after World War II. Laws restricting opportunities for African Americans, Jews, Japanese, and other groups were eliminated, and many minority citizens moved into the mainstream of United States society.

Social practices also changed. Religious and ethnic intermarriage became common, and racial intermarriage became less rare. By the 1980s, more than three-quarters of all young Irish, German, and Polish American men were marrying outside of their respective ethnic groups (Sowell 1978a; Alba 1990).

One effect of these changes, however, was to make it clear that the melting pot had its limits. Many members of the various minority groups prefer not to be too assimilated within dominant patterns in the larger culture, and in any case millions of minority citizens who are economically and racially isolated from the larger society did not realistically have the option of assimilation. It thus became clear that socially or economically disadvantaged groups would have to organize within their own communities to work for improved economic and social opportunity.

Difficulties in Maintaining Subcultural Identities

As many individuals from innumerable minority groups and ethnic subcultures succeeded in entering the mainstream of U.S. society, members of each group have had to decide whether or how to try to retain some of the distinctive language patterns, religious practices, family socialization arrangements, food and clothing preferences, and other aspects of their various subcultures. Dilemmas were posed by the wish to participate fully in the larger society and culture on the one hand and desires to maintain the integrity of one's cultural background on the other. Such dilemmas have been an important part of U.S. history for hundreds of years. Whether in the form of parents worried about how to transmit their values to their children or children uncertain whether or how much they should retain the cultural patterns of their parents, each generation has had to struggle with the same underlying issues.

The poignancy inherent in dilemmas involving maintenance versus rejection of subcultural identity has provided the basis for countless historical and literary works that document their importance in a nation composed of immigrants from all parts of the world. To illustrate these dilemmas, we quote from a recent article in which Jonathan Raban (1990) reflected on a conversation he had with a Korean American father (Mr. Han) who had been in the United States fewer than twenty years. Mr. Han worried whether he would succeed in ensuring that his increasingly Americanized daughter would continue to reflect the attitudes and behaviors that he viewed as essentially Korean:

How, growing up in English, could she hug "Koreanness" to herself as the essence of her identity, while all the time her parents talked Columbia, talked medical school.... "Ah," said Mr. Han, "This is what we are wondering. Wondering, wondering, all the time.... We have example of Chinese. Look at Chinese!—in two—three generation the Chinese people here, they cannot even read the characters! Chinese is only name *... all in the melting pot!"*.... *The way he said it, it was a Mel Ting Pot, and I saw it as some famous cast-iron oriental cooking utensil, in which human beings were boiled over a slow fire until they broke down in to a muddy fibrous stew....*

On the street across from the restaurant I could see a rambling black-painted chalet surrounded by a [billboard] which said Look What We Got! 30 Nude Showgirls! Table Dancing! *It was a sign to chill the heart of a Korean father of young daughters. (Raban 1990, 240–241)*

The Rise of Cultural Pluralism

The idea of the melting together of many diverse cultures into a single culture was not widely approved by leaders of American thought, nor was it clear that it was actually happening. Horace M. Kallen criticized the melting pot theory in his book *Culture and Democracy in the United States* (1924). He used the term *cultural pluralism* to describe his program for the United States as a democracy of nationalities cooperating voluntarily. Other social philosophers, social scientists, and popular writers favored this concept. Among educators, the field of *intergroup relations* assumed considerable importance. Teaching units on intergroup relations and recommendations for more favorable treatment of minority groups found their way into high-school studies and history courses. The late 1940s and early 1950s saw much activity along these lines, supported by such organizations as the National Conference of Christians and Jews and the American Jewish Committee.

Then came the 1954 Supreme Court decision against racially segregated public schools, followed in the 1960s by the Civil Rights Act and by the Civil Rights movement, which broke down many political and economic barriers against African Americans. As noted in Chapter 9, however, black Americans were not brought into the melting pot. With the exception of a few middle-class families, they were segregated residentially in the large cities and their children continued to be segregated in school. Nevertheless, the 1960s saw substantial improvement in the economic, educational, and political situation of the black population.

The relative success of the early civil rights movement stimulated other minority groups to organize for group action—especially the Mexican American and Puerto Rican and American Indian groups. The middle 1960s saw the creation of several Hispanic groups: Cesar Chavez developed the United Farm Workers Organizing Committee in California; Reies Lopez Tijerina started the Alianza Federal de Mercedes in New Mexico. These groups worked for better housing, better wages, better health and educational services. Among the Puerto Ricans, ASPIRA worked for better educational and social conditions. Several important Native American groups were organized, including the American Indian

Movement, which came to public attention with the occupation of the Bureau of Indian Affairs building in Washington in 1972. Meanwhile, the Black Muslims also grew strong in a number of cities, with separate schools and separate business activities alongside their religious institutions.

Integration, Pluralism, Separatism

Cultural pluralism lies between integration on the one hand and separatism on the other. The boundaries are not clear. Although the melting pot concept is the extreme of integration, cultural pluralism can shade into a stable form of integration in which various subcultures are quite distinct in some areas of life but are merged together in other areas of life. At the other extreme is a multigroup society characterized by separatism in which each group keeps itself apart through laws and customs that prevent intermarriage and through a rigid limitation on the extent of its relations with other groups. Individuals and groups that advocate or lean toward separatist policies include the following:

1. Those who want to be left alone to work out their own lifestyles, which they see as superior to others. This position is characteristics of certain small religious sects such as the Amish, the Hutterites, the Seventh Day Adventists, and the Black Muslims. They attempt to keep separate schools and to do as little business as possible with the mainstream society. In 1884, when the Roman Catholic bishops made a decision that Catholic children were not receiving proper religious education and called for every parish in the country to set up and operate its own parish school, this was a separatist act.

2. Those with a distinct and visible racial-ethnic identity, who participate fully in the educational and economic mainstream but tend to maintain a separate social life. Some Asian Americans have taken or been pushed into this condition.

3. Many American Indians and Eskimos—a numerically small but historically significant group, who have been kept in a separate status by

historical events and by basic cultural differences from the European majority.

4. Those who want to use separatism as a temporary means for building strength and identity within the minority group, after which the group will be ready to move into a pluralistic situation with power and confidence. This is the position of spokespersons for some subgroups of African Americans. It grows out of a conviction that the existing form of pluralism is not satisfactory and will not become more satisfactory unless minority groups can gain the power and the self-assurance with which to negotiate with other groups for a fair distribution of the opportunities and privileges of the larger society (Coughlin 1990).

European Ethnic Identification and Affiliations

Some recent research indicates that ethnic identification continues to be an important consideration for many Americans from European background and other ethnic groups (Kristo 1989). For example, Andrew Greeley and his colleagues at the National Opinion Research Center have been collecting data on ethnic groups in the United States and have found that the majority of Irish, Italian, and Jewish respondents rank their ethnic background as either "extremely important" or "very important," and that the adolescent members of these ethnic groups are more likely than their parents to rank their ethnicity as important. Greeley concludes that "the NORC research shows that both unconscious transmissions of ethnic subcultures and conscious ethnic identification are important features of American life" (1980, 148–149). Research also indicates that ethnic identification can be variable across generations, rising or falling in accordance with a variety of political, economic, social, and other factors (Kristo 1989).

However, other research suggests that ethnic affiliations and loyalties have become relatively shallow and inconsequential among many people in the United States with European ancestry. For example, Richard Alba (1990) collected data on Irish, Italian, and Polish Americans residing in the Albany, New York, area and found that only about 20 percent "feel a special sense of relationship to someone else because that person has their ethnic background," and fewer still say they communicate much about their ethnic heritage to their children. Almost none are fluent in the European languages of their ancestors. Other than at least occasionally consuming food associated with their ethnic background, most respondents reported little or no participation in activities involving or reflecting their ethnic origins. After examining these data and other information regarding affiliations of Americans with European ancestors, Andrew Hacker (1990) concluded that postimmigrant generations historically and still today generally have been drawn into a prevailing "trans-national" culture that discourages maintenance of affiliations and loyalties involving a person's particular ethnic background (also see Wolfe 1990).

Historic Importance of Cultural Pluralism

As suggested, it is not easy to find a productive and workable balance between assimilation into a common culture and separation, between cooperative participation in a society and maintenance of a distinctive heritage or identity. Many social and political forces operate to create antagonism among racial/ethnic and cultural subgroups and to generate power struggles and conflict that may result in either subjugation of minorities or harmful fragmentation in the larger society. In this context, John Higham (1990), Emeritus Professor of History at Johns Hopkins University, has emphasized the long-range importance of U.S. movement toward cultural pluralism:

> *In the twentieth century . . . [a] new, multiethnic tolerance [began] spreading from intellectual circles to ever wider segments of the population . . . [and] gave militant minorities a latitude they had never before enjoyed. Dur-*
>
> *ing the middle decades of the twentieth century the relation of ethnic groups to America was gradually redefined. The claim that the U.S. was the great melting pot of the world was heard less and less following World War II and now is seldom made. Instead, in the rhetoric of civic rituals and public education, America was increasingly represented as a nation of enduring subcultures, through which an amiable diversity would and should prevail. . . .*
>
> *As a blueprint for America . . . [cultural pluralism] had just enough truth to undermine the preeminence of an Anglo-Protestant elite and just enough plausibility to cast a patina of idealism over the ensuing struggles for ethnic power. Objectively speaking, the invention of cultural pluralism was an extraordinary ethnic achievement: an exercise of mind that abolished any claims of white Protestants to constitute a rightful majority and defined us all as minorities and all minorities as equal. (Higham 1990, 13)*

Hispanic Separatism?

Separatist tendencies among Hispanics—primarily among Mexican Americans in the Southwest—may turn out to be much stronger than they have been among black Americans. The emphasis that many Mexican Americans place on retention of Spanish within their homes and communities, together with the growing size of predominantly Mexican-American communities in the Southwest, may result in a greater relative stress on separate development. Carlos Arce of the Institute for Social Research has been studying data on the attitudes of Mexican Americans and has found that respondents typically cited Spanish as the single most important aspect of Mexican culture for their families to maintain and were "virtually unanimous in wanting their children to know and speak Spanish." He concluded that the data show a "movement toward ethnicity and away from the 'melting pot'" (Arce 1982, 7). Similar developments have been described by Seth Mydans (1991).

Movement away from melting pot concepts does not, of course, in and of itself mean that Mexican Americans will move very far toward separatism rather than cultural pluralism (Portes and Rumbaut 1990). On the other hand, it is possible that insistence on bilingual as against desegregated education, isolation from the mainstream of large numbers of Mexican Americans in relatively self-contained "barrios," and political antagonism between Mexican Americans and other groups may result in systematic movement toward separatism. Such a movement might resemble separatist tendencies that have been developing among the French in Canada (Garreau 1982). The next two or three decades will determine whether such tendencies become a major force among Mexican Americans in the United States.

AFRICAN AMERICANS AND EDUCATION

Relations between blacks and whites have been a major problem for society throughout United States history. These relations have been changing rapidly since the mid-1950s, when African American migration to the cities began to reach massive proportions and the U.S. Supreme Court outlawed government-imposed segregation in the historic case *Brown* v. *Topeka Board of Education*. In one way or another, these changes have affected every major social institution, including family, business, industry, education, religion, government, sports, and communications. Education has been particularly critical in defining and reflecting the status and problems of the black population.

To understand the educational situation of a minority group, we need to know something about the group in terms of numbers, residence, and socioeconomic status. The black population has been growing at a slightly more rapid rate than the white population. It was 9.9 percent of the total United States population in 1950, 10.5 percent in 1960, 11.1 percent in 1970, 11.6 percent in 1980, and slightly more than 12 percent in 1990.

During the period since World War I, the black population has become urbanized, and it is now more urbanized than the white. In 1910, 73 percent of African Americans lived in rural or semirural settings. This situation is now reversed, with 82 percent living in metropolitan areas in 1988 (Table 10-2.) The urbanization of black Americans has posed new problems in intergroup relations. As long as most lived at a subsistence level in the rural South, African Americans generally were ignored by the rest of the country. When they moved into the cities, they became more highly visible. Many became integrated into the social and economic life of the cities. They followed the familiar pattern of other immigrant ethnic groups. They worked hard and saved their money; they secured as good an education as possible for their children; their children moved up the socioeconomic ladder into professional and business occupations (Lewis 1990). Thus a sizable black middle class developed. More than 40 percent of working-age African Americans can now be classified as middle-class, compared with less than 5 percent in 1910 (Business-Higher Education Forum 1990).

However, a large proportion of African Americans have not been able to succeed in this way; instead, they have become a sizable underclass in concentrated poverty neighborhoods. They and their children are still set aside from the mainstream of life. They are segregated residentially, they are discriminated against with regard to housing and jobs, and their children attend segregated schools (National Research Council 1989; Lemann 1991b). Thus the overall status of black Americans can be viewed in terms of a glass that is either half full (enormous progress since 1940) or half empty (increase in and worsening conditions regarding the large underclass segment).

Also note that a significant proportion of black Americans consists of immigrants from other countries. Nearly 2 million African Americans were born in Africa, Central or South America, the Caribbean, or elsewhere outside the United States. The percentage of foreign-born immigrants in the black population is higher than the comparable figure for the U.S. population as a whole.

TABLE 10-2　*Selected Characteristics of African American, Hispanic, and White Populations in the United States*

Characteristics	African American	Hispanic	White
Median family income (dollars in 1988)	19,329	21,769	33,915
Poverty rate, children under 18 (1989)	44	36	14
Percentage children and youth in female-headed families (1989)	51	30	17
Lifetime fertility expectation (1988)	2.1	2.3	2.1
Average age (1987)	27	25	30
Occupational distribution (1988 percentages)			
White collar	42	40	58
Blue collar	32	37	27
Service	23	18	12
Farm	02	06	03
Metropolitan location (1988)			
Central city	57	56	27
Suburban	25	35	50
Nonmetropolitan	19	09	23
Years of education (1987 medians)	12.4	12.0	12.7

Sources: U.S. Bureau of the Census; Duaney and Pittman 1990; *Statistical Abstract of the United States* 1990.
Note: White-collar grouping includes professional and technical, managers and administrators, sales, and clerical; blue collar includes crafts and kindred, operatives, and nonfarm laborers; service includes private household and other. Persons of Hispanic origin may be of any race. Occupational distribution percentages vary from 100 due to rounding.

Status of African Americans

The occupational distribution of whites and blacks in 1988 can be compared from the data in Table 10-3. Smaller proportions of African Americans are found in the higher-status occupations (professionals and managers) and higher proportions in the lower-status occupations.

Another index of the relatively disadvantaged position of blacks is the fact that unemployment has long been, and continues to be, higher than among whites. Since 1950, the unemployment of blacks aged twenty and over has been about twice as high—roughly 8 to 10 percent as compared to 4 to 6 percent for whites. The differences have been particularly striking among young people aged sixteen to nineteen, where unemployment among whites since 1960 has fluctuated from 10 to 15 percent, but among blacks, from 25 to 45 percent. The unemployment rate among black teenagers averaged about 30 percent in the late 1980s (Brimmer 1990).

In addition, the percentage of blacks classified as below the poverty level continues to be much higher than the corresponding figure for whites. In 1989, 30 percent of blacks were classified as poor under U.S. Department of Labor income guidelines, as compared with 10 percent of whites. The median income of African American families relative to white families declined slightly from 61 percent in 1973 to 57 percent in 1988. In addition, the average income of households of black college graduates is only about two-thirds of that of their white counterparts (Wilkerson 1990c).

On the other hand, the occupational status of African Americans has improved markedly from 1958 to 1990. As we see in Chapter 7,

TABLE 10-3 *Changes in the Occupational Distribution of African American and Non-Hispanic White Workers, 1958 and 1988*

Occupational Grouping	African American		White	
	1958	1988	1958	1988
Managers, professionals, proprietors	06	18	24	30
Clerical, sales, technical, and administrative support	07	26	22	31
Service workers, including unskilled household	33	23	10	10
Precision workers, including crafts and foremen	06	09	14	13
Operators, including semiskilled laborers	35	23	22	14
Farming-related, forestry, and fishing	13	01	08	03

Sources: U.S. Bureau of the Census; *Statistical Abstract of the United States* 1990.
Note: Percentage totals vary from 100 due to rounding. Data for African Americans in 1958 include a small percentage of nonwhites other than blacks. A small percentage of technical workers, whom the Census Bureau now tabulates with clerical and sales, historically were tabulated with professionals.

studies of the 1962–1973 time period showed a clear increase in occupational and educational attainment among blacks, as a sizable black middle class formed and the status attainment process for blacks became much more similar to that of the white population. This result also is clear in Table 10-3, which shows that the proportion of black workers in higher-status occupations tripled between 1958 and 1988. After declining in the early 1980s, the number of black Americans earning more than $50,000 per year (in constant 1979 dollars) increased rapidly during the remainder of the decade (O'Hare 1989). Between 1950 and 1990 the African American population doubled, but the number of African Americans in white-collar jobs increased by 920 percent (Edsall and Edsall 1991).

How should one interpret the data indicating that blacks have been gaining in occupational status but falling farther behind whites in median family income since 1971? Several major developments help account for these differences.

1. Income gains that were registered in the 1950s and 1960s for the black population as a whole were not sustained in the 1970s and 1980s (National Research Council 1989).
2. Economic recession slowed or reversed trends toward socioeconomic improvement among African Americans.

3. Dissolution of two-parent families has placed an increasing percentage of the black population in low-income, female-headed families (Sternlieb and Hughes 1988; Waldrop 1990).
4. The black population apparently became more polarized into middle-class and underclass components than it had been before (Landry 1987; Muwakkil 1990).

Growth of the underclass occurred in conjunction with the urbanization of the black population, which located large numbers of black children and youth in big-city poverty neighborhoods characterized by a high percentage of female-headed families and unattached (single, separated, divorced) males (Brimmer 1990). This interpretation is supported by the following data:

- The income of two-earner black families has increased to 85 percent of the average of similar white families and is still increasing in relative terms (Raspberry 1990), but the relative income of female-headed black families has declined (Waldrop 1990).
- In 1990, more than 50 percent of black children under age eighteen were in families headed by females, as compared with 39 percent in 1970. In central cities of metropolitan

areas with more than 3 million people, more than 60 percent of black families with children were single-parent families (Brimmer 1990).

- Between 1970 and 1982, the percentage of black men classified as not in the labor force increased from 5 to 13 percent. The comparable increase for white men was from 3 to 5 percent (Farley 1984). This disproportion continued in the 1980s (Brimmer 1990).

Thus, recent demographic trends among African Americans seem to have further magnified a 1970 trend that Federal Reserve Board member Andrew Brimmer referred to then as a "deepening schism" among blacks, "between the well-prepared and those with few skills." Although the black middle class has been growing more rapidly than any other segment of the U.S. population (Brodie 1990), problems described in 1975 by Eleanor Norton clearly became even more severe in the late 1970s and 1980: "Raising black children in today's cities, fraught with social danger, requires the maximum in physical and psychological support. Particularly in the ghettos, where blacks are increasingly concentrated, it is simply too much to ask a black mother without a husband at home to raise the children of the black nation" (quoted in Auletta 1982, 263). For the sizable inner-city segment of the black population, according to the Business-Higher Education Forum (1990), the Kerner Commission's 1968 "stark prediction of a divided America, separate and unequal" has become "disturbingly accurate" (p. 17).

Also, the African American middle class may have experienced greater problems in the 1980s and early 1990s than in the 1970s, and much of the black middle class is in a precarious position (Reed 1990). Due partly to economic recessions, many middle-class African Americans have encountered serious problems maintaining their income and social status. On the average, having attained middle-class status much more recently than whites, many are more severely in debt, possess fewer assets, and have

much greater financial responsibilities for low-income relatives than does the typical middle-class white (Pear 1991). As pointed out by Andrew Billingsly of the University of Maryland, much is at stake for the United States as a whole: If middle-class African Americans are unable to maintain their income and security, "they will fall into the lower classes and not be able to pay their bills, their fair share of taxes, and will use a larger share of public services" (quoted in Wilkerson 1990b, 11).

The Plight of Underclass Black Males

Evidence supports the conclusion that the plight of urban black underclass has much of its roots in the problems experienced by males in the inner city (Wilson 1987, 1990; Bennett, Bloom, and Craig 1989; Mincy 1990). Recent data indicate that social disorganization among black males has reached new highs. For example, available data show that the percentage of black males between twenty-five and thirty-four years of age who are married and living with their wives declined from 74 percent in 1940 to 56 percent in 1980, compared with a decline from 72 percent to 69 percent for white males (U.S. Commission on Civil Rights 1987). The marriage rate for younger black males twenty to twenty-four years old) has fallen from 29 percent to 10 percent in less than twenty years (Business-Higher Education Forum 1990). Related data show that the percentage of females in the adult population of the inner city is much higher than the percentage of males (Edmondson and Cutler 1989), because many black males drop out of the labor force, are incarcerated, enter the military, or otherwise are excluded or exclude themselves from mainstream institutions and thus can be viewed as "casualties of the streets" (Sanchez 1990). Recent research also indicates that about two-thirds of young men (both black and white) in the inner city believe they can earn more from crime than from legitimate work, compared with approximately one-third in the early 1980s (Koretz 1991).

Among the indicators and results of this exclusion are the facts that more than 60 percent of black students completing college are female (Hatchett 1986; Carter and Wilson 1989), that the percentage of black male doctorate-degree recipients has declined but the black female percentage has increased (Hess, Ottinger, and Lippincott 1990), that the percentage of adult black females in managerial and professional occupations is more than 50 percent higher than the comparable percentage for adult black males, and that there are fewer than sixty employed black males per one hundred employed black women between the age of twenty and thirty-four (Christensen 1987). These aspects of imbalance between black men and women further exacerbate social disorganization (National Research Council 1989) by generating divorce and separation in families composed of relatively successful women and relatively unsuccessful men, by placing black women in competition with each other for a limited supply of relatively successful men, and by making it more difficult for black men to assume or discharge family responsibilities. (For extended discussion of these dynamics, see *Too Many Women?* by Marcia Guttentag and Paul Secord, 1983, and "The Divergence of Black and White Marriage Patterns," by Bennett, Bloom, and Craig, 1989). Thus research indicates that a 1-percent increase in the ratio of black women to black men results in an increase of more than 6 percent in the odds that black families will be female-headed (Darity and Myers 1984) and that "the problems of male joblessness . . . could be the single most important factor underlying the rise in unwed motherhood among poor black women" (Wilson and Neckerman 1984, 15).

Many concerned citizens and civic leaders are considering or exploring actions that might be particularly responsive to the plight of underclass black males. Proposals for reform include action in the areas of family policy, governmental tax policy, job training, and housing (e.g., Gibbs 1990). Regarding education, some advocates of comprehensive reform in social institutions are discussing possibilities such as the following, which David Hatchett described in a review of some recent thinking among black social scientists and community leaders:

> *Most of the authorities I interviewed concluded that the solution to the black male's difficulties in the educational process lies with . . . [the establishment of] black educational facilities. Perkins says that churches and other institutions need to begin a process where older black men help to teach black male teenagers how to conduct themselves as men. The Hares advocate the development of alternative schools similar to those in Jewish and Asian communities, where after the conclusion of the regular school, black children can be trained in a more specialized manner by black professionals. (Hatchett 1986, 46–47)*

As the crack epidemic spread havoc and conditions in the inner city continued to deteriorate in the late 1980s, concern with the plight of young black males also continued to grow. This situation was summarized by New York Congressman Major Owens, who observed that there is

> *a crisis within the African American community, and a large proportion of an entire generation—full of hope, full of promise—is being destroyed before our eyes. . . . the race between education and catastrophe is now upon us. To fail to educate yet another generation of African American males means that we not only continue to foreclose opportunities for individual lives, but that we continue to pay for our failure over and over again in unnecessary social costs. (Quoted in Conciatore and Hughes 1990, 6.)*

By 1991, several national conferences had focused on the plight of young African American men, mentoring programs designed to connect adult black men with male youth had been established or reinvigorated in a number of cities, sizable government and foundation grants had been awarded to support activities designed to help young black males, and private and government commissions had released action plans to provide support for inner-city youth. For example, the chairman of the association of historically black colleges declared that he and his colleagues had listened too passively to recitals of the observation that "there are more black men in prison than in college," and announced plans to involve the colleges' 3.5 million graduates in efforts to work with young African American males throughout the United States (Schmidt 1990b). In general, there is now widespread recognition of possibilities for enlisting middle-class black men to provide guidance for inner-city youth and of the necessity to involve and coordinate the work of many types of organizations in helping young African American males.

Some educators investigated possibilities for providing special help for young black males through the public schools. In Washington, DC, for example, a public commission recommended that separate classes be organized for black males, to be taught by adult black men. Milwaukee established two African American immersion schools. Emphasis in these schools is on African American curriculum, development of responsible masculinity, and contact every day with an adult African-American mentor (Chmelynski 1990; Johnson 1990; Karp 1991). Comparable projects also are being explored or initiated in Baltimore, Detroit, Miami, New York City, and other locations (Holland 1989; Karp 1991; Traub 1991). Proponents of these projects stress their potential value in providing structured discipline, support for the development of positive cultural identity, and active-learning experiences thought to be compatible with the learning styles of low-income black males (Traub 1990; Karp 1991). Following controversies involving the segregative aspects (both racial and socioeconomic) and alleged sexism in this approach, proposals for separate schools for black males have been rejected in several school districts and modified to allow for participation of females and other racial/ethnic groups in several others (Chmelyn-

ski 1990; Cohen 1990; Stevens 1990; Karp 1991). Careful evaluation of projects will help assess their potential for improving opportunities for young black males.

Is There a Black Subculture?

In thinking about the educational situation of the black population in the United States, it is important to understand the relative importance of two bases for grouping: one based on social class and the other based on race. According to one view, blacks and whites of a given social-class level are very similar in many aspects of life-style, and therefore social class is the major determinant of subcultural differences. The contrasting view is that color or race is a primary factor; that blacks behave and think differently from whites, no matter what their economic status, and thus that race is a major determinant of subcultural differences.

Systematic research has not been conducted on this issue, but data from several sources suggest that low-income African Americans are more pessimistic about opportunities to succeed and feel a greater sense of powerlessness than do low-income whites. For higher-income or higher-status segments of the population, the attitudes and values of blacks and whites are very similar, especially those that have to do with the education of children (Johnson and Sanday 1971; Berry and Asamen 1989).

John Ogbu (1978, 1982, 1990) has pointed out that the "castelike" history of blacks in the United States has had an effect in producing cultural patterns that diverge from the mainstream. Ogbu defined a "castelike minority" as a group in which membership "is acquired more or less permanently at birth. Members . . . generally have limited access to the social goods of society by virtue of their group membership" (1982, p. 125). Enslavement and, later, forced segregation of black Americans prevented them from taking advantage of social opportunities; as a result, cultural patterns arose that reflected their oppressed status. Ogbu indicated that some of these patterns arising out of many decades of blocked opportunity include development of

> a coping lifestyle shared by members of all social classes but most pronounced among lower-class blacks because of extreme poverty and fewer chances for advancement. . . . [Castelike minority children] live in a world in which they daily observe unemployed and underemployed adults as well as drug abuse, alcoholism, and crime. Although ghetto black parents tell their children that it is important to get a good education, they may also subtly convey to them the idea that society does not fully reward blacks. . . . The children increasingly learn to blame the system as their parents do. Eventually the children become disillusioned about their ability to succeed . . . [and] become less and less interested in school, less serious about their schoolwork, and less willing to exert the efforts necessary to do well in school. (Ogbu 1982, 125, 128, 132)

Some consequences of these cultural patterns have been described in a study that Signithia Fordham (1988) conducted at an inner-city high school in Washington, DC. After analyzing the attitudes and behaviors of high achievers at this mostly low-achieving school, Fordham concluded that they used "racelessness" as a strategy to succeed in their academic endeavors. Students striving to succeed in school were ridiculed as being "un-Black" and sometimes as "brainiacs" who identified with the dominant society; in turn, they "adopted personae that indicate a lack of identification" with their peers and with "indigenous Black American culture" (1988, 57–58). Fordham further concluded that this situation creates considerable ambivalence that "drains the energy" of both high and low achievers, and that although racelessness may be a pragmatic strategy that works for some people, it is not producing acceptable academic performance for most students (1988, 81–82). Indeed, as articulated by a black professor at Ford-

ham University, this situation can be viewed as distressingly dysfunctional:

> The notion that someone with a hunger for knowledge would be regarded as a "traitor to his race" would not only be incomprehensible to a Frederick Douglass, Marcus Garvey or Malcom X, it would seem like some kind of sinister white plot. In a society where blacks had to endure jailings, shootings and lynchings to get an education, it seems utterly unbelievable that some black youngsters now regard ignorance and academic failure as a sign of pride. (Naison 1990, 40, 42)

Additional evidence indicating that many low-income African American students acquire attitudes that are counterproductive in terms of academic achievement has been provided in a study of eight Los Angeles high schools conducted by Roslyn Mickelson (1990). Data collected in this study indicated that while they strongly endorsed the general value of education as a means to succeed later in life, working-class black adolescents were more likely than middle-class blacks or working-class whites to agree with items stating that "All I need to learn for my future is to read, write, and make change," and "Based on their experiences, my parents say people like us are not always paid or promoted according to our education." (Working-class white students also agreed with these items more frequently than did middle-class whites.) Mickelson also found that association with peers who did not plan to attend a four-year college was strongly related to both grade-point average and to agreement with items stating that education would not help one succeed personally. She concluded that a "critical factor" affecting the achievement of black students "may well be the students' perceptions of what her or his efforts and accomplishment in school ultimately will bring from the larger society" (Mickelson 1990, 59).

Attitudes opposing the school as portrayed by Ogbu, Fordham, and Mickelson appear to be widespread among students not only at inner-city black schools but also at working-class white schools (e.g., see Willis 1979; Mickelson 1990). On the other hand, rejection of traditional school curricula and academic demands does not appear to be typical of black students elsewhere or of working-class students in other types of schools (Mydans 1990). Gerald Grant (1988) recently studied a desegregated school in Syracuse and found that black students who study no longer are called "whitey" by other blacks, as their predecessors were in the late 1970s. Similarly, Peshkin and White (1990) and Hemmings (1991) interviewed black students attending desegregated high schools in California and Indiana. They concluded that the attitudes and behavior patterns of these students were diverse. Many seemed to be learning how to function well in both their minority culture and mainstream culture, although others did seem to exemplify the attitudes and behaviors described by Fordham. Middle-class black students are less likely to exemplify such attitudes or to succumb to ridicule then are their working-class peers, and desegregation presumably can help reduce perceptions of hopelessness arising from caste barriers and thus can enhance minority students' motivation to succeed in school and society.

On the other hand, desegregation may reinforce unproductive reactions among black students if they are low achievers and do not receive adequate assistance to meet rigorous academic demands in desegregated settings; in this case, black students might be inclined to reject academic values and school work as a psychological defense mechanism in an effort to alleviate feelings of personal failure or ambivalence. One implication is that educators should find ways to demonstrate respect for minority students' background and culture while also strengthening their self-esteem and capacity to succeed in school. An example of such an approach has been described by E. Wayne Harris (1988), who initiated a successful approach to accomplish these goals in the Fairfax County Public Schools, Virginia. Another implication, as pointed out by Ogbu, is that "minorities cannot simply rely on

public policy" to overcome disadvantaged status, but must begin to accept more responsibility for improvement "if they want to succeed" (quoted in Hill 1990).

Black English

One area of behavior in which the existence of a black subculture is apparent involves the use of so-called Black English—a particular dialect that differentiates many black people in the United States from other cultural groups (Dillard 1972; Wyatt and Seymour 1990). Like other aspects of black culture, Black English appears to be much more characteristic of working-class than middle-class blacks (Hale-Benson 1989). African Americans who have grown up in middle-class homes or attained middle-class status typically speak standard English most of the time but occasionally use some elements of Black English. Constructive school desegregation also appears to be helpful in building Standard English skills among African American students (Peshkin and White 1989). On the other hand, studies conducted by William Labov and his colleagues indicate that use of Black English has not been declining among black Americans, probably in part because so many live in highly segregated environments (Cooke 1989). Research also indicates that dialect has little association with school performance in the absence of social-class disadvantage (Schacter 1979; Williams 1987). However, Black English may be viewed as one important factor in turning socioeconomic disadvantage into educational disadvantage.

Because Black English appears to be the basic form of speech for many working-class African American children who are not succeeding in reading and other academic subjects, it frequently has been proposed that the school teach such students in Black English until the students learn to read and can shift to standard English (Pai 1990). Other proposals have suggested teaching English as a foreign language to students who speak Black English, capitalizing on similarities between Black English and Standard English, emphasizing students' personal experience in teaching language, helping students develop *code-switching* techniques, and various other transitional teaching techniques. These types of proposals generally reflect a belief that complete insistence on Standard English for students who are not prepared for it interferes with cognitive development and also communicates nonacceptance of one's culture to students who grow up speaking Black English (Shields and Shaver 1990).*

In line with these conclusions, Lynda Campbell (1990) identified the following principles that are important in helping Black-English speakers acquire competence in Standard English:

1. If students are not motivated, the teacher must help them understand the advantages of acquiring another dialect.
2. Second dialect instruction is most effective when features of Black and Standard English are compared explicitly.
3. Learning Standard English does not require elimination of a native dialect.
4. Teachers should not stigmatize students for using Black English.

Harber and Bryan (1976) reviewed the research dealing with Black English and language interference and found that the existence of this phenomenon has not been sufficiently demonstrated to support a systematic effort to use teaching techniques other than direct instruction in standard English. The authors reached the following three conclusions:

First, even though there is substantial evidence that black low-SES children experience dialect interference when reading orally in Standard English, there is no clear-cut evidence that the children's use of Black English interferes with the entire reading process.

Second, there is, as yet, no conclusive empirical evidence in the literature supporting the belief that using any of the methods which purport to minimize the interference of Black English on reading performance . . . is more successful than the traditional standard instructional materials. . . .

Third, experimentation with beginning reading materials that purport to minimize . . . [interference] has been resisted by many community leaders and parents. (pp. 397–398)

In 1979 a federal judge ruled that the Ann Arbor, Michigan, school district must recognize that students who speak Black English may need special help in learning standard English. Following lengthy court hearings including the testimony of numerous experts in teaching, psychology, and linguistics, Judge Charles Joiner ruled that though speaking Black English may not constitute a language barrier in and of itself, "If a barrier exists . . . it exists because in the process of attempting to teach the students how to speak standard English the students are somehow made to feel inferior." Judge Joiner ordered the school district to submit a plan to identify children who speak Black English and then to take their dialect into consideration in teaching them to read. In general, educational researchers who have analyzed instructional problems encountered by students speaking Black English believe that teachers should avoid overcorrecting or overcompensating for errors in Standard English. Thus, an extensive review of research on literacy instruction concluded that reading teachers should not assume that dialect-related errors indicate an inability to benefit from regular instruction and that they should avoid repetitive reteaching of narrow Standard English skills. The authors of this review also concluded that overly "persistent correction of dialect-based errors" is a "major stumbling block confronting literacy education for this student population" (Knapp and Needels 1991, 115).

---

*Some educators favor special instructional approaches that take into account the Mountain English dialect of disadvantaged white students in Appalachia. In this regard, Adler (1979) has reported some success with a *bidialectical* approach in which Head Start students were taught to understand differences between Mountain English and Standard English.

Difficulties that African American students who speak Black English may experience in school also have received some attention in connection with the special problems they may encounter learning math and science. For example, Orr (1987) studied the performance of black students in Washington, DC and concluded that many of their errors in math and science involved difficulty using such terms as *than*, *of*, and *as*, which function differently in Black English and Standard English. However, other scholars, such as Pollatsek (1989), are not convinced that these errors differed substantially from those of white students or that the problems encountered by black students in Orr's study were due primarily to interference between Black and Standard English rather than inadequate preparation with respect to vocabulary, concepts, and problem solving in math and science.

Educational Attainment and Achievement

As shown in Table 10-4 and Figure 10-1, African American, Hispanic, and Native American students have the lowest average achievement scores among major racial-ethnic groups in the United States. These achievement patterns are closely related to the fact that black and Hispanic Americans tend to be disproportionately concentrated in poverty neighborhoods in big cities, as described in Chapters 1 and 2 and elsewhere in this book. As noted later in this chapter, many Native American students also grow up socially and geographically isolated from mainstream society.

Dropout rates among black and Hispanic students are relatively high (see Chapter 2) and, as shown in Figure 10-1, the average black (or Hispanic) seventeen-year-old has a reading proficiency score about the same as the average white thirteen-year-old. These patterns constitute an important part of the crisis in selecting and sorting that has developed in postindustrial metropolitan society (see Chapter 2).

However, important gains have been registered in the educational attainment and achievement of black Americans. In 1960, only 13 percent of African Americans over age twenty-four

TABLE 10-4 *Percentages of Eighth Graders in the National Education Longitudinal Study Who Were Proficient in Reading and Mathematics at Designated Proficiency Levels and Percentages Reporting Enrollment in Algebra or Other Advanced Mathematics Classes, by Race/Ethnicity**

Race/Ethnicity**	Reading Proficiency Level***			Mathematics Proficiency Level****			Enrolled in Algebra or Other Advanced Math Classes
	Below Basic	Basic	Advanced	Below Basic	Basic	Intermediate or Advanced	
African American	24	58	18	29	49	22	26
Asian American	15	47	38	13	31	57	46
Hispanic	21	59	21	28	49	26	24
Native American	27	57	15	32	50	18	26
White	10	51	39	16	38	47	34

Source: Adapted from Hafner, Ingels, Schneider, and Stevenson 1990.

*Percentages sometimes do not add to 100 due to rounding.

**African American refers to non-Hispanic black students. White refers to non-Hispanic white students. Native American refers to American Indians and Alaskan Eskimos and Aleuts.

***Basic reading proficiency is defined in terms of literal comprehension, including reproduction of detail and/or the author's main thought. Advanced proficiency involves inferential comprehension beyond the author's main thought and/or understanding of relatively abstract concepts.

****Basic mathematics proficiency involves successfully carrying out simple arithmetical operations on whole numbers. Intermediate proficiency involves mastery of simple operations with decimals, fractions, and roots. Advanced proficiency requires conceptual understanding and problem solving.

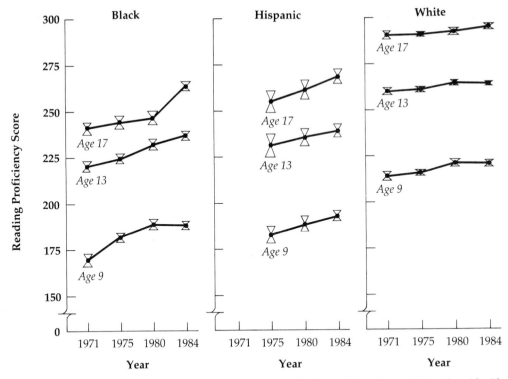

$\underline{\underline{X}}$ = Estimated population mean reading proficiency and 95% confidence interval. It can be said with 95 percent certainty that the mean reading proficiency of the population of interest is within this interval.

FIGURE 10-1 *Average Reading Proficiency Scores for Black, Hispanic, and Non-Hispanic White Students, 1971 to 1989 by Age* (Source: *National Assessment of Educational Progress [NAEP] 1985; Mullis and Jenkins 1990).*

had completed high school; by 1980, slightly more than half (51 percent) had done so. This compares with an increase from 26 percent to 71 percent among non-Hispanic whites during the same time period. And, as shown in Table 10-5, more than half the black-white gap in educational attainment was eliminated between 1940 and 1980 among Americans under forty-five years of age.

In addition, achievement gains among African American and Hispanic students have been substantial. As shown in Figure 10-1, NAEP reading scores of both groups improved impressively between 1971 and 1988. As shown in Tables 10-6 and 10-7, in most comparisons the math and science scores of African American and Hispanic

TABLE 10-5 *Differences in Average Educational Levels (in Years of School) of Non-Hispanic Whites and Blacks, 1940 to 1980*

	Year		
Age Group	1940	1960	1980
26–35	3.9	2.5	1.4
36–45	3.8	3.1	1.8
46–55	3.7	3.5	2.4
56–64	3.7	3.6	3.0

Source: Smith and Welch 1986.

students also improved substantially during the 1970s and 1980s. On the other hand their performance levels in reading, science, math, and other subjects are still far below those of white students. Data presented in Chapter 2 and elsewhere in this book indicate that many black and Hispanic students are concentrated in large central-city school districts with very low achievement and very high dropout rates.

In addition, educational attainment among black students and other disadvantaged groups may not represent as much achievement as it does for white students (see Chapter 7). The somewhat conflicting patterns indicating that the educational attainment and achievement of African Americans have increased substantially while the overall levels of attainment and achievement are still relatively low is consistent with the inference that the gains have been most pronounced for a subgroup of the black population—those who have attained or are beginning to attain middle-class status (Smith 1989; Waldrop 1990).

Family Differences between High- and Low-Achievement Minority Students

Several researchers have tried to determine whether there are differences related to family background between high- and low-achieving minority students. For example, Greenberg and Davidson (1972) and Clark (1983) examined home and family environment differences between academically successful and unsuccessful African American students and found that the families of the high-achieving group were more supportive with respect to orderliness of the home, provision of stimulating learning opportunities, encouragement to achieve, and related variables discussed in Chapters 3, 4, 7, and 8. Levine and his colleagues (Levine 1972; Levine, Eubanks, and Roskoski 1980) collected data

TABLE 10-6 *Average NAEP Mathematics Proficiency Scores (1978 and 1986) and NAEP Science Proficiency Scores (1977 and 1986) of African American, Hispanic, and White Students, by Age Group*

Age Group and Race/Ethnicity*	Mathematics** Proficiency		Science*** Proficiency	
	1978	*1986*	*1977*	*1986*
Nine				
African American	192	202	175	196
Hispanic	203	205	191	199
White	224	227	220	232
Thirteen				
African American	230	249	208	222
Hispanic	238	254	213	226
White	272	274	256	259
Seventeen				
African American	268	279	240	253
Hispanic	276	283	262	259
White	306	308	297	298

Sources: Adapted from Dossey 1988; Mullis and Jenkins 1988; and Mullis, Owen and Phillips 1990.
*White refers to non-Hispanic whites.
**Mathematics proficiency levels: 150—knows some basic addition and subtraction facts; 200—can add and subtract two-digit numbers; 250—can add, subtract, multiply, and divide using whole numbers; 300—can compute with decimals, fractions, and percents, recognize geometric figures, and solve simple equations; 350—can solve multistep problems and use basic algebra.
***Science proficiency levels: 150—knows everyday science facts; 200—understands some basic principles; 250—understands basic life and physical sciences information; 300—has some detailed scientific knowledge; 350—can infer relationships and draw conclusions using detailed scientific knowledge.

TABLE 10-7 *Percentages of Students at or above Designated NAEP Mathematics and Reading Proficiency Levels, Various Years by Race/Ethnicity and Age Group*

| Age Group and Race/Ethnicity* | Mathematics** | | | | | | Reading*** | | | | | |
| | At or above Beginning Skills/ Understanding Level | | At or above Beginning Skill/ Understanding Level | | At or above Moderate-Complex Procedures Levels | | At or above Basic Level | | At or above Intermediate Level | | At or above Adept Level | |
	1978	1986	1978	1986	1976	1978	1975	1988	1975	1988	1975	1988
Nine												
African American	43%	53%	5%	5%	0%	0%	33%	39%	2%	6%	0%	0%
Hispanic	54	59	11	8	1	1	36	47	2	8	0	0
White	76	79	23	25	1	1	9	8	18	20	1	1
Thirteen												
African American	80	96	29	49	2	4	71	91	26	39	2	4
Hispanic	86	88	36	55	4	5	82	86	30	35	2	4
White	98	99	73	79	21	19	96	97	65	63	12	12
Seventeen												
African American	99	100	70	86	18	22	81	79	42	76	8	26
Hispanic	100	99	77	91	22	27	88	96	52	73	13	24
White	100	100	96	98	57	58	99	100	86	89	44	46

Source: Adapted from Dossey 1988; Mullis and Jenkins 1988.

*White refers to non-Hispanic whites.

**Mathematics proficiency levels represent the following: 150—knows some basic addition and subtraction facts; 200—can add and subtract two-digit numbers; 250—can add, subtract, multiply, and divide using whole numbers; 300—can compute with decimals, fractions, and percents, recognize geometric figures, and solve simple equations; 350—can solve multistep problems and use basic algebra.

**Reading proficiency levels represent the following: 150—can carry out simple, discrete reading tasks; 200—can comprehend specific or sequentially related information; 250—can search for information, interrelate ideas, and generalize; 300—can find, understand, summarize, and explain relatively complicated information; 350—can synthesize and learn from specialized reading materials.

indicating that families of relatively high-achieving black students in big-city magnet and parochial schools score mugh higher on these kinds of home environment variables than do students in the same neighborhood who attend nearby public schools that have low achievement levels. Gordon and Musser (1990) recently compared family background characteristics of high- and low-achieving African American students and high- and low-achieving Hispanic students in a large suburban district and found that the home environment differences were exactly in line with those that have differentiated between middle-class and working-class families in decades of research we reviewed in earlier chapters. Although parents of both groups of suburban black and Hispanic students wanted and encouraged their children to succeed in school, the parents of high achievers were higher in social class and also differed from parents of low achievers as follows:

- Encouraged their children to participate in more intellectually stimulating activities, such as hobbies, use of libraries, and family visits to museums.

- Considered "conformity on academic tasks" to be much less important and "curiosity" to be more important than did parents of low achievers. Conversely, parents of low achievers placed more emphasis on "rote memorization of facts," following directions, and turning in neat homework (Gordon and Musser 1990, 53–54).

Higher Education

As pointed out earlier, there has been a substantial improvement in the educational attainment of African Americans. As part of this trend, black enrollment in colleges and universities increased substantially after 1964. The percentage of black students among college and university undergraduates increased from 5 percent in 1966 to 10 percent in 1974 and has since remained a little below this level. The difference that still exists between African Americans and whites in college attendance and completion can be accounted for by differences in socioeconomic status (National Research Council 1989). In fact, some research has indicated that when account is taken of socioeconomic differences, African American students have higher aspirations to attend college than do white students (Portes and Wilson 1976; Smith 1989). Thus, the increase in black attendance in institutions of higher education probably reflects the increase in the size of the black middle-class as well as efforts made by colleges and universities to recruit more minority students and a reduction in the barriers that limit black access to higher education (National Research Council 1989).

However, we also note that some encouraging trends for African American students in higher education most evident in the 1960s and 1970s did not continue in the 1980s. The proportion of black youth eighteen to twenty-four years of age who had enrolled in college peaked at 30 percent in 1978 and then fell slightly to 27 to 28 percent throughout the 1980s. Similarly, the college completion rate for African Americans rose

rapidly from 2 percent in 1940 to 13 percent in 1975 but since then has remained at about this level, and the percentage of African American students in graduate-education enrollment increased in the 1970s and then stabilized at 5 to 7 percent during the 1980s (Mortenson 1991). Among the causes that appear to be responsible (National Research Council 1989; Jaschik 1990a; DeLoughry 1991) for these indications of lack of additional progress in the higher-education participation of African American students (and other disadvantaged groups) are these:

- Shifts in federal aid from grants to loans combined with rising tuition have disproportionately impacted disadvantaged students.
- Many colleges and universities have reduced or eliminated special recruiting and counseling programs and remedial services.
- Entrance standards have been raised at many institutions.
- Some students may have concluded that higher education will not help them obtain high-paying jobs.
- Reduced federal emphasis on affirmative action may have inhibited minority enrollment.
- Difficulties in transferring from community colleges to four-year institutions may have increased.
- The percentage of African American youth entering the military may have increased.
- Deteriorating conditions in the inner city may be discouraging college enrollment.

The Declining Significance of Race?

In 1978, University of Chicago sociologist William Julius Wilson published a book titled *The Declining Significance of Race*, in which he noted occupational gains among blacks and concluded, from these and other data, that economic barriers now constitute central barriers to further black progress:

In earlier years the systematic efforts of whites to suppress blacks were obvious to even the most insensitive observer. Blacks were denied access to valued and scarce resources through various ingenious schemes of racial exploitation, discrimination and segregation. . . . [But in] the period of modern industrial race relations, it would be difficult indeed to comprehend the plight of inner-city blacks by exclusively focusing on racial discrimination. For in a very real sense, the current problems of lower-class blacks are substantially related to fundamental structural changes in the economy. . . .

As a result, for the first time in American history class issues can meaningfully compete with race issues in the way blacks develop or maintain a sense of group position. (Wilson 1978, 1, 21–23)

Wilson's book set off a storm of controversy among social scientists. For example, fourteen members of the Association of Black Sociologists voted to condemn the book because they believed it to be a "misrepresentation of the black experience" that "obscures the problem of the persistent oppression of blacks." They also expressed the fear that opponents of programs to help black Americans would use Wilson's argument to influence government policy (quoted in Willie 1979, 71).

Although most critics granted that Wilson did not claim race to be unimportant in affecting the status and mobility of black Americans, many felt that his emphasis was misleading and dangerous. Harvard sociologist Charles V. Willie (1979) argued that because a high percentage of blacks now live in underclass poverty neighborhoods that are both racial and economic ghettos, Wilson's title actually should have been *The Inclining Significance of Race.*

There are many data and arguments that might be used to support the conclusion that race is or is not declining as a factor in affecting opportunity for black Americans. For example, Wilson argues that the rise in underclass female-headed families among blacks reflects relatively low levels of training and education (i.e., low

social-class indicators) among black males who have increasingly restricted opportunities for high-income employment as structural changes in the economy require higher levels of skill. Other considerations that might be used to support Wilson's position on the growing importance of class relative to race include the following points.

1. Analysis by Jencks (1972, 1979) and by Featherman and Hauser (1978) indicates that the status attainment process for blacks is becoming more like that for whites. For example, Featherman and Hauser found that after controlling for socioeconoimc background, race had less than half as much an effect on occupational status of adult men in 1962 as in 1973. They concluded that black families "seem increasingly able to transfer their socioeconomic statuses to sons," and that occupational and earnings benefits to schooling—especially college education—have risen sharply for blacks (1978, p. 381).

2. After analyzing the information collected in 1966 and 1971, Gottfredson (1979) concluded that "social background is becoming more important *compared* to race in determining the fate of blacks." In addition, studies of academic achievement indicate that social class status largely accounts for low achievement patterns among blacks and some other minority groups (Coleman 1966, 1990a; National Research Council 1989).

On the other hand, a variety of data and arguments support the conclusion that race remains a fundamental factor in blocking progress among black Americans (Reed 1990). Considerations that can be cited here include the following points.

1. Segregation of many black children and youth within the schools and other institutions such as the metropolitan labor market makes it difficult or impossible for them to acquire mainstream cultural patterns and personal contacts that play an important part in affecting mobility (Hacker 1988; Cotton, K. 1991).

2. A review of the literature by Pettigrew (1985) found support for the conclusion that the interaction between race and social class has become an increasingly important determinant of socioeconomic and educational opportunities and outcomes. Pettigrew concluded that

> *the main effects of race and class together do not adequately account for the growing complexity of modern race relations. . . . Racial phenomena generally operate differently across class lines just as class phenomena generally operate differently across racial lines. (Pettigrew 1985, 337)*

No matter what position one takes on the class-caste controversy, it is clear that the largest part of the problem posed for black Americans as a group involves the development of a large black underclass in big cities. From this point of view, whether race or class was originally or continues to be most potent in affecting opportunity is less important than is the fact that the two have become inextricably intertwined in the evolution of metropolitan areas. Stated differently, racism has become "institutionalized" in the functioning of modern urban society. Bayard Rustin has remarked on this new form of racism:

> *The old form of racism was based on prejudging all blacks as somehow inherently undeserving of equal treatment. What makes the new form more insidious is its basis in observed sociological data. The new racist equates the pathology of the poor with race, ignoring the fact that family dissolution, teenage pregnancy, illegitimacy, alcohol and drug abuse, street crime, and idleness are universal problems of the poor. They exist wherever there is economic dislocation and deterioration—in the cities, for example, dotting Britain's devastated industrial north. They are rampant among the white jobless in Liverpool as well as among unemployed blacks in New York. (Rustin 1987, 21)*

Once racism has become institutionalized in this way, social policies that appear to be racially neutral will tend to have a clear racial impact (Hacker 1988; Reed 1990; Murray 1991). For example, social welfare policies that encourage family break-up (by reducing payments when males are in the home), and reductions in expenditures for social welfare are not racially discriminatory in a direct manner. However, since a disproportionate percentage of black Americans is below the poverty level, such developments may have a disproportionate racial impact in terms of limiting black mobility. Similarly, reductions in federal support for public schools can be expected to disproportionately harm black Americans.

An additional conclusion that can be drawn from the race-class controversy is that the well-publicized statement of the National Advisory Commission on Civil Disorders (the Kerner Commission) probably should be reworded. The commission's final report in 1968 warned that "Our nation is moving toward two societies, one black, one white—separate and unequal." To some degree, events since 1967 indicate that this admonition would now be more accurate reworded to read "To a significant extent, the United States has become two separate nations, one white, plus minority middle class, and one minority underclass (largely black and Hispanic)." The future will indicate whether this type of division is more viable than one based entirely on race.

HISPANIC AMERICANS AND EDUCATION

After blacks, the largest minority group in the United States is the Spanish origin or Spanish surname group, more generally referred to as Hispanic. The term *Hispanic* refers to persons whose ancestry is primarily Iberian or Latin American.* Hispanics officially comprised

---

*The U.S. Census uses the phrase *Spanish origin* for people in the states of California, Arizona, New Mexico, Texas, and

almost 9 percent of the total U.S. population in 1990 (Barringer 1991). The estimated numbers of people and, in parentheses, their percentages in the overall U.S. population among the ethnic groups that made up this Hispanic minority in the late 1980s are as follows:

Mexican	12,110,000	(5)
Puerto Rican**	2,471,000	(1)
Cuban	1,035,000	(.5)
Central and South American	2,242,000	(1)
Other Spanish descent	1,579,000	(.6)

However, these population percentages underestimate the actual size of the Hispanic minority. Demographers believe there may be as many as 3 million illegal migrants in the United States (Suro 1990). A high proportion of these undocumented aliens are Mexicans, due in part to the facts that Mexico has one of the fastest growing populations in the world, a high unemployment rate, and a border shared with the United States. Many of these aliens are becoming U.S. citizens as a result of 1986 changes in immigration law. Recent estimates indicate that the Hispanic population of the United States increased by 56 percent between 1980 and 1990 (Barringer 1991).

In addition, the Hispanic population of the United States is much younger than the total population. In 1987, almost 33 percent of the Hispanic population was under sixteen years of age, as compared with 23 percent of the non-Hispanic population. Fertility rates among Hispanics also are higher than those in the total population (see Table 10-2). This high rate means that there will be proportionately more Hispanic children growing up and forming families during the 1990s than is true for the United States population as a whole.

Long-term results of these developments will have a significant impact on the composition of the United States population. The federal government is trying to reduce illegal immigration from Mexico and other countries, but difficulties in border security make it unlikely that this effort will be completely successful. Illegal, as well as legal, immigration together with natural growth in the Hispanic population make it certain that its percentage in the U.S. population will increase in the future (Reinhold 1990). Some authorities predict that the census will show Hispanics as constituting 11 or 12 percent of the population in the year 2000 and much more than that in future years (Exter 1991). The percentage of Spanish-origin population in California increased from 12 percent in 1970 to more than 25 percent in 1991. Growth of this magnitude among the Hispanic minority underlines the increasing importance of government-designated "minority" groups in the United States. Some demographers believe that Hispanics will constitute a majority of the population in California within the next twenty years (Reinhold 1990; Stevenson 1991).

Socioeconomic and Educational Development

As shown in Table 10-2, Hispanics as a group are more highly concentrated in metropolitan areas than are blacks and whites but less highly concentrated in central cities than is the African American population. Family size among the Hispanic group is larger than among blacks and whites, reflecting its relatively young age distribution and high fertility rates; and average family income, although higher than for blacks, is much lower than for whites. The occupational distribution of Hispanic workers is somewhat similar to that of blacks, except that a higher proportion of Hispanics are skilled workers and a lower proportion are service workers.

Colorado who report a Spanish or Mexican family relationship. The Census category "Spanish surname" applies to people, wherever they reside, with such surnames. The latter category therefore omits people who may have a parent or grandparent of Spanish-American lineage but who have non-Spanish names because of intermarriage, just as it includes people who have no such parental lineage but who are married to persons with Spanish surnames.

**Unless otherwise indicated, the term *Puerto Rican* is used in this chapter to refer to Puerto Ricans on the U.S. mainland.

As might be expected given the relatively low socioeconomic status of the Hispanic population, school attainment and achievement levels among Hispanic students are lower than average for U.S. schools. As shown in Table 10-4, achievement levels of Hispanic students generally are similar to those of black students and far below those of white students.

Some data indicate that educational attainment and achievement have been increasing among Hispanic Americans. For example, national surveys conducted by the National Assessment of Educational Progress (see Figure 10-1), showed that reading scores of Hispanic students improved substantially between 1971 and 1988. The number of Hispanics in undergraduate institutions and graduate schools rose steadily through most of the 1970s and 1980s.

However, the 1988 data collected by NAEP (see Figure 10-1) show that the average reading proficiency score of Hispanic seventeen-year-olds is still only slightly above that of white thirteen-year-olds. In addition, some data indicate that little or no gain has been recorded in the Hispanic educational attainment in recent years. For example, the percentage of Hispanic students completing high school did not improve substantially in the 1980s, and the percentage of Hispanics (aged eighteen to twenty-four) enrolled in college increased by only a few points (Mortenson 1991). In 1987, only 750 Hispanic students among 27,446 U.S. citizens received doctorate degrees.

Part of the problem that Hispanic students encounter in school involves the fact that many are classified as non-English speaking or proficient (NES or NEP), or limited-English speaking or proficient (LES or LEP). (In recent years, greater emphasis sometimes has been placed on English *proficiency* as compared with English *speaking*, because many students who speak English are not sufficiently proficient to succeed in school.) Studies conducted by the National Center for Education Statistics and other agencies indicate that there are more than 6 million children whose primary language at home is not En-glish, and that about 3.5 million of these children are sufficiently limited in English to require special assistance in language learning. After studying the situation of LEP children, the majority of whom are Hispanic, the Council of Chief State School Officers reached the following conclusions:

- Large numbers of LEP children do not receive the special services they need to succeed in school. Some do not receive any at all. In particular, many LEP students are not receiving benefits of categorical programs, other than bilingual education, for which they may be eligible. These include compensatory education, special education, and vocational education, among others.

- There is a gap between what researchers have learned about the dynamics of second language acquisition, and the practices in effect in our schools. One example of this is that although research suggests that it takes from five to seven years to become proficient in a second language, LEP students who do receive bilingual education or ESL [English as a second language] services are generally mainstreamed into English classrooms after no more than two to three years without additional language support services.

- Some SEAs [State Education Agencies] have developed initiatives—both administrative and pedagogical—designed to improve the achievement of LEP students, but most of these are relatively new and relatively limited. In some states, statewide reform including the establishment of achievement norms has been the catalyst for developing new approaches to educating LEP children. But it appears that many states have not yet made the commitment to remedial programs many LEP children require to meet the new standards. (Council of Chief State School Officers 1990b, 52).

Nationally, Hispanic students are as segregated in predominantly minority schools as are black students (see Table 9-2). Moreover, the percentage of Hispanic students attending predominantly minority schools increased between

1968 and 1984 in all sections of the United States, so that by 1984 71 percent of Hispanics compared with 64 percent of blacks were in schools 50 percent or more minority (Orfield and Monfort 1987). Thus, it appears that Hispanic students in big cities are segregated in much the same way as are black students. Gary Orfield reviewed the data for both blacks and Hispanics and concluded that to a significant degree, "The remaining problems of segregation are really problems of large metropolitan areas in the large states" (1982, 10).

This pattern of segregation of the Hispanic group reflects the fact that many of its members are part of the big-city underclass (Passell 1991). Many Puerto Rican families live in inner-city neighborhoods, such as East Harlem in New York, and crime, drug use, and other indicators of social disorganization are very high in many Mexican American communities in big cities (Rodriquez 1989). As is true with respect to the African American population, the existence of an underclass among Hispanic Americans poses grave problems for the educational system and other social institutions in the United States.

Segregation of Hispanic students also raises questions about how they should be treated in desegregation plans. Some plans, such as that in San Francisco, have required representation of every major group (white, black, Hispanic, Asian) in formulating the definition of a desegregated school; but in other cases (e.g., Los Angeles), Hispanics have been combined with blacks as a minority to be desegregated or have not been classified as a minority at all for purposes of racial balance. Desegregation may be particularly important for LEP students because it provides them with opportunities to participate in mainstream language and cultural environments (Fillmore 1991).

Due partly to the relatively high percentage of Hispanic students in Los Angeles, Judge Paul Egly employed several social scientists to help him consider important issues including the definition and treatment of Hispanic students in desegregation planning. One of the experts who struggled with this issue concluded that Hispanic and other minority students might be given preference for desegregation according to whether they were connected or disconnected with mainstream society. He also concluded that desegregation might be best accomplished in the future by desegregating working-class and middle-class Hispanic students. In the absence of a metropolitan remedy that would include more non-Hispanic whites, assigning working-class minority students to socioeconomically desegregated minority schools might help "put minority members into the larger networks of opportunity, whereupon *their* children can provide the vital network links for future generations of minority children in America" (Pettigrew 1978, 54, 135).

Several national studies tend to support the conclusions that status and mobility patterns for the Hispanic population are much like those for the African American population, and that growth of an underclass group is an important characteristic of these patterns for both groups. Featherman and Hauser's study (1978) of the occupational status and earnings of United States men in 1962 and 1973 showed that Hispanic Americans are at a greater disadvantage than are other major ethnic groups, after taking account of education, father's occupation, and generational status (see Table 7-3).

Subgroups

The Hispanic minority is made up of a number of subgroups that differ in some important respects such as age, income, and regional location. This section describes the most visible of these groups, with emphasis placed on their socioeconomic characteristics and the educational situation of their children. Following these descriptions, attention is given to the topic of bilingual/bicultural education and to related issues involving segregation of the Hispanic minority and its place within United States schools and society.

"Old" Americans of Spanish Descent in the Southwest. Within fifty years of the discovery of North America by Columbus, expeditions of Spanish soldiers and priests explored the Rio

Grande country. Later, the Spaniards moved north from Mexico along the coast of California, setting up missions and military outposts, as well as large *haciendas* owned by wealthy families. What is now the southwestern corner of the United States was a part of Mexico until the Mexican War of 1848. After the war, which resulted in annexation of Texas and the southwestern territory to the United States, the Spanish and Mexican settlers who remained there became United States citizens.

Thus, there is an "old" population of Spanish origin that has as long a history of residence in this country as the New England colonists. Cities such as Albuquerque, Santa Fe, San Antonio, El Paso, Los Angeles, and San Diego indicate by their names the Spanish influence; and many Spanish surnames are carried on the rosters of the Chamber of Commerce, the upper middle-class service clubs, and the country clubs. In New Mexico, Spanish and English are both official languages. This "old" population of Spanish origin constitutes a large proportion of the group labeled "Other" in Table 10-8.

Also, a few isolated Spanish communities did not move into the mainstream but led an impoverished existence in the mountains of New Mexico and on the dry farms of the areas near the Mexican border. They retained their language and religious customs and have only recently come into close contact with the Anglo culture.

Mexican Americans (Chicanos). By far the largest group of Spanish Americans are those who identify themselves to the census taker as being of Mexican origin. More than 12 million strong by 1990, they provided nearly two-thirds of the approximately 600,000 students in the Los Angeles public schools. Most Mexican Americans live in the Southwest, but there also are large numbers on the West Coast and in the Midwest. A large majority are United States citizens, but many are illegal immigrants and are liable to deportation if discovered by immigration officials.

The name *Chicano* probably comes from the colloquial term *mechicano* (Mexican), which frequently has been used by Mexican Americans in the Southwest to refer to themselves. Many Mexican Americans now use the term to refer to their ethnic group (Jaen 1990), but some others reject it because they believe it has working-class connotations or introduces other stereotypes. In some cases, Chicano is used to refer to first-generation Mexican Americans, but not later generations (Cloud 1990).

The majority of the adults of this group are semiskilled and unskilled workers (see Table 10-8). In many cases, their parents have had experience as agricultural workers, often as migratory workers following the crop cycle through the states of the west coast and mountain regions. In the past thirty years, they have tended to settle permanently in the large and middle-sized cities of the Southwest. The Mexican American group is the most rural of the Spanish American population.

In earlier decades, when many Mexican Americans were migratory laborers, our system of education did not provide regular schooling for their children. The local school districts tended either to set up temporary classes for these children for a few months each year, or to ignore them. Before school desegregation began in the 1950s, there was a tendency to place these children in segregated schools. For example, Mexican American children were formally segregated in California until 1947, and in Texas until 1948.

Since a considerable proportion of Mexican American families use Spanish as their home language, many of their children come to school with little or no facility in English. Many school authorities in the Southwest responded to this situation initially by barring Spanish speech from the school classes and playgrounds as much as possible (Ovando 1990). They argued that pupils would benefit from the no-Spanish rule. However, due to strong objections of parents and pupils and changing attitudes on the part of educators, this rule has now been dropped in most districts.

TABLE 10-8   *Selected Characteristics of Hispanic Groups in the United States*

| | Metropolitan Location (1979 percentages) | |
	Central City	Suburban
All Hispanic Origin	48	32
Mexican American	43	34
Puerto Rican	75	15
Other Hispanic (includes Cuban)	44	37

	Mean Family Income (1988)	Percentage of Families in Poverty (1987)	Percentage of Families Female Head (1988)
All Hispanic Origin	$20,306	26	23
Mexican American	19,968	26	19
Puerto Rican	15,185	38	44
Cuban	27,294	14	16
Central and South American	22,939	19	24
Other Hispanic	21,196	26	25

| | Percentage Distribution in Occupational Groupings of Employed Persons 16 Years of Age or More (1985) | | | |
	White Collar	Blue Collar	Service	Farm
All Hispanic Origin	55	21	22	1
Mexican American	55	21	22	2
Puerto Rican	56	20	23	1
Cuban	56	27	16	0
Non-Hispanic	70	11	18	1

	Percentage 4 years or More College (1988)	Percentage under 21 Years Old (1988)	Percentage Adults Married (1985)
All Hispanic Origin	10	41	58
Mexican American	7	44	60
Puerto Rican	10	42	50
Cuban	17	22	63
Central and South American	17	34	58
Other Hispanic	14	33	55
Non-Hispanic	21	30	59

Sources: U.S. Bureau of the Census; Duaney and Pittman 1990; *Statistical Abstract of the United States* 1990.
Notes: Percentage sums differ from 100 due to rounding. White-collar grouping includes professional and technical, managers and administrators, sales and clerical; blue collar includes crafts and kindred, operatives, and nonfarm laborers; service includes private household and other.

Puerto Ricans.   The socioeconomic status of Puerto Ricans in the United States reflects the economy of the island. That economy has grown greatly over recent decades due to the investment of mainland capital and rapid industrialization. Nevertheless, the per capita income of the island is much less than that of the United States as a whole. There has been a relatively high unemployment rate among the working classes in Puerto Rico, due largely to the modernization of agriculture, which resulted in large numbers of rural people moving to the cities in search of work. Thus, the average Puerto Rican immigrant to the mainland has been a rural person with relatively little education. Racially, Puerto Ricans include persons with 100 percent Spanish ancestry to persons (a minority) with African ancestry (Rodríguez 1989).

As has been true with many other immigrant groups, including Italians, Jews, Mexican Americans, Poles, and Slovaks, accommodation to life in the United States has involved difficult problems that call into question traditional cultural patterns and tend to cleave the generations. These problems probably have been accentuated among Puerto Ricans because so high a proportion of them are located in big-city poverty neighborhoods (Wiley 1990) in which traditional family patterns have become increasingly difficult to maintain. Joseph P. Fitzpatrick has described these difficulties in discussing the efforts of Puerto Rican parents to maintain traditional practices such as chaperonage of young girls and emphasis on respect for age and adult authority:

> *Puerto Rican families have frequently lamented the patterns of behavior of even good boys in the United States. . . . American children are taught to be self-reliant, aggressive, and competitive, to ask "why," and to stand on their own two feet. A Puerto Rican child is generally much more submissive. When the children begin to behave according to the American pattern, the parents cannot understand it. A priest who had worked for many years with migrating Puerto Ricans remarked*

> *to the writer: "When these Puerto Rican families come to New York, I give the boys about 48 hours on the streets of New York, and the differences between his behavior and what the family expects, will have begun to shake the family."*
> *. . . The parents are living in the Puerto Rican culture in their homes. The children are being brought up in an American school where American values are being presented. The parents will never really understand their children; the children will never really understand the parents. (Fitzpatrick 1972, 116–117)*

The problems Puerto Rican children encounter in school appear to be related most closely to their low socioeconomic status, with some intensification due to ethnic and cultural differences (Rodríguez 1989). This mixture of socioeconomic and ethnic factors is clear in the following description of problems in predominantly Puerto Rican schools with which Francisco Cordasco and Eugene Bucchioni introduce their book *The Puerto Rican Community and Its Children on the Mainland*:

> *To many Puerto Rican students, much of North American middle class teaching is uninteresting and unrealistic. . . . In the high school there may be talk of future work as doctors or lawyers. But Puerto Rican students are not always motivated by these techniques, partly because of the seeming impossibility of attainment of these goals. . . . For many Puerto Rican students the urban school becomes a marketplace of unreality and alienation. (Cordasco and Bucchioni 1972, 17)*

Cubans.   Emigration of Cubans to the United States was small until the Castro-led revolution in the late 1950s put property owners at an economic disadvantage and led to a major migration to the United States. Many of the 1960s immigrants from Cuba were well-educated middle-class persons who generally settled in the Miami metropolitan area. In later years, however, Cuba expelled significant numbers of working-class citizens with criminal records, who then were granted asylum in the United States.

Nearly half a million Cuban Americans were living in the area of South Florida by 1980. Other groups of Cubans numbering in the thousands are living in New York, Philadelphia, Chicago, Milwaukee, and Indianapolis. Their median age as of 1980 was thirty-six, considerably older than the other Spanish-surname groups. Approximately 56 percent of employed Cuban adults were in white-collar jobs in 1985 compared with more than 70 percent for Anglos. Even though the Cubans as a group may have economic handicaps, many have business and professional skills, and many have become relatively prosperous in the United States economy. The median income for a Cuban family is considerably higher than that for all Hispanic families.

Bilingual/Bicultural Education

One primary goal of education for Hispanic students with little or no knowledge of English is to teach them to function in English so they can take advantage of opportunities available in the larger society. This goal is now being pursued to a large extent through bilingual education, which provides instruction in students' native languages at least until such time as they are able to learn in English. Federally sponsored bilingual education has expanded fairly rapidly since being initiated for low-status children with limited English skills in Title VII of the Elementary and Secondary Education Act of 1965 and the Bilingual Education Act of 1968, with appropriations increasing from $7.5 million in 1969 to $168 million in 1992. Revisions of the Bilingual Education Act in 1974 opened participation to nonpoverty students.

Although the federal government sponsors bilingual projects for scores of language groups speaking various Asian, Indo-European, and Native American languages, the majority of children in these projects are Hispanic (Schmidt 1991a). California, Colorado, Massachusetts, and other states as well as local school districts also fund a variety of bilingual programs.

Bilingual education has been expanding partly because the federal Office of Civil Rights (OCR) has been insisting that opportunities be improved for limited English-proficient (LEP) and non-English-proficient (NEP) students, and the Supreme Court has backed up this insistence in the 1974 *Lau* v. *Nichols* case (Porter 1990). Since 1970, OCR has required that schools take "affirmative steps" to correct English language deficiencies of minority children in order to receive federal funds in accordance with the Civil Rights Act of 1964. Its authority to enforce this requirement was upheld by a unanimous Supreme Court vote in the *Lau* case, which involved language problems experienced by Chinese students in San Francisco. The Court held that steps had to be taken to help students who "are certain to find their classroom experiences wholly incomprehensible" because they do not understand English. However, it did not spell out a solution but instead stated, "Teaching English to the students of Chinese ancestry is one choice. Giving instruction to this group in Chinese is another. There may be others."

Since 1975, federal guidelines for protecting the rights of LEP and NEP children have required that schools provide special bilingual opportunities where a school district has twenty or more students who have a primary language other than English, unless a school district could demonstrate that another approach would be effective in providing a meaningful opportunity to learn. Until the mid-1980s, the vast majority of programs funded under federal guidelines for LEP and NEP students have used the Transitional Bilingual Education (TBE) approach, in which students are to be taught wholly or partly in their native language until they can function adequately in English. Since 1975, other approaches also have been funded (Schmidt 1991b).

Approaches other than bilingual variants (discussed later) that are used most frequently in educating students with limited English skills or background include Teaching English as a Second Language (TESL) and Immersion, in which students are placed full-time in an English-learning environment. Some scholars believe that these approaches should not be treated or defined as fully or necessarily antithetical. For example, TESL components can be combined with bilingual or partial-immersion, and students' learning assignments can be divided between bilingual and immersion experience (Troike 1981; Porter 1990).

As indicated earlier, considerable uncertainty exists over the kinds of bilingual programs that can or should be offered. Josué González, former director of the U.S. Office of Bilingual Education, has described major alternatives in bilingual programming as ranging from relatively short-term programs aimed at transitional preparation of LEP and NEP students for study in English, to continuing programs requiring that all students learn to function in two languages and cultures.

Some characteristics of five of these alternatives are as follows:

- Type A—*Transitional Bilingual Education* programs, which provide native language instruction to help non–English-speaking students learn to function in English.
- Type B—*Bilingual Maintenance* programs in which there is an additional emphasis on maintaining or developing the native languages skills of LEP and NEP students.
- Type C—*Bilingual/Bicultural Maintenance* programs in which there also is an emphasis on maintaining the culture and teaching the history of the language group of the participating students.
- Type D—*Bilingual/Bicultural Restorationist* programs that also enroll students who have lost their native language due to assimilation, in order to "restore . . . the language and culture of their ancestry."
- Type E—*Bilingual/Bicultural Culturally Pluralistic* programs in which all students regardless of their ethno-linguistic group

learn to function in two languages and benefit from "an active participation in and appreciation of each others' backgrounds." (Adapted from González 1975, 14–15)

It should be noted that there are two types of bilingual programs and three types of bilingual/bicultural programs according to González's definitions, which he points out are themselves oversimplifications of the overlapping goals and characteristics of differing approaches. It also should be noted that other definitions frequently are explicitly or implicitly formulated by other observers, so that it is very important to examine any given program in order to identify its major goals and characteristics. One of the most widely used definitions of bilingual/bicultural education is that offered by a group of bilingual education leaders in May 1973: "a process of total self-development by which a person learns and reinforces his or her own language and culture while at the same time acquiring the ability to function in another language and behave on occasion according to patterns of the second culture" (Rodriguez 1975, 3). This definition is most similar to González's Type C.

Controversies Regarding Bilingual/ Bicultural Education

Bilingual/bicultural education has become one of the most controversial topics in United States education. Decisions made regarding its future are likely to play a major part in determining the subsequent history of the United States. The magnitude of the immediate problem it deals with is suggested by the fact that the Council of Chief State School Officers (1990b) estimated that more than 3 million LEP children are in U.S. elementary and secondary schools. (Most are Hispanic, but more than 100 language groups are represented.) The underlying problem is much larger, involving general social policy toward linguistic minority groups. Although it is impossible to summarize briefly all the interrelated arguments made by various observers, the following pages provide a general overview of some of the most essential issues.

What type of program should be offered? The type of program advocated by a particular observer depends partly on one's ideology concerning the kinds of experience that will be most helpful in preparing children to function productively in society, and on one's views concerning the government's responsibility for fostering such experience.

Toward one end of the continuum on this issue are people who believe that preservation of the language and culture of minority-language groups is a vital necessity that must be systematically attended to in public education if children from these groups are to maintain or develop positive individual and group identity and to cooperate productively with other groups in building an equitable society. This point of view regarding the Mexican-American minority has been summarized by Leonard C. Pacheco:

> *The thousands of Spanish-speaking people of the United States—concentrated for the most part in the American Southwest—are beginning to give voice to feelings that are only barely understood by the dominant Anglo-Saxon culture of the United States. These people feel that their culture should not be submerged or assimilated beyond recognition by American society. The language of these people is a facet, and an important one, of a culture that seeks to be an equal partner in the dominant culture. (1977, 170)*

Toward the other end of the continuum are people who believe that minority children will be better prepared to compete in society if they are immersed as soon as possible in English-language instruction, or that public schools should provide transitional bilingual education but should not require participation in programs emphasizing the maintenance of minority language and culture. This type of position has been taken by Noel Epstein, whose 1977 analysis of bilingual/bicultural education concluded that

maintenance programs are neither necessary nor effective in preparing cultural minorities for participation in United States society and should not be sponsored by the federal government because they may be socially separatist and divisive:

> *If developing and maintaining literacy in the native language is the goal, that would not require giving the native tongue the kind of equal status in the curriculum envisioned by many bilingual/bicultural supporters. It could be accomplished by continuing to teach these pupils one or two classes in the native language for the rest of their school careers. . . . The central issue . . . [is not] the unquestioned importance of ethnicity in individuals' lives . . . [nor] the right or the desirability of groups to maintain their languages and cultures . . . [but] the federal role. Is it a federal responsibility to finance and promote student attachments to their ethnic languages and cultures, jobs long left to families, religious groups, ethnic organizations, private schools, ethnic publications and others? (1977, 7)*

Tension between these two types of positions has appeared in local communities in which minority parents disagree among themselves on whether their children will be best prepared to participate in United States society through immersion-type experiences that force them rapidly to acquire competence in English or through programs that conduct instruction in their native language. In Chicago, for example, residents of Greek-speaking neighborhoods have been bitterly divided on this issue, and in some other communities, Chinese, Puerto Rican, Mexican-American, and Native American parents have been similarly divided internally (Schmidt 1991a).

Uncertainty on this issue also extends to the language used in federal legislation (Rotberg 1982). The Bilingual Education Act of 1974 emphasizes the transitional goal of "providing for children of limited English-speaking ability instruction designed to enable them, while using their native language, to achieve competence in the English language" but also defines bilingual education as instruction given "with appreciation for the cultural heritage of such children." The legislation allows for instruction in the native language "to the extent necessary to allow a child to progress effectively through the educational system." Since no time limit is specified and programs may continue indefinitely if English is introduced slowly and standards for English proficiency are set high, it is possible to establish what are basically language and cultural maintenance programs under the Bilingual Education Act.

What types of programs are being offered? Partly due to lack of adequate data and partly due to difficulties in defining terms and classifying programs, it is not certain how many of the hundreds of bilingual projects supported through federal and state funds are mainly transitional and how many have a predominant language- or culture-maintenance emphasis (Porter 1990). González concluded that the most "cursory examination of bilingual education programs created through legislation" shows "in general, they are *transitional* in their emphasis and regard the learning of English as the ultimate goal. Little elmphasis is placed on language *maintenance* and the corollary assumption that cultural and linguistic pluralism is a desirable condition in the society" (1975, p. 12). However, Epstein also examined a variety of programs and concluded that there is "no question that Washington has been financing language and cultural maintenance programs at least through elementary school" (1975, 25–26). Similar conclusions have been reached by Porter (1990) and other observers.

Research has not completely settled this question. As of 1990, the major national study on participation in bilingual education was a 1977 report prepared by the American Institutes for Research (AIR) on 150 schools and 11,500 students, 75 percent of whom were of Spanish descent. Teachers in the study judged that about 70 percent of their Hispanic students were dominant in English, not Spanish, thus indicating that many of them may be in programs that are pri-

marily maintenance-type rather than transitional. However, many experts in bilingual education, such as José A. Cárdenas (1977) and Carlos Ovando (1990), dispute this conclusion and criticize the AIR study on various grounds including reliance on classification of students by non-Spanish-speaking teachers "in spite of a body of research which points to the unreliability of teacher judgment as an indicator of the language characteristics of students" (1977, p. 74). Cárdenas, Ovando, and others also argue that instruction in the native language constitutes so small a part of the day in most bilingual programs that it is incorrect to consider them maintenance-type.

To what extent do students who might benefit from special language instruction actually receive such services? A 1985 study for the Educational Testing Service found that only 16 percent of Spanish-dominant fourth graders and only 9 percent of Spanish-dominant eighth graders were receiving bilingual or TESL services (Olson 1986a). Officials of the U.S. Department of Education responded by providing data indicating that the number of LEP students between the ages of five and fourteen had declined from 3.6 million in the late 1970s to less than 1.7 million, thus suggesting that special programs to help students acquire English were proving basically sufficient. However, many observers were skeptical about the adequacy and interpretation of these data, and some believed that the department's definition of English proficiency incorrectly minimized the extent of the problem (Crawford 1986a, Ovando, 1990).

Does bilingual/bicultural education improve student academic performance? The situation regarding bilingual research appears to be similar to that regarding desegregation research: it may be misleading to reach a general conclusion based on mixing together a large number of unsuccessful programs with a few that may be particularly well designed and implemented and, consequently, unusually successful. Practically every observer agrees that many bilingual education projects have not been very well implemented. Qualified teachers are scarce, appropriate materials are in short supply, and diagnostic instruments to help in teaching are still somewhat primitive. For this reason, federal legislation has placed substantial emphasis on training staff and on the development and dissemination of exemplary approaches to bilingual education, but it is not now possible to determine whether superior programs can be successfully developed and implemented on a widespread scale in the future.

Research on bilingual education, immersion, and other techniques for teaching students a second language has been complicated, controversial, and, to say the least, contentious. Research on immersion indicates that middle-class students generally perform well when immersed in a second-language environment, provided this approach is well implemented. (Much of this research has involved Anglo students in French schools in Canada.) However, other research has indicated that disadvantaged students generally do not learn well when thrust into a totally new language setting, that mental development is more advanced when students learn higher-order skills in their native language rather than rudimentary skills in a second language (Eddy 1978; Troike 1981; De Avila and Ulibarri 1980; Krashen 1981; Hakuta 1986; Ovando 1990), and that bilingual approaches have been more successful for disadvantaged students than has immersion (Dobson 1985).

On the other hand, one systematic review of research on immersion concluded that it can be helpful for students from "lower socioeconomic backgrounds and from minority ethnic groups" when it is designed and implemented well (Genesee 1985, 359). Also, data on *structured immersion* (in which care is taken to ensure that instruction is understood by students) suggest that "immersion can and does work with low-income Hispanic and Asian children and that the effects seem to endure even after students enter the mainstream" (Gersten and Woodward 1985, 78).

Various reviews of the literature on research dealing explicitly with bilingual approaches have reached radically different conclusions. For example, a review prepared for the U.S. Department of Education (Baker and de Kanter 1981) concluded that based on the results of twenty-eight studies that met the reviewers' standards for methodological adequacy, bilingual approaches were not consistently successful and structured immersion sometimes was more successful than TBE. The authors concluded that the "commonplace observation that children should be taught in a language they understand does not necessarily lead to the conclusion that they should be taught in their home language" (Baker and de Kanter 1981, 13).

Similarly, Christine Rossell (1990b) reviewed thirty-six studies that she had classified as "methodologically sound" and concluded that "there is no consistent research support for transitional bilingual education as a superior instructional practice for improving the English language achievement" of LEP students. She also concluded that bilingual education has not improved the attitudes or self-esteem of students whose native language is not English (Rossell 1990b, 30–32).

Preliminary results of the most recent government-sponsored study of bilingual education also indicated that maintenance and transitional approaches do not generally produce higher achievement than does immersion, and that all three approaches can be successful in helping disadvantaged Spanish-speaking students become fluent in English (van Broekhuizen 1991). However, even before the full study was released critics on all sides expressed negative views concerning its methods and adequacy (Padilla 1991; Schmidt 1991b).

On the other hand, Dulay and Burt (1982) also reviewed studies on the effectiveness of bilingual education; after identifying twelve methodologically acceptable studies on bilingual programs conducted in the United States in the 1970s, they concluded that "despite the recentness of this complex innovaton, more than half of the findings show that bilingual education worked significantly better than monolingual programs" (p. 2). Willig (1985) reviewed and synthesized the results of twenty-three studies and concluded that "participation in bilingual education programs consistently produced small to moderate differences favoring bilingual education for tests of reading, language skills, mathematics, and total achievement when the tests were in English, and for reading, language, mathematics, writing, social studies, listening comprehension, and attitudes toward school or self when tests were in other languages." She also cautioned, however, that "methodological inadequacies in the synthesized studies render the results less than definitive" (p. 269).

Controversies over the findings of research on bilingual education have continued into the 1990s. Hakuta and Gould (1987), for example, systematically analyzed the available research and concluded that "programs with substantial native-language components may be very effective" (p. 40). Their conclusions included the following observations:

1. Even though NEP and LEP students may acquire some English proficiency through instruction in their native language in as little as two years, it may take five to seven years to master the "decontextualized" language skills necessary to function well in English.
2. Prematurely mainstreamed students "run the risk of being diagnosed as slow, disabled, or even retarded because of their language handicap" (p. 41).
3. Both immersion* and bilingual programs vary widely in the extent to which they provide support in English, the instructional methods used and the quality of instruction, and effectiveness of implementation.
4. Children learning a second language will need several years before their English "is

---

*Hakuta and Gould have distinguished between *immersion*, which they define as carefully planned English-only instruction in classes composed entirely of NEP and LEP students, and *submersion*, in which language-minority students attend classes with native English-speaking students. Also see Wong (1987) for additional distinctions between immersion and submersion.

as good as that of children who have been speaking it since birth . . . [although] starting to speak English as late as high school is no barrier to learning to speak it very well" (p. 42).

Iris Rotberg (1982) examined both positive and negative studies dealing with bilingual education and offered the following partial explanation of their frequently conflicting results:

Programs that teach initially in the second language may be more likely to succeed when:

- *Children come from middle- or upper-class homes*
- *Children's linguistic development in the native language is high*
- *There is a strong incentive for the children to learn a second language. . . .*
- *Program quality is high and is specifically designed for children who are learning a second language.*

Conversely, some observers suggest that initial learning in the native language might be more desirable, both academically and psychologically, for children who come from low-income families and also are not proficient in their native language. . . . These generalizations, if not taken too literally, can be helpful to communities considering alternative educational programs for language-minority children. (Rotberg 1982, 35)

Regardless of whether one concludes that bilingual education in the United States has been more or less effective or ineffective, it is clear that bilingual programs for linguistic-minority students from economically disadvantaged families will have to do more than simply provide transitional or continuing instruction in the native language if it is to improve their achievement substantially in English and other subjects. Bilingual education research indicates that LEP and NEP students who have the greatest problem learning

English or another second language in the school also tend to have problems mastering their native language. Conversely, children who perform well in their own language—many Chinese and Mexican-American students, for example—tend to learn English and other school subjects very rapidly (Schacter 1979; Porter 1990). If working class subcultures among Anglo, Chicano, Filipino, Puerto Rican, and other groups impede learning in the school, then bilingual instruction may make little difference. Joshua Fishman of Yeshiva University has studied the research on bilingual education and reached essentially this determination. "On the whole," he concluded, bilingual education is

> *too frail a device in and of itself, to significantly alter the learning experiences of the minority-mother-tongue-poor in general or their majority-language-learning-success in particular. It is of course true that foisting a language other than their own upon such children is equivalent to imposing an extra burden upon those least able to carry it. However, precisely because there are so many other pervasive reasons why such children achieve poorly . . . removing the extra burden . . . does not usually do the trick, particularly when the teachers, curricula, and materials for bilingual education are as nonoptimal as they currently usually are. (Fishman 1977, 5)*

Recent Research on Instruction for LEP and NEP Students

Both the skeptics and the proponents of bilingual/bicultural approaches tend to agree that a good deal more research and experimentation are needed if such programs are to be more successful in the future. Research is needed particularly to identify the specific bilingual and bicultural approaches that work best with differing groups of children and to avoid possible mistakes such as using "Standard" Spanish to teach low-status Puerto Rican students whose dialect is quite different. To be effective, bilingual approaches should be planned in accordance with the school and community contexts in which they operate (Hornberger 1990). In particular, research is beginning to examine the characteristics of schools and/or classrooms in which bilingual education appears to have had considerable success in improving the academic performance of disadvantaged language-minority students (van Broekhuizen 1991).

For example, Tikinoff (1985, 1991) has reported the results of a systematic effort (the Significant Bilingual Instructional Features Study) to identify successful bilingual classrooms enrolling Puerto Rican, Cuban, Mexican, Navajo, and Chinese students and to assess the reasons for their success. The SBIF study found that successful bilingual instruction involves:

1. "Active teaching" in which teachers communicated subject matter and tasks clearly, obtained and maintained students' engagement on instructional tasks, and monitored students' progress while providing appropriate feedback.
2. Effective use of both the native language and the second language, "alternating between the two when necessary."
3. Coordination and integration of English-language development with academic skills development.
4. Appropriate use of information about the students' home culture.
5. Communication of high expectations to students.
6. Adaptation of instruction within the classroom in accordance with the language problems and deficiencies of different students.
7. Variation in the frequency and use of language alternation with the instructional context.
8. Placing more importance on the quality of instruction in basic skills than on the amount.
9. The use of TESL strategies while still coordinating bilingual language development strategies with regular instruction in content areas (Tikinoff 1985).

Many of these SBIF conclusions about successful bilingual education are strikingly similar to those provided by general research (summarized in Chapter 13) on effective teaching and effective schools. Of course, it is not surprising that factors associated with successful instruction in regular classrooms are also present in bilingual classrooms. Further confirmation that key considerations in providing effective instruction in regular classes are also important for bilingual education can be found in an analysis of SBIF data. In this analysis, Courtney Cazden (1985) concluded that great heterogeneity in the bilingual classroom makes it difficult to teach effectively, that the pace of instruction can be unproductively slowed by concurrent translation, and, in particular, that many bilingual classrooms are not successful because they minimize stress on comprehension and thinking skills. Similar conclusions have been reported by Padron and Knight (1990 and van Broekhuizen (1991).

Following up on SBIF results, researchers at the Southwest Regional Educational Laboratory and cooperating organizations conducted a three-year study dealing with significant features of exemplary Special Alternative Instructional Programs (SAIP) for LEP students. After collecting and analyzing data on nine programs/sites at which Spanish-speaking students' academic performance and gains were unusually high, SAIP researchers reported that eight of the sites enrolled students who generally had been in the United States fewer than two or three years and that all nine had developed successful instructional arrangements by reallocating funds and modifying existing instructional programs in accordance with local needs and circumstances (Lucas and Katz 1991; van Broekhuizen 1991). The nine sites varied greatly in their approaches and combinations of approaches, including ESL; transitional bilingual educational (TBE) with mainstreamed instruction in few or many subjects; Sheltered English, which provided extra English-language help in academic subjects for TBE students; school-within-a-school arrangements at the high school level; and special assis-

tance for students exiting TBE. Despite this diversity, the nine programs generally were similar in exemplifying the following characteristics:

- Assistance was open ended—help was provided until it was no longer needed rather than being eliminated at some arbitrary English-proficiency score.
- Innovative methods (e.g., opportunity to repeat courses or receive additional help after exiting TBE) were used to respond to differing students' needs.
- Whenever possible, enrollment continuity was maintained over several years for a given student.
- Student progress was monitored frequently so that appropriate adjustments could be made in the intensity and type of assistance provided.
- Teachers tended to use principles of effective instruction (see Chapter 13) in a manner that facilitated English-language development. Thus, the researchers concluded that the exemplariness of the nine sites was associated with teachers' emphasis on such practices as careful monitoring of student progress, adjusting English usage to make content comprehensible, providing immediate individual feedback, creating and structuring opportunities to use English, frequent checking of students' comprehension, and allowing students to work on assigned tasks with others (van Broekhuizen 1991, pp. 10–16).
- In programs designed to use English as the primary language for instruction, teachers used a variety of methods to draw on and take account of students' native-language "linguistic resources." Leading researchers thus concluded that bilingual and English-emphasis approaches need not be polar opposites (Lucas and Katz 1991, p. 20).

Will bilingual/bicultural education impede school desegregation or be otherwise socially divisive? Uncertainty about the degree to which emphasis on bilingual/bicultural education may impede school desegregation follows partly from the fact that educators have not been able to work out systematic plans for successfully combining the two approaches, as well as recognition that there is likely to be continuing tension between their major objectives. On the one hand, it is clear that placing students of a given language group in separate classes for native language instruction all or part of the school day effectively segregates them even if they are enrolled in a racially and ethnically mixed school (Porter 1990). On the other hand, it also is clear that desegregation plans may limit opportunities for bilingual/bicultural education by dispersing LES and NES students in a large number of schools at which it is difficult to deliver native language instruction economically (Wells 1989b).

Many advocates of bilingual/bicultural education believe it is possible and desirable to devise programs that can be implemented in a desegregated setting. For example, José A. Cárdenas, executive director of the Intercultural Development Research Center in San Antonio, has stated (1975) that in-class grouping of students according to their individual needs, exchange or regrouping of students and teachers across classes for special instruction part of the school day, and staffing patterns that draw on resources other than the regular classroom teacher should all be part of a bilingual program. Such approaches also could facilitate the implementation of bilingual education in desegregated settings. School administrators in Los Angeles and other cities are trying to develop ways of doing this. Castellanos (1980) assessed the tensions that arise between bilingual and desegregation goals and concluded that "bilingual education and school desegregation will conflict only to the extent that the staffs of both programs do not take cognizance of each other, are inflexible in their demands, or insist on quarreling over turf" (p. 8).

The situation with respect to bilingual/bicultural education and desegregation is complicated by the differing conditions and legal rulings that govern developments in differing communities. In many school districts, particularly those in the Southwest, Hispanics are counted as minority in drawing up a student desegregation plan, but in others such as Cleveland they have not been designated by the courts as minority victims of *de jure* segregation. Some school districts count Hispanics along with blacks in developing a desegregation plan, but others have developed plans specifying a multi-ethnic balance in every school. In some locations such as Denver and Detroit bilingual programs have been mandated as part of court desegregatoin remedies in either desegregated or ethnically isolated schools (Wells 1990b), but in some other districts this has not been true. In addition, Hispanic leaders differ from district to district on whether to push hardest for bilingual alternatives or desegregation, or for both equally.

Related to the desegregation issue is the possibility that bilingual/bicultural education will reinforce or stimulate separatist trends that may prove divisive and harmful to the development of a pluralistic society. Some observers, such as Epstein (1977) and (Porter 1990), fear that bilingual or bicultural maintenance programs may contribute to greater emphasis on ethnic separateness and thereby reduce movement toward desegregation in the future. On the other hand, there is little evidence to support the conclusion that bilingual/bicultural maintenance programs generally have had much of an independent effect in stimulating separatist tendencies among racial or ethnic groups in the United States or elsewhere (Padilla 1991). Joshua Fishman has reached the following conclusions concerning the potentially divisive effects of bilingual approaches:

Very few, if any, secessionist movements have been spawned thereby or related thereto, and it would seem to me to be more wicked than wise to raise any such bugaboo in conjunction with discussions of bilingual education in the U.S.A. today.... When coterritorial groups move toward separatism, it is almost never because of conflicts over bilingual education. (1977, p. 6)

Two-Way Bilingual Education

It also should be noted that many scholars such as Fishman (1977), Iiams (1977), González (1975), Hakuta (1986), Orfield (1977), and Ovando (1990) believe that bilingual education ideally should be provided for almost or all students whatever their ethnic background, and that participation in such programs could reduce social divisiveness by bringing students into contact with one another and their respective cultures. Helping all students acquire sufficient skill to function successfully in another language might be an important step toward maintaining a constructive pluralistic society in the United States. Thus, a group of government officials and civic leaders concerned with bilingual education has recommended the following actions and emphases to make bilingual education a positive force for constructive pluralism in the 1980s (Academy for Educational Development 1982):

1. Overall emphasis on development of a "language-competent" society.
2. A "no-holds-barred insistence on full mastery of English."
3. Emphasis on multilingual competence rather than English remediation.
4. Bilingual programs expanded to include English-speaking children, so that non-English speakers and English speakers can help each other learn.
5. Increased attention to the international political and economic advantages of multilingual competence.

This type of two-way bilingual education has been formally endorsed in California. The State Board of Education has established a goal stating that all students should have encouragement and opportunity to become bilingual. Curricula to help students acquire communications skills (not just grammar) in two languages have been developed for both elementary and secondary schools.

Bicognitive Development

In recent years, attention has been given to developing instructional approaches that take into account possible differences in learning styles and preferences among students of differing cultural background. Manual Ramirez III and Alfredo Castañeda have been particularly systematic in examining such possibilities with respect to Mexican-American children and have written a book (1974) in which they describe instructional approaches designed to help students function "bicognitively" (i.e., using more than one cognitive style).

The basis for the Ramirez and Castañeda approach is the finding that Hispanic children are more "field-dependent" or "field-sensitive" than are Anglo children. Field dependence-independence usually is measured with perceptual tests that ask a respondent to identify subpatterns within a larger pattern. Field-sensitive students are described as being more influenced by personal relationships and by praise or disapproval from authority figures than are field-independent students. Based on their own as well as other research, Ramirez and Castañeda argued that instruction for field-sensitive Mexican American students will be more successful if it is adapted to their cognitive style. Among the many suggestions they make for conducting instruction in this way are to humanize the curriculum through use of humor and drama and to emphasize concrete rather than abstract subject matter.

A bicognitive approach such as that advocated by Ramirez, Castañeda, and some other educators is not yet of proven value in working to improve the performance of low-status students of Mexican-American or other background. Some instructional components such as emphasis on friendly, understanding teacher behavior have been regarded as important for decades, but educators still have trouble translating this admonition into effective teacher behavior. De Avila and Ulibarri (1980) have examined the research on field dependence and concluded that it is not consistently related to academic achievement among either urban or rural Hispanic students, and that Mexican-American students are not consistently more field dependent than are non-Hispanic whites. They also worry about the possibility that too much stress on using one teaching style with Hispanic students may be educationally destructive.

ASIAN AMERICANS AND EDUCATION

Seven sizable groups of immigrants from Asia and the Pacific Islands are present in substantial numbers in the United States, although they represent only a small percentage of the total population. These groups are Asian Indians, Chinese, Filipinos, Hawaiians, Japanese, Koreans, and Vietnamese. There also are approximately seventy-five other smaller Asian American subgroups, such as the Hmong, Laotians, and Taiwanese (Schmidt 1991a). In 1990, Asian Americans comprised almost 3 percent of the U.S. population (Butterfield (1991a).

The number of Asian Americans increased from less than 1 million in 1950 to more than 7 million in 1990, almost doubling in the 1980s (Butterfield 1991a). Asians have constituted a substantial proportion of immigration to all regions of the United States since 1950, and their increase in some locations has been explosive. Nearly 1 million Vietnamese refugees entered the United States between 1975 and 1990 (Lyman 1990). The Asian American population is continuing to grow rapidly and is expected to exceed 10 million by the end of the century. By the year 2000, more than 13 percent of California's population probably will be Asian American (Fost 1990; Lev 1991).

Status

Asian Americans have tended to settle in urban areas on the West Coast, but since about 1950 there has been significant distribution of Asian population in all regions of the United States. The Japanese Americans, Korean Americans, and Chinese Americans have a higher percentage in white-collar jobs than the national average. All three groups are relatively high in educational attainment compared to other ethnic groups in the United States. For example, nearly 90 percent of third-generation Japanese Americans have attended college (Takei 1981). Although some problems have been evident with respect to in-migration of low-status population from Cambodia, China, Hong Kong, and other locations (Kifner 1991), most of the once-sordid Chinatowns in big cities have become relatively prosperous and stable communities.

Asian Americans now constitute more than 30 percent of undergraduate enrollment at the Berkeley and UCLA campuses of the University of California, and they also are disproportionately well represented in the enrollments of several highly selective big-city high schools. For example, Stuyvesant High School in New York City had 41 percent Asian students in 1988 (Schwartz 1988). Nearly half of the high-school seniors identified in the Westinghouse Science Talent Search in recent years have been Asian Americans (Simon 1991).

The status of Asian American subgroups is shown in Table 10-9. The fact that these subgroups generally score relatively high on indicators of socioeconomic status and education does not mean that they do not experience special problems as do other nonwhite minority groups (Tachibana 1990). A 1980 study by the U.S. Commission on Civil Rights indicated that "Asian Americans as a group are not the successful minority that the prevailing stereotype suggests. Individual cases of success should not imply that the diverse peoples who make up the Asian American communities are uniformly successful. . . . Asian Americans earn far less than majority Americans with comparable education." (p. 24)

Some of this disadvantage probably is due to the relatively recent in-migration status of many Asian Americans and to language barriers associated with immigration, but some probably can be attributed to discrimination in employment and to lack of political power (Takaki 1990). In addition, there is reason to believe that many

TABLE 10-9   *Selected Characteristics of Asian American Subgroups, 1980*

Subgroup	Annual Household Income	Percentage Graduated from High School (age 25 or older)	Percentage Reported to Speak English Well
Cambodian	12,500	43	37
Chinese	23,700	71	76
Filipino	25,600	74	91
Guamanian	19,700	68	87
Hawaiian	19,500	68	98
Hmong	9,100	22	34
Indian	25,000	80	87
Indonesian	21,000	90	69
Japanese	22,900	82	90
Korean	22,500	78	75
Laotian	8,300	31	27
Melanesian	19,200	47	—
Pakastani	23,800	87	84
Samoan	16,500	61	88
Thai	20,500	72	86
Tongan	18,400	66	65
Vietnamese	15,300	62	60

Source: Adapted from Brier 1990.

Asian American families and students stress success in the educational system in part *because* their English skills are poor and/or they perceive or encounter discrimination in employment (Sue and Okazaki 1990).

Data on Asian students are generally positive. For example, although they constituted 4 percent of public school enrollment in 1980, Asian students accounted for much less than 2 percent of suspensions from school. Conversely, approximately 5 percent of Asian students were participating in instructional programs for the gifted and talented, compared with less than 3 percent of white students. In addition, information from the High School and Beyond data set shows that Asian students are earning significantly more credit in science and math than are students from other racial-ethnic groups (Tsang and Wing 1985). After entering college, the percentages of Asian students majoring in engineering, life science, and physical science are respectively twice, four times, and twice as great as those for white students (Peng 1985).

However, many Asian American students experience special school problems arising from their distinctive cultural patterns (Pai 1990). For example, as pointed out in a paper prepared for the Education Commission of the States, children from Vietnamese families frequently have been encouraged to learn by rote memory and thus may find it difficult to apply analytic skills in the classroom, and students from each Asian group may find it difficult to express their own opinions when asked to do so by their classroom teacher because this might be viewed as disrespect toward adults. Some have academic problems in part because their families came to the United States from isolated mountain communities in which there was no written native language (Lai 1990).

In addition, the concept of counseling has not been a part of Asian cultures, thus making it unusually difficult to conduct counseling programs for Asian students. Mizokawa and Moroshima (1979), Brier (1990), Lai (1990), and Pang (1990) have identified other school-related problems that many Asian American students have encountered:

1. Low self-concept possibly related to lack of material on Asians in the curriculum.
2. Lack of native-speaker fluency in English.
3. Linguistic differences such as the greater emphasis on intonation in Asian languages.
4. Speech anxiety.
5. "Loaded" words, images, and stereotypes such as those that portray Asians as exotic, overly passive, inscrutable, or sinister.
6. Lack of attention to or recognition of differences between various Asian- and Pacific-origin groups, including groups from differing parts of China.
7. Relatively nonassertive and nonverbal behavior in the classroom, particularly in the presence of authority figures.
8. Debilitating experience in pre-immigration camps, leading to later mental-health problems.
9. Relatively low levels of parent contact with schools.
10. Strong sexist traditions that limit the aspirations of girls in some Asian American subgroups.
11. Unusually demanding family responsibilities among several recently arrived subgroups.
12. Perceptions that high-achieving students are nerds.

Southeast Asians

Representation of Asians in the U.S. population has been increased substantially by in-migration since 1975 of more than 1 million persons from Southeast Asia. Among these immigrants, more than two-thirds were from Vietnam; the remainder were from Laos and Cambodia (Fass 1989).

Nearly half of Southeast Asians have settled in California and Texas.

The first wave of Vietnamese immigrants in 1975 and 1976 consisted primarily of well-educated persons of high socioeconomic status. Many in this group could speak English. The Southeast Asian immigration since 1976 has been of refugees heterogeneous in cultural, linguistic, and educational background. Relatively few in this group knew English (Lai 1990).

Given the low social-class background and the language barriers experienced by many Southeast Asian in-migrants in the 1970s and 1980s, it is not surprising that many also experienced economic problems. Nearly two-thirds who arrived after 1980 were receiving public assistance in 1986. Data collected by the federal government indicate that the subsequent status and success of Southeast Asian immigrants to the United States have been highly correlated with proficiency in English. Among those who possessed or had acquired fluency in English, the unemployment rate in 1985 was 19 percent, compared with 32 percent for those speaking no English. Overall, however, the data provided encouraging indications that most were acquiring some English and also were improving in economic status (Jaeger and Sandhu 1985).

As a group, the children of Southeast Asian in-migrants have done well—frequently exceedingly well—in U.S. public schools. For example, a study conducted by Nathan Caplan and his colleagues (Caplan 1985; Caplan, Whitmore and Choy 1990) found that among children of Southeast Asian families who entered the United States after 1978, 47 percent had a math grade point average above 3.5 (on a scale of 4), 27 percent scored at or above the 90th percentile in math achievement, and 79 percent had an overall grade point average above 2.5. The authors also found that the "highest-achieving children are from families that embodied what are traditional Confucian cultural values, emphasizing the family as a cohesive unit working to achieve shared goals, and encouraging a strong respect for education" (Caplan 1985, 7). Although the children and their parents ranked far below the U.S. average in adherence to competitive individualism (i.e., stress on independence of competing individuals), their emphasis on hard work, education, and "steadfast purpose" has helped them succeed because it is compatible with traditional American values (Caplan, Whitmore, and Choy 1990, 145).

School Performance

As shown in Table 10-4, Asian American pupils do as well as or better than white pupils on standard tests of school achievement. They do much better in mathematics. Their performance on tests of reading and of vocabulary is about equal to that of white pupils, despite the fact that many Asian pupils speak little or no English at home. These data are particularly impressive given that approximately 15 percent of Asian students were classified as limited-English-speaking in the early 1980s (Tsang and Wing 1985). Research on the classroom performance of Asian American students indicates that as a group their grades are much higher than would be pre-

dicted by scores on mastery tests, probably because they "work harder" and behave in a manner that pleases teachers (Farkas, Sheehan, and Grobe 1990, 824).

Academic Performance of Subgroups. Because large numbers of immigrants of Asian countries have settled in California, achievement data in that state make it possible to analyze performance of subgroups while taking account of background characteristics that affect achievement. Morris Lai (1990) and his colleagues have carried out analysis of this kind using data on eighth-grade reading scores from the California Assessment Program. As shown in Table 10-11, second-generation Asian American students in five of the subgroups (Asian Indian, Chinese, Filipino, Japanese, and Korean) scored considerably higher than did first-generation students (i.e., relatively recent immigrants) from their respective subgroup. Only in the case of Vietnamese students were scores of the first- and second-generation students similar. The discrepancy may be related to the fact that only thirty-seven Vietnamese students were in the second-generation sample.

TABLE 10-10 *Average Reading Performance of Asian American Subgroups on the California Assessment Program Eighth-Grade Reading Test, by Generation in the United States and Parental Education*

	Asian Indian	Cambodian	Chinese	Filipino	Hmong	Japanese	Korean	Laotian	Vietnamese
First generation	245	180	217	229	201	205	279	161	236
Second generation	358	—	312	276	—	303	348	—	235
Third generation	—	—	304	283	—	325	—	—	—
Parental Education									
College graduate	347	—	305	260	—	319	308	—	238
Some college	—	—	282	252	—	303	278	—	249
High-school graduate	—	—	238	216	—	215	269	147	245
Less than high school	—	166	198	186	202	—	252	159	213
All students	291	183	239	246	208	294	292	165	234

Source: Adapted from Lai 1990.

Note: Average scores are shown only when there were twenty-five or more students in a subgroup. Data are from six large California school districts.

As regards parental education, the general pattern (predictably) shows that students whose parents have high levels of education have higher reading scores than students whose parents have less education. The major exceptions to this pattern involve the relatively low scores of Laotian students whose parents are high-school graduates and of Vietnamese students whose parents are college graduates. These discrepancies probably are related to the relatively recent immigrant status of Laotian and Vietnamese students and to the consequently high proportions of first-generation of LEP and NEP students present in these subgroups. In addition to providing support for this interpretation, Lai and his colleagues expressed the following observations:

> Writers who use phrases such as "performance of Asian (or Asian-American) students was . . ." are probably guilty of unwarranted stereotyping. Furthermore, we suggest that it is even inappropriate to refer to the "achievement of Chinese-American (non-immigrant) students," for example, without taking into account factors such as generation in the U.S., parents' education, or amount of time spent on homework each weekday. . . .
>
> Immigrants from Asia and the Pacific are operating out of different identity systems that are in conflict more often than they overlap. . . . The relatively lower performance of first-generation students from Southeast Asia . . . is consistent with this observation. Another possibly important factor . . . is whether immigrants and their families came to the U.S. because they wanted to or whether they were in the U.S. largely because they had been forced to leave their native country. (Lai 1990, 10–11)

Discrimination in Higher Education

Because Asian American students as a group have high educational aspirations and achievement, their college application rates also are high. Inasmuch as many score very high on ability tests (particularly in math) and aspire to obtain

degrees at highly regarded colleges and universities, the percentage of Asian Americans who apply for entrance to and meet academic admissions criteria at such institutions frequently is higher than is true for other large racial-ethnic groups in the United States.

At the same time, many prestigious colleges and universities use admissions criteria and procedures designed to produce, insofar as possible, a diverse student body with respect to race and ethnicity, region of origin, social-class background, extracurricular activities, and other considerations. Many also give some degree of preference to athletes, children of alumni, and/or relatives of persons who donate large sums of money. When a variety of such criteria are applied in the admissions process, Asian Americans who are qualified for acceptance academically may be refused admission in order to make room for other students with similar ability and achievement scores.

This situation frequently has resulted in disproportionately high rates of rejection and, concomitantly, perceptions of discrimination against Asian American students who apply to attend respected colleges and universities. Whether and in what circumstances relatively high rejection rates may exemplify unconstitutional discrimination has been and remains somewhat unclear because of the many legitimate considerations that can affect the admissions process and uncertainties regarding the application of antidiscrimination laws.

Several recent developments may lead to clarification of illegal practices and resolution of allegations of discrimination against Asian Americans in higher education in the future. For example, in 1990, U.S. Department of Education officials investigated eighty-four graduate-admissions programs at the University of California at Los Angeles and determined that seventy-five had not been discriminating illegally against Asian Americans, eight had not kept information adequate to allow for a determination and would have to improve their recordkeeping, and one (the mathematics department) was guilty of a constitutional violation because there was a "statistical disparity in the rates of admission . . . on the basis of race, an inconsistency in how Asian and white applicants . . . [with] the same evaluation ratings were treated, and insufficient evidence to show a non-discriminatory basis for this pattern" (quoted in Jaschik 1990b, A24). The federal Office of Civil Rights was directed to monitor math department procedures for three years to ensure that no formal or informal quotas are being applied against Asian Americans.

The Department of Education also investigated complaints against Harvard University at about the same time and concluded that although Asian American applicants have been admitted at a lower rate than whites, a constitutional violation had not occurred because the disproportion was caused by preferences (e.g., to recruit athletes and children of alumni) that are permissible as part of a set of policies designed to achieve legitimate institutional objectives without using quotas to restrict admission according to race (De Wittb 1990). Although these rulings may help to clarify legal issues involving college admissions of Asian American students, many relevant issues remain somewhat uncertain. For example, it is not clear whether or how admission of foreign students from Asian countries should enter into analysis of acceptance/rejection rates, how preferences given to African American or other minority students as part of affirmative action plans should enter into calculations, or whether students with ancestors from India, Pakistan, and some other Asian locations should be classified as Asian American in assessing charges of discrimination. In addition, litigation through the court system may change or complicate policies and practices regarding higher-education participation of Asian American students in the future.

NATIVE AMERICANS (AMERICAN INDIANS AND ESKIMOS)

The 1980 census reported that there are now nearly 2 million American Indians. (However, approximately 7 million people in the United States report that they have some Indian ancestry.) There are also approximately 100,000 Eskimos and Aleuts, mostly in Alaska, who are placed in a similar classification (i.e., Native American) with Indians by the federal government (Johnson 1991a). The Native American population has grown rapidly in recent decades, due partly to the fact that the U.S. Public Health Service has brought modern health services to most Native American communities.

Native Americans are diverse in tribal customs, religious beliefs, and ways of earning a living. When white men first came into contact with Indians in the various geographical areas that are now the United States, there were hundreds of tribes that formed several different language groups encompassing more than 200 languages. The Eastern Indians were generally farmers; the Plains Indians were buffalo hunters; the Southwest Indians were dry-land farmers, food gatherers, or small-game hunters. Along the Pacific coast, the people were fishermen; and in Alaska, they were hunters of seal and caribou and salmon fishers.

When the warfare between Indians and whites came to an end about 1870, the government took the role of guardian over the Indian people. It recognized each tribe's ownership of land but tried to teach the adults better farming and cattle- and sheep-growing practices. At the same time, Indian children were placed in boarding schools, where they were expected to learn white American culture. It was hoped that Indians would soon become like other Americans and would become assimilated into the surrounding society.

This policy did not work. Although some American Indians accepted the ways of white society, many held to Indian ways and to tribal identifications. Because they were confined to reservations and ruled by agents of the federal government, their ways of life changed and frequently were no longer Indian in the traditional sense, but neither were their ways of life American. Indians became marked by poverty, primarily because they were generally given poor and infertile land for their reservations (Sandefur 1989).

Native Americans have a moral claim on the public conscience somewhat different from the moral claims of other minority groups because they are the original Americans, whose lands were taken from them by force or by shady bargaining. For this reason, the American Indians might now expect the best possible treatment from the wealthy society that surrounds them. There is a real desire on the part of most government leaders in the United States to make up for past mistakes by giving the Indians better treatment. But there is no general agreement on what is the best program for improvement of Indian life.

Status of American Indians

American Indians today are a disadvantaged minority group. On the average they are low in income, educational level, and occupational levels, and their children are low on school achievement (see Table 10-9). Poverty rates on many reservations exceed 40 percent, and unemployment rates for Indians, particularly for those on reservations, frequently exceed 50 percent (Karoniaktatie 1986). Among some tribes, such as the Navajo, less than 20 percent of students complete high school (Crawford 1986b), and only 104 American Indians received doctorate degrees in 1987. In addition, nearby urban development and pollution have severely hampered many traditional activities involving farming, hunting, and fishing (Hedges 1990). On the other hand, large gains have been made in such professions as law; the number of Indian attorneys increased from less than a dozen to about 600 in the past few decades (A. Cohen 1990).

As noted, the low socioeconomic status of American Indians is attributable in part to the fact that during the nineteenth century many Indians were forcibly moved to reservations distant from economically developed communities. Since that time many Indians have sought social and economic opportunities away from the reservations, and the percentage of Indians residing on reservations declined from more than 50 percent in 1950 to approximately 25 percent in 1990.

Many American Indians who remain live on reservations where the poverty rate is 40 percent or higher. Gary Sandefur (1989) has analyzed the situation of reservation inhabitants and concluded that social arrangements and opportunities there have several positive aspects and advantages:

> *First, the reservation is a cultural base. Indians in the United States do not share a native language as do the different Hispanic groups. There are hundreds of different Indian languages and traditional cultures. . . . [For most Indians] the reservation is the only place where one can speak to others in one's own native language and share in a traditional way of life.*
>
> *Second, life on the reservation is characterized by a strong sense of family and community. . . . [And complex kinship structures] add to daily existence a meaning and context that are missing when one leaves the reservation.*
>
> *Third, . . . [many free social services] are administered through tribal governments and special federal agencies. . . . The Indian Health Services, or tribally run health clinics, for example, provide free health care. (Sandefur 1989, 40)*

Sandefur also concludes, however, that these advantages are counterbalanced by the difficulties of economic development. Many tribes have tried to develop or attract businesses, and in recent years some have organized small gambling operations (e.g., Bingo) that are not legally available in nearby communities or have sold tax-free cigarettes and gasoline (Shabecoff 1990). Some economic gains have resulted, but many efforts have failed due to lack of business experience, difficulties in marketing goods produced on reservations, reluctance of businesses to locate without the protection of state legislation that is superseded by tribal laws, long distances for suppliers, and, in some cases, problems in tribal administration associated with local politics, nepotism, hereditary tribal leadership, and/or difficulties in determining how to use communal property

(Sandefur 1989; Velk 1990). Many of these problems involve what Sandefur characterized as

> *economic, social, and physical isolation from the majority society. . . . [which] has produced extreme poverty, high unemployment, unstable families, low rates of high school graduation, and/or high rates of alcoholism and/or drug abuse. . . . [and which occur even though] other aspects of social organization, such as kinships and community systems seem strong. So the key . . . [to improvement] may lie in reducing . . . physical, social, and economic isolation. (Sandefur 1989, 41)*

Recent Trends in Economic Development among American Indians

Despite the variety of obstacles enumerated here that hamper economic and social development, some American Indian tribes and communities have been making substantial progress in recent years. Health standards, educational opportunities (see later), housing, and other indicators of well-being have improved on many reservations, and a number of tribal efforts to initiate or bolster business, commercial, and industrial enterprises have registered impressive success or promise (Cohen 1990; Denny 1991). Examples of such tribal enterprises include the following:

- The Passamaquoddy tribe in Maine sold New England's only cement plant for $60 million—triple the price they had paid a few years earlier using funds from a land-claims settlement. Economic gains that are being realized by the 2,700 member tribe have been made possible by a communal-investment strategy, as contrasted with the traditional distribution to individuals of proceeds from claim settlements. The Passamaquoddy also have purchased two profitable radio stations and one of Maine's largest blueberry farms.
- The Choctaw Indians in Mississippi operate five auto-parts factories and a greeting-card

operation. The tribe has sponsored members in acquiring various business-related skills and has increased its employment rate to 80 percent.
- Some tribes have increased their prospects for participating in and profitting from development of mineral resources (e.g., coal, natural gas, oil, uranium) that are located in relative abundance on their reservations.

Summarizing the complex situation that exists nationally with respect to economic development among American Indians, Cohen pointed out that only a minority of tribes currently have sufficient capacity to generate substantial revenues. In addition to isolation, low educational levels, poverty, and related obstacles that hamper development, tribal members frequently have little or no experience with or knowledge of marketing plans, investment strategies, accounting and pricing systems, and other skills and practices required for success in business. Equally or more detrimental, there frequently is confusion whether the tribe is a business corporation that should or must use competitive financial and employment practices or a government that should concentrate on providing employment and on equally distributing resources to all members. In addition, many tribes are uncertain about the best ways to settle pending land claims and to build new relationships with state and federal governments (Hedges 1990).

Economic Development among Alaska Natives

December 18, 1971, marked the most comprehensive and favorable legal settlement of native people's claims to land and its resources yet seen—the Alaska Native Claims Settlement Act. For the first time, large economic resources were placed in the hands of Native Americans with very few external controls over how they use these resources. The United States Congress recognized the right of Alaskan natives to land and mineral resources, restored 44 million acres of land to native ownership, and agreed to pay $967 million for land taken over by the federal government and the states (Egan 1990).

As of the date of passage of the Act, there were approximately 76,500 Alaskan natives of all ages entitled to equal shares of the land and money. They did not receive large individual grants. Over the twenty-year period from 1971 to 1991, most of them received less than $1,500 apiece. The valuable thing they did receive was 100 shares in one of thirteen Native Regional Corporations that took title to the land and that keep, for investment purposes, 90 percent of the money paid under the Act. Also, the regional corporations must distribute almost half of their income to some 200 native villages, which form corporations to select land, possibly invest money, or use income to provide services to village residents.

The regional corporations were formed as quickly as possible after the passage of the Act. Most used the approximately $200 million they received from the government in the first five years to invest in productive enterprises, such as mineral exploration, reindeer herds, fish canneries, hotels, and supermarkets.

The stock in the regional corporations could not be sold in the market until 1991, twenty years after the passage of the Act. The money value of the stock depends on the investment experience of the corporations, just as it does for any other business corporation. This means that every Aleut, Eskimo, and Indian in Alaska has become a capitalist by virtue of the Claims Settlement Act.

Educational effects of the Act have included the establishment of several vocational schools like the one at Barrow, the northernmost settlement in the United States and capital city of the Arctic Slope Regional Corporation. Furthermore, an Eskimo university, Inupiaq University, was founded at Barrow to serve as a community college, with representatives in a dozen villages on the Arctic Slope, and with courses given by correspondence for people who could not get to a class.

Informed opinion is divided concerning the cultural and educational consequences of the Land Claims Settlement. Some say that this inevitably means the assimilation of the Alaska native people into the economic and cultural mainstream. Others say that the Eskimo culture, with its emphasis on community action and cooperation, will be active in the form of a cooperative society and culture and that the Eskimo language will be kept alive in the villages, which will not grow very much because life in them requires hunting, fishing, and adjustment to the arctic climate, a life-style that few Anglos will choose.

As might be expected, economic outcomes among 13 regional corporations and more than 200 village corporations have been varied. Some have thrived, others have investments that are not yet successful, and still others are in grave trouble following questionable financial investments. For example, the Cook Inlet Region and the Arctic Slope corporations have profitted handsomely from investments in radio and television stations, fishing, timber, and real estate, and are now among the richest companies in the western part of the United States. Others have suffered severely from declines in energy prices in the 1980s, although some have counteracted financial problems through federal tax laws allowing them to sell their operating losses to national corporations, such as Disney, Marriott, and Pillsbury (Egan 1990).

Experiencing serious economic challenges, some Alaskan Native Corporations recently have initiated or are considering initiation of enterprises that may have negative environmental consequences. Thus, one corporation has joined with the Chevron Oil Company in the first major exploration of the Arctic wildlife area, another has developed plans to log uncut forests bordering Prince William Sound, and a third is planning to build an airstrip in the world's largest refuge for brown bears. Participation in such enterprises poses dilemmas for Alaskan Natives who do not want to sell or lease their land and believe that modern development may harm their traditional means of livelihood (e.g., hunting, fishing) and may undercut their culture's close relationship with nature, but who also must avoid bankruptcy of their communal corporations (Egan 1990). In this respect recent economic developments among Native Americans in Alaska mirror those among Indians in the lower states, who also are struggling with issues of the future of organized economic development and its implications for traditional tribal practices and cultures.

Indians in Urban Centers

Since 1950, there has been substantial migration of Indians into urban centers of the United States. Like other urban migrants, many Indians leave their home communities because of limited employment opportunities. And like many other migrant groups, Indians frequently find urban communities to be alien environments. Their cultural background, with its strong emphasis on close personal interrelationships and strong traditional family and tribal values, does not prepare Indians for depersonalized and sometimes hostile encounters with other urban residents (Little Soldier 1990). Their educational and vocational skills are often inadequate or inappropriate for the available job opportunities. When they seek jobs for which they are prepared, they often face bigotry and discrimination. However, with increasing numbers of Indians already in the city, with improved job training and housing, and with personal advisory services provided by the Bureau of Indian Affairs and private agencies, many Indians are making good adjustments. Off-reservation Indians are more than 50 percent more likely to earn $20,000 a year than are Indians on reservations (Velk 1990).

One special problem confronted by educators who work with Indian students in urban schools is that their pupils may come from twenty or thirty different tribes. Such diversity in tribal background can make it difficult to take account of students' unique culture and language in planning instruction and in trying to work with parents who have diverse expectations and customs (West 1990).

Educational Policy before 1934

As part of nearly 400 treaties with Indian tribes, the federal government ceded about 1 billion acres in return for services providing education, health care, and other benefits. Because official government policy after 1870 was for the assimilation of Indians into the dominant white culture, both in schools run by the federal government's Bureau of Indian Affairs (BIA) and in schools run by churches and missionaries, the aim usually was to teach Indian children to be like white children. Consequently, the schools at first were almost entirely boarding schools, with the Indian child living away from the family and tribe. The Carlisle Indian School founded in 1878 at Carlisle, Pennsylvania, to serve children from midwestern and western tribes was typical. The curriculum was designed to teach Indian children to speak, read, and write English, to live like white people, and to practice a trade. Part of the educational program was the "outing system," which provided an Indian youth a three-year apprenticeship with a white family after completion of school training. The government paid $50 a year for his or her medical care and clothing; his or her labor in the home or on the farm was expected to compensate for his or her room and board.

By the early 1900s, there was a good deal of opposition to the boarding school as the principal institution for educating Indian children, opposition based partly on the resistance of Indian parents to having their children moved away from the family. Accordingly, a number of federally operated day schools were opened on the reservations. At the same time, many Indian children were encouraged to attend local public schools on or near the reservations. By 1920, more Indian pupils were in local public schools than in federal schools.

Indian Education, 1934–1970

The New Deal of the 1930s saw a change in Indian education toward relating schools more closely to Indian life, with the new commissioner of Indian Affairs, John Collier, exerting a decisive influence. In 1934, the Indian Reorganization Act was passed, giving more power and more responsibility for self-government to Indian Tribal Councils. A large number of day schools were built by the federal government on reservations, and the native language was used in the early grades. More emphasis was placed on learning about native Indian culture and history, and on arts and crafts.

World War II had a great influence on Indian life. Some 25,000 Indians served in the armed forces. Older Indian men and women left reservations to take jobs in war industries or other jobs in towns and cities. The end of the war brought Indians back to the reservations with more knowledge of outside affairs and more interest in education, especially high school and vocational education. For example, the Navaho tribe, containing about one-fifth of all Indians and previously the most isolated tribe, moved explicitly to get literacy training for its teenage youth, many of whom had never been to school.

Contemporary Policy of Education for Indians

The federal government moved during the 1960s toward official adoption of a policy of Indian self-determination. This was laid out in detail in President Nixon's message to Congress on July 8, 1970, and was then incorporated in the Indian Education Act of 1972 (Gollnick 1990). The president's message began "It is long past time that the Indian policies of the Federal government begin to recognize and build upon the capacities and insights of the Indian people." The message recommended that Indian tribes should have self-determination over their own affairs without termination of their reservation status and their tribal unity and should have the right to control and operate federal programs, including schools. Following passage of the 1972 Act, the federal government began to close BIA schools and instead contracted school operations to tribes.

This policy continued until 1988, when a moratorium was placed on additional closings but contracting was simplified and requirements were established for more consultation with tribes regarding future federal education regulations (Gollnick 1990). Policies in the future may follow a precedent established in 1990, when Choctaw Indians in southeastern Mississippi established a tribal department to operate all educational programs from preschool through adult learning, thus becoming the first tribe to assume complete control of all such programs on a reservation (Walker 1990b).

Having evolved in several differing directions over more than a century, policy and practice regarding American Indian education eventually had produced the following educational arrangements and distribution of students at the end of the 1980s:

BIA schools operated by the BIA	26,000 students
BIA schools contracted to tribes	12,000 students
Public schools on reservations	70,000 students
Public schools near reservations	105,000 students
Public schools distant from reservations	175,000 students
Private and parochial schools	20,000 students

Available data indicate that the Indian Education (IEA) of 1972 has had significant success in improving educational opportunities for Indian Americans. Evaluation of IEA activities dealing with elementary and secondary education concluded that many programs have been effective in responding to students' special needs, and evaluation of the higher education section concluded that it has been effective in improving opportunity for Indians. These evaluations specifically have indicated that much has been accomplished in providing tutoring, bilingual/bicultural education, guidance counseling, basic skills remediation, dropout prevention, and career education for Indians at all levels in the educational system (Ryan 1982).

Status Problems and Education

As shown in Table 10-4, a central fact about Native American education is that pupils as a group fall well below the national averages on standardized tests of school achievement. This has been true ever since school tests were first given in Native American schools.

This low school achievement is *not* because Native American children are less intelligent than white children. Several studies based on intelligence tests that do not require reading ability show Native American children to be at or slightly above the level of white children. For example, on the Goodenough Draw-a-Man Intelligence Test, a test of mental alertness that does not require language facility, Native American children show about the same level of achievement as white children. The 1,700 Indian children who took this test in 1969 under the auspices of the National Study of American Indian Education showed an average IQ of 101.5, slightly superior to the average of white children (Fuchs and Havighurst 1972).

The problems of Native American education have a good deal in common with the problems of education of other economically disadvantaged minorities. Many Native American children live in homes and communities where the cultural expectations are different and discontinuous from the expectations held by school teachers and school authorities. To be effective, educators must find ways to stimulate learning among students whose cultural backgrounds differ greatly from those of mainstream students.

Dropping out of school also is a major problem at many schools with a high proportion of Native American students. Although the overall incidence of dropping out does not appear to be much greater than among other severely disadvantaged groups, the extremely high poverty and unemployment rates at some reservations and in some Native American urban communities are associated with similarly very high dropout rates (O'Brien 1989). The dropout problem seems to be particularly difficult to alleviate at some schools to which students must travel long distances from isolated rural locations or where students must live away from their families.

One of the most important problems with which educators and community leaders struggle in attempting to improve schools for Native American students is the high rate of alcoholism and, in some communities, drug abuse among adolescents and young adults. Substance abuse has long been a serious problem among Native Americans and has been described as "the primary reason" for Indian students dropping out of high school and college (Monaghan 1987).

More than forty Native American tribes and bands from across North America have joined together since 1982 to initiate the Four Worlds Development Project, which aims to reduce alcoholism and drug abuse among Native American youth by the turn of the century. This project, based largely on community development techniques compatible with traditional values, includes an emphasis on providing children with an improved awareness and understanding of their heritage as Native Americans (Monaghan 1987).

Other important problems confronting Native American education involve several practical difficulties associated with federal operation of reservation schools as well as the high poverty rates and isolation that generally hamper socioeconomic development of many reservations. In part due to financial difficulties experienced by the federal government during the past two decades, BIA schools generally have been poorly funded, and budgets at many tribal-run schools are equally inadequate. Whether BIA operated or tribally administered, schools at isolated locations also find it difficult to attract and retain qualified teachers (O'Brien 1989; Little Soldier 1990).

Probably the most important and difficult problem faced by educators working with Native American students involves the general challenge to take cultural background into account in order to provide effective instruction. Not so much a specific problem or set of problems as an overriding necessity to recognize differences in students' cultural environments and learning styles, this challenge to Native American education has much in common with similar necessities present in working with many culturally different students from African American, Asian American, Hispanic, or other disadvantaged minority groups. In each case, educators must find ways to stimulate learning among students whose cultural backgrounds differ greatly from those of mainstream students.

However, this challenge probably is even more difficult in the case of Native American students because many Native American parents are "adamant that their children be raised *as Indian children. . . .* [preserving their] culture, language, and traditions" (Gollnick 1990, 36). Pointing to educated youth who hardly speak with their elders and, in some cases, remembering how teachers washed their mouths with soap for using their native language, parents who stress preservation of traditional culture may even refuse to let their children attend school (McDonald 1989). Concerned with maintaining the integrity of traditional culture against the attractions and inroads of mainstream society, tribal leaders and other residents of several reservations have severely criticized parents who send their children to off-reservation schools attended by non-Indian students (Barringer 1990b). Because public education aims to provide Native American children with English fluency and other skills required to function effectively in the larger society, public-school educators thus face a dilemma because they must try to design programs that recognize and build on but go beyond aspects of traditional culture (Cantrell, Pete, and Fields 1990). Other sections of this chapter describe bilingual education approaches, ethnic-heritage and multi-ethnic curriculum materials, responsiveness to students' learning-style differences, and related possibilities for recognizing students' ethnic background in delivering effective education for

Native American students as well as other minority children and youth.

Confronting various serious problems such as those already enumerated, educators working with Native American students appear to be making significant progress at many locations. Little Soldier (1990) and McDonald (1989) have identified some examples and activities in which gains have been registered:

- Indian participation has increased at all levels of school system administration and governance.
- More training is being provided for teachers and school board members at reservation schools.
- Curriculum materials and instructional practices reflecting Native American culture are being developed and introduced at all grade levels.
- Large declines in dropout rates and increases in high-school graduates' college entry have taken place at some reservation schools.
- Systematic efforts to hire Native American teacher aides and then help them become certified teachers have been initiated to provide positive role models and reduce the cultural distance between faculties and students.
- Bilingual programs are being developed and conducted at many reservation schools, although this approach frequently is difficult due to the lack of qualified teachers fluent in many of the scores of Indian languages.
- As described next, efforts are underway to improve postsecondary opportunities for Native American students.

Native Americans and Higher Education. As in the case of elementary and secondary education, the situation with respect to Native Americans in higher education presents a mixed picture of positive developments and serious problems and obstacles that hamper further progress. Encouraging aspects and developments include the following:

• The number of (two-year) associate degrees obtained annually by American Indians increased rapidly from 2,953 in 1985 to 3,197 in 1987. In 1961, only 66 American Indians received bachelor's degrees, compared with an average of about 4,000 each year from 1984 to 1988. Between 1976 and 1987, the number of master's degrees awarded annually to Native Americans increased from 987 to 1,104 (Evangelauf 1990).

• Very impressive gains were registered in establishing and operating tribal-run colleges. The first tribal college opened on the Navajo Reservation in Arizona in 1968. By 1990, 27 such colleges had been established (Marriott 1991b). Mostly two-year institutions, tribal colleges now enroll more than 10,000 students. As documented in a major report prepared for the Carnegie Foundation for the Advancement of Teaching, tribal colleges try to reinforce Native American traditions and values that stress building of supportive relationships among individuals who form a cohesive community. They also offer courses in traditional arts, literature, and philosophy and systematically attempt to make education more relevant and accessible to students (Boyer 1990a, 1990b). Graduates who transfer to four-year institutions are more likely to attain degrees than are Native Americans who begin their postsecondary education at these institutions (Mooney 1990).

Despite the considerable progress that seems to be occurring in some aspects of Native American higher education, serious problems and challenges are still apparent. In particular, scholars assessing the status of postsecondary education available to American Indians and Alaskan Natives have stressed the following considerations:

• Financial and related problems are widespread. After reviewing financial limitations, the Carnegie Foundation's report on tribal colleges offered a set of recommendations urging that: (1) the federal government provide the full funding authorized by Congress; (2) libraries, science laboratories, and classroom facilities be significantly improved through federal appropriations; (3) state governments help provide adequate support; and (4) endowment funds for tribal colleges be greatly expanded (Boyer 1990b).

• Although increases in postsecondary enrollment and degree attainment have occurred (see earlier), there also has been a large increase in the Native American college-age population, so that little or no gain was registered during the 1980s in terms of percentages. Much of this problem involves difficulties that low-income Indian students confront in obtaining funds for higher education (Boyer 1990a).

APPALACHIAN STUDENTS

Although not conventionally considered a minority group, rural students in Appalachia (and other economically debilitated rural communities in the Ozarks and elsewhere) can be viewed as a disadvantaged minority group in the sense that their social environment is isolated from mainstream society and helps generate poor performance in the education system.

Many rural students in Appalachia are the descendants of Anglo-Saxon and Scotch-Irish pioneer families that settled in mountainous or hilly parts of the region in the eighteenth and nineteenth centuries (Keefe, Reck, and Reck 1983; De Young 1991). Like other racial-ethnic minority groups discussed in this chapter, their performance in school has been hampered by language and/or dialect differences as well as by other cultural patterns that led to their being defined as distinctively outside the larger society. Thus Keefe, Reck, and Reck (1983) have reviewed the limited data available on ethnic background and its interaction with other factors in the lives of rural Appalachian students and concluded that cultural considerations related to ethnicity combine with socioeconomic and demographic characteristics in hampering their progress in traditional educational settings. For example, cultural patterns stressing resistance to authority, sex-segregation, and suspicion of modern life that are reinforced by poverty and rural location place Appalachian students at a severe disadvantage in the typical classroom.

A number of educators and social scientists who work with Appalachian schools and communities have been trying to identify ways in which teachers can adapt curriculum and instruction constructively in accordance with the cultural and social background of rural Appalachian students. David Mielke (1978), for example, has edited a volume to help teachers modify commercial materials and traditional classroom practices in an effort to take account of Appalachian culture and circumstances. Also, the well-known *Foxfire* approach (Wiggington 1986; Meek 1990; Puckett 1989; Smith 1990–1991) has been designed to use oral history and other local cultural materials to help improve students' motivation and understanding. In addition, possibilities exist for matching instruction with students' learning styles, initiating cooperative learning techniques, and using other interventions discussed elsewhere in this chapter and in Chapter 8.

As many families from rural Appalachia moved to cities seeking improved economic opportunities in the twentieth century, neighborhoods consisting largely or substantially of urban Appalachians have formed in Chicago, Cincinnati, Louisville, Detroit, and other locations in the East and Midwest. Given their disadvantaged economic background, many urban Appalachian students have experienced serious educational problems similar to those encountered by other working-class groups. Possibilities for establishing community-improvement organizations and for working to improve the education of urban Appalachians are described in a paper by Sullivan and Miller (1990) dealing with formation and operation of an Urban Appalachian Council in Cincinnati.

EMPLOYMENT OF MINORITY TEACHERS

As documented in Chapter 1 and elsewhere in this book, the minority population of the United States and its public school system is increasing rapidly and is expected to continue increasing for the foreseeable future. At the same time, however, an alarming decline has been occurring in the percentage of minority teachers in the nation's teaching force.

The percentage of African American enrollment in the public schools is expected to rise to nearly 20 percent by 1995, but the percentage of black public-school teachers has declined from 8 percent throughout the 1970s and 1980s to less than 7 percent in 1990 and is projected to fall even more in the future (Dorman 1990). The situation is similar for Hispanic students and teachers, thus raising serious questions regarding the availability of positive role models for African American and Hispanic students (Wiley 1991).

Major reasons for the declining percentage of minority teachers include the following:

1. As discussed earlier in this chapter, college-attendance rates for black students have not improved in the 1980s.
2. Opportunities for minority students and for women have expanded in such fields as business, law, natural sciences, and engineering, thus reducing the percentage of black students preparing to be teachers.
3. The growing movement to use standardized tests in selecting candidates for teacher education and in licensing both new and currently employed teachers has had a disproportionate impact in terms of eliminating minority candidates.

The latter development—widespread testing for teacher education and for employment in teaching—appears to have had a particularly negative impact in terms of reducing the percentage of minority teachers in the teaching force (McCarthy 1990; Wiley 1991). Available data on passing rates for licensing a new teacher indicate, for example, that only 41 percent of black candidates and 36 percent of Hispanic candidates passed Arizona's test for new teachers in 1983, compared with 70 percent for whites. Similar patterns have been reported in Alabama, California, Connecticut, Florida, Georgia, Louisiana, Mississippi, New Mexico, Oklahoma, Texas, and other states (Chira 1990a; Wiley 1991).

G. Pritchy Smith (1986), Arthur Dorman (1990), and others have provided analyses of the developing crisis in preparation and employment of minority teachers and its implications for all levels of education. These four suggestions are among the actions identified as constituting positive and perhaps necessary responses to the problem:

1. Improve the academic achievement of minority students in elementary and secondary schools, in order to increase the percentage entering college and the likelihood that they will pass tests for new or prospective teachers.
2. Recruit more minority candidates for teacher education, including adults with or without a college degree, and provide sufficient academic and financial assistance to help them succeed in obtaining teaching certificates.
3. Review and modify testing policies and practices, particularly in order to reduce or eliminate cultural inequities in standardized tests used to select candidates for teacher education and new teachers.
4. Ensure that teacher salaries and other aspects of employment are sufficiently attractive to recruit minority candidates.

ADAPTING INSTRUCTION IN ACCORDANCE WITH CULTURE AND LEARNING STYLES

There is reason to believe that adapting instruction to the cultural background of students—particularly disadvantaged minority students—can help improve their performance in school. As we point out in Chapter 8, disadvantaged black students may benefit by considering what some observers perceive to be an unusually high activity

level (Boykin 1983, Willis 1989, Shields and Shaver 1990), and promising opportunities may exist to match students' learning styles with teachers' instructional practices (Hunt 1975; Tharp 1989). Chapter 9 cites evidence that cooperative learning arrangements may be particularly beneficial for economically disadvantaged black students, and earlier in this chapter we describe the bicognitive theory offered by Ramirez and Castañeda.

Probably the best-known example of adaptation of instruction to recognize the cultural background of minority students is the Kamehamaha Early Educational Program (KEEP) initiated in 1971. Designed to improve reading among disadvantaged Hawaiian students in kindergarten through grade three, KEEP has been refined and modified to include the middle grades. Following unsuccessful initial attempts to teach through phonics, KEEP instruction was redesigned to emphasize comprehension of text, criteria-referenced objectives and questioning, integration of language development and reading instruction, small reading groups, and classroom learning centers. In addition, program personnel developed and introduced the experience-text-relationship method to help students learn to function independently of the teacher by drawing on their cultural experience, language, and personal knowledge (Au and Kawakami 1985; Tharp and Gallimore 1988; Anderson, Armbruster, and Roe 1990).

By 1985, KEEP was being implemented in six schools by nearly seventy teachers working with approximately 1,800 students. Data on the reading performance of KEEP minority students indicate that they have been achieving at about the national average through the third grade, compared with much lower scores for similar students in control classes (Jordan 1984; Au 1985; Tharp and Gallimore 1988). Program personnel have stated that "there is now good evidence that with two years of in-service training and consultation, most teachers can learn to operate the program effectively so that their Hawaiian pupils achieve at norm levels," and schools can improve the achievement of "at-risk ethnic minority children by training teachers to use methods designed for and suited to the particular student population" (Jordan 1984, 69).

Other promising practices also have been proposed or reported concerning possibilities for adapting instruction in accordance with cultural background. Regarding the education of Native American students, for example, Havighurst (1971a), Cole (1985), and Padron and Knight (1990) have pointed out that American Indian students are more considerate than Anglo students of peer reactions in the classroom, to the extent that Indian children may not respond to a teacher for fear of shaming other children. In addition, research suggests that some Native American students are not familiar with the concept of competition in the classroom (Cantrall, Pete, and Fields 1990). Similarly, Erickson and Mohatt (1982) have found that Indian students tend to reject being singled out as individuals for public praise or censure and so remain silent when asked to answer questions in the classroom. Little Soldier (1989) concluded that cooperative learning methods (discussed elsewhere in this book) can be effective with Native American students who exemplify these characteristics.

Erickson and Mohatt also have proposed classroom rules of participation consisting of a functional blend of traditional U.S. practice and Native American discourse styles that they believe will enhance instruction in Indian classrooms. Erickson (1985) subsequently reported on the results of an effort to introduce native teachers in schools for Alaskan village children. Participant observation and videotape analysis indicated that achievement rose "dramatically" after closer rapport was established with parents, and the native teachers

> organized instruction and interacted with students in ways that were culturally appropriate. Exercise of social control was for the most part very indirect, and the teachers usually avoided public reinforcement—not only avoiding negative reinforcement ... [but]

> positive reinforcement as well. These patterns are typical of child-rearing in the community. (Erickson 1985, 55)

Many educators working with Native American children also are attempting to integrate their culture into the curriculum. For example, some teachers are teaching the shape of the triangle by comparing it to a tepee, having students read stories with Indian characters, and using symbols from Indian culture in mathematics story problems (NWREL 1987). Educators at the Northwest Regional Educational Laboratory (NWREL 1990) have prepared an entire Indian Reading Series that incorporates these kinds of curriculum innovations and also emphasizes use and acceptance of a child's native language and inclusion of ethnic heritage literatures and Wisconsin and several other states now require instruction on Indian history and culture in all public schools (Gollnick 1990). Introduction of materials that provide information about the history and achievements of their ancestors are particularly important for Native American students because, as in the case of African American, Asian American, Hispanic, and other disadvantaged minority students, media treatment of their group historically was prone to repetitive negative stereotypes. William Gollnick (1990) has summarized some of this negative media treatment of American Indians:

> The movie industry, from the first days of "talkies," portrayed Indians as Pidgin English-speaking nomads. They were on the losing side of glorious battles that resulted in the "Winning of the West." There was seldom mention of treaties and trade. In Hollywood's case, stereotypes sell; the truth would provide a fascinating story, but it probably wouldn't create box office success. Movies and schools have thus provided an inaccurate, fixed-frame view of America's indigenous peoples. (Gollnick 1990, 32)

Similar observations also have been offered regarding some other ethnic groups (Tharp

1989). Kim (1977), for example, has pointed out that Korean children are taught at home not to be "overly expressive with their emotions, feeling and thoughts" and consequently "find it extremely difficult to express them in American classrooms. They would consider it rather rude to challenge a teacher by asking questions" (p. 16). Cultural characteristics of this kind can lead to failure if teachers are not familiar with their origins and meaning.

Pluralistic education that recognizes cultural differences among racial and ethnic minorities will not be easy to implement. Relatively little is known about how teachers can adapt instruction to such differences (Hilliard 1989/1990). Above all, it is not at all clear how the schools can respond to cultural differences without further segregating or isolating students of a given minority group. Conversely, working out methods and approaches to give minority youth a chance to participate in the larger culture while helping them maintain ethnic pride and identity will require an extraordinary effort on the part of U.S. educators and public officials (Tharp 1989).

CONSTRUCTIVE CULTURAL PLURALISM IN EDUCATION

The democratic goal of fair shares needs to be combined with the right of each subgroup to refuse to assimilate itself in the mainstream of economic and cultural life. This combination is constructive cultural pluralism. It respects the right of a cultural subgroup to hold itself aloof from the rest of the society even if this means giving up some of the advantages of full participation in the social mainstream.

Critical aspects of cultural pluralism in the United States also focus significantly on the economic and educational systems. Economic opportunity must be increased for the economically disadvantaged groups in the society, especially blacks, Hispanics, and American Indians. These groups will work through political activity to enhance their access to jobs and to welfare benefits. At the same time, they will seek better education and more education to give them access to better jobs.

Constructive pluralism faces the major problem of working through education to help minority-group members retain their identity and their pride in cultural group membership, and at the same time to increase the socioeconomic status of the economically disadvantaged minority groups (Banks 1988). Helping minority children retain a positive identity may be achieved to some degree through the schools by working to ensure that instruction reflects their racial or ethnic heritage and does not require them to reject their background in order to succeed. As we discuss in this chapter, it is possible that bilingual/bicultural education will help achieve this goal for some groups. However, it is far from certain that minority group members will retain an ethnic identity as they improve their social status except in communities or regions of the United States where they participate in almost a separate culture, as among Mexican Americans in some parts of the Southwest or Eskimos in Alaska.

In addition to bilingual/bicultural approaches discussed earlier in this chapter, there has been growing interest in providing multiethnic studies and curriculum as a means to help advance the goals of cultural pluralism in the United States (Willis 1990). For example, several big-city districts have developed and introduced systematic curricula to help students recognize and understand the importance and meaning of equal opportunity, racial and ethnic tolerance, migration and immigration, contributions to society of members of diverse racial/ethnic groups and women, and other aspects of multi-ethnic studies (Lee 1989; Mercer 1990). In particular, educators and social scientists in Portland (OR), Atlanta, and other large school districts have been introducing materials and methods designed to incorporate African American content into the regular curriculum (Schmidt 1989). Asa Hilliard of Georgia State University has pointed out that we now have a "much broader and deeper foundation" of research and experience to draw on in order to "go beyond the black-studies" approaches that emerged in the 1960s and 1970s (quoted in Schmidt 1989, 8).

However, the goal of improving academic performance and thereby promoting socioeconomic mobility among economically disadvantaged minority students probably will not be accomplished solely through bilingual/bicultural approaches and/or multi-ethnic studies. At present there is little solid evidence suggesting that transitional approaches for teaching low-status black students in Black English, teaching non- or limited-English-speaking students in their native language, or emphasizing multi-ethnic studies are sufficient to improve their academic performance very much. Rather, the major changes needed to improve the performance of low-status students of whatever group also include those outlined in Chapters 8 and 9—namely, early intervention to improve their preparation for school together with desegregation and reform of the school to improve its effectiveness with low-achieving students.

Constructive educational pluralism as described in this chapter is similar to a concept that Nicholas Appleton refers to as the "new pluralism" in an important treatise titled *Cultural Pluralism in Education* (1983). Appleton describes this approach as one in which schools and government agencies should acknowledge the relevance of ethnicity but should not

> *actively promote or reinforce ethnic associations. . . . Individuals [should] determine for themselves to what extent they wish to remain as members of a group and partake of its cultural offerings. . . . Schools would play an important part in this process by teaching students to respect and tolerate diversity; to develop understanding of their own ethnicity, as well as alternate life styles, values, and beliefs; and to decide for themselves how they wish to assert or accept their ethnicity or if they should do so. (Appleton 1983, 92)*

Appleton also proceeds to point out that pluralism in education should not be viewed as requiring exactly the same mixture of policies and practices in all communities or for all students. This means that how schools should respond to learning style differences, how and how much they should stress multi-ethnic curriculum and intergroup-relations activities, and other educational responses to issues involving cultural pluralism necessarily will vary in their development and application depending on local and temporal circumstances. "It should be evident," he concludes, that the "contextual variables" in Puerto Rico differ radically from those in San Francisco, that settings for native Americans in urban areas differ from those for native Americans on reservations, and that the problems of urban blacks are not exactly the same as those of Mexican Americans. But however policies and practices differ with community context, he further concludes, pluralistic multicultural education should follow a general set of guiding principles that include the following eight ideas (1983, 208–217):

1. Interethnic hostility and conflict should be defused and depolarized.
2. Implementation should be treated as a long-range process.
3. Multicultural concepts and perspectives should be incorporated in the total curriculum.
4. Changes should be produced not just in the curriculum but in teaching methods and classroom social structure.
5. Emphasis should be on affective as well as cognitive aims of education.
6. Teaching approaches and materials should be sensitive to students' background and experiences.
7. Parents' involvement in education of their children should be increased.
8. Students should gain a better understanding of such issues as racism, sexism, and social class inequality.

Transformative Multicultural Education

Related to Appleton's point regarding understanding of racism, sexism, and social class inequality, Frederick Erickson (1990) has argued for a "transformative" approach to multicultural education that emphasizes developing commitment to productive cultural pluralism. Multicultural education, according to Erickson, should not just affirm a range of ethnic cultures and identities, but should also help learners acquire "increasingly rich understandings" that extend rather than displace the "old voices and sensemakings" (p. 42). "This is not to say," he concludes, that

> *folk culture festivals and covered dish suppers are anathema for schools with multicultural student populations, nor that ethnic history, language, and culture are necessarily irrelevant in the classroom. . . . Ethnic studies, and even cooking classes, as oral history indigenous to the school community can be a powerful situation for reflection on the past and on today's world. But multicultural education cannot be simply nostalgic and uncritical. It must be actively anti-racist. . . . Simply to have Frederick Douglass present on the classroom wall as a picture of a hero from the past is not much better than just to have George Washington on the wall by himself. The fundamental issue for transformative education lies not in the presence of Douglass or Washington as pictures in the classroom, but in what teachers and students do with them, in critical reflection, exploration, and dialogue. (Erickson 1990, 35)*

Recent Multicultural Education Developments and Controversies

As noted above, educators in Portland, Oregon, and other urban districts have been introducing materials and methods designed to emphasize content related to the history, culture, and concerns of African Americans. In addition to these *Afrocentric* approaches, materials and methods emphasizing the history and situation of other minority groups also are being developed and incorporated in some districts (Winkler 1991). Many developers and advocates of such

minority-oriented approaches believe that the traditional school program is primarily *Eurocentric* and thereby excludes historical and other materials that can help improve the self-confidence, motivation, and performance of low-achieving minority students (Mercer 1991; Winkler 1991).

Efforts to introduce Afrocentric and other minority-oriented materials and approaches and otherwise reduce Eurocentric emphases became particularly controversial after school officials in California and New York initiated projects to review and revise statewide requirements and practices in order to make them more consistently multicultural. In both states, proposed changes focused on inclusions of more and revised materials involving the background and concerns of black and Hispanic students, but representatives of Asian American, Native American, and other racial/ethnic groups, as well as Islamic, Jewish, and other minority religions, objected to perceived omissions and/or distortions concerning their particular subgroup in the population. Critics of the initial products of these efforts offered a number of additional (frequently vocal) objections that included the following (Ravitch 1990; Searle 1990; Sewell 1990; Sullivan 1990; Leo 1991a; Mercer 1991; Siegel 1991; Taylor 1991):

- Much of the key material being introduced is historically inaccurate. For example, after noting that some of the curriculum content used and/or being developed in Portland, the District of Columbia, and other school districts is based on the conclusion that the population and culture of ancient Egypt were predominantly African and that ancient Greece derived its culture mostly from Egypt, John Leo (1991a) reported that Egyptologists and other classical scholars generally disagree with this generalization and believe it greatly exaggerates the accomplishments and influence of ancient African civilizations.

- Many of the content and background materials being used or recommended for use advocate an overly comprehensive rejection of both the traditional curriculum and existing efforts to make the schools constructively multicultural. Regarding this accusation, Leo asserted that although resource documents for developing Afrocentric curriculum in Atlanta and several other cities call for "understanding, respect, and appreciation" of the history and contributions of all groups, the documents constantly criticize Europeans and the traditional content of Western civilization courses. The result, he concluded, is a "sure-fire formula for separation and endless racial animosity" (Leo 1991a, 26).

Diane Ravitch (1990) also has argued that some recent approaches for emphasizing minority-group history and culture constitute an extreme rejection of traditional ideals and existing curriculum. After recognizing the value and importance of efforts to advance cultural pluralism through introduction of materials on the cultures of Africa, Asia, and Latin America, Ravitch concluded that the new "particularist" approach is spurring a "separatist ethic" that rejects the concept and ideal of a common culture. Ravitch views the new particularists as espousing a "version of history in which everyone is either the descendant of victims or of oppressors," thereby fanning and recreating "ancient hatreds" in each new generation (Ravitch 1990, A44).

▪ Many supporters of Afrocentric and other related approaches are intolerant of competing ideas and frequently try to intimidate and silence opposing viewpoints. For example, after citing such incidents as the elimination of a college course taught by a leading race-relations expert who was accused of insensitivity for discussing the southern defense of slavery, John Taylor expressed concern that a growing "demagogic and fanatical" demand for "intellectual conformity" on issues involving racism constitutes a new form of political indoctrination (Taylor 1991, 35). Taylor, Fred Siegel (1991), and others have criticized what they view as similar trends regarding discussion of sexism in history and culture and perceive intolerance regarding examination of race and sex issues as part of a broader *deconstructionist*

attack on scholars who disagree with politically correct positions. Although recognizing that efforts to stifle open discussion have been most common and visible at colleges and universities, these observers also worry that comparable developments are occurring with respect to curriculum and instruction in elementary and secondary schools.

▪ Views said to represent the attitudes and beliefs of minority racial and ethnic groups are not accurate; many group members have diverse viewpoints related to their social class, degree of assimilation, and other factors.

▪ Emphasis on minority culture and history is sometimes being pursued in place of the difficult actions required to improve minority students' performance in reading, math, science, and other subjects. Critics who articulate this position believe that improvement of self-esteem through study of the history and culture of one's ethnic group thus is being overemphasized at the cost and to the neglect of academic growth and rigor (Ravitch 1990; Winkler 1991).

Responding to the type of attacks summarized here, supporters of Afrocentric and other approaches that emphasize the history and culture of minority groups have taken exception to criticisms they view as generally exaggerated and misguided. Among the counterarguments and rebuttals they offer have been the following (Mercer 1991; Winkler 1991):

▪ Few Afrocentrists advocate or support elimination of the history and documents of Western culture from the curriculum. Contrary to critics who charge that such advocacy is widespread and is based largely on the work of ill-informed nonspecialists, according to Molefi Asante of Temple University, the Afrocentric movement is "based on the work of scholars who are trained in the ancient classics of both Europe and Africa and are simply trying to de-bias its curriculum. We are not taking out Europe altogether because it does play a major role in society" (quoted in Sims 1990).

▪ Few if any supporters of Afrocentric or related approaches minimize the importance of academic achievement or advocate its de-emphasis in the curriculum. Instead, stress on the meaning and contributions of one's ethnic gruop is advocated as a means to improve motivation while challenging "every child to strive to develop his or her mind to the fullest" (Peek 1991, 61). This point also was made in a 1991 statement by the executive board of the Organization of American Historians, which viewed some of the critics' accusations as creating a false dichotomy between raising the self-esteem of students by acquainting them with their heritage and teaching students to think critically (Winkler 1991).

Although academic effects of emphasizing minority culture and history in order to improve the performance of low-achieving minority students have not been researched systematically, anecdotal reports from educators at minority schools and a few sources of empirical data support the potential utility of this approach. For example, some inner-city educators have been finding that inclusion of materials on minority history and culture can enhance students' interest and participation in their studies (Wilkerson 1990a; Putka 1991a), and an assessment of college students who participated in an Afrocentric studies program for one year found that their grades improved substantially (Dervarics 1990). However, until additional, careful studies are conducted to assess the outcomes of Afrocentric or similar approaches to curriculum and instruction, it will not be possible to determine whether or how much they can help improve the achievement levels of disadvantaged minority students.

Despite predictable uncertainties regarding how to proceed and probable outcomes, many leading educators believe it is imperative to develop and implement more comprehensive multicultural school programs that emphasize and reflect minority concerns and experience. New York State Commissioner of Education Thomas Sobol summarized one essential reason for moving vigorously in this direction:

Critics ask why we are fretting over multicultural curriculums instead of getting back to the basics. What they miss is the interconnection. . . . If children are to do well academically, school and family and community must work within a context of shared values and expectations; the child must experience the school as an extension, not a rejection, of home and community. (Sobol 1990, 28)

Sobol and his colleagues responsible for the development of multicultural approaches in New York also have tried to identify guidelines for productive implementation. After recounting specific controversies that involved critics and supporters of Afrocentric emphasis and other aspects of initial plans for enhancing multicultural education in New York, Sobol delineated the following considerations to guide subsequent development and implementation:

Revising syllabi . . . is not just a matter of adding information. . . . [but of perspective. From his perspective, Columbus discovered America, but from that] of the Native Americans who greeted his arrival, it was Columbus who was lost, not they. . . .

We need both the whole and its parts. . . . [A central goal] is to develop a shared set of values and a common tradition. . . . [while also helping] each child find his or her place within the whole.

Our Western tradition must be maintained. . . . [It] has been much changed and enriched by the cumulative participation of the sons and daughters of Africa, of Asia, of Central America, of Native Americans. . . . We have not always lived up to our ideals, but . . . we would be shortchanging our children if we failed to ground them in the values of our democratic society. . . .

Whatever we do must be characterized by a high level of scholarship and historical accuracy. We do not want to rewrite history; we want to teach it better. (Sobol 1990, 29–30)

CONCLUSION

We see in this chapter that in the United States, African Americans have made substantial progress toward equality as regards mobility in the economic system and attainment in the educational system. Thus, the Black Revolution of the 1960s and 1970s has had some impact in improving opportunity for many members of the nation's largest minority group. However, gains that have been made frequently are precarious and are not sufficiently widespread to ensure continuing positive developments in the future. Economic gains signify the development of a substantial black middle class, but many blacks are locked into a destructive underclass environment.

The growing Hispanic minority is in much the same position educationally as is the black minority. A relatively large percentage of its Mexican-American and Puerto Rican members are working class, and many are segregated in concentrated poverty schools and neighborhoods in much the same way as are blacks. In addition to disadvantages associated with socioeconomic background, many low-status Hispanic students also experience problems related to linguistic and cultural discrepancies between the school and the home. It is logical to believe that bilingual/bicultural education and other approaches that take these cultural differences into account may help Hispanic students succeed in school and society, but relatively little is known concerning the approaches that might be most effective or how to implement them in the public schools.

In general, many Hispanic youngsters are likely to experience considerable strain between their ethnic and national cultures. Underlying this situation is the paramount need to provide effective education for low-status Hispanic students without isolating them in segregated bilingual programs but also without ignoring their needs as members of a culturally different ethnic minority. This dilemma is similar to that faced by blacks, American Indians, and other minority groups trying to build viable communities as a base for productive participation in the larger society. In trying to do this, minorities face the problem of deciding how to combine emphasis on group identify with stress on individual and group participation in a society composed of a variety of competing and cooperating groups.

Cultural pluralism in the United States is now at a point at which it can be used constructively to make a great improvement in intergroup relations in this country and at the same time to increase the economic and civic opportunity of the minority groups with lowest socioeconomic status. Movement in this direction will require careful educational planning, particularly in the large cities. What is needed is a complex system of pluralism adapted to each of a variety of subcultures and maintaining a strong opportunity structure that facilitates economic success for members of low-income groups.

EXERCISES

1. Write a paper that either supports or opposes a program of bilingual education aimed to assist the children of a particular non-English-speaking minority. What are the advantages and disadvantages?

2. Collect information on a bilingual program in a nearby school district. Is it primarily a transitional or a maintenance program? What criteria can be applied in making this determination? How do local administrators and teachers classify the program?

3. What ethnic groups besides the Hispanic minority are included in nearby bilingual programs? What other ethnic groups are included nationally? Consult local or federal government sources to obtain additional

information on the variety of ethnic groups for which bilingual education programs are being offered.

4. *Hunger of Memory* by Richard Rodriguez describes his early years in a Spanish-speaking home in California and the personal uncertainties he experienced later in becoming an intellectual. Rodriguez has said he hopes these memoirs "can serve as preface to future deliberations" about policy in bilingual education. Read *Hunger of Memory* and discuss its implications for bilingual policy.

5. What are the principal intergroup conflicts (economic, ethnic, religious, or racial) in your community? In your school or college? Interview members of each of the groups in question and obtain their views regarding the ways in which conflict could be alleviated.

6. Write a paper describing your own position on the integration-pluralism-separatism continuum and indicating how you think this area of human relations will develop over the next ten years.

7. Select a particular minority group in which you are interested and write a paper on the treatment of this group in the public schools in your community. Include a description of the strategy (explicit or implicit) of this group for achieving its goals in the community.

8. If you are a member of a minority ethnic group, describe your own experience in the schools.

9. Andrew Greeley (1980) cites evidence indicating that ethnicity and ethnic culture continue to be important considerations for many white ethnic groups in the United States. Stephen Steinberg summarizes evidence indicating that ethnicity is of declining importance in the lives of white Americans, particularly in comparison with social class influences. To what extent do these two scholars disagree? Which point of view is closer to the truth about ethnicity in United States society today?

10. What progress has been made at local colleges and universities in increasing the enrollment of black and Hispanic students? What are the major obstacles preventing further progress?

SUGGESTIONS FOR FURTHER READING

1. To get some perspective on the extent of democratic pluralism in the United States at various times within the past century, read one of the following: *Up from Slavery*, by Booker T. Washington; *The Americanization of Edward T. Bok*, by Edward T. Bok; *Giants in the Earth*, by Rölvaag; *Twenty Years at Hull House*, by Jane Addams; *The Newcomers*, by Oscar Handlin.

2. Students with an interest in white European ethnic groups will be interested in Michael Novak's book, *The Rise of the Unmeltable Ethnics*, which is a spirited defense of the "hardhat ethnics," who he feels are put down by the middle-class intellectuals.

3. The book by Milton Gordon, *Assimilation in American Life,* gives a good historical and sociological treatment of intergroup relations in the United States.

4. An extensive study of American Indian education is given in the book by Estelle Fuchs and Robert J. Havighurst, *To Live on This Earth: American Indian Education.*

5. A useful treatment of cultural pluralism from the point of view of education is provided in the book *Cultural Pluralism*, edited by Edgar G. Epps. His concluding essay on "Schools and Cultural Pluralism" is especially good for clarification of the issues.

6. The last section of *Philosophy and the American School* by Van Cleve Morris and Young Pai provides a philosophical analysis of cultural pluralism in education.

7. *Multicultural Education: Issues and Perspectives* by James Banks includes materials and strategies for teaching children from diverse ethnic groups about diverse ethnic groups. *Multicultural Teaching* (Pamela and Iris Tiedt 1990) and *Comprehensive Multicultural Education* (Christine Bennett 1990) also provide a wealth of useful materials and ideas.

8. The last five chapters of *American Ethnicity*, by Bahr, Chadwick, and Strauss, review and discuss the history and future of cultural pluralism in the United States.

9. The *Comparative Education Review* regularly includes papers on bilingual education in the United States and other countries.

10. *Educating English-Speaking Hispanics*, edited by Leonard Valverde, Rosa Feinberg, and Esther Marquez, provides information and discussion on a topic that received little explicit attention before 1980.

11. *Clamor at the Gates*, edited by Nathan Glazer, discusses many contemporary aspects of immigration and its implications for the United States. The chapter by Peter Rose, "Asian Americans: From Pariahs to Paragons," is particularly recommended.

12. The entire issue of the *American Journal of Education* for November 1986 is devoted to the education of Hispanic Americans.

13. Nicholas Appleton's thoughtful book *Cultural Pluralism in Education* is well worth reading for its insightful analysis and the breadth of its concepts and documentation.

14. A paper by Sau-ling Wong (1987), "The Language Needs of School-Age Asian Immigrants," provides much excellent material on several topics discussed in this chapter.

15. A paper by Shirley Stennis Williams (1987), "The Politics of the Black Child's Language," provides a useful history and analysis of Black English and its implications for education.

16. *The New Black Middle Class* by Bart Landry provides an unusually well written and thought-provoking analysis of data on this important topic.

17. A 1982 paper and a 1978 book by John U. Ogbu provide detailed explanations of the racial (as contrasted with the socioeconomic) disadvantages experienced by low-status blacks in segregated schools and communities.

18. *Maggie's American Dream* is a moving account in which James Comer (1990) describes how his family migrated from the rural South and coped with urban life in the North.

19. The meaning (or lack of meaning) of ethnic identity in contemporary U.S. society is discussed brilliantly in "The Return of the Melting Pot," a 1990 essay by Alan Wolfe.

20. Edited by Gordon La Vern Berry and Joy Keiko Asamen (1989), *Black Students: Psychsocial Issues and Academic Achievement* includes chapters dealing with motivation, family background, black culture, and other topics related to the achievement of African American students.

21. *The Ethnic Enigma*, edited by Peter Kvisto (1989), includes chapters dealing with immigrants from Croatia, Greece, Finland, Hungary, Italy, The Netherlands, and Sweden.

22. *Immigrant America* (Portes and Rumbaut 1990) emphasizes spatial mobility of immigrants, occupational and economic adaptation, identity and political participation, mental health and acculturation, and bilingual performance.

23. Lily Wong Fillmore (1991) provides a poignant description and analysis of the negative consequences that can occur when the children of non-English-speaking parents lose their native language skills and parents thereafter are unable to communicate effectively. Some analysts, such as Rosalie Porter (1991), criticized Fillmore's data and conclusions.

24. The December 1991/January 1992 issue of *Educational Leadership* concentrates on various aspects of multicultural education. The July 1, 1992, issue of *Black Issues in Higher Education* focuses on minority students in graduate and professional education.

Women and Education

In recent years, people in the United States have experienced a resurgence of interest in feminism unparalleled in scope and fervor since the first major wave of concern for women's rights, which developed concurrently with the abolitionist movement of the nineteenth century. Indeed, now, as before, feminists can trace their changing perceptions of the position of women in society partly to their experience in the civil rights movement.

The first major surge of feminism in the United States occurred in the 1840s, when the movement to abolish black slavery was becoming an important political force. The Women's Rights Convention held at Seneca Falls, New York, in 1848, passed twelve resolutions that included statements that "woman is man's equal" but has "too long rested satisfied in the circumscribed limits which corrupt customs . . . have marked off for her." The Convention also resolved that "the speedy success of our course depends upon the . . . untiring efforts of both men and women . . . for the securing to women an equal participation with men in the various trades, professions, and commerce." It thus inaugurated a national effort to counteract belief in the inferiority of women and the confinement of women to domestic roles (the "cult of domesticity").

After the Civil War, Elizabeth Cady Stanton, Susan B. Anthony, and other leaders of the feminist movement founded the National Women's Loyal League (1865) and worked to gain support for women's rights—particularly the vote—along with constitutional amendments (13, 14, and 15) designed to enfranchise black Americans. When some leading opponents of slavery refused to support voting rights for women out of fear that this would detract from the movement to help blacks, feminist leaders formed separate groups to improve the status of women (e.g., the National American Woman's Suffrage Association, 1869). Efforts along these lines finally reached fruition with ratification in 1920 of the Nineteenth Amendment, giving voting rights to 26 million women.

However, the vote proved of limited value in improving the status of women in the United States; and after World War II, many women became increasingly dissatisfied with their situation and opportunities. Civil rights and other strains of social activism again served as a spur for the women's movement: as women participated in efforts to eliminate discrimination against blacks or took part in student movements to gain greater control over educational institutions during the 1960s, feminists became sensitive also to inequities between men and women. Betty Friedan's 1963 book *The Feminine Mystique*, which eloquently described the problems in many women's lives associated with their virtual confinement to home and family roles, marked the emergence to prominence of the modern feminist movement.

Many complex factors come together to affect the contemporary women's movement. One is the increase in level of education of women; another, the changes in concepts of marriage and parenthood, hastened by the development of modern methods of contraception and the increased control over fertility. Changing concepts of sex roles have brought with them an increasing minority of women who no longer look to motherhood as the necessary core of feminine identity (Walsh 1986). Also, there has been an increasing demand for women in the labor force, particularly as the service occupations have expanded.

Now, a majority of women work outside the home at one or more periods in their lives, and a growing proportion enter and stay in the work force throughout their adults lives, thereby creating new role models for their daughters.

The women's movement has given rise to a wide range of advocacy positions focusing on a variety of issues, and there has been rapid growth of literature, both scientific and popular, written by, for, and about women. Some feminist organizations have worked primarily for changes in education, in the law, and in the workplace to create more equality of opportunity for women. Others have taken more extreme views, calling for new sex roles and new forms of family organization. The latter groups believe that important changes in the direction of equality between the sexes cannot be accomplished without fundamental changes in society whereby women will be freed from their primary responsibility for childcare.

Despite the wide range of views it has produced, the feminist movement that took shape in the late 1960s focused overall on the special characteristics and needs of women and the promotion of social, economic, and political changes that will support their development. Most leaders in the feminist movement agree that women occupy a minority status in contemporary society. They also tend to agree that the so-called feminine traits and motivations so widely accepted in the past are due only in small part to underlying biological differences, but instead are due in large part to our socialization practices—that is, to what girls are taught directly or indirectly as they grow up.

Although perhaps the sharpest criticisms are reserved for the socialization experiences that occur within the family, most feminists also see the schools as part of the problem, and they accordingly look to the schools to become part of the solution. It is often alleged, for instance, that most of our educational institutions maintain a division between masculine and feminine subject matter, encouraging women to enter the humanities and certain social sciences, while encouraging men to enter science and technology, the ma-

jor professions, business, and engineering (Keating 1990). Many people believe that this is only one of the ways our formal education system, as it carries out both its socialization and its sorting and selecting functions, helps create what they perceive as the sexist society. Even though such allegations ignore or blur over the very real changes in the education of women that have been occurring over the past century, there is evidence, some of it presented in this chapter, that supports these views in their general outline.

Whatever the speed of social change that lies ahead, and whatever the opinions set forth, the feminist writers and their supporters have clearly succeeded in bringing to public attention a range of issues that have broad implications for educational theory and practice. In turn, educators are looking to the broader social context when they deal with the changing educational needs and demands of women. The latter point is well illustrated in the opening statement of the report by the Carnegie Commission on Higher Education, *Opportunities for Women in Higher Education* (1983, 2):

> *The second most fundamental revolution in the affairs of mankind on earth is now occurring. The first came when man settled down from hunting, fishing, herding, and gathering to sedentary agricultural and village life. The second is now occurring as women, no longer concentrated on and sheltered for their childbearing and childrearing functions, are demanding equality of treatment in all aspects of life, are demanding a new sense of purpose.*

WORK ROLES

Women who devote their time to homemaking and mothering are workers, no less than women who work outside the home. Yet the terms *women workers* or *women in the labor force* have come to refer only to the latter group, those who work outside the home for remuneration. For the sake of convenience only, we shall use the terms in the ways that have become customary.

Fifty years ago, one out of five persons in the labor force was a woman; now, it is nearly half. The woman of today as compared to her mother or grandmother has many more years of life when she is free from the responsibilities of childcare. On the average, mothers are now in their midthirties when they see their last child off to school, and they then have more than forty years ahead of them, or more than half their lives. Increasingly, they use their time to work outside the home. Research indicates that more than nine out of ten women are in the labor force at one or more times in their lives, although whether a given woman will be working outside the home in any given year depends on her age, level of education, racial or ethnic background, marital status, age of her children, and, if she is married, her husband's income. In 1990, 76 percent of women between sixteen and fifty-five years of age were part of the labor force (Fullerton 1989; Uchitelle 1990c).

Not only the numbers but also the characteristics of women workers have changed dramatically. For one thing, in addition to single women, it is now married women, and women with children, who are working outside the home. In 1940, one out of ten mothers in the United States was in the labor force; in 1990, it was approximately five out of ten. The ages at which women are most likely to be working have also changed. If we look at the composition of the labor force in 1920 and compare it with 1990, then at both periods women are most apt to be working when they were age twenty to twenty-four. But then the patterns diverge. In 1920, only a small percentage of women age forty-five to fifty-four were employed, whereas in 1990, it was approximately two-thirds of this group. Today, middle-aged women are working in proportions about as high as younger women (Fullerton 1989; Uchitelle 1990c).

All this means that increasing millions of women have chosen to marry, raise children *and* work, and to work at more than one time in their lives. This change is part of what Neugarten and Neugarten (1987) call the "fluid life cycle" and describe as follows:

Adults of all ages are experiencing changes in the traditional rhythm and timing of events of the life cycle. More men and women marry, divorce, remarry and divorce again up through their seventies. More stay single. More women have their first child before they are fifteen, and more do so after thirty-five. The result is that people are becoming grandparents for the first time at ages ranging from thirty-five to seventy-five. More women, but also increasing numbers of men, raise children in two-parent, then one-parent, then two-parent households. More women, but also increasing numbers of men, exit and reenter school, enter and reenter the work force and undertake second and third careers up through their seventies. It therefore becomes difficult to distinguish the young, the middle-aged and the young-old. (Neugarten and Neugarten 1987, 30)

NEW FAMILY PATTERNS

In addition to changes in timing and increased fluidity, significant numbers of women coming to maturity are moving away from traditional family patterns in other ways (Townsend and O'Neil 1990). New forms of the family unit include the couple who live together without marriage, the husband and wife who have had previous marriages, the couple who choose to remain childless, the never-married or divorced parent raising children alone, and the communal family group. It is true that nearly 80 percent of all families in 1990 were husband-wife families, and only a fraction of all couples had been identified as living together and maintaining a quasi-familial relationship outside marriage. Still, the percentage of female-headed households has increased substantially (see Chapter 4). In addition, the number of women living alone increased rapidly during the 1970s and 1980s, reflecting the increasing numbers of women who postpone marriage, the increasing divorce rate, especially for first marriages, and the increasing numbers of older widowed women who live alone.

We cannot yet assess the long-term effects of the women's movement, of improved methods of family planning, of changes in the education of women, or of changing economic conditions and work patterns as these factors affect the family cycle. This assessment is difficult because social change seems to be affecting younger women more than older women and because we cannot predict the eventual patterns for women who are presently young. Nevertheless, it is clear that more women of all ages are spending more and more time in work roles and in community roles that lie outside the traditional roles of mother and homemaker. Since 1967, more than 16 million women have joined the labor force (Bernstein 1989). The percentage of married couples that include a male worker and a female homemaker declined from 61 percent in 1961 to a little more than 20 percent in 1990 (Riche 1990).

OCCUPATIONAL STATUS

Table 11-1 indicates what percentage of all workers in various occupational groups in 1988 were women. Table 11-2 shows the changing proportions of women in various occupational categories since 1950. Although the overall proportion of women workers has increased substantially, a few major occupational groups still have a concentration of women. More than half of all women were working in relatively low-paying clerical, operative, or service positions in 1988 (see Table 11-2). In fact, a higher proportion of

employed women were clerical or service workers in 1988 than in 1910.

It is worth taking a closer look at the professional-managerial category, since it includes occupations that are closely tied to higher education and are frequently used as the barometer of the status of women workers. As suggested in Table 11-2, the majority of women in the professional and managerial category are employed in the normally lower-paying occupations within the category—for example, as registered nurses and as elementary and secondary schoolteachers. Women have made substantial inroads in some specific occupations; for example, as accountants, lawyers, physicians, bank officials, sales managers. Two occupations that remain heavily male are engineering and architecture (Reskin and Blau 1990).

Women's employment patterns described here do not as yet fully reflect the impact of the educational changes occurring in recent years. The proportions of women now entering medical, law, or business school, and the numbers being awarded degrees in such fields as the physical sciences and mathematics have been increasing. Similarly, data on the career choices of entering college freshmen show that women are increasingly choosing to enter the fields traditionally regarded as men's fields (Nasar 1990). Thus, the occupational distribution of men and women is shifting markedly, as younger women—those who are probably being most affected by the feminist movement—finish their schooling and move into the labor force.

TABLE 11-1 *Women as a Percentage of All Workers, by Occupational Group, 1988*

Occupational Grouping	Percentage
Managers, professionals, proprietors	45
Clerical, sales, technical and administrative support	65
Service workers, including unskilled household	61
Precision workers, including crafts and foremen	08
Operators, including semiskilled and unskilled laborers	26
Farming-related, forestry, and fishing	16
All occupations	45

Source: U.S. Bureau of the Census; *Statistical Abstract of the United States* 1990.
Note: Percentage totals vary from 100 due to rounding.

TABLE 11-2   *Women in Selected Professional and Managerial Occupations, 1950 to 1988*

Occupation	Percentage of All Workers in Occupation			
	1950	*1970*	*1980*	*1988*
Accountants	15	25	36	50
Engineers	1	2	4	7
Lawyers, judges	4	5	13	20
Physicians, osteopaths	7	9	14	20
Registered nurses	98	97	96	95
Teachers	74	70	71	73
College faculty	23	28	34	39

Sources: U.S. Bureau of Labor Statistics; *Statistical Abstract of the United States*, 1990.

But just as is true of predictions regarding rates of marriage and childbearing, it is too soon to assess fully the effects of the women's movement as it interacts with other social and economic factors in influencing the work lives of women. It can be said with certainty, however, that insofar as work decisions are governed by educational preparation, women will no longer be handicapped to the extent they have been in past years. On the other hand, data on the career goals of adolescents indicate that a large proportion of girls continue to aim at and perhaps prefer careers in traditionally female occupations, such as nurse, teacher, and salesclerk. For example, a 1989 study of nearly 6,000 ninth graders from all parts of Pennsylvania concluded that "there still is not widespread acceptance of nontraditional occupations by ninth graders" (Ferrero, Lungstrum, and McKenna 1989). The authors of this study also reported data indicating that relative lack of interest in nontraditional occupations among girls may have been due in part to their placing greater weight than boys on whether the work to be performed interests them. Males were less likely than females to cite interest in the work as a most important consideration in choosing a career. Instead, males were relatively more concerned with job security.

In addition, although major shifts have occurred, data on the occupation structure still show a high amount of sex segregation, with women concentrated in relatively low-paid occupations. In the 1980s, more than half of women would have had to change occupations in order to eliminate sex segregation in occupational placement (Reskin and Blau 1990).

THE EARNINGS GAP

In spite of a relatively optimistic outlook for women who will be working in the future, at the present time women workers make much less money than men do. Fully employed women earn only about seventy-two for every one hundred dollars earned by fully employed men (Crispell 1991; Saltzman 1991).

It is not clear to what extent the earnings gap between women and men reflects discrimination, and to what extent it reflects other factors—for instance, that in many occupations, women work more sporadically than men and therefore accumulate less seniority (Lloyd and Niemi, 1979; Koretz 1990). The gap is present, however, even among women and men with the same amount of education. Women fare best in professional and technical occupations and worst in sales, where their earnings are considerably less than men's (Waite 1981; Schwartz 1988; Sorensen 1991).

Careful studies indicate that the earnings gap between women and men is closely associated with the segregation and concentration of women in less skilled, low-paying, dead-end jobs (Sorensen 1991). The fact that women are concentrated in low-paying jobs appears to be partly a product of discrimination, both institutional and individual (Bergmann 1986; Sorensen 1991).

Institutional discrimination includes recruitment policies and informal networks of hiring and advancement. Discrimination by individuals—who discriminates (personnel officers, managers, others) and why (because of personal preference, assumptions about female turnover rates, or others reasons)—is difficult to assess, but it undoubtedly plays a role, also.

At the same time, the fact that women are concentrated in low-paying jobs is voluntary in part, at least insofar as traditional socialization patterns have led women to set low levels of aspiration for themselves as workers (Corcoran and Courant 1985). Thus, motivational factors constitute another important factor in understanding why large numbers of women fail to move up the occupational ladder. As women become educated for and move into higher-level occupations, and particularly as they begin to think in terms of careers, building up consistent and strong attachment to work in a single or related occupation over long time periods, their earnings vis-à-vis men's should continue to change for the better (Crispell 1991).

THE CONTINUING PLIGHT OF DISPLACED HOMEMAKERS

The situation of nonworking mothers whose work as homemakers is *displaced* by marital dissolution or death of their husbands became a matter of widespread concern in the 1960s and 1970s. As divorce and separation rates escalated rapidly during this period, many women who lacked preparation or experience for rewarding jobs were unemployed or worked in poorly paid jobs that provided inadequate income and security. However, social analysts expected that the problems posed by and for displaced homemakers would substantially diminish as younger women became better prepared for employment and entered the labor force permanently at an earlier age.

Although there may have been some reduction in the percentage of women victimized by the displaced homemaker syndrome, issues involving their situation still pose serious prob-

lems. Thus, data collected in the late 1980s indicated that the number of displaced homemakers increased by about 12 percent in the 1980s, more than half lived in poverty, and 20 percent resided with unrelated people in doubled-up households. Such data led the president of the National Displaced Homemakers Network to state that "like everyone else . . . [we thought] that with so many women entering the work force . . . the number of displaced homemakers would be declining. We were really shocked to find that so many homemakers who are divorced or widowed, and lose the source of support they counted on, still have problems achieving economic self-sufficiency" (quoted in Lewin 1990b, 13).

SEX DIFFERENCES IN ACHIEVEMENT AND ABILITY

Overall sex differences in achievement and attainment appear to be diminishing, but there is considerable controversy concerning the degree to which differences in specific subjects such as mathematics may be due to differences in biological functioning as contrasted with socialization and sex-role stereotyping.

Achievement and Participation

Cross-national studies providing data on educational achievement show that on an international basis males have had higher overall achievement and have attained more years of schooling than have females. For example, Finn, Dulberg, and Reis (1979) surveyed the research in this area and concluded that "on a global basis, the deficiencies in the educational achievement of women are obvious. According to 1970 figures, an estimated 34.2 percent of the world's population is illiterate; 28.0 percent of the male population and 40.3 percent of the female population" (p. 496). Females comprise about 30 percent of elementary and secondary enrollment in low-income countries and a little more than 40 percent in middle- and high-income countries (Haddad, Carney, Rinaldi, and Regel 1990).

Among the best sources of United States data on school achievement by sex are the surveys and reports prepared by the National Assessment of Educational Progress (NAEP). Recent reports released by the NAEP provide data on achievement by sex and age from a number of national surveys conducted since 1971. These assessments indicate that females have slightly higher reading achievement than do males at all three ages tested. As shown in Tables 11-3 and 11-4, the NAEP reports also indicate that males have higher scores in science; the mathematics achievement of males differs very little from that of females at ages nine and thirteen, but males have slightly higher scores than do females at age seventeen. As have several other large-scale

studies, the NAEP surveys indicate that by age seventeen, males score slightly higher than do females on higher-order cognitive skills in mathematics, though females score as high in computation and other lower-order skills (see Table 11-4).

However, the NAEP and other data sources also indicate that sex differences in performance involving reading and mathematics, as well as other subject areas, generally declined in the 1970s and 1980s (Table 11-3). Thus, Linn and Hyde (1989) reviewed longitudinal trends during the past three decades and concluded that there is now little difference by gender in achievement in reading, math computation, and science processes, though boys still have average scores a little higher than girls in math problem solving and science knowledge.

TABLE 11-3 *Average Proficiency Scores of Nine-, Thirteen-, and Seventeen-Year-Olds on National Assessment of Educational Progress (NAEP) Reading, Mathematics, and Science Exams, Various Years by Sex**

Age Group and Sex	Reading			Mathematics			Science		
	1971	1980	1988	1973	1978	1986	1970	1977	1986
Nine									
Female	214	220	216	220	220	222	223	218	221
Male	201	210	208	218	217	222	228	222	227
Thirteen									
Female	261	263	263	267	265	268	253	244	247
Male	250	254	252	265	264	270	257	251	256
Seventeen									
Female	292	290	294	301	297	299	297	282	282
Male	279	282	286	309	304	305	314	297	295

Sources: Adapted from Mullis and Jenkins 1988; Applebee 1990; Mullis and Jenkins 1990; and Mullis, Owen, and Phillips 1990.

*Reading proficiency levels represent the following: 150—can carry out simple, discrete reading tasks; 200—can comprehend specific or sequentially related information; 250—can search for information, interrelate ideas, and generalize; 300—can find, understand, summarize, and explain relatively complicated information; 350—can synthesize and learn from specialized reading materials.

Mathematics proficiency levels represent the following: 150—knows some basic addition and subtraction facts; 200—can add and subtract two-digit numbers; 250—can add, subtract, multiply, and divide using whole numbers; 300—can compute with decimals, fractions, and percents, recognize geometric figures, and solve simple equations; 350—can solve multistep problems and use basic algebra.

Science proficiency levels represents the following: 150—knows everyday science facts; 200—understands some basic principles; 250—understands basic life and physical sciences information; 300—has some detailed scientific knowledge; 350—can infer relationships and draw conclusions using detailed scientific knowledge.

TABLE 11-4 *Percentages of Students at or above NAEP Anchor Points (Proficiency Levels) in Mathematics (1986) and Reading (1988), by Sex and Age Group* *

Age Group and Anchor Point	Mathematics		Reading	
	Female	Male	Female	Male
Nine				
150	98	98	95	91
200	74	74	67	58
250	21	21	18	16
300	01	01	02	01
Thirteen				
200	99	98	97	94
250	73	74	65	51
300	14	18	13	08
Seventeen				
250	96	97	89	83
300	48	54	46	37
350	05	08	06	04

Sources: Adapted from Dossey 1988; Mullis and Jenkins 1990.
*Mathematics proficiency levels represent the following: *150*—knows some basic addition and subtraction facts; *200*—can add and subtract two-digit numbers; *250*—can add, subtract, multiply, and divide using whole numbers; *300*—can compute with decimals, fractions, and percents, recognize geometric figures, and solve simple equations; *350*—can solve multistep problems and use basic algebra.
Reading proficiency levels represent the following: *150*—can carry out simple, discrete reading tasks; *200*—can comprehend specific or sequentially related information; *250*—can search for information, interrelate ideas, and generalize; *300*—can find, undersand, summarize, and explain relatively complicated information; *350*—can synthesize and learn from specialized reading materials.

Differential achievement patterns favoring males in advanced mathematics reflect the fact that females are less likely than males to take math and science courses in high school and college and thereafter less likely to choose and enter careers in engineering, physics, and other fields that depend on math (Keating 1990). This pattern not only represents a diversion of women (compared with men) from relatively well-paid to relatively low-pay occupations, but also functions to restrict development of the nation's pool of scientific talent and skill.

Research indicates that remaining sex differences in mathematics performance and careers are due mostly to the complex and poorly understood interaction of variables involving mo-tivation and attitudes toward math and science, previous performance, exposure to learning opportunities, socialization and sexual stereotyping, verbal and quantitative abilities, and other factors (Chipman, Brush, and Wilson 1985; Ethington and Wolfle 1986; Linn and Hyde 1989; Fennema and Leder 1990; Oakes 1990b). Motivational and attitudinal considerations include greater math anxiety among females than among males, higher confidence in math and science ability among males, lower expectations for females on the part of teachers, and girls' perceptions that math is relatively unimportant for their future careers (Tobias and Weissbrod 1980; Linn and Hyde 1989; Keating 1990; Oakes 1990b). Summarizing the meaning of some of these research findings, Chipman and Wilson (1985) pointed out that implications go beyond the problem of improving math opportunities for girls and women:

> *Poor preparation in mathematics is not just a problem of women: many believe that it is a very general problem in the United States today. . . . Most students know only that mathematics is required to enter the career they desire, not why it is required or how it will be used. . . . There are indications that something about the style of teaching or classroom interaction in high school mathematics may be unattractive to students. Lecturing, with low student involvement, appears to be more common in mathematics classes. . . . In addition, student confidence in ability to learn mathematics declines in high school. Thus, many of the changes that seem to be needed to improve opportunities for female students actually seem to be needed for all students. (Chipman and Wilson 1985, 325)*

Ability

Regarding general academic ability, sex differences are nonexistent or inconsequential. Stated differently, males and females differ little or not at all in total IQ scores (Feingold 1988). This conclusion is not surprising inasmuch as IQ tests are deliberately constructed so as to eliminate sex differences (Stockard 1980).

Much of the recent controversy concerning possible sex differences in ability has centered on whether a higher percentage of males than females have very high aptitude in mathematics or in higher-order cognitive skills in general (Stanley 1990). A widely cited comprehensive review of research on sex differences (Maccoby and Jacklin 1974) indicated that there is more variability in ability among males than females: males are more likely than females to be either very low or very high in ability. Several later reviews of research have concluded that there probably is a greater percentage of mental "defectives" among males than females, and that this pattern may occur because young boys are more vulnerable to serious disease and other physical prob-

lems than are girls (Sherman 1977; Featherstone 1988). In addition, research indicates that males have higher scores than females on tests of spatial ability (Bock and Moore 1986; Kimura 1989) and that these differences are related to males' higher scores in mathematics (Halpern 1986).

As regards the possibility that more males than females may have very high intellectual ability, much of the support for this position in recent years has been provided in longitudinal analysis of SAT mathematics scores (Feingold 1988) and in the Study of Mathematically Precocious Youth (SMPY) conducted at Johns Hopkins University. Data on the SMPY indicate that among more than 10,000 seventh- and eighth-graders who scored higher than 660 on the mathematics section of the Scholastic Aptitude Test, the ratio of boys to girls was approximately fourteen to one (Benbow and Stanley 1980). Males and females in the study were approximately equal in verbal ability. Partly because males and females in those grades generally have had similar participation in mathematics instruction, the authors concluded that there is is a substantial difference in the percentages of males and females who are high in mathematical reasoning ability. After reporting that students' attitudes toward math and its importance were related to their achievement but not their ability scores, the researchers summarized their conclusions:

> *We favor the hypothesis that sex differences in achievement in and attitude toward mathematics result from superior male mathematical ability, which may in turn be related to greater male ability in spatial tasks. This male superiority is probably an expression of both endogenous and exogenous variables. We recognize, however, that our data are consistent with numerous alternative hypotheses. (Benbow and Stanley 1980, 1264)*

Some other researchers, however, have disputed the conclusion that the SMPY patterns probably are due to biologically rooted sex differences. Pointing to differences in socialization and expectations for boys and girls other than differential participation in classroom mathematics instruction, they believe that factors such as greater opportunity to engage in active manipulation of concepts among males than females may account for differences found in the Hopkins data (Kolata 1980; Pallas and Alexander 1983; Linn and Hyde 1989). In addition, gender differences involving spatial visualization and related skills have declined substantially in recent decades (Friedman 1989; Linn and Hyde 1989).

Possible Biological Causes

A number of psychobiological causes have been proposed to account for possible sex differences favoring females in verbal ability or achievement and favoring males in spatial ability or mathematics ability and achievement. Sherman (1977) examined several possible causes, including (1) hereditary differences linked to the X-chromosome, (2) sex differences in serum uric acid (the "gout" hypothesis), (3) hormone differences, and (4) differences in brain lateralization and cerebral organization (e.g., specialization in left- and right-hemisphere functioning). It should be noted that causes grouped under these headings are not necessarily exclusive. For example, differences in brain lateralization may be due to hormonal influences, and both may be generated by the X-chromosone.

After examining each explanation in some detail, Sherman concluded that the only one that has solid research support involves sex differences in brain lateralization. Among right-handed persons, females appear to handle spatial functions more with the left hemisphere (relative to males), whereas males show less hemispheric specialization. There is also some evidence that females may "have more right hemisphere involvement in verbal function," as compared with males. It is "a very viable hypothesis," she concluded, that "more females than males may be ooververbalized and lean too heavily on left-hemisphere, verbal analytic functioning to solve tasks that would benefit from more right hemispheric participation. . . . [This preference] may have a biological basis in the earlier development . . . of linguistic facility and

left-hemisphere dominance for verbal function in women . . . [and in] later maturation that may favor right hemisphere development" in males (Sherman 1977, 181–182).

Anne Petersen (1980) also has reviewed the research on biological processes and sex differences in ability, with specific attention to the role that hormones may play with regard to brain functioning. Her general conclusion is somewhat similar to Sherman's:

The manifestation of genetic potentials may also require certain moderate levels of androgen influence (or perhaps the appropriate ratio of androgen to estrogen or some other endocrine mechanism). These sexually-differential levels may be important at the so-called critical period of development (prenatal in humans) to function in brain organization, hemispheric lateralization, and perhaps prefrontal development. . . . Brain organization may in turn serve to extend cognitive differences to verbal-versus-spatial skills. . . . The appearance at adolescence of sex differences in these skills may be caused by increased sexually differential socialization at this time and/or by the activational influences of hormones at puberty, perhaps on the termination of brain lateralization. (Petersen 1980, 45)

Research on hormones and their possible association with brain-related sex differences in ability is continuing (Gallagher 1988). For example, research indicates that low levels of testosterone are associated with lower spatial skills among men, and high levels of estrogen are associated with higher verbal fluency among women (Kimura 1989). In addition, research on laboratory animals has shown that male-female differences in the organization of neurons reflect the functioning of sex hormones (Diamond 1988). This finding fits well with research indicating that sex hormones affect the brain in producing sex-differentiated and sex-typed behaviors in a variety of species (Weintraub 1981; Witelson and Swallow 1987). Research on prenatal development in human beings indicates that the effects of sex hormones are "dramatic," but also that effects on ability depend greatly on what abilities are being considered (Kimura 1985; 1989).

However, caution should be exercised in assessing the meaning and implications of possible sex differences involving biology and intellectual ability. As pointed out by Shepherd-Look (1982), hormone research is beset with difficult problems involving measurement of hormone levels and their effects, and researchers in this area are beginning to give more emphasis to interactions and contingencies. In many cases, sex hormones may not have a universal influence but may have an effect dependent on situational factors. There is evidence, for example, that the relationship between high levels of testosterone and aggression in males is mediated by psychological stress. Furthermore, there appears to be wide variation across individuals in the effects of hormones, brain lateralization, and other biological factors, so that sex is a "poor screening device for intellectual assessment" (Kimura 1985, 58). Research on possible sex differences in spatial abilities indicates that such differences tend to be relatively small and inconsistent across subskills (Caplan, MacPherson, and Tobin 1985; Benderly 1989). In addition, several studies indicate that spatial abilities scores of girls and women can be improved through education (Halpern 1986; Linn and Hyde 1989).

Implications of Trends Involving Sex Differences

As noted here, studies conducted during the past few decades have indicated that sex differences on measures assessing achievement and ability have been declining and are now small or nonexistent with respect to most areas examined. Marcia Linn and Janet Hyde (1989) reviewed the data available from these studies, as well as related research on trends indicating reduced differentials in math and science participation and interest, and reached the following conclusions regarding their meaning and implications:

Declines in gender differences [have been] consistent with changing educational opportunities, changing social roles, and the changing demands of the workplace. Workers need more communication skills and technical skills as society moves from a manufacturing to an automation and service economy. . . . Just as females are now more likely to use technical skills such as programming, so are males more likely to participate in verbal activities such as report writing. . . .

Because the magnitude of gender differences is so clearly a function of context or situation, we need to focus on situations that minimize gender differences. . . . Environments that instill confidence in all participants offer considerable promise . . . [as do situations in which there are teachers who provide] all students with feedback on the use of problem-solving strategies rather than memorized algorithms; environments that encourage expression of ideas from all students, not just the most confident or aggressive; curricula where the relevance of learning mathematics and science is apparent; and classes that reward both the individual achievement and the cooperative behavior necessary in scientific investigation. (Linn and Hyde 1989, 24–26)

THE EDUCATION OF WOMEN

The changing patterns of work and family life for women have been both the cause and the effect of changes in the education of women that have occurred over the past century. In focusing now on the educational system and on the role of education in shaping women's lives, we should look first at socialization experiences that occur within the school setting.

Socialization

It should be said first that there is an enormous scientific literature on sex differences and socialization practices, a literature that grows out of biology, psychology, sociology, and anthropology as well as education, and a literature that cannot possibly be summarized here. Suffice it to say that while nobody doubts the presence of important biological differences between the sexes, there is a wide variety of interpretations regarding which, if any, of these biological differences make a significant difference in the way boys and girls learn or in the abilities that are needed to fulfill most occupations of modern society. Whatever the inherent biological differences, much of the difference in behavior observed between boys and girls, and later between men and women, stems from differences in the socialization experiences that occur from early infancy onward (Lever 1988; Keating 1990). In short, in most families boys are treated differently from girls from their first days of life, when hospitals give boy babies a blue bracelet and girl babies a pink one (Fagot 1991). Not much later, girls generally are playing with dolls whereas boys are more likely to play aggressively with action figures and war games (Lawson 1989). Such differences become reinforced over time as the child meets the expectations of parents, teachers, and peers, and as these expectations become internalized (Hoffman 1988; Fagot 1991).

For example, one study of differential socialization experiences involved mother-infant interactions during the first and third months of life. Mothers tended to stimulate male infants signficantly more than female infants and to arouse them to a higher activity level. On the other hand, they imitated girl babies significantly more frequently than boy babies, especially their vocalizations (Moss 1967). In another study in which women were asked to interact with six-month-old infants, girl and boy infants each were alternately given a female or a male name and clothes. The researchers found that regardless of biological sex, infants presented as females generally were given dolls and those presented as males were given hammers or rattles (Lever 1988; Keating 1990; Lloyd and Duveen 1990). Perhaps such differences in the treatment of infants in the nursery are involved in the differences observed later when youngsters reach school age, when boys show higher general activity levels than girls and when

girls frequently demonstrate greater verbal skills than boys (Fagot 1991).

One author summarized some of the studies concerning parents' differential socialization of boys and girls, as follows:

> *Mothers maintain physically close and affectionate relationships with girls for a longer period of time. Mothers expect girls to be more dependent and give them more physical attention. On the other hand, boys are given more independence training, more punishment and are encouraged more in intellectual curiosity. Mothers place a greater degree of pressure for achievement and punish dependency more in boys than in girls of pre-school age. In addition, boys' aggression is rewarded as appropriate masculine behavior while girls' aggression is never rewarded, though indirect expressions are tolerated. Mothers place pressures on girls for "feminine" neatness, obedience and conformity, while pressure on boys is for independence and achievement. Mothers of girls . . . demand obedience and control verbal protests by using withdrawals of love, while mothers of boys use negative sanctions (deprivation of privileges) to control verbal protests from boys. (Constantina Safilios-Rothschild, quoted in the report of the Advisory Committee on the Rights and Responsibilities of Women 1975, 34)*

Parental and childhood experiences feed into society's attitudes toward men and women; and schools tend to reflect these attitudes in the ways teachers and counselors deal with students, and in the choice of curriculum materials. We return to socialization and gender roles in the schools later in this chapter.

Vocational Education

Until the 1970s, students reaching the high school level frequently found themselves segregated by sex, either in different schools or within a given school. In some large cities, for example, a specialized science and math school would admit only boys; and boys' vocational schools taught electronics, plumbing, carpentry, printing, and other supposedly male trades, whereas girls' schools prepared students to be homemakers, secretaries, beauticians, and health aides. Although sex discrimination in enrollment is now illegal and the patterns of vocational preparation can be expected to change, it is still the case that more than 80 percent of female enrollment in vocational courses is in business, marketing, and home economics. Women still constitute only a small part of the enrollment in agricultural, technical, and trade and industrial courses (Wirt, Muraskin, Goodwin, and Meyer 1989). Many educators thus believe it is important to guide more women into these so-called nontraditional fields in which they will have improved opportunities to earn higher incomes (Landers 1988; Alpert and Breen 1989; Burge and Culver 1990).

College Attendance

In 1910, approximately 10 percent of students graduated from high school; in 1940, almost 50 percent; and by 1990, nearly 80 percent. Through most of this period, a higher percentage of women than of men graduated from high school. Until recently, the opposite was true for college entrants, for through the years a noticeably higher proportion of men than of women entered and completed college. Beginning in the 1970s, however, the percentage of women among college students has been slightly higher than the percentage of men, and in the 1980s the percentage

TABLE 11-5 *Percentage of Academic Degrees Awarded to Women*

	1964	1983	1989
Bachelor's degrees	42	51	53
Master's degrees	34	50	52
Doctor's degrees	11	33	37
First professional degrees	4	30	36

Source: Adapted from Randour, Strasburg, and Lipman-Blumen 1982; *Statistical Abstract of the United States* 1990; National Research Council 1990a; Chronicle editors 1991.

of women among persons graduating from college surpassed that for men (Schmitt 1989). Although women have made enormous progress toward achieving educational parity, equality in higher education has not yet been fully attained inasmuch as women are still much less likely than men to earn an advanced graduate degree. Differences between the sexes at various levels of attainment in higher education are shown in Table 11-5.

Fields of Study

Women have been moving in increasing numbers into traditionally men's fields (Raymond 1989; Reskin and Blau 1990). Although women continue to be overrepresented in such fields as education and the health professions, their educational interests are rapidly becoming more diversifield. The percentage majoring in mathematics and statistics has increased, as also has been true in business administration and management, in the physical sciences, and in agriculture and forestry (Nasar 1990).

Women have also begun to enroll in educational institutions to which they have never had access in the past. In 1975, legislation was enacted to permit women to apply for appointment to the Army, Naval, and Air Force Academies for the first time, and the U.S. Coast Guard and Merchant Marine Academies have recently been opened to women. All but a few of the private schools that formerly limited enrollment to men, including Yale, Princeton, Dartmouth, and Notre Dame, are now coeducational.

As college women continue to move into nontraditional educational programs, especially those that increase their eligibility for graduate or professional school programs, they are clearly increasing their options for the future. We can expect that women graduating from college in the 1990s will follow more heterogeneous career lines than have the women of the past (Jacobs 1989; Nasar 1990).

Graduate and Professional Education

As seen in Table 11-5, sex differences at the graduate level traditionally were much greater than those at the college level. These differences persist today at the doctoral level, even though women are improving their position. By 1989, women earned 52 percent of master's degrees but only 37 percent of doctorates. (National Research Council 1990a; Chronicle editors 1991).

Women in graduate schools are more likely than men to be single, more likely to be in their thirties or older, and more likely to be enrolled as part-time students. A large proportion expect to take terminal M.A. degrees rather than to proceed toward the doctorate, a function of the fact that more women than men are taking graduate work in such fields as education and social work, where the M.A. is the important credential (Hess, Ottinger, and Lippincott 1990).

With regard to other professional degrees, recent changes in enrollment have resulted in increased proportions of degrees granted to women. For example, the percentage of women among business-school graduates increased from 10 percent in 1970 to 44 percent in 1988; in medical schools, the corresponding increase was from 9 percent in 1970 to 33 percent in 1989.

Graduate school attrition rates for women historically have been higher than for men. It is difficult to document the extent of discrimination against women in graduate and professional schools, but many researchers who have studied the problem believe it has existed to a significant degree, not only in admissions practices, but also in financial aid practices and in the rigidity of institutional reguations that fail to accommodate the needs of many women for flexible schedules. The situation is complicated; applicants are usually selected and rules made by individual departments, making it difficult to maintain a common standard across a university; the cost of educating a graduate student in many universities (especially in such fields as medicine) greatly exceeds the tuition charge and creates a greater concern lest places be taken by women who will not finish because of marriage or motherhood or who will not pursue subsequent careers as effectively as men; some faculty believe women graduate students are therefore not as "dedicated" as men; and so on.

Even though such attitudes are changing, and recent laws prohibiting discrimination are having their effects, it is probably still fair to say that women are somewhat disadvantaged as compared with men in pursuing higher degrees. In part, the disadvantage stems from factors that taken together can be called discrimination, but in part it stems also from the personal decisions made by women themselves. Even though the latter are often explained by the fact that women have been taught to set their standards unnecessarily low, it must also be said that most women in their twenties and thirties face a genuine range of options regarding the balance they wish to create between family and career responsibilities, and related thereto, the financial commitments they wish to make to continued education. Thus, the lack of motivation for graduate work may be a more significant factor for women than for men.

Motivation is, of course, a complicated question. Attention has been given to the possibility that women students, rather than fearing failure, fear success (Horner 1969; Tobias and Weissbrod 1980). Some studies indicate that in addition to the obvious social rejection that a competitive and achieving girl may experience, there is also an internal anxiety and a fear, conscious or unconscious, that outstanding academic or other achievement may be equated with a loss of femininity (Safilios-Rothschild 1979). Girls who have this fear are less likely to pursue higher education.

At the same time, there is good reason to believe that women's gains in higher education will continue and perhaps be accelerated. For one thing, young women are facing less social and institutional resistance in their efforts to gain access to advanced education than did earlier cohorts of women. In addition, older women are finding themselves welcomed back on campus as universities face future enrollment declines that will result from smaller cohorts of college-age persons. More women can be expected to continue their education for longer periods than ever before in our history, and more women will achieve graduate and professional degrees, particularly if encouragment and support are provided to enter nontraditional fields, such as science and math (Hess, Ottinger, and Lippincott 1990).

Instructional Materials

A number of studies have indicated that instructional materials frequently have reflected sexual stereotypes and that such materials have played a part in generating and maintaining disadvantages that girls and women experience in schools and society (Keating 1990). For example, one study conducted in the 1970s showed that among 134 stories in children's reading texts, men were shown in 147 different jobs, but women in only 26; all the work done by women in the stories fell into the traditional concept of women's jobs. The texts included biographies of 88 different men but only 17 women, suggesting that the authors found fewer interesting women to write about. And the central figures in stories dealing with ingenuity, creativity, bravery, perseverance, achievement, adventuresomeness, curiosity, autonomy, and self-respect were boys four times as often as they were girls (U.S. Dept. of HEW, "Sex Stereotyping in Children's Readers" 1975).

Kathryn Scott and Candace Schau (1985) reviewed the literature on instructional materials and sex bias and reached the following four general conclusions:

1. Sex-biased language distorts students' perceptions of reality.
2. Sex-equitable instructional materials can broaden attitudes about sex roles and also increase motivation to learn.
3. Sex-equitable instructional materials influence students' sex-role behaviors. "When children hear stories or see films that contain sex role behaviors, both traditional and nontraditional, they may imitate these behaviors" (p. 224).
4. Many commonly used instructional materials are sex biased.

The problem of sexism in elementary and secondary textbooks has been significantly alleviated since 1972, when Scott, Foresman and Company was the first publisher to take action by issuing "Guidelines for Improving the Image of Women in Textbooks." By 1978, the National Education Association reported that almost all major textbook publishers, nearly forty, had issued such guidelines. Although much progress has been made, more remains to be done (Sadker, Sadker, and Klein 1991). Scott and Schau (1985) have offered a number of recommendations for pursuing further reduction of sex bias and inequity in instructional materials, including guidelines for publishers, consumers, and researchers.

Testing

Testing policies and practices also can lead to or reinforce and support sex inequities. We discussed issues involving sex equity and ability testing in Chapter 2. In addition, there is much concern about potentially inequitable or otherwise negative effects of interest inventories and vocational guidance instruments used in education and counseling. Esther Diamond and Carol Tittle (1985) examined the research on this issue and reported the following general conclusions:

> *Since the early 1970s . . . more research has been done on the question of gender differences in interest inventory responses and the extent to which they contribute to sex inequities in education, than in the 50 years preceding. . . . It is difficult to tell to what extent the bias exists in the inventories themselves—the item content and context—and to what extent their results reflect the bias in society, including that of parents, the media, and other societal influences. It may be a long time before the socialization process catches up with the social changes that have taken place at the legal, theoretical, and legislative levels. (Diamond and Tittle 1985, 182)*

Socialization and Gender in the Schools

As noted earlier in this chapter, gender-related socialization of children and youth beginning in the home and family extends to and affects the treatment and performance of both boys and girls in the educational system. Research (e.g., Eccles and Blumenfeld 1985; Brophy 1985; Irvine 1986; Sadker and Sadker 1985, 1990; Keating 1990; Jones 1991) supports the following conclusions regarding differentials in gender roles and treatment in the schools:

1. Teachers interact more with boys than with girls. Much of this differential interaction involves greater negative feedback given to boys and boys' greater success, compared to girls, in gaining the attention of teachers (Jones 1991). According to Sadker and Sadker, these patterns indicate that boys thereby are "being trained to be assertive; girls are being trained to be passive—spectators relegated to the sidelines of classroom discussion" (1985, 513). However, Eccles and Blumenfeld have reviewed research on differences in gender-related interactions and cautioned that most such differences are small, that greater similarity in treatment "may not yield equitable outcomes for both boys and girls," and that differential treatment seems to be as much a consequence of preexisting differences in student behavior as of teacher bias. Nevertheless, they conclude that when differences do occur, they appear to be "reinforcing sex-stereotyped expectations and behavior" (1985, 112). Somewhat similar conclusions were reached in a recent study (Hart 1989) of interactions in mathematics classes, and in a review of the literature by Sadker, Sadker, and Klein (1991).

2. Sex interacts with race, age, grade level, and other factors in generating differentials in instructional practice and treatment. For example, one sizable study of elementary schools found that although white females in both the lower- and upper-elementary grades received less feedback from teachers than did other students classified by sex and race, black females particularly stood out as receiving fewer opportunities to respond in the classroom as they proceed through the grades (Irvine 1986).

3. Differences in teaching style associated with sex of the teacher probably play a part in reinforcing differential treatment of boys and girls in the classroom. Brophy reviewed the literature on this topic and concluded that female teachers tend to be less teacher-centered and more supportive of students than are male teachers. He also specualted that these patterns may have different consequences for the achievement of boys and girls. However, he also concluded that "the data continue to indicate that male and female teachers are much more similar than different," that teachers "do not systematically discriminate against students of the opposite sex," and that "teachers do not seem to be major reasons in causing or broadening student sex differences (1985, 137).

Sex-role stereotypes are present in the schools in other ways, also; in the arrangement of physical space, as when kindergartens have a corner for the dollhouse, which girls are expected to use, and another corner for building blocks, which boys are expected to use; in music activities, when boys are offered the drums to play and girls are offered the triangles; in social studies, when only traditional family roles are portrayed; and so on. The stereotypes are also reinforced when children see that it is only women teachers who deal with the youngest children and that men teachers are usually to be found only in the higher school grades, and then usually as teachers of science or vocational courses, or as athletic coaches, or as principals (Keating 1990; Jones 1991).

One should also keep in mind the speical sex-related problems that males experience in elementary and secondary schools. As pointed out above, many studies indicate that males have lower verbal achievement than do females, and the school's emphasis on verbal learning places many boys at a serious disadvantage beginning in the early grades. Restak (1979) has noted that high percentages of hyperactive children and of learning disabled children are male and has linked this phenomenon to school expectations that require boys to display fine motor coordination and to sit attentively for long periods at an age when many are not physically ready or able to meet such demands: "the classrooms in most of our nation's primary grades," he concludes, "are geared to skills that come naturally to girls but develop very slowly in boys" (p. 235). McGuiness (1979) has pointed out that the greater distractibility of boys—whether due to biology, socialization, or some combination of the two—interferes with the concentration required to learn to read and write, and Skovholt (1978) concluded that male aggressiveness is frequently associated with behavioral problems and poor performance in the schools. Findings such as these suggest that schools should do much more than they do now to provide instruction in a manner that takes account of both male and female disadvantages in ability and behavior (Keating 1990).

Using participant observer methods, Raphaela Best (1983) studied peer-group dynamics in a group of children moving from the second through the fifth grades and then into junior high school in an affluent but increasingly diverse suburban community. After reviewing research underlining the importance of peer groups in the development of children's attitudes and behaviors, Best distinguished among three different curricula that students learn at school: a first or academic curriculum, a second or "gender-role" curriculum that teaches children the traditional role behavior for their sex, and a third curriculum that involves how boys and girls relate to each other. Best referred to the third curriculum as "self-taught" because the children worked on it by themselves with little help from adults.

After noting that the first curriculum is particularly troublesome for boys, in part because they have relatively more difficulty than do girls in meeting classroom expectations for passive behavior, Best concentrated on studying and then trying to intervene in the second and third curricula.

We've All Got Scars, Best's report on her research, describes the somewhat separate and differing expectations and experiences of boys and girls in their peer groups. One of the clearest patterns in the second grade was that boys began learning the "most fundamental second-curriculum rule for male sex-role behavior" (p. 13): they distanced themselves from the girls, and they began to attach more importance to acceptance by male-oriented peer groups than to rewards and affection from the teacher. Best also found that the boys' reading scores were strongly associated with their peer status, and that causality worked in both directions: rejection harmed academic performance and, in some cases, high performance seemed to help generate acceptance.

Best (1983) proceeded to describe what she termed the positive and negative "canons" that peer relationship and behaviors helped teach boys inside and outside the classroom. The positive canon emphasized a need to "be strong" and "be first," while the negative canon stressed "don't associate with a sissy," "don't play with a cry-baby," "don't do housework," and "don't show affection." Girls, Best found, also learned sex roles through the peer group, but "entering the girls' world was like moving from a dark and fearful forest into a sunny valley" (p. 88) where there was little or nothing that stressed or reinforced fighting and winning; instead, emphasis was on having fun rather than winning and on cooperation more than competition. Best also was struck by the greater leeway allowed to girls; that is, girls could compete and otherwise emulate some aspects of boys' roles without being rejected by other girls, but boys who violated the negative canons were strongly rejected.

The concluding chapters in *We've All Got Scars* describe Best's efforts to reduce and overcome sex-role stereotyping through discussion with her students and the changes that appeared to occur as they moved through elementary school and later, after some intensification in the seventh grade of gender stereotypes involving boy-girl relationships, through junior high school. To "clear the way," she reported, " it was essential that the children learn to see the world around them as it really was rather than . . . the stereotypes . . . [denoting] the passive, incompetent girls they saw in their textbooks, library books, and the media" (p. 130). Although Best is uncertain whether her efforts had much or any impact compared with changes in social influences taking place outside her classroom, she believes that the boys and girls she studied made real progress in overcoming gender stereotyping and its frequently pernicious effects that limit the aspirations of girls, restrict the emotional growth of boys, and establish a nonegalitarian pattern of relationship between the sexes (p. 6).

INTERVENTIONS TO IMPROVE SEX EQUITY IN EDUCATION

During the past thirty years a variety of actions and programs have been initiated to improve sex equity in education. Some of these efforts involve policies and practices to counter discrimination and improve the status of women in general; others involve interventions targeted specifically at the educational system.

Among the most fundamental changes that have taken place are those involving public policy, which provides the legal framework for further situational modification. These changes include legislative and administrative actions such as the federal Equal Pay Act of 1963 and Title VII of the 1964 Civil Rights Act (Keating 1990). Of direct importance to educators is the Higher Education Act of 1972, which provides in its Title IX for sex equality both in employment in educational institutions and in education itself. The Act applies to all schools receiving federal grants and loans—preschools, elementary and secondary schools, vocational and professional schools, and both public and private undergraduate and graduate institutions.

The National Advisory Council on Women's Educational Programs (1982) reviewed developments in education following passage of Title IX and concluded that real progress has been made nationwide in improving educational opportunity for women. In addition to changes such as those described in the preceding pages, the

Council cited improvements in student services (counseling, health, financial aid) and in conducting athletics and other extracurricular activities on an equitable basis. The number of women participating in college sports programs increased from 32,000 in 1972 to 130,000 in 1989 (Horowitz and Lafferty 1990).

Some other developments that facilitate the participation of women in educational programs and support them as they attempt to cope with multiple roles include continuing education programs, the "open" university and "external degrees," women's committees or caucuses in professional associations, and women's studies programs.

Continuing education programs have had special benefits for women who have interrupted their education to marry and rear children but who wish to prepare to enter the labor force. Although the design and focus of such programs vary from college to college, they generally include one or more of the following features: enrollment on a part-time basis, flexible course hours, short-term courses, counseling services for adults, financial aid for part-time study, limited residence requirements, removal of age restrictions, liberal transfers of course credits, curriculum geared to adult experiences, credit by examination, refresher courses, reorientation courses, information services, child-care facilities, relaxation of time requirements for degrees, and job placement assistance.

Many activities have been initiated to extend women's entrance into the so-called male professions as well as to strengthen women's status in all professional fields. For example, many professional associations have established official committees concerned with the status and special problems of women in their respective fields. Generally, these associations seek to abolish dual standards of admission and quota systems and to increase financial assistance to women who wish to acquire a professional education.

In the past twenty years, women's studies have emerged as a special field in higher education (Smithson 1990). Hundreds of institutions of higher education have established formal women's studies programs, and many others offer a variety of courses and services that emphasize women's roles in education and society. Howe (1982) studied the development of feminist scholarship in higher education and identified the major curriculum emphases emerging in the women's studies movement as involving an understanding of the following topics:

1. Patriarchy in historical perspective.
2. The "still chaotic area" of biological and psychological sex differences.
3. Socialization and sex roles.
4. Women in history.
5. Women as represented in the arts they have produced.
6. The impact of post-Freudian psychology on women.
7. Female sexuality.
8. The history and function of education related to women.
9. The history and function of the family.
10. Women in the workforce.
11. Legal and social changes affecting women.

In addition, many activities have been initiated to counter sex-stereotyping and to raise the career and occupational aspirations of girls and women (Carelli 1988; Klein 1990). For example, teacher-training approaches such as the Gender Expectations and Student Achievement Program have been developed to improve classroom participation of female students and to enhance their aspirations and have been used in both pre-service and in-service teacher training (Grayson and Martin 1986). Jacquelynne Eccles (1986) has reviewed the theory and research dealing with efforts to broaden the occupational and educational aspirations of girls and women and pointed out that their

perceived career options can be increased by programs targeted to their beliefs that train them to (1) associate different attributions and expectations with various occupations,

(2) assess the value they attach to occupations, (3) reevaluate their stereotypes of various occupations and life-roles; and (4) reassess the compatibility between various career options and one's adult-role plans. Actively socializing young women and men to recognize the need to be able to support oneself and one's family is probably as important as helping them select the most 'appropriate' profession. (Eccles 1986, 19)

Antisexist Teaching Discourse

Sex equity can be advanced not only through policies to improve women's participation in education and society, but also by working to counteract sexism in all aspects of curriculum and instruction. Much of what teachers can do involves their potential contribution in helping students understand how traditional and current concepts and practices regarding gender limit opportunities available to girls and women. Through regular and on-going classroom discourse, teachers can help overcome and eliminate gender-related barriers to equal opportunity.

Closely related to and usually part of a larger movement we describe in Chapter 7 as aiming to develop critical theory and critical pedagogy to combat social and educational inequities involving social class and race, antisexist teaching approaches similarly focus on enhancing students' "critical consciousness" of social dynamics that inequitably restrict opportunity (Ewell 1990). A useful description and analysis of how teachers can work to counteract sexism and gender-related inequities through classroom discourse has been provided by Kathleen Weiler (1988). She observed several female teachers attempting to achieve these goals in several high schools and summarized her perceptions of their efforts:

They take two interrelated approaches that I think are essential to the kind of critical feminist teaching they hope to achieve. First, they expand the limits of discourse, by directly addressing the forces that shape their students' lives . . . [and by legitimizing] their students' voices . . . [through] acknowledging their students' own experiences and by calling for their students' own narratives. They frequently comment directly on classroom interaction and attempt to create relationships within the class that challenge accepted behavior and attitudes of men and women. Second . . . [they present] themselves as gendered subjects with a personal perspective on issues of gender and race . . . [and thus] reveal their own subjectivity and interests, while at the same time within certain limits legitimating the subjectivity of their students. . . . We can see in the practice of these teachers . . . [the outline of a pedagogy that is] transformative work in which what is most significant is the building of the capacity for critique and self-critique. (Weiler 1988, 131–149)

Weiler also carefully and repeatedly emphasized the difficulties teachers confront in orchestrating a classroom discourse aimed at developing students' critical consciousness regarding gender-related inequities in society and education. In particular, she reported that white feminist teachers frequently conducted a seemingly successful discourse with respect to white, middle-class girls, but their lessons were much more problematic with respect to the participation of minority students and working-class students. Regarding the latter subgroups, she further concluded, there were "conflicts between the essentially middle-class subjectivity of the teacher and the working-class and ethnic cultures of her students" (Weiler 1988). For example, many working-class students did not necessarily agree with feminist criticism of "machoistic" behaviors, and minority students frequently wanted to divert discourse from an emphasis on sexism to a focus on racism. "What we see" in such classrooms, Weiler finally concluded, are "complex redefinitions and constructions of meaning, conflicts between loci of power

that have their root in the class, race and gender divisions of U.S. society as a whole." But precisely for this reason, teachers should recognize conflicting views and accommodate them as part of classroom discourse, so that underlying conflicts and inequities can be "addressed and transformed" (Weiler 1988, 143, 145).

Innovative Instructional Approaches

Much of the effort to enhance sex equity in education involves new or modified instructional approaches that can help overcome girls' traditional obstacles to performance and participation. For example, Operation Smart emphasizes active-learning techniques, such as experimentation with motors and manipulation of hands-on puzzles, that girls historically have had less opportunity to use than boys. Sponsored by Girls, Inc. (formerly the Girls Clubs of America), Operation Smart appears to have improved motivation to learn science and math among participating girls between the ages of nine and fourteen (Nicholson and Hamm 1991).

DEVELOPMENT OF ANDROGYNY

The changing occupational structure of the U.S. society plus what may be loosely called the Feminist Movement have generated consideration of a theoretically and practically important concept called *androgyny*. The world *androgyny* comes from two Greek words—*andros* (male) and *gyne* (female)—and might be defined as "being both male and female" or "being sex-role flexible." Researchers in this developing field suppose that nearly all adults are either masculine, feminine, or androgynous in personal-social characteristics.

A self-rating method for the measurement of androgyny has been created by Sandra Bem (1974). She compiled a list of 200 personality characteristics that seemed to her and some of her students to be socially desirable and either masculine or feminine in tone. A personality characteristic qualified as masculine if it was independently judged by both males and females to be significantly more desirable for a man than for a woman. Similarly, a personality characteristic qualified as feminine if it was judged by both males and females to be significantly more desirable for a women than for a man. Of those characteristics that satisfied these criteria, twenty were selected for the Femininity Scale and twenty were selected for the Masculinity Scale. Another twenty items judged to be neutral also were included. These sixty items comprise the Bem Sex Role Inventory (BSRI).

The BRSI asks a person to indicate on a 7-point scale how well each of the 60 masculine, feminine, and neutral personality characteristics describes himself or herself. The scale ranges from 1 (Never or almost never true) to 7 (Always or almost always true), with a descriptive label for each of the 7 points. On the basis of the responses, each person receives three major scores: a Masculinity score, a Femininity score, and an Androgyny score. The Androgyny score is a measure of the relative amounts of masculinity compared with femininity that the person includes in his or her self-description. People who are high on both Masculinity and Femininity are Androgynous.

To secure data on a representative sample of college students aged about eighteen to twenty, Bem administered the BSRI to students at Stanford University and at the neighboring Foothill Junior College. The results indicated that only a few persons of both genders rate themselves higher on the opposite-sex characteristics than on the characteristics of their own gender.

Androgyny as an Ideal

A powerful essay with the foregoing title has been written by Ann Ferguson (1977). Ferguson criticized the Natural Complement Theory of male/female human nature. This theory rests on the biologically based differences between men and women. Because men are stronger than women and have higher amounts of the male hormone androgen, which is linked to aggressive behavior, it is natural for men to produce the physical commodities needed by society and to make war when necessary. Women should stay at home, raise their children, and minister to the emotional needs of their men and children.

Instead of this simplistic theory, Ferguson argued that it is useful to recognize that human nature is plastic, and that we should ask: "What traits are desirable and possible to teach people in order for them to reach their full individual human potential? And how would our society have to restructure its productive and reproductive relations in order to allow people to develop in this way?" (p. 57).

Elise Boulding (1979; 1987) has pointed out that strong trends toward androgyny have been present in the later stages of the life cycle, at which time the "androgyny of aging" is apparent when men "become gentler, more person- and family-oriented, and women become more assertive, more ready to test out what they know about how the world works" (1987, 131). Boulding believes that further movement toward androgyny would be desirable at earlier ages, but she also points out that such transitions do not occur on a smooth path and are affected by many social and historical influences.

RECENT DIRECTIONS IN FEMINISM

Modifications in the sex roles and related reductions in sex-differentiated norms that viewed aggressiveness as ideally masculine and passivity as ideally feminine have constituted major changes in United States society during the past thirty years. Associated with the feminist movement, these changes involved a combination of interrelated economic and cultural developments. Political developments in the early 1980s have been forcing redirection in the philosophy and goals of the feminist movement. Failure to ratify the Equal Rights Amendment in enough states to modify the U.S. Constitution and political fragmentation among various segments of the feminist movement have generated changes in emphasis among many of its leaders and supporters (Kramer 1986).

One of the best-known statements of some of these changes has been provided by Betty Friedan, whose influential earlier writings in *The Feminine Mystique* played an important part in enlarging opportunities for women and freeing them from the "cult" of domesticity. Friedan's 1981 book, *The Second Stage,* described the agenda she believes should be most important in working to advance women's rights in the future. She argued that the feminist movement will be most successful if it deemphasizes issues that divide liberals and conservatives and men and women and instead places greater emphasis on developing and supporting policies that help women (and men) pursue success in both the family and the labor market.

Friedan calls this direction the "second stage" because she believes it can help overcome some of the disquietiing developments in first-stage efforts to improve opportunities for women. Thus, she stated that supporters of women's rights should avoid "getting locked into obsolete power games and irrelevant sexual battles" and, by emphasizing family policy, should recognize the reality of each woman's "childbearing, her roots and life connection in the family" (pp. 29, 51). Much of the discussion in *The Second Stage* deals with possibilities for making job arrangements more flexible, modifying housing design to reduce homemaking burdens, instituting maternity and paternity leaves, and providing day care and other family services in order to accommodate parents' difficulties in juggling economic and family goals. After describing research indicating that enlarged opportunities for employment have been associated with improved mental health among United States women but that many women are having difficulty reconciling job and "family choices" in contemporary circumstances, she concluded that

> *part of the conflict over motherhood today—
> and part of the conflict that feminists feel
> about family and that younger women feel
> about feminism . . . is a hangover from the
> generations when too great a price was paid.*

> *But part of the conflict is realistic: the price
> of motherhood is still too high for most
> women, the stunting of abilities and earning
> power is a real fear. . . . The enemies of
> feminism insist that woman's move to
> equality, self-realization and her own power
> in society is destroying the family, which they
> feel is woman's real locus of power. Many
> feminists insist that the family was, and is, the
> enemy, the prime obstacle to women's self-
> realization. There are pieces of truth in these
> interlocking fears. . . . Part of the problem
> comes from the lack of real economic mea-
> sures or political attention to the previously
> private woman's work, in home and family,
> an irreducible minimum of which is necessary
> for human and society's survival. (Friedan
> 1981, 87, 95, 111)*

It should be noted that emphasis on family considerations in the women's rights movements fits in well with recent thinking regarding the social psychology of sex differences. In particular, Carol Gilligan (1982; Gilligan, Lyons, and Hanmer 1989) and other social scientists (e.g., Mansbridge 1990) have been re-examining data on female development and concluded that some important generalizations in social science do not quite fit for female respondents because they are based largely or entirely on male samples. Thus, Gilligan concluded that women tend to emphasize "ongoing attachment" with others and "interdependence of self and other" to a greater extent than do men (p. 170). According to Gilligan, this emphasis tends to create problems for women because in modern society it may lead to self-definition through "relationships with others" and then to severe midlife crises when such relationships prove fragile or vulnerable. Gilligan further concluded that women tend to exemplify a "different voice" that construes

> *social reality differently from men and that
> these differences center around experiences of
> attachment and separation . . . the major
> transitions in women's lives would seem to*

involve changes in the understanding and activities of care. When the distinction between helping and pleasing frees the activity of taking care from the wish for approval by others, the ethic of responsibility can become a self-chosen anchor of personal integrity and strength. . . . The inclusion of women's experience brings to developmental understanding a new perspective on relationships that changes the basic constructs of interpretation. The concept of identity expands to include the experience of interconnection. The moral domain is similarly enlarged by the inclusion of responsibility and care in relationships. (Gilligan 1982, 171, 173)

In a related and somewhat similar analysis, Jane Martin (1986) has advocated joining Plato's view that gender roles are not fixed by nature with Rousseau's insight that behavioral traits have been genderized. After pointing out that constructive sexual equity may not be attainable merely by placing more emphasis on the masculine virtues of "rationality and independent judgment" in educating women, she concluded that education also should include development of feminine virtues involving nurturance and care. In addition to counteracting in this way the "negative messages [about women and their roles] transmitted by the standard curriculum," the curriculum should advance equity by attending to "women's lives, work, experiences, and relationships" and should help diffuse "generation love" by joining "reason to feeling and self to other" (Martin 1986, 10).

Dianne Scott-Jones (1991) reviewed the arguments and associated research offered by Gilligan and her colleagues and concluded that their views concerning the female "care voice" have been instructive but require a "more thorough presentation of empirical evidence" to justify their widespread acceptance. In particular, Scott-Jones noted that Gilligan's analysis involved mostly high-status white girls and women and may not fit well for low-status and/or minority females, in part because development of racial

identity may be more important than gender-identity issues for black girls. In addition, she warned against equating "divergence from the care voice with abnormality or maladjustment in females," assuming the "utility of the care orientation across situations," or postulating that "only females have a care orientation." She also concluded that implications of Gilligan's and her colleagues' views for the schools are not very clear and that these views could have negative effects through "maximizing and romanticizing differences between males and females" in a manner that tends to maintain "women's traditional subordinate status" (Scott-Jones 1990, 31–32).

Recent Theory

A broad analytic perspective on the evolution of feminist theory also has been developed by Nel Noddings (1990) of Stanford University. After noting that the thinking of individual women, as well as feminist analysis as a whole, seems to evolve through stages that represent a progression across generations, Noddings portrays the first generation as seeking equality with men, the second generation as rejecting "uncritical assimilation into the male world" in favor of emphasis on bringing the "best female qualities into the public world," and the third generation as critiquing what was "sought and accomplished in the first two phases" and seeking "solutions that arise out of a careful synthesis of old and new questions" (pp. 393–394).

Believing that feminism recently has been moving into the third stage, Noddings agrees with some other feminist theorists (e.g., MacKinnon 1987) whose critiques of previous developments question whether the sameness/difference (i.e., first generation/second generation) debates have produced satisfactory results. Most important in assessing the situation, Noddings concludes, is that arguing sameness/difference issues does not focus adequately on central problems involving the functioning of "hierarchical structures" in the larger social system: "Just as men have dominated, and still dominate, women, so the wealthy and better educated dominate the poor and less educated. Hierarchical structures serve the continuance of domination," and therefore reduction or elimination of hierarchy itself should become the goal of feminist theory (Noddings 1990, 396). It may not be enough, Noddings thus concludes, to make room for Gilligan's "different voice"; because the psychological patterns and perspectives of women have been produced by oppression and subservience, "whatever good it [the 'different voice'] has to express will be denigrated by its association with females" (p. 397). Stated differently, the values and perspectives of women will not be much attended to because women lack power and status. To avoid this outcome, feminist theory should attend to power and its redistribution and to changing the dynamics of traditional power-based hierarchies (also see Gore 1990).

Although third-stage feminists seem to agree on the importance of modifying and restricting the operation of traditional hierarchies, there is not much agreement on how to deal with the complex issues involved in doing so. Should feminists work closely to coordinate their policies and analysis with critical theorists (see Chapter 7) who concentrate on the workings of social-class hierarchies, or would such cooperation inevitably lead to a dilution of feminist concerns and perspectives? Should feminists work to bring about reforms that focus on improving opportunities for women individually, or would such reforms make it more difficult to build support for more comprehensive changes throughout the political and social structure? To what extent, if any, can or should accommodations be sought to recognize the different voices described by Gilligan and Jane Martin (see earlier) before changing the operation of traditional hierarchies?

Noddings was concerned with several such questions when she proceeded to analyze the situation with respect to women in law, nursing, and education. Her discussion of women in the teaching profession portrayed recent analysis as still dealing mainly with sameness/difference issues. Noddings described one example of the paradox faced at this stage as follows:

On the one hand, women teachers want to be recognized as professionals, that is, they want to be recognized as committed, effective teachers . . . but, on the other hand, they recognize that someone must do the care giving in this society. . . . Their fear is that . . . [recent trends in professionalization of teaching will require them to] move further from actual contact with children. . . . [Feminist critics thus are not convinced] that the professionalization of teaching will benefit children. Their agenda would require beginning with families and children . . . [and might concentrate on addressing such goals as provision of] child care on school campuses . . . flexible teaching schedules and partnerships that will allow men and women who wish to spend more time parenting to do so without losing professional status . . . and more time for teachers to be with their students and develop caring relationships. . . . [These goals incorporate a different, feminist] perspective on teaching and on life than those raised by advocates of professionalization. (Noddings 1990, 415)

Feminist Theory in Education and Social Science

Recent feminist writing in education draws from a larger base of feminist social science analysis of which it is a constituent part. Sondra Farganis (1989) has portrayed and assessed some of the outstanding work in this area of analysis in an essay titled "Feminism and the Reconstruction of Social Science." After noting that feminist critiques of science generally resemble other "radical critiques" in challenging the social consequences of "scientization, rationalization, and bureaucratization," Farganis highlights how feminist social science perspectives reject simplistic dualities that assume rigid distinctions, such as those between "subject and object, nature and nurture, biology and environment, individual and community . . . [and] detachment/attachment." Closely related to and frequently inspired by the writing of Carol Gilligan, her analysis postulates that women traditionally engaged in work that led them to "feel and care" for what they produced and thereby generated "a new way of seeing the world" (Farganis 1989, 212). Also synthesizing perspectives developed by Dorothy Smith (1987) and other analysts, Farganis (1989, 213–214) concluded that feminist social scientists tend to stress:

- Understanding of people's daily experience,
- Understanding of "ordinary social consciousness" before it is shaped by scientific theories, and
- Introduction of an "emancipatory dimension" into their writing and research.

In general, according to this analytic framework, science "as now practiced" should be rejected because it "contributes to and even constitutes a political ideology of domination" in that it treats "physical and social entities as objects to be described, measured, and classified, . . . [thus training] us to think of controlling and, in this sense, dominating the people around us." Instead, feminists should view science "as a discourse, as a way of speaking about the world," and should "deconstruct the intricate relationship between science and power, bringing to the surface the ways in which scientific discourse reinforces power" and power actively shapes scientific discourse (Farganis 1989, 214).

One manifestation of traditional discourse that is particularly important to feminists involves definitions and consequences of *gender* categories. As with conceptions of social class, a person's gender (i.e., "the particular cultural way" in which a person's sexual traits and biology are "presented, understood, and played out") affects his or her perceptions: "Gender creates a person who has a whole array of characteristics and the person and the characteristics are in history, not above or outside it"; as such, gender is defined within a "framework that interacts with biological considerations," but is "not unalterably controlled or contained by that biology." But because the "way in which one is esteemed . . . is

not pregiven in any deterministic or mechanistic way but rather is a consequence of historical factors shaped by human agency" (Farganis 1989, 215), one function of feminist social science is to examine the extent to which values attached to gender categories and characteristics are arbitrary and undesirable. Is too much value placed on the ability to lift heavy materials? Is it somehow deviate to choose not to have children? Why, if at all, should performance on a mechanical test be valued more than the ability to draw or sing or dance? Such questions should be of obvious concern to educators who are working to promote more equal opportunities in schools and society for the disadvantaged in general, and for girls and women in particular.

CONCLUSION

A stable and relatively unchanging society uses the process of socialization to teach its young members the social roles they must perform in order to maintain the society in generally satisfactory shape. With respect to sex roles, they are taught the socially appropriate masculine and feminine roles, by their family, school, neighborhood, and community.

Attitudes and behavior regarding sex roles in U.S. society have been changing significantly in the period since 1950. Women have been entering the labor force to an extent that would have been almost unimaginable fifty years ago, and they also have been pursuing higher education in unprecedented numbers. Although the majority of women still are preparing for and entering traditionally so-called white-blouse occupations, a growing proportion are entering traditionally male fields.

Both as a cause and a result of these changes regarding occupational and educational opportunities for women, attitudes and practices involving the socialization of children—particularly girls—also have been changing. For example, parents are less likely today than forty or fifty years ago to stress future homemaking roles in raising girls, and they are more likely to insist that their daughters receive a good education so they can compete on an equal basis in the economy. There is some evidence that middle-class youngsters are somewhat in advance of working-class youngsters in stressing equal opportunity for girls and women (Holland 1980; Christensen 1987; Fox-Genovese 1991), but opportunities opening up for women certainly have not been limited to the middle class. Over the past forty years or so, our society has redefined what is meant by masculinity and feminity.

The first chapter of this book began with a recognition of the fact that the United States has become a postindustrial society in which provision of services—particularly information—is replacing manufacturing and extraction of goods as the primary economic activity. This change in the economy has been one factor generating changes in sex roles in U.S. society, but it is difficult to predict whether future economic change will hinder or further improve opportunities for women. From one point of view, the movement to a postindustrial economy benefits women because women can carry out most tasks in such an economy as well as men. On the other hand, computerization and other forms of advanced technological change may reduce the availability of many jobs such as teacher and secretary that are now filled by women. Much will depend on the educational opportunities available to women and on how well women take advantage of these opportunities to prepare for highly skilled jobs in the economy of the future.

EXERCISES

1. Obtain copies of the readers used in the first and second grades of a nearby school system. Analyze their content with regard to images of women and men.

2. Interview your mother and your grandmother regarding their life histories. What were the attitudes toward women's roles that prevailed when they were young women? What were their own views? Have those views changed recently?

3. Interview several of your instructors. What do they report regarding the status of faculty women in your institution?

4. Talk with three or four mothers of young children. What are their aspirations for their sons? For their daughters? Do these mothers report agreement or disagreement with their husbands on these issues?

5. Construct a sociogram of a fifth-grade class. Do boys have "gangs" whereas girls have "best friends"?

6. Read Charles Derber's *The Pursuit of Attention.* How do men and women differ in conversation?

SUGGESTIONS FOR FURTHER READING

1. Schneir's *Feminism: The Essential Historical Writings* is, as indicated by the title, a collection of major writings on the history of the feminist movement.

2. For historical perspective, Mabel Newcomer's *A Century of Higher Education for American Women* is an excellent reference.

3. The women's liberation movement of the 1960s and 1970s gave rise to a flood of books and magazine articles setting forth a wide range of views. Friedan's *The Feminine Mystique* was an early and highly influential book. Others include Firestone's *The Dialectic of Sex: The Case for Feminist*

Revolution, Morgan's *Sisterhood Is Powerful,* Millett's *Sexual Politics,* Komisar's *The New Feminism,* Chafe's *The American Woman,* and Friedan's *The Second Stage.*

4. *Comparative Perspectives of Third World Women* edited by Beverly Lindsay includes papers dealing with the status and role of women in racial minority groups.

5. *Beyond Her Sphere* by Barbara Harris traces the development of the feminist movement in the United Stated from precolonial times to the present.

6. *The Economics of Sex Differentials* by Lloyd and Niemi and *The Economic Emergence of Women* by Bergmann provide a thorough review and well-balanced assessment of research on why women earn less than men and of the implications of this research for social policy.

7. Constantina Safilios-Rothschild's *Sex Role Socialization and Sex Discrimination* includes a comprehensive review of the research on sex differences in socialization. Particular emphasis is given to the family and the school.

8. *Too Many Women?,* by Marcia Guttentag and Paul Secord, argues that the ratio of men to women in society has an important influence on social, economic, cultural, and political developments. If there are many more men than women, the authors argue, men compete for women by emphasizing marriage and the family, and women have more opportunity to participate fully in society. If there are many more women than men, marriage and the family are deemphasized and women are devalued. Guttentag and Secord support their conclusions with data from ancient and medieval as well as contemporary societies. Their conclusions also received support from an international study conducted by South and Trent (1988).

9. *Women and Mathematics: Balancing the Equation,* edited by Chipman, Brush, and Wilson, reviews a wide range of previous research and also presents and analyzes original research dealing with mathematics achievement and participation of girls and women.

10. *The Handbook for Achieving Sex Equity through Education,* edited by Susan Klein (1990), incudes chapters on curriculum and instruction, school organization and administration, early through postsecondary education, teacher education, testing, and other topics. The volume concludes with eighteen pages of recommendations for improving sex equity through the educational system.

11. Diane Halpern's thoughtful review of research in *Sex Differences in Cognitive Abilities* examines and assesses a number of studies dealing with differentials in performance and their possible causes.

12. Based on interviews with women, Mary Belenky and her colleagues *(Women's Ways of Knowing* 1986) speculate that "educators can help women develop their own authentic voices" by emphasizing "connection over separation, understanding and acceptance over assessment, and collaboration over debate" and by according respect to the "knowledge that emerges from first-hand experience" (p.229).

13. An intriguing study by Janet Lever reports data indicating that boys' play and games tend to be more complex than is true among girls. The author speculates that "boys' greater exposure to complex games may give them an advantage in occupational milieus that share structured features with those of games" (Lever 1988, 341).

14. An essay on "Feminism and Democracy" by Jane Mansbridge (1990) explores general implications of feminist thought in working to improve social policies and institutions.

Additional Topics Focusing on Educational Equity

This chapter provides information on and discussion of three important topics that have major implications for attainment of educational equity: computers in elementary and secondary schools, rural education, and nonpublic schools. Each topic constitutes a large and specialized field of study in itself. We do not try to discuss or analyze all of the important considerations involving these themes; instead, we are concerned largely with recent developments that have direct implications in terms of providing equal and adequate educational opportunity and, perforce, the public policies that might or should be formulated to ensure provision of equitable opportunity.

COMPUTERS AND EQUITY IN ELEMENTARY AND SECONDARY SCHOOLS

Between 1981 and 1990, the number of instructional computers in elementary and secondary schools increased from less than 25,000 to more than 1 million (Becker 1990b). John Lipkin of the Bureau of Social Science Research reviewed the data on computers in education and found that developments in information technology appeared to be advancing what he called the "Matthew Effect": "For whosoever hath, to him shall be given." Lipkin reported that schools and school districts enrolling mostly wealthy students were much more likely to have obtained microcomputers and to be teaching computer literacy than were schools and districts with mostly poverty students (Lipkin 1982, 7). Worse, Lipkin also

found data indicating that where computers were being used to deliver instruction, there was a tendency for middle-class students to concentrate relatively more on higher-order skills and for working-class students to concentrate relatively more on lower-level skills. Lipkin summarized the situation:

It is the urban, low-income minority student who is most likely to be provided with drill and practice usage of computers while middle class students are more likely to use it for more creative purposes relating to problem-solving and discovery. . . .

It has been suggested that the effect of this distinction in computer use is to produce benefits of a different kind along class lines, with the upper classes cast in the mold of leaders and the lower classes, followers.

Evidence of an analogous dichotomy of computer instruction at the secondary level is beginning to appear with the emergence of a vocationally oriented curriculum for innercity or low-income students which is set apart from the higher level uses of the computer which pertain in the precollege curriculum. (Lipkin 1982, 7)

Later studies conducted by the U.S. Office of Technology Assessment indicated that although the hardware gap favoring middle-class over working-class schools had diminished somewhat in the 1980s, schools with high proportions of disadvantaged students are still relatively lacking in computers. Equally or more important, low-income schools generally have less software, fewer qualified instructors, and less funding to repair machinery, purchase computer-related text materials, and provide relevant staff development (DeVillar and Faltis 1991).

It should be noted that both commercial and school-initiated resources and projects that involve home use of the computer also favor wealthier students, who are most likely to possess a personal computer (Teske 1988). For example, many excellent computer programs dealing with thousands of educational topics can now be purchased for home use, and several school districts have introduced arrangements that allow students to use home computers to review vocational guidance information obtained by the district. Many more projects of this kind will be introduced in the future. Students whose families cannot afford a computer will be at a serious disadvantage in competing with those who have access to a microcomputer at home (Rothman 1988; Higgins 1990).

Although developments involving computers and technological change thus threaten to widen achievement gaps between middle-class and working-class students (Kleifen 1989), it is possible that these developments can have the opposite effect. For example, the results of a major pilot project that assessed several approaches using computer-based instruction (CBI) in the New York City schools indicated that the reading scores of disadvantaged students can be significantly enhanced. As shown in Table 12-1, the average reading score for participating students in elementary Chapter 1 and other remedial classes increased from 33.5 in 1987 to 41.7 in 1988, and participating Chapter 1 and remedial students in junior high and middle schools improved from 53.2 to 58.1. However, disadvantaged senior-high students improved hardly at all. The authors of this study provided the following discussion of these results:

It is not clear why the patterns of relationships among student categories . . . seem to change with changes in grade levels. . . . The expla-

nation for this inverse relationship may simply be that CBI is a more effective delivery system for students at low instructional levels. It is more likely that the design of current programs better supports the type of content addressed at lower instructional levels. While the simple tutorial and drill and practice routines common to most systems seem particularly effective, not only for developing needed skills, but for diagnosing skill deficiencies at such levels, the problem-solving skills inherent in higher level reading comprehension and mathematical problem solving may neither be so easily developed, nor the lack of such skills effectively diagnosed, by instructional models of this sort. (Swan, Guerrero, Mitrani, and Schoener 1989, 17–18).

It should not be concluded, however, that computer technology is unsuitable for helping disadvantaged or other students improve in comprehension, problem-solving, and other higher-order skills. Although relatively little software has been developed for this purpose, and there generally is a grave danger that computers will reinforce rather than counteract teachers' tendencies to emphasize low-level drill and memorization, computers have the potential to support

TABLE 12-1 *Average 1987 and 1988 Reading Scores for Elementary, Intermediate, and Senior-High Students from Chapter 1 and Other Remedial Classes Participating in the Computer-Based Instruction Pilot Program in New York City**

Level	1987	1988
Elementary	33.5	41.7
Intermediate (Junior High and Middle School)	53.2	58.1
Senior High	56.5	58.7

Source: Adapted from Swan, Guerrero, Mitrani, and Schoener 1989.

*Reading scores are for students with pre- and postscores on the Degrees of Reading Power test. Gains for elementary and intermediate but not senior-high students appear to have exceeded their previous rate of growth in earlier grades.

and enhance higher-order learning. (Several examples are briefly described in Chapter 13.) After reviewing the results of research dealing with computer technology and development of advanced literacy, Kleifgen (1989, 2) and DeVillar and Faltis (1991, 130) concluded that the following considerations are important in using computers to improve higher-order learning:

- Cognitively challenging software involving text construction, thinking skills, and other intellectual functions.
- Collaborative learning environments in which language is used to solve meaningful problems.
- Skilled teachers who can introduce challenging tasks and who know how to make computers a learning tool.
- Discovery-oriented curricula that are coordinated within and across grade levels.

Similar observations can be made concerning the education of girls and women: females have been disadvantaged in learning math and some other subjects in the past; introduction of the computer may either magnify this disadvantage or help reduce it, depending on how the computer is used and the efforts made to improve opportunity for females (Kiesler, Sproull, and Eccles 1983; Kleifgen 1989). Much will depend on how well and how widely the new technologies are introduced in schools and classrooms, and on how great an effort is made to advance rather than retard the goals of equity for low-income students and for women.

The data on disproportionate use by sex and the differentials reported above by socioeconomic status, race/ethnicity, and ability suggest that serious equity problems have been developing and that schools should do more to ensure productive and equitable results for disadvantaged students and girls (DeVillar and Faltis 1991). The National Task Force on Educational Technology (1986) considered how the schools could productively transform elementary and secondary education in general in order to improve learning and increase "equity of opportunity, access, and quality" through computers and technology. The Task Force reported that schools should begin to plan for a "computer-managed learning environment . . . [that] will allow students to progress at varying speeds according to their individual abilities" and should plan for the "orderly acquisition of both the hardware and software needed to serve the school's educational goals" (p. 14).

RURAL EDUCATION

Statistics compiled by the National Education Association indicate that approximately one-fourth of elementary and secondary students attend rural schools (Newman 1989, 1990; Schwartz 1990). Even though rural schools enroll a substantial proportion of students in the United States, their status and problems have received relatively little attention during the twentieth century. For example, rates of substance abuse, teenage pregnancy, and other indicators of youth problems that detract from school performance are relatively high in rural areas (Weisman 1990b), but difficulties these problems pose for rural schools and communities are often ignored. However, such neglect has been corrected to some extent during the past few years by groups and individuals endeavoring to analyze the problems of rural education and to identify approaches for improving the quality of education in rural schools.

As we point out in Chapter 10, many students in rural areas are from low-income families and have relatively low achievement, particularly in such economically impoverished regions as Appalachia and the Ozarks. In addition to eductional disadvantages associated with poverty background and dialect differences (Keefe, Reck, and Reck 1983; DeYoung 1991), many rural students historically have had relatively low educational aspirations in circumstances in which advanced eduation was not perceived as necessary or even desirable for youth preparing to become farmers or farm laborers (Fuller 1985; DeYoung, Huffman, and Turner 1989; Weisman 1990b).

Although academic performance is high in some rural communities, and students' aspirations certainly have escalated as farming has become highly technological, the relatively low status and economic difficulties experienced by many rural youth probably still function to generate relatively low aspirations. Thus, Oneida Martin (1987) found that a sample of rural high-school students had lower educational aspirations than did a comparison group of disadvantaged urban students. Low aspirations among rural youth may be due partly to internalization of media images and stereotypes that portray rural populations as hicks and hillbillies (Weisman 1990b).

Community Orientation

One distinguishing characteristic of many rural schools and districts is the unusual extent to which they are oriented toward and interact with their surrounding communities. In part because rural schools historically have been one of the largest and most visible local social institutions, and because rural citizens have had relatively few sources of information, recreation, and other services easily accessible in the cities, many rural schools have been an integral part of social life in their communities. With the advent of improvements in transportation and communications, rural populations no longer are as dependent on local schools for such services as was formerly the case, but in many locations schools continue to function as centers for a wide variety of community activities. Patricia and Richard Schmuck (1990) spent six months visiting and examining the contemporary role of small-town schools in the Midwest and West. They reached the following conclusions regarding the broad social functions they serve and their related potential for enhancing educational opportunities available to their students:

The small-town school is like a vortex drawing everyone into it and serving as a foundation for the community. The school engages virtu-

ally everyone, regardless of age, because . . . it irresistibly draws the community's residents into it. . . . Administrators and teachers are public figures; they must be concerned with propriety and public relations because the people's thoughts about the community center on the school. People go to the school for education, entertainment, social life, and community identity. In one town of 5,000 it was reported that the Christmas pageant draws 6,000 spectators. Much more than the church, city hall, or even the tavern, the school occupies the townspeople for considerable time in its classes, sports events, club meetings, potluck dinners, recreational events, musical concerts, open houses, and theatrical presentations. . . .

[But despite serving as the vortex for social life, the small-town school too frequently] misses the opportunity to harness the energy of the academic and intellectual life of the community. Students, teachers, and administrators remain separate from each other rather than unified in a shared purpose. Whether they are aware of it or not, small-town educators and parents seem to be mimicking a mass-production model of academic life that many of their urban counterparts are striving to give up. . . . The small-town school . . . [should in the future] include more than support for the football team, the band, and other forms of community entertainment. It must go beyond that to include the pursuit of the intellect and a genuine respect for democracy as a way of life in the school. (Schmuck and Schmuck 1990, 6–7)

Recent Socioeconomic and Demographic Trends

Because there has been a long-range movement of persons from rural to urban areas in the United States, the problems and challenges facing rural educators frequently have been different than those in large towns and cities. For example, rural schools frequently have suffered from depopulation at the same time that urban schools were crowded beyond capacity. In recent years some aspects of manufacturing (e.g., mining) have declined in rural communities, as in the cities, but rural areas probably have had a harder time attracting so-called high tech replacements (Reid 1990). Specialists in rural education recently met at a symposium to identify contemporary socioeconomic and demographic trends that are having a strong impact on rural schools. Some of their conclusions were summarized as follows:

> *Although the size of the nonmetropolitan population is stagnant or declining, its composition is changing in ways that will reduce demand for conventional educational services. The population is aging: by the year 2030, there will be as many elderly people as school-age children. Rural areas have proportionately more youth than urban ones, but the overall aging of the population will affect both areas alike, cutting demand for elementary and secondary education.*
>
> *The industrial transformation of rural economies and associated worker dislocation will increase the need to retrain workers and assist employees. In fact, the mix of needed educational services will undoubtedly change in the decades to come. Formal classroom education will decline as the need for continuing education and worker retraining grows. The pace of industrial transformation will probably increase in the future. Workers can no longer expect to apply the same skills throughout their professional lives. Continual retraining will be necessary if workers are to avoid downward mobility. Accordingly, nonmetropolitan communities might consider redirecting some of their resources from traditional formal education to continuing education, job retraining, and lifetime learning programs. (Brown 1989, 28–30)*

Diversity

One problem that analysts encounter in trying to delineate and find solutions to educational prob-

lems in rural areas is that rural locations are very diverse and the characteristics of rural schools and society are difficult to define and generalize (DeYoung 1987). This problem was addressed by educators trying to build a network to share information on common problems through the National Rural and Small Schools Consortium. Members of the consortium attending a national conference agreed that rural school districts could be defined as districts that have fewer than 150 residents per square mile and are located in counties in which at least 60 percent of the population lives in communities with fewer than 5,000 inhabitants. They also pointed out that more than 300 separate rural subcultures have been identified, based on such characteristics as ethnic composition, degree of remoteness, and economic infrastructure (Montague, 1986). The diversity of rural schools has been illustrated and underlined by Jonathan Sher:

> *Reliable hard data about the quality of small rural schools are scarce. . . . The fact that small rural schools are so diverse, especially when viewed internationally, only compounds the problem. Indeed, one can find evidence to support nearly any characterization. Someone who wishes to describe these institutions as ineffective, stifling, third-rate, or worse will have little trouble finding schools that fully deserve such criticism. However, another person who wishes to portray rural schools as innovative, high-performing, delightful places will have equal ease in justifying such a glowing assessment. (Sher 1983, 259)*

Despite the great diversity found in rural schools and society, several key problems appear to be particularly widespread. Among the most severe of these contemporary educational problems in rural areas are lack of financial resources (Yatvin 1980), which has been intensified by economic recession in recent years; shortages of teachers; and difficulty in meeting the higher academic standards that increasingly have been mandated by state governments throughout the

United States (Miller and Sidebottom 1985; Montague 1986; Newman 1989, 1990).

Financial Limitations

Given their small population and frequently impoverished economic base, rural districts historically have had a difficult task obtaining the financial resources needed to provide a comprehensive educational program (Stern 1989; Newman 1990). Severe financial limitations thus constitute a recurring theme throughout histories of rural education (Fuller 1985; Tyack 1990). In addition to the inadequate financial base in many rural communities, according to Wayne Fuller, difficulties in supporting public education also arose from farmers' social situation in an industrializing society. Farmers

> could scarcely help feeling that educating their sons and daughters would either lure them away from the farm, where their labor was needed, or make them discontented with a life in which the monotony of morning and evening chores was broken mainly by bone-wearying work. . . . They [also] seemed instinctively to fear that education, at least too much education, went hand in hand with wealth, luxury, and leisure and ended in corruption and decadence. (Fuller 1985, 37–38)

Recent economic trends affecting rural areas appear to have magnified the financial difficulties that historically have hampered the operation of many rural districts (Johnson 1989; Stern 1989). Thus, a case study conducted in rural areas in Minnesota found that low commodity prices, falling land values, and curtailed mining operations have produced negative effects beyond "normal business cycle fluctuations" and are producing both decline in enrollment and "reduced capacity for local tax support" of rural education (Sederberg 1986, 19–20). Conversely, various observers have pointed out that economic recession has made public education an even more important force than it has been tra-

ditionally in providing jobs and skilled personnel for rural areas and in promoting the development of rural communities (e.g., Hobbs 1990).

Teacher Shortage

Due in part to financial difficulties and concomitantly low salaries, many rural districts face recurrent problems in attracting and retaining qualified teachers, even when there is a nationwide oversupply in most subject areas (Miller and Sidebottom 1985). According to a study conducted by the National Rural Project, for example, nearly half of seventy-five rural school districts polled in seventeen states reported problems in recruiting and keeping teachers. In addition to low salaries, cultural and social isolation was noted frequently as a reason for high rates of turnover and insufficient numbers of candidates for teaching positions in rural areas (Helge and Marrs 1981; Miller and Sidebottom 1985). A recent national study of fourth-grade students and their teachers reported that more than one-fifth of rural teachers have four years or less experience—almost twice the rate for the nation as a whole. Given their relative inexperience, rural teachers in this study ranked low as a group in attainment of advanced degrees and professional certificates (Langer, Applebee, Mullis, and Foertsch 1990).

On the other hand, many rural communities also have distinctive features that can be advantageous in attracting and retaining teachers. As Miller and Sidebottom (1985) pointed out, these features include friendly relationships in the community and high potential for achieving respect, scenic and easygoing environments with little traffic or pollution and attractive recreational opportunities, small enrollments that allow teachers to give individual attention to students, and availability of libraries and university extension branches (pp. 15–16).

William Mathes and Robert Carlson (1986) have studied differences among newly certified teachers who accepted positions in differing types of communities and found that many of those teachers in rural school districts were particularly concerned with settling and fitting in to their new communities and work environments. Mathes and Carlson concluded that successful recruitment of rural teachers depends not just on competitive salaries but also on "a sense of support and the presence of a pleasant school climate" (p. 9). Based on similar data and considerations, Miller and Sidebottom recommended a number of actions, such as the seven following, that might help rural schools acclimate their staff and improve professionally:

1. Initiate a colleague support program by pairing new and established teachers.
2. Provide district services or referrals to help with personal problems.
3. Publicly recognize new staff members and their accomplishments.
4. Help teachers obtain external grants for scholarships, travel, and other professional development.
5. Assign faculty only in their areas of certification.
6. Provide such staff development incentives as university credit, released time, and certification renewal.
7. Promote activities to reduce stress, including social functions and exercise.

District Cooperatives

One way rural school districts have tried to overcome limitations associated with inadequate financing, unavailability of specialized teachers, and small size is to form or participate in cooperatives in which they work together to provide improved educational opportunities (Stephens 1991). Andy Sommer (1990) of the Northwest Regional Educational Laboratory studied the organization and functioning of such cooperatives, defined as entities in which two or more districts voluntarily share resources through "an informal or formal agreement providing for the negotiated resolution of conflicts." After describing cooperatives that have a governing board that enables

participating districts to share the costs of special services and other independent cooperatives that have their own facilities, administration, and financing, Sommer identified some services and benefits that frequently are made possible through the operation of cooperatives:

- Sharing equipment, materials, and supplies.
- Reinvigoration of teaching staff through staff development.
- Facilitation of joint efforts with institutions of higher education and other external agencies.
- Sharing of personnel costs.
- Cost savings through insurance pools, joint purchasing agreements, consolidation of transportation, and other cooperative arrangements.
- Improvement or preservation of educational programs that could not be offered economically for a few students in a single district.
- Sharing of expertise contributed by district employees and decision makers or external specialists.
- Improvement of equity through cooperative provision of support services (e.g., counselors, school psychologists) and curriculum specialists (e.g., reading teachers, special education teachers).

Noting that collaborative efforts traditionally have been important in providing for fire protection, electrification, and other cooperative activities, such as barn-raising in rural areas, Sommer concluded that the "formation, maintenance and strengthening of rural educational cooperatives is one method of ensuring the continued effectiveness and vitality of small, rural school districts" (1990, 3). When such prerequisites as commitment to common goals, regular communication, geographic proximity, willingness to work with so-called outsiders, and strong leadership are present, he further concluded, rural district cooperatives can help maintain or increase the attractiveness of rural communities in an era in which many cities are perceived as undesirable places to live because they are unsafe and overly congested.

Instructional Improvement

Due partly to resource limitations and to their low enrollment, rural districts traditionally have had difficulty in providing comprehensive, high-quality programs of curriculum and instruction and in meeting state government standards for minimal programming and services. This problem has become particularly acute as education has come to play an increasingly central role in postindustrial society and as state governments have increased minimum standards during the 1980s (Nelson 1991).

Distance Education.   Improvements in transportation, government initiatives to reduce inequalities, growing awareness of the limitations of extremely small schools and districts, and other forces have coalesced to bring about an enormous reduction in the numbers of rural school districts and one-room schools (see Table 12-2). However, many rural districts with low enrollment and very small schools still find it difficult to provide a full range of instructional services and a comprehensive curriculum. To address this problem, rural educators are trying to make use of advanced technology. This approach, frequently referred to as *distance education,* includes use of such technological developments as the following (Wall 1986; Jordahl 1991):

1. Videotape lessons.
2. Audio teleconferencing, using telephones or other one-way or two-way audio technologies.
3. Interactive television, involving real-time, two-way audio, and visual contact.
4. Interactive video, blending microcomputers with video storage units.
5. Computer networks.

Used effectively, distance education can serve a variety of functions, including provision of specialized courses and instructors to isolated schools, facilitation of interaction among students at differing schools, dissemination of timely information, and delivery of staff development services. Recent examples of the promising use of distance education include development of an Agri Data Network for students studying agriculture at fifteen rural schools in Wyoming; systematic staff development in Missouri; delivery via satellite of instruction in Spanish, Japanese, and precalculus to eighteen school districts in Washington state; provision through teleconferencing of required foreign-language instruction at rural schools in Nebraska; and delivery of foreign language and physics instruction in Oklahoma, Texas, and Utah through multistate telecommunications networks (Wall 1986; Batey and Cowell 1987; Gudat 1988; Holznagel and Olson 1990; Milone and Brady 1991).

Washor and Coutre (1990) have pointed out that distance education can be very cost effective and also can draw on the best and most current resources to deliver outstanding and exciting

TABLE 12-2 *Numbers and Sizes of School Districts Since 1930*

	1931–32	1961–62	1967–68	1973–74	1982–83	1988–89
Number of public school districts	127,244	35,555	22,010	16,730	15,747	15,376
Number of public schools	270,000	107,000	97,890	90,976	82,039	83,165
Total public school enrollment below college level (in thousands)	26,300	38,253	44,140	45,652	39,328	40,408
Average enrollment per school district	207	1,075	2,000	2,700	2,479	2,628

Source: U.S. Department of Education; McDowell and Morgan 1990.

instruction. However, analysis by Holznagel (1990) indicates that substantial start-up costs and state regulations involving class size, certification, and other matters tend to inhibit introduction of distance education in many school districts.

Innovative Instructional Approaches. Paul Nachtigal (1982, 1989) has examined several innovative efforts made to improve instruction in rural schools. Nachtigal concluded that some approaches, such as the Teacher Corps and the Experimental Schools Project, did not work well in rural locations, primarily because they did not take adequate account of the special circumstances that differentiate rural from urban situations and the diverse circumstances that make one rural situation different from others. Some other projects, however, do appear to be effective because they allow for extensive adaptation to local rural settings. Nachtigal concluded that one such project is the National Diffusion Network, which provides school districts with information and follow-up support in selecting among and then implementing successful approaches for improving curriculum and instruction.

Cooperative Projects. As mentioned earlier, one way that rural school districts are attempting to overcome problems associated with shortages of specialized teachers, financial limitations, inadequate equipment and technologies, low enrollment for advanced courses, and related difficulties is to work together in providing expanded services and opportunities. A good example of such cooperation with respect to instruction is apparent in the Biomedical Sciences Preparation Program (BioPrep) initiated in Alabama in 1982. Originally designed to help remedy a severe shortage of health-care personnel in rural parts of Alabama, BioPrep has evolved into a comprehensive honors program that prepares high-school students to pursue a wide range of academic studies. With leadership from the University of Alabama, BioPrep provides teacher training, summer college-campus opportunities for students, a mobile laboratory that visits rural high schools, prep-

aration of student writing portfolios, emphasis on higher-order learning, and other forms of support and stimulation for students and teachers (Rainey 1990). More than 2,000 students participated in 1991, and a high proportion of participants have been obtaining college scholarships.

Effective Schools Projects. One of the most vigorous movements in U.S. education during the 1980s involved efforts to improve students' achievement through *effective schools* projects intended to develop characteristics thought to be important at unusually effective schools. (The effective schools approach is described in Chapter 13.) Among the characteristics most often emphasized are high expectations for students, outstanding leadership, and orderly/productive climate. Effective schools projects have been carried out in all types of school districts—city, suburban, and rural. Because much of the research on usually effective schools has been concerned primarily with poverty schools in big cities, some observers have been skeptical concerning the relevance of effective schools projects for rural schools. Levine and Lezotte (1990) reviewed the relatively scant literature available on this question and reached the following conclusion:

> *In general, there currently is little or no reason to believe that correlates . . . identified as characterizing unusually effective schools are less important or relevant in rural than urban settings. . . . [Although] resource limitations typical of many rural schools may constrain implementation of effective schools projects, this disadvantage may be counterbalanced by considerations facilitating communications and student involvement at small schools in rural areas. Overall . . . effective schools approaches should be as useful in improving education in rural as in urban schools. (p. 67)*

NONPUBLIC SCHOOLS AND PUBLIC POLICY

Church-supported and other nonpublic schools have been an important part of the education system in the United States, both at the elementary-secondary levels and the higher education level. In some towns and rural areas with a population relatively homogeneous in religion, such schools have outshadowed the public schools. They also have constituted a very large enterprise in cities with a high proportion of Catholics. In the Chicago area, for example, enrollment in Catholic elementary schools peaked at 182,262 in the city in 1960 and grew to 127,295 in the suburbs in 1965 (Sanders 1977, 4–5; Walsh 1990c). In 1987 nearly 700,000 students attended Catholic elementary and secondary schools in the five systems operated in Brooklyn, Chicago, Los Angeles, Manhattan, and Philadelphia (National Catholic Education Association 1987).

As shown in Table 12-3, a majority of students in nonpublic elementary and secondary schools are in Catholic schools, and a large majority are in church-related schools. The number of nonpublic students declined by 17 percent between 1966 and 1988. This decrease was accounted for largely by Catholic schools, in which enrollment dropped primarily because of the decline in the size of the youth population, the

movement of population out of central cities, and increased operating costs. The percentages of elementary and secondary students enrolled in Catholic schools ranged from a high of 31 percent in the Mideast region to a low of 7 percent in New England. Enrollment in church-related schools other than Catholic schools generally increased rapidly in the 1970s. Reasons for increasing enrollment in church-related schools frequently involved dissatisfaction with the public schools (including unhappiness with achievement levels, discipline, and perceived lack of teaching of moral values) and/or desegregation of public school districts (Lines 1986). Enrollment in nonpublic elementary and secondary schools represented approximately 12 percent of total public and nonpublic enrollment in 1988, compared with 14 percent in 1964.

In part due to the relatively high socioeconomic status of most students attending prestigious independent private schools and to the withdrawal of many middle-class families from some urban public schools, the average social class of students in nonpublic schools is higher than that of students in public schools. More than

TABLE 12-3 *Enrollment Trends in Nonpublic Elementary and Secondary Schools, 1966 and 1988, by Type of School*

Type of School	Enrollment 1966	Enrollment 1988	Percentage Change
Assembly of God	NA	89,424	NA
Baptist	25,000	335,223	1,230
Calvinist	NA	43,080	NA
Christian	NA	233,094	NA
Episcopal	48,600	85,373	76
Friends (Quakers)	10,600	19,457	84
Jewish	52,600	158,381	201
Lutheran	188,500	247,128	31
Roman Catholic	5,481,300	2,822,585	−49
Seventh Day Adventist	62,600	80,184	28
Other church-related	94,100	299,289	218
Not church-related	341,300	812,879	138
Total nonpublic	6,304,800	5,226,097	−17

Source: National Center for Education Statistics 1981; McMillen and Gerald 1990.
Note: Enrollment in 1966 was not reported separately for Assembly of God, Calvinist, and Christian schools, but instead was included in Other church-related.

30 percent of public-school students were from families with annual income less than $15,000 in 1985, compared with 12 percent of nonpublic-school students. Related data on parents' education also show that in 1982, 94 percent of students whose parents did not have high-school diplomas attended public schools, compared with only 81 percent for students whose parents have four or more years of college (*Statistical Abstract of the United States*, 1987). More recent data (Hafner, Ingels, Schneider, and Stevenson 1990) show that nonpublic schools are disproportionately low in enrollment of students low in socioeconomic status and of African American, Hispanic, and Native American students, compared with public schools (see Table 12-4).

One notable trend in nonpublic schools involves their increasing enrollment of minority students. Although enrollment in Catholic schools declined by more than 40 percent between 1971 and 1987, the number of minority students (black, Hispanic, Asian, American Indian) increased slightly, and the percentage of minority students increased from 11 percent to 22 percent (National Catholic Education Association 1987). Growth in minority enrollment of Catholic schools was largest in the big cities. By 1982, for example, minority students constituted 44 percent of the enrollment in Catholic schools in Chicago (Lanier 1982). Nationally, nearly a quarter of a million black students were enrolled in Catholic schools in 1989 (Walsh 1991). In line with public-nonpublic differences reported here, the families of minority students in nonpublic schools generally are higher in social class than are those of minority students in public schools (Goldberg 1986). This is not surprising inasmuch as nonpublic schools charge tuition—frequently, a substantial amount. On the other hand, many nonpublic schools provide scholarships or have low tuition because they receive church subsidies, pay relatively low salaries, and/or have relatively high pupil-teacher ratios. Thus, they frequently do have a significant enrollment of students from low-income families (Cibulka, O'Brien, and Zewe 1982). Nearly 15 percent of the students in church-related elementary and secondary schools were from families with less than $15,000 income in 1985.

Some observers view the trend toward increased nonpublic enrollment of minority students in big cities as a "new strategy for upward mobility" among parents dissatisfied with low achievement levels and severe discipline problems at many urban schools enrolling high proportions of poverty students (Goldberg 1986; Walsh 1991). As noted above, much of the Catholic school enrollment is in big cities, and students who are black or Hispanic now constitute more than 20 percent of Catholic enrollment. Only about one-third of the black students in Catholic schools are Catholic—an indication that many black students fled the public schools and also that Catholic and other nonpublic schools appear to be providing important educational services for many urban minority students.

TABLE 12-4 *Percentages of Eighth Graders Enrolled in Public Schools, Catholic Schools, and Other Nonpublic Schools, by Race/Ethnicity and Socioeconomic Status**

	Type of School		
	Public	Catholic	Other Nonpublic
All students	88	08	05
*Race/Ethnicity***			
African American	93	06	01
Asian/Pacific Islander	84	09	07
Hispanic	91	08	02
Native American	92	03	05
White	87	08	06
*Socioeconomic status****			
Lowest quartile	96	03	01
Highest quartile	78	11	11

Source: Adapted from Hafner, Ingels, Schneider, and Stevenson, 1990.
*Percentages sometimes do not add to 100 due to rounding.
**African American refers to non-Hispanic black students. White refers to non-Hispanic white students. Native American refers to American Indians and Alaskan Eskimos and Aleuts.
***Socioeconomic status is measured in terms of mother's and father's occupations, mother's and father's educational levels, and family income.

Achievement in Nonpublic Schools

Whether nonpublic schools are more effective than public schools in raising academic achievement and accomplishing other educational goals has become an important issue in the past decade. The debate was spurred particularly by publication of research conducted by James Coleman, Thomas Hoffer, and Sally Kilgore (1981). This research analyzed 1980 data collected from 58,728 students in 1,016 high schools as part of the High School and Beyond study sponsored by the National Center for Education Statistics (also see Coleman 1990a). After comparing data on achievement and other variables for students in public and nonpublic schools, Coleman, Hoffer, and Kilgore reached these conclusions:

1. *Private schools provide better cognitive outcomes than do public schools. . . . When family background factors that predict achievement are controlled, students in both Catholic and other private schools are shown to achieve at a higher level than students in public schools. . . .*
2. *Private schools provide a safer, more disciplined, and more ordered environment than do public schools. . . .*
3. *Private schools encourage interest in higher education and lead more of their students to attend college than do public schools with comparable students. (Coleman, Hoffer, and Kilgore 1981, 224–233)*

Following publication of the major report, Coleman summarized his interpretation of the data on differences between public and nonpublic schools:

The major measured differences . . . [are] in disciplinary climate, in academic demands, and in student behavior. Further, even when the backgrounds of students are statistically controlled, much of these differences remains—differences in homework, in student
attendance and in-school behavior, and differences in the disciplinary climate perceived by students. These differences can reasonably be attributed to differences in school policy rather than student background.

When we examined, wholly within the public sector, the performance of . . . the average public school sophomore, [at schools] with the levels of homework and attendance . . . and disciplinary climate and student behavior attributable to school policy in the Catholic or other private schools, the levels of achievement are approximately the same as those found in the Catholic and other-private sectors. (Coleman, Hoffer, and Kilgore 1981, 19–20)

Because the data analyzed by Coleman, Hoffer, and Kilgore were part of a major government-financed study, they are available for further analysis and reanalysis by other researchers. Several researchers did this and reported results that differ from those of Coleman and his colleagues. In addition, a number of social scientists and educators have challenged conclusions of the study on a variety of technical research grounds and on the basis that it did not fully take account of home background and other differences between public and nonpublic students and schools. For example, Samuel Peng (1982) has analyzed data from the High School and Beyond study and found that controlling for students' ability on entering high school eliminates achievement differences between seniors in public and nonpublic high schools, thus indicating that differences in "input" are responsible for measured achievement differentials.

Similarly, Page and Keith (1981) took account of estimated differences in family background not measured in High School and Beyond and found that this explained the achievement difference between public and nonpublic students. Willms (1982) reanalyzed data from High School and Beyond and reported that when one takes account of family background, there is no difference in achievement of public and nonpublic students in "academic courses of study," though there is a small difference between those in the general track. Goldberger and Cain (1982) carefully reexamined the data and methods used by Coleman, Hoffer, and Kilgore and concluded that there is "no basis for accepting their conclusions and no merit in their analysis" (p. 121). Keith and Page (1985) reanalyzed the data further and concluded that after accounting for background differences, black and Hispanic students have achievement scores little if any higher in Catholic schools than in public schools. Raudenbush and Bryk (1986) reported that although students low in socioeconomic status who attend Catholic schools have achievement somewhat higher than those in public schools, for high-status students the pattern is reversed. A later study by Driscoll (1990) found that nonpublic high schools are more communal (i.e., staff and students share a commitment to the ideal of community and to one another) than public schools and that communal schools rank higher than noncommunal schools on achievement, morale, and other outcomes; most of the difference in favor of the nonpublic schools is associated with their smaller size, however.

Thus critics of the research reported by Coleman and his colleagues generally have concluded that unmeasured home background variables involving greater motivation and home support are higher among nonpublic students whose parents are willing to pay tuition than among public school students of the same social class and income level. They believe that these and other noninstructional differences account for most or all of the achievement differences between public and nonpublic schools (Witte 1990). Finally, they conclude that the reason nonpublic schools are more orderly and disciplined is that they do not have to accept disorderly or difficult students, and that other research, such as a study by the National Assessment of Educational Progress (1981), indicates little or no difference in achievement between public and nonpublic students after taking account of background differences (Lemann 1991a).

However, Coleman and his colleagues as well as other researchers also have carried out additional analyses that they believe confirm and extend some of the original conclusions. For example, Coleman and Hoffer (1987), Lee and Bryk (1988), Chubb and Moe (1990), Coleman (1990a), and Marsh and Grayson (1990) have reported that nonpublic schools enhance achievement by placing a higher proportion of students in academic tracks than do public schools; and Bryk, Holland, Lee, and Carriedo (1984) as well as Chubb and Moe (1990) found that students in nonpublic schools had higher achievement associated with such factors as positive discipline, greater emphasis on academics, and less separate grouping of students low in socioeconomic and/or minority status. The latter variable in turn is related to the smaller concentration of poor and minority students in Catholic and other nonpublic schools than in public schools. In addition, Coleman and Hoffer (1987) analyzed data on the performance of High School and Beyond (HSB) students after 1980 and concluded that Catholic schools produce greater achievement gains and lower dropout rates among low-income, black, and Hispanic students than do other nonpublic schools or public schools. However, these analyses and conclusions also are being severely criticized by other researchers who believe they are methodologically and logically inadequate for reasons similar to those raised with respect to the earlier studies (e.g., Rothman 1990d; Thernstrom 1990; Glass and Matthews 1991; Lemann 1991a; Rosenberg 1991).

One major reason so much difference of opinion exists concerning achievement differentials between nonpublic and public schools is that it is so difficult to determine whether family and home environment differences in student's background, social-class mixture in student bodies, and other input factors have been adequately identified, measured, and statistically taken account of in assessing school outcomes. The research provides strong evidence that orderly school environment, homework, emphasis on college prep courses, internal tracking, and other related school variables are associated with differences in student performance, but these variables are themselves related to student background and social-class mixture variables that may not have been adequately accounted for in a given data set (Lemann 1991a). In addition, the small magnitude of the average achievement gains registered by students in either public or nonpublic schools makes it difficult to identify effects associated with schools or sectors (i.e., public/nonpublic) or to attach much importance to such effects when they are detected (Haertel 1985; Lemann 1991a). Thus, researchers probably will continue to argue over the relative effectiveness of public and nonpublic schools.

If nonpublic schools really are more successful than public schools in promoting high achievement among comparable students and student bodies, one important reason may be that they tend to function with more independence and less bureaucracy than do many public schools. This latter generalization has received support from research by John Chubb and Terry Moe (1985, 1990) of the Brookings Institution. Based on data from the National Administrator—Teacher Survey, which collected follow-up data and expanded on the High School and Beyond Study, Chubb and Moe found that "public schools, relative to private, live in environments that are complex, demanding, powerful, constraining, and uncooperative. As a result, their policies, procedures, and personnel are more likely to be imposed from the outside" (1985, 41).

In particular, as reported by Chubb and Moe, principals of public schools are much more constrained than are nonpublic principals in hiring and firing teachers. In addition, constraints on public-school principals result in their providing "less instructional leadership for teachers and less clear signals about school objectives," as well as less opportunity for teachers to work collegially and exert influence over their own work (1985, 42). These latter characteristics, Chubb and Moe point out, have been associated with

effectiveness of instruction in research on successful schools.

However, in subsequent writings based on their analysis of HSB data, Chubb and Moe (1986, 1990) also recognized that organizational and bureaucratic problems that impede the effective functioning of public schools cannot be solved simply by demanding or somehow requiring these schools to operate more like nonpublic schools. Their concluding comments in this regard include the following remarks:

> *Those who exercise public authority . . . [confront] strident demands from all sides to "do something" concrete . . . [and] to create new administrative rules and monitoring requirements . . . [intended to] ensure that schools behave in ways consistent with programmatic and budgetary intentions. This is especially true when state and federal governments are drawn into problem-solving . . . [and when schools are so problem-ridden that decision makers fear they] cannot be relied on or entrusted with substantial discretion. Why set them loose to fail again? (Chubb and Moe 1990, 63–64)*

> *The public schools . . . are subordinates in a hierarchic system . . . in which myriad interests and actors use the rules, structure, and processes of democracy to impose their preferences on the local school. It is no accident that public schools are lacking in autonomy, that principals have difficulty leading, and that school goals are heterogeneous, unclear, and undemanding . . . [nor that] weak principals are tenured. . . . [This organizational syndrome is] deeply anchored in democratic control as we have come to know it. . . .*

> *If this is essentially correct, the standard proposals for reforming public schools are misconceived. It is easy to say, for instance, that schools should have greater autonomy or that principals should be stronger leaders, but these sorts of reforms cannot simply be imposed. . . . A maverick principal who comes on as a strong leader . . . would quickly tend*

*to get into hot water with political and bu-
reaucratic superiors, teachers, and unions.
(Chubb and Moe 1986, 43–46)*

From one point of view, the question of whether minority students in nonpublic schools have better achievement than those in public schools is analogous to issues involving the establishment of public magnet schools. Magnet schools frequently have been viewed (see Chapter 9) as a means to retain middle-class nonminority and minority students in big-city school districts with high concentrations of poverty students and to provide opportunity for upwardly mobile working-class students who do not want to attend poverty schools. As Denis Doyle has pointed out, private schools in big cities also have provided an "escape" from the problems perceived to be prevalent in big-city districts: "The issue . . . is educational quality, for it is precisely 'good' [private] schools that enroll those students that the 'bad' [public] schools 'push' into the market. . . . It appears that in the 1980s, at least, private schools are increasingly being viewed as the good alternative, and urban public schools as schools of last resort" (Doyle 1982, 17).

In part, the argument that private schools, like public magnet schools, provide an important alternative for middle-class and upwardly mobile working-class students depends on the assertion that they have a more productive and effective educational environment than do the public schools. As we have seen with respect to studies cited above on private and public high schools, private schools do seem to provide a more conducive environment for learning than do public schools, but there is no agreement that this advantage is due to superior educational policies and practices rather than to greater selectivity. The same point can be made comparing magnet and nonmagnet public schools. Just as research on a nonpublic elementary school enrolling high-achieving poverty students indicated that these students had much higher home environment scores than did low-achieving poverty students at a nearby public school after taking account of

social class (Levine 1972), so research on poverty students in an elementary magnet school indicated that they have higher home environment scores than do poverty students of similar social class who elected to remain in their neighborhood schools (Levine, Eubanks, and Roskoski 1980). Such research supports the conclusion that it is extremely difficult to disentangle "selectivity" effects from "school quality" effects in trying to determine whether private schools are more effective than public schools.

Tuition Tax Credits

The debate over the relative effectiveness of public and nonpublic schools has taken place in a larger social context in which political leaders have considered providing tuition tax credits for the parents of students in nonpublic schools. A tax credit allows for a reduction in taxes according to the percent of tuition deductible for federal income tax. In 1982, President Reagan proposed that families earning less than $50,000 per year be allowed a tax reduction equal to 50 percent of nonpublic school tuition, with a maximum limit of $100 per nonpublic student in 1983, $300 in 1984, and $500 in 1985 and thereafter.

Public policy debates concerning tuition tax credits for nonpublic students have been vigorous and emotional. Opponents have argued that such credits would provide unconstitutional support for church-related schools, would undermine the public school system by supporting and encouraging the movement of students to nonpublic schools, would result in a large drain on the U.S. Treasury, would reduce the likelihood of obtaining voter support for public-school tax increases, and/or would contribute to additional racial and socioeconomic segregation and isolation of low-status students in the public schools.

Debate over provision of tax credits and other forms of aid for nonpublic schools also is concerned with policies and practices at the state level. Only two states (Louisiana and Minnesota) currently provide general tax benefits to assist students in nonpublic schools, but many states do provide other assistance in the form of transportation and/or loans or grants to help nonpublic schools provide instructional materials and testing or counseling.

Supporters of tuition tax credits argue that such credits are not unconstitutional (e.g., McGarry 1982) and would not severely reduce federal revenues or hamper public-school tax levy efforts. Often pointing to the research of Coleman and his colleagues (above), they also argue that tax credits would provide wider opportunities for disadvantaged students and would not contribute to and might even reduce racial and socioeconomic isolation. In addition, many supporters believe that tax credits not only would provide parents with a choice in selecting schools but also would stimulate reform efforts in the public schools. This latter point of view has been articulated by Robert Hawkins, Jr., as follows:

> *President Reagan's support for tuition tax credits has again raised the issue of educational reform. The outcry from the education establishment has been both intense and predictable: tuition tax credits will destroy public education and aid the rich. . . . The very notion that tuition tax credits can destroy public education says something about the state of public education. Cynics might well say that public education is doing an adequate job of destroying itself, needing no help from tax credits. . . . Increasing numbers of parents are choosing, at great cost to themselves, to send their children to private schools. These two factors demonstrate how important education is to parents and that they will withhold support from public education until they begin to receive the type of education they want from their public schools. (Hawkins 1982, 9–10)*

As we point out in the preceding section, research does not allow for a confident conclusion regarding the question of whether nonpublic school students have higher achievement than do public school students with the same family and home background. Therefore, it is difficult to predict achievement or other output effects of a tax credit that might shift some or many students from public to nonpublic schools. Similarly, researchers disagree on whether tax credits would increase or decrease racial and socioeconomic isolation in the public schools, and the effects of a tax credit with respect to segregation certainly would depend on the policies (if any) instituted to guard against negative outcomes. For example, a policy requiring that transportation be provided free along with a tax credit would enhance the likelihood that poverty parents would send their children outside the inner city to mixed-class schools, as would policies stipulating that poverty families that paid no taxes would receive the tax credit as an income payment.

Lacking agreement concerning the validity of available data, proponents and opponents will continue to cite findings and conclusions favorable to their own position. Meanwhile, research can help identify some of the probable effects of tax credits and their implications for the educational system. For example, David Longanecker (1982) has calculated that given current enrollment, a maximum credit of $250 per student would reduce federal tax revenues by about 1 billion dollars per year in 1982 dollars. Data collected by the Council of Great City Schools indicate that President Reagan's proposal would have increased federal aid per nonpublic school student from $43 in 1980–81 to $329 in 1984–85, at the same time that aid per public school student would have declined from $206 to $105. On the other hand, any associated movement of students from public to nonpublic schools could increase the amount of local and state revenue available per student in the public schools. Needless to say, we believe that additional research is necessary to help policy makers struggling with the larger issue of public support for students who attend nonpublic schools. We return to the topic of tax credits in the larger context of national movements to increase choice and improve instruction described in the following chapter on reform of U.S. schools.

Education Vouchers

Another way by which nonpublic schools may receive public financial support is through the use of *education vouchers*, a device that has been much discussed and debated since about 1968. This idea grew in part out of the movement for *alternative schools*, which had developed vigorously in the big cities. With much dissatisfaction over the existing school system, it was natural to ask for experimentation with new schools, and this might be better done by people outside the present school system than by those who have adjusted and perhaps are tied to the usual procedures (Raywid 1987, 1990, 1991; Hume 1988).

One obvious way to promote experimentation and new methods is to support with public funds an array of new schools developed by innovators. This led to the voucher idea. Basically, this idea is that parents and students are best judges of the kind of education they need, and that public funds should be entrusted to them, to use in an open market where they have a choice among schools. This should provide better education than the present system, which gives the educational bureaucracy a monopoly. Much of the argument in favor of systematically expanding choice throughout the educational system has been summarized by Peter Flanigan, who contrasted relatively successful parochial schools with problem-ridden public schools in one big city as follows:

Among the most fundamental explanations of the achievement of the Archdiocese system is that it is based on educational choice. The principal has chosen to be at his or her school, and has chosen the school's educational program and faculty. Each teacher has chosen to work at that particular school. Each student has chosen to study there. Everyone involved in the enterprise has "bought into" it, has become involved by choice. In the zoned inner-city school, the principal is assigned to the school, the curriculum is determined in detail by the central bureaucracy, the teachers

are assigned and finally the students are required by law to attend. Nobody has "bought into" such a school—nobody has made a choice. Every aspect of the school is dictated from above. . . . [The public system] is like the Soviet economy, where everything is also dictated from above, and both are failures. (Flanigan 1991, A12)

The voucher method would give a family a voucher for each school-age child, which is worth a certain amount of money—approximately the amount that is spent on the average pupil in the public schools. The family then shops around among schools that meet certain criteria and assigns the voucher to the school of their choice. The school is supported by the vouchers it collects, plus any other money it can obtain from private sources. Parents could send their children to the local public school by giving their vouchers to that school, but the public schools would have to compete in the market with a variety of nonpublic schools as well as with other public schools.

This idea aroused active support and active opposition from people with a wide variety of attitudes toward education. Vouchers were approved by very conservative people, and also by very radical people, because the scheme could presumably free them to find or create the kind of education they most desired.

The federal Office of Economic Opportunity, in its role as supporter of educational experiments designed to reduce poverty and to increase educational opportunity, made several grants of money to support tryouts of the voucher idea in the 1970s. Also, the OEO supported an analysis by Professor Christopher Jencks of Harvard University of the pros and cons of the voucher concept. This analysis explored seven possible voucher plans, or sets of ground rules for distributing money to voucher schools. Jencks points out the probable advantages and disadvantages of each plan. The simplest plan, advocated by free-market conservatives, would provide every child with a flat grant, which his or her family could use to pay tuition at the school of its choice. The school could select pupils freely among applicants and therefore could reject applicants because of low IQ, behavior problems, ethnicity, or other criteria.

The OEO made grants for feasibility studies of vouchers to school systems in Seattle, Gary (Indiana), San Francisco, and San Jose (California). The only study that concluded that the plan was feasible was the San Jose study. An elementary school district (Alum Rock) in that metropolitan area concluded that a plan limited to public schools was worth trying. Accordingly, the OEO made a grant to fund the Alum Rock voucher program for two years (1972–1974). This experiment was limited to public schools in the Alum Rock School District. Parents chose between twenty-one competing school programs, not schools. They allocated their vouchers (equal to the average per-pupil expenditure in the district, plus a supplement of one-third for children who are eligible for school lunch programs and who come from low-income families). Several schools offered three or four different programs, giving some choice to parents who prefer the local neighborhood school. Children were bused (at OEO expense) to any other school with a program they wanted. Names of some of the school programs were Cultural Arts, Multicultural (bilingual), Math-Science, Open-Activity Centered, Individual Learning, Continuous Progress Nongraded, Three R's Plus, Basic Skills, and School 2000. The voucher program was made available to 4,000 pupils, and some 40 percent chose nontraditional programs for the 1972–73 school year.

The OEO also provided substantial funding to evaluate the results of the Alum Rock experiment. Cohen and Farrar (1977) and Levinson (1975, 1990) have reviewed the data on the voucher experiment at Alum Rock and reached the conclusion that as an effort to reform a school system, the voucher demonstration left much to be desired. Relatively few parents took advantage of the opportunity to select an innovative school for their children, and students' academic performance did not improve. On the other hand, Cohen and Farrar also point out that "Alum Rock increased professionals' ability to choose and design their work settings, and made it possible for parents to select among alternatives. If choice and diversity are good, then schools in Alum Rock were better places" (1977, 96–97).

The Alum Rock demonstration constituted only one small test of one version of the voucher approach in one small school district. After the Office of Economic Opportunity was abolished by President Richard Nixon, the voucher approach received relatively little attention until a movement arose to introduce vouchers in California. Led by Professors John Coons and Stephen Sugarman, the California movement attempted to collect sufficient voter signatures and approval to introduce vouchers on a statewide basis.

Education by Choice: The Case for Family Control, by Coons and Sugarman (1978), analyzed many of the issues and possibilities regarding the delivery of vouchers to parents for their children's education and resulted in the preparation of a specific plan that would have established two new types of schools in California: "New Private Schools," which would be eligible for government vouchers, and "New Public Schools," which school districts, higher education institutions, or other public agencies could establish or designate to receive vouchers. As long as the New Schools met state requirements for hiring, employment, admissions policies, curriculum, and facilities and reserved at least 25 percent of their places for enrollment of low-income students on a nondiscriminatory basis, they would be eligible to redeem government vouchers.

Although California efforts to introduce vouchers failed in 1981 and 1982, the topic has received increasing attention in the 1980s and 1990s (see the following chapter). The arguments put forth by Coons and Sugarman and their supporters address several fundamental issues involving the relationships between families, schools, and other government and nongovernmental agencies, and the issues involved cannot be expected to disappear from public debate

(Nathan 1985, 1990). Coons and Sugarman called attention to some of these issues:

> *Family choice for the nonrich could lead to an end to the American double standard. Among those who can afford private school, society leaves the goals and means of education to the family; for the rest of society, the informing principles are politically determined and implemented through compulsory assignments to a particular public school. . . . [If society moves] in a variety of ways toward freedom and responsibility for the family, the present world of schools will increasingly appear an anachronism. . . . The significance of the current political favor for the family is that it provides a respite—a breathing space in history—during which arguments about the family as a responsible political unit can expect a serious hearing for the first time in a century. (1978, 2-3, 200-203)*

Voucher possibilities were raised again in 1985 when U.S. Secretary of Education William Bennett helped prepare legislation that would have provided parents of children served by Chapter 1 with vouchers equal to the amount spent on disadvantaged Chapter 1 students in their local public-school district. The proposed legislation generated some support but also widespread and vocal opposition and criticism. The Council of Chief State School Officers, for example, voted unanimously to oppose it, and the president of the American Association of School Administrators stated, "this proposal is just another way to give public money to private schools" (Stimson 1986, 26). Other major reasons for opposition included complaints that the legislation would not ensure that private schools receiving vouchers used these funds to provide special help for disadvantaged students, would constitute an administrative burden for public schools, and would tend to drain relatively well motivated students from the public schools (Stimson 1986; Bastian 1986). Secretary Bennett subsequently abandoned the proposed legisla-

tion in November 1986, stating that the administration would seek to pursue expanded choice in education through other means. President George Bush offered a somewhat similar 1991 proposal to allow federal funds to follow students who transfer to or enroll in nonpublic schools.

Privatization and Contracting Out

Many services (e.g., policing, airport management, trash removal, railroads) that traditionally or previously have been provided by public agencies are sometimes being contracted out or sold to businesses and other nonpublic institutions. Similarly, some analysts believe that services now performed by public schools could be provided more effectively and efficiently if contracted out or shifted to private agencies (Spicer and Hill 1990). Usually referred to as *privatization*, possibilities of this kind have been examined in great detail by Myron Lieberman (1989). After considering a variety of potential advantages and disadvantages of movement toward the privatization of public-school services, Lieberman concluded that school officials should explore possibilities for contracting out some instructional and other services to nonpublic agencies. Major potential advantages cited by Lieberman include reduction in inflexibility associated with union contracts, possibilities for initiating reforms less dependent on slow changes in state law, minimization of bureaucracy, and opportunities to reduce costs through competition. Lieberman also concluded that previous contracting out and voucher experiments, such as the Alum Rock demonstration, did not provide a good test of possibilities for improvement through privatization.

The first important educational privatization experiment of the 1990s was initiated in the Dade County (FL) schools. Operation of a 550-student elementary school was contracted to Education Alternatives, Inc. (Pipho 1991). Beginning in 1991, the company will work for five years to demonstrate that it can "produce quantifiable improvement in academic performance regardless of the students' educational or economic background" (Holmes 1990, A16). Similar possibilities are being pursued in a number of other school districts (Conlin 1991).

Home Schooling

During the past two decades, there has been a significant increase in home schooling, that is, in the number of students who do not attend schools but instead receive most or all of their education at home (Knowles, Marlow, and Muchmore 1992). Although estimates vary widely concerning the number of students who are educated primarily at home during any given year, several informed and careful observers place this number between 200,000 and 300,000 (Lines 1986, 1987, 1990; Kohn 1989; Lamb 1990). Recent analysis and research support the following conclusions regarding characteristics and effects of home schooling in the United States:

- Although both liberal parents who believe that schools are too authoritarian and conservative parents who are dissatisfied with a perceived lack of moral values in public education are represented among home schoolers, the latter group accounts for much of the growth and enrollment in home schooling. In particular, home schooling has grown rapidly among families that adhere to fundamentalist religious positions (e.g., literal interpretation of the bible) and that utilize religiously oriented material from large Christian publishing houses (Arras 1988; Kohn 1989; Ray 1989a, 1991; Mayberry 1990).

- Although home schooling is nowhere illegal, state governments generally have imposed various requirements dealing with such matters as minimal time for instruction in basic subjects, recordkeeping, administration of standardized tests, and inspection of facilities. Since 1982, however, more than thirty states have reduced or removed some of their constraints on home schooling (Woltman 1989; Zirkel 1991).

- The average parent who home schools is slightly higher in income and education level than is true for the U.S. population as a whole (Ray 1989a; Guterson 1990).

- In line with their relatively high socioeconomic status, home-schooling students have relatively high average scores on standardized tests of academic achievement (Ray 1989a, 1989b, 1991; Knowles, Marlow, and Muchmore 1992).

- Although critics and skeptics worry that home-schooled students may suffer from reduced opportunities for social interaction with peers and for affective development, the limited research available on this issue indicates that they do not generally have low scores on measures of self-concept, leadership, or other aspects of personal development (Ray 1989b, 1991; Knowles, Marlow, and Muchmore 1992).

- Many students schooled at home are withdrawn from public or nonpublic schools for only one or two years (Kohn 1989; Ray 1989a).

- The typical family engaged in home schooling draws on various resources, such as local libraries, churches, other home schoolers, and organizations that provide special materials (Lines 1990).

The increase of home schooling raises significant policy issues involving the structure, goals, and provision of education in the United States. On the one hand education has become increasingly important for personal success and national development, thus leading critics to question whether parents have a right to place their children in environments that may leave them poorly educated or miseducated. For this reason, the National Education Association has advocated rules requiring that adults who school at home demonstrate their teaching competence and submit to extensive and regular scrutiny, and the National Association of Elementary School Principals has fundamentally opposed home schooling (Kohn 1989).

On the other hand, advocates of home schooling and others supportive of its goals and practices, emphasize parental rights to control their children's education and, particularly, to protect them from perceived immoral or otherwise damaging influences in modern society (Ray

1989a; Provenzo 1990). According to this view, whether home-school parents are fundamentalist Christians, so-called New Age young adults, Mormons, or any of numerous other religious and philosophical subgroups, they exemplify a commendable determination to guide their daughters and sons through the many obstacles that impede positive development of children and youth (Mayberry 1990). Thus, one informed observer has speculated that one motivation of home schoolers is to re-establish or maintain the kind of positive adult influence that seems to have been present in many villages and small urban neighborhoods in earlier periods of U.S. history (Doll 1987). In addition, after noting that Mark Twain did not attend school and quoting Twain's advice to "never let your schooling get in the way of your education," Guterson (1990) has pointed out that home schooling may give some children and youth excellent opportunities to develop independent learning skills and to pursue their studies in greater depth than might be possible in most schools.

Perspectives on the Role of Public and Nonpublic Schools

As noted in the preceding sections, advocates of financial assistance and other forms of support for nonpublic schools argue that such encouragement is desirable in order to enhance diversity in the educational system and expand choice for parents and students, to provide improved opportunities for economically disadvantaged students and minority students who attend ineffective public schools, and to enable nonpublic schools to continue offering an alternative for parents who believe that public schools do not place sufficient stress on religious or moral values.

Among the concerns most frequently expressed by opponents of assistance to nonpublic schools are the worries that such assistance would reduce enrollment and support for public schools and that social goals they believe have been historically well served by the public schools thereby would suffer serious erosion (Raywid 1987, 1990, 1991). Many opponents also believe

that growth of the nonpublic system will magnify negative trends toward increasingly greater concentration of disadvantaged students in the public schools. This latter point of view has been articulated by federal Judge Thomas Wiseman:

> *Why should we be concerned about erosion of support for the public schools? Why should it bother us if there appears to be a trend toward a sharp division of society, in which the children of the affluent attend private schools and the public school system exists for the poor and black? . . . The answer to these questions lies in the recognition—the realization that public education has been the leavening agent by which our multi-ethnic, multi-racial society has been able to rise and become a whole loaf.*
>
> *It is* because *we had public schools, which most children attended, that we were able to assimilate so rapidly the great influx of immigrants. . . .*
>
> *It is largely* because *we had public schools, in which children from the most diverse of backgrounds learned to live and work together at an early age, that we have been able to maintain social harmony in such a heterogeneous conglomerate of people. (quoted in Price and Woodard 1985, 251)*

The conclusions one reaches concerning government assistance to nonpublic schools in the United States should be informed at least in part by analysis of the potential and probable positive and negative impacts on the public as well as the nonpublic system. The functions performed historically and currently by the public schools and possibilities for attaining them through nonpublic schools also should be considered. One useful example of an attempt to initiate this type of analysis has been provided by Charles Kniker (1985). He maintains that the public or "common" system of education traditionally was "expected" to serve five major goals:

1. Training in common citizenship.
2. Transmitting of a common set of values.

3. Promoting unity through common experiences for students of diverse background.
4. Providing common opportunities for students with differing social and economic backgrounds.
5. Developing widely accepted views of reforms to solve social problems.

After extensive discussion of changes that have occurred in schools and society, Kniker concluded that nonpublic schools now serve or can serve the functions involving common citizenship, values, and viewpoints regarding reform as well as the public schools do, but that the public schools are better situated to provide common experiences for building "unity from diversity" and for providing "common opportunities" to the disadvantaged. He concluded his essay with these comments:

> The term "common school" has a proud history and . . . intent which is still valid. . . . We are more than individuals. Each of us is a member of many publics. Sooner or later, we must learn how to communicate with those publics as we face intimate personal problems and urgent social concerns. Self-contained educational systems, whether they are religious, economic, racial, geographical, forfeit that necessary function of the "common" school.
>
> A special word needs to be said to readers who are professional educators in the public sector. . . . The openness of the public schools is one test of whether it is truly a "common" school. If your needs must be met at the expense of the students, if you ignore valid criticisms from patrons, if you blame others for all your problems, then society can legitimately ask others to become our next common school. (Kniker 1985, 198)

As regards the extent to which nonpublic schools are in a position to help provide common educational experiences for a diverse student body, data cited earlier in this chapter indicate that Catholic schools frequently have enrollment that is diverse racially and even socioeconomically, but that most other nonpublic schools do not appear to be nearly as diverse as the Catholic system. Of course it also is true that tax credits, vouchers, and other forms of assistance might help nonpublic schools attract many more minority students and severely disadvantaged students, provided they are not excluded by admissions criteria and other obstacles to enrollment. Many advocates of assistance to nonpublic schools would like to encourage such diversity through legislative guidelines for participation in an aid program.

Catholic and other nonpublic schools also might play a larger role than they do now in providing improved education for disadvantaged students if they received substantial financial assistance to facilitate such an effort. Our summary of research on achievement in public and nonpublic schools indicated that many nonpublic schools already are providing excellent opportunities for disadvantaged students, even though their capacity for doing so appears to be linked to or dependent on selection of students relatively high in motivation and home environment. On the other hand, governmental or other enhancement of the nonpublic system might harm the public schools by facilitating further withdrawal of middle-class and upward-mobile students, thus also reinforcing and increasing the problems associated with concentrated poverty in urban school districts.

It also should be noted that one's conclusions regarding the important issues involved in public policy toward nonpublic schools might be determined largely in accordance with interpretations regarding research on their differential characteristics and effectiveness. For example, if it is true that nonpublic schools are more successful and that the reasons for this success primarily involve more effective policies and practices (as argued by Coleman, Hoffer, and Kilgore 1981) and/or greater autonomy and independence (Chubb and Moe 1986), then the responses that seem desirable might include financial assistance for nonpublic schools and efforts to reduce unproductive organizational arrangements in public schools. If, on the other hand, nonpublic schools either are not more effective or are more effective primarily due to advantages in selecting students, then an analyst would be relatively more inclined to oppose public aid for nonpublic schools and to view such aid as potentially harmful to the public system.

EXERCISES

1. Are minority students significantly enrolled in nonpublic schools in your community? What is their social class background? Is there reason to believe they are learning more than they might in the public schools?

2. Visit a church-affiliated elementary or secondary school in your community and prepare a class report describing how its approach to education reflects its religious orientation.

3. To what extent do proposals for education vouchers and tuition tax credits reflect political and economic philosophies and positions? What political goals may influence the arguments of supporters and opponents?

4. After reading Wayne Fuller's book on *The Old Country School*, outline the advantages and disadvantages of the movement that consolidated rural school districts.

5. Discuss computer use in schools with teachers or administrators from a local school district. Do they believe it is helping to improve student achievement? How much are computers used in educating disadvantaged students?

SUGGESTIONS FOR FURTHER READING

1. The voucher concept and its educational applications are described and analyzed in a book by Mecklenburger and Hostrup entitled *Education Vouchers: From Theory to Alum Rock*. A useful history and analysis of the voucher movement is available in a 1977 article by David K. Cohen and Eleanor Farrar in *The Public Interest.*

2. The fascinating history of the Chicago Catholic schools is told in James W. Sander's *The Education of an Urban Minority: Catholics in Chicago, 1833–1965.*

3. *Religious Schooling in America*, edited by James C. Carper and Thomas C. Hunt, includes chapters on Catholic, Lutheran, Calvinist, Seventh-Day Adventist, and Christian as well as Jewish Day Schools.

4. As indicated in its subtitle, *The Old Country School* by Wayne Fuller tells "The Story of Rural Education in the Middle West." Traditional rural education also is described in several sections of *Main Street on the Middle Border* by Lewis Atherton.

5. *God's Choice*, by Alan Peshkin, is a case study of a fundamentalist Christian school.

6. *Privatization and Educational Choice* (1989) by Myron Lieberman provides a comprehensive analysis of possibilities for contracting educational services and functions out to nonschool organizations, vouchers for elementary and secondary students, and various kinds of choice plans and arrangements.

7. A variety of intervention efforts and programs to improve instruction for female and minority students in computer science, math, and science are described in a national survey conducted by Clewell, Thorpe, and Anderson.

8. A nontechnical discussion and analysis of technical problems in the work of Chubb and Moe and other researchers who report achievement differentials between public and nonpublic schools is provided in a 1991 essay by Nicholas Lemann.

School Reform and Effectiveness

The conclusion of Chapter 2 points out that education in our postindustrial, metropolitan society is in a state of crisis related to the deepening problems posed by international economic competition, introduction of high technology as a fundamental consideration in social and economic development, and inadequate functioning of the educational system for a large proportion of students, particularly minority students in concentrated poverty neighborhoods. Economists at the U.S. Bureau of Labor Statistics estimate that minority students will constitute about one-third of new entrants in the labor force in the 1990s. A significant proportion of these students do not possess adequate skills to succeed on the job or to progress beyond initial low-level jobs. Many of the white youth entering the labor force also perform poorly with respect to reasoning, problem-solving, and other higher-order skills. One result is that two-thirds of personnel officers report trouble finding workers with satisfactory technical skills (Boo 1991). To build a labor force prepared to function well in tomorrow's world, opportunities and outcomes in the educational system will have to substantially improved.

The emergence of this crisis has not gone unnoticed or unremarked. As we describe later in this chapter, the general challenge to improve the effectiveness of education has had center-stage recognition since 1983, when a series of national reports focused public attention on indicators of low academic achievement, substantial adult illiteracy, significant high school dropout rates, and other problems involving education. Subsequent developments have continued to re-

flect and generate both serious concern at all levels of government and a variety of efforts to bring about reform of the educational system, particularly through action at the state level.

By the latter part of the 1980s, the sense of urgency being expressed about the crisis in U.S. schools and society had reached an unprecedented level. In 1987, for example, Arkansas Governor William Clinton told members of the American Association of Colleges of Teachers Education, "We don't have as much time as people think" to reform the schools. Without fundamental reform, he proceeded to point out, there will be a constantly widening gulf between the highly educated, well-paid segment of the work force and those who have not received an adequate education (Education Daily 1987, 4). Little had changed three years later, when Clinton observed that "We are miserably failing the half of our high school students who will not go on to college" (quoted in Broder 1990). Similarly, a 1991 report to the U.S. Labor Department concluded that half of the youth population is not acquiring the skills required to earn a decent living or to keep the United States economically competitive (Commission on Achieving Necessary Skills 1991).

Participation of business and civic leaders in calling for and supporting educational reform also has reached an unprecedented level, particularly as regards the challenge of improving the performance of students disadvantaged by economic status and/or minority background. Thus, in 1987 business leaders appeared for the first time before congressional committees considering reauthorization and expansion of Chapter 1 and other federal programs to assist low-achieving students. Also, a group of corporate-leaders representing the American Can Company, the Aluminum Company of America, the State Street Bank and Trust Company, AT&T, and the Pacific Telesis Group provided this testimony:

> Our collective appearance here today is intended to underscore the importance we attach to national efforts to provide educational opportunities for disadvantaged and low-income children and our specific support for the renewal of the Chapter 1 program of federal education aid for disadvantaged and low-income children.

One of the best examples of growing national recognition of the need for massive efforts to improve education for disadvantaged students has been provided by the Forum of Educational Organization Leaders (FEOL). Bringing together the leaders of eleven major national organizations dealing with various aspects of education, the FEOL issued a statement that included the following observations:

> As we have carried forward our grand experiment in universal free public education, we have largely fashioned a system that has served well those who are white, middle to upper income, well motivated, and from relatively stable families. As students have deviated more and more from that norm, the system has served them less and less well. We sometimes seem to say to them, "We've provided the system. It's not our fault if you don't succeed." Whether that attitude is right or wrong, the critical mass of at-risk children and youth has grown so large proportionately that we are in some danger of being toppled by our sense of rightness and righteousness. Instead of blaming the students for not fitting the system, we must design and implement a structure that provides appropriate educational services to those most at risk. . . .
>   To accomplish those objectives will require: changes in federal, state, and local educa-
> tional policies; curriculum modifications; alterations in the time and place where education occurs; different relationships between the schools and a host of other institutions and agencies in the community; strengthening of parent/school relationships; more extensive and different pupil services; more measureable accountability for student learning; greater fiscal resources; and changes in the expectations of education throughout the schooling hierarchy. (Forum of Educational Organization Leaders 1987)

ACHIEVEMENT LEVELS AND TRENDS IN ELEMENTARY AND SECONDARY SCHOOLS

Much of the available data on achievement levels and patterns in U.S. elementary and secondary schools has been collected through National Assessment of Education Progress (NAEP) tests administered periodically since the early 1970s. Recent NAEP reports have provided the basis for identifying and assessing long-range patterns and problems involving students' achievement levels. Table 13-1 summarizes data drawn from several NAEP reports. Some major conclusions that can be drawn from these and related data sets are described here.

1. Average performance levels have been mostly stable for the past two decades. Despite nationwide school reform efforts in the 1980s (see subsequent sections of this chapter), changes from one testing to the next have been small and not consistently positive. For example, mathematics scores of nine-year-olds improved by only three points from 1973 to 1986, reading scores of thirteen-year-olds improved by only three points from 1971 to 1988, and science scores of all three age groups tested by NAEP declined from 1970 to 1986. Only in the case of reading scores among nine- and seventeen-year-olds did performance increase by as much as five points.

Although problems involving sampling of students, equating and scaling of items and performance levels from one test to another,

TABLE 13-1 *Average Proficiency Scores of Nine-, Thirteen-, and Seventeen-Year-Olds on National Assessment of Educational Progress (NAEP) Reading, Mathematics, Science, Civics, and Writing Exams, 1970 to 1989 **

Age Group**	Reading			Mathematics			Science			Civics	Writing	
	1971	1980	1988	1973	1978	1986	1970	1977	1986	1988	1984	1988
Nine	207	215	212	219	219	222	225	220	224	214	171	173
Thirteen	255	259	258	266	264	269	255	247	251	260	212	208
Seventeen	285	286	290	304	300	302	305	290	289	296	223	221

Source: Adapted from Mullis and Jenkins 1988; Applebee 1990; Applebee, Langer, Mullis, and Jenkins 1990; Mullis and Jenkins 1990; and Mullis, Owen, and Phillips 1990.

*Reading proficiency levels represent the following: 150—can carry out simple, discrete reading tasks; 200—can comprehend specific or sequentially related information; 250—can search for information, interrelate ideas, and generalize; 300—can find, understand, summarize, and explain relatively complicated information; 350—can synthesize and learn from specialized reading materials.

Mathematics proficiency levels represent the following: 150—knows some basic addition and subtraction facts; 200—can add and subtract two-digit numbers; 250—can add, subtract, multiply, and divide using whole numbers; 300—can compute with decimals, fractions, and percents, recognize geometric figures, and solve simple equations; 350—can solve multistep problems and use basic algebra.

Science proficiency levels represent the following: 150—knows everyday science facts; 200—understands some basic principles; 250—understands basic life and physical sciences information; 300—has some detailed scientific knowledge; 350—can infer relationships and draw conclusions using detailed scientific knowledge.

Civics proficiency levels represent the following: 200—recognizes the existence of civic life; 250—understands the nature of political institutions and relationships between the citizens and government; 300—understands specific government structures and functions; 350—understands a variety of political institutions and processes.

Writing proficiency levels represent the following: 100—unsatisfactory papers that are very abbreviated, circular, or disjointed; 200—minimally adequate papers that use elements necessary to complete the task, but do not manage them well enough to achieve the task; 300—adequate papers that include information and ideas necessary to accomplish the task and use them well enough to achieve the desired purpose; 400—elaborated papers that go beyond the essential and provide higher levels of coherence and supporting detail.

**Writing scores are reported for fourth, eighth, and eleventh graders, rather than by age group. Scores by grade are very similar to those for corresponding age groups.

consistency in test administration, and other technical issues make it necessary to interpret NAEP (and other national) data sets cautiously (Linn and Dunbar 1990), it is not possible to view the patterns shown in Table 13-1 as indicating that consistent and impressive gains have occurred in student achievement levels. However, it should be kept in mind that African American and Hispanic students have registered substantial gains in reading, mathematics, and science during the past two decades (see Figure 10-1 and Tables 10-6 and 10-7).

2. As shown in Table 13-2, relatively low percentages of students reach high performance levels on NAEP tests. For example, in mathematics less than 60 percent of seventeen-year-olds are at or above the 300 proficiency level (can compute with decimals, fractions, and percents, recognize geometric figures, and solve simple equations), and in reading only 42 percent are at or above the 300 level (can find, understand, summarize, and explain relatively complicated information). In addition, within the generally stable achievement patterns reported for mathematics, reading, and science for the past two decades, small gains appear to have occurred at lower proficiency levels, but these gains have been counterbalanced by small losses at higher achievement levels. As shown in Table 13-2, for example, the percentages of nine- and thirteen-year-olds scoring above the 150, 200, and 250 proficiency levels generally have increased, but generally there have been slight declines or no gains in the percentages of thirteen- and seventeen-year-olds scoring above the 300 proficiency levels.

TABLE 13-2 *Recent Percentages and Longitudinal Changes in Percentages of Students above NAEP Anchor Points (Proficiency Levels) in Mathematics, Reading, and Science, Various Years by Age Group.**

Age Group and Anchor Points	Percentages at or above Designated Anchor Points (Proficiency Levels)			Changes in Percent at or above Designated Anchor Points (Proficiency Levels)		
	1986 Mathematics	*1988 Reading*	*1986 Science*	*Mathematics 1973–1986*	*Reading 1973–1988*	*Science 1970–1986*
Nine						
150	98	93	96	01	03	03
200	74	63	71	04	04	03
250	21	17	28	01	02	01
300	01	01	03	00	00	00
Thirteen						
200	99	95	92	04	02	06
250	73	58	53	08	00	04
300	16	11	09	− 02	− 01	− 02
Seventeen						
200	100	99	97	00	03	− 01
250	96	86	81	04	00	− 01
300	51	42	41	00	03	00
350	06	05	08	− 01	− 02	− 02

Sources: Adapted from Dossey 1988; Mullis, Owen, and Phillips 1990.

*Reading proficiency levels represent the following: 150—can carry out simple, discrete reading tasks; 200—can comprehend specific or sequentially related information; 250—can search for information, interrelate ideas, and generalize; 300—can find, understand, summarize, and explain relatively complicated information; 350—can synthesize and learn from specialized reading materials.

Mathematics proficiency levels represent the following: 150—knows some basic addition and subtraction facts; 200—can add and subtract two-digit numbers; 250—can add, subtract, multiply, and divide using whole numbers; 300—can compute with decimals, fractions, and percents, recognize geometric figures, and solve simple equations; 350—can solve multistep problems and use basic algebra.

Science proficiency levels represent the following: 150—knows everyday science facts; 200—understands some basic principles; 250—understands basic life and physical sciences information; 300—has some detailed scientific knowledge; 350—can infer relationships and draw conclusions using detailed scientific knowledge.

As we point out in Chapter 2, the low performance levels of U.S. students on higher-order mathematics skills place them at the bottom rank among students from seventeen countries that participated in international comparisons (Rothman 1989; Stigler and Stevenson 1991). Similarly in science, one-third of U.S. schools registered science scores below the *lowest* achieving Japanese school at the same grade levels (International Association 1988).

Numerous explanations may help account for levels and trends in student achievement reported by the NAEP. Because the percentage of low-income youths who graduate from high school increased slightly from 1970 to 1980 (Mortenson and Wu 1990), some of the overall trend may be attributable to achievement patterns that seem more characteristic of seventeen-year-olds whose parents had not attended college than of those whose parents had attended or graduated from college (see Table 2-5 in this text). Part of the explanation probably involves a strong tendency for teachers to emphasize instructional practices that can (and apparently did) enhance students' lower-level skills. Analysts working with NAEP data considered the latter possibility, and reported that 59 percent of eighth-grade English teachers in their surveys admitted to focusing on "the mechanics of English" more than half the time. Similarly, fourth-grade teachers stressed skill-sheet assignments, and few seventh-grade teachers reported access to a scientific laboratory (Mullis, Owen, and Phillips 1990). Viewing such data in conjunction with the general patterns and trends shown in Tables 13-1 and 13-2, NAEP investigators concluded that most classrooms currently rely on

teacher presentations, textbooks, and workbook or teacher-prepared exercises. Such patterns of instruction appear to have been successful in helping large numbers of students attain basic levels of proficiency in each subject . . . [but] do not seem to have been successful . . . [in developing higher-order skills involving complex reasoning and problem solving]. For gains in higher-order skills to occur the goals of instruction need to be reconsidered. Teaching decisions were once guided by a hierarchy suggesting that students must first learn the facts and skills and later learn to apply them. Yet many educators now recognize the limitations of this stepping-stone view of education. Educational theory and research suggest a different pattern . . . [in which content mastery and learning of higher-order skills occur together]. . . .

For more thoughtful learning to occur, teachers will need to orchestrate a broader range of instructional experiences . . . providing students with opportunities to prepare for, review, and extend their new learning. . . . [This] will require teachers to move away from traditional authoritarian roles and, at the same time, require students to give up being passive recipients of learning. . . . These modifications will undoubtedly be difficult. (Applebee, Langer, and Mullis 1990, 40–41)

Many other observers, as well as numerous organizations concerned with the quality of educational programs and opportunities, have offered analyses and recommendations similar to those provided by the NAEP. For example, rep-

resentatives from the Education Commission of the States, the Collaborative for Humanities and Arts Teaching (thirteen projects designed to improve instruction in various subject areas), and twenty other national educators' associations met in August 1990 and agreed on the imperative to improve teaching and learning with respect to critical thinking and problem solving (Viadero 1990c). Several weeks later, the National Academy of Sciences released a three-year study on the teaching of biology, which the study group's chairman said currently is based largely on "exercises in memorization rather than an intellectual voyage of exploration" (quoted in Leary 1990). The study also concluded that a permanent national effort is required to make instruction more meaningful and effective in every major scientific field. Similarly, the National Council of Teachers of Mathematics (1991) has proposed a massive effort to train and retrain teachers who will be willing and able to place emphasis on "conjecturing" and problem solving to replace the current stress on "mechanistic answer-finding." Several other studies also indicate that emphasis on rote learning helps account for the generally low math performance level in the United States, compared with Japan and other Asian countries (Schaub and Baker 1991; Stigler and Stevenson 1991).

Educators thus have joined researchers in calling for reexamination and massive transformation and reform of traditional arrangements for delivering instruction in elementary and secondary schools. Based as much or more on acquaintance with what typically takes place in classrooms as on research, they point out that in many respects the educational system has been stagnant, and fundamental improvements in practice have not been introduced to the extent that has been true in health care and some other social systems. One of the most lucid statements of this position has been provided by American Federation of Teachers President Albert Shanker:

Every child in a given community still starts school by virtue of having passed a certain birthday. Children arrive together on the same day at the beginning of school and leave on the same day at the end. They still are organized into large classes where, at the elementary level, they spend most of the day listening to a teacher who must push or pull them through the various lessons so they can all get more or less to the same point at the end of the year. At the secondary level, students still are passed as a group from classroom to classroom, teacher to teacher and subject to subject about every 40 to 50 minutes. Instruction still is organized by curriculum, and curriculum is organized into units to be "covered" and tested by a certain time. We live in a technologically sophisticated society, but "chalk and talk" still is the main technology of schooling from K through 12. We give lip service to the idea that individuals learn in different ways and at different rates, but, in fact, everyone still is expected to learn in the same way—by listening to the teacher talk, by reading books and by reciting and answering questions—and learn at the same rate in order to be considered "normal."

In other words, most schools still act as though education is something done to a child—poured in or glued on—rather than something the child, with the help of the school, makes happen. (Shanker 1990, H4756)

Importance of Numeracy

For obvious reasons, educators and civic leaders have expressed increasing concern as literacy levels reported in NAEP reading assessments and other national data sets have failed to keep pace with the growing importance of comprehension and other higher-order skills in postindustrial society. In recent years recognition of the enhanced importance of *numeracy* also has been increasing. According to Lynn Steen (1990, 212), numeracy refers to the mathematics skills that "enable an individual to cope with the practical demands of everyday life." (Some analysts use the alternate term *quantitative literacy*.) Steen summarized research indicating that numeracy has become the "gatekeeper" to many desirable jobs: the "fraction of new jobs needing mathematical skills" provided in four years of study at the high-school level will be 60 percent "higher in the 1990s than in the 1970s" (Steen 1990, 213). She also pointed out that difficult as it may be substantially to improve literacy, improving numeracy is

> *the more daunting challenge. For each person who never learned to read, there must be a hundred who boast that they were never any good at math. That imbalance is especially troublesome in an age of data and measurement, of computers and statistics. (Steen 1990, 228)*

Evidence of the contemporary importance of numeracy has been provided in several studies using data on the skill levels and initial careers of youth and young adults (Idol and Jones 1991). For example, Francisco Rivera-Batiz (1990a) analyzed relationships between quantitative literacy and employment patterns and found that it is strongly associated with full-time employment status for both men and women. Numeracy appears to be particularly important for black youth and young adults. In this study relatively low levels of quantitative literacy mostly accounted for the "sharply higher probability of non-employment among young Black Americans" (Rivera-Batiz, 1990a, 13). In a separate analysis, Rivera-Batiz found that numeracy is not much related to the earnings of females in the Hispanic sample, but it had a "strong positive impact on wages" among young Hispanic males, who were concentrated in blue-collar jobs and had relatively low reading scores. The author interpreted this pattern as suggesting that quantitative literacy may be important in "substituting for inadequate English language proficiency" among male Hispanic youth from low-status families (Rivera-Batiz 1990b, 23, 25).

NATIONAL REPORTS AND DEVELOPMENTS SINCE 1983

National concern for improvement of the educational system in the United States was greatly stimulated in 1983 when the National Commission on Excellence in Education, appointed by U.S. Secretary of Education Terrel Bell, released its report and recommendations under the title *A Nation at Risk*. The United States is threatened, the National Commission concluded, by a "rising tide of mediocrity" in education. Stating that the United States has been moving toward "unthinkable, unilateral educational disarmament," the National Commission also concluded that "if an unfriendly foreign government had attempted to impose on America the mediocre educational performance that exists today, we might well have viewed it as an act of war" (National Commission 1983, 14).

A Nation at Risk documented many aspects of what Commission members perceived to be decline or inadequacy in the educational system, including weakening of high-school graduation requirements, high rates of illiteracy, declining achievement scores, and unsatisfactory graduation rates. The Commission proceeded to recommend more stringent requirements and higher expectations for students in the "Five New Basics" (English, mathematics, science, social studies, computer science). Recommendations for improving achievement in the New Basics included assignment of more homework, emphasis on study skills, a longer school day and a longer school year, and improvements in management and organization of schools. Regarding teachers and teaching, the Commission recommended that:

1. Teacher preparation programs should have higher standards.
2. Salaries for teachers should be professionally competitive and performance-based.*

School districts should establish career ladders for teaching personnel.
3. Teacher contracts should be for eleven months a year.
4. Grants and loans should be available to attract students into teaching.
5. New teachers should be supervised by master teachers.
6. Alternative routes to teacher certification should be established.

A number of other national reports on the status of education and recommendations for improving it also were published in 1983 and 1984. For example, the Education Commission of the States published the report of its Task Force on Education for Economic Growth (1983), which echoed *A Nation at Risk* in calling for higher academic standards and improvements in discipline, curriculum, teaching, and the status of teachers. Similarly, the College Board (1983) recommended that school officials substantially increase requirements and standards for high-school graduation and entry into postsecondary education.

Major national reports calling for radical reform and improvement in elementary and secondary schools continued to be published and publicized in the late 1980s and 1990s. In general, such reports have increasingly stressed the mismatch between national requirements for a more highly skilled workforce on the one hand and current performance levels in the schools on the other; the importance of launching a comprehensive response that involves

---

*Performance-based remuneration usually refers to arrangements for paying teachers in accordance with extra contributions beyond regular classroom teaching, assumption of additional responsibilities involving classroom instruction, and/ or highly rated performance in carrying out instruction or other tasks. Among the most common arrangements for performance-based remuneration are *career ladders*, which facilitate and reward teachers for undertaking more responsibilities and for improving their preparation; *master teacher programs*, which differentiate teachers' roles and responsibilities; and *mentor programs*, in which outstanding senior teachers provide leadership for other teachers. One particularly controversial approach to performance-based remuneration is *merit pay*, in which basic salary is dependent on teachers' evaluation ratings.

school districts, business, labor, public-interest groups, and all levels of government; and the requirements that schools be thoroughly restructured in order to bring about major gains in student performance. Following are quotes from several such reports:

> *[The current crisis] is a self-inflicted wound that threatens to destroy the U.S. competitive edge unless healed by prompt and drastic actions. . . . [Based on abundant] evidence generated by myriad commissions and study groups over the past decade, the solution to the technical manpower crisis is clear enough, but it is also politically explosive. The U.S. education system needs to be overhauled. . . . Indeed, perestroika would not go far enough; the U.S. education system needs a cultural revolution. (Aerospace Education Foundation 1989, i–ii).*
>
> *Increased demand for higher skilled workers, combined with an aging workforce, has already created shortages of skilled workers. . . . Employers report that alarming numbers of young job applicants have such poor reading and computation skills that it is impossible to provide them with job-specific training. . . . [Moreover, large] numbers of experienced workers have skills that are now obsolete or soon will be. . . . Eliminating the skills gap and enhancing our nation's competitive position will require a substantial, ongoing national commitment to investment in human resources. . . . The time has come for this country to make a commitment to education, a commitment as ambitious and aggressive as our past commitment to space exploration. . . . The U.S. Department of Education, in cooperation with state departments of education, should encourage experimentation involving fundamental restructuring of schools. Encouragement should include grants, technical assistance, and regulatory flexibility. (Commission on Workforce Quality and Labor Market Efficiency 1989, 1–7: 714)*

The Governors Say It Is "Time for Results"

In 1986, the National Governors' Association also published an important and influential report. Titled *Time for Results*, this report incorporated the findings of seven gubernatorial task forces organized to draw up to five-year plans and action agendas dealing respectively with teaching, leadership and management, parent involvement and choice, readiness for school, technology, facilities, and college quality. Some of the recommendations of the task forces are shown in Table 13-3. Tennessee Governor Lamar Alexander's introduction to *Time for Results* included the following comments and explanations:

> *The governors are ready for some old-fashioned horse trading. We'll regulate less, if schools and school districts will produce better results. . . . Have all the governors agreed on this report? No.* Time for Results *has as its sole purpose helping governors be better governors. It is our best advice to each other. . . . Why are the governors getting involved? Because without their leadership, most of what needs to be done won't get done. American public eduction has fallen into some deep ruts. . . . Governors want a new compact with professional educators in America, so that we can lead a coalition of everyone interested in schools and take the next steps together. (Alexander 1986, 202–204)*

As is apparent in Table 13-3, *Time for Results* incorporated and sometimes elaborated on earlier reform reports and initiatives. Regarding teaching, for example, the gubernatorial task force chaired by Thomas Kean of New Jersey stated that "the public must offer teachers a professional work environment and all that goes with it . . . [including] a real voice in decisions . . . [and] the chance to design the standards that define professional performance and ways to assess that performance (Kean 1986, 205). The Task Force on Readiness for school placed very strong emphasis on the problems of disadvantaged students, and

TABLE 13-3   *Selected Recommendations of Gubernatorial Task Forces That Prepared Sections of* Time for Results

---

Teaching

---

1. Support the creation of a national board of professional teacher standards.
2. Develop state initiatives to encourage professional environments.
3. Build the case for sustained real-dollar increases in education spending.

Leadership and Management

---

1. Develop a system to evaluate principals effectively and accurately.
2. Provide incentives and technical assistance to promote school-site management and improvement.
3. Reward principals and schools for performance and effectiveness.

Parent Involvement and Choice

---

1. Provide incentives to school districts.
2. Adopt legislation permitting families to select from among public schools in the state.

Readiness of At-Risk Students

State Initiatives to Assure That At-Risk Children and Youth Meet the New Educational Standards:

---

1. Reward schools for making progress in educating all children.
2. Establish programs . . . [to help parents] learn how to support their children's teachers.
3. Develop incentive programs or direct state aid to reduce class sizes of kindergarten and the lower grades.
4. Establish alternative programs to work with high-school dropouts.
5. Establish a mechanism for state interventions when progress is not being made with low-achieving students.

State Initiatives to Help At-Risk Young Children Become Ready for School:

---

1. Provide assistance for first-time, low-income parents of high-risk infants.
2. Provide kindergarten for all 5-year-old children.
3. Provide quality early-childhood-development programs for at-risk 4-year-olds, and, where feasible, 3-year-olds.
4. Provide parents of preschool children with information on successful parenting.
5. Stress continued improvement of developmental and education programs in day-care centers for preschool children.

Technology

---

1. Encourage and assist school districts that are willing to experiment with ways to restructure school environments to increase productivity by using various forms of technology.
2. Make technology more available for students from low-income families.

Source: National Governors' Association 1986.

its recommendations, like those of the Task Force on Leadership and Management, were much more precise and detailed than comparable recommendations in most earlier reports. Thus, *Time for Results* identified specific steps and goals that governors and other supporters of reform can examine in the future to determine whether substantial progress actually has taken place.

Five years later the governors' association took stock of what had and had not been accomplished in efforts to improve the schools. Its report, *Results in Education: 1990* (National Governors' Association 1991), generally concluded that some progress had been made but much more needed to be done with respect to each area in which *Time for Results* had offered recommendations (Pipho 1991).

For example, the 1991 report noted that many states had initiated testing policies to screen preservice and practicing teachers but relatively little movement has occurred toward enhancing professional environments within schools, and that most states had taken some action to improve opportunities for at-risk students but most such efforts have been "marginal" and few have been "institutionalized." The chair of the association's education panel (Colorado Governor Roy Romer) reviewed the overall implications of the 1991 report and concluded that the governors had learned much about "what doesn't work," particularly with respect to "piecemeal" reform efforts; therefore, future initiatives would have to be more comprehensive and collaborative (quoted in De Witt 1991). In line with this point of view, the governors already had begun to work more closely with the federal government (see subsequent section on national education goals), and resolved to consider the initiatives recommended in *Time for Results* in conjunction with future collaborative activity involving the president and the Congress of the United States. Results henceforth are to be viewed as dependent in part on nationwide efforts to improve the effectiveness of the educational system.

CED, CCSSO, and Other Reports Emphasizing Disadvantaged Students

In addition to such reports as *A Nation Prepared* and *Time for Results*, which dealt with reform of schools for all students, several reports have been particularly concerned with disadvantaged students. One of the most impressive and influential of these reports is *Children in Need*, prepared by the Committee for Economic Development (CED). A nonprofit organization representing many large corporations and higher-education institutions, the Committee noted low achievement and high dropout rates among economically and socially disadvantaged students and concluded that the United States "can ill afford such an egregious waste of human resources. . . . Allowing this to continue will not only impoverish these children, it will impoverish our nation— culturally, politically, and economically" (Committee for Economic Development 1987).

After concluding that education reforms are "doomed" without much more effective early childhood education for disadvantaged students, *Children in Need* proceeded to recommend massive improvements in programs to help preschool students, increase cooperation between schools and families, provide assistance for pregnant teenagers and other "high-risk" mothers, create alternate school settings, reduce the size of schools and classes, and introduce "radical" redefinitions in school purposes and structures. Chairman Owen Butler spoke for many of his committee colleagues in further concluding that business should respond by leading another "wave of reform" to improve education for the disadvantaged (Olson 1987c).

Four years later, the CED published a follow-up report, *The Unfinished Agenda: A New Vision for Child Development and Education*. After calling attention to the substantial increase in the percentage of children in poverty, the Committee called for large increases in Headstart programming and funding as well as early-childhood programs for three- and four-year-olds. It also urged that schools and other agencies work together to provide parental education in child rearing, coordination of social services, provision of preventive health and nutrition services, improvement in school-home relations, and other aspects of ecological intervention for disadvantaged children described here in Chapters 4 and 8 (Committee for Economic Development 1991). Referring to the level of effort and financing required to improve the family and educational environments of poverty children as "massive," one primary author of *An Unfinished Agenda* stated that we are "only at the beginning stages of addressing the problem" (quoted in Celis 1991, A14).

The Council of Chief State School Officers (CCSSO) also has indicated vigorous support for massive efforts to improve the education of disadvantaged students. In a policy paper entitled "Assuring Educational Success for Students at Risk" that its members endorsed unanimously, the CCSSO stated that "state law should provide the supporting health, social welfare, employment, housing, safety, transportation, and other human services which, together with the educational programs, are reasonably calculated to enable all persons to graduate from high school."

As regards education, the CCSSO said that every student should be *guaranteed* "enrollment in a school with systematically designed and delivered instruction of demonstrable effectiveness, and with adequate and up-to-date learning technologies and materials of proven value" (Council of Chief State School Officers 1987, 7). Other reports issued by the CCSSO indicated that implementation of its policy regarding guarantees may require support for students to transfer from low-achieving schools or districts to "successful" locations elsewhere, "state takeovers" of school districts that are financially or educationally "distressed," reduction in the concentration of low achievers at low achieving schools, and introduction of a system of school-site planning and decision making (Burch 1988). According to several CCSSO reports, large increases in funding for education will be required to bring about these and other reforms in the schools (Jones 1988).

Teacher Preparation and Tomorrow's Teachers and Schools

Three years after the publication of *A Nation at Risk*, the Carnegie Task Force on Teaching As a Profession (1986) released *A Nation Prepared: Teachers in the 21st Century*. Representing the views and recommendations of a fourteen-member task force of business, civic, and educational leaders, *A Nation Prepared* portrayed a world economy in the middle of a "profound transformation" that requires much more stress on learning (as contrasted with schooling) through an educational system sufficiently challenging and rigorous to ensure that students acquire "complex, non-routine intellectual" skills. Central recommendations in *A Nation Prepared* included the following suggestions:

1. Create a hierarchical teaching profession to include a corps of lead teachers who will have leadership responsibilities in the schools.

2. Give teachers more control over what happens in schools, and in turn hold them more accountable for student performance.
3. Establish a national board, as in law and medicine, to set higher standards for teachers and to certify those who meet them.
4. Require that future teachers obtain a bachelor's degree *before* participating in professional training; replace undergraduate education majors with a new professional curriculum at the graduate level.
5. Increase the pool of minority teachers by providing incentives and better general education for minority students.

A first major step toward implementation of recommendations in *A Nation Prepared* was taken in May 1987 when the Carnegie Forum on Education and the Economy announced the establishment of the National Board for Professional Teaching Standards (NEPTS) a nonprofit organization that will issue certificates to teachers who demonstrate mastery of prescribed standards of professional knowledge and ability. The sixty-four-member board, which includes more than forty teachers, works in cooperation with research-and-development personnel at Stanford University and other institutions at which efforts have been underway to improve assessment of teachers' skills and knowledge (Olson 1986b; Payzant 1988). Major developments that have occurred since the National Board was established have included the following (National Board for Professional Teaching Standards 1989; Goodlad 1989; Bradley 1990a, 1991a; Diegmueller 1990c; Viadero 1990a):

• The Board received 5 million dollars from the Carnegie Foundation to begin its work and decided to seek an additional 45 million dollars from the federal government and other sources.
• Aiming to introduce its initial national assessment/licensing tests in 1993, the Board appointed committees to create standards for its first three certificates to be offered respectively for middle-school generalists, high-school mathematics teachers, and middle-school English

teachers. It also identified twenty-six other sub-ject specialities for which licensing tests are to be prepared and certificates are to be awarded. Testing methods are to include use of portfolios, interviews, video or computer simulations, or other innovative assessment methods.

• As part of a report that rejected the so-called egg-crate model of schools that isolate teachers in separate classrooms, the Board identified ge-neric teaching standards that candidates must meet to obtain certificates. In addition to subject-area knowledge and skill in teaching, competen-cies stressed in the standards include those in-volved in working with other professionals in curriculum development, making decisions about how to use a variety of instructional strat-egies, and mentoring of students.

• Education officials in several states an-nounced that they intend to provide significant salary increases to teachers who pass NBPTS cer-tificate exams.

• In July 1989, the Board announced that eli-gibility for NBPTS certification would require possession of a baccalaureate degree from an ac-credited college or university and prior comple-tion of three years of successful teaching in ele-mentary or secondary schools.

• The Board's annual report for 1989 stressed that candidates for national certification will have to meet "high and rigorous" standards that go considerably beyond the minimum standards typical of state-government certificate tests.

• In September 1989, the Board of Directors of the American Association of Colleges for Teacher Education (AACTE) voted unani-mously to oppose NBPTS policies on prerequi-sites for certification. Emphasizing the view that failure to require a professional degree from an accredited school or college of education weak-ens rather than strengthens the National Boards' commitment to high standards, the president of AACTE's Board said that state certification re-quirements (which must be met to obtain teaching experience) are uneven and frequently unsatisfac-tory. One probable effect of AACTE opposition has been to reduce the likelihood that the NBPTS

will obtain much of the tens of millions of dollars it has been seeking in federal financial support.

• The Association of Teacher Educators and the National Educational Association joined the AACTE in asking the National Board to recon-sider policies that omit requirements for posses-sion of an accredited degree in education and a state teaching certificate.

• In 1990 and 1991, the NBPTS began to award contracts for development of certificate tests. Among the initial awards were a $393,000 contract to develop a "video portfolio" assess-ment of teaching, a $343,333 contract to develop "performance-based" exercises to gauge teach-ers' skills and knowledge in working with diverse groups of students, a $67,000 contract to summa-rize information on available tests for assessing the teaching of mathematics, and a $1.5 million con-tract to develop and pilot test methods for assess-ing middle- and junior-high-school teachers in cen-tral city, rural, and suburban school districts.

Reforms in teaching and in the teaching profession also are being pursued by the Holmes Group, a consortium of deans of many of the best-known schools and colleges of education throughout the United States. Its first major re-port, *Tomorrow's Teachers* (The Holmes Group 1986), highlighted the goals of making the edu-cation of teachers intellectually sound; recogniz-ing differences in knowledge, skill, and commit-ment among teachers; creating relevant, defensible standards of entry into the teaching profession; connecting education schools more closely with elementary and secondary schools; and making schools better places for teachers to work and learn. In particular, *Tomorrow's Teachers* echoed *A Nation Prepared* in recommending that the teacher-training sequence should eliminate the undergraduate education major and replace it with a fifth year of graduate-level preparation.

The Holmes group operated for several years with fluid membership of about 125 institu-tions from all fifty states and then, in January 1987, formally established its structure and oper-ating practices. It also received severe criticism from many quarters, including teacher-education faculty who perceived it as an elitist organization trying to ensure supervisor status for new teachers graduating from its relatively small number of prestigious members. Many critics particularly challenged the wisdom and feasibility of its recommendation to limit teacher education to a fifth year of graduate-level study, which they perceived as a self-serving maneuver reflecting the relatively severe problems involved in operating a coherent undergraduate teacher-education program at prominent research-oriented institutions.

Obstacles encountered by the Holmes Group have been and continue to be enormous. Teacher education in the United States takes place at thousands of locations subject to diverse state and local regulations and influences. Shortages of funding and other support, variations in the ability of students and faculty, lack of cooperation between higher education and school districts, student desires to complete an inexpensive program quickly, and many other considerations hamper movement toward a fifth-year approach as well as other recommendations of the Holmes Group, the Carnegie Task Force on Teaching, and other organizations concerned with reform in teacher education. Given these difficulties, it is not surprising that membership in the Holmes Group (which entails a significant annual membership fee) has shrunk to less than 100 and that the Group has backed off its emphasis on limiting teacher education to graduate-level study. Some members have moved or are still trying to move in this direction, and several states including Texas have mandated it statewide, but many or most Holmes institutions (as well as most other colleges and universities) are emphasizing alternate possibilities for improving teaching and teacher education.

Among the important developments with respect to the recent history of the Holmes Group have been the following (The Holmes Group 1989; Devaney 1990, 1991; Bradley 1991b):

- A 1989 Holmes Group report refined earlier recommendations for programs to prepare future teachers by specifying that the following

"commonalities" should be present: (1) a disciplinary or interdisciplinary undergraduate major (other than education); (2) early exposure to schools beginning in the sophomore year; (3) education coursework in the junior and senior years; and (4) clinical experiences that may begin in the junior or senior year and extend into a fifth year incorporating an internship supervised by mentor teachers and university faculty. After noting that many Homes Group institutions had "rather bravely, exhaustively, and no doubt exhaustingly addressed" challenges in moving toward "comprehensive, coherent" programs built on these commonalities, the report endorsed promising possibilities at campuses that have begun to assign teacher education students to "small, continuing cohorts," create "blocks" of interrelated methods courses, conduct "practica at campus laboratories providing video and computer simulations of learning," and/or combine field experiences with "reflective" seminars.

- In 1990, the Holmes Group specified four "policy directions" to guide its subsequent efforts. The directions deal respectively with the following goals: (1) center the "whole school of education . . . around issues of teaching and learning as these are conceptualized and enacted in the preparation curricula and practica for teachers, administrators and other school professionals"; (2) "infuse the values of equity and cultural diversity into liberal arts and education curricula, education school staffing, and research"; (3) "reconstitute faculty research activity so it contributes more powerfully to school improvement, engaging the participation of observers"; and (4) hold the Group "to account" by creating a "panel of outside experts" to assess its effectiveness (Devaney 1990, 1–2).

- The Group's second major report, *Tomorrow's Schools* (Young, Sykes, Featherstone, and Elmore 1990), encouraged teacher-education institutions to move beyond *Tomorrow's Teachers* by "entering and sustaining partnerships with schoolpeople to create new forms for teacher education and for inquiring about teaching and learning."

• In 1991, the Group approved a proposal to create a Holmes Center for Faculty Leadership and Renewal. Located at Ohio State University, the Center will work to ensure that teacher-preparation programs use the best available pedagogical knowledge and technology.

• In 1991, the Holmes Group announced three new initiatives in connection with its goals involving movement toward equity and cultural diversity in teaching and teacher education: (1) formation and support of a group of minority "Holmes Scholars" who will receive tuition and other assistance at schools or colleges of teacher education and will form a network to provide learning experiences not available at individual campuses; (2) an effort to help institutions with high minority enrollment "join the Holmes Group and enact its agenda"; and (3) formation of an "equity critique and review panel" to help plan and carry out a variety of activities aimed at improving equity.

The Holmes Group's efforts to improve the preparation and functioning of teachers increasingly have focused on the creation and operation of Professional Development Schools (PDSs) designed to provide close connections between schools and colleges of education on the one hand and elementary and secondary schools on the other. Similar to but offering more comprehensive programs and more intimate linkages than traditional so-called clinical schools and laboratory schools at which higher-education institutions have provided actual classroom experience for future teachers, PDSs as described in *Tomorrow's Schools* are to emphasize the following "design" goals:

1. Teaching for understanding for everybody's children.
2. Creation of learning communities.
3. Continuing learning to be engaged in by teachers, teacher educators, and administrators.
4. Thoughtful long-term inquiry into teaching and learning.

Facilitated through joint operation by higher-education institutions and school districts, Professional Development Schools are to provide a location at which college faculty can conduct research and work with teachers and future teachers in learning how to provide effective education for diverse groups of students; elementary and secondary teachers can serve as college faculty and mentor future teachers and new teachers; and all participants can work together to "invent new institutions" capable of meeting the educational challenges of the future.

There has been no shortage of either support or skepticism for Holmes Group proposals aimed at establishing Professional Development Schools to improve the educational system. Supporters point to the potential value and importance of linking public schools with colleges and universities in a comprehensive effort to create new institutions that both discover and use the most effective methods for teaching diverse students, while also providing sequenced and carefully supervised preparation for new and future teachers who function as part of a dedicated professional community (Johnson 1990). For their part, skeptics—who generally are sympathetic with PDS goals and characteristics—point to the great costs together with the limited funding available for operating such schools, the numerous obstacles and divergent interests that hamper collaborative efforts between higher education institutions and school districts, the limited number of future teachers who could be expected to gain placements at PDSs, the "clash of cultures" between university personnel who emphasize inquiry learning and school faculties that, for one or another reason, are unable or unwilling to depart from low-level instruction, the tremendously increased demands likely to be placed on already overburdened teachers appointed to PDSs, and other problems involved in establishing these schools as a significant force in our educational system (Viadero 1990b; Bradley 1991b). Obviously, it is not certain that many such schools actually will be established or will operate successfully over a period of time to demonstrate possibilities for bringing about reform in the larger system.

It should be noted that the American Federation of Teachers, the National Education Association, the American Association of Colleges and Teacher Education, and other organizations also have been working on plans for operating schools that are similar to PDSs in that they involve colleges and universities or other external organizations in working with school facilities to provide improved preservice and inservice teacher education along with inquiry-oriented learning for students. In addition, leading teacher educators, such as John Goodlad (1990), have provided detailed arguments and plans for creating "partner schools" to take the lead in revitalizing the educational system. It is unknown—and probably unknowable—how much impact these efforts are having on a national basis, but encouraging developments include an AACTE survey indicating that a large majority of teacher-training institutions have strengthened their relationships with elementary and secondary schools (Diegmueller 1991b). If many of these relationships prove productive, a start will have been made toward improving the performance of tomorrow's teachers working in tomorrow's schools.

Assessment of Student Performance and "The Nation's Report Card"

Another particularly important document that has helped shape reform of education is the 1987 report on improving assessment of student achievement prepared by the Study Group, a twenty-two-member committee chaired by former Tennessee Governor Lamar Alexander and supported by funds from several private foundations. The report, *The Nation's Report Card*, assessed the "accomplishments and short-comings" of the National Assessment of Educational Progress (NAEP) and endeavored to determine whether and how a national assessment of achievement in elementary and secondary schools should be carried out in the future. After pointing out that some data previously disseminated by the U.S. Department of Education have been 'wretchedly inadequate," the Study Group

recommended that work should proceed on developing better national assessments for the future. Specific recommendations (Study Group 1987, 7–10) included the following:

1. Maintain continuity with the NAEP data base.
2. Include regular assessment of reading, writing, literacy, mathematics, science, technology, history, geography, and civics.
3. Provide for "add-on" assessments so that states, districts, and even buildings can be assessed on a voluntary basis.
4. Increase federal funding so that annual spending on national assessment rises from the 4 to 6 million dollar level of the NAEP to the range of 20 to 30 million dollars.

The Study Group's recommendations dealing with "Content and Coverage" placed special emphasis on avoiding the pitfalls and negative consequences of much previous minimum competency testing that has focused on mechanical skills and factual knowledge, thereby encouraging districts and schools to concentrate on low-level instruction. Before recommending that the NAEP should "make the assessment of higher-order thinking a central concern of future assessments," *The Nation's Report Card* stated:

> *One theme that will continually reappear in this report is a concern for the measurement of more complex levels of thinking and reasoning. We are convinced that it is time for the national assessment to devote closer attention to the measurement of more complex skills. . . . Until recently . . . careful definition and measurement of these skills has taken second place to a more limited measurement of factual knowledge based largely upon memory or very simple reasoning tasks . . . .*
>
> *We recognize of course that the effort to define, assess, and teach this level of skill is a well-established one in education. . . . What is new, however, is the emergence of a commitment in recent years to develop and assess*

these skills among all members of the national community. Such a challenging objective had to await the development of new insights into the exact nature of these skills, and the best ways to measure and evaluate them.

Recent developments in the many allied disciplines that study thinking and learning have now placed the accomplishment of this goal within our reach. The past two decades have witnessed an explosion of new ideas about how human beings learn and what happens in higher-order thinking. At the same time powerful new computer technologies now make available a range of measurement tools sophisticated and sensitive enough to measure complex thinking with some accuracy. (Study Group 1987, 15–16)

Many other prominent and influential organizations also have registered dissatisfaction with existing testing practices and called for a greater emphasis on assessment of higher-order skills. For example, more than three dozen groups (including the American Association of Colleges for Teacher Education and the National Association of Elementary School Principals) joined in releasing a 1990 "Statement on Genuine Accountability," which said that "Standardized multiple-choice tests are not an adequate means to measure educational progress" (editors of *Fair Test Examiner* 1989–90, 1). The National Commission on Testing and Public Policy (composed largely of leading educators, civic officials, and social scientists) issued a report that included the recommendation that "Testing programs should be redirected from overreliance on multiple-choice tests toward alternative forms of assessment . . . [based] where feasible . . . on multiple sources of information, especially direct evidence of actual performance" (National Commission on Testing and Public Policy 1990, 8). Again in 1991, dozens of organizations, including the NEA, the NAACP, and the PTA, joined in protesting the prevalence of standardized tests and the prospects that any type of test might soon be introduced for the first time on a required basis na-

tionally (Stout 1991). Joining the many other organizations that released antitesting statements in recent years, the National Association of Secondary School Principals (1988) asserted that "Performance on standardized tests is a poor indicator of performance on tasks that require disciplined inquiry," and The National Council of Teachers of English (1990) concluded that "Standardized testing continues to distort and debase many aspects of the language arts program."

Numerous studies that support the preceding conclusions have been conducted with respect to virtually every major subject taught in elementary and secondary schools. For example, the National Research Council (1991) summarized contemporary research on the effects of standardized tests in biology, concluding that existing tests "rely on recall" and thereby "reduce and distort" teaching for concepts by "testing for words and definitions instead," and a systematic study of state practices in assessing science performance concluded that they generally "foster fragmentation of shallow knowledge rather than mastery of central science principles in depth" and "provide no reliable assessment of process or thinking skills" (Gong, Lahart, and Courtney 1990, 7). Such studies have played an important part in building a wide constituency for improving testing practices as part of the national reform movement.

Reflecting broad support from many sources and a sizable research base, educators and lay leaders as well as testing specialists have moved to develop and introduce approaches to overcome the many deficiencies outlined here with respect to minimum competency testing and standardized tests. Among the most important testing developments that have taken place or are being pursued with significant intensity and resources are the following:

- In accordance with recommendations in *The Nation's Report Card* and other reports, the NAEP Board of Directors decided in 1990 to add performance-based items and measurements to future versions of its various tests. Specifically, the Board voted to assess writing partly in terms of a portfolio that students already have produced, to include open-ended questions in reading and math, and to require essay responses in answering some science questions. It also decided to develop scoring methods that will portray students' scores as proficient or lacking in adequate proficiency in mastering specific standards students should meet in grades four, eight, and twelve. In addition, the Board proposed to expand its samples so that, for the first time, scores would be available state by state and for individual schools and districts, rather than just for broad geographic regions (Rothman 1991a, 1991b; 1991c; Finn 1991). However, participation will be on a voluntary basis (Haertel 1991).

However, the American Association of School Administrators, the Council of Chief State School Officers, and some other influential organizations opposed the decision to collect and report data that identified states, schools, or districts, arguing that NAEP tests still would not be sufficiently broad and performance-based to overcome tendencies toward overemphasis on teaching narrow skills included in the test. Critics also believe that state and district testing conducted by the NAEP will not be useful in determining how to improve the schools (Koretz 1991). Policies regarding the future role and scope of NAEP testing will be made largely in accordance with Congressional budget decisions to support or limit expansion in the future (Boysen 1990; Martinez 1990).

- Alternate and/or complementary possibilities for national testing have been pursued by the National Governor's Association, the National Education Goals Panel (see later), the U.S. Department of Labor, and other organizations and institutions (Finn 1991; Rothman 1990c; 1991b). For example, the Labor Department's Commission on Achieving Necessary Skills has been working to identify skills that would be included on a national test of high-school students' job readiness; the National Center on Education and the Economy obtained foundation funds to develop a plan for creating a "certificate of initial mastery" test that would qualify or disqualify

sixteen-year-olds for subsequent education or employment; and civic leaders who formed an organization called Education America asked Congress to fund and require national administration of a comprehensive test of the performance of high-school seniors. Decisions regarding pursuit of these and other proposals have become highly controversial as supporters pointed to the need for improved tests that might motivate students to work harder to acquire important skills, and opponents objected that adequate testing methods focused on higher-order skills are not yet available and administration of tests on a national basis would only further exacerbate problems created by low-level testing. In this context, a co-director of a federally sponsored testing-research center warned that it will require five to ten years just to develop and validate appropriate new tests, not to mention enormous amounts of teacher training during and after this period. The Director of the Council for Educational Research and Development said that many government and civic leaders were mistakenly adopting a "Field of Dreams" mentality—because we want better tests, they will magically come to use (Rothman 1991c).

- Some state departments of education have been adopting improved tests or developing tests of their own. For example, Connecticut and New York now administer the Degrees of Reading Power test on a statewide basis at some grades because it provides a much better measure of students' comprehension levels than do traditional standardized tests. Illinois, Michigan, and several other states have been developing or introducing tests for assessing students' mastery of higher-order skills in reading, math, critical thinking, history, and other subjects (Valencia 1989; Ivens and Koslin 1991; Linn 1991).

- In June 1991, the Oregon legislature adopted the Certificate of Initial Mastery approach described in Chapter 6. Tenth graders will take a basic-skills exam that will qualify them to continue their education in either a college-preparation track or a job-training tack. Students who fail will be retained in the tenth grade for remedial assistance until they pass and obtain a certificate. Educational leaders in Oregon predict that it may take ten years and billions of dollars to reform elementary and secondary schools to allow for successful functioning of the new system (Kantrowitz and Wingert 1991).

▪ Educators in many schools and districts are experimenting with and developing various approaches to performance-based assessment of students' achievement levels and progress. In general, performance-based approaches assess outcomes in terms of what students produce in responding to challenging assignments that require much more than selecting among multiple-choice alternatives or true-false responses. Performance-based assessment also gives more attention to the process through which assignments are carried out and the quality of the work that students produce than to narrow assessments of responses in terms of right or wrong or the quantity of correct responses. As mentioned earlier, the NAEP is beginning to emphasize essays and other aspects of performance-based assessment and numerous other approaches are being used or developed to assess students in terms of portfolios, exhibitions, or other compilations of varied work products through which they attain and/or demonstrate mastery of diverse higher-order skills. These kinds of assessments involving students' performance with reference to a major work product frequently are discussed using terminology such as *authentic* testing and *instructionally-defensible* assessment (Wolf 1989; Mitchell 1990; Wiggins 1990; Paulson, Paulson, and Meyer 1991; Russell 1991).

Performance-based assessment approaches already have been introduced successfully at many locations. Portfolios, for example, are being used to assess and improve students' performance in writing. Several scholars who have examined implementation of this approach have concluded that it can provide "powerful educational tools for encouraging students to take charge of their own learning." After identifying eight guidelines for the constructive use of portfolios, these authors further concluded that "portfolio assessment offers the opportunity to observe students in taking risks, developing creative solutions, and learning to make judgements about their own performances....[and thereby can provide] a complex and comprehensive view of student performance in context" (Paulson, Paulson, and Meyer 1991, 61, 63).

However, performance-based assessment approaches are still far from being adequately developed and may never provide a feasible alternative for preparing regular summaries of how well students or schools are performing in most subject areas on a statewide or national basis. For one thing, portfolios and similar approaches consume large amounts of assessment time. (Cizek 1991). In addition, even the most careful performance-based assessments may result in subjective and unreliable evaluation, and teachers can find ways to assign passing scores to very low achievers in a manner analogous to what they do in teaching the content of standardized tests (Rothman 1990c). Thus, even a strong advocate of portfolio assessments has described them as "messy" products that teachers must "struggle to make sense of" in trying to evaluate students' performance (Wolf 1989, 37). Most important, performance-based assessment probably cannot generate large gains in achievement in and of itself, but can have substantial, long-range impact only when part of a much larger effort to bring about comprehensive reform in the schools (Wiggins 1990).

▪ Testing specialists also have been developing innovative approaches that may help to bring about educational reform in the future. For example, several researchers are working to refine "dynamic assessment" methods that enable students to demonstrate what and how they are learning as they respond to a paper-and-pencil test, inventories to assess students' "metacognitive" performance are being tried in numerous schools, and computerized problem simulations are being developed at the Educational Testing Service and elsewhere (Linn 1991). However, these approaches currently are designed primarily to provide diagnostic information about students' learning patterns and problems. It probably will be a long time before they can be used to assess performance levels across schools or districts in a manner that contributes to productive school reform.

Some observers who have been studying achievement trends in U.S. schools are relatively positive about the emphasis placed on testing and teaching for minimum competency in the 1970s and 1980s. For example, Barbara Lerner (1990) reviewed NAEP data indicating that substantial gains have occurred in basic (but not higher-order) skills (see the first part of this chapter) and concluded that these gains were due largely to the minimum competency movement's preoccupation with helping poor achievers acquire low-level skills needed for subsequent success. Similarly, Linda Winfield (1990) studied NAEP achievement patterns for eighth graders and concluded that students at schools with minimal competency testing programs gained more in reading proficiency than those at schools without such programs.

However, neither Lerner nor Winfield suggested that minimum competency testing and teaching should be viewed as a way to raise performance with respect to higher-order skills in the future. Instead, they concluded that the main lesson to be learned from the minimum competency movement of the past two decades is that appropriate testing as part of a larger reform effort can affect both practice and outcomes in schools and classrooms. If this conclusion is correct, it is encouraging to note that some states that previously were strong exponents of minimum competency programs "moved on" in the late 1980s to focus their testing and school reform efforts on more advanced skills (Russell 1991).

The Rise and Stagnation of Teacher Merit-Pay and Career-Ladders

As we mention earlier, *A Nation at Risk* (along with other prominent national education reports) recommended performance-based remuneration approaches that would stimulate teachers to improve their effectiveness as part of merit-pay, career-ladder, or related incentives plans. This proposal was well received by many readers because common sense suggests that paying or otherwise rewarding teachers in accordance with their performance should stimulate them to become or remain productive.

Unfortunately, common sense is not a useful guide for assessing the desirability or feasibility of merit-pay or other remuneration proposals in the absence of careful and comprehensive analysis. A 1981 review of the history and status of merit-pay plans concluded that many such plans have been introduced in U.S. schools in the twentieth century, particularly in the early 1980s, but few if any seem to have worked well because of the "host of practical problems" associated with their implementation. Among the most important problems are:

- The difficulties that arise in measuring teachers' output and effectiveness.
- The concomitant need for complicated evaluation systems, and requirements for substantial funding to increase pay for meritorious teachers.
- Negative or demotivating reactions on the part of teachers who receive little or no reward.
- Disruption or destruction of working relationships between teachers who are or are not rewarded (Clearinghouse on Educational Management editors 1981).

Subsequent analyses and research reviews (e.g., Soar and Soar 1984; Bushardt and Fowler 1987; Smylie and Smart 1990) have continued to document the inherent complexities and severe problems involved in devising and implementing workable merit-pay plans, and the perhaps predictable demise of most merit-remuneration schemes that have been tried in the schools.

Rather than defining and rewarding merit in accordance with some measure of teacher output, career-ladder plans provide remuneration according to the responsibilities teachers are assigned or discharge within a heirarchy that differentiates between such positions as certified teacher or beginning teacher on the one hand and more responsible positions (e.g., master teacher, mentor teacher, lead teacher) higher on the ladder. Most career-ladder plans provide for increased teacher involvement in schoolwide or district-level tasks and for reconfiguration in teachers' work and authority patterns (Hart and Murphy 1990).

Although hierarchical differentiation in teachers' responsibilities tends to make career-ladder plans even more complicated than merit-pay plans, career ladders frequently have been viewed as a relatively easy way to identify and reward productive teachers and thereby stimulate professional effectiveness. For this reason career-ladder possibilities received increasing attention and support in the 1970s and 1980s. The federal government allocated funds in 1984 to help school districts develop career-ladder and merit-pay plans, and numerous states either provided similar assistance to districts or developed, and in some cases introduced, some form of these teacher-incentive approaches on a statewide basis. By 1990, more than forty states either were considering or had developed or implemented various "career enhancement initiatives" (Smylie and Smart 1990).

Research on the implementation and outcomes of career ladders has been somewhat limited, but it is clear that many have created or at least encountered obstacles and problems similar to those already enumerated with respect to merit pay. The available research on career-ladder plans indicates that they frequently generate considerable resistance and disrupt working relationships among teachers and they have diverse effects from teacher to teacher and school to school. In general, it is clear that career-ladder and merit-pay plans are difficult to design and implement effectively, do not quickly or consistently produce gains in teacher, student, or school performance, and probably will not succeed unless they address complicated larger is-

sues involving the professionalization of teaching, empowerment of teachers, the nature of teaching and learning, and the change process in organizations (Freiberg 1987; Hart and Murphy 1990; Smylie and Smart 1990).

As problems became apparent in some states that had initiated career-ladder or merit-pay plans in the first half of the 1980s, recognition also grew that performance-based remuneration approaches are not a quick and easy panacea to improve the schools. For example:

- Officials in Florida found that adequate tests were not available in most subject areas to assess teachers as part of that state's system for linking pay and performance.
- Legislators substantially narrowed the career-ladder plan in Texas after they discovered it might cost a quarter of a billion dollars a year to implement fully.
- Observers in these and other states described problems with respect to lack of staff development and preparation and absence of evaluation components that may be required for effective implementation of performance-based teacher incentives.

The overall result, according to one reporter, was that "Very few states are now moving forward with the kind of centralized, statewide teacher-incentive plans that appeared in the first few years of the school-reform movement" (Olson 1987b, 16).

However, the fact that merit-pay and career-ladder incentive plans have been stagnant during the past few years does not mean that these approaches cannot have positive results or necessarily will play little or no role in future reform efforts. Some educational officials are tracking developments in connection with the merit plan introduced in the Fairfax, Virginia, public schools. The Fairfax approach to merit pay has encountered numerous snags, including much higher-than-predicted costs associated with the large proportion of teachers who initially earned a substantial salary increase, but some developments in Fairfax have been encouraging and collection of positive data on outcomes in the future could stir new interest in merit plans nationally (Heath 1988; Spillane 1991). Regarding career ladders, school districts in Arizona, Tennessee, Utah, and several other locations are proceeding with and learning from the implementation of sophisticated plans that seem to be registering some success (Pipho 1988; Bellon 1989; Braver and Helmstadter 1990; Hart 1990; Hart and Murphy 1990). Successful evaluation reports from a few of these locations might reinvigorate state and district-level interest in possibilities for improving education through performance-based remuneration of teachers.

School Performance Incentives and Differential Treatment

In part because career-ladder, merit-pay, and other teacher-incentive approaches have not been successfully initiated on a widespread basis, state policymakers have been increasingly willing to experiment with approaches that provide incentives or disincentives or otherwise allow for differential treatment based on the performance of entire schools. In addition, the federal government has initiated efforts to reward schools that "demonstrate improved achievement among students" (Bush 1991, 2).

By 1990, nearly twenty states had introduced or were formulating some type of incentive program intended to boost productivity by rewarding schools for high performance. As analyzed by Richards and Shujaa (1990), some of these programs involved predefined *fixed* performance standards that schools strive to meet in order to attain rewards; others use *competitive* standards that reward a designated number of percentage of schools that attain the highest performance. School incentive plans also differ with respect to whether standards are based largely or entirely on quantitative data regarding student performance or more qualitative measures that assess improvement in diverse areas, such as faculty, student, and parental attitudes or teachers'

self-assessments and reports. Rewards also can and do vary greatly, from programs that award Flags of Progress or other forms of public recognition to programs providing primarily monetary awards ranging from a few thousand to hundreds of thousands of dollars for high-performing schools.

Richards and Shujaa further noted that rather than focusing only on rewards for high-performing schools, some approaches either substitute or also use sanctions or other disincentives. Both incentives and disincentives can be viewed as forms of differential treatment of schools within a district or state. After presenting several brief case studies of the operation and, sometimes, cessation of differing kinds of school incentives programs in various states, Richards and Shujaa concluded that numerous problems and questions exist with respect to their effects and successful implementation. Some important issues that have emerged are the following:

1. Because schools' achievement levels are so closely associated with their students' socio-economic status, it is difficult to find and/or identify schools with unusually high or low achievement (see Chapters 2 and 8 in this text).
2. Little is known about how school personnel respond or can be encouraged or assisted to respond positively to building-level incentives.
3. Incentive funding can undermine state equalization formulas designed to reduce the impact of disparities in community capacity to finance education.
4. Little is known about the types or amounts of incentives that can make a difference in improving student achievement.
5. As we discuss elsewhere in this chapter, accountability emphasis on student test scores can distort instruction in unproductive directions.
6. It is always difficult and frequently impossible to separate incentive effects from those of simultaneous school reforms.

Other studies also have questioned the efficacy of specific school-level performance incentive programs. For example, Stephenson and Levine (1987) analyzed data used by a big-city school district to meet a Florida mandate requiring districts to identify "merit" schools that were unusually successful in raising achievement. Their analysis showed that very few if any schools had superior achievement gains after taking account of students' socioeconomic background, and that identification of merit schools was highly dependent on the grade level and subject area tested and was not stable from year to year. In this context, it is difficult to see how rewarding a school for being meritorious could stimulate subsequent improvement in the future.

There are many ways differing schools can be treated differentially in trying to improve their effectiveness. Susan Fuhrman and Patti Fry (1991) have prepared a topology of various differential approaches, along with a preliminary assessment of the problems likely to be encountered in working to implement them. After noting that states historically have treated districts differentially with respect to such matters as provision of extra funding for low-wealth communities and granting of exemptions regarding teacher certificate requirements in the case of very small districts, these authors identified the following "emerging approaches" (in addition to rewards incentives described above) that some states recently have been developing explicitly to link "outcome measures to differential treatment" (Fuhrman and Fry 1991, 259–264):

▪ *"Performance-based accreditation,"* which expands "categories of accreditation or certification . . . to discriminate more discretely among districts" and to incorporate student outcome measures. Districts receiving low ratings are targeted for "more intensive oversight and assistance."

▪ *Provision of sanctions* against schools with low performance scores. Sanctions being considered or adopted in various states go beyond traditional penalties for noncompliance with state regulations and can range from severe punishments (e.g., loss of financial aid, takeover by the state) to milder reactions, such as imposition of additional requirements or oversight. At least six states have developed programs for strong but temporary state intervention or takeover in "academically bankrupt" or "educationally impaired" districts.

▪ *Targeting of assistance to low-performing districts* apart from accreditation procedures, typically in the form of provision of technical and other support to help such districts develop and implement improvement plans.

▪ *Regulatory waivers more comprehensive than traditional exemptions from state requirements*, which are granted in order to encourage flexibility and innovation.

Fuhrman and Fry also concluded that "problems and issues" have become apparent as states have expanded differential treatment as a means to bring about improvement in schools. Among the difficulties that make differential treatment a problematic mechanism for reform are the following (Fuhrman and Fry 1991, 265–275):

1. Lack of adequate measures of school and student performance.

2. Uncertainty whether waivers should be granted to high-performing schools on the ground that they require less supervision, or to low-performing schools on the grounds that exemption from bureaucratic regulation can help their faculties improve their programs.

3. Failure and/or inability to distinguish between low-performing districts that are or are not likely to benefit from various incentives and disincentives.

4. Tendencies and possibilities for districts or schools to manipulate data in order to improve their performance ratings. For example, low-achieving students can be placed in special education classes where they are not tested, tests can be administered when low achievers tend to be absent, and outright cheating can occur in the case of high-stakes tests that determine whether a school is accredited or classified as eligible for takeover.

5. Lack of knowledge of local problems on the part of state or other external officials involved in a state takeover of poorly performing schools. In addition, the process wherein state governments place local schools in receivership can be mostly unproductive. Thus, one educator who was involved in the State of New Jersey takeover of the Jersey City Schools summarized that experience as follows:

> *During the four years . . . [during which the state and the district] were at loggerheads before the actual takeover, human energy and financial resources focussed on compliance and not on satisfying student needs. (Tewel 1991, 29)*

6. Inability of the state to provide adequate financial, technical, or other support for low-performing schools or districts.

7. Failure of schools to identify or use waiver possibilities. (This potential development is discussed in the following section on restructuring and deregulation.)

Restructuring, Deregulation, Waivers, and School-Based Management

In recent years many recommendations and demands for school reform have called for a restructuring of one or another aspect of the educational system. Restructuring can be and indeed has been used in reference to just about every conceivable aspect of education: assessment and testing, curriculum, financial accountability and support systems, instructional methods, governance arrangements, scheduling and assignment of students to classes, school choice plans, teacher training or retraining, and countless others. One carefully thought through and instructive definition of restructuring is provided by staff of the National Governors' Association, who view it as a "systemic approach that acknowl-

edges the complexity of fundamentally changing the way schools are organized to significantly increase student learning. . . . [and thus] requires many pieces of the system to change" (David, Cohen, Honetschlager, and Traiman 1990, 1). Similarly, the Council of Chief State School Officers (1989) views restructuring as a comprehensive process that can and should extend to all facets of the "structure, operation, and responsibilities" of schools (p. 1). Officials of the Education Commission of the States have emphasized that the entire educational system—from "schoolhouse to statehouse"—is involved in restructuring and must change (Armstrong 1990).

Much of the available discussion and analysis about restructuring deals in some way with alternatives for deregulating teachers and schools. And as mentioned in the preceding section and elsewhere in this chapter, many states and school districts are exploring or introducing various possibilities for reducing rules and regulations that impede school reform efforts. (Many observers also point out that external regulations frequently provide teachers and administrators with an excuse to neglect promising but inconvenient or difficult changes.) Whether in connection with counterproductive testing that emphasizes low-level skills, district or state policies that protect incompetent teachers, attendance policies that assign students to dysfunctional poverty schools, or numerous other external requirements or forces that function to limit teacher or school effectiveness, deregulation increasingly is being perceived as a key consideration in working to restructure and reform the schools. The remainder of this section reviews recent developments with respect to two major approaches to deregulative restructuring—*conditional deregulation with waivers* and *school-based management*—and then concludes with a brief summary of several significant attempts to bring about *comprehensive restructuring* of many aspects of a local and a state educational system.

Conditional Deregulation with Waivers. By 1990, more than twenty states had introduced or adopted some form of legislation to reduce regulation of local schools and districts. In some cases deregulation is across the board, as happens when a state eliminates restrictions dealing with textbook requirements or limitations on the employment of teachers from nonaccredited colleges. In other cases deregulation involves granting waivers to schools that successfully meet predefined standards specified by the state or, conversely, to schools that are functioning or performing poorly and may benefit from deregulation. In the latter situation, deregulation through waivers and other forms of relief tends to be conditional—it is granted on a temporary basis while assistance is (or should be) provided to encourage improvement. Failure to improve may result in systematic deregulation, a state takeover, loss of state funds, or other penalties.

The linkages between waivers, provision of help, and possible imposition of penalties provide a means to try to make schools accountable for their output. Thus, conditional deregulation, according to one leading advocate, can put "teeth into accountability." According to this analyst (Dale Mann of Columbia University), conditional deregulation should incorporate the following steps and components (Mann 1990, 26, 28):

- *Tailor-made goals* through which school faculties negotiate priorities with state and district officials.
- *Flexible compliance* procedures that involve the suspension, reduction, or removal of unproductive regulations.
- *Biennial reviews* of student progress toward the negotiated learning goals.
- *Discretionary budgets* that loosen restrictions on how schools can expend their funds.
- *Contract waivers* that suspend or invalidate teacher contract provisions that a faculty perceives as hampering improvement.
- *Reorganized services* that the faculty receives after determining what type of help it requires from the central office.

Possibilities for introducing conditional deregulation with waivers have been attracting growing interest and acceptance from high-level local, state, and federal officials, and several states and districts have been designing or initiating pilot programs using this approach to restructuring (Natale 1990). However, a variety of problems are likely to arise with respect to conditional waivers, as is also true regarding other types of waivers, whether granted unconditionally or semipermanently as part of school-based management (see below) or as rewards for success rather than inducements to improve dysfunctional schools. Major questions and issues regarding waiver approaches in general include the following (Bowers 1990; Fuhrman and Fry 1991):

- Will many or most schools take advantage of waiver possibilities? Some observers have expressed disappointment with the frequent failure of schools participating in deregulation experiments to request waivers, and many observers are not sure that decision makers at the school level generally are able and/or willing to identify and conceptualize productive waivers.
- What types of technical assistance and other support should be made available to help faculties identify and use waivers productively? Most observers agree that waiver approaches will not work well if treated as an opportunity for central officials to abdicate their responsibilities for school improvement, but little is known concerning what kinds of help central units should provide to participating schools.

School-Based Management. Near the end of Chapter 4, we mention that many school districts are trying to enhance parent and community involvement through the establishment of building-level governance councils that have considerable decision-making authority. Formation of such councils, which depending on the district may or may not have significant parent representation, is part of a more widespread effort to move toward deregulation by forming and operating councils, committees, or alternate mechanisms that give teachers an increased role in determining what happens in their schools. Most frequently labeled *school-based management*, but sometimes referred to as *shared governance, site-based decision making* and *intradistrict decentralization*, this approach seeks to improve educational programs through advancing *teacher empowerment* and *faculty collaboration* at each participating school. Empowerment and collaboration, in turn, are widely thought to have much potential for improving teacher and school effectiveness (Maeroff 1988; Smith and Scott 1990; Moore 1991; Lane and Epps 1992).

A significant effort to introduce school-based management has been under way in the Dade County (FL) public schools, where teachers and other staff at participating schools are elected to form a Shared Decision-Making (SDM) committee. The SDM committee, which seeks input from other staff, parents, and students, has considerable authority in designing instructional arrangements and programs, selecting and assigning staff, determining allocations from the school's budget, and other aspects of school operation. In addition, schools using the school-based management approach are encouraged to request and assisted in obtaining waivers from real or imagined regulations and restrictions that faculty believe hamper their effectiveness.

The Dade SDM project began with 33 schools participating in 1987 and has since expanded to include more than 130 of the district's 263 schools. Although it is too early to determine whether school-based management in Dade will have a substantial impact in terms of improving student performance, participating schools have made numerous changes, such as initiation of after-school programs, revisions in class size, use of peer teacher evaluation methods, increase in staff development, expansion of parent contacts, and provision of counseling or other special services for students. Most SDM schools concentrate on implementing from four to twelve

changes or programs in a given year, and some have asked for and received one or more regulatory waivers (Strusinski 1990; Collins 1991).

Substantial attempts at implementing school-based management approaches also are taking place in Boston, Detroit, Indianapolis, Los Angeles, Memphis, San Diego, and hundreds of other school districts, both large and small, urban and rural. One of the best known and most closely watched efforts has been initiated in Chicago, where 1988 state legislation now provides for the election at every school of councils comprised of both parents and staff. Building councils in Chicago have broad authority in assigning faculty responsibilities and selecting new teachers and administrators, determining methods and materials in curriculum and instruction, designing schedules and educational services, allocating budget funds, and other matters (Bernard 1990; Doherty and Wilson 1990; Hess and Addington 1990; Rist 1990; Moore 1991).

Because Dade County, Chicago, and many other districts have only introduced school-based management during the past few years, it is too soon to reach firm conclusions regarding the extent to which this approach to restructuring will produce widespread improvement in the educational system. Meanwhile, there is much to be learned from initial developments. Various analysts and researchers have reported problems and obstacles that frequently hamper the work and effectiveness of participants in school-based management projects, including the following (Glickman 1990; Henderson and Marburger 1990; Meadows 1990; Malen, Ogawa, and Kranz 1991; Taylor and Levine 1991; Levine and Eubanks 1992):

1. *Inadequate time, training, and technical assistance* to engage in comprehensive analysis and decision making concerning possible educational improvements.
2. *Lack of resources and, in particular, discretionary funds* to initiate promising changes and improvements.

3. *Restrictions and regulations* that hamper flexibility.

4. *Unwillingness to request regulatory waivers* when they are available.

5. *Difficulties in stimulating consideration and/ or gaining acceptance of inconvenient or difficult changes*, such as policies that require experienced teachers to work with low achievers or assign larger classes or fewer resources to certain teachers.

6. *Dilemmas and lack of clarity regarding the distribution of authority and power* between administrators, teachers, school councils, and central officials.

7. *Confusion between school-based management and effective schools approaches*, that is, assuming that teacher empowerment automatically produces improvements while neglecting necessities to raise expectations for student performance, improve instructional arrangements for low achievers, and address other characteristics of unusually effective schools (see the section later on Effective Schools Research).

8. *Withholding or unavailability of shared information required to make wise decisions.*

9. *Constraints on teacher participation in decision making,* including lack of interest on the part of some or many teachers and lack of consensus.

10. *Reluctance of administrators* to give up traditional prerogatives.

11. *Failure of top-level decision makers* to provide the leadership and support necessary to make school-based management (or any other innovation) workable.

Comprehensive District Restructuring: Rochester. Probably the best-known attempt to bring about comprehensive restructuring at the school district level has been taking place in Rochester, New York. Developments arising from efforts to bring about fundamental reform of the Rochester Public Schools since 1987 have included the following (Bradley 1989, 1990b; E. Graham 1989; Buckley 1990):

- School-based management procedures and councils were established in every school.

- In return for a substantial increase in the basic salary schedule, teachers agreed to work longer hours and accept other additional responsibilities.

- Key business and civic leaders played an integral part in encouraging restructuring, initiating school partnerships, and providing financial support for innovative projects. In discussing business responsibilities for reform of the Rochester Schools, Eastman Kodak President Kay Whitmore advised other executives, "Be prepared to work very hard and for a long time. The more time I spend on it [education reform], the more complicated it gets" (quoted in Buckley 1989, 58).

- Based on models described in *A Nation Prepared*, a career-ladder approach was adopted that provides for four levels of positions: (1) *intern* (new) teachers working under the supervision of experienced colleagues; (2) *resident* teachers who have completed an internship but have only provisional certification; (3) *professional* teachers with permanent certification; and (4) *lead* teachers with at least ten years experience who work longer hours and devote at least half their time to serving as mentors, planning instructional improvements, and discharging other leadership roles. Lead teachers, who are selected by panels consisting of four teachers and three administrators, can earn more than three times as much as typical beginning teachers.

- Building on Rochester's already sizable magnet program, all schools became "schools of choice" that offer specialized learning opportunities and compete with each other for students.

- Instead of following traditional seniority practices, the district introduced new procedures wherein a faculty committee at each school interviews teachers who wish to transfer in or out, examines their records, and makes decisions based on local problems and considerations.

- Regarding teacher accountability, the district introduced procedures for increasing peer review in teacher evaluation and then negotiated a new union contract that, in return for additional large salary increases and expansion in the number of lead teachers, provided for performance-based assessment and remuneration of teachers, removal of teachers rated as unsatisfactory without going through traditional (and nearly universal) due-process proceedings, elimination of restrictions on the length of the teacher's workday, and other changes. Rochester teachers voted to reject this contract, which then was renegotiated to retain most aspects of the existing teacher evaluation system, with some modification based in part on introduction of criteria being developed by the National Board for Professional Teaching Standards. However, in 1991 the Board of Education unanimously rejected the proposed contract, partly because board members concluded it would not correct existing practices that hardly ever remove unsatisfactory teachers. The resulting bitterness and conflict among parents, teachers, and civic leaders seriously hampered the reform effort in Rochester (Chira 1991c).

Comprehensive State Restructuring: Kentucky. No state has moved to restructure and reform its educational system as thoroughly as has Kentucky. In 1989, the Kentucky Supreme Court declared the existing "system of common schools" unconstitutional, on the grounds that it was inequitable and exemplified other deficiencies. The court then directed the executive and legislative branches to change and improve the "entire sweep of the system—all its parts and parcels." Less than a year later, the Kentucky General Assembly approved and the governor signed a massive education bill (consisting of nearly 1,000 pages and weighing about 20 pounds) that among numerous other provisions introduced the following changes and innovations to be phased in by 1996 (Harp 1990; Pipho 1990; Foster 1991):

▪ Monetary and other rewards including teachers' pay bonuses will be given to successful schools, and unsuccessful schools will be identified so that "distinguished Kentucky educators"

and other forms of support can be assigned to help them.

▪ Faculty at unsuccessful schools who do not improve can be replaced by state-appointed teachers and administrators, and parents can receive state support to remove their children if the building is not subsequently closed.

▪ Parents will be able to withdraw their children from schools they deem unsatisfactory.

▪ Curriculum, instruction, and student assessment will become performance-based with emphasis on criterion-referenced (i.e., mastery-oriented) learning.

▪ Staff development will be increased substantially statewide.

▪ Family and youth service centers will be established in communities where 20 percent or more of students quality for subsidized lunches.

▪ All positions in the Kentucky Department of Education will be abolished and replaced with appointments in an agency reconstituted to reduce regulation and bureaucracy and instead provide more technical and assistance support.

▪ Strong antinepotism provisions will be introduced with regard to school-board elections and functioning.

▪ All schools are to adopt site-based management and establish building governance councils with substantial authority in redesigning curriculum and instruction and allocating their budgets to carry out improvement plans.

▪ Instead of traditional school accreditation based largely on minutes of instruction per lesson or subject, Carnegie units, and other input measures, state assessment of schools will be in terms of student achievement and other output (performance) indicators.

▪ New testing programs will be installed to facilitate productive implementations of the requirements regarding performance-based assessment of students, teachers, and schools.

▪ The compulsory school attendance age will be raised from sixteen to eighteen.

▪ All elementary schools will operate ungraded primary units for students now in grades K through 4.

- All districts will offer at least half-day preschool programs for disadvantaged four-year-olds.
- The state's financial formula has been changed to provide additional funds for low-wealth districts.
- If the legislature approves gubernatorial recommendations, taxes are to be increased (by more than 1 billion dollars during just the first two years) to pay for improvements and reforms.

National Goals: Agreements and Developments

Another way governors of the fifty states have endeavored to work toward educational reform has involved cooperation with the president and the federal government in defining and pursuing goals for the educational system. Cooperation for this purpose reached an unprecedented level in September 1989 when the governors met in Charlottesville, Virginia, with President George Bush to discuss establishment of national goals and directions for accomplishing them. After two days of deliberations, the president noted the historic importance of the meeting, which may vastly expand the federal role in shaping the future of local schools and districts, and then said that "A social compact begins today in Charlottesville, a compact between parents, teachers, principals, superintendents, state legislators, governors, and the Administration. Our compact is founded not on promises, but on challenges. . . . The American people are ready for radical reforms" (quoted in Miller 1989). Subsequent discussion and negotiations led to agreement on the following six national goals that were identified (along with twenty-one objectives distributed across the goals) in a February 1990 statement released by the governors:

1. By the year 2000, all children will start school ready to learn.
2. By the year 2000, the high school graduation rate will increase to at least 90 percent.
3. By the year 2000, American students will leave grades four, eight, and twelve having demonstrated competency over challenging subject matter including English, mathematics, science, history, and geography, and every school in America will ensure that all students learn to use their minds well, so they may be prepared for responsible citizenship, further learning, and productive employment in our modern economy.
4. By the year 2000, U.S. students will be first in the world in mathematics and science achievement.
5. By the year 2000, every adult American will be literate and will possess the knowledge and skills necessary to compete in a global economy and exercise the rights and responsibilities of citizenship.
6. By the year 2000, every school in America will be free of drugs and violence and will offer a disciplined environment conducive to learning.

One central issue addressed frequently by participants at the Charlottesville meeting and by concerned observers elsewhere has involved the source and potentially large scope of funding to support substantial movement toward the ambitious goals identified in the 1990 agreement (Walker 1990a). The president of the Carnegie Foundation for the Advancement of Teaching represented the views of many when he said that if national goals are not accompanied by substantial financial commitments, then "we should scrap the whole idea" (quoted in Lewis 1989a). However, other participants and observers, particularly President Bush and members of his administration, maintained that much can be accomplished through redirection and improvement in the use of existing expenditures as well as expansion of student-choice plans (see our section later) and other reforms they believe may involve little additional cost.

Many participants and observers also have expressed strong reservations concerning governmental capacity to register much progress in the absence of historically nonexistent policies, structures, and agencies that might initiate and help carry out the difficult reforms required to accomplish the six national goals. For example, one prominent educator observed that the president basically has "ordered the cars to drive faster . . . [but he] didn't say how the engine was going to be souped up, or whether the tires had to be fixed, or whether the road should be any different." An official of the American Association for the Advancement of Science questioned the seriousness of efforts that he viewed as lacking concrete plans and means for their attainment: "When President Kennedy said we had to beat the Russians to the moon and get a person there, we didn't just strap some rockets on the side of an airplane" (quoted in Olson 1990b).

Having established long-range goals that clearly will be very difficult to accomplish, the governors and the president confronted numerous challenges in trying to translate goals into action and results. Major developments involving efforts to move toward attainment of the goals have included the following (Miller 1991b; Olson and Miller 1991):

▪ The governors and the president agreed to establish a National Education Goals Panel to issue annual reports and offer recommendations regarding the progress of the school reform movement. The panel has six voting members appointed by the National Governors' Association (NGA) and four appointed by the president. Congressional leaders from both political parties also serve on the panel.
▪ The president formed an administration team including cabinet officials charged with planning follow-up activities related to attainment of the national goals.
▪ The Committee for Education Funding, an umbrella organization with more than 100 member organizations, called on the president and Congress to double the federal education budget between 1991 and 1996. An accompanying statement by the 1991 chair of the Committee warned that "If we do not invest more now . . . [the na-tional education goals] will become just a mirage that we will still be pursuing in the year 2000."

▪ Officials at the White House released a 1990 report enumerating federal actions that were being proposed or carried out in order to limit paperwork and reduce restrictions on state and local spending of federal funds, in line with NGA recommendations for eliminating unproductive regulation that hampers the attainment of the national goals. One year later, the president asked Congress to fund development of national tests in English, geography, history, and science and to help establish a national network of demonstration schools in cooperation with business and industry (Chira 1991a).

▪ By 1991, numerous observers were offering criticisms concerning what they perceived as an absence of leadership in initiating or furthering national goals-related activities and reforms, particularly on the part of the president. For example, the chief editor of the Gallup Poll said that "We've asked several different times what is Bush's most important accomplishment so far, and no one ever mentions education"; a former director (until 1990) of the NGA's education programs said that the president "hasn't done nearly as much" as he could have to keep the goals "in front of the American people and to promote that agenda"; the president of the National Education Association said that nobody has "put together a plan for how we're going to meet the goals"; and the president of the Council for Basic Education expressed the view that the president "hasn't really done much except talk, and talk is cheap." Responding to such criticisms, the president's domestic-policy adviser said that "Changing our education system is going to take an extended period of time to see dramatic results" (quoted in Olson and Miller 1991, 1, 30–31).

Impact of National Reform Efforts

The various national, state, and local reports on the status of education have received considerable and continuing attention throughout the United States and undoubtedly have played an important part in stimulating and reinforcing efforts to improve the schools, particularly at the level of state government. Many states had established or were moving to establish new policies, such as state supervision of deficient schools or school districts and competency testing of new teachers and administrators. Many governors, state legislators, and local school officials used the national reports as support to redouble these efforts to establish accountability mechanisms through which they hoped to assure the public that maintaining or increasing taxes for education actually resulted in effective or improved educational programming. Additional or accelerated movement toward increased state testing, stronger graduation requirements, introduction of performance-based teacher evaluation, and other actions recommended in the national reports thus occurred in many states and school districts. By 1990, school-improvement initiatives included the following (Barton and Coley 1990; Fuhrman and Elmore 1990):

- Forty-two states had raised high-school graduation requirements.
- Forty-seven states had introduced, refined, or institutionalized statewide student testing programs.
- Numerous states had introduced teacher testing programs, so that thirty-nine states required new teachers and/or teacher-education applicants to pass a test. In addition, many schools and colleges of education had either introduced or strengthened admissions and exit requirements.
- A number of states had introduced programs that reward teachers or schools partly on the basis of high performance.
- At least twenty-five states had initiated programs to identify and stimulate change at schools with low performance scores.
- Seventy-three percent of high schools had set stricter attendance standards.
- Seventy percent of high schools had set stricter standards for participation in athletics and other extracurricular activities.

- Forty percent of high schools had lengthened the school day.

Frequent Criticisms of Reports and Efforts Dealing with Reform

Many observers have questioned the adequacy of some or most of the national reports and recommendations dealing with problems and reform possibilities in education, as well as the actions that have been taken in attempting to bring about recommended improvements. Few quarrel with the emphasis on reversing a so-called rising tide of mediocrity, but many perceive the major accomplishments to date as constituting more a rising pile of reports than a serious or promising attempt to bring about meaningful improvements in the educational system. Several of the most common and trenchant criticisms and doubts are summarized below.

1. Many of the reports largely ignored the practical problems involved in improving the performance of low-achieving students—particularly disadvantaged students in urban areas (Bastian 1986; Shanker 1988; Patterson 1990). This criticism has been expressed by A. Harry Passow as follows:

> The reports of the eighties . . . fail to attend to the particular problems and needs of schools with large populations of poor and minority children. . . . If there is a real crisis in education, it is in the urban schools. . . . Simply recommending that school personnel set tougher, stiffer academic demands, and crack down on discipline problems without effecting necessary changes in pedagogy, curriculum, and personnel is an inadequate solution. (Passow 1984, 680)

2. The reports are not likely to have much positive impact because they mostly have ignored important school governance issues that will determine whether reform efforts succeed or fail (Chubb 1988, Chubb and Moe 1990). Myron Lieberman (1986) has expressed and summarized this point of view:

Competent media treatment of A Nation at Risk . . . *would probably have consigned it to oblivion. Its failure to deal with such critical issues as the inefficient governance structure, collective bargaining, and teacher-tenure law are only part of the explanation of its futilitarian nature. Significantly, the national commission that sponsored the report deliberately avoided several issues in order to have a unanimous report. There would be nothing necessarily wrong with this if the commission had informed the American people of this important fact. (Lieberman 1986, 20)*

3. In concentrating on actions that lend themselves to legislative mandates (e.g., increased graduation requirements, a longer school day), many of the reports thereby not only minimized the need for fundamental changes in teaching and learning but also generally neglected and even obscured the kinds of change efforts required to bring about major reform in the functioning of schools. (A later section in this chapter discusses research and analysis on the change process and requirements for fundamental reform). Many observers thus concluded that *A Nation at Risk* and other reports were unlikely to accomplish any more real improvement in the schools than had previous calls for improvement in education in earlier decades (Spady 1983). This point of view was expressed by Glen Harvey:

A number of policy-related changes designed to respond to recent recommendations are particularly likely to result in only illusory school improvement. Raising the graduation requirements from three to four years of English, for example, without improving the content of instruction . . . only gives the impression of improving the level of educational attainment. (Harvey 1984, 9)

A somewhat similar viewpoint was articulated by former National Education Association President Mary Futrell (1986; Edmundson 1989), with special reference to recommendations for improving the quality and output of the teaching force:

Policymakers are giving new meaning to the term myopia. Policymakers, by and large, do not want to hear that reform efforts, to be effective, must target a complex constellation of problems . . . [or that] real reform must address the everyday realities of the learning workplace. Above all, policymakers do not want to hear that educational reform is hard work. . . .

Our schools today are structurally decrepit, still shaped by an organizational model appropriate to nineteenth century industry. This model does little to enliven the imagination . . . [or to] encourage collegial cooperation. It does much to intensify isolation.

. . . We must reform the reform movement. And the reform of reform must begin with releasing all educations from the structural straightjackets in which they are now strapped. Without this change, all the reform documents that have been written will become no more than faded reminders of what might have been. (Futrell 1986, 6)

We cannot continue to assume that a system which has allowed 25–30% of the children to fall through the cracks will be the system that will take us into the twenty-first century. (Quoted in Edmundson 1989, 6)

4. The reports both built on and extended actions in many states to define and test students' minimum competency skills, and in so doing they reinforced rather than countered tendencies to emphasize mechanical, low-order skills that are easiest to teach and test. The effects of minimum competency testing sometimes are destructive, particularly in concentrated poverty schools in which students can spend years memorizing and regurgitating factual material to pass competency tests, whereas students in middle-class schools quickly pass the tests and proceed to instruction placing more emphasis on higher-order skills (Allington 1991).

After many states had introduced or expanded student competency testing in accordance with recommendations in *A Nation and Risk* and other reports, Clune, White, and Patterson (1989) examined and assessed the resulting developments at a national sample of high schools. The researchers reported that schools generally were under pressure simultaneously to place higher proportions of students in relatively advanced courses (such as algebra) and to ensure that they receive passing grades and test scores. In part because substantial funds for improvement usually were not available and little had been done fundamentally to improve teaching and learning so as to help students master difficult content, the result in many schools has been to emphasize memorization of low-level skills and knowledge sufficient to pass the tests. Janice Patterson of the research team summarized this general outcome as follows:

> The education reforms of the 1980s focused on increased number of courses for high school graduation as well as minimum performance on competency-based tests. These reforms had little effect on middle- and upper-level achievers but important effects on at-risk students. . . . The findings reveal that although schools increased the number of math and science courses, these courses were primarily low-level content . . . teachers of at-risk students tended to teach the test in a variety of ways that went beyond test-taking skills. . . . [Thus competency tests] served as the driving force on curriculum in ways that were not envisioned by policymakers seeking increased conceptual skills. (Patterson 1990, 21–22)

Bruce Wilson and H. Dickson Corbett (1990) also examined the competency testing movement and concluded that negative effects are most likely when the tests are used to determine whether students pass or fail courses or graduate and/or results by school and district are widely disseminated. After intensively studying developments in two states that had introduced these kinds of high stakes testing practices, Wilson and Corbett reported that teachers previously had been somewhat skeptical about the value of state tests but many had re-examined and modified curriculum and instruction in an effort to help improve student performance. However, after the stakes were raised by publishing district scores or linking student performance to graduation, a turning point was reached at which:

> the modest positive effects associated with having additional diagnostic information available was overwhelmed by perversion of local practice *[italics added]*, with primary goal becoming to improve test scores. Many of the negative behaviors associated with "teaching to the test" thus emerged. . . .
>
> [If statewide testing programs are of little benefit for students, why their] popularity? Statewide tests are primarily a political device; they are easily legislated and . . . easily interpreted. . . . [By way of contrast, substantial school improvement requires] generous dollops of technical assistance and staff interaction within a three-to-five-year time span. (Wilson and Corbett 1990, 261–262)

5. Related to its dependence on bureaucratic and legislative mandates and its emphasis on minimum competency testing, the reform movement has functioned in conjunction with other developments to deprofessionalize or "de-skill" the teaching force. Deprofessionalization of teachers refers to administrative control policies and practices that stimulate or force teachers to simplify curriculum and instruction for the purpose of ensuring that students demonstrate a specified level of mastery on easy-to-grade tests (Sykes 1990).

Linda McNeil (1986; 1988; 1990) has characterized the behavior of many teachers subject to such policies and practices in terms of "defensive teaching," "fragmentation" of the curriculum to fit the tests, "omission" of important material and topics not tested, "mystification" of topics in the sense that regurgitation takes precedence over understanding, and "defensive simplification," through which teachers back off from in-depth instruction in order to gain minimal compliance from students. These kinds of dynamics are discussed in more detail in a later section of this chapter.

Many observers believe that administrative control associated with the reform movement has exacerbated the tendencies described by McNeil, which appear to be clearly antithetical to the task of improving student performance in critical thinking and other higher-order skills. For example, researchers who observed classroom lessons at elementary and secondary schools in North Carolina found that introduction of an approach to increase teacher accountability was associated with a large decline in teachers' emphasis on higher-order learning. The approach in question uses the Teacher Performance Appraisal Instrument (TPAI), which is similar to teacher assessment instruments introduced in a number of other states and emphasizes teacher-centered delivery of structured lessons following prescribed steps in a sequence. (This is the direct instruction model discussed later in this chapter.) Data collected in the study indicated that the percentage of teachers who placed at least some emphasis on "conjectural" exploration of concepts and questioning behavior by students rather than teacher-centered delivery of information fell from 40 percent to 11 percent over the three-year period during which teachers received training and encouragement to behave in accordance with the TPAI (Milner 1991).

Numerous other observers also believe that teacher evaluation/accountability instruments and procedures introduced in many states as part of the reform movement have had negative effects on instruction (Rowan 1990; Sykes 1990). Thus, Harriet Tyson-Bernstein examined the Texas Teacher Appraisal System (TTAS) and concluded that it "rewards teachers who lecture and question a relatively passive class but not teachers who help students struggle through difficult tasks." She further concluded that though

the TTAS may help in removing some incompetent teachers and in raising basic-skills test scores in the short run, the long-range effect will be to "inhibit the development of curiosity and higher realms of thinking" (Tyson-Bernstein 1987, 29). Similarly, an associate director of the American Federation of Teachers has been severely critical of the teacher evaluation system introduced in Louisiana in 1988 on the grounds that it is a "formulaic" instrument that rewards "didactic" teachers who emphasize mastery of "organized lists of information" (Diegmueller 1991a, 18).

6. Few national reports have provided adequate estimates or information about the costs of making reform a reality. In this regard, the American Association of School Administrators (1984) estimated that implementing just two proposals from *A Nation at Risk*—raising beginning teachers' salaries to a market-sensitive level and lengthening the school term to 200 days a year, 7 hours a day—would require a 27 percent increase in existing school budgets. One report that did provide estimates was that of the Quality Education for Minorities (1990) project, which estimated that for the twenty-two largest, predominantly-minority school districts, it would cost about 2.7 billion dollars over a five-year period to extend the school year, add 5 percent supplemental raises to teacher salaries, greatly expand early childhood education, and add adequate personnel in math and science.

7. Reforms that have been introduced on a widespread basis have not constituted a coherent approach for improving the schools. To the contrary, initiatives frequently have worked at cross purposes and sometimes actually made it more difficult to attain the goals of reform. For example, even when tests introduced to assess the performance of students and schools have not overemphasized low-level, mechanical skills, they sometimes have placed enormous record-keeping burdens on teachers. Tests introduced to assess applicants for teacher education have eliminated some incompetent candidates, but they also have resulted in invalid rejection of

minority applicants already in short supply. Campaigns to reduce dropping out of school frequently have increased retention rates but, in the absence of substantial funds to improve curriculum and instruction, they have overloaded teachers with additional numbers of low-achieving students. These kinds of incoherence in the reform movement have been criticized by Richard Elmore and Susan Fuhrman (1990) as follows:

> *Over the longer term, reform policies could fail, not because they are individually flawed or poorly implemented, but because, in combination, they make good teaching and learning more difficult in schools. This finding suggests that the next task of education reform is to design policies on curriculum, teacher preparation and professional development, testing and assessment, and school organization and governance that work together in a coherent way, rather than simply imposing new, disparate demands on schools. (Elmore and Fuhrman 1990, 161)*

Conclusions Regarding National Reform

Although little systematic research is available and it obviously is extremely difficult if not impossible to determine what has been taking place in fifty states and more than fifteen thousand school districts, educators must try to identify and delineate the major problems that have emerged in the past. Tentative and preliminary though one must be in drawing conclusions, some sense of the status of the reform movement and the critical issues with which it is grappling is a necessary prerequisite in trying to determine what should be done to solve the central problems facing the educational system in the United States. Our assessment of some of the most important developments and issues currently confronting the reform movement is provided below.

1. The reform movement to date has not sufficiently addressed the necessity of bringing about fundamental reform of organizational structures and governance as well as of instructional arrangements and practices in the schools. While it is true that a few states, such as Colorado, Kentucky, and Maryland, have encouraged and helped districts plan for fundamental reform, most states have avoided the difficult and expensive issues involved in moving beyond mandated bureaucratic initiatives.

At the building and district levels, the situation is very uneven. Many schools and districts are exploring or even implementing fundamental changes in organizational and instructional arrangements and structures. However, most schools apparently are not yet doing so, and directions for the future are not clear. (Possibilities for fundamental reform, particularly at the high-school level, are discussed later in this chapter.)

2. Dilemmas involving perceived needs for testing and accountability on the one hand and emphasis on higher-order skills and independent learning on the other are still far from being resolved. Although there is increased recognition of the dangers of low-level testing that drives instruction toward further stress on memorization and regurgitation of factual material, minimum competency testing that may be having this effect also has continued to increase. Efforts to introduce and improve testing of higher-order skills will accelerate in the future, but this trend is likely to require years of development, and financial as well as other forms of support may not be adequate.

3. Efforts to change preparation and remuneration arrangements for teachers have been proceeding through the work of the Carnegie Task Force on Teaching as a Profession, the Holmes Group, and other organizations, but there is disagreement on key issues, such as whether a teaching certificate should require postbachelor's degree preparation and whether teaching careers, responsibilities, and pay should be differentiated for master teachers, regular teachers, teacher aides, and other teaching positions. For example, the National Education Association has consistently opposed proposals to create lead teachers, as proposed by the Carnegie Task Force. Also, active opposition from teachers' groups along with very high costs and other problems encountered in conceptualizing and implementing career ladders and other performance-based approaches in Florida, Tennessee, Texas, and elsewhere have blocked development and further implementation in many states (Jacobson 1986; Olson 1987a, 1987b; Buckley 1989; Frase and Poston 1990).

4. Dilemmas and tensions involving the general promotion of excellence on the one hand and of educational equity on the other have not been systematically confronted and resolved. Many analysts believe that the two types of goals can be harmonized provided that adequate attention and resources are devoted to each one, and that the schools can and should improve the performance of all student groups at the same time that massive efforts are under way to help the disadvantaged. Contradictions are likely to arise in practice, however, particularly when reform programs are sporadic and superficial, and do not satisfactorily address the most serious underlying problems in the educational system.

With regard to expansion of graduation requirements, for example, introduction of rigorous requirements may help improve instruction for the average student, but implemented in isolation these reforms may increase failure and dropout rates for disadvantaged students (McDill, Natriello, and Pallas 1986; Wilson 1990). Regarding testing of teachers, similarly, the reform movement may be exacerbating an incipient crisis in the availability of minority teachers. Testing of teachers as advocated in *A Nation Prepared* and numerous other reform reports may lead to improvements in the overall quality of the teaching force, but grave, negative consequences may follow if this goal is attained without ensuring an adequate supply of minority teachers (Chira 1990a).

The tension between excellence and equity also is evident with respect to proposals for move-

ment toward a national test. On the one hand, supporters of national testing generally believe that student motivation and achievement will improve if there are real penalties for lack of effort and poor performance, and many argue that opportunities for low achievers will be improved if tests channel them into strong employment preparation programs rather than, as at present, menial unskilled jobs or low-level community colleges (see Chapters 2 and 6). On the other hand, opponents believe that national testing of high-school seniors or graduates will eliminate many low achievers' higher-education opportunities that are increasingly important in postindustrial societies (see Chapter 7), thereby counteracting or eliminating a distinctive, historical strength of the social and educational system in the United States—more than in any other country, young people have had multiple opportunities to become "late bloomers" who overcome or reverse personal histories of low achievement or attainment (Chira 1991b; O'Neal 1991). In the midst of this debate, one conclusion seems irrefutable: Unless vast improvements are *first* brought about in the functioning of inner-city schools and/or in arrangements for improving the transition from school to work, national testing will further constrict the life chances of many disadvantaged youth whose low performance will disqualify them from either higher education or good entry-level jobs in the economy.

5. Rather than continuing to reinforce trends toward further deskilling of teachers, the reform movement must be basically transformed to empower and assist them in making productive decisions concerning effective delivery of instruction in their classrooms (Maeroff 1988; Foster 1991). Empowerment is important in part because instructional goals involving the development of students' higher-order thinking and comprehension skills are not likely to be attained through continued dependence on narrow prescriptions for teacher-centered delivery of instruction (Sykes 1990; Foster 1991).

PARTICIPATION OF EXTERNAL ORGANIZATIONS IN IMPROVEMENT AND REFORM

In addition to the contributions some business and other community leaders have made in helping to initiate and support demands for reform of the educational system, corporations and other organizations are playing a growing role in working directly with the schools to bring about improvement (Lewis 1990; Weisman 1990b). Nearly half of the elementary and secondary schools in the United States now receive help from an external partner (usually a business), and most large corporations provide assistance to public schools or groups of schools, usually as part of an Adopt-A-School program (McNeil 1990). Types of assistance most often provided include speakers and resource people for instruction, sponsorship of achievement awards, career days and conferences, tutoring, and equipment donations.

The best-known approach for joining business and the public schools in a substantial effort to improve education is the Boston Compact initiated by business, civic, governmental, and civic leaders in 1982 (Walker 1990b). In forming the compact, business and public-school officials committed themselves to the attainment of annual goals. For the first year, business leaders agreed to recruit at least 200 companies to participate in programs for hiring public-school graduates and for providing employment for students. School officials agreed to reduce absenteeism and the dropout rate by 5 percent, to introduce competency requirements for graduation, and to increase the placement rate of graduates into higher education or full-time employment by 5 percent. "The message the Compact now sends to Boston's young people," according to Robert Schwartz and Jeannette Hargroves, is that "if you stay in school, work hard, and master the basics, you will be helped to find a job" (1986–87, 15).

As of 1990, nearly 400 companies were participating in the Boston Compact, and the project had expanded to involve a number of agencies, activities, and components that include the following (Diesenhouse 1989; Lewis 1990):

1. Establishment of an Action Center for Educational Services and Scholarships, which provides eligible graduates with financing to attend college.
2. Provision of staff to coordinate the contributions of companies and provide job counseling and career education in high schools.
3. Inclusion of more than twenty local colleges and universities in efforts to expand higher-education opportunities for graduates and to provide various forms of assistance to schools in Boston. These institutions pledged to help place at least 75 percent of 1989 high-school graduates in higher education.
4. Establishment of Support for Early Education Development (SEED) to improve education for Boston's preschool and primary children.
5. Creation of Compact Ventures to work with potential dropouts.

Early results associated with the partnerships forged among the Boston Compact, the public schools, and other institutions have been mostly encouraging. Data collected by Compact officials indicate that very high proportions of high-school graduates either enter college or are employed full time and most college entrants are persisting to graduation (Lacayo 1986; Diesenhouse 1989). Meanwhile, the National Alliance of Business and other organizations have initiated projects similar to the Boston Compact in numerous other big cities (Lewis 1990).

Responding to plentiful indications that improvement of the educational system has become a critical national priority, civic and community leaders have resolved to participate more actively in local, state, and national school-reform efforts throughout the United States. Among the actions and projects initiated by corporations, foundations, and other organizations in the late 1980s and early 1990s are the following:

- RJR Nabisco allocated 30 million dollars to help implement improvements in the educational system between 1990 and 1995.
- General Electric allocated nearly 20 million dollars to assist disadvantaged college-bound youth.
- The MacArthur Foundation provided 40 million dollars to facilitate reform in the Chicago Public Schools over a ten-year period.
- Community leaders organized a 25 million dollar endowment to help finance improvements in educational opportunities for students in Baltimore.
- Citibank committed 20 million dollars to help improve elementary and secondary schools.
- IBM committed 25 million dollars for school-reform projects.
- The Coca Cola Foundation announced it will donate 50 million dollars to improve education in the 1990s.

Higher Education Students as Tutors

Much of what higher education institutions have tried to contribute to school improvement efforts has involved programs in which college and university students tutor elementary and secondary pupils. Contributions of this kind were assessed in a national survey conducted for the U.S. Department of Education by Policy Study Associates (Reisner, Petry, and Armitage 1990). The investigators found that "mentoring" programs that provide tutoring for elementary and secondary students were being conducted by nearly 1,000 of the nation's approximately 3,200 colleges and universities. Although more than 63,000 tutors and mentors were working with nearly 200,000 students, local demand for such services generally was much greater than could be satisfied. Confirming earlier studies (e.g., Slavin and Madden 1989) that supported the potential value of tutors in improving student achievement, the investigators found reasons to conclude that tutoring by higher education stu-

dents frequently is beneficial for low-achieving elementary and secondary students. They also concluded (Reisner, Petry, and Armitage 1990, ii) that the most effective programs tend to exemplify the following characteristics:

- Time commitments of tutors/mentors are clearly defined.
- There is systematic screening of prospective tutors/mentors and "matching" with tutored students that takes account of "shared traits and interests."
- "Thorough training" is provided for tutors and mentors.
- Close relationships are maintained between participating school systems and institutions of higher education.

Assured College Access for High School Graduates

As mentioned earlier, a major component in the Boston Compact (and other cities in which similar approaches have been introduced) involves enhancement of student motivation through guaranteeing postsecondary education for low-status students who complete high school. In many communities, such guarantees now are being provided and/or financed through assistance from wealthy individuals, community agencies, colleges and universities, and/or philanthropic foundations (Freedman 1991). Among the best known of these efforts are the following:

- The I Have a Dream Program originated by Eugene Lang in 1981 for sixty-one sixth graders graduating from P.S. 121 in New York City. Counseling and various educational services also were provided for students as they proceeded through secondary schools. In 1991, thirty-eight of these inner-city students were attending colleges and universities (Berger 1989; Freedman 1991; Nieves 1991).
- Project Choice in Kansas City, Kansas, and Kansas City, Missouri, where a foundation organized by Ewing and Marion Kauffman is

providing guaranteed college funding plus relevant services for 1988, 1989, and 1990 freshmen proceeding through one high school and 150 students at five other schools. Participating students must pass random drug tests, maintain acceptable standards in behavior and academic performance, and accept tutoring help if needed (Rhone 1992).

▪ The Taylor Plan, through which the State of Louisiana provides free tuition at state colleges and universities for qualified low- and moderate-income students. Initiated in 1990, this program is named after an oil producer (Paul Taylor) who started a New Orleans project similar to Lang's I Have a Dream approach and then worked hard to convince the Louisiana legislature of the need for a statewide program on the grounds that either "we have to expand the pool of recruits" for college or "we will cease to exist as an industrial nation" (quoted in Walsh 1990a).

▪ Indiana's 21st Century Scholars program, which was initiated in 1990 and contributes the difference between federal and other financial aid for which a low-income applicant is eligible for tuition costs at state colleges and universities.

▪ New York State's Liberty Scholarship Program, similar to the 21st Century Scholars program but which began in 1988 with an emphasis on provision of counseling to help participating students succeed in high school.

▪ The Rhode Island Children's Crusade, which offers full scholarships at state colleges and universities to low-income students and also provides academic assistance, mentoring, and other services to support the participation of eligible students beginning in the third grade. In return, students sign agreements in which they reject illegal drugs and other dysfunctional behaviors.

Programs such as these proliferated rapidly in the 1980s and early 1990s. By 1991, 141 sponsors were helping to support programs similar to I Have a Dream in 41 cities, and at least 40 additional comparable projects elsewhere were identified by researchers at the federal government's General Accounting Office (GAO). A GAO na-

tional evaluation of efforts to assure college access for low-income youth also identified thirteen "last dollar" programs that guarantee the "final amount a student needs to attend college (or other eligible postsecondary school) after efforts to obtain all other aid have been exhausted" (Chelimsky 1990, 29). The GAO evaluation concluded that of the guaranteed-tuition programs it surveyed, sixty-six differ from earlier programs in that they constitute "comprehensive efforts, starting early in the school career, to increase the chances of academic success for disadvantaged youth. . . . [by combining] a financial aid guarantee, personal, often intense mentoring, and a wide range of program elements aimed at increasing both motivation and academic skills" (Chelimsky 1990, 2). The report also found that although such programs reach only a small percentage of the nation's disadvantaged students and usually encounter serious problems involving insufficient funding, staff overload and burnout, lack of cooperation from some parents, and other considerations, they do

appear to be achieving an important success in keeping the selected student groups intact and in school. This is a critical precondition for any other effects. Some program components—especially the early intervention, personal mentoring, and intensive academic help in "sponsorship" programs—seem to have the potential to markedly increase motivation and achievement. (Chelimsky 1990, 2)

RECENT SCHOOL CHOICE PROPOSALS AND DEVELOPMENTS

Proposals for giving students more choice concerning the schools they attend have been receiving considerable and growing attention since the mid-1980s. Some support for increased choice has been provided by proponents identified with the magnet/alternative schools movement (see Chapter 10) and proposals for tuition tax credits and education vouchers (see Chapter 12), but in recent years choice plans have been advocated by a much larger collection of individuals and groups who perceive choice as a way to reform schools by bringing about greater accountability and flexibility throughout the educational system. In addition to magnet-school plans and other choice-related activities already described in preceding chapters, important developments regarding enhancement of students' opportunities to choose where they will enroll and what they will study have included the following:

▪ After citing choice as "perhaps the single most promising idea" for advancing national efforts to reform the schools and for helping bring about "empowerment of disadvantaged citizens," President Bush stated his intention to "provide every feasible assistance—financial and otherwise—to states and districts interested in further experience with choice plans." In line with this statement of intent, the president asked Congress to allow federal funds to follow students who transfer to nonpublic schools and the secretary of the U.S. Department of Education created an "outreach" unit (i.e., The Center for Choice in Education) to sponsor workshops and seminars, operate an information hotline, organize a "resource bank" of consultants, and carry on other activities to promote expansion of school-choice arrangements (Pitsch 1990; Chira 1991a).

▪ Through legislation following up on CCSSO recommendations (described earlier in this chapter) to broaden enrollment opportunities for disadvantaged students, the state of Washington and several other states introduced "open enrollment" plans allowing transfer across and/or within school districts. Considered by many observers to be the most far-reaching of these open enrollment initiatives, Washington's 1990 legislation provides students who experience a "special hardship or detrimental condition" with an absolute right to leave their home districts and enter another in which space is available. Students requesting a transfer to a district "more accessible to a parent's workplace or child-care site also must be allowed to enter the new district. Other students can be denied transfers if their withdrawal would reduce desegregation or if these parents cannot show that a transfer would be beneficial for educational, financial, or health or safety-related reasons. In addition, all school districts must adopt policies allowing for internal transfers (Snider 1990b).

▪ Colorado enacted a law requiring that all districts permit students to transfer freely within their boundaries. Transfer requests can be refused only on the grounds of insufficient space (Snider 1990a).

▪ City officials in Epsom, New Hampshire, provided $1,000 tax reductions per year for each family in which students attend a high school other than their local school. Because these reductions extend to families whose children attend nonpublic schools, the Epsom law was considered a test of the tax-credit approach. Opponents of the law successfully challenged its constitutionality in the courts (Butterfield 1991b).

▪ Legislation enacted in Wisconsin in 1990 permits up to 1 percent of Milwaukee public school students to attend nonsectarian private schools, which then receive state reimbursement, provided that the students are from low-income families. Wisconsin thus became the first state to promote choice for disadvantaged students through a voucher program that extends to nonpublic schools. After surviving initial court challenges, the legislation (called the Milwaukee Choice Plan) resulted in payment to private schools for nearly 400 students during the 1990–91 school year (Farrell 1990; Peterkin 1991).

▪ Minnesota initiated the first statewide requirement introducing certain aspects (discussed later) of choice and open enrollment and completed phase-in of these arrangements in 1991. Except for several districts operating under desegregation guidelines, students can change schools or districts for any reason, with partial transportation provided for interdistrict transfer. Districts can refuse to admit applicants but cannot deny permission to leave. By 1992, more than 6,000 students had transferred to schools in another district.

In addition to open enrollment provisions, Minnesota's school choice laws established a Postsecondary Enrollment Options program that enables high-school juniors and seniors to take college courses with no tuition charge, an Area Learning Center program and Graduation Incentives funds that allow unsuccessful students older than eleven to enroll in alternative-school units outside their districts, and a program that helps finance alternative learning opportunities at nonsectarian private schools (Pearson 1989; Olson 1991b).

Data collected between 1988 and 1991 supported a variety of conclusions and inferences, including the following, regarding the operation and effects of choice arrangements in Minnesota: (1) significant numbers and percentages of participating students had returned to school after dropping out; (2) many high schools had introduced or expanded advanced placement courses in order to avoid losing students to higher education institutions; (3) thousands of students from nonpublic schools returned to public schools to take advantage of choice opportunities; (4) some schools and districts reported a disproportionate loss of their most motivated and/or high-achieving students; (5) nearly half the students who transferred to another district reported doing so primarily for convenience, that is, to attend a school closer to home or one with a day-care program; (6) some administrators in districts losing enrollment feared that their schools might be hurt by a vicious circle in which such loss resulted in reduced state aid followed by elimination of educational services and still more transfers out; and (7) students in alternative programs improved in academic performance and aspirations (Pearson 1989; Shanker 1989; Olson 1991b).

As a variety of proposals have been offered and diverse steps have been taken to expand school choice, vast numbers of supporting and opposing opinions and recommendations for and against further action have been promulgated. Among those who support magnetization of entire school districts and regions, tax credits or vouchers to attend nonpublic schools, fully open enrollment within and across district boundaries, creation of networks of alternative schools, or other options for expanding students' opportunities to select among schools, the following assertions and arguments have been most prominent (Coons and Sugarman 1978, 1991; Nathan 1985, 1990; Chubb and Moe 1990; Leo 1991c; Raywid 1990, 1991; Wells 1990; Clinchy 1992).

- Providing choice for disadvantaged students will enable them to escape from poorly functioning schools and transfer to effective schools.
- Because public schools generally are not very successful in working with low achievers, there is little to lose through introducing arrangements facilitating their transfer to schools different than those they now attend.
- Achievement, aspirations, and other outcomes will improve for many students because they will be more motivated at schools they have selected and/or will be more interested in instruction emphasized at their new schools.
- Both existing public schools and alternate learning institutions (whether public or nonpublic) will provide improved educational opportunities because their staffs will be competing to attract students.
- Increased opportunities will be available to match school programs and services with students' needs.
- Parents will be empowered and encouraged to play a larger role in their children's education.

Critics of proposals to introduce choice arrangements rapidly on a wide scale question the assumptions and conclusions offered by the advocates, particularly in cases that involve subsidized participation of nonpublic schools. Arguments advanced most frequently by opponents and skeptics include the following (Shanker 1989; 1991; Bastian 1990; Evans 1990; Witte 1990; Heckman 1991; Leo 1991c):

- Choice arrangements will reinforce and increase stratification and segregation because highly motivated and/or high-achieving white and minority students will be disproportionately likely to participate and transfer out of schools that already are predominantly minority or low income in enrollment.

- Much of the movement of students will involve damaging transfer of middle-class students to nonpublic schools. This point of view was expressed by Wisconsin Commissioner of Education Herbert Grover: "You'll allow the informed and influential . . . the economic royalty of this country to get subsidies . . . [and in so doing] you'll absolutely nuke the public support for the institution that serves the predominant majority of young people" (quoted in Olson 1990a, 11).

- Public financial support for nonpublic schools through various choice mechanisms is unconstitutional.

- Competition among schools seeking to attract transfer students will not in itself ensure that improvements will occur; other proposed or emerging reforms described and discussed in this chapter are more important and promising than choice.

- Opening and closing of numerous schools based on their competitive attractiveness will disrupt the fundamental operation of the entire educational system.

- There is little or no reason to believe that most schools that presently enroll relatively few low-achieving, disadvantaged students would be more successful with such students than are their present schools.

- Even if one assumes that schools capable of substantially improving the performance of low achievers are widely available to participants in a choice plan, many or most parents lack the knowledge and experience necessary to select schools, and these outstanding schools may not accept many low achievers.

- Complications involved in massive movement of students from one school or district to another will hamper effective implementation of other recent or emerging reform efforts that are beginning to register significant success.

- Participation of nonpublic institutions will result in the establishment or growth of "cult" schools based on divisive racist or religious ideologies (Honig 1990, A13).

- Although desirable for various reasons, greater parent involvement in education associated with choice plans will not in itself result in large improvements in school effectiveness.

- Although accountability may increase in the sense that unattractive schools will lose students and may even be closed, overall accountability will be reduced because nonpublic schools and, possibly, small alternative schools will not be subject to existing public standards and scrutiny of their operation.

Advocates of choice rebut the assertions of opponents and argue that deficiencies that may have been identified in Alum Rock, elitist magnet plans, or other choice arrangements are not inevitable; they can be avoided through careful design and implementation of choice plans based on learning from past mistakes and assessment of probable dangers. In particular, they view experience with well-designed magnet plans and data on the accomplishments of nonpublic schools (see Chapters 9 and 12) as indications of gains that can be attained through intelligent development and implementation of proposals to expand choice (Raywid 1991).

In this context, some national organizations as well as influential citizens who have analyzed recent developments and proposals urge cautions in moving toward expanded choice. For example, the Forum of Educational Organization Leaders (described early in this chapter) has opposed proposals to provide widespread choice through vouchers, tax credits, or other government subsidies on the grounds that such choice arrangements may circumvent existing provisions for quality control and accountability and may magnify social-class and racial stratification and segregation. Similarly, some prominent business leaders have argued that federal officials' emphasis on choice threatens to divert attention, energy, and resources from other more important reforms. A study group established by the Association for Supervision and Curriculum Development concluded that whereas choice "may be one factor" in bringing about improvement in education, it is "largely unproven" and does not in itself "guarantee quality schools for all students"; therefore "district and state policymakers contemplating choice should carefully consider the concerns raised by choice critics" (Berreth 1991, 13).

Such qualms are shared by many advocates of proposals to substantially and systematically expand choice. One observer believes that choice is "reform's best choice" but also is education's "new 600-pound gorilla" that may "balkanize" U.S. society by in effect funding schools with a "strong separatist tint" (Leo 1991c, 17). Given that both advocates and opponents—not to mention a large spectrum of more neutral observers—recognize potential dangers as well as possible benefits in moving to expand choice, it is not surprising that numerous analysts have been trying to delineate policies and practices for implementing choice plans that could be introduced as productively as possible. Policies frequently proposed to accomplish this purpose include the following (Bastian 1986, 1990; Nathan 1990; Wells 1990; Coons and Sugarman 1991; Heckman 1991):

- Make sure that parents and students have adequate and relevant information and counseling.
- Provide free transportation, scholarships, and other material support to ensure that choices are fully available and do not depend on income and social status.
- Include components and guidelines (such as are found in "controlled choice" plans) to avoid segregation and resegregation.
- Ensure that enrollment and admissions procedures are equitable and do not exclude large proportions of students from the most desirable schools.
- Include provisions to free government-operated schools from regulations not imposed on private schools.

- Do not neglect other necessary reform possibilities and necessities; instead, treat choice as part of a comprehensive reform agenda.
- Provide for parent involvement at their children's new schools.

MANIFEST/LATENT FUNCTIONS AND UNFORESEEN CONSEQUENCES

Much of the school reform movement of the past decade is of interest to sociologists because of the many ways it frequently illustrated the large gaps between *manifest* and *latent* functions in a social system. Developed in most detail by Robert Merton (1967), these terms distinguish between the stated (manifest) intentions that accompany a system's actions and underlying, unstated (latent) intentions that in some respects may be more important than the articulated reasons and goals. When latent functions outweigh manifest ones, consequences of the system's actions may be very different from those identified publicly in initiating the actions. A good example of a latent function involves the so-called cooling-out effects of community colleges discussed in Chapter 2. Federal aid to students at proprietary schools, also discussed in Chapter 2, illustrates how unforeseen consequences can contribute to deterioration in a system one is trying to improve. A classic example is provided by Brinkerhoff and Hopkins (1990). They describe how agricultural extension agents were given a fixed budget to maintain their vehicles. Maintenance costs declined substantially, but only because the agents avoided hard-to-reach locations in order to reduce wear and tear on their vehicles.

School reform seems to constitute fertile ground for generating unforeseen consequences associated with differences between manifest and latent functions. On the one hand, fundamentally improving schools is a complex and difficult undertaking likely to require large amounts of human, financial, and other resources, not the least of which is years of hard and frustrating work directed at long-range goals. On the other hand, government units at all levels were (and are) under pressure to bring about substantial, rapid gains in student performance, usually with only a small fraction of the resources required to do so in a systematic and reliable fashion. In this situation legislators and other participants in policymaking tend to promulgate relatively small changes in rules and regulations that they nevertheless can portray as having been initiated to bring about improvement on the part of teachers and students. Such methods have the latent purpose of deflecting or blunting criticism and demands for change by pointing to actions and responses that give the appearance of seriously addressing problems. Actual consequences, however, can be very different from those originally articulated. Examples of school reform policies that in some cases fit this description include the following:

- As indicated earlier, minimum competency testing and related policies that sometimes have stimulated (additional) overemphasis on low-order skills and have deskilled teachers.
- Career-ladder plans that discouraged rather than stimulated teachers.
- Requirements that students who fail one academic course cannot participate in athletics or other extracurricular activities, which in the absence of comprehensive efforts to improve teaching and learning sometimes have resulted in awarding inflated grades to allow students to continue to participate. Alternatively, some students have avoided rigorous courses in order to maintain their eligibility (Harp 1991).
- Requirements that low-achieving students must take advanced academic courses to graduate from high school, which in the absence of systematic improvement in curriculum and instruction frequently have resulted in lowered standards in classes composed of unprepared students. Alternatively, in some cases standards have been maintained but low-achieving students have failed and dropped out of school (Morris 1991).
- Requirements that low-achieving students below a given performance level be retained in

grade, which in the absence of special assistance to improve their learning frequently have resulted only in further demotivating already unsuccessful students.

In such examples as these, unforeseen—though frequently forseeable—consequences may have done more to limit than improve educational services and opportunities available to students, especially low-achieving students. Unable or unwilling to bring about difficult and costly educational reforms, policymakers instead frequently responded with cosmetic changes. (As described by Ralph Kilmann in *Managing beyond the Quick Fix* [1989], this type of response, i.e., the "Band-Aid" solution to serious problems, is common in all types of organizations and institutions, not just in schools.) Such a response is particularly unfortunate in education because a great deal has been learned in recent decades concerning possibilities for actually bringing about fundamental improvements through systematic planning and implementation of promising ideas and practices. Much of this research and knowledge is briefly summarized in the remainder of this chapter.

EFFECTIVE SCHOOLS RESEARCH

As we note in Chapters 7 and 8, schools with high proportions of poverty students usually have had low achievement. Many educators, following research reported by James Coleman (1966) and his colleagues believed that schools could not become much more effective than they already are in working with large numbers of disadvantaged low achievers. However, research and experience in the 1980s have been much more encouraging about the possibilities for making inner-city schools and, indeed, most or all schools substantially more successful than they have been historically (Levine and Lezotte 1990; Raudenbush 1990; Levine 1991a; Stringfield and Teddlie 1991). Examples of research and analysis that support such a conclusion are described and discussed in this and the following sections.

Elementary Level

A Phi Delta Kappa-sponsored study (1980) of successful urban (i.e., big-city) elementary schools concluded that these schools shared the following characteristics in addition to outstanding leadership: (1) clearly stated goals and objectives; (2) reductions in adult/child ratios; (3) structured learning environments; and (4) high levels of parental contact with the school and parental involvement with school activities. Similarly, Ronald Edmonds (1979) and his colleagues studied elementary schools in New York and Michigan in which low-income students were achieving at a level comparable to more advantaged students and concluded that the "most tangible and indispensable characteristics" of these schools were (1) strong administrative leadership; (2) a climate of expectation in which no children are permitted to fall below minimum levels of achievement; (3) an orderly and quiet rather than rigid and oppressive atmosphere; (4) a strong emphasis on acquisition of basic skills; (5) concentration of school resources and energy on attainment of fundamental objectives; and (6) frequent monitoring of student progress.

At the same time, researchers have been trying to identify the characteristics of unusually effective schools in general, not just those in big cities or in concentrated poverty neighborhoods. As one might expect, the results of their studies are similar to those concerned more specifically with inner-city schools. The characteristics of effective schools as portrayed in this already large and growing literature have been summarized by staff of the Connecticut School Effectiveness Project (Shoemaker 1982):

1. A *safe and orderly environment* that is not oppressive and is conducive to teaching and learning.
2. A *clear school mission* through which the staff shares a commitment to instructional goals, priorities, assessment procedures, and accountability.

3. *Instructional leadership* by a principal who understands and applies the characteristics of instructional effectiveness.
4. A climate of *high expectations* in which the staff demonstrates that all students can attain mastery of basic skills.
5. High *time on task* brought about when a high percentage of students' time is spent engaged in planned activities to master basic skills.
6. Frequent *monitoring of student progress* using the results to improve individual performance and also to improve the instructional program.
7. Positive *home-school relations* in which parents support the schools' basic mission and play an important part in helping to achieve it.

More detail regarding the characteristics of unusually effective elementary schools—in this case, inner-city elementary schools—was provided in a study (Levine and Stark, 1982) of instructional and organizational arrangements at high-achieving inner-city elementary schools in Chicago, Los Angeles, and Community District 19 in Brooklyn, New York. District 19 schools had introduced a comprehensive reading approach that placed emphasis on the Chicago Mastery Learning Reading Program (CMLRP), which is explicitly designed to teach reading comprehension and other higher-order skills in kindergarten through eighth grade. Several of the Los Angeles schools included in the study had participated in the Curriculum Alignment Project (Niedermeyer and Yelon 1981), in which school faculties attend workshops that help them coordinate instructional materials and methods with frequent tests on specific skills selected for emphasis at each grade and classroom. When the training is successful, teachers are less likely to rely on basal texts regardless of whether they are too advanced for some students or too simple for others; instead, their goal is to select sections from texts and other available materials or to create new materials that are most appropriate for teaching a specific skill to a particular group of students. Drawing on these and other approaches, the unusually effective inner-city schools in this study exemplified the following characteristics:

Instructional Processes and Arrangements

1. Curriculum objectives, teaching materials, and testing were being painstakingly aligned with each other, whether through the Curriculum Alignment Project in Los Angeles, the introduction of the CMLRP in District 19, or some other less formal approach.
2. Arrangements more effective than the customary Chapter 1 "pullout" approach had been introduced for dealing with the learning problems of low-achieving students. In general, this means that rather than removing students for additional instruction uncoordinated with the regular classroom, arrangements were made to coordinate fully compensatory and regular instruction. In some cases, achievement improvements were produced through grouping of the lowest achieving students in very small classes.
3. Relatively great emphasis was placed on higher-order cognitive skills.
4. Explicit efforts had been made to minimize teachers' record-keeping chores.

Organizational Processes and Arrangements

1. Supervision had become much more outcome-based, in part because teachers had devised a schedule for introducing specific skills.
2. Comparative monitoring of classroom progress (i.e., charting and comparing student performance across classrooms) was carried out, partly for the purpose of setting minimum goals for introduction and pacing of lessons.

Leadership Characteristics and Emphases

1. Administrators were both supportive of teachers and skilled in providing a structured institutional pattern in which teachers could function effectively.
2. Administrators were willing and able to bend rules and regulations in a manner that enhanced school effectiveness.

Conclusions from the research on successful schools are being used in working to improve the effectiveness of instruction in the public schools, both in the inner city and elsewhere. By 1990 more than 6,000 school districts had initiated projects designed to improve educational effectiveness through emulating the characteristics of unusually successful schools (General Accounting Office 1989). In addition, state officials in Connecticut, Florida, New Jersey, and several other states are providing a variety of support services to help low-performing schools establish more effective practices. Among eighteen Milwaukee elementary schools that have been participating in a project to raise achievement in the inner city, the percentage of fifth-grade students reading in the lowest performance category decreased from 55 percent in 1979 to 30 percent in 1985. Maureen McCormack-Larkin (1985) has studied developments in this group of Milwaukee schools and has identified five important practices in schools with the greatest achievement gains:

1. Continuous faculty planning for full content coverage of the most important learning skills and objectives.
2. Development of a schoolwide homework policy requiring daily completion of assignments. Teachers enforced the policy by monitoring exits at dismissal and sending empty-handed students back to their rooms.
3. Introduction of daily and weekly schedules and other mechanisms to accelerate the pacing of instruction.
4. Flexible practices to avoid rigid homogeneous grouping.
5. Departure from social promotions.

Thus, it appears that while in the past infrequently encountered successful inner-city elementary schools were mavericks attributable mainly to the efforts of an atypical principal, it now is possible to create such schools through careful planning and implementation of improved arrangements for curriculum and instruction (Levine and Leibert 1987; Levine and Lezotte 1980; Levine 1991a). Success in this effort in turn would mean that disadvantaged students, particularly those at big-city poverty schools, will have a much better chance to succeed in schools and society.

A number of analysts have gone much further in trying to identify characteristics of unusually effective schools. For example, David Squires, William Huitt, and John Segars (1983) prepared a list of fifty characteristics they used to construct a school-diagnosis questionnaire. After reviewing more than twenty years of research on this topic, Levine and Lezotte (1990) identified eight correlates and twenty-five subcorrelates that have been associated with unusual effectiveness. In particular, Levine and Lezotte's review of the literature identified the following characteristics that had not been emphasized adequately in previous formulations:

- Active/enriched learning.
- Focus on higher-order learning in assessing instruction.
- Vigorous selection of teachers and replacement of incompetents.
- Availability of instructional support personnel.

Intermediate Level

Relatively few studies have succeeded in identifying the distinctive characteristics of effective secondary schools. One reason for the shortage of research is the small number of secondary schools that stand out as having high achievement compared to other schools similar in socioeconomic composition. Difficult as it has been to find unusually successful elementary schools (in terms of academic achievement), finding successful secondary schools has been even more difficult.

A few intermediate schools, however, have demonstrated that their students' achievement can be raised to relatively high levels. Following a search for high-achieving inner-city intermediate schools (defined as junior high schools including grades 7, 8, and 9 or middle schools including grades 7 and 8), Levine and his colleagues (1984) identified five such schools in four big cities. They concluded that effective inner-city intermediate schools exemplified these four common characteristics:

1. Organizational arrangements facilitated improved reading performance among low-achieving students.
2. Teachers emphasized achievement of higher-order cognitive skills.
3. Guidance and personal development of students were emphasized.
4. Expectations and requirements for student performance were high.

Each successful intermediate school described in this study had a different approach and mixture of approaches for attaining the goals implicit in these four characteristics. Some approaches used by these schools included:

I. Effective organizational arrangements for low achievers
   a. Small classes of low achievers taught by highly skilled teachers
   b. More time devoted to reading, language, and math
   c. Individual and small-group tutoring
   d. School-within-a-school units for low achievers
II. Emphasis on higher-order skills
   a. Availability of elective courses emphasizing these skills
   b. Instructional materials designed to teach higher-order skills
   c. Improved coordination between electives and regular courses
   d. Instructional strategies designed to develop thinking and comprehension

III. Emphasis on guidance and personal development
   a. Large numbers of counselors and guidance personnel
   b. Elective courses emphasizing personal development
   c. Use of community agencies
   d. Group counseling
IV. High expectations and requirements
   a. Contracts with students and parents
   b. Required summer school for failure in any subject
   c. Schoolwide point systems for students
   d. Weekly or biweekly report cards

Each of the five schools described in the study had made structural changes to improve the performance of their students, particularly their low achievers. By structural change, we mean major modifications in the school schedule as well as in how students and teachers are assigned to classes. For example, one school had changed the typical pattern so that classes of low achievers were much smaller than average classes; another had reduced the time devoted to science and social studies in order to increase the allocation for reading and math. Such changes appear to be prerequisite to school effectiveness at the secondary level (Firestone and Herriott 1982).

Senior High Level

Because there are far fewer successful inner-city schools at the senior high level than at the elementary and intermediate levels and because high schools usually are much more complex than are the lower schools, relatively little is known about the characteristics of unusually successful senior high schools. Among the few inner-city high schools for which there are data indicating that substantial gains have been made in improving student performance is South Boston High School. In 1975, South Boston became a desegregated high school attended by predominantly low-income and low-achieving white and black students. Reform of South Boston took several years to accomplish during a time of continuing turmoil related to desegregation and political upheaval in the Boston school system, but by 1980 data on improvement in the performance of students were encouraging and impressive.

Between 1979 and 1980, for example, average reading scores improved from the 16th percentile to the 40th percentile in the ninth grade and from the 18th to the 32nd percentile in the tenth grade. In addition, the percentage of graduates attending postsecondary education institutions increased from less than 8 percent in 1976 to 40 percent in 1980. Considerations that appear to have been most important in accounting for these and other improvements at South Boston included the following (Kozberg and Winegar 1981; personal observations of the authors):

- A new principal and administrative team made major changes in traditional organizational patterns and practices and insisted that staff members re-examine their instructional methods in order to develop more effective approaches for educating disadvantaged adolescents and youth.
- Associated with these changes, more than two-thirds of the previous faculty were replaced by teachers willing to discard traditional methods and practices that were largely ineffective.
- A number of in-school and out-of-school alternatives were initiated to address the learning problems and preferences of students. These alternatives included a self-contained school-within-a-school emphasizing academic learning, a minischool emphasizing experiential learning and individualized instruction, and a Transportation Learning Center.
- Nearly all ninth and tenth graders were placed in reading and writing courses rather than in traditional English classes, and methods used to teach reading and writing were drawn from sound theory and research regarding learning among disadvantaged adolescents.
- Students were placed in mathematics courses rather than in business mathematics, which primarily repeated beginning arithmetic.

- Work-study programs based on learning opportunities in the community were made available to many students after the ninth grade. In particular, paid work-study assignments were focused at selected sites such as Boston City Hospital, and participating students received coordinated instruction in subjects jointly planned by the academic staff and the work-study staff.
- Discipline throughout the school was very firm but also fair. Stricter attendance and tardiness policies were introduced with the assistance of parents, the Student Council, and community representatives.
- Strong security measures were imposed as needed to ensure the safety of students. Measures of this kind included the appointment of a youth-oriented security patrol and the partitioning of dangerous locations.
- School spirit and pride were systematically emphasized.
- Systematic guidance in personal development of students was emphasized. In part, this approach is carried out through a required Career Exploration course in the ninth grade. In addition, emphasis is placed on providing structured assistance for ninth graders through the selection of youth-oriented personnel to serve as homeroom teachers. In addition, the fact that South Boston is a small school allowed all administrators and counselors to know every student by name.
- An effective in-school suspension program was introduced. The South Boston approach differs from those at most other inner-city schools in that participating students are fully isolated from the remainder of the school in order to emphasize the severity of their rules violations.
- A conscious and explicit effort has been made to draw on resources in the local neighborhood and the larger community in order to provide better educational opportunities and to overcome the many educational and personal problems that hinder learning among inner-city adolescents and youth. For example, arrangements with Tufts University psychologists and psychiatrists have provided important help to emotionally disturbed students, and local social-work agencies have provided individual and family counseling services.

Because no two schools have exactly the same problems and situations, one cannot conclude that other senior high schools would be successful if they introduced the same programs and changes as did South Boston. However, some of the South Boston characteristics, such as systematic emphasis on school spirit, firm but fair discipline, small schools and classes, and emphasis on development of reading and math skills, have received considerable support in research on effective high-school approaches for improving student performance, particularly among low achievers (National Institute of Education 1978; Featherstone 1987; Levine and Sherk 1990, 1991).

In addition, South Boston illustrates structural changes that can be used to improve the delivery of education in senior high schools. After studying the literature on high schools that are trying to improve the performance of low achievers in reading and other subjects, Levine (1991b) and his colleagues identified several promising structural changes that included the following:

1. *School-within-a-school for low achievers.* Students who can read but are more than two or three years below grade level are assigned to a school-within-a-school serving from 80 to 120 students and staffed by 4 or 5 teachers (English, reading, math, science, and social studies) and a coordinator. If teachers in this type of program are specially selected for their ability and willingness to work with low achievers, participating students can make very large gains in reading and other basic skills (Gooden, Lane, and Levine 1989; Levine and Sherk 1990).

2. *Achievement centers.* The achievement center is a promising approach developed at Cleveland Heights (Ohio) High School. After specific learning objectives are identified for a given grade and subject area (for example, tenth-grade

English), an achievement center is established for both remedial and developmental purposes. Students who do not have skills prerequisite for a particular unit or who need special assistance in developing their full potential will attend the achievement center instead of or in addition to the regular class. Achievement center placement generally replaces the regular class for no more than two or three weeks (Levine and Eubanks 1989).

3. *A longer and different school day.* Possibilities for changing the school day to facilitate student achievement in various subjects are exemplified by the John Dewey High School in Brooklyn, New York. Dewey appears to have successfully provided effective educational opportunities for its diverse student body through such interrelated changes as a lengthened school day, provision of smaller classes and extra assistance for low-achieving students, and establishment of independent learning centers in every major subject.

Considerations Affecting Interpretation of Research

Readers of effective schools research and analysis should be aware of a number of considerations that may affect interpretation and conclusions. First, various definitions of school effectiveness are widely divergent. Some persons refer to a school with unusually high academic achievement, usually after taking account of social class; others may be referring to a self-renewing school that continuously identifies and solves internal problems, or to a school that promotes students' personal growth, or to a school that has had increases in academic performance, or to a school that concentrates on independent learning.

Second, most research on effective schools is correlational. Researchers have identified characteristics (correlates) of unusually effective schools, but only a few have manipulated a particular variable, such as expectations for students or leadership of the principal, to assess effects on

achievement. Dependence on correlational research makes it difficult to be certain that efforts to improve a given characteristic will make any real difference in students' performance (Preece 1990).

Third, other methodological problems have left much of the research vulnerable to criticism (Good and Brophy 1986). For example, schools identified as effective in a given subject (e.g., reading) during a given year may not be effective on other measures or on the same measure in subsequent years. In addition, statistical controls for students' social class and family background frequently have not been adequate to attribute high achievement to school characteristics (Stephenson and Levine 1987; Levine and Lezotte 1990; Levine 1991a).

Fourth, the identification of general characteristics cited in the effective schools research does not provide teachers and principals with much specific guidance about what they should do in the schools. For example, saying that a school requires a productive climate and good leadership does not provide much direct help in determining how to accomplish these goals.

Fifth, it should be noted that several writers (e.g., Sowell 1974) who have tried to identify unusually effective inner-city high schools have cited schools that either constituted high-dropout environments in which only a relatively small and selective group of students advanced beyond the ninth or tenth grade or used extremely rigorous discipline policies that led many students to leave and thus provided a better learning environment for those who remained. The latter strategy may be defensible on several grounds, particularly if a school district establishes small alternative schools for students eliminated from regular high schools. However, schools using this strategy offer little guidance for identifying the characteristics of senior high schools that successfully serve a population consisting of mostly disadvantaged low achievers.

Finally, most research has been concerned entirely or largely with inner-city schools. Schools identified as unusually effective in such studies generally have been poverty schools in which academic achievement is higher than that at most other schools with similarly disadvantaged students. It is more difficult to identify unusually effective schools outside the inner city, where high achievement is more common. In addition, the key components of effectiveness outside the inner city probably differ in some respects from those at poverty schools. Research conducted by Stringfield and Teddlie (1987, 1991), for example, found that principals of unusually effective middle-class schools were less active in the teacher-hiring process than were principals of effective poverty schools.

RESEARCH ON THE DELIVERY OF EFFECTIVE INSTRUCTION

Much research has been conducted during the 1970s and 1980s, and much as been learned about delivery of effective instruction. Although there naturally is considerable overlap between research on effective schools and research dealing with effective instruction or effective teaching, the two areas of study can be thought of as conceptually distinct: studies of effective instruction are concerned with classroom-level implementation, whereas effective schools research as most frequently defined deals with schoolwide characteristics (Levine and Lezotte 1990). Of course, it is apparent that a school cannot be unusually successful unless its teachers deliver instruction effectively, but schools that are not particularly successful compared to other schools with similar students can and frequently do have some outstanding teachers.

Classroom Management

Studies of classroom instruction indicate that effective teachers tend to be particularly successful with respect to classroom management and that teachers who merit this description exemplify a variety of behaviors, such as the following (Brophy 1982; Doyle 1986, 1990; McCartney and Jordan 1990; Waxman and Walberg 1991), to establish and enhance discipline and motivation. These teachers:

1. Arrange the physical environment to avoid disruption or misbehavior.
2. Establish clear routines and rules at the beginning of the academic term.
3. Make sure students understand what will be tolerated and know what to do if they need help.
4. Provide smooth and efficient transitions between activities.
5. Provide a variety of assignments and learning experiences.
6. Constantly monitor the class for indications of inattention or confusion.
7. Use a variety of approaches, such as eye contact and verbal directions, to focus attention during lessons.
8. Avoid responding emotionally to problems.

Effective Teaching

Thousands of studies have been conducted on various aspects of instructional delivery, and hundreds of formulations have been offered to describe the major aspects of effective teaching based on this large research literature (Stallings and McCarthy 1990). Although it is not possible to summarize this body of knowledge fully or to take account of all important findings in a brief capsulization, Jere Brophy and Thomas Good (1986) have provided a representative summary in their chapter on "Teacher Behavior and Student Achievement in the *Handbook of Research on Teaching* edited by Merlin Wittrock (1986). Highlights of their summary indicate that student learning is related to such instructional variables as these five:

1. High opportunity to learn and time for learning; pacing of instruction to ensure high contact coverage.
2. Academic instruction emphasis with high expectations for students and high allocation of available time for instruction.

3. High student engagement rates and effective classroom management.

4. Appropriate levels of difficulty in activities suited to students' current level of needs and interests.

5. High or at least moderate rates of success for students as they progress through the curriculum.

In providing this summary and integration of research, Brophy and Good also note that there is a tension between the goal of maximizing content coverage by pacing students as rapidly as possible and the goal involving

> the needs to (a) move in small steps so that each new objective can be learned readily and without frustration; (b) see that the students practice the new learning until they achieve consolidated mastery . . . and (c) where necessary, see that the students learn to integrate the new learning with other concepts and skills and to apply it efficiently in problem-solving situations. The pace at which the class can move will depend on the students' abilities and developmental levels, the nature of the subject matter, the student-teacher ratio, and the teacher's managerial and instructional skills. (Brophy and Good 1986, 361)

Brophy and Good also found that research indicates that students achieve more when there is "active teaching" through which the teacher "presents information and develops concepts through lecture and demonstration, elaborates this information in the feedback given following responses, . . . prepares the students for follow-up seatwork activities by giving instructions and going through practice examples, monitors progress on assignments after releasing the students to work independently and follows up with appropriate feedback and reteaching when necessary" (p. 361). Brophy and Good also proceed to discuss the findings of research with regard to such teaching variables as giving information, questioning the students, reacting to student re-

sponses, and handling seatwork and homework assignments.

Other representative formulations of some effective-instruction research have been provided by Herbert Walberg (1990) and by Barak Rosenshine and Robert Stevens (1986; Rosenshine 1990). The latter authors identified six "fundamental instructional functions" that constitute a structured teaching approach "particularly useful when teaching younger students, slower students, and students of all ages and abilities during the first stage of instruction with unfamiliar material" (p. 378). The six functions Rosenshine and Stevens identify and then analyze in much more detail are (1) daily review and checking homework, (2) presentation, (3) guided practice, (4) corrective and feedback, (5) independent practice (seatwork), and (6) weekly and monthly reviews. This type of approach also has been referred to frequently as "direct instruction" or "explicit teaching" (Rosenshine 1986; Dole, Duffy, Roehler, and Pearson 1991).

TEACHING FOR COMPREHENSION AND PROBLEM SOLVING

Even the strongest proponents of active teaching, direct instruction, and similar research-based effective teaching formulations recognize that teacher-centered instruction that provides structured learning activities to teach discrete skills is an incomplete and sometimes unsuitable approach for developing comprehension and reasoning, problem-solving, critical thinking, and other higher-order skills and competencies (Anderson, Hiebert, Scott, and Wilkinson 1985; Berg and Clough 1991; Brophy 1991). Rosenshine (1986, 1990), for example, has observed that effective teaching research is more pertinent to the teaching of discrete skills, such as decoding of words and computation in math, than to the understanding of complex material. Marzano and his colleagues (1987) have reviewed research dealing with development of students' cognitive functioning and concluded that direct-instruction formulations are too restrictive to accommodate the variety of teaching and learning activities and strategies required to develop dynamic knowledge focusing on higher-order mental processes. They summarized some of this research as follows:

> *Prescriptive teaching of skills can actually inhibit the learning process because it does not allow students to progress through the important "shaping" and "personalizing" stage of learning dynamic information. . . . [The direct instruction model] can foster an inaccurate and unhealthy tone which suggests that the teacher should be monitoring students to make sure they are "doing it right."...When knowledge is static in nature, the instructional goal is for students to be able to assimilate the information into their existing knowledge base. . . . [But when the goal shifts to dynamic use of static knowledge the teacher should] encourage and foster personal and quite divergent connections made by individual students. . . . The above discussion argues against the use of a single model of instruction and emphasizes the need for a repertoire of instructional models and strategies. (Marzano et al. 1987, 240–244)*

During the past decade, much progress has been made in identifying a range of skills and cognitive functions that should or could be addressed and in devising instructional methods and materials to provide effective instruction focusing on thinking and other higher-order mental processes. By the mid-1980s, more than thirty instructional programs with sets of materials had been developed that focus on improving students' thinking capabilities (Chance 1986; Jones and Idol 1990; Idol and Jones 1991).

To systematize the work being done in this important field, Robert Marzano and his colleagues (1987) prepared a typology of thinking dimensions for use in the planning of curriculum and instruction to improve students' cognitive functioning. Published for the Association Collaborative for Teaching Thinking (an umbrella group representing twenty-eight national organizations) by the Association for Supervision and Curriculum Development, the typology describes five major dimensions of thinking, three of which are subdivided into subdimensions of cognitive skills and processes that in turn include many additional more discrete aspects of cognitive functioning. Emphasis throughout this and other similar typologies is on learning-to-learn strategies and skills and on development of capacity for self-directed and independent learning. (Marzano, Pickering, and Brandt 1990; Idol and Jones 1991). The five major dimensions of thinking specified in this project are:

1. Metacognition (involving self-regulation of one's own learning).
2. Creative thinking.
3. Critical thinking.
4. Thinking processes.
5. Thinking skills.

Within the wide range of cognitive processes and skills subsumed under such headings as "Teaching of Thinking," the aspect that has received the most attention in educational research and development has been comprehension in reading. Many instructional methods and approaches for improving students' ability to read with understanding have been either devised or refined during the past two decades (Harris and Cooper 1985; Jones and Idol 1990; Dole, Duffy, Roehler, and Pearson 1991). Surveying these developments, David Pearson (1985) of the University of Illinois Center for the Study of Reading has referred to the increase in our knowledge of teaching for comprehension as a "revolution" in pedagogy. Some of the many comprehension-enhancement strategies and methods that have demonstrated positive results in terms of student achievement are the following:

1. Concept mapping, story mapping, graphic organizers, and other approaches for providing schema to help students comprehend what they read (Harris and Cooper 1985; Jones and Idol 1990; Levine and Sherk 1991).

2. Reciprocal teaching and other forms of co-operative learning through which students are helped to take active responsibility for understanding material and for helping each other carry out comprehension tasks (Palincsar 1987; Belmont 1989; Brophy 1990; Idol and Jones 1991).

3. Questioning techniques to develop higher-order learning through prereading, reading process, and postreading strategies and activities (Anthony and Raphael 1987; Manzo and Manzo 1990; Idol and Jones 1991).

4. Directed reading-thinking activities that guide students in developing an understanding of the presentation and content of written and oral discourse (Harris and Cooper 1985; Manzo and Manzo 1990).

5. Prediction techniques that systematically ask students to predict what they will encounter in reading based on previous knowledge and on activation of their previous knowledge (Presseisen 1987; Manzo and Manzo 1990).

6. Scaffolding approaches through which teachers model thought processes and then help students gradually accept responsibility for formulating questions and hypotheses (Jones 1986; Jones and Idol 1990; Pressley and Harris 1990; Rosenshine 1990).

7. Metacognitive strategies for helping students learn to understand and regulate their own reading and learning. (Harris and Cooper 1985; Duffy 1986; Duffy, Roehler, and Putnam 1987; Palincsar 1987; Pressley and Harris 1990; Levine and Sherk 1991).

8. Learning-to-learn strategies such as are incorporated in Chicago Mastery Learning Reading (Jones, Friedman, Tinzman, and Cox 1985) and other sets of materials (Presseisen 1988; Idol and Jones 1991).

9. Mediation activities to stimulate growth in understanding, as in the Instrumental Enrichment program developed by Reuven Feuerstein (1980; Link 1985; Presseisen 1988; Pechman 1990; Idol and Jones 1991).

10. Concept development methods that help students understand and apply concepts and related vocabulary (Klausmeier 1985; Marzano et al. 1987; Manzo and Manzo 1990; Idol and Jones 1991).

In addition, scholars specializing in instructional design have been working to determine how lessons should be planned, sequenced, and taught in order to help students acquire greater mastery of higher-order skills. For example, Barak Rosenshine (1990) reviewed research on this topic and devised a "tentative general model" for teaching relatively unstructured skills through the use of "eight major elements" that "scaffold" instruction for the student. Noting that his model has some resemblance to the six instructional functions he had earlier identified as helpful in teaching highly structured skills (see earlier), Rosenshine concluded that the eight elements (and subelements) thus may provide the basis for more effective delivery of instruction with respect to both types of skills (1990, 6):

1. Initiate instruction at a level students can understand.

2. Identify and use "procedural facilitators" that help students learn the skill. Procedural facilitators are suggestions that can help students "bridge or scaffold the gap" between the task and their current abilities. Examples include "questions words," such as "Who, What, When, Where, Why, How," summarization guides, and question-generation techniques.

3. Regulate the difficulty by gradually increasing the complexity of the task.

4. In presenting the lesson, demonstrate use of the skill, "think aloud" as the lesson proceeds, and anticipate and "precorrect" student difficulties.

5. Guide student practice with cue cards and other practice aids as well as activities that require students to increase their active participation.

6. Provide for feedback and student "self-checking" activities.

7. Provide independent practice with new examples.
8. Facilitate application to new examples.

The many strategies, materials, and programs now available to help deliver more effective instruction dealing with comprehension in reading and other subjects, problem-solving in math, and thinking processes in general provide a stark contrast to the patterns of instruction historically and currently still typical of many or most elementary and secondary classrooms. Research has amply documented that very little classroom time in the United States (or elsewhere) is devoted to instruction focusing on or supportive of enhanced comprehension, problem-solving, or thinking and higher-order mental processing (Boyer 1983; Cuban 1983; Goodlad 1984; MacGinitie and MacGinitie 1986; Putnam, Lampert, and Peterson 1990).

For example, Thomas Good and Douglas Grouws (1987) and other researchers (e.g., Porter 1991) have reported that only a small proportion of time in math classes is spent introducing and explaining concepts or teaching higher-order skills and understandings; most math instruction is devoted to drill, practice, and procedural detail. Good and Grouws also point out that much is known about how to teach problem-solving and other higher-order math skills more effectively and that staff development can be successful in helping teachers improve math instruction for this purpose.

ISSUES IN IMPROVING COMPREHENSION AND COGNITIVE DEVELOPMENT

Possessing the technical knowledge to provide much more effective instruction focusing on higher-order mental processes does not ensure that meaningful change to accomplish this objective will actually occur. Educators also must recognize and take action to overcome the major impediments to successful change and must devise and implement workable and realistic plans that can overcome these obstacles. Central issues

in developing such plans are discussed in the following sections.

Considerations and Obstacles in Delivery of Instruction

Many obstacles encountered in attempting to provide effective instruction with respect to higher-order mental processes and cognitive development involve the regularities of schooling (Goodlad 1984) and the tendencies for instruction to become fixated on low-level learning, particularly in classes or schools with many disadvantaged, low achievers (Levine and Cooper 1991). Several of the most important of these tendencies are described in this section.

Institutional Realities and Classroom Management Requirements. Philip Jackson (1968), John Goodlad (1984), Linda McNeil (1986), John Mergendoller (1988), and many others have pointed out that the realities perceived by teachers and administrators responsible for the welfare and behavior of many students result in an emphasis on obedience to rules and regulations designed to ensure orderly conduct. Walter Doyle (1985; 1990) has documented how emphasis on order in turn works against a focus on higher-order learning because tasks involving "recall or predictable algorithms, such as those found in vocabulary or grammar assignments," tend to proceed most "smoothly and efficiently" (Doyle 1985, 12). Doyle also has pointed out that "higher level tasks are often difficult to carry out" because

> the flow of activity slows down in the class when students find the work difficult or risky to accomplish . . . and student error rates go up. . . . When this happens, problems of student attention and motivation to work can occur. These conditions create tension in a classroom between the academic task system and the demands for pace and momentum inherent in the management of classroom groups. (Doyle 1985, 60)

Student Preference for Lower-Order Skills. Many students prefer low-level learning activities that they can complete easily and quickly rather than more challenging work that requires much more physical and mental exertion and that also exposes them to more risk of failure (Herndon 1968). This pattern has been described in the work of Walter Doyle (1983, 1985, 1990) and other researchers. Doyle also has pointed out that tasks emphasizing understanding and reasoning are "high in inherent ambiguity and risk for students" so that the probability of failure also is high (Doyle 1985, 12). Many students respond to the challenge or higher-order assignments by attempting to

> *increase the explicitness of a teacher's instructions. . . . [For example, two researchers] met with strong resistance . . . when they attempted to shift information-processing demands in a mathematics class from routine or procedural tasks to understanding tasks. The students refused to cooperate and argued that they had a right to be told what to do. . . . [After their experience, the researchers] commented that "it is no longer a mystery why so many teachers and so many textbooks present ninth-grade algebra as a rote algorithmic subject." (Doyle 1983, 184–185)*

Bargains, Accommodations, and Compromises. As described by Walter Doyle (1983, 1990), the realities of classroom interaction generate a tendency for many students to resist challenging, intellectual tasks. A series of studies conducted in the 1970s and 1980s has described how this tendency helps generate bargains and treaties through which teachers and students agree to the establishment of minimal standards and passive, mechanical learning. Although an agreement of this kind is apparent in many elementary schools, it is particularly characteristic of intermediate and senior high schools. In addition to Doyle, Ernest Boyer (1983), Philip Cusick (1983), John Goodlad (1984), Theodore Sizer (1984, 1991), Arthur Powell (1985), Robert Hampel (1986),

Annette Hemmings (1991), and many others have studied and described the genesis and effects of arrangements that lead to or involve a focus on minimal standards and low-level learning. Michael Sedlak and his colleagues (Sedlak, Wheeler, Pullin, and Cusick 1986) have described some major aspects of the situation in secondary schools:

> *For a variety of reasons . . . [many students] invest their time and energy outside the school in activities that reward them financially, offer them some semblance of adult responsibility, or treat them as valued consumers . . . .*
>
> *In most high schools, there exists a complex, tacit conspiracy to avoid rigorous, demanding, academic inquiry. A "bargain" of sorts is struck that demands little academically of either teachers or students . . . .*
>
> *[Several studies have shown how] students sought to minimize requirements, delay or postpone assignments, and receive the highest grades they could for the least amount of effort. . . . The negotiation process often invalidated efforts to evaluate achievement. (Sedlak, Wheeler, Pullin, and Cusick 1986, 13, 5 101–102)*

Low Expectations and Learning Scripts for Low Achievers. As we point out in Chapters 7 and 8, low expectations and requirements appear to play an important part in generating and reinforcing low performance levels among many disadvantaged students (Payne 1984, 1989; Levine and Lezotte 1990). We also concluded that high standards are particularly difficult to establish and maintain in concentrated poverty schools with high proportions of low achievers. Thus, raising of standards and expectations has been a key component in the effective schools movement.

Tendencies for instruction to concentrate on low-level learning skills in both elementary and secondary schools appear to be magnified in the case of low-achieving students, in part because some teachers do not believe many of their poorly functioning students can perform much better. In line with those beliefs and perceptions, some teachers apparently develop a script that confines low achievers to passive, mechanical learning assignments and experiences (Allington 1991). For example, Richard Shavelson (1985) found indications of low-level scripts for low achievers in a case study of an elementary teacher who was asked to use her "high-ability student script" with her low-ability group. According to Shavelson, the high-ability script involved changing to a more difficult textbook, emphasizing discussion of the meaning of the stories, asking questions for which more than one answer might be acceptable, and switching from highly constrained formats to unconstrained papers. Shavelson reported that the behavior and performance of students in the low-ability group greatly improved.

In addition, there are indications that disadvantaged black students (and perhaps other minority students as well) sometimes internalize low-level learning scripts that significantly impede their school progress. Thus, Ray Hammond and Jeffrey Howard have observed a tendency among black youth in the inner city to "avoid engagement in intellectual competition." Hammond and Howard believe that this avoidance behavior represents a self-fulfilling prophecy that "arises when the larger society projects an image of black intellectual inferiority *and* when that image is internalized at a less-than-conscious level by black people over a number of generations" (Hammond and Howard 1986, 61). They also point to frequent derogatory nicknaming (e.g., nerd, egghead) of school-oriented students as evidence of widespread avoidance behavior among disadvantaged black students.

Teachers' Preferences and Handicaps. Emphasis on passive, lower-order learning and mechanical skills also arises in part from factors involving teachers' preferences and characteristics. Low-level material and skills are easier to teach and test than are higher mental processes. Tendencies to stress lower-order learning understand-

ably are particularly prevalent among teachers who have large classes, are overloaded with paperwork or other organizational burdens, and/or work in difficult schools with a high proportion of low-achieving students (Levine and Cooper 1991). Preparing lessons to help students acquire higher-order skills and understandings, assigning and grading more complex written assignments and independent research, and/or working in other ways to provide active learning experiences are difficult undertakings that require time and energy on the part of the teacher (Pechman 1990). In addition, some teachers are not intellectually or personally capable or prepared to function effectively in a classroom that stresses cognitive development and movement toward independent learning.

Mediated Development to Assist Low Achievers

As described above, research and development personnel have devised and refined many instructional approaches and programs for helping students progress with respect to cognitive functioning and higher-order mental processes. We also have emphasized that the provision of explicit assistance to enhance cognitive growth in a step-by-step framework is particularly important for disadvantaged low achievers, whose previous experience has provided limited preparation for functioning at a high level in processing abstract knowledge in the classroom. Thus, recent research has emphasized the importance of providing systematic, mediated assistance in helping students—particularly low-achieving students—acquire metacognitive controls, learning-to-learn strategies, and other skills and understandings required to improve cognitive functioning (Levine 1988; Presseisen 1988; Idol and Jones 1991).

Sema Brainin (1985) has reviewed the research on Feuerstein's Instrumental Enrichment program and other mediated learning approaches to improve the cognitive development of low-achieving adolescents and reported that such mediation appears to have had positive results when it has attended adequately to such "essential conditions" as sharing with the learner "an intentional and analytic approach to the learning process itself," developing an "awareness of the meaning of stimuli and their relevance in ever-larger contexts increasingly remote from direct experience," and enabling learners to "experience and express cognitive growth in productive ways." She also cautions, however, that there has been little investigation to determine what approaches work best and how they can be implemented most effectively in specific situations, and that a particularly "critical facet" of meaningful efforts involves "taking realistic account of the professional growth required for teachers to become effective cognitive educators" (Brainin 1985, 139, 144).

Failure to Move beyond Order and Structure

Despite the particular importance of providing continuing mediated support to help low-achieving students develop higher-order skills, teachers working with disadvantaged lower-achievers frequently tend to become fixated on the structured learning aspects of this challenge and to ignore the imperative to move toward more active, independent learning. This mistake is particularly easy to make because highly structured learning combined with effective classroom management tends to produce a more orderly environment, which teachers, administrators, parents, and students rightly perceive to be a prerequisite for successful instruction. Sedlak and his colleagues have described this tendency as a "social trap" in which success in classroom management can "delude" teachers into thinking they are meeting their responsibilities "at the expense of the formal objective of maximizing academic learning" (Sedlak, Wheeler, Pullin, and Cusick 1986, 102). And as we noted in Chapter 3, attempts to move rapidly toward independent learning in schools enrolling many disadvantaged students frequently have involved misguided efforts that produced little more than chaos in the classroom.

It is difficult to find a proper and productive balance between low achievers' needs for mastering initial basic skills and the challenge to help them proceed beyond low-level mechanical learning (Doyle 1990). Because students functioning far below grade do have severe deficiencies in such skills as word identification and computation, it generally is important to correct these deficiencies in the primary grades if possible and in later grades if necessary (Sizemore 1985; 1990). On the other hand, research also indicates that movement toward higher-order learning can help students master and retain mechanical skills because it provides them with schema for organizing information and that effective instruction emphasizing higher-mental processes results in as much or more growth in lower-level learning as does instruction limited primarily to lower-mental processes (Soled 1987, 1988; Bloom 1988; Passow 1990; Allington 1991).

High Costs of Effective Instruction

Amid much uncertainty concerning the selection and implementation of instructional approaches for improving students' cognitive development and functioning, one conclusion seems apparent: The financial costs of moving in this direction successfully on a widespread basis will be large. In part, this is because providing mediated instruction requires considerable personal contact and individualized attention from teachers and other faculty, particularly in the case of low achievers who have not yet learned to work well independently.

In addition, the costs of training and retraining teachers to be what Brainin called "cognitive educators" will be much higher than generally have been expended or even contemplated in teacher training (Pechman 1990). This conclusion was one lesson reported by Ruth Kurth and Linda Stromberg (1984), who worked with a small group of teachers in an effort to provide more teaching of comprehension and to "promote independent reading" in a suburban elementary school. Kurth and Stromberg concluded that although these goals can be attained and have a positive impact on achievement, success depended on "continuous, almost Herculean efforts" (p. 22). Similarly, Putnam, Roehler, and Duffy (1987) have been working to help elementary teachers implement more effective comprehension instruction and have concluded that "the development of cognitive skills and independent decision making" demands "elaborate staff development . . . [during which time there must be] sensitive, individual assistance that is responsive to each teacher's particular background, current context, and emerging understandings of what is being learned" (p. 24).

EXEMPLARY APPROACHES FOR IMPROVING INSTRUCTION

A number of approaches have been developed that appear to be successful in improving cognitive functioning and other aspects of achievement when they are implemented well. To illustrate the possibilities being tried in school districts throughout the United States, this section describes some of the approaches that have helped improve the achievement of disadvantaged students.

Teacher Expectations and Student Achievement Training

Developed by personnel at the office of the Los Angeles County Superintendent of Schools, Teacher Expectations and Student Achievement (TESA) training is being widely used and has had considerable success in raising expectations for low-achieving students and in improving teacher-student interactions (Kerman 1979). Consisting initially of five workshops scheduled about one month apart, TESA training emphasizes fifteen important teaching behaviors, including higher-order questioning, provision of individual support for students, and equitable distribution of

opportunity. Participants observe each other four times following each workshop, and data from these observations are provided to help them examine their interactions with students. Implementation of TESA thus is based on research indicating that staff development tends to be most effective when teachers observe and assist one another in actual classrooms.

Technology-Based Approaches

As we note in Chapter 12, computers and other modern technologies can make an important contribution toward improving the effectiveness of instruction and enhancing students' learning in comprehension and other higher-order skills. Research indicates that computer-assisted instruction can produce a variety of achievement gains (Liao 1991). One good example of a technology-based approach designed specifically to help students acquire the "confidence, skills, and knowledge necessary to solve problems and become independent thinkers and learners" is the "anchored instruction" approach being developed by The Cognition and Technology Group. Anchored instruction aims to create "problem-solving environments" based on the use of videodisc and computer technologies that provide a framework for focusing on sustained exploration of "authentic" tasks (The Cognition and Technology Group 1990, 2).

Initial work of the Group involves painstaking creation of videodiscs and related instructional materials designed to improve problem-formulation and problem-solving capacities and various comprehension and communications skills among average and low-achieving students. Students work cooperatively much of the time in small groups, and guidance in learning-to-learn is provided by both the teacher and the technology. Videodisc and computer technologies in the Group's projects allow for simulation of realistic situations that can motivate students and challenge them to use higher-order skills in solving problems. Based on student and teacher reactions during pilot stages of the projects, Group researchers concluded that students with varied backgrounds were participating actively and becoming more proficient at complex problem solving.

The wide variety of technology-based instructional projects now being developed is almost bewildering. Many of these projects involve multimedia packages incorporating computers, videodiscs and television, film, books, pamphlets, and other types of technologies and materials. In future years, hypermedia technologies involving interactive compact discs that combine advanced video, audio, and computing capabilities also will become important in education (Paske 1990). Projects undergoing intensive development and testing include:

1. The Global Laboratory, in which students and teachers from many countries will conduct ecological research.
2. The DynaBook system for accessing multiple sources of information.
3. The LabNet microcomputer and telecommunications system through which high school teachers provide hands-on laboratory experiences for students.
4. The French Assistant software for translating English to French.
5. The Personal Science Laboratory for teaching physics and chemistry topics on microcomputers.
6. The Visual Almanac videodisc encyclopedia.
7. The Dynagrams system for using computers to present science simulations.
8. The Earth Lab network that promotes cooperating learning in studying ecology.
9. The Journey in Mathematics package for improving the elementary-school curriculum.
10. The Simulation City approach for teaching urban development.
11. The MediaWorks and Musicland systems to help students create multimedia presentations (Kinnaman 1990; Sneider and Barber 1990; Hansen 1991; Pearlman 1991; Salpeter 1991; Van Horn 1991).

Apart from such specific projects, interactive computer networks are being developed and/or expanded to provide students and teachers with opportunities for rapidly acquiring and exchanging information and ideas from all parts of the world. Many already participate in electronic bulletin boards and other computerized communications services; many more will do so in the future as technological changes allow easier and less costly access (Grunwald 1990; Watson 1990; Pearlman 1991). Educators will face a great challenge in working to implement such approaches productively within the schools of the future.

Accelerated Schools

Initiated in 1986 as a cooperative project involving Stanford University and an inner-city elementary school in San Francisco, the Accelerated Schools approach aims to bring about fundamental restructuring and improvement at schools with a high proportion of disadvantaged students. After receiving training in problem-solving and group process skills, participating faculties address schoolwide issues involving selection of curriculum, grouping of students, delivery of instruction, improvement of climate and expectations held for students, and other major aspects of school organization and operation. Particular emphasis is on accelerating the pace of instruction through reduction of repetitious, low-level learning experiences that are unnecessary or counterproductive for many students. By 1992, more than fifty elementary schools in several states (including California, Illinois, and Missouri) were participating in Accelerated Schools projects, and plans were to extend the approach to middle schools. Encouraging preliminary results at many participating schools indicate that improvements are occurring with respect to climate, attendance, achievement, and other indicators of school effectiveness (LeTendre 1991; McCarthy, Hopfenberg, and Levin 1991).

Higher-Order Thinking Skills (HOTS) Program

Developed by Stanley Pogrow (1990a, 1990b) and his colleagues at the University of Arizona, the Higher-Order Thinking Skills (HOTS) program is specifically designed to replace remedial Chapter 1 laboratories and other so-called drill-and-practice, compensatory education and/or special education arrangements in grades four through seven. However, HOTS also can be used to improve thinking skills and learning-to-learn among all students. Pogrow (1990a) has described HOTS as encompassing four major components:

1. Use of computers for problem solving.
2. Emphasis on dramatization techniques that require students to verbalize and thereby stimulate language development.
3. Systematic inclusion of Socratic questioning techniques.
4. Stress on thinking skills.

The computer component draws on software that introduces Socratic questioning, learning games and simulations, active language use, and other assignments and experiences designed to engage students in active learning and higher-order thinking. The HOTS thinking skills curriculum stresses metacognitive learning, drawing inferences from context, and other comprehension-enhancement strategies and methods of the kind described in preceding parts of this chapter.

Participation in HOTS usually involves assignment of nine or fewer previously low-achieving students to a specially trained teacher for 35 minutes a day, 4 or 5 days a week, for a period of 2 years per student. Regular classroom teachers are asked to support the HOTS approach by also placing some emphasis on questioning techniques, verbalization, and thinking skills. Evaluations indicate that the average HOTS student registers large gains in reading and math even though the program does not explicitly teach or stress discrete basic skills that usually are stressed in testing. Pogrow (1990b)

has summarized some of these outcomes and described the overall goals as well as general implications as follows:

The activities were designed to be intellectually challenging. Students would have to struggle to be successful, but every effort was made to make the activities stimulating and motivational . . . teachers were trained to maintain proper levels of ambiguity in discussions so that students would have to . . . construct meaning, and articulate complete ideas and strategies. Teachers also were trained to guide students without simplifying problems . . . or telling students what to do. . . . [The results support the conclusion that at-risk] students have tremendous levels of intellectual and academic potential . . . *[but many do not]* understand "understanding." . . . *[This]* fundamental learning problem can be eliminated if enough time and enough resources are made available. . . . *[Given that the basic problem is that students do not understand "understanding," then the usual]* remedial approaches are likely to make long-term learning problems worse . . . *[by treating information as discrete facts to be memorized and thereby producing]* a vicious cycle wherein the more remediation, the less students . . . are able to apply their learning. (Pogrow 1990b, 390–394)

Mastery Learning

Chapter 8 provides a brief description of the mastery learning approach developed by Benjamin Bloom and his colleagues and cites several sources indicating that it appears to have been successful in raising the achievement of disadvantaged students in some locations. The five major steps in the mastery-learning sequence defined by Bloom and his colleagues (e.g., Block and Anderson 1975; Guskey 1985) are to:

1. Define a specific learning objective.
2. Teach the understanding or skills embodied in the objective.

3. Use a criterion-referenced test to assess mastery.
4. Provide corrective instruction for nonmasters and enrichment or acceleration for students who did master the objective.
5. Retest the students who received corrective instruction.

Bloom and his colleagues advocate whole-group instruction during the initial teaching phase, whereas some other mastery-learning developers (e.g., Hyman and Cohen 1979) emphasize small-group and individual instruction throughout the mastery sequence. Many approaches other than mastery learning also concentrate on student mastery of specific learning skills. Such approaches can be viewed as mastery-type learning, but more often are referred to as outcomes-based instruction (Rubin and Spady 1984).

Data on the implementation of mastery learning indicate that it can bring about large gains in student achievement, particularly among low achievers (Burns and Kojimoto 1989; Kulik and Kulik 1990). When well implemented, mastery learning can raise the student now at the fiftieth percentile to the ninetieth percentile or higher, and the low achiever now at the fifteenth percentile can improve to the fortieth percentile or above. Gains of this magnitude are possible when mastery learning is combined with enhancement of students' initial skills on concepts prerequisite to the instruction, provision of appropriate cues and feedback, emphasis on students' active participation, and/or work with parents to improve the home learning environment. Bloom (1984) concludes, moreover, that these gains can be attained for higher-order learning not just for mechanical learning of factual information.

The research by Bloom and his colleagues has been conducted mostly with individual classes using teacher-made tests, but research indicates that comparable results can be attained on a schoolwide basis using standardized tests. Jones and Spady (1985) have examined mastery learning in Johnson City, New York; Red Bank, New Jersey; and in several other school districts.

They conclude that very large gains in academic achievement have been registered when mastery learning has been implemented effectively.

However, as also is true with respect to other approaches that emphasize teacher-centered delivery of instruction on specific skills, mastery learning is particularly susceptible to misimplementation caused in part by overemphasis on narrow, mechanical skills that are easiest to teach and test. In addition, teachers frequently have been overloaded with record-keeping chores. In general, effective implementation of mastery learning requires systematic attention to prerequisites for success, such as manageable class size, large amounts of planning time for teachers, substantial staff development, and provision of adequate time for corrective instruction (Levine 1985; Burns and Kojimoto 1989; Koslovksy 1990).

Student Team Learning and Other Cooperative Learning Approaches

Chapter 9 refers to research indicating that cooperative learning arrangements have contributed to achievement gains in desegregated classrooms, in part because such arrangements appear to fit the learning styles of many minority students. Probably the best known example of a cooperative learning approach is Student Team Learning (STL) developed by Robert Slavin and his colleagues at The Johns Hopkins University. Student Team Learning is being widely used because it has demonstrated impressive success in helping improve classroom participation and achievement of many groups of students in various settings, not just minority students in desegregated classes (Slavin 1980; 1989/1990; 1990b; Hilke 1990).

The STL approach uses a number of techniques in which students work in four- or five-member learning teams and receive recognition based on the extent to which all team members complete and master a common set of skills. Students' scores are based on their performance in comparison with other students who start at the same level or on improvement over their own previous performance, thus making it possible for all students to score well if they work diligently. Studies of STL have shown positive outcomes in reading, math, social studies, science, and other subjects. When implemented well, STL also has produced significant gains in students' attitudes toward school and self-concept.

The developers of Student Team Learning also have been testing several modified versions called Team Accelerated Individualization (TAI) and Cooperative Integrated Reading and Composition (CIRC). Research on TAI, which combines team learning, individualization, and mastery learning in teaching math in the middle grades, indicates that it can produce large improvements in student attitudes as well as in achievement (Slavin, Madden, and Stevens 1989/1990; Slavin 1991). Research on CIRC, which combines team learning with specially prepared materials and use of comprehension-development strategies to improve instruction in reading and language arts, indicates that CIRC has produced substantial achievement gains among both regular students and special-education students in the middle grades (Slavin, Madden, and Stevens 1989/1990; Hilke 1990, Slavin 1990a).

Success for All

Possibly the most comprehensive approach developed in recent years to improve the performance of disadvantaged students is Success for All, which provides intensive preschool and kindergarten instruction and family support that stress language development and learning-to-learn skills, followed by individualized assistance in primary-grades reading and math delivered to small classes and groups of students at inner-city elementary schools (Madden et al. 1990; 1991). Success for All also emphasizes cooperative learning, mastery-oriented instruction, and development of thinking skills, with technical support and staff development provided by coordinators and resource persons assigned to

each participating school. Results after the first two years of this important project indicated that reading and language performance was much better among Success for All students than was true at comparison schools, particularly in the case of initially low achievers. Developers of Success for All view these results as supportive of their approach to "comprehensive schoolwide restructuring" designed to ensure that "*every* child" has a good opportunity to learn well from the earliest grades and avoid subsequent placement in special education or long-term remediation (Slavin 1990; Madden 1991).

Reading Recovery

Reflecting linguistic-based theories originally developed in New Zealand, Reading Recovery emphasizes intensive assistance in beginning reading for children who experience serious problems learning to read. Participating students receive one-on-one tutoring for 30 minutes a day from a highly trained teacher. Tutoring usually is provided for 12 to 20 weeks in the first grade, but some students who still have reading problems may receive additional tutoring in the second or third grades. Emphasis in tutoring is on use of short paperback books with only a few lines per page, learning to read through writing and oral expression, diagnosis and correction of individual learning problems associated with a student's particular learning style, and detailed recording of student behavior and performance when producing language independently (Pinnell 1990).

Now being implemented or initiated in hundreds of school districts, Reading Recovery aims to ensure that all students will learn by overcoming initial reading problems before they become debilitating. Assessments of results in early-adopting districts are very encouraging. Unlike many early childhood approaches in which participants registered strong gains in preschool or kindergarten classes and then deteriorated in performance in later grades (see Chapter 8), Reading Recovery students generally have maintained gains (in comparison with similar students not in the program) into the fourth grade (Pinnell 1990). Although these evaluation data have been hard to collect and must be treated cautiously because they are not comprehensive, several nationally respected reading experts have viewed initial results as unusually promising (e.g., Adams 1990; Anderson and Armbruster 1990). However, developers of the Reading Recovery approach also stress that it is a difficult intervention that will require significant time and resources to implement effectively (Pinnell 1990).

Degrees of Reading Power Comprehension Development Approach

Another promising approach is the comprehension development framework built in part on the Degrees of Reading Power (DRP) test developed by the College Board. Unlike mastery learning and Student Team Learning, which generally have been accepted most readily and implemented most effectively on a schoolwide basis in elementary and intermediate schools, the DRP comprehension development approach is frequently being introduced most successfully at the senior-high level.

The first step in this approach is to obtain comprehension scores for all students by administering the DRP test. Unlike other standardized tests of reading comprehension, the DRP provides an assessment that indicates how well a student actually can comprehend prose he or she encounters inside and outside of school. It also is criterion-referenced in the sense that it assesses students' actual level of comprehension, not just whether a high or low achiever is above or below some abstract grade level as designated by other standardized reading tests.

After determining students' comprehension levels, the second step is to align instructional materials with the comprehension level of one's students. The aim at this point and subsequently is to provide materials that do not frustrate students in completing homework and other independent learning activities, while using materials slightly beyond students' current

functional level during instruction designed to help students gain in comprehension. Because this approach aims at improving comprehension in social studies, science, and other subjects, which presumably is a central goal of education in all subject areas, the DRP comprehension development framework is intended to enhance comprehension throughout the curriculum.

The third and most extensive step in the DRP approach is to help faculty introduce comprehension-development teaching and learning strategies in line with students' current functional levels and problems (Harris and Cooper 1985; Levine 1991b). At this stage, teachers are assisted in selecting and using appropriate strategies from among the many available possibilities, such as higher-order questioning, directed thinking activities, concept mapping, cooperative team learning, and others mentioned elsewhere in this chapter. Successful results in terms of improving student achievement have been reported in Levittown, New York, Orlando, Florida, and several other school districts (Levine and Sherk 1990, 1991).

Combinations of Approaches

Promising instructional approaches such as those described here are not mutually exclusive. Drawing on a larger research base concerned with the characteristics of effective schools and effective instruction, they can be and frequently are combined with each other and with other promising approaches involving change in testing, instructional and organizational arrangements and policies, staff development, and other interventions to improve education. Thus, as in the examples noted above, STL is being combined with mastery learning as part of TAI, HOTS incorporates both computers and comprehension-development strategies (such as those used in the DRP approach), the DRP approach can draw on STL, computers are being used to teach comprehension-development strategies such as concept mapping (Cronin, Meadows, and Sinatra 1990), TESA can be an important component in introducing mastery learning or STL, and DRP testing can be used to help keep mastery learning focused on higher-order skills development. Levine and Sherk (1990) have described how outstanding secondary schools have helped disadvantaged students register very large gains in reading comprehension using a combination of DRP testing and instructional strategies, cooperative learning, and other approaches; Arredondo and Block (1990) have provided examples of successful instruction combining mastery learning with an emphasis on thinking skills; and Guskey (1990) has explained how educators can and should proceed to integrate and coordinate TESA, cooperative learning, critical thinking curricula, mastery learning, and other promising approaches.

ACCOMPLISHING SCHOOL IMPROVEMENT AND REFORM

Identifying instructional and organizational changes that may improve schools is not the same as actually bringing about successful change. Analysis of efforts to improve schools has provided information and understanding concerning the issues that should be addressed and the steps that should be taken to enhance the likelihood of successful reform. Among the themes that research indicates should be emphasized are the ten described below.

Problem-Solving Orientation and Critical Inquiry

The introduction of an innovation frequently has little or no effect on student achievement because a variety of problems arise to hinder practical implementation. For example, specialists may prepare an outstanding math curriculum for sixth graders and school districts may purchase the new curriculum materials, but teachers may choose not to use the materials, may use them improperly because they do not fit the testing schedule, or may not know how to use them. Innovations are not likely to be implemented suc-

cessfully unless the organization introducing them focuses continually on identifying and solving day-to-day implementation problems (Goodlad 1987; Joyce 1990; Levine and Lazotte 1990). In addition, the attitude exemplified by faculty in a school participating in a successful reform effort is of critical inquiry or critical reflection aimed at re-examining current goals and practices and of search for improved ways of organizing and delivering instruction more effectively (Fullan 1990, 1991; Levine and Cooper 1990; Louis and Miles 1990).

School-Level Emphasis

Because the innovating organization must identify and solve day-to-day problems, the focus in bringing about change must be at the level of the individual school building where many of the problems occur (Goodlad 1987; Fullan 1990, 1991; Joyce 1990). Site-level improvement in turn requires considerable planning time, technical assistance, and other resources expended to help faculty improve the effectiveness of their instructional program (Smith and Scott 1990).

Staff Development

Schoolwide staff development focusing on improved delivery of instruction is a core activity in the school improvement process (Joyce and Showers 1988; Joyce, Murphy, Showers, and Murphy 1989; Levine and Ornstein 1989; Joyce 1990; Louis and Miles 1990; Richardson 1990). In the case of an elementary school, the entire staff should participate; in secondary schools, departments may be the appropriate unit for some activities. Kenneth Sirotnik (1987) concluded that the amount of time required for productive change through staff development possibly will amount to the equivalent of one full day per week and two paid months during the summer. Staff development usually is most successful when it takes place during the regular school day.

Collection of Data

One particularly important activity in implementing major change involves collection of data to identify problems in a school's instructional arrangements and outcomes (Levine and Lezotte 1990). Other things being equal, faculty will be more likely to change their behavior and practices if data clearly indicate a need for such change. For this reason, many successful change efforts have emphasized the collection of appropriate data to help set directions for instructional improvements. Questionnaires, interviews, and documents can be analyzed to identify problems and issues that impede implementation of more effective instruction (Schmuck and Runkel 1990).

Faculty Involvement and Collegial Collaboration

Many studies support the conclusion that teacher involvement in decisions about how to implement an innovation can be important in determining whether it is successful (Joyce 1990; Levine 1991). This is not surprising inasmuch as people who are expected to alter their working patterns will be more likely to accept change if they have a part in selecting and shaping it than if it is imposed by others. In addition, teachers as grass-roots workers are in the best position to identify the practical obstacles that will hinder successful implementation.

Furthermore, research supports the conclusion that collegial collaboration and planning for improvement are two of the most important and productive aspects of faculty involvement in school reform efforts (Zahorik 1987; McLaughlin 1990). Collegial collaboration, including staff development activities in which teachers observe and critique each other's work and address obstacles to effective delivery of instruction, may be indispensable in improving instructional and organizational arrangements and school culture (Fullan 1990, 1991; Joyce 1990; Levine and Lezotte 1990; Smith and Scott 1990).

Combined Bottom-Up and Top-Down Approach

Because research had emphasized the importance of faculty participation in decisions, analysts in the 1960s and 1970s tended to emphasize a bottom-up approach in order to develop a sense of ownership among teachers. However, research in the 1980s has supported the importance of top-down and external components in initiating change successfully (McLaughlin 1990). Insistence on and support for change by administrators, school board members, and others at the district and state levels frequently are required if successful implementation is to occur at the classroom level (Levine and Ornstein, 1989). Thus, two comprehensive, independent studies of innovation (Huberman and Miles 1982; Marsh and Berman 1984) have concluded that top-down initiation and support frequently are required to effectuate and institutionalize long-term improvements. Matthew Miles has described the stance of top-level administrators who communicate to principals and teachers an understanding that "we are going to try a new approach, you are going to implement it, and we are going to help you." Miles believes that administrative pressure and support frequently lead teachers to develop mastery of an innovation. Mastery then helps them develop the commitment to implement the change effectively (Miles 1983). But where there is top-down pressure to bring about change, it "had better be accompanied by plenty of support" (Louis and Miles 1990, 291).

Implementability

The success of school improvement and reform efforts also depends on whether the changes introduced are implementable in the sense that they have high potential for being adopted and used effectively by teachers (Levine and Cooper 1991). David Crandall, Jeffrey Eiseman, and Karen Louis (1986) have summarized five of the key dimensions that affect implementability:

1. *Compatibility* with the social context of prospective users.
2. *Accessibility* to prospective users who do not already share the conceptual framework of the designers.
3. *Observability* that enables prospective users to assess the innovation in terms of their own reality.
4. *Craft legitimization* that indicates the innovation has been workable in field testing or actual school situations.
5. *Adaptability* that allows users to engage in local adaptation.

Regarding adaptability, Crandall, Eiseman, and Louis have examined the research on implementation of educational innovations and further concluded that a difficult-to-attain balance must be achieved between making necessary changes to fit particular schools or classrooms on the one hand and ensuring implementation of the most central core components of the innovation on the other hand (1986, 32–33).

Development of Shared Agreements

Successful implementation of a major innovation requires change in many institutional arrangements, including scheduling of staff and student time, development of new behaviors and attitudes on the part of teachers and students, and selection and use of instructional methods and materials. The building principal, who is responsible for arrangements throughout the institution, usually is the key person in successfully implementing change. In addition, the faculty must have a shared culture, or shared vision of the kinds of changes that are possible and necessary to improve their instructional practice; otherwise the staff is unlikely seriously to consider proposals that require significant changes in existing arrangements and behaviors (Fullan 1990, 1991; Levine 1991a).

Some schools require much more time and effort to develop shared agreements than do others (Goodlad 1987; Louis and Miles 1990; Carl-

son 1991). At some schools there is considerable agreement that achievement must be improved and that this requires change in many current arrangements; here, the problems of change management are largely technical. At many other schools, however, verbal recognition of the need for improvement does not denote any real willingness to change current practices (Joyce 1990). In these schools, the initial emphasis must be on the very difficult task involved in developing and shaping a new set of agreements and understandings concerning the school's purpose and everyday practices (Driscoll 1990).

Nonbureaucratic Implementation

Successful implementation of fundamental reforms in the delivery of instruction cannot be accomplished primarily through bureaucratic approaches that overemphasize filling out of forms and collection of data—even computerized data—to determine whether teachers and schools are responding to central directives (Levine and Lezotte 1990; Sykes 1990; Hamilton 1991).

As we discussed earlier in this chapter, much of the national reform effort has taken the form of mandated change involving course requirements, instructional schedules, teacher presentation of specified subject matter following prescribed steps for delivering instruction, and other aspects of school operation, together with accountability and appraisal systems to ensure that the directives are being carried out. However, decades of research and experience indicate that substantial improvement depends on technical assistance from support personnel working closely with teachers on a personal basis, not on piles of forms, detailed deadlines, and other bureaucratic control mechanisms (Levine and Leibert 1987; Levine and Lezotte 1990).

Instructional Resource Personnel

As noted earlier, successful school reform requires continuous and intensive staff development, as well as re-examination and modification of existing policies and practices in a school, collaboration throughout the faculty, and technical assistance provided to teachers by knowledgeable persons rather than written directives and bureaucratic regulations. Given these kinds of requirements for carrying out successful reform efforts, it is not surprising that research points to the importance of providing instructional resource personnel responsible for the conduct of such activities at the building level (Levine and Lezotte 1990). Whether designated as instructional coordinators, directors of instruction, staff developers, assistant principals for instruction, or by numerous other titles, instructional resource persons constitute an indispensable component in working to bring about major improvements in student performance.

AT-RISK OR MARGINAL STUDENTS AND DROPOUTS

Attention to the problems of students who are low achieving or have been encountering other problems in school has been coalescing under such designations as at-risk students, marginal students, and potential dropouts. In general, such designations refer to the significant proportion of students whose educational performance and opportunities probably will not be improved significantly simply by adding more rigorous course requirements or otherwise imposing external standards such as are present in minimal competency tests (Wilson 1990; Boyd 1991).

The term *at-risk student* can denote a general category that sometimes has been applied broadly to students whose disadvantaged economic or social background is associated with lack of success in the public schools. (This seems to be the usage favored in the statement by the Forum of Educational Leaders cited earlier in this chapter.) Other definitions, such as the following one by Gary Wehlage, Robert Rutter, and Anne Turnbaugh (1987), specifically cite low achievement and alienation from the school as elements in the underlying formulation:

The at-risk student is . . . a young person who comes from a low socioeconomic background which may include various forms of family stress or instability. If the young person is consistently discouraged by the school because he or she receives signals about academic inadequacies and failures, perceives little interest or caring from teachers, and sees the institution's discipline as both ineffective and unfair, then it is not unreasonable to expect that the student will become alienated and uncommitted to getting a high school diploma. (Wehlage, Rutter, and Turnbaugh 1987, 71)

Gary Wehlage and his colleagues have been developing and assessing educational programs for at-risk students as defined here (Wehlage 1989). As a result of these activities, they have described a general model for delivering improved education for at-risk students either in school-within-a-school units or in alternative schools. The four parts of this model (Wehlage, Rutter, and Turnbaugh 1987) include the following aspects:

1. *Administration and organization.* A learning unit ideally should include 25 to 100 students with 2 to 6 faculty, small enough to provide "face-to-face relationships on a continuing basis" and to enable teachers to express a caring relationship as well as to "personalize and individualize" their instruction.
2. *Teacher culture.* Teachers must believe that at-risk students "deserve a renewed opportunity" to learn and must be willing to deal with "problems in the home, community, or peer groups" that affect their students' behavior in school.
3. *Curriculum.* Teaching must incorporate individualization, clear objectives, provision of prompt feedback and concrete evidence of progress, and an active role for students. Initial emphasis should be on improving basic skills deficits, but learning activities emphasizing such topics as sex education, parenting instruction, and nutrition also should be included.

4. *Experiential learning.* Planned, experiential learning activities should include tasks such as volunteer at a day-care center, nursing home, newspaper office, or law enforcement agency. (Wehlage, Rutter, and Turnbaugh 1987, 71–73).

Marginal Students

A formulation somewhat similar to the at-risk category has been provided by Robert Sinclair and Ward Ghory (1987, 1990; Sinclair 1991), who have analyzed problems and possibilities for improving educational programs for marginal students. Sinclair and Ghory define *marginality* with reference to such behaviors as low achievement, truancy, class cutting, tardiness, disciplinary infractions, and dissatisfaction with school among a "shadow population . . . of young people who are not being well served by the American public schools" (1987, 41). After noting that "becoming marginal" generally proceeds through four "levels of seriousness" from "testing" to "coasting," "retreating," and finally, "rebelling," Sinclair and Ghory (1987, 53, 62) identify "counterproductive regularities" that contribute to the difficulties of marginal learners:

1. Large-group instruction that results in uncorrected errors in learning.
2. Narrowness of traditional instruction favoring advanced students.
3. Inflexibility in school schedules.
4. Differential treatment by ability group or track.
5. "Misuses of evaluation that reinforce a student's status" as unsuccessful.
6. Teacher organizations that limit reform efforts.
7. "Insufficient and inequitable funding."

Dropouts

Growing national dissatisfaction with the quality of education in general has both generated and reflected concern for the high school dropout rate and the career limitations that will be encountered by many young people who do not complete high school. As we point out in Chapter 2, most non-Hispanic white students complete high school and the dropout rate for black students has declined, but the dropout rate for minority students still is disproportionately high and half or more of the students in inner-city neighborhoods in big cities are not completing high school.

Some of the concern with recent dropout rates may be unjustified inasmuch as many dropouts return to school and obtain diplomas or pass graduation-equivalency exams (Finn 1987). However, the high correlation between dropping out and socioeconomic status as well as the high rates among disadvantaged students in the inner city indicate that failure to complete high school is a serious national problem (Rumberger 1987; Hinds 1990).

Many interventions have been proposed, and many programs have been or are being implemented to reduce the dropout rate. Among the possible (and not mutually exclusive) steps most often advocated and emphasized are the following:

1. *Early intervention* to help potential dropouts experience more success in school and develop more positive attitudes in elementary and intermediate schools (McPartland and Slavin 1990; Finn 1991).
2. *Alternative* opportunities such as schools-within-a-school, magnet schools, career academies, in-school suspension programs, street academies, high-school outposts, and storefront schools (Wehlage, Rutter, and Turnbaugh 1987; Gooden, Lane, and Levine 1989; Levine and Sherk 1990; Levine 1991b).
3. *Smaller schools and classes* that can facilitate more personal contact between students and teachers (Reinhard 1987; Wehlage et al. 1989; Wilson 1990).
4. *Vocational education* opportunities that might enhance motivation and provide

more experience of success for potential dropouts (Barton 1990; McPartland and Slavin 1990).

5. *Employment linkages* to provide part-time employment and skill training (Hamilton 1986, 1990b; Gage 1990), along with other possibilities (discussed at the conclusion of Chapter 6) to improve the transition to work and adulthood.

6. *Independent study* and *alternative credit* opportunities to complete high-school subjects outside of regular classes and hours (Herbert 1991).

7. *Counseling* and *special services and programs*, such as those for delinquents or pregnant girls (National Governors' Association 1987; Quality Education for Minorities Project 1990).

8. *Revisions in curriculum and instruction* to make education more relevant, motivating, and successful for disinterested and/or alienated students (Wilson 1990).

9. *Experiential learning* opportunities that facilitate active learning outside the regular classroom (McPartland and Slavin 1990).

10. *Contact with successful adult mentors* with similar racial/ethnic and socioeconomic backgrounds (Abi-Nader 1991).

11. *Assignment to tutoring tasks* and other responsibilities for helping younger students (Nettles 1990).

Each general approach for reducing the dropout rate and making schools more effective for potential dropouts has some support in research. For example, Stephen Hamilton (1986) and N. L. Gage (1990) surveyed the research on antidropout programs emphasizing vocational education and other aspects of learning outside of regular academic classes and concluded that experiential learning along these lines can increase holding power when it is implemented well and coordinated with regular instruction. Nevertheless, others who have surveyed the research on antidropout programs have concluded that we do not now clearly understand what in-

terventions and mixtures of interventions work best in differing circumstances and how they should be implemented optimally in the schools (Mann 1990; Finn 1991).

CRUCIAL ISSUES IN MOVING FURTHER TOWARD SCHOOL REFORM

Throughout this book, and particularly throughout this chapter, we identify important issues and problems in considering possibilities for improving education in elementary and secondary schools. We do not attempt to review or summarize all of the relevant themes introduced and discussed; instead, we highlight three issues that deserve more explicit attention if the school reform movement is to be successful in radically improving the effectiveness of instruction. These three issues involve grouping and tracking in elementary and secondary schools, the growing imperative to undertake substantial reorganization of secondary schools, and the need to increase students' engagement in learning focused on higher-order skills.

Grouping and Tracking

Our initial discussions of grouping and tracking in Chapters 2 and 8 conclude that assigning students to classes or tracks according to previous achievement or ability scores frequently has had detrimental effects for low achievers but that the issues involved in devising effective organizational arrangements for instruction are complex and difficult (Passow 1988b; Gamoran 1990). Earlier in this chapter, and in Chapter 8, we also cite evidence (from research on unusually effective inner-city schools) indicating that some grouping by previous achievement can be productive if it results in improved arrangements for teaching low achievers.

Part of the problem in reaching conclusions about grouping and tracking involves the fact that heterogeneous assignment of students to very diverse classes usually has not been successful unless it has used effective individualized and small-group methods that allow students to proceed at their own pace (continuous-progress instruction). Unfortunately, individualized, continuous-progress instruction requires an enormous amount of planning, effort, and instructional resources (Scriven 1975; Cohen 1986; Bennett and Desforges 1988). When teachers in this situation do not receive sufficient resources for implementing individualized, continuous-progress instruction, students often spend much of their time in unproductive seatwork (Stallings and McCarthy 1990). Large classes with very diverse composition are difficult to work with effectively even when teachers use Student Team Learning and other techniques that can help them deal with diversity (Barr and Anderson 1991).

For reasons described in Chapters 2 and 8, however, alternatives to heterogeneous assignment, such as ability grouping and tracking, usually have been unsuccessful, at least for low achievers (Gamoran 1990). In cases in which some degree of homogeneous grouping of low-achieving students has been relatively successful, emphasis has been on maintaining full content coverage and a rapid pace of instruction, on bolstering students' self-concept, and on otherwise working to overcome problems inherent in homogeneous assignment (Leinhardt and Pallay 1982; Sizemore 1985, 1987, 1990; Slavin 1990a). One potential advantage of homogeneous grouping of the lowest-achieving students is that it can make the job of teachers throughout the school much more manageable (Eubanks and Levine 1987a; Slavin 1990a).

In general, we believe it is best to avoid or minimize homogeneous grouping to the extent possible, particularly in racially and socioeconomically mixed settings where such grouping may generate segregation within or across classrooms. In many schools, however, strictly heterogeneous organization may not be feasible, and some amount of homogeneous grouping may be more workable provided that appropriate special assistance is available to the lowest achievers. In the latter situation, we agree with recent reviews of research in which Robert Slavin (1986, 1987,

1988) identified the following "general principles for making ability grouping an effective practice" at the elementary level:

> *Students should remain in heterogeneous classes at most times, and be regrouped by ability only in subjects in which reducing heterogeneity is particularly important (for example, math and reading). . . . Grouping plans must reassess student placements frequently and allow for easy reassignments based on student progress. (Slavin 1986, 4)*

Beyond these principles, we believe that some new terminology is desirable for partially circumventing the frequently emotional controversy between those who support and those who oppose homogeneous grouping. The best language we have identified for this purpose involves the concept of leveling, which advocates making a broad distinction between readers and nonreaders, or, sometimes, between good readers, poor readers and nonreaders (Sizemore 1985; Levine and Sherk 1990; Levine 1991b). Once this distinction is made, special assistance can be provided for poor readers and nonreaders. A similar distinction probably should be made between students who are above and below some level of minimally adequate functioning in mathematics.

As regards tracking of students into separate programs for the college-bound, business education, vocational studies, general education, or other categories, research we cite in Chapters 2, 7, and 8 indicates that such differentiation plays an important part in limiting or hampering the achievement and aspirations of students in nonacademic tracks (e.g., Gamoran 1990). In addition, many researchers who have examined the data on differences between public and nonpublic schools (see Chapter 12) have concluded that the relatively widespread tracking in the public system functions to depress the horizons and performance of many students. After studying tracking and its effects in U.S. secondary schools Ernest Boyer (1983), Theodore Sizer (1984), Jomills Braddock (1990), Robert Slavin (1990a) and other educators have strongly recommended that schools should minimize or reduce their tracking systems and initiate improvements to allow for effective instruction in an expanded common curriculum.

Reorganization of Secondary Schools

Previous sections of this chapter cite secondary-school studies in which observers have concluded that intermediate and senior high schools in the United States generally are not providing adequate education for many of their students. Martin Lazerson (1986) reviewed a number of these studies and was struck by the "awesome mindlessness" they found present at the high-school level, and Michael Sedlak and his colleagues (1986) have pointed out that the reform movement's typical concentration on raising standards and requirements without seriously addressing underlying problems threatens the secondary school's historic mission to provide equal and effective opportunities for all groups of students in the United States. If we do not find a way to deliver meaningful "academic learning for everyone," these authors concluded, the new standards either will become a "crueler form of screening and pushing" students out of the schools or "they will be rescinded and watered down in the name of practicality" (Sedlak, Wheeler, Pullin, and Cusick 1986, 23).

Some indication of the pervasiveness of the problems has been provided in a study of ninth graders that the National Association of Secondary School Principals conducted in a representative sample of 141 secondary schools in 48 states and the District of Columbia. Based partly on data collected by observers who followed a randomly selected ninth grader in each school on March 7, 1984, the authors of the study (Lounsbury and Johnston 1985) concluded that there is a "clear lack of meaningful intellectual interaction between students and teachers," that the curriculum is highly fragmented, and that most students sit passively for long periods of time (p. 73). As shown in Table 13-4, students were seldom recognized individually by teachers, did not initiate much conversation with teachers inside or outside of class, and had relatively little involvement in critical thinking or in selecting learning activities. Similar results were reported in a later nationwide study of eighth graders (Lounsbury and Clark 1990).

As suggested by the authors and studies cited as well as by other sources, problems in U.S. secondary schools are so pervasive and entrenched that they probably will not be successfully addressed without major reform in how schools are organized and operated. Earlier in this chapter we note the example of South Boston and also describe several kinds of major organizational changes (e.g., schools-within-a-school,

TABLE 13-4 *Observers' Ratings of Ninth Graders' Experience in School*

Statement	Average Rating by Observers*
Was the student recognized individually by at least one teacher?	1.25
Was the student involved in situations calling for value discrimination, critical thinking, or analysis of options?	1.65
Did the student have opportunity to elect or select anything in his or her learning activities?	1.67
Did the student initiate conversation with a teacher during class or outside of class?	1.39

Source: Adapted from Lounsbury and Johnston 1985.
*1 = little or no evidence of the phenomenon
 2 = some evidence
 3 = a great deal of evidence.
(See the text of this chapter for additional information.)

achievement centers, and a longer and different school day) that can help enhance the performance of low achievers and improve the functioning of urban high schools. As is apparent from other material in this chapter, however, reorganization probably will be required to improve secondary education not only in the cities but also throughout the United States. National possibilities for making secondary education more meaningful and more oriented toward higher mental processes should receive priority attention in the future.

Among the suggestions to guide reorganization and reform of secondary schools are those offered by Ernest Boyer, Arthur Powell, Theodore Sizer, and other educators who have participated with them in studying high schools. Related to their proposals about reduced tracking and greater emphasis on thinking and cognitive development, these authors and studies have offered a variety of recommendations for major reorganization. Boyer (1983), for example, called for breaking up large high schools into smaller units, for flexibility to permit larger blocks of instructional time, and for a class size limit of twenty in basic English/writing courses taught by teachers with no more than two such classes per term. Sizer (1984, 1991) recommended that high-school teachers should work in teams of 7 or 8 with about 100 students each.

Arthur Powell (1985), in a comparable analysis, compared the typical high school to a "shopping mall" in which students do their "own thing," learning is "just another consumer choice," and "unspecial" students easily become lost. He concluded this portrayal by saying:

> Changes [to engage teenagers seriously in school studies] will require major structural reform. . . . Teachers need a more flexible day . . . to get away from the exhausting routine of large-group instruction . . . [and to] spend time with students in different formats. . . . Students need to have their class time reduced because so many classes are wholly boring and without educational purpose, because

students need other kinds of contact with teachers, and because they need more time to work on their own. (Powell 1985, 261)

Active and Engaged Learning Focused on Higher-Order Skills

Many educators and other observers have recognized the need to increase engagement in learning. Among the suggestions most frequently emphasized are to provide students' with more successful and challenging learning environments in the early grades so they will not bring a history of failure to secondary schools, to build in opportunities for more active learning focused on themes that engage students' interests, to provide a better match between classroom instruction and students' conceptual levels and learning styles (see Chapters 8 and 10), to take better account of peer and community influences in delivering instruction (see Chapter 5), to introduce more experiential learning opportunities for adolescents (Chapter 6), to support the establishment of magnet and alternative schools (Chapters 10 and 12), and to modify school arrangements in order to establish school-within-a-school units or other approaches to reorganization as described in preceding sections. It is doubtful whether the school reform movement ultimately will be successful unless suggestions of these kinds are addressed systematically and comprehensively throughout the educational system.

But learning must be more than just active and engaged if it is to provide young people with the higher-order comprehension and thinking skills required to function well in postindustrial society. It also must be mediated (i.e., carefully guided) by skillful teachers and other adults who help students improve their cognitive performance and their capacity for mastering and applying higher-order skills. As emphasized repeatedly in this concluding chapter and in several preceding chapters, education—particularly for currently low-achieving students—must be redesigned and restructured to guide students successfully toward acquisition of higher-order cognitive skills.

Much of the new terminology and methodology recently introduced by learning analysts is aimed at improving the educational system's capacity to attain these overriding goals for schooling in a prosperous, democratic society. For example, various instructional-development specialists have been devising a wide range of approaches for providing:

- "Cognitive apprenticeships" through which students improve thinking skills in a motivating, real-world setting (Garcia and Pearson 1990; Resnick 1990; Idol and Jones 1991).
- "Scaffolded" instruction that temporarily provides step-by-step modeling and other forms of assistance to improve cognitive capacity that are gradually withdrawn as learners become more independent (Garcia and Pearson 1991; Rosenshine 1990).
- "Explicit comprehension instruction" to improve reading skills through a mixture of active student learning and direct instruction emphasizing comprehension-improvement strategies (Pearson 1985).
- "Cognitively guided instruction" that builds on existing knowledge and intuitive reasoning in "developing understanding of problem solving" (Putnam, Lampert, and Peterson 1990b).
- "Anchored" instruction (or "situated cognition") involving multimedia simulations designed to motivate and develop independent learning skills (The Cognition and Technology Group 1990).
- "Mediated" learning that stresses personal assistance to help low achievers master increasingly difficult skills (Brainen 1985; Presseisen 1988; Pechman 1990).

Some of these or other related terms probably will become standard terminology in educational analysis in the next decade; others may be quickly forgotten or superseded by later versions. Whatever terms and approaches eventually gain widespread acceptance, the underlying challenge will remain the same: to provide children and youth with the knowledge and skills to function successfully on an equitable basis in future society.

CONCLUSION: SCHOOL REFORM AND THE CRISIS IN METROPOLITAN SOCIETY

In Chapter 2, we describe how the developing educational crisis in postindustrial metropolitan society centers on the emergence of an underclass in socioeconomically and frequently racially isolated inner-city neighborhoods. Other sections of this book also describe related developments involving low school achievement, crime and delinquency, teenage pregnancy, unemployment, and other problems particularly acute among children and youth in concentrated poverty neighborhoods in big cities.

Recent data indicate that real improvements in students' performance are being registered in schools enrolling disadvantaged students in some big cities. In some cases, as we point out in Chapter 7 and earlier in this chapter, such gains seem to have been produced in part through the implementation of unusually successful effective schools projects, along with other instructional improvement activities. As shown in Table 13-5, for example, the average reading scores of elementary students in the Kansas City (Missouri) Public Schools improved markedly between 1980 and 1990, at which time they had reached or were only a little below national norms. (Gains in the mechanics of language and in math computation in the three districts shown in Table 13-5 have been even larger than the reading gains.) Data not shown in Table 13-5 also demonstrate comparable gains in achievement at the district's predominantly black elementary schools. In San Diego, data for that district's minority-isolated schools show large achievement gains in reading through the eleventh grade, and Washington, DC—which has long been more than 90 percent minority—also has had large gains at all grade levels.

TABLE 13-5   *Improvement in Average Reading Scores in Three Big-City School Districts*

Kansas City, MO (median grade equivalent)			
Grade	1978	1985	1990	National Norm*
3	3.1	3.3	3.4	3.8
6	5.5	5.8	5.8	6.8
8	6.7	7.2	8.3	8.7

San Diego Minority Isolated Schools (percentage of students above national median)		
Grade	1980	1990	National Norm*
5	17	32	50
9	22	35	50
11	32	44	50

Washington, DC (median grade equivalent)			
Grade	1978	1982	1990	National Norm*
3	3.0	3.8	3.7	3.8
6	5.1	6.2	6.4	6.8
9	6.8	7.9	9.1	9.8

Source: Anderson 1987; Behnke 1986; Kansas City, Missouri, Public Schools; Nagel 1986; Nagel and Mittleholtz 1991; Washington, DC, Public Schools.
*National norms citied for 1990.

Although a significant part of the achievement gains registered in Kansas City, Washington, DC, and some other cities (e.g., Atlanta) probably are spurious effects of more rigorous promotions policies,** it appears that these gains partly reflect improved delivery of instruction in the classroom (Levine and Ornstein 1989). Kansas City, for example, has implemented a number of important changes, including provision of an assistant to the principal for instruction, reduction of Chapter 1 pullout arrangements, sponsorship of TESA training in many schools, and introduction of Chicago Mastery Learning Reading (Levine 1992). As part of a court-ordered desegregation plan, San Diego's minority-isolated schools have participated in an effective schools project (the Achievement Goals Program) that stresses mastery learning, improved classroom management, direct instruc-

tion, increased time on task, greater emphasis on higher-order skills and language learning, and staff development (Courter and Ward 1983; Nagel and Mittleholtz 1991). The San Diego schools also have introduced a radical curriculum alignment that inhibits teachers from proceeding page-by-page through texts at the pace of the slowest students (Nagel and Mittleholtz 1991).

Despite improvements that appear to have taken place in some cities, many measures and considerations involving the performance of disadvantaged urban students nationally are primarily negative. Six such indicators include the following:

1. NAEP and other data continue to show inadequate achievement levels among disadvantaged urban students.
2. Dropout rates at many inner-city schools and in some big cities exceed 40 or 50 percent.
3. Even urban districts that have registered large achievement gains at the elementary level generally continue to report very low

**Retaining students in grade generally increases longitudinal scores as those shown in Table 13-5, even when there is no improvement in students' annual rate of growth.

achievement at the secondary level. As shown in Table 13-5, for example, eighth- and ninth-grade reading scores in Kansas City and Washington, DC, are still far below the national average. Nationwide, achievement in big-city high schools can only be viewed as abysmally low. (For an example, see Figure 2-3.)

4. As indicated in this chapter and elsewhere in this book, schools in the United States place relatively little stress on the development of thinking skills and higher mental processes, particularly in schools with many disadvantaged low achievers. The ideal of a high-level, academically-oriented common curriculum for all students is far from realization.

5. Most national and state school reform reports and efforts have not systematically addressed or generated the massive changes needed in U.S. secondary schools in general and in inner-city secondary schools in particular (Reed 1990).

6. Innovations such as mastery learning and effective schools projects are not being implemented effectively in many urban school districts and elsewhere (Levine 1985, 1988, 1991a, 1992).

Thus, the situation with respect to the academic performance of poverty students in big cities continues to be generally unsatisfactory with respect to such key learning skills as comprehension in reading. Comparable generalizations can be offered about the goal of reducing racial isolation for urban minority students. As we show in Chapter 9, much desegregation has been achieved in small towns and cities and rural areas, as well as in a few larger cities that have had some success in implementing plans on a regional basis. Overall, however, large numbers and proportions of minority students still attend socioeconomically and racially isolated schools that reinforce the disadvantages these students experience growing up in segregated poverty environments.

Recognizing the difficulties involved in bringing about radical improvement in the academic performance of disadvantaged children, Oliver Wendell Holmes once pointed out that a child's education begins generations before it is born. But today we no longer have the luxury of depending on evolutionary changes in families and society to generate an increase in the proportion of disadvantaged youth who are well prepared to succeed in school; instead, schools must become much more effective than in the past. The impressive attainments of a relatively small proportion of unusually successful schools and projects cited in this chapter illustrate what could be accomplished in the future on a widespread basis.

The problems involved in improving education for disadvantaged children and youth intersect with the larger national challenge to improve the functioning of schools with respect to students' cognitive development and mastery of higher-order learning skills. As we note at the beginning of this chapter and in Chapter 2 and elsewhere, massive improvements are needed throughout our educational system. Some observers perceive strong parallels with the early part of the twentieth century, when compulsory education was expanded and reforms in curriculum and instruction were introduced to provide a higher proportion of young people with the basic skills and certificates required for success in an industrial-era economy. Drawing on the social analysis of John Dewey, educators at that time endeavored to make the schools more meaningful for working-class children and youth who previously attained only rudimentary skills in reading and computation. This effort succeeded in the sense that increasingly higher percentages of students have entered secondary schools and now earn high-school diplomas, but as we have seen, standards for performance have not been rigorous and many students attain only relatively low achievement levels. Now, developments involving international economic competitiveness similarly require fundamental reforms to improve the cognitive performance of masses of students currently at low levels of academic performance.

Solutions to problems that challenge the educational system to provide more effective instruction for disadvantaged students and to enhance higher-order skills among all groups of students will depend on the system's success in implementing lessons learned from research and analysis dealing with improvement and reform in elementary and secondary education. Various comprehensive reforms described in preceding sections, such as ecological intervention in early childhood, coordination of education with other social services for children and youth, establishment of better linkage between the employment system and the schools, and initiation of effective schools projects that aim at fundamental reform throughout each participating school, may bring about massive improvement in educational opportunities and outcomes. Reminiscent as they are of educators' efforts early in this century to help larger numbers of children and youth participate in an industrial economy, comprehensive reform approaches now being initiated or already operating may similarly reposition the educational system to function successfully in accordance with the escalating demands placed on it in the postindustrial era of a new century.

EXERCISES

1. Interview teachers in a nearby school district concerning the school reform movement of the 1980s. Do they believe that national and state reform reports and efforts have had a positive impact? Which actions or changes do they perceive have been useful? Which do they think have been nonproductive or damaging?

2. Observe instruction in a high school class for college-bound students and then in a class for students who probably will not attend college. What differences appear to be present in teacher and school expectations for students? What do you think might be done to raise expectations successfully in either or both classes?

3. What are school districts in your community doing to prevent or reduce dropouts? Are these efforts succeeding? Are evaluation reports available? What do district officials believe are the major obstacles to success?

4. Why is there tension between the aims of educational excellence and educational equity? What efforts that contribute to one goal might detract from the other? What might be done to enhance the attainment of both goals?

5. Compare and contrast the recommendations of *A Nation at Risk*, prepared by the National Commission on Excellence in Education, with *Time for Results*, prepared by the National Governors' Association.

6. If you live in or near a big city, examine data on student performance to determine whether or how much academic achievement has improved during the past five or ten years. If gains have been registered, what changes in instruction and educational programming do school officials believe have been most responsible?

7. What do faculty in your school or college think about the Holmes Report? Do they believe its recommendations are likely to be implemented?

8. Have negative, unforeseen consequences occurred in connection with school-reform efforts in your community? How might these outcomes have been foreseen or avoided?

SUGGESTIONS FOR FURTHER READING

1. The Spring 1985 issue of *Teachers College Record* and the Fall 1986 issue of *Metropolitan Education* are devoted largely to discussion and analysis of the dropout problem.

2. *The Great School Debate*, edited by Beatrice and Ronald Gross, presents a wide variety of perspectives and viewpoints on school reform reports and proposals.

3. *Creating Effective Schools*, by Wilbur Brookover and his colleagues, describes an intensive in-service training program to improve achievement and learning climate in elementary and secondary schools.

4. The February 1971 issue of the *Phi Delta Kappan* describes several successful inner-city elementary schools in which academic achievement was higher than usual for such schools. Material in this issue includes an analysis of actions that might help accomplish this goal in other inner-city schools.

5. The Summer 1985 issue of *The Journal of Negro Education* is a theme issue describing successful policies, practices, and programs at inner-city schools.

6. Much of the material in the May 1986 issue of *Educational Leadership* deals with the teaching of thinking.

7. The March 1987 issue of *Educational Leadership* is devoted largely to the education of at-risk students.

8. *Reading, Thinking, and Concept Development*, edited by Theodore Harris and Eric Cooper, describes a variety of instructional strategies for improving students' thinking skills and comprehension.

9. *Improving Student Achievement through Mastery Learning Programs* (D. U. Levine, ed., 1985) provides analysis and illustrations regarding successful implementation of mastery learning.

10. Analysis of and reactions to the Holmes Group report and recommendations are provided in *Reforming Teacher Education*, edited by Jonas F. Soltis.

11. Many of the forces leading to low standards and emphasis on low-level learning in U.S. schools are described, illustrated, and analyzed by Linda McNeil in *Contradictions of Control*.

12. The developments and detours, twists and turns, claims and counterclaims, and pronouncements and renunciations of the school reform movement can be followed week by week and month by month in *Education Week*, the *Phi Delta Kappan*, and other periodicals.

13. The U.S. Department of Education (1987) has prepared an excellent summary of much of the effective schools and related research. Titled *Schools That Work, Educating Disadvantaged Children*, single copies have been available free of charge by writing to *Schools That Work*, Pueblo, Colorado 81009.

14. A report entitled *Saving Urban Schools* (Carnegie Foundation for the Advancement of Teaching 1988) proposes radical improvement and reform in the financing, organization, and operation of urban schools.

15. *At-Risk Students and Thinking*, edited by Barbara Presseisen, includes eight chapters dealing with research findings and instructional approaches for improving the cognitive performance of low achievers.

16. *Educational Values and Cognitive Instruction: Implications for Reform*, edited by Lorna Idol and Beau Fly Jones, includes chapters dealing with instruction in critical thinking and other higher-order skills, cognitive apprenticeships, grouping of students, motivation, teaching writing and mathematics, the school change process, and inquiry-centered learning.

17. Numerous aspects and implications of research and analysis involving school choice are explored in *Choice and Control in American Education*, edited by William Clune and John Witte (1991).

18. *The Educational Reform Movement of the 1980s* edited by Joseph Murphy (1990) includes chapters on student competency tests, teacher testing, national reports and commissions, career ladders, and other relevant topics.

19. The theme of the January/February 1992 issue of *Journal of Teacher Education* is professional development schools.

20. The May 1992 issue of *Educational Leadership* reports on recent efforts to improve testing and assessment of students.

21. *Restructuring the Schools* edited by John Lane and Edgar Epps (1992) includes chapters on school choice, site-based management, state policies, and related topics.

Bibliography

Aaron, H. J. 1977. *Healthy, wealthy, and wise: Backdoor approaches to education.* Cambridge, MA: Aspen Institute for Humanistic Studies. (p. 247)

Abi-Nader, J. 1991. Creating a vision of the future. *Phi Delta Kappan* 72 (7): 546–549. (p. 529)

Abrahams, R. D. 1970. *Deep down in the jungle. Negro narrative folklore from the streets of Philadelphia* Chicago: Aldine. (p. 104)

Abrams, C. 1965. *The city is the frontier.* New York: Harper and Row. (p. 86)

Abrams, J. D. 1988. Outcomes and basics reinforce each other. *The School Administrator* 45 (2): 47–49. (p. 268)

Academy for Educational Development. 1982. A new direction for bilingual education in the 1980's. *Focus of the National Clearinghouse for Bilingual Education* No. 10: 1–4. (p. 381)

Adams, M. J. 1990. *Beginning to read: Thinking and learning about print.* Urbana: University of Illinois at Urbana-Champaign Center for the Study of Reading. (pp. 112, 258, 263, 281, 283, 523)

Addams, J. 1938. *Twenty years at Hull House.* New York: Macmillan. (p. 405)

Aerospace Education Foundation, 1989. *America's next crisis.* Arlington, VA: Aerospace Education Foundation. (p. 509)

Ahlstrom, W. M., and Havighurst, R. J. 1971. *Delinquent boys in high school.* San Francisco: Jossey-Bass. (p. 210)

Alba, Richard D. 1988. Cohorts and the dynamics of ethnic change. In *Social structures and human lives*, edited by M. White Riley. Beverly Hills, CA: Sage. (pp. 216, 217)

———. 1990. *Ethnic identity: The transformation of white America.* New Haven: Yale University Press. (pp. 346, 348)

Alexander, K. L.; Cook, M.; and McDill, E. L. 1977. *Curriculum tracking and educational stratification: Some further evidence.* Baltimore: The Johns Hopkins University Center for Social Organization of Schools, Report No. 237. (p. 161)

Alexander, K. L., and McDill, E. L. 1976. Selection and allocation within schools: Some causes and consequences of curriculum placement. *American Sociological Review* 41: 963–981. (pp. 161, 162, 237)

Alexander, L. 1986. Time for results: An overview. *Phi Delta Kappan* 68 (3): 202–204. (p. 468)

Allington, R. 1991. How policy and regulation influence instruction for at-risk learners. In *Educational values and cognitive instruction: Implications for reform*, edited by Lorna Idol and Beau Fly Jones. Hillsdale, NJ: Erlbaum. (pp. 491, 516, 517)

Almeida, P. M. 1977. Children's television and the modeling of proreading behaviors. *Education and Urban Society* 10 (November): 55–60. (p. 135)

Alpert, D., and Breen, D. T. 1989. 'Liberality' in children and adolescents. *Journal of Vocational Behavior* 34: 154–160. (p. 421)

Alwin, D. F. 1988. From obedience to autonomy. *Public Opinion Quarterly* 52: 33–52. (p. 233)

———. 1989. Changes in qualities valued in children in the United States, 1964 to 1984. *Social Science Research* 18: 195–236. (pp. 89, 218, 232, 233)

American Academy of Pediatrics. 1990. Children, adolescents, and television. *Pediatrics* 85: 1119. (p. 119)

American Association of School Administrators. 1984. *The cost of reform.* Arlington, VA: American Association of School Administrators. (p. 493)

Ames, C., and Felker, D. W. 1977. Children's achievement attributions and reinforcing behaviors in relation to self-concept and reward structure. Paper presented at the annual meeting of the American Education Research Association, Los Angeles, April.

Ames, C. A. 1990. Motivation: What teachers need to know. *Teachers College Record* 91 (3): 409–421. (p. 261)

Ames, R., and Ames, C. 1991. Motivation and effective teaching. In *Educational values and cognitive instruction: Implications for reform*, edited by Lorna Idol and Beau Fly Jones. Hillsdale, NJ: Erlbaum. (p. 260)

Amir, Y. 1969. Contact hypothesis in ethnic relations. *Psychological Bulletin* 71: 319–342. (p. 315)

Anderson, D. R., and Collins, P. A. 1988. *The impact on children's education: Television's influence on cognitive development.* Washington, DC: U.S.

Department of Education Office of Educational Research and Improvement. (p. 137)

Anderson, E. 1978. *A place on the corner*. Chicago: University of Chicago Press. (p. 17)

———. 1989. Sex codes and family life among poor inner-city youths. In *The ghetto underclass: Social science perspectives*, edited by William Julius Wilson. V. 501. The Annals of the American Academy of Political and Social Science. Newbury Park, CA: Sage. (p. 17, 18, 166)

Anderson L. W., and Pellicer, L. O. 1990. Synthesis of research on compensatory and remedial education. *Educational Leadership* 48 (1): 10–16. (pp. 283, 284, 285, 286)

Anderson, N. 1959. *The urban community: A world perspective*. New York: Holt, Rinehart & Winston. (p. 94)

Anderson, R. B. 1977. *The effectiveness of follow-through: What have we learned?* Paper presented at the annual meeting of the American Education Research Association, Los Angeles. (p. 283)

Anderson, R. C., and Armbruster, B. B. 1900. Some maximums for learning and instruction. *Teachers College Record* 91 (3): 396–408. (p. 516)

Anderson, R. C.; Armbruster, B. B.; and Roe, M. 1990. Improving the education of reading teachers. *Daedalus* 119 (2): 187–210. (p. 397, 523)

Anderson, R. C.; Hiebert, E. H.; Scott, J. A.; and Wilkinson, J. A. G. 1985. *Becoming a nation of readers: Report of the Commission on Reading*. Washington, DC: National Institute of Education. (p. 511)

Anderson, S. 1987. Personal communication with compilation of unpublished data. (p. 534)

Anthony, H. M., and Raphael, T. E. 1987. Using questioning strategies to promote students' active comprehension of content area material. Michigan State University Institute for Research on Teaching, Occasional Paper No. 109. (p. 513)

Anyon, J. 1983. Social class and the hidden curriculum of work. In *The hidden curriculum and moral education*, edited by Henry Giroux and David Purpel. Berkeley, CA: McCutchan. (p. 238)

———. 1988. Social class and the hidden curriculum of work. In *Childhood socialization*, edited by Gerald Handel. New York: Aldine de Gruyter. (pp. 238, 239)

Apple, M. W. 1981. Reproduction, contestation, and curriculum. In *New directions in education: Critical perspectives*. Buffalo: Department of Social Foundations and Comparative Education Center, State University of New York. (p. 253)

———. 1985. *Education and power*. Boston: Ark. (p. 253)

———. 1990. *Ideology and curriculum*. 2nd ed. New York: Routledge. (pp. 247, 253)

———. 1991. Series editor's introduction. In *Growing-up modern*, by Bruce Falmer. New York: Routledge. (p. 253)

———, ed. 1982. *Cultural and economic reproduction in education*. Boston: Routledge and Kegan Paul. (pp. 247, 253)

Apple, M. W., and Jungck, S. 1990. 'You don't have to be a teacher to teach this unit': Teaching, technology and gender in the classroom. *American Educational Research Journal* 27 (2): 227–251. (pp. 244, 253)

Apple, M. W., and Weis, L., eds. 1983. *Ideology and practice in schooling*. Philadelphia: Temple University. (p. 254)

Applebee, A. N., et al. 1990. *Learning to write in our nation's schools*. Princeton, NJ: Educational Testing Service. (pp. 415, 463)

Applebee, A. N.; Langer, J. A.; and Mullis, I. V. S. 1990. *Crossroads in American education*. Princeton, NJ: Educational Testing Service. (p. 463)

Applebee, A. N.; Langer, J. A.; Mullis, I. V. S.; and Jenkins, L. B. 1990. *The writing report card, 1984–88*. Princeton, NJ: Educational Testing Service. (pp. 463, 465)

Applebome, P. 1991. Although urban blight worsens, most people don't feel its impact. *The New York Times* January 28: A1, A12. (p. 82)

Appleton, N. 1983. *Cultural pluralism in education*. New York: Longman. (pp. 400, 406)

Arce, C. H. 1982. Maintaining a growing culture. *ISR Newsletter* 10 (4): 7–8. (p. 349)

Archambault, F. X., et. al. 1990. Some findings on the nature of physical abuse runaways experience on the street. Paper presented at the annual meeting of the American Educational Research Association, Boston. (p. 141)

Aries, P. 1965. *Centuries of childhood: A social history of family life*. New York: Random House. (p. 90)

———. 1989. Introduction. In *A history of private life. Passions of the Renaissance*, edited by Roger Chartier. Cambridge, MA: Belknap. (p. 91)

Armor, D. J. 1988. School busing: A time for change. In *Eliminating racism*, edited by Phyllis A. Katz and Dalmas A. Taylor. New York: Plenum. (p. 306)

———. 1989. After busing: Education and choice. *The Public Interest* No. 95: 24–37. (p. 332)

Armstrong, J. 1990. A road map for restructuring schools. *Education Week* 9(26):24. (p. 483)

Aronson, E., and Gonzalez, A. 1988. Desegregation, jigsaw, and the Mexican-American experience. In *Eliminating racism*, edited by Phyllis A. Katz and Dalmas A. Taylor. New York: Plenum. (p. 315)

Arrarte, A. M. 1990. The corporate classroom. *U.S. News and World Report* 109 (5): 42–43. (p. 126)

Arras, B. 1988. Update on home schooling. *National Monitor of Education* 11 (0): 1–3. (p. 456)

Arredondo, D. E., and Block, J. H. 1990. Recognizing the connections between thinking skills and mastery learning. *Educational Leadership* 47 (5): 4–10. (p. 524)

Ascher, C. 1988. Improving the school-home connection for low-income urban parents. *ERIC Clearinghouse on Urban Education* No. 41: 1–4. (p. 143)

———. 1989. Urban school finance: The quest for equal educational opportunity. *ERIC Clearinghouse on Urban Education* No. 55: 1–4 (p. 295)

———. 1990a. Linking schools with human service agencies. *Clearinghouse on Urban Education Digest* No. 62: 1–2. (p. 209)

———. 1990b. Using magnet schools for desegregation: Some suggestions from the research. In *Magnet schools*, edited by Nolan Estes, Daniel U. Levine, and Donald R. Waldrip. Austin, TX: Morgan. (pp. 306, 309)

Asher, S. R., and Coie, J. D., eds. 1990. *Peer rejection in childhood*. New York: Cambridge University Press. (pp. 119, 151, 152, 153, 154, 156, 157, 164, 325)

Associated Press. 1989. Children pour into foster care. *Newsday* December 12: 15. (p. 141)

Astin, A. W. 1969. Folklore of selectivity. *Saturday Review* December 20: 57–59. (p. 288)

———. 1985. *Achieving educational excellence*. San Francisco: Jossey-Bass. (pp. 52, 53, 288)

———. 1990. Educational assessment and educational equity. *American Journal of Education* 98 (4): 458–478. (pp. 52, 303)

Atherton, L. 1984. *Main street on the middle border*. Bloomington: Indiana University Press. (p. 459)

Au, K. H. 1985. Developing and implementation of the KEEP reading program. In *Reading comprehension: From research to practice*, edited by J. Orassanu. Hillsdale, NJ: Erlbaum. (p. 397)

Au, K. H., and Kawakami, A. J. 1985. Research currents: Talk story and learning to read. *Language Arts* 62 (4): 406–411. (p. 397)

Auletta, K. 1982. *The underclass*. New York: Random House. (pp. 19, 353)

Austin, R. L. 1980. Adolescent subcultures of violence. *The Sociological Quarterly* 21: 545–561. (p. 196)

Bacchus, M., and Marchiafava, B. 1991. Implementing school reform in Chicago: The system perspective. Paper presented at the annual meeting of the American Educational Research Association, Chicago.

Bachen, C. M.; Hornby, M. C.; Roberts, D. F.; and Hernandez-Ramos, P. F. 1982. Television viewing behavior and the development of reading skills: Survey evidence. Paper presented at the annual meeting of the American Educational Research Association, New York. (p. 137)

Bacon, K. H. 1990. Many educators view involved parents as key to children's success in school. *The Wall Street Journal* July 31: B1. (p. 136, 142)

Bahr, H. M.; Chadwick, B. A.; and Strauss, J. H. 1979. *American ethnicity*. Lexington, MA: D.C. Heath. (p. 406)

Bailey, T. 1990. *Changes in the nature and structure of work: Implications for skill requirements and skill formation*. Columbus, OH: National Center for Research in Vocational Education. (pp. 23, 71)

———. 1991. Jobs of the future and the education they will require: Evidence from occupational forecasts. *Educational Researcher* 20 (2): 11–20. (p. 23)

Bailyn, B. 1986. *Voyagers to the West*. New York: Knopf. (p. 104)

Baker, J. 1989. Programs that can make a difference. *Newsweek* 114 (11): 28. (p. 290)

Baker, K. A. 1985. Research evidence of a school discipline problem. *Phi Delta Kappan* 66 (7): 482–487. (p. 276)

———. 1991. *Bilingual education: Time to take a second look?* Bloomington, IN: Phi Delta Kappa. (p. 376)

Baker, K. A., and de Kanter, A. A. 1981. Effectiveness of bilingual education: A review of the literature. Paper prepared for the U.S. Office of Education Office of Planning, Budget, and Evaluation, September. (p. 376)

Baltzell, E. G. 1958. *Philadelphia gentleman: The making of a national upper class*. Glencoe, IL: Free Press. (p. 35)

Bandow, D. 1990. National service: 'Idea whose time will never come?' *Education Week* 9 (36): 32. (p. 205)

Bane, M. J. 1976. *Here to stay: American families in the twentieth century*. New York: Basic Books. (p. 122)

Banks, J. A. 1988. *Multicultural education: Issues and perspectives*. 2nd ed. Boston: Allyn and Bacon. (pp. 379, 406)

Banks, R. R. 1991. Bias is embedded in all standardized aptitude tests. *Education Week* 10 (19): 32, 34. (p. 69)

Barden, J. C. 1990a. Foster care system reeling, despite law meant to help. *The New York Times*. September 21: A1, A10. (p. 141)

———. 1990b. Toll of troubled families: Flood of homeless youth. *The New York Times* February 5: A1, 87. (pp. 140, 141)

———. 1991. When foster care ends, home is often the streets. *The New York Times* January 6: 1, 15. (p. 141)

Barnett, W. S. 1985. Benefit-cost analysis of the Perry Preschool program and its policy implications. *Educational Evaluation and Policy Analysis* 7 (4): 333–342. (p. 281)

Barnett, W. S., and Escobar, C. M. 1987. The economics of early educational intervention: A review. *Review of Educational Research* 57 (4): 387–414. (p. 281)

———. 1989. Research on the cost-effectiveness of early educational intervention: Implications for policy, practice, and research. Paper presented at the annual meeting of the American Educational Research Association, San Francisco. (p. 281)

Barney, J. 1990. Stepfamilies: Second chance or second-rate? *Phi Delta Kappan* 72 (2): 144–147. (p. 129)

Barr, R., and Anderson, C. S. 1991. Grouping students for instruction in elementary schools. In *Educational values and cognitive instruction: Implications for reform*, edited by Lorna Idol and Beau Fly Jones. Hillsdale, NJ: Erlbaum. (pp. 43, 44, 262, 530)

Barrett, T. C. 1989. Evaluating suicide-prevention programs. *Education Week* 9 (12): 28. (p. 185)

Barringer, F. 1989. Waiting is over: Births near 50's level. *The New York Times* October 31: 13. (p. 117)

———. 1990a. After 18-year decline, teen-age births are up. *The New York Times* August 17: A1, A9. (p. 202)

———. 1990b. Pueblo parents feel generation gap. *The New York Times* October 24: B9. (p. 394)

———. 1991. Census shows profound change in racial makeup of the nation. *The New York Times* March 11: A1, A12. (p. 366)

Barth, R. 1979. Home-based reinforcement of school behavior: A review and analysis. *Review of Educational Research* 49 (3): 436–458. (p. 115)

Barton, P. E. 1990. *From school to work*. Princeton, NJ: Educational Testing Service Policy Information Center. (pp. 55, 191, 194, 195, 529)

Barton, P. E., and Coley, R. J. 1990. *The education reform decade*. Princeton, NJ: Educational Testing Service. (p. 490)

Barton, P. E., and Kirsch, I.S. 1990. *Workplace competencies: The need to improve literacy and employment readiness*. Washington, DC: U.S. Government Printing Office. (pp. 23, 24, 47, 71)

Bastian, A. 1990. School choice: Unwrapping the package. In *Choice in Education*, edited by W. W. Boyd and H. J. Walberg. Berkeley, CA: McCutchan. (pp. 500, 502)

Bastian, A., et al. 1986. *Choosing equality*. Philadelphia: Temple University Press. (pp. 455, 490, 502)

Bates, P. 1990. Desegregation: Can we get there from here? *Phi Delta Kappan* 72 (1): 8–16. (p. 307)

Batey, A., and Cowell, R. N. 1987. *Distance education: An overview*. Portland, OR: The Northwest Regional Educational Laboratory. (p. 444)

Battistich, V., et al. 1989. Effect of an elementary program to enhance prosocial behavior on children's cognitive-social problem-solving skills and strategies. *Journal of Applied Developmental Psychology* 10 (2): 147–170. (p. 157)

Beatty, J. 1990. A post-cold war budget. *The Atlantic Monthly* 265 (2): 74–82. (pp. 278, 284)

Beck, M. 1990. The geezer boom. *Newsweek* Winter/Spring: 62–68. (p. 27)

Becker, H. J. 1979. Personal networks of opportunity in obtaining jobs: Racial differences and effects of segregation. Paper presented at the annual meeting of the American Educational Research Association, San Francisco. (p. 317)

———. 1990a. Curriculum and instruction in middle-grade schools. *Phi Delta Kappan* 71 (6): 450–457. (p. 239)

———. 1990b. Use of computers in United States schools: 1989. Paper presented at the annual meeting of the American Educational Research Association, Boston. (p. 437)

Becker, W. C. 1977. Teaching reading and languages to the disadvantaged: What we have learned from field research. *Harvard Educational Review* 47: 518–543. (p. 298)

Behnke, G., et al. 1986. *Testing results for minority isolated schools, Spring 1986*. San Diego: San Diego City Schools. (p. 534)

Behr, G. E., and Hanson, R. A. 1977. Differential access to instruction: A source of educational inequality. Paper presented at the annual meeting of the American Educational Research Association, Los Angeles.

Bejar, I. I. 1981. Does nutrition cause intelligence? A reanalysis of the Cali Experiment. *Intelligence* 5: 49–68. (p. 132)

Belenky, M. F.; Clinchy, B. M.; Goldberger, N. R.; and Tarule, J. M. 1986. *Women's ways of knowing*. New York: Basic Books. (p. 435)

Bell, D. 1973. *The coming of post-industrial society*. New York: Basic Books. (pp. 21, 182)

———. 1976. *The cultural contradictions of capitalism*. New York: Basic Books. (p. 182)

Bellon, J. J. 1989. Refocusing state reform: The Tennessee experience. Paper presented at the annual meeting of the American Educational Research Association, San Francisco. (p. 481)

Belmont, J. M. 1989. Cognitive strategies and strategic learning. *American Psychologist* 44 (2): 142–148. (p. 513)

Bem, S. 1974. The measurement of psychological androgyny. *Journal of Consulting and Clinical Psychology* 42: 155–162. (p. 428)

Benbow, C. P., and Stanley, J. C. 1980. Sex differences in mathematical ability: Fact or artifact: *Science* 210 (12): 1262–1264. (p. 417)

Benderly, B. L. 1989. Don't believe everything you read. *Psychology Today* 23: (1): 67–69. (p. 419)

Bendix, R., and Lipset, S. 1953. *Class status and power: A reader in social stratification*. New York: The Free Press. (p. 34)

Beniger, J. R. 1986. *The control revolution*. Cambridge, MA: Harvard University Press. (p. 22)

Bennett, C. I. 1990. *Comprehensive multicultural education*. Boston: Allyn and Bacon. (p. 406)

Bennett, D. A. 1979. The impact of court ordered desegregation: A defendant's view. Paper presented at an ERIC conference on Impact of Courts on Schools, Washington, DC. (p. 332)

Bennett, N., and Desforges, C. 1988. Matching classroom tasks to students' attainments. *The Elementary School Journal* 88 (2): 221–234. (pp. 262, 530)

Bennett, N. G.; Bloom, D. E.; and Craig, P. H. 1989. The divergence of black and white marriage patterns. *American Journal of Sociology* 95 (3): 692–722. (pp. 203, 353, 354)

Benson, C. S. 1979. Household production of human capital: Time uses of parents and children as inputs. Paper presented at the annual meeting of the American Educational Research Association, San Francisco. (p. 132)

Berg, C. A., and Clough, M. 1991. Hunter lesson design: The wrong one for science teaching. *Educational Leadership* 48 (2):73–78. (p. 511)

Berger, B. M. 1960. *Working class suburb*. Berkeley: University of California Press. (p. 35)

Berger, B. M., and Berger, P. L. 1983. *The war over the family: Capturing the middle ground*. New York: Doubleday. (p. 148)

Berger, J. 1989. East Harlem students clutch a college dream. *The New York Times* August 27: 1, 21. (p. 497)

———. 1990. Indifference to meanness and the price. *The New York Times* August 13: A16. (p. 21)

Berger, P. L. 1979. The worldview of the new class: Secularity and its discontents. In *The New Class?*, edited by B. Bruce-Briggs. New Brunswick, NJ: Transaction. (p. 5)

Bergmann, B. 1986. *The economic emergence of women*. New York: Basic Books. (pp. 413, 435)

Bernard, A. 1990. Democracy in Chicago schools. *Network for Public Schools* 16 (2): 3–7. (p. 485)

Bernstein, A. 1989. What's dragging productivity down? Women's low wages. *Business Week* No. 3135: 171. (p. 412)

Bernstein, B. 1961. Social class and linguistic development: A theory of social learning. In *Education, economy and society*, edited by A. H. Halsey, J. Floud, and C. A. Anderson. New York: The Free Press. (p. 234)

———. 1975. *Class, codes and control*. London and Boston: Routledge and Kegan Paul. (pp. 102, 234)

———. 1986. On pedagogic discourse. In *Handbook of theory and research in the sociology of education*, edited by John G. Richardson. New York: Greenwood. (p. 234)

———. 1990. *The structuring of pedagogic discourse*. New York: Routledge. (p. 102, 234, 239)

Berreth, D. 1991. From ASCD's perspective. *Educational Leadership* 48 (4): 13. (p. 502)

Berry, G. L. V., and Asamen, J. K., eds. 1989. *Black students. Psychosocial issues and academic achievement.* Newbury Park, CA: Sage. (pp. 112, 131, 356)

Best, R. 1983. *We've all got scars: What boys and girls learn in elementary school.* Bloomington: Indiana University Press. (p. 425)

Bianchi, S. M., and Spain, D. 1986. *American women in transition.* New York: Russell Sage. (p. 116)

Biddle, B. J.; Bank, B. J.; and Marlin, M. M. 1980. Parental and peer influence on adolescents. *Social Forces* 58: 1057–1079. (p. 155)

Binzen, P. 1970. *Whitetown.* New York: Random House. (pp. 101, 260)

Bishop, J. H. 1989. Why the apathy in American high schools? *Educational Researcher* 18 (1): 6–10, 42. (p. 192, 193)

———. 1990. The productivity consequences of what is learned in high school. *Journal of Curriculum Studies* 22 (2): 101–126. (p. 192)

Bishop, K. 1989. Fear grows over effects of a new smokable drug. *Education Week* September 16: 1, 6.

Blackwell, J. W. 1990. Ethnic inequality and the rate of homicide. *Social Forces* 69 (1): 53–70. (p. 199)

Blair, S. J. 1990. Congress should reject 'separate but equal' aid programs. *The Chronicle of Higher Education* 36 (25):A52. (p. 62)

Blake, J. 1989a. *Family size and achievement.* Berkeley: University of California Press. (p. 130)

———. 1989b. Number of siblings and educational attainment. *Science* 245: 32–36. (p. 130)

Blakeslee. S. 1989. Crack's toll among babies. *New York Times* September 17: 1, 12. (pp. 21, 118, 130, 292)

Blank, R. K. 1984. Magnet schools offer diversity and quality. *Educational Leadership* 42 (7): 72. (p. 321)

———. 1990. Analyzing educational effects of magnet schools using local district data. *Sociological Practice Review* 1 (1): 40–51. (pp. 321, 324)

Blechman, E. A. 1982. Are children with one parent at psychological risk? A methodological review. *Journal of Marriage and the Family* 44: 179–195.

Blits, J. H., and Gottfredson, L. G. 1990. Employment testing and job performance. *The Public Interest* No. 98 (Winter): 18–25.

Block, J. H., and Anderson, L. W. 1975. *Mastery learning in classroom instruction.* New York: Macmillan. (p. 520)

Bloom, B. S. 1964. *Stability and change in human characteristics.* New York: John Wiley. (p. 108)

———. 1976. *Human characteristics and school learning.* New York: McGraw-Hill. (p. 267)

———. 1984. The search for methods of group instruction as effective as one-to-one tutoring. *Educational Researcher* 13 (6): 4–16. (p. 521)

———. 1988. All our children learning well in elementary school and beyond. *Principal* 67 (4): 12–17. (pp. 268, 517)

Bluestone, B.; Clayton-Mathews, A.; Havens, J.; and Young, H. 1990. Generational alliance: Social security as a bank for education and training. *The American Prospect* No. 2: 15–29. (p. 206)

Bluestone, B., and Harrison, B. 1987. The grim truth about the job 'miracle.' *The New York Times* February 1: 5.3, 3. (p. 24)

Blumenstyk, G. 1990a. Federal court ruling that public disclosure of tests violates copyright law seen a blow to 'truth in testing' movement. *The Chronicle of Higher Education* 36 (20): A1, A25. (p. 70)

———. 1990b. House, Senate agree on legislation to promote community service. *The Chronicle of Higher Education* 37 (8): A20. (p. 206)

Bock, D. F., and Moore, E. G. J. 1986. *Advantage and disadvantage: A profile of American youth.* Hillsdale, NJ: Erlbaum. (p. 417)

Boger, J. M. 1990. The mental health team: A process of maximizing human potential in schools. Paper presented at the annual meeting of the American Educational Research Association, Boston. (p. 145)

Bollens, J. C., and Schmandt, H. J. *The metropolis.* New York: Harper & Row. (p. 86)

Boo, K. 1991. Beyond beauty schools. *The Washington Monthly* 23 (3): 26–31. (pp. 62, 88, 461)

Boocock, S. S. 1976. *Students, schools, and educational policy: A sociological view.* Cambridge, MA: Aspen Institute forHumanistic Studies. (p. 155)

Borger, G. 1989. Why the catastrophic care fight will change generational policies. *U.S. News & World Report* 107 (14): 18. (p. 31)

Borjas, G. J. 1990. *Friends or strangers: The impact of immigrants on the U. S. economy.* New York: Basic Books. (p. 344)

Boswell, J. 1988. *The kindness of strangers. The abandonment of children in Western Europe from late antiquity to the Renaissance.* New York: Pantheon. (pp. 90, 91)

Boudon, R. 1973. *Education, opportunity, and social inequality: Changing prospects in western society.* New York: John Wiley. (p. 228)

Boulding, E. 1979. *Children's rights in the wheel of life*. New Brunswick, NJ: Transaction, (p. 429)

——. 1987. Changing gender roles in familial, occupational, and civic settings. In *Society as educator in an age of transition*, edited by Kenneth D. Benne and Steven Tozer. Eighty-sixth yearbook of the National Society for the Study of Education, Part II. Chicago: University of Chicago Press. (p. 429)

Bourgois, P. 1989. Just another night on crack street. *The New York Times Magazine* November 12: 53–65, 94. (pp. 18, 21)

Bowers, B. C. 1990. State efforts to deregulate education. *ERIC Digest Series* No. EA 51: 1–2. (p. 484)

Bowles, S. 1975. Unequal education and the reproduction of the social division of labor. In *Schooling in a corporate society*, edited by Martin Carnoy, New York: David McKay. (p. 243)

Bowles, S., and Gintis, H. 1976. *Schooling in capitalist America*. New York: Basic Books. (p. 243)

——. 1981. Education as a site of contradictions in the reproduction of the capital labor relationship: Second thoughts on the "correspondence principle." *Economic and Industrial Democracy* 2: 223–242. (p. 244)

Bowman, B. T. 1989. Educating language-minority children: Challenges and opportunities. *Phi Delta Kappan* 71 (2): 118–120. (pp. 234, 258)

Boyd, W. L., et al. 1991. *Policy dilemmas in urban education*. Washington, DC: National Association of State Urban Land Grant Colleges. (pp. 295, 309, 527)

Boyer, E. 1983. *High school*. New York: Harper and Row. (pp. 514, 515, 530, 532)

Boyer, P. 1990a. Native Americans and higher education. *Change* 22 (1): 27–30. (p. 395)

——. 1990b. *Tribal colleges: shaping the future of Native America*. Princeton, NJ: Princeton University Press. (p. 395)

Boykin, A. W. 1978. Psychological/behavioral verve in academic/task performance: Pretheoretical considerations. *The Journal of Negro Education* 47: 343–354. (pp. 258, 397)

——. 1983. On academic task performance and Afro-American children. In *Achievement and achievement motives*, edited by J. R. Spencer. Boston: W. H. Freeman. (pp. 258, 397)

Boylan, Ann M. 1988. *Sunday School. The transformation of an American institution 1790–1880*. New Haven: Yale University Press. (p. 175)

Boys Clubs of America. 1985. *Boys Clubs Alumni Survey*.New York: Boys Clubs of America. (p. 171)

Boysen, T. C. 1990. Support NAEP's expansion: End the 'tyranny of patchwork testing.' *Education Week* 10 (6): 36. (p. 477)

Braccidiferro, G. 1991. Federal grants bolstering aid programs. *The New York Times* January 6: R3. (p. 140)

Braddock, J. H. II. 1981. Race, athletics, and educational attainment: Dispelling the myths. *Youth and Society* 12 (March): 335–350. (p. 163)

——. 1987. Social and academic consequences of school desegregation. Paper prepared for the Conference on Future Designs for Educational Equity, St. Louis. (pp. 317, 318)

——. 1990. *Tracking*. Baltimore, MD: The Johns Hopkins University Center for Research on Effective Schooling for Disadvantaged Students. (p. 530)

Braddock, J. H. II., and McPartland, J. M. 1987. How minorities continue to be excluded from equal employment opportunities: Research on labor market and institutional barriers. *Journal of Social Issues* 43 (1): 5–39. (p. 317)

Bradley, A. 1989. 'This is damned hard.' *Teacher Magazine* 1 (3): 12–14. (p. 486)

——. 1990a. Request for developing teacher assessment prepared. *Education Week* 9 (24): 11. (p. 471)

——. 1990b. Rochester board unanimously rejects teacher's pact. *Education Week* 10 (19): 4. (p. 486)

——. 1991a. Standards board awards three contracts to develop teacher assessments. *Education Week* 3 (24): 5. (p. 471)

——. 1991b. Teaching our teachers. *Education Week* 10 (25): 17–28. (pp. 473, 474)

Bradley, L. A., and Bradley, G. W. 1977. The academic achievement of black students in desegregated schools: A critical review. *Review of Educational Research* 47: 399–444. (p. 311)

Brainin, S. S. 1985. Mediated learning: Pedagogic issues in the improvement of cognitive functioning. In *Review of Research in Education* 12, edited by Edmund W. Gordon. Washington, DC: American Educational Research Association. (pp. 516, 517, 533)

Brake, M. 1980. *The sociology of youth culture and subcultures*. Boston: Routledge and Kegan Paul. (p. 97)

Brandt, R. 1989. On parents and schools: A conversation with Joyce Epstein. *Educational Leadership* 47 (2): 24–27. (p. 144)

———. 1989/1990. On cooperative learning: A conversation with Spencer Kagan. *Educational Leadership* 47 (4): 8–11. (p. 316)

Braver, M. W., and Helmstadter, G. C. 1990. Incentive pay for teachers: Does it impact student achievement? Paper presented at the annual meeting of the American Educational Research Association, Boston. (p. 481)

Bredo, E.; Henry, M.; and McDermott, R. P. 1990. The cultural organization of teaching and learning. *Harvard Educational Review* 60 (2): 247–258. (pp. 234, 258)

Bridgman, A. 1984. Schools urged to seek solutions to troubles of latch-key children. *Education Week* 3 (36): 10, 15. (p. 138)

Brier, D. M., et al. 1990. *Asian Americans. A status report*. Washington, DC: U.S. Government General Accounting Office. (pp. 383, 384)

Brimmer, A. F. 1990. 45 years in business and employment. *Ebony* 46 (1): 122–124. (pp. 351, 352, 353)

Brinkerhoff, D. W., and Hopkins, R. L. 1990. *Institutional dimensions of education sector lending*. Washington, DC: World Bank. (p. 502)

Brint, S., and Karabel, J. 1989. *The diverted dream*. New York: Oxford University Press. (pp. 56, 57, 58)

Brittain, C. V. 1963. Adolescent choices and parent-peer cross pressures. *American Sociological Review* 28: 385–391. (p. 154)

Broder, D. S. 1990. Addressing America's 'skill crisis.' *The Kansas City Star* December 12: C-9. (p. 461)

Broderick, P. C., and Sewell, T. E. 1983. Learned helplessness and attributions for success and failure in children of different social class. Paper presented at the annual meeting of the American Educational Research Association, Montreal. (p. 260)

Brodie, J. M. 1990. References to class distinctions concern black scholars. *Black Issues in Higher Education* 7 (17): 10–13. (p. 353)

Brody, G. H.; Neubaum, E.; and Forehand, R. 1988. Serial marriage: A heuristic analysis of an emerging family form. *Psychological Bulletin* 103 (2): 211–222. (p. 118)

Bronfenbrenner, U. 1974. *Is early intervention effective? Report on longitudinal evaluations of pre-school programs*. DHEW No. (OHD) 74–25. Washington, DC: U.S. Department of Health, Education and Welfare. (pp. 268, 289)

———. 1977. The calamitous decline of the American family. *Congressional Record-Extension of Remarks* January 4, E40–E43. (p. 10)

———. 1979. *The ecology of human development*. Cambridge, MA: Harvard University Press. (p. 289)

Brookover, W. B., et al. 1982. *Creating effective schools*. Holmes Beach, FL: Learning Publications. (p. 537)

Brophy, J. E. 1982. Classroom organization and management. *The Elementary School Journal* 82: 265–285. (p. 510)

———. 1985. Interactions of male and female students with male and female teachers. In *Gender influences in classroom interaction*, edited by Louise Cherry Wilkinson and Cora B. Marrett. Orlando, FL: Academic Press. (p. 424)

———. 1991. Effective schooling for disadvantaged students. In *Better schooling for the children of poverty: Alternatives to conventional wisdom*, edited by Michael S. Knapp and Patrick M. Shields. Berkeley, CA: McCutchan. (p. 511)

Brophy, J. E., and Good, T. L. 1986. Teacher behavior and student achievement. In *Handbook of research on teaching*, 3rd ed., edited by Merlin C. Wittrock. New York: Macmillan. (pp. 260, 510, 511)

Brotman, B. 1982. Facing up to the underclass in America. *Chicago Tribune* September 26: 1. (p. 19)

Brown, B. B.; Kohrs D.; and Lazarro, C. 1991. The academic costs and consequences of extracurricular participation in high school. Paper presented at the annual meeting of the American Educational Research Association, Chicago. (p. 163)

Brown, B. F. 1980. A study of the school needs of children from one-parent families. *Phi Delta Kappan* 61 (April): 537–540. (p. 129)

Brown, C. 1969. *Manchild in the promised land*. New York: Macmillan. (pp. 49, 104)

Brown, D. L. 1989, Demographic trends relevant to education in nonmetropolitan America. In *Rural education. A changing landscape*, edited by Joyce D. Stern. Washington, DC: U.S. Department of Education Office of Educational Research. (p. 441)

Bruce-Briggs, B. 1979. An introduction to the idea of the new class. In *The new class?*, edited by B.

Bruce-Briggs. New Brunswick, NJ: Transaction. (pp. 4, 5)

Bryk, A. S.; Holland, P. B.; Lee, V. E.; and Carriedo, R. A. 1984. *Effective Catholic schools: An exploration*. Washington, DC: National Catholic Education Association. (p. 449)

Bryk, A. S.; Lee, V. E.; and Smith, J. B. 1990. High school organization and its effects on teachers and students: An interpretive summary of the research. In *Choice and control in American education*, edited by W. H. Clune and J. F. Witte. Vol. 1. London: Falmer. (p. 162)

Buckley, J. 1990. The hard lessons of school reform. *U.S. News and World Report* 106 (25): 58–60. (pp. 486, 495)

Buie, J. 1987. Pregnant teen-agers: New view of old solution. *Education Week* 6 (28): 32. (p. 204)

Burbridge, L. C. 1983. *Employment and training programs for youth: An interpretation and synthesis of measured outcomes*. Washington, DC: The Urban Institute. (p. 294)

Burch, S. 1988. Commission reports on children at risk. *Black Issues in Higher Education* 4 (20): 15. (p. 471)

Burge, P. L., and Culver, S. M. 1990. Sexism, legislative power, and vocational education. In *Gender in the classroom*, edited by Susan L. Gabriel and Issiah Smithson. Urbana: University of Illinois. (p. 421)

Burghardt, J., and Gordon, A. 1990. *More jobs and higher pay*. New York: The Rockefeller Foundation. (p. 188)

Burke, G., and Rumberger, R. W. 1987. *The future impact of technology on work and education*. Philadelphia: Falmer. (p. 23)

Burns, R., and Kojimoto, C. 1989. Demystifying mastery learning. *Outcomes* 8 (3): 7–16. (p. 521)

Burr, W. R., et al. 1979. *Contemporary theories about the family*. New York: Free Press. (p. 148)

Burrill, L. E. 1987. How well should a high school graduate read? *NASSP Bulletin* 71 (497): 61–72. (p. 408)

Buscemi, M. 1985. What schools are doing to prevent alcohol and drug abuse. *The School Administrator* 42 (9): 11–14. (pp. 201, 202)

Bush, G. 1991. Remarks by the President. White House Press Statement, February 27. (p. 481)

Bushardt, S. C., and Fowler, A. R., Jr. 1987. Improving teaching effectiveness: Merit pay vs. organizational culture. *Capstone Journal of Education* 7 (2): 28–38. (p. 479)

Business-Higher Education Forum. 1990. *Three realities. Minority life in the United States*. Washington, DC: Business-Higher Education Forum. (pp. 350, 353)

Butterfield, F. 1991a. Asians spread across a land, and help change it. *The New York Times* February 24: 14. (p. 382)

———. 1991b. Tax rebate in New Hampshire town poses test for school-choice issues. *The New York Times* January 30: B8. (p. 499)

Butts, R. F. 1974. Public education and political community. *History of Education Quarterly* 14: 165–184. (p. 247)

Byrne, J. A. 1990. Profiting from the nonprofits. *Business Week* No. 3151: 66–78. (p. 170)

Cage, M. C. 1990. Tougher regulations for for-profit trade schools gain support in a growing number of states. *The Chronicle of Higher Education* 36 (32): A22–A24. (p. 62)

Caldas, S. J. 1991. Understanding teenage pregnancy and childbearing in the United States. Paper presented at the annual meeting of the American Educational Association, Chicago. (pp. 202, 203)

Caldwell, B. M. 1991. Continuity in the early years: Transitions between grades and systems. In *The care and education of America's young children: Obstacles and opportunities*, edited by Sharon Lynn Kagan. Chicago: University of Chicago Press. (pp. 279, 280, 281, 282, 283)

California Assessment Program. 1982. *Survey of sixth grade school achievement and television viewing habits*. Sacramento: California State Department of Education. (p. 137)

Camburn, E. M. 1990. College completion among students from high schools located in large metropolitan areas. *American Journal of Education* 98 (4):551–569. (pp. 241, 242)

Campbell, L. 1990. Ebonics-The black dialect. Paper prepared at St. Louis University for the STEPS/ SWAS annual conference, Kansas City. (p. 358)

Cantrall, B.; Pete, L.; and Fields, M. 1990. Navajo culture: A bridge to the rest of the world. Paper presented at the annual meeting of the American Educational Research Association, Boston. (pp. 394, 398)

Caplan, N. 1985. Working toward self-sufficiency. *ISR Newsletter* 13 (1): 4–5, 7. (pp. 384, 385)

Caplan, N.; Whitmore, K.; and Choy, M. H. 1989. *The boat people and achievement in America*. Ann

Arbor: University of Michigan Press. (pp. 218, 220, 384, 385)

Caplan, P. J.; MacPherson, G. M.; and Tobin, P. 1985. Do sex differences in spatial abilities exist? *American Psychologist* 40 (7): 786–799. (p. 419)

Capron, C., and Duyme, M. 1989. Assessment of effects of socio-economic status on IQ in a full-cross fostering study. *Nature* 340 (August 17): 552–554. (p. 115)

Cardenas, J. A. 1977. Bilingual education, segregation, and a third alternative. *Inequality in Education* 19 (February): 19–22. (pp. 375, 380)

Carelli, A. O., ed. 1988. *Sex equity in education.* Springfield, IL: Thomas. (p. 427)

Carew, J. V. 1976. Environmental stimulation: A longitudinal observation study of how people influence the young child's intellectual development in his everyday environment. Paper presented at the Annual Meeting of the American Educational Research Association, San Francisco. (pp. 114, 115)

Carlson, A. C. 1987. Children in poverty and other legacies of the redistributive state. *Persuasion at Work* 19 (1): 1–5.(p. 31)

———. 1990. By the decades: The troubled course of the family, 1945–1900 . . . and beyond. *The Family in America* 4 (5): 1–8. (p. 116)

Carlson, R. V. 1991. Culture and organization planning. In *Educational planning*, edited by Robert V. Carlson and Gary Awkerman. New York: Longman. (p. 526)

Carnegie Commission on Higher Education. 1983. *Opportunities for women in higher education.* New York: McGraw-Hill. (p. 410)

Carnegie Corporation. 1977. Postscript from an interview with Kenneth Keniston. *Carnegie Quarterly* 25 (4): 10–12. (pp. 123, 124)

Carnegie Council on Policy Studies in Higher Education. 1979. *The federal role in post-secondary education: Unfinished business, 1975–1980.* San Francisco: Jossey-Bass.

Carnegie Foundation for the Advancement of Teaching. 1988. *Saving urban schools.* Princeton, NJ: Princeton University Press. (p. 537)

Carnegie Task Force on Teaching as a Profession. 1986. *A nation prepared: Teachers in the 21st century.* New York: Carnegie Corporation. (p. 471)

Carnoy, M. 1974. *Education as cultural imperialism.* New York: David McKay. (p. 243)

———. 1982. Education, economy, and the state. In *Cultural and economic reproduction in education*, edited by Michael Apple. Boston: Routledge and Kegan Paul. (p. 244)

———. 1989. Education, state, and culture in American society. In *Critical pedagogy, the state, and cultural struggle*, edited by Henry A. Giroux and Peter McLaren. Albany: State University of New York Press. (p. 244)

Carnoy, M., and Levin, H. M. 1985. *Schooling and work in the democratic state.* Stanford, CA: Stanford University Press. (p. 244)

Carper, J. C., and Hunt, T. C., eds. 1984. *Religious schooling in America.* Birmingham, AL: Religious Education Press. (p. 459)

Carter, D. J. 1990. Community and junior colleges: A recent profile. *Research Briefs* 1 (4): 1–8. (p. 57)

Carter, D. J., and Wilson, R. 1989. *Minorities in higher education.* Washington, DC: American Council on Education. (pp. 51, 354)

Carter, L. F. 1984. The sustaining effects study of compensatory and elementary education. *Educational Researcher* 13 (7): 4–13. (p. 284)

Carter, M. C., and Levine, D. U. 1977. *Ethnicity, home environment, and reading achievement.* Kansas City: University of Missouri at Kansas City Center for the Study of Metropolitan Problems in Education. (p. 131)

Caruso, D. R., and Detterman, K. K. 1981. Intelligence research and social policy. *Phi Delta Kappan* 63 (3): 183–187. (p. 279)

Casserly, M., and Kober, N. 1990. *Results 2000.* Washington, DC: The Council of the Great Cities Schools. (pp. 81, 295, 296)

Castellanos, C. 1980. Bilingual education versus school desegregation: Resolving the conflict. *NJEA Review* 53 (6): 7–16. (p. 386)

Castells, M. 1985. High technology, economic restructuring, and the urban-region process in the United States. In *High technology, space, and society*, edited by Manuel Castells. Beverly Hills, CA: Sage. (pp. 23, 85)

Cavallo, D. 1981. *Muscles and morals.* Philadelphia: University of Pennsylvania Press. (p. 252)

Cazden, C. B. 1985. Effectiveness of instructional features in bilingual education classrooms. Paper presented at the annual meeting of the American Educational Research Association, Chicago. (p. 379)

———. 1988. *Classroom discourse: The language of teaching and learning*. Portsmouth, NH: Heinemann. (p. 258)

Celis, W. 3d. 1991. Study urges a preschool role for businesses. *The New York Times* March 1: A14. (p. 470)

Center to Prevent Handgun Violence. 1990. *A generation under the gun*. Washington, DC: Center to Prevent Handgun Violence. (p. 185)

Chafe, W. H. 1972. *The American woman: Her changing social, economic, and political roles, 1920-1970*. New York: Oxford University Press. (p. 435)

Chall, J., and Mirsky, A., eds. 1978. *Education and the brain*. Seventy-Seventh Yearbook of the National Society for the Study of Education. Chicago: University of Chicago Press. (p. 148)

Chance, P. 1986. *Thinking in the classroom: A survey of programs*. New York: Teachers College Press. (p. 512)

Charren, P. 1990. What's missing in children's TV. *World Monitor* 3 (12): 28-34. (p. 138)

Charters, W. W., Jr., and Gage, N. L., eds. 1963. *Readings in the social psychology of education*. Boston: Allyn and Bacon. (p. 87)

Chartier, R., ed. 1989. *A history of private life: Passions of the Renaissance*. Cambridge, MA: Belknap. (pp. 89, 90, 91, 121, 165).

Chelimsky, E., et al. 1990. *Promising practice*. Washington, DC: General Accounting Office. (p. 498)

Cherlin, A. J., and Furstenberg, F. F., Jr. 1986. *The new American grandparent*. New York: Basic Books.

Cherlin, A. J., et al. 1991. Longitudinal studies of effects of divorce on children in Great Britain and the United States. *Science* 252 (5011): 1386-1389. (p. 127, 128)

Chinoy, E. 1955. *Automobile workers and the American dream*. New York: Doubleday. (p. 34)

Chipman, S. F.; Brush, L. R.; and Wilson, D. M., eds. 1985. *Women and mathematics: Balancing the equation*. Hillsdale, NJ: Erlbaum. (p. 416)

Chipman, S. F., and Wilson, D. M. 1985. Understanding mathematics course enrollment and mathematics achievement: A synthesis of the research. In *Women and mathematics: Balancing the equation*, edited by Susan F. Chipman, Lorelei R. Brush, and Donna M. Wilson. Hillsdale, NJ: Erlbaum. (pp. 416, 417)

Chira, S. 1990a. Efforts to reshape teaching focus on finding new talent. *The New York Times* August 28: A1, A14. (pp. 397, 495)

———. 1990b. Preschool aid for the poor: How big a head start? *The New York Times* February 14: A1, B8. (pp. 268, 279,281)

———. 1991a. Bush presses bill allowing parents to choose schools. *The New York Times* April 19: A1, A10. (pp. 489, 499)

———. 1991b. How to translate the talk about school reform into action? *The New York Times* March 24: E1. (p. 495)

———. 1991c. Rochester: An uneasy symbol of school reform. *The New York Times* April 10: B8. (p. 487)

Chmelynski, C. 1990. Controversy attends schools with all-black, all-male classes. *The Executive Educator* 12 (10): 16-18. (p. 355)

Chosky, P. 1989. Proprietary schools: Judged by bad examples. *The Chronicle of Higher Education* 36 (10): B4. (p. 62)

Christensen, B. J. 1987. "The white woman's burden": The cultural clash between American feminists and ethnic minorities. *The Family in America* 1 (2): 1-I0. (pp. 354, 434)

———. 1990. Boardroom blunder: American business and the family. *The Family in America* 4 (3): 1-8 (pp. 23, 25)

———. 1991a. Imperiled infants: A legitimate concern. *The Family in America* 5 (1): 1-8. (p. 132)

———. 1991b. The grandparent gap: Why ties between the generations are unraveling in America. *The Family in America* 5 (3): 1-8.

Chronicle editors. 1991. Facts on file. *The Chronicle of Higher Education* 37 (23): A42 (pp. 421, 422)

Chubb, J. E. 1988. Why the current wave of school reform will fail. *The Public Interest* No. 90: 28-49. (p. 450)

Chubb, J. E., and Moe, T. M. 1985. Politics, markets, and the organization of schools. Paper presented at the annual meeting of the American Political Science Association, New Orleans. (pp. 450)

———. 1986. *Politics, markets, and the organization of schools*. Washington, DC: The Brookings Institution. (pp. 450, 451, 458)

———. 1990. *Politics, markets, and America's schools*. Washington, DC: The Brookings Institution. (pp. 237, 238, 449, 450, 500)

Cibulka, J. G.; O'Brien, T. J.; and Zewe, D. 1982. *Inner-city private elementary schools: A study*. Milwaukee: Marquette University Press. (p. 447)

Cizek, G. I. 1991. Innovation or enervation? *Phi Delta Kappan* 72 (9): 695-699. (p. 478)

Clark, B. 1960. The cooling-out function in higher education. *American Journal of Sociology* 65: 569–576. (p. 59)

Clark, R. 1983. *Family life and school environment*. Chicago: University of Chicago Press. (pp. 113, 361)

Clarke-Stewart, A. 1977. *Child care in the family: A review of research and some propositions for policy*. New York: Academic Press. (pp. 127, 148)

Clasen, D. R., and Brown, B. B. 1986. The relationship between adolescent peer groups and school performance. Paper presented at the annual meeting of the American Educational Research Association, San Francisco. (p. 159)

Clausen, J. A. 1966. Family structure, socialization and personality. In *Review of child development research*, Vol. 2, edited by M. L. Hoffman and L. W. Hoffman. New York: Russell Sage Foundation. (pp. 149–150)

Clausen, J. A., and Williams, J. R. 1963. Sociological correlates of child behavior. In *Child Psychology*, edited by Harold W. Stevenson. Sixty-Second Yearbook of the National Society for the Study of Education, Part 1. Chicago: University of Chicago Press. (p. 148)

Clay, P. L. 1981. Single parents and the public schools. *How does the partnership work?* Columbia, MD: National Committee for Citizens in Education. (p. 129)

Clearinghouse on Educational Management editors. 1981. Merit pay. *Research Action Brief* No. 15: 1–4.

Clewell, B. C., and Joy, M. F. 1990. Evaluation of a magnet school system. In *Magnet Schools*, edited by Nolan Estes, Daniel U. Levine, and Donald R. Waldrip. Austin, TX: Morgan. (p. 327)

Clewell, B. C.; Thorpe, M. E.; and Anderson, B. T. 1987. *Intervention programs in math, science, and computer science for minority and female students in grades four through eight*. Princeton, NJ: Educational Testing Service. (p. 460)

Clinchy, E. 1992. Public schools of choice. In *Restructuring the Schools*, edited by John J. Lane and Edgar G. Epps. Berkeley, CA: McCutchan. (p. 500)

Cloud, N. 1990. Measuring level of acculturation in bilingual, bicultural children. Paper presented at the annual meeting of the American Educational Research Association, Boston. (p. 369)

Cloward, R. A., and Ohlin, L. E. 1960. *Delinquency and opportunity: A theory of delinquent gangs*. New York: The Free Press.

Clune, W. H.; White, P.; and Patterson, J. 1989. *The implementation and effects of high school graduation requirements*. New Brunswick, NJ: Rutgers University Center for Policy Research in Education. (p. 492)

Clune, W. H., and Witte, J. F. 1991. eds. *Control and Choice in American Education*. 2 Volumes. London: Falmer. (p. 538)

Coale, A. J., and Zelnik, M. 1963. *New estimates of fertility and population in the United States*. Princeton, NJ: Princeton University Press. (p. 117)

Cocaine use rising. 1985–86. *ISR Newsletter* Winter: 578.

Cohany, S. 1986. What happened to the high school class of 1985? *Monthly Labor Review* 109 (10): 28–30. (p. 39)

Cohen, A. M. 1977. The social equalization fantasy. *Community College Review* 5 (Fall): 74–82. (p. 253)

———. 1989. Reconsidering the community college contribution. Paper presented at the annual meeting of the American Educational Research Association, San Francisco. (pp. 59, 60, 290)

———. 1990. The case for the community college. *American Journal of Education*. 98 (4): 426–442. (pp. 59, 60, 290, 355, 388)

Cohen, C. 1990. Tribal enterprise. *The Atlantic* 264 (4): 32–43. (p. 389)

Cohen, D. K. 1991. San Diego agencies join to ensure 'new beginnings' for families. *Education Week* 10 (18): 16–19. (p. 290)

Cohen, D. K., and Farrar, E. 1977. Power to the parents? The story of educational vouchers. *The Public Interest* No. 48 (Summer): 72–97. (p. 454)

Cohen, D. L. 1990. $10 million for parenting programs set. *Education Week* 9 (20): 7. (p. 290)

Cohen, E. G. 1980. Design and redesign of the desegregated school. In *School desegregation: Past, present and future*, edited by W. G. Stephan and J. Feagin. New York: Plenum. (p. 316)

———. 1986. On the sociology of the classroom. In *The contributions of the social sciences to educational policy and practice*, edited by J. Hannaway and M. E. Lockheed. Berkeley, CA: McCutchan. (pp. 157, 316, 530)

———. 1990. Continuing to cooperate: Prerequisites for persistence. *Phi Delta Kappan* 72 (2): 134–138. (pp. 157, 316)

Cohen, G. 1981. Culture and educational attainment. *Harvard Educational Review* 51: 270–285. (pp. 92, 232, 233)

Cohen, R. 1990. Imagination without walls. *The Washington Post Magazine* October 7: 11. (p. 355)

Cohen, S. 1976. The history of American education, 1990–1976: The uses of the past. *Harvard Educational Review* 46: 298–330. (p. 247)

Coie, J. D., and Kupersmidt, J. 1983. A behavioral analysis of emerging social status in boy's groups. *Child Development* 54: 1400–1416. (p. 157)

Coie, J. D., and Whidby, J. 1986. Gender differences as the basis for social rejection in childhood. Paper presented at the annual meeting of the American Educational Research Association, San Francisco. (p. 157)

Cole, M. 1985. Mind as a cultural achievement: Implications for IQ testing. In *Learning and teaching the ways of knowing*, edited by Elliot Eisner. Eighty-Fourth Yearbook of the National Society for the Study of Education, Part II. Chicago: University of Chicago Press. (p. 398)

Cole, N. S. 1990. Gender differences and admissions policies: Implications for test use. Paper presented at the annual meeting of the American Educational Research Association, Boston. (p. 70)

Coleman, J. S. 1959. Academic achievement and the structure of competition. *Harvard Educational Review* 29: 331–351. (p. 159)

———. 1961. *The adolescent society*. New York: The Free Press. (p. 159)

———. 1982. Public schools, private schools, and the public interest. *American Education* 18 (1): 17–22.

———. 1990a. *Equality and achievement in education*. Boulder, CO: Westview. (pp. 95, 237, 305, 364, 448, 449)

———. 1990b. *Foundations of social theory*. Cambridge, MA: Harvard University Press. (pp. 32, 117)

———. 1990c. How worksite schools and other school reforms can generate social capital. *American Educator* 14 (2): 35–36, 45. (p. 126)

Coleman, J. S., and Hoffer, T. 1987. *Public and private high schools: The impact of communities*. New York: Basic Books. (pp. 95, 449)

Coleman, J. S.; Hoffer, T.; and Kilgore, S. 1981. *Public and private schools*. Washington, DC: National Center for Education Statistics. (pp. 448, 458)

Coleman, J. S., and Husen, T. 1985. Becoming adult in a changing society. Paris: Organization for Economic Co-operation and Development. (pp. 207, 208)

Coleman, J. S., et al. 1966. *Equality of educational opportunity*. Washington, DC: U.S. Government Printing Office. (pp. 237, 274, 305, 503)

———. 1974. *Youth: Transition to adulthood*. Report of the Panel on Youth of the President's Science Advisory Committee. Chicago and London: University of Chicago Press. (p. 177)

Colman, R. P., and Neugarten, 1971. *Social status in the city*. San Francisco: Jossey-Bass. (pp. 8, 34, 254)

College Board. 1983. *Academic preparation for college*. New York: The College Board. (p. 467)

Collins, R. 1991. Projectwide impact of school-based management on selected indicators over 3 years. Paper presented at the Annual Meeting of the American Educational Research Association, Chicago. (p. 485)

Collomp, A. 1989. Families: habitations and cohabitations. In *A history of private life. Passions of the Renaissance*, edited by Roger Chartier. Cambridge, MA: Belknap. (p. 90)

Colman, W. G. 1977. Schools, housing, jobs, transportation: Interlocking metropolitan problems. In *School desegregation in metropolitan areas: Choices and prospects*, edited by Ronald D. Henderson and Mary von Euler. Washington, DC: National Institute of Education. (p. 84)

Comer, J. P. 1980. *School power*. New York: Free Press. (p. 145)

———. 1988. Educating poor minority children. *Scientific American* 2259 (5): 42–48. (p. 145)

———. 1990. *Maggie's American dream*. New York: Plume. (p. 145)

Comer, J. P., and Haynes, N. M. 1991. Parent involvement in schools: An ecological approach. *The Elementary School Journal* 91 (3): 271–278. (pp. 143, 145)

Commission on Achieving Necessary Skills. 1991. *What work requires of schools*. Washington, DC: U. S. Department of Labor. (p. 461)

Commission on the Skills of the American Workforce: 1990. *America's choice: High skills or low wages*. Rochester, NY: National Center for Education and the Economy. (p. 191)

Commission on Workforce Quality and Labor Market Efficiency. 1989. *Investing in people*. Washington, DC: U.S. Department of Labor. (pp. 24, 188, 294, 468)

Committee for Economic Development. 1985. *Investing in our children*. Washington, DC: Committee on Economic Development. (p. 71)

———. 1987. *Children in need: Investment strategies for the disadvantaged*. Washington, DC: Committee for Economic Development. (p. 470)

———. 1991. *The Unfinished agenda: A new vision for child development and education*. Washington, DC: Committee for Economic Development. (p. 470)

Committee on Ability Testing. 1982. *Ability testing: uses, consequences, and controversies*. Washington, DC: National Academy Press. (p. 68)

Compton, N.; Duncan, M.; and Hruska, J. 1986. *Student pregnancy*. Washington, DC: National Education Association. (p. 204)

Comptroller General of the United States. 1977. *Preventingmental retardation—more can be done*. Washington, DC: Comptroller General of the United States. (p. 132)

Comstock, G. 1977. Types of portrayal and aggressive behavior. *Journal of Communication* 27 (Summer): 189-198. (p. 135)

Conciatore, J., and Hughes, M. 1990. The race between education and catastrophe. *Black Issues in Higher Education* 7 (17): 6-7. (p. 354)

Condry, J. C., and Siman, M. A. 1974. Characteristics of adult- and peer-oriented children. *Journal of Marriage and the Family* 36: 543-554. (p. 156)

Congressional Budget Office. 1986. *Trends in educational achievement*. Washington, DC: Congress of the United States. (p. 31)

———. 1991. *Student aid and the cost of post- secondary education*. Washington, DC: Congressional Budget Office. (pp. 64, 66)

Conlin, E. 1991. Educating the market. *INC.* 13 (7): 62-67. (p. 456)

Connell, R. W. 1989. Curriculum politics, hegemony, and strategies for social change. In *Popular culture, schooling, and everyday life*, edited by Henry A. Giroux and Roger Simon. Granby, MA: Bergin and Garvey. (p. 250)

Connell, R. W.; Ashenden, D. J.; Kessler, S.; and Dowsett, G. W. 1982. *Making the difference*. Boston: George Allen & Unwin. (p. 250)

Cooke, P. 1989. Hey, dude: Like neh-oh-way! *The New York Times Magazine* November 19: 50, 52, 54, 60. (p. 357)

Coons, J. E., and Sugarman, S. D. 1978. *Education by choice. The case for family control*. Berkeley: University of California Press. (pp. 454, 455, 500)

———. 1991. The private school option in systems of educational choice. *Educational Leadership* 48 (2): 54-56. (pp. 500, 502)

Cooper, E. J. 1986. Excerpts from testimony. *Outcomes* 6 (1): 10-12. (p. 48)

———. 1992. Curriculum reform and testing. In *Literacy among Afro-American youth*, edited by Vivian Gadsden. Philadelphia: Ablex. (p. 477)

Corcoran, M., and Courant, P. 1985. *Sex-role socialization and occupational segregation: An exploratory investigation*. University of Wisconsin-Madison IRP Discussion Paper DP #797-85. (p. 414)

Cordasco, F., and Bucchioni, E. 1972. Introduction. In *The Puerto Rican community and its children on the mainland: A sourcebook for teachers, social workers and the professionals*, edited by F. Cordasco and E. Bucchioni. Metuchen, NJ: Scarecrow. (p. 371)

Cotton, J. P. 1991. Recent changes in the structure and value of African-American occupations. *The Trotter Review* 4 (3): 6-11. (pp. 15, 51)

Cotton, K. 1991. *Educating urban minority youth: Research on effective practices*. Portland, OR: Northwest Regional Educational Laboratory. (p. 364)

Cotton, K., and Conklin, N. F. 1989. *Research on Early Childhood Education*. Portland, OR: Northwest Regional Educational Laboratory. (p. 280)

Coughlin, E. K. 1990. Research notes. *The Chronicle of Higher Education* 36 (45): A5. (p. 348)

Coulson, J. E. 1976. *National evaluation of the Emergency School Aid Act (ESAA): Survey of the second-year studies*. Santa Monica, CA: System Development Corporation. (p. 312)

Council of Chief State School Officers. 1987. *Assuring educational success for students at risk*. Policy statement approved by the members of the Council, Asheville, NC. (p. 471)

———. 1989. *Restructuring schools*. Washington, DC: Council of Chief State School Officers. (p. 483)

———. 1990a. *Family support, education, and involvement*. Washington, DC: Council of Chief State School Officers. (p. 142)

———. 1990b. *The challenge and state response*. Washington, DC: Council of Chief State School Officers. (pp. 363, 373)

Courter, R. L., and Ward, B. A. 1983. Staff development for school improvement. In *Staff development*, edited by Gary A. Griffin and Kenneth J. Rehage. Eighty-Second Yearbook of the National Society for the Study of Education, Part II. Chicago: University of Chicago Press. (p. 534)

Crain, R. L. 1970. School integration and occupational achievement of Negroes. *American Journal of Sociology* 75: 593–606. (p. 317)

Crain, R. L., and Mahard, R. E. 1982. *Desegregation plans that raise black achievement: A review of the research*. Santa Monica, CA: Rand. (pp. 274, 312)

Crandall, D. P.; Eiseman, J. W.; and Louis, K. 1986. Strategic planning issues that bear on the success of school improvement efforts. *Educational Administration Quarterly* 22 (3): 21–53. (pp. 525, 526)

Crawford, J. 1986a. Lawmakers, lobbyists challenge E.D.'s bilingual-education data. *Education Week* 5 (32): 13. (p. 375)

———. 1986b. One-third of Navajos drop out annually, new study finds. *Education Week* 6 (13): 1, 14. (p. 388)

Cremin, L. A. 1977. *Traditions of American education*. New York: Basic Books. (pp. 165, 166)

Crisis. 1986. Interview. Dr. Nathan Hare. *The Crisis* 93 (3): 30–35, 45–46.

Crispell, D. 1989. High hopes on the ropes. *American Demographics* 11 (1): 14. (p. 25)

———. 1990. Workers in 1990. *American Demographics* 12 (3): 36–40. (p. 22)

———. 1991. Women's earning gap is closing—slowly. *American Demographics* 13 (2): 14. (pp. 413, 414)

Crittenden, D. 1990. You've come a long way, moll. *The Wall Street Journal* January 25: A14. (p. 197)

Cronin, H.; Meadows, D.; and Sinatra, R. 1990. Integrating computers, reading, and writing across the curriculum. *Educational Leadership* 48 (1): 57–62. (p. 523)

Crook, D. B., and Lavin, D. E. 1989. The community-college effect revisited: The long-term impact of community-college entry on B.A. attainment. Paper presented at the annual meeting of the American Educational Research Association, San Francisco. (pp. 60, 287)

Crosswhite, F. J., et al. 1985. *Second international mathematics study summary report for the United States*. Champaign, IL: Stipes. (p. 48)

Crouse, J. 1985. Does the SAT help colleges make better selection decisions? *Harvard Educational Review* 55: 198–219. (p. 69)

Crouse, J., and Trusheim, D. 1988. The case against the SAT. *The Public Interest* No. 93: 97–110. (p. 69)

———. 1991. How colleges can correctly determine selection benefits from the SAT. *Harvard Educational Review* 61(2): 125–146. (p. 69)

C.S.R. 1985. *The impact of Head Start on children, families, and communities*. Washington, DC: U.S. Department of Health and Human Services (p. 286)

Cuban, L. 1983. *How teachers taught*. New York: Longman. (p. 514)

———. 1990. Reforming again, again, and again. *Educational Researcher* 19 (1): 3–13. (p. 245)

Curnan, S. P. 1990. Field experiences of youth: In school, in transition, and in service. Paper presented at the annual meeting of the American Educational Research Association, Boston. (p. 188)

Currie, E. 1985. *Confronting crime. An American challenge*. New York: Pantheon. (p. 199)

Curtis, R. Q., Jr. 1975. Adolescent orientations toward parents and peers: Variations by sex, age, and socioeconomic status. *Adolescence* 10: 483–494. (p. 154)

Cusick, P. A. 1983. *The egalitarian ideal and the American high school*. New York: Longman. (pp. 159, 515)

Cutler, B. 1990. Man of the '90s. *American Demographics* 12 (10): 18 (p. 180)

Daley, S. 1991. Born on crack, and coping with kindergarten. *The New York Times* February 7: A1, A13. (p. 142)

Danzig, R., and Szanton, P. 1986. *National service: What would it mean?* New York: The Ford Foundation. (p. 205)

Dar, Y., and Resh, N. 1986. Classroom intellectual composition and academic achievement. *American Educational Research Journal* 23 (3): 357–374. (p. 43)

Darity, W. A., and Myers, S. L. 1984. Does welfare dependency cause female headship? The case of the black family. *Journal of Marriage and the Family* 46: 765–779. (p. 354)

Darlington, R. B., et al. 1980. Preschool programs and later school competence of children from low-income families. *Science* 208 (April): 202–204. (p. 280)

Dauber, S. L., and Epstein, J. L. 1989. *Parent attitudes and practices of parent involvement in inner-city elementary and middle schools*. Baltimore, MD: The Johns Hopkins University Center for Research on Elementary and Middle Schools. (pp. 143, 144)

Dave, R. H. 1963. *The identification and measurement of environmental process variables that are related to educational achievement.* Unpublished Ph.D. dissertation, University of Chicago. (p. 110)

David, J. L.; Cohen, M.; Honetschlager, D.; and Traiman, S. 1990. *State action to restructure schools: First steps.* Washington, DC: National Governors' Association. (p. 483)

Davidson, H. H., and Greenberg, J. W. 1969. *School achievers from a deprived background.* New York: City College of the City University of New York. (p. 107)

Davies, D. 1991. Schools reaching out. *Phi Delta Kappan* 72 (5): 376–382. (p. 145)

Davis, A. 1948. *Social-class influences upon learning.* Cambridge, MA: Harvard University Press. (p. 35)

Davis, A., and Havighurst, R. J. 1947. *Father of the man.* Boston: Hougton Mifflin. (p. 147)

Davis, K. 1980. A theory of teenage pregnancy in the United States. In *Adolescent pregnancy and childbearing: Findings from research*, edited by Catherine S. Chilman. Washington, DC: U.S. Government Printing Office. (pp. 202, 203)

Dawson, D. A. 1990. Family structure and children's health and well-being: Data from the 1988 National Health Interviews Survey on child health. Paper presented at the annual meeting of the Population Association of America, Toronto. (p. 126)

Day, R. D. 1988. The mother-state-child "family": Cul-de-sac or path to the future? *The Family in America* 2 (3): 1–8. (p. 121)

De Avila, E. A., and Ulibarri, D. M. 1980. Theoretical perspectives on the selection of instructional techniques for Hispanic students. In *Educating English-speaking Hispanics*, edited by Leonard A. Valverde, Rose Castro Feinberg, and Esther M. Marquez. Washington, DC: Association for Supervision and Curriculum Development. (pp. 376, 381)

Deets, H. 1990. All ages must work for economic equity. *AARP Bulletin* 31 (10): 3. (p. 33)

Delaney, P. 1975. System is blamed for delinquency. *The New York Times* May 5: B7. (p. 277)

DeLoughry, T. J. 1991. Report highlights gap in college-completion rates of rich and poor. *The Chronicle of Higher Education* 37 (20): A20. (p. 363)

Demos, J. 1983. *Past, present, and personal.* New York: Oxford University Press. (p. 104)

Dennis, R. E. 1990. Pathways to violence: Focus on the African American male. *Challenge* 1 (1): 47–56. (pp. 196, 197)

Denny, R. 1991. Indians all over North America battle for treaty rights. *Utne Reader* No. 43: 24–26. (p. 389)

Dentler, R. A. 1990. Conclusions from a national study. In *Magnet schools*, edited by Nolan Estes, Daniel U. Levine, and Donald R. Waldrip, Austin, TX: Morgan. (pp. 324, 325)

DePalma, A. 1990. The culture question. *The New York Times Education Life* November 4: 22–23. (p. 259)

DeParle, J. 1990a. Crux of tax debate: Who pays more? *The New York Times* October 15: C15. (p. 25)

———. 1990b. Senate report finds major flaws in the regulation of trade schools. *The New York Times* September 12: A13. (p. 62)

———. 1991. Suffering in the cities persists as U.S. fights other battles. *The New York Times* January 27: 1, 15. (pp. 14, 77)

DeParle, J., and Applebome, P. 1991. Ideas to aid poor abound, but consensus is wanting. *The New York Times* January 29: A1, A12. (pp. 25, 62)

Derber, C. 1979. *The pursuit of attention.* New York: Schenkman. (p. 434)

Dervarics, C. 1985. Panel report lauds success of job corps, seeks continued funding. *Higher Education Daily* 13 (158): 5. (p. 294)

———. 1990. Afro-centric program yields academic gains. *Black Issues in Higher Education* 7 (20): 1, 34. (p. 403)

Desai, S.; Chase-Lansdale, P. L.; and Michael, R. T. 1989. Mother or market? Effects of maternal employment on the intellectual ability of 4-year-old children. *Demography* 26 (4): 545–561. (pp. 126, 128, 130, 138)

Deutsch, M., et al. 1964. *Communication of information in the elementary classroom.* New York: Institute for Developmental Studies. (p. 263)

Devaney, K. 1990. Holmes board plans national panel to assess progress. *The Holmes Group Forum* 4 (3): 1–2. (p. 473)

———. 1991. 'Holmes Scholars' net set as national equity initiative. *The Holmes Group Forum* 5 (2): 1–2. (p. 473)

DeVillar, R. A., and Faltis, C. 1991. *Computers and cultural diversity.* Albany: State University of New York. (pp. 438, 439)

DeVos, G. 1982. Adaptive strategies for U.S. minorities. In *Minority mental health*, edited by Enrico E. Jones and Sheldon J. Korchin. New York: Praeger. (p. 220)

De Witt, K. 1990a. Emigres, charging stigmata, move on. *The New York Times* September 4: A12. (p. 219)

———. 1990b. Harvard cleared in inquiry on bias. *The New York Times* October 7: 18. (p. 387)

———. 1991. Head of monitoring panel reports progress by states on education. *The New York Times* January 6: 17. (pp. 395, 470)

DeYoung, A. J. 1987. The status of American rural education research: An integrated review and commentary. *Review of Educational Research* 57: 123–148. (p. 441)

———. Economic development and its effects on formal schooling in Appalachia. *American Educational Research Journal* 28 (2): 297–315. (p. 439)

DeYoung, A. J.; Huffman, K.; and Turner, M. E. 1989. Dropout issues in rural America, with a case study of one Central Appalachian school district. In *Dropouts from school*, edited by Lois Weis, Eleanor Farrar, and Hugh G. Petrie. Albany: State University of New York. (p. 440)

Diamond, E. E., and Tittle, C. K. 1985. Sex equity in testing. In *Handbook for achieving sex equity through education*, edited by Susan S. Klein. Baltimore: The Johns Hopkins University Press. (p. 423)

Diamond, M. C. 1988. *Enriching heredity*. New York: Free Press. (pp. 259, 418, 423)

Diegmueller, K. 1991a. N.E.A. launches teacher-training initiative in three states. *Education Week* 10 (24): 5. (p. 493)

———. 1991b. Teacher-education reform slow, deans say in study. *Education Week* 10 (25): 9. (p. 475)

———. 1991c. University of GA wins contract for teaching tests. *Education Week* 10 (25): 11. (p. 471)

Diesenhouse, S. 1989. Harvest of diplomas for Boston poor. *The New York Times* May 24: 25. (p. 496)

DiIulio, J. J., Jr. 1989. The impact of inner-city crime. *ThePublic Interest* No. 96: 28–46. (pp. 21, 292)

Dillard, J. L. 1972. *Black English*. New York: Random House. (p. 357)

Division of Vocational and Technical Education. 1979. *Status of vocational education in 1979*. Washington, DC: U.S. Department of Health, Education and Welfare.

Dobriner, W. M. 1963. *Class in suburbia*. Englewood Cliffs, NJ: Prentice-Hall. (p. 35)

Dobson, D. P. 1985. *The application of immersion education in the United States*. Rosslyn, VA: National Clearinghouse for Bilingual Education. (p. 376)

Doeringer, P. B., and Piore, M. J. 1971. *Internal labor markets and manpower analysis*. Lexington, MA: Heath-Lexington. (p. 35)

Doherty, E. J., and Wilson, L. S. 1990. The making of a contract for education reform. *Phi Delta Kappan* 71 (10): 791–796. (p. 485)

Dole, J. A., Duffy, G. G., Roehler, L. R., and Pearson, P. D. 1991. Moving from the old to the new: Research on teaching comprehension instruction. *Review of Educational Research* 61 (2): 239–264 (pp. 54, 512)

Doll, R. C. 1987. Presenting. *Home School Researcher*. 3 (3): 4–5. (p. 457)

Doll, R. C., and Levine, D. U. 1972. Toward a definition of "structure" in the education of disadvantaged students. In *Opening opportunities for disadvantaged learners*, edited by A. Harry Passow. New York: Teachers College Press. (p. 98)

Dorman, A. 1990. Recruiting and retraining minority teachers. *NCREL Policy Briefs* No. 8: 1–2. (p. 396)

Dornbusch, S. M., and Gray, K. D. 1988. Single-parent families. In *Feminism, children, and the new families*, edited by Sanford A. Dornbusch and Myra H. Stober. New York: Guilford Press. (p. 128)

Door, A. 1986. *Television and children*. Beverly Hills, CA: Sage. (pp. 135, 136, 137)

Dorr-Bremme, D. W. 1991. Culture, practice, and change: School effectiveness reconsidered. *The Elementary School Journal* (in press). (p. 261)

Dossey, J. A., et al. 1988. *The mathematics report card*. Princeton, NJ: Educational Testing Service. (pp. 48, 49, 361, 362, 416, 464)

Dougherty, K. 1987. The effects of community colleges: Aid or hindrance to socioeconomic attainment? *Sociology of Education* 60: 86–103. (p. 53)

Doyle, D. P. 1982. A den of inequity: Private schools reconsidered. *American Education* 18 (8): 11–17. (p. 451)

Doyle, W. 1983. Academic work. *Review of Educational Research* 53: 159–199. (p. 515)

———. 1985. Effective secondary classroom practices. In *Reaching for excellence*, edited by Regina M. J. Kyle. Washington, DC: The National Institute of Education. (pp. 514, 515)

———. 1986. Classroom organization and management. In *Handbook of research on teaching*, edited by Merlin C. Wittrock. New York: Macmillan (p. 510)

———. 1990. Classroom knowledge as a foundation for teaching. *Teachers College Record* 91 (3): 347–360. (pp. 510, 514, 515, 517)

Dreeben, R., and Barr, R. 1988. Classroom composition and the design of instruction. *Sociology of Education* 61: 29–142. (p. 263)

Dreier, P., and Hulchanski, J. D. 1990. Affordable housing: lessons from Canada. *The American Prospect* No. 1: 119–125. (p. 25)

Discoll, M. E. 1990. The formation of community in public schools: Findings and hypotheses. *Administrator's Notebook* 34 (4): 1–4. (pp. 449, 526)

Drucker, P. F. 1989. *The new realities*. New York: Harper and Row. (pp. 5, 169, 170)

Duaney, L., and Pittman, K. 1990. *Latino youth at the crossroads*. Washington, DC: DF Publications. (pp. 351, 370)

Duffy, G. G., et al. 1986. The relationship between explicit verbal explanation during reading skill instruction and student awareness and achievement. *Reading Research Quarterly* 21: 237–282. (p. 513)

Duffy, G. G.; Roehler, L. R.; and Putnam, J. 1987. Putting the teacher in control: Basal reading textbooks and instructional decision making. *The Elementary School Journal* 87 (3): 357–366. (p. 513)

Dulay, H., and Burt, M. 1982. Bilingual education: A close look at its effects. *Focus of the National Clearinghouse for Bilingual Education* 1: 1–4. (p. 376)

Dunivant, N. 1982. The relationship between learning disabilities and juvenile delinquency: Brief summary of research findings. Paper published by the National Center for State Courts, Williamsburg, VA. (p. 198)

Durkheim, E. 1956. *Education and Sociology*. Glencoe, IL: Free Press. (p. 184)

Dwyer, K. M. 1990. Characteristics of eighth-grade students who initiate self-care in elementary and junior high schools. *Pediatrics* 86: 448–454. (p. 138)

Easterlin, R. A. 1980. *Birth and fortune. The impact of numbers on personal welfare*. New York: Basic Books. (p. 117)

Eccles, J. S. 1986. Gender-roles and women's achievement. *Educational Researcher* 15 (6): 15–19. (p. 427)

Eccles, J. S., and Blumenfeld. 1985. Classroom experiences and student gender: Are there differences and do they matter? In *Gender influences in classroom interaction*, edited by Louise Cherry Wilkinson and Cora B. Marrett. Orlando, FL: Academic Press. (p. 424)

Eckert, P. 1989. *Jocks and burnouts*. New York: TeachersCollege Press. (pp. 160, 161)

Eckland, B. E.; Henderson, L. B.; and Kolstad, A. J. 1981. *College attainment four years after high school*. Washington, DC: National Center for Education Statistics. (p. 41)

Eckroade, G.; Salehi, S.; and Wode, J. 1991. An analysis of the long-term effects of the extended elementary education prekindergarten program. Paper presented at the annual meeting of the American Educational Research Association, Chicago. (pp. 279, 280)

Eddy, P. 1978. Does foreign language study aid native language development? *ERIC/CLL News Bulletin* No. 1: 1–2. (p. 376)

Eder, D., and Parker, S. 1987. The cultural production and reproduction of gender. *Sociology of Education* 60: 200–213. (p. 153)

Editors of FairTest Examiner. 1989–90. Coalition calls for 'genuine' accountability. *FairTest Examiner* 4 (1): 1, 6. (p. 476)

Editors of Harper's. 1991. She wants her TV! He wants his book! *Harper's* 282 (1690): 44–55. (p. 119)

Editors of ISR. 1985–1986. Cocaine use rising. *ISR Newsletter* Winter: 5, 7–8. (p. 200)

Edmonds, R. 1979. Effective schools for the urban poor. *Educational Leadership* 38: 15–24. (p. 504)

Edmondson, B. 1990. Help desperately wanted. *American Demographics* 12 (1): 60, 62. (p. 25)

Edmondson, B., and Cutler, B. 1989. Where the boys are. *The Atlantic Monthly* 263 (2): 67. (p. 353)

Edmundson, P. J. 1989. *Educating educators*. Washington, DC: American Association of Colleges of Teacher Education. (p. 491)

Edsall, T. B., and Edsall, M. D. 1991. Race. *The Atlantic Monthly* 267 (5): 53–86. (pp. 16, 352)

Education Advocates Coalition. 1980. Misclassification of minorities in "educable mentally retarded classes." *Integrateducation* 18 (1–4): 113–115. (p. 134)

Education Daily. 1987. Governor warns of polarization in society without Education reforms. *Education Daily* 20 (29): 4. (p. 461)

Education Forum. 1984. Education reports prompt state reform. *CDF Reports* December: 10. (p. 491)

Educational Testing Service. 1980. *Test use and validity: A response to charges in the Nader/Nairn report on ETS*. Princeton, NJ: Educational Testing Service.

Eells, K., et al: 1951. *Intelligence and cultural differences*. Chicago: University of Chicago Press. (p. 66)

Egan, T. 1988. Proposal to curb busing in Seattle seeks to attract whites to schools. *The New York Times* March 28: A17. (p. 327)

———. 1990. Mired in poverty, Alaska Natives ponder how much land to spend. *The New York Times*. June 1: A1, A11. (pp. 390, 391)

Eisenhart, M. 1989. Reconsidering cultural differences in American schools. *Educational Foundations* 3 (2): 51–68. (p. 143).

Elardo, R.; Bradley, R.; and Caldwell, B. M. 1975. The relation of infants' home environments to mental test performance from six to thirty-six months: A longitudinal analysis. *Child Development* 46: 71–76. (p. 113)

Ellickson, P. L., and Bell, R. M. 1990. Drug prevention in junior high:A multi-site longitudinal test. *Science* 247: 1299–1305. (p. 202)

Elliott, D. S.; Huizinga, D.; and Ageton, S. S. 1985. *Explaining delinquency and drug use*. Beverly Hills, CA: Sage. (pp. 155, 197, 198)

Ellis, J. E. 1990 What black families need to make the dream come true. *Business Week* No. 3142: 29. (p. 203)

Elmore, R. F., and Fuhrman, S. H. 1990. The national interest and the federal role in education. *The Journal of Federalism* 20 (Summer): 149–162. (p. 494)

England, R. E.; Stewart, J., Jr.; and Meier, K. L. 1990. Excellence in education. *Equity and Excellence* 24 (4): 35–40. (p. 134)

Epps, E. G. 1974. Schools and cultural pluralism. In *Cultural pluralism*, edited by Edgar G. Epps. Berkeley, CA: McCutchan. (p. 405)

Epstein, E. H. 1972. Social class, ethnicity, and academic achievement: A cross-cultural approach. *The Journal of Negro Education* 14: 202–215. (p. 131)

Epstein, J. L. 1990. Effects of teacher practices of parent involvement on student achievement in reading and math. In *Literacy through family, community, school interaction*, edited by Steven Slivern. Greenwich, CT: JAI. (p. 142)

———. 1991. Paths to partnership. *Phi Delta Kappan* 72 (5): 344–349. (pp. 142, 143)

Epstein, J. L., and Dauber, S. L. 1991. School programs and teacher practices of parent involvement in inner-city elementary and middle schools. *The Elementary School Journal* 91 (3): 288–305. (pp. 143, 144, 231)

Epstein, N. 1977. *Language, ethnicity, and the schools: Policy alternatives for bilingual-bicultural education*. Washington, DC: The George Washington University Institute for Educational Leadership. (pp. 374, 380)

Erickson, F. 1985. *Qualitative methods in teaching*. Lansing: Michigan State University Institute for Research on Teaching. (p. 398)

———. 1990. Culture, policies and educational practice. *Educational Foundations* 4 (2): 21–45. (p. 401)

Erickson, F., and Mohatt, G. 1982. The cultural organization of participation structures in two classrooms of Indian students. In *Doing the enthography of schooling*, edited by George Spindler. New York: Holt, Rinehart and Winston. (p. 398)

Estes, N.; Levine, D. U.; and Waldrip, D. R., eds. 1990. *Magnet schools*. Austin, TX: Morgan. (pp. 323, 339)

Ethington, C. A., and Wolfle, L. M. 1986. A structural model of mathematics achievement for men and women. *American Educational Research Journal* 23 (1): 65–75. (p. 416)

Eubanks, E. E., and Levine, D. U. 1977. The PUSH program for excellence in big-city schools. *Phi Delta Kappan* 58: 383–388. (pp. 100, 167)

———. 1987a. Administrative and organizational arrangements and considerations. In *Educating the black child*, edited by Dorothy S. Strickland and Eric J. Cooper. Washington, DC: Howard University Press. (p. 530)

———. 1987b. Ancillary relief components in urban school desegregation.The University of Chicago National School Desegregation Project Working Paper No. 8. (p. 311)

Evangelauf, J. 1987. Students' borrowing quintuples in decades, raising the specter of a 'debtor generation.' *The Chronicle of Higher Education* January 7: 1, 18. (pp. 62, 63)

———. 1990. 1988 enrollments of all racial groups hit record levels. *The Chronicle of Higher Education*. 36 (30): A1, A37. (p. 395)

Evans, D. E. 1990. The mythology of the marketplace in school choice. *Education Week* 10 (7): 32. (p. 500)

Everhart, R. B. 1983. *Reading, writing, and resistance*. Boston: Routledge and Kegan Paul. (pp. 250, 251)

Ewell, B. C. 1990. Empowering otherness: Feminist criticism and the academy. In *Reorientations*, edited by B. Henricksen and T. Morgan. Urbana: University of Illinois Press. (pp. 247, 427)

Exter, T. 1991. One million Hispanic club. *American Demographics* 13 (2): 59. (p. 366)

Fagot, B. 1991. Using knowledge from play research to expand sex-typing options. Paper presented at the annual meeting of the American Educational Research Association, Chicago, (p. 420).

Farber, N. 1990. The significance of race and class in marital decisions among unmarried adolescent mothers. *Social Forces* 37 (1): 51–63. (p. 203)

Farganis, S. 1989. Feminism and the reconstruction of social science. In *Gender/body/knowledge*, edited by Alison M. Jaggar and Susan R. Bordo. New Brunswick, NJ: Rutgers University Press. (pp. 432, 433)

Farkas, G.; Sheehan, D.; and Grobe, R. P. 1990. Coursework mastery and school success: Gender, ethnicity, and poverty groups within an urban school district. *American Educational Research Journal* 27 (4): 807–827. (p. 385)

Farley, R. 1984. *Blacks and whites*. Cambridge, MA: Harvard University Press. (p. 353)

Farnsworth, M., and Leiber, M. J. 1989. Strain theory revisited: Economic goals, educational means, and delinquency. *American Sociological Review* 54: 263–274. (p. 197)

Farnsworth, M.; Schweinhart, L. J.; and Berrueta-Clement, J. R. 1985. Preschool intervention, school success and delinquency in a high-risk sample of youth. *American Educational Research Journal* 22: 445–464. (p. 280)

Farrell, W. C. 1990. School choice and the educational opportunities of African American children. *The Journal of Negro Education* 59 (4): 529–537. (p. 499)

Fass, S. 1989. Innovations in the struggle for self- reliance. *International Migration Review* 20 (2): 351–380. (p. 384)

Feagans, L. 1982. The development and importance of narratives for school adaptation. In *The language of children reared in poverty*, edited by Lynne

Feagans and Dale Clark Farran. New York: Academic Press. (p. 235)

Feagans, L., and Farran, D. C., eds. 1982. *The language of children reared in poverty*. New York: Academic Press. (p. 254)

Featherman, D. L., and Hauser, R. M. 1976. Changes in the socioeconomic stratification of the races, 1962–1973. *American Journal of Sociology* 82: 621–651. (p. 241)

———. 1978. *Opportunity and change*. New York: Academic Press. (pp. 220, 222, 227, 241, 364, 368)

Featherstone, H. 1987. Orderly classrooms and corridors: Why some have them and others don't. *The Harvard Educational Letter* 3 (5): 1–5. (p. 417)

Feinblatt, J. 1991. Teach kids to 'talk it out?' *The New York Times* January 4: A13. (p. 277)

Feingold, A. 1988. Cognitive gender differences are disappearing. *American Psychologist* 43 (2): 95–103. (p. 417)

Fennema E., and Leder, G. 1990. *Mathematics and gender*. New York: Teachers College Press. (p. 416)

Ferguson, A. 1977. Androgyny as an ideal for human development. In *Feminism and philosophy*. Totewa, NJ: Littlefield, Adams. (p. 429)

Ferndandez, R., and Vellez. 1985. Race, color, and language in the changing public schools. In *Urban ethnicity in the United States*, edited by Lionel Maldonado and Joan Moore. Beverly Hills, CA: Sage. (p. 51)

Ferrero, G. W.; Lungstrum, R. M.; and McKenna, A. E. 1989. Ninth-grade students' attitudes toward nontraditional occupations. Paper presented at the annual meeting of the American Educational Research Association, San Francisco. (p. 413)

Feuerstein, R. 1980. *Instrumental enrichment*. Baltimore: University Park Press. (p. 513)

Fiddmont, Norman. 1976. Achievement in inner-city schools. Paper prepared at the School of Education, University of Missouri-Kansas City. (p. 274)

Fillmore, L. W. 1991. Language and cultural issues in the early education of language minority children. In *The care and education of America's young children: Obstacles and opportunities*, edited by Sharon Lynn Kagan. Chicago: University of Chicago Press. (p. 368)

Finn, C. E., Jr. 1987. The high school dropout puzzle. *The Public Interest* No. 87: 3–22. (p. 528)

———. 1991. National testing, no longer a foreign idea. *The Wall Street Journal* March 11: A11. (p. 477)

Finn, J. D. 1991. How to make the dropout problem go away. *Educational Researcher* 20 (1): 28–30. (pp. 477, 528, 529)

Finn, J. D., and Achilles, C. M. 1990. Answers and questions about class size: A statewide experiment. *American Educational Research Journal* 27 (3): 557–577. (p. 264)

Finn, J. D.; Dulberg, L.; and Reis, J. 1979. Sex differences in educational attainment: A cross-national perspective. *Harvard Educational Review* 49: 477–503. (p. 414)

Firestone, S. 1970. *The dialect of sex: The case for feminist revolution*. New York: William Morrow and Co. (p. 434)

Firestone, W. A., and Herriott, R. E. 1982. Prescriptions for effective elementary schools don't fit secondary schools. *Educational Leadership* 40: 51–53. (p. 507)

Fishman, J. A. 1977. Bilingual education—A perspective. *IRCD Bulletin* 12 (Spring): 1–12. (pp. 378, 380, 381)

Fishman, R. 1990. Megalopolis unbound. *Wilson Quarterly* 14 (1): 25–45. (pp. 72, 83)

Fiske, E. B. 1989a. Can money spent on schools save money that would be spent on prisons? *The New York Times* September 23–27.(p. 198)

———. 1989b. Impending U.S. jobs 'disaster': Work force unqualified to work. *The New York Times* September 25: 1, 12. (pp. 24, 198)

Fitzpatrick, J. P. 1972. Transition to the mainland. In *The Puerto Rican community and its children on the mainland: A sourcebook for teachers, social workers and other professionals*, edited by Francesco Cordasco and Eugene Bucchioni. Metuchen, NJ: Scarecrow. (p. 371)

Flanigan, P. M. 1991. A school system that works. *The Wall Street Journal* February 12: A12. (p. 453)

Flax, E. 1990a. Researchers see early signs of adolescent problems. *Education Week* 9 (39): 16. (pp. 197, 201)

———. 1990b. Work to eliminate use of 'gateway drugs,' report urges. *Education Week* 10 (12): 27. (p. 202)

Flynn, J. R. 1980. *Race, IQ, and Jensen*. London: Routledge and Kegan Paul. (p. 67)

———. 1987. Massive IQ gains in 14 nations: What IQ tests really measure. *Psychological Bulletin* 101: 171–191. (p. 67)

Fodeeraro, L. W. 1990. Catholic schools close as costs outpace parishes. *The New York Times* February 18: 38. (p. 447)

Foley, D. 1990. Danger: School zone. *Teacher* 1 (8): 57–63. (pp. 276, 277)

Foley, J.; Manaker, M.; and Schwartz, J. L. 1984. *National service and America's future*. Washington, DC: Youth Policy Institute. (p. 205)

Footlik, J. K. 1990. What happened to the family? *Newsweek* Winter/Spring: 14–20. (p. 115)

Fordham, S. 1988. Racelessness as a factor in black students' school success: Pragmatic strategy or Pyrrhic victory? *Harvard Education Review* 58 (1): 54–84. (p. 356)

Forehand, G.; Ragosta, M.; and Rock, D. A. 1977. *School conditions and race relations*. Princeton, NJ: Educational Testing Service. (p. 314)

Forum of Educational Organization Leaders. 1987. *Statement on meeting the needs of children and youth at risk of school failure*. Washington, DC: Forum of Educational Organization Leaders. (p. 462)

Fost, D. 1990. California's Asian-market. *American Demographics* 12 (10): 34–37. (p. 382)

Foster, J. D. 1991. The role of accountability in Kentucky's education reform act of 1990. *Educational Leadership* 48 (5): 34–36. (pp. 487, 495)

Foster, S. G. 1982. Success of minority engineering programs may have promise for secondary schools. *Education Week* 2 (9): 1, 17. (p. 289)

Fox, K. 1990. *Metropolitan America*. New Brunswick, NJ: Rutgers University Press. (pp. 76, 78)

Fox-Genovese, E. 1991. *Feminism without illusions*. Chapel Hill: University of North Carolina Press. (p. 434)

Frances, C. 1990. Student aid. *Change* 22 (4): 35–43. (pp. 25, 62)

Frase, L. E., and Poston, W. K., Jr. 1990. Teacher incentive programs. *The Clearing House* 64(2): 95–98. (p. 495)

Frazier, F., et al. 1990. *The urban underclass*.Washington, DC: U.S. General Accounting Office. (pp. 280, 294)

Frechtling, J. A., and Nyitray, M. S. 1977. The structure and content of compensatory education programs: A research strategy for evaluating Title I's effects on services and effects on students. Paper presented at the annual meeting of the American Educational Research Association, Los Angeles. (p. 278)

Freedman, M. 1991. Mentoring: New help for kids and schools. *The Harvard Education Letter* 7 (2): 1–3. (p. 497)

Freeman, R. B., and Holzer, H. T. 1985. Young blacks and jobs—what we now know. *The Public Interest* No. 78: 18–31. (p. 187)

———. 1986. *The black unemployment crisis*. Chicago: University of Chicago Press. (p. 187)

Freiberg, H. J. 1987. Career ladders: Messages gleaned from experience. *Journal of Teacher Education* 38 (4): 49–56. (p. 480)

Frey, Walt. 1990. Metropolitan America: Beyond the transition. *Population Bulletin* 45 (2): 1–51. (pp. 76, 83)

Friedan, B. 1963. *The feminine mystique*. New York: Dell. (pp. 409, 430)

———. 1981. *The second stage*. New York: Random House. (pp. 430, 435)

Friedenberg, E. Z. 1959. *The vanishing adolescent*. Boston: Beacon Press. (p. 174)

Friedman, L. 1989. Mathematics and the gender gap: A meta-analysis of recent studies on sex differences in mathematical tasks. *Review of Educational Research* 59 (2): 185–213. (p. 418)

Friedman, L., and Christiansen, G. 1990. *Shut out: Denial of education to homeless children*. Washington, DC: National Law Center on Homelessness and Poverty. (p. 140)

Friedrich, O. 1985. The changing face of America. *Time* July 8: 26–33. (p. 342)

Fuchs, E., and Havighurst, R. J. 1972. *To live on this earth: American Indian education*. Garden City, NY: Doubleday Anchor Books. (pp. 393, 405)

Fuerst, J. S. 1976. Report from Chicago: a program that works. *The Public Interest* 43 (Spring): 59–69. (p. 281)

———. 1977. Child-parent centers: An evaluation. *Integrated Education* 15 (May–June): 17–20. (p. 281)

Fuhrman, S., and Fry, P. 1991. Diversity amidst standardization: State differential treatment of districts. In *Choice and control in American education*, Vol. 2., edited by William F. Clune and John F. Witte. London: Falmer. (pp. 482, 484)

Fuhrman, S. H., and Elmore, R. F. 1990. Understanding local control in the wake of state education reform. *Educational Evaluation and Policy Analysis* 12 (1): 82–96. (p. 490)

Fullan, M. G. 1990. Staff development, innovation and institutional development. In *Changing school culture through staff development*, edited by Bruce Joyce. Alexandria, VA: Association for Supervision and Curriculum Development. (pp. 524, 525, 526)

———. 1991. *The new meaning of educational change*. New York: Teachers College Press. (pp. 524, 525, 526)

Fuller, W. E. 1985. *The old country school*. Chicago: The University of Chicago Press. (pp. 440, 442, 459)

Fullerton, H. N., Jr. 1989. New labor force projections, spanning 1988 to 2000. *Monthly Labor Review* 112 (11): 3–11. (pp. 27, 411)

Furstenberg, F. F., Jr. 1977. *Unplanned parenthood*. New York: Free Press. (p. 204)

———. 1988. Bringing back the shotgun wedding. *The Public Interest* No. 90: pp. 121–127. (p. 204)

Furstenberg, F. F.; Jr., Brooks-Gunn, J.; and Morgan, S. P. 1987. *Adolescent mothers in later life*. New York: Cambridge University Press. (p. 204)

Furstenberg, F. F., Jr.; Levine, J. A.; and Brooks-Gunn, J. 1990. The children of teenage mothers. *Family Planning Perspectives* 22 (2): 54–61. (p. 204)

Futrell, M. H. 1986. Restructuring teaching: A call for research. *Educational Researcher* 15 (10): 5–8. (p. 491)

Gabarino, J., and Plantz, M. C. 1980. *Urban environments and urban children*. New York: Institute for Urban and Minority Education, Teachers College, Columbia University. (p. 92)

Gage, N. L. 1990. Dealing with the dropout problem. *Phi Delta Kappan* 72 (4): 280–285. (p. 529)

Gaines, D. 1991. *Teenage wasteland*. New York: Pantheon. (p. 105)

Galbraith, J. 1982. *Emergency interim survey: Fiscal condition of 48 large cities*. Washington, DC: U.S. Government Printing Office. (p. 77)

Gallagher, W. 1988. Sex and hormones. *The Atlantic Monthly* 261 (4): 77–82. (p. 418)

Gallaher, A. 1961. *Plainville fifteen years later*. New York: Columbia University Press. (p. 34)

Gamoran, A. 1986a. Instructional and institutional effects of ability grouping. *Sociology of Education*, 59: 185–198. (p. 44)

———. 1986b. The stratification of high school learning opportunities. Paper presented at the annual meeting of the American Education Research Association, San Francisco. (p. 44)

———. 1990. Instructional organizational practices that affect equity. In *Leadership, equity, and school effectiveness*, edited by H. Prentice Baptiste, Jr., Hersholt Wasman, Judith Walker de

Felix, and James E. Anderson. Newbury Park, CA: Sage. (pp. 43, 44, 529, 530)

Gans, H. J. 1962. *The urban villagers*. New York: The Free Press. (p. 93)

———. 1967. *The Levittowners* New York: Pantheon. (p. 35)

———. 1976. The role of education in the escape from poverty. In *Education, inequality, and national policy*, edited by N. Ashline, T. R. Pazzullo, and C. I. Norris. Lexington, MA: D.C. Heath. (p. 20)

Gappert, G., and Knight, R. V., eds. 1982 *Cities in the 21st century*. Beverly Hills, CA: Sage. (p. 87)

Garber, H. L. 1988. *The Milwaukee project*. Washington, DC: American Association on Mental Retardation. (pp. 291, 292).

Garcia, G., and Pearson, D. 1991. Modifying reading instruction to maximize its effectiveness for 'all' students. In *Better schooling for the children of poverty: Alternatives to conventional wisdom*, edited by Michael Knapp and Patrick Shields. Berkeley, CA: McCutchan. (pp. 270, 533)

Gardner, L., and Shoemaker, D. J. 1989. Social bonding and delinquency: A comparative analysis. *The Sociological Quarterly*. 30 (3): 481–500. (p. 198)

Garreau, J. 1982. *The nine nations of North America*. New York: Avon. (p. 350)

Garrison, M., and Hammil, D. 1971. Who are the retarded? *Exceptional Children* 38: 13–20. (p. 134)

Gelis, J. 1989. The child: From anonymity to individuality. In *A history of private life. Passions of the Renaissance*, edited by Roger Chartier. Cambridge, MA: Harvard University Press. (pp. 91, 120)

General Accounting Office. 1989. *Effective schools programs*. Washington, DC: U.S. General Accounting Office. (p. 505)

Genesee, F. 1985. Second language learning through immersion: A review of U.S. programs. *Review of Educational Research* 55 (4): 541–561. (p. 376)

Gerson, R. P., and Damon, W. 1978. Moral understanding and children's conduct. *New Directions for Child Development* 2: 41–59. (p. 153)

Gersten, R., and Woodward, J. 1985. A case for structured immersion. *Educational Leadership* 43 (1): 75–79. (p. 376)

Getzels, J. W. 1978. The school and the acquisition of values. In *From youth to constructive adult life: The role of the public school*, edited by Ralph W. Tyler. Berkeley, CA: McCutchan. (p. 180)

Gibbs, J. T. 1990. *Young, black, and male in America: An endangered species*. Dover, MA: Auburn House. (p. 354)

Gillerman, M. 1991. St. Louis magnet schools fill fast. *St. Louis Post-Dispatch* March 24: 11D. (p. 334)

Gilligan, C. 1982. *In a different voice: Psychological theory and women's development*. Cambridge, MA: Harvard University Press. (pp. 430, 431)

Gilligan, C.; Lyons, N. P.; and Hanmer, T. J., eds. 1989. *Making connections*. Troy, NY: Emma Willard School. (p. 430)

Giroux, H. A. 1983. Theories of reproduction and resistance in the new sociology of education: A critical analysis. *Educational Review* 53: 253–297. (p. 251)

———. 1988a. *Schooling and the struggle for public life*. Minneapolis: University of Minnesota Press. (pp. 248, 249)

———. 1988b. *Teachers as intellectuals*. Granby, MA: Bergin and Garvey. (p. 248, 251)

———. 1991. Modernism, postmodernism, and feminism: Rethinking the boundaries of educational discourse. In *Postmodernism, feminism, and cultural politics*, edited by Henry A. Giroux. Albany: State University of New York Press. (pp. 248, 251)

Giroux, H. A., and McLaren, P. 1986. Teacher education and the politics of engagement: The case for democratic schooling. *Harvard Educational Review* 56: 213–238. (p. 251)

Giroux, H. A., and Purpel, D. 1983. *The hidden curriculum and moral education*. Berkeley, CA: McCutchan. (p. 254)

Giroux, H. A., and Simon, R. I., eds. 1989. *Popular culture, schooling, and everyday life*. Granby, MA: Bergin and Garvey. (pp. 248, 249)

Gisi, L. G., and Forbes, R. H. 1982. *The information society: Are high school graduates ready?* Denver: Education Commission of the States. (p. 23)

Glaberson, William, 1989. U.S. court says awards based on S.A.T.'s are unfair to girls. *The New York Times* February 4: 1, 50. (p. 70)

Glaser, D. 1979. Economic and sociocultural variables affecting rates of youth unemployment, delinquency, and crime. *Youth and Society* 11 (1): 53–82. (p. 196)

Glaser, E. M., and Ross, H. L. 1970. *A study of successful persons from seriously disadvantaged backgrounds*. Washington, DC: U.S. Dept. of Labor Office of Special Manpower Programs. (p. 19)

Glasgow, D. G. 1980. *The black underclass. Poverty, unemployment, and entrapment of ghetto youth.* San Francisco: Jossey–Bass. (p. 18)

Glass, D. V., ed. 1954. *Social mobility in Britain.* London: Routledge and Kegan Paul. (p. 224)

Glass, G. V., and Matthews, D. A. 1991. Are data enough? *Education Researcher* 20 (3): 24–27. (p. 449)

Glazer, N., ed. 1985. *Clamor at the gates.* San Francisco: ICS Press. (p. 406)

Gleckman, H. 1990. Social Security's days as a sacred cow are numbered. *Business Week* No. 3153: 33. (pp. 31, 32)

Glen, C. L. 1991. Will Boston be the proof of the choice pudding? *Educational Leadership* 48 (2): 41–43. (p. 327)

Glickman, C. 1990. Pushing school reform to the edge: The seven ironies of school empowerment. *Phi Delta Kappan* 72 (1): 68–75. (p. 485)

Glidewell, J. C.; Kantor, M. B.; Smith, L. M.; and Stringer, L. H. 1966. Socialization and social structure in the classroom. In *Review of research in child development.* Vol. 2, edited by Martin and Lois Hoffman. New York: Russell Sage Foundation. (p. 174)

Goldberg, K. 1986. Blacks push strategies to improve their education. *Education Week* 6 (13): 1–15. (p. 447)

———. 1987. Many homeless children reported out of school. *Education Week* 6 (26): 6.

Goldberg, S. 1990. Numbers don't lie: Men do better than women. *The New York Times* July 5: 23. (p. 70)

Goldberger, A., and Cain, G. 1982. The causal analysis of cognitive outcomes in the Coleman, Hoffer, and Kilgore report. *Sociology of Education* 55 (2): 103–122. (p. 449)

Goldman, A. 1991. Poll shows Jews both assimilate and keep tradition. *The New York Times* June 7:A8. (p. 222)

Goldsmith, W. W. 1982. Poverty and profit in urban growth and decline. In *Race, poverty and the urban underclass,* edited by Clement Cottingham Lexington, MA: D.C. Heath. (p. 15)

Goldthorpe, J. H. 1980. *Social mobility and class structure in modern Britain.* Oxford: Clarendon Press. (pp. 224, 225)

———. 1987. *Social mobility and class structure in modern Britain.* 2nd ed. Oxford: Clarendon Press (p. 224)

Goleman, D. 1988. Studies of latchkey children say effects need not be bad. *The New York Times* September 22: 1, 25. (p. 138)

———. 1989. Sensing silent cues emerges as key skill. *The New York Times* October 10: 21, 24. (pp. 138, 135, 152)

———. 1990. The link between birth order and innovation. *The New York Times* May 8: B1, B9. (p. 130)

———. 1991. New ways to battle bias: Fight acts, not feelings. *The New York Times* July 16: B1, B9. (p. 315)

Gollnick, W. A. 1990. The reappearance of the vanishing American. *The College Board Review* No. 155: 30–34. (pp. 392, 394, 398)

Gong, B.; Lahart, C.; and Courtney, R. 1990. Current state science assessments: Is something better than nothing? Paper presented at the annual meeting of the American Educational Research Association, Boston. (p. 476)

Gonzalez, G. A. 1980. The non-Spanish speaking Hispanic child: Curriculum concerns/supervisory initiatives. In *Educating English-speaking Hispanics,* edited by Leonard A. Valverde, Rosa Castro Feinberg, and Esther M. Marquez. Washington, DC: Association for Supervision and Curriculum Development.

Gonzalez, J. 1975. Coming of age in bilingual/bicultural education: An historical perspective. *Inequality in Education* 19: 5–17. (pp. 373, 375, 381)

Good, T. L. 181. Teacher expectations and student perceptions: A decade of research. *Educational Leadership* 38: 415–422. (p. 261)

Good, T. L., and Brophy, J. E. 1986. School effects. In *Handbook of research on teaching,* edited by Merlin C. Wittrock. New York: Macmillan. (p. 509)

Good, T. L., and Grouws, D. A. 1987. Increasing teachers' understanding of mathematical ideas through inservice training. *Phi Delta Kappan* 68: 778–783. (p. 514)

Good, T. L., and Marshall, S. 1984. Do students learn more in heterogeneous or homogenous groups? In *The social context of instruction,* edited by Margaret T. Hallinan and Aage B. Sorensen. New York: Academic Press. (p. 43)

Gooden, F.; Lane, M. A.; and Levine, D. U. 1989. A school-within-a-school for at-risk urban students. *The Journal of Negro Education* 58 (3): 367–371. (pp. 508, 528)

Goodlad, J. I. 1984. *A place called school.* New York: McGraw-Hill. (pp. 85, 151, 514, 575)

———. 1987. Structure, process, and an agenda. In *The ecology of school renewal*, edited by John I. Goodlad. Eighty-Sixth Yearbook of the National Society for the Study of Education, Part I. Chicago: University of Chicago Press. (pp. 524, 526)

———. 1989. Keeping the gates. *American Association of Colleges for Teacher Education Briefs* 10 (6): 3, 9. (p. 471)

———. 1990. *Teachers for our nation's schools*. San Francisco: Jossey-Bass. (p. 475)

Goodman, E. 1990. 'War of the Roses' line may serve as footnote of no-fault divorce era. *The Kansas City Star* January 2: A9. (p. 128)

Goodman, G. 1979. *Choosing sides*. New York: Schocken Books. (p. 252)

Goodson, B. D., and Layzer, J. I. 1991. Effects of Project Giant Step. Paper presented at the annual meeting of the American Educational Research Association, Chicago. (p. 291)

Goodyer, I. M. 1990. Family relationships, life events and childhood psychopathology. *Journal of Child Psychology and Psychiatry* 31: 161–181. (p. 126)

Gordon, C. W. 1957. *The social system of the high school*. New York: The Free Press. (p. 174)

Gordon, E. W. 1976. Equal opportunity in education. *IRCD Bulletin* 11 (Winter): 1–15. (p. 289)

Gordon, E. W., and Musser, J. M. 1990. *A study of minority achievement in Montgomery County Public Schools*. Pomona, NY: Gordon and Gordon Associates in Human Development. (pp. 362, 363)

Gordon, M. 1964. *Assimilation in American life: The role of race, religion and origins*. New York: Oxford University Press. (pp. 35, 345)

Gore, J. M. 1990. What can we do for you! What *can* "we" do for "you"? *Educational Foundations* 4(3): 5–26. (pp. 244, 432)

Gottfredson, L. S. 1979. Racial differences in the evolution of educational and occupational aspirations. Paper presented at the annual meeting of the American Educational Research Association, San Francisco. (p. 364)

———. 1984. *The role of intelligence and education in the division of labor*. Baltimore: Center for Social Organization of Schools. (p. 71)

Gottfredson, M., and Hirschi, T. 1989. Why we're losing the war on crime. *The Washington Post* September 10: C3. (p. 196)

Gottman, J. 1961. *Megalopolis: The urbanized northeastern seaboard of the United States*. New York: Twentieth Century Fund. (pp. 86–87)

Gould, S. J. 1980. Jensen's last stand. *The New York Review of Books* 27 (7): 38–44. (p. 68)

———. 1981. *The mismeasure of man*. New York: Norton. (p. 68)

Graham, E. 1989a. Motivation in Afro-Americans. In *Black students: Psychosocial issues and academic achievement*, edited by G. L. Berry and J. K. Asamen. Newbury Park, CA: Sage. (p. 266)

Graham, E. 1989b. Starting from scratch. *The Wall Street Journal* March 31: R4, R6. (p. 486)

Grant, C. A. 1990. Desegregation, racial attitudes, and intergroup contact: A discussion of change. *Phi Delta Kappan* 72 (1): 25–32. (p. 315)

Grant, G. 1988. *The world we created at Hamilton High 1953-1987*. Cambridge, MA: Harvard University Press. (p. 357)

Graue, M. E.; Weinstein, T.; and Walberg, H. J. 1982. *The effects of family-intervention programs on learning in early childhood: A meta-evaluation*. Unpublished manuscript. University of Illinois-Chicago Circle Office of Evaluation Research. (p. 115)

Grayson, D. A., and Martin, M. D. 1986. Gender expectations and student achievement. Paper presented at the annual meeting of the American Educational Research Association, San Francisco. (p. 427)

Greeley, A. M. 1963. *Religion and career*. New York: Sheed and Ward. (p. 35)

———. 1980. School desegregation and ethnicity. In *School desegregation: Past, present, and future*, edited by Walter G. Stephan and Joseph R. Feagin. New York: Plenum. (p. 348, 405)

Green, J. L. 1983. Research on teaching as a linguistic process. A state of the art. In *Review of research in education 10*, edited by Edmund W. Gordon. Washington, DC: American Educational Research Association. (p. 258)

Greenberg, H., and Davidson, H. 1972. Home background and school achievement of black urban ghetto children. *American Journal of Orthopsychiatry* 42: 803–810. (p. 259, 361)

Greene, M. S. 1989. Abuse, neglect rising in DC—Drugs ravage home life. *The Washington Post* September 10: A1. (p. 296)

Greider, W. 1988. The Rolling Stone survey. *Rolling Stone* No. 523: 34–54. (p. 180)

Gross, B., and Gross, R., eds. 1985. *The great school debate*. New York: Simon & Schuster Touchstone. (p. 537)

Gross, J. 1990. Bystander deaths reshape city lives. *The New York Times* August 12: 14. (pp. 21, 275)

Grunwald, P. 1990. The new generation of information systems. *Phi Delta Kappan* 72 (2): 113–114. (p. 519)

Gudat, S. 1988. Satellite network helps keep rural schools open. *Phi Delta Kappan* 69 (7): 533–534. (p. 444)

Guidubaldi, J. 1984. Adjusting to divorce. Paper presented at the annual meeting of the American Educational Research Association, New Orleans. (p. 126)

Guinagh, B. J., and Gordon, I. J. 1976. *School performance as a function of early stimulation*. Gainesville, FL: University of Florida Institute for Development of Human Resources. (p. 280)

Gurr, T. R., ed. 1989. *Violence in America*. Vol. 1. Newbury Park, CA: Sage. (pp. 196, 197)

Gursky, D. 1990. A plan that works. *Teacher Magazine* 1 (9): 46–54. (p. 145)

Guskey, T. R. 1985. *Implementing mastery learning*. Belmont, CA: Wadsworth. (p. 520)

———. 1990. Integrating innovations. *Educational Leadership* 47 (5): 11–15. (p. 524)

Guterson, D. 1990. When schools fail children. *Harper's* 281 (1686): 58–64. (p. 457)

Guttentag, M., and Ross, M. 1972. Movement responses in simple concept learning. *American Journal of Orthopsychiatry* 42: 657–665. (p. 259)

Guttentag, M., and Secord, P. F. 1983. *Too many women? The sex ratio question*. Beverly Hills. CA: Sage. (pp. 354, 435)

Guyer, B., et al. 1989. Intentional injuries among children and adolescents in Massachusetts. *New England Journal of Medicine* 321 (23): 1584–1589. (p. 196)

Hacker, A. H. 1979. Two "new classes" or none? In *The new class?*, edited by B. Bruce-Briggs. New Brunswick, NJ: Transaction. (p. 5)

———. 1988. Black crime, white racism. *The New Yorker Review of Books* 35 (3): 36–42. (pp. 15, 21, 219, 242, 364, 365)

———. 1990. Trans-national America. *The New York Review of Books* 37 (18): 19–24. (p. 349)

Haddad, W. D.; Carnoy, M.; Rinaldi, R.; and Regel, O. 1990. *Education and development*. Washington, DC: World Bank. (p. 415)

Haertel, E. 1985. *Comparing achievement in public and private schools*. Palo Alto, CA: Stanford University Institute for Research on Educational Finance and Governance. (p. 450)

———. 1991. Should the National Assessment of Educational Progress be used to compare the states? *Educational Researcher* 20 (3): 17. (p. 477)

Hafner, A.; Ingels, S.; Schneider, B.; and Stevenson, D. 1990. *A profile of the American eighth grader: NELS: 88 student descriptive summary*. Washington, DC: U.S. Government Printing Office (pp. 127, 172, 260, 359, 447)

Hafner, A. L. 1985. Gender differences in college students' educational and occupational aspirations: 1971–1983. Paper presented at the annual meeting of the American Educational Research Association, Chicago.

Hahn, A., and Lerman, R. 1985. *What works in youth employment policy?* Washington, DC: National Planning Association. (p. 186)

Hakuta, K. 1986. *Mirror of language*. New York: Basic Books. (pp. 376, 381)

Hakuta, K., and Gould, L. J. 1987. Synthesis of research on bilingual education. *Educational Leadership* 44 (6): 38–45. (p. 377)

Hale, P. D. 1990. Kansas City, Missouri: A comprehensive magnet plan. In *Magnet schools*, edited by Nolan Estes, Daniel U. Levine, and Donald R. Waldrip. Austin, TX: Morgan. (p. 326)

Hale-Benson, J. 1989. The school learning environment and academic success. In *Black students: Psychosocial issues and academic achievement*, edited by G. L. Berry and J. K. Asamen. Newbury Park, CA: Sage. (pp. 257, 357)

Hall, A. J. 1990. Immigration today. *National Geographic* 178 (3): 103–105. (p. 342)

Hall, S. J., and Henderson, A. 1990. Restructuring schools through parent involvement. *Network for Public Schools* 15 (6): 1, 3–8. (p. 145)

Hallinan, M. T., and Smith, S. S. 1989. Classroom characteristics and student friendship cliques. *Social Forces* 67 (4): 898–919. (p. 158)

Hallinan, M. T., and Teixeira, R. A. 1987. Students' interracial friendships: Individual characteristics, structural effects, and racial differences. *American Journal of Education* 95: 563–583. (p. 315)

Hallinan, M. T., and Williams, R. A. 1990. Students' characteristics and the peer-influence process. *Sociology of Education* 63 (2): 122–132. (pp. 116, 237, 317)

Halperin, S. 1988. *The forgotten half: Pathways to success for America's youth and young families*.

Washington, DC: William T. Grant Foundation Commission on Work, Family, and Citizenship. (p. 124)

Halpern, D. F. 1986. *Sex differences in cognitive abilities*. Hillsdale, NJ: Erlbaum. (pp. 417, 419, 435)

Halsey, A. H. 1976. Towards meritocracy? The case of Britain. In *Power and ideology in education*, edited by Jerome Karabel and A. H. Halsey. New York: Oxford University Press. (p. 230)

Halsey, A. H.; Heath, A. F.; and Ridge, J. M. 1980. *Origins and destinations: Family class and education in modern Britain*. New York: Oxford University Press. (p. 228)

Hamilton, D. N. 1991. An alternative to the rational planning model. In *Educational planning*, edited by Robert V. Carlson and Gary Awkerman. New York: Longman. (p. 526)

Hamilton, S. F. 1986. Raising standards and reducing dropout rates. *Teachers College Record* 87: 410–429. (p. 529)

———. 1990a. *Apprenticeship for adulthood*. New York:Free Press. (pp. 56, 195, 195)

———. 1990b. Calling for an American system of apprenticeship. *Education Week* 9 (37): 36. (p. 529)

Hammond, R., and Howard, J. P. 1986. Doing what's expected of you: The roots and the rise of the dropout culture. *Metropolitan Education* No. 2: 53–71. (p. 516)

Hampel, R. L. 1986. The last little citadel: *American high schools since 1940*. Boston: Houghton Mifflin. (p. 515)

Handlin, O. 1951. *The uprooted*. Boston: Little Brown. (p. 104)

———. 1959. *The newcomers*. Cambridge, MA: Harvard University Press. (pp. 104, 405)

Hanford, G. H. 1991. *Life with the SAT*. New York: The College Board. (p. 70)

Hanks, M. 1979. Race, sexual status and athletics in the process of educational achievement. *Social Science Quarterly* 60 (3): 482–496. (p. 163)

Hansen, D. A. 1986. Family-school articulations: The effects of interaction rule mismatch. *American Educational Research Journal* 23: 643–659. (p. 63)

Hansen, J. S. 1986. Student loans: Are they overburdening a generation? Paper prepared for the Joint Economic Committee of the U.S. Congress.

Hanson, D. J. 1980. Drug education: Does it work? In *Drugs and the youth culture*, edited by Frank R. Scarpitti and Susan K. Datesman. Beverly Hills, CA: Sage. (p. 201)

Harber, J. R., and Bryan, D. N. 1976. Black English and the teaching of reading. *Review of Education Research* 46: 387–405. (p. 358)

Harp, L. 1990. Ky. districts seen jumping on reform bandwagon. *Education Week* 9 (40): 36. (p. 487)

———. 1991. Texas drive to modify no-pass, no-play policy stalls. *Education Week* 10 (36): 16. (p. 503)

Harper's editors. 1985. Images of fear. *Harper's* 270 (No. 2620): 41. (p. 120)

Harris, B. 1978. *Beyond her sphere: Women and the professions in American history*. Westport, CT: Greenwood. (p. 435)

Harris, E. W. 1988. An "up" experience with minority achievement. *The School Administrator* 45 (4): 34–35. (p. 357)

Harris, N., et al. 1975. *The integration of American schools: Problems, experiences, solutions*. Boston: Allyn and Bacon. (p. 338)

Harris, T. L., and Cooper, E. J. 1985. *Reading, thinking, and concept development*. New York: College Entrance Examination Board. (pp. 512, 513, 523)

Harrison, B. 1972a. Education and underemployment in the urban ghetto. *American Economic Review* 62: 796–812. (p. 241)

———. 1972b. *Education, training, and the urban ghetto*. Baltimore: The Johns Hopkins University Press. (p. 18)

Harrison, C. H. 1987. *Student service*. Princeton, NJ: The Carnegie Foundation for the Advancement of Teaching.

Hart, A. W. 1987. A career ladder's effect on teacher career and work attitudes. *American Educational Research Journal* 24 (8): 479–503.

———. 1990. Impacts of the school social unit on teacher authority during work redesign. *American Educational Research Journal* 27 (3): 503–532. (p. 481)

Hart, A. W., and Murphy, M. J. 1990. Career ladders and work in schools. In *The educational reform movement of the 1980s*, edited by Joseph Murphy. Berkeley, CA: McCutchan. (pp. 480, 481)

Hart, G. 1987. Education: The key to America's third century. *Congressional Record—Senate* February 3: S1527–S1530. (p. 71)

Hart, L. E. 1989. Classroom processes, sex of student, and confidence in learning mathematics. *Journal for Research in Mathematics Education* 20 (3): 242–260. (p. 424)

Hartle, T. 1990. Federal support for higher education in the 90's. *Change* 22 (4): 3–41. (p. 62)

Hartup, W. W. 1989. Social relationships and their developmental significance. *American Psychologist* 44: 120–126. (pp. 153, 157)

Harvey, G. 1984. Recent reports concerning education or the road to Nirvana: You can't get there from here. Paper presented at the annual meeting of the American Educational Research Association, New Orleans. (p. 491)

Haskins, R. 1989. Beyond metaphor. The efficacy of early childhood education. *American Psychologist* 44 (2): 274–282. (pp. 279, 280)

Hatchett, D. 1986. A conflict of reasons and remedies. *The Crisis* 93 (3): 36–41, 46–47. (p. 354)

Haveman, R. 1988. *Starting even: An equal opportunity program to combat the nation's new poverty.* New York: Simon & Schuster. (p. 206)

Havighurst, R. J. 1964. *The public schools of Chicago.* Chicago: Chicago Public Schools. (p. 239)

———. 1966. Overcoming value differences. In *The inner city classroom: Teacher behaviors,* edited by Robert D. Strom. Columbus, OH: Merrill. (p. 99)

———. 1971a. Minority subcultures and the law of effect. In *Educating the disadvantaged,* edited by Allan C. Ornstein et al. New York: AMS Press. (p. 398)

———. 1971b. Nurturing the cognitive skills in health. *Journal of School Health* 42 (2): 73–76. (p. 132)

———. 1976. The relative importance of social class and ethnicity in human development. *Human Development* 19: 56–64. (p. 132)

Havighurst, R. J.; Bowman, P. H.; Liddle, G. F.; Mathews, C. V.; and Pierce, J. V. 1962. *Growing up in River City.* New York: John Wiley. (pp. 8, 214)

Havighurst, R. J., and Morgan, H. G. 1951. *The social history of a war-boom community.* New York: Longmans, Green. (p. 7)

Hawkins, R. B., Jr. 1982. Tuition tax credits: Another voice. *American Education* 18 (8): 9–10. (p. 452)

Hawley, R. A. 1990. The bumpy road to drug-free schools. *Phi Delta Kappan* 72 (4): 310–314. (p. 201)

Hawley, W. D. 1983. Achieving quality integrated education with or without federal help. *Phi Delta Kappan* 64 (5): 334–338. (p. 303)

Hawley, W. D., and Smylie, M. A. 1988. The contributions of school desegregation to academic achievement and racial integration. In *Eliminating racism,* edited by Phyllis A. Katz and Dalmas A. Taylor, New York: Plenum. (pp. 303, 307, 311)

Hawley, W. D., et al. 1982. *Strategies for effective desegregation: Lessons from research.* Lexington, MA: Lexington Books. (p. 303)

Healy, J. M. 1990. Chaos on Sesame Street. *American Educator* 14 (4): 22–27, 39. (p. 136)

Heath, S. B. 1983. *Ways with words: Language, life, and work in communities and classroom.* New York: Cambridge University Press. (p. 234)

Heath, S. B., and McLaughlin, M. W. 1987. A child resource policy: Moving beyond dependence on school and family. *Phi Delta Kappan* 68 (8): 576–580. (pp. 112, 170, 234)

———. 1991. Community organizations as family. *Phi Delta Kappan* 72 (8): 623–627. (p. 175)

Heath, T. 1988. Fairfax teachers endorse merit pay. *The Washington Post* September 30: B8. (p. 481)

Heckman, P. E. 1991. Evidence, values, and the revitalization of schools. *Educational Leadership* 48 (2): 14–15. (pp. 500, 502)

Hedges, C. 1990. The violent debate over tribal sovereignty. *The New York Times* September 23: ES 9 (pp. 388, 389)

Heffernan, D., and Tarlov, S. 1989. *Service opportunities for youth.* Washington, DC: Children's Defense Fund. (p. 206)

Helge, D., and Marrs, L. 1981. *Personal recruitment and retention in rural America.* Bellingham: Western Washington University. (p. 442)

Helgesen, S. 1990. *The female advantage.* New York: Doubleday. (p. 169)

Hemmings, A. 1991. High-achieving black high school students and model student image. Paper presented at the annual meeting of the American Educational Research Association, Chicago. (pp. 357, 515)

Henderson, A., and Marburger, C. 1990. Ten pitfalls of school-based improvement. *Network for Public Schools* 15 (5): 3–5. (p. 485)

Henderson, R. D., and von Euler, M., eds. 1977. *School desegregation in metropolitan areas: Choices and prospects.* Washington, DC: U.S. Government Printing Office. (p. 338)

Hendrickson, G. L. 1977. Review of Title I evaluation studies. Paper presented at the annual meeting of the American Educational Research Association, Los Angeles. (p. 284)

Henricksen, B., and Morgan T. E., eds. 1990. *Reorientations.* Urbana: University of Illinois Press. (pp. 247, 254)

Hentoff, N. 1977. *Does anybody give a damn?* New York: Knopf. (p. 306)

Herbers, J. 1986. *The new heartland*. New York: New York Times Books. (p. 87)

———. 1987. Poverty of blacks spreads to cities. *The New York Times* January 26: AI, A27. (p. 75)

Herbert, V. 1991. Alternatives can be the answer to at-risk students. *The Executive Educator* 13 (12): 30, 35. (p. 529)

Herndon, J. 1968. *The way it spozed to be*. New York: Bantam. (pp. 98, 297, 515)

Herrnstein, R. J. 1982. IQ testing and the media. *The Atlantic* 250 (2): 68–74. (p. 67)

———. 1990. Still an American dilemma. *The Public Interest* No. 98 (Winter): 3–17. (p. 67)

Hess, A. G., Jr., and Addington, H. 1990. *Chicago school reform: What it is and how it came to be*. Chicago: Chicago Panel on School Policy and Finance. (p. 485)

Hess, A. G., Jr., and Laubec, D. 1985. *Dropouts from the Chicago public schools*. Chicago: Chicago Panel on Public Schools Policy and Finance. (p. 81)

Hess, A. G., Jr.; Lewis, J.; Laine, R. D.; and Gilbert, A. M. 1991. *The inequity in Illinois school finance*. Chicago: EdEquity Coalition. (pp. 75, 485)

Hess, J.; Ottinger, C.; and Lippincott, J. 1990. A decade of change: The status of U.S. women doctorates, 1978–88. *American Council on Education Research Briefs* 1 (6): 1–8. (pp. 354, 422, 423)

Hess, R. D., and McDevitt, T. M. 1984. Some cognitive consequences of maternal intervention techniques: A longitudinal study. *Child Development* 55: 2017–2030. (p. 112)

Hess, R. D., and Shipman, V. C. 1965. Early experience and the socialization of cognitive modes in children. *Child development* 36: 869–886. (pp. 107, 235)

Hess, R. D., and Torney, J. 1967. *The development of political attitudes in children*. Chicago: Aldine. (p. 148)

Hewlett, S. A. 1991. Running hard just to keep up. *Time* 136 (19): 54. (p. 156)

Higgins, J. J. 1990. Computer report card. *Business Week* No. 3191: 40ED. (p. 438)

Higham, J. 1990. The pot that didn't melt. *The New York Review of Books* 37 (6): 11–13. (p. 349)

Hilke, E. V. 1990. *Cooperative learning*. Bloomington, IN: Phi Delta Kappa. (pp. 156, 316, 521, 522)

Hill, D. 1990. A theory of success and failure. *Teacher* 1 (9): 40–45. (p. 357)

Hillard, A. G. III. 1989/1990. Teaching and cultural styles in a pluralist society. *Rethinking schools* 4 (2): 3. (pp. 259, 399)

Hilts, P. J. 1990a. Birth-control backlash. *The New York Times Magazine* December 16: 41, 55, 70–74. (p. 203)

———. 1990b. U.S. opens a drive on lead poisoning in nation's young. *The New York Times* December 20: A1, A16. (p. 132)

Hindelang, M. J. 1981. Variations in sex-race-age-specific incidence rates of offending. *American Sociological Review* 46: 461–474. (p. 120)

Hinds M. 1990. Cutting the dropout rate: High goal but low hopes. *The New York Times* February 17: 1, 11. (p. 528)

Hobbs, D. J. 1990. *Education reform and rural economic health: Policy implications*. Charleston, WV: Appalachia Educational Laboratory. (p. 442)

Hobinger, P. C., and Offer, D. 1982. Prediction of adolescent suicide: A population model. *American Journal of Psychiatry* 139: 302–307. (p. 184)

Hodges, H. M., Jr. 1968. Peninsula people: Social stratification in a metropolitan complex. In *Permanence and change in social class*, edited by Clayton Lane. Cambridge, MA: Schenkman. (pp. 8, 10)

Hoffer, T. B., and Coleman, J. S. 1990. Changing families and communities: Implications for schools. In *Educational leadership and changing contexts of families, communities*, edited by B. Mitchell and L. Cunningham. Chicago: University of Chicago Press. (p. 126)

Hoffman, L. W. 1988. Changes in family roles, socialization, and sex differences. In *Childhood socialization*, edited by Gerald Handel. New York: Aldine de Gruyter. (p. 420)

Hogan, D. 1982. Education and class formation: The peculiarities of the Americans. In *Cultural and economic reproduction in education*, edited by Michael Apple. Boston: Routledge and Kegan Paul.

Holland, A., and Andre, T. 1988. Participants in extracurricular activities in secondary school: What is known, what needs to be known? *Review of Educational Research* 57 (4): 437–466. (pp. 162, 164)

Holland, C. 1988. Doctor of sexology. *Psychology Today* 22 (5): 45–48.

Holland, J. 1980. *Women's occupational choice*. Stockholm, Sweden: Stockholm Institute of Education. (p. 434)

——. 1981. Social class and changes in orientation to meaning. *Sociology* 15 (February): 1–18. (p. 234)

Holland, S. H. 1989. Fighting the epidemic of failure. *Teacher Magazine* 1 (1): 88–89. (p. 356)

Hollifield, J. 1990. State education finance systems inequitable, immoral and illegal. *RTD Review* 5 (1): 1–3. (p. 295)

Hollingshead, A. B. 1949. *Elmtown's youth*. New York: John Wiley. (pp. 7, 35)

——. 1957. *Two factor index of social position*. New Haven, CT: Yale Station. (p. 2)

Holmes, M. 1988. A pessimistic conclusion—education and the public school. In *Cultural literacy and the idea of general education*, edited by Ian Westbury and Alan Purves. Chicago: University of Chicago Press. (pp. 107, 112, 230, 240)

Holmes, S. A. 1990. In Florida, a private company will operate a public school. *The New York Times* December 7: A1, A16. (p. 436)

Holznagel, D. 1990. *A depiction of distance education in the Northwest Region*. Portland. OR: Northwest Regional Educational Laboratory. (p. 445)

Holznagel, D. C., and Olson, T. 1990. *A study of distance education policies in state education agencies*. Portland, OR: Northwest Regional Educational Laboratory. (pp. 444, 445)

Honig, B. 1990. School vouchers: Dangerous claptrap. *The New York Times* June 29: A13. (p. 501)

Hoover, E. M., and Vernon, R. 1959. *Anatomy of a metropolis*. Cambridge, MA: Harvard University Press. (p. 86)

Hoover-Dempsey, K. V.; Bassler, O. C.; and Brissie, J. S. 1987. Parent involvement: Contributions of teacher efficacy, school socioeconomic status and other school characteristics. *American Educational Research Journal*. 24 (3): 417–437. (p. 143)

Hope, K. 1982. A liberal theory of prestige. *American Journal of Sociology* 87: 1011–1031. (p. 2)

Hornberger, N. H. 1990. Creating successful learning contexts for bilingual literacy. *Teachers College Record* 92 (2):212–229. (p. 378)

Horner, M. A. 1969. Fail: Bright women. *Psychology Today* 3 (6): 36–38. (p. 422)

Horowitz, J. M., and Lafferty, E. 1990. Work that body! *Time* 136 (19): 68. (p. 426)

Hout, M. 1988. More universalism, less structural mobility: The American occupation structure in the 1980s. *American Journal of Sociology* 93 (6): 1358:1400. (pp. 225, 226, 229)

Howe, F. 1982. Feminist scholarship. *Change* 14 (3): 12–20.

Howe, H. II. 1990. Thinking about the forgotten half. *Teachers College Record* 92 (2): 293–305. (pp. 124, 183)

Howe, W. J. 1988. Education and demographics. *Monthly Labor Review* 111 (1): 3–9. (pp. 15, 23, 25)

Howell, F. M., and McBroom, L. W. 1982. Social relations at home and at school: An analysis of the correspondence principle. *Sociology of Education* 55 (1): 40–52. (p. 239)

Huba, G. J., and Bentler, P. M. 1980. The role of peer and adult models for drug taking at different stages in adolescence. *Journal of Youth and Adolescence* 9: 449–465. (p. 200)

Huberman, A. M., and Miles, M. B. 1982. *Motivation up close: A field study in 12 school settings*. Andover, MA: The Network. (p. 525)

Hughes, J. W., and Sternlieb, G. 1990. Home steep home. *American Demographics* 12 (1): 40–43, 64. (p. 25)

Hulbert, A. 1984. Children as parents. *The New Republic* 191 (11): 15–22. (p. 204)

——. 1990. Poor conceptions. *The New Republic* 203 (20): 21–23. (pp. 203, 204)

Hume, M. 1988. Presidential commission reviews education voucher proposals. *Education Daily* 21 (54): 1–2. (p. 453)

Hunt, D. E. 1965. *Indicators of developmental change in lower class children*. Cooperative Research Project S–166. Syracuse, NY: Syracuse University. (p. 269)

——. 1975. Person-environment interaction: A challenge found wanting before it was tried. *Review of Educational Research* 45: 209–230. (pp. 269, 397)

Hunt, D. E., et al. 1974. Students conceptual level and models of teaching: Theoretical and empirical coordination of two models. *Interchange* 5 (3): 19–30. (p. 269)

Hunt, J. M. 1979. Psychological development: Early experience. *Annual Review of Psychology* 30: 103–143. (pp. 108, 133)

Hurn, C. J. 1978. *The limits and possibilities of schooling*. Boston: Allyn and Bacon. (p. 253)

Hyman, J. S., and Cohen, S. A. 1979. Learning for mastery: Ten conclusions after 15 years and 3,000 schools. *Educational Leadership* 37: 104–109. (p. 521)

Ianni, F. A. J. 1980. A positive note on schools and discipline. *Educational Leadership* (March): 452–458. (p. 277)

———. 1989a. Providing a structure for adolescent development. *Phi Delta Kappan* 70 (9): 673–689. (pp. 152, 154, 164, 207)

———. 1989b. *The search for structure*. New York: Macmillan. (pp. 94, 153, 154, 164, 166, 168, 169)

Idol, L., and Jones, B. F., eds. 1991. *Educational values andcognitive instruction: Implications for reform*. Hillsdale, NJ: Erlbaum. (pp. 269, 466, 512, 513, 516, 533)

Iiams, T. M. 1977. The gathering storm over bilingual education. *Phi Delta Kappan* 59: 226–230. (p. 381)

Inciardi, J. A. 1980. Youth, drugs, and street crime. In *Drugs and the youth culture*, edited by Frank R. Scarpitti and Susan K. Datesman. Beverly Hills, CA: Sage. (p. 201)

Inglehart, R. 1990. *Culture shift in advanced industrial society*. Princeton, NJ: Princeton University. (pp. 180, 181, 182)

Inkeles, A., et al. 1983. *Exploring individual modernity*. New York: Columbia University Press. (p. 236)

Inkeles, A., and Smith, D. H. 1974. *Becoming modern: Individual change in countries*. Cambridge, MA: Harvard University Press. (p. 236)

International Association for the Evaluation of Education Achievement. 1988. *Science Achievement in Seventeen Countries*. Oxford: Pergamon. (p. 464)

Irvine, J. J. 1986. Teacher-student interactions: Effects of student race, sex, and grade. *Journal of Educational Psychology* 78 (1): 14–21. (p. 424)

Ivens, S. H., and Koslin, B. L. 1991. *Demands for reading literacy require new accountability methods*. Brewster, NY: Touchstone Applied Science Associates. (p. 477)

Jackson, P. W. 1968. *Life in classrooms*. New York: Holt. (p. 514)

Jacobs, J. A. 1989. *Revolving doors: Sex segregation in women's careers*. Palo Alto, CA: Stanford University Press. (p. 421)

Jacobson, R. L. 1986. Teacher unions give qualified backing to Carnegie proposals on school reform. *The Chronicle of Higher Education* 32 (20): 1, 22. (p. 495)

Jaeger, S., and Sandhu, H. 1985. Southeast Asian refugees: English language development and acculturation. *Focus* No. 21: 1–4. (p. 384)

Jaen, V. 1990. Chicano discrimination. *Equity and Excellence* 24 (4): 21–22. (p. 369)

Jaffe, F. S., and Dryfoos, J. G. 1980. Fertility control services for adolescents: Access and utilization. In *Adolescent pregnancy and childbearing: Findings from research*. Washington, DC: U.S. Government Printing Office. (p. 204)

Jaroff, L. 1991. Controlling a childhood menace. *Time* 137 (8): 68–69. (p. 132)

Jaschik, S. 1990a. Student-aid changes affect blacks more, a UCLA study finds. *The Chronicle of Higher Education* 37 (7): A21, A28. (pp. 62, 64, 363)

———. 1990b. U.S. accuses UCLA of bias against Asian Americans. *The Chronicle of Higher Education* 32 (6): A1, A24. (p. 387)

———. 1991. Record number of freshmen plan to join protests on campuses, survey prior to Gulf War shows. *The Chronicle of Higher Education* 37 (20): A1, A32. (p. 180)

Jencks, C. 1979. *Who gets ahead? The determinants of economic success in America*. New York: Basic Books. (pp. 227, 228)

———. 1991. Is violent crime increasing? *The American Prospect* No. 4: 98–109. (pp. 120, 185, 196, 364)

Jencks, C., et al. 1972. *Inequality: A reassessment of the effects of family and schooling in America*. New York: Basic Books. (pp. 227, 364)

———. 1987. Genes and crimes. *The New York Review of Books* 34 (2): 33–41. (pp. 67, 198)

Jencks, C., and Mayer, S. 1989. *The social consequences of growing up in a poor neighborhood: A review*. Evanston, IL: Northwestern University Center for Urban Affairs and Policy Research. (p. 313)

Jennings, L. 1989. Shootings cause 11% of youths' deaths, study finds. *Education Week* 9 (10): 20. (p. 185)

———. 1990. Parents as partners. *Education Week* 9 (40): 23–32. (pp. 142, 143, 144)

Jensen, A. R. 1968. Social class, race, and genetics: Implications for education. *American Educational Research Journal* 5: 1–42. (p. 67)

———. 1969. How much can we boost IQ and scholastic achievement? *Harvard Education Review* 39: 1–123. (p. 67)

———. 1980. *Bias in mental testing*. New York: The Free Press. (pp. 67, 68)

———. 1981. *Straight talk about mental tests*. New York: The Free Press. (p. 68)

Jessor, R.; Chase, J. A.; and Donovan, J. E. 1980. Psychosocial correlates of marijuana use and problem drinking in a national sample of adolescents. *American Journal of Public Health* 70: 604–613. (pp. 155, 200)

Jessor, R., and Jessor, S. L. 1977. *Problem behavior and psychosocial development: A longitudinal study of youth.* New York: Academic Press. (p. 210)

Johnson, D. 1990a. Milwaukee creating 2 schools just for black boys. *The New York Times* September 30: 1, 18. (p. 355)

———. 1990b. Move to suburbs spurs the poor to seek work. *The New York Times* May 1: A9. (p. 336)

———. 1991a. Census finds many claiming new identity: Indian. *The New York Times* March 5: A1, A10. (pp. 76, 387)

———. 1991b. Discovered, at edge of known civilization, the sub-suburb. *The New York Times* April 29: E6. (p. 76)

Johnson, D. W., and Johnson, R. T. 1981. The key to healthy development and socialization. *Character* 2 (11): 1–8. (p. 166)

———. 1984. *Cooperative learning.* New Brighton, MA: Interaction Books. (p. 157)

———. 1989/1990. Social skills for successful group work. *Educational Leadership* 47 (4): 29–33. (p. 316)

———. 1990. *Cooperation and competition: Theory and research.* Hillsdale, NJ: Erlbaum. (pp. 157, 316)

Johnson, K. 1989. Recent population redistribution trends in nonmetropolitan America. Paper prepared at Loyola University of Chicago. (pp. 72, 442)

Johnson, L. B. 1965. Message from the President of the United States relative to the problems and future of the central city and its suburbs, March 2. (p. 337)

Johnson, N. J., and Sanday, P. R. 1971. Subcultural variations in an urban population. *American Anthropologist* 73: 128–143. (p. 355)

Johnson, W. R. 1990. Inviting conversations: The Holmes Group and tomorrow's schools. *American Educational Research Journal* 27 (4): 581–588. (p. 474)

Johnston, L. D.; O'Malley, P. M.; and Bachman, J. G. 1990. *Drug use, drinking, and smoking.* Rockville, MD: National Institute on Drug Abuse. (p. 189)

Jones, B. F.; Friedman, L. B.; Tinzmann, M.; and Cox, B. F. 1985. Enriched mastery learning: A model of enriched comprehension instruction. In *Improving student achievement through mastery learning programs,* edited by Daniel U. Levine. San Francisco: Jossey-Bass. (p. 513)

Jones, B. F., and Idol, L., eds. 1990. *Dimensions of thinking and cognitive instruction.* Hillsdale, NJ: Erlbaum. (pp. 512, 513)

Jones, B. F., and Spady, W. G. 1985. Enhanced mastery learning as a solution to the two sigma problem. In *Improving student achievement through mastery learning programs,* edited by Daniel U. Levine. San Francisco: Jossey-Bass. (p. 521)

Jones, E. 1988. Students at risk in a global society. *The School Administrator* 45 (1): 31–32. (pp. 315, 471)

Jones, E. F., et al. 1986. *Teenage pregnancy in industrialized countries.* New Haven, CT: Yale University Press. (pp. 203, 513)

Jones, J. M. 1988. Racism in black and white. In *Eliminating racism,* edited by Phyllis A. Katz and Dalmas A. Taylor. New York: Plenum. (p. 329)

Jones, M. G. 1991. Gender issues in teacher education. In *Education 91/92* edited by F. Schultz. Guilford, CN: Dushkin. (p. 424)

Jordhal, G. 1991. Breaking down classroom walls: Distance learning comes of age. *Technology and learning.* 11 (5): 72–78. (p. 444)

Jordan, C. 1984. Cultural compatibility and the education of Hawaiian children: Implications for mainland educators. *Education Research Quarterly* 8 (4): 59–69. (pp. 397, 398)

Joyce, B., ed. 1990. *Changing school culture through staff development.* Arlington, VA: Association for Supervision and Curriculum Development. (pp. 524, 525, 526)

Joyce, B.; Murphy, C.; Showers, B.; and Murphy, J. 1989. *School renewal and cultural change.* 47 (3): 70–77. (p. 524)

Joyce, B., and Showers, B. 1987. The power of school. *Phi Delta Kappan* 68: 352–355. (p. 95)

———. 1988. *Student achievement through staff development.* New York: Longman. (p. 524)

Kagan, J. 1984. *The nature of the child.* New York: Basic Books. (p. 147)

Kagan, J., and Klein, R. E. 1973. Cross-cultural perspectives on early development. *American Psychologist* 28: 947–961. (p. 133)

Kagan, S. 1989/1990. The structural approach to cooperative learning. *Educational Leadership* 47 (4): 12–15. (p. 316)

———. ed. 1991. *The care and education of America's young children: Obstacles and opportunities.* Chicago: University of Chicago Press. (p. 298)

Kahl, J. A. 1957. *The American class structure.* New York: Holt, Rinehart & Winston. (p. 34)

Kallen, H. M. 1924. *Culture and democracy in the United States.* New York: Boni and Liveright. (p. 347)

Kamarck, E. A., and Galston, W. A. 1990. *Putting children first: A progressive family policy for the 1990s.* Washington, DC: Progressive Policy Institute. (pp. 16, 129, 145, 156, 165, 183, 197)

Kamerman, S. B. 1991. Starting right. What we owe to children under three. *The American Prospect* No. 4: 63–68. (p. 116)

Kantrowitz, B., and Wingert, P. 1991. Putting values in diplomas. *Newsweek* 118 (3): 62. (p. 478)

Kaplan, G. 1991. Suppose they gave an intergenerational conflict and nobody came. *Phi Delta Kappan* 72 (9): K1–K12. (pp. 31, 35)

Karabel, J., and Halsey, A. H. 1977. Educational research: A review and interpretation. In *Power, ideology and education,* edited by J. Karabel and A. H. Halsey. New York: Oxford University Press. (p. 253)

Karen, R. 1990. Becoming attached. *The Atlantic Monthly* 265 (2): 35–70. (p. 113)

Karoniaktatie. 1986. Indian unemployment commentary. *Awkesasne Notes* 18 (5): 11–13. (p. 388)

Karp, S. 1991. Reflections on African American immersion schools. *Rethinking Schools* 5 (4): 18–19. (p. 355)

Kasarda, D. J., and Billy, J. O. G. 1985. Social mobility and fertility. In *Annual review of sociology,* edited by Ralph H. Turner and James F. Short, Jr. Palo Alto, CA: Annual Reviews. (p. 219)

Kass, J. 1990. Magnet schools discriminate against poor, Kimbrough says. *Chicago Tribune* August 4: 1, 5. (pp. 51, 330)

Katz, I. 1964. Review of evidence relating to effects of desegregation on the intellectual performance of Negroes. *American Psychologist* 19: 381–399. (p. 290)

Katz, M. B. 1968. *The irony of early school reform.* Cambridge, MA: Harvard University Press. (p. 247)

———. 1975. *Class, bureaucracy, and schools.* New York: Praeger. (p. 247)

Kaus, M. 1990. For a new equality. *The New Republic* 202 (19): 18–27. (p. 229)

Kean, T. H. 1986. Who will teach? *Phi Delta Kappan* 68 (3): 205–207. (p. 468)

Keating, P. 1990. Striving for sex equity in schools. In *Access to knowledge,* edited by John I. Goodlad and Pamela Keating. New York: College Entrance Examination Board. (pp. 410, 416, 420, 423, 424, 425, 426)

Keefe, S. E.; Reck, U. M. L.; and Reck, G. 1983. Ethnicity and education in Southern Appalachia: A review. *Ethnic Groups* 5: 199–226. (pp. 395, 439)

Keith, T. Z., and Page, E. B. 1985. Do Catholic high schools improve minority students achievement? *American Educational Research Journal* 22 (3): 337–349. (p. 449)

Keniston, K. 1972. *Youth and dissent.* New York: Harcourt Brace Jovanovich. (p. 178)

Keniston, K., and Carnegie Council on Children. 1977. *All our children. The American family under pressure.* New York: Harcourt Brace Jovanovich. (p. 123)

Kennedy, E. 1991. School readiness act. *Congressional Record—Senate* April 24: S4986–S5002. (pp. 279, 280)

Kennedy, M. M. 1987. *The effectiveness of Chapter 1 services.* Washington, DC: U.S. Government Printing Office. (p. 284)

Kennedy, M. M.; Jung, R. K.; and Orland, M. E. 1986. *Poverty, achievement and the distribution of compensatory education services.* Washington, DC: U.S. Government Printing Office. (p. 284)

Kerman, S. 1979. Teacher expectations and student achievement. *Phi Delta Kappan* 60: 716–718. (p. 518)

Kerr, P. 1989. Suburbs and a blighted city foresee a future in common. *The New York Times* September 7: 1, 11. (p. 76)

Kessler, C., and Quinn, M. E. 1977. Child-language development in two socio-economic environments. Paper presented at the annual meeting of the American Educational Research Association, Los Angeles. (p. 268)

Kett, J. F. 1977. *Rites of passage: Adolescence in America 1970 to the present.* New York: Basic Books. (p. 174)

Kiesler, S.; Sproull, L.; and Eccles, J. S. 1983. Second-class citizens? *Psychology Today* 17 (3): 42–48. (p. 439)

Kifner, J. 1991. Abducted Chinese illegal aliens rescued. *The New York Times* January 8: B3. (p. 382)

Kilborn, P. T. 1990. Youths lacking special skills find jobs leading nowhere. *The New York Times* November 27: 1, 11. (pp. 21, 23, 185, 229)

Killmann, R. H. *Managing beyond the quick fix*. San Francisco: Jossey-Bass. (p. 503)

Kim, H. 1977. Education of the Korean immigrant child. *Integrated Education* 15 (Jan.-Feb.): 15–18. (p. 399)

Kimmel, M. 1988. Ms. Scoutmaster. *Psychology Today* 22 (5): 64–65. (p. 170)

Kimura, D. 1985. Male brain, female brain: The hidden difference. *Psychology Today* 19 (11): 50–58. (pp. 418, 419)

———. 1989. How sex hormones boost—or cut—intellectual ability. *Psychology Today* 23 (1): 62–66. (pp. 417, 418)

King, W. 1990. From angry city streets to green lawns and back. *The New York Times* March 16: A16. (p. 94)

Kingston, P. W., and Lewis, L. S. 1990. Undergraduates at elite institutions: The best, the brightest, and the richest. In *The high-status track*, edited by Paul William Kingston and Lionel S. Lewis. Albany: State University of New York Press. (pp. 11, 52)

———. eds. 1990. *The high-status track*. Albany: State University of New York Press. (p. 52)

Kingston, P. W., and Smart, J. C. 1990. The economic pay-off of prestigious colleges. In *The high-status track*, edited by Paul William Kingston and Lionel S. Lewis. Albany: State University of New York Press. (pp. 52, 53)

Kinnamen, D. E. 1990. The next decade: What the future holds. *Technology and Learning* 11 (1): 42–44, 46–49. (p. 519)

Kirsch, I. S., and Jungeblut, A. 1986. *Literacy: Profiles of America's young adults*. Princeton, NJ: Educational Testing Service. (pp. 47, 71)

———. 1978. *Opening and closing*. Cambridge: Cambridge University Press.

Klapp, O. E. 1969. *Collective search for identity*. New York: Holt, Rinehart & Winston. (p. 96)

Klausmeier, H. J. 1985. *Educational psychology*. New York: Harper and Row. (p. 513)

Kleifgen, J. A. 1989. Computers and opportunities for learning development. *ERIC Clearinghouse on Urban Education Digest* No. 54: 1–2. (pp. 438, 439)

Klein, J. 1990. Russians aren't coming. *New York* 23 (31): 16, 19.

Klein, N. D. 1977. *Special education: Definition, law and policy*. Cleveland: Cleveland State University, mimeographed. (p. 134)

Klein, S. F., ed. 1990. *Handbook for achieving sex equity through education*. 2nd ed. Baltimore: The Johns Hopkins University Press. (pp. 343, 427)

Klein, Z., and Eshel, Y. 1980. *Integrating Jerusalem's schools*. New York: Academic Press. (p. 313)

Klingelhofer, E. L., and Longacre, B. J. 1972. A case in point. *The Research Reporter* 7 (3): 5–7. (p. 288)

Knapp, M. S., and Needels, M. 1991. Review of research on curriculum and instruction in literacy. In *Better schooling for the children of poverty: Alternatives to conventional wisdom*, edited by Michael S. Knapp and Patrick M. Shields. Berkeley, CA: McCutchan. (p. 358)

Knapp, M. S., and Shields, P. M., eds. 1991 *Better schooling for the children of poverty: Alternatives to conventional wisdom*. Berkeley, CA: McCutchan. (p. 298)

Knapp, M. S., et al. 1991. *What is taught, and how, to the children of poverty*. Washington, DC: U.S. Department of Education. (pp. 261, 262)

Knepper, P. R. 1991. Do seniors from schools with higher academic scores have superior life outcomes? Paper presented at the annual meeting of the American Educational Research Association, Chicago. (p. 41)

Knight, R. V. 1982. City development in advanced industrial societies. In *Cities in the 21st century*, edited by Gary Gappert and Richard V. Knight. Beverly Hills, CA: Sage. (p. 82)

Kniker, C. R. 1985. Reflections on the continuing crusade for common schools: Glorious failures, shameful harvests, or . . . ? In *Religious schooling in America*, edited by James C. Carper and Thomas C. Hunt. Birmingham, AL: Religious Education Press. (pp. 457, 458)

Knowles, J. G.; Marlow, S. E.; and Muchmore, J. A. 1992. From pedagogy to ideology: origins and phases of home schools in the United States, 1970–1990. *American Journal of Education* February, in press. (p. 456)

Kohlberg, L. 1966. Moral education in the schools: A developmental view. *School Review* 74: 1–29. (p. 174)

Kohn, A. 1989. Home schooling. *The Atlantic Monthly* 261 (4): 20–25. (p. 456)

———. 1990. The ABC's of caring. *Teacher Magazine* 1 (4): 52–58. (pp. 157, 232)

———. 1991. Caring kids. *Phi Delta Kappan* 72 (7): 496–506. (p. 157)

Kohn, M. L. 1969. *Class and conformity: A study in values.* Homewood, IL: Dorsey. (pp. 231, 236)

———. 1987. Cross-national research as an analytic strategy. *American Sociological Review* 52: 713–731. (pp. 231, 236)

Kohn, M. L.; et al. 1990. Position in the class structure and psychological functioning in the United States, Japan, and Poland. *American Journal of Sociology* 95 (4): 864–1008. (pp. 231, 236)

Kohn, M. L., and Schooler, C. 1973. Occupational experience and psychological functioning: An assessment of reciprocal effects. *American Sociological Review* 38: 97–118. (p. 232)

Kolata, G. 1990. Program helped underweight babies, study shows. *The New York Times* June 13: A10. (p. 290)

Kolata, G. B. 1980. Math and sex: Are girls born with less ability? *Science* 210 (12): 1234–1235. (p. 418)

Kolstad, A. J., and Owings, J. A. 1986. *High school dropouts who change their minds about school.* Washington, DC: U.S. Department of Education. (p. 51)

Komisar, L. 1972. *The new feminism.* New York: Warner Books. (p. 435)

Konopka, G. 1977. *Young girls: A portrait of adolescence.* Englewood Cliffs, NJ: Prentice-Hall. (p. 170)

Koretz, D. 1991. State comparisons using NAEP: Large costs, disappointing benefits. *Educational Researcher* 20 (3): 19–21. (p. 477)

Koretz, D., and Vantresca, M. 1984. *Poverty among children.* Washington, DC: U.S. Congressional Budget Office.

Koretz, G. 1990. Not everyone is so worried about the r-word. *Business Week* No. 3193: 14. (p. 413)

———. 1991a. Economic trends. *Business Week* No. 3199: 16. (pp. 116, 117, 353)

———. 1991b. The crisis of hopelessness grows in the inner city. *Business Week* No. 3220: 20. (p. 353)

Kosters, M. H., and Ross, M. N. 1988. A shrinking middle class? *The Public Interest* No. 90: 3–27. (p. 25)

Kotkin, J. 1989. America's rising sun. *Reason* 20 (8): 22–27. (p. 344)

———. 1991a. A passage to Sunnyvale. *California* 16 (5): 26–27. (p. 344)

———. 1991b. The 'spacemen' have landed. *California* 16 (3): 20–21. (p. 344)

Kotkin, J., and Kishimoto, Y. 1988. *The third century.* New York: Crown. (pp. 68, 220, 344)

Kotlowitz, A. 1991. *There are no children here.* New York: Doubleday. (p. 105)

Kozberg, G., and Winegar, J. 1981. The South Boston story: Implications for secondary schools. *Phi Delta Kappan* 62 (April): 565–569. (p. 507)

Kozlovsky, J. D. 1990. Integrating thinking skills and mastery learning in Baltimore County. *Educational Leadership* 47 (5): 6. (p. 521)

Kozol, J. 1967. *Death at an early age.* Boston: Houghton Mifflin. (p. 297)

Kramer, R. 1986. The third wave. *Wilson Quarterly* 10 (4): 110–129. (p. 429)

Krashen, S. 1981. *Second language acquisition and second language learning.* Oxford: Pergamon. (p. 376)

Krol, R. A. 1980. A meta analysis of the effects of desegregation on academic achievement. *The Urban Review* 12: 211–224. (p. 312)

Kulieke, M. J.; Rosenbaum, J. E.; Rubinowitz, L. S.; and McCareins, A. C. 1985. The effects of residential integration on mother's educational and occupational expectations for their children. Paper presented at the annual meeting of the American Educational Research Association, Chicago. (p. 336)

Kulik, C. C., and Kulik, J. A. 1982. Effects of ability grouping on secondary school students. *American Educational Research Journal* 19 (3): 415–428. (p. 43)

Kulik, C. C.; Kulik, J. A.; and Bangert-Downs, R. L. 1990. Effectiveness of mastery learning programs: A meta-analysis. *Review of Educational Research* 60 (2): 265–299. (p. 521)

Kulik, C. C.; Kulik, J. A.; and Schwalb, B. J. 1982. College programs for high-risk and disadvantaged students: A meta-analysis of findings. Paper presented at the annual meeting of the American Educational Research Association, New York. (p. 289)

Kulik, J. A., and Kulik, C. C. 1987. Effects of ability grouping on student achievement. *Equity and Excellence* 23 (1–2): 22–30. (p. 43)

Kurth, R. J., and Stromberg, L. J. 1984. Improving the teaching of comprehension in elementary schools: A second year report. Paper presented at the annual meeting of the American Educational Research Association, New Orleans. (p. 517)

Kutner, L. 1990. Parent and child. *The New York Times* August 16: B6. (pp. 139, 152, 153)

Kuttner, R. 1987. The patrimony society. *The New Republic* 196 (19): 18–21. (p. 25)

———. 1989. The labor market is a lot looser than it looks. *Business Week* No. 3097: 18. (p. 18)

Kvaraceus, W. D., and Miller, W. B. 1959. Delinquent behavior: Culture and the individual. Washington, DC: National Education Association. (p. 197)

Kvisto, P. ed. 1989. *The ethnic enigma*. Philadelphia: Black Institute. (pp. 220, 406)

Labaton, S. 1990. Glutted probation system puts communities in peril. *The New York Times* June 19: A1, A10. (p. 275)

Lacayo, R. 1986. Spreading the wings of an idea. *Time* 128 (12): 61. (p. 496)

Lai, M. K., et al. 1990. Reading and written expression performance of ten Asian/Pacific Islander ethnic groups on the eighth grade California Assessment Program. Paper presented at the annual meeting of the American Educational Research Association, Boston. (pp. 383, 384, 385, 386)

Lake, R. W. 1981. *The new suburbanites. Race and housing in the suburbs*. New Brunswick, NJ: Rutgers University. (pp. 76, 107)

Lamb, L. 1990. Do-it-yourself schools. *Utne Reader* No. 38: 32, 34. (p. 456)

Lamm, R. D. 1990. Again, age beats youth. *The New York Times* December 2: E19. (p. 31)

Land, K. C.; McCall, P. L.; and Cohen, L. E. 1990. Structural covariates of homicides rates: Are there any invariances across time and social space? *American Journal of Sociology* 95 (4): 922–963. (p. 185)

Landers, L. A. 1988. Nontraditional vocational education leads women toward economic gain, PEER says. *Educational Daily* 27 (64): 3. (p. 421)

Landry, B. 1987. *The new black middle class*. Berkeley: University of California Press. (pp. 240, 352)

Lane, John J., and Edgar G. Epps, eds. 1992. *Restructuring the schools*. Berkeley, CA: McCutchan. (pp. 485, 538)

Lane, R. 1989. On the social meaning of homicide trends in America. In *Violence in America*, edited by Ted Robert Gurr. Newbury Park, CA: Sage. (p. 199)

Lang, D. 1987. Equality, prestige, and controlled mobility in the academic hierarchy. *American Journal of Education* 95 (3): 441–466. (p. 52)

Langbein, J. H. 1991. The inheritance revolution. *The Public Interest* No. 102: 15–31. (pp. 31, 32)

Langer, J. A.; Applebee, A. N.; Mullis, I. V. S.; and Foertsch, M. A. 1990. *Learning to read in our nation's schools*. Princeton, NJ: Educational Testing Service. (pp. 137, 442)

Lanier, A. S. 1982. Let us now praise Catholic schools. *Chicago* 31 (10): 147–153. (p. 447)

Lanier, J. E. 1987. Letter from the president. *The Holmes Group Forum* No. 1: 1.

Laosa, L. M. 1977. Maternal teaching strategies in Mexican-American families: Socioeconomic factors affecting intra-group variability in how mothers teach their children. Paper presented at the annual meeting of the American Educational Research Association, Los Angeles. (p. 131)

Lapointe, A. 1987. Test results provide data useful to educators planning to improve schools. *NASSP Bulletin* 71 (497): 73–78. (p. 47)

Lareau, A. 1989. *Home advantage*. London: Falmer. (pp. 231, 257)

Larson, M. A., and Dittmann, F. E. 1975. *Compensatory education and early adolescence: Reviewing our national strategy*. EPRC 2158-7. Menlo Park, CA: Stanford Research Institute. (p. 285)

Lasch, C. 1977. *Haven in a heartless world: The family besieged*. New York: Basic Books. (pp. 182, 183)

———. 1978. *The culture of narcissism: American life in an age of diminishing expectations*. New York: Warner Books. (p. 182)

———. 1990. *The true and only heaven*. New York: Norton. (pp. 4, 95, 136, 182)

———. 1991. The new class controversy. *Chronicles* 14 (6): 21–25. (p. 182)

Lavin, D.; Alba, R. D.; and Silberstein, R. A. 1981. *Right vs. privilege*. New York: The Free Press. (pp. 287, 288)

Lavin, D. E., and Crook, D. B. 1990. Open admissions and its outcomes. *American Journal of Education* 98 (4): 389–425. (p. 288)

Lavin, D.; Murtha, J.; Kaufman, B.; and Hyllegard, D. 1986. Long-term educational attainment in an open-access university system: Effects of ethnicity, economic status, and college type. Paper presented at the annual meeting of the American Educational Research Association, San Francisco. (p. 287)

Lawson, C. 1989. Girls still apply makeup, boys fight wars. *The New York Times* June 15: 15–19. (p. 420)

———. 1990. In Missouri, schools open their doors to day care. *The New York Times* October 4: B1, B5. (pp. 138, 290)

Lawton, M. 1991. Teenage males said more apt to die from gunshots than natural causes. *Education Week* 10 (26): 4. (p. 185)

Layzer, J. I.; Goodson, B. D.; and Layzer, J. A. 1990. *Evaluation of Project Giant Step*. Cambridge, MA: Abt. (p. 291)

Lazar, I., et al. 1977. Preliminary findings of the developmental continuity longitudinal study. Paper presented at the Office of Child Development Conference on "Parents, Children, and Continuity." Washington, DC. (p. 280)

Lazerson, M. 1986. Review of "A study of high schools." *Harvard Educational Review* 56: 37–48. (p. 531)

Leary, W. E. 1990. Stinging criticism offered on way biology is taught. *The New York Times* September 7: A10. (p. 465)

Lee, F. R. 1989. Required classes on intolerance begin, amid doubts, in New York. *The New York Times* September 18: 12. (p. 399)

———. 1990. Can a change in rules alter young lives? *The New York Times* March 11: 11. (p. 276)

Lee, H. 1960. *To kill a mockingbird*. Philadelphia: Lippincott. (p. 104)

Lee, R. H. 1955. *The city*. Philadelphia: Lippincott. (p. 107)

Lee, V. E., and Bryk, A. S. 1988. Curriculum tracking as mediating the social distribution of high school achievement. *Sociology of Education* 61: 78–94. (p. 449)

Leff, L. 1980. In inner-city schools, getting an education is often a difficult job. *The Wall Street Journal* February 5: 1, 18.

Leifer, A. D.; Gordon, N. J.; and Graves, S. B. 1975. Children's television: More than mere entertainment. *Harvard Educational Review* 44: 213–245. (p. 135)

Leinhardt, G., and Pallay, A. 1982. Restrictive educational settings: Exile or haven? *Review of Educational Research* 54 (4): 557–578. (pp. 262, 530)

Lemann, N. 1989. Stressed out in suburbia. *Harper's* 264 (5): 36–48. (p. 76)

———. 1991a. A false panacea. *The Atlantic Monthly* 267 (1): 101–105. (pp. 15, 449, 450)

———. 1991b. *The promised land*. New York: Knopf. (pp. 15, 16)

Lemlech, J. K. 1977. *Handbook for successful urban teaching*. New York: Harper & Row.

Lenski, G. 1961. *The religious factor*. New York: Doubleday. (p. 35)

Leo, J. 1991a. A fringe history of the world. *U.S. News and World Report* 109 (19): 25. (pp. 401, 402)

———. 1991b. Community and personal duty. *U.S. News and World Report*. 110 (3): 17. (p. 182)

———. 1991c. School reform's best choice. *U.S. News and World Report* 110 (1): 17. (pp. 500, 502)

Leontief, W. 1985. The choice of technology. *Scientific American* 252 (6): 37–45.

Lerman, R. I., and Pouncy, H. 1990. The compelling case for youth apprenticeships. *The Public Interest* No. 101: 62–77. (p. 194)

Lerner, B. 1990. Rethinking education's Cinderella reform—A cure for those end-of-century blues. Paper presented at the annual meeting of the American Educational Research Association, Boston. (p. 479)

Lerner, R. M., and Shea, J. A. 1982. Social behavior in adolescence. In *Handbook of developmental psychology*, edited by Benjamin Wolman. Englewood Cliffs, NJ: Prentice-Hall. (p. 153)

LeTendre, B. 1991. Missouri's accelerated schools. *Accelerated Schools* 1 (1): 8–9. (p. 519)

Lev, M. 1991. Advertising. *The New York Times* January 14: E9. (p. 382)

Lever, J. 1988. Sex differences in the complexity of children's play and games. In *Childhood socialization*, edited by Gerald Handel. New York: Aldine de Gruyter. (pp. 420, 435)

Levin, H. M. 1976. Educational opportunity and social inequality in western Europe. *Social Problems* 24: 148–172. (p. 243)

Levin, H. M.; Guthrie, J. W.; Kleindorfer, G. B.; and Stout, R. T. 1971. School achievement and postschool success: A review. *Review of Educational Research* 41: 1–16. (p. 39)

Levine, D. U. 1966. *Raising standards in inner-city schools*. Washington, DC: Council for Basic Education. (p. 267)

———. 1968. Cultural diffraction in the social system of the low-income school. *School and Society* 96 (2306): 206–210. (pp. 98, 99)

———. 1972. The unfinished identity of metropolitan man. In *Teaching about life in the city*, edited by Richard Wisniewski. The Forty-Second Yearbook of the National Council for the Social Studies. Washington, DC: National Council for the Social Studies. (pp. 102, 361)

———. 1985. Key considerations for achieving success in mastery learning programs. In *Improving student achievement through mastery learning pro-grams*, edited by Daniel U. Levine. San Francisco: Jossey-Bass. (pp. 268, 521, 535)

————. 1988. Teaching thinking to at-risk students: Generalizations and speculations. In *At-risk students and thinking: Perspectives from research*, edited by Barbara Z. Presseisen. Washington, DC: National Educational Association. (pp. 516, 535)

————. 1991a. Creating effective schools: Findings and implications from research and practice. *Phi Delta Kappan* 72 (5): 389–393. (pp. 503, 509, 526, 535)

————. 1991b. Implementation of an urban school-within-a-school approach. Draft, title tent. In *Improving the education of at-risk students*, edited by J. W. de Felix, J. Anderson, P. Baptiste, and H. Waxman. Newbury Park, CA: Sage. (pp. 508, 523, 525, 528, 530)

————. 1992. Notes on recent achievement patterns in Kansas City and Milwaukee. Paper prepared at the Center for the Study of Metropolitan Problems in Education (draft). (pp. 271, 273, 534)

Levine, D. U., ed. 1985. *Improving student achievement through mastering learning programs*. San Francisco: Jossey-Bass. (p. 537)

Levine, D. U., et al. 1972. The home environment of students in a high achieving inner-city parochial school and a nearby public school. *Sociology of Education* 45: 435–445. (pp. 361, 451)

————. 1979. Concentrated poverty and reading achievement in seven big cities. *The Urban Review* 11 (2): 63–80. (p. 270)

Levine, D. U., and Campbell, C. 1978. Magnet schools. In *Citizens guide to quality education: A report of the Citizen's Council for Ohio Schools*, edited by Rachel B. Tompkins. Cleveland: Citizens' Council for Ohio Schools. (p. 325)

Levine, D. U., and Cooper, E. J. 1991. The change process and its implications in teaching thinking. In Lorna Idol and Beau F. Jones, eds., *Educational Values and Cognitive Instruction*. Hillsdale, NJ: Erlbaum. (pp. 516, 524, 525)

Levine, D. U., and Eubanks, E. E. 1989. Organizational arrangements in effective secondary schools. In *Organizing for learning*, edited by Herbert J. Walberg and John J. Lane. Reston, VA: National Association of Secondary School Principals. (p. 509)

————. 1990a. Achievement disparities between minority and nonminority students in suburban schools. *Journal of Negro Education* 59 (2): 186–194. (p. 50)

————. 1990b. Desegregation and regional magnetization. In *Magnet schools*, edited by Nolan Estes, Daniel U. Levine, and Donald R. Waldrip. Austin, TX: Morgan. (pp. 332, 333, 334)

————. 1992. Site-based management: Engine for reform or pipedream? In *Local school reform*, edited by John J. Lane and Edgar G. Epps. Berkeley, CA: McCutchan. (pp. 145, 485)

Levine, D. U., and Havighurst, R. J., eds. 1977. *The future of big city schools: Desegregation policies and magnet alternatives*. Berkeley, CA: McCutchan. (p. 338)

Levine, D. U., and Leibert, R. E. 1987. Improving school improvement plans. *The Elementary School Journal* 87 (4): 397–412. (p. 526)

Levine, D. U., and Levine, R. F. 1977. The social and instructional setting for metropolitan integration. In *Social desegregation in metropolitan areas: Choices and prospects*, edited by Ronald D. Henderson and Mary von Euler. Washington, DC: The National Institute of Education, (p. 330)

Levine, D. U., and Lezotte, L. W. 1990. *Unusually effective schools*. Madison, WI: National Center for Effective Schools Research and Development. (pp. 144, 262, 267, 445, 503, 504, 509, 510, 515, 524, 526, 527)

Levine, D. U., and Meyer, J. K. 1977. Level rate of desegregation and white enrollment decline in a big city school district. *Social Problems* 24: 451–462. (p. 309)

Levine, D. U., and Ornstein, A. C. 1989. Research on classroom and school effectiveness and its implications for improving big city schools. *The Urban Review* 21 (2): 81–94. (pp. 268, 524, 534)

Levine, D. U., and Sherk, J. K. 1990. *Effective implementation of a comprehension-improvement approach in secondary schools*. Kansas City: University of Missouri-Kansas City School of Education. (pp. 268, 508, 523, 524, 528, 530)

————. 1991. Implementation of reforms to improve comprehension skills at an unusually effective inner-city intermediate school. *The Peabody Journal of Education* (in press). (pp. 268, 508, 512, 513)

Levine, D. U., and Stark, J. 1982. Instructional and organizational arrangements that improve achievement in inner-city schools. *Educational Leadership* 40 (3): 41–48. (pp. 262, 504)

Levine, D. U.; Eubanks, E. E.; and Roskoski, L. S. 1980. *Social class and home background of magnet and non-magnet students*. Kansas City: University of Missouri-Kansas City School of Education. (pp. 147, 361, 451)

Levine, D. U.; Levine, R. F.; and Eubanks, E. E. 1984. Characteristics of effective inner-city intermediate schools. *Phi Delta Kappan* (65): 707–711. (pp. 504, 506)

———. 1985. Successful implementation of instruction at inner-city schools. *Journal of Negro Education* 54: 313–331. (p. 262)

Levine, D. U.; Mitchell, E. S.; and Havighurst, R. J. 1970. Family status, type of high school and college attendance. Kansas City: Center for the Study of Metropolitan Problems in Education. (pp. 161, 245)

Levinson, E. 1975. *The Alum Rock voucher demonstration*. Santa Monica, CA: Rand. (p. 454)

———. 1990. Will technology transform education or will the schools co-opt technology? *Phi Delta Kappan* 72 (2): 121–126. (p. 454)

Levitan, S. A., and Mangum, G. L. 1969. *Federal training and work programs in the sixties*. Ann Arbor, MI: Institute of Labor and Industrial Relations. (p. 294)

Levitan, S. A.; Magnum, G. L.; and Pines, M. W. 1989. *A proper inheritance*. Washington, DC: The George Washington University Center for Social Policy Studies. (p. 117)

Levy, F., and Michel, R. C. 1985. Are baby boomers selfish? *American Demographics* (4): 38–41. (p. 25)

———. 1991. *The economic future of American families*. Washington, DC: The Urban Institute. (pp. 23, 24, 25, 229)

Lewin, T. 1990a. Father's vanishing act called common drama. *The New York Times* June 4: A15. (p. 119)

———. 1990b. Plight of displaced homemakers is growing as many face poverty. *The New York Times* June 2: 13. (p. 414)

Lewis, A. C. 1986. ED's 'pro-choice' plan: If at first you don't succeed. *Phi Delta Kappan* 67 (5): 331–332. (p. 455)

———. 1989a. A box of tools but no blueprint. *Phi Delta Kappan* 71 (3): 180–181. (p. 488)

———. 1989b. Played out? *The New York Times* January 7: Educ 42–43. (p. 162)

———. 1991a. Business as a real partner. *Phi Delta Kappan* 72 (6): 420–422. (p. 191)

———. 1991b. Coordinating services: Do we have the will? *Phi Delta Kappan*. 72 (5): 340–341. (p. 209)

Lewis, A. L. 1990. Business gets serious about saving our schools. *Human Capital* 1 (3): 28–31. (p. 496)

Lewis, E. 1990. African-Americans and the great migration. *Crisis* 98 (2): 18–22, 44–45. (p. 350)

Lewis, J. L., and Moore, J. W. 1990. The impact on student achievement gains of classroom compositions ranging from heterogeneous to homogeneous groupings in elementary schools. Paper presented at the annual meeting of the American Educational Research Association, Boston. (p. 263)

Lewis, O. 1961. *Children of Sanchez*. New York: Random House. (pp. 103, 259)

———. 1966. *La vida*. New York: Random House. (p. 103)

Liao, Y-K. 1991. Effects of computer assisted instruction and computer programming on students' cognitive performance: A meta-analysis. Paper presented at the annual meeting of the American Educational Research Association, Chicago. (p. 518)

Lieberman, M. 1986. Why reform was 'dead on arrival.' *Education Week* 5 (20): 20. (pp. 490, 491)

———. 1989. *Privatization and educational choice*. New York: Saint Martin's Press. (p. 455)

Liebow, E. 1967. *Tally's corner*. Boston: Little, Brown. (pp. 17, 94)

Liebman, J. S. 1990. Implementing Brown in the nineties: Political reconstruction, liberal recollection, and litigatively enforced legislative reform. *Virginia Law Review* 76 (3): 349–435. (p. 317)

Lindsay, B., ed. 1983. *Comparative perspectives of third world women*. 2nd ed. New York: Praeger. (p. 435)

Lines, P. M. 1986. The new private schools and their historic purpose. *Phi Delta Kappan* 67 (5): 373–379. (pp. 446, 456)

———. 1987. An overview of home instruction. *Phi Delta Kappan* 68 (7): 510–517. (p. 456)

———. 1990. *Home instruction: Size, characteristics, and growth*. Norwood, NJ: Ablex. (p. 456)

Link, F. R., ed. 1985. *Essays on the intellect*. Alexandria, VA: Association for Curriculum Development. (p. 513)

Linn, M. C., and Hyde, J. S. 1989. Gender, mathematics, and science. *Educational Researcher* 18 (8): 17–19, 22–27. (pp. 415, 416, 418, 419)

Linn, R. L. 1991. Dimensions of thinking: Implications for testing. In *Educational values and cognitive implications for reform*, edited by Lorna Idol and Beau Fly Jones. Hillsdale, NJ: Erlbaum. (pp. 477, 478).

Linn, R. L., and Dunbar, S. B. 1990. The nation's report card goes home. *Phi Delta Kappan* 72 (2): 127–133. (p. 463)

Lipkin, J. 1982. The troubling equity issue in computer education: Is computer literacy the answer or the problem? *Education Times* 3 (38): 7. (p. 437)

Lipsitz, J. 1977. *Growing up forgotten: A review of research and programs concerning early adolescence.* Lexington, MA: Lexington Books. (p. 170)

Liston, D. P. 1990. *Capitalist schools.* New York: Routledge. (pp. 255, 261)

Liston, D. P., and Zeichner, K. M. 1990. Teacher education and the social context of schooling: Issues for curriculum development. *American Educational Research Journal* 27 (4): 610–636. (p. 261)

Little Soldier, L. 1989. Cooperative learning and the Native American student. *Phi Delta Kappan* October 71 (2): 161–163. (p. 398)

———. 1990. The education of Native American students. *Equity and Excellence* Summer 24 (4): 66–69. (pp. 392, 393, 394)

Lloyd, B., and Duveen, G. 1990. A semiotic analysis of the development of social representations of gender. In *Social representations and the development of knowledge*, edited by Gerald Duveen and Barbara Lloyd. New York: Cambridge University Press. (p. 420)

Lloyd, C. B., and Niemi, B. T. 1971. *The economics of sex differentials.* New York: Columbia University Press. (pp. 413, 435)

Locust, C. 1988. Wounding to the spirit: Discrimination and traditional American Indian belief systems. *Harvard Educational Review* 58 (3): 315. (p. 386)

London, R. 1991. Judge's overruling of crack law brings turmoil. *The New York Times* January 11: B9. (pp. 21, 141)

Longanecker, D. 1982. What will it cost? *IFG Policy Perspectives* Winter: 1–2. (p. 452)

Longman, P. 1985. Justice between generations. *The Atlantic* 255 (6): 73–81. (p. 31)

———. 1989. Elderly, affluent—and selfish. *The New York Times* October 10: 27. (p. 32)

Lorch, D. 1989. Homeless reported doing poorly in class. *The New York Times* September 12: 14. (p. 140)

Lotto, L. S. 1985. The unfinished agenda: Report from the National Commission on Secondary Vocational Education. *Phi Delta Kappan* 66: 568–573. (p. 65)

Louis, K. S., and Miles, M. B. 1990. *Improving the urban high school.* New York: Teachers College Press. (pp. 524, 525, 526)

Lounsbury, J. H., and Clark, D. C. 1990. *Inside grade eight: From apathy to excitement.* Reston, VA: National Association of Secondary School Principals. (p. 531)

Lounsbury, J. H., and Johnston, J. H. 1985. *How fares the ninth grade? A day in the life of a ninth grader.* Washington, DC: National Association of Secondary School Principals. (p. 531)

Lucas, T., and Katz, A. 1991. The roles of students' native languages in exemplary SAIPs. Paper presented at the annual meeting of the American Educational Research Association, Chicago. (p. 379)

Ludtke, M. 1990. Answers at last. *Time* 136 (26): 44–49. (p. 139)

Lueder, D. 1989. Tennessee parents were invited to participate—and they did. *Educational Leadership* 47 (2): 15–17. (p. 290)

Luke, C. 1989. *Pedagogy, printing, and Protestantism.* Albany: State University of New York Press. (p. 165)

Lyman, P. N. 1990. Boat people and U.S. *The New York Times* January 30: A14. (p. 382)

Lynn, L. E., Jr. 1973. *The effectiveness of compensatory education: Summary and review of the evidence.* Report of the Assistant Secretary for Planning and Evaluation, U.S. Department of Health, Education and Welfare, Washington, DC.

———. 1977. A decade of policy developments in income maintenance systems. In *A decade of federal anti-poverty programs*, edited by Robert H. Haveman. New York: Academic Press. (p. 16)

Lytle, J. 1988. Is special education serving minority students? *Harvard Educational Review* 58 (1): 116–120. (p. 134)

Maccoby, E. E. 1985. *Readings in social psychology.* New York: Holt, Rinehart & Winston. (p. 232)

Maccoby, E. E., and Jacklin, C. N. 1974. *Psychology of sex differences.* Palo Alto, CA: Stanford University Press. (p. 417)

MacGinitie, W. H., and MacGinitie, R. K. 1986. Teaching students not to read. In *Literacy, society, and schooling*, edited by Suzanne de Castell. Cambridge: Cambridge University Press. (p. 514)

MacIver, D. J., and Epstein, J. L. 1990. *How equal are opportunities for learning in disadvantaged and advantaged middle grade schools?* Baltimore:

Center for Research on Effective Schooling for Disadvantaged Students. (p. 238)

MacKinnon, C. A. 1987. *Feminism unmodified*. Cambridge, MA: Harvard University Press. (p. 431)

MacLeod, D. I. 1983. *Building character in the American boy*. Madison: The University of Wisconsin Press. (pp. 169, 175)

Madden, N. A. et al. 1990. Success for all: First-year outcomes of a comprehensive plan for reforming urban education. *American Educational Research Association* 27 (2): 255–278. (p. 522)

———. 1991. Success for all. *Phi Delta Kappan* 72 (8): 593–599. (pp. 522)

Maeroff, G. I. 1988. *The empowerment of teachers: Overcoming the crisis on confidence*. New York: Teachers College Press. (pp. 485, 495)

Magner, D. K. 1991. Hispanics remain 'grossly underrepresented' on campuses, report says. *The Chronicle of Higher Education* 37 (19): 2. (p. 51)

Magnet, M. 1987. America's underclass: What to do? *Fortune* 115 (10): 130–150. (p. 19)

Mahoney, M. A. 1976. The American family: Centuries and decades of change. *National Elementary School Principal* 55 (May–June): 6–11. (p. 122)

Malcolm, A. H. 1990. Going beyond jails in drives to make U.S. a safer place. *The New York Times* October 10: A1, A9. (p. 199)

Malen, B.; Ogawa, R. T.; and Kranz, J. 1991. What do we know about school-based management? In *Choice and control in American education*, Vol. 2., edited by William Clune and John Witte. London: Falmer. (p. 485)

Mallozzi, V. M. 1989. Dimwit jocks: Maybe not. *The New York Times* November 5: Educ. 7. (p. 163)

Mancini, J. K. 1981. *Strategic styles. Coping in the inner city*. Hanover, NH: University Press of New England. (p. 35)

Mandell, M. J. 1990. Does America need more 'huddled masses'? Yes. *Business Week* No. 3149: 20. (p. 344)

Manges, M. 1990. The dead-end kids. *The Wall Street Journal* February 9: R32–33. (p. 195)

Mann, D. 1990. It's time to trade red tape for accountability in education. *The Executive Educator* 12 (1): 26, 28. (pp. 484, 529)

Mansbridge, J. 1990. Feminism and democracy. *The American prospect* No. 1: 126–139. (pp. 430, 435)

Manzo, A., and Manzo, U. 1990. *Content area reading*. Columbus, OH: Merrill. (p. 513)

Marino, C. D., and McCowan, R. J. 1976. The effects of parent absence on children. *Child Study Journal* 6 (March): 165–182. (p. 127)

Marjoribanks, K. 1972. Ethnic and environmental influences on mental abilities. *Journal of American Sociology* 78: 323–336. (p. 131)

Marriott, M. 1990. Videodisc joining the book as new tool in the classroom. *The New York Times* September 12: A1, B7. (p. 120)

———. 1991a. A wide range of help for minority students who try engineering. *The New York Times* March 6: B7. (p. 25)

———. 1991b. Tribal network is nurturing minds. *The New York Times* January 23: B9. (p. 395)

Marsh, D. D., and Berman, P. 1984. Conceptualizing the problems of increasing the capacity of schools to implement reform efforts. Paper presented at the annual meeting of the American Educational Research Association, New Orleans. (p. 525)

Marsh, H. W., and Grayson, D. 1990. Public/Catholic differences in the high school and beyond data: A multigroup structural equation modeling approach to testing mean differences. *Journal of Educational Statistics* 15 (3): 199–235. (p. 449)

Marshak, R. E. 1981. Open access, open admissions, open warfare. Part one. *Change* 13 (8): 12–19, 51–53. (p. 287)

Martin, J. 1986. Redefining the educated person: Rethinking the significance of gender. *Educational Researcher* 15 (6): 6–10. (p. 431)

Martin, O. L. 1987. A comparative analysis of the educational plight of urban black and rural white high school students: Are their needs similar? Paper presented at the annual meeting of the American Educational Research Association, Washington, DC. (p. 440)

Martin, R. 1990. When 'helping' really hurts. *A Heartland Perspective* December 17: 1–5. (p. 16)

Martinez, M. G. 1990. Proposal for NAEP is 'recipe for disaster.' *Education Week* 9 (25): 27–28. (p. 447)

Marvin, M. et al. 1976. *Planning assistance programs to reduce school violence and disruption*. Washington, DC: U.S. Department of Justice, National Institute for Juvenile Justice and Delinquency Prevention.

Marzano, R. J., et al. 1987. *Dimensions of thinking*. Alexandria, VA: Association for Supervision and Curriculum Development. (pp. 511, 512, 513)

Marzano, R. J.; Pickering, D. J.; and Brandt, R. S. 1990. Integrating instructional programs through dimensions of learning. *Educational Leadership* 47 (5): 17–24. (p. 512)

Massey, C. G.; Scott, M. V.; and Dornsbusch, A. 1975. Racism without racists: Institutional reform in urban schools. *The Black Scholar* 7 (March): 3–11. (p. 265)

Massey, D. S., and Denton, N. A. 1989. Hypersegregation in U.S. metropolitan areas: Black and Hispanic segregation along five dimensions. *Demography* 26 (3): 373–391. (pp. 74, 75)

Massey, D. S., and Eggers, M. L. 1990. The ecology of inequality: Minorities and the concentration of poverty, 1970–1980. *American Journal of Sociology* 95: 1153–1188. (pp. 74, 76)

Mathes, W. A., and Carlson, R. V. 1986. Conditions for practice: The reasons teachers selected rural schools. Paper presented at the annual meeting of the American Educational Research Association, San Francisco. (p. 442)

Mayberry, M. 1990. Cultural cleavages and commonalities within and surrounding home education. Paper presented at the annual meeting of the American Educational Research Association, Boston. (pp. 456, 457)

Mayer, K. 1963. The changing shape of the American class structure. *Social Research* 30: 458–468. (p. 9)

Mayer, S. E., and Jencks, C. 1989. Growing up in poor neighborhoods: How much does it matter? *Science* 243: 489–497. (p. 196)

Mayeske, G. W., et al. 1971. *A study of our nation's schools*. Washington, DC: U.S. Government Printing Office. (p. 237)

McCarthy, J.; Hopfenberg, W. S.; and Levin, H. M. 1991. Accelerated schools—Evolving thoughts on the evaluation of an innovative model. Paper presented at the annual meeting of the American Educational Research Association, Chicago. (p. 519)

McCarthy, M. M. 1990. Teacher-testing programs. In *The educational reform movement of the 1980s*, edited by Joseph Murphy. Berkeley, CA: McCutchan. (p. 396)

McCartney, K., and Jordan, E. 1990. Parallels between research on child care and research on school effects. *Educational Researcher* 19 (1): 24–27. (p. 510)

McCormack-Larkin, M. 1985. Ingredients of a successful school effectiveness project. *Educational Leadership* 42: 31–37. (p. 505)

McDill, E. L.; Natriello, G.; and Pallas, A. M. 1986. A population at risk: Consequences of tougher school standards for student dropouts. *American Journal of Education* 94: 135–181. (p. 495)

McDowell, L., and Morgan, F. B. 1990. *Public elementary and secondary schools and agencies in the United States and outlying areas: School year 1988–1989*. Washington, DC: U.S. Department of Education. (p. 444)

McGarry, D. D. 1982. The advantages and constitutionality of tuition tax credits. *Educational Freedom* 15 (2): 1–52. (p. 452)

McGue, M. 1989. Nature-nurture and intelligence. *Nature* 340 (August 17): 507–508. (pp. 67, 231)

McGuiness, D. 1979. How schools discriminate against boys. *Human Nature* February: 87–88. (p. 425)

McGuire, D. 1990. Missouri early childhood program catches on throughout nation. *The Kansas City Star* January 2: 3A. (p. 290)

McIntyre, R. S. 1991. The Reaganites and the renegade. *The American Prospect* No. 4: 12–16. (p. 25)

McKinney, S., and Schnare, A. B. 1987. *Trends in residential segregation by race: 1960–1980*. Washington, DC: The Urban Institute. (p. 77)

McKnight, C. C., et al. 1987. *The underachieving curriculum*. Champaign, IL: Stipes. (p. 48)

McLaughlin, M. W. 1990. The Rand change agent study revisited: Macro perspectives and micro realities. *Educational Researcher* 19 (9): 11–16. (p. 525)

McLure, W. P., and Pence, A. M. 1971. Early childhood and basic elementary and secondary education. In *Planning to finance education*, edited by Roe Johns, et al. Gainsville, FL: National Education Project. (p. 294)

McMillen, M. M., and Gerald, E. 1990. *Characteristics of private schools: 1987–88*. Washington, DC: U.S. Department of Education. (p. 446)

McMurrin, L. R. 1985. Magnet schools achieve excellence and racial balance. *The School Administrator* 42, No. 9: 28, 32. (p. 333)

McNeil, L. M. 1986. *Contradictions of control: School structure and school knowledge*. New York: Routledge and Kegan Paul. (pp. 492, 514, 537)

———. 1988. Contradictions of control. *Phi Delta Kappan* 69 (6): 432–438. (p. 492)

———. 1990. What America's public schools really need. *Human Capital* 1 (3): 34–39. (pp. 492, 496)

McPartland, J. M., and Slavin, R. E. 1990. *Increasing achievement of at-risk students at each grade level.* Washington, DC: U.S. Government Printing Office. (pp. 528, 529)

McPherson, M. 1982. Open access, open admissions, open warfare. Part two. *Change* 14 (1): 30–42. (p. 287)

———. 1986. Who should pay for college and when? *Change* May/June: 9. (p. 63)

Mead, L. M. 1989. The limitations of structural analysis. *The Public Interest* 97: 105–111. (p. 21)

———. 1991. The new politics of the new poverty. *The Public Interest* No. 103: 3–20. (p. 21)

Mead, M., and Wolfenstein, M. 1955. *Childhood in contemporary cultures.* Chicago: University of Chicago Press. (p. 148)

Meadows, B. J. 1990. The rewards and risks of shared leadership. *Phi Delta Kappan* 71 (7): 545–548. (p. 485)

Mecklenburger, J. A., and Hostrup, R. W., eds. 1972. *Education vouchers: From theory to Alum Rock.* Homewood, IL: ETC Publications.

Medrich, E. A. 1982. Time use outside school: Community services and facilities in the lives of young adolescents. In *3:00 to 6:00 p.m.: Young adolescents at home and in the community,* edited by Leah M. Lefstein, et al. Carrboro: Center for Early Adolescence, University of North Carolina at Chapel Hill. (p. 172)

Meek, A. 1990. On 25 years of Foxfire: A conversation with Eliot Wiggington. *Educational Leadership* 47 (6): 30–36. (p. 396)

Menacker, J.; Hurwitz, E.; and Weldon, W. 1988. Parent-teacher cooperation in schools serving the urban poor. *The Clearing House* 62 (3): 108–111. (p. 143)

Menacker, J.; Weldon, W.; and Hurwitz, E. 1990. Community influences on school crime and violence. *Urban Education* 25 (1): 68–80. (pp. 276, 277)

Mercer, J. 1991. Nile Valley scholars bring new light to controversy on African studies. *Black Issues in Higher Education* 7 (26): 1, 12–16. (pp. 401, 402)

Mercer, J. R. 1973. *Labeling the mentally retarded.* Berkeley, CA: University of California Press. (pp. 67, 131)

Mergendoller, J., et al. 1988. Task demands and accountability in middle-grade science classes. *The Elementary School Journal* 88 (2): 251–265. (p. 514)

Merton, R. K. 1967. *Social theory and social structure.* New York: Free Press. (p. 502)

Messner, S. F. 1989. Economic discrimination and societal homicide rates: Further evidence of the cost of inequality. *American Sociological Review* 54: 597–611. (p. 199)

Metz, M. H. 1986. *Different by design.* New York: Routledge and Kegan Paul. (p. 339)

Michael, B., ed. 1990. *Volunteers in public schools.* Washington, DC: National Academy Press. (p. 148)

Mickelson, R. A. 1990. The attitude-achievement paradox among black adolescents. *Sociology of Education* 63: 44–61. (pp. 356, 357)

Mickelson, R. A., and Smith, S. S. 1989. Inner-city social dislocations and school outcomes: A structural interpretation. In *Black students: Psychosocial issues and academic achievement,* edited by G. L. Berry and J. K. Asamen. Newbury Park, CA: Sage. (pp. 17, 18, 198)

Mielke, D. 1978. *Teaching mountain children.* Boone, NC: Appalachian Consortium Press. (p. 396)

Mihalik, M. 1990. The lure of the paycheck. *Teacher Magazine* 1 (4): 36–39. (pp. 204, 205)

Miles, M. B. 1983. Unraveling the mystery of institutionalization. *Educational Leadership* 41 (3): 14–19. (p. 525)

Miller, D. F. 1990. *The case for school-based clinics.* Bloomington, IN: Phi Delta Kappa. (pp. 204, 205, 211)

Miller, D. R., and Swanson, G. E. 1958. *The changing American parent.* New York: Wiley. (p. 148)

Miller, H. P. 1964. *Rich man, poor man: The distribution of income in America.* New York: Thomas Y. Crowell Company. (p. 13)

Miller, J. A. 1988. G. A. O. analysis says anti-drug efforts poorly evaluated. *Education Week* 7 (22): 16. (p. 201)

———. 1989. Summit's promise: 'Social compact' for reforms. *Education Week* 9 (5): 1, 10–11. (p. 488)

———. 1990. Faced with cuts in funds, Seattle postpones rules. *Education Week* 10 (3): 1, 23. (p. 327)

———. 1991a. Chapter 1: An educational revolution. *Educational Week* 10 (35): C1–C113. (pp. 284, 285)

———. 1991b. School groups ask Bush to back up goals with increased spending. *Education Week* 10 (12): 22. (p. 489)

Miller, J. M., and Sidebottom, D. 1985. *Teachers. Finding and keeping the best in small and rural districts*. Washington, DC: The American Association of School Administrators. (p. 442)

Miller, L. S. 1986, Nation-building and education. *Education Week* 5 (34): 52. (p. 84)

Miller, W. 1973. *Violence by youth groups as a crime problem in major American cities*. Washington, DC: U.S. Government Printing Office. (p. 277)

Miller-Jones, D. 1989. Culture and testing. *American Psychologist* 44 (2): 360–366. (p. 66)

Millett, K. 1971. *Sexual politics*. New York: Avon. (p. 435)

Mills, C. J., and Noyes, H. L. 1984. Patterns and correlates of initial and subsequent drug use among adolescents. *Journal of Consulting and Clinical Psychology* 52: 231–243. (p. 200)

Mills, C. W. 1951. *White collar*. New York: Oxford University Press. (p. 35)

Milne, A.; Myers, D.; Rosenthal, A.; and Ginsburg, A. 1986. Single parents, working mothers, and the educational achievement of school children. *Sociology of Education* 59: 125–139. (p. 126)

Milner, J. O. 1991. Suppositional style and teacher evaluation. *Phi Delta Kappan* 72 (6): 464–467. (p. 493)

Milone, M. N., Jr., and Brady, H. 1991. The rich potential of educational television. *Technology and Learning* 1 (4): 21–29. (p. 444)

Mims, R., and Lewis, E. 1989. A portrait of the boss. *Business Week* October 20: 23–25, 28. (p. 11)

Mincy, R. B. 1990. No underclass solution can ignore young males. *The Urban Institute Policy and Research Report* 20 (3): 28. (p. 353)

Mincy, R. B.; Sawhill, I. V.; and Wolf, D. A. 1990. The underclass: definition and measurement. *Science* 248: 450–453. (pp. 14, 15, 353)

Mirga, T. 1983. Busing will not help to desegregate Chicago schools, federal judge rules. *Education Week* 2 (17): 9, 19. (p. 329)

Mitchell, R. 1990. Performance assessment: An emphasis on activity. *Education Week* 9 (18): 36, 25. (p. 478)

Mizokawa, D. T., and Moroshima, J. K. 1979. The education for, by, and of Asian/Pacific Americans, I and II. *Research Review of Equal Education* 3 (3 & 4): 1–33, 1–39. (p. 384)

Monaghan, P. 1987. A model project combats Indians educational crisis. *The Chronicle of Higher Education* 38 (31): 3. (p. 393)

Montague, B. 1986. Rural educators say "networking" key. *Education Week* 6 (6): 5, 17. (pp. 441, 442)

Monti, D. J. 1985. *A semblance of justice*. Columbia: University of Missouri Press. (p. 338)

Mooney, C. J. 1990. Colleges for American Indians said to need money and recognition. *The Chronicle of Higher Education* 36 (11): A20. (p. 395)

Moore, D. 1991. Voice and choice in Chicago. In *Choice and control in American education*, Vol. 2., edited by William H. Clune and John F. Witte. London: Falmer. (p. 485)

Moore, D., and Davenport, S. 1989. *The new improved sorting machine*. Madison, WI: National Center for Effective Secondary Schools. (p. 325)

Moore, K. A.; Simms, M. C.; and Betsey, C. L. 1986. *Choice and circumstance*. New Brunswick, NJ: Transaction. (p. 203)

Morgan, G. 1989. Drastic changes for management. *Business Month* 133 (3): 67–70.

Morgan, H. 1980. How schools fail black children. *Social Policy* 10 (4): 49–54. (p. 259)

Morgan, J. 1991. Magnet schools. *Black Issues in Higher Education* 8 (4): 1, 14–15. (p. 323)

Morgan, R., ed. 1970. *Sisterhood is powerful: An anthology of writings from the women's liberation movement*. New York: Random House. (p. 435)

Morgenthau, T. 1989. Children of the underclass. *Newsweek* 114 (11): 16–24. (p. 141)

Morris, C. R. 1989. The coming global boom. *The Atlantic Monthly* 264 (4): 51–64. (p. 23)

Morris, D. R. Structural patterns and change in grade retention rates. Paper presented at the annual meeting of the American Educational Research Association, Chicago. (p. 503)

Morris, V. C., and Pai, Y. 1976. *Philosophy and the American school*. Boston: Houghton Mifflin. (p. 406)

Mortenson, T. G. 1990. *The impact of increased loan utilization among low family income students*. Iowa City: American College Testing Program. (p. 43)

———. 1991. *Equity of higher educational opportunity for women, black, Hispanic, and low income students*. Iowa City: American College Testing Program. (pp. 42, 43, 363, 367)

Mortenson, T. G., and Wu, Z. 1990. *High school graduation and college participation of young adults by family income backgrounds, 1970 to 1989*. Iowa City: American College Testing Program. (pp. 42, 63, 64, 464)

Moss, H. A. 1967. Sex, age, and stage as determinants of mother-infant interaction. *Merrill-Palmer Quarterly* 13 (1): 19–36. (p. 420)

Mosteller, F., and Moynihan, D. P., eds. 1972. *On equality of educational opportunity*. New York: Random House. (p. 237)

Moynihan, D. P. 1989. Promise to the mentally ill has not been kept. *The New York Times* May 22: 22. (p. 139)

Mullin, S. P., and Summers, A. A. 1983. Is more better? The effectiveness of spending on compensatory education. *Phi Delta Kappan* (5): 330–343. (p. 284)

Mullis, I. V. S., and Jenkins, L. 1988. *The science report card*. Princeton, NJ: Educational Testing Service. (pp. 361, 415, 463)

———. 1990. *The reading report card, 1971–88*. Princeton, NJ: Educational Testing Service. (pp. 46, 48, 111, 360, 415, 416, 463)

Mullis, I. V. S.; Owen, E. H.; and Phillips, G. W. 1990. *Accelerating academic achievement*. Princeton, NJ: Educational Testing Service. (pp. 71, 361, 415, 463, 464, 465)

Mumford, L. 1961. *The city in history*. New York: Harcourt Brace Jovanovich. (p. 107)

Mundy, L. 1989. The success story of the war on poverty. *The Washington Monthly* 21 (11): 26–31. (p. 279)

Murphy, J., ed. 1990. *The educational reform movement of the 1980s*. Berkeley, CA: McCutchan. (p. 538)

Murphy, K., and Welch, F. 1989. Wage premiums for college graduates. *Educational Researcher* 18 (4): 17–26. (p. 229)

Murray, C. 1990. The British underclass. *The Public Interest* No. 99: 4–29. (p. 14)

Murray, N. 1991. Is the playing field really level? *Rethinking Schools* 5 (2): 7. (p. 365)

Musgrove, F. 1966. *The family, education, and society*. London: Routledge and Kegan Paul. (p. 91)

Musumeci, M., and Szczypkowksi, R. 1991. *New York State magnet schools evaluation study*. Larchmont, NY: Magi Educational Services. (p. 324)

Muuss, R., ed. 1971. *Adolescent behavior and society: A book of readings*. New York: Random House. (p. 174)

Muwakkil, S. 1990. The rap gap: Class divisions divide the black community. *Utne Reader* No. 37: 52. (p. 352)

Mydans, S. 1989. School offers day-care for teen-age mothers. *The New York Times* December 27: 12. (p. 202)

———. 1990. Black identity vs. success and seeming white. *The New York Times* April 25: 36. (p. 357)

———. 1991. They're in a new home, but feel tied to the old. *The New York Times* June 30: 8. (p. 349)

Myers, D. E.; Milne, A. M.; Baker, K.; and Ginsburg, A. 1987. Student discipline and high school performance. *Sociology of Education* 60: 18–33. (p. 126)

Myers, S. L., Jr. 1990. Drugs and market structure: Is there really a drug crisis in the black community? *Challenge*. 1 (1): 1–223. (p. 196)

Nachtigal, P. M. 1982. *Rural education*. Boulder, CO: Westview. (p. 445)

———. 1989. The McREL approach to rural school improvement. In *Rural education*, edited by Joyce D. Stern. Washington, DC: U.S. Department of Education. (p. 445)

Nagel, T. 1986. A longitudinal study of systematic efforts to raise standardized test scores using factors from school effectiveness research. Paper presented at the annual meeting of the American Educational Research Association, San Francisco. (p. 534)

Nagel, T., and Mittleholtz, D. 1991. San Diego school effectiveness program produces large gains in standardized achievement scores of minority elementary schools. Paper presented at the annual meeting of the Association of Teacher Educators, New Orleans. (p. 534)

Nairn, A., et al. 1980. The reign of ETS: The corporation that makes up minds. Washington, DC: Nader and Associates. (p. 69)

Naison, M. 1990. Blacks blocking the school door. *Newsday* April 2: 40, 42. (p. 356)

Nasar, S. 1989. Economic outlook. *U.S. News and World Report* 107 (23): 56. (p. 24)

———. 1990. Women's gains will keep coming. *U.S. News and World Report* 108 (13): 45. (pp. 412, 421)

———. 1991. American revival in manufacturing seen in U.S. report. *The New York Times* February 5: A1, C17. (p. 21)

Nasaw, D. 1985. *Children of the city*. New York: Oxford University. (p. 104)

Natale, J. A. 1990. The drive for deregulation gathers steam. *The Executive Educator* 12 (1): 27. (p. 484)

———. 1991. Promotion or retention? Ideas are changing—again. *The Executive Educator* 13 (1): 15–18. (p. 267)

Nathan, J. 1985. The rhetoric and the reality of expanding educational choices. *Phi Delta Kappan* 66 (7): 476–481. (pp. 455, 500)

———. 1990. Progress, problems, and prospects of state education choice plans. In *Choice in education*, edited by W. L. Boyd and H. J. Walberg. Berkeley, CA: McCutchan. (pp. 455, 502)

Nathan, R. R. 1991. Where the minority middle class lives. *The Wall Street Journal* May 22: A14. (p. 76)

National Academy of Sciences. 1982a. *Families that work: Children in a changing world*. Washington, DC: National Academy Press.

———. 1982b. *Placing children in special education: A struggle for equity*. Washington, DC: National Academy Press. (p. 134)

National Advisory Commission on Civil Disorders. 1968. *Report of the National Advisory Commission on Civil Disorders*. Washington, DC: U.S. Government Printing Office.

National Advisory Council on Women's Educational Programs. 1982. *Educational equity: A continuing quest*. Washington, DC: U.S. Department of Education. (p. 426)

National Assessment of Educational Progress. 1981a. *Has Title I improved education for disadvantaged students? Evidence from three national assessments of reading*. Report No. SY-DS-50. Denver: National Assessment of Educational Progress. (p. 449)

———. 1981b. Private students read better, but . . . *NAEP Newsletter* 14 (1): 3.

———. 1985. *The reading report card*. Princeton, NJ: Educational Testing Service. (pp. 45, 137, 360)

National Association of Secondary School Principals. 1988. *Beyond standardized testing*. Reston, VA: National Association of Secondary School Principals. (p. 476)

National Board for Professional Teaching Standards. 1989. *1989 annual report*. Detroit: National Board for Professional Teaching Standards. (p. 471)

National Catholic Education Association, 1987. *United States Catholic elementary and secondary schools, 1986-87*. Washington, DC: National Catholic Education Association. (pp. 446, 447)

National Center for Education Statistics. 1981. *The condition of education*. Washington, DC: U.S. Government Printing Office. (p. 446)

———. 1984. *Two years after high school*. Washington, DC: U.S. Government Printing Office. (p. 63)

———. 1985. *The condition of education*. Washington, DC: U.S. Government Printing Office.

———. 1990. *Characteristics of private schools: 1987-88*. Washington, DC: U.S. Department of Education. (p. 446)

National Commission on Excellence in Education. 1983. *A nation at risk: The imperative for educational reform*. Washington, DC: U.S. Government Printing Office. (pp. 467, 536)

National Commission on Secondary Vocational Education. 1984. *The unfinished agenda*. Columbus, OH: National Center for Research in Vocational Education.

National Commission on Testing and Public Policy. 1990. *From gatekeeper to gateway: Transforming testing in America*.Executive Summary. Chestnut Hill, MA: National Commission on Testing and Public Policy. (p. 476)

National Commission on The Role of the School and the Community in Improving Adolescent Health. 1990. *Code blue*. Alexandria, VA: National Association of State Boards of Education, (p. 208)

National Council of Teachers of English. 1990. Report on trends and issues. Paper released by the National Council. (p. 476)

National Council of Teachers of Mathematics. 1991. *A call for change*. Washington, DC: National Council of Teachers of Mathematics. (p. 465)

National Governors' Association. 1986. *Time for results: The governors' report on education*. Washington, DC: National Governors' Association. (pp. 468, 469, 536)

———. 1987. *Bringing down the barriers*. Washington, DC: National Governors' Association Center for Research. (pp. 469, 529)

———. 1991. *Results in education: 1990*. Washington, DC: National Governors' Association. (p. 506)

National Institute of Education. 1978. *Violent schools—safe schools*. Washington, DC: U.S. Government Printing Office. (p. 508)

National Institute on Drug Abuse. 1977. *Marijuana and health*. Sixth annual report to the U.S. Congress. Washington, DC: U.S. Government Printing Office.

National Law Center on Homelessness and Poverty. 1990. McKinney Act education amendments update. *In Just Times* 1 (8): 2. (p. 140)

National Monitor staff. 1988. Classroom child abuse programs may be harmful. *National Monitor of Education* 11 (9): 6-7. (p. 117)

National Research Council, 1989. *Common Destiny. Blacks and American society*, edited for the National Academy of Science by Gerald David Jaynes and Robin M. Williams, Jr. Washington, DC: National Academy Press. (pp. 51, 219, 300, 301, 311, 313)

———. 1990a. *Summary report: Doctorate recipients from United States Universities*. Washington, DC: National Research Council. (pp. 421, 422)

———. 1990b. *Who cares for America's children: Child care policy for the 1990's*. Washington, DC: National Research Council. (p. 279)

———. 1991. *Fulfilling the promise: Biology education in the nation's schools*. Washington, DC: National Research Council. (p. 465)

National Science Foundation. 1982. *Teletext and videotext in the United States*. New York: McGraw-Hill. (p. 119)

National Task Force on Educational Technology. 1986. *Transforming American education: Reducing the risk to the nation*. Washington, DC: U.S. Department of Education Office of Educational Research and Improvement. (p. 439)

Navarro, M. 1991. Rights panel likens school plan to segregation. *The New York Times* January 13: 15. (p. 500)

Nazario, S. L. 1990. Bearing the brunt. *The Wall Street Journal* February 9: R29. (p. 60)

Neinhuis, M. 1986. Early-intervention plan's effects mixed.*Education Week* 6 (13): 9. (p. 280)

Nelson, J. 1989. Why some children opt for sidelines. *The New York Times* November 6: 21. (p. 164)

Nelson, S. 1991. Small, rural schools use innovative ideas to renew curricula. *The Northwest Report* May 1991: 1, 4–5. (p. 444)

Nettles, S. M. 1990. *Community involvement and disadvantaged students: A review*. Baltimore: The Johns Hopkins Center for Research on Effective Schooling for Disadvantaged Students. (pp. 163, 166, 204, 266, 529)

Neugarten, B. L. 1949. The democracy of childhood. In *Democracy in Jonesville*, edited by W. Lloyd Warner and associates. New York: Harper and Row. (p. 154)

Neugarten, B. L., and Neugarten, D. A. 1987. The changing meanings of age. *Psychology Today* 21 (5): 29–33. (pp. 169, 411)

Nevi, C. 1987. In defense of tracking. *Educational Leadership* 44 (66): 24–26. (p. 44)

Newcomb, T. H. 1970. Open admissions: Before the deluge. Paper prepared for distribution at the Closing General Session of the National Conference on Higher Education sponsored by the American Association for Higher Education, Washington, DC.

Newcomer, M. 1959. *A century of higher education for American women*. New York: Harper & Row. (p. 434)

Newitt, J., et al. 1984. *School-to-work transition programs: A policy analysis*. Croton-on-Hudson, NY: Hudson Institute.

Newman, M. 1989. School consolidation garnering legislators' attention. *Education Week* 9 (16): 15, 19. (pp. 439, 442)

———. 1990. Too many districts? *Teacher* 1 (56): 12–13. (p. 442)

Newson, J., and Newson, E. 1976. *Seven years old in the home environment*. London: Unwin. (pp. 235, 439)

New Republic editors. 1986. The split-level economy. *The New Republic* No. 3712: 5–6. (p. 25)

Nicholson, H. J., and Hamm, J. K. 1990. Measurement and evaluation in Girls Clubs of America's Operation SMART: What's in it for schools? Paper presented at the annual meeting of the American Educational Research Association, Boston. (p. 428)

Niederberger, M. 1990. Schools trying to get more students to go to college. *The Pittsburgh Press* March 26: A6. (p. 55)

Niedermeyer, F., and Yelon, S. 1981. Los Angeles aligns instruction with essential skills. *Education Leadership* 38 (8): 618–620. (p. 504)

Nieves, E. 1991. College was the carrot, but not all went for it. *The New York Times* July 12: B10 (p. 497)

Nilsen, S. R., et al. 1990. *Preparing noncollege youth for employment in the U.S. and foreign countries*. Washington, DC: U.S. General Accounting Office. (p. 191)

Nock, S. L, and Kingston, P. W. 1988. Time with children: The impact of couples' work-time commitments. *Social Forces* 67 (1): 59–85. (p. 116)

Noddings, N. 1990. Feminist critiques in the professions. In *Review of Research in Education 16*, edited by Courtney Cazden. Washington, DC: American Educational Research Association. (pp. 431, 432)

Nordheimer, J. 1990. 'War of the Exes': Season of anxiety for divorced fathers. *The New York Times* July 12: B1. (p. 119)

Nottelmann, E. D. 1982. Children's adjustment in school: The interaction of physical maturity and school transition. Paper presented at the annual meeting of the American Educational Research Association, New York. (p. 158)

Novak, M. 1971. *The rise of the unmeltable ethnics*. New York: Macmillan. (p. 405)

Nazario, S. L. 1990. Bearing the brunt. *The Wall Street Journal* February 9: R20–R21. (p. 35)

Nuttall, E. V., et al. 1976. The effects of family size, birth order, sibling separation and crowding on the academic achievement of boys and girls. *American Educational Research Journal* 13: 217–223. (p. 130)

NWREL. 1987. Principals praise the effective practices in Indian education training. *The Northwest Report* February: 5. (p. 398)

———. 1990. *Indian reading series*. Portland, OR: Northwest Regional Educational Laboratory. (p. 398)

Oakes, J. 1985. *Keeping track*. New Haven, CT: Yale University Press. (p. 44)

———. 1990a. *Multiplying inequalities*. Santa Monica, CA: Rand. (p. 416)

———. 1990b. Opportunities, achievement, and choice: Women and minority students in science and mathematics. In *Review of Research in Education 16*, edited by Courtney Cazden. Washington, DC: American Educational Research Association. (pp. 246, 271)

Oakes, J., and Lipton, M. 1990. Tracking and ability grouping: a structural barrier to access and achievement. In *Access to knowledge*, edited by John I. Goodlad and Pamela Keating. New York: College Entrance Examination Board. (p. 44)

O'Brien, E. M. 1989. The demise of Native American education. *Black Issues in Higher Education* 7 (1): 15–22. (p. 393)

Oden, S., and Ricks, J. 1990. Follow-up study of Head Start's role in the lives of children and families. Paper presented at the annual meeting of the American Educational Research Association, Boston. (p. 279)

Ogbu, J. U. 1978. *Minority education and caste: The American system in cross-cultural perspective*. New York: Academic Press. (pp. 221, 355)

———. 1982. Social forces as a context of ghetto children's school failure. In *The language of children reared in poverty*, edited by Lynne Feagans and Dale Clark Farran. New York: Academic Press. (pp. 221, 355, 356)

———. 1990. Minority status and literacy in comparative perspective. *Daedalus* 119 (2): 141–168. (pp. 219, 221, 355)

O'Hare, W. 1989. In the black. *American Demographics* 11 (1): 25–29. (p. 352)

O'Keefe, M. 1986. College costs. *Change* May/June: 6–8. (p. 64)

Olmsted, P. P., and Szegda, M. J. 1988. Long-term effects of Follow Through participation. Paper presented at the annual meeting of the American Educational Research Association, New Orleans. (p. 280)

Olneck, M. R., and Bills, D. B. 1980. What makes Sammy run? An empirical assessment of the Bowles-Gintis correspondence theory. *American Journal of Education* 89 (1): 27–61. (p. 246)

Olson, D. H., and Miller, B. C., eds. 1983. *Family studies review yearbook*. Beverly Hills, CA: Sage. (p. 148)

Olson, L. 1986a. Many bilingual pupils unaided, study finds. *Education Week* 5 (17): 1, 17. (p. 375)

———. 1986b. Carnegie report: A 'powerful synthesis' that raises both hopes and questions. *Education Week* 5 (31): 1, 18. (p. 471)

———. 1987a. Certification panel gets cool reception from some administrators. *Education Week* 6 (35): 1, 16. (p. 495)

———. 1987b. Performance-based pay systems for teachers are being re-examined. *Education Week* 6 (29): 1, 16–17. (pp. 480, 495)

———. 1987c. Reforms 'doomed,' says panel, without early family aid. *Education Week* 7 (1): 1, 43. (p. 470)

———. 1990a. Federal agencies sound the alarm over the 'school-to-work transition.' *Education Week* 9 (35): 1, 19. (pp. 191, 501)

———. 1990b. Lessons learned? Old goal-setting stirs new doubts. *Education Week* 9 (21): 1, 23. (p. 142)

———. 1990c. Parents as partners. *Education Week* 9 (28): 17–24. (pp. 142, 489)

———. 1991a. Proposals for private-school choice reviving at all levels of government. *Education Week* 10 (22): 1, 10–11. (p. 500)

———. 1991b. Study documents impact of four Minn. choice plans. *Education Week* 10 (16): 19. (p. 500)

Olson, L., and Miller, J. A. 1991. The 'education president' at midterm: Mismatch between rhetoric, results? *Education Week* 10 (16): 1, 30–31. (p. 489)

O'Neal, J. 1991. Drive for national standards picking up steam. *Educational Leadership* 48 (5): 4–8. (p. 495)

O'Reilly, R. P. 1969. *Racial and social class isolation in the schools*. New York: New York State Department of Education Division of Research Office of Research and Evaluation. (p. 274)

Orfield, G. 1977. Response II. In *Language ethnicity, and the schools: Policy alternatives for bilingual-bicultural education*. Washington, DC: The George Washington University Institute for Educational Leadership. (p. 381)

———. 1981. *Toward a strategy for urban integration. Lessons in school and housing policy from twelve cities*. New York: Ford Foundation. (p. 335)

———. 1982. Desegregation of black and Hispanic students from 1968 to 1980. Paper prepared for the Joint Center for Political Studies. (pp. 302, 368)

———. 1987. Racial change in U.S. enrollment, 1968–1984. The University of Chicago National School Desegregation Project Working Papers, No. 1. (pp. 29, 303)

———. 1990. Public policy and college opportunity. *America Journal of Education* 98 (4): 317–350. (p. 63)

Orfield, G., and Monfort, F. 1987. Are American schools desegregating in the Reagan era? The University of Chicago National School Desegregation Project Working Papers, No. 14. (pp. 302, 303, 368)

Orland, M. E. 1990. Demographics of disadvantage: Intensity of childhood poverty and its relationship to educational achievement. In *Access to knowledge*, edited by John I. Goodlad and Pamela Keating. New York: College Entrance Examination Board. (pp. 237, 273, 247)

Ornstein, A. O.; Levine, D. U.; and Wilkerson, D. A. 1975. *Reforming metropolitan schools*. Pacific Palisades, CA: Goodyear. (p. 298)

Orr, E. W. 1987. *Twice as less: Black English and the performance of black students in mathematics and science*. New York: Norton. (p. 359)

Orr, J. B., and Nichelson, P. F. 1970. *The radical suburb*. Philadelphia: Westminster Press. (p. 96)

Ortega y Gassett, J. 1958. *Man and crisis*. New York: Norton. (p. 96)

Ottinger, C. 1990. College graduates in the labor market: Today and the future. *American Council on Education and Research Briefs* 1 (5): 1–8. (p. 229)

Otto, L. B. 1982. Extracurricular activities. In *Improving educational standards and productivity*, edited by Herbert J. Walberg. Berkeley, CA: McCutchan. (pp. 163, 164)

Ovando, C. J. 1990. Politics and pedagogy: The case of bilingual education. *Harvard Educational Review* 60 (3): 341–356. (pp. 369, 375, 376, 381)

Pacheco, L. C. 1977. Educational renewal: A bilingual-bicultural imperative. *Educational Horizons* 55: 168–176. (p. 374)

Padilla, A. M., et al. 1991. The English-only movement. *American Psychologist* 46 (2): 120–130. (pp. 376, 380)

Padron, Y. N., and Knight, S. L. 1990. Linguistic and cultural influences on classroom instruction. In *Leadership, equity, and school effectiveness*, edited by H. Prentice Baptiste, Jr., Hersholt C. Waxman, Judith Walker de Felix, and James E. Anderson, Newbury Park, CA: Sage. (pp. 379, 398)

Page, E. B., and Grandon, G. M. 1979. Family configurations and mental ability: Two theories contrasted with U.S. data. *American Educational Research Journal* 16: 257–272. (p. 130)

Page, E. G., and Keith, T. Z. 1981. Effects of U.S. private schools: A technical analysis of two recent claims. *Harvard Educational Review* 51 (4): 497–509. (p. 448)

Page, R., and Valli, L. 1990. *Curriculum differentiation*. Albany: State University of New York. (pp. 44, 261, 262)

Pai, Y. 1990. *Cultural foundations of education*. Columbus, OH: Merrill. (pp. 357, 383)

Palinscar, A. S. 1987. Reciprocal teaching: Field evaluations in remedial and content area reading. Paper presented at the annual meeting of the American Educational Research Association, Washington, DC. (p. 513)

Pallas, A. M., and Alexander, K. L. 1983. Sex differences in quantitative SAT performance. New evidence on the differential coursework hypothesis. *American Educational Research Journal* 20 (2): 165–182. (p. 418)

Palmer, F. H. n.d. *The effects of minimal early intervention on subsequent IQ scores and reading achievement*. Stony Brook, NY: State University of New York. (p. 280)

Palmer, J. L. 1990. *Who cares for America's children?* Washington, DC: National Academy Press. (p. 279)

Palmer, J. L.; Smeeding, T.; and Torrey, B. B., eds. 1988. *The vulnerable*. Washington, DC: The Urban Institute. (p. 180)

Panel on Adolescent Pregnancy and Childbearing. 1986. *Risking the future: Adolescent sexuality, pregnancy, and childbearing.* Washington, DC: National Research Council. (p. 205)

Panel on Policies and Prospects for Metropolitan and Nonmetropolitan America. 1980. *Urban America in the eighties: Perspectives and prospects.* Washington, DC: U.S. Government Printing Office. (p. 78)

Panel on Secondary School Education for the Changing Workplace. 1984. *High schools and the changing workplace.* Washington, DC: National Academy Press. (p. 24)

Pang, V. O. 1990. Asian-American children: A diverse population. *The Educational Forum* 55 (1): 49–66. (p. 384)

Parker, J. G., and Asher, S. R. 1986. Predicting long-term outcomes from peer rejection: Studies of dropping out, delinquency, and adult psychopathology. Paper presented at the annual meeting of the American Educational Research Association, San Francisco. (p. 152)

———. 1990. Friendship adjustment, group acceptance, and feelings of loneliness and social dissatisfaction in childhood. Paper presented at the annual meeting of the American Educational Research Association, Boston. (p. 152)

Pascal, A. 1977. *What do we know about school desegregation?* Santa Monica, CA: The Rand Corporation, P-5777. (p. 313)

Paske, R. 1990. Hypermedia: A progress report part 3: CD-ROM, CD-I, DVI, etc. *T. H. E. Journal* 18 (3): 93–97. (p. 519)

Passell, P. 1990. College tuition: A better idea? *The New York Times* July 4: 22. (p. 229)

———. 1991. Chronic poverty, black and white. *The New York Times* February 24: 14. (p. 368)

Passow, A. H. 1984. Tackling the reform reports of the 1980s. *Phi Delta Kappan* 65 (10): 674–683. (p. 490)

———. 1988a. *Curriculum and instruction in Chapter 1 programs: A look back and a look ahead.* New York: Teachers College ERIC Clearinghouse on Urban Education. (p. 284)

———. 1998b. Issues of access to knowledge. In *Critical issues in curriculum*, edited by Laurel N. Tanner and Kenneth J. Rehage. Chicago: University of Chicago Press. (pp. 42, 529)

———. 1990. Enriching the compensatory education curriculum for disadvantaged students. *Clearinghouse on Urban Education Digest* No. 61: 1–2. (pp. 268, 293, 519)

Patchen, M. 1982. *Black-white contact in schools: Its social and academic effects.* West Lafayette, IN: Purdue University Press.

Paternoster, R. 1989. Absolute and restrictive deterrence in a panel of youth: Explaining the onset, persistence/desistence, and frequency of delinquent offending. *Social Problems* 36 (3): 289–309. (p. 197)

Patterson, J. H. 1990. Minorities gain, but gaps remain. Paper presented at the annual meeting of the American Educational Research Association, Boston. (pp. 490, 492)

Patterson, O. 1979. The black community: Is there a future? In *The third century: America as a post-industrial society*, edited by Seymour Martin Lipset. Stanford, CA: Hoover Institution. (p. 77)

Paulson, F. L.; Paulson, P. R.; and Meyer, C. A. 1991 What makes a portfolio a portfolio? *Educational Leadership* 48 (5): 60–63. (p. 478)

Payne, C. M. 1984. *Getting what we ask for.* Westport, CT: Greenwood. (pp. 238, 261, 515)

———. 1989. Urban teachers and dropout-prone students: The uneasy partners. In *Dropouts from school*, edited by Lois Weis, Eleanor Farrar, and Hugh G. Petrie. Albany: State University of New York. (pp. 238, 261, 515)

Payzant, T. W. 1988. Standards board makes significant gains. *The School Administrator* 45 (2): 29–31. (p. 471)

Pear, R. 1990a. Bush is sent bill to increase entry of skilled immigrants. *The New York Times* October 29: A11. (p. 344)

———. 1990b. Congress acts to admit more skilled immigrants. *The New York Times* August 15: A12. (pp. 342, 344)

———. 1990c. U.S. reports poverty is down but inequality is up. *The New York Times* September 27: A10. (pp. 24, 25, 31)

———. 1991. Rich got richer in 80's; Others held even. *The New York Times* January 11: A1, A13. (pp. 24, 353)

Pearce, D. 1980. *Breaking down barriers: New evidence on the impact of metropolitan school desegregation on housing patterns.* Washington, DC: National Center for Desegregation Policy. (p. 335)

Pearcey, N. 1990. Is love enough? Recreating the economic base of the family. *The Family in America* 4 (1): 1–8. (pp. 89, 90, 120, 121)

Pearlman, R. 1991. Restructuring with technology: A tour of schools where it's happening. *Technology and Learning* 11 (4): 31–36. (p. 519)

Pearsall, P. 1990. *The power of the family: strength, comfort, and healing.* New York: Doubleday. (p. 197)

Pearson, J. 1989. Myths of choice: The governor's new clothes? *Phi Delta Kappan* 70 (10): 821–823. (p. 500)

Pearson, P. D. 1985. *The comprehension revolution: A twenty-year history of process and practice related to reading comprehension.* University of Illinois at Urbana-Champaign Center for the Study of Reading Report No. 57. (pp. 270, 512, 533)

Pechman, E. M. 1990. The child as meaning maker: The organizing theme of professional practice schools. In *Professional practice schools: Building a model II,* edited by Marsha Levine. Washington, DC: American Federation of Teachers. (pp. 513, 516, 517, 533)

Peek, B. C. 1991. Race and violence in the schools. *The New York Review of Books* 38 (1 & 2): 60–61. (p. 403)

Pell, C. 1990a. Carl D. Perkins Vocational Applied Technology Education Act amendments—conference report. *Congressional Record—Senate* August 2: S12011–S12014. (p. 56)

———. 1990b. Report of the National Center for Education and the Economy. *Congressional Record— Senate.* October 18: S16012–S16014. (pp. 192, 194)

Peng, S. S. 1982. *Effective high schools: What are their attributes?* Washington, DC: National Center for Education Statistics. (p. 448)

———. 1985. Enrollment patterns of Asian American students in post-secondary education. Paper presented at the annual meeting of the American Educational Research Association, Chicago. (p. 383)

———. 1990. Some selected statistics on higher education: What do they signify? Paper presented at the annual meeting of the American Educational Research Association, Boston. (pp. 41, 42)

Perlmann, J. 1988. *Ethnic differences. Schooling and social structure among the Irish, Italians, Jews, and Blacks in an American City, 1880–1935.* New York: Cambridge University Press. (pp. 219, 220)

Perry, J. C. 1991. Children at risk: The case against day care. *The Family in America* 5 (2): 1–10. (pp. 116, 138)

Personik, V. A. 1985. A second look at industry output and employment trends to 1985. *Monthly Labor Review* 108 (11): 26–41. (p. 22)

Peshkin, A. 1986. *God's choice.* Chicago: The University of Chicago Press. (p. 459)

Peshkin, A., and White, C. J. 1990. Four black American students: Coming of age in a multiethnic high school. *Teachers College Record* 92 (1): 21–38. (p. 357)

Peterkin, R. S. 1990. Restructuring America's school systems. *Clipboard* No. 3: 1–2. (p. 327)

———. 1991. What's happening in Milwaukee? *Educational Leadership* 48 (2): 50–52. (pp. 327, 499)

Peterman, F. P. 1990. The effects of an increased ratio of high- to low-aptitude students on academic tasks and teacher communications. Paper delivered at the annual meeting of the American Educational Research Association, Boston. (p. 44)

Petersen, A. C. 1980. Biopsychosocial processes in the development of sex-related differences. In *The psychobiology of sex differences and sex roles,* edited by J. E. Parson. New York: Hemispheric Publishing Corporation. (p. 418)

Peterson, D. 1989. Parental involvement in the educational process. *ERIC Clearinghouse on Educational Management* No. EA43: 1–2. (p. 144)

Peterson, P. E. 1985. *The politics of school reform 1870–1940.* Chicago: University of Chicago Press. (p. 254)

Peterson, P. G. 1990. The budget, from comedy to tragedy. *The New York Times* September 16: 23. (p. 32)

Peterson, R. A., and DeBord, L. 1966. *Supportiveness of the home and academic performance of disadvantaged boys.* Nashville: George Peabody College for Teachers Institute of Mental Retardation and Intellectual Development. (p. 131)

Pettigrew, T. F. 1973. Busing: A review of the evidence. *The Public Interest* Winter: 81–118. (p. 313)

———. 1978. *Report to the Superior Court of the State of California for the County of Los Angeles, November 14.* (pp. 317, 368)

———. 1985. New black-white patterns: How best to conceptualize them? In *Annual review of sociology,* edited by Ralph H. Turner and James F. Short, Jr. Palo Alto, CA: Annual Reviews. (p. 365)

Pfeifer, J. K. 1986. *Teenage suicide: What can the schools do?* Bloomington, IN: Phi Delta Kappa. (p. 185)

Phelps, E. B. 1980. Youth groups and agencies. In *Toward adolescence: The middle school years,* edited by Mauritz Johnson. Seventy-Ninth Yearbook of the National Society for the Study of

Education, Part I. Chicago: University of Chicago Press. (p. 170)

Phi Delta Kappa. 1980. *Why do some urban schools succeed?* Bloomington, IN: Phi Delta Kappa. (p. 504)

Philadelphia Public Schools. 1977. Test scores continue to rise. *Perspective: An In-Depth Look at the Philadelphia Public Schools* June. (p. 281)

Piaget, J. 1932. *The moral judgment of the child.* New York: Harcourt Brace Jovanovich. (p. 174)

Pierce, C. M.; Carew, J. V.; and Willis, D. 1977. An experiment in racism: TV commercials. *Education and Urban Society* 10 (November): 61–87. (p. 136)

Pincus, F. L. 1980. The false promises of community colleges: Class conflict and vocational education. *Harvard Educational Review* 50: 332–361. (p. 87)

Pincus, F. L., and Archer, E. 1989. *Bridges to opportunity.* New York: Academy for Educational Development and College Entrance Examination Board. (pp. 57, 59, 61)

Pinnell, G. S. 1990. Success for low achievers through reading recovery. *Educational Leadership* 48 (1): 17–21. (pp. 522, 523)

Pipho, C. 1988. Career ladders are changing. *Phi Delta Kappan* 69 (8): 550–551. (p. 481)

———. 1990. Reflecting on the Kentucky State Court decision. *Education Week* 9 (32): 28. (p. 487)

———. 1991. Tents and pushy camels. *Phi Delta Kappan* 72 (7): 494–495. (pp. 126, 455, 469)

Pitsch, M. 1990. Cavazos creates outreach office to promote choice. *Education Week* 10 (15): 30. (p. 499)

Plagens, P. 1991. Violence in our culture. *Newsweek* 117 (13): 46–52. (pp. 135, 136, 197)

Plisko, V., and Stern, J. D. 1985. *The condition of education.* Washington, DC: National Center for Education Statistics.

Plomin, R. 1989. Environment and genes. *American Psychologist* 44 (2): 105–111. (p. 67)

Pogrow, S. 1990a. A Socratic approach to using computers with at-risk students. *Educational Leadership* 47 (5): 61–66. (p. 520)

———. 1990b. Challenging at-risk students: Findings from the HOTS program. *Phi Delta Kappan* 71 (5): 389–397. (p. 520)

Pollatsek, A. 1989. Does Black English stand between black students and success in math and science? Perhaps. *Contemporary Psychology* 34 (10): 908–909. (p. 359)

Pollitt, K. 1991. The smurfette principle. *The New York Times Magazine* April 7: 22–24. (p. 136)

Pollock, L. A. 1983. *Forgotten children.* Cambridge: Cambridge University Press. (p. 91)

Popenoe, D. 1988. *Disturbing the nest. Family change and decline in modern societies.* New York: Aldine de Gruyter. (pp. 119, 124, 125, 183)

———. 1991. Family decline in the Swedish welfare state. *The Public Interest* No. 102: 65–77. (pp. 124, 130)

Porat, M. 1977. *Information economy: Definition and measurement.* Washington, DC: U.S. Department of Commerce. (p. 22)

Porter, A. 1991. Good teaching of mathematics to disadvantaged students. In *Better schooling for the children of poverty: Alternatives to conventional wisdom,* edited by Michael S. Knapp and Patrick M. Shields. Berkeley, CA: McCutchan. (p. 514)

Porter, A. G., et al. 1986. Content determinants. Michigan State University Institute for Research on Teaching Research Series Paper No. 179.

Porter, P. R. 1976. *The recovery of American cities.* New York: Two Continents. (pp. 83, 86)

Porter, R. P. 1990. *Forked tongue: The politics of bilingual education.* New York: Basic Books. (pp. 372, 373, 375, 378, 380)

———. 1991. The false alarm over early English acquisition. *Education Week* 10 (37): 32. (p. 407)

Portes, A., and Rumbaut, R. G. 1990. *Immigrant America.* Berkeley, CA: University of California Press. (pp. 343, 350, 406)

Portes, A., and Wilson, K. L. 1976. Black-white differences in educational attainment. *American Sociological Review* 41: 414–431. (pp. 241, 363)

Poulos, R. W.; Rubenstein, E. A.; and Liebert, R. M. 1975. Positive social learning. *Journal of Communications* 25 (Autumn): 90–97. (p. 136)

Powell, A. G. 1985. Being unspecial in the shopping mall high school. *Phi Delta Kappan* 67: 255–261. (pp. 515, 532)

Powell, B., and Steelman, L. C. 1990. Beyond sibling size: Sibling density, sex composition, and educational outcomes. *Social Forces* 698 (1): 181–206. (p. 130)

Powell, G. J. 1989. Defining self-concept as a dimension of academic achievement for inner-city youth. In *Black students: Psychosocial issues and academic achievement,* edited by G. Berry and J. Asamen. Newbury Park, CA: Sage. (p. 266)

Prager, J.; Longshore, D.; and Seeman, M. 1986. *School desegregation research*. New York: Plenum. (p. 339)

Preece, P. 1990. Pitfalls in research on school and teacher effectiveness. *Research Papers in Education* 4 (3): 47–69. (p. 509)

Presseisen, B. Z. 1987. *Thinking skills throughout the curriculum*. Bloomington, IN: Pi Lambda Theta. (p. 513)

———. ed. 1988. *At-risk students and thinking: Perspectives from research*. Washington, DC: National Education Association. (pp. 513, 516, 533)

Pressley, M., and Harris, K. R. 1990. What we really know about strategy instruction. *Educational Leadership* 48 (1): 31–34. (p. 513)

Preston, S. H. 1984. Children and the elderly in the U.S. *Scientific American* 251 (6): 44–49. (p. 32)

Price, C. A., and Woodard, D. 1985. *The burden of busing*. Knoxville: The University of Tennessee Press. (p. 457)

Proctor, S. D. 1989. To the rescue: A national youth academy. *The New York Times* September 16: 15. (p. 95)

Provenzo, E. F., Jr. 1990. *Religious fundamentalism and American education*. Albany: State University of New York. (p.457)

Puckett, J. L. 1989. *Foxfire reconsidered*. Urbana: University of Illinois Press. (p. 396)

Purkey, S., and Smith, M. S. 1983. Effective schools: A review. *The Elementary School Journal* 83 (4): 427–452.

Purpel, D. 1988. *The moral and spiritual crisis in education*. South Hadley, MA: Bergin and Garvey. (p. 254)

Putka, G. 1991a. Curricula of color. *The Wall Street Journal* July 1: A1, A4. (p. 403)

———. 1991b. Education reformers have new respect for Catholic schools. *The Wall Street Journal* March 28: A1, A8. (p. 438)

Putnam, J.; Roehler, L. R.; and Duffy, G. R. 1987. The staff development model of the teacher explanation project. Michigan State University Institute for Research on Teaching Occasional Research Paper No. 108. (p. 518)

Putnam, R. T.; Lampert, M.; and Peterson, P. L. 1990. Alternative perspectives on knowing instruction in elementary schools. In *Review of Research in Education 16*, edited by Courtney Cazden. Washington, DC: American Educational Research Association. (pp. 514, 533)

Quality Education for Minorities Project. 1990. *Education that works: An action plan for the education of minorities*. Cambridge, MA: Massachusetts Institute of Technology. (pp. 265, 294, 493, 529)

Quantz, R. A. 1981–82. Mild mental retardation and race. *Educational Studies* 12: 387–393. (p. 134)

Raban, J. 1990. New world (part four). *Granta* 32: 231–255. (p. 347)

Rainey, L. 1990. BioPrep: An academic honors program for rural students. *Phi Delta Kappan* 72 (2): 170–171. (pp. 347, 445)

Rainwater, L. 1970. *Behind ghetto walls: Black families in a federal slum*. Chicago: Aldine. (pp. 94, 103)

Rainwater, L.; Coleman, R. P.; and Handel, G. 1959. *Workingman's wife*. New York: Oceana Publications. (p. 35)

Ramirez, J. D.; Yuen, S. D.; and Ramey, D. R. 1991. *Final report: Longitudinal study of structured English immersion strategy, early-exit, and late-exit transitional bilingual programs for language-minority children. Executive Summary*. San Mateo, CA: Aquirre International. (p. 376)

Ramirez, M. III. 1976. Cultural democracy through bilingual education. *Consortium Currents* 3 (Spring-Summer): 11–15.

Ramirez, M. III, and Castañeda, A. 1974. *Cultural democracy, bicognitive development, and education*. New York: Academic Press. (p. 381)

Ramos, M. 1980. The hippies: Where are they now? In *Drugs and the youth culture*, edited by Frank R. Scarpitti and Susan K. Datesman. Beverly Hills, CA: Sage (p. 201)

Randour, M. L.; Strasburg, G. L.; and Lipman-Blumen, J. 1982. Women in higher education: Trends in enrollments and degrees earned. *Harvard Educational Review* 52 (2): 189–202. (p. 421)

Raspberry, W. 1976. The discipline revival. *Washington Post* February 2: A16. (p. 167)

———. 1990. Why blacks 'poor-mouth' their status. *PittsburghPost-Gazette* May 18: 6. (p. 352)

———. 1991. The ecology of urban recovery. *The Washington Post* February 13: A19. (p. 20)

Raudenbush, S. W. 1990. New evidence in the search for effective primary schools. *American Journal of Education* 98 (2): 175–183. (p. 503)

Raudenbush, S. W., and Bryk, A. S. 1986. A hierarchical model for studying school effects. *Sociology of Education* 59 (1): 1–17. (p. 449)

Ravitch, D. 1977. *The revisionists revised: Studies in the historiography of American education.* Proceedings of the National Academy of Education 4, Palo Alto, CA. pp. 1–84. (p. 247)

———. 1990. Multiculturalism yes, particularism no. *The Chronicle of Higher Education.* 37 (8): A44. (pp. 401, 402)

Ray, B. D. 1989a. An overview of home schooling in the United States: Its growth and development and future challenges. Paper presented at the annual meeting of the American Educational Research Association, San Francisco. (pp. 456, 457)

———. 1989b. Research on home education. *Private School Monitor* 11 (1): 7–9. (p. 456)

———. 1991. Religious orthodoxy and student achievement in home education. Paper presented at the annual meeting of the American Educational Research Association, Chicago. (pp. 456, 501)

Raymond, C. 1989. Shift of many traditionally male jobs to women. *The Chronicle of Higher Education* 36 (6): A4, A6. (p. 421)

Raywid, M. A. 1987. Public choice, yes; Vouchers, no! *Phi Delta Kappan* 68 (10): 762–769. (pp. 453, 457, 458)

———. 1990. The accomplishments of schools of choice. In *Magnet schools,* edited by Nolan Estes, Daniel U. Levine, and Donald R. Waldrip. Austin, TX: Morgan. (pp. 453, 457, 500)

———. 1991. Is there a case for choice? *Educational Leadership* 48 (4): 4–12. (pp. 453, 457, 500)

Read, M. S. 1976. *Malnutrition, learning, and behavior.* Washington, DC: National Institute for Child Health and Human Development, Center for Research for Mothers and Children. DHEW Publication No. 76–1036. (pp. 132, 133)

Reed, I. 1991. Living at ground zero. *The Utne Reader* No. 54: 60–63. (p. 141)

Reed, W. L., ed. 1990. *Critiques of the NRC study, A Common Destiny: Blacks and American Society.* Vol. 1. Boston: Trotter Institute. (pp. 353, 364, 365, 535)

Rehberg, R. A., and Rosenthal, E. 1975. *Class and merit in the American high school: A multistudy analysis.* Binghamton State University of New York at Binghamton Center for Comparative Political Research, Paper no. 27. (p. 162)

Reich, R. B. 1989. As the world turns. *The New Republic* 200 (18): 23–28. (pp. 5, 6)

———. 1990. Why the rich are getting richer and the poor poorer. *Utne Reader* No. 37: 42–49. (p. 5)

———. 1991. The REAL economy. *The Atlantic Monthly* 267 (2): 35–52. (pp. 5, 6, 23)

Reid, J. N. 1990. Education and rural development: A review of recent evidence. Paper presented at the annual meeting of the American Educational Research Association, Boston. (p. 441)

Reinhard, B. 1987. Sex, drugs, and dropping out: Governors come face to face with real world. *Education Daily* 20 (132): 3–4. (p. 528)

Reinhold, R. 1990. California is proving ground for multiracial vision in U.S. *The New York Times* June 16: 1, 7. (p. 366)

Reisner, E. R.; Petry, C. A.; and Armitage, M. 1990. *A review of programs involving college students as tutors or mentors in grades K–12.* Washington, DC: Policy Studies Associates. (p. 497)

Reiss, A. J., Jr. 1961. *Occupations and social status.* New York: The Free Press. (p. 2)

Rendon, L. I., and Taylor, M. T. 1990. Hispanic students action for success. *AACJC Journal* 60 (3): 18–23. (p. 289)

Reppucci, N. D., and Herman, J. 1991. Sexuality education and child sexual abuse prevention programs in the schools. In *Review of Research in Education 17,* edited by Gerald Grant. Washington, DC: American Educational Research Association. (pp. 117, 149)

Reskin, B. F., and Blau, F. D. 1990. *Job queues, gender queues.* Philadelphia: Temple University Press. (pp. 412, 413, 421)

Resnick, D. P., and Resnick, L. B. 1985. Standards, curriculum, and performance. *Educational Researcher* 14 (4): 5–20. (pp. 85, 86, 293)

Resnick, L. B. 1990. Literacy in school and out. *Daedalus* 119 (2): 169–186. (pp. 85, 293, 533)

Restak, R. M. 1979. The other differences between girls and boys. *Educational Leadership* 37: 232–235. (p. 424)

Rhine, R. W. 1981. *Making schools more effective: New directions from Follow Through.* New York: Academic Press. (p. 198)

Rhone, T. 1992. Personal communication. (p. 498)

Rice, E. E. 1981. Should the family protection act be passed? Yes. *Update on Law-Related Education* 5 (2): 19–20, 65.

Richards, C. E., and Shujaa, M. 1990. School performance standards. In *Teachers and their workplace,* edited by Pedro Reyes. Newbury Park, CA: Sage. (p. 481)

Richardson, R. C., Jr. 1985. How are students learning? *Change* 17 (3): 43–49. (p. 240)

———. 1990. Community colleges: Democratizing or diverting? *Change* 22 (4): 52–53. (p. 57)

———. 1991. Promoting fair college outcomes. *Policy Perspectives* 3 (3): B7–B8. (p. 289)

Richardson, V. 1990. Significant and worthwhile change in teaching practice. *Educational Researcher* 19 (7): 10–18. (p. 524)

Riche, M. F. 1990. The boomerang age. *American Demographics* 12 (5): 28–30. 52. (pp. 117, 177, 412)

———. 1991. The future of the family. *American Demographics* 13 (3): 44–46. (pp. 117, 412)

Riesman, D., et al. 1950. *The lonely crowd*. New Haven, CT: Yale University Press. (pp. 10, 21)

Riessman, F. 1962. *The culturally deprived child*. New York: Harper & Row. (p. 104)

Rist, M. C. 1990a. Race and politics rip into the urban superintendency. *The Executive Educator* 12 (12): 12–15. (pp. 81, 318)

———. 1990b. Walter Marks. *The Executive Educator* 12(6): 12–14. (p. 326)

———. 1990c. In Chicago, school reform gives real power to the people. *The Executive Educator* 12 (10): 25–27. (p. 485)

Rist, R. C. 1973. *The urban school: A factory for failure*. Cambridge, MA: MIT Press. (p. 262)

———. 1981. Walking through a house of mirrors: Youth Education and employment training. *Education and Urban Society* November: 3–14. (p. 185)

Rivera-Batiz, F. 1986. *Finding work*. New York: Falmer. (p. 210)

———. 1990a. Quantitative literacy and the likelihood of employment. Paper presented at the annual meeting of the American Educational Research Association, Boston. (p. 466)

———. 1990b. The effects of literacy on the earnings of Hispanics in the United States. Paper presented at the annual meeting of the American Educational Research Association, Boston. 9 (p. 466)

Roberts, J. L. 1982. Boston schools worry about costs and crime as much as education. *The Wall Street Journal* May 13: 1, 22. (p. 296)

Roberts, M. 1988. Schoolyard menace. *Psychology Today* 22 (2): 52–56. (p. 157)

———. 1990. Turning boycotts of 2 Korean greengrocers in Brooklyn into green power. *The New York Times* June 7: A16. (p. 220)

Robinson, T. 1990. Truancy crackdown. *Chicago Sun-Times* May 30: 1, 12. (p. 277)

Robinson, V. 1981. Community colleges: Education's biggest growth industry has an uncertain mission. *Education Times* November 23.

Rockwell, J. 1990. Why rock remains the enemy. *The New York Times* January 21: 24. (p. 136)

Rodgers, W. L., and Backman, J. G. 1988. *The subjective well-being of young adults*. Ann Arbor: University of Michigan Survey Research Center. (pp. 180, 183)

Rodriguez, A. 1975. Introduction. *Inequality in Education* 3 (February): 4–6. (p. 373)

Rodriguez, C. E. 1989. *Puerto Ricans*. London: Unwin Hyman. (pp. 368, 371)

Rodriguez, R. 1982. *The hunger of memory*. Boston: Godine. (p. 104)

Rollings, E. M., and Nye, F. I. 1979. Wife-mother employment, family, and society. In *Contemporary theories about the family*, edited by Wesley R. Burr, Reuben Hill, F. Ivan Nye, and Ira L. Reiss, Vol. 1. New York: The Free Press. (p. 138)

Rollins, B. C., and Thomas, D. L. 1979. Parental support, power, and control techniques in the socialization of children. In *Contemporary theories about the family*, edited by W. R. Burr, et al. New York: Free Press. (p. 112)

Rolvaag, O. E. 1927. *Giants in the earth*. New York: Harper. (p. 405)

Ropers, R. H. 1985. The rise of the urban homeless. *Public Affairs Report* 26 (5–6): 1–14. (pp. 139, 140)

Rose, E. 1986. Drug-education programs widespread, but vary greatly in content. *Education Week* 5 (26): 7. (p. 202)

Rose, H. 1982. The future of black ghettos. In *Cities in the 21st century*, edited by Gary Gappert and Richard V. Knight. Beverly Hills, CA: Sage. (p. 76)

Rosen, B. C. 1959. Race, ethnicity, and the achievement syndrome. *American Sociological Review* 24: 47–60. (p. 218)

Rosenbaum, J. E. 1976. *Making inequality*. New York: John Wiley. (p. 87)

Rosenbaum, J. E.; Kulieke, M. J.; and Rubinowitz, L. S. 1987. Low-income black children in white suburban schools. *The Journal of Negro Education* 56 (1): 35–43. (p. 336)

Rosenbaum, J. E., and Popkin, S. J. 1991. Employment and earnings of low-income blacks who move to middle-class suburbs. In *The Urban Underclass*, edited by Christopher Jencks and Paul E. Peterson. Washington, DC: The Brookings Institution. (p. 336)

Rosenbaum, J. E.; Rubinowitz, L.; and Kulieke, M. 1985. *Low-income black children in white suburban schools*. Evanston, IL: Northwestern University. (p. 336)

Rosenberg, B. 1991. Not a case for market control. *Educational Leadership* 48 (2): 64–65. (p. 449)

Rosenberg, M. S. 1987. Directions for research on the psychological maltreatment of children. *American Psychologist* 42 (2): 166–171.

Rosenberger, L. 1985. Letting in 'latchkey' children. *The New York Times* August 18: 17–18. (p. 138)

Rosenholtz, S. 1977. *The multiple abilities curriculum: An intervention against the self-fulfilling prophecy*. Unpublished Ph.D. dissertation, Stanford University. (p. 316)

Rosenshine, B. V. 1986. Synthesis of research on explicit teaching. *Educational Leadership* 43 (7): 60–69. (p. 268)

———. 1990. Scaffolds for teaching content-specific higher-level skills. Unpublished paper, University of Illinois at Champaign-Urbana. (pp. 268, 511, 513, 533)

Rosenshine, B. V., and Stevens, R. 1986. Teaching functions. In *Handbook of research on teaching*, edited by Merlin C. Wittrock. New York: Macmillan. (p. 511)

Rosenthal, E. 1990. U.S. is by far the leader in homicide. *The New York Times* June 27: A9. (p. 185)

Rosewater, A. 1989. *Down these mean streets: Violence by and against America's children*. Fact sheet prepared for the U.S. House of Representatives Select Committee on Children, Youth, and Families. (p. 197)

Rossell, C. H. 1978. Magnet schools as a desegregation tool. *Urban Education* 14: 303–320. (p. 325)

———. 1990a. *The carrot or the stick for school desegregation policy*. Philadelphia: Temple University. (p. 306)

———. 1990b. The research on bilingual education. *Equity and choice* 6 (2): 29–36. (p. 376)

Rossi, P. H. 1989. *Down and out in America: The origins of homelessness*. Chicago: University of Chicago Press. (pp. 139, 140)

Rossi, P. H., and Rossi, A. S. 1961. Some effects of parochial school education in America. *Daedalus* 90 (Spring): 300–328.

Rotberg, I. D. 1982. Some legal and research considerations in establishing federal policy in bilingual education. *Harvard Educational Review* 52 (2): 149–168. (pp. 374, 377)

Roth, B. M. 1990. Social psychology's 'racisim.' *The Public Interest* No. 98 (Winter): 26–36. (p. 308)

Rothchild, J., and Wolf, S. B. 1976. *The children of the counterculture*. Garden City, NY: Doubleday. (p. 105)

Rothman, R. 1986. Raise status of teaching, colleges told. *Education Week* 6 (9): 7.

———. 1987. Mathematics scores show U.S. is a nation of underachievers. *Education Week* 6 (17): 1, 20–21. (p. 49)

———. 1988. 'Computer competence' still rare among students, assessment finds. *Education Week* 7 (29): 1, 20. (p. 438)

———. 1989. U.S. pupils earn familiar low scores on international science, math tests. *Education Week* 8 (20): 5. (pp. 49, 464)

———. 1990a. NAEP to create three standards of performance. *Education Week* 9 (35): 1, 8. (p. 477)

———. 1990b. NAEP will make its most extensive use of performance items. *Education Week* 9 (18): 1, 21. (p. 477)

———. 1990c. New tests based on performance raise questions. *Education Week* 10 (2): 1, 10, 12. (p. 477, 478)

———. 1990d. Paper launches academic attack on Chubb-Moe book on education. *Education Week* 10 (11): 1, 20. (p. 449)

———. 1991a. Group unveils plan for national test for all high-school seniors. *Education Week* 10 (20): 5. (p. 477)

———. 1991b. Promise, pitfalls seen in creating national exams. *Education Week* 10 (19): 17, (p. 477)

———. 1991c. Supply of new testing methods said trailing behind strong demand. *Education Week* 10 (26): 11. (p. 477)

Rowan, B. 1990. Commitment and control: Alternative strategies for the organizational design of schools. In *Review of Education 16*, edited by Courtney Cazden. Washington, DC: American Educational Research Association. (p. 493)

Rubel, R. J. 1980. Extent, perspectives, and consequences of violence and vandalism in public schools. In *Violence and crime in the schools*, edited by Keith Baker and Robert J. Rubel. Lexington, MA: D.C. Heath. (p. 276)

Rubin, L. G. 1976. *Worlds of pain: Life in the working-class family*. New York: Basic Books. (pp. 93)

Rubin, S. E., and Spady, W. G. 1984. Achieving excellence through outcome-based instructional delivery. *Educational Leadership* 41 (8): 37–44. (p. 528)

Rumberger, R. W. 1987. High school dropouts: A review of issues and evidence. *Review of Educational Research* 57: 101–121. (p. 528)

Russell, W. J. 1991. Interview on assessment issues with James Popham. *Educational Researcher* 20 (2): 24–27. (pp. 478, 479)

Rustin, B. 1987. The King to come. *The New Republic* 196 (10): 19–21. (p. 365)

Ryan, F. A. 1982. The federal role in American Indian education. *Harvard Educational Review* 52 (4): 423–430. (p. 393)

Ryan, J. A. 1973. *White ethnics: Their life in working-class America*. Englewood Cliffs, NJ: Prentice-Hall. (p. 105)

Ryder, N. B. 1974. The family in developed countries. *Scientific American* 231 (3): 123–132. (p. 121)

Sadker, M., and Sadker, D. 1985. Sexism in the classroom: From grade school to graduate school. *Phi Delta Kappan* 67 (7): 512–515. (p. 424)

———. 1990,. Confronting sexism in the college classroom. In *Gender in the classroom*, edited by Susan L. Gabriel and Isaiah Smithson. Urbana: University of Illinois. (p. 424)

Sadker, M.; Sadker, D.; and Klein, S. 1991. The issue of gender in elementary and secondary education. In *Review of research in education 17*, edited by Gerald Grant. Washington, DC: American Educational Research Association. (pp. 423, 424)

Safilios-Rothschild, C. 1979. *Sex role socialization and sex discrimination: A synthesis and critique of the literature*. Washington, DC: National Institute of Education. (pp. 420, 422, 435)

St. John, N. H. 1975. *School desegregation: Outcomes for children*. New York: Wiley. (p. 311)

Salpeter, J., 1991. Compact discs in the multimedia classroom. *Technology and learning*. 11 (5): 33–40, 66–67. (p. 519)

Saltzman, A. 1991. Trouble at the top. 1991. *U.S. News and World Report* 110 (23): 38–48. (p. 413)

Sampson, R. J., and Groves, W. B. 1989. Community structure and crime: Testing social-disorganization theory. *American Journal of Sociology* 95 (4): 774–802. (p. 197)

Sanchez, T. 1990. Adding gentle but firm persuasion. *The Washington Post* February 2: A1, A18–19. (p. 353)

Sanday, P. R. 1972. *On the causes of IQ differences between groups and the implications for social policy considerations*. Pittsburgh: School of Urban and Public Affairs, Carnegie-Mellon University. (p. 67)

Sandefur, G. D. 1989. American Indian reservations: The first underclass areas? *Focus* 12 (1): 37–41. (pp. 387, 388, 389)

Sanders, J. W. 1977. *The education of an urban minority: Catholics in Chicago, 1833–1965*. New York: Oxford University Press. (p. 446)

Saunders, M. T. Alcohol can be a dead end for teenagers. *The New York Times* November 7: 22. (pp. 199, 200)

Saxe, G. B.; Guberman, S. R.; and Gearhart, M. 1987. Social processes in early number development. *Monographs of the Society for Research in Child Development* 52 (2). (p. 113)

Saxon, B. 1991. Tally's corner revisited. *Harvard Educational Review* 61 (1): 88–95. (p. 35)

Scarr, S. 1981a. Implicit messages. *American Journal of Education* 89: 330–338. (pp. 67, 68)

———. 1981b. IQ: *Race, social class and individual differences. New studies of old problems*. Hillsdale, NJ: Erlbaum. (p. 67)

Schacter, F. F. 1979. *Everyday mother talk to toddlers: Early intervention*. New York: Academic Press. (pp. 357, 378)

Schaefer, E. S. 1991. Goals for parent and future-parent education: Research on parental beliefs and behavior. *The Elementary School Journal* 91 (3): 239–247. (pp. 107, 108, 231, 235)

Schaeffer, E. 1989. Forging a worklink for youth. *Work*America* 6 (12): 4. (p. 193)

Schapiro, R. 1990. Assignment: Make a difference. *Teacher* 1 (5): 60–65. (p. 205)

Schaub, M., and Baker, D. B. 1991. Solving the math problem: Paper presented at the annual meeting of the American Educational Research Association, Chicago. (p. 465).

Schevtschuk-Armstrong, L. 1991. Draft O.C.R. memo outlines grounds for probing ability-grouping practices. *Education Week*. 10 (22): 21–22. (p. 43)

Schinke, S. P.; Botvin, G. J.; and Orlandi, M. A. 1991. *Substance abuse in children and adolescents*. Newbury Park, CA: Sage. (p. 211)

Schmidt, P. 1989. Educators foresee 'Renaissance' in African studies. *Education Week* 9 (7): 8. (p. 402)

———. 1990a. Debate over 'Follow Through' program reopens. *Education Week* 9 (23): 23. (pp. 282, 372)

———. 1990b. Movement grows to rescue black males 'in crisis.' *Education Week*. 10 (4): 9. (pp. 355, 378)

———. 1991a. After slow start, Asian-Americans beginning to exert power on education-policy issues. *Education Week* 10 (23): 1, 18–20. (pp. 374, 382)

———. 1991b. Three types of bilingual education effective, E. D. study concludes. *Education Week* 10 (22): 1–23. (p. 376)

Schmidt, W. E. 1989. Some Chicagoans are moved out of projects into a future. *The New York Times* February 3: 1, 10. (pp. 336, 399, 400)

———. 1990. Lead paint poisons children despite 1971 law on removal. *The New York Times* August 26: 1, 20. (p. 134)

Schmitt, C. 1989. *Changes in educational attainment: A comparison among 1972, 1980, and high school seniors*. Washington, DC: U.S. Department of Education Office of Educational Research and Improvement. (p. 421)

Schmitt, E. 1988. New York suburbs struggle to cope with steep increase in the homeless. *The New York Times* December 26: 15. (pp. 39, 140)

Schmuck, P., and Schmuck, R. 1990. Democratic participation in small-town schools. *UCEA Review* 31 (3): 6–7. (p. 440)

Schmuck, R. A., and Runkel, P. J. 1990. *The Handbook of Organization Development in Schools*. 3rd ed. Palo Alto, CA: Mayfield. (p. 525)

Schneir, M., ed. 1972. *Feminism: The essential historical writings*. New York: Vintage Books. (p. 434)

Schofield, J. W. 1991. School desegregation and intergroup relations. In *Review of research in education 17*, edited by Gerald Grant. Washington, DC: American Educational Research Association. (pp. 314, 315)

Schorr, L. B. 1989. *Within our reach. Breaking the cycle of disadvantage*. New York: Doubleday Anchor. (pp. 108, 133, 138, 257, 279, 289, 290)

Schramm, W.; Lyle, J.; and Parker, E. E. 1960. *Television in the lives of our children*. Palo Alto, CA: Stanford University Press.

Schumer, F. 1990. Star-crossed. *New York* 23 (13): 32–38. (p. 222)

Schunk, D. H. 1987. Peer models and children's behavioral change. *Review of Educational Research* 57: 149–174. (p. 152)

Schwartz, J. 1988. Closing the gap. *American Demographics* 10 (1): 29, 41. (pp. 382, 413)

———. 1990. Catch-22. *American Demographics* 12 (2): 10. (p. 439)

Schwartz, J., and Exter, T. 1990. Crime stoppers. *American Demographics* 12 (11): 24–30. (p. 199)

Schwartz, R., and Hargroves, J. 1986–87. The Boston compact. *Metropolitan Education* No. 3: 14–24. (p. 496)

Schwartz, T. 1988. Daisy Tsui. *New York* 21 (17): 115, 117.

Schweinhart, L. J. 1987. What is and is not implied in the study of three preschool curriculum models. Paper presented at the annual meeting of the American Educational Research Association, Washington, DC. (p. 281)

Schweinhart, L. J., and Weikart, D. P. 1977. Research report—can preschool education make a lasting difference? *Bulletin of the High/Scope Foundation* 4 (Fall): 1–4. (pp. 279, 280)

———. 1980. *Young children grow up: The effects of the Perry Preschool Program on youths through age 15*. Ypsilanti, MI: High/Scope Educational Research Foundation. (p. 280)

———. 1989. Education for young children living in poverty: Child-initiated learning or teacher-directed instruction? *The Elementary School Journal* 89 (2): 213–239. (p. 280)

Scott, K. P., and Schau, C. G. 1985. Sex equity and sex bias in instructional materials. In *Handbook for achieving sex equity through education*, edited by Susan S. Klein. Baltimore: The Johns Hopkins University Press. (p. 423)

Scott, R. R., and McPartland, J. M. 1982. Desegregation as national policy. Correlates of racial attitudes. *American Educational Research Journal* 19 (3): 397–414. (p. 315)

Scott-Jones, D. 1990. From "voice" to "fugue" in females' development. *Educational Researcher* 20 (2): 31–32. (p. 431)

Scriven, M. 1975. Problems and prospects for individualization. In *Systems of individualized education*, edited by Harriet Talmadge. Berkeley, CA: McCutchan. (p. 530)

Searle, J. 1990. The storm over the university. *The New York Review of Books*. 37 (19): 34–42. (p. 401)

Sears, R. R.; Maccoby, E. E.; and Levin, H. 1957. *Patterns of child rearing*. Evanston, IL: Row, Peterson, (p. 148)

Sederberg, C. H. 1986. Economic role of school districts in rural communities. Paper presented at the annual meeting of the American Educational Research Association, San Francisco. (p. 442)

Sedlak, M. W.; Wheeler, C. W.; Pullin, D. C.; and Cusick, P. A. 1986. *Selling students short*. New York: Teachers College Press. (pp. 515, 517, 531)

Select Committee on Children, Youth, and Families. 1986. *Teen pregnancy: What is being done?* Washington, DC: U.S. Government Printing Office. (pp. 202, 205)

————. n.d. *Teen pregnancy in the U.S. A fact sheet*. Washington, DC: U.S. House of Representatives. (p. 206)

Seligman, J. 1990. Variations on a theme. *Newsweek* Winter/Spring: 38–46. (p. 118)

Sennet, R. 1973. Middle-class families and urban violence. The experience of a Chicago community in the nineteenth century. In *The American family in social-historical perspective*, edited by Michael Gordon. New York: St. Martin's Press. (p. 97)

Sewell, R. L. 1990. Out of Africa. *The New Republic* 203 (27): 6. (p. 401)

Shabecoff, P. 1990. Indian gambling spreads, upsetting some. *The New York Times* July 23: A6. (p. 388)

————. 1991. Role of taxes debated in adding to income gap. *The New York Times* February 23: 23. (p. 24)

Shade, B. J. 1982. Afro-American cognitive style: A variable in school success? *Review of Educational Research* 52 (2): 219–244. (p. 260)

————. 1986. Is there an Afro-American cognitive style? *The Journal of Black Psychology* 13 (1): 13–16. (p. 260)

Shanker, A. 1988. Opting out of the old stuff. *The New York Times* April 3: E–9. (p. 490)

————. 1989. But it's no cure-all. *The New York Times* January 22: E9. (p. 500)

————. 1990. Incentives for reform. *Congressional Record—House* July 16: H4756–H4757. (p. 466)

————. 1991. A conservative questions choice. *The New York Times* February 10: E7. (p. 500)

Shavelson, R. T. 1985. Schemata and teaching routines: A historic perspective. Paper presented at the annual meeting of the American Educational Research Association, Chicago.

Shea, B. M. 1976. Schooling and its antecedents: Substantive and methodological issues in the status attainment process. *Review of Educational Research* 46: 463–526. (pp. 237, 242)

Shearer, D. 1989. In search of equal partnerships: Prospects for progressive urban policy in the 1990s. In *Unequal partnerships*, edited by Gregory D. Squires. New Brunswick, NJ: Rutgers University Press. (p. 78)

Sheff, D. 1988. Portrait of a generation. *Rolling Stone* No. 525: 46–65. (p. 183)

Shepherd-Look, D. L. 1982. Sex differentiation and the development of sex roles. In *Handbook of developmental psychology*, edited by B. Wolman. Englewood Cliffs, NJ: Prentice-Hall. (pp. 127, 419)

Sher, J. P. 1983. Education's ugly duckling: Rural schools in urban nations. *Phi Delta Kappan* 65 (4): 257–262. (p. 441)

Sherman, J. 1977. Effects of biological factors on sex-related differences in mathematics achievement. In *Women and mathematics: Research perspectives for change*, edited by L. H. Fox and E. Fennema. Washington, DC: National Institute of Education. (pp. 417, 418)

Sherry, P.; Gomez, G.; Rush, M.; and Sobocinski, M. 1991. Factors affecting teenage alcohol use. Paper presented at the annual meeting of the American Educational Research Association, Chicago. (pp. 198, 200)

Shields, P. M., and Shaver, D. M. *The mismatch between the school and home cultures of academically at-risk students*. Menlo Park, CA: SRI International. (pp. 234, 258, 358, 397)

Shipman, V. C., et al. 1976. *Disadvantaged children and their first school experiences*. Princeton, NJ: Educational Testing Service. (p. 113)

Shoemaker, J. 1982. Effective schools: Putting the research to the ultimate test. *Pre-Post Press* 2: 1–2. (p. 504)

Shorter, E. 1975. *The making of the modern family*. New York: Basic Books. (pp. 91, 121)

Shostak, A. B., and Gomberg, W., eds. 1964. *Blue-collar world*. Englewood Cliffs, NJ: Prentice-Hall. (p. 35)

Shulman, L. S. 1987. Knowledge and teaching foundations of the new reform. *Harvard Educational Review* 57 (1): 1–22.

Siegal, A. E. 1975. Communicating with the next generation. *Journal of Communication* 25 (Autumn): 14–24. (p. 119)

Siegel, F. 1991. The cult of multiculturalism. *The New Republic* 204 (7): 34–40. (pp. 401, 402)

Silvern, S. B. 1988. Continuity/discontinuity between home and early childhood education environments. *The Elementary School Journal* 89 (2): 147–159. (p. 144)

Simon, J. L. 1990. *The economic consequences of immigration.* London: Basil Blackwell. (p. 344)

———. 1991. The case for greatly increased immigration. *The Public Interest* No. 102: 89–103. (pp. 344, 382)

Simon, P. 1989. Reducing violence on television. *Education Week.* 9 (5): 28. (pp. 135, 184)

———. 1990. Summary of labor committee substitute to S. 543 Job Training and Basic Skills Act of 1990. *Congressional Record—Senate* October 25: S18127–S18133. (pp. 51, 190)

Sims, C. 1990. World views. *The New York Times* November 4: Educ. 23. (p. 402)

Sinatra, R. 1990. Semantic mapping: A thinking strategy for improved reading and writing development. *Teaching Thinking and Problem Solving* 12 (1): 1–4. (p. 512)

Sinclair, R. 1991. Issues related to identifying at-risk students. In *Improving the education of at-risk students,* edited by Judith Walker de Felix, James Anderson, Prentice Baptiste, and Hersholt Waxman. Newbury Park, CA: Sage. (p. 528)

Sinclair, R. L., and Ghory, W. J. 1987. *Reaching marginal students.* Berkeley, CA: McCutchan. (p. 528)

———. 1990. Last things first: Realizing equality by improving conditions for marginal students. In *Access to knowledge,* edited by John I. Goodlad and Pamela Keating. New York: College Entrance Examination Board. (p. 528)

Singer, R. N. 1977. To err or not to err: A question for the instruction of psychomotor skills. *Review of Educational Research* 47: 479–498. (p. 293)

Sirotnik, K. A. 1987. Evaluation in the ecology of schooling: The process of school renewal. In *The ecology of school renewal,* edited by John I. Goodlad. Eighty-Sixth Yearbook of the National Society for the Study of Education, Part I. Chicago: University of Chicago Press. (p. 524)

Sizemore, B. A. 1985. Pitfalls and promises of effective schools research. *Journal of Negro Education* 54: 269–288. (pp. 517, 530)

———. 1987. The effective African American elementary school. In *Schooling in social context. Qualitative studies,* edited by George W. Noblit and William T. Pink. Norwood, NJ: Ablex. (pp. 144, 530)

———. 1990. The Madison Elementary School: A turn around case. In *Going to school,* edited by Kofi Lomotey. Albany: State University of New York. (pp. 517, 530, 532)

Sizer, T. R. 1984. *Horace's compromise.* Boston: Houghton Mifflin. (p. 532)

———. 1991. No pain, no gain. *Educational Leadership* 48 (8): 32–34. (pp. 515, 532)

Skeels, H. M. 1966. Adult status of children with contrasting early life experiences. *Monograph of the Society for Research in Child Development* 31, no. 6, Serial 105. Chicago: University of Chicago Press. (pp. 110, 133)

Skeels, H. M., and Dye, H. B. 1939. A study of the effects of differential stimulation on mentally retarded children. *Proceedings and Addresses of the American Association of Mental Deficiency* 44 (1): 114–136. (pp. 108, 109)

Skerry, P. 1991. Individualist America and today's immigrants. *The Public Interest* No. 102: 104–119. (pp. 220, 344)

Skolnick, A., and Skolnick, J. H., eds. 1971. *Family in transition.* Boston: Little, Brown. (p. 148)

Skovholt, J. 1978. Feminism and men's lives. *Counseling Psychologist* April: 3–10. (p. 425)

Slavin, R. E. 1977a. *Student team learning techniques: Narrowing the achievement gap between the races.* Baltimore: The Johns Hopkins University Center for Social Organization of Schools, Report No. 228. (p. 316)

———. 1977b. *Student learning team and scores adjusted for past achievement: A summary of field experiments.* Baltimore: The Johns Hopkins University Center for Social Organization of Schools, Report No. 227. (p. 316)

———. 1980. Cooperative learning. *Review of Educational Research* 50: 315–342. (pp. 316, 521)

———. 1986. How ability grouping affects student achievement in elementary schools. *CREMS Bulletin* June: 2–4. (p. 530)

———. 1987. Grouping for instruction in the elementary school. *Educational Psychologist* 22 (2): 109–127. (p. 157)

———. 1988. Synthesis of research on grouping in elementary and secondary schools. *Educational Leadership* 45 (4): 67–77. (p. 530)

———. 1989. A theory of school and classroom organization. *Educational Psychologist* 24: 89–108. (p. 157)

———. 1989/1990. Research on cooperative learning: Consensus and controversy. *Educational Leadership* 47 (4): 52–54. (pp. 316, 521)

———. 1990a. Achievement effects of ability grouping in secondary schools: A best-evidence synthesis. *Review of Educational Research* 60 (3): 471–499. (pp. 43, 262, 522, 530)

———. 1990b. *Cooperative learning. Theory, research and practice*. Englewood cliffs, NJ: Prentice-Hall. (pp. 157, 316, 521)

———. 1991. Synthesis of research on cooperative learning. *Educational Leadership* 48 (5): 72–82. (pp. 42, 157, 522)

Slavin, R. E., et al. 1990. Success for all: Effects of variations in duration and resources of a schoolwide elementary restructuring program. Paper presented at the annual meeting of the American Educational Research Association, Boston. (p. 522)

Slavin, R. E., and Madden, N. A.; 1989. What works for students at risk: A research synthesis. *Educational Leadership* 46 (5): 4–12. (p. 497)

Slavin, R. E.; Madden, N. A.; and Stevens, R. J. 1989/1990. Cooperative learning models for the 3 r's. *Educational Leadership* 47 (4): 22–28. (p. 522)

Smilansky, M. 1991. *Friendship and adolescence in young adulthood*. Gaithersburg, MD: Psychological and Educational Publications. (pp. 153, 154, 159, 175)

Smith, A. W. 1989. Educational attainment as a determinant of social class among Black Americans. *The Journal of Negro Education* 58 (3): 416–429. (pp. 242, 361, 363)

Smith, B. 1965. *They closed their schools. Prince Edward County, Virginia, 1951-64*. Chapel Hill: University of North Carolina Press. (p. 338)

Smith, D. 1990. *Caught in the crossfire*. Washington, DC: Center to Prevent Handgun Violence. (p. 276)

Smith, D. E. 1987. *The everyday world as problematic. A feminist sociology*. Boston: Northeastern University. (p. 433)

Smith, G. P. 1986. Unresolved issues and new developments in teacher competency testing. *Urban Educator* 8 (1): 1–16. (p. 397)

Smith, H. 1990–1991. Authentic work via the Foxfire approach. *National Center on Effective Schools Newsletter* 5 (3): 7–9. (p. 396)

Smith, J., and Exter, T. 1990. Crime stoppers. *American Demographics* 12 (11): 24–30. (p. 199)

Smith, J. K., and Wick, J. W. 1976. Practical problems of attempting to implement a mastery learning program in a large city school system. Paper presented at the annual meeting of the American Educational Research Association, San Francisco. (p. 268)

Smith, J. P. 1982. Race and human capital. Paper prepared for a conference of the National Academy of Education, Chicago. (p. 242)

Smith, J. P., and Welch, F. R. 1986. *Closing the gap*. Santa Monica, CA: Rand. (pp. 360, 397)

Smith, S.; Blank, S.; and Bond, J. T. 1990. *One program, two generations*. New York: Columbia University National Center for Children in Poverty. (pp. 189, 289, 290)

Smith, S. C., and Scott, J. C. 1990. *The collaborative school*. Eugene, OR: ERIC Clearinghouse on Educational Management. (pp. 485, 524, 525)

Smithson, I. 1990. Introduction. In *Gender in the classroom*, edited by Susan L. Gabriel and Isaiah Smithson. Urbana: University of Illinois. (p. 426)

Smittle, P. 1990. Assessment's next wave. *The College Board Review* No. 156: 22–28. (p. 289)

Smylie, M. A., and Smart, J. C. 1990. Teacher support for career enhancement initiatives: Program characteristics and effects on work. *Educational Evaluation and Policy Analysis* 12 (2): 139–155. (pp. 479, 480)

Sneider, C., and Barber, J. 1990. The new probeware: Science labs in a box. *Technology and Learning* 11 (2): 32–39. (p. 519)

Snider, W. 1987. New York's dropout data reanalyzed. *Education Week* 6 (24): 17. (p. 81)

———. 1990a. 'Choice' proposals make headway in statehouses in 1990. *Education Week* 10 (1): 26, 33. (p. 499)

———. 1990b. Wash. lawmakers adopt school-choice package. *Education Week* 9 (29): 14. (p. 499)

Snow, C. E. 1991. The theoretical basis of the home-school study of language and literacy development. Paper presented at the annual meeting of the American Educational Research Association, Chicago. (p. 258)

Snow, C. E.; Dubber, C.; and De Blauw, A. 1982. Routines in mother-child interaction. In *The language of children reared in poverty*, edited by Lynne Feagans and Dale Clark Farran. New York: Academic Press. (p. 235)

Soar, R. S., and Soar, R. M. 1984. Teacher merit pay: Can research help? *Journal of Human Behavior and Learning* 1 (1): 3–13. (p. 479)

Sobol, T. 1990. Understanding diversity. *Educational Leadership* 48 (3): 27–30. (p. 403)

Soled, S. W. 1987. Teaching processes to improve both higher as well as lower mental process achievement. Paper presented at the annual meeting of the American Educational Research Association, Washington, DC. (p. 517)

———. 1988. Does mastery learning improve higher order thinking as well as rote learning? Paper presented at the annual meeting of the American Educational Research Association, New Orleans. (p. 517)

Solomon, D., et al. 1988. Enhancing children's prosocial behavior in the classroom. *American Educational Research Journal* 25: 527–554. (p. 157)

Solomon, M. B. 1991. It's the way out of our multiple-choice mentality. *Education Week* 10 (19): 32, 34. (p. 70)

Soltis, J. F. 1987. *Reforming teacher education: The impact of the Holmes Group Report.* New York: Teachers College Press.

Sommer, A. 1990. *Rural school district cooperatives.* Portland, OR: Northwest Regional Educational Laboratory. (p. 443)

Sorensen, A. B., and Hallinan, M. T. 1986. Effects of ability grouping on growth in academic achievement. *American Educational Research Journal* 23: 529–542. (p. 43)

Sorensen, E. 1991. *Exploring the reasons behind the narrowing gender gap in earnings.* Lanham, MD: Urban Institute Press. (p. 413)

Sorin, G. 1990. *The nurturing neighborhood.* New York: New York University Press. (p. 175)

South, S. J., and Trent, K. 1988. Sex ratios and women's roles: A cross-national analysis. *American Journal of Sociology* 93 (5): 1096–1115. (p. 435)

Sowell, T. 1974. Black excellence: The case of Dunbar high school. *The Public Interest* Spring: 5–12. (p. 509)

———. 1978a. Ethnicity in changing America. *Daedalus* 107: 213–237. (pp. 68, 219, 346)

———. 1978b. *American ethnic groups.* Washington, DC: Urban Institute. (p. 219)

———. 1981. *Ethnic America.* New York: Basic Books. (pp. 216, 217, 219, 222)

Spady, W. G. 1983. The illusion of reform. *Educational Leadership* 41 (1): 31–32. (p. 491)

Spectorsky, A. C. 1955. *The exurbanites.* Philadelphia: J. B. Lippincott. (p. 35)

Spicer, M. W., and Hill, E. W. 1990. Evaluating parental choice in public education: Policy beyond the monopoly model. *American Journal of Education* 98 (2): 97–113. (p. 455)

Spillane, R. 1991. Not all merit-pay models have been unsuccessful. *Education Week* 10 (23): 34–35. (p. 481)

Spitz, H. R. 1986. *The raising of intelligence. A selected history of attempts to raise retarded intelligence.* Hillsdale, NJ: Erlbaum. (pp. 110, 280)

Squires, D. A.; Huitt W. G.; and Segars, J. K. 1983. *Effective schools and classrooms: A research-based perspective.* Washington, DC: Association for Supervision and Curriculum Development. (p. 506)

Stafford, F. P. 1987. Women's work, sibling competition, and children's school performance. *The American Economic Review* 77 (5): 972–980. (pp. 122, 130)

Stallings, J. A., and McCarthy, J. 1990. Teacher effectiveness research and equity issues. In *Leadership, equity, and school effectiveness,* edited by H. Prentice Baptiste, Jr., Hersholt C. Waxman, Judith Walker de Felix, and James E. Anderson. Newbury Park, CA: Sage. (pp. 261, 510, 530)

Stanley, J. C. 1990. We need to know why women falter in math. *The Chronicle of Higher Education* 36 (17): B.4. (p. 417)

Starr, P. 1991. The cultural enemy within. *The American Prospect* No. 4: 9–11. (p. 519)

Steel, L., and Schubert, J. G. 1983. The effectiveness of Upward Bound in preparing disadvantaged youth for postsecondary education. Paper presented at the annual meeting of the American Educational Research Association, Montreal. (p. 285)

Steelman, L. C. 1985. A tale of two variables: A review of the intellectual consequences of sibship size and birth order. *Review of Educational Research* 55: 353–386. (p. 130)

Steelman, L. C., and Doby, J. T. 1983. Family size and birth order as factors in the IQ performance of black and white children. *Sociology of Education* 56: 101–109. (p. 130)

Steen, L. A. 1987. Mathematics education: A predictor of scientific competitiveness. *Science* 237: 251–252, 303. (p. 49)

———. 1990. Numeracy. *Daedalus* 119 (2): 211–231. (p. 466)

Stein, J. A.; Newcomb, M. D.; and Bentler, P. M. 1987. An 8-year study of multiple influences on drug use and drug use consequences. *Journal of Personality and Social Psychology* 53 (6): 1094–1105. (p. 200)

Steinberg, S. 1981. *The ethnic myth. Race, ethnicity, and class in America*. New York: Anteneum. (p. 221)

Steinmetz, G., and Wright, E. O. 1989. The fall and rise of the petty bourgeoisie: Changing patterns of self-employment in the postwar United States. *American Sociological Review* 94: 973–1018. (p. 4)

Stendler, C. B. 1949. *Children of Brasstown*. Urbana: Bureau of Research and Service of the College of Education, University of Illinois. (p. 35)

Stephan, W. G., and Feagin, J. R., eds. 1980. *School desegregation: Past, present, and future*. New York: Plenum. (p. 338)

Stephens, E. R. 1991. State planning for interdistrict coordination. In *Educational planning*, edited by Robert V. Carlson and Gary Awkerman. New York: Longman. (p. 443)

Stephenson, R. S., and Levine, D. U. 1987. Are effective or meritorious schools meretricious? *The Urban Review* 19 (1): 25–34. (pp. 482, 509)

Stern, D., et al. 1990. Quality of students' work experience and orientation toward work. Paper presented at the annual meeting of the American Educational Research Association, Boston. (pp. 195, 196)

Stern, J. D. 1989. *Rural education. A changing landscape*. Washington, DC: U.S. Department of Education Office of Educational Research and Development. (p. 442)

Sternlieb, G. 1974. The city as sandbox. In *Suburban dynamics and the future of the city*, edited by James W. Hughes. New Brunswick, NJ: Rutgers University Center for Urban Policy Research. (p. 75)

Sternlieb, G., and Burchell, R. W. 1973. *Residential abandonment*. New Brunswick, NJ: Rutgers University. (p. 73)

Sternlieb, G., and Hughes, J. W. 1988. Black households. *American Demographics* 10 (4); 35–37. (p. 352)

Stevens, L. B. 1990. 'Separate but equal' has no place. *Education Week* 10 (9): 32. (p. 366)

Stevenson, R. W. 1991. Hispanic population grows by 70 percent in California. *The New York Times* February 26: A13. (pp. 355, 366)

Stigler, J. W., and Stevenson, H. W. 1991. How Asian teachers polish each lesson to perfection. *American Educator* 15 (1): 12–20, 43–48. (pp. 49, 464, 465)

Stimson, J. 1986. Battlelines on vouchers are drawn clearly. *The School Administrator* 43 (2): 25–26. (p. 455)

Stinchcombe, A. L.; Medill, M. J.; and Walker, D. 1969. Is there a racial tipping point in changing schools? *Journal of Social Issues* 25: 127–136. (p. 309)

Stockard, J. 1980. Sex inequities in the experiences of students. In *Sex equity in education*, edited by J. Stockard et al. New York: Academic Press. (p. 417)

Stone, J. R.; Stern, D. Hopkins, C.; and McMillion, M. 1990. Adolescents' perceptions of their work. *Journal of Vocational Education Research* 15 (15): 31–53. (p. 195)

Stone, L. 1974. The massacre of the innocents. *The New York Review of Books* 21 (November 14): 25–31. (pp. 92, 120)

———. 1991. *Road to divorce: England 1530–1987*. New York: Oxford University Press. (pp. 89, 92, 120)

Stone, M. 1989. Three lives. *New York* 22 (5): 35–42. (p. 98)

Stonehill, R. M., and Anderson, J. I. 1982. *An evaluation of ESEA Title I program operations and education effects*. Washington, DC: U.S. Government Printing Office. (p. 284)

Stout, H. 1991. Groups seek to bar a national test for school children. *The Wall Street Journal* March 28: A5. (p. 476)

Stringfield, S., and Teddlie, C. 1987. A time to summarize: Six years and three phases of the Louisiana school effectiveness study. Paper presented at the annual meeting of the American Educational Research Association, Washington, DC. (p. 570)

———. 1991. Schools as affectors of teacher effects. In *Effective teaching: Current research*, edited by Hersholt C. Waxman and Herbert J. Walberg. Berkeley, CA: McCutchan. (pp. 503, 510)

Strodtbeck, F. L. 1958. Family interaction, values and achievement. In *Talent and society*, edited by David C. McClelland, Alfred L. Baldwin, Urie Bronfenbrenner, and Fred L. Strodtbeck. Princeton, NJ: Van Nostrand. (p. 218)

Stronge, J. H. 1991. Emerging service delivery models for educating homeless children and youth: A sociological perspective. Paper presented at the annual meeting of the American Educational Research Association, Chicago. (p. 140)

Strother, D. B. 1984. Latchkey children: The fastest-growing special interest group in the schools. *Phi Delta Kappan* 66 (4): 290–293. (p. 139)

Strusinski, M. 1990. The evolution of shared decision making in school-based management. Paper presented at the annual meeting of the American Educational Research Association, Boston. (p. 485)

Study Group. 1987. *The nation's report card.* Cambridge, MA: National Academy of Education. (pp. 475, 475)

Sue, S., and Okazaki, S. 1990. Asian-American educational achievement. *American Psychologist* 45 (8): 913–920. (pp. 113, 383)

Sullivan, A. 1990. Racism 101. *The New Republic* 203 (23): 18–21. (p. 401)

Sullivan, M. and Miller, D. 1990. Cincinnati's urban Appalachian council and Appalachian identity. *Harvard Educational Review* 60 (1): 106–124. (p. 396)

Sullivan, M. L. 1990. *Getting paid: Youth, crime and work in the inner city.* Ithaca: NY: Cornell University Press. (p. 196)

Suro, R. 1990. Behind the census numbers, swirling tides of movement. *The New York Times* September 16: E4. (pp. 15, 76, 366)

———. 1991. Where have all the jobs gone? Follow the crabgrass. *The New York Times* March 4: E5. (p. 16)

Suttles, G. D. 1968. *The social order of the slum. Ethnicity and territory in the inner city.* Chicago: University of Chicago Press. (p. 35)

Svanum, S.; Ringle, R. G.; and McLaughlin, J. E. 1982. Father absence and cognitive performance in a large sample of six- to eleven-year-old children. *Child Development* 53: 136–143. (pp. 126, 129)

Swan, K.; Guerrero, F.; Mitrani, M.; and Schoener, J. 1989. Honing in on the target: Who among the educationally disadvantaged benefits most from what CBI? Paper presented at the annual meeting of the American Educational Research Association, San Francisco. (p. 438)

Sweet, D. A. 1986. Extracurricular activity participants outperform other students. *OERI Bulletin* September: 1–2. (p. 163)

Sykes, G. 1990. Organizing policy into practice: Reactions to the cases. *Educational Evaluation and Policy Analysis* 12 (3): 243–247. (pp. 492, 493, 495, 526)

Tachibana, J. 1990. Model minority myth presents unrepresentative portrait of Asian Americans, many educators say. *Black Issues in Higher Education* 6 (24): 1, 11. (p. 382)

Taeuber, K. 1990. Desegregation of public school districts: Persistence and change. *Phi Delta Kappan* 72 (1): 18–24. (pp. 77, 301, 305, 330)

Taggart, R. 1982. Lessons from experience with employment and training programs for youth. In *Education and work*, edited by Harry F. Silberman. Eighty-First Yearbook of the National Society for the Study of Education, Part II. Chicago: University of Chicago Press. (p. 187)

Takaki, R. 1990. The harmful myth of Asian superiority. *The New York Times* June 16: 15. (p. 382)

Takei, Y. 1981. Asian-Pacific education after Brown and Lau. Paper presented at the annual meeting of the American Educational Research Association, Los Angeles. (p. 382)

Tallman, I., and Morgner, R. 1970. Life-style differences among urban and suburban blue-collar families. *Social Forces* 48: 334–348. (p. 93)

Task Force on Education for Economic Growth. 1983. *Action for excellence.* Denver: Education Commission of the States.

Taylor, B. O., and Levine, D. U. 1991. Effective schools projects and school-based management. *Phi Delta Kappan* 72 (5): 394–397. (p. 485)

Taylor, E. 1989. Time is not on their side. *Time* 133 (9): 74. (p. 234)

Taylor, J. 1991. Are you politically correct? *New York.* 24 (3): 32–40. (pp. 401, 402)

Terry, D. 1991. Project tenants see island of safety washing away. *The New York Times* February 4: A1, C10. (pp. 14, 15)

Teske, S. 1987. Governor warns of polarization of society without education reforms. *Education Daily* 20 (29): 4. (p. 72)

———. 1988. Students lack knowledge and training to use computers, NAEP says. *Education Daily* 21 (65): 1–2.

Tewel, K. J. 1991. Do state takeovers hasten reforms—or impede progress? *The Executive Educator* 13 (3): 14–29. (p. 483)

Tharp, R. G. 1989. Psychocultural variables and constants. *American Psychologist* 44 (2): 349–359. (pp. 258, 397, 399)

Tharp, R. G., and Gallimore, R. 1988. *Rousing minds to life.* Cambridge: Cambridge University Press. (p. 397)

The Cognition and Technology Group at Vanderbilt. 1990. Anchored instruction and its relationship to situated cognition. *Educational Researcher* 19 (6): 2–10. (p. 533)

The Holmes Group. 1986. *Tomorrow's teachers*. East Lansing, MI: The Holmes Group. (p. 473)

———. 1989. *Work in progress: The Holmes Group one year on*. East Lansing, MI: The Holmes Group. (p. 473)

The National Commission on the Role of the School and the Community in Improving Adolescent Health. 1990. *CODE Blue: Uniting for healthier youth;*. Alexandria, VA: National Association of State Boards of Education. (p. 208)

Thernstrom, A. 1990. Is choice a necessity? *The Public Interest* No. 101: 124–131. (p. 500)

Therrien, L. 1989. Nightmare on video street. *Business Week* No. 3123: 34. (p. 119)

Thomas, P. 1967. *Down these mean streets*. New York: New American Library. (pp. 35, 259)

Thomas, T. C., and Pelavin, S. H. 1976. *Patterns in ESEA Title I reading achievement*. Project 4537. Menlo Park, CA: Stanford Research Institute. (p. 284)

Thornberry, T. 1987. Toward an interactional theory of delinquency. *Criminology* 25 (4): 863–891. (p. 198)

Thornburg, H. D. 1979. Can the middle school adapt to the needs of its students? *Colorado Journal of Educational Research* 19 (1): 26–29. (p. 158)

Tiedt, P. L., and Tiedt, I. M. 1990. *Multicultural teaching*. Boston: Allyn and Bacon. (p. 405)

Tikinoff, W. J. 1985. *Applying significant bilingual instructional features in the classroom*. Rosslyn, VA: InterAmerica Research Associates. (p. 378)

———. 1991. Modifying instructional environments. Paper presented at the annual meeting of the American Educational Research Association, Chicago. (p. 378)

Tinto, V. 1981. Higher education and occupational attainment in segmented labor markets: Recent evidence from the United States. *Higher Education* 10: 499–516. (p. 230)

Tobias, S., and Wiessbrod, G. 1980. Anxiety and mathematics: An update. *Harvard Educational Review* 50 (1): 63–70. (pp. 416, 422)

Toch, T. 1990. Plugging the school tax gap. *U.S. News and World Report* 108 (25): 58–59. (p. 295)

Tolchin, M. 1990. U.S. panel declares child abuse represents 'national emergency.' *The New York Times* June 28: A13. (p. 117)

Tompkins, G. M. 1990. The St. Louis plan. *Equity and Excellence* 24 (4): 71–73. (p. 334)

Tony, M. 1990. Bullying. *Network for Public Schools* 16 (1): 3. (pp. 157, 158)

Townsend, B., and O'Neil, K. 1990. Women get mad. *American Demographics* 12 (8): 26–32. (p. 411)

Traub, J. 1991. Ghetto blasters, *The New Republic* 204 (15): 21–22. (p. 355)

Treaster, J. B. 1990. Programs find adolescents' use of cocaine can be curtailed. *The New York Times* June 2: 10. (p. 202)

———. 1991. Cocaine use found on the way down among U.S. youths. *The New York Times* January 25: A1, A10. (p. 201)

Treiman, D. J. 1977. *Occupational prestige in comparative perspective*. New York: Academic Press. (p. 3)

Troike, R. C. 1981. Synthesis of research on bilingual education. *Educational Leadership* 38 (6): 498–504. (pp. 373, 376)

Trovato, F., and Vos, R. 1990. Domestic/religious individualism and youth suicide in Canada. *Family Perspectives* 224: 68–81. (p. 184)

Tsang, S-L., and Wing, L. C. 1985. *Beyond Angel Island: The education of Asian Americas*. Oakland, CA: ARC Associates. (pp. 383, 385)

Tucker, E. 1977. The follow through planned variation experiment: What is the pay-off? Paper presented at the annual meeting of the American Educational Research Association, Los Angeles. (p. 282)

Tucker-Ladd, P. R. 1990. Alienated adolescents: How can the school help? *Clearing House* 64 (2): 112–115. (p. 159)

Turow, J. 1981. *Entertainment, education, and the hard sell. Three decades of network children's television*. New York: Praeger. (p. 137)

Tussing, A. D. 1975. Emergence of the new unemployment. *Intellect* 103: 303–311.

Tyack, D. 1990. 'Restructuring' in historical perspective: Tinkering toward Utopia. *Teachers College Record* 92 (2): 170–191. (p. 442)

Tye, K. A. 1985. *The junior high school. School in search of a mission*. Lanham, MD: University Press of America. (p. 160)

Tyler, R. W., ed. 1978. *From youth to constructive adult life: The role of the public school*. Berkeley, CA: McCutchan. (p. 210)

———. 1991. General statement on program evaluation. In *Evaluation and education: At quarter century*, edited by Milbrey McLaughlin and D. C. Phillips. Chicago: University of Chicago Press. (pp. 102, 105)

Tyson-Bernstein, H. 1987. The Texas Teacher Appraisal System: What does it really appraise? *American Educator* 11 (1): 26–31. (p. 493)

Uchitelle, L. 1990a. Reviving a role for apprenticeships. *The New York Times* June 18: C2. (p. 56)

———. 1990b. Unequal pay widens in U.S. *The New York Times* August 14: 1, 17. (p. 25)

———. 1990c. Women's push into work force seems to have reached plateau. *The New York Times* November 24: 1, 18. (pp. 116, 411)

United States Bureau of the Census. 1960. *U.S. census of population: 1960 final report PC–1B*. Washington, DC: U.S. Government Printing Office. (p. 179)

———. 1970. *U.S. census of population: 1970 final report, PC (1A)*. Washington, DC: U.S. Government Printing Office.

———. 1975. *Current population reports*. Series P–25, No. 601. Washington, DC: U.S. Government Printing Office.

———. 1977. *Social indicators. 1976*. Washington, DC: U.S. Government Printing Office.

———. 1980. *Current population reports*. Series P–20, No. 354. Washington, DC: U.S. Government Printing Office.

———. 1981. *Current population reports*. Series P–20, No. 347; Series P–60, No. 124. Washington, DC: U.S. Government Printing Office.

———. 1984. *Projections of the population of the United States, by age, sex and race: 1983 to 2080*. Washington, DC: U.S. Government Printing Office. (p. 29)

———. 1985. *Current population reports*. Series P–20, No. 403. Washington, DC: U.S. Government Printing Office.

———. 1986. *Current population reports*. Series P–25, No. 998. Washington, DC: U.S. Government Printing Office.

———. 1987. *After-school care of school-age children: December 1984*. Series P–23, No. 149. Washington, DC: U.S. Government Printing Office. (p. 138)

United States Commission on Civil Rights. 1982. *Youth unemployment*. Washington, DC: U.S. Government Printing Office. (p. 189)

United States Department of Education. 1982. *Digest of education statistics*. Washington, DC: U.S. Government Printing Office.

———. 1987. *Schools that work. Educating disadvantaged children*. Washington, DC: U.S. Government Printing Office. (p. 353)

United States Department of Health, Education and Welfare. 1975. *Sex stereotyping in children's readers*. Washington, DC: U.S. Government Printing Office. (p. 423)

United States Department of Health and Human Services. 1982. *Television and behavior: Ten years of scientific progress and implications for the eighties*. Vol 1. Summary report. Washington, DC: U.S. Government Printing Office. (p. 135)

United States Department of Labor. 1977. *Employment and training report of the president*. Washington, DC: U.S. Government Printing Office.

———. 1981. *Employment and earnings*. Washington, DC: U.S. Department of Labor.

United States General Accounting Office. 1980. *CETA demonstration provides lessons on implementing youth programs*. Washington, DC: U.S. Government Printing Office.

———. 1986. *School dropouts*. Washington, DC: U.S. Government Accounting Office.

United States Office of Education. 1975. *Digest of education statistics*. Washington, DC: U.S. Government Printing Office.

———. 1977. *Instructional strategies in schools with high concentration of low-income pupils*. Washington, DC: U.S. Office of Education. (pp. 261–262)

United States Public Health Service, Panel of Scientists. 1972. *Report to the Surgeon-General on television violence*. Washington, DC: U.S. Government Printing Office. (p. 135)

United States Senate Subcommittee to Investigate Juvenile Delinquency. 1977. *Our nation's schools—a report card: "A" in school violence and vandalism*. Washington, DC: U.S. Government Printing Office. (p. 277)

Valdivieso, R. 1991. Disadvantaged urban eighth graders. *The Research Bulletin* 11 (1): 1–16. (p. 246)

Valencia, S. W., et al. 1989. Theory and practice in statewide reading assessment: Closing the gap. *Educational Leadership* 46 (7): 57–63. (p. 477)

Valverde, L.; Feinberg, R. C.; and Marquez, E. 1980. *Educating English-speaking Hispanics*. Washington, DC: Association for Supervision and Curriculum Development.

van Broekhuizen, L. D. 1991. Addressing limited English proficient students' needs. Paper presented at the annual meeting of the American Educational Research Association, Chicago. (pp. 376, 379)

Van Horn, R. 1991. Educational power tools: New instructional delivery systems. *Phi Delta Kappan* 72 (7): 527–533. (p. 519)

Vanfossen, B. E., Jones, J. D.; and Spade, J. Z. 1987. Curriculum tracking and status maintenance. *Sociology of Education* 60: 104–122. (pp. 43, 44, 162)

Velk, T. 1990. Welfare, not cowboys, kills Indians. *The Wall Street Journal* September 7: A12. (pp. 389, 391)

Venezky, R. L.; Kaestle, C. F.; and Sum, A. M. 1987. *The subtle danger*. Princeton, NJ: Educational Testing Service. (p. 47)

Verhovek, S. E. 1990. Girls win 51.3% in regents series. *The New York Times* March 4: 1 (p. 69)

Vernon, R. 1961. *Metropolis, 1985*. Cambridge, MA: Harvard University Press. (p. 86)

Veroff, J.; Douvan, E.; and Kulka, R. A. 1981. *The inner American: A self-portrait*. New York: Basic Books. (pp. 180, 183)

Viadero, D. 1986. Drug education: Search for success continues. *Education Week* 6 (5): 1, 11. (p. 202)

———. 1987a. Detroit student's murder provokes angry outcry. *Education Week* 6 (32): 1, 17. (p. 276)

———. 1987b. More and more students are juggling conflicting demands of school, work. *Education Week* 6 (2): 1, 17. (p. 195)

———. 1990a. A.T.E. joins chorus of concern over eligibility for certification. *Education Week* 9 (24): 11. (p. 471)

———. 1990b. Holmes Group outlines 'clinical schools' network. *Education Week* 9 (20): 5. (p. 474)

———. 1990c. Subject-matter groups convene historic 'congress.' *Education Week* 10 (1): 16. (p. 465)

Vinovskis, M. A. 1986. *The origins of public high schools*. Madison: University of Wisconsin Press. (p. 254)

Violas, P. C. 1978. *The training of the urban working class. A history of twentieth-century American education*. Chicago: Rand McNally. (pp. 247, 253)

Wachs, T. D.; Uzgiris, I. C.; and Hunt, J. McV. 1971. Cognitive development in infants of different age levels and from different environmental backgrounds. *Merrill-Palmer Quarterly* 17: 282–317. (p. 113)

Wacquant, L. J. D., and Wilson, W. J. 1989. The cost of racial and class exclusion in the inner city. In

The ghetto underclass: Social science perspectives, edited by William Julius Wilson. V. 501. The Annals of the American Academy of Political and Social Science. Newbury Park, CA: Sage. (pp. 15, 21, 77)

Wagenaar, T. C. 1981. High school seniors' view of themselves and their schools: A trend analysis. *Phi Delta Kappan* 63 (1): 29–32.

Waite, H. J. 1981. U.S. women at work. *Population Bulletin* 36 (2): 3–43. (p. 413)

Walberg, H. J. 1990. Productive teaching and instruction: Assessing the knowledge base. *Phi Delta Kappan* 71 (6): 470–478. (p. 511)

Walberg, H. J., and Marjoribanks, K. 1976. Family environment and cognitive development: Twelve analytic models. *Review of Educational Research* 46: 527–551. (p. 130)

Walberg, H. J., and Tsai, S. 1985. Correlates of achievement and attitudes: A national assessment study. *Journal of Educational Psychology* 78: 159–167. (p. 137)

Waldinger, R. 1990. Immigrant enterprise in the United States. In *Structures of capital*, edited by Sharon Zukin and Paul DiMaggio. New York: Cambridge University Press. (pp. 219, 220, 511)

Waldrop, J. 1990. Shades of black. *American Demographics* 12 (9): 30–34. (pp. 115, 116, 352, 361)

Walker, C. R., and Guest, R. H. 1952. *The man on the assembly line*. Cambridge, MA: Harvard University Press. (p. 35)

Walker, R. 1990. Governors aim to make schools, '2nd to none.' *Education Week* 9 (24): 1, 17. (p. 488)

———. 1990a. School built by Miss. Indian tribe 'breaks new ground' *Education Week* 10 (8): 11. (pp. 392, 496)

———. 1990b. The education of business. *Teacher Magazine* 1 (4): 66–68. (p. 496)

Wall, M. 1986. Technological options for rural schools. *Educational Leadership* 43 (6): 50–52. (p. 444)

Waller, A. E.; Baker, S. P.; and Szoucka, A. 1989. Childhood injury deaths: National analysis and geographic variations. *American Journal of Public Health* 79 (3): 310–315. (p. 184)

Wallerstein, J. A. 1989. *Second chances. Men, women, and children a decade after divorce*. New York: Ticknor and Fields. (p. 129)

Walmsley, S. A., and Allington, R. L. 1990. Redefining and reforming instructional support programs for at-risk students. In *Organizing and supervising a reading/language program*, edited by J. Cassidy and D. R. Hittleman. Newark, DE: International Reading Association. (p. 284)

Walsh, D. I. 1986. What women want. *American Demographics* 8 (6): 60. (p. 409)

———. 1989. 'National schoolhouse' rings in its 2nd generation. *Education Week* 9 (5): 1, 24–25. (p. 135)

Walsh, M. 1990a. La. oilman hits the road to promote 'Taylor' plans assuring college access. *Education Week* 9 (29): 16. (p. 498)

———. 1990b. Media. *Education Week* 9 (20): 8. (pp. 137, 138)

———. 1990c. School closings, tuition hikes in store for Chicago Archidiocese. *Education Week* 9 (19): 1, 10. (p. 446)

———. 1991. Black private academics are held up as filling void. *Education Week* 10 (25): 1, 28–29. (pp. 309, 447)

Wang, M. C. 1988. A promising approach for reforming spec. ed., *Education Week* 7 (32): 34. (p. 282)

Warner, W. L. 1953. *American life: Dream and reality.* Chicago: University of Chicago Press. (p. 34)

Warner, W. L., et al. 1949. *Democracy in Jonesville.* New York: Harper & Row. (pp. 7, 34)

Warner, W. L., and Lunt, P. S. 1941. *The social life of a modern community.* New Haven, CT: Yale University Press. (pp. 8, 34)

Warner, W. L.; Meeker, M.; and Eells, K. 1960. *Social class in America.* New York: Harper Torchbooks. (pp. 1, 2, 7, 35)

Wartes, J. 1989. Home schooler outcomes within Washington state. *Private School Monitor* 11 (1): 13–15. (p. 456)

Washington, B. T. 1963. *Up from slavery.* Garden City, NY: Doubleday. (p. 405)

Washor, E., and Coutre, D. 1990. A distance learning system that pays its own costs. *T. H. E. Journal* 18 (5): 62–64. (p. 444)

Wasserman, H. L. 1972. A comparative study of school performance among boys from broken and intact black families. *The Journal of Negro Education* 41: 137–141. (p. 129)

Waste, R. J. 1989. Federal urban policy in the 1980's. *Urban Resources* 5 (2): 21–24. (p. 81)

Waters, H. F. 1990. Watch what kids watch. *Newsweek* 115 (2): 50–52. (p. 137)

Watkins, B., and Montgomery, A. B. 1989. Conceptions of athletic excellence among children and adolescents. *Child Development* 60: 1362–1372. (p. 164)

Watkins, B. T. 1990. 2-year institutions under pressure to ease transfers. *The Chronicle of Higher Education* 36 (21): A1, A37. (pp. 56, 58)

Watson, B. 1990. The wired classroom: American education goes on-line. *Phi Delta Kappan* 72 (2): 109–112. (p. 519)

Watson, M., et al. 1989. The child development project: A values education program that combines traditional and developmental approaches. Paper presented at the annual meeting of the American Educational Research Association, San Francisco. (p. 157)

Waxman, H. C., and Walberg, H. J. eds. 1991. *Effective teaching: Current research.* Berkeley, CA: McCutchan. (p. 510)

Weaver, R. C. 1964. *The city and its suburbs.* New City 2 (March): 4–6. (p. 82)

Webb, M. 1987. Peer-helping relationships in urban schools. *Clearinghouse on Urban Education Digest* 37: 1–2. (p. 156)

Webster-Stratton, C. W. 1989. The relationship of marital support, conflict, and divorce to perceptions, behaviors, and childhood conduct problems. *Journal of Marriage and the Family* 51 (May): 417–430. (p. 128)

Wehlage, G. G., et al. 1989. *Reducing the risk. Schools as communities of support.* New York: Falmer. (pp. 527, 528)

Wehlage, G. G.; Rutter, R. A.; and Turnbaugh, A. 1987. A program model for at-risk high school students. *Educational Leadership* 44: 70–73. (pp. 527, 528)

Weidenthal, M. D. 1989. *Who cares about the inner city?* Washington, DC: American Association of Community and Junior Colleges. (pp. 60, 61)

Weiler, K. 1988, *Women teaching for change.* South Hadley, MA: Bergin and Harvey. (pp. 427, 428)

Weinberg, M. 1977. *Minority students: A research appraisal.* Washington, DC: U.S. Government Printing Office. (p. 311)

Weinberg, R. A. 1989. Intelligence and IQ. *American Psychologist* 44 (2): 98–104. (pp. 69, 110)

Weiner, B. 1976. An attributional approach for educational psychology. In *Review of research in education 4,* edited by Lee S. Shulman. Itasca, IL: Peacock.

Weintraub, P. 1981. The brain: His and hers. *Discover* 2 (4): 15–20. (p. 418)

Weis, L. 1987. The 1980s: De-industrialization and change in white working class male and female use of cultural forms. *Metropolitan Education* no. 5: 82–117. (p. 251)

———. 1990. *Working class without work*. New York: Routledge. (p. 251)

Weisman, J. 1990a. 'Latchkey' 8th graders likely to possess emotional 'risk factors,' study discloses. *Education Week* 10 (3): 6. (p. 139)

———. 1990b. Rural America is quietly 'hurting,' educators warn. *Education Week* 10 (6): 10. (pp. 439, 440, 496)

———. 1991a. 'Jobs' program hailed for preparing students for success at work. *Education Week* 10 (18): 1, 20. (p. 186)

———. 1991b. Report cautiously optimistic on school-business ties. *Education Week* 10 (24): 19. (p. 496)

Wells, A. S. 1989a. Educating homeless children. *ERIC Clearinghouse on Urban Education Digest* No. 54: 1–2. (p. 140)

———. 1989b. Hispanic education in America: Separate and unequal. *Clearinghouse on Urban Education Digest* November 15: 1–2. (p. 380)

———. 1990. Public school choice: Issues and concerns for urban educators. *ERIC Clearinghouse on Urban Education* No. 63: 1–4. (pp. 380, 500, 502)

———. 1991a. Asking what schools have done, or can do, to help desegregation. *The New York Times* January 16: B7. (p. 335)

———. 1991b. Once a desegregation tool, magnet schools becoming schools of choice. *The New York Times* January 9: B9. (pp. 323, 325)

Wells, E., and Prindle, C. 1986. *'Where's room 185?' How schools can reduce their dropout problem*. Chicago: Chicago Panel on Public School Policy and Finance. (p. 277)

Wentzel, K. R. 1990. The relationship between parental childrearing practices, socio-emotional adjustment, and academic achievement. Paper presented at the annual meeting of the American Educational Research Association, Boston. (p. 113)

West, J. 1945. *Plainville, U.S.A.* New York: Columbia University Press. (p. 7)

West, P. 1990. Head of E.D.'s Indian-education office aims to build schools' 'Indian-ness.' *Education Week* 10 (2): 23. (p. 391)

Westerfelt, H. 1987–1988. Tracking the homeless. *Focus* 10 (4): 20–24. (p. 140)

Westoff, C. F. 1981. Some speculations on the future of marriage and fertility. In *Teenage sexuality, pregnancy, and childbearing*, edited by Frank F.

Furstenberg, Jr., Richard Lincoln, and Jane Menken. Philadelphia: University of Pennsylvania. (p. 117)

Whitehead, R., Jr. 1990. Class acts: America's changing middle class faces polarization and problems. *Utne Reader* No. 37: 50–53. (pp. 9, 13, 24)

Whitman, D. 1989/1990. The surprising news about the underclass. *U.S. News and World Report* 107 (25): 73, 76. (p. 14)

———. 1991. Beyond thrift and loyalty. *U.S. News and World Report* 110 (1): 50–52. (pp. 170, 171)

Whyte, W. F. 1943. *Street-corner society*. Chicago: University of Chicago Press. (p. 35)

Wichess, S. F. 1984. Jobs for America's graduates: A youth employment program that means business. *The Clearing House* 57: 197–200. (p. 186)

Widom, C. S. 1989. The intergenerational transmission of violence. In *Pathways to criminal violence*, edited by Neil A. Weiner and Marvin E. Wolfgag. Newbury Park, CA: Sage. (p. 117)

Wiggington, E. 1986. *Foxfire 7–9*. Garden City, NJ: Anchor. (p. 396)

Wiggins, G. 1990. 'Standards' should mean 'qualities,' not quantities. *Education Week* 9 (18): 36, 25. (p. 478)

Wilcox, K. A. 1978. *Schooling and socialization for work roles: A structural inquiry into cultural transmission in an urban American community*. Unpublished Ph.D. dissertation, Harvard University. (p. 238)

Wiley, E. III. 1990. Educational dilemma result of tendency to ignore Latino family problems. *Black Issues in Higher Education* 7 (5): 6, 14. (pp. 17, 371)

———. 1991. Teacher exams still wreaking havoc on minority teachers. *Black Issues in Higher Education* 8 (6): 1, 12–14. (pp. 396, 397)

Wilkerson, I. 1990a. Blacks look to basics. *The New York Times* November 4: Educ 26. (pp. 15, 403)

———. 1990b. Detroit desperately searches for its very lifeblood: People. *The New York Times* September 6: A1, A12. (pp. 73, 353)

———. 1990c. Middle-class blacks try to grip a ladder while lending a hand. *The New York Times* November 26: 1, 11. (p. 351)

———. 1991. How Milwaukee boomed but left its blacks behind. *The New York Times* March 19: A1, A12. (p. 16)

Wilkerson, R. M., and White, K. P. 1988. Effects of the 4MAT system of instruction on students' achievement, retention, and attitudes. *The Elementary School Journal* 88 (4): 357–368.

Will, G. F. 1989. The servants of the strong. *Newsweek* 114 (17): 90. (p. 32)

Williams, P. A. 1987. *Standardizing school dropout measures*. New Brunswick, NJ: Rutgers University Center for Policy Research in Education. (p. 357)

Williams, S. S. 1987. The politics of the black child's language. In *Ethnicity and language*, edited by Winston A. Van Horne and Thomas V. Tonnesen. Madison: The University of Wisconsin System Institute on Race and Ethnicity. (p. 406)

Williams, T. M., and Kornblum, W. 1985. *Growing up poor*. Lexington, MA: Lexington. (pp. 18, 166, 187, 196)

Willie, C. V., ed. 1979. *The caste and class controversy*. New York: General Hall. (p. 364)

Willie, C. V., and Uchitelle, S. 1987. County and city transfers: Central city black students and suburban white students. The University of Chicago National School Desegregation Project Working Paper No. 9. (p. 338)

Willig, A. C. 1985. A meta-analysis of selected studies on the effectiveness of bilingual education. *Review of Educational Research* 55 (3): 269–317. (p. 376)

Willis, B. H.; Thomas, S. N.; and Hoppe, M. H. 1985. *Changing minds in a changing world*. Research Triangle Park, NC: Southeastern Regional Council for Educational Improvement. (p. 136)

Willis, M. G. 1989. Learning styles of African American children: A review of the literature and interventions. *The Journal of Black Psychology* 16 (1): 47–65. (pp. 260, 397)

Willis, P. 1979. *Learning to labour: How working class kids get working class jobs*. Westmead, England: Saxon House. (pp. 174, 357)

Willis, S. 1990. The inclusive curriculum. *ASCD Update* 32 (2): 1, 6, 8. (p. 399)

Willms, D. 1982. Is there any private school advantage? *IFG Policy Perspectives* Winter: 1–2. (p. 448)

Wilms, W. W. 1987. Proprietary schools. *Change* January/February: 10–22. (p. 61)

Wilson, A. B. 1959. Residential segregation of social classes and aspirations of high school boys. *American Sociological Review* 24: 836–845. (pp. 161, 308, 309)

———. 1967. Educational consequences of segregation in a California community. In *Racial isolation in the public schools*. Vol. 2. U.S. Commission on Civil Rights. Washington, DC: U.S. Government Printing Office, Appendix C3, pp. 165–206. (p. 237)

Wilson, B. L., and Corbett, H. D. 1990. Statewide testing and local improvement: An oxymoron? In *The educational reform movement of the 1980s*, edited by Joseph Murphy. Berkeley. CA: McCutchan. (p. 492)

Wilson, D. 1990. *Effective schools research and dropout reduction*. Austin, TX: Texas Education Agency. (pp. 18, 20, 495, 527, 528, 529)

Wilson, J. Q. 1983. *Thinking about crime*. 2nd ed. New York: Basic Books. (p. 210)

Wilson, J. Q., and Herrnstein, R. J. 1985. *Crime and human nature*. New York: Simon and Schuster. (pp. 197, 198)

Wilson, R. 1989. Many states seek tougher regulation of for-profit schools. *The Chronicle of Higher Education* 35 (21): A1, A18, A19. (p. 62)

Wilson, W. J. 1978. *The declining significance of race: Blacks and changing American institutions*. Chicago: University of Chicago Press. (p. 364)

———. 1979. The declining significance of race: Revisited but not revised. In *The caste and class controversy*, edited by Charles V. Willie. New York: General Hall. (p. 364)

———. 1987. *The truly disadvantaged: The inner-city, the underclass, and public policy*. Chicago: University of Chicago Press. (pp. 14, 15, 275)

———. 1990. Race-neutral policies and the democratic coalition. *The American prospect*. No. 1: 78–81. (pp. 14, 15, 353)

Wilson, W. J., and Aponte, R. 1985. Urban poverty. In *Annual review of sociology*, edited by Ralph H. Turner and James F. Short, Jr. Palo Alto, CA: Annual Reviews.

Wilson, W. J., and Neckerman, K. M. 1984. Poverty and policy: Retrospect and prospects. University of Wisconsin-Madison Institute for Research on Poverty Conference Paper. (p. 354)

Winard, A. I. 1970. Delineation of current poverty areas in big cities. Paper delivered at the annual meeting of the Population Association of America, Atlanta. (p. 15)

Winfield, I., et al. 1989. Career processes in Great Britain and the United States. *Social Forces* 68 (1): 284–308. (p. 228)

Winfield, L. F. 1990. School competency testing reforms and student achievement: Exploring a national perspective. *Educational Evaluation and Policy Analysis* 12 (2): 157–173. (p. 479)

Wingert, P., and Kantrowitz, B. A. 1990. The day care generation. *Newsweek* Winter/Spring: 86. (p. 116)

Winkler, K. J. 1991. Organization of American historians backs teaching of non-Western culture and diversity in schools. *The Chronicle of Higher Education* 37 (21): A5-A7. (pp. 402, 403)

Winn, M. 1977. *The plug-in drug: Television, children, and the family.* New York: Viking. (p. 136)

———. 1989. The VCR: A new and improved babysitter? *The New York Times* August 27: 29, 32. (p. 136)

Wirt, J. G.; Muraskin, L. D.; Goodwin, D. A.; and Meyer, R. H. 1989. *National Assessment of Vocational Education summary of findings and recommendations.* Washington, DC: U.S. Department of Education. (pp. 54, 55, 421)

Witelson, S. F., and Swallow, J. A. 1987. Individual differences in human brain function. *National Forum* 67 (2): 17–24. (p. 418)

Witkins, G. 1991. Kids who kill. *U.S. News and World Report* 110 (13): 26–32. (p. 277)

Witte, J. 1990. *Choice in American education.* Madison: The University of Wisconsin-Madison Robert M. La Follette Institute of Public Affairs. (pp. 449, 500)

Witte, J., and Walsh, D. J. 1990. A systematic test of the effective schools model. *Educational evaluation and policy analysis* 12 (2): 188–212. (pp. 78, 79, 80, 81, 275)

Wittrock, M. C., ed. 1986. *Handbook of research on teaching.* New York: Macmillan. (p. 510)

Wolf, D. P. 1989. Portfolio assessment: Sampling student work. *Educational Leadership* 46 (7): 35–39. (p. 478)

Wolf, R. M. 1964. *The identification and measurement of environmental process variables related to intelligence.* Unpublished Ph.D. dissertation, University of Chicago. (p. 110)

Wolfe, A. 1990. The return of the melting pot. *The New Republic* 203 (27): 27–34. (p. 349)

Wolman, J. 1976. Black flight adds to cities' problems. *Kansas City Star* December 28: 16. (p. 309)

Wolters, R. 1984. *The burden of Brown.* Knoxville: The University of Tennessee Press. (p. 338)

Woltman, J. 1989. Home schooling debates in N. D. since deregulation. *Education Week* 9 (10): 15. (pp. 76, 456)

Wong, S. C. 1987. The language needs of school-age Asian immigrants and refugees in the United States. In *Ethnicity and language,* edited by Winston A. VanHorne and T. V. G. Madison: The University of Wisconsin System Institute on Race and Ethnicity. (p. 377)

Woodward, K. L. 1990. Young beyond their years. *Newsweek* Winter/Spring: 54–60. (p. 195)

Word, E., et al. 1990. *Student/teacher achievement ratio (STAR) Tennessee' K–3 class size study.* Nashville: Tennessee State Department of Education. (p. 264)

Wright, E. O. 1985. *Classes.* London: New Left Press. (p. 4)

Wright, J. D., and Wright, S. R. 1976. Social class and parental values for children: A partial replication and extension of the Kohn thesis. *American Sociological Review* 41: 527–537. (p. 232)

Wrigley, J. 1982. A message of marginality: Black youth, alienation, and unemployment. In *Education and work,* edited by Harry F. Silberman. Eighty-First Yearbook of the National Society for the Study of Education, Part II. Chicago: University of Chicago Press. (pp. 189, 265)

Wyatt, T. A., and Seymour, H. H. 1990. The implications of code-switching in Black English speakers. *Equity and Excellence* 24 (4): 17–20. (p. 357)

Wycliff, D. 1990. Help is given in the pursuit of education dreams. *The New York Times* June 20: B9. (p. 498)

Wynne, E. A., and Hess, M. 1986. Long-trends in youth conduct and revival of traditional value patterns. *Educational Evaluation and Policy Analysis* 8: 294–308. (pp. 184, 185, 196)

Yankelovich, D. 1972. *Changing values on the campus.* New York: Simon & Schuster. (p. 180)

———. 1981. Searching for self-fulfillment in a world turned upside down. *American Demographics* 4 (3): 27–32, 43–44.

Yatvin, J. 1990. The superintendent. *Educational Leadership* 48 (1): 87. (p. 441)

Young, L.; Sykes, G.; Featherstone, J.; and Elmore, R. 1990. *Tomorrow's schools: Design for Professional Development Schools.* East Lansing, MI: The Holmes Group. (p. 473)

Young, M., ed. 1973. *The American family in social-historical perspective.* New York: St. Martin's Press. (p. 147)

Young, M., and Willmott, P. 1973. *The symmetrical family.* New York: Random House. (pp. 91, 93)

Zabin, L. S. et al. 1986. Evaluation of a pregnancy prevention program for urban teenagers. *Family Planning Perspectives* 18: 119–126. (p. 204)

Zahorik, J. A. 1987. Teachers' collegial interaction: An exploratory study. *Elementary School Journal* 87: 385–396. (p. 525)

Zajonc, R. B. 1976. Family configuration and intelligence. *Science* 192: 227–336. (p. 130)

———. 1986. Family factors and intellectual test performance: a reply to Steelman. *Review of Educational Research* 56: 365–371. (p. 130)

Zangwill, I. 1909. *The melting pot.* New York: Macmillan. (pp. 345, 346)

Zelizer, V. A. 1985. *Pricing the priceless child.* New York: Basic Books. (pp. 89, 91, 105)

Zemsky, R. 1990. Breaking the mold. *Policy Perspectives* 2 (2): 1–8. (p. 56, 62)

Zigler, E. 1970. Social class and the socialization process. *Review of Educational Research* 40: 87–110. (pp. 148, 234)

———. 1973. Project Head Start: Success or failure? *Children Today* 2 (November–December): 2–71. (p. 279)

———. 1991. Using research to inform policy: The case of early intervention. In *The care and education of America's young children: Obstacles and opportunities*, edited by Sharon Lynn Kagan. Chicago: University of Chicago Press. (pp. 289, 293, 294)

Zill, N. 1982. The condition of American children and youth: The need for a balanced appraisal. Paper presented at the annual meeting of the Association for the Advancement of Science, Washington, DC. (p. 122)

Zill, N., and Schoenborn, C. A. 1990. Developmental, learning and emotional problems: Health of our nation's children. National Center for Health Statistics Advance Data Paper No. 190. (pp. 126, 233)

Zimmerman, B. J. 1990. Self-regulated learning and academic achievement: An overview. *Educational Psychologist* 25 (1): 3–17. (p. 269)

Zinsmeister, K. 1990. Growing up scared. *The Atlantic Monthly* 265 (6): 49–66. (pp. 122, 275)

Zirkel, P. A. 1991. Home schooling. *Phi Delta Kappan* 72 (5): 408–409. (p. 456)

Zuboff, S. 1988. *In the age of the smart machine.* New York: Basic Books. (pp. 6, 23, 35)

Zuckerman, M. 1990. Some dubious premises in research and theory on racial differences. *American Psychologist* 45 (12): 1297–1303. (pp. 66, 198, 201)

Zwerling, L. S. 1988. The Miami-Dade story. *Change* 20 (1): 10–23. (p. 289)

Index